WITHDRAWN

WITHDRAWN

THE BOOK
OF
THE PLAY

Courtesy of John Cranford Adams, from a photograph by Wendell Kilmer

THE STAGE OF THE GLOBE THEATER, LONDON
A scale-model reconstruction by John Cranford Adams, illustrating the
Elizabethan multiple-space stage.

PN
6112
W2.5

808.82
W15b

71935

THE BOOK

OF

THE PLAY

An Introduction
to Drama

BY

Harold R. Walley

PROFESSOR OF ENGLISH
OHIO STATE UNIVERSITY

CHARLES SCRIBNER'S SONS

NEW YORK

GOSHEN COLLEGE LIBRARY
GOSHEN, INDIANA.

Copyright, 1950, by
CHARLES SCRIBNER'S SONS
B-12.60[V]
Printed in the United States of America

*All rights reserved. No part of this book
may be reproduced in any form without
the permission of Charles Scribner's Sons*

Preface

The Book of the Play is intended to be something more than an exhibit of dramatic masterpieces accompanied by the conventional gallery guide. As its subtitle indicates, it is a systematically planned introduction to drama. Composed of several distinct but complementary parts, each of which is designed to perform a definite function, it is conceived as a combined source-book of information and laboratory manual to implement self-instruction by the process of personally conducted experiment. Its subject is the body of dramatic achievement which represents the theatrical tradition of western Europe. It is addressed to the beginner who is undertaking his first systematic study of dramatic art, and especially to the beginner who is perforce obliged to serve much of this apprenticeship in reading plays rather than in seeing them performed on the stage. Furthermore, although it recognizes that within the breast of many a beginner beats the heart of an aspiring actor, director, or playwright, and trusts that such aspirations will derive substantial benefit from the matters here set forth, it is addressed primarily to the consumer rather than the practitioner of drama; its point of view is consistently that of the audience. Within these limits its aim is to provide the knowledge and understanding which are essential to an intelligent enjoyment of drama and fundamental to any more advanced study of the subject. Consequently, while its approach is always elementary, its scope is not restricted to mere rudiments; it endeavors to be as comprehensive as is necessary for adequate comprehension.

As more desirable for introductory purposes, the approach adopted is analytical rather than historical. There are several reasons for this choice. While the historical approach to drama affords a cumulative synthesis of its salient qualities in terms of their progressive development, for the beginner it incurs a serious risk of losing the woods of essential drama among the trees of ephemeral fashion. In addition, it tends to obscure the distinction between purely historic and intrinsic values, between interesting experiment and significant achievement. The analytical approach, on the other hand, by subordinating matters of chronology to a collective and retrospective view of the subject, considers drama as an organic whole and thus tends to examine its various functions, procedures, and values in the light of its enduring achievement. In doing so, it enjoys the advantage of approximating the naturally retrospective approach of the beginner himself. Quite understandably a beginner's prime interest in drama, as in any new experience, is in its immediate value. While he may concede a certain academic significance to the fact that a Greek tragedy, a Renaissance comedy, or, for that matter, a modern problem play once moved multitudes, what strikes him as really pertinent is its impact upon one alive today. Since this initial attitude is not only natural but also eminently intelligent, it offers a logical point of departure. Its major liability is not so much a failure to distinguish nicely between past and present virtues as its all too common failure to recognize present virtue because of limited acquaintance. The average beginner is prone to estimate relevance solely by conformity with familiar preconceptions. The chief function, therefore, of an introduction to drama is to correct this bias, to extend systematically the experience of the beginner, and to provide him with a broader and deeper appreciation of the human values resident in drama's various achievements.

In pursuit of this function, the somewhat ambitious purpose of the present book is to place at the student's disposal in concise form all the essential materials for an understanding of the human interests which have prompted dramatic expression, the various effects aimed at by dramatic art, the characteristic methods whereby drama has attained its objectives, and the significant results of the whole enterprise. The presentation of these materials is guided by two fundamental principles. The first of these is that the proper milieu of drama is not the page but the stage: that drama is primarily an art of the theater, inseparable from the physical conditions of stage production, and to be interpreted in terms of theatrical effect. The second is that the best introduction to drama is an introduction to the best drama. Whatever may be gained by tempering the wind to the shorn lamb, through a gradual exposure to drama in its less exacting forms, is more than offset by the unfortunate impression of mediocrity likely to result. If the beginner is ever to be convinced that the game of drama is worth the candle, it is strategically important that he derive his first impressions from the game at its best. The difficulties inherent in this procedure the book endeavors to alleviate by the organization of its materials. Its scheme is designed to reduce the complexity of the problem to factors which can be dealt with one at a time. By segregating the major aspects of drama it seeks to clarify the nature and significance of each separately. At the same time, by integrating the several parts of the design logically it provides a systematic method for interpreting the whole. In the organization of this scheme, however, attention should be called to two deliberate omissions. No effort is made to spare the student the mental anguish of doing his own thinking, and there is no attempt to usurp the function of the teacher. Among the thousand natural shocks that pedagogical flesh is heir to perhaps none is more conducive to blasphemy than the textbook which leaves a teacher no function but to applaud its wisdom or to quarrel with its judgment. *The Book of the Play* strives earnestly to avoid such obtrusion. Its function is simply to supply, to explain, and to organize the materials for study. Its purpose is to facilitate more profitable classroom discussion. Its sole ambition is to combine lucidity with an accuracy and precision which will sustain exacting critical scrutiny. The application and interpretation of its materials it reserves scrupulously, and properly, for the teacher and student themselves.

The first two sections of the book are concerned with preliminaries. Of these, the one dealing with the Art of Drama is largely technical. To the extent that such matters enter into an intelligent reading or witnessing of drama, it endeavors to explain what drama is, what it is trying to do, how it goes about doing it, why it does so, and what it all amounts to. While every effort has been exerted to keep this discussion as simple and lucid as possible, the need for combining comprehensiveness with brevity dictates that it also be succinct and compact. It is intended not for cursory reading but for careful study, and will yield its full value to nothing less. The section devoted to The Development of Drama by no means pretends to be a history of drama, even in miniature. It merely supplies enough historical orientation to enable the student to conceive of the plays which he reads in a rudimentary context rather than a total vacuum. Its function is to relate the significant achievements of drama to the general circumstances of their origin, to indicate the process whereby they came into existence, and in so doing to summarize the major phases through which drama has passed. Although brief and highly selective, it is at the same time solicitous to provide an accurate and balanced synopsis of the cardinal developments which have made drama what it is.

The core of the book is the section designated as The Achievement of Drama. Here are reprinted twelve plays chosen to illustrate the principal kinds of dramatic endeavor which have resulted over the centuries in a positive and enduring artistic achievement. Each play is preceded by an introductory discussion of the dramatic type which it exemplifies. These introductions are designed not so much to supply information about the dramatist and his works or a critical interpretation of the specific play as to elucidate a variety of drama—to explain its nature, its purpose, its origin, its theatrical premises, its technical peculiarities, and its general human implications. Each play is further provided with enough annotation to make the text intelligible to the modern reader and with an apparatus of questions and suggestions to serve as a guide for intensive study. The plays themselves have been selected on the basis of several definite specifications. In the first place, each is a supreme example of successful dramatic art, an integral part of the world's permanent theatrical repertory, a work of continuing significance for a modern audience, and thus a constituent of the knowledge desirable for any cultivated individual. In the second place, each represents a distinctive and important concept of drama; it is a masterpiece of its kind; and it is drawn from the dramatic epoch which is most closely identified with the establishment of the type. Finally, each is a characteristic work of a major world dramatist, who is an acknowledged master of the genre and owes his reputation largely to his achievement therein. Collectively, the plays illustrate all the major types and epochs of drama, and the principal varieties of dramatic technique, in so far as these have produced enduring results. Included among them are the four basic types of tragedy, the four most important types of comedy, and the four main types of intermediate drama. Half of the plays are drawn from drama prior to the eighteenth century; the remaining plays are modern. For the sake of those who prefer an historical approach, the various types of drama have been arranged roughly in the chronological order of their establishment, and thus provide, together with their respective introductions, a selective survey of the chief dramatic developments from ancient times to the present. Also, for those who desire to emphasize matters of literary style, a considerable stylistic diversity has been supplied in the five plays which wear their native English and thus escape the inherent liabilities of translation.

In this connection a word should be said about the seven plays which appear in borrowed clothing. Few experiences are quite so disconcerting to a student as to encounter an alleged foreign masterpiece in a version which either is a patent libel of the original or else raises serious doubts about the acumen of those who profess to admire this sort of thing. In the case of drama, it is particularly disastrous to be confronted with dialogue which could not possibly be spoken on the stage without provoking incredulity or ribaldry. For this reason exceptional care has been exercised in the selection of translations, and the editor owes a special debt to the translators and owners of copyright whose fine coöperation has made available in every instance the version which he has preferred. Wherever possible this is one which has stood the test of successful use on the stage. Several appear for the first time in a book of this character. Since in the nature of the case no translation can ever be an exact replica of its original, the present ones have been chosen on the following credentials. They retain the essential form and substance of the original. They also preserve its general tone, intent, and spirit. If they do not succeed in adequately transmitting, at least they do not wholly pervert its literary quality. And, last but most important, they are couched in language which a student can conceive as compatible with dramatic utterance on an actual stage.

The remaining features of the book represent mechanical aids to study. On the principle that one illustration is worth pages of explanation, the discussions of theatrical matters are supplemented with reproductions of the four basic types of stage for which drama has been designed. As a means of extending systematically the student's acquaintance with drama, the introduction to each dramatic type is concluded with specific suggestions for further reading which will illustrate the chief variations of the type and its possible ramifications. To implement such reading, a formal bibliography is replaced by two special book-lists. The first contains representative collections of drama which afford access to the plays most frequently desired and thus supply a comprehensive and convenient working library of drama. The second is an annotated and rigorously selective list of books about drama which will serve to expand the present introduction. Since the student's time is limited, and he is only confused by a multiplicity of unfamiliar titles, the practical purpose of this list is to direct him to one useful and dependable first book on each major aspect of the subject. His further interests will find abundant aid in the larger bibliographies provided by these books. As a guide for intensive study of the plays in this volume, each play is supplied with a set of detailed questions and suggestions designed to promote systematic analysis by the Socratic method. The use of this indirect approach is prompted by a desire both to avoid ready-made interpretations and to advance the student's understanding by helping him to form his own conclusions. The questions are frankly leading questions. Often, when points of special significance are at issue, they are deliberately phrased in such a manner as to indicate the general nature of the answer. Furthermore, in each instance they are carefully adapted to illuminate the special character of the play and to emphasize the distinctive features of the type to which it belongs. At the same time they are intended to expound no specific interpretation of the play, but rather to raise the questions which need to be answered before any satisfactory interpretation can be arrived at. Hence they are to be regarded primarily as aids to reflection, devised to assist the student in applying to specific problems the miscellaneous information provided elsewhere in the book. To afford convenient access to these materials, the book, finally, contains a detailed index, which will readily bring into any desired focus its various dispersed resources.

In conclusion there remains but the pleasure of recording my obligation to those whose aid has contributed immeasurably to whatever merit this volume may possess. Where assistance has been so generous and gracious, acknowledgment is less a duty than a welcome privilege. I have already indicated my general debt to the publishers and owners of copyright whose coöperation has made this book possible, and the details of this indebtedness are recorded specifically in their proper place elsewhere. More particularly, however, I wish to express my gratitude to Professor Thomas Marc Parrott for his signal kindness in permitting me to reprint the texts of *Hamlet* and *Twelfth Night* prepared for his own edition of Shakespeare, and to Mr. Robert Henderson for his equal kindness in placing at my disposal his translation of Racine. To Dr. John Cranford Adams, President of Hofstra College, and to his collaborator, Mr. Irwin

Smith of Garden City, I am indebted for a generosity beyond the call of courtesy which has made it possible for me to reproduce here for the first time their superb reconstruction of the Globe Theater. To my friend and colleague Professor John H. McDowell, Director of the Ohio State University Theater, I return thanks for his unsparing aid and counsel in matters of stagecraft and theatrical history. My sincere thanks are also due to Professor Joe Lee Davis, of the University of Michigan, who read much of this book in manuscript, for the substantial benefits which it has derived from his sympathetic and astute criticism. Finally, it is a particular pleasure to express to my daughter, Miss Katharine Walley, my appreciation of her invaluable assistance in the laborious task of preparing the manuscript.

Harold R. Walley

Columbus, Ohio
September 1, 1949

Contents

THE ART OF DRAMA

THE DEVELOPMENT OF DRAMA

THE ACHIEVEMENT OF DRAMA

List of Illustrations

THE BOOK
OF
THE PLAY

THE ART
OF
DRAMA

The Art of Drama

DRAMA AND THE THEATER

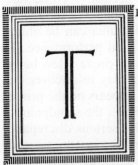HERE IS PERHAPS no form of literary art more popular in its appeal and more immediate in its impact than drama. Also, as one meets it in the theater, there is none which apparently requires less effort for its enjoyment. Yet actually no form of literature is more complex in its nature, more intricate and subtle in its artistic technique, or inherently more difficult both to execute and to comprehend. The reasons for this paradox are the hybrid nature of drama and the artistic medium in which it exists. For drama is not only a form of literature but also an art of the theater. Whereas most literature is designed for the printed page and for private reading, drama is designed primarily for the stage and for public exhibition. Its mode of expression always includes more than language, and its final effect always depends upon a synthesis of related arts.

The truth of the matter is that drama becomes a complete work of art only when it is created upon the stage. To be exact, it exists only while it is in the actual process of presentation. This basic fact is the source of very real problems for both the dramatist and the audience. Because the mechanism of the theater is exceedingly complex and difficult to control, drama is singularly at the mercy of its artistic medium. Its success is always contingent upon numerous intermediaries who come between the dramatist and his audience. Since the effect of any play can be no better than the competence of its director and its actors, the inescapable fate of drama is to wear the livery of its production. But so many and so variable are the factors which enter into theatrical production that any uniform effectiveness is bound to be uncertain. Just as a mediocre play can be inflated by excellent presentation, a dramatic masterpiece can be hopelessly crippled by inept production and incompetent acting. The significance of these facts may be readily perceived by consulting one's honest opinion of Shakespeare's dramatic ability; it is quite likely to reflect the quality of the performances one has seen. Indeed, not only the quality of the production but the mere availability

3

of a theater can be for drama a matter of life or death. The stage is by no means so ubiquitous as books or magazines or the motion-picture screen. For many people the opportunity to witness a play in the theater is rare; and even when it does exist, it is usually subject to severe limitations. In the theater one can rarely select a play to suit one's immediate preference, as one may a novel in a library; one is obliged to accept perforce what the theater happens to offer.

To circumvent at least some of these difficulties an obvious expedient is the reading of drama. Certainly for anyone who desires more than a casual acquaintance with the rich store of the world's dramatic literature it is an expedient invested with the virtue of necessity. To be sure, it can never be more than a substitute for the living magic of the theater itself; nevertheless, for the initiate this reading of drama can be almost as colorful and exciting as the witnessing of an actual performance. To an inexperienced reader, unfortunately, it is likely to prove a less happy alternative. For one need merely read the text of a play to discover that between a vivid experience in the theater and what appears on the printed page there is an almost irreconcilable difference. From the standpoint of one who wishes to read drama pleasurably, it is this serious discrepancy which necessitates some practical assistance and impels a systematic study of the art. It also explains the existence of such a book as this.

ON SEEING AND READING A PLAY

The discrepancy between seeing a play on the stage and reading its printed text arises from the fact that, despite certain superficial similarities, the two experiences are of radically different kinds. On the stage a play presents a fusion of many elements, each of which performs a special function and adds to the total effect a subtle quality of its own. Spoken dialogue conveys not only ideas but a modulation of voice which reënforces meaning and imparts interpretative emphasis. Dialogue is complemented with the synchronized action of real people, which is often as expressive as speech. Pantomime and stage business are sometimes embellished with dances or ballet. Customarily this action is so organized that it produces the pictorial effect of merging tableaux and at times, with the plastic values of its mass movements, an effect which is almost architectural. The action itself is reënforced with appropriate stage settings. Design and décor supply a counterpoint to word and deed; lighting reflects the nuances of dramatic value; music insinuates the contours of a mood. And all these devices perform their appointed functions simultaneously in one concerted enchantment of the spectator's sensibilities.

Of this total experience the printed text of a play preserves only a meager vestige. Beyond an impersonal record of dialogue little survives. The condensed indications of stage setting and business barely suggest the elaborate texture of presupposed action and spectacle, while the very intrusion of such stage directions is distracting to the reader and tends to disrupt the smooth flow of drama. As for the rest, nearly everything which gives substance and vitality to a stage performance is conspicuously absent. Indeed, what remains does not possess even the virtue of disembodied voices, for printed dialogue lacks the vitalizing intonations of speech. Like Hamlet one reads words, words, words, yet, ironically, words not devised to be read but to fall on the ear with the accents of a living voice.

To make matters worse, reading a play is not only unlike seeing it in the theater but quite different from reading any other kind of literature. Novels, short stories, and poems are ordinarily designed to be read. Their natural medium of communication is the printed page. Consequently a reader may assume that everything essential to his comprehension of such literature is contained in the text before him. For example, a novel provides not only a full account of all pertinent action, speech, and thought, but a running commentary of explanation and analysis designed to clarify their significance. As a work of art it is self-contained and complete in itself, requiring no supplement but the reader's intelligence and experience. The script of a play, on the contrary, makes no pretense of being a finished product addressed to the ultimate consumer. It is a working blueprint designed for those whose expert interpretation can give it final substance. Without that supplement of interpretation it is incomplete, and its existence as a work of art is only potential.

The difference between a play on the stage and the same play in print is substantially the difference between the text of a novel and that of a play. In the theater even an inexperienced spectator can usually follow the purport of a play without special effort or preparation because he is the beneficiary of special attention. His ease is the product of others' labor. Since the play exists for the express purpose of attracting and maintaining his interest and, if possible, impressing him, every effort has been exerted to insure his favorable response. Playwright, director, designer, actor, all the miscellaneous functionaries of the theater, have lavished their ingenuity upon him. Countless hours of countless individuals have concentrated upon one systematic conspiracy of interpretation to the sole end that he may comprehend and enjoy. The reader of a play benefits from no such special attention; dramatic interpretation is the business of the stage. Bereft also of the artistic completeness to which he is accustomed in poetry and the novel, he is obliged to be his own interpreter. Satisfactory reading of drama, therefore, becomes an art of projecting upon the stage of one's imagination the finished production implied by the printed text. In order to practice the art successfully, it is necessary for the reader to take upon himself the multiple responsibilities of director, designer, and actor. Following the intimations of the script, he must be able to visualize the appearance of the stage at all times and the flow of action across it. Unceasingly alert to the significant gesture and the essential detail of stage business, he must be able with his mind's eye to define each character as a living personality. With his inner ear he must be able to hear the voices which speak the lines and record the subtle variations of their volume, inflection, and tempo. Meanwhile he must himself be the actor of every rôle. In short, the reader must undertake all the comprehensive study and elucidation of the script without which a theatrical production cannot succeed, and add sufficient versatility to be an impressionable witness of his own interpretative acting.

In many respects the reading of a play is like reading the score of a symphony. Everything essential to the performed work is imbedded in the script, but it requires technical knowledge to understand the notation and a creative imagination to conceive the intended effect. The most practical assistance in developing these faculties is afforded by at least a rudimentary understanding of the conditions which determine and the principles which govern customary dramatic procedure.

THE DRAMATIC MEDIUM

Any attempt to understand a play and to evaluate it critically raises three leading questions. What is the play trying to accomplish? How effectively do the methods employed serve their purpose? And what is the final human significance of the whole enterprise? Because the last of these questions involves fundamental problems of philosophy it is too broad to be dealt with here except by implication. The first two, however, relate more narrowly to dramatic theory and practice. Together they provide the subject matter of this book.

What a play attempts to do and how well it does it are matters inseparable from the artistic medium in which it works. All art is a technical effort to solve the problems inherent in its chosen medium. The measure of its success, as well as the distinctive quality of its achievement, is largely determined by what *can* be achieved within that medium. For every artistic medium combines with its special advantages certain limitations which severely restrict its product.

The artistic medium of drama is the theater. Because of this fact drama is obliged to be quite as much a business as an art. Production of plays is an expensive undertaking, which cannot be indulged without adequate financial support. A poet, taking advantage of what is known as prestige, may be able to write for the chosen few while his publisher makes up the deficit from more profitable sales. A playwright has a more vital stake in the box office. In the theater, if a play is to exist at all, it must be capable of mustering an audience. Moreover, it must perform this feat with the resources available to it. Regardless of a playwright's ambitions, there are some things which can be done in the theater very well and some which cannot be done so effectively. A play is always bounded by the mechanical limitations of the stage and by the human limitations of the actors; for these comprise a playwright's only means of expression.

Although in a general sense drama is a form of narrative, its distinguishing mode of expression is not narration but representation. That is to say, drama does not tell about what has occurred in the past; it exhibits before one's eyes an occurrence at the precise moment of its occurring. In point of vividness and immediate impact the method is unsurpassed. Art can approach no closer to reality without becoming life. Nevertheless, the method also has its disadvantages. If direct presentation is to be effective, it is obliged to be interesting at all times and to maintain a continuous forward movement. Perhaps Homer may occasionally nod, but a dramatist cannot afford to. Furthermore, if the presentation is to be effective immediately and cumulatively, it must be immediately clear and comprehensible. In the theater there is no time to reflect or to reconsider the evidence; one has to read as one runs. Finally, this clarity has to be achieved, not by discursive explanation and analysis, but through the speech and conduct of the actors. Thought and feeling have to be revealed; explanation and meaning have to be conveyed by inference.

The actor is at once drama's greatest and most hazardous asset. Characters in a novel are figments of the imagination, which can be elaborated or sketched, emphasized or suppressed as the novelist chooses to manipulate the reader's attention. Characters on the stage are real people, always present in their totality even when they have nothing of importance to do. They do not appear or vanish as convenience dictates, but have to be moved about and on and off the stage adroitly and unobtrusively. Above all, they possess the asset and the liability of being unmistakably human. Whatever they do or say, whatever they represent, consequently refers itself to comprehensible human nature. But an actor is not merely human; he is a specific individual with a physical appearance and traits of personality which inevitably transfer themselves to the character he represents. One's conception of Hamlet is bound to reflect the appearance and mannerisms of the actor who plays the rôle; and if these tangible elements do not coincide with what the play provides for him to do and say, the whole character becomes incomprehensible and incredible. For these reasons a dramatist is uniquely bound to his actors, and the fate of his play is circumscribed by their capacities.

Drama also has to take into account the mechanical limitations of the stage. For one thing, the stage is stringently limited in space. The stupendous spectacles so dear to the motion picture—the vast panorama of massed humanity, the clash of embattled armies, the cataclysm of nature—simply cannot be housed on the stage. It is equally limited in time. The number and elaborateness of stage sets are contingent upon the amount of time and effort required to set them up and to change them. Also the stage has its limits in verisimilitude. Not all the resources of modern invention can invest every situation with an air of reality. The staging of the storm scene in *King Lear* is rarely very convincing.

The bullet-riddled hubbub of the battle in *Cyrano de Bergerac* remains strictly papier-mâché. And many sequences in *The Dream Play* can result in only a working compromise. It is upon its skill in getting around these limitations of the stage that the success of a play depends.

The factor of the dramatic medium perhaps most difficult to control is the audience. Drama is an art not only of expression but of successful communication. Unless it produces its intended effect upon the audience it is impotent and fails, and without a satisfied audience it ceases to exist. But dealing with an audience is a complicated problem. To solve it satisfactorily, a play must be interesting, must be understood, and must evoke a proper response; and it must accomplish these ends upon a mass basis. A novel can ordinarily presuppose one reader at a time under conditions of relative privacy. A play, on the other hand, addresses a heterogeneous aggregation of individuals composed of anyone with the price of admission and subject to all the distractions and pressures of public concourse. Under these circumstances a play has to make itself understood without for a moment abating its interest. Otherwise, while the play is expounding, the audience may walk out. One does not usually go to the theater to be instructed but to be entertained.

In order to accomplish this exacting feat, a play must be adept in mass psychology. From beginning to end it must be designed to exploit the known or suspected capacities of an audience—the scope of its knowledge and experience, its probable convictions or prejudices, its common attitudes of mind and emotional sensibilities. For a dramatist the beginning of wisdom is study of his audience. Because a play can communicate no more than an audience can understand, and can accomplish no more than an audience will accept, the character of all drama is to a large extent conditioned by the prevailing interests and tastes of the audience for which it was originally created. Even the conventional playing time of approximately two hours is dictated by the capacity of an average audience for sustained concentration, while the intermissions are a concession to its need for mental and physical relaxation.

Because of this dependence upon the audience, drama is obliged to insure its effects. A cold audience is the advertisement of dramatic failure. Therefore, if a play professes to deal with matters of interest, it must convince the audience that they are interesting. If it intends a scene to be ludicrous, it must move the audience to laughter. If it endeavors to reveal the poignant pathos of life, it must contrive that the audience is emotionally touched. Moreover, these reactions must be sufficiently general and contagious that they create an effect of unanimity in the audience. A minority of death's-heads can ruin the feast of laughter, and an ill-timed guffaw will snap the tensity of the deepest emotion. Fortunately, the insuring of dramatic effects is not governed solely by the existing capacities of an audience. These capacities are susceptible to expansion.

An audience can understand whatever it can be made to understand, and it will accept whatever it can be brought to accept. Consequently a large share of dramatic art consists in controlling the audience, in guiding it unobtrusively to the specific understanding which a dramatist desires and in molding it gently but firmly into the reaction which he decrees.

THE NATURE OF DRAMATIC ART

The art of drama is the technical skill of using the theater's resources to provide an experience which has beauty and human significance. Its characteristic technique consists of those mechanical devices which a process of trial and error and the test of time have demonstrated to be most efficacious in exploiting the advantages and avoiding the disadvantages of its medium. Since the basis of this technique is exhibition of human beings engaged in speech and action, its product appears to be an attempted replica of human life. Certainly one is obliged to interpret a stage presentation in much the same fashion as one interprets life—by observing events and by drawing inferences from the appearance and manner of people, from their conversation, and from the consequences of their behavior. One's natural impulse, therefore, is to view what appears on the stage as substantially equivalent to what one meets off the stage.

Despite superficial resemblances, however, drama, being an art, is not at all the same as life. The experiences afforded by life are haphazard and conditioned by natural processes which are often beyond human control or even human awareness. One can never be certain about their relative importance. In any case, whatever significance they possess is likely to be obscured by irrelevant factors. The experiences provided by drama, on the contrary, are not natural but artificial; they are not the result of chance but of artistic selection. The situations of drama do not simply occur; they are deliberately fabricated. And both selection and fabrication are dictated by a definite purpose and meaning, for the clarification of which every irrelevancy is eliminated and every relevant factor is arranged functionally. Drama, to paraphrase Pope, is nature methodized. From beginning to end it is a product of conscious artifice. To equate it with life is to confuse the issue at the outset.

For the spectator or reader this artificial aspect of drama has important implications. While one is obliged to interpret drama as one does life, the process is much simpler than an interpretation of life. In all well-articulated drama one can always be sure that everything one encounters contributes to a specific meaning and is so ordered as to make that contribution clear. Whatever does not bear upon the final meaning is scrupulously omitted. So stringent is the economy of drama that no good dramatist can afford to squander precious time upon irrelevancies, which, if permitted, would only mislead his audience. One's interpretation, therefore, is constantly guided both by what is introduced in a play and by what is left out. For this reason one must be wary of hypotheses erected upon matters about which a play is silent. The first principle of dramatic interpretation is that everything specifically set forth or implied in a play is relevant to its meaning, and nothing else either pertains to it or even exists.

The purpose of dramatic artifice is not only to impose a design of unity and coherence upon the confused welter of life but to endow it with an irresistible human connotation. Because it thus aspires to impress and to move its audience, drama is essentially an art devoted to the creation of theatrical effects. The purpose of *Hamlet,* for instance, is to give an audience the effect of actually being in Hamlet's situation. *The Way of the World* makes vivid the brittle brilliance of sophisticated affectation. *The Sea Gull* subjects one to the creeping paralysis of spiritual triviality. This preoccupation of drama applies not only to the totality of its effect but to the theatrical impact of individual scenes and incidents. What is known as "good theater" is the tense situation, the telling gesture, the stroke of vivid revelation, in short the *coup de théâtre,* which is striking in itself and stirs an audience to reaction. Thus in *Twelfth Night* Shakespeare deliberately contrives for its effect the moment when Malvolio bursts upon the audience with his preposterous gaudiness. And Rostand builds a calculated *tour de force* in the famous duel in which Cyrano de Bergerac concludes his ballade and the life of Valvert with one brilliantly timed thrust. As Cyrano says elsewhere, "What a gesture!"

By concentrating upon effects drama endeavors to enlist the active participation of an audience in meaningful human experience. Its function is not to tell about joy and sorrow but to exhibit the embodiment of them so vividly and so movingly that their reality is transmitted alive into the consciousness of the audience. To the accomplishment of this effect all the component elements of drama are subsidiary. Story, characters, situations are but means to an end and have dramatic value in direct proportion to the effects which they are able to create. It should, therefore, be noted that a simple ability to follow the events of a story does not constitute either an understanding or an appreciation of drama. As a matter of fact, the story which a play tells is usually but the springboard from which drama takes off. For this reason the novelty of a story or situation has relatively little bearing upon its final dramatic effectiveness. Actually its familiarity may be a help rather than a hindrance. In *Oedipus the King, Hamlet,* and *Phædra,* the dramatists deliberately chose to deal with well-worn situations. Indeed, their very familiarity is counted on to aid in clarifying the dramatic treatment. The originality and interest of the plays reside, as the dramatists intended, in what they did with their story materials.

DRAMATIC ILLUSION

Since the effects of drama are the products of artifice, what drama purveys is not reality but illusion. The theater is notoriously the home of make-believe, and the commodity which it dispenses is wholesale pretense. No audience goes to a theater to encounter reality; it goes to beguile itself with a waking dream. From the first rise of the curtain it pretends to be somewhere else. It pretends that all space is conformable to the dimensions of a stage and that any vagary of time is consistent with the hours elapsed in a theater. It pretends that a painted flat is a solid wall, even when it ripples in an off-stage wind, that a cyclorama is a vista of sky or sea, and that a blue spot is a flood of moonlight. Encouraged by the audience, the actors in turn pretend to be quite other people. They pretend to love or quarrel or die with sublime disregard of their actual sentiments or capacity for chronic resurrection. On the face of it, the whole performance is as palpably unreal as the magician's familiar illusion of sawing a woman in half.

Now this is precisely the point of the whole matter. Actually the art of drama is a form of theatrical magic—a magic of illusion created for an audience which is accustomed to check its disbelief at the box office. This does not mean, however, that dramatic illusion is tantamount to fraud; for, like the magician's art, drama never professes to be anything but illusion. Neither does it mean that dramatic illusion embraces every vagary of the irresponsible fancy or that a theater audience will swallow anything at all. Like the magician's illusion of sawing a woman in two, the success of dramatic illusion depends upon its verisimilitude: that is, upon its ability to create by an admitted pretense an effect of apparent reality. Thus, regardless of the materials it employs or their remoteness from common experience, satisfactory dramatic illusion is always an illusion of reality. Unless it creates this semblance of reality there is no valid stimulus to which an audience can respond. For a human audience to react positively to that which has no real existence within the scope of its experience is as impossibly fatuous as it is psychologically impossible.

The illusions which drama creates, however, may represent widely different orders of reality, all of which are equally legitimate. O'Neill's *Desire Under the Elms,* for example, endeavors to provide an objective picture of the grim physical and spiritual state of those who must wrest a meager subsistence from stubborn soil. *An Enemy of the People* concentrates upon the shabby social compromises in which average humanity demonstrates its genius for being commonplace. *The Misanthrope* and *The Way of the World* portray stylized patterns of social behavior which represent human life not as it naturally is but as it endeavors to be under the impetus of conventional codes. *Twelfth Night* and *Cyrano de Bergerac* project the substance of humanity's perennial romantic impulse to remold its world nearer to the heart's desire. And *The Dream Play,* while attempting to reproduce the bizarre verisimilitude of a dream, symbolizes the abstract truths which underlie the dream-like insubstantiality of human experience. In one way or another all these represent aspects of human reality; but as there is a difference in their quality, there is a corresponding difference among the illusions in which drama endeavors to incorporate their reality. One must be cautious, therefore, not to estimate the validity of a dramatic illusion simply on the ground of one's personal preference for one kind of reality over another.

Whatever may be the aspect of reality reflected in a dramatic illusion, one must never lose sight of the fact that reproduction of reality and creation of a convincing illusion are two quite different things. The canons of dramatic art are dictated neither by scientifically established fact nor by absolute philosophical truth but by verisimilitude. Consequently the illusion created by plays like *Desire Under the Elms* and *The Playboy of the Western World* is no more real than the illusion produced by *Phædra* or *Twelfth Night*; both are equally artificial. On the other hand, whatever sustains the verisimilitude of an illusion is dramatically legitimate, no matter how inconsistent with reality it may actually be. Since drama is an art of illusion, its technique is always a conscious artifice in which the ends justify the means.

THE PROBLEM OF PLAUSIBILITY

In order to be successful a dramatic illusion has to be convincing. That is, it must be of such a nature that, for its duration at least, an audience is able to believe in its reality. Actually, the creation of this effect is usually aided by the coöperation of the audience itself. Since it has no sane reason for being present at all unless it expects to derive satisfaction from what is going on, every audience brings into the theater a positive will to believe. From the start it is predisposed to accept without question anything which is not downright incredible. In view of this fact, the practical obligation of drama is not so much to promote belief as simply to avoid incredulity.

The chief requisite of a convincing dramatic illusion is self-consistency. Without a perfect coherence of all component parts the fabric of illusion collapses like a house of cards. Therefore, any occurrence or conduct which denies the premises upon which an illusion rests naturally arouses the suspicion of an audience and destroys the credibility of the whole illusion. For example, in *The Sea Gull* it is necessary that Trepleff be seriously affected by his discovery of Nina's essential triviality or his behavior would violate the realistic basis of the play. Should Cyrano de Bergerac, on the other hand, experience a similar revulsion from the superficiality of Roxane, his reaction would do equal violence to the romantic sentiment which informs Rostand's play. In the theater it is impossible to be successfully realistic and romantic at the same time. Like oil and water, the characteristic elements of different illusions do not mix; incongruous association merely emphasizes their irreconcilable antagonism.

Because of this need for self-consistency drama habitually obeys more arbitrary laws than life. Truth is always stranger than fiction. Although in the course of ordinary life many events may be quite inappropriate to the circumstances, totally unexpected, and theoretically illogical, in a play an audience regularly expects everything to be accounted for on a more orderly basis. It demands that events follow a strict pattern of cause and effect, that the behavior of stage characters be strictly in accord with recognizable human impulses and with the specific personality attributed to them, that the whole order of life with which the play deals exhibit a comprehensible logic, and that even the irrational have a rational explanation. It demands, in short, that drama, as an art, impose upon life an artistic rationale.

Under the pressure of these arbitrary demands, the conviction carried by a dramatic illusion derives not so much from its coincidence with demonstrable fact or eternal truth as from its conformity with what the audience expects. Primarily an audience expects the circumstances of a play to appear natural. Its conception of what is natural, however, is usually a generalization which reduces the normal experiences of average humanity to a rough system of logical principles. Whatever is normally characteristic of any situation comes to be expected and therefore can be accepted as natural and convincing; but any departure from this norm obviously requires special explanation before its naturalness can be accepted. In order to be convincing, drama is obliged to operate upon this general plane of natural expectation. As Aristotle long ago pointed out, drama is most convincing when it deals, not with that which is historically actual or scientifically possible, but with that which is humanly probable. Correspondingly, it is this concentration upon a probability rooted in common human experience which imparts to drama its universal appeal and application.

Since, however, drama is designed not for leisurely study and critical analysis but for immediate acceptance in a theater at its face value, proper effectiveness demands that its inherent probability also be apparent. That is to say, drama is obliged to be both probable and plausible. As a practical consideration, in keeping with the illusory nature of drama, this appearance of probability is actually more important than the fact. For, in general, an audience can be induced to accept anything so long as it does not outrage credulity, whereas it is disposed to accept nothing, not even truth itself, unless it wears the guise of plausibility. Consequently a large part of dramatic technique is addressed to this specific need. As a matter of fact, the art of drama is in no small measure a form of legerdemain whereby incredulities are anticipated, inconsistencies or impossibilities are covered up or explained away, and improbabilities are given a specious plausibility. For this reason dramatic plausibility can be a highly ambiguous virtue, which needs to be viewed with appropriate caution. Necessary as it is to convincing effect, it may or may not have much to do with either reality or truth. It is not at all uncommon for a theatrical effect to be clothed in a superficial plausibility which has no legitimate justification in dramatic logic or human experience, but which serves merely as a factitious pretext for an immediate sensation. Everyone has encountered at one time or another the scene of spurious pathos concocted as a deliberate "tear-jerker," the arbitrary crisis fabricated for the sake of a momentary thrill, the heroic gesture flaunted to milk easy applause, or the mawkish sentiment mouthed to exploit a ready-made prejudice. Such so-called "cliff-hanging" and "flag-waving" usually do possess a sort of immediate plausibility, but their kind of plausibility calls attention to an important difference among theatrical values. In final value there is a vast difference between effects which are genuinely dramatic and those which are simply theatrical.

The quality of dramatic plausibility, particularly its relation to the broad foundations of human experience, constitutes an important measure of drama's ultimate value. While in general this is a matter of degree which admits of infinite gradation, it also serves to differentiate certain common orders of drama. Farce and melodrama, for example, possess a factitious plausibility derived from their own arbitrary premises; but as these premises frankly have little bearing upon common human experience, the forms of drama which they produce have no greater bearing upon life. Burlesque and satire have the plausibility of exaggerated truth and an admittedly partial view; therefore they have value in proportion to their special interests and the validity of their bias. Tragedy and high comedy, on the other hand, possess an immediate plausibility which is confirmed by the most exacting analysis of human experience. The plausibility of great drama always possesses the validity of demonstrable truth to life. Because of this fact such drama makes a direct and important contribution to an understanding of life itself.

DRAMATIC CONVENTIONS

Since drama is obliged to achieve its plausible effect of reality by limited and artificial means, its success obviously involves more than meets the eye and ear in the theater. The difficulty with an art of make-believe is that an adult audience, even though it may be diverted by a spectacle which it recognizes to be artificial and false, cannot be expected to be genuinely moved by it without feeling foolish. As a matter of fact, no audience ever is much affected, directly, by the artificial pretenses of the stage. No audience in possession of its faculties is impressed by the feigned death of a perfectly healthy actor pretending to be Hamlet, or by the spurious folly of a clever actress pretending to be the absurd Lady Wishfort. What actually occurs in every successful play is a subtle psychological substitution. Stimulated by what appears on the stage, the imagination of the audience automatically translates these pretenses into the realities which they are designed to suggest. It is to this authentic reality, alive in the imagination, that an audience responds: to the actual death of a real Hamlet, and to the actual folly of a real Lady Wishfort, superimposed by the imagination upon the artifices of the stage.

Because this psychological transmutation is imperative for effective drama, the prime function of dramatic art is to stimulate and guide the imagination of the audience; and the validity of its technique is proportional to the contribution which it makes to this end. The more closely stage practices correspond to the reality which is to be imagined, the easier it is, of course, for an audience to make the transition from one to the other. The limitations of the theater, however, rarely permit close verisimilitude. Fortunately, the wide discrepancy which often exists between stage practice and imagined reality is actually less important than it appears to be. Every audience recognizes the limitations of the stage and, in order that the show may go on, is quite ready to compromise about methods so long as they make clear exactly what it is supposed to imagine. In other words, it makes a virtue of necessity and agrees to accept the will for the deed. As a result, drama regularly repairs its lapses from verisimilitude by the substitution of *dramatic conventions*.

A dramatic convention is simply a tacit agreement between the audience and those responsible for a play that, for the sake of mutual benefit, a dramatic device will be accepted not on the ground of its naturalness but on the ground of its purpose. Like every convention, it is a concession to expediency which justifies itself by its practical utility. Like all conventions, it is strictly artificial and bears little relationship to natural human experience beyond its need and desirability. Yet because it is a convention, sanctioned within its own sphere by established custom, it tends to possess the naturalness conferred by familiarity.

So accustomed is the average audience to this conventionality of drama that it is rarely conscious of the unnaturalness of what it accepts as a matter of course. It is the practice of actors, for instance, even though they may be in the intimacy of drawing-room conversation, to speak with abnormally loud voices in order that the audience may be able to understand them. They also have the extraordinary habit of always performing important stage business so that the spectators will have an unobstructed view. A stage whisper accomplishes the miraculous feat of being at the same time audible in the far reaches of the balcony and inaudible to persons within a few feet of the speaker on the stage. In similar defiance of physical law, a dimming of stage lights can plunge actors into such stygian darkness that they cannot distinguish one from another, yet leave them sufficiently illuminated for the audience to follow the action. Time conveniently leaps any specified interval or doubles back upon itself with the mere lowering of a curtain. And the mercurial aplomb with which the stage itself changes locality confounds alike geography and possibility.

Although these commonplaces of dramatic convention are patently unnatural, so familiar and so obviously necessary are they that they in no way detract from the illusion of reality. Of similar constitution is the whole body of dramatic technique. Dramatic art is founded upon conventions which are automatically accepted as appropriate and natural to the extent that they are familiar and their purpose is understood.

Thus, as a concession to the spectator's need for immediate comprehension and his limited capacity for sustained attention, it is conventional for drama to concentrate its action most unnaturally, to strip its picture of life to its essentials, and to prefer broad, rather obvious effects. Much of an actor's costuming and deportment is designed to exploit recognizable commonplaces as clues to his personality or social status. Since characters in a play vary widely in their function and relative importance, it is conventional to vary the degree of their development accordingly. Some are endowed with a well-rounded, complex individuality; some are sketched only as familiar types; and some, whose function is simply that of cogs in the machinery of plot or stage presentation, have only the impersonality of stock figures, who possess no more identity than is required to explain their function. In the same way situations, stage business, and emotional reactions are often deliberately stereotyped in order to produce economically a conventional effect. Because information must be conveyed to an audience with a minimum loss of time, scenery and lighting are contrived to supplement action and dialogue; action is conceived in terms of its expressiveness; and dialogue is more given to explanation than the occasion strictly warrants. Because the inner thoughts and emotions of a character often require an expression beyond the adequacy of pantomime or normal dialogue, lay figures like the confidant are introduced to serve as a sounding-board for an actor's self-revelation, or the actor himself, in a parenthetical aside or soliloquy, speaks directly to the audience and takes it into his confidence. In order that the audience may be entertained while it is being informed, dramatic characters regularly converse with a wit, felicity, and eloquence rarely to be met except on the stage. Finally, in certain kinds of drama, it is conventional for all sorts of people to express themselves in verse: not with any intention of persuading an audience that some people do speak verse rather than prose, but simply as a concession to the fact that for certain kinds of human experience poetry is the most appropriate form of expression.

The acceptability of a dramatic convention, and therefore its artistic legitimacy, ordinarily rests upon its fulfillment of four major requirements: it must be necessary; it must be effective; it must be appropriate to the illusion of which it forms a part; and it must be either familiar or unmistakable in its purport. Because these requirements are closely interrelated and include certain variable factors, not all dramatic conventions are universally valid. Furthermore, from time to time theatrical conditions change; and as they change, some dramatic conventions change with them. In this connection, however, one must be cautious, particularly when dealing with an unfamiliar kind of drama, not to assume that the momentary strangeness of a departure from familiar convention necessarily indicates an actual ineptitude. Mere difference by no means signifies inferiority.

The point may be illustrated by the dramatic use of scenery, which is always a matter of convention. On the modern stage it is conventional to provide a play with localized pictorial settings. At other times and under other conditions it was conventional to employ little or no scenery. For example, *Twelfth Night* was designed for a relatively bare stage, *The Misanthrope* for a conventionalized stage with little special scenery, and *The Sea Gull* for several fairly elaborate stage sets. Each employs scenery according to the normal conventions of its time. Each sets its stage and acts upon the imagination of the audience in its own way and for its own purposes. Each carefully integrates its particular form of scenery with the total dramatic illusion. Any exchange of scenic methods among the plays would materially alter this integration. It is, therefore, an error to assume that the more detailed scenery of the one play makes it inherently more natural and effective than the other two. Scenery is never more than an expedient; even in its most circumstantial elaboration it can only approximate reality in canvas, paint, and lighting. One set for *The Sea Gull*, as an example, stipulates the background of a lake, which obviously can exist as no more than a suggestion. Thus where all is merely a choice among artificialities, the virtue of scenic convention is largely relative, and the actual presence or absence of tangible scenery makes little difference in a play's final effectiveness. As a matter of fact, scenery, if it is so conspicuous as to direct attention to itself, can be actually detrimental to dramatic effect and thus forfeit its value as a useful convention.

In the light of these facts, it is evident that the supreme requisite of every effective convention is appropriateness. Indeed, in so conventional an art as drama the strict appropriateness of all parts is essential to self-consistency. The observance of this dramatic principle is what is known as *decorum*. In general, decorum simply means suitability to the occasion; but this suitability may be interpreted in a variety of ways. For Aristotle, in ancient times, tragic decorum demanded an action conducive to pity and awe, characters of heroic proportions, and rhetorically embellished dialogue. To many critics and dramatists of the Renaissance decorum meant adherence to prescribed dramatic rules. To a later naturalistic age it meant conformity with the scientific laws which presumably govern human behavior. Regardless of varying interpretations, however, the basic principle remains the same: since the plausibility of every dramatic illusion depends upon its self-consistency, every participating convention must be appropriate to the essential nature of the illusion. Decorum is the strict observance of this principle. In many respects it is the most comprehensive property of good drama. Certainly it is the mortar which binds together the elements of sound dramatic structure. Without its proper observance drama is unconvincing, and its illusion of reality vanishes.

DRAMATIC ACTION

Up to this point we have been concerned chiefly with the artistic nature of drama and the conventionality imposed upon it by its medium of expression. It is now time to consider some of the means which drama regularly uses to achieve its ends. Because many of these are practically obligatory, and thus give a certain basic uniformity to all plays, a working knowledge of dramatic principles and practices affords perhaps the best preparation for an intelligent reading of drama. But because we are here concerned with the reader rather than the writer of plays, we shall confine our attention to the more general aspects of this dramatic technique.

Since the aim of drama is to interest and move an audience by a spectacle of human beings in action, its raw material is humanity in its natural and social environment. The substance, therefore, of all drama is simply what people do, say, and are: in other words, human action, dialogue, and character. To be dramatically effective, of course, these materials must be selected so that they possess interest in themselves and human significance in their implications. The coherent organization of such selected materials into a dramatically effective design constitutes what is known as *dramatic action*. The dramatic action is the formally integrated substance of every play.

Broadly speaking, dramatic action is a working out of the potentialities in a dramatic situation. But not every situation nor every kind of action is dramatic and therefore suitable for a play. The nature of what is dramatic may be indicated by a simple illustration. Suppose one observes two people conversing on a street corner. The incident may attract one's casual interest momentarily but probably will not sustain interest very long. Even though one should be informed who the people are, what sort of personality and background they represent, and how they happened to engage in conversation, the interest of the situation is not materially enhanced or prolonged. But now suppose the conversation develops into a violent argument, and the two individuals ultimately fall to blows. At once the situation takes on a different interest. The curiosity of even a detached bystander impels one to wonder what the row is about and to see what is going to happen. The chances are that one will at least await the final outcome. It is possible that, upon discovering the cause of the controversy, one's own sympathies may be aroused, one may take sides, and eventually one may even become personally involved.

The difference between the two situations arises from the new factors which have been added. To begin with, there is introduced an opposition of forces not present before. This clash of opposites in turn raises an issue, which is bound to have consequences. The exact nature of these consequences, however, as well as the final victor in the controversy, is a matter of uncertainty. On the other hand, the opposition of forces is evidently so serious that no resolution of the difficulty appears possible without either a decision in favor of one or a reconciliation of the two. Finally, there are the general merits of the case, which naturally have a bearing upon the justice of the final outcome. To put it another way, the second situation adds to the first the elements of conflict, inevitable consequences, suspense, climactic decision, and a general human significance which promotes empathy, or emotional response. It is the introduction of these elements which arouses interest and sustains attention. It is the presence or absence of these elements which makes the difference between a dramatic and an undramatic situation.

Dramatic action is the formal development of a dramatic situation to its logical conclusion. Because of its formal nature this development follows an invariable pattern. It begins with the introduction of a fundamental conflict which involves the opposition of individuals, principles, emotional impulses, social standards, or any combination of these or other factors. It proceeds, by a selection of appropriate and revelatory incidents, to clarify the exact nature of the conflict and the consequences which issue from it. The cumulative effect of these it pursues to a climax, or point beyond which the conflict can no longer be held in suspension but must be resolved by a decision one way or another. And it concludes with an exhibition or indication of the results produced by the climactic decision. This schematic development constitutes the real substance of every play. In its course it usually tells some sort of story; nevertheless, dramatic action embraces more than simple story or even stage business. These are, of course, important elements; but, besides external incident and physical activity, dramatic action also includes the motility of the mind and spirit, psychological reactions, emotional responses, the struggle of idea with idea, the intangible tensions of moments charged with stress—in short, everything which imparts to human experience dramatic force. Indeed, some of the most powerful dramatic action has little outward manifestation at all.

DRAMATIC STRUCTURE

The structural device used to give unified form, coherence, and meaning to a dramatic action is the *plot*. A dramatic plot performs its function by selecting the specific incidents to be given dramatic representation and arranging them in a climactic order so that they lead to a logical conclusion. The plot of a play, therefore, is not the same thing as the story which a play tells; it is the mechanical means of utilizing that story to produce a desired effect. Plot always involves an artificial arrangement of means for a particular end. For this reason it often serves as an index to the *theme*, or abstract meaning, of a play. And in some plays, where the theme is really a *thesis*, the plot constitutes the argument advanced to prove the truth of the proposition.

An effective dramatic plot can be constructed in either of two ways. It may comprise a series of episodes, loosely related to each other but having a coherence because they illustrate successive phases in the development of a theme or the interaction of a common group of characters. This is known as an *episodic plot*, which may be illustrated by *The Dream Play* or *Cyrano de Bergerac*. Its principal virtues are its flexibility, its variety, and its effect of naturalness. The alternative form consists of a series of scenes, each growing out of the preceding and bound in a causal relationship to the others. Every scene represents a specific stage in the development of a single closely integrated pattern of action. This is known as an *organic plot*, and is variously illustrated in *Hamlet, An Enemy of the People*, and *Desire Under the Elms*. Its virtues are solidity of structure and an effect of logical inevitability.

Closely related to these basic forms of plot structure are the two conventional methods of conducting a plot. The difference between them is occasioned by the dramatist's *point of attack*: that is, the exact point in the whole story at which the dramatist chooses to begin his dramatic action. The first of these methods concentrates upon the exploitation of what is essentially a single complex situation. It begins its dramatic action at a point close to the climax. At its beginning most of the relevant dramatic factors already exist as potentialities of the situation. It is the function of the plot to bring these inherent factors to light and to clarify their dramatic significance by a process of progressive revelation or discovery. Such a plot may be called an *unfolding plot*. Its classical example is *Oedipus the King,* although it appears also in *Phædra, The Misanthrope,* and *An Enemy of the People,* and is the usual method employed in ancient drama and its many modern derivatives. The second method makes its point of attack with the initial incident which logically precipitates the dramatic action, and then proceeds to accumulate the consequences of this incident until they produce a climax. At the beginning of the dramatic action only some of the decisive factors exist; the remainder are introduced cumulatively as the action itself develops them. This type of plot may be called an *accretive plot*. It is the characteristic plot method of most romantic drama and appears in *Hamlet, The Dream Play, Cyrano de Bergerac,* and *Desire Under the Elms.*

Whichever method a plot may employ, its basic function is to provide the structure of a unified and complete dramatic action. Such a complete action is one marked by a genuine beginning, middle, and end, which Aristotle has defined as follows: "A beginning is that which is not itself necessarily after anything else, and which has naturally something else after it; an end is that which is naturally after something itself, either as its necessary or usual consequent, and with nothing else after it; and a middle, that which is by nature after one thing and has also another after it." To put it another way, before the beginning of a sound plot there is nothing in the existing situation to necessitate any particular dramatic action, and at its conclusion no further development can alter the significance of its specific dramatic action. A good plot begins and ends in a state of equilibrium; its course marks the progress from an initial disturbance to a final restoration of this equilibrium.

Since the general function of a plot is always the same, its structure tends to follow a fairly regular formula. In order that the audience may understand the circumstances existing at the start of the dramatic action, a plot necessarily begins with an *exposition* of these circumstances, which usually includes an introduction and brief characterization of the principal characters. In the course of this preliminary exposition it is customary to introduce the incident which posits an opposition of forces and precipitates the dramatic action. The second stage, often referred to as the *complication,* traces the development of this initial conflict through a constantly increasing complexity and tension until a climax is reached and some decisive action is necessary. This *climax,* also sometimes called the *crisis,* brings the dramatic conflict to a head and marks the highest point of complexity and emotional intensity in the dramatic action. Often it is represented on the stage by an open clash between the two chief opponents in what is known as the *obligatory scene.* The final part of the plot is the *dénouement*: the "unknotting" or resolution of the complexity. It presents the direct consequences of the decisive climax, brings the dramatic conflict to a logical end, and in concluding the dramatic action produces a new equilibrium of forces. The dénouement may vary greatly in duration: in some serious plays it is protracted; in others it is almost coincident with the climax; but usually it forms the shortest part of the plot.

The effectiveness of dramatic structure depends chiefly upon three factors. The first of these is the *selection* of the materials to be dramatized. Because the economy of drama demands that everything in a play be strictly functional, it is necessary that the incidents chosen for presentation on the stage successfully concentrate and clarify the essential dramatic action. At the same time they must be of such a nature that they possess interest in themselves. To the extent that dramatic selection fulfills these needs it serves as an invaluable guide to an audience by diverting it from irrelevancies and by distributing emphasis among what is relevant in such a manner that each segment of action is seen in its proper relation to the whole.

The second factor may be called *incremental progression*. This is an arrangement of selected materials in such a way that each successive scene of a play builds upon those which have preceded and in turn adds a new increment to the cumulative progress of the plot. Its effect is that of a steady forward movement in the dramatic action toward a logical climax and conclusion. Whenever this forward surge falters, the plot tends to sag and the dramatic action to fall apart. If it breaks down at its climactic point, the result is anti-climax and an impression of fiasco. But as long as it is successfully sustained, incremental progression is the major factor in imparting to plot a convincing effect of inevitability.

The final factor, and the one most instrumental in maintaining the interest of an audience, is *suspense*. Suspense is an arrangement of dramatic materials in such a manner that the curiosity which they stimulate about their consequences is constantly baffled by an indecisive tension between anticipation and doubt. The average human being is likely to find an immediate interest, and often a distinct pleasure, in the novelty of a totally unexpected occurrence; and, to take advantage of this fact, drama makes abundant use of surprise. Ultimately one derives the greatest satisfaction from a result which is prepared for and fulfills a definite expectation; and, for this reason, drama usually strives for an appearance of inevitability. But what continues to whet one's curiosity and constrains one to pursue a complication to its conclusion is uncertainty about the outcome. This is the tantalizing feature which preserved the neck of Scheherazade during her *Thousand and One Nights' Entertainments* and prolongs the day-to-day agony of listeners to radio serials. Suspense is the deliberate cultivation of dramatic uncertainty.

The presence of this factor, however, does not mean that the final outcome of a play is totally unpredictable. Were the final outcome of comedy and tragedy actually unpredictable, all the preceding circumstances would be so ambiguous that they would lose their value; and even such an absolute fabric of suspense as melodrama leaves no doubt that ultimately our hero will triumph and escape unscathed. Suspense is concerned, not with logical probability, but with certainty. Between it and the inevitable logic of good plot progression there is no irreconcilable conflict. As a matter of fact, much of the real effect of suspense derives from logical anticipation. All that suspense does is inject into a reasonable expectation a possibility of doubt, and thus deprive the probable of any degree of certainty. It is the tantalizing vacillation between an anticipation of what is reasonably to be expected and a final uncertainty as to actually whether, or exactly when, or precisely how it will come about which constitutes the peculiar quality of suspense. It is an uncertainty which can be resolved only by the outcome itself. To hold the attention of an audience until this outcome is revealed is, of course, its technical function.

EXPOSITION

The ability of an audience to follow and understand a dramatic action depends largely upon the dramatist's skill in making clear the circumstances which give rise to it. This explanation is known as *dramatic exposition*. Since, in a sense, the whole of a dramatic action is an exposition of the plot or theme, formal exposition may appear anywhere in a play as it is needed. But since it is at the outset of the action that most explanation is necessary, the opening of a play usually concentrates upon exposition. To this initial exposition most plays devote the greater part of the first act.

The chief problem of exposition is to provide adequate information as economically and as unobtrusively as the resources of the stage permit. By the use of appropriate stage settings, particularly in plays which stress environment, it is often possible to indicate a great deal about economic and social backgrounds, interests, tastes, and personalities. In plays designed for little or no scenery, passages of descriptive dialogue often set an imaginary stage for similar expository purposes. Since, as a rule, few characters in a play are central to the action, the principal function of the other characters is usually to provide exposition. Of this sort are *background characters,* like the townsmen in *An Enemy of the People* or the theater patrons in *Cyrano de Bergerac,* who perform a service not unlike that of stage properties; or *stock characters* like servants, companions, or family friends; or *type characters,* whose lack of personal individuality emphasizes the generic human traits and attitudes which they represent. The less individualized a character is, the more easily he can be associated with a familiar classification. By using such familiar stereotypes it is possible for a dramatist to tap the knowledge already in the possession of his audience and thus avoid lengthy explanations.

The most common means of exposition is, of course, the spoken word. Dramatic dialogue differs from ordinary conversation in that it is created to advance the action and thus to reveal information about the plot and characters. Particularly at the beginning of a play it is talk with a purpose. Here the curiosity and garrulity of characters reach epidemic proportions so that the audience may overhear what it needs to know, while the comings and goings on the stage are largely a pretext for introducing essential information. Often a play opens with a conventional prologue or an expository dialogue between servants or other secondary characters. Throughout the action it is conventional to provide various lay figures to whom the more important characters may speak and thus have a natural excuse for expressing themselves. This is the regular rôle of the so-called *confidant,* who usually appears as the confidential servant or intimate friend of a principal character. In classical drama and its derivatives the *chorus* performs a comparable function.

Dramatic exposition encounters a special problem when it is required to make clear the inner state of a character. Upon such occasions, since open rehearsal of self-analysis is scarcely a normal human practice, drama is again obliged to abandon naturalness for convention. It is thus conventional for dramatic characters to speak about themselves with preternatural fullness and astuteness. Frequently this is done in *monologue,* under the pretext of imparting confidential information to a companion. Where it is dramatically appropriate, monologue is sometimes supplemented by a *soliloquy* or an *aside.* A soliloquy is a monologue which, instead of being directed to a lay figure on the stage, is addressed directly to the audience. It is a convention by means of which a character momentarily suspends the normal dramatic action while he takes the audience into his confidence; that is, it is not a device whereby a character talks to himself, but one whereby an audience for the time being assumes the rôle of confidant. An aside is a brief parenthetic remark addressed in similar fashion either to the audience or to certain characters on the stage. In plays where neither of these devices is appropriate to the dramatic illusion a semblance of greater naturalness is gained by substituting conversations, often highly confidential and improbable, in which assorted characters discuss each other for the benefit of the audience. The fundamental difficulty, of course, is that the nature of drama precludes the opportunities which a novelist possesses for personal comment and interpretation; therefore, when it is necessary to expound personalities and ideas, a dramatist is obliged to resort to subterfuges. A common example is the character known as a *raisonneur,* who is introduced into a play for the express purpose of speaking for the dramatist and supplying the comment which he deems desirable. Regardless of the subterfuge employed, however, one characteristic of all expository devices is essential: since their sole purpose is to inform the audience, whatsoever information they convey is always to be accepted at its face value as a trustworthy revelation of the truth.

Although speech is the most comprehensive means of providing exposition, much can also be contributed by direct action on the stage. A good deal of stage business, pantomime, gesticulation, and facial expression has this purpose. The somewhat exaggerated gestures and postures traditional in acting form a sort of conventional sign-language to express the reactions of a character. Often a simple incident brings with it so many familiar associations that its mere existence produces a rich context of meaning. There is, for instance, the ghost in the opening scene of *Hamlet.* All it does is appear; yet to anyone with even a rudimentary acquaintance with ghost lore that appearance conveys an amazing amount of information. One knows that no respectable ghost walks without a specific reason; that the reason is always a matter of unfinished business, usually connected with secret crime and justice unfulfilled; that the ghost can be given rest only by a rectification of the wrongs; and that, in this particular presage of "something rotten in the state of Denmark," although the armor of the ghost bodes ill for someone, the raised beaver and benevolent countenance indicate friendliness toward those to whom it appears. This is a fairly comprehensive explanation of affairs as the play opens; yet all the essential information is implicit in a single crossing of the stage by a completely silent ghost.

There are definite limits, however, to what can be conveyed by action. Even when action is most expressive, its meaning is always implicit and has to be understood by inference. For this reason, effective expository action is usually obliged to employ special devices to draw attention to itself and guide the inferences of the audience. These are chiefly devices of structural arrangement, of which the most common are repetition, parallelism, and contrast. *Repetition* of any elements in a dramatic action naturally singles them out by emphasis and directs attention to their common features. This device is especially useful when it combines with a duplication of general features a slight deviation in particulars. For example, if one considers the three scenes of wooing in *The Way of the World,* involving Millamant and Mirabell, Millamant and Sir Willful, and Lady Wishfort and the disguised Waitwell, one cannot help noticing a similarity among them which invites comparison, as the dramatist intends. At the same time, a comparison of them immediately draws attention to certain striking dissimilarities, so that the total effect is paradoxically one of simultaneous difference and sameness, again as the dramatist intends. This device of *significant variation* is particularly valuable for directing attention to specific details in a context which gives them significance. It is used for serious purposes throughout the second act of *Hamlet,* where it provides an essential clue to Hamlet's progressive disillusionment.

Parallelism and *dramatic contrast* are special extensions of the device just discussed. Both are based upon a juxtaposition of scenes, actions, or characters which are obviously comparable. The first, by arranging two instances so that their general outlines parallel each other, and by emphasizing the features which they have in common, calls attention to inherent similarities between them which might otherwise pass unnoticed. Thus the vengeance of Laertes for his murdered father parallels that of Hamlet, and the latter's mental disturbance is paralleled by Ophelia's derangement because of her father's death. In similar fashion, the relations of Trepleff and Nina, in *The Sea Gull,* are paralleled by the relations of Nina and Tregorin. Dramatic contrast, which is the most widely used device of expository action, uses the juxtaposition of roughly comparable instances so that their partial resemblance may serve to emphasize their significant differences. For example, immediately after Hamlet has staged his play and feels ripe for vengeance on the guilty, he is successively exhibited in two contrasting scenes, each of which concerns one of the partners in guilt

—an encounter with Claudius at prayer and a visit to his mother in her chamber. The contrast between his reactions to these two situations does much to clarify the real state of his feelings and to explain the nature of his spiritual conflict. So widely used and useful for purposes of exposition and emphasis is this particular device that it is wise to be constantly alert for it. Dramatic contrast is perhaps the most ubiquitous guide to what a dramatist is trying to say.

Closely related to dramatic contrast is a device which is so fundamental to drama that it is less an artifice than an integral part of dramatic conflict. This is *dramatic irony*. In general, irony is a contrast between semblance and reality, between what the truth is assumed to be and what it actually proves to be. Ordinarily human behavior tends to be governed by what, at the moment and in the prevailing circumstances, seems to be most advantageous. In keeping with this tendency, the conflicts of drama regularly arise either from a contrast between what characters in a specific situation believe to be expedient and what in the light of absolute fact actually is expedient, or from a contrast between divergent estimates of expediency. Since no rational individual deliberately sets out to make himself ludicrous or wretched, the contrasts between purpose and result which produce both comedy and tragedy involve fundamental ironies of human life. For this reason, the spirit of irony impregnates the whole texture of drama, and the irony of its contrasts is drama's most characteristic emphasis. Under the genial auspices of comedy, the ironic spectacle of humanity laboring to be ridiculous is highly amusing. Under the critical scrutiny of satire, the ironic complacency of fools and knaves gives laughter the barb of censure. Under the grave compassion of tragedy, the ironic defeat of life by itself probes the profoundest mystery of human experience.

Whatever its methods, good dramatic exposition always fulfills two exacting requirements. In the first place, it is intrinsically interesting. No play can afford to bore its audience while it is explaining itself. For this reason expository action, because of its relative vividness and speed, holds a natural advantage over expository dialogue unless the latter is spiced with wit, humor, or emotional tensity. A famous instance of intrinsic expository interest is the opening scene of *Hamlet,* with its masterly combination of striking action, eerie atmosphere, and tense dialogue. In the second place, good dramatic exposition is always inconspicuous. It never obtrudes upon the flow of action, but, disguised beneath the cloak of normal behavior and dispersed among the natural probabilities of a situation, it is inserted casually as occasion offers. Neither is it dragged in by the hair simply because it is needed to explain a sudden turn of the action, but is introduced as early as possible so that it may have served its purpose by the time it is needed. The ideal of exposition is to inform an audience while it is unaware of the full significance of what is happening. Like the art of magic it performs the mechanics of its tricks while one's attention is diverted elsewhere. But because it is most effective when it is least apparent, a reader is obliged to pay close attention to what is said and done in a play or he may very well miss the point of much adroit dramatic exposition.

MOTIVATION

Effective dramatic action is not only comprehensible but also convincing. Drama either persuades an audience to accept what occurs on the stage as consistent with human experience or it forfeits its illusion of reality. In order to achieve this acceptance, however, it is unnecessary that incidents and characters on the stage be an exact counterpart of life. What is requisite is that the conduct of a dramatic action, in whole and in part, accord with the operative principles of human life as the audience has deduced them from its own experience. The dramatic technique of securing this conformity is known as *motivation*.

As we noted earlier, drama enjoys the initial advantage of an audience which, expecting to be satisfied, is ordinarily neither hostile nor skeptical but disposed to accept anything not patently preposterous. The dramatist's chief task, therefore, is to insure that this "willing suspension of disbelief" is not interfered with. Now, the members of a theater audience, like most human beings, are inclined to look upon themselves as reasonable creatures, whose perception of truth is guided by reasonable principles. In affirmation of this view, they normally subscribe to the proposition that every occurrence ought to have an ascertainable cause and every human action a conscious or unconscious motive. The credibility of any dramatic incident they accordingly tend to estimate in terms of its conformity with these reasonable premises. What disturbs an audience is its inability to account satisfactorily for what happens on the stage. On the other hand, it will accept without demur practically any occurrence which appears to have an adequate explanation.

Motivation is the systematic process of supplying acceptable reasons for whatever occurs in a dramatic action. Such reasons are acceptable when they concur with the laws of probability which an audience expects of drama. In this respect every audience makes an intuitive artistic distinction between drama and life. Whatever may be its views about the latter, the former it holds to stringent canons of order and logic. In acceptable drama nothing occurs without a specific cause, no one speaks or acts without a sufficient motive, life observes a rational order, and whatever exists has a logical reason for its existence. Satisfactory motivation is obliged to abide by these rules of the game. Its basic assumption is a dramatic world of logical order. Its practice is an art of subtle preparation and foreshadowing by means of which every occurrence is anticipated by an explanatory cause. Its perfection is an inevitable sequence of cause and effect.

In such a systematic scheme of life the introduction of chance or coincidence always tends to weaken a dramatic action. While undeniably both chance and coincidence do play a real part in common experience, their appearance in drama always creates a serious hazard. The reason is that inherently both constitute a breach of logical order and do violence to normal probability. Because in themselves they represent a departure from the usual, it follows that any sequence of events dependent on them becomes equally exceptional and accordingly loses its general validity. The basing of any important dramatic action upon chance or coincidence, therefore, always weakens the logic of its motivation, diminishes its probability, and reduces the force of its general human application.

Motivation is successful to the extent that it is promptly confirmed by the experience of the audience. In general practice this confirmation depends upon the answer which a play supplies to certain questions tacitly posed by every audience. Do the events of the play conform with a pattern of causation to which the audience is accustomed? Does the behavior of the characters on the stage reflect human impulses and reactions identical with those of the audience under comparable circumstances? When the answer to such questions is in the affirmative, motivation succeeds immediately; it is verified by common experience. When, on the other hand, the answer is not so certain, the essential question shifts its ground. If the circumstances of the play do not exemplify a customary pattern, then what specific justification exists for the departure? Or, to rephrase the question, precisely what sort of human beings would reasonably perform the actions set forth in the play? The tenor of this latter question indicates two of the most important principles of all motivation. The first is that any dramatic action whatsoever is satisfactorily motivated when it is shown to be appropriate to the characters involved in it. The second follows from the first: namely, that the most flexible and generally valuable source of satisfactory motivation is dramatic character. For example, any typical action is at once sufficiently motivated by simply associating it with an appropriate and familiar type of human nature. This is the method employed by Ibsen for much of the motivation in *An Enemy of the People* and by Congreve in *The Way of the World*. On the other hand, as in *Hamlet, Cyrano de Bergerac,* or *The Playboy of the Western World,* even the most extraordinary behavior can be motivated convincingly by deriving it from the idiosyncrasies of a character, so long as the singularity of the character is shown to be merely a special synthesis of common human traits. In either case the motivation is rooted in human nature, and the result is a dramatic action validated by common human experience.

It is motivation, as much as anything, which relates drama to life. To the extent that motivation issues from character, and dramatic action is a logical expression of human nature, the impingement of drama upon the meaning of life is inescapable. For this reason the ultimate significance of drama varies according to the nature and quality of its motivation.

Farce and melodrama are essentially trivial because they are more concerned with ephemeral effects than with irrefutable causes and rely more on factitious incidents than on the natural expression of character. High comedy and tragedy endeavor to account convincingly for their effects. They conceive of dramatic action as a projection of fundamental human nature with a psychologically sound motivation. Consequently they provide a vicarious experience of authentic human life. It is this particular aspect of motivation which prompts the dictum that character is drama.

TEMPO

Perhaps the least conspicuous essential of dramatic action is its timing. Any art which owes its existence to a successful creation of effects has to take into account the psychological moment most appropriate for achieving those effects. A surprise is a surprise only before one has come to expect it, and a halting jest comes lamely off. In addition, it needs to take into account the rate of movement at which a specific kind of action attains its maximum effectiveness; for such rhythms exert a subtle influence upon the sensibilities of an audience. Repartee and rapier-play alike demand nimble heels, whereas sorrow moves best at a slower pace. Finally, it must take into account the fact that the amount of time consumed by any dramatic action has a direct bearing upon its relative emphasis and its emotional connotations. The more time an action consumes, the more important it appears to be. That which is light and relatively trivial moves naturally with swift ease; that which is grave moves more ponderously because of its intrinsic weight. The pellmell piling-up of absurdities which one meets in farce has much to do with its hilarious effect. A staccato cacophony of headlong erratic actions and simultaneous broken ejaculations produces automatically an effect of confusion. On the other hand, the slow, somber throb of suffering induces an almost inevitable mood of solemnity. With a fairly constant amount of time at his disposal, it is up to the dramatist to make that time appear to fly or crawl according to the best interests of his dramatic action. This manipulation of time effects, of the speed and rhythm of a play, is known as its *tempo*.

The tempo of a play is controlled by the particular effects at which it aims and by the assimilative capacities of its audience. Thus the tempo of comedy and melodrama is usually faster than that of tragedy or serious problem drama. Often, for the sake of bringing dramatic incidents into close juxtaposition, stage time is foreshortened or telescoped or practically made to stand still; so that the actual playing time of a scene bears little relation to the time which supposedly has elapsed. Similarly the tempo of a scene is often dictated less by the time which it would naturally consume than by the amount of attention which it deserves or the amount of time which an audience requires to understand it. Although action may be rapid-fire or deliberate and slowed down by calculated pauses, to the extent that it involves intricate stage business its speed must always allow for proper comprehension. On the other hand, since its appeal is inherently more direct than that of speech, physical action naturally tends to increase tempo whereas dialogue tends to retard it. The fact of the matter is that merely following the general drift of dialogue presupposes an intellectual effort which requires a certain amount of time. The more complex the thought is, the more time it requires for comprehension. Also, as a general rule, the more time the thought requires, the more impressed an audience is likely to be with its importance. Nevertheless, dialogue itself possesses considerable latitude of tempo: characters may chatter or converse ponderously. Its tempo is controlled by weight of subject matter and rhetorical artifice. Glib recitals of the commonplace, fluent syllables, short phrases, and simple sentences make for rapid tempo. Abstruse thought, density of meaning, involved phraseology, and complex sentence structure, as they retard both enunciation and comprehension, also have the effect of slowing tempo.

Tempo is, of course, most apparent on the stage, where it forms an essential part of effective production. For this reason it is the one feature of drama most likely to be overlooked in reading a play. Tempo, however, is integral to dramatic effect; it is implicit in the script of every play; it can be ignored only at the cost of serious loss. The reader must, therefore, be cautious to follow the indications of tempo which a dramatist has built into the structure of his dialogue, incorporated in his stage directions, and implied between the lines. Unless the reader is careful to vary his pace as indicated, to visualize the relative speed of events, to give pauses their due and silence its proper eloquence, tempo fails of effect and the play loses a valuable adjunct.

TONE

Our consideration of the technical means by which drama becomes articulate may be concluded with a few remarks concerning the matter of dramatic *tone*. This intangible and somewhat elusive feature of all drama is more readily recognized than described. Essentially tone is the quality imparted to a play by the dramatist's manner of dealing with his materials—a quality which in turn endows the play with its distinctive emotional connotation. It is the spirit which pervades a dramatic action, giving it unity of effect and an emotional tincture suitable to its context. As such, it is a subtle essence distilled not from any single dramatic artifice but from the whole treatment of a situation. It is at once the overt expression of implicit dramatic meaning and the principal means of inducing in an audience a properly receptive attitude. Since the core of its value is appropriateness to the occasion, tone may be said to be the manifestation in a play of essential dramatic decorum.

The function of tone in drama is always the ancillary one of reën- forcing other dramatic elements. Thus it may serve to clarify exposition, to strengthen the credibility of motivation, to regulate tempo, or to enhance theatrical effect. Its most characteristic and valuable use is to exert a subtle control over the reactions of an audience by impregnating drama with an emotional connotation which is conducive to its proper interpretation. Without such specific guidance the responses of an audience are uncontrolled and likely to be erratic, and the chances of securing an intended dramatic effect consequently dubious. Especially in differentiating between comedy and tragedy it is important to apprise an audience as early and as definitely as possible how seriously it is to view the circumstances. The manner in which the tone of dramatic treatment contributes to this sort of control may be observed by comparing the opening scenes of *Twelfth Night* with the corresponding scenes of *Hamlet*.

The immediate object of dramatic tone is the establishment of a mood which is appropriate to the dramatic action. For the attainment of this end, it endeavors to create systematically an atmosphere which, by enveloping both play and audience in one permeating influence, will bring into harmony the dramatic action and the sensibilities of the spectators. In doing so, it levies upon resources as extensive as drama itself. Scenery, properties, costume, gesture, lighting, music, sound effects, collectively and severally, are brought to impinge upon the senses of the audience and thus to stimulate unobtrusively its sensations. Perhaps the greatest single asset is the attitude which may be imputed to dramatic characters regarding the situations in which they find themselves; for by skillfully manipulating such expressed attitudes it is often possible, through a sort of contagion, to induce a corresponding attitude in the audience. In addition, the heavy dependence of drama on dialogue makes available a resource which is so distinctive in character and so subtle in effect that it deserves special notice. As the structure and texture of dramatic speech produce variations in dramatic tempo, its manner and content also affect dramatic tone. But whereas the atmospheric pressures exerted by simple sight and sound act upon the senses of an audience from without, dramatic dialogue operates upon the sensibilities of an audience by means of pressures from within its own consciousness. The significant factor in this process is the proclivity of language for metaphorical or figurative expression: that is, for couching ideas in the form of images or symbols. Since the psychological effect of this practice is to transfer such images bodily from the spoken word into the consciousness of the hearer, linguistic imagery both acts as a powerful stimulant upon the imagination of an audience and at the same time supplies it with a ready-made store of mental images. By deliberately controlling this process, therefore, through judicious selection and systematic organization of imagery, it is possible for dramatic discourse to implant in the mind of an audience vivid incitements to a desired mood which are so indirect and subtle that they leave scarcely any awareness of what is taking place.

To illustrate this tonal use of imagery, a few examples from *Hamlet* will indicate the general method. Broadly speaking, the tragedy of *Hamlet* is the disintegration and destruction of an individual and a society under the corrosive influence of evil. This progress of destruction Shakespeare envisages as equivalent to the ravages of a virulent disease. In order to reënforce this conception, he subjects his audience to what is in effect the atmosphere of a sick-room by building into the fabric of his dialogue a whole series of images which call to mind the physical evidences of sickness and decay. These images apply both to his characters and to the world which they inhabit; for not only is Hamlet represented as a victim of malignant melancholia, but the earth itself is "thought-sick" with the malady of life. Thus, at the very beginning of the play, life appears as "an unweeded garden" gone to seed and consumed utterly by "things rank and gross in nature." The o'erhanging firmament is "a foul and pestilent congregation of vapours" beneath which men propagate in a "nasty sty . . . stew'd in corruption" as "the sun breeds maggots in a dead dog." Man himself is but a "quintessence of dust" fatted for the final banquet of politic worms or, like the dead Polonius, a potential stench of putrescent decomposition. And the play moves to its end through the charnel atmosphere of the graveyard with its grisly images of ignoble dust, rotting flesh, and malodorous bone. To supplement this general impression of decay, numerous specific details of action are also translated into the imagery of disease. For example, the murder of Hamlet's father is brought about by a "tetter" which "bark'd about" his body, "Most lazar-like, with vile and loathsome crust." Hamlet, specifically warned against letting his mind become "tainted," feels contaminated by "some vicious mole of nature" from which his whole being may "take corruption," proclaims his "wit's diseased," and plays out his rôle amid the fevers of neurasthenia, hysteria, and suspected insanity. To Claudius the peril associated with Hamlet is both a festering "ulcer" and a "hectic" raging in the blood, which "like the owner of a foul disease" he has concealed and permitted to "feed even on the pith of life." As for Gertrude, her soul is "sick" and her sense of decency "apoplex'd"; her conduct "sets a blister" on the forehead of innocent love; and her evasions of guilt but "skin and film the ulcerous place, Whiles rank corruption, mining all within, Infects unseen." The whole scheme of this imagery is brought to a focus in the scene in which Hamlet confronts his mother in her chamber with the representations of her two husbands. Here, in sharply defined contrast, the play poses the central meaning of its imagery—the tragic discrepancy between virtue's radiant health and the mildewed blight of pustulent corruption which follows the infection of evil. The use of such a focal scene, to sum up and mirror the essential thematic purport of a play, occurs frequently in drama. It may be paralleled, for instance, in such diverse plays as *The Sea Gull, The Playboy of the Western World, Cyrano de Bergerac,* and *Desire Under the Elms,* where similar schemes of imagery are also employed effectively to emphasize the dominant tone.

In addition to its own inherent significance, the tone of a play also reflects the individuality of its dramatist and the spirit of its age. It is, for example, the peculiar signature which distinguishes a play by Congreve from one by Chekhov, and it is the hallmark which differentiates the kinds of tragedy cultivated by Sophocles, Shakespeare, and O'Neill. In this respect it is closely affiliated with the *style* of a playwright and his age. Now, style is simply a conscious or unconscious manifestation of personality. It is a distinctive synthesis of background, temperament, point of view, and habit of expression. To a certain extent it is unique, and to a certain extent conventional; for style is always influenced by prevailing fashions. Because convention occupies so important a place in the theater, dramatic style preponderantly tends to be conventional and to follow contemporary fashion. Consequently, in this sense, the drama of any particular period may be said to be *stylized*: that is, it is conceived and executed in conformity with the dramatic style in vogue at the time. *Oedipus, The Misanthrope, An Enemy of the People,* and *The Dream Play* produce widely different dramatic effects. It should be noted, however, that the variance is due, not to any essential difference in dramatic truth or artistic skill, but to the striking difference in their respective style and tone. As a result of this stylizing inherent in all drama, the proper effect of any play is inseparable from its particular style. The capturing of this appropriate style is the basis of all effective production in the theater, as its sensitive recognition is the secret of all satisfactory reading of drama in the library.

THE CONTINGENCIES OF AN ATTITUDE

In the last analysis, dramatic technique is as good as the effects which it produces, and dramatic art is as valuable as the human experience which it provides. Both effect and value, however, are contingent upon the attitude one takes toward the whole dramatic experience. No play can possibly succeed in its avowed aim unless one's attitude is favorable to its success. For example, Chekhov describes *The Sea Gull* as a comedy; but, depending upon whether one actually views the situation as comic or tragic, the fate of Treplest can produce diametrically opposite effects, with a corresponding disparity of significance. And the plight of Alceste in *The Misanthrope* is quite likely to arouse indignation unless one finds him ridiculous, as Molière intends.

In order to achieve its intended effect, therefore, drama is obliged to insure an appropriate attitude in its audience. Now, essentially, the attitude of an audience indicates how it *feels* about a dramatic situation; that is, it expresses the emotional equation which an audience makes between what happens on the stage and its personal sense of values. Consequently, control over the attitude of an audience entails a control over its feelings. Should its reaction be other than that intended, the effect produced by a play is grotesque and unsatisfactory. Should there be no reaction, or at best one which indicates little feeling one way or another, the result is fatal. Indifference is the one attitude which a play cannot survive. An indifferent audience is prima-facie evidence that a play has failed—a fact promptly confirmed by an anemic box office and an empty theater. Every successful play promotes a reaction and induces an attitude hospitable to its intended effect. This state of emotional participation in a dramatic action is technically known as *empathy*.

Because drama is based upon conflict, much of its appeal is that inherent in any contest. Now, whether the specific contest be a football game, a chess match, or a play, the interest and excitement one derives from it are usually proportional to one's personal stake in the outcome. The intensity of one's emotional reaction increases as one takes sides in the contest and feels a personal triumph or defeat in the result. Furthermore, such an allegiance naturally disposes one to favor one side and to oppose the other. To restate this in technical terminology: empathy is rarely neutral; by identifying itself with certain components of a dramatic action and opposing others, it normally expresses *sympathy* for the former and *antipathy* toward the latter.

Every dramatic conflict presupposes such a distribution of sympathy and antipathy on the part of the audience. In order to promote a correct allocation of sympathy, drama conventionally builds its action around one character, or a group of characters functioning as a unit, whom it singles out to serve as a sort of standard-bearer for interests presumably congenial to the audience. This character, often inaccurately referred to as the hero of the play, is technically known as the *protagonist,* a term which literally means "the principal contestant." His status as the principal contestant he owes, not to the fact that he is conspicuously heroic or provocative of admiration or affection, but to the fact that he is the proponent of interests with which the audience is identified. Consequently he and his associates stand in a special relationship to the sympathies of the audience, and his fortunes epitomize the significance of the contest. Whatsoever sets itself against him and his interests, be it another individual, a social force, environment, or destiny, constitutes his dramatic *antagonist,* or "opposed contestant." Because the protagonist thus crystallizes the issues of the conflict and focuses the attention and sympathy of the audience, his function also establishes the point of view from which the play is to be evaluated.

Because an audience tends to measure actions on the stage by the same general rule of thumb which it uses in its daily life, its attitude primarily reflects its own experience. On the other hand, this natural attitude is constantly subjected to, and inevitably colored by, the attitude which the dramatist himself adopts toward life and his dramatic materials. Between this attitude of the dramatist and the final effect of a play there is always a very close correlation. For example, if a playwright's attitude toward his subject is one of simple amusement, the effect of his play is that of pure entertainment. If it is one of scientific curiosity, the effect is that of methodical analysis. If it is critical and censorious, the result is satire. If it is didactic, its edifying effect may range from dispassionate discussion or defense of a thesis to open preachment or propaganda. Thus many common varieties of drama owe their origin and purpose to the attitude of the dramatist. They achieve their effects by imposing his attitude upon the audience.

A dramatist's attitude toward life has a special bearing upon the kind of dramatic illusion which he chooses to create. Dramatic illusions of reality naturally vary in accordance with the concept of reality which underlies them. In general, concepts of reality differ from one another according to the degree in which they equate reality with the perceptible phenomena of physical existence. At one extreme reality may be conceived to be that which has a demonstrable physical existence validated by common sensuous perception. At the opposed extreme such physical phenomena may be regarded as constituting no more than partial or superficial manifestations of a reality which can be conceived only as an intellectual abstraction. And between these materialistic and idealistic extremes exist many possible gradations.

Within the province of drama, a playwright who seeks reality in the commonplaces of ordinary human life is said to be a *realist,* and his effort to reproduce a semblance of familiar experience results in an illusion of *realism.* Sometimes this interest in "things as they are," or rather as they appear to be, is concerned less with the simple evidences of their existence than with the natural or social processes which they illustrate. This essentially scientific preoccupation is known as *naturalism* and results in a naturalistic illusion in which life appears as a mechanism dominated by inexorable natural laws. At other times a realistic dramatist's impatience with the mere facts of existence may extend to the mechanistic principles which engage the naturalist. In such instances he often seeks refuge in *symbolism* and strives for an illusion in which familiar realities are endowed with a transcendental significance by exemplifying aspects of abstract philosophic truth.

Approaching the problem somewhat differently, a dramatist may find reality not so much in the objective phenomena which one perceives as in the subjective concepts derived from these perceptions. He may hold, for instance, that the reality revealed by human experience is actually the organic design implicit in the flux of appearances; that, stripped of superficial irrelevancies and reduced to the dominant outlines of essential form and significance, it is basically an idea of structural order and proportion. A dramatist who holds this view of reality adopts the attitude of *classicism* established by the ancient Greeks, and the illusion for which he strives is one of abstract reality embodied in a pattern of classical decorum. In contradistinction to this generic view, a dramatist may take the position that, as far as human consciousness is concerned, reality is primarily an individual matter; that, in effect, it is substantially whatever an individual conceives it to be. On the ground that every human individual necessarily inhabits a world which is circumscribed by his own sensibilities, he may hold that, in the nature of the case, reality is simply whatsoever in individual experience possesses human significance. According to this conception, reality comprises the external environment of an individual to the extent that he is aware of it, but it also includes his awareness of those inner aspirations and impulsions, those ideals, convictions, and even delusions which give human significance to individual life. Essentially this is the attitude of *romanticism*, which endeavors to capture in its illusion the reality of man's subjective life. Sometimes this illusion stresses the romantic idiosyncrasies of individual impulse to such a degree that imagination is divorced from both common experience and rational restraint, and the result is *fantasy*. At other times it concentrates so exclusively upon the inner life of the individual mind and emotions that it deliberately distorts its representation of external environment to conform with the impression which that environment makes upon an individual consciousness. The result is an eclectic and arbitrary illusion which attempts to project concretely the reality of a highly subjective experience. The attitude and methods involved in this procedure constitute what is known as *expressionism*.

THE EVALUATION OF DRAMA

The attitude one adopts toward a dramatic experience is inseparable from the value one places upon it. As the proof of a pudding is in the eating, the value of a play is in the human nourishment one derives from it. But in estimating such nutritional values one has to deal with a highly miscellaneous fare adapted to heterogeneous tastes. From time to time in its checkered career the theater has been variously a place of evil resort, a haven for idle dalliance, a public forum, a temple of the arts, and a sanctuary of religious devotion. Its works present a comparable motley to the view. Judicious appraisal of them, therefore, is always obliged to weigh the relative values of widely divergent human interests.

Evaluation of drama, whether it proceed from systematic critical analysis or simple instinctive reaction, hinges upon two major considerations: the technical skill with which a play strives to achieve its appointed effect and the final human significance of what it accomplishes. The first is an esthetic consideration which estimates a play's success as a work of art. Since it applies to technical matters already discussed at length, it requires no further notice here beyond calling attention to the fact that its basic criteria are effectiveness in terms of the prevailing dramatic medium, naturalness of method, and appropriateness to the desired illusion of reality.

The second consideration is broadly philosophical and as complex as human life. Like all value judgments it is bound to be highly personal; yet ultimately it calls into question the validity of one's own judicial standards. For this reason judgments of final human value have to be made with great caution. In particular, one must be cautious about pre-judging a play arbitrarily by applying a standard of absolute values to conditions which are fundamentally relative. For example, one may decide that *Hamlet* has greater human value than *The Way of the World* on the grounds that tragedy is a form of drama superior to comedy, that depiction of the passions is nobler than the portrayal of manners, and that disaster is more important than amusement. While these grounds are, of course, arguable, any assumption of their universal validity raises some pertinent questions. For what purposes is tragedy superior to comedy? Why is suffering a more commendable spectacle than rational behavior? Is not the importance of disaster precisely its interference with the enjoyment of life, and if so, how can this enjoyment be less important than disaster? Undoubtedly there are qualitative distinctions to be observed here, but the final human values concerned are necessarily relative.

The evaluation of any play in terms of absolute standards always involves a confusion among categories of experience and a perspective too narrow for the scope of life. There is no cogent reason why *The Way of the World* should be judged by *Hamlet,* or why the value of every play should be measured by either. There is a time for laughter and a time for tears; and not everything that swims need be a whale. Intrinsically a good tragedy is not more valuable than a good comedy. Even drawing-room entertainment can be unexcelled in its kind. And among kinds, who is to say which is invariably the most valuable? As a matter of fact, one can never be certain that any established standard of values is adequate for every occasion. Plays are designed to present their own credentials, and often the evidence supporting these credentials both expands one's experience and alters one's basis of judgment. Consequently, because the conditions continually change, one's evaluation of a play usually amounts less to an absolute judgment based upon nebulous universal criteria than to a simple acceptance or rejection of the specific value which the dramatist himself places upon his play.

This value is implicit in a dramatist's attitude toward his materials and his treatment of them. The prevailing seriousness of Shakespeare's attitude toward *Hamlet* is eloquent of the grave importance which he attaches to the play. The dispassionate compassion of Chekhov reflects the inconclusive irony which he sees in *The Sea Gull.* Synge's ribald integrity closely parallels the paradox which in *The Playboy of the Western World* buoyantly floats lusty farce upon the ground swell of authentic folk temperament. To the extent that one's own attitude coincides with that of the dramatist one automatically approves the values which it implies. When one's attitude differs, one registers a disagreement on values which impugns the justice of the dramatist's attitude. Thus, in the last analysis, the evaluation of a play is a pronouncement upon the acceptability of the playwright's attitude.

Now, as a rule, the acceptability of a dramatist's attitude depends upon its appropriateness to the occasion and upon the intellectual maturity which it reveals. Therefore, in addition to discriminating among the kinds of attitude discussed earlier, dramatic evaluation also appraises the essential quality of an attitude. For instance, it is necessary to take into account whether a dramatist's attitude is sincere or not, whether it is serious or playful, profound or superficial. What does it indicate of broad human experience, of psychological astuteness, of philosophic depth, of ethical sensitivity? Is it pragmatic or idealistic? Is it consistent with reasonable common sense, or is it sentimental? Does it reflect the self-conscious worldly wisdom of the sophisticate, or is it naïve? These qualities impart not only widely divergent values to a dramatist's attitude, but values which inherently vary according to the circumstances. For example, the human value of plays like *The Misanthrope* and *The Way of the World* is measured in degrees of sophistication. The validity of *An Enemy of the People* derives from its practical appraisal of social problems, its psychological acuity, and its ethical idealism. Without psychological accuracy and philosophical truth *The Dream Play* is only a bewildering mirage. Divorced from its idealistic sentiment, *Cyrano de Bergerac* is a preposterous charade of wax figures. On the other hand, the sentimental tenderness appropriate to Cyrano's love for Roxane is by no means equally appropriate to Malvolio's wooing of Olivia in *Twelfth Night*. A transference of Molière's elegant sophistication to *The Playboy of the Western World* reduces the latter play to vulgar buffoonery. And an application of Synge's detached irreverence to *Desire Under the Elms* dissolves its poignant frustrations into uncouth barnyard melodrama. As the circumstances change, the quality of an attitude changes its value.

What constitutes the appropriateness and the qualitative value of a dramatist's attitude is, in short, its critical maturity. It is the comprehensiveness of human experience, the capacity for precise and profound understanding, and the judicial wisdom and integrity reflected in it which argue validity and inspire confidence. To the extent that these qualities are revealed in a play one has no alternative but to accept the value of its testimony. This propriety and cogency of valuation is the aim of all good drama. The measure of its success in attaining this end is the final measure of its artistic and human greatness.

THE DEVELOPMENT
OF
DRAMA

The Development of Drama

TYPES OF DRAMA

S A PART of the cultural tradition of western Europe the art of drama has been practiced for more than two thousand years. With only one major interruption during this span, a host of dramatists—famous, obscure, and often anonymous—have labored under all sorts of social and theatrical conditions to provide dramatic experiences which possess human value. Spurred by changing theatrical facilities, veering tastes, and the constant demand for novelty, they have experimented tirelessly in an effort to perfect their methods and to extend the boundaries of their art. The surviving result has been a profusion of dramatic literature which, at first glance, appears to be as varied as it is bewildering.

Upon closer examination, however, the greater part of this variety turns out to be more superficial than significant. In many instances it represents no more than abortive experimentation, the net accomplishment of which has been but to demonstrate the stringent limitations of the theatrical medium. More often it reflects simply a modification or refinement of established techniques; for drama is adept at changing its costumes without altering its real identity. As a matter of fact, because its possibilities are contingent upon the nature of its artistic medium, much of drama is bound to remain invariable regardless of time or place or intention. A play is always restricted to what can be presented effectively in action, speech, and spectacle. Since the human capacities of actor and audience are not subject to radical change, the general scope and structure of drama, together with its basic principles of exposition and appeal, are obliged to remain roughly constant. Mere mechanical variations amount to no more than alternative means of employing the same technique. Thus such apparently diverse comedies as Terence's *The Brothers,* Molière's *School for Wives,* and Somerset Maugham's *The Circle,* in spite of superficial differences in technique, actually use the same methods to achieve the same end, and in *Lysistrata* and *Arms and the Man* Aristophanes and Shaw have written substantially the same kind of play. Constrained by the nature of its art to progress cautiously and

41

tentatively, drama has always tended to be conservative and singularly tenacious of traditional practices. It has preferred a growth of gradual mutation and accretion rather than radical innovation. Even its most revolutionary developments have been little more than an accommodation of new interests or facilities to customary dramatic uses. Consequently, the two thousand years of drama from the *Oresteia* of Aeschylus to Eugene O'Neill's *Mourning Becomes Electra* have produced less significant variety in purpose and technique than at first appears or one might expect.

Occasionally, on the other hand, amid the superficial versatility of the theater there have appeared certain differences in dramatic intention which are both genuine and fundamental. These variations take on significance because they involve divergent conceptions of the function of dramatic art. Differing in their basic premises, they have impelled drama to exploit different categories of human interest and to employ distinctive techniques for the purpose of producing essentially different kinds of effect. As these variations have become deliberate and have been brought to a point of genuine artistic achievement, they have resulted in the creation of substantially different *types of drama.*

The commonly recognized types of drama are largely the product of two variable factors in the theatrical medium. Of these, the first and perhaps more influential is the audience, especially in its capacity of index to the prevailing tastes and preoccupations of its time. Over the centuries, from Periclean Athens to modern Broadway, theatrical audiences have altered considerably, if not in individual human nature, at least in collective personality, current interests, and point of view. Because of this alteration drama has been under the constant necessity of establishing fresh points of contact with its supporters. The boisterous satirical extravaganzas with which Aristophanes delighted an Athenian populace were ill adapted to the more self-conscious decorum of the audience for which Molière wrote his greatest comedies. During the latter nineteenth century the scientific and sociological preoccupations of the audience introduced an emphasis in human experience which demanded a new method of dramatic interpretation. In order to keep pace with these periodic changes in interest and expectation, drama has been obliged to shift its own ground accordingly. And sometimes the shift has been radical enough to evolve a new type of play.

The second factor which affects the basic character of drama is the theater itself and the appointments of its stage. If human nature is the soul of drama, the theater is its body, from which the whole form and personality of the art can never be divorced. But theaters have sprung from the most heterogeneous origins—from temple precincts, inn-yards, schoolrooms, tennis courts. In size they have ranged from the vast amphitheater of the ancient Greeks to the intimate studio theater. The stage itself, at one time or another, has been a bare platform. a massive architectural façade, a framed picture of flats and wings and backdrops, an elaborately furnished room, or a geometrical design anchored in space. Its resources have ranged from crude machines and rudimentary properties to the most elaborate equipment for the production of theatrical effects. Inevitably these variant facilities have exerted an influence upon the plays designed to utilize them. Often, as in the substitution of electric lighting for the earlier illumination by gas or candle, the chief effect of the change has been merely to improve the mechanics of performing an established function. Not infrequently, however, such innovations have also enhanced the flexibility and control of stage effects to such an extent that they have modified the character of drama. Some have added new dimensions to the scope of theatrical art. Some, by contributing new material resources, have altered the form and texture of the artistic product. And some, by revising the basic concept of the stage and its integral relationship to drama, have transformed its whole dramatic function.

Variations in the theater and the audience affect both the form and the content of drama, although not always at the same time or in the same degree. Ordinarily a change in one without a corresponding change in the other is insufficient to produce a radical difference in the dramatic result. For example, in specific content, point of view, and stage facilities Shakespeare's *Richard II* and Shaw's *Saint Joan* differ considerably; yet so alike are they in form and technique that they remain essentially the same kind of play. Conversely, although Sophocles' *Oedipus the King* and Ibsen's *Ghosts* differ in facilities, form, and mechanics, their basic similarity of content and purpose unites them in the same dramatic category. In neither case does the difference in form or content alone result in a fundamentally different type of drama. On the other hand, the structure and facilities of the ancient Greek theater did combine with the propensities of its audience to produce a theatrical spectacle which, in its appropriateness to the special circumstances, is unique in both form and substance. In the theater of Shakespeare's England a similar combination produced equally unique results. And each of these combinations is as alien to the other as both are to the theaters of Ibsen or O'Neill. It is from such fortuitous matings of stage and audience, of form and substance, that the significant types of drama have been born.

The more important of these dramatic types are illustrated in the plays reprinted in this volume and considered specifically in the remaining discussion. Actually the commonly recognized types of drama fall into two somewhat different categories. The first consists of general types, which represent a logical and analytical endeavor to differentiate broad aspects of human experience and to express an appropriate attitude toward their significance. These types are apparently indigenous to drama and have existed continuously from its earliest appearance without respect to place or time. To this category belong such generic types as tragedy, comedy, melodrama, and farce. The second category comprises types of drama which are in effect special adaptations of the more general types. These types are primarily historical; that is, they have come into existence from time to time during the historical development of drama in response to special conditions and in order to exploit special interests. Sporadic by nature, they are neither inherent nor universal in drama. They have continued or recurred as the special circumstances which originally evoked them have either repeated themselves in the theater or have succeeded in perpetuating their general appeal.

COMEDY AND TRAGEDY

The general types of drama represent perennial human reactions to the significance of life. Broadly speaking, they reflect either of two possible attitudes. The one is an attitude of detached amusement, which views human life as essentially an agreeable experience, vexed at times, to be sure, by transitory vicissitudes, but, when considered in proper perspective, not to be taken too seriously. The other sees in human life a not altogether satisfactory experience involving fundamental difficulties and maladjustments grave enough to warrant serious personal concern. From these contrasting views derive the two basic types of drama, known respectively as *comedy* and *tragedy*.

There is an often-quoted remark by Horace Walpole to the effect that "The world is a comedy to those that think, a tragedy to those who feel." However true or false this general observation may be, the fact remains that comedy is essentially an intellectual type of drama. Rationality is the basis of its attitude toward life, as its appeal is ultimately to the judicious reason. Its aim is to examine the circumstances of human life in just perspective and to evaluate them in the light of common sense. To this end it habitually cultivates an attitude of detachment, endeavors to treat its materials objectively, and implies a process of critical discrimination and judgment. Its initial premise is that impotent agitation over conditions which lie beyond human control, being futile, is wholly irrational; that, on the contrary, the secret of human success and happiness is intelligent adaptation to the conditions which prevail. Consequently it confines its attention to those areas of individual and social behavior which are appropriate to such an adaptation and are presumably, therefore, under human jurisdiction.

Within this deliberately restricted sphere comedy makes the logical assumption that any enterprise rationally conceived and executed is bound to conclude in a manner commensurate with reasonable human desires and standards of propriety. Hence the normal culmination of comedy is the so-called happy ending. Any interruptions of this rational and satisfactory process are manifestly the result of temporary confusion or an irrational lapse into stupidity or folly. While momentarily disconcerting, and perhaps even distressing to those actually involved, such aberrations scarcely subvert the rational basis of human life or impugn its essential justice. Inadvertent errors readily yield to truth and common sense, while persistence in folly richly deserves its reward of absurdity. In this critical perspective the blundering of humanity becomes more amusing than alarming. Indeed, common sense dictates that it be treated with proper levity. To a detached observer its incongruity with human capacities and pretensions is as ludicrous as it is diverting. Even its experiments in iniquity appear less a symptom of elemental depravity than a misguided abandonment of good sense meriting the censure of ridicule. For these reasons the spirit of comedy is the spirit of laughter: not because comedy concentrates exclusively upon the hilarious, but because it reflects an attitude toward human life in which laughter is the natural and most appropriate expression of critical good sense.

Tragedy represents a radically different approach. Rejecting compromises of expediency and common sense, it stresses the fact that life embraces more than strictly rational considerations and that most compelling human experiences involve emotional pressures which preclude an attitude of serene detachment. It observes that the most characteristic aspirations of humanity, as well as many of its most admirable actions, spring from intense personal feeling and often reflect quite irrational impulses. Finally, it recognizes that, as the vital meaning of any experience is registered in its emotional impact upon those concerned, its relative importance is bound to be an individual matter. For better or for worse, man is obliged to live and die as an individual within the scope of his unique capacity. Regardless of hypothetical perspectives or objective critical standards, his actual happiness or misery is defined by his own subjective experience. But in order to appreciate the full significance of these truths it is necessary to identify oneself with the specific individuals affected, to put oneself into their precise situation, and to share their point of view and unique reactions.

Such a vicarious participation in human experience is the purpose of tragedy. In the light of this purpose, what is most important about human life is not so much an objective appraisal of its rationality as a sympathetic comprehension of its emotional reality. Consequently tragedy concentrates upon what happens to an individual rather than upon what he does; its concern is more with passion than with action; its characteristic substance is a spectacle of human suffering. From this point of view the vicissitudes of mortal experience appear less reassuring than is customary in comedy. As tragedy sees it, human life is no holiday excursion amid charted inland waters, but a hazardous venture upon treacherous seas which man is ill equipped to navigate. It is a voyage vexed by adverse winds and unexpected tempests and hidden reefs, in which too often the hapless mariner hears the sirens singing, and disaster is the inexorable penalty of shipwreck. Particularly it is the ironic

GOSHEN COLLEGE LIBRARY
GOSHEN, INDIANA

pathos of the shipwreck which engages the attention of tragedy. For tragedy recognizes the paradox that perhaps never is man's mortal adventure so magnificent and awe-inspiring as in its terrible capacity for destruction. Moreover, it perceives that man's own capacity for greatness rarely shows to better advantage than in extremity or appears more noble than when pitted against insuperable odds. It is the austere irony of this sublimity in disaster which tragedy endeavors to communicate with a compassion too poignant for laughter and an awe too profound for tears.

Comedy and tragedy represent formal and somewhat arbitrary attempts to interpret human experience logically on the basis of contrasting premises. It is these premises, rather than any marked divergence in subject matter, which differentiate the two types. While it is true that some subjects, more than others, lend themselves naturally to comic or tragic treatment, in the main the raw materials of life tend to be neutral; they acquire their immediate connotation from the contingent circumstances and are therefore susceptible to either comic or tragic interpretation. Marital infidelity, for example, serves equally well as a common subject for such polar extremes as high tragedy and bedroom farce, while even death can provide both the somber anguish of Synge's *Riders to the Sea* and the hilarity of Noel Coward's *Blithe Spirit*. The difference in value is one of interpretation. It is this difference in interpretation which comedy and tragedy endeavor to formalize. Psychologically the process is justified by the fact that no audience can be grave and gay at the same time. Logically it derives from the principle that, while a dramatic effect may be either amusing or profoundly moving, it cannot be both at the same time without ambiguity and a consequent loss of force.

Because, however, the subject materials of comedy and tragedy do overlap, and because human experience itself rarely conforms with strictly logical principles, drama not infrequently rebels against artificial restraint in a desire for more flexible interpretation. Especially in periods concerned with realism there is a tendency to insist that the strands of human experience form a variegated pattern neither wholly bright nor dark, and that any attempt to impose upon them an arbitrary uniformity is simply not true to life. The result has been a series of recurring experiments to evolve some intermediate type of drama which would combine the characteristic features of comedy and tragedy and balance serious interests with pleasant entertainment. Too indeterminate in scope and nature for any very precise designation, this somewhat amorphous type has appeared from time to time under various names—*pastoral, tragicomedy, comedy drama, heroic comedy,* and sometimes, for want of more adequate description, simply as a *play* or *drama*. Essentially a compromise designed to exploit the virtues of both comedy and tragedy while avoiding their restrictions, it endeavors to make up in variety and flexibility what it loses in sustained effect. Throughout the history of drama it reflects a persistent search for a third mode of interpreting human experience, and in the modern theater it is perhaps the most characteristic type.

The three types just discussed exhaust the logical possibilities of dramatic interpretation. They constitute the basic types of all drama. Closely associated with them, however, are two derivative types known as *farce* and *melodrama*. These latter bear to comedy and serious drama about the same relationship as shadow to substance. Their distinguishing features are their frank dedication to superficial entertainment and their indifference to any genuine interpretation of human life. Farce employs the mechanics of comedy to produce laughable situations with little regard for their normal plausibility or their reflection of actual human nature. Melodrama combines the suspense, conflict, and emotional intensity of serious drama with the facile resolutions of comedy to fabricate theatrical thrills under a specious semblance of reality. Both types emphasize plot and situation at the expense of character and social context. Essentially both are exercises in technical virtuosity, which, when performed with skill, can be vastly entertaining but which neither pretend nor provide any further emolument.

The distinctive types of drama which comprise the artistic achievement of the European theater are all historical adaptations of the foregoing general types to special theatrical conditions. The more important of these specialized types are discussed elsewhere in this book in connection with the plays chosen to illustrate them. Meanwhile, however, since the types themselves are historical in origin, it may be useful to give some brief attention to the historical context of which they are a part. Therefore, while it is neither feasible nor necessary to undertake here a detailed account of theatrical history, the following pages provide an outline sketch of the major dramatic developments in western Europe which may serve as a background for the individual plays to be considered later.

ANCIENT DRAMA

In the cultural tradition of western Europe there are four major epochs of notable dramatic achievement. The first of these is the period of ancient classical drama, which flourished in Greece during the fifth and fourth centuries and in Rome during the third and second centuries before Christ. The second is the Renaissance, which found its most effective expression in the drama of Elizabethan England. The third is the latter half of the seventeenth century, which saw the perfection of French neo-classical drama. And the fourth is the period of modern drama extending from the last quarter of the nineteenth century to the present time. In each of these epochs distinctive theatrical conditions resulted in the creation of plays which not only contributed significantly to the development of dramatic art but have retained their effectiveness in the repertory of enduring dramatic literature.

The ancient drama of Greece had its inception in religious ritual, probably in honor of the god Dionysus, and never entirely lost its religious tincture. Originally it was of a processional nature and consisted chiefly of choral odes. With the gradual addition of individualized actors to supplement the chorus, emphasis shifted to dialogue and mimetic action until eventually the result became the earliest form of authentic drama, *classical tragedy*. By the time of its golden age, in the fifth century B.C., Greek tragedy had evolved into an impressive communal spectacle subsidized by the state and presented during special spring festivals in vast open-air amphitheaters. Something of its splendor is preserved in the surviving plays of its greatest masters, Aeschylus (524–455), Sophocles (495–406), and Euripides (c. 480–c. 407), which amply indicate its rich variety of human connotation.

Greek tragedies were regularly presented in groups of three, followed by a lighter after-piece known as a satyr-play. The four plays constituted an entire day's entertainment provided by a single dramatist in a prize competition which was open to the public. Usually the three tragedies possessed only very loose affiliations with each other, like the several movements of a symphony; but sometimes they were coördinated into a closely knit trilogy, as in the sole surviving example, the *Oresteia* of Aeschylus. In deference to the semi-religious auspices, classical tragedy was prevailingly serious and dealt with themes drawn from familiar mythology. Designed for performance on a simple stage before a huge audience, its action was broad, formal, and deliberately stylized. The burden of its dramatic effect fell largely on the declamatory poetry of its dialogue. With this dialogue it mingled antiphonal passages accompanied by music, choral chants, and interpretative dances, to produce a dramatic spectacle not unlike modern grand opera. In structure and technique it inaugurated one of the basic forms of world drama, established many of the artistic principles of serious drama, and has served as a model for generations of admirers and imitators.

Somewhat later than tragedy, and as a counterbalance to it, Greece also developed two varieties of comedy. The earlier, which is preserved in the so-called Old Comedy of Aristophanes (c. 445–c. 385), was a boisterous extravaganza compounded about equally of ribald farce, ingenious fancy, robust realism, rugged common sense, and hard-hitting personal satire. Casual in methods, intimate in manner, and addressed specifically to a homogeneous audience of freethinking, outspoken Athenian citizens, it was an admirable vehicle for contemporary comment and local allusion. But, once the special conditions which fostered it altered, its general effectiveness quickly declined, and it has survived more as a pungent historical memory than as an active dramatic force.

For this reason it is not represented in this volume. A distant echo of its spirit may be found in such dissimilar places as the Gilbert and Sullivan operettas and some of Shaw's comedies.

Its successor, known as New Comedy, survives only in a few fragments from the work of its greatest exponent, Menander (c. 342–292). Its general characteristics, however, are reflected in the frank imitations produced by the Roman comic playwrights, Plautus (c. 254–184) and Terence (c. 195–159). New Comedy provided a coördinated series of lively scenes based upon mistake, misadventure, and intrigue. It introduced an integrated plot dealing with the affairs of ordinary human beings and often built around a love story of sorts. Motivating its confusions by misapprehension and deliberate deception, it made liberal use of disguise, mistaken identity, trickery, and surprising disclosures to create an effect of suspense and comic irony. Its basic mechanics were those of intrigue, of the contrived error, of plot and counterplot, usually under the manipulation of a clever servant. Employing conventionalized character types and stereotyped situations, it ranged from broad farce to deft character delineation and amusing social satire. In general, it reduced comic entertainment to a flexible and easily imitated formula, and as such laid the foundation for centuries of European comic practice.

Historically Roman drama was little more than an appendage of Greek drama, to which it owed most of its inspiration and substance. Indeed, Plautus and Terence are important less because of their innate dramatic genius than because of their capacity for successful imitation and the accident that their plays preserve an otherwise vanished form of drama. Seneca (died 65 A.D.), the sole surviving representative of Roman tragedy, is even less impressive in his rhetorical, often undramatic dilution of his Greek tragic models. On the other hand, Roman drama enjoys an historical importance out of all proportion to its intrinsic merit by virtue of the fact that in time it became the chief agent in transmitting the influence of classical drama to the later theater of western Europe. While the Roman playwrights themselves have not succeeded in holding the stage, they and their drama have been reincarnated in the work of more fortunate successors. It is in these more durable reincarnations that they are represented in this volume.

During the years of the empire Roman drama, which had always been obliged to maintain a precarious competition with cruder forms of entertainment, rapidly degenerated into vulgar and sensational spectacle. Artistically debauched and increasingly opposed by the growing power of the Christian church, it ultimately expired in the general disintegration of the empire. For centuries afterward there existed in Europe no living drama. When by the ninth century the dramatic impulse began to revive, it was to make a fresh start and to follow a course of development which in many respects repeated that of ancient drama.

RENAISSANCE DRAMA

Like the Greek before it, medieval drama originated in the celebration of religious festivals. From simple mimetic embellishments of the liturgy connected with the Easter and Christmas services arose the practice of enacting brief episodes drawn from Biblical history or the lives of the saints. The purpose, which was strictly didactic, was to provide a kind of visual aid in the religious instruction of unlettered minds. The auspices were amateur; the technique remained primitive and naïve; and the total effect was more narrative and expository than genuinely dra-- matic. But the practice gained in popularity and soon began to acquire apocryphal additions designed for pure entertainment. Yielding to secular pressures, it gradually passed out of the church and the control of the clergy into the hands of the medieval guilds. At the same time the plays, although remaining individually short and episodic, rapidly increased in number and in correlation. In certain instances they finally coalesced into large cycles of episodes, which summarized the salient features of Christian doctrine from the Fall of Lucifer to the Day of Judgment and which required several days for their complete presentation. Commonly enacted with simple furnishings upon multiple stages or a procession of "pageants," or floats, the plays correspondingly grew more pretentious and spectacular in their staging. Essentially naïve and crudely articulated, anachronistically realistic, and rudimentary in dramatic conception, these little fragments of drama, known variously as *miracles* and *mysteries,* for centuries provided dramatic sustenance to a growing audience, and in doing so established a basis for later dramatic conceptions.

As the miracle play was an embodiment of Scriptural narrative, the second important development of medieval drama was a didactic extension of the sermon. Exploiting the medieval fondness for allegory, the *moral play,* or *morality,* endeavored to give concrete and symbolic expression to the problem of human salvation. In terms of personified abstractions it exemplified the pilgrimage of Everyman toward the grave, the perpetual struggle of Virtues and Vices for the possession of Man's Soul, and the dispute between Justice and Mercy in the ultimate judgment of Mankind. By virtue of the conflict implicit in its themes and the concreteness of its methods, the morality was inherently dramatic and immediate in its contact with familiar life. But because it was also severely restricted in scope, it was soon forced to adapt itself to miscellaneous, and sometimes incongruous, uses in order to survive. Diverted to religious controversy, secular history, humanistic culture, and heterogeneous social commentary, it enjoyed a highly versatile career until finally it became the native stock upon which was grafted much of subsequent popular drama.

Although of great importance historically, medieval drama produced few plays of much intrinsic value. Its abiding contribution to European drama was certain dramatic forms and methods which could be, and have been, adapted to more impressive uses. For example, the miracle supplied the mold for most historical drama from Shakespeare to Sherwood's *Abe Lincoln in Illinois*. In its turn, the morality has fathered such diverse offspring as Goethe's *Faust*, Ibsen's *Peer Gynt*, and Strindberg's *The Dream Play*. More immediately, however, the artistic fruition of medieval drama came in the Renaissance.

During the sixteenth and seventeenth centuries western Europe witnessed its second great epoch of dramatic achievement. These centuries saw the culmination of a sustained dramatic development which took its particular character from a convergence of the medieval tradition with a reawakened interest in ancient drama. Generally speaking, this development followed two main courses. In Italy and France a humanistic preoccupation with classical drama became the dominant factor and promoted an ambition to reproduce the artistic effects of the ancients. The result was an abundance of dramatic theory and critical principle buttressed with elaborate experimentation in stage architecture and theatrical practice; but the theory-ridden drama itself unfortunately failed to rise above stiff academic imitation which was more notable for antiquarian zeal than for inherent vitality. It was not until after two centuries of fanning dead ashes that in France, during the late seventeenth century, the embers of antiquity were finally rekindled to a second flame. Meanwhile in Spain and England a lusty native tradition laid irreverent hands upon the classics and merged the medieval and the ancient with a unique Renaissance flamboyance to produce something new under the sun of drama. Although practically independent of one another, the dramatic developments of the two countries followed amazingly similar courses, to culminate, on the one hand, in the prodigious genius of Lope de Vega (1562–1635) and, on the other, in the universal art of William Shakespeare (1564–1616). In Spain, however, drama closely identified itself with idiosyncrasies of taste and interest peculiar to the Spanish temperament and culture of the period. Its singularity of spirit tended toward isolation, and, not being readily transportable, it came to exert only a minor influence upon the rest of Europe. The drama of England was both less isolated in its interests and more universal in its appeal. For this reason the distinctive dramatic genius of the Renaissance found its most effective and influential expression in the drama of Elizabethan England.

Abounding in vigor and often uncritical versatility, Elizabethan drama explored a wide range of human interests and dramatic manners. If in the course of its varied experiments it produced much that was abortive or of trivial significance, at its best its impressive galaxy of playwrights achieved a technical skill and a dramatic power which have remained a permanent theatrical heritage. In its early days Christopher

Marlowe transformed the vanishing miracle cycle into majestic historical pageantry and infused the moribund morality with a passion and poetry such as the stage had not known for over a thousand years. Later the alchemy of Shakespeare transmuted a second-hand technique and an Autolycus pack of twice-told tales into some of the world's most genial comedy and most moving tragedy. Ben Jonson combined the methods of Plautus and the spirit of Aristophanes with contemporary psychological theory to create a satirical comedy whose lively and pungent anatomizing of human nature and its social milieu begot whole generations of theatrical descendants and is excelled by Molière alone. And after the drama had passed its zenith Francis Beaumont and John Fletcher, with· unflagging ingenuity, graceful sentiment, and sparkling wit, elevated sophisticated entertainment to a facile but exquisite art in a long series of elegant tragicomedies and tragedies and impudent comedies of intrigue and manners.

Amid all its variety of mingled old and new, Elizabethan drama contributed one major achievement to the theater of western Europe. By bringing to artistic fulfillment a practice initiated in medieval drama, it established a new concept of dramatic art. Working with a relatively bare platform stage, which lent itself to maximum flexibility of space and time and to the utmost freedom of the imagination, Elizabethan drama mastered the art of translating a romantic narrative of adventure and intrigue into a cumulative synthesis of swift-paced dramatic action. It is this art which produced the two most characteristic achievements of Renaissance drama: the suspense, gayety, and poetic charm of *romantic comedy,* and the somber violence and passion of *romantic tragedy.* In both types the work of Shakespeare is unsurpassed. The special features of each are considered elsewhere in connection with the appropriate play.

SEVENTEENTH-CENTURY DRAMA

While in England the theater was creating a new order of romantic drama and in Spain was delighting a national audience with lively comedies of intrigue and tragicomedies of love and honor, Italian and French humanists continued the unrewarding effort to revive classical drama. In Italy a few elegant adaptations of Terentian comedy achieved sporadic effectiveness. Much more successful was a popular second derivative of Roman comedy known as *commedia dell'arte* or comedy-of-masks. This was a broad form of farce, based upon conventional intrigue plots, stock situations, and stereotyped characters, which employed improvised dialogue and stage business. Popular because of its elementary appeal and the resourceful skill of its actors, it joined with traditional native farce in exerting an important influence on the development of continental comedy. But the unsuccessful effort to produce satisfactory classical tragedy gradually dwindled away into a theoretical attempt to codify and illustrate the correct principles for producing satisfactory classical tragedy. Perhaps the chief handicap of these neo-classical ambitions was the fact that their fulfillment demanded a homogeneity of interests, tastes, and cultural standards which simply did not exist in the heterogeneous Renaissance.

Such a favorable cultural climate did, however, come into existence briefly in seventeenth-century France. During the reign of the Grand Monarch, Louis XIV, the turbulent life of Europe poised for a fleeting interval of exquisite self-consciousness. Under the warming rays of the Sun King flowered a fragile society of fastidious artifice. Manners took on the properties of a fine art; wit became a profession; and social codes supplanted the laws of nature. In this rarefied atmosphere the theater was transformed into an elegant salon dedicated to the intercourse and diversion of the sophisticated. It was its happy fortune that, before the sun set forever, this theater also found dramatists capable of lengthening the postures of affectation into shadows of enduring human significance and of imparting to the wings of a butterfly the flight of an eagle.

This third important epoch of drama produced the masterpieces of French classicism. It was heralded by the uneven and somewhat recalcitrant genius of Pierre Corneille (1606–1684), who combined an inherited formalism with disturbing overtones from Spanish cloak-and-sword drama and a certain personal tincture of Renaissance exuberance, to strain the seams of stage decorum with unprecedented power. It reached its apogee in the versatile genius of Molière (Jean Baptiste Poquelin, 1622–1673), who wove from miscellaneous strands of Roman comedy, *commedia dell'arte,* Spanish intrigue, Italian *intermezzi,* and native farce a glittering web to catch the immortal absurdities·of human nature in its hapless encounters with sense and society. Finally, it found in Jean Racine (1639–1699) a genius sufficiently attuned to the spirit of the age to appreciate the psychological and ethical purport of social affectations, and sufficiently refined to give fastidious expression to the delicacies of sensibility. The highly specialized types of analytical drama which these men evolved to serve their purposes added a significant new dimension to the theater of Europe. Its precise nature is discussed at greater length later.

The triumph of romantic drama in Elizabethan England and of neo-classical drama in seventeenth-century France both fulfilled and exhausted the dramatic impulses inherent in the Renaissance. For nearly two centuries thereafter the drama of Europe subsisted under the shadow of these twin giants and did little but imitate, adapt, modify, and recombine their characteristic principles and practices. During a brief period of intense activity, at the very end of the seventeenth century, the playwrights of Restoration England merged the native tradition of Jonson and Fletcher with the alien urbanity of Molière to create a unique confection for sophisticated tastes. Sufficiently distinctive and effective to deserve a small but brilliant niche in the dramatic pantheon, this took the form of a barbed *comedy of manners,* narrow and artificial in interest, cynical and unmoral in spirit, but glittering with brittle wit and impudent sophistication. Especially in the comedies of William Congreve (1670–1729) it established an English criterion for the dazzling bagatelle, a diminished reflection of which has appeared from time to time in the plays of Sheridan, Wilde, Maugham, and Noel Coward.

Elsewhere, throughout the eighteenth century, tragedy became a pallid ghost of either Racine or Shakespeare, and comedy rang the changes on Jonson and Fletcher or Molière. In the realm of comedy two minor innovations provided the sole variety. The first substituted for wit and the spirit of laughter an emphasis upon delicacy of feeling, and thus evolved *sentimental comedy.* The second, by shifting its subject matter from the intrigues of fashionable society and the roguery of low life to the commonplace vicissitudes of middle-class domesticity, created a prevailingly serious *bourgeois drama.* Both tended to replace gayety with sober sentiment and to exchange laughter for a concern with social problems. Only rarely, as in the work of Beaumarchais in France, Goldoni in Italy, and Holberg in Denmark, was the dead level of uninspired medocrity redeemed by an authentic echo of Molière's comic force. Late in the century, and continuing in the early part of the next, some relief from the monotony was afforded by a romantic revolt, which was largely inspired by the Elizabethans with some aid from Renaissance Spanish drama. In Germany this revolt burgeoned into the historical plays of Schiller and the more florid excursions of Goethe. In France it impelled Victor Hugo to invest cloak-and-sword melodrama with a not entirely warranted impressiveness by the power of his poetic imagination. In the sequel, the synthetic sound and fury of its tatterdemalion camp-followers inundated practically every theater of Europe, including the Scandinavian, until it collapsed into the cardboard sensationalism of nineteenth-century melodrama. To compensate for its dramatic deficiencies, the age tinkered with the mechanics of theatrical production, modifying the shape of the stage, improving machinery and lighting, and experimenting with the possibilities of scenery and stage spectacle. The throne left vacant by the dramatist was preëmpted by the actor, and the age became one of distinguished acting. Eventually the art of drama degenerated to a frank tailoring of rôles to fit the contours of popular actor-managers.

MODERN DRAMA

By the middle of the nineteenth century certain new factors began to operate in both the theater and the life of western Europe. In one way or another these were all an outgrowth of the century's rapid expansion in scientific discovery and scientific habits of thought. Eventually they precipitated a fourth theatrical epoch, that of modern drama.

Although each affected dramatic practice in its own particular way, so close was the interaction of the several factors that no one can properly be given priority over the others. Each tended to supplement and confirm the others until the influences became so ubiquitous and concerted that they moved drama irresistibly in one direction.

In the theater, for example, an increasing invention of mechanical devices materially enlarged the resources of stage production. At first these enhanced resources were employed chiefly to supply traditional plays with an appropriate historical setting or to produce ingenious and lavish spectacle for its own sake. Improvements in lighting, however, exerted a more significant influence. As stronger and better diffused lighting afforded greater visibility, it became possible for the acting area to shift from its customary place forward on the projecting apron of the stage and to withdraw behind the proscenium arch. Here it took on the aspect of a framed and illuminated picture, and subsequently of an enclosed room, lacking its fourth wall but separated from the audience by footlights. Methods of acting also underwent a change. Bathed in sufficient illumination to reveal facial expression and give force to intimate gestures, the actor was able to forgo exaggerated attitudinizing for a style of greater restraint and naturalness. With this new accent upon naturalness of action came the inevitable corollary, scenic verisimilitude; the available scenic machinery was used to transform the recessed and compact stage into a setting appropriate to the specific dramatic action which it housed. And with this retreat of drama into a specified precinct of its own there followed a subtle change in the whole concept of its nature. A play ceased to be simply a histrionic performance addressed to its audience; it became instead an independent segment of human life with an illusory reality of its own, circumscribed by the boundaries of the stage, and segregated from an audience which was, in effect, merely permitted to eavesdrop so long as it remained unobtrusive.

These developments effectually transformed the whole character of drama. Although for more than two thousand years drama and the stage had shared a close partnership, the two had always remained essentially separable entities. In all its mutations the stage had never constituted more than an area upon which dramatic action took place or a formalized background for such action. Drama, on the other hand, had always been a self-contained matter of action and dialogue; independent of place or time, it had created its imagined setting by word of mouth and had transported that setting with the movements of its actors; its predominant artistic virtues had been mimetic and literary. The closest bond had always been between drama and the audience, not between drama and the stage. In the nineteenth century, for the first time, this ancient relationship was radically altered. The audience was banished, quite literally, into the outer darkness of the auditorium. Specific physical settings anchored drama to the stage. Scenery and lighting effects became integral parts of the total dramatic illusion. What had formerly fallen within the comprehensive function of dialogue was distributed among the ancillary devices of more detailed stage business, interpretative pantomime, and scenic exposition. In short, drama ceased to be primarily a literary art and became instead a fusion of theatrical arts.

As mechanical innovation transformed methods of staging, a corresponding mechanization in life and thought altered the basic conception of drama. It is the nature of drama to concentrate upon the inherent conflicts of human existence. In the eyes of the nineteenth century, entangled as it was in the complications of an increasingly mechanized industrial society, the most urgent human conflicts were those produced by social maladjustment. Indeed, the central conflict of the age appeared to be the conflict between the individual and his social environment. The scientific materialism of contemporary thought pushed the matter a step further. It pointed out that, if the individual was a component of human society, he was even more inextricably part of a natural universe, and thus in no small degree a creature of his physical constitution and environment. In the light of this consideration, the fundamental conflict of human drama was the unremitting struggle of man, individually and collectively, with the material facts of existence, with the inexorable laws of nature, and with the mysterious forces of his own psychology. No drama could purport to deal with reality which failed to take these problems into account. Consequently in the thinking of the age, as in the practice of play production, dramatic action came to be integrated with the setting of action, and character and environment became inseparable.

The result was revolutionary. Prior to the nineteenth century, drama dealt with a world dominated by human nature. It assumed that human life was essentially subject to human control and expressive of human will. It therefore considered human behavior in terms of human responsibility, and concerned itself with the properties most appropriate to human beings, reason and morality. Moreover, it conceived of humanity as a universal constant everywhere reducible to the same common elements, irrespective of time or place. Hence it tended to think of human life in terms of recurring patterns and to seek in the individual character a reflection of general archetypes. Viewing the superficial variations of custom and environment as largely irrelevant, it concentrated upon the universal and the essential, eternally manifest in changeless human nature. The nineteenth-century identification of the individual with his environment destroyed at one stroke the possibility of drama on such universal terms. Its submergence of man in nature shattered equally the notion that drama could be founded on strictly human considerations. In the theater the concrete environment of explicit stage sets, clamoring tacitly for proper attention, made obvious the fact that drama possessed a local habitation as well as a name. When the question at issue was a social problem, it was equally evident that the problem was inseparable from the conditions which produced it. Inevitably human conduct and human nature took on a relative value, contingent upon the circumstances of particular environment, and dramatic action became a localized inter-action between man and the complex conditions of his natural existence.

The change made necessary a new method of dramaturgy. The impact of environment upon personality could have little real meaning unless the environment was presented with scrupulous versimilitude. Problems of society or individual behavior lost most of their force unless the analysis of the circumstances observed a scientific precision and accuracy. Moreover, the general significance of such a scientific examina-tion was likely to be meager unless it dealt with the familiar, the factual, and the natural. In order to satisfy these requirements, drama during the later nineteenth century became prevailingly realistic. It endeavored to select its subject matter from the observable facts of familiar experience. It restricted itself to dramatic methods compatible with an effect of naturalness and truth to life. It undertook a clinical analysis of the social and psychological problems involved in man's effort to cope with his nature and his environment. Avoiding factitious manipulations of plot or character, it strove for an illusion of life consistent with common reality.

The new manner in drama instituted at least a technical beginning by mid-century. In the hands of the French playwright Eugène Scribe, the so-called *well-made play*—a lineal descendant of Racine's compact tragic technique—cultivated a specious naturalness by stressing a tightly knit structural pattern of explicit cause and effect. During the succeeding years the method was applied tentatively to contemporary interests and social questions by Émile Augier and the younger Dumas. Eventually the compact and logical technique provided an admirable instrument for the genius of Henrik Ibsen (1828–1906), who in the next-to-last decade of the century practically founded modern drama with his realistic *problem plays*. The sociological approach of Ibsen, the apparent realism of his methods, and the intellectual challenge of the problems with which he dealt set powerful echoes reverberating throughout Europe and America. A whole generation of playwrights set about illuminating their own particular premises with torches lit from the rising sun of Norway. Not the least of these illuminations were the pyrotechnics of good theater, pungent wit, and social comment exploded by George Bernard Shaw.

Meanwhile the realistic impulse of the new mode begot a deliberate effort to transform drama into a mirror of "things as they are." Initial attempts to banish theatricalism and reproduce without distortion a "slice of life" unfortunately accomplished little beyond an effective demonstra-tion that the theater is not a laboratory and that science and art are two different things. The basic difficulty was that purely descriptive realism tended to reflect merely the surface appearance of life and was singularly deficient in drama. Only in the work of a few dramatists, of whom the Russian Anton Chekhov (1860–1904) was the most accomplished, were the commonplaces of human experience conceived of in terms of an inherent pattern which could combine artistic interpretation with an illusion of ordinary life. The attempt did stimulate, however, in an otherwise rather uniform European theater, a widespread examination of regional characteristics and an exploration of folk nature, such as one finds in the Irish drama of John Millington Synge (1871–1909). But for the most part the realistic treatment of common life found its most effective expression in some form of the social problem play.

Besides exploiting the social problem, modern drama has evolved two other general methods of dealing with the truth beneath appearances. In the first instance, some dramatists, like Zola, Strindberg, Hauptmann, Gorki, and O'Neill, have explored the organic nature of human experience. Reflecting the ascendancy of natural science in contemporary thought, they have conceived of drama as a complex struggle of natural and social forces upon the stage of human destiny. The so-called naturalism of their plays is designed to provide a scientific inquiry into the nature of the phenomenon and a clarification of the processes which it illustrates. The method has been particularly effective, as in notable plays by Strindberg, Pirandello, and O'Neill, in producing penetrating psychological studies of the sources of human behavior. The second broad expedient of modern drama is closely related to this psychological interest. In certain of their plays dramatists like Strindberg, Maeterlinck, Pirandello, and O'Neill have adopted the view that external realities are significant chiefly as symbolical manifestations of an inner reality, and that the true concern of drama, as of life, is with this inner reality. They have therefore combined the materials of realism with the mechanics of symbolism to create an eclectic representation of familiar experience in terms of its philosophical implication. As a general means of endowing the crude facts of existence with a spiritual value, symbolism has been a recognized device of modern drama since the days of Ibsen; in the theater it has been operative since the time of the medieval morality plays; and as a method of interpretation it is doubtless as old as human thought. Its peculiar significance in modern drama is twofold. In the first place, it afforded a compromise whereby drama might preserve its fidelity to realism and yet escape the peril of expiring under the dead weight of material fact. In the second place, it provided a means of employing the scientific inquiries of modern psychology to reveal dramatically the hidden realities of subjective consciousness. Probing into the unique experience of the individual mind, and even into the dark recesses of the subconscious, it has striven to lay bare the drama of man's inner life. By means of the symbolistic technique known as expressionism, it has attempted to set forth upon the stage with realistic accuracy an objective embodiment of that fantasia of the conscious and unconscious which constitutes subjective experience.

Such, in brief, have been the major developments in the drama of western Europe and America to the present date. The preceding pages have endeavored to sketch in barest outline the salient features of a rich and vital human activity. At the sacrifice of oversimplification, and perhaps of partial distortion, they have selected for notice only those crests of achievement which mark the ground swell of dramatic development and define its essential character. Taken as a whole, the prodigal annals of dramatic experiment reveal much that was abortive and much more that was repetitious and uninspired. Over the centuries also, as cultures have flowered and perished, as customs have come and gone, human interests and tastes have altered; and with these changes the theater has veered like a weather vane in the wind. Nevertheless, the generations of men continue, and the struggle of man with his destiny is timeless. Here and there, in the march of two thousand years, the sparks struck off by that struggle kindled in the theater a flame which the passing centuries have not extinguished. For wheresoever man has once set up the living image of his essence, he leaves a memorial which can never wholly die. Such memorials are the signature of the great dramatists. They mark how each in his own way, laying hold upon time, has broken off for his fellow men a fragment of eternity. The hoarded treasure of these rare fragments constitutes the abiding achievement of drama. In the following pages are presented the more memorable instances of this achievement. Let us now turn to these specific examples, always bearing in mind two important truths about the art which they exemplify: dramatic manners and methods are merely interchangeable fashions, but the substance of human drama knows no time or change.

THE ACHIEVEMENT
OF
DRAMA

Margarete Bieber, "A History of the Greek and Roman Theater"

THE THEATER OF DIONYSUS AT ATHENS

A reconstruction, from a drawing by Heinrich Bulle, illustrating the unit stage of the classical theater.

Classical Tragedy

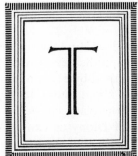HE EARLIEST TYPE OF DRAMA to achieve a permanent place in the theater of western Europe is classical tragedy. So called because it is the characteristic form of serious drama developed by the classical culture of the ancient world, it reached its perfection in Greece during the fifth century B.C. Originally no more than a working compromise with contemporary theatrical conditions, like every successful art it made such a virtue of its necessities that the resulting product both outlived the original conditions and has maintained a high artistic value to the present day. For centuries it was widely admired; it has served as a model for repeated imitation; and in the modern theater it still exerts a very considerable influence. Among its more notable contributions, it is responsible for one of the two basic structural forms which underlie the whole of European drama.

Classical tragedy came into existence as a religious and cultural function of ancient Greek community life. Comprising part of the annual spring festival in honor of the god Dionysus, it was a public spectacle sponsored by the state. At the peak of its development in Athens it constituted an elaborate and impressive ceremonial. To accommodate it was built the huge open-air Theater of Dionysus. Here annually three dramatists, chosen by a careful process of elimination, offered original plays in public competition for awards decided by official judges. To each dramatist was allotted a separate day in which to present a sequence of three tragedies followed by a lighter after-piece known as a satyr-play. To each were also assigned three professional actors paid from the public purse and a chorus of citizens furnished by a selected patron. With these resources at his disposal, the dramatist undertook the challenge of impressing a critical audience of fellow citizens with a performance which combined the features of a civic ceremony, a cultural experience, and a competitive contest.

The conditions incident to such a performance naturally affected the character of the plays. Two factors were particularly influential. In the first place, there was the Greek conception of what constituted a normal dramatic performance. Traditionally the nucleus of classical tragedy was a chorus designed to chant hymns and perform ceremonial dances. The inception of Greek drama was, therefore, more analogous to a combination of cantata or oratorio with ballet than to a modern play. As episodes of spoken dialogue came to be added, these were regarded as extensions and embellishments of the choral element which differed from it in degree more than in kind. Even in these episodes certain passages were regularly designed to be sung with a musical accompaniment, either as a monody by a single actor or responsively by actors and chorus. The result was that, although dramatic dialogue and action increased in importance, to a Greek audience classical tragedy always connoted a theatrical performance not unlike modern opera.

In the second place, classical tragedy was obliged to take into account the exigencies of production in an open amphitheater of vast proportions. Something of what these were can be surmised by examining the illustration facing page 63. Since information about the Greek theater of this period is somewhat sketchy and opinions vary considerably, this conjectural reconstruction of the Theater of Dionysus cannot be taken as wholly accurate in detail. For example, the actual stage was probably more simple and primitive, and the semicircular open space shown before it was probably a complete circle with an altar to the god occupying its center. On the other hand, the illustration affords a substantially correct notion of how the theater appeared during the lifetime of Sophocles. This Theater of Dionysus, one will observe, was a huge bowl-like structure open to the sky. Except for the segment occupied by the stage, it consisted of eighty raised tiers of seats with accommodations for approximately 17,000 spectators. Its focus was a central open space, which was known as the *orchestra*. This orchestra circle was the space occupied throughout the play by the chorus and used for its formal dances. Immediately behind it, and separated from the spectators by passageways, which were used for the entrance and exit of the chorus and occasional actors, was a shallow rectangular area approximately 100 feet wide and possibly raised by several low steps. This area was surrounded on three sides by permanent stage buildings and was backed by an architectural façade, known as the *proscenium*, which screened the *scene*, or main stage house. It was the area ordinarily used by the actors in the play, although the flat roof surmounting the proscenium was also used occasionally as an auxiliary acting level. The proscenium itself was pierced with three doors, which provided the normal entrances and exits for the actors. In *Oedipus*, the great central door represented, of course, the palace of Thebes. Taken altogether, the Greek stage, it will be seen, created an effect which was at once simple, plastic, and massive.

The difficulties of dramatic production in a theater of such proportions will be apparent to anyone who has witnessed a football game in a large modern stadium. Problems of visibility and acoustics impose inescapable restrictions. Where actors are dwarfed by their surroundings, their speech and actions become comprehensible only through exaggeration, and theatrical effects are impressive only when bold of outline and massive in structure. In large measure classical tragedy is what it is because it evolved an artistic solution for these problems. Adjusting to a scale commensurate with its theater, it strove habitually for dimensions larger than life; in order to escape the diminutive it deliberately cultivated the imposing. By drawing liberally upon the chorus it lent mass to its mimetic action. To impart stature and bulk to its actors it mounted them upon *cothurni* (which were boots with raised platform soles), padded their contours, garbed them statuesquely in flowing costumes, and equipped them with tall conventionalized masks which served the double purpose of supplying features recognizable at a distance and amplifying the voice. Since in this state of encumberment neither abundance nor intimacy of physical action was feasible, stage business was reduced to a stately minimum, and acting became a broadly interpretative matter of conventional posture, stylized pantomime, and symbolic gesture. In compensation, drama relied heavily upon speech and choral song. But dramatic speech itself, for much the same reason, also tended to be formal, declamatory, and, as often as possible, intoned or merged with chant. Under theatrical conditions wholly disproportionate to naturalness or nicety of detail, the effects aimed at were those of heightened simplicity with little regard for realistic verisimilitude.

In exploiting these theatrical conditions to artistic advantage, Greek playwrights usually preferred to dramatize stories familiar to the audience. As befitted the occasion and the unrealistic style of production, these stories were drawn mainly from traditional mythology. The practice had certain definite advantages. For one thing, it readily established an initial common ground of understanding with the audience and thus obviated the need for elaborate exposition, which might be difficult to follow in the theater. Then, too, the fact that such stories concerned episodes and personages of an heroic age remote from contemporary life served to place the incidents of the play in a desirable perspective. On the other hand, familiarity with the general outlines of the story precluded any real suspense about its outcome. The effect was to divert attention from the simple facts in the case and to center it on the treatment and significance of the facts, which are, after all, the chief concerns of drama. In particular, this acquaintance with the general outcome promoted the use of such effective dramatic devices as foreshadowing of events, peripety (a sudden reversal in the significance of a situation), and that irony which is the core of tragic effect but which is impotent unless the audience possesses some foreknowledge.

Because the continuous presence of the chorus throughout a classical tragedy tended to limit the scope of action, place, and time, Greek playwrights also found it expedient to concentrate dramatic treatment upon a single complex situation. In order to fulfill its purpose satisfactorily, such a situation needed to be one which contained within itself various elements of conflict, brought these opposed forces to a focus, and accordingly precipitated a dramatic crisis. The basic situation of classical tragedy was, therefore, essentially a situation of crisis. All the significant elements of dramatic conflict were implicit in it from the start. It was the function of the plot to expose these inherent elements progressively, to transform the potential into the actual, and thus to exhibit their effective force. The customary point of attack was that point of precarious suspension immediately before a wave of dramatic action breaks. The development of the plot dealt with the breaking of that wave upon the victims in its path, with their struggles in the torrent, and with the resulting debris left on the shore as the wave finally recedes.

The effect of this technique is evident in the characteristic emphasis of classical tragedy. Concentrating as it does upon the climax of traditional stories, classical tragedy tends to stress the climactic and traditional aspects of its dramatic situations. Since it deals in large measure with the consequences of acts performed before the play's opening, it necessarily dwells more upon what happens to the characters than upon their antecedent deeds. Its emphasis falls upon the reactions to an existing situation and primarily upon responses of thought and feeling. As a result, the center of dramatic action is within the characters, and dramatic action itself takes the form of a psychological struggle between conflicting emotional impulses. The purpose of the play is to give adequate expression to this inner drama. But since mimetic representation of emotional states is automatically limited to rudimentary and symbolic acts, the most eloquent expression is obviously speech, which was also the most comprehensive medium of expression in the Greek theater. It is accordingly the practice of classical tragedy to concentrate upon the facilities of dialogue, declamation, and choral song to reveal the intricacies of a psychological drama which is only implied by the stage action. Subordinating the function of physical action, it explores the rhetorical and imaginative resources of poetry to illuminate the fluctuating tensions of inner conflict. Even in its most climactic phases it prefers to place deeds of violence offstage and to report them through the mouth of a messenger, not alone that proper decorum may be observed, but deliberately to emphasize the connotation of the deed rather than the deed itself. And the artistic aim of this poetic expression is, not the realism with which it achieves a dramatic effect, but the effectiveness with which it reveals a dramatic reality.

The use of traditional subject matter also encourages an emphasis upon those broad general effects promoted by the exigencies of theatrical production. To a Greek audience mythology provided a sifted synthesis of a common cultural tradition. Endowed with the symbolic quality of myth, these stories of gods and heroes represented not so much the isolated fortunes of unique individuals as aspects of generic human experience. In keeping with this point of view, classical tragedy treats its mythological subjects less in terms of their singularity than in terms of their universal implications. It conceives of its dramatic situations as both specific and general. It represents its characters not as isolated individuals but as types of familiar humanity concerned with man's common lot. For the immediate occasion Oedipus may serve to point an instance; but Oedipus, drawn larger than life, is less the likeness of one man in an extraordinary dilemma than he is a type of all men caught in the meshes of inscrutable life, menaced by their own fallibility, and unwittingly bent upon their own destruction. By stripping away the singularities of ephemeral detail classical tragedy divorces its embodiment of life from the entanglements of immediate place and time. In thus reducing human life to the bold contours of universal experience, it endeavors to present the drama of essential humanity in its eternal struggle with destiny and thereby to reveal the pathos and the dignity of its heroic passion.

In the opinion of Aristotle, drama's first and perhaps greatest critic, one of the supreme examples of classical tragedy is Sophocles' *Oedipus the King.* Its author, together with his contemporaries Aeschylus and Euripides, was largely responsible for the golden age of ancient drama and remains in many respects the most representative, as he was the most popular, dramatist of his time. Artistically his long life (*c.* 495–406 B.C.) was both prolific and consistently successful. A fine poet, a consummate dramatic craftsman, a man of serene and comprehensive wisdom, Sophocles was a singularly happy expression of the temperament and ideals which created classical tragedy. *Oedipus the King,* which is the generally acknowledged masterpiece of his seven surviving plays, was first produced about 430 B.C. While it is not entirely typical of all classical tragedy, if any one play could epitomize so various an achievement, it does illustrate the salient features of the type in a play which has lost little of its original dramatic impact.

Oedipus the King dramatizes an episode from one of the principal Greek myths, the tragic history of Thebes, which also provided the subject of Sophocles' other masterpiece, *Antigone.* Its technique illustrates admirably both the mechanics and the effectiveness of classical dramaturgy. Beginning *in medias res,* the play at once introduces a situation in which every component of the final tragedy is already held in suspension. Swiftly and relentlessly the plot precipitates these fatal particles until they form a cumulative design of inescapable catastrophe. In the process a progressive enlightenment brings one character after another to a perception of the truth and goads Oedipus to an increasing desperation as he struggles to allay a dawning horror. Meanwhile the audience, acquainted with the destined end, watches with a horrible fascination the tightening of the noose and receives a vivid demonstration of the grim irony of which tragic life is capable.

The play opens conventionally with a *prologue,* the function of which is to set forth succinctly the salient features of the dramatic situation. It is followed immediately by the *parodos,* or processional entry of the chorus, which in its first formal song establishes the tone of the play and gives expression to its emotional context. Thereupon follows a series of *episodes* devoted to dramatic action and dialogue. Each episode presents a unified phase of the developing dramatic action and a corresponding aspect of Oedipus' attitude toward the situation. This dialogue is carried on by the three actors provided for classical tragedy, with occasional participation by the *coryphaeus,* or leader of the chorus. Although there are actually eight speaking rôles in the play, a change of costumes and masks makes it possible for the available actors to play all the parts; for there are never more than three speakers on the stage at the same time. On the other hand, since it was probably the need for trained voices which originally limited the number of actors, the spreaking rôles are freely supplemented by the use of mute characters. The dialogue itself, which is skillfully orchestrated to provide a rhetorical counterpoint to the emotional content, ranges from swift dramatic colloquies to set passages of declamation and at times, as in the *kommos* of the second episode, rises with the mounting tension into responsive chant. Each episode concludes with a *stasimon,* or choral interlude, which sums up the significance of the preceding action, comments upon it, or generalizes its application. The whole play culminates in the *exodus,* which brings the action to its climax and the passion to its crest of intensity. This consists of three conventional parts: the long descriptive speech of the messenger which recounts the off-stage death of Jocasta and the blinding of Oedipus, the revealed catastrophe of Oedipus' final anguish, and the epilogue of the chorus as it withdraws from the stage.

In the total economy of the play the function of the chorus requires particular notice as perhaps the most distinctive feature of classical tragedy. As used by Sophocles, the chorus consists of fifteen singers and dancers sometimes divided into two antiphonal semi-choruses and headed by a coryphaeus, who speaks for it when the chorus participates in dialogue. Its general theatrical purpose is to contribute spectacle, song, and poetic beauty to the total effect of the play. In a more strictly dramatic sense it performs a peculiar double function. As a group of Theban elders, it constitutes an integral part of the dramatic setting and provides a stabilizing frame of reference for the specific incidents of the action. Intimately concerned in the events of the play, it reflects the fluctuations of their significance and serves as a sounding-board for the individual responses of Oedipus. In this capacity it supplies a localizing atmosphere for the action and a general context for Oedipus' personal fortunes. On the other hand, occupying an intermediate position between the actors and the audience, the chorus stands both within and outside the dramatic action of the play. It is almost as though in the chorus classical tragedy presented to the audience its own ideal group of spectators, sensitive to the involutions of the play, completely under the dramatist's control, and exquisitely responsive to the appropriate implications. As such, the chorus is an invaluable mediator between the play and the audience. Vicariously, and most subtly, it serves to establish a point of view, to guide the understanding, to articulate precisely emotional responses, and to enlarge the particular instance to universal connotation. Since it is identified with the audience by their common rôle of interested spectator, its participation in the play is tantamount to a participation of the audience itself. In performing this important function, the chorus is one of the most delicate and valuable instruments of artistic effect ever evolved by drama.

Classical tragedy is one of the world's most enduring dramatic achievements. Besides *Oedipus the King* it produced such masterpieces of the Greek theater as the *Antigone* of Sophocles, the *Agamemnon* of Aeschylus, and the *Medea* and *Alcestis* of Euripides. It underlies the great tragedies of Corneille and Racine. It is the matrix of such diverse plays as Goethe's *Iphigenia in Tauris*, Ibsen's *Ghosts*, and Maxwell Anderson's *The Wingless Victory*. It has inspired such fine closet dramas as Milton's *Samson Agonistes* and Shelley's *Prometheus Unbound*. And it is largely responsible for one of the most impressive plays of the twentieth century, Eugene O'Neill's *Mourning Becomes Electra*.

OEDIPUS
THE
KING

by SOPHOCLES

TRANSLATED BY

CLARENCE W. MENDELL

Characters in the Play

OEDIPUS, *King of Thebes*

PRIEST OF ZEUS

CREON, *brother of* JOCASTA

TIRESIAS, *a blind seer*

JOCASTA, *wife of* OEDIPUS *and widow of* KING LAIUS

FIRST MESSENGER, *from Corinth*

A SHEPHERD

SECOND MESSENGER, *a member of the royal household*

CHORUS OF THEBAN ELDERS

Mutes

A Group of SUPPLIANTS

The Children ANTIGONE *and* ISMENE, *daughters of* OEDIPUS *and* JOCASTA

SCENE: *Before the royal palace at Thebes.*

Copyright 1941 and reprinted with the permission of the Yale University Press. The spelling of certain proper names has been altered to bring them into conformity with familiar usage, and a few stage directions have been supplied.

PROLOGUE

[*Enter a* PRIEST OF ZEUS, *followed by group of* SUPPLIANTS. *From the palace enter* OEDIPUS.]

OEDIPUS. My children, ancient Cadmus'[1] newest brood,
What is this embassy that waits impatient
Bedecked with suppliant branches? All our town
Is filled with sound of holy sacrifice
And paeans too and wailing misery.
These things, my children, I have deemed it wrong
To learn from others: I went forth myself,
I, famed on the lips of all men, Oedipus.
But tell me, sire—for thou art fit to speak
For these—in what mood stand ye there? In fear
Or loyalty? Stony of heart the man
Who finds no pity for such embassy.
PRIEST. O Oedipus, that rulest o'er my land,
Thou seest us, how of every age we sit
Before thy altars, some not yet endowed
With strength of distant flight, and some
Heavy with age who serve as priests (myself
The priest of Zeus) and other some elect
From all the tribes. Within the market-place
Sits the whole populace in suppliant garb
By Pallas' twofold shrine revered, or where
Ismenus' sacred soil speaks prophecy.
For, as thou seest too, our commonwealth
Labors full sore nor yet avails to lift
Its head above the billowing surge of death,
Wasting alike in the rich crops of earth
And in her grazing herds, while women suffer
The pangs of barren childbirth. Through her midst
The fire-bearing god, mad pestilence,
Hurling his shafts, scourges relentlessly
Our city till, beneath his hand, the home
Of Cadmus is made void and Hades black
With groans and lamentations is enriched.
Not with the gods do I now make thee one
Nor these thy children seated at thy gate,

But first of all mankind we reckon thee
In ways of men and in perplexities
Haling from heaven above. 'Twas thou that camest
Loosing our Cadmean city from the toll
We paid the singer of harsh harmonies,[2]
Learning no clue from us: no other man
Instructed thee but by the lore of god,
Men say, believing, thou didst right our life.
Now too, O Oedipus, that rulest all,
Turning to thee we all petition thee:
Discover straight some remedy for us.
It may be thou shalt hearken to the voice
Of god or of some man, thou knowest whose.
For yesterday's experience methinks
Best validates the counsel of today.
Up then, and save thy city, thou who art
Best of mankind; up, gird thyself, for thee
This country calls its savior, honoring
Thy past devotion. Never let memory
Recall thy rule, how once erect we stood
Upraised only to fall. Nay save the state.
A happy rescue from the cursed Sphinx
Thou gavest us long since: be now the same.
And thou wouldst rule this city as thou dost,
Better to rule o'er men than emptiness.
Fortress and ship alike become as naught
Bereft of humankind to dwell therein.
OEDIPUS. My children pitiable, not strange to me,
Familiar rather are the things ye ask.
Full well I know your anguish—yet, howe'er
Ye suffer all, there is no one of you
Whose suffering equals mine. Your several griefs
Touch each one man, no other than yourselves:
My spirit groans for all the city—ay,
For me and you alike. Ye rouse me not
From sleep, for, be assured, I have shed tears
Uncounted; many a path my mind has traced,

---

[1] Cadmus was the traditional founder of Thebes.

[2] The Sphinx. Oedipus was originally chosen King of Thebes because, by solving the famous riddle of the Sphinx, he saved the city from the winged monster's depredations.

73

And that which I have found—one only means
To remedy our lot—that have I followed,
Sending Menoeceus' son, my brother Creon,
Unto Apollo's Pythian shrine to learn
What word or act of mine might save the state.
Already with the loitering length of days
Time tortures me in wonder how he fares.
For well beyond what old experience
Bids us expect he still is absent. When
He comes, I shall not then be derelict
In my fulfilment of god's whole behest.
PRIEST.   Timely thy word, O King, for these but now
Point me to where already Creon comes.

[Enter CREON.]

OEDIPUS.   O Lord Apollo, may he come endued
With bright good fortune, as his eye is bright.
PRIEST.   'Tis safe to hazard that his news is good:
Else not with fruited laurel were he decked.
OEDIPUS.   Soon shall we know for he can hear us now.
My lord and kinsman, son of Menoeceus,
What message dost thou bring us from the god?
CREON.   Good news, for I declare that even ills,
If they but end aright, may all be well.
OEDIPUS.   What news is this? For neither bold of heart
Nor fearful am I at thy present word.
CREON.   If thou wouldst hear in presence of these men
I am prepared to speak—or else within.
OEDIPUS.   Speak to them all. Heavier the grief I bear
For them than for my own heart's suffering.
CREON.   Speak then I will my message from the god.
Lord Phoebus bade us all outspokenly
Drive forth the pestilence that's bred within
Our land nor fatten it beyond control.
OEDIPUS.   And with what exorcism? What is the means?

CREON.   Exile or death, repaying ancient death.
For blood it is that overwhelms our state.
OEDIPUS.   Upon what man does god decree this chance?
CREON.   Laius, my lord, was one time sovereign here
Over our land, ere ever thou didst come.
OEDIPUS.   I know by hearsay, for I saw him not.
CREON.   And he being dead, comes clear god's high command
Forthwith to punish those his murderers.
OEDIPUS.   And they are where? Where shall be found the clue
Hard to unravel of such ancient crime?
CREON.   Within this land he said. That which is sought
Is found; the unconsidered vanishes.
OEDIPUS.   At home or in the country or abroad
Did Laius happen on his bloody fate?
CREON.   Faring upon a mission, as he said,
Laius returned no more from his emprise.
OEDIPUS.   No comrade of the road, no messenger
Beheld the deed that one might learn from him?
CREON.   Dead are they all save one who terrified
Fled with one word alone of all he saw.
OEDIPUS.   And what was that? One thing may lead to much
If we but gain some slight foothold of hope.
CREON.   Robbers he said encountered on the way,
Not one but many, killed him ruthlessly.
OEDIPUS.   How could a robber save by gold suborned
From Thebes, attain to such bold arrogance?
CREON.   Suspicion spake as much but, Laius dead,
No champion was there in our misery.
OEDIPUS.   What dread disaster could restrain the state
From learning all, its master so destroyed?
CREON.   The riddling Sprinx compelled us to resign
Mystery remote for questions close at hand.

OEDIPUS. From the beginning then I'll prove it clear.
For just is Phoebus, rightly too thyself
Hast laid on me this duty to the dead.
So shalt thou find me rightly an ally
Unto this land obedient to the god.
For not alone as boon to distant friends
But for myself I'll scotch this pestilence.
Seeing that whoso slew him, he likewise
Fearing my venging hand, might slay me too.
Hence if I fail him not I benefit
Myself. Up then, my people, speedily
Stand from these altars, raise your suppliant staves.
Let someone gather here the citizens
Of Thebes, assured that I shall compass all
And we shall stand revealed all fortunate
Under god's guiding help—or fallen quite.
PRIEST. My children, let us rise. It was for this
Which now he tells us that we gathered here
And so may Phoebus with his oracle
Be savior too and end the pestilence.

[*Exeunt.*]

PARODOS

[*Enter* CHORUS OF THEBAN ELDERS, *singing.*]

FIRST STROPHE

O thou Word, sweet spoken, of Zeus
  How shall I name thee?
Forth from the Pythian shrine
Gleaming with gold art come
  Unto glorious Thebes.
And my quivering heart is taut and I shudder with fear,
    Thou Delian God,
  As low on my knees I pray.
Comes there a fate unknown
Or again with the circling years
  Recurring woe?
Tell me, thou child of golden Hope, Word
  ever living.

FIRST ANTISTROPHE

First to thee, O daughter of Zeus,
  Deathless Athena,
Make I my suppliant prayer;
Artemis too I call
  She who ranges the hills
And she sits on the throne high raised in
    the gathering place;
  And Phoebus who shoots
  Afar over earth his darts:
  Threefold defenders, come
  As of old at our city's need
    Ye came to save,
Banishing far the flame of woe: come now
  to save us.

SECOND STROPHE

Woe, woe is me, countless the pains I
    bear;
  All that is mine is doomed:
    No shaft of wit
  Brings me deliverance;
  No generations new
  To cherish my fatherland
No more do the mothers of Thebes, bearing their sons
  Suffer the pain and live,
But soul on soul, like birds, ye may see
    them fly
    Swifter than fire
On to the distant strand, home of the western god.

SECOND ANTISTROPHE

Beyond our ken, countless the city's
    dead;
  Foul on the plain they lie
    In cruel ranks;
  Mothers bereft, gray haired,
  In supplication bent
  And wives by the altar side,
They groan for the ills that are ours: sorrows untold:
  Paeans of woe that burst

From aged lips that moan for a city
    doomed.
  Wherefore for these
Send us some bulwark fair, golden daugh-
    ter of Zeus.

THIRD STROPHE

Ares too, god of the raging death:
  Helmet nor shield are his
But the flame and the shouting.
Back, turn him back, far from our father-
    land,
  Back on a favoring breeze
  To Amphitrite's couch [3]
Or the harbor welcomeless of the Thracian
    surge.
  For now if the night leave aught
  Day comes apace to consume.

O, father above, on him,
Lord of the lightning flash,
Hurl now thy thunderbolt.

THIRD ANTISTROPHE

Lord of light, god of the golden bow [4]
  Scatter thy shafts untamed
  To defend us, we pray thee.
Aye and the fire gleaming of Artemis
  Which on the Lycian hills,
  She flashes peak by peak;
And the golden mitered god of our native
    land
Whose face with the wine is red,
Bacchus, I call, with thy rout
Of maenads attended, come.
Come with the flaming torch,
Smite thou the god disowned.

FIRST EPISODE

[*Enter* OEDIPUS *during the last lines of the choral ode.*]
OEDIPUS. Ye pray, and what ye pray for—
  if straightway
Ye hearken to my words and give me aid
Against the pestilence—ye may attain:
Deliverance and surcease from your woes—
Words of a stranger to this history,
A stranger to the deed. Not far alone
Could I without a hint pursue the quest.
Wherefore, your latest citizen, do I
Make proclamation to the Cadmean land:
Whoso of you knows by whose hand as-
  sailed
Laius the son of Labdacus was slain
I bid him tell me all. But if he fear
For his own self, then let him none the less
Denounce himself, for he shall suffer naught
Save banishment. So too if any man
Knows that the culprit came from other
  lands
Let him not hold his tongue, for whoso
  speaks
Reward is his and gratitude beside.

But if ye will not speak, if dumb with fear
Ye seek to shield or friend or self from
  harm
Then hearken to the purpose that is mine.
No man soever from this sovereign realm
Whose rule is mine, by shelter or by word
Shall aid the murderer, or e'er admit
His presence at the litany or shrine
Of sacrifice or at the lustral fire,
But thrust him from his home, knowing
  full well
He is the accursed thing as now the god
By Pythian oracle hath made us know.
So do I purpose to ally myself
With god and with the dead. Here I invoke
This curse upon the guilty one or all
Wretched to plumb the depths of misery.
Likewise upon myself if knowingly
I harbor in my house the murderer
I imprecate the curses I have named.
So upon each of you I lay a charge
To heed these words—for my sake and the
  god's
And for our city in its barrenness

---

[3] *I.e.,* the Mediterranean Sea, of which the nymph Amphitrite was queen.

[4] Apollo. As a god traditionally interested in the establishment of cities, he was regarded as a special guardian of civic welfare.

Abandoned of the gods and perishing.
For even if it were not sent from heaven,
This plague upon us, yet, 'twere unthinkable
To leave still unavenged the death
Of one so noble and your king withal
Nor track it down. Now since I hold the power
That once was his, and am the heir as well
Of his own marriage couch, possess the wife
That lay with him and would have borne to us
A common offspring had not fate ill timed,
Striking him down, forbidden, I pronounce
Myself his champion, even as his son,
And I shall leave no single thing untried
To find and seize that man who put to death
The son of Labdacus, heir to the line
Of Polydorus and of Cadmus too,
Ancient Agenor's latest progeny.
Meantime for such as see not eye to eye
With this my purpose, I invoke the gods
To grant them harvest neither in their fields
Nor in their homes, but with this petilence
Or some more terrible, to end their line.
But citizens of this Cadmean realm
That hearken to my words, on them I pray
May Justice smile forever and the gods.

CHORUS.[5] O King, upon my oath as thou dost ask
I speak: I did not kill the man, nor know
The murderer. To say who did the deed
Was Phoebus' task who laid on us the quest.

OEDIPUS. Right is thy judgment, but to force the gods
Unwilling, that may no man undertake.

CHORUS. Fain would I say what seemeth second best.

OEDIPUS. If there be yet a third best, speak it out.

CHORUS. After lord Phoebus [6] he who seeth most
In harmony, our lord Tiresias,
Might best reward our present questioning.

OEDIPUS. Nor has this thought escaped me. I have sent
At Creon's bidding twice to summon him,

Nor understand why he came not long since.

CHORUS. All other hints were vague and ancient tales.

OEDIPUS. What hints then are there? I would know each word.

CHORUS. 'Twas said some travelers had murdered him.

OEDIPUS. So have I heard, but none saw him who saw.

CHORUS. Nor if he knows what fear is will he stay
When he has heard thy curses now invoked.

OEDIPUS. Words may not frighten him who fears no deed.

[*Enter* TIRESIAS, *led by a boy.*]

CHORUS. But lo he comes who shall convict the man.
For these are bringing now the godlike seer   ,
In whom alone of men is born the truth.

OEDIPUS. Tiresias, whose mind doth ponder all
Things known and things unspeakable on earth
And in the heavens above, though seeing naught
Thou knowest in what plight our city stands
Wherefrom, my lord, we find in thee alone
Our sole deliverer. For Phoebus' word
(Perchance thou hast not heard from messengers)
Comes back in answer to our questionings
Telling of one release from petilence
And only one, if we by searching out
Should find and slay forthwith the murderers
Of Laius or should drive them from our land.
Wherefore begrudge us not thy counseling
Whether from augury or from the lore
Of other ways prophetic thou knowest aught.
But save alike thyself, the city, me,
And fend from all the taint of murder done.
For we are in thy hands: man's noblest toil
Is helping others to the uttermost.

---

[5] When the Chorus participates in dramatic dialogue, the lines are conventionally spoken by individual members, usually by the *coryphaeus*, or leader of the Chorus.

[6] Apollo, among whose various attributes was patronage of poetry, music, and prophecy.

TIRESIAS. Alas, alas, how frightful to be wise
Where wisdom brings no gain. I knew this well
But had forgotten. Else had I never come.

OEDIPUS. What sayest thou? How downcast art arrived.

TIRESIAS. Release me to my home. Most easily
Shall we two bear our fates, if thou consent.

OEDIPUS. Strange are thy words nor friendly to the state
That gives thee sustenance, if thou speak not.

TIRESIAS. Not so: for thine own words as I perceive
Come not in season. Be not mine the same.

OEDIPUS. By all the gods I beg thee, leave us not,
If thou knowest aught, me and these suppliants.

TIRESIAS. Aye for ye all are ignorant. Mine own
Misfortunes shall I hide, to speak not thine.

OEDIPUS. What is this word? Thou knowest and wilt not speak
But wouldst betray thy city unto death?

TIRESIAS. Neither myself nor thee shall I distress.
Why ask in vain? Thou shalt not learn from me.

OEDIPUS. Basest of all base men, that wouldst enrage
The hardest rock, wilt never speak, but still
Present thyself unmoved in stubbornness?

TIRESIAS. My wrath thou blamest but thine own so near
Thou seest not, and yet upbraidest me.

OEDIPUS. Who would not rage to hear such words as thine
Wherewith even now thou dost outrage the state?

TIRESIAS. 'Twill come though by my silence hidden deep.

OEDIPUS. Then what will come thou too must speak to me.

TIRESIAS. I'll speak no further; wherefore if thou wilt,
Vent to the full thy wildest storm of rage.

OEDIPUS. Truly I'll leave unsaid no single word
Of all I think. Such is my rage. Know then
What I believe: that thou didst plot this deed.
Performed it too save only that thy hands
Wrought not the act. And hadst thou now thy sight
I'd say the murder too was all thine own.

TIRESIAS. Is't true? I charge thee then from thy decree
Swerve not, nor from this day forevermore
Speak unto these or me: thou art the man
That bringest on this land the curse of guilt.

OEDIPUS. Thus shameless wouldst thou speak and still expect
Somewhere to find a refuge from thy fate?

TIRESIAS. Safety is mine. I speak the all powerful truth.

OEDIPUS. Who taught thee then? 'Twas not thy priestly art.

TIRESIAS. I learned of thee, that forced my unwilling speech.

OEDIPUS. What speech? Lest I should err, speak it once more.

TIRESIAS. Hast thou not known or wouldst thou spread a net?

OEDIPUS. Unknowable it seems—speak it again.

TIRESIAS. I say thou art the slayer that thou wouldst find.

OEDIPUS. Not to thy joy hast spoken twice such words.

TIRESIAS. Shall I say more then that shall irk thee more?

OEDIPUS. Say what thou wilt, for thou shalt say in vain.

TIRESIAS. I say that thou has lived most shamefully
Unwitting with thy kin, nor knowest thy plight.

OEDIPUS. Dost think unharmed still to repeat such things?

TIRESIAS. Aye, if there be in truth protecting strength.

OEDIPUS. There is, for all save thee—but not for thee
For thou art blind in ear and mind and eye.

TIRESIAS. These jeerings prove thee wretched for e'er long
Each man of these shall hurl them back at thee.

OEDIPUS. Thou dwellest in continuous night, nor canst
Hurt me or any man that sees the day.

TIRESIAS. 'Tis not thy fate to fall by hand of mine.
Apollo shall suffice, the charge is his.

OEDIPUS. Was't Creon's thought or thine this treachery?

TIRESIAS. Creon ne'er did thee harm but thou thyself.

OEDIPUS. O Wealth and Power and Craft outreaching craft
Throughout our jealous life. What envious thrust
Can we be safe from if for this throne's sake
Whereof by gift I ne'er solicited
Thebes made me master, if for this my lord
Creon the faithful, friend since first I came,
Secretly plotting seeks to thrust me forth,
Suborning for his end this muddling priest
That knows the wiles of wealth, sees faultlessly
Where gain is for the getting, yet straightway
Sought for his priestcraft stumbles and is blind.
For tell me when hast thou shown prophecy?
Why when the riddling bitch bedeviled us
Didst thou not speak some safety to the state?
'Twas hardly for a chance arrival then
To spell that riddle, prophecy forsooth
Was needed then. Yet from thy twittering birds
Thou spakest naught, nor knewest aught from god.
'Twas I who came, I, Oedipus, that had
No knowledge of it all, and yet prevailed
By simple wisdom with no lore of birds.
Whom thou wouldst exile in the expectancy
Of high position close to Creon's throne.
Sorrow shall be the harvest—thine and his—
Of this prophetic sowing. Wert not old
Such thought as thine should bring thee violence.

CHORUS. Oedipus, both his words and thine appear
Spoken in anger, so at least I judge.
Such words we need not: be it our concern
How best we may fulfill god's oracle.

TIRESIAS. Tyrant thou art—yet cannot so refuse
The right to answer. That much lies within
My power. No slave am I to thee or any man
Beside—only to Loxias.[7] Wherefore
Write me not down to Creon's patronage.
Thou chidest me with blindness. Hear me say
That eyes thou hast but seest not thy plight,
Not even where thou livest nor with whom.
Dost know from whom thou'rt born? Nay, ignorant,
Thou hast made thyself the foe of thine own kin
That dwell with Hades or yet tread the earth.
Thee shall thy mother's curse, thy father's too,
Swift footed, two edged, drive from out this land
With eyes that see now, seeing then no more.
What refuge there that shall not echo back
Thy piteous cry—what haunt of desolate
Cithaeron [8]—when thou seest the anchorage
Whither on favoring breeze, into this home
Thou hast sailed in to shipwreck. Other ills

[7] "The Interpreter" or "Oracle"—a title applied to Apollo as the prophetic spokesman for Zeus.

[8] A mountain reputed to be the dwelling of the avenging Furies.

Countless (thou seest them not) shall level
   thee
With thine own self and thy begotten seed.
Revile thou as thou wilt the word I speak
And Creon too, for in the whole wide
   world
No man shall be so smitten as thyself.

OEDIPUS.   Can such things then be borne
   from such as he?
Begone to thy perdition—get thee gone—
Out of this house—begone I say, begone.

TIRESIAS.   I had not come hadst thou not
   summoned me.

OEDIPUS.   I knew thee not, that thou
   wouldst speak the fool
Or I had never brought thee to my house.

TIRESIAS.   I am but as I am—to thee a
   fool,
Yet wise indeed to those that gave thee
   birth.

OEDIPUS.   Who? Stay. Canst say who 'twas
   that gave me birth?

TIRESIAS.   This day shall give thee birth
   and give thee death.

OEDIPUS.   Forever riddles, riddles, dost
   thou speak.

TIRESIAS.   And art not thou the best to
   answer these?

OEDIPUS.   Chide me with that. Thou'lt find
   me fortunate.

TIRESIAS.   That was the fortune that hath
   ruined thee.

OEDIPUS.   I care not if the city so be saved.

TIRESIAS.   Then do I go—come boy and
   lead me home.

OEDIPUS.   Aye, let him lead thee, lingering
   here thou art
A nuisance, 'twere relief to have thee gone.

TIRESIAS.   I go for I have spoken that for
   which
I came, nor feared thy face; thou hast no
   power
Over my lips. But hark to what I say.
He whom thou seekest issuing thy threats
And heralding the death of Laius—he
Dwells here within—an alien visitor—
So is the tale—but shall appear at last

Native born Theban—yet no joy be his
At that discovery. For blind where once
He saw, a rich man beggared, he shall go
Forth to a foreign land feeling his way
With helpless staff, proving at last to be
Brother and sire to his own progeny.
And unto her that bore him in the womb
Both son and husband, to his aged sire
Betrayer first and then his murderer.
Go thou within and on these prophecies
Think well—if in one single circumstance
Thou find me false, denounce my prophet's
   role.

[TIRESIAS *is led out by the boy;*
OEDIPUS *withdaws into the palace.*]

FIRST STASIMON [9]

[CHORUS, *singing.*]

FIRST STROPHE

Voice, god-sent from Delphi's rock,
   Whose was the deed
   Ill-wrought with blood-stained hands
   Unspeakable? To lands
Afar with the speed wind-swift of the
   winged steed
Now must he take his flight nor longer
   mock
The embattled son of Zeus that leaps
   Swift following
With the brandished flame that never
   sleeps
And Fate insatiate unpitying.

FIRST ANTISTROPHE

Flashing from Parnassus' peaks
   Gleaming with snow
   Behest imperative
   To find the fugitive
That far through the trackless wood and
   the caves below
Wanders alone distraught and ever seeks
To avert the doom whose heartless Fate
   Relentlessly
From Apollo's shrine immaculate
Pursuing shapes unmoved his destiny.

[9] The several *stasima*, or choral interludes, which punctuate the stages of dramatic action, are chanted, often antiphonally, by the Chorus as it executes the formal figures of an interpretative dance.

Dread is the word, dread is the augury
  And the truth who knows?
Words have I none: fluttering hopes I
  see
And anon fear in their place. For the
  morrow shows
  Darkness deep as today.
  What old grief can I say
Breeding hate of our royal line
Now might sully the fame long won
  By Polybus' son [10]
Or fasten on him the doom of the word
  divine.

Zeus knoweth all, Zeus and the Delphian
  lord
  With all-seeing eye.
Yea, but of man, priests with prophetic
  word
Why unto them yield we credulity?
  Though in wisdom of mind
  Man may humble mankind,
Never shall I till the truth be clear
Grant his guilt who released our state
  From ruinous Fate
Outwitted the riddling monster and ban-
  ished fear.

SECOND EPISODE

[Enter CREON.*]*

CREON. My fellow citizens, I am informed
That Oedipus the King hath uttered here
Grave charges against me. And so I
  come
Resentful, seeing that in our present plight
If he believe that aught in word or deed
From me hath injured him, I have no will
Under suspicion to prolong my life.
Not simple is the harm that such a charge
Does me but manifold if I am thought
False to my city and to you, my friends.
CHORUS. Such was the charge he made
  perchance
Not in cool wisdom but in bitter wrath.
CREON. And said he also that by my ad-
  vice
The seer put forth his lying prophecies?
CHORUS. So spake he but with what intent,
  who knows?
CREON. But with a mind unclouded and
  clear eye
Brought he this charge against me? Tell me
  that.
CHORUS. I know not. For I am not wont
  to see
What kings perform. But look, he comes
  himself.

[10] Oedipus. Polybus was the King of Corinth
whom Oedipus believed to be his father.

[Enter OEDIPUS*]*

OEDIPUS. Thou? Thou? How art thou
  come? Such brazen front
Of daring hast thou as to approach my
  house,
The murderer proven of this man and
  now
Usurper manifest of this my throne?
Come tell me by the gods, was't cowardice
Or folly seen in me that tempted thee
To such a plotting or didst think the act
Would not betray thy stealthy treachery
Or even perchance that I might wittingly
Ignore it? Is it not a fool's attempt
With neither force nor friends to seek a
  throne
That only numbers and great wealth can
  win?
CREON. Knowest then what must be?
  Hearken thou shalt
To answering words: and so with knowl-
  edge judge.
OEDIPUS. Trickster with words I know
  thee—yet am I
Not quickly taught, knowing thy deadly
  hate.
CREON. First hear from me one word that
  I shall speak.
OEDIPUS. So be thou'lt not assert thou art
  not base.

CREON. And thou conceive some gain in stubbornness
Unyoked with wisdom, then thou art not wise.

OEDIPUS. And thou conceive escape from punishment,
Doing a kinsman ill, thou art not wise.

CREON. Therein thou speakest true, I grant it thee;
Yet show what wrong from me thou hast endured.

OEDIPUS. Didst thou advise or not that I must send
To fetch forthwith this prophesying priest?

CREON. Aye and now too approve such policy.

OEDIPUS. How long ago was it that Laius hence—

CREON. Did what? I follow not thy questioning.

OEDIPUS. Was spirited by fatal violence?

CREON. Long span of years must fill that reckoning.

OEDIPUS. And was this priest a priest in those days too?

CREON. As wise as now and honored equally.

OEDIPUS. Made he then any mention of my name?

CREON. He did not—or at least when I was nigh.

OEDIPUS. And of the murdered king— made ye no search?

CREON. Assuredly we searched but learned no clue.

OEDIPUS. Why then did not this wise man speak these things?

CREON. I know not; knowing not I hold my tongue.

OEDIPUS. This much thou knowest and wouldst be wise to speak.

CREON. What thing? For if I know it, I'll not deny.

OEDIPUS. That had Tiresias not conferred with thee
He had not named me Laius' murderer.

CREON. If he says so, thou knowest. I too have right
To question thee as thou hast questioned me.

OEDIPUS. Ask what thou wilt: thou shalt not prove my guilt.

CREON. How then, hast thou my sister for thy wife?

OEDIPUS. That question surely may not be denied.

CREON. And dost thou rule on equal terms with her?

OEDIPUS. All that her heart desires she has from me.

CREON. And am I not a third with equal power?

OEDIPUS. Thou art in truth and so art proven base.

CREON. Nay, if thou usest reason with thyself
Consider first: would any choose to rule
Encompassed round with terror if the same
Authority might rest in perfect peace?
For I at any rate have never sought
To be a king rather than have the right
Of kingly powers—nor any man of sense.
And now from thee with naught to terrify
I have all favor; ruled I here alone
Much must I do perforce against my will.
How then should any crown appear to me
Sweeter than royal privilege secure?
Not yet am I so foolish as to seek
For other goal than honor linked with gain.
Now all men greet me, all men wish me well
And those that would reach thee bespeak my ear
Since there alone lies prospect of success.
Why then should I, abandoning the sure
Advantage that is mine, seek otherwhere?
No mind that harbors wisdom can be false.
And I have neither loved folly myself
Nor could I join another in such act.
Wherefore send now to Pytho for the proof
Of these my words: find out the oracle:
Ask if I told it true. And furthermore
If thou canst prove that with Tiresias
I ever have connived, then not with one
But with a twofold vote, thine own and mine,
Take me and slay me. Only charge me not
In secret with dark counsels. Justice ne'er
Lightly deems bad men good or good men bad.

To cast away a faithful friend I deem
No wiser than to fling aside one's life.
This truth in time thou'lt learn, since time
alone
Reveals the just. A single passing day
Amply suffices to disclose the base.

CHORUS. Wise words, my lord, for one
that would not slip;
The swift in counsel rarely counsel best.

OEDIPUS. When he who plots in secret
moves apace
I too must counsel swiftly. Else my ends,
The while I linger sleeping foolishly,
Are lost forever, his forever gained.

CREON. What wilt thou then? Wouldst
drive me from the land?

OEDIPUS. That least of all: my will is
death not flight,
Proclaiming to the world base envy's power.

CREON. These are the words of stubborn
unbelief.

OEDIPUS. Thou hast not acted to inspire
belief.

CREON. Thou seemst not sane.

OEDIPUS. Yet am in my affairs.

CREON. Thou shouldst be so in mine.

OEDIPUS. But thou art base.

CREON. What if thou knowest naught?

OEDIPUS. Yet must I rule.

CREON. Not if thy rule be wrong.

OEDIPUS. O city mine!

CREON. Not thine alone—for Thebes is
mine as well.

[*Enter* JOCASTA.]

CHORUS. Desist, my lords. Most happily
for you
I see Jocasta coming from the house.
Her help should end this present quarreling.

JOCASTA. What foolish strife of words, all
ill-advised,
Is this ye raise? Are ye not then ashamed,
Your country perishing, to air abroad
Your private wrongs? Nay, rather come
within
Nor magnify your petty difference.

CREON. Nay sister, for thy husband
Oedipus
Makes twofold threat against me—either
death
By violence or exile from this land.

OEDIPUS. 'Tis so for, woman, with base
treachery
I caught him plotting ill against my life.

CREON. Never may joy be mine but death
accursed
If I am guilty of thy lightest charge.

JOCASTA. Now by the gods believe him,
Oedipus,
For his oath's sake that he has sworn and
for
My sake as well and these that stand by
thee.

KOMMOS [11]

CHORUS. Yield thee, my King, hearken I
pray.

OEDIPUS. What is thy will?

CHORUS. Grant him belief, wise hitherto,
pledging his oath.

OEDIPUS. Knowest thou what thou wilt?

CHORUS. Aye.

OEDIPUS. Then declare it me.

CHORUS. Never should friend by friend,
sworn under oath,
Lightly be thrust aside.

OEDIPUS. Know then assuredly asking of
me this boon
Exile for me or death
Follows thy prayer.

CHORUS. Nay by the god of light
By Helios' self, first of the gods above,
May I in misery
Friendless of god and man
Wretchedly die,
If in my inmost breast lurks such desire.
Yearns now my sorrowing heart
Torn by my country's plight
Mocked by thy strife.

OEDIPUS. Let him then go, even though it
mean my death

[11] A *kommos* is a lyrical passage introduced into the midst of a dramatic episode to heighten the emotional tension. The lines are chanted to a musical accompaniment. Unlike the *stasimon*, the *kommos* does not mark a pause in the draamtic action, but indicates a peak of intensity. Note that the two *kommoi* in this episode, each ending in a short choral lyric, deliberately follow the same metrical pattern.

Or if dishonored into banishment
I must depart. Thy words, not his, prevail.
For him where'er he be my hate pursues.
CREON.   Grudging is thy surrender, arrogant
Thy wrath. Natures like thine by Fate's decree
Are ever to themselves hardest to bear.
OEDIPUS.   Wilt thou not leave me and begone?
CREON.   I go.
Thou canst not comprehend—these know me just.

[*Exit* CREON.]

KOMMOS

CHORUS.   Why, O my Queen, why dost delay?
Lead him within.
JOCASTA.   First I must know what hath entailed strife such as this.
CHORUS.   Groundless suspicion here: rankling injustice there.
JOCASTA.   Nurtured by both?
CHORUS.   Aye.
JOCASTA.   And the cause?
CHORUS.   More than enough to me
Seems now the harm that's done, while yet my country bleeds.
OEDIPUS.   Seest thou then thy zeal
Whither it leads?
CHORUS.   Not only once, my King—
I say again, fool should I be and worse
Witless and reft of sense
Should I be false to thee
Thou that didst come
Bringing new life to me, saving the state
Tossed on a raging sea
Aye and again to be
Savior and guide.
JOCASTA.   Tell me, my lord, I charge thee by the gods,
Whence came to thee this wrath unquenchable?
OEDIPUS.   Thee will I tell—I love thee more than these—
'Twas Creon and his plots against my life.
JOCASTA.   Speak plainly if indeed thou hast plain cause.

OEDIPUS.   He plainly names me Laius' murderer.
JOCASTA.   Speaking his own words or some other man's?
OEDIPUS.   Making a bastard priest spokesman for him
To keep unsoiled his own lips, craftily.
JOCASTA.   Then think no more of it— hearken to me
And know that never yet hath mortal man
Shared in prophetic art. I'll show to thee
Sure proof of these my words. There came of old
A prophecy to Laius, I say not
From Phoebus' self but from his ministers,
How death should come to him by his son's hand
That should be born to Laius and to me.
Yet—so the rumor hath it—Laius died
Murdered by robbers—strangers—where forsooth
The triple crossroads meet. The child of ours
Not three days old, its ankles bound with thongs,
By others' hands, Laius had left exposed
Far on the trackless hillside. So, I ween,
Apollo did not make of that poor child
His father's murderer nor did fulfill
The fears of Laius that his fate should come
At his child's hand. So did the words of priests
Foretell. Give them no heed. For what god needs
He can himself most easily disclose.
OEDIPUS.   What restless thoughts of terror, O my wife,
Hast thou engendered in my troubled mind?
JOCASTA.   What hath disturbed thee that thou speakest so?
OEDIPUS.   Methought I heard thee say that Laius' death
O'ertook him where the triple crossroads meet.
JOCASTA.   So ran the story and hath never ceased.
OEDIPUS.   Where is the spot that saw the murder done?
JOCASTA.   Phocis the land is called—a branching road

Leads there from Delphi and from Daulia.

OEDIPUS. How long the time from that event till now?

JOCASTA. 'Twas just before thy coming that the word
Was brought to us—ere thou wast King of Thebes.

OEDIPUS. O Zeus, what is thy will to do with me?

JOCASTA. Why, Oedipus, should this so trouble thee?

OEDIPUS. Ask me not yet—but tell me this instead.
Laius, what was his form, what years were his?

JOCASTA. His stature tall, silver just streaked his hair,
And in appearance not unlike to thee.

OEDIPUS. Woe, woe, is me: it seems that I have hurled,
Unwitting, dreadful curses on myself.

JOCASTA. How sayest; my lord, I tremble at thy word.

OEDIPUS. I fear in truth Tiresias still hath sight.
But thou mayst show. Tell me this one thing more.

JOCASTA. I tremble, yet I'll answer and thou wilt.

OEDIPUS. Did Laius go alone, or like a king,
Surrounded by his spearmen royally?

JOCASTA. Five men in all, a herald one, the King
Rode in his chariot, the rest afoot.

OEDIPUS. Alas, 'tis all too clear. Who was the man
That here returning made report to thee?

JOCASTA. A servant that escaped, alone of all.

OEDIPUS. And now perchance is in the palace here?

JOCASTA. Not so, for when he came to Thebes and found
Thee on the throne, with Laius dead, he pled,
Seizing my hand, to be dispatched far hence
Into the fields, the pastures of our flocks,
That so he might not see the city more.

And I consented. Faithful service given
Deserved such favor, aye and greater too.

OEDIPUS. Might someone bring him here without delay?

JOCASTA. 'Tis possible. Why dost thou wish it so?

OEDIPUS. I fear that I have spoken overmuch.
And for this reason I would see the man.

JOCASTA. The man shall come anon, yet O my lord,
I too deserve to know what troubles thee.

OEDIPUS. Nor shalt thou be denied when such dread fear
Possesses me. For whither should I turn
If not to thee, fast in misfortune's clutch?
My father was King Polybus, the lord
Of Corinth, and my mother Merope.
Dorian she. And I was held the first
Of all the citizens, till there befell
A chance surprising yet not meriting
My great concern thereat. A banqueter
Befuddled with much wine, hurled in my face
The taunt that I was not my father's son.
Much angered, for that day I held my peace
Though hardly: on the next I questioned straight
My parents both who flamed with instant wrath
At him who spake the insult. From their scorn
I took some comfort, but anon the taunt
Rankled unceasing, while the rumor spread.
Wherefore without their knowledge I betook
Myself to Pytho. Whence, touching the quest
That brought me thither, Phoebus caring naught
Sent me away unanswered, yet himself
Vouchsafing other knowledge, bade me know
Dread horror past believing: 'twas my fate
By wedlock with my mother to beget
Offspring abhorrent in the eyes of all
Mankind and be besides the murderer
Of mine own father. When I heard these words
Guided by heaven's stars I fled apace

Corinth and all her land that so I might
Escape fulfilment of the oracle.
Making my way I came unto the spot
Where thou dost say this King of thine was
    slain.
The truth I'll tell thee, for thou art my wife:
Nearing this triple crossways as I went,
A herald met me and a traveler
Drawn in a carriage, as thou saidst, by colts.
Straightway the herald and the old man too
Were both for pushing me aside. I struck
In righteous anger at the charioteer
Who jostled me; the old man when he saw,
Watching the moment when I passed him
    close,
Reached from the car and with his two-
    pronged goad
Smote me upon the head. Unequally
He paid that debt, for with quick reckon-
    ing
Struck by the staff in this my hand, he
    plunged
Headlong from out the chariot. All the rest
I killed, forthwith. Now if there chanced
    to be
Twixt Laius and this stranger any bond
Of kinship, who in all this wretched world
More wretched than myself? What man
    more cursed:
Whom not a soul may welcome in the
    home,
Stranger nor friend, nor speak a word to
    me
But all must thrust me out. No other man
Invoked this curse but I myself decreed
Such things against myself. The dead man's
    couch
I have polluted with the self-same hands
That slew him. Am I cursed in very truth?
Am I not all unholy? I must flee
And fleeing may not look upon my own
Nor tread the pathways of my fatherland,
Fearing that Fate foretold, that I should
    wed
My mother and become the murderer
Of Polybus my father who begat
And reared me. Surely one may well be-
    lieve
'Tis from some cruel god that on my head
Such fate hath fallen. Never, O gods above

August and holy, never may I see
That day. Rather from sight of all man-
    kind
May I be hidden far, nor e'er behold
The stain of such a doom clinging to me.
CHORUS. Dreadful to me, my lord, these
    things, yet till
Thou hearest from that witness, nurse thy
    hope.
OEDIPUS. So much of hope is all that's left
    me now:
To await the herdsman and to hear his tale.
JOCASTA. And when he comes, what
    wouldst thou hear from him?
OEDIPUS. I'll tell thee: if his story still
    remain
Consistent with thine own, then I am
    cleared.
JOCASTA. What word of mine hath so im-
    pressed thee then?
OEDIPUS. By thine account he said in tell-
    ing thee
Robbers killed Laius. If he still persist
Nor change the number, then I killed him
    not.
For one and many tally not; but if
He now maintain 'twas but a single man
Surely the deed can only be mine own.
JOCASTA. Nay but he told it so, be well
    assured,
Nor can deny it now, the city heard,
Not I alone. And if he now deny
Or change his story, he can never prove
That Laius' murder came as prophesied.
Since Loxias said that by his own son's
    hand
Laius must die. And surely 'twas not he,
That wretched child, that slew him. Nay,
    himself
Did perish long before. Wherefore hence-
    forth
I'll look not here nor there for oracles.
OEDIPUS. Just is thy reasoning. Yet do not
    fail
To give thine orders that the peasant come.
JOCASTA. I'll send in haste, but let us go
    within—
Naught would I do that fits not with thy
    will.

[*Exeunt* OEDIPUS *and* JOCASTA.]

SECOND STASIMON

[CHORUS *singing*]

Come whensoe'er it will may Fate o'ertake
    me still
Guarding each word and act with reverent
    awe
For swift are the laws of Fate
That have fared from heaven's gate
And god on Olympus' height hath made
    each law.
No mortal brought them forth, no lethal
    breath
Awaits them: hall-marked with divinity
    they know not death.

But arrogance breeds force, swift on its
    course
When glutted full, proud arrogance climbs
    high,
Snatches the cornice—then, clutching foot-
    hold in vain
Plunges, far down on heartless crags to
    lie.
But the strife that leads to good I shall
    ever ask,
And to god who rules on high perform my
    task.

Whoso'er in word or deed
Acts with arrogance
Whoso will not justice heed,
Godward looks askance,
Him may justice overtake
Him may Fate unhappy shake
If he get not gain with praise
If he keep not all his ways
Pure from stain of guilt.
Else why this offering here of love,
This worship of dance to the gods above?

Never again to Delphi's shrine
Shall I go with heart's desire,
Never again to Abbae's pine
Nor Olympus' altar fire,
If there be not here
Such music clear
As proveth divinity.
But O thou god if thou hearest aught,
Thou Zeus that rulest on high,
May our impious acts with evil wrought
Scape not thy watchful eye.
For the prophet's word
By our dead King heard,
With holy horror fraught,
Has vanished like air
And Apollo's care
Is held as naught.

THIRD EPISODE

[*Enter* JOCASTA.]

JOCASTA. Lords of this land, my purpose
    is resolved
To visit now the temples of the gods
Bearing this wreath and gifts for sacrifice.
For Oedipus' emotions run too high
Beneath his sufferings. Not like a man
Of wisdom doth he judge these new
    events
By what is old, yielding to each new voice
So be it speak of terrors. Therefore, since
My counseling is vain, to thee I come,
Lycian lord Apollo, suppliant,
(For thou art nearest) to petition thee:
Grant us release without defilement: now
Terror possesses us as who behold
Smitten with fear the captain of their ship.

[*Enter the* FIRST MESSENGER, *as* JOCASTA
    places her offerings upon the altar.]

MESSENGER. Strangers, I fain would learn
    from you where dwells
King Oedipus—or better, where is he?
CHORUS. Here stands his palace and him-
    self within.
This is his wife, the mother of his brood.
MESSENGER. Happy be she forever, may
    she dwell
Always in happiness, being his Queen.
JOCASTA. Blessed be thy lot too whoe'er
    thou art
For so thy words deserve. But speak:
    wherefore
Dost thou now come: what news wouldst
    thou impart?

MESSENGER.   Good news unto this house and to the King.

JOCASTA.   What is it and from whom thine embassy?

MESSENGER.   From Corinth, and the word that I shall speak
Shall bring thee happiness, and grief as well.

JOCASTA.   What word is that that hath such twofold power?

MESSENGER.   The dwellers of the Isthmian land will make
Him King of Corinth, so the rumor ran.

JOCASTA.   How so? Is not old Polybus their king?

MESSENGER.   Nay, for Death holds him fast within the tomb.

JOCASTA.   How sayest thou? Is Polybus then dead?

MESSENGER.   If I speak not the truth then let me die.

JOCASTA.   Maiden, run swift and tell thy master this.
Where are ye then, ye oracles of god?
This was the man that, long since, Oedipus
Feared and avoided lest he be constrained
To murder him, and now the self-same King
Lies dead, outdone by Fate and not by him.

[*Enter* OEDIPUS.]

OEDIPUS.   O dearest wife, Jocasta, why, I pray,
Hast thou now summoned me from out the house?

JOCASTA.   Hearken to this man's word, then judge thyself
The outcome of the dreaded oracles.

OEDIPUS.   Who is the man? What would he say to me?

JOCASTA.   Coming from Corinth he brings messages
Of Polybus thy father, and his death.

OEDIPUS.   How sayest thou, stranger, speak now for thyself.

MESSENGER.   If this must be my first report then know
That he has gone indeed the way of Death.

OEDIPUS.   By violence, or died he by disease?

MESSENGER.   Slight matters turn the scale when one is old.

OEDIPUS.   Illness it was then that hath brought him low?

MESSENGER.   Aye, and the long tale of passing years.

OEDIPUS.   Alas, alas, why therefore, O my wife,
Should one look ever to the Pythian shrine
Or hearken to the cry of birds? 'Twas they
That would have made me murderer of him
My father, yet it seems he now is dead
While here I stand unarmed and innocent—
Unless he died of longing for his son:
So only could one blame me. And in truth
Polybus lies in Hades and hath swept
With him the oracles and proved them
   naught.

JOCASTA.   And said I not long since it would be so?

OEDIPUS.   Thou didst, and yet by fear I was misled.

JOCASTA.   Now therefore give them not a single thought.

OEDIPUS.   Surely I still must fear my mother's couch.

JOCASTA.   What fear should be for mortal man whose life
Fate rules supreme, nor can he aught foresee?
Better to live by chance as best ye may.
Nor shouldst thou fear this wedlock horrible
With thine own mother: many men there be
That in their dreams have done this act. He best
Supports his life who counts these things as naught.

OEDIPUS.   Well spoken were thy words save that she lives
Who bore me: since she lives she still compels
Terror in me, fair though thy counselings.

JOCASTA.   And yet thy father's death should give thee pause.

OEDIPUS. 'Tis true I grant thee, but my mother lives.

MESSENGER. What woman is it whom thou fearest so?

OEDIPUS. Merope, who was wife to Polybus.

MESSENGER. And what the fear that she inspires in thee?

OEDIPUS. An oracle that came, stranger, from god.

MESSENGER. Mayst tell it, or must others know it not?

OEDIPUS. Truly I may. Loxias spoke of old
How I must marry with my mother, then
Shed with these hands of mine, my father's blood.
Corinth and I have therefore been long since
Strangers and happily too save that it's sweet
To look on those who brought us to the light.

MESSENGER. Such was the fear that wrought thy banishment?

OEDIPUS. Aye, that I might not work my father's death.

MESSENGER. How then have I not freed thee from thy fear
Coming, my lord, with welcome messages?

OEDIPUS. And truly thou shalt have thy just reward.

MESSENGER. I will confess that was my secret hope
That I might profit by thy coming home.

OEDIPUS. Home will I never come while she yet lives.

MESSENGER. My son, 'tis clear thou knowest not what thou dost.

OEDIPUS. How so, old man? Tell me now by the gods.

MESSENGER. If for this cause thou wilt not now return.

OEDIPUS. 'Tis cause enough, lest Phoebus prove his word.

MESSENGER. And from thy parents thou incur some guilt?

OEDIPUS. Just so, for that shall always be my fear.

MESSENGER. Dost know, then, that thy fears are all for naught?

OEDIPUS. How can that be and I a child of theirs?

MESSENGER. For Polybus was never kin of thine.

OEDIPUS. What sayest thou? Polybus not my sire?

MESSENGER. No more than I myself, as much, no more.

OEDIPUS. Why match thyself with him who caused my birth?

MESSENGER. Nay, he begat thee not, nor he nor I.

OEDIPUS. Wherefore, if this be so, called he me son?

MESSENGER. Delivered by these hands, a gift thou wert.

OEDIPUS. And could he love me so when gotten thus?

MESSENGER. He could by virtue of long childlessness.

OEDIPUS. Thou, hadst thou bought me or didst find this gift?

MESSENGER. I found thee in Cithaeron's wooded glades.

OEDIPUS. Purposing what didst wander to this land?

MESSENGER. In charge of flocks that ranged these mountainsides.

OEDIPUS. Thou wert a shepherd and a hireling then?

MESSENGER. My son, I was thy savior in those days.

OEDIPUS. How so, what suffering didst thou save me from?

MESSENGER. Whereof thine ankles give thee evidence.[12]

OEDIPUS. Alas, why call to mind that ancient woe?

MESSENGER. I loosed thine ankles fastened with a thong.

OEDIPUS. An outrage from my days in swaddling clothes.

MESSENGER. And from that outrage thou hast still thy name.

[12] The name Oedipus means "swollen foot." The swollen ankles of Oedipus afford an interesting early example of one of drama's most long-lived devices—the establishment of identity by means of a distinguishing mark.

OEDIPUS. Speak, by the gods; was that a parent's deed?

MESSENGER. I know not, he knows best that gave thee me.

OEDIPUS. Thou didst not find me? I was given thee?

MESSENGER. Another shepherd placed thee in my hands.

OEDIPUS. What man is that? Dost know? Canst point him out?

MESSENGER. 'Twas one of Laius' shepherds, so 'twas said.

OEDIPUS. His who was King in Thebes in days gone by?

MESSENGER. Aye, his indeed, a herdsman of that King.

OEDIPUS. Lives the man still that I might look on him?

MESSENGER. Ye men of Thebes should know that best of all.

OEDIPUS. Knows any man of you of whom he speaks
Or have ye seen this shepherd in the town
Or on the upland pastures? Let such speak.
The time is come that these things be revealed.

CHORUS. Methinks it is no other than the man
Thou hast desired to see. Jocasta now
Surely might best reveal to thee the truth.

OEDIPUS. O wife and Queen, knowest thou whom but now
We summoned hither? Speaks he of the same?

JOCASTA. What matters whom he mentioned? Give no thought
To what he said, for all such thoughts are vain.

OEDIPUS. It may not be. With such proofs in my grasp
I must discover now my lineage.

JOCASTA. No, by the gods, if thou hast any care
For thine own life, ask not. My woe's enough.

OEDIPUS. Fear not, for though from triple servitude
I find my line thou shalt not so be base.

JOCASTA. Believe me none the less: touch not this thing.

OEDIPUS. I may not so believe thee, I must learn.

JOCASTA. For thine own sake I speak and counsel well.

OEDIPUS. These counselings have long since vexed my soul.

JOCASTA. O hapless man, god grant thee ignorance.

OEDIPUS. Let someone bring this shepherd to me straight:
This woman, let her boast her royal line.

JOCASTA. Alas, most wretched man; for this one word
I speak thee now, none else forevermore.
[JOCASTA *rushes into the palace.*]

CHORUS. Why has she gone, thy Queen, O Oedipus,
In frenzied grief? I fear that from this deep
Silence of hers misfortune shall break forth.

OEDIPUS. Let come what will. Low though my lineage
Be proven, yet I'll know it. She perchance
Womanlike in her pride may fear in shame
To face mine origin. I hold myself
Own child of Fortune; she beneficent
Shall never cause me shame. Her child am I
Brother of all the months whose passing course
Made me now small, now great, and being such
In parentage pray god I never prove
False to that mother Fortune nor desert
The search that shall yet prove my lineage.
[*Exeunt* OEDIPUS *and* MESSENGER.]

THIRD STASIMON

[CHORUS *singing.*]

STROPHE

Now by Olympus high
If aught of phophecy
    Or wisdom lie
    Within this breast
Tomorrow's moon shall see
    Our Oedipus stand confessed
Thy countryman, Cithaeron, and thy son,

This dance a duty done
    In loyalty.
Lord god, Apollo, let these our deeds be
    blessed.

Whose was the goddess' womb
That unto Pan bore thee
Through wooded coomb
    And grass-grown run
Pursued relentlessly?
    Or art thou Apollo's son?
For dear to him is every upland way.
    Or Hermes'—who shall say?
        Or was it he
Great Bacchus, loved of the nymphs on
    Helicon?

FOURTH EPISODE

[*Enter* OEDIPUS *and the* FIRST MESSENGER.]

OEDIPUS.   Sir, if I too who never met the
    man
May yet venture a guess, yonder, methinks
I see the herdsman whom we seek. In years
He matches well this stranger and besides
Servants they are of mine conducting him.
Yet better is thy knowledge than mine own
Since thou hast seen the fellow ere today.
CHORUS.   I know him, have no doubt, of
    Laius' men
Shepherd of all most faithful to the King.

[*The* HERDSMAN *is led in.*]

OEDIPUS.   Thee first I question; didst thou
    mean this man,
Stranger from Corinth?
MESSENGER.   Aye, the man thou seest.
OEDIPUS.   Thou too, old man, look hither,
    answer me
My question: wast thou ever Laius' man?
HERDSMAN.   I was, a house-born slave, no
    market prize.
OEDIPUS.   What task was thine? How didst
    thou spend thy life?
HERDSMAN.   The larger part in following
    the herds.
OEDIPUS.   What were the regions thou
    didst most frequent?
HERDSMAN.   Cithaeron mostly and its
    neighborhood.
OEDIPUS.   This fellow here, hast ever seen
    him there?
HERDSMAN.   What doing, sir, and what
    man dost thou mean?
OEDIPUS.   Who stands before thee: hast
    met him before?

HERDSMAN.   Not so that I might say at
    once from memory.
MESSENGER.   Nor any wonder. Yet, my
    lord, I can
Clearly recall what now he has forgot.
I doubt not he remembers well the time
When for three summers clear from spring
    until
Arcturus' rising we together roamed
These stretches of Cithaeron, he with two
Herds while I tended one. When winter
    came
I drove my flocks to Corinth home, he his
To Laius' folds. Is this the truth I speak
Or do I tell of things that never were?
HERDSMAN.   The truth indeed, and yet
    'twas long ago.
MESSENGER.   Come tell me then, canst
    thou recall how once
Thou gavest me a child to rear as mine?
HERDSMAN.   How now? Why dost thou
    question me of that?
MESSENGER.   For this is he who was a
    baby then.
HERDSMAN.   Destruction take thee, wilt
    thou hold thy tongue?
OEDIPUS.   Old man, revile him not, thy
    words, not his,
Seem most to need amendment, chide him
    not.
HERDSMAN.   And what, good master, have
    I done amiss?
OEDIPUS.   Refusing thus to answer what
    he asks.
HERDSMAN.   He asks in ignorance, and
    all in vain.
OEDIPUS.   Thou speak not freely, thou
    shalt speak in pain.

HERDSMAN. By all the gods, force not an aged man.

OEDIPUS. Will someone quickly bind the fellow's hands?

HERDSMAN. Ah wretched me, for what, what wouldst thou know?

OEDIPUS. The child, didst give it to him as he says?

HERDSMAN. I did, and would to god I had died then.

OEDIPUS. Thou shalt die now and thou speak not the truth.

HERDSMAN. And if I do, more surely shall I die.

OEDIPUS. The fellow seems determined to delay.

HERDSMAN. Not I, I told you that I gave the child.

OEDIPUS. Whence hadst thou it, was't thine or someone's else?

HERDSMAN. 'Twas not mine own, I had it from a man.

OEDIPUS. A Theban? One of these? And from what home?

HERDSMAN. No, by the gods, my lord, ask me no more.

OEDIPUS. Thou art a dead man if I ask again.

HERDSMAN. Well then, it was a child of Laius' house.

OEDIPUS. A slave, or one free born of his own race?

HERDSMAN. Alas, I tremble on the brink of speech.

OEDIPUS. And I of hearing, yet perforce I must.

HERDSMAN. His own the child was called. The Queen within,
Thy wife, may best confirm to thee the fact.

OEDIPUS. Was it she gave the child?

HERDSMAN.   'Twas she, my lord.

OEDIPUS. What was her purpose?

HERDSMAN.   I should kill the child.

OEDIPUS. Unnatural mother.

HERDSMAN.   Oracles she feared.

OEDIPUS. What?

HERDSMAN. He should kill his parent, so 'twas said.

OEDIPUS. How then didst thou bestow him on this man?

HERDSMAN. In pity, sire, thinking that he would take
The child to his own country, yet it seems
He saved him to misfortune. If thou art
The man he says, then dreadful is thy doom.

OEDIPUS. Alas, alas. It must then all be true.
O light of day, may I ne'er look on thee
Again, who now am found cursed at my birth,
Wedded in incest, steeped in mine own blood.

[OEDIPUS *flees into the palace. The* FIRST MESSENGER *and* HERDSMAN *withdraw.*]

FOURTH STASIMON

[CHORUS *singing.*]

FIRST STROPHE

Alas, alas for the years of mortality:
　　I count ye as naught.
　Who is he that hath ever found
　More than a vision of empty sound
　　By fancy wrought?
And ever the vision ends in calamity.
　For now, my King, soul wracked and
　　　sore distressed,
　　Thy fate do I behold
　　Woes manifold
　And I count no mortal blessed.

FIRST ANTISTROPHE

Beyond man's skill did he speed his unerr-
　　ing shaft
　　And won to his goal
　Fortune's prize of prosperity
　Slaying the Sphinx with her mystery
　　And stopped the toll
Of that death she levied: foully she
　　　wrought and laughed
　　Till thou didst come, champion and
　　　tower of might.
　　Henceforth all conquering
　　　Art hailed as king
　　In this land of god's delight.

SECOND STROPHE

And now on the lips of all
  Whose fate so black?
While the Furies of madness in hungry
    pack
  Cry for thy fall.
For into a harbor strange thou hast sailed
Where the deathless laws of the gods have
    failed,
Where the same unhallowed love prevailed
On sire and son in the self-same hall.
  What god bestowed
This poisonous boon, this fatal goad
  To sow where his father sowed?

SECOND ANTISTROPHE

But time that is never blind
  Hath now disclosed
What the dwellers of earth, to the light
    exposed,
  Shudder to find.
Seed of begetter and him begot
In the self-same furrow that sensed them
    not
And I would to god thy thrice-cursed lot
Were hidden darkly from all mankind.
  I mourn thy plight
That unto me brought sudden light
  To end in eternal night.

EXODUS

[*Enter* SECOND MESSENGER [13] *from the palace.*]

MESSENGER. Ye ever-honored most in Thebes, what deeds
Shall smite your ears, what sights shall ye behold
What grief is yours if to tradition true
Ye still revere the house of Labdacus.
Waters of Ister, streams of Phasis ne'er
Can cleanse this dwelling, such the dreadful deed
It hides but shall disclose, no deed of chance
But wittingly contrived. Always those griefs
Hurt most whose choice the world shall mark our own.
CHORUS. Already we have witnessed here such deeds
As might call forth such cry; what hast thou more?
MESSENGER. To take the shortest course for him who speaks
And him who hears: the Queen Jocasta is dead.
CHORUS. O lady of ill fortune, by what means?

MESSENGER. By her own hand. The part most horrible,
The sight of it, is spared thee. What remains
Of all her woe within my memory
Straight shalt thou hear. Frantic with mad despair
She came within the antechamber. Then
Rushed to the wedding couch, with both her hands
Tearing her hair, dashed shut the doors behind
Invoking Laius, dead these many years,
And called to mind that son that he begot
So long ago by whom he died and left
Her that had borne him wretched to produce
Offspring to share with his. She cried against
That marriage which to her misfortune raised
A double brood, husband by husband got
And children by her child. How after that
She perished I know not, for Oedipus
Burst in with shouting who allowed us not
Further to look upon her misery
Since on his frenzy rested all our eyes.

[13] Strictly speaking, the Second Messenger is not a messenger at all, but a sort of announcer or expositor. He is a stock figure regularly employed at this point in classical tragedy to recount the violent happenings off-stage. His set speech provides the dramatist with an opportunity for both sustained poetry and an interpreted effect by means of dramatic narrative and vivid description.

Madly he raged, asking of us a sword
And calling for the wife that was no wife
The mother's womb that bore alike himself
And his own children. In his madness some
Divinity did guide him for 'twas none
Of us poor mortals who were standing by.
Then with a dreadful shout, as beckoned
    on
He hurled himself upon the double doors—
Back from their sockets bent the yielding
    bolts—
And rushed within. There we beheld his
    wife
Hanged by a twisted cord still swaying
    there.
And when he saw her, with a mighty cry
He loosed the rope that held her. As she
    lay
Stretched on the ground, followed a grue-
    some sight.
For from her dress he tore the golden
    brooch
That held it. Raising it aloft he smote
Full on his eyeballs shouting as he struck
That they should nevermore behold what
    he
Had suffered nor the evil he had wrought.
Darkened forever they might never look
Again on what they had no right to see,
Failing to recognize what most they ought.
And with such imprecations 'twas not once
But many times he beat upon his eyes.
The bloody eyeballs burst upon his beard
Not in slow drops of blood but in one black
Down-rushing stream of blood, like shower
    of hail.
Such are the woes that issue from these
    twain,
Husband and wife commingled. What was
    once
Their happy lot, and happiness in truth,
This day is turned to wailing, madness,
    death
And all the woes that are, are theirs today.
CHORUS. Hath now the wretched man
    some rest from pain?
MESSENGER. He shouts aloud that some-
    one draw the bolts
And show to all in Thebes the murderer
Of his own father and his mother too.

With blasphemies that I may not repeat
He swears to hurl himself forth from this
    land
Nor still remain a curse unto the house,
Under the curse he spoke. Yet someone's
    strength
And guidance too he needs, his agony
Is more than human strength can bear.
    Thou too
Shalt see, for now the unbolted palace
    gates
Open to show a sight that can but win
Thy fierce abhorrence but thy pity too.

[*Enter* OEDIPUS *supported by attendants,*
    his face stained with blood.]

CHORUS.[14]   O agony too sore for sight
Beyond the utmost range
Of human agony.
What madness, hapless man, assailed thy
    soul?
What angered god
O'erleaping space
Struck down thine ill-starred Fortune?
Woe is me,
Much as I fain would learn,
Frozen with horror, impotent,
I dare not ask nor look but overwhelmed
Shudder and hold my peace.
OEDIPUS.   Woe, woe is mine.
Where in mine agony
Shall I be borne?
Fluttering words are naught.
Where, god, the end?
CHORUS.   Where there is no relief for ear
    or eye.
OEDIPUS.   O cloud of the nether night,
Abhorrent, unspeakable,
Wafted on following breezes fraught with
    death
Alas the goad of memory strikes
Piercing my heart
Cruelly joined in one with the stabs
Of the golden brooch.
CHORUS.   No wonder in thy plight there
    comes to thee
A double grief, a twofold pain to bear.
OEDIPUS.   O friend that art steadfast still
Thou only art left to me.

[14] The following dialogue in lyrical measures is
chanted responsively to a musical accompaniment.

Pity for suffering blindness makes thee
  kind.
Alas thy presence speaks to me
Blind though I am.
Darkness like death is mine, yet I know
Thou hast left me not.
CHORUS. O doer of dread deeds, how
  couldst thou dare
Destroy thine eyes? What god compelled
  that act?
OEDIPUS. Lord of the Delphian shrine,
Apollo, god of the taut strong bow,
Wrought for me woe on woe:
His was the curse
But the hand that struck was mine;
Mine was the blow.
God! Would I see again
Whose opened eyes
Could naught behold that held not mem-
  ory's curse?
CHORUS. True is that word of thine.
OEDIPUS. What should I see? Shall I ever
  know
Love or a welcoming word?
Banish me ere ye too
Fall neath the blight that clings
Round me accursed
Hated of god, damned through eternity.
CHORUS. Twofold thy misery: for, being
  damned,
Thou still canst feel. Would god I knew
  thee not.
OEDIPUS. Cursed forever be
The hand that loosed from my feet the
  thong
Striking the shackles off
Giving me life
When I lay a helpless babe.
Graceless the deed;
Better were death for me
Than live a curse
To mine own self and all that touches
  me.
CHORUS. Better were death indeed.
OEDIPUS. Then had I not with the curse
  of god
Drenched in my father's blood
Mounted the couch of her,
Mother and queen to me.
Outlaw from earth

Outlaw from heaven, woe beyond woe is
  mine.
CHORUS. I cannot say thy counsel was the
  best
For death would be to thee a very boon.
OEDIPUS. Instruct me not that all is evilly
Contrived. I cannot bear more counseling
For had I now my sight could I endure
To face my father in the halls of hell,
To look upon my mother? I have wrought
Such wrongs against those two as would
  make death
By hanging seem as nothing. Can ye think
Beside that sight of mine own progeny
Begotten as they were could give me
  joy?
Not in mine eyes at least. Not Thebes
  herself,
Not all her parapets, her sculptured gods
Seeing that I of all her citizens
Fairest of promise, now accursed, have won
The doom of seeing these no more, myself
The spokesman of the curse bidding men
  thrust
Forth from the city the unholy one,
Disclosed by god of Laius' royal line.
Could I with such a brand upon me look
Upon my fellow citizens? Not I,
And were there means to dam the fountain
  head
Of hearing, I had not withheld to close
This wretched body fast that neither sight
Nor sound should penetrate. Our thoughts
  should dwell
Beyond the reach of evil. O Cithaeron, why
Didst thou accept my life? Why didst thou
  not
Slay me at once? So had I never shown
Myself unto the world and whence I
  sprang.
O Polybus and Corinth and that home
Once called mine own, how fair the object
  seemed
Of thy kind nurture, and how foul beneath
Proven at last both base and basely born.
O triple crossroads and that hidden glade
Narrowing through the oak trees where
  those three
Roads met that drank mine own blood by
  my hand

Drawn from my father's veins, do ye then still
Remember me, the deed I showed you there
And coming hither wrought again? O rites
Of wedlock, ye that brought me forth and gave
Harvest to me sown in the self-same field
Confounding name of father, brother, son,
Of mother, bride, and wife to consummate
All that is held most shameful of mankind.
Yet what is foul to do is foul to speak.
Wherefore by all the gods with utmost speed
Hide me in some far hiding place or slay
Outright or cast me in the sea where none
May e'er behold me more. Come, scruple not
To touch this wretched man. Ye need not fear.
No mortal but myself may bear this guilt.

[*Enter* CREON, *followed by the children* ANTIGONE *and* ISMENE.]

CHORUS. Lo at thy words comes Creon who may best
Grant thy request or counsel thee for he
Alone is left our guardian in thy place.
OEDIPUS. Alas what word is left for me to speak
To him? What truth shall he behold in me
Who proved myself to him in all things false?
CREON. I am not come to mock thee, Oedipus,
Nor speak reproaches for thy evil past.
But if ye here respect no more the race
Of man at least show reverence to the flame
All nourishing of Helios nor expose
Pollution such as this which neither light
Of day, nor earth, nor rains of heaven may bear.
With all your speed lead him within. The woes
Of kindred they alone should see and hear
To whom the bonds of kinship give the right.
OEDIPUS. Nay, by the gods, since thou hast quelled my fear

Coming thus nobly to a man so base
Grant me one boon. For thine own sake I'll speak.
CREON. What favor dost thou ask so eagerly?
OEDIPUS. Cast me forth swiftly from this land, where I
May share no more in human intercourse.
CREON. That had I done, be well assured, save that
I would be taught of god what's best to do.
OEDIPUS. God hath already spoken bidding us
Destroy the unholy man that slew his sire.
CREON. Such was his word, yet seeing where we stand
'Tis best to learn anew our proper course.
OEDIPUS. Wilt ask advice about one so accursed?
CREON. Aye for thyself wilt now believe god's word.
OEDIPUS. One charge I lay on thee, one last request.
To her that lies within give burial
As seemeth best to thee. So shalt thou give
Last rites unto thine own. But never doom
This city of my fathers to receive
Me as a citizen to dwell therein.
Nay send me forth to live where rises steep
Cithaeron, called mine own, the living tomb
My father and my mother gave to me:
Thus at their hands who willed it I may die.
Yet this I know. Never shall dread disease
Nor human ill destroy me. I was snatched
From death, to serve some stranger will of god.
For me let Fate lead where it will. And more
I ask no favor, Creon, for my sons.
They are now men and wheresoe'er they are
Shall win their livelihood. I crave thy care
For my two daughters. Piteous is their lot
Who know no table but mine own, have shared
All things with me. Grant too, most noble lord,
That I may touch them once again and mourn

With them this evil plight. Could I but place
My hands on them methinks I could believe
That they were mine as when I saw them here.
O god, what shall I say? Do I not hear
Their weeping voices? Hast thou pitied me
And brought my daughters, Creon? Is it so?

CREON. 'Tis so. 'Twas I that brought them, knowing well
From thy past joy what comfort they might give.

OEDIPUS. God give thee blessing and a happier fate
Than mine for this good act. Where are ye there,
My children? Hither, hither come and take
These hands that are in truth a brother's hands,
Hands which wrought havoc with your father's eyes
That saw so clearly once. Yet seeing naught
Nor gaining wisdom's light, he gave you life
By his own mother. 'Tis for you I weep
Whom now I may not see. But I perceive
What bitterness of life amongst mankind
Henceforth is yours. What friendly gatherings
Will you attend, what feasts whose end for you
Shall not be weeping in the place of joy?
And when you reach the years of womanhood
With thoughts of marriage, who will then assume
Reproaches that must ever fall alike
On my descendants and on yours? What woe
Exists that is not ours? Your father slew
His sire, quickened the womb that gave him life
To bring you forth. Such is your heritage.
Who then shall wed you? There is none that lives.
Unwedden, barren, 'tis your doom to die.
But O Menoeceus' son, since thou alone
Art left to father these—for she and I
That brought them to the light are lost indeed—
Suffer them not—thy kin—to wander lone
Beggared and husbandless nor make them one
With this my misery. Nay, pity them
Seeing their youth deprived of everything
Save what may come from thee. Take thou this hand
And grant my wish. To you my children much
I should bequeath of counsel were your minds
Mature. Now let this be your constant prayer
That wheresoe'er chance place your lot, ye live
With happier fate than was your father's share.

CREON.[15] All sufficient now thy mourning. Thou must go within the house.

OEDIPUS. Yield I must, though yield I would not.

CREON. Aye, for all things have their time.

OEDIPUS. Knowest how I might go freely?

CREON. If thou sayest I shall know.

OEDIPUS. If thou wouldst but grant me exile.

CREON. That lies on the knees of god.

OEDIPUS. Yet to god am I most hateful.

CREON. Hence may win thy wish perchance.

OEDIPUS. Thou dost will it?

CREON. Nay, 'tis never mine to speak what I mean not.

OEDIPUS. Send me then within the palace.

CREON. Go, but leave thy children here.

OEDIPUS. Rob me not of them, I pray thee.

CREON. Seek not to prevail in all.
For the power thou once hast wielded has not followed to the end.

CHORUS. Ye that dwell in Thebes behold him. Oedipus thy King is this,
He who solved the far-famed riddle, mightiest in all Thebes was he.
On his fortune who that dwelt here gazed not once with envious eye?
Now behold what surge of evil hath encompassed him about.

[15] This final lyrical passage is again chanted.

So the while we wait the outcome of the
fateful final day
We may call no mortal happy till his course
of life is done

And he reach the goal of darkness, find his
heaven free from pain.

[Exeunt.]

Romantic Tragedy

F THE TWO BASIC PATTERNS which underlie the structure of most European drama, one was given its currency by classical tragedy. Two thousand years elapsed before the second achieved a comparable artistic status in that product of the Renaissance known as romantic tragedy. During these intervening centuries occurred fundamental changes in both the character of the theater and the attitude of those who frequented it. Romantic tragedy is the heir of those changes. Specifically, it is the offspring of medieval religious pageantry and the romantic spirit of the high Renaissance. It represents a technique accumulated from episodic historical spectacle and pieced out with eclectic borrowings from Roman drama. Among its accomplishments is the conversion of drama into a popular commercial entertainment designed for presentation in a public playhouse by companies of professional actors. Although this distinctively romantic form of art has appeared throughout Europe since the sixteenth century, its most effective and enduring expression is still to be found in the drama of Elizabethan England. Unquestionably its finest exponent is William Shakespeare (1564–1616), the chief ornament of the Elizabethan age, the most popular playwright of his time, and the greatest dramatist of the English stage. In his works the type has remained a living force in the theater and has exerted an incalculable influence upon subsequent drama. His masterpiece, *Hamlet* (c. 1601), enjoys the unique distinction of being not only the supreme example of romantic tragedy but perhaps the most widely known and influential single play of modern times.

Classical tragedy, as we have seen, is a more or less operatic exhibition of a single concentrated dramatic crisis. Romantic tragedy, on the contrary, is a mode of telling an extended story in terms of the stage. It is an embodiment in speech and action of a sequence of incidents which cumulatively constitute a climactic narrative. Whereas the technique of classical tragedy is like the unfolding of a single bud, petal by petal, until it is revealed in full bloom, that of romantic tragedy embraces a more comprehensive process from seed-time to harvest with due attention to all the intermediate stages of growth, pollination, and ripening. For this reason the entire conception of romantic tragedy exhibits an inherent narrative bias. Its plot consists of a series of individuated scenes related to one another by a chronological and causal sequence. It is characteristic of this plot to describe a complete cycle of dramatic action from its initiating cause, through the various complications which develop a crisis, to its conclusion in catastrophe. Unlike the analytical concentration of classical tragedy, this synthetic and narrative technique encourages a multiplicity of incident in the play and fills the stage with physical action. The real drama of romantic tragedy concerns not only the nature but the making of a catastrophe. Hence little of what goes into that making can be assumed or merely implied; the incremental importance of the contributing incidents demands that they actually appear upon the stage. Furthermore, since so much of the dramatic interest accrues from the process through which a catastrophe occurs, the matter of motivation acquires special importance and necessitates scene after scene to clarify the precise causes of human behavior and of the events which progressively modify it. As a result, the elucidation of a story like that of *Hamlet* involves so many details of incident and stage business that its dramatic action is much more copious and complex than that of *Oedipus the King.*

An important feature of this narrative process of plot development is the emphasis which it throws upon the individual scene. Although in *Hamlet* the scenes of the play have been grouped into acts by later editors, these act divisions do not represent Shakespeare's original intention and are, as a matter of fact, foreign to the organic structure of the dramatic type to which the play belongs. Romantic tragedy, like the modern motion picture, is organized on the principle of a linked procession of scenes, either unbroken from beginning to end or, at most, broken by a single intermission about midway. These scenes may be many or few, long or short, as the circumstances of the narrative require; but they gain their effect by a sustained forward movement, in the course of which the dramatic situation is built up within the confines of the play by a process of gradual accretion. In such a scheme the real unit of dramatic structure and interest is the individual scene. Each scene successively possesses its own decisive importance and is charged with suspense by the possible consequences which it implies. The dramatic action is characteristically a swift and fluent movement from one contributory incident to another. The total effect is a cumulative suspension of these dynamic and ambivalent incidents until the last draws them all into focus and discharges their accumulated force.

The narrative technique of romantic tragedy also affects the nature and function of dramatic dialogue. A form of drama which enacts so much of its subject upon the stage has obviously less need for extended speeches of explanation or recapitulation than classical tragedy. Its dialogue accordingly tends to become ancillary to stage business and to grow directly out of the immediate action. The general effect is a greater informality and naturalness of speech which often simulates the quality of ordinary conversation. This change, however, is dictated by strictly technical considerations and is not to be interpreted as an effort to gain realistic verisimilitude. For the purposes of romantic tragedy speech and action are no more than instruments in setting forth a narrative. As the play is designed to make this narrative explicit and concrete, speech and action are designed to make it comprehensible and effective. Since the major emphasis falls upon representative action, the function of speech is chiefly to complement this action by supplying whatever cannot be represented satisfactorily on the stage. Thus dialogue serves to link separated incidents, to provide supplementary information, to interpret the significance of events, to indicate the setting, and to guide the audience toward proper understanding. Inherently capable of a more subtle variety than action, it also serves to invest the bare form of events with an enriching texture of appropriate thought and phrase. To these ends it employs prose or verse as the requirements of adequate expression advise. Although at times colloquial and quite realistic in tone, it does not hesitate to use all the artifices of monologue, aside, soliloquy, declamation, and expository discourse to describe, confide, or expatiate according to the needs of the occasion. So comprehensive and so absolute is this function of dialogue that actually no further supplement to action is needed. Indeed, because of this fact, romantic tragedy is a singularly self-sufficient form of drama which exists practically independent of stage facilities. Its effect is based entirely upon its own speech and action.

From what has just been said it is evident that romantic tragedy requires little in the way of special stage setting. In point of fact, it was originally designed for a very simple stage and for a theater much smaller and more compact than the Greek. The Elizabethan theater was a polygonal structure consisting of a stage building and three contiguous tiers of roofed galleries surrounding a central pit which was open to the sky. The seats in the galleries and the standing-room in the pit accommodated about 2,500 spectators. The main stage projected from the façade of the stage building midway into the pit and was surrounded on three sides by the audience. Its general appearance may be seen in the conjectural reconstruction (see frontispiece) of the Globe Theater, where Shakespeare's *Hamlet* was first produced.

At first glance, the original stage of romantic drama appears to be nothing but a bare platform. Substantially that is what it was. Its construction afforded small opportunity for the erection or use of scenery. Its lack of curtains to screen the main stage militated against setting that area with heavy properties. Its neutral and invariable appearance precluded much visual stimulation of realistic illusions. Nevertheless, its structure was skilfully devised to serve its appointed purpose. This purpose was to provide an architectural arrangement of playing areas and acting levels. Its foundation was the outer platform stage, which served as the principal scene of action. This was partially roofed and furnished with several trap doors to facilitate the use of machinery from above and below. Behind the main platform was a shallow recessed alcove, or inner stage, which could be screened by curtains. The presence of these curtains made possible a shift of simple properties, so that the inner stage might be set either as a separate locality or as a background for the outer stage. Immediately above this alcove a screened upper stage, with its shallow balcony and flanking windows, afforded similar opportunities with the added advantage of elevation. The total effect was that of a permanent multiple stage upon which action could be revealed with unbroken continuity in a rapid succession of shifting scenes or in several areas simultaneously.

For a type of theatrical presentation dedicated to speech and action, one concerned less with painting pictures than with telling a story, the spare simplicity of this stage was perhaps its greatest virtue. In many respects it was not unlike the modern motion-picture screen. Just as the screen is a bare plane upon which pictures can be brought to life, the Elizabethan stage was a structural area upon which action could be exhibited and invested with the vivid context of poetic imagination. In itself it was nowhere in particular but could in an instant become anywhere that circumstances demanded. With its appointments designed to serve this emphasis on pure dramatic action, it was primarily a place where incidents could occur and lines could be spoken with a maximum of flexibility and a minimum of restraint. It was a place across which action could flow freely and on which could be mounted the spectacle of costumes and banners, the pageantry of marching men, and the pictorial effects of stage tableaux. Its forestage was clear and spacious to accommodate the swift passage of actors and lively stage business. Projecting into the midst of the theater, it brought action so close to the spectators that drama became an intimate and highly personalized experience, in which direct communication with the audience by means of asides and soliloquies was altogether natural. The recessed inner stage provided a setting for interiors and with its curtain facilitated the use of necessary properties. When action flowed outward from it on to the forestage, as was often the practice, the inner stage both augmented and automatically shifted the scene of the whole main stage. The upper stage could either segregate a unit of action from the rest of the stage or effect any juxtaposition involving height. Strategic use of the traverses, or alcove curtains, made possible a change of locality as smooth and rapid as that of a motion picture, a merging of scene with scene, and a transition from one unit of dramatic action to another without awkward interruptions. With no formal scenery to distract attention from the human drama, no cumbersome properties to clog the free movement of action, and no proscenium arch or stage curtain to come between play and audience, everything about the Elizabethan stage was flexible, plastic, intimate, and admirably suited to the furtherance of story in action.

The distinctive character of romantic tragedy is a direct outgrowth of its narrative bias, its intimacy of staging, and its Renaissance heritage. Concerned with the progress of a narrative, romantic tragedy stresses the circumstantial details which account for that progress. Assuming an intimate contact between actors and audience, it couches drama in terms of those particulars which individualize personality at close range. Temperamentally individualistic and romantic, it prefers subject matter which lies off the beaten path of the typical and the commonplace. This preference for the circumstantial, the individual, and the exceptional carries with it a dramatic emphasis which is diametrically opposed to that of classical tragedy. For any emphasis upon the exceptional is bound to be an emphasis upon those peculiarities which differentiate it from the customary, and these differences are always bound to be not general but specific. It is impossible, for example, to treat the story of *Hamlet* as simply a typical instance of common human experience; for it is nothing of the sort. It is the unique case history of a specific adultery, murder, and revenge. The aim of romantic tragedy is to give dramatic value to such a specific experience. In order to do so, it is obliged to make clear the precise nature of the circumstances which are responsible for the situation and for its progressive development; or, in other words, it is obliged to stress the special and the individual in both circumstance and human nature. Thus the object of *Hamlet* is to show exactly what sort of individuals are involved in the situation, exactly what factors govern their behavior, and exactly why their behavior turns out to be disastrous. The play accordingly examines in detail the causes of Hamlet's disillusionment and psychological turmoil, the nature of his relations with his mother and Ophelia, and the reasons for the interference of Polonius and Rosencrantz and Guildenstern. It dissects the personal dilemmas of Hamlet, Claudius, and Laertes. It demonstrates the ironic disparity between specific intention and general result, and the consequent process whereby the whole situation gets out of control. And in the course of the demonstration it endeavors to define the peculiar quality of tragedy in terms of the explicit evidence.

In keeping with its emphasis on the particular, this type of drama conceives of tragedy as a highly personal experience. The tragedy of *Hamlet* is primarily the tragedy of a unique individual. While the events of the play might conceivably be interpreted as the tragedy of Claudius or Gertrude or Ophelia, from the point of view actually adopted they take on meaning solely as they bear upon the subjective experience of Hamlet. The aim of the play is to view events through his eyes, to experience life with his sensibilities, to suffer from his insufficiencies, and to appreciate tragedy as he comes to know it. Consequently it concentrates upon the special details which give Hamlet his peculiar identity and make his situation unique. In this respect a play like *Hamlet* differs from classical tragedy much as the heterogeneous complexity of a Gothic cathedral differs from the selective simplicity of a Greek temple. *Hamlet* is designed to present the tragedy of the individual human being at odds with his world and isolated from his fellows by the very qualities which make him an individual. As such, it becomes, in a larger sense, the essential tragedy of individuality itself.

In order to convey the general implications of so individual a case, successful romantic tragedy is obliged to exercise special care in establishing a common ground of relationship between the experience of its tragic protagonist and that of the audience. On the principle that to understand thoroughly is to share, it endeavors to effect this rapport by an elaborate technique of detailed dramatic analysis. The purpose of this technique, however, is not to identify the unique tragic individual with the common experience of the audience, but to enable the audience to conform to the particular dimensions of the tragic individual. By its process of systematic analysis romantic tragedy endeavors to reduce the complex of individual personality, motive, and conduct to those basic elements which it holds in common with all human nature. Subjected to such an analysis, even so complex an individual as Hamlet is seen to be but a special synthesis of universal human traits, and his peculiar situation but a special product of universally operative forces. The point of contact, therefore, lies, not in the totality of the play, which makes *Hamlet* a separate and highly specialized experience, but in the component elements, which mold the life of play and audience alike. These significant elements the technique of romantic tragedy endeavors to throw into relief. By doing so, it transforms the unique tragedy of *Hamlet* into the potential tragedy of every man: not because Hamlet himself is everyman or because his dilemma is everyman's dilemma, but because whatever he is or whatever befalls him is compounded of the same elements which comprise every man's nature and experience. From this analytical reduction of the particular and special to common human terms derive the universal appeal and validity of romantic tragedy. From this practice also derives the interesting fact that, whereas classical tragedy has a natural affinity with the generalized truths of myth, romantic tragedy has always been the most successful dramatic form in dealing with the particularized materials of history.

Since the Renaissance, romantic tragedy has held a permanent place in the European theater, lending its general form and methods to a variety of purposes which are not always tragic. Its pure form appears to best advantage in Shakespeare's great tragedies, ranging from *Romeo and Juliet* to *Macbeth,* as well as in such lesser English plays of the seventeenth century as *The Duchess of Malfi* by John Webster, *The Changeling* by Thomas Middleton and William Rowley, and *The Cardinal* by James Shirley. Under various modifications it appears in the dramatic work of

Lope de Vega, Calderon, and Goethe, in Schiller's *Wilhelm Tell* and *Wallenstein's Death*, in Hugo's *Hernani* and *Ruy Blas*, and in Shelley's *The Cenci*. As noted above, the type has been especially valuable for the treatment of historical and biographical subjects, as in Shakespeare's English history plays or his *Julius Caesar* and *Antony and Cleopatra*, in Pushkin's Russian chronicle *Boris Godunov*, or in Alfred de Vigny's biographical study *Chatterton*. This is the purpose to which it is chiefly adapted in drama of the twentieth century, as may be seen in such miscellaneous examples as Shaw's *Saint Joan*, O'Neill's *Marco Millions*, Anderson's *Elizabeth the Queen*, and Sherwood's *Abe Lincoln in Illinois*.

THE TRAGEDY OF
HAMLET
PRINCE OF DENMARK

by

WILLIAM SHAKESPEARE

Dramatis Personæ

CLAUDIUS, *King of Denmark*
HAMLET, *son to the late, and
    nephew to the present King*
POLONIUS, *Lord Chamberlain*
HORATIO, *friend to* HAMLET
LAERTES, *son to* POLONIUS
VOLTIMAND,
CORNELIUS,
ROSENCRANTZ,
GUILDENSTERN, } *courtiers*
OSRIC,
A GENTLEMAN,
MARCELLUS, } *officers.*
BERNARDO,

FRANCISCO, *a soldier*
REYNALDO, *servant to* POLONIUS
A PRIEST
PLAYERS
Two CLOWNS, *grave-diggers*
FORTINBRAS, *Prince of Norway*
A CAPTAIN
ENGLISH AMBASSADORS

GERTRUDE, *Queen of Denmark,
    and mother to* HAMLET
OPHELIA, *daughter to* POLONIUS

GHOST *of* HAMLET's *Father*

*Lords, Ladies, Officers, Soldiers, Sailors, Messengers,
and other Attendants.*

SCENE: *Elsinore, Denmark.*

The texts of *Hamlet* and *Twelfth Night* which appear in this volume are the texts prepared by Thomas Marc Parrott for his edition of Shakespeare, copyright 1938 by Charles Scribner's Sons. They are here reprinted through the gracious generosity of their editor.

ACT I

Scene I

Elsinore. A platform before the castle.

[FRANCISCO *at his post. Enter to him*
BERNARDO.]

BERNARDO.   Who's there?

FRANCISCO.   Nay, answer me. Stand,
and unfold yourself.

BER.   Long live the king!

FRAN.   Bernardo?

BER.   He.

FRAN.   You come most carefully upon
your hour.

BER.   'T is now struck twelve: get thee
to bed, Francisco.

FRAN.   For this relief much thanks; 't is
bitter cold,
And I am sick at heart.

BER.   Have you had quiet guard?

FRAN.   Not a mouse stirring.

BER.   Well, good-night.
If you do meet Horatio and Marcellus,
The rivals [1] of my watch, bid them make
haste.

[*Enter* HORATIO *and* MARCELLUS.]

FRAN.   I think I hear them. Stand, ho!
Who is there?

HORATIO.   Friends to this ground.

MARCELLUS.   And liegemen to the Dane.

FRAN.   Give you good-night.

MAR.   O, farewell, honest soldier:
Who hath reliev'd you?

FRAN.   Bernardo has my place.
Give you good-night.   [*Exit* FRANCISCO.]

MAR.   Holla! Bernardo!

BER.   Say—
What, is Horatio there?

HOR.   A piece of him.

BER.   Welcome, Horatio; welcome,
good Marcellus.

HOR.   What, has this thing appear'd
again to-night?

BER.   I have seen nothing.

MAR.   Horatio says 't is but our fantasy

[1] Partners.

And will not let belief take hold of him
Touching this dreaded sight, twice seen of
us;
Therefore I have entreated him along
With us to watch the minutes of this night,
That if again this apparition come,
He may approve [2] our eyes and speak to it.

HOR.   Tush, tush, 't will not appear.

BER.   Sit down a while,
And let us once again assail your ears,
That are so fortified against our story,
What we have two nights seen.

HOR.   Well, sit we down,
And let us hear Bernardo speak of this.

BER.   Last night of all,
When yond same star that 's westward
from the pole
Had made his course t' illumine that part
of heaven
Where now it burns, Marcellus and myself,
The bell then beating one,—

[*Enter the* GHOST.]

MAR.   Peace, break thee off! Look,
where it comes again!

BER.   In the same figure, like the King
that 's dead.

MAR.   Thou art a scholar; speak to it,
Horatio.

BER.   Looks it not like the King? Mark
it, Horatio.

HOR.   Most like; it harrows me with fear
and wonder.

BER.   It would be spoke to.

MAR.   Question it, Horatio.

HOR.   What art thou that usurp'st this
time of night,
Together with that fair and warlike form
In which the majesty of buried Denmark
Did sometimes march? By heaven I charge
thee, speak!

MAR.   It is offended.

BER.   See, it stalks away!

HOR.   Stay! Speak, speak! I charge thee,
speak!   [*Exit* GHOST.]

[2] Confirm.

109

MAR.   'T is gone, and will not answer.

BER.   How now, Horatio? you tremble and look pale;

Is not this something more than fantasy?

What think you on 't?

HOR.   Before my God, I might not this believe

Without the sensible and true avouch

Of mine own eyes.

MAR.   Is it not like the King?

HOR.   As thou art to thyself.

Such was the very armour he had on

When he the ambitious Norway combated;

So frown'd he once, when, in an angry parle,[3]

He smote the sledded Polacks on the ice.

'T is strange.

MAR.   Thus twice before, and jump at this dead hour,

With martial stalk hath he gone by our watch.

HOR.   In what particular thought to work I know not;

But, in the gross and scope [4] of my opinion,

This bodes some strange eruption to our state.

MAR.   Good now, sit down, and tell me, he that knows,

Why this same strict and most observant watch

So nightly toils the subject [5] of the land,

And why such daily cast of brazen cannon,

And foreign mart for implements of war;

Why such impress of shipwrights, whose sore task

Does not divide the Sunday from the week;

What might be toward, that this sweaty haste

Doth make the night joint-labourer with the day,

Who is 't that can inform me?

HOR.   That can I;

At least, the whisper goes so. Our last king,

Whose image even but now appear'd to us,

Was, as you know, by Fortinbras of Norway,

Thereto prick'd on by a most emulate pride,

Dar'd to the combat; in which our valiant Hamlet—

For so this side of our known world esteem'd him—

Did slay this Fortinbras; who, by a seal'd compact

Well ratified by law and heraldry,

Did forfeit, with his life, all those his lands

Which he stood seiz'd of, to the conqueror;

Against the which, a moiety competent

Was gaged [6] by our king; which had return'd

To the inheritance of Fortinbras,

Had he been vanquisher; as, by the same co-mart,

And carriage of the article design'd,[7]

His fell to Hamlet. Now, sir, young Fortinbras,

Of unimproved mettle [8] hot and full,

Hath in the skirts of Norway here and there

Shark'd up a list of lawless resolutes,

For food and diet, to some enterprise

That hath a stomach in 't [9]; which is no other—

As it doth well appear unto our state—

But to recover of us, by strong hand

And terms compulsatory, those foresaid lands

So by his father lost; and this, I take it,

Is the main motive of our preparations,

The source of this our watch, and the chief head

Of this post-haste and romage [10] in the land.

BER.   I think it be no other but e'en so;

Well may it sort [11] that this portentous figure

Comes armed through our watch, so like the King

That was and is the question of these wars.

HOR.   A mote it is to trouble the mind's eye.

In the most high and palmy state of Rome,

A little ere the mightiest Julius fell,

---

[3] Parley.

[4] General drift.

[5] Causes toil for the subjects.

[6] A comparable amount was pledged.

[7] As, by the same bargain, and the conveyance of the agreement drawn up.

[8] Untempered ardor.   [9] Calls for valor.

[10] Chief origin of this hurry and bustle.

[11] Be appropriate.

The graves stood tenantless and the sheeted
    dead
Did squeak and gibber in the Roman
    streets.

   .   .   .   .   .

As stars with trains of fire and dews of
    blood,
Disasters in the sun; and the moist star [12]
Upon whose influence Neptune's empire
    stands
Was sick almost to doomsday with eclipse:
And even the like precurse [13] of fear'd
    events,
As harbingers preceding still the fates
And prologue to the omen coming on,
Have heaven and earth together demon-
    strated
Unto our climatures [14] and countrymen.

            [*Re-enter* GHOST.]

But soft, behold! Lo, where it comes again!
I 'll cross it,[15] though it blast me. Stay, illu-
    sion!
If thou hast any sound, or use of voice,
Speak to me;   [*It spreads its arms.*]
If there be any good thing to be done
That may to thee do ease and grace to me,
Speak to me;
If thou art privy to thy country's fate,
Which, happily, foreknowing may avoid,
O speak!
Or if thou hast uphoarded in thy life
Extorted treasure in the womb of earth,
For which, they say, you spirits oft walk in
    death,
Speak it; stay, and speak!
            [*The cock crows.*]
            Stop it, Marcellus.
MAR.   Shall I strike at it with my parti-
    san? [16]
HOR.   Do, if it will not stand.
BER.   'T is here!
HOR.   'T is here!
MAR.   'T is gone!   [*Exit* GHOST.]
We do it wrong, being so majestical,

To offer it the show of violence;
For it is as the air, invulnerable,
And our vain blows malicious mockery.
    BER.   It was about to speak, when the
    cock crew.
    HOR.   And then it started like a guilty
    thing
Upon a fearful summons. I have heard,
The cock, that is the trumpet to the morn,
Doth with his lofty and shrill-sounding
    throat
Awake the god of day; and, at his warning,
Whether in sea or fire, in earth or air,
Th' extravagant and erring spirit [17] hies
To his confine; and of the truth herein
This present object made probation.[18]
    MAR.   It faded on the crowing of the
    cock.
Some say that ever 'gainst that season
    comes
Wherein our Saviour's birth is celebrated,
This bird of dawning singeth all night long;
And then, they say, no spirit dare stir
    abroad;
The nights are wholesome; then no planets
    strike,
No fairy takes, nor witch hath power to
    charm,
So hallow'd and so gracious is that time.
    HOR.   So have I heard and do in part
    believe it.
But, look, the morn, in russet mantle clad,
Walks o'er the dew of yon high eastward
    hill:
Break we our watch up; and, by my advice,
Let us impart what we have seen to-night
Unto young Hamlet; for, upon my life,
This spirit, dumb to us, will speak to him.
Do you consent we shall acquaint him
    with it,
As needful in our loves, fitting our duty?
    MAR.   Let 's do 't, I pray; and I this
    morning know
Where we shall find him most convenient.

                [*Exeunt.*]

---

[12] The moon. The syntax of the passage is confused by the apparent loss of a line.
[13] Foreshadowing.
[14] Territories.
[15] Cross its path.

[16] A spear tipped with a blade somewhat like a
bayonet.
[17] The truant spirit wandering abroad.
[18] Gave proof.

Scene II

A room of state in the castle.

[*Flourish. Enter* CLAUDIUS, *King of Denmark,* GERTRUDE, *the Queen, Councillors* (VOLTIMAND *and* CORNELIUS), POLONIUS, *and his son* LAERTES, HAMLET, *Lords Attendant.*]

KING.   Though yet of Hamlet our dear brother's death
The memory be green, and that it us befitted
To bear our hearts in grief, and our whole kingdom
To be contracted in one brow of woe,
Yet so far hath discretion fought with nature
That we with wisest sorrow think on him
Together with remembrance of ourselves:
Therefore our sometimes sister, now our queen,
Th' imperial jointress to this warlike state,
Have we, as 't were with a defeated joy,—
With an auspicious and a dropping eye,
With mirth in funeral and with dirge in marriage,
In equal scale weighing delight and dole,—
Taken to wife; nor have we herein barr'd
Your better wisdoms, which have freely gone
With this affair along. For all, our thanks.
Now follows that you know: young Fortinbras,
Holding a weak supposal of our worth,
Or thinking by our late dear brother's death
Our state to be disjoint and out of frame,
Colleagued with this dream of his advantage,
He hath not fail'd to pester us with message
Importing the surrender of those lands
Lost by his father, with all bonds of law,
To our most valiant brother. So much for him.
Now for ourself and for this time of meeting,

Thus much the business is: we have here writ
To Norway, uncle of young Fortinbras,—
Who, impotent and bed-rid, scarcely hears
Of this his nephew's purpose,—to suppress
His further gait herein, in that the levies,
The lists and full proportions, are all made
Out of his subject [1]; and we here dispatch
You, good Cornelius, and you, Voltimand,
For bearing of this greeting to old Norway;
Giving to you no further personal power
To business with the king, more than the scope
Of these delated articles [2] allow.
              [*Giving a paper.*]
Farewell, and let your haste commend your duty.
CORNELIUS. ⎰In that and all things will we
VOLTIMAND. ⎱   show our duty.
KING.   We doubt it nothing; heartily farewell.
     [*Exeunt* VOLTIMAND *and* CORNELIUS.]
And now, Laertes, what 's the news with you?
You told us of some suit; what is 't, Laertes?
You cannot speak of reason to the Dane,
And lose your voice [3]: what wouldst thou beg, Laertes,
That shall not be my offer, not thy asking?
The head is not more native to the heart,
The hand more instrumental to the mouth,
Than is the throne of Denmark to thy father.
What wouldst thou have, Laertes?
LAERTES.   My dread lord,
Your leave and favour to return to France;
From whence though willingly I came to Denmark
To show my duty in your coronation,
Yet now, I must confess, that duty done,
My thoughts and wishes bend again towards France
And bow them to your gracious leave and pardon.
KING.   Have you your father's leave? What says Polonius?

---

[1] *I.e.,* all the recruits are subjects of Norway.
[2] Specified instructions.

[3] You cannot waste your breath when making any reasonable request of the King of Denmark.

POLONIUS. He hath, my lord, wrung
  from me my slow leave
By laboursome petition, and at last
Upon his will I seal'd my hard consent:
I do beseech you, give him leave to go.
  KING. Take thy fair hour, Laertes: time
  be thine,
And thy best graces spend it at thy will!
But now, my cousin [4] Hamlet, and my
  son,—
  HAMLET. [*Aside.*] A little more than
  kin, and less than kind.
  KING. How is it that the clouds still
  hang on you?
  HAM. Not so, my lord; I am too much
  in the sun.[5]
  QUEEN. Good Hamlet, cast thy nighted
  colour off,
And let thine eye look like a friend on
  Denmark;
Do not for ever with thy vailed lids
Seek for thy noble father in the dust;
Thou know'st 't is common; all that lives
  must die,
Passing through nature to eternity.
  HAM. Ay, madam, it is common.
  QUEEN.   If it be,
Why seems it so particular with thee?
  HAM. Seems, madam! Nay, it is; I know
  not "seems."
'T is not alone my inky cloak, good mother,
Nor customary suits of solemn black,
Nor windy suspiration of forc'd breath,
No, nor the fruitful river in the eye,
Nor the dejected haviour of the visage,
Together with all forms, moods, shapes of
  grief,
That can denote me truly: these indeed
  seem,
For they are actions that a man might play;
But I have that within which passeth show,
These but the trappings and the suits of
  woe.
  KING. 'T is sweet and commendable in
  your nature, Hamlet,
To give these mourning duties to your
  father:

But you must know, your father lost a
  father,
That father lost, lost his; and the survivor
  bound
In filial obligation for some term
To do obsequious sorrow; but to persever
In obstinate condolement is a course
Of impious stubbornness; 't is unmanly
  grief;
It shows a will most incorrect to heaven,
A heart unfortified, a mind impatient,
An understanding simple and unschool'd;
For what we know must be, and is as com-
  mon
As any the most vulgar [6] thing to sense,
Why should we in our peevish opposition
Take it to heart? Fie! 't is a fault to heaven,
A fault against the dead, a fault to nature,
To reason most absurd, whose common
  theme
Is death of fathers, and who still hath cried,
From the first corse till he that died today,
"This must be so." We pray you, throw to
  earth
This unprevailing woe, and think of us
As of a father; for, let the world take note,
You are the most immediate to our throne,
And with no less nobility of love
Than that which dearest father bears his
  son,
Do I impart towards you. For your intent
In going back to school in Wittenberg,
It is most retrograde to our desire;
And we beseech you, bend you to remain
Here in the cheer and comfort of our eye,
Our chiefest courtier, cousin, and our son.
  QUEEN. Let not thy mother lose her
  prayers, Hamlet:
I prithee, stay with us; go not to Witten-
  berg.
  HAMLET. I shall in all my best obey
  you, madam.
  KING. Why, 't is a loving and a fair re-
  ply:
Be as ourself in Denmark. Madam, come;
This gentle and unforc'd accord of Hamlet
Sits smiling to my heart; in grace whereof,

---

[4] Kinsman.
[5] A pun on *son*, alluding to the King's earlier
remark, and *sun, i.e.,* the glare of the court. Note
that Hamlet's remarks frequently carry a double
meaning.
[6] Common.

No jocund health that Denmark drinks
to-day,
But the great cannon to the clouds shall
tell,
And the King's rouse [7] the heaven shall
bruit again,
Re-speaking earthly thunder. Come away.
          [*Flourish. Exeunt all but* HAMLET.]
  HAMLET.   Oh, that this too too sullied
  flesh would melt,
Thaw, and resolve itself into a dew!
Or that the Everlasting had not fix'd
His canon [8] 'gainst self-slaughter! O God!
  God!
How weary, stale, flat, and unprofitable,
Seem to me all the uses of this world!
Fie on 't! ah fie! 'T is an unweeded garden,
That grows to seed; things rank and gross
  in nature
Possess it merely.[9] That it should come
  thus!
But two months dead; nay, not so much,
  not two,
So excellent a king; that was, to this,
Hyperion to a satyr; so loving to my
  mother
That he might not beteem [10] the winds of
  heaven
Visit her face too roughly—heaven and
  earth!
Must I remember? Why, she would hang
  on him,
As if increase of appetite had grown
By what it fed on; and yet, within a
  month,—
Let me not think on 't!—Frailty, thy name
  is woman!—
A little month, or e'er those shoes were old
With which she followed my poor father's
  body,
Like Niobe, all tears,—why she, even
  she—
O God! a beast, that wants discourse of
  reason,[11]
Would have mourn'd longer—married with
  my uncle,
My father's brother, but no more like my
  father

Than I to Hercules; within a month,
Ere yet the salt of most unrighteous tears
Had left the flushing in her galled eyes,
She married. O, most wicked speed, to post
With such dexterity to incestuous sheets! [12]
It is not, nor it cannot come to good:
But break my heart, for I must hold my
  tongue.

          [*Enter* HORATIO, MARCELLUS, *and*
                    BERNARDO.]

  HORATIO.   Hail to your lordship!
  HAMLET.   I am glad to see you well.
Horatio!—or I do not forget myself.
  HOR.   The same, my lord, and your poor
  servant ever.
  HAM.   Sir, my good friend; I 'll change
  that name with you;
And what make you from Wittenberg, Ho-
  ratio?
Marcellus.
  MARCELLUS.   My good lord!
  HAM.   I am very glad to see you. [*To*
  BERNARDO.] Good even, sir.—
But what, in faith, make you from Witten-
  berg?
  HOR.   A truant disposition, good my
  lord.
  HAM.   I would not hear your enemy say
  so,
Nor shall you do my ear that violence,
To make it truster of your own report
Against yourself: I know you are no truant;
But what is your affair in Elsinore?
We 'll teach you for to drink ere you de-
  part.
  HOR.   My lord, I came to see your
  father's funeral.
  HAM.   I prithee, do not mock me, fel-
  low-student;
I think it was to see my mother's wedding.
  HOR.   Indeed, my lord, it followed hard
  upon.
  HAM.   Thrift, thrift, Horatio! The fu-
  neral bak'd-meats
Did coldly furnish forth the marriage
  tables.
Would I had met my dearest foe in heaven

---

[7] Draining of a bumper.   [8] Law.
[9] Entirely.   [10] Could not tolerate.
[11] Lacks the reasoning faculty.

[12] In Shakespeare's day marriage with the
brother of a deceased husband was considered incestuous.

Or ever I had seen that day, Horatio!
My father!—methinks I see my father.

HOR.   Where, my lord?

HAM.   In my mind's eye, Horatio.

HOR.   I saw him once; 'a was a goodly
king.

HAM.   'A was a man, take him for all in
all,
I shall not look upon his like again.

HOR.   My lord, I think I saw him yester-
night.

HAM.   Saw? Who?

HOR.   My lord, the King your father.

HAM.   The King my father!

HOR.   Season your admiration [13] for a
while
With an attent ear, till I may deliver,
Upon the witness of these gentlemen,
This marvel to you.

HAM.   For God's love, let me hear.

HOR.   Two nights together had these
gentlemen,
Marcellus and Bernardo, on their watch,
In the dead waste and middle of the night,
Been thus encounter'd. A figure like your
father,
Armed at point exactly, cap-a-pe,[14]
Appears before them, and with solemn
march
Goes slow and stately by them: thrice he
walk'd
By their oppress'd and fear-surprised eyes,
Within his truncheon's length; whilst they,
distill'd
Almost to jelly with the act of fear,
Stand dumb and speak not to him. This to
me
In dreadful [15] secrecy impart they did,
And I with them the third night kept the
watch.
Where, as they had deliver'd, both in time,
Form of the thing, each word made true
and good,
The apparition comes: I knew your father;
These hands are not more like.

HAM.   But where was this?

MAR.   My lord upon the platform where
we watch.

HAM.   Did you not speak to it?

HOR.   My lord, I did;
But answer made it none: yet once me-
thought
It lifted up it [16] head and did address
Itself to motion, like as it would speak;
But even then the morning cock crew
loud,
And at the sound it shrunk in haste away,
And vanish'd from our sight.

HAM.   'T is very strange.

HOR.   As I do live, my honour'd lord,
't is true,
And we did think it writ down in our duty
To let you know of it.

HAM.   Indeed, indeed, sirs, but this troubles me.
Hold you the watch to-night?

ALL.   We do, my lord.

HAM.   Arm'd, say you?

ALL.   Arm'd, my lord.

HAM.   From top to toe?

ALL.   My lord, from head to foot.

HAM.   Then saw you not his face?

HOR.   O, yes, my lord; he wore his
beaver [17] up.

HAM.   What, look'd he frowningly?

HOR.   A countenance more in sorrow
than in anger.

HAM.   Pale, or red?

HOR.   Nay, very pale.

HAM.   And fix'd his eyes upon you?

HOR.   Most constantly.

HAM.   I would I had been there.

HOR.   It would have much amaz'd you.

HAM.   Very like, very like. Stay'd it
long?

HOR.   While one with moderate haste
might tell a hundred.

MAR. ⎫
        ⎬ Longer, longer.
BER. ⎭

HOR.   Not when I saw 't.

HAM.   His beard was grizzled, no?

HOR.   It was, as I have seen it in his life,
A sable silver'd.

HAM.   I will watch to-night;
Perchance 't will walk again.

HOR.   I war'nt it will.

---

[13] Moderate your astonishment.
[14] To the last detail, from head to foot.
[15] Awe-struck.   [16] An early form of *its*.
[17] Visor of a helmet.

HAM. If it assume my noble father's person,

I 'll speak to it, though hell itself should gape

And bid me hold my peace; I pray you all,

If you have hitherto conceal'd this sight,

Let it be tenable in your silence still;

And whatsomever else shall hap to-night,

Give it an understanding, but no tongue;

I will requite your loves. So, fare you well.

Upon the platform 'twixt eleven and twelve,

I 'll visit you.

ALL.   Our duty to your honour.

HAM. Your loves, as mine to you; farewell.   [Exeunt all but HAMLET.]

My father's spirit—in arms! all is not well;

I doubt some foul play; would the night were come!

Till then sit still, my soul: foul deeds will rise,

Though all the earth o'erwhelm them to men's eyes.   [Exit.]

Scene III

A room in the house of Polonius.

[*Enter* LAERTES *and* OPHELIA, *his sister.*]

LAERTES. My necessaries are embark'd, farewell;

And, sister, as the winds give benefit

And convoy is assistant,[1] do not sleep,

But let me hear from you.

OPHELIA.   Do you doubt that?

LAERTES. For Hamlet and the trifling of his favour,

Hold it a fashion and a toy in blood,[2]

A violet in the youth of primy [3] nature,

Forward, not permanent, sweet, not lasting,

The perfume and suppliance of a minute;

No more.

OPH.   No more but so?

LAER.   Think it no more;

For nature crescent does not grow alone

In thews and bulk, but, as this temple waxes,

The inward service of the mind and soul

Grows wide withal. Perhaps he loves you now,

And now no soil nor cautel [4] doth besmirch

The virtue of his will; but you must fear,

His greatness weigh'd, his will is not his own;

For he himself is subject to his birth.

He may not, as unvalued [5] persons do,

Carve for himself, for on his choice depends

The sanity and health of this whole state;

And therefore must his choice be circumscrib'd

Unto the voice and yielding of that body

Whereof he is the head. Then, if he says he loves you,

It fits your wisdom so far to believe it

As he in his particular act and place

May give his saying deed; which is no further

Than the main voice of Denmark goes withal.

Then weigh what loss your honour may sustain

If with too credent ear you list his songs,

Or lose your heart, or your chaste treasure open

To his unmaster'd importunity.

Fear it, Ophelia, fear it, my dear sister,

And keep you in the rear of your affection,

Out of the shot and danger of desire.

The chariest maid is prodigal enough,

If she unmask her beauty to the moon:

Virtue itself scapes not calumnious strokes:

The canker galls the infants of the spring

Too oft before their buttons be disclos'd,[6]

And in the morn and liquid dew of youth

Contagious blastments are most imminent.

Be wary then, best safety lies in fear;

Youth to itself rebels, though none else near.

OPH. I shall the effect of this good lesson keep,

As watchman to my heart: but, good my brother,

Do not, as some ungracious pastors do,

Show me the steep and thorny way to heaven,

Whiles, like a puff'd and reckless libertine,

[1] Means of conveyance are available.
[2] A pastime and a caprice of passion.
[3] Springlike.   [4] Deceit.
[5] Of unimportant station.
[6] Too often the canker-worm blights the early blossoms before their buds have opened.

Himself the primrose path of dalliance treads,
And recks not his own rede.[7]

LAER.   O, fear me not;

[*Enter* POLONIUS]

I stay too long: but here my father comes.
A double blessing is a double grace,
Occasion smiles upon a second leave.

POLONIUS.   Yet here, Laertes? Aboard, aboard, for shame!
The wind sits in the shoulder of your sail,
And you are stay'd for. There; my blessing with thee!
And these few precepts in thy memory
Look thou character.[8] Give thy thoughts no tongue,
Nor any unproportion'd thought his act;
Be thou familiar, but by no means vulgar;
Those friends thou hast, and their adoption tried,
Grapple them unto thy soul with hoops of steel;
But do not dull thy palm with entertainment
Of each new-hatch'd, unfledg'd courage.[9] Beware
Of entrance to a quarrel; but being in,
Bear 't that th' opposed may beware of thee.
Give every man thy ear, but few thy voice;
Take each man's censure,[10] but reserve thy judgement.
Costly thy habit as thy purse can buy,
But not express'd in fancy; rich, not gaudy;
For the apparel oft proclaims the man,
And they in France of the best rank and station
Are of a most select and generous chief [11] in that.
Neither a borrower nor a lender be;
For loan oft loses both itself and friend,
And borrowing dulleth edge of husbandry; [12]
This above all: to thine own self be true,
And it must follow, as the night the day,
Thou canst not then be false to any man.
Farewell; my blessing season this in thee!

LAER.   Most humbly do I take my leave, my lord.

POL.   The time invites you; go, your servants tend.

LAER.   Farewell, Ophelia, and remember well
What I have said to you.

OPH.   'T is in my memory lock'd,
And you yourself shall keep the key of it.

LAER.   Farewell.   [*Exit* LAERTES.]

POL.   What is 't, Ophelia, he hath said to you?

OPH.   So please you, something touching the Lord Hamlet.

POL.   Marry, well bethought.
'T is told me, he hath very oft of late
Given private time to you, and you yourself
Have of your audience been most free and bounteous.
If it be so—as so 't is put on me,
And that in way of caution—I must tell you,
You do not understand yourself so clearly
As it behoves my daughter and your honour.
What is between you? Give me up the truth.

OPH.   He hath, my lord, of late made many tenders
Of his affection to me.

POL.   Affection! pooh! You speak like a green girl,
Unsifted in such perilous circumstance.
Do you believe his tenders, as you call them?

OPH.   I do not know, my lord, what I should think.

POL.   Marry, I will teach you: think yourself a baby
That you have ta'en these tenders for true pay,
Which are not sterling. Tender yourself more dearly,
Or—not to crack the wind of the poor phrase,
Running it thus—you 'll tender me a fool.

[7] Does not heed his own counsel.
[8] Inscribe.
[9] Young gallant.
[10] Opinion.
[11] Well-bred eminence.
[12] Thrift.

OPH.   My lord, he hath importun'd me
   with love
In honourable fashion.
   POL.   Ay, fashion you may call it: go
   to, go to!
   OPH.   And hath given countenance to
   his speech, my lord,
With almost all the holy vows of heaven.
   POL.   Ay, springes [13] to catch wood-
   cocks. I do know,
When the blood burns, how prodigal the
   soul
Lends the tongue vows. These blazes,
   daughter,
Giving more light than heat, extinct in both
Even in their promise, as it is a-making,
You must not take for fire. From this time
Be somewhat scanter of your maiden pres-
   ence,
Set your entreatments [14] at a higher rate
Than a command to parley: for Lord
   Hamlet,
Believe so much in him, that he is young,
And with a larger tether may he walk
Than may be given you: in few, Ophelia,
Do not believe his vows, for they are
   brokers, [15]
Not of that dye which their investments [16]
   show,
But mere implorators of unholy suits,
Breathing like sanctified and pious bawds,
The better to beguile. This is for all:
I would not, in plain terms, from this time
   forth,
Have you so slander any moment leisure
As to give words or talk with the Lord
   Hamlet.
Look to 't, I charge you: come your ways.
   OPH.   I shall obey, my lord.   [*Exeunt.*]

Scene IV

The platform.

[*Enter* HAMLET, HORATIO, *and* MARCELLUS.]

   HAMLET.   The air bites shrewdly; it is
   very cold.
   HORATIO.   It is a nipping and an eager
   air.

---

[13] Snares. Woodcocks were reputedly stupid
birds.
[14] Interviews.   [15] Procurers.   [16] Attire.

HAM.   What hour now?
HOR.   I think it lacks of twelve.
MARCELLUS.   No, it is struck.
HOR.   Indeed? I heard it not; it then
   draws near the season
Wherein the spirit held his wont to walk.
   [*A flourish of trumpets, and two
      pieces goes off within.*]
What does this mean, my lord?
   HAM.   The King doth wake to-night and
   takes his rouse,
Keeps wassails, and the swagg'ring up-
   spring [1] reels;
And, as he drains his draughts of Rhenish
   down,
The kettle-drum and trumpet thus bray out
The triumph of his pledge.
   HOR.   Is it a custom?
   HAM.   Ay, marry, is 't,
But to my mind, though I am native here
And to the manner born, it is a custom
More honour'd in the breach than the
   observance.
This heavy-headed revel east and west
Makes us traduc'd and tax'd [2] of other
   nations:
They clepe us drunkards, and with swinish
   phrase
Soil our addition; [3] and indeed it takes
From our achievements, though perform'd
   at height,
The pith and marrow of our attribute. [4]
So oft it chances in particular men,
That for some vicious mole of nature in
   them,
As, in their birth—wherein they are not
   guilty,
Since nature cannot choose his origin—
By their o'ergrowth of some complexion [5]
Oft breaking down the pales [6] and forts of
   reason,
Or by some habit that too much o'er-
   leavens
The form of plausive [7] manners, that these
   men,
Carrying, I say, the stamp of one defect,
Being nature's livery or fortune's star,—
His virtues else---be they as pure as grace,
As infinite as man may undergo—

---

[1] A lively dance.   [2] Censured.   [3] Honor.
[4] Reputation.   [5] Innate tendency.   [6] Enclosures.
[7] Pleasing.

Shall in the general censure [8] take corruption

From that particular fault: the dram of e'il [9]

Doth all the noble substance often dout [10]

To his own scandal.

[*Enter* GHOST.]

HOR.   Look, my lord, it comes!

HAM.   Angels and ministers of grace defend us!

Be thou a spirit of health or goblin damn'd,

Bring with thee airs from heaven or blasts from hell,

Be thy intents wicked or charitable,

Thou com'st in such a questionable [11] shape

That I will speak to thee. I 'll call thee Hamlet,

King, father, royal Dane. O, answer me!

Let me not burst in ignorance, but tell

Why thy canoniz'd bones, hearsed in death,

Have burst their cerements; why the sepulchre,

Wherein we saw thee quietly interr'd,

Hath op'd his ponderous and marble jaws,

To cast thee up again. What may this mean,

That thou, dead corse, again in complete steel

Revisits thus the glimpses of the moon,

Making night hideous, and we fools of nature

So horridly to shake our disposition

With thoughts beyond the reaches of our souls?

Say, why is this? Wherefore? What should we do?   [GHOST *beckons* HAMLET.]

HOR.   It beckons you to go away with it,

As if it some impartment did desire

To you alone.

MAR.   Look, with what courteous action

It waves you to a more removed ground.

But do not go with it.

HOR.   No, by no means.

HAM.   It will not speak; then will I follow it.

HOR.   Do not, my lord.

HAM.   Why, what should be the fear?

I do not set my life at a pin's fee,

And for my soul, what can it do to that,

Being a thing immortal as itself?

It waves me forth again; I 'll follow it.

HOR.   What if it tempt you toward the flood, my lord,

Or to the dreadful summit of the cliff

That beetles o'er his base into the sea,

And there assume some other horrible form,

Which might deprive your sovereignty of reason

And draw you into madness? Think of it.

The very place puts toys [12] of desperation,

Without more motive, into every brain

That looks so many fathoms to the sea

And hears it roar beneath.

HAM.   It waves me still.

Go on, I 'll follow thee.

MAR.   You shall not go, my lord.

HAM.   Hold off your hands.

HOR.   Be rul'd; you shall not go.

HAM.   My fate cries out,

And makes each petty artery in this body

As hardy as the Nemean lion's nerve.

Still am I call'd: unhand me, gentlemen;

By heaven, I 'll make a ghost of him that lets [13] me!

I say, away!—Go on, I 'll follow thee.

[*Exeunt* GHOST *and* HAMLET.]

HOR.   He waxes desperate with imagination.

MAR.   Let 's follow; 't is not fit thus to obey him.

HOR.   Have after—to what issue will this come?

MAR.   Something is rotten in the state of Denmark.

HOR.   Heaven will direct it.

MAR.   Nay, let 's follow him.

[*Exeunt.*]

Scene V

Another part of the platform.

[*Enter* GHOST *and* HAMLET.]

HAMLET.   Where wilt thou lead me? Speak, I 'll go no further.

GHOST.   Mark me.

HAM.   I will.

[8] Public opinion.   [9] Evil.   [10] Cancel.

[11] Inviting question.   [12] Whims.   [13] Hinders.

GHOST.   My hour is almost come,
When I to sulph'rous and tormenting
    flames
Must render up myself.
    HAM.   Alas, poor ghost!
    GHOST. Pity me not, but lend thy seri-
    ous hearing
To what I shall unfold.
    HAM.   Speak; I am bound to hear.
    GHOST. So art thou to revenge, when
    thou shalt hear.
    HAM. What?
    GHOST. I am thy father's spirit,
Doom'd for a certain term to walk the
    night,
And for the day confin'd to fast in fires,
Till the foul crimes done in my days of
    nature
Are burnt and purg'd away: but that I am
    forbid
To tell the secrets of my prison-house,
I could a tale unfold whose lightest word
Would harrow up thy soul, freeze thy
    young blood,
Make thy two eyes, like stars, start from
    their spheres,
Thy knotty and combined locks to part
And each particular hair to stand an end,
Like quills upon the fretful porpentine.[1]
But this eternal blazon [2] must not be
To ears of flesh and blood. List, list, O, list!
If thou didst ever thy dear father love—
    HAM. O God!
    GHOST. Revenge his foul and most un-
    natural murder.
    HAM. Murder!
    GHOST. Murder most foul, as in the
    best it is,
But this most foul, strange, and unnatural.
    HAM. Haste me to know 't, that I, with
    wings as swift
As meditation or the thoughts of love,
May sweep to my revenge.
    GHOST.   I find thee apt;
And duller shouldst thou be than the fat
    weed
That roots itself in ease on Lethe wharf,[3]
Wouldst thou not stir in this. Now, Hamlet,
    hear:

'T is given out that, sleeping in my orchard,
A serpent stung me; so the whole ear of
    Denmark
Is by a forged process of my death
Rankly abus'd [4]; but know, thou noble
    youth,
The serpent that did sting thy father's life
Now wears his crown.
    HAM.   O my prophetic soul!
My uncle!
    GHOST. Ay, that incestuous, that adul-
    terate beast,
With witchcraft of his wit, with traitorous
    gifts,—
O wicked wit and gifts, that have the power
So to seduce!—won to his shameful lust
The will of my most seeming-virtuous
    queen;
O Hamlet, what a falling-off was there!
From me, whose love was of that dignity
That it went hand in hand even with the
    vow
I made to her in marriage, and to de-
    cline
Upon a wretch whose natural gifts were
    poor
To those of mine!
But virtue, as it never will be moved,
Though lewdness court it in a shape of
    heaven,
So lust, though to a radiant angel link'd
Will sate itself in a celestial bed
And prey on garbage.
But, soft! methinks I scent the morning air,
Brief let me be. Sleeping within mine or-
    chard,
My custom always of the afternoon,
Upon my secure hour thy uncle stole,
With juice of cursed hebona in a vial,
And in the porches of mine ears did pour
The lep'rous distilment; whose effect
Holds such an enmity with blood of man
That swift as quicksilver it courses through
The natural gates and alleys of the body,
And with a sudden vigour it doth posset [5]
And curd, like eager [6] droppings into milk,
The thin and wholesome blood: so did it
    mine,
And a most instant tetter bark'd about,

---

[1] Porcupine.   [2] Revelation of eternity.
[3] The bank of Lethe, the river of oblivion.
[4] Grossly deceived.   [5] Curdle.
[6] Acid.

Most lazar-like,[7] with vile and loathsome
    crust,
All my smooth body.
Thus was I, sleeping, by a brother's hand
Of life, of crown, of queen, at once dis-
    patch'd;
Cut off even in the blossoms of my sin,
Unhouseled, disappointed, unanel'd,[8]
No reckoning made, but sent to my ac-
    count
With all my imperfections on my head.
O, horrible! O, horrible! most horrible!
If thou hast nature in thee, bear it not;
Let not the royal bed of Denmark be
A couch for luxury [9] and damned incest.
But, howsomever thou pursuest this act,
Taint not thy mind, nor let they soul con-
    trive
Against thy mother aught: leave her to
    heaven
And to those thorns that in her bosom
    lodge,
To prick and sting her. Fare thee well at
    once!
The glow-worm shows the matin to be
    near,
And 'gins to pale his uneffectual fire.
Adieu, adieu, adieu! remember me.

                              [*Exit* GHOST.]
HAM. O all you host of heaven! O
    earth! What else?
And shall I couple hell? O, fie! Hold, hold,
    my heart,
And you, my sinews, grow not instant old,
But bear me stiffly up. Remember thee?
Ay, thou poor ghost, while memory holds
    a seat
In this distracted globe.[10] Remember thee?
Yea, from the table [11] of my memory
I 'll wipe away all trivial fond [12] records,
All saws [13] of books, all forms, all pres-
    sures past,
That youth and observation copied there,
And thy commandment all alone shall live
Within the book and volume of my brain,
Unmix'd with baser matter; yes, by heaven!
O most pernicious woman!
O villain, villain, smiling, damned villain!

My tables!—Meet it is I set it down
That one may smile and smile, and be a vil-
    lain,
At least I 'm sure it may be so in Denmark.
So, uncle, there you are. Now to my word;
It is "Adieu, adieu! remember me."
I have sworn it.
    HORATIO. [*Within.*] My lord, my lord!
    MARCELLUS. [*Within.*] Lord Hamlet!
    HOR.   [*Within.*] Heaven secure him!
    HAM. So be it!
    MAR. [*Within.*] Illo, ho, ho, my lord!
    HAM. Hillo, ho, ho, boy! Come, bird,
    come.

    [*Enter* HORATIO *and* MARCELLUS.]

    MAR. How is 't, my noble lord?
    HOR.   What news, my lord?
    HAM. O wonderful!
    HOR. Good my lord, tell it.
    HAM.   No, you will reveal it.
    HOR. Not I, my lord, by heaven.
    MAR.   Nor I, my lord.
    HAM. How say you, then, would heart
    of man once think it?—
But you 'll be secret?
    HOR.   )
               Ay, by heaven, my lord.
    MAR.   )
    HAM. There 's ne'er a villain dwelling
    in all Denmark
But he 's an arrant knave.
    HOR. There needs no ghost, my lord,
    come from the grave
To tell us this.
    HAM. Why, right, you are in the right.
And so, without more circumstance [14] at
    all,
I hold it fit that we shake hands and part;
You, as your business and desire shall
    point you,
For every man has business and desire,
Such as it is; and for mine own poor part,
I will go pray.
    HOR. These are but wild and whirling
    words, my lord.
    HAM. I 'm sorry they offend you,
    heartily;
Yes, faith, heartily.

---

[7] Like a leper.
[8] Without the final rites of the eucharist, abso-
lution, and extreme unction.

[9] Lust.   [10] *I.e.,* his head.   [11] Tablet.
[12] Foolish.   [13] Choice sayings.
[14] Details.

HOR.   There 's no offence, my lord.

HAM.   Yes, by Saint Patrick, but there is, Horatio,

And much offence too—touching this vision here,

It is an honest [15] ghost, that let me tell you—

For your desire to know what is between

O'ermaster 't as you may. And now, good friends,

As you are friends, scholars, and soldiers,

Give me one poor request.

HOR.   What is 't, my lord? We will.

HAM.   Never make known what you have seen to-night.

BOTH.   My lord, we will not.

HAM.   Nay, but swear 't.

HOR.   In faith,
My lord, not I.

MAR.   Nor I, my lord, in faith.

HAM.   Upon my sword.

MAR.   We have sworn, my lord, already.

HAM.   Indeed, upon my sword, indeed.

GHOST.   [Beneath the stage.] Swear!

HAM.   Ha, ha, boy! say'st thou so? Art thou there, truepenny?

Come on; you hear this fellow in the cellarage;

Consent to swear.

HOR.   Propose the oath, my lord.

HAM.   Never to speak of this that you have seen.

Swear by my sword.

GHOST.   [Beneath.] Swear.

HAM.   Hic et ubique? [16] Then we 'll shift our ground.

Come hither, gentlemen,

And lay your hands again upon my sword:

Swear by my sword

Never to speak of this that you have heard.

GHOST.   [Beneath.] Swear by his sword.

HAM.   Well said, old mole! Canst work i' th' earth so fast?

A worthy pioner! [17] Once more remove, good friends.

HOR.   O day and night, but this is wondrous strange!

HAM.   And therefore as a stranger give it welcome.

There are more things in heaven and earth, Horatio,

Than are dreamt of in your philosophy.

But come;

Here, as before, never, so help you mercy,

How strange or odd some'er I bear myself,—

As I perchance hereafter shall think meet

To put an antic disposition on [18]—

That you, at such times seeing me, never shall,

With arms encumber'd [19] thus, or this headshake,

Or by pronouncing of some doubtful phrase

As "Well, well we know," or "We could, an if we would,"

Or "If we list to speak," or "There be, an if they might,"

Or such ambiguous giving out, to note

That you know aught of me,—this do swear,

So grace and mercy at your most need help you.

GHOST.   [Beneath.] Swear.

HAM.   Rest, rest, perturbed spirit! [They swear.] So, gentlemen,

With all my love I do commend me to you;

And what so poor a man as Hamlet is

May do, t' express his love and friending to you,

God willing, shall not lack. Let us go in together;

And still your fingers on your lips, I pray.

The time is out of joint; O cursed spite,

That ever I was born to set it right!

Nay, come, let 's go together.   [Exeunt.]

ACT II

Scene I

A room in the house of Polonius.

[Enter POLONIUS and REYNALDO.]

POLONIUS.   Give him this money and these notes, Reynaldo.

REYNALDO.   I will, my lord.

POL.   You shall do marvellous wisely, good Reynaldo,

[15] Authentic.   [16] Here and everywhere.
[17] Pioneer, sapper.
[18] Affect a fantastic manner.
[19] Folded.

Before you visit him, to make inquire
Of his behaviour.

REY.   My lord, I did intend it.

POL.   Marry, well said, very well said.
Look you, sir,
Inquire me first what Danskers are in Paris,
And how, and who, what means, and where
     they keep,
What company, at what expense; and
     finding
By this encompassment and drift of ques-
     tion
That they do know my son, come you more
     nearer
Than your particular demands will touch
     it: [1]
Take you, as 't were, some distant knowl-
     edge of him,
As thus, "I know his father and his friends,
And in part him." Do you mark this,
     Reynaldo?

REY.   Ay, very well, my lord.

POL.   "And in part him; but," you may
     say, "not well.
But, if 't be he I mean, he 's very wild,
Addicted so and so;" and there put on
     him
What forgeries you please; marry, none so
     rank
As may dishonour him,—take heed of
     that;
But, sir, such wanton, wild, and usual slips
As are companions noted and most known
To youth and liberty.

REY.   As gaming, my lord?

POL.   Ay, or drinking, fencing, swear-
     ing, quarreling,
Drabbing [2]; you may go so far.

REY.   My lord, that would dishonour
     him.

POL.   Faith, no, as you may season it in
     the charge.
You must not put another scandal on
     him,
That he is open to incontinency,[3]
That 's not my meaning; but breathe his
     faults so quaintly

That they may seem the taints of liberty,
The flash and outbreak of a fiery mind,
A savageness in unreclaimed blood,
Of general assault.[4]

REY.   But, my good lord,—

POL.   Wherefore should you do this?

REY.   Ay, my lord,
I would know that.

POL.   Marry, sir, here 's my drift,
And, I believe, it is a fetch of warrant: [5]
You laying these slight sullies on my son
As 't were a thing a little soil'd i' th' work-
     ing,
Mark you,
Your party in converse, him you would
     sound,
Having ever seen in the prenominate [6]
     crimes
The youth you breathe of guilty, be assur'd
He closes with you in this consequence; [7]
"Good sir," or so, or "friend," or "gentle-
     man,"
According to the phrase or the addition
Of man and country—

REY.   Very good, my lord.

POL.   And then, sir, does 'a this—'a
does—What was I about to say? By the
mass, I was about to say something. Where
did I leave?

REY.   At "closes in the consequence,"
at "friend or so," and "gentleman."

POL.   At "closes in the consequence,"
ay, marry—
He closes thus: "I know the gentleman.
I saw him yesterday, or th' other day,
Or then, or then, with such and such; and,
     as you say,
There was 'a gaming; there o'ertook in 's
     rouse;
There falling out at tennis;" or, perchance,
"I saw him enter such a house of sale,"
Videlicet, a brothel, or so forth.
See you now—
Your bait of falsehood takes this carp of
     truth;
And thus do we of wisdom and of reach,
With windlasses and with assays of bias,

---

[1] *I.e.,* you will learn more by indirect suggestions than by direct questions.
[2] Consorting with prostitutes.
[3] Debauchery.   [4] To which everyone is subject.

[5] Justifiable subterfuge.
[6] Aforementioned.
[7] He will agree with you in the following manner.

By indirections find directions out; [8]
So by my former lecture and advice,
Shall you my son. You have me, have you
    not?
    REY. My lord, I have.
    POL.   God buy you; [9] fare you well.
    REY. Good my lord.
    POL. Observe his inclination in yourself.
    REY. I shall, my lord.
    POL. And let him ply his music.
    REY.   Well, my lord.
    POL. Farewell.   [*Exit* REYNALDO.]

          [*Enter* OPHELIA.]

How now, Ophelia! what 's the matter?
    OPHELIA. O, my lord, my lord, I have
    been so affrighted!
    POL. With what: i' th' name of God?
    OPH. My lord, as I was sewing in my
    closet,
Lord Hamlet, with his doublet all unbrac'd,
No hat upon his head, his stockings fouled,
Ungarter'd, and down-gyved [10] to his ankle,
Pale as his shirt, his knees knocking each
    other,
And with a look so piteous in purport
As if he had been loosed out of hell
To speak of horrors,—he comes before me.
    POL. Mad for thy love?
    OPH.   My lord, I do not know.
But truly, I do fear it.
    POL.   What said he?
    OPH. He took me by the wrist and held
    me hard;
Then goes he to the length of all his arm,
And, with his other hand thus o'er his
    brow,
He falls to such perusal of my face
As 'a would draw it. Long stay'd he so.
At last, a little shaking of mine arm,
And thrice his head thus waving up and
    down,
He rais'd a sigh so piteous and profound
That it did seem to shatter all his bulk
And end his being; that done, he lets me
    go;
And, with his head over his shoulder
    turn'd,

He seem'd to find his way without his eyes,
For out o' doors he went without their
    help,
And, to the last, bended their light on me.
    POL. Come, go with me, I will go seek
    the King.
This is the very ecstasy [11] of love,
Whose violent property fordoes itself [12]
And leads the will to desperate undertak-
    ings
As oft as any passion under heaven
That does afflict our natures: I am sorry,—
What, have you given him any hard words
    of late?
    OPH. No, my good lord, but, as you
    did command,
I did repel his letters and denied
His access to me.
    POL.   That hath made him mad.
I am sorry that with better heed and judge-
    ment
I had not quoted [13] him. I fear'd he did but
    trifle
And meant to wreck thee; but beshrew my
    jealousy! [14]
By heaven, it is as proper to our age
To cast beyond ourselves in our opinions
As it is common for the younger sort
To lack discretion. Come, go we to the
    King.
This must be known, which, being kept
    close, might move
More grief to hide than hate to utter love.
Come.   [*Exeunt.*]

Scene II
A room in the castle.

[*Flourish. Enter* KING, QUEEN, ROSEN-
CRANTZ, GUILDENSTERN, *with others.*]

    KING. Welcome, dear Rosencrantz and
    Guildenstern!
Moreover that we much did long to see
    you,
The need we have to use you did provoke
Our hasty sending. Something have you
    heard

---

[8] Thus we wise and resourceful people with
subterfuges and tangential approaches find out the
right direction indirectly.
[9] God be with you, good-bye.
[10] Hanging down like fetters.   [11] Madness.
[12] Whose inherent violence destroys itself.
[13] Observed.
[14] Confound my suspicious nature!

Of Hamlet's transformation; so I call it,
Sith nor th' exterior nor the inward man
Resembles that it was. What it should be,
More than his father's death, that thus hath
    put him
So much from th' understanding of himself,
I cannot dream of: I entreat you both,
That, being of so young days brought up
    with him
And sith so neighbour'd to his youth and
    haviour,
That you vouchsafe your rest here in our
    court
Some little time; so by your companies
To draw him on to pleasures, and to gather
So much as from occasions you may glean,
Whether aught, to us unknown, afflicts him
    thus,
That, open'd, lies within our remedy.

    QUEEN. Good gentlemen, he hath much
    talk'd of you;
And sure I am two men there is not living
To whom he more adheres. If it will please
    you
To show us so much gentry [1] and good
    will
As to expend your time with us a while
For the supply and profit of our hope,
Your visitation shall receive such thanks
As fits a king's remembrance.

    ROSENCRANTZ. Both your Majesties
Might, by the sovereign power you have of
    us,
Put your dread pleasures more into com-
    mand
Than to entreaty.

    GUILDENSTERN. But we both obey,
And here give up ourselves, in the full
    bent [2]
To lay our service freely at your feet,
To be commanded.

    KING. Thanks, Rosencrantz and gentle
    Guildenstern.

    QUEEN. Thanks, Guildenstern and gen-
    tle Rosencrantz;
And I beseech you instantly to visit
My too much changed son. Go, some of
    you,

And bring these gentlemen where Hamlet
    is.

    GUIL. Heavens make our presence and
    our practices
Pleasant and helpful to him!

    QUEEN. Ay, amen!

    [*Exeunt* ROSENCRANTZ, GUILDENSTERN,
    and some Attendants.]

    [*Enter* POLONIUS.]

    POLONIUS. Th' ambassadors from Nor-
    way, my good lord,
Are joyfully return'd.

    KING. Thou still hast been the father
    of good news.

    POL. Have I, my lord? I assure you, my
    good liege,
I hold my duty as I hold my soul,
Both to my God and to my gracious king;
And I do think, or else this brain of mine
Hunts not the trail of policy so sure [3]
As it hath us'd to do, that I have found
The very cause of Hamlet's lunacy.

    KING. O, speak of that; that do I long
    to hear.

    POL. Give first admittance to th' am-
    bassadors.
My news shall be the fruit to that great
    feast.

    KING. Thyself do grace to them, and
    bring them in. [*Exit* POLONIUS.]
He tells me, my dear Gertrude, he hath
    found
The head and source of all your son's dis-
    temper.

    QUEEN. I doubt it is no other but the
    main,[4]
His father's death and our o'erhasty mar-
    riage.

    [*Re-enter* POLONIUS, *with* VOLTIMAND
    and CORNELIUS.]

    KING. Well, we shall sift him.—Wel-
    come, my good friends!
Say, Voltimand, what from our brother
    Norway?

    VOLTIMAND. Most fair return of greet-
    ings and desires.
Upon our first, he sent out to suppress

---

[1] Courtesy.
[2] Complete willingness.
[3] Is not so adroit in politic finesse.
[4] Chief concern.

His nephew's levies, which to him appear'd
To be a preparation 'gainst the Polack,
But, better look'd into, he truly found
It was against your Highness; whereat
    griev'd,
That so his sickness, age, and impotence
Was falsely borne in hand,[5] sends out
    arrests
On Fortinbras; which he, in brief, obeys,
Receives rebuke from Norway, and in fine
Makes vow before his uncle never more
To give th' assay of arms against your
    Majesty:
Whereon old Norway, overcome with joy,
Gives him threescore thousand crowns in
    annual fee,
And his commission to employ those sol-
    diers,
So levied as before, against the Polack;
With an entreaty, herein further shown,
                    [*Giving a paper.*]
That it might please you to give quiet pass
Through your dominions for this enterprise,
On such regards of safety and allowance
As therein are set down.
    KING.   It likes us well;
And at our more considered time we 'll
    read,
Answer, and think upon this business:
Meantime we thank you for your well-took
    labour.
Go to your rest; at night we'll feast to-
    gether:
Most welcome home!
                    [*Exeunt Ambassadors.*]
    POLONIUS. This business is well ended.
My liege, and madam, to expostulate
What majesty should be, what duty is,
Why day is day, night night, and time is
    time,
Were nothing but to waste night, day, and
    time;
Therefore, since brevity is the soul of wit
And tediousness the limbs and outward
    flourishes,
I will be brief. Your noble son is mad.
Mad call I it; for, to define true madness,

What is 't but to be nothing else but mad?
But let that go.
    QUEEN.   More matter, with less art.
    POL. Madam, I swear I use no art at all.
That he is mad, 't is true; 't is true 't is pity,
And pity 't is 't is true—a foolish figure![6]
But farewell it, for I will use no art.
Mad let us grant him then; and now re-
    mains
That we find out the cause of this effect,
Or rather say, the cause of this defect,
For this effect defective comes by cause.
Thus it remains, and the remainder thus.
Perpend.
I have a daughter—have while she is
    mine—
Who, in her duty and obedience, mark,
Hath given me this; now gather, and sur-
    mise.
                    [*Reads the letter.*]

"To the celestial and my soul's idol, the most
    beautified Ophelia,—"

That 's an ill phrase, a vile phrase; "beauti-
fied" is a vile phrase. But you shall hear.
Thus:

"In her excellent white bosom, these."

    QUEEN. Came this from Hamlet to her?
    POL. Good madam, stay a while; I will
    be faithful.   [*Reads.*]

    "Doubt thou the stars are fire,
        Doubt that the sun doth move,
    Doubt truth to be a liar,
        But never doubt I love.
O dear Ophelia, I am ill at these numbers,[7] I
have not art to reckon my groans; but that I
love thee best, O most best, believe it. Adieu.
    Thine evermore, most dear lady,
    Whilst this machine [8] is to him,
                    HAMLET."

This in obedience hath my daughter shown
    me,
And more above, hath his solicitings,
As they fell out by time, by means, and
    place,

---

[5] Taken advantage of.
[6] Figure of rhetoric. Polonius has a weakness
for rhetorical flourishes, in which he frequently

bogs down and loses the thread of his discourse.
[7] Poor at writing verses.
[8] Body.

All given to mine ear.

KING. But how hath she Receiv'd his love?

POL. What do you think of me?

KING. As of a man faithful and honourable.

POL. I would fain prove so. But what might you think,
When I had seen this hot love on the wing,—
As I perceiv'd it, I must tell you that,
Before my daughter told me,—what might you,
Or my dear Majesty your queen here, think,
If I had play'd the desk or table-book,[9]
Or given my heart a winking, mute and dumb,
Or look'd upon this love with idle sight,
What might you think? No, I went round to work,
And my young mistress thus I did bespeak:
"Lord Hamlet is a prince out of thy star.
This must not be;" and then I prescripts gave her,
That she should lock herself from his resort,
Admit no messengers, receive no tokens.
Which done, she took the fruits of my advice;
And he, repell'd,—a short tale to make—
Fell into a sadness, then into a fast,
Thence to a watch, thence into a weakness,
Thence to a lightness, and, by this declension,
Into the madness wherein now he raves,
And all we mourn for.

KING. Do you think 't is this?

QUEEN. It may be, very like.

POL. Hath there been such a time—I would fain know that—
That I have positively said, " 'T is so,"
When it prov'd otherwise?

KING. Not that I know.

POL. Take this from this,[10] if this be otherwise:
If circumstances lead me, I will find
Where truth is hid, though it were hid indeed
Within the centre.[11]

KING. How may we try it further?

POL. You know, sometimes he walks four hours together
Here in the lobby.

QUEEN. So he does, indeed.

POL. At such a time I 'll loose my daughter to him:
Be you and I behind an arras [12] then;
Mark the encounter, if he love her not
And be not from his reason fall'n thereon,
Let me be no assistant for a state,
But keep a farm and carters.

KING. We will try it.

[*Enter* HAMLET, *reading on a book.*]

QUEEN. But look where sadly the poor wretch comes reading.

POL. Away, I do beseech you, both away.
I 'll board him presently.[13] O, give me leave.

[*Exeunt* KING, QUEEN, *and Attendants.*]
How does my good Lord Hamlet?

HAMLET. Well, God-a-mercy.

POL. Do you know me, my lord?

HAM. Excellent well; you are a fishmonger.[14]

POL. Not I, my lord.

HAM. Then I would you were so honest a man.

POL. Honest, my lord?

HAM. Ay, sir; to be honest, as this world goes, is to be one man picked out of ten thousand.

POL. That 's very true, my lord.

HAM. For if the sun breed maggots in a dead dog, being a good kissing carrion—Have you a daughter?

POL. I have, my lord.

HAM. Let her not walk i' th' sun: conception [15] is a blessing, but as your daughter may conceive—Friend, look to 't.

POL. [*Aside.*] How say you by that?

---

[9] Simply filed away the information.
[10] *I.e.,* his head from his shoulders.
[11] Center of the earth. [12] Tapestry curtain.
[13] Accost him at once.
[14] The word means both fish-dealer and pander. Throughout this colloquy, as elsewhere, Hamlet's remarks have a double meaning. The primary meaning impresses Polonius as incoherent and insane; the secondary meaning, which escapes him, is quite lucid.
[15] Understanding, with a later pun on the meaning of pregnancy.

Still harping on my daughter: yet he knew me not at first; 'a said I was a fishmonger; 'a is far gone; and truly in my youth I suffered much extremity for love; very near this. I 'll speak to him again.—What do you read, my lord?

HAM.   Words, words, words.

POL.   What is the matter, my lord?

HAM.   Between who?

POL.   I mean, the matter that you read, my lord.

HAM.   Slanders, sir; for the satirical rogue says here that old men have grey beards, that their faces are wrinkled, their eyes purging thick amber and plum-tree gum, and that they have a plentiful lack of wit, together with most weak hams: all which, sir, though I most powerfully and potently believe, yet I hold it not honesty to have it thus set down; for yourself, sir, shall grow old as I am, if like a crab you could go backward.

POL.   [Aside.] Though this be madness, yet there is method in 't.—Will you walk out of the air, my lord?

HAM.   Into my grave?

POL.   Indeed, that is out of the air. [Aside.] How pregnant sometimes his replies are! a happiness that often madness hits on, which reason and sanity could not so prosperously be delivered of. I will leave him, and suddenly contrive the means of meeting between him and my daughter.— My lord, I will take my leave of you.

HAM.   You cannot, sir, take from me anything that I will not more willingly part withal,—except my life, except my life, except my life.

POL.   Fare you well, my lord.

HAM.   These tedious old fools!

[Enter ROSENCRANTZ and GUILDENSTERN.]

POL.   You go to seek the Lord Hamlet? There he is.

ROSENCRANTZ.   [To POLONIUS.] God save you, sir!   [Exit POLONIUS.]

GUILDENSTERN.   My honoured lord!

ROS.   My most dear lord!

HAM.   My excellent good friends! How dost thou, Guildenstern? Ah, Rosencrantz!

Good lads, how do you both?

ROS.   As the indifferent [16] children of the earth.

GUIL.   Happy in that we are not over-happy. On Fortune's cap we are not the very button.

HAM.   Nor the soles of her shoe?

ROS.   Neither, my lord.

HAM.   Then you live about her waist, or in the middle of her favours?

GUIL.   Faith, her privates we.

HAM.   In the secret parts of Fortune? Oh, most true; she is a strumpet. What news?

ROS.   None, my lord, but that the world 's grown honest.

HAM.   Then is doomsday near; but your news is not true. Let me question more in particular: what have you, my good friends, deserved at the hands of Fortune, that she sends you to prison hither?

GUIL.   Prison, my lord?

HAM.   Denmark 's a prison.

ROS.   Then is the world one.

HAM.   A goodly one, in which there are many confines, wards, and dungeons, Denmark being one o' th' worst.

ROS.   We think not so, my lord.

HAM.   Why, then, 't is none to you; for there is nothing either good or bad, but thinking makes it so: to me it is a prison.

ROS.   Why, then, your ambition makes it one: 't is too narrow for your mind.

HAM.   O God, I could be bounded in a nutshell and count myself a king of infinite space, were it not that I have bad dreams.

GUIL.   Which dreams indeed are ambition, for the very substance of the ambitious is merely the shadow of a dream.

HAM.   A dream itself is but a shadow.

ROS.   Truly, and I hold ambition of so airy and light a quality that it is but a shadow's shadow.

HAM.   Then are our beggars bodies, and our monarchs and outstretched heroes the beggars' shadows. Shall we to th' court? for, by my fay, I cannot reason.

BOTH.   We 'll wait upon you.

[16] Ordinary.

HAM. No such matter. I will not sort you with the rest of my servants, for, to speak to you like an honest man, I am most dreadfully attended. But in the beaten way of friendship, what make you at Elsinore?

ROS. To visit you, my lord; no other occasion.

HAM. Beggar that I am, I am even poor in thanks, but I thank you; and sure, dear friends, my thanks are too dear a half-penny. Were you not sent for? Is it your own inclining? Is it a free visitation? Come, come, deal justly with me: come, come; nay, speak.

GUIL. What should we say, my lord?

HAM. Why, anything, but to th' purpose. You were sent for; and there is a kind of confession in your looks which your modesties have not craft enough to colour. I know the good king and queen have sent for you.

ROS. To what end, my lord?

HAM. That you must teach me: but let me conjure you, by the rights of our fellowship, by the consonancy [17] of our youth, by the obligation of our ever-preserved love, and by what more dear a better proposer can charge you withal, be even and direct with me, whether you were sent for or no!

ROS. [Aside to GUILDENSTERN.] What say you?

HAM. [Aside.] Nay, then, I have an eye of you.—If you love me, hold not off.

GUIL. My lord, we were sent for.

HAM. I will tell you why; so shall my anticipation prevent your discovery,[18] and your secrecy to the King and Queen moult no feather. I have of late—but wherefore I know not—lost all my mirth, forgone all custom of exercises; and indeed it goes so heavily with my disposition that this goodly frame, the earth, seems to me a sterile promontory, this most excellent canopy, the air, look you, this brave o'erhanging firmament, this majestical roof fretted with golden fire, why, it appeareth nothing to me but a foul and pestilent congregation of vapours. What a piece of work is a man! How noble in reason! How infinite in faculties! In form and moving how express and admirable! In action how like an angel! In apprehension how like a god! The beauty of the world! The paragon of animals! And yet, to me, what is this quintessence of dust? Man delights not me—nor woman neither, though by your smiling you seem to say so.

ROS. My lord, there was no such stuff in my thoughts.

HAM. Why did ye laugh then, when I said, "Man delights not me"?

ROS. To think, my lord, if you delight not in man, what lenten entertainment [19] the players shall receive from you. We coted [20] them on the way, and hither are they coming to offer you service.

HAM. He that plays the king shall be welcome; his majesty shall have tribute on me; the adventurous knight shall use his foil and target; the lover shall not sigh gratis; the humorous man shall end his part in peace; the clown shall make those laugh whose lungs are tickle o' th' sere [21]; and the lady shall say her mind freely, or the blank verse shall halt for 't. What players are they?

ROS. Even those you were wont to take such delight in, the tragedians of the city.

HAM. How chances it they travel? Their residence,[22] both in reputation and profit, was better both ways.

ROS. I think their inhibition comes by the means of the late innovation.[23]

HAM. Do they hold the same estimation they did when I was in the city? Are they so followed?

ROS. No, indeed, they are not.

HAM. How comes it? Do they grow rusty?

ROS. Nay, their endeavour keeps in the wonted pace; but there is, sir, an aery of

[17] Similitude.
[18] Forestall your own admission.
[19] Poor reception. [20] Overtook.
[21] Quick on the trigger.
[22] Remaining in the city.
[23] The interference with the players refers to an innovation of Shakespeare's time. For a time companies of child actors—the "aery of eyases," or brood of young hawks, spoken of below—became tremendously popular and jeered at the common stage in satires from the goose-quill pens of their dramatists.

children, little eyases, that cry out on the top of question, and are most tyrannically clapped for 't: these are now the fashion, and so berattle the common stages—so they call them—that many wearing rapiers are afraid of goose-quills and dare scarce come thither.

HAM. What, are they children? Who maintains 'em? How are they escoted? [24] Will they pursue the quality [25] no longer than they can sing? Will they not say afterwards, if they should grow themselves to common players,—as it is most like, if their means are no better—their writers do them wrong, to make them exclaim against their own succession?

ROS. Faith, there has been much to do on both sides, and the nation holds it no sin to tarre [26] them to controversy. There was for a while no money bid for argument [27] unless the poet and the player went to cuffs in the question.

HAM. Is 't possible?

GUIL. O, there has been much throwing about of brains.

HAM. Do the boys carry it away?

ROS. Ay, that they do, my lord; Hercules and his load too. [28]

HAM. It is not very strange; for my uncle is king of Denmark, and those that would make mouths at him while my father lived, give twenty, forty, fifty, a hundred ducats apiece for his picture in little. 'Sblood, there is something in this more than natural, if philosophy could find it out.   [Flourish within.]

GUIL. There are the players.

HAM. Gentlemen, you are welcome to Elsinore. Your hands, come, then. Th' appurtenance of welcome is fashion and ceremony: let me comply with you in this garb, lest my extent to the players, which I tell you, must show fairly outwards, should more appear like entertainment than yours. You are welcome; but my uncle-father and aunt-mother are deceived.

GUIL. In what, my dear lord?

HAM. I am but mad north-north-west: when the wind is southerly I know a hawk from a handsaw. [29]

[Enter POLONIUS.]

POLONIUS. Well be with you, gentlemen!

HAM. [Aside to them.] Hark you, Guildenstern, and you too, at each ear a hearer: that great baby you see there is not yet out of his swaddling-clouts.

ROS. Happily [30] he is the second time come to them, for they say an old man is twice a child.

HAM. I will prophesy he comes to tell me of the players; mark it. [Aloud.] You say right, sir; a Monday morning; 't was then indeed.

POL. My lord, I have news to tell you.

HAM. My lord, I have news to tell you. When Roscius was an actor in Rome—

POL. The actors are come hither, my lord.

HAM. Buzz, buzz!

POL. Upon mine honour,—

HAM. "Then came each actor on his ass,"—

POL. The best actors in the world, either for tragedy, comedy, history, pastoral, pastoral-comical, historical-pastoral, scene individable, or poem unlimited. [31] Seneca cannot be too heavy, nor Plautus too light for the law of writ and liberty. These are the only men.

HAM. O Jephthah, judge of Israel, what a treasure hadst thou!

POL. What a treasure had he, my lord?

HAM. Why,
"One fair daughter, and no more,
    The which he loved passing well."

POL. [Aside.] Still on my daughter.

HAM. Am I not i' th' right, old Jephthah?

POL. If you call me Jephthah, my lord, I have a daughter that I love passing well.

---

[24] Supported.
[25] Acting profession.
[26] Incite.   [27] Dramatic subject.
[28] A reference to the Globe Theater and its sign: Hercules supporting the globe on his shoulders.

[29] I.e., Hamlet is mad only when it suits his convenience.   [30] Perhaps.
[31] These terms, and the following "law of writ and the liberty," refer respectively to plays which conform to the classical rules and those which follow the more free Renaissance pattern.

HAM.   Nay, that follows not.

POL.   What follows, then, my lord?

HAM.   Why,

"As by lot, God wot,"

and then, you know,

"It came to pass as most like it was,"—
the first row [32] of the pious chanson will
show you more, for look where my abridge-
ment comes.

[*Enter four or five* PLAYERS.]

You are welcome, masters, welcome all. I
am glad to see thee well. Welcome, good
friends. O, old friend! Why, thy face is
valanced [33] since I saw thee last; com'st
thou to beard me in Denmark? What, my
young lady and mistress! By 'r Lady, your
ladyship is nearer to heaven than when I
saw you last, by the altitude of a chopine.[34]
Pray God, your voice, like a piece of uncurrent gold, be not cracked within the
ring.[35] Masters, you are all welcome. We 'll
e'en to 't like French falconers—fly at anything we see; we 'll have a speech straight.
Come, give us a taste of your quality;
come, a passionate speech.

FIRST PLAYER.   What speech, my good
lord?

HAM.   I heard thee speak me a speech
once, but it was never acted; or, if it was,
not above once; for the play, I remember,
pleased not the million; 't was caviare to
the general; [36] but it was—as I received it,
and others, whose judgement in such matters cried in the top of mine [37]—an excellent play, well digested in the scenes, set
down with as much modesty as cunning.
I remember one said there were no sallets [38]
in the lines to make the matter savoury,
nor no matter in the phrase that might in-
dict the author of affection; [39] but called it
an honest method, as wholesome as sweet,
and by very much more handsome than
fine.[40] One speech in 't I chiefly loved; 't
was Æneas' tale to Dido, and thereabout of

it especially when he speaks of Priam's
slaughter. If it live in your memory, begin
at this line: let me see, let me see—
"The rugged Pyrrhus, like th' Hyrcanian
    beast," [41]
—'T is not so; it begins with Pyrrhus:—
"The rugged Pyrrhus, he whose sable arms,
Black as his purpose, did the night resem-
    ble
When he lay couched in th' ominous
    horse,[42]
Hath now this dread and black complexion
    smear'd
With heraldry more dismal: head to foot
Now is he total gules, horribly trick'd [43]
With blood of fathers, mothers, daughters,
    sons,
Bak'd and impasted with the parching
    streets,
That lend a tyrannous and a damned light
To their lords' murder. Roasted in wrath
    and fire,
And thus o'er-sized [44] with coagulate gore,
With eyes like carbuncles, the hellish Pyr-
    rhus
Old grandsire Priam seeks."
So, proceed you.

POL.   'Fore God, my lord, well spoken,
with good accent and good discretion.

FIRST PLAY.   "Anon he finds him
Striking too short at Greeks; his antique
    sword,
Rebellious to his arm, lies where it falls,
Repugnant to command; unequal match'd,
Pyrrhus at Priam drives, in rage strikes
    wide,
But with the whiff and wind of his fell
    sword
Th' unnerved father falls. Then senseless
    Ilium,
Seeming to feel this blow, with flaming top
Stoops to his base, and with a hideous crash
Takes prisoner Pyrrhus' ear; for, lo! his
    sword,
Which was declining on the milky head

---

[32] Stanza.   [33] Fringed with a beard.
[34] Thick-soled shoe.
[35] The witticism plays with the two facts that
a coin damaged within the circle surrounding the
sovereign's head was unfit for currency and that
the boy actor was unfit for female rôles when his
voice changed.

[36] A delicacy too exceptional for the common
taste.
[37] Excelled mine.   [38] Salads, *i.e.,* spicy jests.
[39] Affectation.   [40] Ornate.   [41] The tiger.
[42] The wooden horse used to end the siege of
Troy.
[43] All red, horribly adorned. [44] Smeared over.

Of reverend Priam, seem'd i' th' air to stick;
So, as a painted tyrant, Pyrrhus stood
And like a neutral to his will and matter,[45]
Did nothing.
But, as we often see, against some storm,
A silence in the heavens, the rack [46] stand still,
The bold winds speechless and the orb below
As hush as death, anon the dreadful thunder
Doth rend the region; so, after Pyrrhus' pause,
Aroused vengeance sets him new a-work;
And never did the Cyclops' hammers fall
On Mars's armour forg'd for proof eterne [47]
With less remorse than Pyrrhus' bleeding sword
Now falls on Priam.
Out, out, thou strumpet Fortune! All you gods,
In general synod take away her power!
Break all the spokes and fellies [48] from her wheel,
And bowl the round nave [49] down the hill of heaven
As low as to the fiends!"

POL. This is too long.

HAM. It shall to the barber's, with your beard. Prithee, say on; he 's for a jig or a tale of bawdry, or he sleeps: say on; come to Hecuba.

FIRST PLAY. "But who, Ah, woe! had seen the mobled [50] queen"—

HAM. "The mobled queen"?

POL. That 's good; "mobled queen" is good.

FIRST PLAY. "Run barefoot up and down, threat'ning the flames
With bisson rheum,[51] a clout about that head
Where late the diadem stood, and for a robe,
About her lank and all o'er-teemed [52] loins,
A blanket, in the alarm of fear caught up;—

Who this had seen, with tongue in venom steep'd,
'Gainst Fortune's state would treason have pronounc'd:
But if the gods themselves did see her then,
When she saw Pyrrhus make malicious sport
In mincing with his sword her husband's limbs,
The instant burst of clamour that she made,
Unless things mortal move them not at all,
Would have made milch [53] the burning eyes of heaven,
And passion in the gods."

POL. Look, whe'er he has not turned his colour and has tears in 's eyes. Prithee, no more.

HAM. 'T is well; I 'll have thee speak out the rest of this soon. Good my lord, will you see the players well bestowed? Do you hear? Let them be well used, for they are the abstract and brief chronicles of the time; after your death you were better have a bad epitaph than their ill report while you live.

POL. My lord, I will use them according to their desert.

HAM. God's bodykins, man, much better! Use every man after his desert, and who shall scape whipping? Use them after your own honour and dignity; the less they deserve, the more merit is in your bounty. Take them in.

POL. Come, sirs. [Exit POLONIUS.]

HAM. Follow him, friends; we 'll hear a play to-morrow. [Exeunt all the PLAYERS but the FIRST.] Dost thou hear me, old friend? Can you play "The Murder of Gonzago"?

FIRST PLAY. Ay, my lord.

HAM. We 'll ha 't to-morrow night. You could, for a need, study a speech of some dozen lines or sixteen lines, which I would set down and insert in 't, could you not?

FIRST PLAY. Ay, my lord.

HAM. Very well. Follow that lord, and

---

[45] His purpose and its fulfilment.
[46] Bank of clouds.
[47] Eternal durability.
[48] Segments of the rim.
[49] Hub.
[50] Muffled: an unusual word which perplexes Hamlet.
[51] Blinding tears.
[52] Exhausted with child-bearing.
[53] Milked tears from.

look you mock him not. [*Exit* FIRST
PLAYER.] My good friends, I 'll leave you
till night: you are welcome to Elsinore.

ROS.   Good my lord!

[*Exeunt* ROSENCRANTZ *and* GUILDEN-
STERN.]

HAM.   Ay, so, God buy to you.—Now
I am alone.

O, what a rogue and peasant slave am I!
Is it not monstrous that this player here,
But in a fiction, in a dream of passion,
Could force his soul so to his own conceit [54]
That from her working all his visage
wann'd,
Tears in his eyes, distraction in his aspect,
A broken voice, and his whole function
suiting
With forms to his conceit? And all for
nothing!
For Hecuba! [55]
What 's Hecuba to him, or he to Hecuba,
That he should weep for her? What would
he do,
Had he the motive and the cue for passion
That I have? He would drown the stage
with tears
And cleave the general ear with horrid
speech,
Make mad the guilty and appal the free,
Confound the ignorant, and amaze indeed
The very faculties of eyes and ears.
Yet I,
A dull and muddy-mettled rascal, peak
Like John-a-dreams, unpregnant of my
cause,[56]
And can say nothing; no, not for a king,
Upon whose property and most dear life
A damn'd defeat was made. Am I a cow-
ard?
Who calls me villain, breaks my pate
across,
Plucks off my beard and blows it in my
face,
Tweaks me by the nose, gives me the lie i'
th' throat
As deep as to the lungs, who does me this?

Ha!
'Swounds, I should take it; for it cannot
be
But I am pigeon-liver'd and lack gall
To make oppression bitter, or ere this
I should ha' fatted all the region kites
With this slave's offal. Bloody, bawdy vil-
lain!
Remorseless, treacherous, lecherous, kind-
less [57] villain!
O, vengeance!
Why, what an ass am I! This is most brave,
That I, the son of a dear father murdered,
Prompted to my revenge by heaven and
hell,
Must, like a whore, unpack my heart with
words,
And fall a-cursing, like a very drab,
A stallion! [58]
Fie upon 't! Foh! About, my brains!
Hum, I have heard
That guilty creatures sitting at a play
Have by the very cunning of the scene
Been struck so to the soul that presently [59]
They have proclaim'd their malefactions;
For murder, though it have no tongue, will
speak
With most miraculous organ: I 'll have
these players
Play something like the murder of my
father
Before mine uncle, I'll observe his looks,
I 'll tent [60] him to the quick; if he but
blench,[61]
I know my course. The spirit that I have
seen
May be a devil; and the devil hath power
T' assume a pleasing shape; yea, and per-
haps
Out of my weakness and my melancholy,
As he is very potent with such spirits,
Abuses me to damn me; I 'll have grounds
More relative [62] than this—the play 's the
thing
Wherein I 'll catch the conscience of the
King.   [*Exit.*]

[54] Imaginative invention.
[55] The wife of Priam and Queen of Troy referred to in the Player's speech.
[56] Mope like a dreamer, unquickened by my
motives for action.
[57] Inhuman.

[58] Stud, or male prostitute. In his disgust Hamlet applies to himself the preceding "very drab,"
i.e., a typical whore.
[59] Forthwith.
[60] Probe.   [61] Wince.
[62] Relevant.

ACT III

Scene I

A room in the castle.

[*Enter* KING, QUEEN, POLONIUS, OPHELIA, ROSENCRANTZ, GUILDENSTERN, *and* Lords.]

KING.   And can you, by no drift of conference,
Get from him why he puts on this confusion,
Grating so harshly all his days of quiet
With turbulent and dangerous lunacy?
ROSENCRANTZ.   He does confess he feels himself distracted;
But from what cause 'a will by no means speak.
GUILDENSTERN.   Nor do we find him forward to be sounded,
But, with a crafty madness, keeps aloof
When we would bring him on to some confession
Of his true state.
QUEEN.   Did he receive you well?
ROS.   Most like a gentleman.
GUIL.   But with much forcing of his disposition.[1]
ROS.   Niggard of question; but, of our demands,
Most free in his reply.
QUEEN.   Did you assay him
To any pastime?
ROS.   Madam, it so fell out, that certain players
We o'er-raught [2] on the way; of these we told him,
And there did seem in him a kind of joy
To hear of it: they are here about the court,
And, as I think, they have already order
This night to play before him.
POLONIUS.   'T is most true.
And he beseech'd me to entreat your Majesties
To hear and see the matter.
KING.   With all my heart; and it doth much content me
To hear him so inclin'd.
Good gentlemen, give him a further edge,
And drive his purpose into these delights.
ROS.   We shall, my lord.

[*Exeunt* ROSENCRANTZ *and* GUILDENSTERN.]
KING.   Sweet Gertrude, leave us two,
For we have closely sent for Hamlet hither,
That he, as 't were by accident, may here
Affront [3] Ophelia.
Her father and myself—lawful espials [4]—
We 'll so bestow ourselves that, seeing unseen,
We may of their encounter frankly judge,
And gather by him, as he is behav'd,
If 't be th' affliction of his love or no
That thus he suffers for.
QUEEN.   I shall obey you.
And for your part, Ophelia, I do wish
That your good beauties be the happy cause
Of Hamlet's wildness; so shall I hope your virtues
Will bring him to his wonted way again,
To both your honours.
OPHELIA.   Madam, I wish it may.
[*Exit* QUEEN.]
POL.   Ophelia, walk you here. Gracious, so please you,
We will bestow ourselves. [*To* OPHELIA.] Read on this book,
That show of such an exercise may colour
Your loneliness. We are oft to blame in this,—
'T is too much prov'd—that with devotion's visage
And pious action we do sugar o'er
The devil himself.
KING. [*Aside.*] O, 't is true!
How smart a lash that speech doth give my conscience!
The harlot's cheek, beautied with plast'ring art,
Is not more ugly to the thing that helps it
Than is my deed to my most painted word:
O heavy burden!
POL.   I hear him coming; let 's withdraw, my lord.
[*Exeunt* KING *and* POLONIUS.]

[*Enter* HAMLET]

HAMLET.   To be, or not to be: that is the question:
Whether 't is nobler in the mind to suffer

---
[1] But only by making a deliberate effort.
[2] Overtook.   [3] Encounter.   [4] Spies.

The slings and arrows of outrageous for-
tune,
Or to take arms against a sea of troubles,
And by opposing end them. To die, to
sleep—
No more; and by a sleep to say we end
The heart-ache and the thousand natural
shocks
That flesh is heir to; 't is a consummation
Devoutly to be wish'd; to die; to sleep;
To sleep, perchance to dream; ay, there 's
the rub; [5]
For in that sleep of death what dreams may
come,
When we have shuffled off this mortal coil,[6]
Must give us pause; there 's the respect
That makes calamity of so long life: [7]
For who would bear the whips and scorns
of time,
Th' oppressor's wrong, the proud man's
contumely,
The pangs of dispriz'd [8] love, the law's de-
lay,
The insolence of office, and the spurns
That patient merit of th' unworthy takes,
When he himself might his quietus make
With a bare bodkin? [9] Who would fardels [10]
bear,
To grunt and sweat under a weary life,
But that the dread of something after death,
The undiscover'd country from whose
bourn
No traveller returns, puzzles the will
And makes us rather bear those ills we
have
Than fly to others that we know not of?
Thus conscience [11] does make cowards of
us all;
And thus the native hue of resolution
Is sicklied o'er with the pale cast of thought,
And enterprises of great pitch and moment
With this regard their currents turn awry,
And lose the name of action.—Soft you
now,
The fair Ophelia!—Nymph, in thy orisons

Be all my sins remember'd.
OPH.   Good my lord,
How does your honour for this many a
day?
HAM. I humbly thank you, well, well,
well.
OPH. My lord, I have remembrances
of yours
That I have longed long to re-deliver.
I pray you, now receive them.
   HAM.   No, not I;
I never gave you aught.
   OPH. My honour'd lord, you know right
well you did,
And, with them, words of so sweet breath
compos'd
As made the things more rich. Their per-
fume lost,
Take these again; for to the noble mind
Rich gifts wax poor when givers prove un-
kind.
There, my lord.
   HAM. Ha, ha! are you honest? [12]
   OPH. My lord!
   HAM. Are you fair?
   OPH. What means your lordship?
   HAM. That if you be honest and fair,
your honesty should admit no discourse to
your beauty.
   OPH. Could beauty, my lord, have bet-
ter commerce than with honesty?
   HAM. Ay, truly; for the power of beauty
will sooner transform honesty from what it
is to a bawd than the force of honesty can
translate beauty into his likeness. This was
sometime a paradox, but now the time
gives it proof. I did love you once.
   OPH. Indeed, my lord, you made me
believe so.
   HAM. You should not have believed me,
for virtue cannot so inoculate our old stock
but we shall relish of it.[13] I loved you not.
   OPH. I was the more deceived.
   HAM. Get thee to a nunnery; why
wouldst thou be a breeder of sinners? I

---

[5] The obstacle that spoils one's aim. A term
taken from bowling.
   [6] Cast off this mortal turmoil.
   [7] It is this consideration which makes calamity
so long-lived.   [8] Scorned.
   [9] Might settle his account with a mere dagger.
   [10] Burdens.

[11] Knowledge or consciousness of all the factors
involved.
   [12] Besides having the general significance of
honorable, the word also specifically means *chaste*.
   [13] No matter how much virtue is grafted on to
our old stock (*i.e.*, of original sin), we shall still
bear the taint of it.

am myself indifferent [14] honest, but yet I could accuse me of such things that it were better my mother had not borne me: I am very proud, revengeful, ambitious, with more offences at my beck than I have thoughts to put them in, imagination to give them shape, or time to act them in. What should such fellows as I do crawling between earth and heaven? We are arrant knaves all; believe none of us, go thy ways to a nunnery. Where 's your father?

OPH.   At home, my lord.

HAM.   Let the doors be shut upon him, that he may play the fool nowhere but in 's own house. Farewell!

OPH.   O, help him, you sweet heavens!

HAM.   If thou dost marry, I 'll give thee this plague for thy dowry: be thou as chaste as ice, as pure as snow, thou shalt not escape calumny. Get thee to a nunnery, farewell! Or, if thou wilt needs marry, marry a fool; for wise men know well enough what monsters you make of them. To a nunnery, go, and quickly too, fare-well!

OPH.   Heavenly powers, restore him!

HAM.   I have heard of your paintings, well enough. God hath given you one face, and you make yourselves another. You jig and amble, and you lisp and nick-name God's creatures and make your wantonness your ignorance. Go to, I 'll no more on 't; it hath made me mad. I say, we will have no moe marriage: those that are married already, all but one, shall live; the rest shall keep as they are. To a nunnery, go.   [*Exit* HAMLET.]

OPH.   O, what a noble mind is here o'er-thrown!

The courtier's, soldier's, scholar's eye, tongue, sword;

Th' expectancy and rose of the fair state,

The glass of fashion and the mould of form,

The observ'd of all observers, quite quite down!

And I, of ladies most deject and wretched,

That suck'd the honey of his music vows,

Now see that noble and most sovereign

reason,

Like sweet bells jangled out of time and harsh:

That unmatch'd form and feature of blown youth [15]

Blasted with ecstasy.[16] O, woe is me,

T' have seen what I have seen, see what I see!

[*Re-enter* KING *and* POLONIUS.]

KING.   Love! his affections do not that way tend;

Nor what he spake, though it lack'd form a little,

Was not like madness. There 's something in his soul

O'er which his melancholy sits on brood,

And I do doubt the hatch and the disclose

Will be some danger; which for to prevent,

I have in quick determination

Thus set it down: he shall with speed to England

For the demand of our neglected tribute.

Haply the seas and countries different

With variable objects shall expel

This something-settled matter in his heart,

Whereon his brains still beating puts him thus

From fashion of himself. What think you on 't?

POL.   It shall do well; but yet do I believe

The origin and commencement of his grief

Sprung from neglected love. How now, Ophelia?

You need not tell us what Lord Hamlet said;

We heard it all. My lord, do as you please,

But, if you hold it fit, after the play

Let his queen mother all alone entreat him

To show his grief; let her be round [17] with him,

And I 'll be plac'd, so please you, in the ear

Of all their conference. If she find him not,

To England send him, or confine him where

Your wisdom best shall think.

KING.   It shall be so.

Madness in great ones must not unwatch'd go.   [*Exeunt.*]

---

[14] More or less.   [15] Youth in full bloom.   [16] Madness.   [17] Blunt.

Scene II
A hall in the castle.

[*Enter* HAMLET *and three of the Players.*]

HAMLET. Speak the speech, I pray you, as I pronounced it to you, trippingly on the tongue; but if you mouth it, as many of our players do, I had as lief the town-crier spoke my lines. Nor do not saw the air too much with your hand thus, but use all gently, for in the very torrent, tempest, and, as I may say, the whirlwind of your passion, you must acquire and beget a temperance that may give it smoothness. O, it offends me to the soul to see a robustious periwig-pated fellow tear a passion to tatters, to very rags, to split the ears of the groundlings,[1] who for the most part are capable of nothing but inexplicable dumbshows and noise: I would have such a fellow whipped for o'erdoing Termagant; it out-herods Herod:[2] pray you, avoid it.

FIRST PLAYER. I warrant your honour.

HAMLET. Be not too tame neither, but let your own discretion be your tutor; suit the action to the word, the word to the action; with this special observance, that you o'erstep not the modesty of nature: for anything so o'erdone is from the purpose of playing, whose end, both at the first and now, was and is, to hold, as 't were, the mirror up to nature; to show virtue her own feature, scorn her own image, and the very age and body of the time his form and pressure. Now this overdone, or come tardy off, though it makes the unskilful laugh, cannot but make the judicious grieve; the censure of the which one[3] must, in your allowance, o'erweigh a whole theatre of others. O, there be players that I have seen play, and heard others praise, and that highly, not to speak it profanely, that, neither having th' accent of Christians nor the gait of Christian, pagan, nor man, have so strutted and bellowed that I have thought some of Nature's journeymen had made men and not made them well, they imitated humanity so abominably.

FIRST PLAY. I hope we have reformed that indifferently with us.

HAM. O, reform it altogether; and let those that play your clowns speak no more than is set down for them; for there be of them that will themselves laugh to set on some quantity of barren spectators to laugh too, though in the mean time some necessary question of the play be then to be considered. That 's villainous, and shows a most pitiful ambition in the fool that uses it. Go, make you ready.

[*Exeunt* PLAYERS.]

[*Enter* POLONIUS, ROSENCRANTZ, *and* GUILDENSTERN.]

How now, my lord! Will the King hear this piece of work?

POLONIUS. And the Queen too, and that presently.

HAM. Bid the players make haste.

[*Exit* POLONIUS.]

Will you two help to hasten them?

ROSENCRANTZ. ⎫
GUILDENSTERN. ⎬ Ay, my lord.

[*Exeunt* ROSENCRANTZ *and* GUILDENSTERN.]

HAM. What ho! Horatio!

[*Enter* HORATIO.]

HORATIO. Here, sweet lord, at your service.

HAM. Horatio, thou art e'en as just a man
As e'er my conversation cop'd withal.[4]

HOR. O, my dear lord,—

HAM.   Nay, do not think I flatter,
For what advancement may I hope from thee
That no revenue hast but thy good spirits
To feed and clothe thee? Why should the poor be flatter'd?
No, let the candied tongue lick absurd pomp,
And crook the pregnant hinges of the knee

---

[1] Patrons who stood in the pit of the theater and usually constituted the least cultured part of the audience.
[2] Termagant and Herod were familiar characters of medieval religious drama who were noted for noisy rant.
[3] *I.e.*, the judgment of one judicious person.
[4] As my acquaintance has encountered.

Where thrift may follow fawning. Dost
  thou hear?
Since my dear soul was mistress of my
  choice
And could of men distinguish her elec-
  tion,
S' hath seal'd thee for herself, for thou hast
  been
As one, in suffering all, that suffers nothing,
A man that Fortune's buffets and rewards
Hast ta'en with equal thanks; and blest are
  those
Whose blood and judgement are so well
  commedled,[5]
That they are not a pipe for Fortune's
  finger
To sound what stop she please. Give me
  that man
That is not passion's slave, and I will wear
  him
In my heart's core, ay, in my heart of heart,
As I do thee.—Something too much of
  this.—
There is a play to-night before the King;
One scene of it comes near the circum-
  stance
Which I have told thee of my father's
  death.
I prithee, when thou seest that act a-foot,
Even with the very comment of thy soul
Observe my uncle: if his occulted [6] guilt
Do not itself unkennel in one speech,
It is a damned ghost that we have seen,
And my imaginations are as foul
As Vulcan's stithy.[7] Give him heedful note;
For I mine eyes will rivet to his face,
And after we will both our judgements join
In censure of his seeming.
   HOR.   Well, my lord.
If 'a steal aught the whilst this play is play-
  ing,
And scape detecting, I will pay the theft.
[*Danish march. A flourish. Enter* KING,
  QUEEN, POLONIUS, OPHELIA, ROSEN-
  CRANTZ, GUILDENSTERN, *and other
  Lords attendant, with his guard carry-
  ing torches.*]

[5] Whose emotional impulses and rational judgment are so well blended.
[6] Concealed.

HAM. They are coming to the play. I
  must be idle;
Get you a place.
  KING. How fares our cousin Hamlet?
  HAM. Excellent, i' faith, of the chame-
leon's dish: [8] I eat the air, promise-
crammed— You cannot feed capons so.
  KING. I have nothing with this answer,
Hamlet; these words are not mine.
  HAM. No, nor mine now. [*To* POLO-
NIUS.] My lord, you played once i' th' uni-
versity, you say?
  POLONIUS. That did I, my lord, and
was accounted a good actor.
  HAM. What did you enact?
  POL. I did enact Julius Cæsar; I was
killed i' th' Capitol; Brutus killed me.
  HAM. It was a brute part of him to kill
so capital a calf there. Be the players
ready?
  ROSENCRANTZ. Ay, my lord, they stay
upon your patience.[9]
  QUEEN. Come hither, my dear Hamlet,
sit by me.
  HAM. No, good mother, here 's metal
more attractive.
      [*Lying down at* OPHELIA'S *feet.*]
  POL. [*To the* KING.] O, ho! do you mark
that?
  HAM. Lady, shall I lie in your lap?
  OPHELIA. No, my lord.
  HAM. I mean, my head upon your lap?
  OPH. Ay, my lord.
  HAM. Do you think I meant country
matters?
  OPH. I think nothing, my lord.
  HAM. That 's a fair thought to lie be-
tween maid's legs.
  OPH. What is, my lord?
  HAM. Nothing.
  OPH. You are merry, my lord.
  HAM. Who, I?
  OPH. Ay, my lord.
  HAM. O God, your only jig-maker.
What should a man do but be merry? for,
look you, how cheerfully my mother looks,
and my father died within 's two hours.

[7] The forge of Vulcan, who was the smith of
the gods.
[8] Chameleons were supposed to feed on air.
[9] Await your pleasure.

OPH.   Nay 't is twice two months, my lord.

HAM.   So long? Nay then, let the devil wear black, for I 'll have a suit of sables.[10] O heavens! die two months ago, and not forgotten yet? Then there 's hope a great man's memory may outlive his life half a year; but, by 'r Lady, 'a must build churches then, or else shall 'a suffer not thinking on, with the hobby-horse,[11] whose epitaph is, "For, O, for, O, the hobby-horse is forgot."

[*The trumpets sounds. The dumb-show enters.*

Enter a King and Queen, the Queen embracing him and he her. She kneels and makes show of protestation unto him; he takes her up and declines his head upon her neck. He lays him down upon a bank of flowers. She, seeing him asleep, leaves him. Anon comes in another man, takes off his crown, kisses it, pours poison in the sleeper's ears, and leaves him. The Queen returns, finds the King dead, makes passionate action. The poisoner, with some three or four, come in again, seem to condole with her. The dead body is carried away. The poisoner woos the Queen with gifts; she seems harsh a while, but in the end accepts his love. Exeunt.]

OPH.   What means this, my lord?

HAM.   Marry, this is miching mallecho;[12] it means mischief.

OPH.   Belike this show imports the argument of the play?

[*Enter* PROLOGUE.]

HAM.   We shall know by this fellow. The players cannot keep counsel, they 'll tell all.

OPH.   Will 'a tell us what this show meant?

HAM.   Ay, or any show that you will show him: be not you ashamed to show,

he 'll not shame to tell you what it means.

OPH.   You are naught, you are naught;[13] I 'll mark the play.

PROLOGUE.

> For us, and for our tragedy,
> Here stooping to your clemency,
> We beg your hearing patiently.

[*Exit.*]

HAM.   Is this a prologue, or the posy of a ring? [14]

OPH.   'T is brief, my lord.

HAM.   As woman's love.

[*Enter two* PLAYERS, KING *and* QUEEN.]

PLAYER KING.   Full thirty times hath Phœbus' cart gone round
Neptune's salt wash and Tellus' orbed ground,
And thirty dozen moons with borrowed sheen
About the world have times twelve thirties been,
Since love our hearts and Hymen did our hands
Unite commutual in most sacred bands.

PLAYER QUEEN.   So many journeys may the sun and moon
Make us again count o'er ere love be done!
But, woe is me, you are so sick of late,
So far from cheer and from your former state,
That I distrust you.[15] Yet, though I distrust,
Discomfort you, my lord, it nothing must;
For women fear too much, even as they love,
And women's fear and love hold quantity,
In neither aught, or in extremity,[16]
Now, what my love is, proof hath made you know;
And as my love is siz'd, my fear is so:
Where love is great, the littlest doubts are fear;
Where little fears grow great, great love grows there.

---

[10] *I.e.,* exchange mourning for gala attire.
[11] A traditional figure in May games and the Morris Dance, at the time frowned on by the righteous.
[12] Sneaking knavery.

[13] Wicked.
[14] A short motto inscribed on a ring.
[15] Am concerned about you.
[16] Women's fear and love are alike in that they either have no existence or run to extremes.

P. KING. Faith, I must leave thee, love, and shortly too.
My operant powers their functions leave to do;
And thou shalt live in this fair world behind,
Honour'd, belov'd; and haply one as kind
For husband shalt thou—

P. QUEEN.   O, confound the rest!
Such love must needs be treason in my breast:
In second husband let me be accurst,
None wed the second but who kill'd the first.

HAM. [*Aside.*] That 's wormwood!

P. QUEEN. The instances that second marriage move
Are base respects of thrift, but none of love:
A second time I kill my husband dead,
When second husband kisses me in bed.

P. KING. I do believe you think what now you speak,
But what we do determine oft we break.
Purpose is but the slave to memory,
Of violent birth, but poor validity;
Which now, the fruit unripe, sticks on the tree,
But fall unshaken when they mellow be.
Most necessary 't is that we forget
To pay ourselves what to ourselves is debt:
What to ourselves in passion we propose,
The passion ending, doth the purpose lose.
The violence of either grief or joy
Their own enactures [17] with themselves destroy:
Where joy most revels, grief doth most lament;
Grief joys, joy grieves, on slender accident.
This world is not for aye, nor 't is not strange
That even our loves should with our fortunes change,
For 't is a question left us yet to prove,
Whether love lead fortune, or else fortune love.
The great man down, you mark his favourite flies;

The poor advanc'd makes friends of enemies:
And hitherto doth love on fortune tend,
For who not needs shall never lack a friend;
And who in want a hollow friend doth try,
Directly seasons him his enemy.
But, orderly to end where I begun,
Our wills and fates do so contrary run
That our devices still are overthrown;
Our thoughts are ours, their ends none of our own:
So think thou wilt no second husband wed;
But die thy thoughts when thy first lord is dead.

P. QUEEN. Nor earth to me give food, nor heaven light!
Sport and repose lock from me day and night!
To desperation turn my trust and hope,
An anchor's cheer [18] in prison be my scope!
Each opposite that blanks the face of joy
Meet what I would have well and it destroy!
Both here and hence pursue me lasting strife,
If, once a widow, ever I be wife!

HAM. If she should break it now!

P. KING. 'T is deeply sworn. Sweet, leave me here a while.
My spirits grow dull, and fain I would beguile
The tedious day with sleep.   [*Sleeps.*]

P. QUEEN.   Sleep rock thy brain,
And never come mischance between us twain!
                    [*Exit* PLAYER QUEEN.]

HAM. Madam, how like you this play?

QUEEN. The lady doth protest too much, methinks.

HAM. O, but she 'll keep her word.

KING. Have you heard the argument? Is there no offence in 't?

HAM. No, no, they do but jest, poison in jest; no offence i' th' world.

KING. What do you call the play?

HAM. The Mouse-trap. Marry, how? Tropically.[19] This play is the image of a murder done in Vienna; Gonzago is the

[17] Proposed actions.

[18] A hermit's fare.   [19] Metaphorically.

duke's name; his wife, Baptista. You shall see anon, 't is a knavish piece of work, but what of that? Your Majesty and we that have free souls, it touches us not: let the galled jade wince, our withers are unwrung.[20]

[*Enter* LUCIANUS.]

This is one Lucianus, nephew to the king.

OPH. You are as good as a chorus, my lord.

HAM. I could interpret [21] between you and your love, if I could see the puppets dallying.

OPH. You are keen, my lord, you are keen.

HAM. It would cost you a groaning to take off mine edge.

OPH. Still better, and worse.

HAM. So you mistake your husbands. Begin, murderer; leave thy damnable faces and begin. Come, "the croaking raven doth bellow for revenge."

LUCIANUS. Thoughts black, hands apt, drugs fit, and time agreeing;
Confederate season, else no creature seeing.
Thou mixture rank, of midnight weeds collected
With Hecate's [22] ban thrice blasted, thrice infected,
Thy natural magic and dire property
On wholesome life usurps immediately.

[*Pours the poison into the sleeper's ears.*]

HAM. He poisons him i' th' garden for his estate, his name 's Gonzago; the story is extant, and writ in very choice Italian; you shall see anon how the murderer gets the love of Gonzago's wife.

OPH. The King rises.

HAM. What, frighted with false fire?

QUEEN. How fares my lord?

POL. Give o'er the play.

KING. Give me some light. Away!

POL. Lights, lights, lights!

[*Exeunt all but* HAMLET *and* HORATIO.]

HAM. Why, let the strucken deer go weep,
The hart ungalled play;
For some must watch, while some must sleep,—
Thus runs the world away.

Would not this, sir, and a forest of feathers —if the rest of my fortunes turn Turk [23] with me—with two Provincial roses on my razed shoes,[24] get me a fellowship in a cry of players, sir?

HOR. Half a share.

HAM. A whole one, I.
For thou dost know, O Damon dear,
This realm dismantled was
Of Jove himself; and now reigns here
A very, very—pacock.[25]

HOR. You might have rhymed.

HAM. O good Horatio, I 'll take the ghost's word for a thousand pound. Didst perceive?

HOR. Very well, my lord.

HAM. Upon the talk of the poisoning?

HOR. I did very well note him.

HAM. Ah, ha! Come, some music! Come, the recorders! [26]
For if the king like not the comedy,
Why then, belike, he likes it not, perdy.
Come, some music!

[*Re-enter* ROSENCRANTZ *and* GUILDENSTERN.]

GUILDENSTERN. Good my lord, vouchsafe me a word with you.

HAM. Sir, a whole history.

GUIL. The King, sir,—

HAM. Ay, sir, what of him?

GUIL. Is in his retirement marvellous distempered.

HAM. With drink, sir?

GUIL. No, my lord, with choler.

HAM. Your wisdom should show itself more richer to signify this to the doctor; for, for me to put him to his purgation would perhaps plunge him into more choler.

[20] Let the nag wince whose withers are rubbed sore; it's no skin off us.
[21] Like a showman explaining the actions of puppets. [22] Hecate was goddess of witchcraft.
[23] Treat me barbarously.
[24] Shoes ornamented with perforations, which,

like the preceding feathers and rosettes, characterized actors' costumes.
[25] In place of *ass*, which completes the rhyme, Hamlet substitutes *peacock*, a symbol of vanity and lust.
[26] Musical pipes similar to the flageolet.

GUIL. Good my lord, put your discourse into some frame, and start not so wildly from my affair.

HAM. I am tame, sir; pronounce.

GUIL. The Queen, your mother, in most great affliction of spirit, hath sent me to you.

HAM. You are welcome.

GUIL. Nay, good my lord, this courtesy is not of the right breed. If it shall please you to make me a wholesome answer I will do your mother's commandment; if not, your pardon and my return shall be the end of my business.

HAM. Sir, I cannot.

ROSENCRANTZ. What, my lord?

HAM. Make you a wholesome answer: my wit 's diseased. But, sir, such answer as I can make, you shall command, or, rather, as you say, my mother. Therefore no more, but to the matter. My mother, you say,—

ROS. Then thus she says: your behaviour hath struck her into amazement and admiration.[27]

HAM. O wonderful son, that can so stonish a mother! But is there no sequel at the heels of this mother's admiration? Impart.

ROS. She desires to speak with you in her closet ere you go to bed.

HAM. We shall obey, were she ten times our mother. Have you any further trade with us?

ROS. My lord, you once did love me.

HAM. And do still, by these pickers and stealers.[28]

ROS. Good my lord, what is your cause of distemper? You do surely bar the door upon your own liberty if you deny your griefs to your friend.

HAM. Sir, I lack advancement.

ROS. How can that be, when you have the voice of the King himself for your succession in Denmark?

HAM. Ay, but "While the grass grows," —the proverb [29] is something musty.

[*Re-enter the* PLAYERS *with recorders.*]

O, the recorders! Let me see one.—To withdraw with you: [30]—why do you go about to recover the wind [31] of me, as if you would drive me into a toil? [32]

GUIL. O, my lord, if my duty be too bold, my love is too unmannerly.

HAM. I do not well understand that. Will you play upon this pipe?

GUIL. My lord, I cannot.

HAM. I pray you.

GUIL. Believe me, I cannot.

HAM. I do beseech you.

GUIL. I know no touch of it, my lord.

HAM. 'T is as easy as lying: govern these ventages with your finger and thumb, give it breath with your mouth, and it will discourse most eloquent music. Look you, these are the stops.

GUIL. But these cannot I command to any utt'rance of harmony; I have not the skill.

HAM. Why, look you now, how unworthy a thing you make of me! You would play upon me, you would seem to know my stops, you would pluck out the heart of my mystery, you would sound me from my lowest note to the top of my compass; and there is much music, excellent voice, in this little organ, yet cannot you make it speak. 'Sblood, do you think that I am easier to be played on than a pipe? Call me what instrument you will, though you can fret me,[33] yet you cannot play upon me.

[*Enter* POLONIUS.]

God bless you, sir.

POLONIUS. My lord, the Queen would speak with you, and presently.[34]

HAM. Do you see yonder cloud that 's almost in shape of a camel?

POL. By th' mass and 't is like a camel indeed.

HAM. Methinks it is like a weasel.

POL. It is backed like a weasel.

HAM. Or like a whale?

POL. Very like a whale.

---

[27] Astonishment. [28] Hands.
[29] "While the grass grows, the horse starves."
[30] In confidence.
[31] Get to the windward (as in hunting).
[32] Snare.
[33] The pun plays on the two meanings of *annoy* and *finger the frets* of a musical instrument.
[34] Immediately.

HAM. Then I will come to my mother by and by. [*Aside.*] They fool me to the top of my bent.[35]—I will come by and by.

POL. I will say so. [*Exit* POLONIUS.]

HAM. "By and by" is easily said. Leave me, friends. [*Exeunt all but* HAMLET.] 'T is now the very witching time of night When churchyards yawn and hell itself breathes out Contagion to this world: now could I drink hot blood, And do such bitter business as the day Would quake to look on. Soft! now to my mother. O heart, lose not thy nature, let not ever The soul of Nero [36] enter this firm bosom; Let me be cruel, not unnatural. I will speak daggers to her, but use none. My tongue and soul in this be hypocrites; How in my words somever she be shent,[37] To give them seals [38] never, my soul, consent! [*Exit.*]

Scene III

A room in the castle.

[*Enter* KING, ROSENCRANTZ, *and* GUILDENSTERN.]

KING. I like him not, nor stands it safe with us To let his madness range. Therefore prepare you: I your commission will forthwith dispatch, And he to England shall along with you. The terms of our estate may not endure Hazard so near's as doth hourly grow Out of his braves.[1]

GUILDENSTERN. We will ourselves provide.

Most holy and religious fear it is To keep those many many bodies safe That live and feed upon your Majesty.

ROSENCRANTZ. The single and peculiar life is bound With all the strength and armour of the mind To keep itself from noyance, but much more That spirit upon whose weal depends and rests The lives of many. The cease of majesty Dies not alone, but, like a gulf,[2] doth draw What 's near it with it: or it is a massy wheel, Fix'd on the summit of the highest mount, To whose huge spokes ten thousand lesser things Are mortis'd and adjoin'd; which, when it falls, Each small annexment, petty consequence, Attends the boisterous ruin. Never alone Did the King sigh, but with a general groan.

KING. Arm you,[3] I pray you, to this speedy voyage, For we will fetters put about this fear, Which now goes too free-footed.

ROS. We will haste us.

[*Exeunt* ROSENCRANTZ *and* GUILDENSTERN.]

[*Enter* POLONIUS.]

POLONIUS. My lord, he 's going to his mother's closet: Behind the arras I 'll convey myself, To hear the process.—I 'll warrant she 'll tax him home; [4] And, as you said, and wisely was it said, 'T is meet that some more audience than a mother, Since nature makes them partial, should o'erhear The speech of vantage.[5] Fare you well, my liege. I 'll call upon you ere you go to bed, And tell you what I know.

KING. Thanks, dear my lord.

[*Exit* POLONIUS.]

O, my offence is rank, it smells to heaven; It hath the primal eldest curse [6] upon 't, A brother's murder. Pray can I not, Though inclination be as sharp as will. My stronger guilt defeats my strong intent, And, like a man to double business bound,

---

[35] They take me for a lunatic, to suit the peak of my inclination.
[36] Who murdered his mother.
[37] Berated. [38] To confirm words with deeds.

[1] Insolences. [2] Whirlpool.
[3] Prepare yourselves. [4] Scold him soundly.
[5] From an advantageous position.
[6] The curse of Cain.

I stand in pause where I shall first begin,
And both neglect. What if this cursed hand
Were thicker than itself with brother's
    blood,
Is there not rain enough in the sweet heav-
    ens
To wash it white as snow? Whereto serves
    mercy
But to confront the visage of offence?
And what 's in prayer but this twofold
    force,
To be forestalled ere we come to fall,
Or pardon'd being down? Then I 'll look
    up;
My fault is past. But, O, what form of
    prayer
Can serve my turn? "Forgive me my foul
    murder"?
That cannot be; since I am still possess'd
Of those effects for which I did the mur-
    der,
My crown, mine own ambition, and my
    queen.
May one be pardon'd and retain th' of-
    fence?
In the corrupted currents of this world
Offence's gilded hand may shove by jus-
    tice,
And oft 't is seen the wicked prize itself
Buys out the law: but 't is not so above;
There is no shuffling, there the action lies
In his true nature; and we ourselves com-
    pell'd,
Even to the teeth and forehead of our
    faults,
To give in evidence. What then? What
    rests? [7]
Try what repentance can.—What can it
    not?
Yet what can it when one cannot repent?
O wretched state! O bosom black as death!
O limed [8] soul, that, struggling to be free,
Art more engag'd! Help, angels! Make
    assay!
Bow, stubborn knees, and, heart with
    strings of steel,
Be soft as sinews of the new-born babe!
All may be well.   [*He kneels.*]

[*Enter* HAMLET.]

HAMLET.   Now might I do it pat, now 'a
    is a-praying,
And now I 'll do 't.—And so 'a goes to
    heaven;
And so am I reveng'd. That would be
    scann'd: [9]
A villain kills my father, and for that,
I, his sole son, do this same villain send
To heaven.
Oh, this is base and silly,[10] not revenge.
'A took my father grossly, full of bread,
With all his crimes broad blown, as flush
    as May;
And how his audit stands who knows save
    Heaven?
But in our circumstance and course of
    thought
'T is heavy with him: and am I then re-
    veng'd,
To take him in the purging of his soul,
When he is fit and season'd for his passage?
No!
Up, sword, and know thou a more horrid
    hent,[11]
When he is drunk asleep, or in his rage,
Or in th' incestuous pleasure of his bed,
At game a-swearing, or about some act
That has no relish of salvation in 't,
Then trip him, that his heels may kick at
    heaven,
And that his soul may be as damn'd and
    black
As hell, whereto it goes. My mother stays.
This physic but prolongs thy sickly days.
                    [*Exit* HAMLET.]
    KING.   [*Rising.*] My words fly up, my
    thoughts remain below:
Words without thoughts never to heaven
    go.   [*Exit.*]

Scene IV
The Queen's closet.

[*Enter* QUEEN *and* POLONIUS.]

POLONIUS.   'A will come straight, look
    you lay home to him:

---

[7] Remains.   [8] Stuck fast, as in bird-lime.
[9] Calls for examination.

[10] Simple-minded, naïve.
[11] Await a more horrible occasion.

Tell him his pranks have been too broad to bear with,

And that your Grace hath screen'd and stood between

Much heat and him. I 'll silence me e'en here.

Pray you, be round with him.

HAMLET. [*Within.*] Mother, mother, mother!

QUEEN. I 'll warrant you, fear me not. Withdraw, I hear him coming.

[POLONIUS *hides behind the arras.*]

[*Enter* HAMLET.]

HAM. Now, mother, what 's the matter?

QUEEN. Hamlet, thou hast thy father much offended.

HAM. Mother, you have my father much offended.

QUEEN. Come, come, you answer with an idle tongue.

HAM. Go, go, you question with a wicked tongue.

QUEEN. Why, how now, Hamlet!

HAM. What 's the matter now?

QUEEN. Have you forgot me?

HAM. No, by the rood,[1] not so. You are the Queen, your husband's brother's wife;

And would it were not so, you are my mother.

QUEEN. Nay, then, I 'll set those to you that can speak.

HAM. Come, come, and sit you down; you shall not budge;

You go not till I set you up a glass

Where you may see the inmost part of you.

QUEEN. What wilt thou do? Thou wilt not murder me?

Help, ho!

POL. [*Behind.*] What, ho! help!

HAM. [*Drawing.*] How now! A rat? Dead, for a ducat, dead!

[*Kills* POLONIUS *through the arras.*]

POL. [*Behind.*] O, I am slain!

QUEEN. O me, what hast thou done?

HAM. Nay, I know not. Is it the King?

QUEEN. O, what a rash and bloody deed is this!

HAM. A bloody deed—almost as bad, good mother,

As kill a king, and marry with his brother.

QUEEN. As kill a king!

HAM. Ay, lady, it was my word.

[*Lifts up the arras and discovers* POLONIUS.]

Thou wretched, rash, intruding fool, farewell!

I took thee for thy better; take thy fortune;

Thou find'st to be too busy is some danger.

—Leave wringing of your hands; peace, sit you down,

And let me wring your heart; for so I shall,

If it be made of penetrable stuff,

If damned custom have not braz'd it so

That it be proof and bulwark against sense.[2]

QUEEN. What have I done, that thou dar'st wag thy tongue

In noise so rude against me?

HAM. Such an act

That blurs the grace and blush of modesty,

Calls virtue hypocrite, takes off the rose

From the fair forehead of an innocent love

And sets a blister [3] there, makes marriage-vows

As false as dicers' oaths; O, such a deed

As from the body of contraction [4] plucks

The very soul, and sweet religion makes

A rhapsody of words. Heaven's face doth glow,

And this solidity and compound mass,[5]

With heated visage, as against the doom,[6]

Is thought-sick at the act.

QUEEN. Ay me, what act,

That roars so loud and thunders in the index? [7]

HAM. Look here, upon this picture, and on this,

---

[1] Cross.   [2] Sensitivity.
[3] Alluding to the practice of branding prostitutes on the forehead.
[4] The marriage-vow; *religion,* in the next line refers to the sacrament of marriage.

[5] The earth.

[6] As at the approach of the Last Judgment.

[7] Prologue; literally, the table of contents at the beginning of a book.

The counterfeit presentment of two
    brothers.
See, what a grace was seated on this brow:
Hyperion's curls, the front of Jove himself,
An eye like Mars, to threaten and com-
    mand,
A station [8] like the herald Mercury
New-lighted on a heaven-kissing hill,
A combination and a form indeed,
Where every god did seem to set his seal,
To give the world assurance of a man:
This was your husband.—Look you now
    what follows:
Here is your husband, like a mildew'd ear,[9]
Blasting his wholesome brother. Have you
    eyes?
Could you on this fair mountain leave to
    feed,
And batten [10] on this moor? Ha! have you
    eyes?
You cannot call it love, for at your age
The hey-day in the blood is tame, it 's
    humble,
And waits upon the judgement; and what
    judgement
Would step from this to this? Sense sure
    you have,
Else could you not have motion; but sure,
    that sense
Is apoplex'd; for madness would not err,
Nor sense to ecstasy was ne'er so thrall'd
But it reserv'd some quantity of choice,
To serve in such a difference. What devil
    was 't
That thus hath cozen'd you at hoodman-
    blind? [11]
Eyes without feeling, feeling without sight,
Ears without hands or eyes, smelling sans
    all,
Or but a sickly part of one true sense
Could not so mope.
O shame! where is thy blush? Rebellious
    hell,
If thou canst mutine in a matron's bones,
To flaming youth let virtue be as wax,
And melt in her own fire. Proclaim no
    shame

When the compulsive ardour gives the
    charge,
Since frost itself as actively doth burn
And reason panders will.[12]
QUEEN.   O Hamlet, speak no more!
Thou turn'st mine eyes into my very soul,
And there I see such black and grained
    spots
As will leave there their tinct.
HAM.   Nay, but to live
In the rank sweat of an enseamed [13] bed,
Stew'd in corruption, honeying and making
    love
Over the nasty sty—
QUEEN.   O, speak to me no more!
These words like daggers enter in mine
    ears.
No more, sweet Hamlet!
HAM.   A murderer and a villain,
A slave that is not twentieth part the tithe
Of your precedent lord! A vice of kings,[14]
A cutpurse of the empire and the rule,
That from a shelf the precious diadem
    stole,
And put it in his pocket!
QUEEN.   No more!
[Enter GHOST in his night-gown.[15]]
HAM. A king of shreds and patches—
Save me, and hover o'er me with your
    wings,
You heavenly guards! What would your
    gracious figure?
QUEEN. Alas, he 's mad!
HAM. Do you not come your tardy son
    to chide,
That, laps'd in time and passion, lets go by
Th' important acting of your dread com-
    mand?
O, say!
GHOST. Do not forget! This visitation
Is but to whet thy almost blunted purpose.
But, look, amazement [16] on thy mother
    sits;
O, step between her and her fighting soul;
Conceit [17] in weakest bodies strongest
    works.
Speak to her, Hamlet.

---

[8] Posture.
[9] As in Pharaoh's dream (*Genesis*, xli, 5–7).
[10] Gorge.   [11] Deluded you at blind-man's buff.
[12] Plays pander to appetite.   [13] Greasy.

[14] A royal rogue. The Vice was a knavish character in the morality plays.
[15] Dressing-gown, as befits the privacy of his
own apartment. [16] Distraction. [17] Imagination.

HAM.   How is it with you, lady?
QUEEN.   Alas, how is 't with you,
That you do bend your eye on vacancy
And with th' incorporal air do hold discourse?
Forth at your eyes your spirits wildly peep,
And, as the sleeping soldiers in th' alarm,
Your bedded hair, like life in excrements,[18]
Start up and stand an end. O gentle son,
Upon the heat and flame of thy distemper
Sprinkle cool patience. Whereon do you look?
HAM.   On him, on him! Look you, how pale he glares!
His form and cause conjoin'd, preaching to stones,
Would make them capable.[19] Do not look upon me,
Lest with this piteous action you convert
My stern effects;[20] then what I have to do
Will want true colour, tears perchance for blood.
QUEEN.   To whom do you speak this?
HAM.   Do you see nothing there?
QUEEN.   Nothing at all, yet all that is I see.
HAM.   Nor did you nothing hear?
QUEEN.   No, nothing but ourselves.
HAM.   Why, look you there! Look, how it steals away!
My father, in his habit as he lived!
Look, where he goes, even now, out at the portal!   [Exit GHOST.]
QUEEN.   This is the very coinage of your brain:
This bodiless creation ecstasy
Is very cunning in.
HAM.   Ecstasy!
My pulse, as yours, doth temperately keep time,
And makes as healthful music: it is not madness
That I have utter'd: bring me to the test,
And I the matter will re-word, which madness
Would gambol from. Mother, for love of grace,

Lay not that flattering unction [21] to your soul,
That not your trespass, but my madness speaks;
It will but skin and film the ulcerous place,
Whiles rank corruption, mining all within,
Infects unseen. Confess yourself to Heaven;
Repent what 's past, avoid what is to come,
And do not spread the compost on the weeds,
To make them ranker. Forgive me this my virtue,
For in the fatness of these pursy times [22]
Virtue itself of vice must pardon beg,
Yea, curb [23] and woo for leave to do him good.
QUEEN.   O Hamlet, thou hast cleft my heart in twain.
HAM.   O, throw away the worser part of it,
And live the purer with the other half.
Good-night; but go not to my uncle's bed.
Assume a virtue, if you have it not.
That monster, custom, who all sense doth eat
Of habits evil,[24] is angel yet in this,
That to the use of actions fair and good
He likewise gives a frock or livery,
That aptly is put on. Refrain to-night,
And that shall lend a kind of easiness
To the next abstinence; the next more easy;
For use almost can change the stamp of nature,
And either curb the devil or throw him out,
With wondrous potency. Once more, good-night;
And when you are desirous to be blest,
I 'll blessing beg of you. For this same lord,
          [Pointing to POLONIUS.]
I do repent; but Heaven hath pleas'd it so,
To punish me with this and this with me,
That I must be their scourge and minister.
I will bestow him, and will answer well
The death I gave him. So, again, good-night.
I must be cruel, only to be kind.

---

[18] Such outgrowths of the body as nails and hair.   [19] I.e., of feeling and action.
[20] Alter the effects of my stern resolve.
[21] Soothing ointment.

[22] In the sluggishness of these bloated times.
[23] Bow.
[24] Who eats away all consciousness of evil habits.

Thus bad begins and worse remains behind.

One word more, good lady.

QUEEN. What shall I do?

HAM. Not this, by no means, that I bid you do:

Let the bloat king tempt you again to bed,

Pinch wanton on your cheek, call you his mouse,

And let him, for a pair of reechy [25] kisses,

Or paddling in your neck with his damn'd fingers,

Make you to ravel all this matter out,

That I essentially am not in madness,

But mad in craft. 'T were good you let him know;

For who, that 's but a queen, fair, sober, wise,

Would from a paddock,[26] from a bat, a gib,[27]

Such dear concernings hide? Who would do so?

No, in despite of sense and secrecy,

Unpeg the basket on the house's top,

Let the birds fly, and like the famous ape,

To try conclusions, in the basket creep,

And break your own neck down.

QUEEN. Be thou assur'd, if words be made of breath,

And breath of life, I have no life to breathe

What thou hast said to me.

HAM. I must to England; you know that?

QUEEN. Alack,

I had forgot. 'T is so concluded on.

HAM. There 's letters seal'd, and my two school-fellows,

Whom I will trust as I will adders fang'd,

They bear the mandate; they must sweep my way,

And marshal me to knavery. Let it work;

For 't is the sport to have the enginer

Hoist with his own petar; [28] and 't shall go hard

But I will delve one yard below their mines,

And blow them at the moon. O, 't is most sweet,

When in one line two crafts directly meet.

This man shall set me packing.

I 'll lug the guts into the neighbour room.

Mother, good-night indeed. This counsellor

Is now most still, most secret, and most grave,

Who was in life a foolish prating knave.

Come, sir, to draw toward an end with you.

Good-night, mother.

[*Exeunt severally,* HAMLET *tugging in* POLONIUS.]

ACT IV

Scene I

A room in the castle.

[*Enter* KING, QUEEN, ROSENCRANTZ, *and* GUILDENSTERN.]

KING. There 's matter in these sighs, these profound heaves;

You must translate, 't is fit we understand them.

Where is your son?

QUEEN. Bestow this place on us a little while.

[*Exeunt* ROSENCRANTZ *and* GUILDENSTERN.]

Ah, mine own lord, what have I seen to-night!

KING. What, Gertrude? How does Hamlet?

QUEEN. Mad as the sea and wind, when both contend

Which is the mightier—in his lawless fit,

Behind the arras hearing something stir,

Whips out his rapier, cries, "A rat, a rat!"

And in this brainish apprehension [1] kills

The unseen good old man.

KING. O heavy deed!

It had been so with us, had we been there.

His liberty is full of threats to all,

To you yourself, to us, to every one.

Alas, how shall this bloody deed be answer'd?

It will be laid to us, whose providence

---

[25] Filthy. [26] Toad. [27] Tomcat.

[28] To have the inventor blown up by his own bomb. [1] Mental delusion.

Should have kept short, restrain'd, and out
of haunt,[2]
This mad young man; but so much was our
love,
We would not understand what was most
fit,
But, like the owner of a foul disease,
To keep it from divulging, let it feed
Even on the pith of life. Where is he
gone?

QUEEN.   To draw apart the body he
hath kill'd,
O'er whom his very madness, like some ore
Among a mineral of metals base,
Shows itself pure; 'a weeps for what is
done.

KING.   O Gertrude, come away!
The sun no sooner shall the mountains
touch,
But we will ship him hence, and this vile
deed
We must, with all our majesty and skill,
Both countenance and excuse. Ho, Guil-
denstern!

[Re-enter ROSENCRANTZ and
GUILDENSTERN.]

Friends both, go join you with some
further aid;
Hamlet in madness hath Polonius slain,
And from his mother's closet hath he
dragg'd him.
Go seek him out, speak fair, and bring the
body
Into the chapel. I pray you, haste in this.
[Exeunt ROSENCRANTZ and GUILDENSTERN.]
Come, Gertrude, we 'll call up our wisest
friends
To let them know both what we mean
to do
And what 's untimely done, so, haply,
slander
Whose whisper o'er the world's diameter,
As level as the cannon to his blank,[3]
Transports his poison'd shot, may miss our
name,
And hit the woundless [4] air. O, come away!
My soul is full of discord and dismay.
[Exeunt.]

[2] Association with others.

Scene II
Another room in the castle.

[*Enter* HAMLET.]

HAMLET.   Safely stowed.
GENTLEMEN.   [*Within.*] Hamlet! Lord
Hamlet!
HAM.   But soft, what noise? Who calls
on Hamlet?
O, here they come.

[*Enter* ROSENCRANTZ *and* GUILDENSTERN]

ROSENCRANTZ.   What have you done,
my lord, with the dead body?
HAM.   Compounded it with dust, whereto 't is kin.
ROS.   Tell us where 't is, that we may
take it thence
And bear it to the chapel.
HAM.   Do not believe it.
ROS.   Believe what?
HAM.   That I can keep your counsel and
not mine own. Besides, to be demanded of
a sponge, what replication should be made
by the son of a king?
ROS.   Take you me for a sponge, my
lord?
HAM.   Ay, sir, that soaks up the King's
countenance, his rewards, his authorities.
But such officers do the King best service
in the end: he keeps them, like an ape an
apple, in the corner of his jaw; first
mouthed, to be last swallowed: when he
needs what you have gleaned, it is but
squeezing you, and, sponge, you shall be
dry again.
ROS.   I understand you not, my lord.
HAM.   I am glad of it: a knavish speech
sleeps in a foolish ear.
ROS.   My lord, you must tell us
where the body is, and go with us to the
King.
HAM.   The body is with the King, but
the King is not with the body. The King is
a thing—
GUILDENSTERN.   A thing, my lord!
HAM.   Of nothing; bring me to him.
Hide fox, and all after.   [*Exeunt.*]

[3] The white center of a target.   [4] Invulnerable.

Scene III

Another room in the castle.

[*Enter* KING *and two or three.*]

KING. I have sent to seek him, and to
find the body.
How dangerous is it that this man goes
loose!
Yet must not we put the strong law on him;
He 's lov'd of the distracted multitude,
Who like not in their judgement, but their
eyes,
And where 't is so, the offender's scourge [1]
is weigh'd,
But never the offence. To bear all smooth
and even,
This sudden sending him away must seem
Deliberate pause.[2] Diseases desperate
grown
By desperate appliance are reliev'd,
Or not at all.

[*Enter* ROSENCRANTZ *and others.*]

How now! What hath befall'n?
ROSENCRANTZ. Where the dead body is
bestow'd, my lord,
We cannot get from him.
KING.   But where is he?
ROS. Without, my lord, guarded, to
know your pleasure.
KING. Bring him before us.
ROS. Ho! bring in the lord.

[*Enter* HAMLET *guarded and*
GUILDENSTERN.]

KING. Now, Hamlet, where 's Polonius?
HAM. At supper.
KING. At supper! Where?
HAM. Not where he eats, but where 'a
is eaten: a certain convocation of politic
worms are e'en at him. Your worm is your
only emperor for diet: we fat all creatures
else to fat us, and we fat ourselves for maggots. Your fat king and your lean beggar
is but variable service, two dishes, but to
one table; that 's the end.
KING. Alas, alas!
HAM. A man may fish with the worm
that hath eat of a king, and eat of the fish
that hath fed of that worm.
KING. What dost thou mean by this?
HAM. Nothing but to show you how a
king may go a progress [3] through the guts
of a beggar.
KING. Where is Polonius?
HAM. In heaven; send thither to see: if
your messenger find him not there, seek
him i' th' other place yourself. But if indeed, you find him not within this month,
you shall nose him as you go up the stairs
into the lobby.
KING. Go seek him there.
                    [*To some* ATTENDANTS.]
HAM. 'A will stay till you come.
                    [*Exeunt* ATTENDANTS.]
KING. Hamlet, this deed, for thine espe-
cial safety,—
Which we do tender,[4] as we dearly grieve
For that which thou hast done,—must send
thee hence
With fiery quickness; therefore prepare thy-
self.
The bark is ready, and the wind at help,
Th' associates tend,[5] and everything is bent
For England.
HAM.   For England?
KING.   Ay, Hamlet.
HAM.   Good.
KING. So is it, if thou knew'st our pur-
poses.
HAM. I see a cherub that sees them.
But, come, for England! Farewell, dear
mother.
KING. Thy loving father, Hamlet.
HAM. My mother: father and mother is
man and wife, man and wife is one flesh,
and so, my mother. Come, for England!
                         [*Exit* HAMLET.]
KING. Follow him at foot,[6] tempt him
with speed aboard,
Delay it not; I 'll have him hence to-night.
Away! for everything is seal'd and done
That else leans on th' affair, pray you,
make haste.
                [*Exeunt* ROSENCRANTZ *and*
                         GUILDENSTERN.]

[1] Punishment.   [2] A planned delay.
[3] A royal journey of state.
[4] Cherish.   [5] Your companions wait.
[6] At his heels.

And, England, if my love thou hold'st at
 aught,—

As my great power thereof may give thee
 sense,

Since yet thy cicatrice [7] looks raw and red

After the Danish sword, and thy free awe

Pays homage to us—thou mayst not coldly
 set

Our sovereign process,[8] which imports at
 full,

By letters congruing to that effect,

The present [9] death of Hamlet. Do it, England;

For like the hectic [10] in my blood he rages,

And thou must cure me: till I know 't is
 done,

Howe'er my haps,[11] my joys were ne'er begun.   *[Exit.]*

Scene IV

A plain in Denmark.

[*Enter* FORTINBRAS, *and a* CAPTAIN, *with
his army over the stage.*]

FORTINBRAS. Go, captain, from me
 greet the Danish king.

Tell him that, by his license, Fortinbras

Craves the conveyance [1] of a promis'd
 march

Over his kingdom. You know the rendez-
 vous.

If that his Majesty would aught with us,

We shall express our duty in his eye;

And let him know so.

CAPTAIN.   I will do 't, my lord.

FOR. Go softly on.

    [*Exeunt* FORTINBRAS *and army.*]

[*Enter* HAMLET, ROSENCRANTZ, GUILDEN-
STERN, *and others.*]

HAMLET. Good sir, whose powers are
 these?

CAP. They are of Norway, sir.

HAM. How purpos'd, sir, I pray you?

CAP. Against some part of Poland.

HAM. Who commands them, sir?

CAP. The nephew to old Norway, Fortinbras.

HAM. Goes it against the main of Poland, sir,

Or for some frontier?

CAP. Truly to speak, and with no addition,

We go to gain a little patch of ground

That hath in it no profit but the name.

To pay five ducats, five, I would not farm it;

Nor will it yield to Norway or the Pole

A ranker rate, should it be sold in fee.[2]

HAM. Why, then the Polack never will
 defend it.

CAP. Yes, it is already garrison'd.

HAM. Two thousand souls and twenty
 thousand ducats

Will not debate the question of this straw.

This is th' imposthume of [3] much wealth
 and peace,

That inward breaks, and shows no cause
 without

Why the man dies. I humbly thank you, sir.

CAP. God buy you, sir.

       [Exit CAPTAIN.]

ROSENCRANTZ. Will 't please you go,
 my lord?

HAM. I 'll be with you straight; go a
 little before.

    [*Exeunt all except* HAMLET.]

How all occasions do inform against me,

And spur my dull revenge! What is a
 man,

If his chief good and market of his time

Be but to sleep and feed? A beast, no more.

Sure He that made us with such large discourse,[4]

Looking before and after, gave us not

That capability and god-like reason

To fust [5] in us unus'd. Now, whether it be

Bestial oblivion, or some craven scruple

Of thinking too precisely on th' event,—[6]

A thought which, quarter'd, hath but one
 part wisdom

And ever three parts coward—I do not
 know

Why yet I live to say, "This thing 's to do,"

---

[7] Scar. [8] Not lightly regard our instructions.
[9] Immediate.   [10] Fever.
[11] Whatever my fortunes.
[1] An escort to signify official permission.

[2] It would not bring a higher amount if sold
outright.
[3] Abscess caused by. [4] Capacity for thought.
[5] Mould.   [6] Outcome.

Sith I have cause and will and strength and
 means
To do 't: examples gross as earth exhort
 me;
Witness this army of such mass and charge
Led by a delicate and tender prince,
Whose spirit with divine ambition puff'd
Makes mouths at the invisible event,
Exposing what is mortal and unsure
To all that fortune, death, and danger dare,
Even for an egg-shell. Rightly to be great
Is not to stir without great argument,
But greatly to find quarrel in a straw
When honour 's at the stake.[7] How stand I
 then,
That have a father kill'd, a mother stain'd,
Excitements of my reason and my blood,
And let all sleep, while to my shame I see
The imminent death of twenty thousand
 men,
That for a fantasy and trick of fame
Go to their graves like beds, fight for a
 plot
Whereon the numbers cannot try the cause,
Which is not tomb enough and continent [8]
To hide the slain? O, from this time forth,
My thoughts be bloody, or be nothing
 worth!   [Exit.]

Scene V

Elsinore. A room in the castle.

[*Enter* QUEEN, HORATIO, *and a* GENTLEMAN.]

QUEEN. I will not speak with her.
GENTLEMAN. She is importunate, in-
 deed distract;
Her mood will needs be pitied.
QUEEN.   What would she have?
GENT. She speaks much of her father;
 says she hears
There 's tricks i' th' world, and hems, and
 beats her heart,
Spurns enviously [1] at straws, speaks things
 in doubt
That carry but half sense. Her speech is
 nothing,

Yet the unshaped use of it doth move
The hearers to collection. They yawn at it
And botch the words up fit to their own
 thoughts; [2]
Which, as her winks, and nods, and ges-
 tures yield them,
Indeed would make one think there would
 be thought,
Though nothing sure, yet much unhappily.
HORATIO. 'T were good she were spoken
 with, for she may strew
Dangerous conjectures in ill-breeding
 minds.
Let her come in.   [*Exit* GENTLEMAN.]
QUEEN. [*Aside.*] To my sick soul, as
 sin's true nature is,
Each toy seems prologue to some great
 amiss; [3]
So full of artless jealousy [4] is guilt,
It spills itself in fearing to be spilt.

[*Enter* OPHELIA, *distracted.*]

OPHELIA. Where is the beauteous maj-
 esty of Denmark?
QUEEN. How now, Ophelia!
OPH. [*Sings.*]

> How should I your true love know
> From another one?
> By his cockle hat and staff,
> And his sandal shoon.

QUEEN. Alas, sweet lady, what imports
 this song?
OPH. Say you? Nay, pray you, mark.
[*Sings.*]

> He is dead and gone, lady,
> He is dead and gone;
> At his head a grass-green turf
> At his heels a stone.

[*Enter* KING.]

QUEEN. Nay, but, Ophelia,—
OPH. Pray you, mark.
[*Sings.*]

> White his shroud as the mountain snow,—

QUEEN. Alas, look here, my lord.

---

[7] Rightly to be great is to make no move without a sufficiently great reason, but at the same
time to find in a trifle a reason great enough for
fighting when honor is at stake.
[8] Container.   [1] Kicks angrily.

[2] Her incoherence prompts hearers to piece together the fragments. They gape at her words and
patch them up to suit their own ideas.
[3] Each trifle seems the introduction to some
great misfortune.   [4] Inept suspicion.

OPH. [*Sings.*]

> Larded [5] all with sweet flowers;
> Which bewept to the ground did not go
> With true-love showers.

KING.   How do you, pretty lady?

OPH.   Well, God 'ild you! [6] They say the owl was a baker's daughter.[7] Lord, we know what we are, but know not what we may be. God be at your table!

KING.   Conceit upon her father.

OPH.   Pray let 's have no words of this, but when they ask you what it means, say you this:

[*Sings.*]

> To-morrow is Saint Valentine's day,
> All in the morning betime,
> And I a maid at your window,
> To be your Valentine.

> Then up he rose and donn'd his clothes,
> And dupp'd [8] the chamber door;
> Let in the maid, that out a maid
> Never departed more.

KING.   Pretty Ophelia!

OPH.   Indeed, without an oath I 'll make an end on 't.

> By gis, and by Saint Charity,
> Alack, and fie for shame!
> Young men will do 't, if they come to 't;
> By Cock, they are to blame.

> Quoth she, "Before you tumbled me,
> You promis'd me to wed."

He answers:

> "So would I ha' done, by yonder sun,
> An thou hadst not come to my bed."

KING.   How long hath she been thus?

OPH.   I hope all will be well. We must be patient; but I cannot choose but weep, to think they should lay him i' th' cold ground. My brother shall know of it; and so I thank you for your good counsel. Come, my coach! Good-night, ladies; good-night, sweet ladies; good-night, good-night.

[*Exit* OPHELIA.]

KING.   Follow her close; give her good watch, I pray you.

[*Exeunt* HORATIO *and* GENTLEMAN.]

O, this is the poison of deep grief; it springs
All from her father's death—and now behold!
O Gertrude, Gertrude,
When sorrows come, they come not single spies,
But in battalions. First, her father slain;
Next, your son gone; and he most violent author
Of his own just remove; the people muddied,
Thick and unwholesome in their thoughts and whispers,
For good Polonius' death; and we have done but greenly
In hugger-mugger to inter him; [9] poor Ophelia
Divided from herself and her fair judgement,
Without the which we are pictures, or mere beasts;
Last, and as much containing as all these,
Her brother is in secret come from France,
Feeds on his wonder, keeps himself in clouds,
And wants not buzzers to infect his ear
With pestilent speeches of his father's death,
Wherein necessity, of matter beggar'd,
Will nothing stick our persons to arraign
In ear and ear. O my dear Gertrude, this,
Like to a murd'ring-piece,[10] in many places
Gives me superfluous death.

[*A noise within.*]

QUEEN.   Alack, what noise is this?

KING.   Attend!   [*Enter a* MESSENGER.]
Where is my Switzers? [11] Let them guard the door.
What is the matter?

MESSENGER.   Save yourself, my lord!
The ocean, overpeering of his list,[12]

---

[5] Garnished.
[6] God reward you!
[7] According to legend, a baker's daughter was transformed into an owl for begrudging bread to Christ.
[8] Opened.
[9] Acted like a novice in hustling him into his grave.
[10] A cannon loaded with shot which spread upon discharge.
[11] Swiss bodyguard.
[12] Shore.

Eats not the flats with more impiteous haste
Than young Laertes, in a riotous head,[13]
O'erbears your officers: the rabble call him
   lord;
And, as the world were now but to begin,
Antiquity forgot, custom not known,
The ratifiers and props of every word,
They cry, "Choose we! Laertes shall be
   king!"
Caps, hands, and tongues applaud it to the
   clouds,
"Laertes shall be king, Laertes king!"
   QUEEN. How cheerfully on the false
   trail they cry!
O, this is counter,[14] you false Danish dogs!

[Noise within. Enter LAERTES *with
other* DANES]

   KING. The doors are broke.
   LAERTES. Where is this king? Sirs, stand
   you all without.
   DANES. No, let's come in.
   LAER. I pray you, give me leave.
   DANES. We will, we will.
      [They retire without the door.]
   LAER. I thank you; keep the door. O
   thou vile king,
Give me my father!
   QUEEN. Calmly, good Laertes.
   LAER. That drop of blood that's calm
   proclaims me bastard,
Cries cuckold to my father, brands the har-
   lot
Even here, between the chaste unsmirched
   brow
Of my true mother.
   KING. What is the cause, Laertes,
That thy rebellion looks so giant-like?
Let him go, Gertrude; do not fear our per-
   son:
There's such divinity doth hedge a king,
That treason can but peep to what it would,
Acts little of his will. Tell me, Laertes,
Why thou art thus incens'd. Let him go,
   Gertrude.
Speak, man.
   LAER. Where is my father?

[13] With an armed force of rioters.
[14] On the wrong scent.
[15] I disregard what happens in this world or the next.

   KING. Dead.
   QUEEN. But not by him.
   KING. Let him demand his fill.
   LAER. How came he dead? I'll not be
   juggled with.
To hell allegiance! Vows to the blackest
   devil!
Conscience and grace to the profoundest
   pit!
I dare damnation. To this point I stand,
That both the worlds I give to negligence,[15]
Let come what comes; only I'll be reveng'd
Most throughly for my father.
   KING. Who shall stay you?
   LAER. My will, not all the world's:
And for my means, I'll husband them so
   well,
They shall go far with little.
   KING. Good Laertes,
If you desire to know the certainty
Of your dear father, is't writ in your re-
   venge
That, swoopstake,[16] you will draw both
   friend and foe,
Winner and loser?
   LAER. None but his enemies.
   KING. Will you know them then?
   LAER. To his good friends thus wide
   I'll ope my arms,
And like the kind life-rend'ring pelican [17]
Repast them with my blood.
   KING. Why, now you speak
Like a good child and a true gentleman.
That I am guiltless of your father's death,
And am most sensibly in grief for it,
It shall as level to your judgement 'pear,
As day does to your eye.
   [A noise within: "Let her come in!"]
   LAER. How now; what noise is that?

[Re-enter OPHELIA.]

O heat, dry up my brains! Tears seven
   times salt
Burn out the sense and virtue of mine
   eye!
By heaven, thy madness shall be paid with
   weight

[16] Sweeping up all the stakes on the board.
[17] The mother pelican was supposed to feed her young with her own blood.

Till our scale turn the beam. O rose of
    May!
Dear maid, kind sister, sweet Ophelia!
O heavens! is 't possible, a young maid's
    wits
Should be as mortal as an old man's life?
Nature is fine in love,[18] and where 't is fine,
It sends some precious instance [19] of itself
After the thing it loves.
    OPHELIA. [*Sings.*]

    They bore him barefac'd on the bier;
        Hey non nonny, nonny, hey nonny;
    And in his grave rain'd many a tear,—

Fare you well, my dove!
    LAER. Hadst thou thy wits and didst
        persuade revenge,
It could not move thus.
    OPH. You must sing, "A-down a-down,
and you call him a-down-a." O how the
wheel becomes it! It is the false steward,
that stole his master's daughter.
    LAER. This nothing 's more than matter.
    OPH. There 's rosemary, that 's for re-
membrance; pray you, love, remember; and
there is pansies, that 's for thoughts.[20]
    LAER. A document in madness, thoughts
and remembrance fitted.
    OPH. There 's fennel for you, and col-
umbines; there 's rue for you, and here 's
some for me; we may call it herb of grace
o' Sundays; O, you must wear your rue
with a difference. There 's a daisy. I would
give you some violets, but they withered all
when my father died; they say 'a made a
good end,—
    [*Sings.*]

    For bonny sweet Robin is all my joy.

    LAER. Thought and affliction, passion,
        hell itself,
She turns to favour and to prettiness.
    OPH. [*Sings.*]

    And will 'a not come again?
    And will 'a not come again?

[18] In love nature becomes refined.
[19] Evidence, here referring to Ophelia's wits.
[20] The language of flowers gives a symbolic
meaning to Ophelia's distribution: to Laertes,
rosemary (remembrance) and pansies (thoughts);
to the King, fennel (flattery) and columbines

    No, no, he is dead;
    Go to thy death-bed;
    He never will come again.

    His beard was as white as snow,
    All flaxen was his poll.
        He is gone, he is gone,
        And we cast away moan.
    God ha' mercy on his soul!

And of all Christian souls, I pray God.
    God buy ye.   [*Exit* OPHELIA.]
    LAER. Do you see this, O God?
    KING. Laertes, I must commune with
        your grief,
Or you deny me right. Go but apart,
Make choice of whom your wisest friends
    you will,
And they shall hear and judge 'twixt you
    and me.
If by direct or by collateral hand
They find us touch'd, we will our kingdom
    give,
Our crown, our life, and all that we call
    ours,
To you in satisfaction; but if not,
Be you content to lend your patience to us,
And we shall jointly labour with your soul
To give it due content.
    LAER.   Let this be so.
His means of death, his obscure burial,
No trophy, sword, nor hatchment [21] o'er
    his bones,
No noble rite nor formal ostentation,
Cry to be heard, as 't were from heaven to
    earth,
That I must call 't in question.
    KING.   So you shall;
And where th' offence is let the great axe
    fall.
I pray you, go with me.   [*Exeunt.*]

Scene VI
Another room in the castle.

[*Enter* HORATIO *with an* ATTENDANT.]

    HORATIO. What are they that would
        speak with me?

(ingratitude); to the Queen and herself, rue,
which had a double significance (for Ophelia, sorrow; for the Queen, penitence). For the Queen
there is also a daisy (unfaithfulness), but the violets (fidelity) are all withered.
[21] Coat of arms.

ATTENDANT. Sea-faring men, sir; they say they have letters for you.

HOR. Let them come in.

[*Exit* ATTENDANT.]

I do not know from what part of the world I should be greeted, if not from Lord Hamlet.

[*Enter* SAILORS.]

FIRST SAILOR. God bless you, sir.

HOR. Let Him bless thee too.

FIRST SAIL. 'A shall, sir, an 't please Him.

There 's a letter for you, sir—it came from th' ambassador that was bound for England —if your name be Horatio, as I am let to know it is.

HOR. [*Reads.*]

"Horatio, when thou shalt have overlooked this, give these fellows some means to the King; they have letters for him. Ere we were two days old at sea, a pirate of very warlike appointment gave us chase. Finding ourselves too slow of sail, we put on a compelled valour and in the grapple I boarded them. On the instant they got clear of our ship, so I alone became their prisoner. They have dealt with me like thieves of mercy, but they knew what they did: I am to do a good turn for them. Let the King have the letters I have sent, and repair thou to me with as much haste as thou wouldest fly death. I have words to speak in thine ear will make thee dumb, yet are they much too light for the bore of the matter. These good fellows will bring thee where I am. Rosencrantz and Guildenstern hold their course for England; of them I have much to tell thee. Farewell.

He that thou knowest thine,

HAMLET."

Come, I will give you way for these your letters;

And do 't the speedier, that you may direct me

To him from whom you brought them.

[*Exeunt.*]

Scene VII
Another room in the castle.

[*Enter* KING *and* LAERTES.]

KING. Now must your conscience my acquaintance seal;

And you must put me in your heart for friend,

Sith you have heard, and with a knowing ear,

That he which hath your noble father slain Pursued my life.

LAERTES   It well appears: but tell me Why you proceeded not against these feats, So criminal and so capital in nature, As by your safety, wisdom, all things else, You mainly were stirr'd up.

KING.   O, for two special reasons, Which may to you, perhaps, seem much unsinew'd,[1]

And yet to me they are strong. The Queen his mother

Lives almost by his looks; and for myself—

My virtue or my plague, be it either which—

She is so conjunctive [2] to my life and soul,

That, as the star moves not but in his sphere,

I could not but by her. The other motive Why to a public count I might not go, Is the great love the general gender [3] bear him;

Who, dipping all his faults in their affection,

Would, like the spring that turneth wood to stone,

Convert his gyves to graces; so that my arrows,

Too slightly timber'd for so loud a wind, Would have reverted to my bow again, And not where I have aim'd them.

LAER. And so have I a noble father lost,

A sister driven into desp'rate terms,

Whose worth, if praises may go back again,

Stood challenger on mount of all the age

For her perfections.[4] But my revenge will come.

KING. Break not your sleeps for that; you must not think

That we are made of stuff so flat and dull

That we can let our beard be shook with danger

And think it pastime. You shortly shall hear more.

---

[1] Lacking in sinew, *i.e.,* weak.
[2] Closely joined.   [3] Common people.

[4] Challenged the whole age to surpass her perfections.

I lov'd your father, and we love ourself,
And that, I hope, will teach you to imagine—

[*Enter a* MESSENGER *with letters.*]

How now! What news?

MESSENGER. Letters, my lord,
from Hamlet.
These to your Majesty; this to the Queen.
KING. From Hamlet! Who brought
them?
MESS. Sailors, my lord, they say; I saw
them not.
They were given me by Claudio. He re-
ceived them
Of him that brought them.
KING. Laertes, you shall hear them.
Leave us. [*Exit* MESSENGER.]
[*Reads.*]
"High and mighty, You shall know I am set
naked on your kingdom. To-morrow shall I
beg leave to see your kingly eyes, when I shall,
first asking you pardon, thereunto recount the
occasion of my sudden and more strange re-
turn.
HAMLET."

What should this mean? Are all the rest
come back?
Or is it some abuse,[5] and no such thing?
LAER. Know you the hand?
KING. 'T is Hamlet's character.[6]
"Naked."
And in a postscript here, he says, "alone."
Can you devise me?
LAER. I'm lost in it, my lord; but let
him come:
It warms the very sickness in my heart
That I shall live and tell him to his teeth,
"Thus didest thou."
KING. If it be so, Laertes,—
And how should it be so? How other-
wise?—
Will you be rul'd by me?
LAER. Ay, my lord,
So you will not o'errule me to a peace.
KING. To thine own peace. If he be now
return'd,

As checking at [7] his voyage, and that he
means
No more to undertake it, I will work him
To an exploit, now ripe in my device,
Under the which he shall not choose but
fall;
And for his death no wind of blame shall
breathe,
But even his mother shall uncharge the
practice [8]
And call it accident.
LAER. My lord, I will be rul'd;
That rather, if you could devise it so
That I might be the organ.[9]
KING. It falls right.
You have been talk'd of since your travel
much,
And that in Hamlet's hearing, for a quality
Wherein, they say, you shine. Your sum of
parts [10]
Did not together pluck such envy from him
As did that one, and that, in my regard,
Of the unworthiest siege.[11]
LAER. What part is that, my lord?
KING. A very riband in the cap of
youth,
Yet needful too; for youth no less becomes
The light and careless livery that it wears
Than settled age his sables and his weeds,
Importing health and graveness. Two
months since,
Here was a gentleman of Normandy;—
I have seen myself, and serv'd against, the
French,
And they can well on horseback; but this
gallant
Had witchcraft in 't; he grew unto his seat.
And to such wondrous doing brought his
horse,
As had he been incorps'd and demi-
natur'd [12]
With the brave beast. So far he topp'd my
thought,
That I, in forgery of shapes and tricks,[13]
Come short of what he did.
LAER. A Norman, was 't?
KING. A Norman.

---

[5] Trick. [6] Handwriting.
[7] Turning aside from.
[8] Absolve the plot from treachery.

[9] Instrument. [10] Accomplishments.
[11] The least in rank. [12] Of one body.
[13] In imagining feats.

LAER. Upon my life, Lamound.

KING. The very same.

LAER. I know him well: he is the brooch indeed
And gem of all their nation.

KING. He made confession of you,
And gave you such a masterly report
For art and exercise in your defence,
And for your rapier most especial,
That he cried out, 't would be a sight indeed
If one could match you. The scrimmers [14] of their nation,
He swore, had neither motion, guard, nor eye,
If you oppos'd them. Sir, this report of his
Did Hamlet so envenom with his envy
That he could nothing do but wish and beg
Your sudden coming o'er to play with you.
Now, out of this—

LAER. What out of this, my lord?

KING. Laertes, was your father dear to you?
Or are you like the painting of a sorrow,
A face without a heart?

LAER. Why ask you this?

KING. Not that I think you did not love your father,
But that I know love is begun by time,
And that I see, in passages of proof,
Time qualifies the spark and fire of it.
There lives within the very flame of love
A kind of wick or snuff that will abate it,
And nothing is at a like goodness still; [15]
For goodness, growing to a plurisy,[16]
Dies in his own too much. That we would do,
We should do when we would; for this "would" changes,
And hath abatements and delays as many
As there are tongues, are hands, are accidents;
And then this "should" is like a spendthrift sigh,
That hurts by easing. But, to the quick of th' ulcer—

Hamlet comes back. What would you undertake,
To show yourself in deed your father's son
More than in words?

LAER. To cut his throat i' th' church.

KING. No place, indeed, should murder sanctuarize; [17]
Revenge should have no bounds. But, good Laertes,
Will you do this, keep close within your chamber.
Hamlet return'd shall know you are come home:
We 'll put on those shall praise your excellence
And set a double varnish on the fame
The Frenchman gave you, bring you in fine [18] together
And wager on your heads; he, being remiss,
Most generous [19] and free from all contriving,
Will not peruse the foils, so that with ease,
Or with a little shuffling, you may choose
A sword unbated [20] and in a pass of practice [21]
Requite him for your father.

LAER. I will do 't;
And, for that purpose, I 'll anoint my sword.
I bought an unction of a mountebank,
So mortal that, but dip a knife in it,
Where it draws blood no cataplasm [22] so rare,
Collected from all simples [23] that have virtue
Under the moon, can save the thing from death
That is but scratch'd withal. I 'll touch my point
With this contagion, that, if I gall him slightly,
It may be death.

KING. Let 's further think of this,
Weigh what convenience both of time and means

---

[14] Fencers.   [15] Always uniformly good.
[16] Excess.
[17] Afford sanctuary, or protection, from murder.
[18] Finally.

[19] Noble in spirit.
[20] Without the tip blunted.
[21] Treacherous thrust.
[22] Poultice.
[23] Medicinal herbs.

May fit us to our shape.[24] If this should fail,
And that our drift look through our bad performance,
'T were better not assay'd; therefore this project
Should have a back or second, that might hold
If this did blast in proof.[25] Soft! let me see:
We 'll make a solemn wager on your cunnings—
I ha 't!
When in your motion you are hot and dry—
As make your bouts more violent to that end—
And that he calls for drink, I 'll have preferr'd him
A chalice for the nonce,[26] whereon but sipping,
If he by chance escape your venom'd stuck,
Our purpose may hold there. But stay, what noise?

[*Enter* QUEEN.]

QUEEN. One woe doth tread upon another's heel,
So fast they follow: your sister 's drown'd, Laertes.

LAER. Drown'd! O, where?

QUEEN. There is a willow grows askant the brook,
That shows his hoar leaves in the glassy stream,
Therewith fantastic garlands did she make
Of crow-flowers, nettles, daisies, and long purples
That liberal [27] shepherds give a grosser name,
But our cold maids do dead men's fingers call them;
There, on the pendent boughs her cronet weeds [28]
Clamb'ring to hang, an envious sliver broke,
When down her weedy trophies and herself
Fell in the weeping brook. Her clothes spread wide,
And, mermaid-like, awhile they bore her up;
Which time she chanted snatches of old lauds,[29]
As one incapable [30] of her own distress,
Or like a creature native and indued [31]
Unto that element. But long it could not be
Till that her garments, heavy with their drink,
Pull'd the poor wretch from her melodious lay
To muddy death.

LAER. Alas, then, she is drown'd.

QUEEN. Drown'd, drown'd.

LAER. Too much of water hast thou, poor Ophelia,
And therefore I forbid my tears; but yet
It is our trick: [32] nature her custom holds,
Let shame say what it will; when these are gone,
The woman will be out.[33] Adieu, my lord;
I have a speech o' fire that fain would blaze,
But that this folly drowns it.

[*Exit* LAERTES.]

KING. Let 's follow, Gertrude.
How much I had to do to calm his rage!
Now fear I this will give it start again,
Therefore let 's follow. [*Exeunt.*]

ACT V

Scene I
A churchyard.

[*Enter two* CLOWNS [1] *with spades and pickaxes.*]

FIRST CLOWN. Is she to be buried in Christian burial when she wilfully seeks her own salvation?

SECOND CLOWN. I tell thee she is, therefore make her grave straight. The crowner [2]

---

[29] Hymns. [30] Without comprehension.
[31] Adapted. [32] Characteristic.
[33] My unmanliness will be gone.
[1] Loutish fellows, here a sexton and his helper. The rôles were designed for the clowns, or low comedians, of the acting company.
[2] Coroner.

[24] Plan. [25] Blow up in the trial.
[26] Occasion.
[27] Outspoken. [28] Chaplet of wild flowers.

hath sat on her, and finds it Christian burial.

FIRST CLO.   How can that be, unless she drowned herself in her own defence?

SECOND CLO.   Why, 't is found so.

FIRST CLO.   It must be *"se offendendo,"* [3] it cannot be else. For here lies the point: if I drown myself wittingly, it argues an act, and an act hath three branches; it is, to act, to do, and to perform; argal,[4] she drowned herself wittingly.

SECOND CLO.   Nay, but hear you, goodman delver,—

FIRST CLO.   Give me leave. Here lies the water; good. Here stands the man; good. If the man go to this water and drown himself, it is, will he, nill he, he goes,—mark you that? But if the water come to him and drown him, he drowns not himself; argal, he that is not guilty of his own death shortens not his own life.

SECOND CLO.   But is this law?

FIRST CLO.   Ay, marry, is 't; crowner's quest [5] law.

SECOND CLO.   Will you ha' the truth on 't? If this had not been a gentlewoman, she should have been buried out o' Christian burial.

FIRST CLO.   Why, there thou say'st; and the more pity that great folk should have countenance in this world to drown or hang themselves, more than their even Christian. Come, my spade! There is no ancient gentlemen but gardeners, ditchers, and grave-makers; they hold up Adam's profession.

SECOND CLO.   Was he a gentleman?

FIRST CLO.   'A was the first that ever bore arms.

SECOND CLO.   Why, he had none.

FIRST CLO.   What, art a heathen? How dost thou understand the Scripture? The Scripture says Adam digged; could he dig without arms? I 'll put another question to thee. If thou answerest me not to the purpose, confess thyself—

SECOND CLO.   Go to.

FIRST CLO.   What is he that builds stronger than either the mason, the shipwright, or the carpenter?

SECOND CLO.   The gallows-maker; for that frame outlives a thousand tenants.

FIRST CLO.   I like thy wit well, in good faith. The gallows does well; but how does it well? It does well to those that do ill. Now, thou dost ill to say the gallows is built stronger than the church, argal, the gallows may do well to thee. To 't again, come.

SECOND CLO.   "Who builds stronger than a mason, a shipwright, or a carpenter?"

FIRST CLO.   Ay, tell me that, and unyoke.

SECOND CLO.   Marry, now I can tell.

FIRST CLO.   To 't.

SECOND CLO.   Mass, I cannot tell.

FIRST CLO.   Cudgel thy brains no more about it, for your dull ass will not mend his pace with beating; and, when you are asked this question next, say "a grave-maker"; the houses that he makes lasts till doomsday. Go, get thee in; and fetch me a stoup of liquor.

[*Exit* SECOND CLOWN. FIRST CLOWN *digs, and sings.*]

In youth, when I did love, did love,
   Methought it was very sweet,
To contract, O, the time for-a-my behove,[6]
   O, methought, there-a-was nothing-a meet.

[*Enter* HAMLET *and* HORATIO.]

HAMLET.   Has this fellow no feeling of his business? 'A sings at grave-making.

HORATIO.   Custom hath made it in him a property of easiness.[7]

HAM.   'T is e'en so: the hand of little employment hath the daintier sense.

FIRST CLO.   [*Sings.*]

   But age, with his stealing steps,
      Hath clawed me in his clutch,
   And hath shipped me into the land,
      As if I had never been such.

[*Throws up a skull.*]

---

[3] In self-offense. What he means is *se defendendo,* in self-defense.
[4] Ergo, therefore.

[5] Coroner's inquest.
[6] Advantage.
[7] Matter of indifference.

HAM. That skull had a tongue in it, and could sing once. How the knave jowls [8] it to the ground, as if it were Cain's jawbone, that did the first murder! This might be the pate of a politician, which this ass now o'erreaches; one that would circumvent God, might it not?

HOR. It might, my lord.

HAM. Or of a courtier, which could say, "Good morrow, sweet lord! How dost thou, sweet lord?" This might be my lord such-a-one that praised my lord such-a-one's horse, when 'a meant to beg it; might it not?

HOR. Ay, my lord.

HAM. Why, e'en so; and now my Lady Worm's; chapless,[9] and knocked about the mazzard [10] with a sexton's spade: here 's fine revolution, an we had the trick to see 't. Did these bones cost no more the breeding, but to play at loggats [11] with 'em? Mine ache to think on 't.

FIRST CLO. [Sings.]

A pick-axe, and a spade, a spade, a spade
  For and a shrouding sheet;
O, a pit of clay for to be made
  For such a guest is meet.

[Throws up another skull.]

HAM. There 's another. Why may not that be the skull of a lawyer? Where be his quiddities now, his quillets,[12] his cases, his tenures, and his tricks? Why does he suffer this mad knave now to knock him about the sconce with a dirty shovel, and will not tell him of his action of battery? Hum! This fellow might be in 's time a great buyer of land, with his statutes, his recognizances, his fines, his double vouchers, his recoveries. Is this the fine of his fines, and the recovery of his recoveries,[13] to have his fine pate full of fine dirt? Will his vouchers vouch him no more of his purchases, and double ones too, than the length and breadth of a pair of indentures? The very conveyances of his lands will hardly lie in this box, and must th' inheritor himself have no more, ha?

HOR. Not a jot more, my lord.

HAM. Is not parchment made of sheepskins?

HOR. Ay, my lord, and of calf-skins too.

HAM. They are sheep and calves which seek out assurance in that. I will speak to this fellow. Whose grave 's this, sirrah?

FIRST CLO. Mine, sir.
[Sings.]

O, a pit of clay for to be made
  For such a guest is meet.

HAM. I think it be thine indeed, for thou liest in 't.

FIRST CLO. You lie out on 't, sir, and therefore it is not yours: for my part, I do not lie in 't, yet it is mine.

HAM. Thou dost lie in 't, to be in 't and say it is thine. 'T is for the dead, not for the quick, therefore thou liest.

FIRST CLO. 'T is a quick lie, sir; 't will away again, from me to you.

HAM. What man dost thou dig it for?

FIRST CLO. For no man, sir.

HAM. What woman, then?

FIRST CLO. For none, neither.

HAM. Who is to be buried in 't?

FIRST CLO. One that was a woman, sir; but, rest her soul, she 's dead.

HAM. How absolute the knave is! We must speak by the card,[14] or equivocation will undo us. By the Lord, Horatio, this three years I have took note of it; the age is grown so picked [15] that the toe of the peasant comes so near the heel of the courtier, he galls his kibe.[16] How long hast thou been a grave-maker?

FIRST CLO. Of all the days i' th' year, I came to 't that day that our last king Hamlet overcame Fortinbras.

HAM. How long is that since?

FIRST CLO. Cannot you tell that? Every fool can tell that. It was that very day that

---

[8] Hurls. [9] Lacking the lower jaw.
[10] Noggin. Slang term for the head.
[11] A game like bowls played with sticks of wood.
[12] His hair-splittings and his quibbles.

[13] The end of his conveyances, and the last transfer of his transfers.
[14] Punctiliously.
[15] Fastidious.
[16] Rubs his chilblain into a blister.

young Hamlet was born; he that is mad, and sent into England.

HAM.   Ay, marry, why was he sent into England?

FIRST CLO.   Why, because 'a was mad: 'a shall recover his wits there; or, if he do not, 't is no great matter there.

HAM.   Why?

FIRST CLO.   'T will not be seen in him there; there the men are as mad as he.

HAM.   How came he mad?

FIRST CLO.   Very strangely, they say.

HAM.   How "strangely"?

FIRST CLO.   Faith, e'en with losing his wits.

HAM.   Upon what ground?

FIRST CLO.   Why, here in Denmark: I have been sexton here, man and boy, thirty years.

HAM.   How long will a man lie 'i th' earth ere he rot?

FIRST CLO.   Faith, if 'a be not rotten before 'a die—as we have many pocky [17] corses now-a-days, that will scarce hold the laying in—'a will last you some eight year or nine year. A tanner will last you nine year.

HAM.   Why he more than another?

FIRST CLO.   Why, sir, his hide is so tanned with his trade that 'a will keep out water a great while, and your water is a sore decayer of your whoreson dead body. Here 's a skull now; this skull hath lien you i' th' earth three and twenty years.

HAM.   Whose was it?

FIRST CLO.   A whoreson mad fellow's [18] it was. Whose do you think it was?

HAM.   Nay, I know not.

FIRST CLO.   A pestilence on him for a mad rogue! 'A poured a flagon of Rhenish on my head once. This same skull, sir, was, sir, Yorick's skull, the King's jester.

HAM.   This?

FIRST CLO.   E'en that.

HAM.   Let me see. [Takes the skull.] Alas, poor Yorick! I knew him, Horatio; a fellow of infinite jest, of most excellent fancy. He hath borne me on his back a thousand times. And now how abhorred in my imagination it is! My gorge rises at it. Here hung those lips that I have kissed I know not how oft. Where be your gibes now, your gambols, your songs, your flashes of merriment, that were wont to set the table on a roar? Not one now, to mock your own grinning? Quite chop-fallen? [19] Now get you to my lady's chamber, and tell her, let her paint an inch thick, to this favour she must come. Make her laugh at that. Prithee, Horatio, tell me one thing.

HOR.   What 's that, my lord?

HAM.   Dost thou think Alexander looked o' this fashion i' th' earth?

HOR.   E'en so.

HAM.   And smelt so? Pah!
[Puts down the skull.]

HOR.   E'en so, my lord.

HAM.   To what base uses we may return, Horatio! Why may not imagination trace the noble dust of Alexander, till 'a find it stopping a bung-hole?

HOR.   'T were to consider too curiously,[20] to consider so.

HAM.   No, faith, not a jot; but to follow him thither with modesty enough [21] and likelihood to lead it; as thus: Alexander died, Alexander was buried, Alexander returneth to dust, the dust is earth, of earth we make loam, and why of that loam whereto he was converted might they not stop a beer-barrel?

Imperious Cæsar, dead and turn'd to clay,
Might stop a hole to keep the wind away.
O, that that earth, which kept the world in awe,
Should patch a wall t' expel the winter's flaw! [22]
But soft, but soft, awhile! Here comes the King.

[Enter KING, QUEEN, LAERTES, and a Coffin, with a PRIEST and LORDS attendant.]

The Queen, the courtiers. Who is this they follow?

---

[17] Consumed by venereal disease.
[18] A comical bastard's. Although *whoreson* strictly means a bastard, the word is chiefly used as a rather colorless vulgar intensive.

[19] Down in the mouth.
[20] Ingeniously.
[21] Without exaggeration.
[22] Blast.

And with such maimed rites? This doth be-
token
The corse they follow did with desp'rate
hand
Fordo it own life: 't was of some estate.²³
Couch we a while, and mark.

                [Retiring with HORATIO.]

LAERTES. What ceremony else?

HAM. That is Laertes, a very noble
youth. Mark.

LAER. What ceremony else?

PRIEST. Her obsequies have been as far
enlarg'd
As we have warranty. Her death was doubt-
ful;
And, but that great command o'ersways the
order,
She should in ground unsanctified have
lodg'd
Till the last trumpet; for charitable prayers,
Shards, flints, and pebbles should be thrown
on her:
Yet here she is allowed her virgin crants,²⁴
Her maiden strewments, and the bringing
home
Of bell and burial.

LAER. Must there no more be done?

PRIEST.   No more be done.
We should profane the service of the
dead
To sing a requiem and such rest to her
As to peace-parted souls.

LAER.   Lay her i' th' earth,
And from her fair and unpolluted flesh
May violets spring! I tell thee, churlish
priest,
A minist'ring angel shall my sister be,
When thou liest howling.

HAM.   What, the fair Ophelia!

QUEEN. Sweets to the sweet; farewell!

                  [Scattering flowers.]

I hop'd thou shouldst have been my Hamlet's wife;
I thought thy bride-bed to have deck'd,
sweet maid,
And not have strew'd thy grave.

LAER.   O, treble woe
Fall ten times treble on that cursed head

Whose wicked deed thy most ingenious
sense
Depriv'd thee of! Hold off the earth a
while,
Till I have caught her once more in mine
arms.

                [Leaps in the grave.]

Now pile your dust upon the quick and
dead,
Till of this flat a mountain you have made
T' o'ertop old Pelion,²⁵ or the skyish head
Of blue Olympus.

HAM. *[Advancing.]* What is he whose
grief
Bears such an emphasis, whose phrase of
sorrow
Conjures the wand'ring stars and makes
them stand
Like wonder-wounded hearers? This is I,
Hamlet, the Dane!

LAER. The devil take thy soul!

              [Grappling with him.]

HAM.   Thou pray'st not well.
I prithee, take thy fingers from my throat,
For, though I am not splenitive and rash,
Yet have I something in me dangerous,
Which let thy wiseness fear. Hold off thy
hand!

KING. Pluck them asunder.

QUEEN.   Hamlet, Hamlet!

ALL.   Gentlemen,—

HOR. Good my lord, be quiet.

        [The ATTENDANTS *part them.]*

HAM. Why, I will fight with him upon
this theme
Until my eyelids will no longer wag.

QUEEN. O my son, what theme?

HAM. I lov'd Ophelia: forty thousand
brothers
Could not, with all their quantity of love,
Make up my sum. What wilt thou do for
her?

KING. O, he is mad, Laertes.

QUEEN. For love of God, forbear him.

HAM. 'Swounds, show me what thou 't
do.
Woo 't weep? Woo 't fight? Woo 't fast?
Woo 't tear thyself?

---

²³ Destroy its own life: 'twas of some high
rank.
²⁴ Wreath of flowers.

²⁵ According to ancient myth, the giants once
piled Mt. Pelion on Mt. Ossa in an effort to reach
the home of the gods at the top of Mt. Olympus.

Woo 't drink up eisel?[26] Eat a crocodile?
I 'll do 't. Dost come here to whine?
To outface me with leaping in her grave?
Be buried quick with her, and so will I;
And, if thou prate of mountains, let them
   throw
Millions of acres on us, till our ground,
Singeing his pate against the burning
   zone,[27]
Make Ossa like a wart! Nay, an thou 'lt
   mouth,
I 'll rant as well as thou.
      QUEEN.   This is mere madness,
And thus a while the fit will work on
   him;
Anon, as patient as the female dove,
When that her golden couplets are dis-
   clos'd,[28]
His silence will sit drooping.
   HAM.   Hear you, sir,
What is the reason that you use me thus?
I lov'd you ever. But it is no matter.
Let Hercules himself do what he may,
The cat will mew and dog will have his day.
                              [*Exit* HAMLET.]
   KING.   I pray thee, good Horatio, wait
      upon him.   [*Exit* HORATIO.]
[*To* LAERTES.] Strengthen your patience
      in our last night's speech;
We 'll put the matter to the present push.[29]
Good Gertrude, set some watch over your
   son.
This grave shall have a living monument.[30]
An hour of quiet shortly shall we see;
Till then, in patience our proceeding be.
                              [*Exeunt.*]

Scene II
A hall in the castle.

[*Enter* HAMLET *and* HORATIO.]

HAMLET.   So much for this, sir; now
   you shall see the other—
You do remember all the circumstance?
   HORATIO.   Remember it, my lord!

---

26 Vinegar.
27 The zone of the sun's orbit.
28 Twin nestlings are hatched.
29 Immediate trial.
30 A lasting memorial, which, the King implies
to Laertes, will also be a live one, *i.e.,* Hamlet.

HAM.   Sir, in my heart there was a kind
   of fighting,
That would not let me sleep; methought I
   lay
Worse than the mutines in the bilboes.[1]
   Rashly,—
And prais'd be rashness for it: let us
   know
Our indiscretion sometime serves us well
When our deep plots do pall; and that
   should learn us
There 's a divinity that shapes our ends,
Rough-hew them how we will—
   HOR.   That is most certain.
   HAM.   Up from my cabin,
My sea-gown scarf'd about me, in the dark
Grop'd I to find out them, had my desire,
Finger'd their packet; and in fine withdrew
To mine own room again, making so bold,
My fears forgetting manners, to unseal
Their grand commission; where I found,
   Horatio,—
Ah, royal knavery!—an exact command,
Larded with many several sorts of reasons
Importing Denmark's health and England's
   too,
With, ho! such bugs and goblins in my life,
That, on the supervise, no leisure bated,[2]
No, not to stay the grinding of the axe,
My head should be struck off.
   HOR.   Is 't possible?
   HAM.   Here 's the commision; read it
      at more leisure.
But wilt thou hear now how I did proceed?
   HOR.   I beseech you.
   HAM.   Being thus be-netted round with
      villainies,—
Ere I could make a prologue to my brains,
They had begun the play,—I sat me down,
Devis'd a new commission, wrote it fair;
I once did hold it, as our statists [3] do,
A baseness to write fair, and labour'd much
How to forget that learning; but, sir, now
It did me yeoman's service. Wilt thou know
Th' effect of what I wrote?
   HOR.   Ay, good my lord.

---

1 Mutineers in fetters.
2 Such bogies and fanciful terrors contingent
on my living that, as soon as read, with no waste
of time.
3 Statesmen, who looked upon good handwriting as plebeian and the mark of a clerk.

HAM. An earnest conjuration from the King,
As England was his faithful tributary,
As love between them like the palm might flourish,
As peace should still her wheaten garland wear
And stand a comma 'tween their amities,
And many such-like "As"-es of great charge,
That, on the view and knowing of these contents,
Without debatement further, more or less,
He should those bearers put to sudden death,
Not shriving time allow'd.

HOR. How was this seal'd?

HAM. Why, even in that was Heaven ordinant.[4]
I had my father's signet in my purse,
Which was the model of that Danish seal;
Folded the writ up in the form of th' other,
Subscrib'd it, gave 't th' impression, plac'd it safely,
The changeling never known. Now the next day
Was our sea-fight; and what to this was sequent
Thou knowest already.

HOR. So Guildenstern and Rosencrantz go to 't.

HAM. Why man, they did make love to this employment;
They are not near my conscience; their defeat
Does by their own insinuation [5] grow:
'T is dangerous when the baser nature comes
Between the pass and fell incensed points
Of mighty opposites.

HOR. Why, what a king is this!

HAM. Does it not, think thee, stand me now upon—
He that hath kill'd my king and whor'd my mother,
Popp'd in between th' election and my hopes,[6]

Thrown out his angle for my proper life,
And with such cozenage [7]—is 't not perfect conscience,
To quit him with this arm? And is 't not to be damn'd,
To let this canker of our nature come
In further evil?

HOR. It must be shortly known to him from England
What is the issue of the business there.

HAM. It will be short; the interim is mine,
And a man's life 's no more than to say "One."
But I am very sorry, good Horatio,
That to Laertes I forgot myself;
For, by the image of my cause, I see
The portraiture of his. I 'll court his favours:
But, sure, the bravery [8] of his grief did put me
Into a tow'ring passion.

HOR. Peace! who comes here?

[Enter young OSRIC.]

OSRIC. Your lordship is right welcome back to Denmark.

HAM. I humbly thank you, sir. [*To* HORATIO.]—Dost know this water-fly?

HOR. No, my good lord.

HAM. Thy state is the more gracious, for 't is a vice to know him. He hath much land, and fertile; let a beast be lord of beasts, and his crib [9] shall stand at the King's mess. 'T is a chough,[10] but, as I say, spacious in the possession of dirt.

OSR. Sweet lord, if your lordship were at leisure, I should impart a thing to you from his Majesty.

HAM. I will receive it, sir, with all diligence of spirit. Put your bonnet to his right use; 't is for the head.

OSR. I thank your lordship, it is very hot.

HAM. No, believe me, 't is very cold; the wind is northerly.

OSR. It is indifferent cold, my lord, indeed.

---

[4] Supervising. [5] Interference.
[6] The choice of Claudius rather than Hamlet by the Danes, whose monarchy was elective.
[7] Fished for my life itself, and with such treachery. [8] Flamboyance.
[9] Trough. [10] Chattering jackdaw.

HAM.   Methinks it is very sultry and hot for my complexion.

OSR.   Exceedingly, my lord; it is very sultry,—as 't were—I cannot tell how. But, my lord, his Majesty bade me signify to you that 'a has laid a great wager on your head. Sir, this is the matter,—

HAM.   I beseech you, remember—

[HAMLET *moves him to put on his hat.*]

OSR.   Nay, good my lord; for my ease, in good faith. Sir, here is newly come to court Laertes, believe me, an absolute gentleman, full of most excellent differences, of very soft society and great showing; indeed, to speak feelingly of him, he is the card or calendar of gentry, for you shall find in him the continent of what parts a gentleman would see.

HAM.   Sir, his definement suffers no perdition in you; though, I know, to divide him inventorially would dizzy th' arithmetic of memory, and yet but yaw neither, in ˢpect of his quick sail. But, in the verity of extolment, I take him to be a soul of great article, and his infusion of such dearth and rareness, as, to make true diction of him, his semblable is his mirror; and who else would trace him, his umbrage, nothing more.[11]

OSR.   Your lordship speaks most infallibly of him.

HAM.   The concernancy, sir? [12] Why do we wrap the gentleman in our more rawer breath?

OSR.   Sir?

HOR.   Is 't not possible to understand in another tongue? You will to 't, sir, really.[13]

HAM.   What imports the nomination of this gentleman?

OSR.   Of Laertes?

HOR.   His purse is empty already; all 's golden words are spent.

HAM.   Of him, sir.

OSR.   I know you are not ignorant—

HAM.   I would you did, sir; yet, in faith, if you did, it would not much approve me. Well, sir?

OSR.   You are not ignorant of what excellence Laertes is—

HAM.   I dare not confess that, lest I should compare with him in excellence; but to know a man well were to know himself.

OSR.   I mean, sir, for his weapon; but in the imputation [14] laid on him by them, in his meed he 's unfellowed.

HAM.   What 's his weapon?

OSR.   Rapier and dagger.

HAM.   That 's two of his weapons; but well.

OSR.   The King, sir, hath wagered with him six Barbary horses, against the which he has impawned, as I take it, six French rapiers and poniards, with their assigns, as girdle, hangers, and so. Three of the carriages, in faith, are very dear to fancy, very responsive to the hilts, most delicate carriages, and of very liberal conceit.[15]

HAM.   What call you the carriages?

HOR.   I knew you must be edified by the margent [16] ere you had done.

OSR.   The carriages, sir, are the hangers.

HAM.   The phrase would be more germane to the matter, if we could carry cannon by our sides; I would it might be hangers till then. But, on: six Barbary horses against six French swords, their assigns, and three liberal-conceited carriages; that 's the French bet against the Danish. Why is all this "impawned," as you call it?

OSR.   The King, sir, hath laid, sir, that in a dozen passes between yourself and him, he shall not exceed you three hits; he hath laid on twelve for nine; and it would come to immediate trial, if your lordship would vouchsafe the answer.

HAM.   How if I answer no?

OSR.   I mean, my lord, the opposition of your person in trial.

HAM.   Sir, I will walk here in the hall; if it please his Majesty, it is the breathing time of day with me.[17] Let the foils be

---

[11] In this deliberate parody of Osric's high-flown rhetoric Hamlet is merely saying that to compute the virtues of Laertes is impossible; his like is to be found only in his mirror, for his nearest rival is but a shadow of him.
[12] What is the point of this praise?
[13] You will catch on, really.
[14] Estimation.
[15] Elaborate design.
[16] Explanatory notes, which usually appeared in the margins of Elizabethan books.
[17] My customary time for exercise.

brought, the gentleman willing, and the King hold his purpose, I will win for him an I can; if not, I will gain nothing but my shame and the odd hits.

OSR. Shall I deliver you so?

HAM. To this effect, sir; after what flourish your nature will.

OSR. I commend my duty to your lordship.

HAM. Yours, yours [*Exit* OSRIC.] He does well to commend it himself; there are no tongues else for 's turn.

HOR. This lapwing runs away with the shell on his head.

HAM. 'A did, sir, comply with his dug [18] before 'a suck'd it. Thus has he—and many more of the same bevy that I know the drossy age dotes on—only got the tune of the time and, out of an habit of encounter, a kind of yeasty collection, which carries them through and through the most fanned and winnowed opinions; and do but blow them to their trial, the bubbles are out.[19]

[*Enter a* LORD.]

LORD. My lord, his Majesty commended him to you by young Osric, who brings back to him, that you attend him in the hall. He sends to know if your pleasure hold to play with Laertes, or that you will take longer time.

HAM. I am constant to my purposes; they follow the King's pleasure. If his fitness speaks, mine is ready, now or whensoever, provided I be so able as now.

LORD. The King and Queen and all are coming down.

HAM. In happy time.

LORD. The Queen desires you to use some gentle entertainment to Laertes before you fall to play.

HAM. She well instructs me.

[*Exit* LORD.]

HOR. You will lose, my lord.

HAM. I do not think so; since he went into France, I have been in continual practice. I shall win at the odds. But thou wouldst not think how ill all 's here about my heart; but it is no matter.

HOR. Nay, good lord,—

HAM. It is but foolery; but it is such a kind of gain-giving,[20] as would perhaps trouble a woman.

HOR. If your mind dislike anything, obey it. I will forestall their repair hither, and say you are not fit.

HAM. Not a whit; we defy augury; there is special providence in the fall of a sparrow. If it be now, 't is not to come; if it be not to come, it will be now; if it be not now, yet it will come; the readiness is all. Since no man of aught he leaves knows, what is 't to leave betimes? Let be.

[*Enter* KING, QUEEN, LAERTES, OSRIC, *and all the State and other* ATTENDANTS, *with foils and daggers; a table and flagons of wine on it. Trumpets, drums, and Officers with cushions.*]

KING. Come, Hamlet, come, and take
    this hand from me.
     [*The* KING *puts* LAERTES' *hand into*
     HAMLET'S.]

HAM. Give me your pardon, sir. I have
    done you wrong,
But pardon 't, as you are a gentleman.
This presence knows, and you must needs
    have heard,
How I am punish'd with a sore distraction.
What I have done
That might your nature, honour, and exception [21]
Roughly awake, I here proclaim was madness.
Was 't Hamlet wrong'd Laertes? Never
    Hamlet!
If Hamlet from himself be ta'en away,
And when he 's not himself does wrong
    Laertes,
Then Hamlet does it not, Hamlet denies it.
Who does it, then? His madness. If 't be so,
Hamlet is of the faction that is wrong'd;
His madness is poor Hamlet's enemy.
Sir, in this audience,

---

[18] Was ceremonious with the nipple
[19] He has picked up the vogue and, by a sort of contagion, a froth of affectations which enable him to get by among even those of most dis-

criminating judgment; but blow up such bubbles to a real test, and they burst.
[20] Misgiving.
[21] Objection.

Let my disclaiming from a purpos'd evil
Free me so far in your most generous
  thoughts,
That I have shot my arrow o'er the house
And hurt my brother.

LAERTES.   I am satisfied in nature,
Whose motive, in this case, should stir me
  most
To my revenge; but in my terms of honour
I stand aloof, and will no reconcilement
Till by some elder masters of known
  honour
I have a voice and precedent of peace,
To keep my name ungor'd. But till that
  time,
I do receive your offer'd love like love,
And will not wrong it.

HAM.   I embrace it freely,
And will this brother's wager frankly play.
Give us the foils.

LAER.   Come, one for me.

HAM.   I 'll be your foil, Laertes; in mine
  ignorance
Your skill shall, like a star i' th' darkest
  night,
Stick fiery off indeed.

LAER.   You mock me, sir.

HAM.   No, by this hand.

KING.   Give them the foils, young Osric.
  Cousin Hamlet,
You know the wager?

HAM.   Very well, my lord.
Your Grace hath laid the odds o' th'
  weaker side.

KING.   I do not fear it, I have seen you
  both;
But since he is better'd, we have therefore
  odds.

LAER.   This is too heavy; let me see another.

HAM.   This likes me well. These foils
  have all a length?

              [*They prepare to play.*]

OSR.   Ay, my good lord.

KING.   Set me the stoups of wine upon
  that table.
If Hamlet give the first or second hit,
Or quit in answer of the third exchange,
Let all the battlements their ordnance fire.

The King shall drink to Hamlet's better
  breath,
And in the cup an union [22] shall he throw,
Richer than that which four successive
  kings
In Denmark's crown have worn. Give me
  the cups,
And let the kettle [23] to the trumpet speak,
The trumpet to the cannoneer without,
The cannons to the heavens, the heaven to
  earth,
"Now the King drinks to Hamlet." Come,
  begin;
And you, the judges, bear a wary eye.

                        [*Trumpets sound.*]

HAM.   Come on, sir.

LAER.   Come, my lord. [*They play.*]

HAM.   One.

LAER.   No.

HAM.   Judgement.

OSRIC.   A hit, a very palpable hit.

LAER.   Well; again.

KING.   Stay, give me drink. Hamlet, this
  pearl is thine;
Here's to thy health! Give him the cup.

      [*Trumpets sound, and shot goes off
        within.*]

HAM.   I 'll play this bout first; set it by
  a while.
Come. [*They play.*] Another hit; what say
  you?

LAER.   A touch, a touch, I do confess 't.

KING.   Our son shall win.

QUEEN.   He 's fat, and scant of
  breath.[24]
Here, Hamlet, take my napkin, rub thy
  brows.
The Queen carouses to thy fortune, Hamlet.

HAM.   Good madam!

KING.   Gertrude, do not drink.

QUEEN.   I will, my lord; I pray you
  pardon me.

KING. [*Aside.*] It is the poison'd cup; it is
  too late.

HAM.   I dare not drink yet, madam; by
  and by.

QUEEN.   Come, let me wipe thy face.

---

[22] Pearl.   [23] Kettle-drum.   [24] Out of condition and panting.

LAER. My lord, I 'll hit him now.

KING. I do not think 't.

LAER. [*Aside.*] And yet it is almost against my conscience.

HAM. Come, for the third, Laertes; you but dally.

I pray you, pass with your best violence.

I am afeard you make a wanton of me.[25]

LAER. Say you so? Come on.

[*They play.*]

OSR. Nothing, neither way.

LAER. Have at you now!

[LAERTES *wounds* HAMLET; *then, in scuffling, they change rapiers.*]

KING. Part them; they are incens'd.

HAM. Nay, come, again.

[HAMLET *wounds* LAERTES. *The* QUEEN *falls.*]

OSR. Look to the Queen there! Ho!

HOR. They bleed on both sides. How is 't, my lord!

OSR. How is 't, Laertes?

LAER. Why, as a woodcock to mine own springe,[26] Osric;

I am justly kill'd with mine own treachery.

HAM. How does the Queen?

KING. She swounds to see them bleed.

QUEEN. No, no, the drink, the drink,— O my dear Hamlet,—

The drink, the drink! I am poison'd.

[*Dies.*]

HAM. O villainy! Ho! let the door be lock'd:

Treachery! Seek it out.

LAER. It is here, Hamlet. Hamlet, thou art slain.

No med'cine in the world can do thee good;

In thee there is not half an hour's life;

The treacherous instrument is in thy hand,

Unbated and envenom'd: the foul practice

Hath turn'd itself on me; lo, here I lie,

Never to rise again. Thy mother 's poison'd.

I can no more:—the King, the King 's to blame.

HAM. The point envenom'd too!

Then, venom, to thy work.

[*Hurts the* KING.]

ALL. Treason! treason!

KING. O, yet defend me, friends; I am but hurt.

HAM. Here, thou incestuous, murd'rous, damned Dane,

Drink off this potion! Is thy union here?

Follow my mother! [KING *dies.*]

LAER. He is justly served;

It is a poison temper'd by himself.

Exchange forgiveness with me, noble Hamlet;

Mine and my father's death come not upon thee,

Nor thine on me! [*Dies.*]

HAM. Heaven make thee free of it! I follow thee.

I am dead, Horatio. Wretched queen, adieu!

You that look pale and tremble at this chance,

That are but mutes or audience to this act,

Had I but time—as this fell sergeant, Death,

Is strict in his arrest—O, I could tell you—

But let it be. Horatio, I am dead;

Thou livest; report me and my cause aright

To the unsatisfied.

HOR. Never believe it:

I am more an antique Roman[27] than a Dane;

Here 's yet some liquor left.

HAM. As thou 'rt a man,

Give me the cup; let go, by heaven, I 'll have 't!

O God, Horatio, what a wounded name,

Things standing thus unknown, shall live behind me!

If thou didst ever hold me in thy heart,

Absent thee from felicity a while

And in this harsh world draw thy breath in pain

To tell my story.

[*March afar off, and shot within.*]

What warlike noise is this?

OSR. Young Fortinbras, with conquest come from Poland,

To th' ambassadors of England gives

[25] Are letting me win, like a child.
[26] Snare.

[27] Referring to the Roman stoics, who preferred suicide to living in an intolerable world.

This warlike volley.

HAM.   O, I die, Horatio;
The potent poison quite o'er-crows my
    spirit:
I cannot live to hear the news from Eng-
    land,
But I do prophesy th' election lights
On Fortinbras; he has my dying voice.
So tell him, with th' occurrents, more and
    less,
Which have solicited [28]—the rest is silence.
                                    [*Dies.*]

HOR.   Now cracks a noble heart. Good-
    night, sweet prince,
And flights of angels sing thee to thy rest!
Why does the drum come hither?

[*Enter* FORTINBRAS *and the English* AMBAS-
    SADORS, *with drum, colours, and* AT-
    TENDANTS.]

FORTINBRAS.   Where is this sight?
HOR.   What is it you would see?
If aught of woe or wonder, cease your
    search.
FORT.   This quarry cries on havoc.[29] O
    proud Death,
What feast is toward in thine eternal cell,
That thou so many princes at a shot
So bloodily hast struck?
FIRST AMBASSADOR.   The sight is dis-
    mal,
And our affairs from England come too
    late:
The ears are senseless that should give us
    hearing,
To tell him his commandment is fulfill'd
That Rosencrantz and Guildenstern are
    dead.
Where should we have our thanks?
HOR.   Not from his mouth,
Had it th' ability of life to thank you.
He never gave commandment for their
    death:
But since, so jump upon this bloody ques-
    tion,

You from the Polack wars, and you from
    England,
Are here arrived, give order that these
    bodies
High on a stage be placed to the view;
And let me speak to th' yet unknowing
    world
How these things came about: so shall you
    hear
Of carnal, bloody, and unnatural acts,
Of accidental judgements, casual slaugh-
    ters,
Of deaths put on by cunning and forc'd
    cause,
And, in this upshot, purposes mistook
Fall'n on th' inventors' heads: all this can I
Truly deliver.
FORT.   Let us haste to hear it,
And call the noblest to the audience.
For me, with sorrow I embrace my fortune:
I have some rights of memory in this king-
    dom,
Which now to claim, my vantage doth in-
    vite me.
HOR.   Of that I shall have also cause to
    speak,
And from his mouth whose voice [30] will
    draw on more:
But let this same be presently perform'd
Even while men's minds are wild, lest more
    mischance,
On plots and errors, happen.
FORT.   Let four captains
Bear Hamlet, like a soldier, to the stage,
For he was likely, had he been put on,
To have prov'd most royal; and, for his
    passage,
The soldiers' music and the rites of war
Speak loudly for him.
Take up the bodies: such a sight as this
Becomes the field,[31] but here shows much
    amiss.
Go, bid the soldiers shoot.
            [*Exeunt marching, after the which a
                peal of ordnance are shot off.*]

[28] Together with the chief occurrences which
have provoked these events.

[29] This heap of slain proclaims a massacre.
[30] Support.   [31] Field of battle.

Romantic Comedy

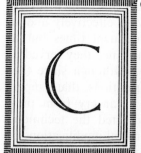OMEDY, BECAUSE of the nature of the entertainment which it provides, makes its appeal to a universal and timeless human instinct; for laughter arises from the amusing incongruities of human life as spontaneously as bubbles from sparkling wine. At the same time, since its natural subject matter is the immediate and familiar, and since its effect depends upon a nice balance between recognition and surprise, comedy is also a form of drama acutely susceptible to changes in custom and point of view. Its Achilles' heel is its ephemerality; for only too often today's wit proves to be tomorrow's inanity, and there is nothing so stale as an outmoded jest. As a result, the comic stage of Europe's past is littered with the debris of tarnished gayety. Varieties of comedy have served their purpose and gone their way, to be absorbed or replaced by more congenial successors. The earliest type to survive these vicissitudes and retain a permanent niche in the European theater is romantic comedy, which is historically a product of the Renaissance. Although in its time it was a type widely cultivated, its survival is largely due to the accident that it supplied the mold into which Shakespeare poured his comic genius. As a matter of fact, not only is Shakespeare the supreme exponent of the type, but his work is almost unique in preserving its pure form. The unrivaled masterpiece of romantic comedy is his *Twelfth Night* (c. 1601), a play which realizes to perfection the artistic possibilities of the type with a craftsmanship so masterly that it practically defies serious damage in production.

In large measure, romantic comedy is the comic counterpart of romantic tragedy. Much of what has been said about the characteristic features of the latter applies equally to romantic comedy. Its primary concern is to set forth the circumstances of a complete and complex story according to a pattern of increasing suspense. Its emphasis is upon the universal context of the exceptional situation and the specific individual. Its dramaturgy and tempo presuppose a simple and highly fluid stage. It exhibits a similar reliance upon the self-sufficiency of speech and action.

And it concentrates in the same way upon the individual scene as the basic unit of dramatic interest. Indeed, it uses its plot chiefly as a framework to support certain big scenes which can be exploited at length for comic entertainment. The principal difference between romantic tragedy and romantic comedy, apart from their divergent views of life, lies in the specialized and highly developed comic technique which the latter inherited from Roman comedy.

As far as the mere machinery of comic effect is concerned, the technique of all European comedy rests upon one common foundation. Substantially this is the technique established by the two Roman comic playwrights Plautus and Terence. Borrowing in their turn from the practices of Greek New Comedy, these two master technicians in their surviving plays have explored the mechanics of comedy so effectively and so comprehensively that little has remained for subsequent times but to adapt and amplify their methods. During the Renaissance they served as the universally acknowledged models for comedy. Although since that time comedy has experienced so many transformations that, superficially at least, the modern varieties may seem a far cry from their ancient progenitors, actually the changes have affected the technique very little. In most instances they involve only superficial modifications or a shift in the purposes for which the technique is used; the basic principles and practices remain the same. As a matter of fact, so fundamental is this truth that Plautus and Terence themselves have suffered the ironic fate of being swallowed by their own offspring. Because of the revolutions of taste, their own comedies no longer hold the stage except in modern adaptations; they have been supplanted by those who have clothed an old art in a new fashion. Nevertheless, the technical genius of the Roman masters continues to live a buried life in the mechanics of nearly every comedy from their own times to the present day.

The structural organization of a play like *Twelfth Night* is lifted bodily from Roman comedy. Plautus conceived of comedy as a ludicrous, often farcical exhibition of the incongruities resident in an absurd situation. These incongruities he based upon the confusions incident to error and misunderstanding. The misapprehensions he contrived with the mechanical devices of concealed identity, disguise, deception, and deliberate intrigue, often at the hands of an ingenious servant. As functional cogs in the machinery of comic confusion, he employed a set of largely conventionalized stock characters, who, because they often reflected familiar social types, occasionally lent themselves to good-humored satire. By means of this facile but effective formula the fertile invention of Plautus filled the stage with bustling action conceived in the spirit of broad farce and boisterous hilarity. To the basic practices of Plautus, Terence added a refinement of technique and taste and a polish of execution. In his hands the simple exploitation of a comic situation developed into a sustained and intricate plot with an emphasis upon suspense. In place of broad farce he chose to elaborate the love interest and the climactic sequence of adventurous incidents. In keeping with this shift of emphasis, he also devoted more attention to character analysis and thus transformed his stock characters into amusing projections of fundamental human nature. Finally, through the cultivation of witty and elegant repartee, he elevated comic dialogue to a plane of conscious art and sophisticated entertainment.

In *Twelfth Night* the technique of Roman comedy is applied to the perennial predilections of romance. The controlling purpose of romantic comedy is to entertain with a spectacle of human life representative of its most prepossessing aspects. In accord with this aim it presents a mode of life in which human experience and human nature are frankly idealized. The basis of this portrayal, it must be understood, is not falsification but special selection of materials. Rejecting all concessions to the mere prevalence of unwelcome fact or commonplace routine, romantic comedy deliberately chooses to confine itself to those aspects of human experience in which both life and humanity appear to best advantage. Thus it sets up as its norm and common denominator a life remolded nearer to the heart's desire—or, perhaps to be more exact, nearer to what the erratic human heart habitually professes to desire. In any case, the result is a scheme of existence as remote from common reality as it is true to human nature. It posits a world given over to love and merriment, without the inconveniences of toil or hardship. In this idyllic world normal life is tuned to a song and a jest. Human creatures are as they should be, and occasionally are. Ladies are invariably lovely and charming, witty and devoted; gentlemen are correspondingly handsome, gallant, and talented; and both possess the happy faculty of rising impeccably to the demands of every occasion. Inferior souls adorn with equal felicity the humbler stations in which it has pleased a benevolent destiny to place them. Even knaves and fools have the virtue of variety and afford the pleasure of their proper disposition. As for incidental misadventures, threats of peril, or clashes of will, these are but ripples on the surface of a placid stream; they constitute no more than a piquant sauce to spice the banquet of enjoyment, a welcome theme for retrospective mirth. For not the least virtue of this best of all possible worlds is its infinite capacity for innocent merriment. The prevailing mood of romantic comedy is one of light-hearted gayety, of graceful sentiment, and of genial laughter. It suffuses a charitable spirit of good humor which is wholly devoid of caustic satire or serious censure. Perhaps its most distinctive characteristics are its bubbling sense of sheer fun and its indulgent delight in the unconscious absurdities of agreeable human nature.

In its comprehensive versatility and its delicately proportioned balance of component parts, *Twelfth Night* is a consummate realization of the resources and effects within the scope of romantic comedy. A symphonic orchestration of amusing dialogue, lively stage business, and comic character revelation, with appropriate overtones of music and song, it creates effects which are most subtly calculated in terms of a dancing tempo, precision timing, and the immediate context of the situation. Because it is so expressly designed for stage effect and because, like all comedy, it relies so heavily upon exact context and timing, the real virtues of *Twelfth Night* become fully apparent only when the play is envisaged as an actual stage performance. So conceived, the play moves swiftly and with unceasing variety through a series of deftly contrived misunderstandings to a climax of mad confusion. The mechanism is a simple enough process of quite natural error arising from a few initial misconceptions, but its artful use produces a most intricate maze of complications. The convergence of these in the hilarious final scene is accomplished by a masterpiece of theatrical construction. Not only is confusion piled upon confusion with kaleidoscopic shifts of sentiment, but its intensity steadily mounts until, at the last possible moment, when chaos seems to be beyond repair, all the pieces are neatly jolted into their proper place by one sudden *coup de théâtre,* which fulfills the cardinal law of good comedy, to ring down the curtain quickly and leave the audience laughing. In the course of these proceedings the play manages to run the whole gamut of comic resources. It exploits the incongruities of situation occasioned by Viola's masquerade and the presence of indistinguishable twins. It employs intrigue and the practical joke for Malvolio's undoing. It levies upon farce for the grotesque duel. Amid a running fire of nimble repartee it balances the rollicking revels of Sir Toby and his companions with the wit of Feste and the amiable imbecilities of Sir Andrew. And everywhere it makes comic capital of those petty treasons in human nature which produce, for example, the sentimental affectations of Orsino, the feminine maneuverings of Voila and Olivia, the complacent day-dreaming of Malvolio, or the circumspect valor of Sir Andrew.

All in all, however, it is the prevailing mood of this type of comedy which is perhaps its most distinctive feature. Essentially this mood is a combination of graceful poetic sentiment with a lively awareness of the lapses from reason that such a sentiment is heir to. Thus its chuckling delight in the ambivalence of human frailty is at once too kindly and too sympathetic for actual censure. Indeed, to this spirit of genial tolerance, diverted but unperturbed by life's little absurdities, human life becomes most engaging precisely because of its incongruities, as human nature appears most comfortable because of its imperfections. As a result, the critical objectivity of its comic judgment is constantly tempered by a subjective predisposition in favor of creatures so delightfully fallible. It is the violation of this prevailing comic spirit which brings down upon Malvolio the most unsympathetic treatment of the play. Egotistical, complacent, and fanatically sober, Malvolio confuses propriety with virtue and conceives of enjoyment as the evidence of an idle mind. Totally destitute of a sense of humor, he lacks both its capacity for amusement and the critical discrimination upon which it rests. His sense of values is accordingly so lacking in proportion and perspective that he remains impervious even to the breaches he himself commits against his own standards. With malice toward all that does not conform to his personal prescriptions, and with charity for none but himself, Malvolio not only forfeits respect for a comic good sense but also places himself beyond the pale of comic indulgence. In a world presided over by the iconoclastic irreverence of the comic spirit his fatuous solemnity is an irresistible target for ribald bombardment.

Because of its highly distinctive combination of elements, romantic comedy reflects to a large degree the spirit of a particular age and the temperament of an individual dramatist. For this reason it has proved to be a type of drama not readily perpetuated, and its pure form is rare in the theater. The best examples are to be found among Shakespeare's romantic comedies, such as *A Midsummer Night's Dream, The Merchant of Venice,* and *As You Like It.* A variation of the type appears among the comedies of Lope de Vega, such as *The Gardener's Dog.* In general, pure romantic comedy has been so much subjected to the shifting tastes of subsequent times that its later incarnations bear slight resemblance to the original. For example, it reappears, somewhat pallidly, in the sentimental comedy of the eighteenth century, such as Goldsmith's *The Good-Natured Man* or *She Stoops to Conquer.* More modern derivatives are found among the comedies of J. M. Barrie and A. A. Milne, such as *Dear Brutus* or *Mr. Pim Passes By,* and among such diverse plays as Molnar's *Liliom,* Anderson's *High Tor,* or even O'Neill's *Ah, Wilderness.* But the most common modern versions of romantic comedy are the operetta and the musical comedy. It is in the Savoy operas of Gilbert and Sullivan, the Victor Herbert operettas, or such musical plays as *The Student Prince, The Chocolate Soldier,* or *Oklahoma,* that romantic comedy retains most of its pristine manner.

TWELFTH NIGHT

OR

WHAT YOU WILL

by

WILLIAM SHAKESPEARE

Dramatis Personæ

ORSINO, *Duke of Illyria.*
SEBASTIAN, *brother to* VIOLA.
ANTONIO, *a sea-captain, friend to*
   SEBASTIAN.
A SEA-CAPTAIN, *friend to* VIOLA.
VALENTINE, } *gentlemen attending*
CURIO,   }   *on the Duke.*
SIR TOBY BELCH, *uncle to* OLIVIA.

SIR ANDREW AGUECHEEK.
MALVOLIO, *steward to* OLIVIA.
FABIAN, *a gentleman,* } *servants to*
FESTE, *a clown,*   }   OLIVIA.
OLIVIA, *a rich countess.*
VIOLA.
MARIA, OLIVIA'S *woman.*

Lords, Priests, Sailors, Officers, Musicians, and other Attendants.

SCENE: *A city in Illyria, and the sea-coast near it.*

Like *Hamlet, Twelfth Night* presents the text prepared by Thomas Marc Parrott. through whose courtesy it is here reprinted. The play derives its title from the twelfth night after Christmas, which traditionally ended the holiday festivities and, in Elizabethan days, was given over to topsy-turvy merrymaking.

ACT I

Scene I

The Duke's palace.

[*Enter* ORSINO, *Duke of Illyria,* CURIO, *and other* LORDS, MUSICIANS *attending.*]

DUKE. If music be the food of love, play on!
Give me excess of it, that, surfeiting,
The appetite may sicken, and so die.
That strain again! It had a dying fall.
O, it came o'er my ear like the sweet sound
That breathes upon a bank of violets,
Stealing and giving odour. Enough! no more!
'T is not so sweet now as it was before.
O spirit of love, how quick and fresh art thou,
That, notwithstanding thy capacity
Receiveth as the sea, nought enters there,
Of what validity and pitch soe'er,
But falls into abatement and low price
Even in a minute! So full of shapes is fancy
That it alone is high fantastical.
CURIO. Will you go hunt, my lord?
DUKE.   What, Curio?
CUR. The hart.
DUKE. Why, so I do, the noblest that I have.
O, when mine eyes did see Olivia first,
Methought she purg'd the air of pestilence!
That instant was I turn'd into a hart;
And my desires, like fell and cruel hounds,
E'er since pursue me.

[*Enter* VALENTINE.]

                 How now! what news from her?
VALENTINE. So please my lord, I might not be admitted,
But from her handmaid do return this answer:
The element itself, till seven years' heat,[1]
Shall not behold her face at ample view;
But like a cloistress she will veiled walk,
And water once a day her chamber round
With eye-offending brine: all this to season

A brother's dead love, which she would keep fresh
And lasting in her sad remembrance.
DUKE. O, she that hath a heart of that fine frame
To pay this debt of love but to a brother,
How will she love when the rich golden shaft
Hath kill'd the flock of all affections else
That live in her; when liver, brain, and heart,[2]
These sovereign thrones, are all supplied, and fill'd
Her sweet perfections with one self king!
Away before me to sweet beds of flowers;
Love-thoughts lie rich when canopied with bowers.   [*Exeunt.*]

Scene II
The sea-coast.

[*Enter* VIOLA, *a* CAPTAIN, *and* SAILORS.]

VIOLA. What country, friends, is this?
CAPTAIN. This is Illyria, lady.
VIO. And what should I do in Illyria?
My brother he is in Elysium.
Perchance he is not drown'd. What think you, sailors?
CAP. It is perchance that you yourself were saved.
VIO. O my poor brother! and so perchance may he be.
CAP. True, madam; and, to comfort you with chance,
Assure yourself, after our ship did split,
When you and those poor number saved with you
Hung on our driving boat, I saw your brother,
Most provident in peril, bind himself,
Courage and hope both teaching him the practice,
To a strong mast that liv'd upon the sea;
Where, like Arion [1] on the dolphin's back,
I saw him hold acquaintance with the waves
So long as I could see.

---

[1] The sky itself, till seven summers have passed.
[2] Seats respectively of passion, intellect, and sentiment.

[1] A Greek poet whose singing charmed dolphins into rescuing him from the sea.

VIO. For saying so, there 's gold.
Mine own escape unfoldeth to my hope,
Whereto thy speech serves for authority,
The like of him. Know'st thou this country?

CAP. Ay, madam, well; for I was bred and born
Not three hours' travel from this very place.

VIO. Who governs here?

CAP. A noble duke, in nature as in name.

VIO. What is his name?

CAP. Orsino.

VIO. Orsino! I have heard my father name him.
He was a bachelor then.

CAP. And so is now, or was so very late;
For but a month ago I went from hence,
And then 't was fresh in murmur—as, you know,
What great ones do the less will prattle of—
That he did seek the love of fair Olivia.

VIO. What 's she?

CAP. A virtuous maid, the daughter of a count
That died some twelvemonth since, then leaving her
In the protection of his son, her brother,
Who shortly also died; for whose dear love,
They say, she hath abjur'd the company
And sight of men.

VIO.   O that I serv'd that lady,
And might not be delivered to the world,
Till I had made mine own occasion mellow,
What my estate is! [2]

CAP.   That were hard to compass,
Because she will admit no kind of suit,
No, not the Duke's.

VIO. There is a fair behaviour in thee, captain;
And though that nature with a beauteous wall
Doth oft close in pollution, yet of thee
I will believe thou hast a mind that suits

With this thy fair and outward character.
I prithee, and I 'll pay thee bounteously,
Conceal me what I am, and be my aid
For such disguise as haply shall become
The form of my intent. I 'll serve this duke.
Thou shalt present me as an eunuch to him.
It may be worth thy pains, for I can sing
And speak to him in many sorts of music
That will allow me very worth his service.
What else may hap, to time I will commit,
Only shape thou thy silence to my wit.

CAP. Be you his eunuch, and your mute I 'll be.
When my tongue blabs, then let mine eyes not see.

VIO. I thank thee. Lead me on.
                                [*Exeunt.*]

Scene III
Olivia's house.

[*Enter* SIR TOBY BELCH *and* MARIA.]

SIR TOBY. What a plague means my niece, to take the death of her brother thus? I am sure care 's an enemy to life.

MARIA. By my troth, Sir Toby, you must come in earlier o' nights. Your cousin, my lady, takes great exceptions to your ill hours.

SIR TO. Why, let her except before excepted.[1]

MAR. Ay, but you must confine yourself within the modest limits of order.

SIR TO. Confine? I 'll confine myself no finer than I am. These clothes are good enough to drink in, and so be these boots too; an they be not, let them hang themselves in their own straps.

MAR. That quaffing and drinking will undo you. I heard my lady talk of it yesterday, and of a foolish knight that you brought in one night here to be her wooer.

SIR TO. Who? Sir Andrew Aguecheek?

MAR. Ay, he.

SIR TO. He 's as tall [2] a man as any 's in Illyria.

MAR. What 's that to the purpose?

---

[2] Created a ripe opportunity to reveal my situation.

[1] A legal tag: exceptions aforesaid noted.
[2] Besides referring to height, the word also means *valiant*.

SIR TO. Why, he has three thousand ducats a year.

MAR. Ay, but he 'll have but a year in all these ducats. He 's a very fool and a prodigal.

SIR TO. Fie, that you 'll say so! He plays o' the viol-de-gamboys,[3] and speaks three or four languages word for word without book, and hath all the good gifts of nature.

MAR. He hath indeed, almost natural;[4] for besides that he 's a fool, he 's a great quarreller; and but that he hath the gift of a coward to allay the gust[5] he hath in quarrelling, 't is thought among the prudent he would quickly have the gift of a grave.

SIR TO. By this hand, they are scoundrels and substractors[6] that say so of him. Who are they?

MAR. They that add, moreover, he 's drunk nightly in your company.

SIR TO. With drinking healths to my niece. I'll drink to her as long as there is a passage in my throat and drink in Illyria. He 's a coward and coystrill[7] that will not drink to my niece till his brains turn o' the toe like a parish-top.[8] What, wench! *Castiliano vulgo!*[9] for here comes Sir Andrew Agueface.

[Enter SIR ANDREW.]

SIR ANDREW. Sir Toby Belch! How now, Sir Toby Belch!

SIR TO. Sweet Sir Andrew!

SIR AND. Bless you, fair shrew.

MAR. And you too, sir.

SIR TO. Accost, Sir Andrew, accost.

SIR AND. What 's that?

SIR TO. My niece's chambermaid.

SIR AND. Good Mistress Accost, I desire better acquaintance.

MAR. My name is Mary, sir.

SIR AND. Good Mistress Mary Accost,—

SIR TO. You mistake, knight. "Accost" is front her, board her, woo her, assail her.

SIR AND. By my troth, I would not undertake her in this company. Is that the meaning of "accost"?

MAR. Fare you well, gentlemen.

SIR TO. An thou let part so, Sir Andrew, would thou mightst never draw sword again.

SIR AND. An you part so, mistress, I would I might never draw sword again. Fair lady, do you think you have fools in hand?

MAR. Sir, I have not you by the hand.

SIR AND. Marry, but you shall have; and here 's my hand.

MAR. Now, sir, "thought is free." I pray you, bring your hand to the buttery-bar and let it drink.

SIR AND. Wherefore, sweetheart? What's your metaphor?

MAR. It 's dry,[10] sir.

SIR AND. Why, I think so. I am not such an ass, but I can keep my hand dry. But what 's your jest?

MAR. A dry[11] jest, sir.

SIR AND. Are you full of them?

MAR. Ay, sir, I have them at my fingers' ends. Marry, now I let go your hand, I am barren. *[Exit MARIA.]*

SIR TO. O knight, thou lackst a cup of canary.[12] When did I see thee so put down?

SIR AND. Never in your life, I think, unless you see canary put me down. Methinks sometimes I have no more wit than a Christian or an ordinary man has; but I am a great eater of beef and I believe that does harm to my wit.

SIR TO. No question.

SIR AND. An I thought that, I 'd forswear it. I 'll ride home to-morrow, Sir Toby.

SIR TO. *Pourquoi,*[13] my dear knight?

SIR AND. What is *"pourquoi"*? Do or not do? I would I had bestowed that time in the tongues that I have in fencing, dancing, and bear-baiting. O, had I but followed the arts!

SIR TO. Then hadst thou had an excel-

---

[3] Bass fiddle.   [4] A pun on *natural*, an idiot.
[5] Dilute the zest.   [6] Detractors.   [7] Knave.
[8] A large top used for community sport and exercise.

[9] Keep a sober face, like a Spaniard!
[10] A moist palm was supposed to indicate an amorous disposition.
[11] Dull.   [12] Canary wine.   [13] Why?

lent head of hair.

SIR AND. Why, would that have mended my hair?

SIR TO. Past question; for thou seest it will not curl by nature.

SIR AND. But it becomes me well enough, does 't not?

SIR TO. Excellent; it hangs like flax on a distaff, and I hope to see a housewife take thee between her legs, and spin it off.

SIR AND. Faith, I 'll home to-morrow, Sir Toby. Your niece will not be seen, or if she be, it 's four to one she 'll none of me. The Count himself here hard by wooes her.

SIR TO. She 'll none o' the Count. She 'll not match above her degree, neither in estate, years, nor wit; I have heard her swear 't. Tut, there 's life in 't, man.

SIR AND. I 'll stay a month longer. I am a fellow o' the strangest mind in the world; I delight in masques and revels sometimes altogether.

SIR TO. Art thou good at these kick-shawses,[14] knight?

SIR AND. As any man in Illyria, whatsoever he be, under the degree of my betters; and yet I will not compare with an old man.

SIR TO. What is thy excellence in a galliard,[15] knight?

SIR AND. Faith, I can cut a caper.

SIR TO. And I can cut the mutton[16] to 't.

SIR AND. And I think I have the back-trick simply as strong as any man in Illyria.

SIR TO. Wherefore are these things hid? Wherefore have these gifts a curtain before 'em? Are they like to take dust, like Mistress Mall's picture? Why dost thou not go to church in a galliard and come home in a coranto?[17] My very walk should be a jig. I would not so much as make water but in a sink-a-pace. What dost thou mean? Is it a world to hide virtues in? I did think, by the excellent constitution of thy leg, it was formed under the star of a galliard.

SIR AND. Ay, 't is strong, and it does indifferent well in a damned coloured stock.[18] Shall we set about some revels?

SIR TO. What shall we do else? Were we not born under Taurus?[19]

SIR AND. Taurus! That 's sides and heart.

SIR TO. No, sir, it is legs and thighs. Let me see thee caper. Ha! Higher! Ha, ha! Excellent! [Exeunt.]

Scene IV

The Duke's palace.

[Enter VALENTINE, and VIOLA in man's attire.]

VALENTINE. If the Duke continue these favours towards you, Cesario, you are like to be much advanced. He hath known you but three days, and already you are no stranger.

VIOLA. You either fear his humour or my negligence, that you call in question the continuance of his love. Is he inconstant, sir, in his favours?

VAL. No, believe me.

[Enter DUKE, CURIO, and ATTENDANTS.]

VIO. I thank you. Here comes the Count.

DUKE. Who saw Cesario, ho?

VIO. On your attendance, my lord; here.

DUKE. Stand you a while aloof. Cesario, Thou know'st no less but all. I have unclasp'd
To thee the book even of my secret soul;
Therefore, good youth, address thy gait unto her.
Be not denied access, stand at her doors,
And tell them, there thy fixed foot shall grow
Till thou have audience.

---

[14] Trifles.

[15] A lively dance which included such exploits as the caper, or leap into the air, and the backtrick, or backward leap.

[16] Often served with caper sauce. Mutton was also a slang term for a prostitute.

[17] This and the following jig and sink-a-pace (cinque-pace) were equally athletic dances.

[18] Stocking.

[19] The sign of the zodiac actually supposed to govern the neck and throat.

VIO.   Sure, my noble lord,
If she be so abandon'd to her sorrow
As it is spoke, she never will admit me.

DUKE. Be clamorous and leap all civil
  bounds
Rather than make unprofited return.

VIO. Say I do speak with her, my lord,
  what then?

DUKE. O, then unfold the passion of
  my love,
Surprise her with discourse of my dear
  faith.
It shall become thee well to act my woes.
She will attend it better in thy youth
Than in a nuncio's of more grave aspect.

VIO. I think not so, my lord.

DUKE.   Dear lad, believe it;
For they shall yet belie thy happy years,
That say thou art a man. Diana's lip
Is not more smooth and rubious; thy small
  pipe
Is as the maiden's organ, shrill and sound;
And all is semblative a woman's part.
I know thy constellation is right apt
For this affair. Some four or five attend
  him,—
All, if you will; for I myself am best
When least in company. Prosper well in
  this,
And thou shalt live as freely as thy lord,
To call his fortunes thine.

VIO.   I 'll do my best
To woo your lady,—[aside] yet, a barful
  strife!
Whoe'er I woo, myself would be his wife.
                          [Exeunt.]

Scene V

Olivia's house.

[Enter MARIA and CLOWN.]

MARIA. Nay, either tell me where thou
hast been, or I will not open my lips so
wide as a bristle may enter in way of thy
excuse. My lady will hang thee for thy
absence.

CLOWN. Let her hang me! He that is
well hanged in this world needs to fear no
colours.[1]

MAR. Make that good.

CLO. He shall see none to fear.

MAR. A good lenten [2] answer. I can tell
thee where that saying was born, of "I fear
no colours."

CLO. Where, good Mistress Mary?

MAR. In the wars; and that may you be
bold to say in your foolery.

CLO. Well, God give them wisdom that
have it; and those that are fools, let them
use their talents.

MAR. Yet you will be hanged for being
so long absent; or, to be turned away, is not
that as good as a hanging to you?

CLO. Many a good hanging prevents a
bad marriage; and, for turning away, let
summer bear it out.[3]

MAR. You are resolute, then?

CLO. Not so, neither; but I am resolved
on two points.

MAR. That if one break, the other will
hold; or, if both break, your gaskins fall.[4]

CLO. Apt, in good faith; very apt. Well,
go thy way. If Sir Toby would leave drinking, thou wert as witty a piece of Eve's
flesh as any in Illyria.

MAR. Peace, you rogue, no more o'
that. Here comes my lady. Make your excuse wisely, you were best.
                          [Exit MARIA.]

[Enter LADY OLIVIA and retinue with
MALVOLIO.]

CLO. Wit, an 't be thy will, put me into
good fooling! Those wits, that think they
have thee, do very oft prove fools; and I,
that am sure I lack thee, may pass for a
wise man; for what says Quinapalus? [5]
"Better a witty fool than a foolish wit."—
God bless thee, lady!

OLIVIA. Take the fool away.

CLO. Do you not hear, fellows? Take
away the lady.

OLI. Go to, you 're a dry fool. I 'll no
more of you; besides, you grow dishonest.

CLO. Two faults, madonna, that drink
and good counsel will amend; for give the

---

[1] Nothing, with a pun on *collar, i.e.,* noose.
[2] Meager.
[3] Make it endurable.

[4] Gaskins (loose breeches) were attached to the
doublet with points (laces).
[5] An invented authority.

dry fool drink, then is the fool not dry: bid the dishonest man mend himself; if he mend, he is no longer dishonest; if he cannot, let the botcher [6] mend him. Any thing that 's mended is but patched; virtue that transgresses is but patched with sin, and sin that amends is but patched with virtue. If that this simple syllogism will serve, so; if it will not, what remedy? As there is no true cuckold but calamity, so beauty 's a flower. The lady bade take away the fool; therefore, I say again, take her away.

OLI. Sir, I bade them take away you.

CLO. Misprision [7] in the highest degree! Lady, *"cucullus non facit monachum";* [8] that 's as much to say as I wear not motley in my brain. Good madonna, give me leave to prove you a fool.

OLI. Can you do it?

CLO. Dexteriously, good madonna.

OLI. Make your proof.

CLO. I must catechise you for it, madonna. Good my mouse [9] of virtue, answer me.

OLI. Well, sir, for want of other idleness, I 'll bide your proof.

CLO. Good madonna, why mourn'st thou?

OLI. Good fool, for my brother's death.

CLO. I think his soul is in hell, madonna.

OLI. I know his soul is in heaven, fool.

CLO. The more fool, madonna, to mourn for your brother's soul being in heaven. Take away the fool, gentlemen.

OLI. What think you of this fool, Malvolio? Doth he not mend?

MALVOLIO. Yes, and shall do till the pangs of death shake him. Infirmity, that decays the wise, doth ever make the better fool.

CLO. God send you, sir, a speedy infirmity, for the better increasing your folly! Sir Toby will be sworn that I am no fox, but he will not pass his word for twopence that you are no fool.

OLI. How say you to that, Malvolio?

MAL. I marvel your ladyship takes delight in such a barren rascal. I saw him put down the other day with an ordinary fool that has no more brain than a stone. Look you now, he 's out of his guard already. Unless you laugh and minister occasion to him, he is gagged. I protest, I take these wise men, that crow so at these set kind of fools, no better than the fools' zanies. [10]

OLI. O, you are sick of self-love, Malvolio, and taste with a distempered appetite. To be generous, guiltless, and of free disposition, is to take those things for birdbolts that you deem cannon-bullets. There is no slander in an allowed [11] fool, though he do nothing but rail; nor no railing in a known discreet man though he do nothing but reprove.

CLO. Now Mercury endue thee with leasing, [12] for thou speak'st well of fools!

[Re-enter MARIA.]

MARIA. Madam, there is at the gate a young gentleman much desires to speak with you.

OLI. From the Count Orsino, is it?

MAR. I know not, madam. 'T is a fair young man, and well attended.

OLI. Who of my people hold him in delay?

MAR. Sir Toby, madam, your kinsman.

OLI. Fetch him off, I pray you. He speaks nothing but madman; fie on him! [*Exit* MARIA.] Go you, Malvolio; if it be a suit from the Count, I am sick, or not at home,—what you will, to dismiss it. [*Exit* MALVOLIO.] Now you see, sir, how your fooling grows old, and people dislike it.

CLO. Thou hast spoke for us, madonna, as if thy eldest son should be a fool; whose skull Jove cram with brains! for—here he comes—

[Enter SIR TOBY.]

one of thy kin has a most weak *pia mater.* [13]

[6] Mender of old clothes.
[7] Misapprehension.
[8] "A cowl does not make a monk": referring to his own fool's motley.
[9] A common term of playful affection.

[10] Stooges.
[11] Professional.
[12] Lying.
[13] Skull-padding. *Pia mater* is the membrane covering the brain.

OLI. By mine honour, half drunk. What is he at the gate, cousin?

SIR TOBY. A gentleman.

OLI. A gentleman! What gentleman?

SIR TO. 'T is a gentleman here—a plague o' these pickle-herring! [14] How now, sot!

CLO. Good Sir Toby!

OLI. Cousin, cousin,[15] how have you come so early by this lethargy?

SIR TO. Lechery! I defy lechery. There 's one at the gate.

OLI. Ay, marry, what is he?

SIR TO. Let him be the devil, an he will, I care not; give me faith, say I. Well, it 's all one. [Exit SIR TOBY.]

OLI. What 's a drunken man like, fool?

CLO. Like a drowned man, a fool, and a madman. One draught above heat makes him a fool, the second mads him, and a third drowns him.

OLI. Go thou and seek the crowner [16] and let him sit o' my coz, for he 's in the third degree of drink, he 's drowned. Go, look after him.

CLO. He is but mad yet, madonna; and the fool shall look to the madman. [Exit CLOWN.]

[Re-enter MALVOLIO.]

MALVOLIO. Madam, yond young fellow swears he will speak with you. I told him you were sick: he takes on him to understand so much, and therefore comes to speak with you. I told him you were asleep: he seems to have a fore-knowledge of that too, and therefore comes to speak with you. What is to be said to him, lady? He 's fortified against any denial.

OLI. Tell him he shall not speak with me.

MAL. Has been told so; and he says, he 'll stand at your door like a sheriff's post, and be the supporter to a bench, but he 'll speak with you.

OLI. What kind o' man is he?

MAL. Why, of mankind.

OLI. What manner of man?

MAL. Of very ill manner. He 'll speak with you, will you or no.

OLI. Of what personage and years is he?

MAL. Not yet old enough for a man, nor young enough for a boy; as a squash [17] is before 't is a peascod, or a codling when 't is almost an apple: 't is with him in standing water,[18] between boy and man. He is very well-favoured and he speaks very shrewishly: one would think his mother's milk were scarce out of him.

OLI. Let him approach. Call in my gentlewoman.

MAL. Gentlewoman, my lady calls. [Exit MALVOLIO.]

[Re-enter MARIA.]

OLI. Give me my veil. Come, throw it o'er my face.
We 'll once more hear Orsino's embassy.

[Enter VIOLA.]

VIOLA. The honourable lady of the house, which is she?

OLI. Speak to me; I shall answer for her. Your will?

VIO. Most radiant, exquisite, and unmatchable beauty,—I pray you, tell me if this be the lady of the house, for I never saw her. I would be loath to cast away my speech, for besides that it is excellently well penned, I have taken great pains to con it.[19] Good beauties, let me sustain no scorn. I am very comptible, even to the least sinister usage.[20]

OLI. Whence came you, sir?

VIO. I can say little more than I have studied, and that question 's out of my part. Good gentle one, give me modest assurance if you be the lady of the house, that I may proceed in my speech.

OLI. Are you a comedian?

VIO. No, my profound heart; and yet, by the very fangs of malice I swear, I am not that I play. Are you the lady of the house?

[14] An apology prompted by the hiccough which has just interrupted him.
[15] Kinsman.
[16] Coroner.
[17] Unripe peapod.
[18] Turn of the tide.
[19] Memorize it.
[20] Sensitive, even to the least snub.

OLI. If I do not usurp myself, I am.

VIO. Most certain, if you are she, you do usurp yourself; for what is yours to bestow is not yours to reserve. But this is from my commission. I will on with my speech in your praise, and then show you the heart of my message.

OLI. Come to what is important in 't. I forgive you the praise.

VIO. Alas, I took great pains to study it, and 't is poetical.

OLI. It is the more like to be feigned. I pray you, keep it in. I heard you were saucy at my gates, and allowed your approach rather to wonder at you than to hear you. If you be not mad, be gone: if you have reason, be brief: 't is not that time of moon with me to make one in so skipping a dialogue.

MARIA. Will you hoist sail, sir? Here lies your way.

VIO. No, good swabber, I am to hull here a little longer. Some mollification for your giant, sweet lady. Tell me your mind. I am a messenger.

OLI. Sure, you have some hideous matter to deliver, when the courtesy of it is so fearful. Speak your office.

VIO. It alone concerns your ear. I bring no overture of war, no taxation [21] of homage: I hold the olive in my hand: my words are as full of peace as matter.

OLI. Yet you began rudely. What are you? What would you?

VIO. The rudeness that hath appeared in me have I learned from my entertainment. What I am, and what I would, are as secret as maidenhead; to your ears, divinity; to any other's, profanation.

OLI. Give us the place alone; we will hear this divinity. [22] [Exit MARIA.] Now, sir, what is your text?

VIO. Most sweet lady,—

OLI. A comfortable doctrine, and much may be said of it. Where lies your text?

VIO. In Orsino's bosom.

OLI. In his bosom! In what chapter of his bosom?

VIO. To answer by the method, in the first of his heart.

OLI. O, I have read it; it is heresy. Have you no more to say?

VIO. Good madam, let me see your face.

OLI. Have you any commission from your lord to negotiate with my face? You are now out of your text, but we will draw the curtain and show you the picture. Look you, sir, such a one I was this present. Is 't not well done?   [Unveiling.]

VIO. Excellently done, if God did all.

OLI. 'T is in grain, [23] sir; 't will endure wind and weather.

VIO. 'T is beauty truly blent, whose red and white
Nature's own sweet and cunning hand laid on.
Lady, you are the cruell'st she alive,
If you will lead these graces to the grave
And leave the world no copy.

OLI. O, sir, I will not be so hard-hearted; I will give out divers schedules of my beauty. It shall be inventoried, and every particle and utensil labelled to my will: [24] as, item, two lips, indifferent red; item, two grey eyes, with lids to them; item, one neck, one chin, and so forth. Were you sent hither to praise [25] me?

VIO. I see you what you are, you are too proud;
But, if you were the devil, you are fair.
My lord and master loves you. O, such love
Could be but recompens'd, though you were crown'd
The nonpareil of beauty!

OLI.   How does he love me?

VIO. With adorations, with fertile tears,
With groans that thunder love, with sighs of fire.

OLI. Your lord does know my mind; I cannot love him.
Yet I suppose him virtuous, know him noble;
Of great estate, of fresh and stainless youth,

21 Demand.
22 Theological discussion: which dictates the form of the following metaphors.
23 A fast color.
24 Itemized in my will.
25 Appraise.

In voices well divulg'd,[26] free, learn'd, and
    valiant,
And in dimension and the shape of nature
A gracious person: but yet I cannot love
    him.
He might have took his answer long ago.

    VIO. If I did love you in my master's
    flame,
With such a suff'ring, such a deadly life,
In your denial I would find no sense.
I would not understand it.

    OLI.   Why, what would you?

    VIO. Make me a willow cabin at your
    gate,
And call upon my soul within the house;
Write loyal cantons [27] of contemned love
And sing them loud even in the dead of
    night;
Halloo your name to the reverberate hills
And make the babbling gossip of the air
Cry out "Olivia!" O, you should not rest
Between the elements of air and earth,
But you should pity me!

    OLI.   You might do much.
What is your parentage?

    VIO. Above my fortunes, yet my state
    is well.
I am a gentleman.

    OLI.   Get you to your lord.
I cannot love him. Let him send no more,—
Unless, perchance, you come to me again
To tell me how he takes it. Fare you well!
I thank you for your pains: spend this for
    me.

    VIO. I am no fee'd post, lady. Keep
    your purse.
My master, not myself, lacks recompense.
Love make his heart of flint that you shall
    love;
And let your fervour, like my master's, be

Plac'd in contempt! Farewell, fair cruelty.
                      [*Exit* VIOLA.]

    OLI. "What is your parentage?"
"Above my fortunes, yet my state is well.
I am a gentleman." I 'll be sworn thou art.
Thy tongue, thy face, thy limbs, actions,
    and spirit
Do give thee five-fold blazon.[28] Not too
    fast! Soft, soft!
Unless the master were the man. How now!
Even so quickly may one catch the plague?
Methinks I feel this youth's perfections
With an invisible and subtle stealth
To creep in at mine eyes. Well, let it be.
What ho, Malvolio!

           [*Re-enter* MALVOLIO.]

    MALVOLIO.   Here, madam, at your
    service.

    OLI. Run after that same peevish mes-
    senger,
The County's man. He left this ring behind
    him,
Would I or not. Tell him I 'll none of it.
Desire him not to flatter with his lord,
Nor hold him up with hopes. I 'm not for
    him.
If that the youth will come this way to-
    morrow,
I 'll give him reasons for 't. Hie thee,
    Malvolio.

    MAL. Madam, I will.
                  [*Exit* MALVOLIO.]

    OLI. I do I know not what, and fear
    to find
Mine eye too great a flatterer for my mind.
Fate, show thy force; ourselves we do not
    owe; [29]
What is decreed must be, and be this so.
                         [*Exit.*]

ACT II

Scene I
The sea-coast.
[*Enter* ANTONIO *and* SEBASTIAN.]

ANTONIO. Will you stay no longer? Nor
will you not that I go with you?

SEBASTIAN. By your patience, no. My
stars shine darkly over me. The malignancy
of my fate might perhaps distemper yours,
therefore I shall crave of you your leave
that I may bear my evils alone. It were a

---

26 Well spoken of.
27 Songs.

28 The coat of arms denoting a gentleman.
29 Own.

bad recompense for your love, to lay any of them on you.

ANT. Let me yet know of you whither you are bound.

SEB. No, sooth, sir: my determinate voyage is mere extravagancy.[1] But I perceive in you so excellent a touch of modesty, that you will not extort from me what I am willing to keep in; therefore it charges me in manners the rather to express myself. You must know of me then, Antonio, my name is Sebastian, which I called Roderigo. My father was that Sebastian of Messaline, whom I know you have heard of. He left behind him myself and a sister, both born in an hour. If the heavens had been pleased, would we had so ended! But you, sir, altered that; for some hour before you took me from the breach [2] of the sea was my sister drowned.

ANT. Alas the day!

SEB. A lady, sir, though it was said she much resembled me, was yet of many accounted beautiful; but, though I could not with such estimable wonder overfar believe that, yet thus far I will boldly publish her: she bore a mind that envy could not but call fair. She is drowned already, sir, with salt water, though I seem to drown her remembrance again with more.

ANT. Pardon me, sir, your bad entertainment.

SEB. O good Antonio, forgive me your trouble.

ANT. If you will not murder me for my love, let me be your servant.

SEB. If you will not undo what you have done, that is, kill him whom you have recovered, desire it not. Fare ye well at once. My bosom is full of kindness, and I am yet so near the manners of my mother, that upon the least occasion more mine eyes will tell tales of me.[3] I am bound to the Count Orsino's court. Farewell.

[*Exit* SEBASTIAN.]

ANT. The gentleness of all the gods go with thee!
I have many enemies in Orsino's court,

Else would I very shortly see thee there.
But, come what may, I do adore thee so,
That danger shall seem sport, and I will go.

[*Exit.*]

Scene II
A street.

[*Enter* VIOLA *and* MALVOLIO, *at several doors.*]

MALVOLIO. Were you not e'en now with the Countess Olivia?

VIOLA. Even now, sir. On a moderate pace I have since arrived but hither.

MAL. She returns this ring to you, sir: you might have saved me my pains, to have taken it away yourself. She adds, moreover, that you should put your lord into a desperate assurance [1] she will none of him; and one thing more, that you be never so hardy to come again in his affairs, unless it be to report your lord's taking of this. Receive it so.

VIO. She took the ring of me. I 'll none of it.

MAL. Come, sir, you peevishly threw it to her; and her will is, it should be so returned. If it be worth stooping for, there it lies in your eye; if not, be it his that finds it.

[*Exit* MALVOLIO.]

VIO. I left no ring with her: what means this lady?
Fortune forbid my outside have not charm'd her!
She made good view of me; indeed so much,
That sure methought her eyes had lost her tongue,
For she did speak in starts distractedly.
She loves me, sure: the cunning of her passion
Invites me in this churlish messenger.
None of my lord's ring! Why, he sent her none.
I am the man: if it be so, as 't is,
Poor lady, she were better love a dream.
Disguise, I see thou art a wickedness

---

[1] Sheer aimless wandering.
[2] Breakers.

[3] *I.e.,* betray his tender feelings by weeping.
[1] Certainty beyond hope.

Wherein the pregnant [2] enemy does much.
How easy is it for the proper-false [3]
In women's waxen hearts to set their
  forms!
Alas, our frailty is the cause, not we!
For such as we are made of, such we be.
How will this fadge? [4] My master loves her
  dearly;
And I, poor monster, fond [5] as much on
  him;
And she, mistaken, seems to dote on me.
What will become of this? As I am man,
My state is desperate for my master's love;
As I am woman,—now alas the day!—
What thriftless sighs shall poor Olivia
  breathe!
O time! thou must untangle this, not I.
It is too hard a knot for me t' untie!

                               [*Exit.*]

Scene III
Olivia's house.

[*Enter* SIR TOBY *and* SIR ANDREW.]

SIR TOBY.   Approach, Sir Andrew. Not
ꝺ be a-bed after midnight is to be up betimes; and *"diliculo surgere,"* [1] thou
know'st,—

SIR ANDREW.   Nay, by my troth, I know
not; but I know, to be up late is to be up
late.

SIR TO.   A false conclusion: I hate it as
an unfilled can. To be up after midnight
and to go to bed then, is early; so that to go
to bed after midnight is to go to bed betimes. Does not our lives consist of the
four elements?

SIR AND.   Faith, so they say; but I think
it rather consists of eating and drinking.

SIR TO.   Thou 'rt a scholar; let us therefore eat and drink. Marian, I say! a stoup
of wine!

[*Enter* CLOWN.]

SIR AND.   Here comes the fool, i' faith.

CLOWN.   How now, my hearts! Did you
never see the picture of "we three"? [2]

SIR TO.   Welcome, ass. Now let 's have
a catch.[3]

SIR AND.   By my troth, the fool has an
excellent breast.[4] I had rather than forty
shillings I had such a leg, and so sweet a
breath to sing, as the fool has. In sooth,
thou wast in very gracious fooling last
night, when thou spok'st of Pigrogromitus,
of the Vapians passing the equinoctial of
Queubus.[5] 'T was very good, i' faith. I sent
thee sixpence for thy leman.[6] Hadst it?

CLO.   I did impeticos thy gratillity; [7] for
Malvolio's nose is no whipstock. My lady
has a white hand, and the Mermidons are
no bottle-ale houses.

SIR AND.   Excellent! Why, this is the best
fooling, when all is done. Now, a song.

SIR TO.   Come on; there is sixpence for
you. Let 's have a song.

SIR AND.   There 's a testril [8] of me too.
If one knight give a—

CLO.   Would you have a love-song or a
song of good life?

SIR TO.   A love-song, a love-song.

SIR AND.   Ay, ay. I care not for good
life.

CLO.   [*Sings.*]

O mistress mine, where are you roaming?
O, stay and hear, your true love 's coming,
  That can sing both high and low.
Trip no further, pretty sweeting;
Journeys end in lovers meeting,
  Every wise man's son doth know.

SIR AND.   Excellent good, i' faith.

SIR TO.   Good, good.

CLO.   [*Sings.*]

What is love? 'T is not hereafter.
Present mirth hath present laughter;
  What 's to come is still unsure.
In delay there lies no plenty;
Then come kiss me, sweet and twenty,
  Youth 's a stuff will not endure.

---

[2] Designing.   [3] Prepossessing deceivers.
[4] Fit together.   [5] Dote.
[1] A schoolbook motto: "To arise early is most
healthful."
[2] A picture of two asses which, added to the
viewer, made three.

[3] A song like a round.
[4] Voice.
[5] More of the Clown's mock learning.
[6] Sweetheart.
[7] Pocket your gratuity.
[8] Sixpence.

SIR AND. A mellifluous voice, as I am true knight.

SIR TO. A contagious breath.

SIR AND. Very sweet and contagious, i' faith.

SIR TO. To hear by the nose, it is dulcet in contagion. But shall we make the welkin dance indeed? Shall we rouse the night-owl in a catch that will draw three souls out of one weaver? Shall we do that?

SIR AND. An you love me, let 's do 't. I am dog at a catch.

CLO. By 'r lady, sir, and some dogs will catch well.

SIR AND. Most certain. Let our catch be, "Thou knave."

CLO. "Hold thy peace, thou knave," knight? I shall be constrained in 't to call thee knave, knight.

SIR AND. 'T is not the first time I have constrained one to call me knave. Begin, fool. It begins, "Hold thy peace."

CLO. I shall never begin if I hold my peace.

SIR AND. Good, i' faith. Come, begin.
                                    [Catch sung.]

[Enter MARIA.]

MARIA. What a caterwauling do you keep here! If my lady have not called up her steward Malvolio and bid him turn you out of doors, never trust me.

SIR TO. My lady 's a Cataian,[9] we are politicians, Malvolio 's a Peg-a-Ramsey,[10] and "Three merry men be we." Am not I consanguineous? Am I not of her blood? Tilly-vally. Lady! [Sings.] "There dwelt a man in Babylon, lady, lady!"

CLO. Beshrew me, the knight's in admirable fooling.

SIR AND. Ay, he does well enough if he be disposed, and so do I too. He does it with a better grace, but I do it more natural.

SIR TO. [Sings.] "O, the twelfth day of December,"—

MAR. For the love o' God, peace!

[Enter MALVOLIO.]

MALVOLIO. My masters, are you mad, or what are you? Have you no wit, manners, nor honesty, but to gabble like tinkers at this time of night? Do ye make an ale-house of my lady's house, that ye squeak out your coziers'[11] catches without any mitigation or remorse of voice? Is there no respect of place, persons, nor time in you?

SIR TO. We did keep time, sir, in our catches. Sneck up![12]

MAL. Sir Toby, I must be round[13] with you. My lady bade me tell you that, though she harbours you as her kinsman, she 's nothing allied to your disorders. If you can separate yourself and your misdemeanours, you are welcome to the house; if not, an it would please you to take leave of her, she is very willing to bid you farewell.

SIR TO. "Farewell, dear heart, since I must needs be gone."

MAR. Nay, good Sir Toby.

CLO. "His eyes do show his days are almost done."

MAL. Is 't even so?

SIR TO. "But I will never die."

CLO. Sir Toby, there you lie.

MAL. This is much credit to you.

SIR TO. "Shall I bid him go?"

CLO. "What an if you do?"

SIR TO. "Shall I bid him go, and spare not?"

CLO. "O no, no, no, no, you dare not."

SIR TO. Out o' tune, sir! Ye lie. Art any more than a steward? Dost thou think, because thou art virtuous, there shall be no more cakes and ale?

CLO. Yes, by Saint Anne, and ginger[14] shall be hot i' the mouth too.

SIR TO. Thou 'rt i' the right. Go, sir, rub your chain with crumbs.[15] A stoup of wine, Maria!

MAL. Mistress Mary, if you prized my lady's favour at anything more than contempt, you would not give means for this uncivil rule. She shall know of it, by this hand.   [Exit MALVOLIO.]

---

[9] Chinaman, meaning rogue.
[10] Sportive heroine of an old song.
[11] Cobblers'.
[12] Go be hanged!

[13] Blunt.
[14] Used to spice ale.
[15] Polish your chain, i.e., stay in your place. A gold chain was a steward's badge of office.

MAR. Go shake your ears.

SIR AND. 'T were as good a deed as to drink when a man 's a-hungry, to challenge him the field, and then to break promise with him and make a fool of him.

SIR TO. Do 't, knight. I 'll write thee a challenge, or I 'll deliver thy indignation to him by word of mouth.

MAR. Sweet Sir Toby, be patient for to-night. Since the youth of the Count's was to-day with my lady, she is much out of quiet. For Monsieur Malvolio, let me alone with him. If I do not gull him into a nay-word,[16] and make him a common recreation, do not think I have wit enough to lie straight in my bed. I know I can do it.

SIR TO. Possess us, possess us. Tell us something of him.

MAR. Marry, sir, sometimes he is a kind of puritan.

SIR AND. O, if I thought that, I 'd beat him like a dog!

SIR TO. What, for being a puritan? Thy exquisite reason, dear knight?

SIR AND. I have no exquisite reason for 't, but I have reason good enough.

MAR. The devil a puritan that he is, or anything constantly, but a time-pleaser; an affectioned ass, that cons state without book [17] and utters it by great swarths; the best persuaded of himself, so crammed, as he thinks, with excellencies, that it is his grounds of faith that all that look on him love him; and on that vice in him will my revenge find notable cause to work.

SIR TO. What wilt thou do?

MAR. I will drop in his way some obscure epistles of love; wherein, by the colour of his beard, the shape of his leg, the manner of his gait, the expressure of his eye, forehead, and complexion, he shall find himself most feelingly personated. I can write very like my lady your niece. On a forgotten matter we can hardly make distinction of our hands.

SIR TO. Excellent! I smell a device.

SIR AND. I have 't in my nose too.

SIR TO. He shall think by the letters that thou wilt drop that they come from my niece, and that she 's in love with him.

MAR. My purpose is, indeed, a horse of that colour.

SIR AND. And your horse now would make him an ass.

MAR. Ass, I doubt not.

SIR AND. O, 't will be admirable!

MAR. Sport royal, I warrant you. I know my physic will work with him. I will plant you two, and let the fool make a third, where he shall find the letter: observe his construction of it. For this night, to bed, and dream on the event. Farewell.

[*Exit* MARIA.]

SIR TO. Good night, Penthesilea.[18]

SIR AND. Before me, she 's a good wench.

SIR TO. She 's a beagle, true-bred, and one that adores me. What o' that?

SIR AND. I was adored once too.

SIR TO. Let 's to bed, knight. Thou hadst need send for more money.

SIR AND. If I cannot recover your niece, I am a foul way out.

SIR TO. Send for money, knight. If thou hast her not i' th' end, call me cut.[19]

SIR AND. If I do not, never trust me, take it how you will.

SIR TO. Come, come, I 'll go burn some sack; [20] 't is too late to go to bed now. Come, knight; come, knight. [*Exeunt.*]

Scene IV
The Duke's palace.

[*Enter* DUKE, VIOLA, CURIO, *and others.*]

DUKE. Give me some music. Now,—
   good morrow, friends,—
Now, good Cesario, but that piece of song,
That old and antic [1] song we heard last
   night.
Methought it did relieve my passion much,
More than light airs and recollected terms
Of these most brisk and giddy-paced times.
Come, but one verse.

CURIO. He is not here, so please your lordship, that should sing it.

---

[16] Trick him until his name is a byword.
[17] An affected ass, that memorizes courtly behavior.

[18] Queen of the belligerent Amazons.
[19] A horse: a common expression of contempt.
[20] Heat some wine.   [1] Quaint.

DUKE. Who was it?

CUR. Feste, the jester, my lord; a fool that the lady Olivia's father took much delight in. He is about the house.

DUKE. Seek him out, and play the tune the while. [*Exit* CURIO. *Music plays.*]
Come hither, boy. If ever thou shalt love,
In the sweet pangs of it remember me;
For such as I am all true lovers are,
Unstaid and skittish in all motions else,
Save in the constant image of the creature
That is belov'd. How dost thou like this tune?

VIOLA. It gives a very echo to the seat
Where Love is thron'd.

DUKE.   Thou dost speak masterly.
My life upon 't, young though thou art, thine eye
Hath stay'd upon some favour [2] that it loves.
Hath it not, boy?

VIO.   A little, by your favour.

DUKE. What kind of woman is 't?

VIO.   Of your complexion.

DUKE. She is not worth thee, then. What years, i' faith?

VIO. About your years, my lord.

DUKE. Too old, by heaven. Let still the woman take
An elder than herself; so wears she to him,
So sways she level in her husband's heart.
For, boy, however we do praise ourselves,
Our fancies are more giddy and unfirm,
More longing, wavering, sooner lost and worn,
Than women's are.

VIO.   I think it well, my lord.

DUKE. Then let they love be younger than thyself,
Or thy affection cannot hold the bent.
For women are as roses, whose fair flower
Being once display'd, doth fall that very hour.

VIO. And so they are; alas, that they are so!
To die, even when they to perfection grow!

[*Re-enter* CURIO *and* CLOWN.]

DUKE. O, fellow, come, the song we had last night.
Mark it, Cesario, it is old and plain.
The spinsters and the knitters in the sun
And the free maids that weave their thread with bones [3]
Do use to chant it. It is silly sooth,[4]
And dallies with the innocence of love,
Like the old age.[5]

CLOWN. Are you ready, sir?

DUKE. Ay; prithee, sing.   [*Music.*]

Song.

[CLOWN.]

Come away, come away, death,
    And in sad cypress let me be laid.
Fly away, fly away, breath;
    I am slain by a fair cruel maid.
My shroud of white, stuck all with yew,
        O, prepare it!
My part of death, no one so true
        Did share it.

Not a flower, not a flower sweet,
    On my black coffin let there be strown.
Not a friend, not a friend greet
    My poor corpse, where my bones shall be thrown.
A thousand thousand sighs to save,
        Lay me, O, where
Sad true lover never find my grave,
        To weep there!

DUKE. There 's for thy pains.

CLO. No pains, sir; I take pleasure in singing, sir.

DUKE. I 'll pay thy pleasure then.

CLO. Truly, sir, and pleasure will be paid, one time or another.

DUKE. Give me now leave to leave thee.

CLO. Now, the melancholy god protect thee, and the tailor make thy doublet of changeable taffeta, for thy mind is a very opal. I would have men of such constancy put to sea, that their business might be everything and their intent everywhere; for that 's it that always make a good voyage of nothing. Farewell.   [*Exit* CLOWN.]

DUKE. Let all the rest give place.

[CURIO *and* ATTENDANTS *retire.*]

---

[2] Lingered on some face. Note the double significance of Viola's reply.

[3] Bone bobbins.
[4] Simple truth.   [5] Good old times.

Once more, Cesario,
Get thee to yond same sovereign cruelty.
Tell her, my love, more noble than the
  world,
Prizes not quantity of dirty lands.
The parts that fortune hath bestow'd upon
  her,
Tell her, I hold as giddily as fortune; [6]
But 't is that miracle and queen of gems
That nature pranks [7] her in attracts my
  soul.
  VIO.   But if she cannot love you, sir?
  DUKE.   I cannot be so answer'd.
  VIO.   Sooth, but you must.
Say that some lady, as perhaps there is,
Hath for your love as great a pang of heart
As you have for Olivia. You cannot love
  her.
You tell her so. Must she not then be
  answer'd?
  DUKE.   There is no woman's sides
Can bide the beating of so strong a passion
As love doth give my heart; no woman's
  heart
So big, to hold so much: they lack reten-
  tion.
Alas, their love may be call'd appetite,
No motion of the liver, but the palate,
That suffer surfeit, cloyment, and revolt;
But mine is all as hungry as the sea,
And can digest as much. Make no compare
Between that love a woman can bear me
And that I owe Olivia.
  VIO.   Ay, but I know—
  DUKE.   What dost thou know?
  VIO.   Too well what love women to men
  may owe.
In faith, they are as true of heart as we.
My father had a daughter lov'd a man,
As it might be, perhaps, were I a woman,
I should your lordship.
  DUKE.   And what 's her history?
  VIO.   A blank, my lord. She never told
  her love,
But let concealment, like a worm i' the
  bud,
Feed on her damask cheek. She pin'd in
  thought,

And with a green and yellow melancholy
She sat, like Patience on a monument,
Smiling at grief. Was not this love indeed?
We men may say more, swear more; but
  indeed
Our shows are more than will, for still we
  prove
Much in our vows, but little in our love.
  DUKE.   But died thy sister of her love,
  my boy?
  VIO.   I am all the daughters of my
  father's house,
And all the brothers too;—and yet I know
  not.
Sir, shall I to this lady?
  DUKE.   Ay, that 's the theme.
To her in haste. Give her this jewel: say
My love can give no place, bide no denay.[8]
                              [Exeunt.]

Scene V
Olivia's garden.

[Enter SIR TOBY, SIR ANDREW, and FABIAN.]

SIR TOBY.   Come thy ways, Signior Fabian.
FABIAN.   Nay, I 'll come. If I lose a
scruple of this sport, let me be boiled to
death with melancholy.
SIR TO.   Wouldst thou not be glad to
have the niggardly rascally sheep-biter [1]
come by some notable shame?
FAB.   I would exult, man. You know, he
brought me out o' favour with my lady
about a bear-baiting here.
SIR TO.   To anger him we 'll have the
bear again, and we will fool him black and
blue. Shall we not, Sir Andrew?
SIR ANDREW.   An we do not, it is pity of
our lives.

[Enter MARIA.]

SIR TO.   Here comes the little villain.
How now, my metal of India! [2]
MARIA.   Get ye all three into the box-
tree; [3] Malvolio 's coming down this walk.
He has been yonder i' the sun practising
behaviour to his own shadow this half hour.

---

[6] I have as little regard for as fortune has.
[7] Adorns.   [8] Endure no denial.

[1] Cur.
[2] *I.e.*, girl of gold.   [3] Hedge.

Observe him, for the love of mockery, for I know this letter will make a contemplative idiot of him. Close, in the name of jesting! Lie thou there [*throws down a letter*], for here comes the trout that must be caught with tickling.

[*Exit* MARIA.]

[*Enter* MALVOLIO.]

MALVOLIO. 'T is but fortune. All is fortune. Maria once told me she did affect [4] me; and I have heard herself come thus near, that, should she fancy, it should be one of my complexion. Besides, she uses me with a more exalted respect than any one else that follows her. What should I think on 't?

SIR TO. Here 's an overweening rogue!

FAB. O, peace! Contemplation makes a rare turkey-cock of him. How he jets [5] under his advanced plumes!

SIR AND. 'S light, I could so beat the rogue!

FAB. Peace, I say.

MAL. To be Count Malvolio!

SIR TO. Ah, rogue!

SIR AND. Pistol him, pistol him.

FAB. Peace, peace!

MAL. There is example for 't. The lady of the Strachy married the yeoman of the wardrobe.

SIR AND. Fie on him, Jezebel!

FAB. O, peace! now he 's deeply in. Look how imagination blows him.

MAL. Having been three months married to her, sitting in my state,—

SIR TO. O, for a stone-bow, to hit him in the eye!

MAL. Calling my officers about me, in my branched [6] velvet gown, having come from a day-bed, where I have left Olivia sleeping,—

SIR TO. Fire and brimstone!

FAB. O, peace, peace!

MAL. And then to have the humour of state; [7] and after a demure travel of regard, telling them I know my place as I would

they should do theirs, to ask for my kinsman Toby,—

SIR TO. Bolts and shackles!

FAB. O peace, peace, peace! Now, now.

MAL. Seven of my people, with an obedient start, make out for him. I frown the while, and perchance wind up my watch, or play with my—some rich jewel. [8] Toby approaches, curtsies there to me,—

SIR TO. Shall this fellow live?

FAB. Though our silence be drawn from us with cars, yet peace.

MAL. I extend my hand to him thus, quenching my familiar smile with an austere regard of control,—

SIR TO. And does not Toby take you a blow o' the lips then?

MAL. Saying, "Cousin Toby, my fortunes, having cast me on your niece, give me this prerogative of speech,"—

SIR TO. What, what?

MAL. "You must amend your drunkenness."

SIR TO. Out, scab!

FAB. Nay, patience, or we break the sinews of our plot.

MAL. "Besides, you waste the treasure of your time with a foolish knight,"—

SIR AND. That 's me, I warrant you.

MAL. "One Sir Andrew,"—

SIR AND. I knew 't was I; for many do call me fool.

MAL. What employment have we here?
[*Taking up the letter.*]

FAB. Now is the woodcock near the gin. [9]

SIR TO. O, peace, and the spirit of humours intimate reading aloud to him!

MAL. By my life, this is my lady's hand. These be her very C's, her U's, and her T's; and thus makes she her great P's. It is, in contempt of question, [10] her hand.

SIR AND. Her C's, her U's, and her T's: why that?

MAL. [*Reads.*] "To the unknown beloved, this, and my good wishes":—her very phrases! By your leave, wax. Soft! And

---

[4] Love. He, of course, is referring to Olivia.
[5] Struts.
[6] Embroidered with branches.
[7] Air of authority.

[8] He is about to say "my steward's chain," but catches himself in time.
[9] Snare.
[10] Beyond a doubt.

the impressure her Lucrece, with which she uses to seal: 't is my lady. To whom should this be?

FAB.   This wins him, liver and all.

MAL.   [*Reads.*]

> "Jove knows I love;
> But who?
> Lips, do not move;
> No man must know."

"No man must know." What follows? The numbers [11] altered! "No man must know!" If this should be thee, Malvolio?

SIR TO.   Marry, hang thee, brock! [12]

MAL.   [*Reads.*]

> "I may command where I adore;
> But silence, like a Lucrece knife,
> With bloodless stroke my heart doth gore.
> M, O, A, I, doth sway my life."

FAB.   A fustian riddle! [13]

SIR TO.   Excellent wench, say I.

MAL.   "M, O, A, I, doth sway my life." Nay, but first, let me see, let me see, let me see.

FAB.   What dish o' poison has she dressed him!

SIR TO.   And with what wing the staniel checks at it! [14]

MAL.   "I may command where I adore." Why, she may command me: I serve her: she is my lady. Why, this is evident to any formal capacity, there is no obstruction in this. And the end,—what should that alphabetical position portend? If I could make that resemble something in me!— Softly! M, O, A, I,—

SIR TO.   O, ay, make up that. He is now at a cold scent.

FAB.   Sowter will cry upon 't for all this, though it be as rank as a fox.[15]

MAL.   M,—Malvolio; M,—why, that begins my name.

FAB.   Did not I say he would work it out? The cur is excellent at faults.

MAL.   M,—but then there is no consonancy in the sequel; that suffers under probation: [16] A should follow, but O does.

FAB.   And O shall end, I hope.

SIR TO.   Ay, or I 'll cudgel him, and make him cry O!

MAL.   And then I comes behind.

FAB.   Ay, an you had any eye behind you, you might see more detraction at your heels than fortunes before you.

MAL.   M, O, A, I; this simulation [17] is not as the former; and yet, to crush this a little, it would bow to me, for every one of these letters are in my name. Soft! here follows prose.

[*Reads.*] "If this fall into thy hand, revolve.[18] In my stars [19] I am above thee, but be not afraid of greatness: some are born great, some achieves greatness, and some have greatness thrust upon 'em. Thy Fates open their hands, let thy blood and spirit embrace them; and, to inure thyself to what thou art like to be, cast thy humble slough [20] and appear fresh. Be opposite with a kinsman, surly with servants; let thy tongue tang arguments of state; put thyself into the trick of singularity: she thus advises thee that sighs for thee. Remember who commended thy yellow stockings, and wished to see thee ever cross-gartered.[21] I say, remember. Go to, thou art made, if thou desir'st to be so; if not, let me see thee a steward still, the fellow of servants, and not worthy to touch Fortune's fingers. Farewell. She that would alter services [22] with thee,

THE FORTUNATE—UNHAPPY."

Daylight and champian [23] discovers not more: this is open. I will be proud, I will read politic authors, I will baffle [24] Sir Toby, I will wash off gross acquaintance, I will be point-device [25] the very man. I do not now fool myself, to let imagination jade [26] me; for every reason excites to this, that my lady loves me. She did commend my yellow stockings of late, she did praise my leg being cross-gartered; and in this she

---

[11] Meter.   [12] Badger, *i.e.*, stinker!
[13] A shoddy puzzle, referring to the obvious acrostic on Malvolio's name.
[14] The untrained hawk is diverted by it.
[15] The stupid hound will bay even though the false scent is unmistakable.
[16] Test.   [17] Disguised meaning.
[18] Consider.   [19] Destiny.
[20] Skin, *i.e.*, like a snake.

[21] In the color symbolism of the time, the yellow stockings would signify a languishing lover. Cross-garters, *i.e.*, garters crossed so as to come both above and below the knee, at the time of the play were going out of fashion and were worn chiefly by the older generation and rustics.
[22] Exchange stations.
[23] Open country.   [24] Treat contemptuously.
[25] To a nicety.   [26] Trick.

manifests herself to my love, and with a kind of injunction drives me to these habits of her liking. I thank my stars I am happy, I will be strange, stout, in yellow stockings, and cross-gartered, even with the swiftness of putting on. Jove and my stars be praised! Here is yet a postscript.

[*Reads.*] "Thou canst not choose but know who I am. If thou entertain'st my love, let it appear in thy smiling. Thy smiles become thee well; therefore in my presence still smile, dear my sweet, I prithee."

Jove, I thank thee. I will smile; I will do everything that thou wilt have me.

[Exit MALVOLIO.]

FAB. I will not give my part of this sport for a pension of thousands to be paid from the Sophy.[27]

SIR TO. I could marry this wench for this device—

SIR AND. So could I too.

SIR TO. And ask no other dowry with her but such another jest.

[Re-enter MARIA.]

SIR AND. Nor I neither.

FAB. Here comes my noble gull-catcher.

SIR TO. Wilt thou set thy foot o' my neck?

SIR AND. Or o' mine either?

SIR TO. Shall I play my freedom at tray-trip,[28] and become thy bond-slave?

SIR AND. I' faith, or I either?

SIR TO. Why, thou hast put him in such a dream, that when the image of it leaves him he must run mad.

MARIA. Nay, but say true: does it work upon him?

SIR TO. Like aqua-vitæ [29] with a mid-wife.

MAR. If you will then see the fruits of the sport, mark his first approach before my lady. He will come to her in yellow stockings, and 't is a colour she abhors, and cross-gartered, a fashion she detests; and he will smile upon her, which will now be so unsuitable to her disposition, being addicted to a melancholy as she is, that it cannot but turn him into a notable contempt. If you will see it, follow me.

SIR TO. To the gates of Tartar,[30] thou most excellent devil of wit!

SIR AND. I 'll make one too. [*Exeunt.*]

ACT III

Scene I

Olivia's garden.

[*Enter* VIOLA *and* CLOWN *with a tabor.*]

VIOLA. Save thee, friend, and thy music! Dost thou live by thy tabor?

CLOWN. No, sir, I live by the church.

VIO. Art thou a churchman?

CLO. No such matter, sir; I do live by the church; for I do live at my house, and my house doth stand by the church.

VIO. So thou mayst say, the king lies by a beggar, if a beggar dwells near him; or, the church stands by thy tabor, if thy tabor stand by the church.

CLO. You have said, sir. To see this age! A sentence is but a cheveril [1] glove to a good wit. How quickly the wrong side may be turned outward!

VIO. Nay, that 's certain. They that dally nicely with words may quickly make them wanton.

CLO. I would, therefore, my sister had had no name, sir.

VIO. Why, man?

CLO. Why, sir, her name 's a word, and to dally with that word might make my sister wanton. But, indeed, words are very rascals since bonds disgraced them.

VIO. Thy reason, man?

CLO. Troth, sir, I can yield you none without words; and words are grown so false, I am loath to prove reason with them.

VIO. I warrant thou art a merry fellow and car'st for nothing.

CLO. Not so, sir, I do care for something; but in my conscience, sir, I do not care for you: if that be to care for nothing.

---

[27] Shah of Persia.　　[28] A dice game.　　[29] Brandy.　　[30] Tartarus: hell.　　[1] Kid.

sir, I would it would make you invisible.

VIO. Art not thou the Lady Olivia's fool?

CLO. No, indeed, sir; the Lady Olivia has no folly. She will keep no fool, sir, till she be married; and fools are as like husbands as pilchards are to herrings, the husband's the bigger. I am indeed not her fool, but her corrupter of words.

VIO. I saw thee late at the Count Orsino's.

CLO. Foolery, sir, does walk about the orb like the sun, it shines everywhere. I would be sorry, sir, but the fool should be as oft with your master as with my mistress. I think I saw your wisdom there.

VIO. Nay, an thou pass upon me,[2] I'll no more with thee. Hold, there's expenses for thee.

CLO. Now Jove, in his next commodity[3] of hair, send thee a beard!

VIO. By my troth, I'll tell thee, I am almost sick for one,—[aside] though I would not have it grow on my chin. Is thy lady within?

CLO. Would not a pair of these have bred, sir?

VIO. Yes, being kept together and put to use.[4]

CLO. I would play Lord Pandarus of Phrygia,[5] sir, to bring a Cressida to this Troilus.

VIO. I understand you, sir; 't is well begged.

CLO. The matter, I hope, is not great, sir, begging but a beggar. Cressida was a beggar. My lady is within, sir. I will conster[6] to them whence you come: who you are and what you would are out of my welkin—I might say "element," but the word is overworn.   [Exit CLOWN.]

VIO. This fellow is wise enough to play the fool,

And to do that well craves a kind of wit.

He must observe their mood on whom he jests,

The quality of persons, and the time,

And, like the haggard,[7] check at every feather

That comes before his eye. This is a practice

As full of labour as a wise man's art;

For folly that he wisely shows is fit;

But wise men, folly-fall'n, quite taint their wit.

[Enter SIR TOBY and SIR ANDREW.]

SIR TOBY. Save you, gentleman.

VIO. And you, sir.

SIR ANDREW. *Dieu vous garde, monsieur.*

VIO. *Et vous aussi; votre serviteur.*

SIR AND. I hope, sir, you are; and I am yours.

SIR TO. Will you encounter the house? My niece is desirous you should enter, if your trade be to her.

VIO. I am bound to your niece, sir; I mean, she is the list[8] of my voyage.

SIR TO. Taste your legs, sir; put them to motion.

VIO. My legs do better understand me, sir, than I understand what you mean by bidding me taste my legs.

SIR TO. I mean, to go, sir, to enter.

VIO. I will answer you with gait and entrance. But we are prevented.[9]

[Enter OLIVIA and MARIA her Gentlewoman.]

Most excellent accomplished lady, the heavens rain odours on you!

SIR AND. That youth's a rare courtier. "Rain odours"; well.

VIO. My matter hath no voice, lady, but to your own most pregnant and vouchsafed[10] ear.

SIR AND. "Odours," "pregnant," and "vouchsafed"; I'll get 'em all three all ready.

OLIVIA. Let the garden door be shut, and leave me to my hearing. [Exeunt all

---

[2] If you thrust at me.   [3] Consignment.
[4] Put out at interest.
[5] Who served as go-between in the love affair of Troilus and Cressida. Subsequently Cressida became a leper forced to beg alms.

[6] Explain.
[7] Untrained hawk.
[8] Destination.
[9] Anticipated.
[10] Receptive and attentive.

but OLIVIA *and* VIOLA.] Give me your hand, sir.

VIO.   My duty, madam, and most humble service.

OLI.   What is your name?

VIO.   Cesario is your servant's name, fair princess.

OLI.   My servant, sir! 'T was never merry world

Since lowly feigning was call'd compliment.

You 're servant to the Count Orsino, youth.

VIO.   And he is yours, and his must needs be yours.

Your servant's servant is your servant, madam.

OLI.   For him, I think not on him: for his thoughts,

Would they were blanks, rather than fill'd with me!

VIO.   Madam, I come to whet your gentle thoughts

On his behalf.

OLI.   O, by your leave, I pray you,

I bade you never speak again of him;

But, would you undertake another suit,

I had rather hear you to solicit that

Than music from the spheres.

VIO.   Dear lady,—

OLI.   Give me leave, beseech you. I did send,

After the last enchantment you did here,

A ring in chase of you; so did I abuse [11]

Myself, my servant, and, I fear me, you.

Under your hard construction must I sit,

To force that on you, in a shameful cunning,

Which you knew none of yours. What might you think?

Have you not set mine honour at the stake

And baited it [12] with all th' unmuzzled thoughts

That tyrannous heart can think? To one of your receiving

Enough is shown. A cypress,[13] not a bosom,

Hides my heart. So, let me hear you speak.

VIO.   I pity you.

OLI.   That 's a degree to love.

VIO.   No, not a grize; [14] for 't is a vulgar proof,[15]

That very oft we pity enemies.

OLI.   Why, then, methinks 't is time to smile again.

O world, how apt the poor are to be proud!

If one should be a prey, how much the better

To fall before the lion than the wolf!

[*Clock strikes.*]

The clock upbraids me with the waste of time.

Be not afraid, good youth, I will not have you;

And yet, when wit and youth is come to harvest,

Your wife is like to reap a proper man.

There lies your way, due west.

VIO.   Then westward-ho!

Grace and good disposition

Attend your ladyship!

You 'll nothing, madam, to my lord by me?

OLI.   Stay!

I prithee, tell me what thou think'st of me.

VIO.   That you do think you are not what you are.

OLI.   If I think so, I think the same of you.

VIO.   Then think you right. I am not what I am.

OLI.   I would you were as I would have you be!

VIO.   Would it be better, madam, than I am?

I wish it might, for now I am your fool.

OLI.   O, what a deal of scorn looks beautiful

In the contempt and anger of his lip!

A murd'rous guilt shows not itself more soon

Than love that would seem hid. Love's night is noon.

Cesario, by the roses of the spring,

By maidhood, honour, truth, and everything,

I love thee so, that, maugre [16] all thy pride,

---

[11] Deal falsely with.
[12] The figure is from the sport of bear-baiting, in which a bear, tied to a stake, was set upon by dogs.
[13] A transparent veiling.
[14] Step.
[15] Common experience.
[16] In spite of.

Nor wit nor reason can my passion hide.

Do not extort thy reasons from this clause,

For that [17] I woo, thou therefore hast no cause;

But rather reason thus with reason fetter,

Love sought is good, but given unsought is better.

VIO. By innocence I swear, and by my youth,

I have one heart, one bosom, and one truth,

And that no woman has; nor never none

Shall mistress be of it, save I alone.

And so adieu, good madam; nevermore

Will I my master's tears to you deplore.

OLI. Yet come again; for thou perhaps mayst move

That heart, which now abhors, to like his love.   [*Exeunt.*]

Scene II
Olivia's house.

[*Enter* SIR TOBY, SIR ANDREW, *and* FABIAN.]

SIR ANDREW. No, faith, I 'll not stay a jot longer.

SIR TOBY. Thy reason, dear venom, give thy reason.

FABIAN. You must needs yield your reason, Sir Andrew.

SIR AND. Marry, I saw your niece do more favours to the Count's serving-man than ever she bestowed upon me. I saw 't i' th' orchard.

SIR TO. Did she see thee the while, old boy? Tell me that.

SIR AND. As plain as I see you now.

FAB. This was a great argument of love in her toward you.

SIR AND. 'S light, will you make an ass o' me?

FAB. I will prove it legitimate, sir, upon the oaths of judgement and reason.

SIR TO. And they have been grand-jurymen since before Noah was a sailor.

FAB. She did show favour to the youth

in your sight only to exasperate you, to awake your dormouse valour, to put fire in your heart, and brimstone in your liver. You should then have accosted her; and with some excellent jests, fire-new from the mint, you should have banged the youth into dumbness. This was looked for at your hand, and this was balked: the double gilt of this opportunity you let time wash off, and you are now sailed into the north of my lady's opinion, where you will hang like an icicle on a Dutchman's beard, unless you do redeem it by some laudable attempt either of valour or policy.

SIR AND. An 't be any way, it must be with valour; for policy I hate: I had as lief be a Brownist [1] as a politician.

SIR TO. Why, then, build me thy fortunes upon the basis of valour. Challenge me the Count's youth to fight with him; hurt him in eleven places; my niece shall take note of it; and assure thyself, there is no love-broker in the world can more prevail in man's commendation with woman than report of valour.

FAB. There is no way but this, Sir Andrew.

SIR AND. Will either of you bear me a challenge to him?

SIR TO. Go, write it in a martial hand. Be curst [2] and brief. It is no matter how witty, so it be eloquent and full of invention: taunt him with the license of ink: if thou thou'st [3] him some thrice, it shall not be amiss; and as many lies as will lie in thy sheet of paper, although the sheet were big enough for the bed of Ware [4] in England, set 'em down: go about it. Let there be gall enough in thy ink, though thou write with a goose-pen, no matter: about it.

SIR AND. Where shall I find you?

SIR TO. We 'll call thee at the cubiculo. Go.   [*Exit* SIR ANDREW.]

FAB. This is a dear manakin to you, Sir Toby.

SIR TO. I have been dear to him, lad, some two thousand strong, or so.

[17] Because.
[1] Member of an extreme Puritan sect.
[2] Ill-tempered.
[3] To address a stranger with the familiar *thou*,

instead of *you*, was to insult him as an inferior.
[4] A famous bed in an inn at Ware; it was more than 10 feet square.

FAB. We shall have a rare letter from him. But you 'll not deliver 't?

SIR TO. Never trust me, then; and by all means stir on the youth to an answer. I think oxen and wainropes cannot hale them together. For Andrew, if he were opened, and you find so much blood in his liver as will clog the foot of a flea, I 'll eat the rest of th' anatomy.

FAB. And his opposite, the youth, bears in his visage no great presage of cruelty.

[Enter MARIA.]

SIR TO. Look, where the youngest wren of mine comes.

MARIA. If you desire the spleen, and will laugh yourselves into stitches, follow me. Yond gull Malvolio is turned heathen, a very renegado; for there is no Christian, that means to be saved by believing rightly, can ever believe such impossible passages of grossness.[5] He 's in yellow stockings.

SIR TO. And cross-gartered?

MAR. Most villanously; like a pedant that keeps a school i' the church. I have dogged him like his murderer. He does obey every point of the letter that I dropped to betray him. He does smile his face into more lines than is in the new map with the augmentation of the Indies. You have not seen such a thing as 't is. I can hardly forbear hurling things at him. I know my lady will strike him: if she do, he 'll smile and take 't for a great favour.

SIR TO. Come, bring us, bring us where he is. [Exeunt.]

Scene III
A street.

[Enter SEBASTIAN and ANTONIO.]

SEBASTIAN. I would not by my will have troubled you;
But since you make your pleasure of your pains,
I will no further chide you.

ANTONIO. I could not stay behind you: my desire,
More sharp than filed steel, did spur me forth,

And not all love to see you, though so much
As might have drawn one to a longer voyage,
But jealousy [1] what might befall your travel,
Being skilless in these parts; which to a stranger,
Unguided and unfriended, often prove
Rough and unhospitable: my willing love,
The rather by these arguments of fear,
Set forth in your pursuit.

SEB. My kind Antonio,
I can no other answer make but thanks,
And thanks, and ever thanks; and oft good turns
Are shuffled off with such uncurrent pay;
But, were my worth as is my conscience firm,
You should find better dealing. What 's to do?
Shall we go see the reliques of this town?

ANT. To-morrow, sir: best first go see your lodging.

SEB. I am not weary, an 't is long to night.
I pray you, let us satisfy our eyes
With the memorials and the things of fame
That do renown this city.

ANT. Would you 'd pardon me.
I do not without danger walk these streets.
Once, in a sea-fight, 'gainst the Count his galleys
I did some service; of such note indeed,
That were I ta'en here it would scarce be answer'd.

SEB. Belike you slew great number of his people.

ANT. Th' offence is not of such a bloody nature,
Albeit the quality of the time and quarrel
Might well have given us bloody argument.
It might have since been answer'd in re-paying
What we took from them, which, for traf-fic's sake,
Most of our city did; only myself stood out,
For which, if I be lapsed [2] in this place,

---

[5] I.e., such gross impossibilities as the letter contained.   [1] Anxiety.   [2] Taken off guard.

I shall pay dear.

SEB.   Do not then walk too open.

ANT. It does not fit me. Hold, sir,
  here 's my purse.

In the south suburbs, at the Elephant

Is best to lodge. I will bespeak our diet,

Whiles you beguile the time and feed your
  knowledge

With viewing of the town. There shall you
  have me.

SEB. Why I your purse?

ANT. Haply your eye shall light upon
  some toy

You have desire to purchase; and your
  store,

I think, is not for idle markets,[3] sir.

SEB. I 'll be your purse-bearer and leave
  you for

An hour.

ANT.   To th' Elephant.

SEB.   I do remember.

                                   [*Exeunt.*]

Scene IV
Olivia's garden.

[*Enter* OLIVIA *and* MARIA.]

OLIVIA. I have sent after him; he says
  he 'll come.

How shall I feast him? What bestow of
  him?

For youth is bought more oft than begg'd
  or borrow'd.

I speak too loud.

Where 's Malvolio? He is sad and civil,[1]

And suits well for a servant with my fortunes.

Where is Malvolio?

MARIA. He 's coming, madam, but in
very strange manner. He is, sure, possessed,
madam.

OLI. Why, what 's the matter? Does he
rave?

MAR. No, madam, he does nothing but
smile. Your ladyship were best to have
some guard about you, if he come; for sure
the man is tainted in 's wits.

OLI. Go call him hither. [*Exit* MARIA.]
                        I am as mad as he,

If sad and merry madness equal be.

[*Enter* MALVOLIO, *with* MARIA.]

How now, Malvolio!

MALVOLIO. Sweet lady, ho, ho.

OLI. Smil'st thou?

I sent for thee upon a sad occasion.

MAL. Sad, lady? I could be sad. This
does make some obstruction in the blood,
this cross-gartering; but what of that? If it
please the eye of one, it is with me as the
very true sonnet is, "Please one, and please
all." [2]

OLI. Why, how dost thou, man? What is
the matter with thee?

MAL. Not black in my mind, though yellow in my legs. It did come to his hands,
and commands shall be executed. I think we
do know the sweet Roman hand.

OLI. Wilt thou go to bed, Malvolio?

MAL. To bed! Ay, sweet heart, and I 'll
come to thee.

OLI. God comfort thee! Why dost thou
smile so and kiss thy hand so oft?

MARIA. How do you, Malvolio?

MAL. At your request? Yes: nightin-
gales answer daws.

MAR. Why appear you with this ridiculous boldness before my lady?

MAL. "Be not afraid of greatness:" 't
was well writ.

OLI. What mean'st thou by that, Malvolio?

MAL. "Some are born great,"—

OLI. Ha?

MAL. "Some achieve greatness,"—

OLI. What say'st thou?

MAL. "And some have greatness thrust
upon them."

OLI. Heaven restore thee!

MAL. "Remember who commended thy
yellow stockings,"—

OLI. Thy yellow stockings!

MAL. "And wish'd to see thee cross-gartered."

OLI. Cross-gartered!

---

[3] Not sufficient for unnecessary purchases.

[1] Sober and sedate.
[2] The refrain of an old ballad.

MAL. "Go to, thou art made, if thou de-sir'st to be so;"—

OLI. Am I made?

MAL. "If not, let me see thee a servant still."

OLI. Why, this is very midsummer madness.

[*Enter* SERVANT.]

SERVANT. Madam, the young gentle-man of the Count Orsino's is returned. I could hardly entreat him back. He attends your ladyship's pleasure.

OLI. I 'll come to him. [*Exit* SERVANT.] Good Maria, let this fellow be looked to. Where' s my cousin Toby? Let some of my people have a special care of him: I would not have him miscarry [3] for the half of my dowry.

[*Exeunt* OLIVIA *and* MARIA.]

MAL. O, ho! do you come near me now? No worse man than Sir Toby to look to me! This concurs directly with the letter: she sends him on purpose, that I may ap-pear stubborn to him, for she incites me to that in the letter. "Cast thy humble slough," says she; "be opposite with a kinsman, surly with servants; let thy tongue tang with argu-ments of state; put thyself into the trick of singularity;" and consequently sets down the manner how; as, a sad face, a reverend carriage, a slow tongue, in the habit of some sir of note, and so forth. I have limed [4] her; but it is Jove's doing, and Jove make me thankful! And when she went away now, "Let this fellow be looked to"; "fellow!" not Malvolio, nor after my de-gree, but "fellow." Why, everything ad-heres together, that no dram of a scruple, no scruple of a scruple, no obstacle, no in-credulous or unsafe circumstance—What can be said? Nothing that can be can come between me and the full prospect of my hopes. Well, Jove, not I, is the doer of this, and he is to be thanked.

[*Re-enter* MARIA, *with* SIR TOBY *and* FABIAN.]

SIR TOBY. Which way is he, in the name

of sanctity? If all the devils of hell be drawn in little, and Legion [5] himself pos-sessed him, yet I 'll speak to him.

FABIAN. Here he is, here he is. How is 't with you, sir? How is 't with you, man?

MAL. Go off; I discard you: let me en-joy my private: go off.

MARIA. Lo, how hollow the fiend speaks within him! Did not I tell you? Sir Toby, my lady prays you to have a care of him.

MAL. Ah, ha! Does she so?

SIR TO. Go to, go to; peace, peace. We must deal gently with him: let me alone. How do you, Malvolio? How is 't with you? What, man, defy the devil! Consider, he 's an enemy to mankind.

MAL. Do you know what you say?

MAR. La you! and you speak ill of the devil, how he takes it at heart! Pray God he be not bewitched!

FAB. Carry his water to the wise woman.

MAR. Marry, and it shall be done to-morrow morning if I live. My lady would not lose him for more than I 'll say.

MAL. How now, mistress!

MAR. O Lord!

SIR TO. Prithee, hold thy peace; this is not the way: do you not see you move him? Let me alone with him.

FAB. No way but gentleness; gently, gently: the fiend is rough, and will not be roughly used.

SIR TO. Why, how now, my bawcock! [6] How dost thou, chuck?

MAL. Sir!

SIR TO. Ay, "Biddy, come with me." What, man, 't is not for gravity to play at cherry-pit with Satan. Hang him, foul collier!

MAR. Get him to say his prayers, good Sir Toby, get him to pray.

MAL. My prayers, minx!

MAR. No, I warrant you, he will not hear of godliness.

MAL. Go, hang yourselves all! You are idle shallow things; I am not of your ele-ment. You shall know more hereafter.

[*Exit* MALVOLIO.]

---

[3] Come to harm. [4] Snared.
[5] The name given to the devils in *Mark* v, 1–19.

[6] Good fellow. Sir Toby pretends to humor Malvolio with wheedling baby talk.

SIR TO. Is 't possible?

FAB. If this were played upon a stage now, I could condemn it as an improbable fiction.

SIR TO. His very genius [7] hath taken the infection of the device, man.

MAR. Nay, pursue him now, lest the device take air and taint.

FAB. Why, we shall make him mad indeed.

MAR. The house will be the quieter.

SIR TO. Come, we 'll have him in a dark room and bound. My niece is already in the belief that he 's mad. We may carry it thus, for our pleasure and his penance, till our very pastime, tired out of breath, prompt us to have mercy on him; at which time we will bring the device to the bar and crown thee for a finder of madmen. But see, but see.

[Enter SIR ANDREW.]

FAB. More matter for a May morning.

SIR ANDREW. Here 's the challenge, read it: I warrant there 's vinegar and pepper in 't.

FAB. Is 't so saucy?

SIR AND. Ay, is 't, I warrant him: do but read.

SIR TO. Give me. [*Reads.*] "Youth, whatsoever thou art, thou art but a scurvy fellow."

FAB. Good and valiant.

SIR TO. [*Reads.*] "Wonder not, nor admire [8] not in thy mind, why I do call thee so, for I will show thee no reason for 't."

FAB. A good note. That keeps you from the blow of the law.

SIR TO. [*Reads.*] "Thou com'st to the lady Olivia, and in my sight she uses thee kindly. But thou liest in thy throat; that is not the matter I challenge thee for."

FAB. Very brief, and to exceeding good sense—less.

SIR TO. [*Reads.*] "I will waylay thee going home; where if it be thy chance to kill me,"—

FAB. Good.

SIR TO. [*Reads.*] "Thou kill'st me like a rogue and a villain."

FAB. Still you keep o' the windy side of the law; good.

SIR TO. [*Reads.*] "Fare thee well, and God have mercy upon one of our souls! He may have mercy upon mine; but my hope is better, and so look to thyself. Thy friend, as thou usest him, and thy sworn enemy,

ANDREW AGUECHEEK."

If this letter move him not, his legs cannot. I 'll give 't him.

MAR. You may have very fit occasion for 't. He is now in some commerce with my lady, and will by and by depart.

SIR TO. Go, Sir Andrew, scout me for him at the corner of the orchard like a bum-baily.[9] So soon as ever thou seest him, draw; and, as thou draw'st, swear horrible; for it comes to pass oft that a terrible oath, with a swaggering accent sharply twanged off, gives manhood more approbation than ever proof itself would have earned him. Away!

SIR AND. Nay, let me alone for swearing.   [*Exit* SIR ANDREW.]

SIR TO. Now will not I deliver his letter; for the behaviour of the young gentleman gives him out to be of good capacity and breeding; his employment between his lord and my niece confirms no less; therefore this letter, being so excellently ignorant, will breed no terror in the youth; he will find it comes from a clodpole.[10] But, sir, I will deliver his challenge by word of mouth, set upon Aguecheek a notable report of valour, and drive the gentleman, as I know his youth will aptly receive it, into a most hideous opinion of his rage, skill, fury, and impetuosity. This will so fright them both that they will kill one another by the look, like cockatrices.[11]

[Re-enter OLIVIA *with* VIOLA.]

FAB. Here he comes with your niece. Give them way till he take leave, and presently after him.

---

[7] Essence.
[8] Marvel.
[9] Like a bailiff with an arrest warrant.
[10] Blockhead.
[11] Fabulous serpents supposed to kill with a glance.

SIR. TO. I will meditate the while upon some horrid message for a challenge.

[*Exeunt* SIR TOBY, FABIAN, *and* MARIA.]

OLIVIA. I have said too much unto a
   heart of stone,
And laid mine honour too unchary [12] on 't.
There 's something in me that reproves my
   fault;
But such a headstrong potent fault it is,
That it but mocks reproof.

VIOLA. With the same 'haviour that
   your passion bears
Goes on my master's grief.

OLI. Here, wear this jewel for me, 't is
   my picture.
Refuse it not; it hath no tongue to vex you;
And I beseech you come again to-morrow.
What shall you ask of me that I 'll deny,
That honour sav'd may upon asking give?

VIO. Nothing but this—your true love
   for my master.

OLI. How with mine honour may I give
   him that
Which I have given to you?

VIO.   I will acquit [13] you.

OLI. Well, come again to-morrow: fare
   thee well!
A fiend like thee might bear my soul to
   hell.   [*Exit* OLIVIA.]

[*Re-enter* SIR TOBY *and* FABIAN.]

SIR TOBY. Gentleman, God save thee!

VIO. And you, sir.

SIR TO. That defence thou hast, betake thee to 't. Of what nature the wrongs are thou hast done him, I know not; but thy intercepter, full of despite, bloody as the hunter, attends thee at the orchard-end. Dismount thy tuck, be yare [14] in thy preparation, for thy assailant is quick, skilful and deadly.

VIO. You mistake, sir, I am sure: no man hath any quarrel to me: my remembrance is very free and clear from any image of offence done to any man.

SIR TO. You 'll find it otherwise, I assure you; therefore, if you hold your life at any price, betake you to your guard; for your opposite hath in him what youth, strength, skill, and wrath can furnish man withal.

VIO. I pray you, sir, what is he?

SIR TO. He is knight, dubbed with unhatched rapier and on carpet consideration; [15] but he is a devil in private brawl: souls and bodies hath he divorced three; and his incensement at this moment is so implacable, that satisfaction be none but by pangs of death and sepulchre. Hob, nob, is his word; give 't or take 't.

VIO. I will return again into the house and desire some conduct of the lady. I am no fighter. I have heard of some kind of men that put quarrels purposely on others, to taste their valour: belike this is a man of that quirk.

SIR TO. Sir, no; his indignation derives itself out of a very competent injury; therefore, get you on and give him his desire. Back you shall not to the house, unless you undertake that with me which with as much safety you might answer him; therefore, on, or strip your sword stark naked; for meddle you must, that 's certain, or forswear to wear iron about you.

VIO. This is as uncivil as strange. I beseech you, do me this courteous office, as to know of the knight what my offence to him is: it is something of my negligence, nothing of my purpose.

SIR TO. I will do so. Signor Fabian, stay you by this gentleman till my return.

[*Exit* SIR TOBY.]

VIO. Pray you, sir, do you know of this matter?

FAB. I know the knight is incensed against you, even to a mortal arbitrement, [16] but nothing of the circumstance more.

VIO. I beseech you, what manner of man is he?

FAB. Nothing of that wonderful promise, to read him by his form, as you are like to find him in the proof of his valour. He is, indeed, sir, the most skilful, bloody, and fatal opposite that you could possibly have found in any part of Illyria. Will you walk

---

[12] Recklessly.   [13] Release.
[14] Draw your sword, be nimble.
[15] A knight created for activities connected not with the battlefield but the royal palace: *i.e.,* a swivel-chair hero.
[16] Decision to the death.

towards him? I will make your peace with him if I can.

VIO. I shall be much bound to you for 't: I am one that had rather go with sir priest than sir knight; I care not who knows so much of my mettle. [*Exeunt.*]

[*Re-enter* SIR TOBY *with* SIR ANDREW.]

SIR TOBY. Why, man, he 's a very devil; I have not seen such a firago.[17] I had a pass with him, rapier, scabbard, and all, and he gives me the stuck in with such a mortal motion, that it is inevitable; and on the answer, he pays you as surely as your feet hits the ground they step on. They say he has been fencer to the Sophy.

SIR ANDREW. Pox on 't, I 'll not meddle with him.

SIR TO. Ay, but he will not now be pacified. Fabian can scarce hold him yonder.

SIR AND. Plague on 't, an I thought he had been valiant and so cunning in fence, I 'd have seen him damned ere I 'd have challenged him. Let him let the matter slip, and I 'll give him my horse, grey Capilet.

SIR TO. I 'll make the motion. Stand here; make a good show on 't: this shall end without the perdition of souls. [*Aside.*] Marry, I 'll ride your horse as well as I ride you.

[*Re-enter* FABIAN *and* VIOLA.]

[*To* FABIAN.] I have his horse to take up [18] the quarrel. I have persuaded him the youth 's a devil.

FABIAN. He is as horribly conceited of him; [19] and pants and looks pale, as if a bear were at his heels.

SIR TO. [*To* VIOLA.] There 's no remedy, sir; he will fight with you for 's oath sake. Marry, he hath better bethought him of his quarrel, and he finds that now scarce to be worth talking of; therefore draw, for the supportance of his vow: he protests he will not hurt you.

VIOLA [*Aside.*] Pray God defend me! A little thing would make me tell them how much I lack of a man.

FAB. Give ground, if you see him furious.

SIR TO. Come, Sir Andrew, there 's no remedy; the gentleman will, for his honour's sake, have one bout with you: he cannot by the duello avoid it; but he has promised me, as he is a gentleman and a soldier, he will not hurt you. Come on; to 't.

SIR AND. Pray God, he keep his oath.

[*Enter* ANTONIO.]

VIO. I do assure you, 't is against my will. [*They draw.*]

ANTONIO. Put up your sword. If this young gentleman
Have done offence, I take the fault on me;
If you offend him, I for him defy you.

SIR TO. You, sir! Why, what are you?

ANT. One, sir, that for his love dares yet do more
Than you have heard him brag to you he will.

SIR TO. Nay, if you be an undertaker,[20] I am for you. [*They draw.*]

[*Enter* OFFICERS.]

FAB. O good Sir Toby, hold! Here come the officers.

SIR TO. I 'll be with you anon.

VIO. Pray, sir, put your sword up, if you please.

SIR AND. Marry, will I, sir; and, for that I promised you, I 'll be as good as my word. He will bear you easily and reins well.

FIRST OFFICER. This is the man; do thy office.

SECOND OFFICER. Antonio, I arrest thee at the suit of Count Orsino.

ANT. You do mistake me, sir.

FIRST OFF. No, sir, no jot. I know your favour well,
Though now you have no sea-cap on your head.
Take him away; he knows I know him well.

ANT. I must obey. [*To* VIOLA.] This comes with seeking you.
But there 's no remedy; I shall answer it.
What will you do, now my necessity
Makes me to ask you for my purse? It grieves me
Much more for what I cannot do for you

---

[17] Virago.
[18] Settle.
[19] He imagines him to be as horrible.
[20] If you insist on taking up the affair.

Than what befalls myself. You stand
   amaz'd,
But be of comfort.

SECOND OFF.   Come, sir, away.

ANT.   I must entreat of you some of that
   money.

VIOLA.   What money, sir?
For the fair kindness you have show'd me
   here,
And, part, being prompted by your present
   trouble,
Out of my lean and low ability
I 'll lend you something. My having is not
   much.
I 'll make division of my present with you.
Hold, there 's half my coffer.

ANT.   Will you deny me now?
Is 't possible that my deserts to you
Can lack persuasion? Do not tempt my
   misery,
Lest that it make me so unsound a man
As to upbraid you with those kindnesses
That I have done for you.

VIO.   I know of none,
Nor know I you by voice or any feature.
I hate ingratitude more in a man
Than lying, vainness, babbling drunken-
   ness,
Or any taint of vice whose strong corrup-
   tion
Inhabits our frail blood.

ANT.   O heavens themselves!

SECOND OFF.   Come, sir, I pray you, go.

ANT.   Let me speak a little. This youth
   that you see here
I snatch'd one half out of the jaws of death,
Reliev'd him with such sanctity of love,
And to his image, which methought did
   promise
Most venerable worth, did I devotion.

FIRST OFF.   What 's that to us? The
   time goes by; away!

ANT.   But, O, how vile an idol proves
   this god!

ACT IV

Scene I
The street before Olivia's house.

[*Enter* SEBASTIAN *and* CLOWN.]

CLOWN.   Will you make me believe that
I am not sent for you?

Thou hast, Sebastian, done good feature
   shame.
In nature there 's no blemish but the mind;
None can be call'd deform'd but the un-
   kind.
Virtue is beauty, but the beauteous evil
Are empty trunks o'erflourish'd by the
   devil.

FIRST OFF.   The man grows mad; away
   with him!
Come, come, sir.

ANT.   Lead me on.
               [*Exit* ANTONIO *with* OFFICERS.]

VIO.   Methinks his words do from such
   such passion fly,
That he believes himself; so do not I.
Prove true, imagination, O, prove true,
That I, dear brother, be now ta'en for you!

SIR TO.   Come hither, knight; come
hither, Fabian; we 'll whisper o'er a couplet
or two of most sage saws.[21]

VIO.   He nam'd Sebastian. I my brother
   know
Yet living in my glass; even such and so
In favour was my brother, and he went
Still in this fashion, colour, ornament,
For him I imitate. O, if it prove,
Tempests are kind and salt waves fresh in
   love.   [*Exit* VIOLA.]

SIR TO.   A very dishonest paltry boy,
and more a coward than a hare. His dishonesty appears in leaving his friend here
in necessity and denying him; and, for his
cowardship, ask Fabian.

FAB.   A coward, a most devout coward,
religious in it.

SIR AND.   'Slid, I 'll after him again and
beat him.

SIR TO.   Do; cuff him soundly, but never
draw thy sword.

SIR AND.   An I do not,—

FAB.   Come, let 's see the event,

SIR TO.   I dare lay any money 't will be
nothing yet.   [*Exeunt.*]

SEBASTIAN.   Go to, go to, thou art a
foolish fellow; let me be clear of thee.

CLO.   Well held out, i' faith! No, I do

---

[21] Wise sayings.

not know you; nor I am not sent to you by my lady, to bid you come speak with her; nor your name is not Master Cesario; nor this is not my nose neither. Nothing that is so is so.

SEB. I prithee, vent thy folly somewhere else. Thou know'st not me.

CLO. Vent my folly! He has heard that word of some great man and now applies it to a fool. Vent my folly! I am afraid this great lubber, the world, will prove a cockney. I prithee now, ungird thy strangeness and tell me what I shall vent to my lady. Shall I vent to her that thou art coming?

SEB. I prithee, foolish Greek,[1] depart from me.
There's money for thee: if you tarry longer,
I shall give worse payment.

CLO. By my troth, thou hast an open hand. These wise men that give fools money get themselves a good report—after fourteen years' purchase.[2]

[*Enter* SIR ANDREW, SIR TOBY, *and* FABIAN.]

SIR ANDREW. Now, sir, have I met you again? There's for you.
[*Striking* SEBASTIAN.]

SEB. Why, there's for thee, and there, and there. Are all the people mad?
[*Beating* SIR ANDREW.]

SIR TOBY. Hold, sir, or I'll throw your dagger o'er the house.

CLO. This will I tell my lady straight. I would not be in some of your coats for two pence. [*Exit* CLOWN.]

SIR TO. Come on, sir. Hold!

SIR AND. Nay, let him alone: I'll go another way to work with him: I'll have an action of battery against him, if there be any law in Illyria. Though I struck him first, yet it's no matter for that.

SEB. Let go thy hand.

SIR TO. Come, sir, I will not let you go.

Come, my young soldier, put up your iron; you are well flesh'd.[3] Come on.

SEB. I will be free from thee. What wouldst thou now?
If thou dar'st tempt me further, dray thy sword. [*Draws.*]

SIR TO. What, what? Nay, then I must have an ounce or two of this malapert blood from you. [*Draws.*]

[*Enter* OLIVIA.]

OLIVIA. Hold, Toby! On thy life I charge thee, hold!

SIR TO. Madam—

OLI. Will it be ever thus? Ungracious wretch,
Fit for the mountains and the barbarous caves,
Where manners ne'er were preach'd! Out of my sight!
Be not offended, dear Cesario.
Rudesby,[4] be gone!
[*Exeunt* SIR TOBY, SIR ANDREW, *and* FABIAN.]
I prithee, gentle friend,
Let thy fair wisdom, not thy passion, sway
In this uncivil and unjust extent
Against thy peace. Go with me to my house,
And hear thou there how many fruitless pranks
This ruffian hath botch'd[5] up, that thou thereby
Mayst smile at this. Thou shalt not choose but go.
Do not deny. Beshrew his soul for me,
He started one poor heart of mine in thee.

SEB. What relish is in this? How runs the stream?
Or I am mad, or else this is a dream.
Let fancy still my sense in Lethe[6] steep.
If it be thus to dream, still let me sleep!

OLI. Nay, come, I prithee. Would thou'dst be rul'd by me!

SEB. Madam, I will.

OLI. O, say so, and so be!
[*Exeunt.*]

---

[1] Prankster.
[2] At a high price. Land values were usually estimated at twelve times their annual rent.
[3] You have had your taste of fighting.
[4] Ruffian.   [5] Patched.
[6] The river of oblivion in Hades.

Scene II
Olivia's house.

[Enter MARIA and CLOWN.]

MARIA. Nay, I prithee, put on this gown and this beard: make him believe thou art Sir Topas the curate: do it quickly; I 'll call Sir Toby the whilst. [Exit MARIA.]

CLOWN. Well, I 'll put it on, and I will dissemble myself in 't; and I would I were the first that ever dissembled in such a gown. I am not tall enough to become the function well, nor lean enough to be thought a good student; but to be said an honest man and a good housekeeper goes as fairly as to say a careful man and a great scholar. The competitors [1] enter.

[Enter SIR TOBY and MARIA.]

SIR TOBY. Jove bless thee, master Parson.

CLO. Bonos dies, Sir Toby: for, as the old hermit of Prague, that never saw pen and ink, very wittily said to a niece of King Gorboduc, "That that is is"; so I, being master Parson, am master Parson; for, what is "that" but "that," and "is" but "is"?

SIR TO. To him, Sir Topas.

CLO. What, ho, I say! Peace in this prison!

SIR TO. The knave counterfeits well; a good knave.

MALVOLIO. [Within.] Who calls there?

CLO. Sir Topas the curate, who comes to visit Malvolio the lunatic.

MAL. Sir Topas, Sir Topas, good Sir Topas, go to my lady.

CLO. Out, hyperbolical fiend! How vexest thou this man! Talkest thou nothing but of ladies?

SIR TO. Well said, master Parson.

MAL. Sir Topas, never was man thus wronged. Good Sir Topas, do not think I am mad. They have laid me here in hideous darkness.

CLO. Fie, thou dishonest Satan! I call thee by the most modest terms, for I am one of those gentle ones that will use the devil himself with courtesy. Say'st thou that house is dark?

MAL. As hell, Sir Topas.

CLO. Why, it hath bay windows transparent as barricadoes, and the clerestories [2] toward the south north are as lustrous as ebony; and yet complainest thou of obstruction?

MAL. I am not mad, Sir Topas. I say to you, this house is dark.

CLO. Madman, thou errest: I say, there is no darkness but ignorance, in which thou art more puzzled than the Egyptians in their fog.[3]

MAL. I say, this house is dark as ignorance, though ignorance were as dark as hell; and I say, there was never man thus abused. I am no more mad than you are: make the trial of it in any constant question.[4]

CLO. What is the opinion of Pythagoras [5] concerning wild fowl?

MAL. That the soul of our grandam might haply inhabit a bird.

CLO. What think'st thou of his opinion?

MAL. I think nobly of the soul, and no way approve his opinion.

CLO. Fare thee well! Remain thou still in darkness. Thou shalt hold the opinion of Pythagoras ere I will allow of thy wits, and fear to kill a woodcock, lest thou dispossess the soul of thy grandam. Fare thee well.

MAL. Sir Topas, Sir Topas!

SIR TO. My most exquisite Sir Topas!

CLO. Nay, I am for all waters.[6]

MARIA. Thou mightst have done this without thy beard and gown. He sees thee not.

SIR TO. To him in thine own voice, and bring me word how thou find'st him. I would we were well rid of this knavery. If he may be conveniently delivered, I would he were, for I am now so far in offence with my niece that I cannot pursue with

---

[1] Confederates.
[2] Upper windows.
[3] One of the plagues visited upon the Egyptians by Moses.
[4] Established subject.
[5] A Greek philosopher whose teaching included the transmigration of souls.
[6] I can handle anything.

any safety this sport to the upshot. Come by and by to my chamber.

[*Exit* SIR TOBY *with* MARIA.]

CLO. [*Singing.*]

"Hey, Robin, jolly Robin,
  Tell me how thy lady does."

MAL. Fool!

CLO. "My lady is unkind, perdy."

MAL. Fool!

CLO. "Alas, why is she so?"

MAL. Fool, I say!

CLO. "She loves another"—Who calls, ha?

MAL. Good fool, as ever thou wilt deserve well at my hand, help me to a candle, and pen, ink, and paper. As I am a gentleman, I will live to be thankful to thee for 't.

CLO. Master Malvolio?

MAL. Ay, good fool.

CLO. Alas, sir, how fell you besides your five wits?

MAL. Fool, there was never man so notoriously [7] abused. I am as well in my wits, fool, as thou art.

CLO. But as well? Then you are mad indeed, if you be no better in your wits than a fool.

MAL. They have here propertied me,[8] keep me in darkness, send ministers to me, asses, and do all they can to face me out of my wits.

CLO. Advise you what you say; the minister is here.[9] Malvolio, Malvolio, thy wits the heavens restore! Endeavour thyself to sleep, and leave thy vain bibble babble.

MAL. Sir Topas!

CLO. Maintain no words with him, good fellow. Who, I, sir? Not I, sir. God buy you, good Sir Topas. Marry, amen. I will, sir, I will.

MAL. Fool, fool, fool, I say!

CLO. Alas, sir, be patient. What say you, sir? I am shent [10] for speaking to you.

MAL. Good fool, help me to some light and some paper. I tell thee, I am as well in my wits as any man in Illyria.

CLO. Well-a-day that you were, sir!

MAL. By this hand, I am. Good fool, some ink, paper, and light; and convey what I will set down to my lady. It shall advantage thee more than ever the bearing of letter did.

CLO. I will help you to 't. But tell me true, are you not mad indeed, or do you but counterfeit?

MAL. Believe me, I am not. I tell thee true.

CLO. Nay, I 'll ne'er believe a madman till I see his brains. I will fetch you light and paper and ink.

MAL. Fool, I 'll requite it in the highest degree. I prithee, be gone.

CLO. [*Singing.*]

I am gone, sir
And anon, sir,
I 'll be with you again,
  In a trice,
  Like to the old Vice,[11]
Your need to sustain;

Who, with dagger of lath,
In his rage and his wrath,
  Cries, ah, ha! to the devil,
Like a mad lad.
Pare thy nails, dad.
Adieu, goodman devil.

[*Exit.*]

Scene III
Olivia's garden.

[*Enter* SEBASTIAN.]

SEBASTIAN. This is the air, that is the glorious sun,
This pearl she gave me, I do feel 't and see 't;
And though 't is wonder that enwraps me thus,
Yet 't is not madness. Where 's Antonio, then?
I could not find him at the Elephant;
Yet there he was, and there I found this credit,[1]
That he did range the town to seek me out.
His counsel now might do me golden service;

---

[7] Notably.
[8] Used me as a property in advancing their schemes.
[9] In the following, note that the Clown speaks sometimes in his own person and sometimes with the voice of Sir Topas.
[10] Rebuked.
[11] The clown of the morality plays.   [1] Belief.

For though my soul disputes well with my
  sense,
That this may be some error, but no mad-
  ness,
Yet doth this accident and flood of for-
  tune
So far exceed all instance, all discourse,[2]
That I am ready to distrust mine eyes
And wrangle with my reason that per-
  suades me
To any other trust but that I am mad
Or else the lady 's mad; yet, if 't were so,
She could not sway her house, command
  her followers,
Take and give back affairs and their dis-
  patch
With such a smooth, discreet, and stable
  bearing
As I perceive she does. There 's some-
  thing in 't
That is deceivable. But here the lady
  comes.

[*Enter* OLIVIA *and* PRIEST.]

OLIVIA.   Blame not this haste of mine. If
  you mean well,
Now go with me and with this holy man
Into the chantry by; there, before him,
And underneath that consecrated roof,
Plight me the full assurance of your faith,
That my most jealous [3] and too doubtful
  soul
May live at peace. He shall conceal it
Whiles [4] you are willing it shall come to
  note,
What time we will our celebration keep
According to my birth. What do you say?
  SEB.   I 'll follow this good man, and go
  with you;
And, having sworn truth, ever will be true.
  OLI.   Then lead the way, good father;
  and heavens so shine
That they may fairly note this act of mine!
                                    [*Exeunt.*]

ACT V

Scene I

Before Olivia's house.

[*Enter* CLOWN *and* FABIAN.]

FABIAN.   Now, as thou lov'st me, let me
see his letter.

CLOWN.   Good Master Fabian, grant me
another request.

FAB.   Anything.

CLO.   Do not desire to see this letter.

FAB.   This is to give a dog and in recompense desire my dog again.

[*Enter* DUKE, VIOLA, CURIO, *and* LORDS.]

DUKE.   Belong you to the Lady Olivia,
friends?

CLO.   Ay, sir! we are some of her trappings.

DUKE.   I know thee well; how dost thou,
my good fellow?

CLO.   Truly, sir, the better for my foes
and the worse for my friends.

DUKE.   Just the contrary; the better for
thy friends.

CLO.   No, sir, the worse.

DUKE.   How can that be?

CLO.   Marry, sir, they praise me and
make an ass of me. Now my foes tell me
plainly I am an ass; so that by my foes, sir,
I profit in the knowledge of myself, and
by my friends I am abused; so that, conclusions to be as kisses,[1] if your four nega-
tives make your two affirmatives, why then,
the worse for my friends and the better for
my foes.

DUKE.   Why, this is excellent.

CLO.   By my troth, sir, no; though it
please you to be one of my friends.

DUKE.   Thou shalt not be the worse for
me. There 's gold.

CLO.   But that it would be double-deal-
ing, sir, I would you could make it another.

DUKE.   O, you give me ill counsel.

CLO.   Put your grace in your pocket, sir,
for this once, and let your flesh and blood
obey it.

DUKE.   Well, I will be so much a sinner,
to be a double-dealer. There 's another.

---

[2] All precedent, all rational explanation.
[3] Misgiving.
[4] Until.

[1] *I.e.*, a double negative is an affirmative, just as
in kissing two refusals are equivalent to a permission.

CLO. Primo, secundo, tertio, is a good play; and the old saying is, the third pays for all. The triplex, sir, is a good tripping measure; or the bells of Saint Bennet, sir, may put you in mind; one, two, three.

DUKE. You can fool no more money out of me at this throw: if you will let your lady know I am here to speak with her, and bring her along with you, it may awake my bounty further.

CLO. Marry, sir, lullaby to your bounty till I come again. I go, sir, but I would not have you to think that my desire of having is the sin of covetousness; but, as you say, sir, let your bounty take a nap, I will awake it anon. [*Exit* CLOWN.]

[*Enter* ANTONIO *and* OFFICERS.]

VIOLA. Here comes the man, sir, that did rescue me.

DUKE. That face of his I do remember well,
Yet when I saw it last, it was besmear'd
As black as Vulcan in the smoke of war.
A bawbling [2] vessel was he captain of,
For shallow draught and bulk unprizable, [3]
With which such scathful [4] grapple did he make
With the most noble bottom [5] of our fleet,
That very envy and the tongue of loss [6]
Cried fame and honour on him. What 's the matter?

FIRST OFFICER. Orsino, this is that Antonio
That took the *Phœnix* and her fraught from Candy,
And this is he that did the *Tiger* board,
When your young nephew Titus lost his leg.
Here in the streets, desperate [7] of shame and state,
In private brabble [8] did we apprehend him.

VIO. He did me kindness, sir, drew on my side,
But in conclusion put strange speech upon me.
I know not what 't was but distraction.

DUKE. Notable pirate! Thou salt-water thief!
What foolish boldness brought thee to their mercies
Whom thou, in terms so bloody and so dear,
Hast made thine enemies?

ANTONIO.   Orsino, noble sir,
Be pleas'd that I shake off these names you give me.
Antonio never yet was thief or pirate,
Though I confess, on base and ground enough,
Orsino's enemy. A witchcraft drew me hither.
That most ingrateful boy there by your side,
From the rude sea's enrag'd and foamy mouth
Did I redeem; a wreck past hope he was:
His life I gave him, and did thereto add
My love, without retention or restraint,
All his in dedication. For his sake
Did I expose myself, pure for his love,
Into the danger of this adverse town;
Drew to defend him when he was beset;
Where being apprehended, his false cunning,
Not meaning to partake with me in danger,
Taught him to face me out of his acquaintance,
And grew a twenty years removed thing
While one would wink; denied me mine own purse,
Which I had recommended to his use
Not half an hour before.

VIO.   How can this be?

DUKE. When came he to this town?

ANT. To-day, my lord; and for three months before,
No interim, not a minute's vacancy,
Both day and night did we keep company.

[*Enter* OLIVIA *and* ATTENDANTS.]

DUKE. Here comes the countess; now heaven walks on earth.
But for thee, fellow; fellow, thy words are madness.
Three months this youth hath tended upon me;

---

[2] Trifling.　　　[3] Of no account.
[4] Destructive.　　[5] Ship.

[6] The voices of even his enemies and the losers.
[7] Reckless.　　　[8] Brawl.

But more of that anon. Take him aside.
OLIVIA. What would my lord, but that
he may not have,
Wherein Olivia may seem serviceable?
Cesario, you do not keep promise with me.
VIO. Madam!
DUKE. Gracious Olivia,—
OLI. What do you say, Cesario? Good
my lord,—
VIO. My lord would speak; my duty
hushes me.
OLI. If it be aught to the old tune, my
lord,
It is as fat and fulsome [9] to mine ear
As howling after music.
DUKE.   Still so cruel!
OLI. Still so constant, lord.
DUKE. What, to perverseness? You un-
civil lady,
To whose ingrate and unauspicious altars
My soul the faithfull'st offerings have
breath'd out
That e'er devotion tender'd! What shall I
do?
OLI. Even what it please my lord, that
shall become him.
DUKE. Why should I not, had I the
heart to do it,
Like to th' Egyptian thief at point of
death,[10]
Kill what I love?—a savage jealousy
That sometimes savours nobly. But hear
me this:
Since you to non-regardance cast my faith,
And that I partly know the instrument
That screws me from my true place in your
favour,
Live you the marble-breasted tyrant still;
But this your minion,[11] whom I know you
love,
And whom, by heaven I swear, I tender
dearly,
Him will I tear out of that cruel eye,
Where he sits crowned in his master's spite.
Come, boy, with me; my thoughts are ripe
in mischief.
I 'll sacrifice the lamb that I do love,
To spite a raven's heart within a dove.

VIO. And I, most jocund, apt, and will-
ingly,
To do you rest, a thousand deaths would
die.
OLI. Where goes Cesario?
VIO.   After him I love
More than I love these eyes, more than my
life,
More, by all mores, than e'er I shall love
wife.
If I do feign, you witnesses above
Punish my life for taining of my love!
OLI. Ay me, detested! How am I be-
guil'd!
VIO. Who does beguile you? Who does
do you wrong?
OLI. Hast thou forgot thyself? Is it so
long?
Call forth the holy father.
DUKE.   Come, away!
OLI. Whither, my lord? Cesario, hus-
band, stay.
DUKE. Husband?
OLI.   Ay, husband! Can he that deny?
DUKE. Her husband, sirrah?
VIO.   No, my lord, not I.
OLI. Alas, it is the baseness of thy fear
That makes thee strangle thy propriety.[12]
Fear not, Cesario; take thy fortunes up.
Be that thou know'st thou art, and then
thou art
As great as that thou fear'st.

[*Enter* PRIEST.]

                    O, welcome, father!
Father, I charge thee by thy reverence,
Here to unfold, though lately we intended
To keep in darkness what occasion now
Reveals before 't is ripe, what thou dost
know
Hath newly pass'd between this youth and
me.
PRIEST. A contract of eternal bond of
love,
Confirm'd by mutual joinder of your hands,
Attested by the holy close of lips,
Strengthen'd by interchangement of your
rings;

_____

[9] Gross and offensive.
[10] In his *Ethiopian History* Heliodorus tells the
story of an Egyptian bandit who, falling in love
with his captive, tried to kill her when he faced
capture.
[11] Darling.   [12] Destroy your true self.

And all the ceremony of this compact
Seal'd in my function, by my testimony;
Since when, my watch hath told me, toward my grave
I have travell'd but two hours.

DUKE. O thou dissembling cub! What wilt thou be
When time hath sow'd a grizzle on thy case? [13]
Or will not else thy craft so quickly grow,
That thine own trip shall be thine overthrow?
Farewell, and take her; but direct thy feet
Where thou and I henceforth may never meet.

VIO. My lord, I do protest—

OLI. O, do not swear!
Hold little faith, though thou hast too much fear.

[*Enter* SIR ANDREW.]

SIR ANDREW. For the love of God, a surgeon! Send one presently [14] to Sir Toby.

OLI. What 's the matter?

SIR AND. Has broke my head across and has given Sir Toby a bloody coxcomb [15] too. For the love of God, your help! I had rather than forty pound I were at home.

OLI. Who has done this, Sir Andrew?

SIR AND. The Count's gentleman, one Cesario: we took him for a coward, but he 's the very devil incardinate.[16]

DUKE. My gentleman, Cesario?

SIR AND. 'Od's lifelings, here he is! You broke my head for nothing; and that that I did, I was set on to do 't by Sir Toby.

VIO. Why do you speak to me? I never hurt you.
You drew your sword upon me without cause;
But I bespake you fair, and hurt you not.

[*Enter* SIR TOBY *and* CLOWN.]

SIR AND. If a bloody coxcomb be a hurt, you have hurt me: I think you set nothing by a bloody coxcomb. Here comes Sir Toby halting: you shall hear more; but

if he had not been in drink, he would have tickled you othergates [17] than he did.

DUKE. How now, gentleman! How is 't with you?

SIR TOBY. That 's all one. Has hurt me, and there 's the end on 't. Sot,[18] didst see Dick surgeon, sot?

CLOWN. O, he 's drunk, Sir Toby, an hour agone. His eyes were set at eight i' the morning.

SIR TO. Then he 's a rogue, and a passy measures pavin.[19] I hate a drunken rogue.

OLI. Away with him! Who hath made this havoc with them?

SIR AND. I 'll help you, Sir Toby, because we 'll be dressed together.

SIR TO. Will you help?—an ass-head and a coxcomb and a knave, a thin-faced knave, a gull!

OLI. Get him to bed, and let his hurt be look'd to.

[*Exeunt* CLOWN, FABIAN, SIR TOBY,
and SIR ANDREW.]

[*Enter* SEBASTIAN.]

SEBASTIAN. I am sorry, madam, I have hurt your kinsman;
But, had it been the brother of my blood,
I must have done no less with wit and safety.
You throw a strange regard upon me, and by that
I do perceive it hath offended you.
Pardon me, sweet one, even for the vows
We made each other but so late ago.

DUKE. One face, one voice, one habit, and two persons,
A natural perspective,[20] that is and is not!

SEB. Antonio, O my dear Antonio!
How have the hours rack'd and tortur'd me,
Since I have lost thee!

ANTONIO. Sebastian are you?

SEB. Fear'st thou that, Antonio?

ANT. How have you made division of yourself?
An apple, cleft in two, is not more twin

[13] Grey hairs on your skin.   [14] Immediately.
[15] Head.   [16] He means *incarnate*.
[17] After another fashion.   [18] Fool.
[19] The pavan was a stately dance which, danced
in so-called "passa-measures," was based on musical units of eight measures.
[20] A picture which revealed two separate images when viewed from different angles.

Than these two creatures. Which is Sebastian?

OLI.   Most wonderful!

SEB.   Do I stand there? I never had a
brother,

Nor can there be that deity in my nature,

Of here and everywhere. I had a sister,

Whom the blind waves and surges have
devour'd.

Of charity, what kin are you to me?

What countryman? What name? What
parentage?

VIO.   Of Messaline; Sebastian was my
father;

Such a Sebastian was my brother too;

So went he suited [21] to his watery tomb.

If spirits can assume both form and suit

You come to fright us.

SEB.   A spirit I am indeed;

But am in that dimension [22] grossly clad

Which from the womb I did participate.

Were you a woman, as the rest goes even,[23]

I should my tears let fall upon your cheek,

And say, "Thrice welcome, drowned
Viola!"

VIO.   My father had a mole upon his
brow.

SEB.   And so had mine.

VIO.   And died that day when Viola
from her birth

Had number'd thirteen years.

SEB.   O, that record is lively in my soul!

He finished indeed his mortal act

That day that made my sister thirteen
years.

VIO.   If nothing lets [24] to make us happy
both

But this my masculine usurp'd attire,

Do not embrace me till each circumstance

Of place, time, fortune, do cohere and
jump [25]

That I am Viola; which to confirm,

I 'll bring you to a captain in this town,

Where lie my maiden weeds; by whose
gentle help

I was preserv'd to serve this noble count.

All the occurrence of my fortunes since

Hath been between this lady and this lord.

SEB.   [To OLIVIA.] So comes it, lady, you
have been mistook;

But nature to her bias drew in that.[26]

You would have been contracted to a maid;

Nor are you therein, by my life, deceiv'd,

You are betroth'd both to a maid and man.

DUKE.   Be not amaz'd, right noble is his
blood.

If this be so, as yet the glass seems true,

I shall have share in this most happy
wreck.

[To VIOLA.] Boy, thou hast said to me a
thousand times

Thou never shouldst love woman like to
me.

VIO.   And all those sayings will I over-
swear;

And all those swearings keep as true in soul

As doth that orbed continent [27] the fire

That severs day from night.

DUKE.   Give me thy hand,

And let me see thee in thy woman's weeds.

VIO.   The captain that did bring me first
on shore

Hath my maid's garments. He upon some
action

Is now in durance, at Malvolio's suit,

A gentleman, and follower of my lady's.

OLI.   He shall enlarge him; fetch Malvolio hither.

And yet, alas, now I remember me,

They say, poor gentleman, he 's much distract.

[Re-enter CLOWN with a letter, and FABIAN.]

A most extracting frenzy of mine own

From my remembrance clearly banish'd
his.

How does he, sirrah?

CLOWN.   Truly, madam, he holds Belze-
bub at the stave's end [28] as well as a man in
his case may do. Has here writ a letter to
you. I should have given 't you to-day
morning, but as a madman's epistles are no
gospels, so it skills not much when they are
delivered.

OLI.   Open 't, and read it.

CLO.   Look then to be well edified when

---

[21] Dressed.   [22] Form.
[23] Coincides.   [24] Prevents.
[25] Agree.

[26] Pulled in the direction of her inclination.
[27] Globed container, *i.e.,* the sun.
[28] He is keeping the fiend at arm's length.

the fool delivers the madman. [*Reads.*] "By the Lord, madam,"—

OLI.   How now, art thou mad?

CLO.   No, madam, I do but read madness: an your ladyship will have it as it ought to be, you must allow Vox.²⁹

OLI.   Prithee, read i' thy right wits.

CLO.   So I do, madonna; but to read his right wits is to read thus; therefore perpend, my princess, and give ear.

OLI.   Read it you, sirrah. [*To* FABIAN.]

FABIAN.   [*Reads.*]

"By the Lord, madam, you wrong me, and the world shall know it: though you have put me into darkness and given your drunken cousin rule over me, yet have I the benefit of my senses as well as your ladyship. I have your own letter that induced me to the semblance I put on; with the which I doubt not but to do myself much right, or you much shame. Think of me as you please. I leave my duty a little unthought of and speak out of my injury.

"THE MADLY-USED MALVOLIO."

OLI.   Did he write this?

CLO.   Ay, madam.

DUKE.   This savours not much of distraction.

OLI.   See him deliver'd, Fabian; bring him hither.   [*Exit* FABIAN.]

My lord, so please you, these things further thought on,

To think me as well a sister as a wife,

One day shall crown the alliance on 't, so please you,

Here at my house and at my proper cost.³⁰

DUKE.   Madam, I am most apt t' embrace your offer.

[*To* VIOLA.] Your master quits ³¹ you; and for your service done him,

So much against the mettle of your sex,

So far beneath your soft and tender breeding,

And since you call'd me master for so long,

Here is my hand. You shall from this time be

Your master's mistress.

OLI.   A sister! You are she.

²⁹ Permit the proper tone of voice.
³⁰ Own expense.

[*Enter* MALVOLIO *and* FABIAN.]

DUKE.   Is this the madman?

OLI.   Ay, my lord, this same.

How now, Malvolio!

MALVOLIO.   Madam, you have done me wrong,

Notorious wrong.

OLI.   Have I, Malvolio? No.

MAL.   Lady, you have. Pray you, peruse that letter;

You must not now deny it is your hand.

Write from it, if you can, in hand or phrase;

Or say 't is not your seal, not your invention.

You can say none of this. Well, grant it then

And tell me, in the modesty of honour,

Why you have given me such clear lights of favour,

Bade me come smiling and cross-garter'd to you,

To put on yellow stockings and to frown

Upon Sir Toby and the lighter people;

And, acting this in an obedient hope,

Why have you suffer'd me to be imprison'd,

Kept in a dark house, visited by the priest,

And made the most notorious geck and gull ³²

That e'er invention played on? Tell me why.

OLI.   Alas, Malvolio, this is not my writing,

Though, I confess, much like the character;

But out of question 't is Maria's hand.

And now I do bethink me, it was she

First told me thou wast mad. Then cam'st in smiling,

And in such forms which here were presuppos'd

Upon thee in the letter. Prithee, be content.

This practice ³³ hath most shrewdly pass'd upon thee;

But when we know the grounds and authors of it,

Thou shalt be both the plaintiff and the judge

Of thine own cause.

³¹ Releases.   ³² Dupe and fool.
³³ Plot.

FAB.   Good madam, hear me speak,
And let no quarrel nor no brawl to come
Taint the condition of this present hour,
Which I have wonder'd at. In hope it shall
    not,
Most freely I confess, myself and Toby
Set this device agaist Malvolio here,
Upon some stubborn and uncourteous
    parts
We had conceiv'd against him. Maria writ
The letter at Sir Toby's great importance,[34]
In recompense whereof he hath married
    her.
How with a sportful malice it was follow'd
May rather pluck on laughter than revenge,
If that the injuries be justly weigh'd
That have on both sides pass'd.

OLI.   Alas, poor fool, how have they
    baffl'd thee! [35]

CLO.   Why, "some are born great, some
achieve greatness, and some have greatness
thrown upon them." I was one, sir, in this
interlude; one Sir Topas, sir; but that 's all
one. "By the Lord, fool, I am not mad."
But do you remember? "Madam, why
laugh you at such a barren rascal? An you
smile not, he 's gagged." And thus the
whirligig of time brings in his revenges.

MAL.   I 'll be reveng'd on the whole
pack of you.   [*Exit* MALVOLIO.]

OLI.   He hath been most notoriously
    abus'd.

DUKE.   Pursue him, and entreat him to
    a peace;

He hath not told us of the captain yet.
When that is known and golden time con-
    vents,[36]
A solemn combination shall be made
Of our dear souls. Meantime, sweet sister,
We will not part from hence. Cesario,
    come;
For so you shall be, while you are a man;
But when in other habits you are seen,
Orsino's mistress and his fancy's queen.

            [*Exeunt all, except* CLOWN.]

CLO.   [*Sings.*]

When that I was and a little tiny boy,
    With hey, ho, the wind and the rain,
A foolish thing was but a toy,
    For the rain it raineth every day.

But when I came to man's estate,
    With hey, ho, &c.
'Gainst knaves and thieves men shut their gate,
    For the rain, &c.

But when I came, alas! to wive,
    With hey, ho, &c.
By swaggering could I never thrive,
    For the rain, &c.

But when I came unto my beds,
    With hey, ho, &c.
With toss-pots [37] still had drunken heads,
    For the rain, &c.

A great while ago the world begun,
    With hey, ho, &c.
But that 's all one, our play is done,
    And we 'll strive to please you every day.

                                [*Exit.*]

[34] Importunity.
[35] Put you to shame.

[36] Is convenient.
[37] Drunkards.

The Grotto Theater at Versailles

A contemporary engraving by Le Pautre, illustrating the picture-frame stage of the late Renaissance and after.

Social Comedy

OMANTIC COMEDY, for all its gay and humorous treatment of life, is not, in the strictest sense, a pure form of comedy. This is so because its comedy is always incidental to the romance. Furthermore, its fondness for the individualistic and the exceptional, its delight in sentiment, and its attitude of indulgent sympathy tend to dilute the pure essence of the comic spirit. The spirit of pure comedy is a spirit of critical laughter expressive of intellectual detachment and witty rationality. It is an emanation of the head rather than the heart. It surveys the human scene objectively and dispassionately; it cultivates the virtues of accurate perception and a just sense of proportion; it dispenses laughing justice according to the canons of wit and rational sanity. Its criteria of judgment are reasonableness and common sense. Since incongruity is the staple of comedy, and incongruity cannot exist without a basis of comparison, the comic spirit is obliged to adopt some general frame of reference congenial to its standard of common sense. This it finds most naturally in the collective experience of society. Hence pure comedy is essentially a social comedy, and its appropriate subjects are those aspects of human behavior which are inconsistent with the harmonious operation of a sane society.

Inherently the comic is a social phenomenon. Whereas tragedy concentrates upon the pathos and terror of man's lonely isolation, comedy is always concerned with his ungainly entanglement in the meshes of society. As a matter of fact, it is impossible to be comic in isolation; for to be comic is to deviate from the normal, and the normal always implies a collective sanction. Thus comic incongruity is fundamentally a social distinction based upon the ability to function effectively as a component element of society. Any departure from this standard of normality constitutes a threat to social stability. But, in the light of common sense, a threat to social stability is both irrational and absurd. The core of comedy, therefore, is a conflict between individual eccentricity and collective harmony, in which the comic spirit stands as a champion of social sanity against irresponsible caprice. This inherent social bias is the foundation of all pure comedy. From it derive the distinguishing characteristics of the type: its profound belief in the importance of society as a human institution, its shrewd observation of contemporary manners, its insistence upon social perspective and a proper sense of proportion, its intellectual detachment and sanity, and its cultivation of a critical serenity capable of viewing disproportion and incongruity as essentially ridiculous. This last is perhaps its cardinal virtue. It is the saving grace which prevents social criticism from descending to querulous censure and a consequent extinction of the pure comic spirit. Comic criticism in the form of satire incurs the danger of an ill temper which may defeat its own corrective purpose, and a lapse into irony blunts the keen edge of laughter with the corrosion of serious alarm. But the serene laughter of true comedy clears the critical atmosphere and inspires confidence in the balanced sanity of its judgment.

As an expression of man's social instincts, social comedy makes its appeal to man's social sensibilities, and entertains by stimulating and refining his social perspicacity. Its favorite means are the shrewd perception and the witty demonstration. Its success depends upon the veracity of its chosen materials and upon the actual absurdity which it is able to expose in them. Because society itself is but a collective manifestation of human nature, social comedy is essentially a comedy of character. Because the standards of society are but a rationalization of common human experience, social comedy arraigns as ridiculous any breach of common sense. Hence it finds its proper scope in those aspects of human behavior which possess social connotation, and founds its point of view upon the exigencies of civilized social intercourse. Its function is to define the appropriate issues, to marshal the pertinent evidence, and for sufficient cause to laugh the culprit out of court.

If the requisites of successful social comedy are astute social consciousness, keen wit, common sense, and a capacity for serene amusement, no dramatist who ever lived exemplified them with greater abundance and felicity than Jean Baptiste Poquelin (1622–1673), the French actor, playwright, and theatrical manager who chose to appear under the professional name of Molière. Molière is the world's supreme master of social comedy. The greatest comic actor of his time, he possessed a superb sense of the theatrically effective. A facile and expert dramatic craftsman, he succeeded in welding the odds and ends of miscellaneous theatrical traditions into a highly skillful and versatile art of civilized entertainment. The spiritual epitome of a socially self-conscious age, he lavished his talents upon a portraiture of society which is as penetrating in its critical insight as it is urbane. Almost single-handed he created French drama upon an international scale and established the most prevalent form of modern comedy. During the fifteen crowded years before his untimely death he wrote and produced more than a score of

highly varied comic entertainments, of which nearly half are to be num-
bered among the world's greatest comedies. His masterpiece, in the
opinion of many, and certainly one of the most brilliant social comedies
ever penned, is *The Misanthrope,* which was first produced in Paris on
June 4, 1666.

For the general technique of his social comedy Molière is largely
indebted to the comedy of masks of his immediate predecessors. This
technique, however, like that of romantic comedy, derives ultimately
from the practices of Roman comedy. In point of fact, the basic mechanism of all social comedy is substantially that of Plautus. It is a mechanism designed to expose selected characters to situations which will throw
into relief their peculiarities and demonstrate their ridiculous incongruity with sane social standards. The characters are chosen to represent
either social types or else generalized aspects of human nature. The
situations are contrived to bring out the salient features of these types
under circumstances which afford a means of evaluating them. When
the characters have been sufficiently exhibited to reveal their absurdity
and its inevitable consequences, the play has fulfilled its purpose and is
over. In this respect social comedy differs notably from its romantic
counterpart. The plot of romantic comedy is devoted to the progress of
a story. The plot of social comedy is concerned with story only inci-
dentally; its function is simply to reveal characters in exemplary situations. Thus in a play like *The Misanthrope* the characters have a social
context but no personal history. We do not know how they happen to be
in their peculiar situation or what finally becomes of them. They simply
appear, exhibit themselves, and are gone. All that is important is the
kind of people they are and the human traits they exemplify. For the
purposes of the play, their existence is arrested at a point of time, and
in that concentrated flash of revelation they play out the whole of their
significant history. Moreover, in the delineation of this synoptic history,
whereas romantic comedy proceeds by an idealization of selective human
realities, social comedy strives for a verisimilitude based upon general
human experience. And whereas the former tends to temper the severity
of criticism with a sympathetic indulgence, the latter is solicitous that
no compromise of critical integrity interfere with the strictures of common sense.

Because of its prevailing interests there is little occasion for much
physical action in social comedy. For the exhibition of character and
human relations its needs are usually satisfied by a mere opportunity for
social intercourse. *The Misanthrope,* for example, is almost entirely a
conversation piece. Drama of this sort demands very little in the way of
special stage setting or facilities for stage business. Actually it grew up
on a quite simple stage and one substantially different from the romantic
stage of Elizabethan England. The Elizabethan stage was a development
of the medieval multiple stage and was designed to facilitate abundant

action. The French stage of Molière's time was an adaptation of the Italian Renaissance stage, which in turn derived from the ancient Roman stage, and was designed to provide an appropriate setting for dramatic conversation. The illustration facing page 217 represents the production of a Molière comedy on such a stage at Versailles. Although the Paris theaters were less ornate than the one illustrated, they also were artificially illuminated rectangular halls with a stage across one end. Spectators occupied the galleries, which ran around the remaining three sides, and the raised tiers of seats in the auditorium, or stood in the *parterre* immediately before the stage. It was also a common, if annoying, custom for fashionable patrons to be seated along both sides of the stage. Much of the general arrangement and atmosphere is accurately recreated in the opening scene of Rostand's *Cyrano de Bergerac*.

The stage, although imposing in effect, was basically simple in conception. Its dominant feature was a proscenium arch which transformed the acting area into a framed picture. A painted back-drop and a series of side-wings arranged in perspective supplied this picture-frame stage with a scenic setting, which was lighted from overhead by chandeliers. The availability of a proscenium curtain also made possible a change of scenery when desired. The scenery itself was largely formal and decorative in function. Neither particularized nor closely integrated with the dramatic action, it was designed simply to create a conventional interior or exterior effect, and bore about the same relation to the play that a frame bears to a picture. So far as the scenery was concerned, drama continued to be a detachable and self-sufficient creation of speech and action. As a matter of fact, the poor diffusion of the candle light obliged the actors to perform so far forward on the stage that the play appeared to take place less within the stage setting than in front of it. At the same time, the presence of an actual setting, like the permanent houses of the Roman and later Italian stage, did serve to concentrate the action of the play in one specific locality. For the purposes of social comedy this concentration was by no means a disadvantage; for society, being a generality, is viewed best collectively and in a place of general resort. Even to the present day social comedy tends to prefer concentrated and generalized settings, with the single-set comedy not at all uncommon. Indeed, the conventional drawing-room set has become practically a cliché of the type.

The social bias of *The Misanthrope* is clearly indicated by its title. Patently any individual at odds with the human race is an anti-social eccentric and a hopeless social misfit. It is true that Alceste has his provocations. As a man of plain dealing and no nonsense, he is righteously offended by the casual expediency of his friend Philinte, by the frivolous coquetry of Célimène, by the envious malice of Arsinoé, by the pretentious foppery of the elegant gallants—in short, by the whole insincere and irresponsible shoddiness of society. In making clear these legitimate grounds for indignation, Molière presents not only a brilliant picture of fashionable society in the Paris of Louis XIV, but a tart satire on the perennial ways of the social world. In one acid etching after another he passes in review the familiar inhabitants of this polite world—the fop, the coquette, the faded belle, the self-centered sophisticate—with all their accustomed frippery of affectation, vanity, envy, cruel wit, malicious gossip, and smug hypocrisy. It is portraiture done with a shrewd eye for the revealing gesture and a keen instinct for the ironic self-trayal. And in this X-ray likeness of society being itself, civilized man cuts about as sorry a figure in his skeleton as in his underwear.

On the other hand, as Philinte repeatedly points out, the derelictions of society, while they may explain, scarcely justify behavior like that of Alceste. For all his pugnacious integrity, indeed because of it, Alceste is as socially reprehensible as anyone else, and in his own way is perhaps most fatuous of all. Undoubtedly his exasperation with folly and hypocrisy makes him a sympathetic figure, but it does not alter the fact that, from any sensible point of view, he is a sympathetic figure gone woefully wrong. It takes all kinds of people, including fools and poltroons, to make up a society, and a certain genius for adaptability if one is not to strangle it at birth. The individual who finds himself too exquisite for normal human contact simply becomes a candidate for sainthood or extinction, neither of which, unfortunately, is conducive to an active social life. This is the predicament into which Alceste maneuvers himself; and one can understand the sociable Célimène's lack of enthusiasm for sharing his desert retreat. From the standpoint of common sense, to shun society is essentially barbarous; to demand of it an impossible perfection is unreasonable; but to make a spectacle of oneself because it fails to conform to one's personal specifications is childish and downright ridiculous.

The central difficulty with Alceste is that he wishes to play an established game according to his own set of rules while standing with one foot on earth and the other in heaven. The awkwardness of this operation involves him in a series of contortions which are as preposterous as they are confused. Insisting on the truth and nothing but the truth in criticizing undistinguished verses, he makes an enemy by pronouncements which are naturally accepted by the victim as simply an exhibition of poor taste and worse manners. Admittedly irrational in his infatuation with a coquetry which he despises, he denounces the unreasonableness of Célimène because she refuses to redeem his own defect by an equal irrationality. Inveighing against the havoc of malicious tongues, he insists upon the prerogative of speaking unwelcome opinions. Truth he demands of all men, but he is outraged when he encounters it in Philinte and Célimène. He ends by preferring to lose 20,000 francs rather than forfeit his grounds for despising mankind, and rejects Célimène because her repentant love does not include a vow of asceticism. Obviously such an attitude is compatible with neither social grace nor common reason. His very probity makes Alceste absurd. He is ridiculous, however, not because of his principles, but because of their confusion and the excesses which they prompt. And, in the constantly shifting perspective of the play, what is true of Alceste is also true in varying degrees of the other characters. From moment to moment they too hover precariously between sound practical sense and erratic absurdity. The maintaining of this delicate balance between the appealing and the ridiculous, together with its strict discrimination between the one and the other, is no small part of Molière's genius for subtle social comedy.

The cultivation of this type of drama has been so widespread that to illustrate its ramifications would be to call the roster of European comedy. Something of its scope, however, can be seen in even a few selected examples. The variety of Molière himself appears in such comedies as *Tartuffe, The Bourgeois Gentleman,* and *The Miser.* Interesting ancient examples may be found in *The Pot of Gold* or *The Captives* by Plautus and in *Phormio* or *The Brothers* by Terence. Among English playwrights of the seventeenth century, Ben Jonson cultivates the type in *The Alchemist* and *Volpone,* and Philip Massinger in the long popular comedy *A New Way to Pay Old Debts.* The direct tradition of Molière is continued by Beaumarchais in *The Barber of Seville* and *The Marriage of Figaro.* Modern English variations may be found in Shaw's *Candida* or *Pygmalion,* in Barrie's *What Every Woman Knows,* and in Maugham's *The Constant Wife.*

THE MISANTHROPE
A COMEDY

by

MOLIERE
(JEAN BAPTISTE POQUELIN)

TRANSLATED BY

CURTIS HIDDEN PAGE

Characters

ALCESTE, *in love with* CÉLIMÈNE
PHILINTE, *friend of* ALCESTE
ORONTE, *in love with* CÉLIMÈNE
CÉLIMÈNE, *a young widow*
ÉLIANTE, CÉLIMÈNE'S *cousin*
ARSINOÉ, *friend of* CÉLIMÈNE

ACASTE ⎱ *marquises*
CLITANDRE ⎰
BASQUE, CÉLIMÈNE'S *servant*
AN OFFICER *of the Marshal's Court*
DUBOIS, ALCESTE'S *valet*

*The Scene is at Paris in the second-floor reception room of
Célimène's house.*

The *Misanthrope*, by Molière, translated by Curtis Hidden Page. Courtesy of
G. P. Putnam's Sons.

ACT I

Scene I [1]

PHILINTE, ALCESTE

PHILINTE.   What is it? What 's the matter?
ALCESTE.   [*Seated.*]   Leave me, pray.
PHILINTE.   But tell me first, what new
fantastic humour . . .
ALCESTE.   Leave me alone, I say. Out of
my sight!
PHILINTE.   But can't you listen, at least,
and not be angry?
ALCESTE.   I will be angry, and I will not
listen.
PHILINTE.   I cannot understand your gusts
of temper;
And though we 're friends, I 'll be the very
first . . .
ALCESTE.   [*Starting to his feet.*] What, I,
your friend? Go strike that off your
books.
I have professed to be so hitherto;
But after seeing what you did just now,
I tell you flatly I am so no longer
And want no place in such corrupted
hearts.
PHILINTE.   Am I so very wicked, do you
think?
ALCESTE.   Go to, you ought to die for very
shame!
Such conduct can have no excuse; it must
Arouse abhorrence in all men of honour.
I see you load a man with your caresses,
Profess for him the utmost tenderness,
And overcharge the zeal of your embrac-
ings
With protestations, promises, and oaths;
And when I come to ask you who he is
You hardly can remember even his name!
Your ardour cools the moment he is gone,
And you inform me you care nothing for
him!
Good God! 't is shameful, abject, infamous,
So basely to play traitor to your soul;
And if, by evil chance, I 'd done as much,

I should go straight and hang myself for
spite.
PHILINTE.   It doesn't seem to me a hang-
ing matter;
And I 'll petition for your gracious leave
A little to commute your rigorous sentence,
And not go hang myself for that, an't
please you.
ALCESTE.   How unbecoming is your pleas-
antry!
PHILINTE.   But seriously, what would you
have me do?
ALCESTE.   Be genuine; and like a man of
honour
Let no word pass unless it 's from the heart.
PHILINTE.   But when a man salutes you
joyfully,
You have to pay him back in his own coin,
Make what response you can to his polite-
ness,
And render pledge for pledge, and oath for
oath.
ALCESTE.   No, no, I can't endure these
abject manners
So much affected by your men of fashion;
There 's nothing I detest like the contor-
tions
Of all your noble protestation-mongers,
So generous with meaningless embraces,
So ready with their gifts of empty words,
Who vie with all men in civilities,
And treat alike the true man and the cox-
comb.
What use is it to have a man embrace you,
Swear friendship, zeal, esteem, and faithful
love,
And loudly praise you to your face, then
run
And do as much for any scamp he meets?
No, no. No self-respecting man can ever
Accept esteem that 's prostituted so;
The highest honour has but little charm
If given to all the universe alike;
Real love must rest upon some preference;
You might as well love none, as everybody.
Since you go in for these prevailing vices,

---

[1] According to the Continental practice of scene division, each scene indicates, not a change of place, but a new stage of dramatic action and a changed grouping of characters occasioned by an entrance or exit. The names listed at the head of each scene indicate the characters who either en- ter or remain.

225

By God, you 're not my kind of man, that 's all;
I 'll be no sharer in the fellowship
Of hearts that make for merit no distinction;
I must be singled out; to put it flatly,
The friend of all mankind 's no friend for me.

PHILINTE. But, while we 're of the world, we must observe
Some outward courtesies that custom calls for.

ALCESTE. No, no, I tell you; we must ruthlessly
Chastise this shameful trade in make-beliefs
Of friendship. Let 's be men; on all occasions
Show in our words the truth that 's in our hearts,
Letting the heart itself speak out, not hiding
Our feelings under masks of compliment.

PHILINTE. There 's many a time and place when utter frankness
Would be ridiculous, or even worse;
And sometimes, no offence to your high honour,
'T is well to hide the feelings in our hearts.
Would it be proper, decent, in good taste,
To tell a thousand people your opinion
About themselves? When you detest a man,
Must you declare it to him, to his face?

ALCESTE. Yes.

PHILINTE. What!—you 'd tell that ancient dame, Emilia,
That she 's too old to play the pretty girl,
And that her painting is a public scandal?

ALCESTE. Of course.

PHILINTE. And Dorilas, that he 's a bore;
And that he 's wearied every ear at court
With tales of his exploits and high extraction?

ALCESTE. By all means.

PHILINTE. You are joking.

ALCESTE. No. I 'll spare

No one. My eyes are far too much offended.
The court and town alike present me nothing
But objects to provoke my spleen; I fall
Into black humours and profound disgust,
To see men treat each other as they do;
There 's nowhere aught but dastard flattery,
Injustice, treachery, selfishness, deceit;
I can't endure it, I go mad—and mean
Squarely to break with all the human race.

PHILINTE. This philosophic wrath 's a bit too savage.
I laugh at the black moods I find you in,
And think that we, who were brought up together,
Are like those brothers in the *School for Husbands,*[2]
Whose . . .

ALCESTE. Heavens, have done your dull comparisons.

PHILINTE. No, really now, have done your own vagaries.
The world will not reform for all your meddling;
And since plain speaking has such charms for you,
I 'll tell you plainly that your strange distemper
Is thought as good 's a play, where'er you go;
Such mighty wrath against the ways o' the world
Makes you a laughing-stock for many people.

ALCESTE. So much the better! Zounds, so much the better!
The very thing I want; I 'm overjoyed;
'T is a good sign. I hate mankind so much,
I should be sorry if they thought me wise.

PHILINTE. You have a great spite against human nature.

ALCESTE. Yes, I 've conceived a frightful hatred for it.

PHILINTE. And are all mortals, quite without exception,
To be included in this detestation?

---

[2] A popular earlier comedy by Molière dealing with the relative merits of two brothers, one austere and the other amiable.

There are some, surely, even now-a-
days . . .

ALCESTE. There 's no exception, and I
hate all men:
A part, because they 're wicked and do
evil;
The rest, because they fawn upon the
wicked,
And fail to feel for them that healthy
hatred
Which vice should always rouse in virtuous
hearts.
You see the rank injustice of this fawning,
Shown toward the bare-faced scoundrel
I 'm at law with.
The traitor's face shows plainly through his
mask,
And everywhere he 's known for what he
is;
His up-turned eyes, his honeyed canting
voice,
Impose on none but strangers. All men
know
That this confounded, low-bred, sneaking
scamp
Has made his way by doing dirty jobs,
And that the splendid fortune these have
brought him
Turns merit bitter and makes virtue blush.
Whatever shameful names you heap upon
him,
There 's no one to defend his wretched
honour;
Call him a cheat, a rogue, a cursed rascal,
And every one agrees, none contradicts
you.
But yet his grinning face is always wel-
comed;
He worms in everywhere, he 's greeted,
smiled on;
And if there is preferment to compete for,
Intrigue will win it for him, from the
worthiest.
Damnation! It offends me mortally
To see how people compromise with vice;
Sometimes I 'm seized upon by sudden
longings
To flee from all mankind, and live in
deserts.

PHILINTE. Don't take the manners of the
time so hard!
Be a bit merciful to human nature;
Let us not judge it with the utmost rigour,
But look upon its faults with some in-
dulgence.
Our social life demands a pliant virtue;
Too strict uprightness may be blame-
worthy;
Sound judgment always will avoid ex-
tremes,
And will be sober even in its virtue.
The stiff unbending morals of old times
Clash with our modern age and common
usage;
They ask of mortal men too much perfec-
tion;
We must yield to the times, and not too
hardly;
And 't is the very utmost height of folly
To take upon you to reform the world.
I see a hundred things each day, as you do,
That might be better, were they different;
And yet, whatever I see happening,
I don't fly in a passion, as you do;
I quietly accept men as they are,
Make up my mind to tolerate their con-
duct,
And think my calmness is, for court or
town,
As good philosophy as is your choler.

ALCESTE. But can this calmness, sir, that
talks so well,
Be moved at nothing? If perchance a friend
Betrays you—tries by fraud to steal your
fortune—
Or if vile slanders are devised against you,
Will you behold all this and not get angry?

PHILINTE. Yes, I can look on faults, at
which your soul
Revolts, as vices linked with human nature;
To put it in a word, I 'm no more shocked
To see a man unjust, deceitful, selfish,
Than to see vultures ravenous for prey,
Or monkeys mischievous, or wolves blood-
thirsty.

ALCESTE. What! see myself betrayed,
robbed, torn in pieces,
And not . . . Good heavens! I won't talk
with you,
Your reasoning is such sheer sophistry!

PHILINTE. In truth, you had far better
hold your tongue.

Storm somewhat less against your adversary,

And give some slight attention to your suit.

ALCESTE. I 'll give it none at all—that
point is settled.

PHILINTE. Who will solicit [3] for you, then,
d' ye think?

ALCESTE. Who? Reason, equity, and my
just rights.

PHILINTE. You won't go call on any of
the judges?

ALCESTE. No. Is my cause unjust, or even
doubtful?

PHILINTE. No, I agree with you. But still,
intrigue . . .

ALCESTE. No. I won't stir a step. My mind
's made up.

My cause is wrong, or right.

PHILINTE.   Don't trust to that.

ALCESTE. I shall not budge.

PHILINTE.   Your adversary 's strong,

And may, through his cabal, bear off . . .

ALCESTE.   No matter.

PHILINTE. You'll find you've made a great
mistake.

ALCESTE.   So be it.

I want to see how this thing will turn out.

PHILINTE. But . . .

ALCESTE.   It will be a joy to lose my suit.

PHILINTE. But surely . . .

ALCESTE.   By this trial I shall see

If men can be sufficiently perverse,

Rascally, villainous, and impudent

To do me wrong before the universe.

PHILINTE. Lord, what a man!

ALCESTE.   No matter what it costs me,

Just for the beauty of the thing, I 'd rather

My suit were lost.

PHILINTE.   People would laugh at you,

Alceste, if they could hear you talk so,
truly.

ALCESTE. So much the worse for those
who laughed.

PHILINTE.   But tell me:

This strict integrity that you demand,

This truthfulness exact and scrupulous—

Say, do you find them here, in her you
iove?

For my part, I 'm amazed that you, while
being

(Or so 't would seem) so utterly at odds

With all the human race, should, spite of
all

That makes it hateful to you, find in it

A charm to stay your eyes. Still more surprising

Is that strange choice your heart has fixed
upon.

Though Éliante, the true, has shown a
kindness

For you, and though Arsinoé, the prude,

Looks on you with an eye of favour, still

Your heart rejects their love, while Célimène,

Whose taste for slander and coquettish
temper

So truly ape the manners of the age,

Holds it, for pastime, captive in her chains.

How happens it that, when you hate our
manners

So bitterly, you bear with them in her?

Are they no longer false when housed so
fairly?

Do you not see, or do you pardon them?

ALCESTE. No, no. The love I feel for this
young widow

Can't make me blind to any of her faults.

For all the passion she 's inspired me with,

I am the first to see them and condemn
them.

Yet none the less—I must confess my
weakness—

Do what I will, she still finds ways to
please me;

In vain I see her faults, in vain I blame
them,

Still in my own despite she makes me love
her;

Her charms prevail; no doubt my love, in
time,

Will purge her of the vices of the age.

PHILINTE. If you accomplish that, you
will do wonders.

You think she loves you, then?

[3] It was a custom of the time to commend oneself to the judge in a lawsuit by a visit and an
appropriate remembrance. Although looked upon
more as a courtesy than a bribe, the practice obviously encouraged abuse. Alceste's attitude, on
the other hand, could appear simply rude.

ALCESTE. By heaven, I do!
I could not love her if I didn't think so.

PHILINTE. But if her fondness for you is confessed,
Why should you fret yourself about your rivals?

ALCESTE. Because a heart that truly loves, demands
To have its loved one wholly to itself.
I 've come here now to tell her all I feel
Upon this point.

PHILINTE. If I could have my way
I should address my suit to Éliante,
Her cousin. She is steadfast and sincere,
Esteems you, and would be a fitter choice.

ALCESTE. Yes, yes, quite true. My reason tells me so
Each day. But reason does not govern love.

PHILINTE. I fear for your affections; and your hope
May well . . .

Scene II

ORONTE, ALCESTE, PHILINTE

ORONTE [To ALCESTE.] I learned below that Éliante
And Célimène have both gone out a-shopping.
But since they told me you were here, I came
Up stairs, to pay you, from my very heart,
My tribute of unlimited esteem,
And tell you of my ardent wish, long-cherished,
To be among the number of your friends.
Yes, I 've a heart that loves to honour merit;
I long to see the bonds of friendship join us;
And I believe a zealous friend, and one
Of my condition, can't well be rejected.

[During this speech, ALCESTE stands musing, and seems not to notice that ORONTE is speaking to him.]

'T is you, by your good leave, that I 'm addressing.

ALCESTE. I, sir?

ORONTE. Yes, you. I hope I don't offend you.

ALCESTE. By no means. But I 'm very much surprised.
I did not look for such an honour, sir.

ORONTE. My great esteem for you should not surprise you,
For you can claim the like from everyone.

ALCESTE. Sir . . .

ORONTE. Nothing in the state can measure up
To that supreme desert men see in you.

ALCESTE. Sir . . .

ORONTE. Yes, for me, I hold you far above
All that 's most eminent in all the nation.

ALCESTE. Sir . . .

ORONTE. Heaven strike me dead, if I am lying!
And for a present witness of my feelings,
Pray let me, sir, most heartily embrace you,
And ask you for a place among your friends.
Your hand, I beg of you. You promise me
Your friendship?

ALCESTE. Sir . . .

ORONTE. What, you refuse it?

ALCESTE. Sir,
'T is too much honour that you wish to do me.
But friendship needs a touch of mystery,
And asks initiation. We profane
Its name, to drag it in on all occasions.
It springs from mutual knowledge, mutual choice;
Before we form this tie, we need to know
Each other better; we might have such natures
That we should both repent our hasty bargain.

ORONTE. 'Pon honour, spoken like a man of sense!
And I esteem you for it all the more.
We 'll let time knit these gentle ties between us;
But meanwhile, I am wholly at your service.
If you need any favour from the court,
'T is known I cut some figure with the king;
I have his ear, and he has always used me,
'Pon honour, like a perfect gentleman.

In short, I 'm yours completely, every way;
And since you 've so much wit, I 've come
  to show you,
Just to inaugurate our charming friend-
  ship,
A sonnet that I wrote not long ago,
And ask you whether I 'd best publish it.
ALCESTE.   Sir, I 'm ill fitted to decide such
  matters;
Pray you, excuse me.
ORONTE.   Why?
ALCESTE.   I have the fault
Of being more sincere than suits the case.
ORONTE.   The very thing I want. Why, you
  would wrong me
If, when I come for your unfeigned opin-
  ion,
You should deceive me, hiding anything.
ALCESTE.   Since that is what you wish, sir,
  I am willing.
ORONTE.   "Sonnet."   It   is   a   sonnet.
"Hope . . ." It is
A lady who had fanned my flame with
  hope.
"Hope . . ." It is none of your grand pom-
  pous lines.
But light familiar verse, soft, languishing.
            [At each interruption he looks
                    toward ALCESTE.]
ALCESTE.   We 'll see, sir.
ORONTE.   "Hope . . ." I don't know
  if its style
Will seem sufficiently clean-cut and facile,
Or if the choice of words will satisfy
  you.
ALCESTE.   Sir, we shall see.
ORONTE.   Besides, I ought to tell you,
It took me but a quarter-hour to write it.
ALCESTE.   Out with it, sir. The time can
  make no odds.
ORONTE. [Reading.]

Hope, it is true, may bring relief
    And rock to sleep awhile our pain;
But, Phyllis, what small gain and brief,
    If nothing follow in its train!

PHILINTE.   I 'm charmed already with this
  little taste.
ALCESTE. [Aside to PHILINTE.]   What! Can
  you have the face to call that fine?

ORONTE.
  You showed me some benevolence,
    But should have shown me less, or none,
  Nor put yourself to such expense
    To give me hope, and hope alone.

PHILINTE.   Ah! In what gallant terms these
  things are phrased!
ALCESTE. [Aside to PHILINTE.]   Good heavens! Vile flatterer! You 're praising rubbish.
ORONTE.

  If I must wait eternally,
  Fordone by love, to death I 'll fly,
    And end my lost endeavour.
  Then vain your care, my Phyllis fair;
  Hope and despair are one, I swear,
    When hope lasts on forever.

PHILINTE.   The ending 's pretty, amorous,
  admirable,
It has a dying fall.
ALCESTE. [Aside.]   Plague take your fall,
You devil's poison-monger! Would you 'd
  had
The dying fall yourself!
PHILINTE.   I never heard
Lines better turned.
ALCESTE. [Aside.]   By heaven!
ORONTE.   You flatter me
And think, perhaps . . .
PHILINTE.   I am not flattering.
ALCESTE. [Aside.]   What are you doing
  then, you vile impostor?
ORONTE. [To ALCESTE.]   But you, sir—you
  remember our agreement.
I pray you speak in all sincerity.
ALCESTE.   This is a ticklish subject always,
  sir;
We 're fond of being flattered for our wit.
But I was saying, just the other day,
To some one—I won't mention any
  names—
On hearing certain verses he had written,
That any gentleman should always keep
In stern control this writing itch we 're
  seized with;
That he must hold in check the great im-
  patience
We feel to give the world these idle pas-
  times;
For, through this eagerness to show our
  works,

'T is likely we shall cut a foolish figure.

ORONTE. And do you mean to intimate by this,
That I am wrong to wish . . . ?

ALCESTE. I don't say that.
But I was telling him, a frigid piece
Of writing bores to death; and this one weakness
Is quite enough to damn a man, no matter
What sterling qualities he have withal;
For men are judged most often by their foibles.

ORONTE. Then do you think my sonnet bad?

ALCESTE. I don't
Say that. But still, as reason for not writing,
I tried to make him see how, right among us,
This lust for ink has spoiled most worthy men.

ORONTE. Do I write badly then? D' ye mean I 'm like 'em?

ALCESTE. I don't say that. But still (said I to him)
What is your urgent need of making verses?
And who the deuce should drive you into print?
Only poor creatures writing for a living
Can ever be excused for publishing
A wretched book. Come, come, resist temptation,
Conceal this sort of business from the public,
And don't, for anything, go and abandon
Your reputation as a gentleman
To get in place on 't, from a greedy printer
That of ridiculous and wretched scribe.
That 's what I tried to make him understand.

ORONTE. All well and good, sir; and I take your meaning.
But may n't I know what there is, in my sonnet . . .

ALCESTE. Candidly, sir, 't is good . . . good closet-verse.
You have been guided by the worst of models,
And your expressions are not true to nature.
Now what is this: "And rock to sleep our pain"?
Or this: "If nothing follow in its train"?
What means: "Nor put yourself to such expense,
To give me hope, and hope alone"? What sense
Is there in this: "Hope and despair are one
When hope lasts on"—or words to that effect?
This style, full of conceits,[4] that we 're so vain of,
Is far from truth to life and genuineness;
'T is merely play on words, sheer affectation,
And nature speaks far otherwise than so.
The wretched taste of this age makes me shudder;
Rude as they were, our fathers judged far better;
And I esteem all that 's admired to-day
Far less than this old song, which I 'll say over.

> If the king had given me
> His Paris town so fair,
> But to have it I must leave
> Loving of my dear, O!
> I would say, "King Henry, pray
> Take back your Paris fair,
> I 'd rather have my dearie, O!
> I 'd rather have my dear."

The rhyme is not exact, the style 's old-fashioned;
But don't you see it 's worth a thousand times
All your new gewgaws that good sense revolts at,
And there true passion speaks its native tongue?

> If the king had given me
> His Paris town so fair,
> But to have it I must leave
> Loving of my dear, O!
> I would say, "King Henry, pray
> Take back your Paris fair,
> I 'd rather have my dearie, O!
> I 'd rather have my dear."

---

[4] Affected fancies, which are, of course, what Alceste objects to. One of the chief characteristics of society in Molière's day was its fondness for elegant language.

That 's what a really loving heart might say.
[*To* PHILINTE, *who laughs.*] Yes, Mr. Wag,
   in spite of all your wits,
I set that far above the flowery fustian
And tinsel stuff that everyone extols.
ORONTE.   And I maintain my lines are ex-
   cellent.
ALCESTE.   You have your reasons, sir, for
   thinking so;
But you must grant me reasons of my own,
And not expect that mine shall bow to
   yours.
ORONTE.   I 'm satisfied to find that others
   prize them.
ALCESTE.   They have the art of feigning.
   I have not.
ORONTE.   D' ye think you are endowed
   with all the brains?
ALCESTE.   Did I but praise your rhymes,
   you 'd grant me more.
ORONTE.   I 'll get along quite well without
   your praise.
ALCESTE.   You 'll have to get along with-
   out it, please.
ORONTE.   I 'd like to have you write, in
   your own style,
Some verses on the subject, just to see.
ALCESTE.   I might, by bad luck, write as
   wretched ones;
But I 'd be mighty careful not to show 'em.
ORONTE.   You talk most high and mighty;
   but your pride . . .
ALCESTE.   Go seek your incense-swingers
   somewhere else.

ORONTE.   Come, little sir, don't take such
   lofty airs.
ALCESTE.   Faith, mighty sir, I 'll take what
   airs I please.
PHILINTE. [*Stepping between them.*] Eh!
   sirs, you go too far. Let be, I pray you.
ORONTE.   I 'm in the wrong, of course; I 'll
   quit the field.
I am your servant, sir, with all my heart.
ALCESTE.   And I, sir, am your most obedient servant.

Scene III

PHILINTE, ALCESTE

PHILINTE.   Well, now you see! For being
   too sincere,
You 've got an ugly quarrel on your hands;
I saw Oronte, on purpose to be flattered . . .
ALCESTE.   Don't speak to me.
PHILINTE.   But . . .
ALCESTE.   I renounce mankind.
PHILINTE.   'T is too much . . .
ALCESTE.   Let me be.
PHILINTE.   If I . . .
ALCESTE.   No talking.
PHILINTE.   But what . . .
ALCESTE.   I 'll hear no more.
PHILINTE.   But . . .
ALCESTE.   Sir!
PHILINTE.   You outrage . . .
ALCESTE.   Zounds! 't is too much. Don't
   follow me, I say.
PHILINTE.   What nonsense! I sha'n't let
   you get away.

ACT II [1]

Scene I
ALCESTE, CÉLIMÈNE

ALCESTE.   Madam, will you allow me to
   speak plainly?
I 'm far from satisfied with your behaviour;
It fills my heart with so much bitterness
I feel 't were better we break off our match;
'T would be deception to speak otherwise;
Sooner or later we must surely break.
Were I to promise you the contrary

A thousand times, I could not keep my
   word.
CÉLIMÈNE.   So—'t was to scold at me, ap-
   parently,
That you were kind enough to bring me
   home?
ALCESTE.   I am not scolding. But your hu-
   mour, madam,
Gives any and everyone too easy access
Into your heart. You have too many lovers

[1] The end of the preceding act clears the stage.   Each succeeding act begins with a new entrance of characters.

Besieging you—a thing I can't endure.

CÉLIMÈNE.   And must you hold me guilty
of my lovers?

How can I hinder men from liking me?

And when they come to pay me pleasant
calls,

Ought I to take a stick and drive them out?

ALCESTE.   No stick is needed, madam, but
a heart

Less tender and less open to their loves.

I know your charms attend you everywhere;

But those your eyes attract are bound to
you

By your kind welcome of them, which completes

The conquest of your beauty o'er their
hearts.

The too fond hope you 're always holding
out

Binds their attendance to you; somewhat
less

Complacence on your part would drive
away

This jostling mob of suitors. Tell me,
madam,

By what kind fate Clitandre can have
pleased you

So much? On what foundation of sublime

Virtue and merit in him do you base

The honour of your high esteem? Perhaps

'T is the long nail upon his little finger [2]

That won your admiration? Or it may be,

The shining merit of his yellow wig

Quite overcame you, as it did the rest

Of high society? Or his broad ruffs

About the knees, have made you love him?
Or

His mass of ribbons charmed you? Or,
perhaps,

The vast proportions of his German
breeches

Conquered your soul, the while he played
your slave?

Or did his laugh, or his falsetto voice,

Find out the secret way of winning you?

CÉLIMÈNE.   How foolishly you take offence
at him!

You know exactly why I treat him kindly;

For he can bring me over all his friends

To help me win my law-suit, as he promised.

ALCESTE.   Then lose your law-suit, madam,
bravely lose it,

And don't retain a rival I detest.

CÉLIMÈNE.   But you grow jealous of the
universe.

ALCESTE.   Because you welcome all the
universe.

CÉLIMÈNE.   This very fact should calm
your foolish terrors,

That I treat all with equal graciousness;

You 'd have more cause, by far, to be
offended,

Were all my favours heaped on one.

ALCESTE.   But, madam,

What have I more than all of them, I pray
you?

—I, whom you blame for too much jealousy!

CÉLIMÈNE.   The happiness of knowing you
are loved.

ALCESTE.   How can my burning heart be
sure of it?

CÉLIMÈNE.   I think that since I 've taken
pains to say so,

Such a confession ought to be sufficient.

ALCESTE.   How shall I know you did n't
say as much

At the same time, perhaps, to all the others?

CÉLIMÈNE.   Truly, a gallant lover's compliment!

You make me out a pretty sort of person.

Well, then, to save you such anxiety,

I take back, here and now, all I have said;

Now nothing can deceive you but yourself;

I hope you 're satisfied.

ALCESTE.   'Sdeath, must I love you!

Oh, if I could but once get back my heart,

How I 'd bless Heaven for such a rare good
fortune!

I strive with all my strength, and don't
conceal it,

To break the cruel bonds by which I 'm
bound;

Still all my greatest efforts come to nothing;

It must be for my sins I love you so.

[2] At the time the wearing of long fingernails
was the vogue among fops.

CÉLIMÈNE. Truly, your passion is unparalleled.

ALCESTE. Yes, on that point I challenge all the world.

My love is inconceivable; be sure

No one has ever loved as I do, madam.

CÉLIMÈNE. That's true, your method is entirely novel,

You love a woman just to quarrel with her;

Only in peevish words you show your passion,

And love was never such a scold before.

ALCESTE. It rests with you to dissipate my anger.

Let us cut short all bickerings, I beg you,

Speak open-heartedly, and put a stop . . .

Scene II

CÉLIMÈNE, ALCESTE, BASQUE

CÉLIMÈNE. What is it?

BASQUE. Here's Acaste.

CÉLIMÈNE. Well, show him up.

Scene III

CÉLIMÈNE, ALCESTE

ALCESTE. What! Can I never have you to myself?

You're always quick to let in everybody,

And can't make up your mind, in all the day,

One moment to deny yourself to people?

CÉLIMÈNE. Must I get up a quarrel with him, too?

ALCESTE. You show a deference that I can't endure.

CÉLIMÈNE. He is a man who never would forgive me,

If he should learn I did n't want to see him.

ALCESTE. What of it? . . . and why put yourself to trouble . . . ?

CÉLIMÈNE. Good lack! From such as he, good-will's important;

These people somehow have their say at court.

They force themselves on every conversation;

And though they cannot help you, they may harm you;

No matter what support you may have elsewhere,

You must not quarrel with these loud-mouthed gentry.

ALCESTE. In any case, and for whatever reason,

You find some cause to let in everybody;

And your discreet and careful policy . . .

Scene IV

ALCESTE, CÉLIMÈNE, BASQUE

BASQUE. Madam, here is Clitandre as well.

ALCESTE. Precisely.

[He makes as if to go.]

CÉLIMÈNE. Now what's this hurry?

ALCESTE. I am going.

CÉLIMÈNE. Stay.

ALCESTE. But what for?

CÉLIMÈNE. Stay.

ALCESTE. I can't.

CÉLIMÈNE. You shall.

ALCESTE. No use.

These conversations only weary me,

It is too much to ask that I endure 'em.

CÉLIMÈNE. You shall, you shall.

ALCESTE. No, 't is impossible.

CÉLIMÈNE. Well then, begone. Off with you. You're quite free.

Scene V

ÉLIANTE, PHILINTE, ACASTE, CLITANDRE, ALCESTE, CÉLIMÈNE, BASQUE

ÉLIANTE [To CÉLIMÈNE.] The marquises are coming up with us.

Have they not been announced?

CÉLIMÈNE. Yes. [To BASQUE.] Chairs for all.

[BASQUE places the chairs, and goes out.]

What! [To ALCESTE.] Not gone yet?

ALCESTE. No; but I shall insist

That you declare yourself, for them or me.

CÉLIMÈNE. Be still!

ALCESTE. You shall declare yourself, to-day.

CÉLIMÈNE. You've lost your senses.

ALCESTE.   No, you shall make known
Your choice.

CÉLIMÈNE.   So ho!

ALCESTE.   You shall decide.

CÉLIMÈNE.   You 're joking.

ALCESTE.   No. You shall choose. I have
  endured too long.

CLITANDRE.   Egad! I 'm just from court.
  At the levee [3]
Cléonte did prove himself a perfect ass;
Has he no friend who could enlighten him
With charitable comments on his manners?

CÉLIMÈNE.   'T is true, he cuts a very sorry
  figure
Before society. He 's always startling;
But when you see him after some brief
  absence,
You find him more fantastical than ever.

ACASTE.   Talk of fantastic characters!
  Egad!
I 've just encountered one of the most tedi-
  ous:
Damon, the talker, kept me, by your leave,
Out of my chair, one hour, in the sun.

CÉLIMÈNE.   He is a marvellous talker—
  one who finds
The art of saying naught with many words.
You can't make head or tail of his dis-
  course,
And what you listen to is only noise.

ÉLIANTE. [To PHILINTE.] Not a bad opening.
  The conversation
Takes a fine start toward slandering our
  neighbours.

CLITANDRE.   Madam, Timante 's another
  perfect type.

CÉLIMÈNE.   From head to foot, of mystery
  compact!
He throws you one wild glance, and hurries
  by;
And without business, is always busy.
All that he says abounds in affectation;
He wearies you to death with mannerisms;
He interrupts the talk at every moment
To whisper you some secret—which is
  nothing!
He makes a marvel of the merest trifle,

And even says "Good morning" in your
  ear.

ACASTE.   And Gerald, madam!

CÉLIMÈNE.   Oh, the boresome boaster!
He stoops to nothing less than lord and
  lady,
Is always moving in the highest circles,
And never mentions aught but duke or
  prince.
"The quality" has turned his head; his talk
Is all of horses, carriages, and dogs.
He *thees* and *thous* the men of highest
  rank,[4]
And just plain *sir* is obsolete with him.

CLITANDRE.   They say he 's on the best
  terms with Bélise.

CÉLIMÈNE.   The poor in spirit! What dull
  company!
The days she calls I suffer martyrdom;
I toil and sweat to keep the conversation
Alive, and constantly the barrenness
Of her expression lets it die again.
In vain attack upon her stupid silence
You summon to your aid all common-
  places;
Rain or fine weather, cold, or heat, are soon
Exhausted, yet her visit, bad enough
To start with, still drags on to frightful
  lengths;
You ask what 't is o'clock, yawn twenty
  times,
And still she 'll budge no more than any
  log.

ACASTE.   What think you of Adraste?

CÉLIMÈNE.   Oh! what a pride!
The man is so puffed up with love of self
He ne'er can rest contented with the court,
And makes a daily trade of cursing it,
Because no office, place, or favour 's
  granted
But what he finds himself unjustly used.

CLITANDRE.   But there 's young Cleon; our
  best sort of people
Frequent his house of late; now what of
  him?

CÉLIMÈNE.   He 's made himself a merit of
  his cook;

---

[3] An intimate morning reception held in the King's bed-chamber and attended by privileged courtiers.

[4] That is, he addresses people of highest rank with the personal pronouns appropriate only to intimates. The distinction in the pronoun of address, common in other languages, has dropped out of modern English.

And 't is his table people go to call on.

ÉLIANTE. He takes great care to serve the daintiest dishes.

CÉLIMÈNE. Yes; if he only did n't serve himself;

His stupid person is a villainous dish

That spoils, to my taste, all his finest dinners.

PHILINTE. Damis, his uncle, is well thought of, madam;

What say you of him?

CÉLIMÈNE.   He 's a friend of mine.

PHILINTE. He seems a gentleman, and full of sense.

CÉLIMÈNE. Yes; but he 's always trying to be witty,

Which drives me wild; in all his talk, he labours

To be delivered of some brilliant saying.

Since he has taken a notion to be clever,

Nothing can hit his taste, he 's grown so nice.

He needs must censure everything that 's written,

And thinks, to praise does not become a wit,

But to find fault will prove your skill and learning,

And to admire and laugh belongs to fools;

He thinks that by approving nothing new

He sets himself above all other men.

Even in conversations he finds fault;

The talk 's too trivial for his condescension;

With folded arms, he looks in pity down

From heights of wit on everything that 's said.

ACASTE. Damme! That 's just his picture, to the life.

CLITANDRE. [To CÉLIMÈNE.] For drawing portraits, you 're incomparable.

ALCESTE. On! On! Stand firm, thrust hard, my good court-friends;

You give each one his turn, spare none at all;

And yet no one of them could show himself,

But what you 'd rush to meet him, give your hand,

And kiss his cheeks, and swear you were his servants.

CLITANDRE. But why blame us? If what is said offends you,

You must address your censures to the lady.

ALCESTE. No, no! To you. 'T is your approving laughter

That wings these slanderous arrows of her wit.

And her satiric humour feeds upon

The guilty incense of your flatteries;

Her heart would find less charm in raillery

Were she to see it pass without applause.

And so 't is always flatterers we find

To blame for vices spread among mankind.

PHILINTE. But why so earnest in behalf of people

In whom you 'd blame yourself the self-same faults?

CÉLIMÈNE. Must not the gentleman needs contradict?

What! Would you have him think like other people,

And not exhibit, in and out of season,

The spirit of gainsaying he 's endowed with?

Others' opinions are not fit for him,

And he must always hold the opposite,

Because he 'd fear to seem like common mortals,

If he were caught agreeing with anyone.

The glory of contradiction charms him so

He often takes up arms against himself,

And falls to combating his own beliefs

If he but hears them from another's lips.

ALCESTE. You have the laughers, madam, on your side;

That 's saying everything. On with your satire!

PHILINTE. But then, 't is true you 're always up in arms

'Gainst everything that anybody says;

And with ill-humour you admit yourself,

You can't let people either blame or praise.

ALCESTE. Zounds! That 's because they 're always in the wrong,

Because ill-humour always is in season

Against them; for they are, in every case,

Praisers impertinent, or critics pert.

CÉLIMÈNE. But . . .

ALCESTE.   Madam, no! I say, though I should die for 't,
You have diversions that I can't put up with;
And people here are in the wrong to nourish
Your inclination to the faults they blame.
CLITANDRE.   'T is not for me to say; still, I 'll declare
That hitherto I 've found the lady faultless.
ACASTE.   I find her full of graces and attractions;
But as for faults, I have n't seen them yet.
ALCESTE.   I 've seen them all, and, far from hiding it,
She knows I make a point to tax her with them.
The more we love, the less we ought to flatter;
True love is proven by condoning nothing;
For my part, I would banish those base lovers
I found agreeing with my own opinions,
And pandering with weak obsequiousness
To my vagaries upon all occasions.
CÉLIMÈNE.   In short, were you to rule men's hearts, they must,
To show true love, renounce all compliments,
And set the high ideal of perfect passion
In railing handsomely at those they love.
ÉLIANTE.   Love is but little subject to such laws,
And lovers always like to vaunt their choice.
Their passion can find naught in her to blame,
For in the loved one, all seems lovable.
They count her faults perfections, and invent
Sweet names to call them by. The pallid maiden
Is like a pure white jasmine flower for fairness;
The frightful dark one is a rich brunette;
The lean one has a figure lithe and free;
The fat one has a fine majestic carriage;
The dowdy, graced with little charm, is called

A careless beauty; and the giantess
Appears a goddess to adoring eyes.
The dwarf is deemed a brief epitome
Of heaven's miracles; the haughty maiden
Is worthy of a crown; the cheat is clever;
The silly dunce, so perfectly good-hearted;
The chatterbox, so pleasantly vivacious;
The silent girl, so modest and retiring.
Thus does a lover, whom true passion fires,
Love even the faults of her whom he admires.
ALCESTE.   For my part, I maintain . . .
CÉLIMÈNE.   Let 's drop this subject,
And walk a little in the gallery.
What! Are you going, gentlemen?
CLITANDRE and ACASTE.   No, madam.
ALCESTE.   You have a mighty fear of their departure.
Go when you please, sirs; but I give you notice
I shall not stir till after you are gone.
ACASTE.   Unless my presence prove importunate
There 's nothing calls me elsewhere all day long.
CLITANDRE.   If I can wait upon the king at bed time
I have no other business to engage me.
CÉLIMÈNE. [To ALCESTE.] You must be joking, surely.
ALCESTE.   Not at all.
We 'll see if I 'm the one you would be rid of.

Scene VI

ALCESTE, CÉLIMÈNE, ÉLIANTE, ACASTE, PHILINTE, CLITANDRE, BASQUE

BASQUE. [To ALCESTE.] Sir, there 's a man who wants to speak to you
On business that, he says, can't be put off.
ALCESTE.   Tell him I know of no such urgent business.
BASQUE.   He 's got a jacket on with plaited coat-tails
And gold all over.
CÉLIMÈNE. [To ALCESTE.] Go see what it is,
Or rather, have him up.

Scene VII

ALCESTE, CÉLIMÈNE, ÉLIANTE, ACASTE,
PHILINTE, CLITANDRE, *An* OFFICER *from
the Marshals' Court* [5]

ALCESTE. [*Stepping forward to meet the*
OFFICER.] What do you want?
Come in, sir.
THE OFFICER. Sir, I want a word with
you.
ALCESTE. Speak out then, sir, and let me
know what 't is.
THE OFFICER. The honourable Marshals,
whom I serve,
Bid you appear before them, sir, at once.
ALCESTE. Who? I, sir?
THE OFFICER. You.
ALCESTE. And what for, may I ask?
PHILINTE. [*To* ALCESTE.] 'T is your ridicu-
lous quarrel with Oronte.
CÉLIMÈNE. [*To* PHILINTE.] What quarrel?
PHILINTE. They had words this morning
here
About some trifling lines he did n't like.
The Marshals want to hush things up at
once.
ALCESTE. I 'll never stoop to any base
compliance.
PHILINTE. You must obey their summons.
Come, get ready . . .

ALCESTE. What sort of terms can they ar-
range between us?
Will they condemn me by a vote to think
The verses good that we disputed over?
I won't take back a single word about them,
I think them wretched.
PHILINTE. But a gentler tone . . .
ALCESTE. I shall not budge an inch;
they're villainous.
PHILINTE. You ought to be the least bit
tractable.
Come, come along with me.
ALCESTE. I'll go, but nothing
Can make me take it back.
PHILINTE. Come show yourself . . .
ALCESTE. Short of a special order from
the king
Commanding me to think their plaguy
verses
Are good, I shall maintain, by heaven,
they 're wretched,
And any man that made them merits hang-
ing.
[*To* CLITANDRE *and* ACASTE, *who laugh.*]
By God's blood, gentlemen, I did n't know
I was so entertaining.
CÉLIMÈNE. Go, go quickly
Where you are summoned.
ALCESTE. Yes, I 'll go; and straight
Be back again to settle our debate.

ACT III

Scene I

CLITANDRE, ACASTE

CLITANDRE. Dear Marquis, you seem quite
self-satisfied;
You 're pleased with everything, annoyed
at nothing.
Now tell me truly, are you sure—don't
flatter
Yourself—you've such great reason to be
joyous?
ACASTE. Egad now! When I look myself
well over,
I can't find any cause for discontent;
I 'm rich, I 'm young, I 'm of a family
That well may give itself the style of noble;

And by the rank which my extraction gives
me,
I can lay claim to almost any office.
In courage, which we all must value most,
The world knows (not to boast) that I 'm
not lacking;
They 've seen me carry an affair of honour
Quite dashingly and cavalierly through.
With wit, of course, I 'm furnished; and
good taste
To judge off-hand, and talk on any subject,
And, when new plays come out (which I
adore),
On the stage-seats to act the knowing
critic,
Decide the drama's fate, and lead the ap-
plause

[5] A court established to settle the disputes of
nobles and soldiers, and thus break up the widespread practice of duelling.

Whenever a fine passage merits bravos.
I 'm dexterous, handsome, have a good complexion,
Especially fine teeth, a slender figure;
And as for dressing well, I think, without
Conceit, 't were foolish to dispute me that.
I find myself as much esteemed as can be,
Loved by the fair sex, favoured by the king.
And with all this, dear Marquis, I should think
That any man might be self-satisfied.

CLITANDRE.   Yes. But, since elsewhere you find easy conquests,
Why waste your sighs upon this lady here?

ACASTE.   I? Gad, not I! I 'm not of make or temper
To bear a fair one's coldness. Let the common
And awkward fellows burn with constancy
For frigid beauties, languish at their feet,
Bear their rebuffs, seek help in sighs and tears,
And try, by long continuance of service,
To win what is denied their scanty merit.
But men like me, dear Marquis, are not made
To love on credit and pay all expenses.
However rare may be the ladies' merits
I think that I 'm as good as they, thank Heaven;
That to be honoured with a heart like mine,
Should not, in any reason, cost them nothing;
And that the least a man like me can ask,
To make things fair, is meeting him half-way.

CLITANDRE.   You think then, Marquis, you 're in favour here?

ACASTE.   I have some reason, Marquis, so to think.

CLITANDRE.   Trust me, divest yourself of that delusion;
Dear fellow, you deceive and blind yourself.

ACASTE.   Quite true, I do deceive and blind myself.

CLITANDRE.   What makes you think your happiness so perfect?

ACASTE.   I do deceive myself.

CLITANDRE.   Upon what grounds . . . ?

ACASTE.   I blind myself.

CLITANDRE.   Have you trustworthy proofs?

ACASTE.   I fool myself, I say.

CLITANDRE.   Can Célimène
Have secretly avowed some love for you?

ACASTE.   No, I 'm ill-used.

CLITANDRE.   But answer me, I beg you.

ACASTE.   I meet with nothing but rebuffs.

CLITANDRE.   Have done
With jesting; say what hope she 's given you.

ACASTE.   I am the luckless one, and you the lucky.
She feels for me a horrible aversion,
And one of these days I must hang myself.

CLITANDRE.   Come, Marquis, let 's arrange our love-affairs,
Will you, by both agreeing on one thing—
If either of us show convincing proof
That he 's preferred by Célimène, the other
Shall give a clear field to the future victor
And free him from assiduous rivalry?

ACASTE.   Egad! I swear I like your propo-sition,
And I agree with all my heart. But hush . . .

Scene II

CÉLIMÈNE, ACASTE, CLITANDRE

CÉLIMÈNE.   Still here?

CLITANDRE.   Love stays our steps.

CÉLIMÈNE.   I heard just now
A carriage driving in. Who can it be?

Scene III

CÉLIMÈNE, ACASTE, CLITANDRE, BASQUE

BASQUE.   Arsinoé is coming up to see you, Madam.

CÉLIMÈNE.   What can the woman want with me?

BASQUE.   She 's talking now to Éliante, downstairs.

CÉLIMÈNE.   What is she thinking of? What brings her here?

ACASTE.   She everywhere is called a perfect prude;
Her zealous ardour . . .

CÉLIMÈNE.   Yes, yes, all put on.

At heart she 's of the world, and does her
utmost
To hook some man, and yet she can't suc-
ceed.
So she can only look with eyes of envy
Upon another woman's train of suitors;
Her sorry charms, in their abandonment,
Are always railing at our age's blindness.
She 'd like to hide, under sham prudery,
The frightful solitude that 's seen about her;
To save the credit of her feeble charms,
She makes a crime of every power they
lack.
The lady, all the same, would like a lover,
And even has a weakness for Alceste.
The court he pays to me insults her beauty;
She claims that I have stolen him from her;
And in her jealous spite, but ill concealed,
She secretly attacks me everywhere.
I 've never in my life seen such an idiot;
Her conduct is the height of silly malice,
And . . .

Scene IV

ARSINOÉ, CÈLIMÈNE, CLITANDRE, ACASTE

CÉLIMÈNE. Oh! What lucky chance has
brought you here?
In truth I was right anxious for you,
madam.
ARSINOÉ. I 've come to speak of something
that I thought
I ought to . . .
CÉLIMÈNE.   Dear! How glad I am to
see you!

[CLITANDRE and ACASTE go out
laughing.]

Scene V

ARSINOÉ, CÉLIMÈNE

ARSINOÉ. Their going away was certainly
most timely.
CÉLIMÈNE. Shall we sit down?
ARSINOÉ.   It is not necessary.
Friendship ought most to show itself, dear
madam,
In things that are of most importance to us;
And since there 's none of greater import,
surely,

Than what concerns propriety and honour,
I 've come to prove my heart-felt love for
you,
By telling you of something that involves
Your honour. Yesterday I called upon
Some very virtuous friends of mine; and
there
The talk was all of you; your conduct,
madam,
That wins you so much notoriety,
Had the misfortune not to be commended.
This motley crowd whose visits you en-
courage,
Your love-affairs, the rumours they give
rise to,
Had censors far more numerous and harsh
Than I could wish. Of course, you well may
know
Which side I took; how I did all I could
To clear you; swore you really *meant* no
harm
And said I 'd vouch for it your *heart* was
right.
But still, you know there are some things
in life
One can't defend, however much one wants
to;
And so I found myself compelled to grant
Your way of living was somewhat against
you;
That to the world it had an ugly look;
That everywhere it makes all sorts of talk,
And that your conduct might, if you but
chose,
Give far less reason for censorious judg-
ment.
Not that I think you 've really failed in
virtue;
Heaven preserve me from that thought, at
least!
But still, the mere appearances of evil
Are quickly credited; 't is not enough
To live uprightly for ourselves alone.
I hope you have too sensible a spirit,
Madam, to take amiss this useful warning,
Or think it due to any other motive
Than my concern for all that touches you.
CÉLIMÈNE. Madam, I owe you many
thanks. This warning
Has put me deeply in your debt; so far

From taking it amiss, I shall insist
Upon repaying it at once in kind
By giving you a warning which concerns
Your honour. Since you prove yourself my
    friend
By telling me the common talk about me,
I 'll follow, in my turn, this good example,
By telling you what people say of you.
Where I was visiting the other day,
I met some people of especial merit,
Who, in discussing true ideals of virtue,
Turned their remarks upon your character,
Dear madam. But your prudery and fer-
    vour
Were not regarded as the best of models;
Your false assumption of a grave de-
    meanour,
Your endless talk of virtue and of honour,
Your mincings and your mouthings at the
    shadow
Of coarseness that some doubtful word may
    have,
The high esteem in which you hold your-
    self
And pitying glances that you cast on others,
Your constant preaching, and your acrid
    judgments
On things quite innocent and honourable:
All this, to be quite frank with you, dear
    madam,
Was blamed with one accord. What is the
    good,
They said, of all this outward show of
    virtue
And modesty, when all the rest belies it?
She 's punctual at her prayers, to a degree,
But beats her servants, and won't pay their
    wages.
At public worship she displays great fer-
    vour,
But paints herself, and tries to play the
    beauty.
She has the nude in pictures covered up,
But the reality, meanwhile, she likes.
I took your part against them, one and all,
Assuring them that this was calumny;
But their opinions all combined against me,
And their conclusion was, that you 'd do
    well
To meddle less with other people's con-
duct,
And look a bit more closely to your own;
That we should scrutinise ourselves no little
Before assuming to condemn our neigh-
    bours,
And add the weight of exemplary living
To any censure that we pass on others;
And even so, if needful, we should leave it
To those whom Heaven appoints to judge
    such matters.
I hope you likewise are too sensible,
Madam, to take amiss this useful warning,
Or think it due to any other motive
Than my concern for all that touches you.
ARSINOÉ. Whatever risk we run in our
    reproofs,
I did not, madam, look for this retort;
And I see plainly, by its bitterness,
That my frank warning cut you to the
    quick.
CÉLIMÈNE. No! Say it pleased me, rather.
    Were folk wise
Such mutual warnings would become the
    fashion.
Given in good faith, they 'd soon dispel that
    blindness
Most of us suffer as regards ourselves.
'T will be your fault if we should not con-
    tinue
This faithful service with unbated zeal,
And take pains privately to tell each other
What you may hear of me, and I of you.
ARSINOÉ. Ah, madam, I can hear no ill of
    you;
It is in me that everything 's to blame.
CÉLIMÈNE. Everything, madam, may be
    praised or blamed,
And each is right, in proper time and sea-
    son.
There is an age for love-affairs, methinks,
And there 's an age that 's fit for prudery.
It may be policy to choose the second
When youth is gone and all its glamour
    faded,
For that may serve to hide a sorry down-
    fall.
Perhaps some day I 'll follow in your foot-
    steps,
For age brings everything; but 't is not time,
As all men know, to be a prude at twenty.

ARSINOÉ. You plume yourself upon a slight advantage,
And make a frightful noise about your age.
The trifling difference between yours and mine
Is no such mighty matter to be proud of,
And I can't see why you 're so angry, madam,
And fall upon me in such bitter fashion.

CÉLIMÈNE. I, madam, likewise cannot see just why
You should let loose against me everywhere.
Must I be blamed for all your disappointments,
And can I help it if the men won't court you?
If they love me, and will persist in paying
To me addresses that you 'd rather have,
Why, I can't help it, and it 's not my fault;
The field is free for you, and I don't hinder
Your having charms to win them, if you can.

ARSINOÉ. Good lack! D' ye think that any-one 's concerned
About the mob of lovers you 're so vain of,
Or that we cannot easily infer
What price is paid to get 'em now-a-days?
D' ye hope, the way things go, to make us think
Your simple merit draws this motley crowd?
That they 're inflamed with honourable passion,
And that they court you only for your virtues?
No one is blinded by such vain pretences;
The world 's no dupe. I know some women, too,
With charms to kindle tender sentiments,
Who don't have lovers always dangling round 'em;
Whereby we may infer that they 're not won
Without some great advances on our part;
That men don't woo us just to look at us,
And all the court they pay is dearly bought.
Then don't be so puffed up with boastful pride
For the cheap tinsel of a paltry triumph;
Don't let your beauty be so self-conceited,

And for so little treat folk haughtily.
For if my charms could envy yours their conquests,
Why, I might do as others do, methinks,
And prove, by being lavish of myself,
That one has lovers if one wants to have 'em.

CÉLIMÈNE. Then have 'em, madam; let us see it done.
Try if by this rare secret you can please;
And don't . . .

ARSINOÉ. Let 's end this conversation, madam,
'T will carry us too far; I should have taken
My leave already, as I ought to do,
If I were n't forced to wait here for my carriage.

CÉLIMÈNE. Stay just as long as suits you, madam. Nothing
Need hurry you. But not to weary you
With my attentions, here 's a gentleman,
Most opportunely come, to take my place
And give you better company than I can.

Scene VI

CÉLIMÈNE, ARSINOÉ, ALCESTE

CÉLIMÈNE. Alceste, I must go write a line or two;
I can't defer it without serious loss.
Please stay with madam; she will be so kind
As gladly to excuse my impoliteness.

Scene VII

ALCESTE, ARSINOÉ

ARSINOÉ. You see she wishes me to talk with you
Just for a moment, till my carriage comes;
Her hospitality could offer nothing
More charming to me than such conversation.
People of lofty merit needs must win
Esteem and love from everyone; your worth
Has some especial charm to make my heart
Espouse your interests in every way.
I wish the court would cast an eye of favour
On you, and do more justice to your merits.

You 've reason to complain; I 'm out of patience
To see them day by day do nothing for you.

ALCESTE. Me, madam! Pray what claim have I upon them?
What service have I rendered to the state?
What brilliant deeds have I achieved to give me
Cause for complaint that they do nothing for me?

ARSINOÉ. Not all those whom the court delights to honour
Have always done such signal services.
The opportunity as well as power
Is needed; and the merit that you show
Ought . . .

ALCESTE. Heavens! I beg you, let my merit be;
How can the court be bothered about that?
'T would have its hands too full, if it attempted
To bring to light the worth of everybody.

ARSINOÉ. But brilliant worth will bring itself to light.
Yours is esteemed by many, and most highly;
Why, I could mention two distinguished houses
Where men of weight extolled you yesterday.

ALCESTE. Eh! madam, now-a-days all men are praised;
The present age has no distinctions left,
And all is equally of dazzling merit;
There is no honour brought you by such praise,
Flung at your head, stuffed down your throat; I see
My valet 's praised too, in the Court Gazette!

ARSINOÉ. For my part, I could wish, to prove your worth,
Some court employment might appeal to you.
If you 'll but show the least desire for it,
We 'll straightway set intrigues at work to serve you;
I 've persons at my beck and call, to help you

And make the pathway smooth to all preferment.

ALCESTE. Madam, what would you have me do at court?
My character demands I keep away,
For heaven did not give me, at my birth,
A soul congenial to court atmosphere.
I know I don't possess the talents needful
To win success, and make my fortune there.
A frank sincerity is my chief merit,
I 've not the skill to hoodwink men with words,
And anyone who lacks the gift of hiding
His thoughts, should make brief stay in such a country.
Away from court, 't is true, we 've not that standing
Or honourable rank which it bestows;
But still, for compensation, we escape
Having to play the part of silly fools,
To bear a thousand pitiless rebuffs,
To laud the rhymes of Mr. So-and-So,
Burn incense at the shrine of Madam Blank,
And bear the shallow wit of hare-brained lordlings.

ARSINOÉ. Then let us drop this matter of the court,
Since you prefer it; but my heart is moved
To pity by your love-affair. To tell you
Just what I think about it, I could wish
Your passion were more fittingly bestowed.
You certainly deserve a kinder fate,
For she who charms you is unworthy of you.

ALCESTE. Madam, in saying this, do you remember,
I pray you, that this person is your friend?

ARSINOÉ. Yes. But it really goes against my conscience
Longer to bear the wrong that 's being done you.
The state I see you in afflicts my soul
Too much. I warn you that your love 's betrayed.

ALCESTE. Madam, you 're showing much concern for me;
Such news is always welcome to a lover!

ARSINOÉ. Yes, though my friend, she is,

and I declare her,
Unworthy to enthrall a true man's heart;
And her affection for you is a sham.

ALCESTE. That 's possible; we can't see people's hearts;
But still, in charity you might refrain,
Madam, from raising such a doubt in mine.

ARSINOÉ. If you prefer not to be undeceived,
I 'll say no more to you; that 's easy enough.

ALCESTE. In such a case, whatever we may learn,

Doubts are more torturing than any truth;
And I had rather I were told of nothing
Except what can be proved with certainty.

ARSINOÉ. That 's right enough; and on this present matter
You shall receive complete enlightenment.
I 'll let your own eyes prove it all to you.
Only escort me home, and there I 'll show you
A faithful proof of her unfaithfulness;
And if your heart can love another fair,
Perhaps you 'll find your consolation there.

ACT IV

Scene I

ÉLIANTE, PHILINTE

PHILINTE. Never was seen a man so hard to manage,
Or compromise so difficult to make;
In vain they tried to move him every way,
They couldn't drag him from his fixed opinion;
And never did so strange an altercation,
Methinks, employ the wisdom of the Marshals.
"No, gentlemen," he said, "I 'll not retract;
I will agree to all you please, except
This one point. What is he offended at?
What does he want of me? Does it reflect
Upon his honour, if he can't write well?
What odds to him is my opinion, which
He took so much amiss; a man may be
A perfect gentleman, and write poor verse.
These matters do not raise the point of honour.
I hold him a true man in all respects,
Brave, worthy, noble, anything you will,
But still, a wretched writer. I will praise,
If you desire, his lavish style of living,
His skill in horsemanship, in arms, in dancing;
But for his verse, I beg to be excused;
And if a man has not the luck to write
Better than that, he ought to give up rhyming,
Unless condemned to it on pain of death.'
In short, the only favour or concession

He could with effort bring himself to grant
Was saying (as he thought, in gentler style):
"I 'm sorry, sir, that I 'm so hard to please,
And for your sake I wish with all my heart
I could have liked your recent sonnet better."
Whereon the Marshals forced them to embrace,
And hastily hushed up the whole affair.

ÉLIANTE. His ways are very strange; yet I must own
That I esteem him above other men;
And this sincerity he makes a point of
Has something noble and heroic in it.
'T is a rare virtue now-a-days. I wish
That everyone took pattern after him.

PHILINTE. The more I see of him, the more amazed
I am to see this passion he 's enslaved to.
With such a character as heaven gave him,
I don't know how he ever came to love
At all; and even less how it could be
Your cousin that his fancy fixed upon.

ÉLIANTE. This only goes to show love doesn't always
Depend on harmony of humours; all
Their theories of sympathetic souls
Are pretty, but the present case belies them.

PHILINTE. But do you think he 's loved, from what we see?

ÉLIANTE. That is a point not easy to determine.
Does she love him or not?—how can we judge,

When her own heart 's not sure of what it
  feels?
She loves sometimes without quite know-
  ing it,
And thinks she loves, too, sometimes, when
  she doesn't.
PHILINTE. I think our friend is very like
  to have
More trouble than he looks for, with your
  cousin;
And, to be frank, if he but felt as I do,
He 'd look in quite a different direction,
And by a fitter choice would take advan-
  tage,
Madam, of that kind favour you accord
  him.
ÉLIANTE. For my part, I don't try to hide
  my feelings,
And think, in such things, we should be
  straightforward.
I don't oppose his ardent love for her,
But rather do my best to forward it;
And if the matter could depend on me,
I should unite him with the one he loves.
But if (since anything is possible)
The fates should thwart him in his choice,
  and if
Another's love be crowned with more suc-
  cess,
I could be glad, then, to receive his hom-
  age;
His having been refused, in such a case,
Would cause me no aversion.
PHILINTE.   For my part,
I likewise don't oppose your kindness,
  madam,
For him; and he can tell you, if he will
What I have said to him upon that point.
But if their marriage once for all prevented
His suit to you, then I should do my utmost
To win that favour which your generous
  heart
Now grants to him; and count myself most
  happy
If what he misses might descend to me.
ÉLIANTE. Philinte, you 're jesting.
PHILINTE.   Madam, I am speaking
Now from my inmost heart. I wait the
  chance
To make this offer unreservedly.

And all my hopes are eager for that moment.

Scene II

ALCESTE, ÉLIANTE, PHILINTE

ALCESTE. Ah! madam, help me to avenge
  a crime
That triumphs over all my strength of soul.
ÉLIANTE. What is the matter? What can
  move you so?
ALCESTE. The matter is . . . 't is death
  to think upon it! . . .
Complete upheaval of the universe
Could not o'erwhelm me more than this dis-
  aster.
All 's over with . . . My love . . . I can-
  not speak.
ÉLIANTE. Try to control yourself some-
  what.
ALCESTE.   Just heaven!
How can so many graces be united
With hateful vices of the basest nature!
ÉLIANTE. But tell us, what can make
  you . . . ?
ALCESTE.   All is ruined.
I am betrayed, destroyed, stricken to death,
For Célimène—ah! who could have be-
  lieved it?—
For Célimène deceives me; she is faithless.
ÉLIANTE. Have you sufficient grounds for
  that belief?
PHILINTE. Perhaps you are too hastily
  suspicious;
Your jealous temper sometimes takes
  chimeras
For . . .
ALCESTE. 'Sdeath! Mind your own busi-
  ness, will you, sir?
[To ÉLIANTE.] I 'm all too certain of her
  treason, madam,
Having it written down in her own hand.
Yes, here 's a letter to Oronte, disclosing
Her shame and my misfortune; to Oronte,
Whose suit I thought she scorned, and
  whom I feared
The least of all my rivals.
PHILINTE.   Letters, sometimes,
Are not so guilty as they may appear.

ALCESTE. Once more, sir, will you please let me alone,
And pay attention to your own concerns?

ÉLIANTE. You ought to calm yourself. The outrage . . .

ALCESTE. Madam,
This rests with you. To you I have recourse
For power to free my heart from galling anguish.
Avenge me on your false ungrateful cousin
Who basely has betrayed my constant love
By such a deed as must arouse your horror.

ÉLIANTE. Avenge you? I? But how?

ALCESTE. Accept my heart.
Accept it, in that faithless woman's place;
Only in that way can I be avenged;
I 'll punish her by the sincere attachment,
Profound affection, worshipful attentions,
Eager devotion, and assiduous service
My heart will henceforth offer at your shrine.

ÉLIANTE. I truly sympathise with what you suffer,
And don't despise the heart you offer me;
But still, perhaps the harm is not so great,
And you may yet give up this wish for vengeance.
For when a charming woman wrongs a man,
He forms a hundred plans, but acts on none;
In vain is even the strongest argument,
A guilty loved one soon seems innocent;
The wish to harm her quickly disappears,
And lover's wrath—we all know how it wears.

ALCESTE. No, madam, no. I 'm mortally offended.
There 's no relenting. I have done with her.
Nothing can change my settled resolution;
If I could love her still, I 'd hate myself.
But here she comes. My anger is redoubled
At sight of her. I 'll taunt her with her treason,
Confound her utterly, then bring to you
A heart quite freed from her delusive charms.

Scene III

CÉLIMÈNE, ALCESTE

ALCESTE. [Aside.] O heaven! Can I be master of my passion?

CÉLIMÈNE. [Aside.] So ho!
[To ALCESTE.] Well, what 's the matter with you now?
And what 's the meaning of your deep-drawn sighs,
And those black looks you cast in my direction?

ALCESTE. That all the horrors which a heart can hold
Have nothing to compare with your dishonour;
That fate and devils and the wrath of heaven
Never produced a creature so perverse.

CÉLIMÈNE. A pretty compliment. I like it vastly.

ALCESTE. Have done with joking. 'T is no time for laughter.
Far rather blush, for you have reason to;
I have full proof here of your perfidy.
'T was this that my presentiments foretold;
Not without reason was my love alarmed,
And through those many doubts that you called hateful
My soul foresaw the truth my eyes have found.
In spite of all your care and clever feigning,
My star predicted what I had to fear.
But do not hope I 'll suffer unavenged
The sting of such a wrong. 'T is true, I know,
That will has no control of our affections,
That love must always come spontaneously,
That never any heart was won by force,
And every soul is free to name its master.
So I could find no reason for complaint
If you had treated me without deceit;
And though you had repulsed me from the first
I could have quarrelled only with my fate.
But to lead on my heart by false avowals,
Why, that is treason, that is perfidy
For which no punishment can be too great;

And I may give free rein to my resentment.
Yes, fear the worst, after such infamy;
I am beside myself, I am all rage.
Pierced by the deadly blow which you have struck,
My reason can no longer rule my senses;
I yield to impulses of righteous anger,
And will not answer for the things I do.

CÉLIMÈNE.   But tell me, whence comes this excess of passion?
Have you quite lost your senses, pray?

ALCESTE.   Yes, yes,
I lost them, when I sucked the murderous poison
Of my misfortune from the sight of you,
And thought to find some slight sincerity
In those deceitful charms that so bewitched me.

CÉLIMÈNE.   Come now, what perfidy can you complain of?

ALCESTE.   How false your heart, how skilled in arts of feigning!
But I have proofs to force its last defence.
Look here, and recognise your character;
This letter is sufficient to convict you,
And there can be no answer made to this.

CÉLIMÈNE.   So that 's the thing you're so worked up about.

ALCESTE.   What! Don't you blush to see this piece of writing?

CÉLIMÈNE.   And why, pray, should I blush at sight of it?

ALCESTE.   What! Add audacity to artifice!
Will you disown it for not being signed?

CÉLIMÈNE.   But why disown a letter that I wrote?

ALCESTE.   And you can look on it without confusion
To see the crime toward me it brands you with!

CÉLIMÈNE.   You are in truth a most fantastic fellow.

ALCESTE.   What! You outbrave unanswerable proof?
The love shown in this letter for Oronte
Does not wrong me, or cover you with shame?

CÉLIMÈNE.   Oronte! Who says the letter is to him?

ALCESTE.   Why, those who put it in my hands just now.
But granting it was written to another,
Have I less reason to complain of you?
Are you less culpable toward me for that?

CÉLIMÈNE.   But if this note was written to a woman,
In what can it offend you? Where 's the guilt?

ALCESTE.   Ah! 't is a clever turn, a fine evasion.
I 'll own I didn't look for such a shift,
And I am quite convinced by it, of course.
How dare you seek such palpable devices?
Or do you think me quite devoid of sense?
Come, show me by what trick, and with what face,
You can maintain so evident a lie;
How you will twist to suit them to a woman
All the expressions of this passionate letter?
Interpret now, to hide your faithlessness,
What I shall read . . .

CÉLIMÈNE.   Not I; I do not care to.
You 're foolish, to assume such domination,
And say the things you dare to, to my face.

ALCESTE.   No, no; now don't get angry; try a little
To justify these words here.

CÉLIMÈNE.   No, I will not.
What you may think of it is nothing to me.

ALCESTE.   But I beseech you, show me how this letter
Can fit a woman, and I 'll be content.

CÉLIMÈNE.   No, it is to Oronte. I 'll have you think so.
I welcome his attentions joyfully,
Admire his talk, esteem his character,
And will confess to everything you please.
Go on, do what you choose, let nothing stop you,
But don't vex me about it any more.

ALCESTE.   [Aside.] Good heavens! Can anything be found more cruel?
Was ever heart so treated? What! I come
All hot with righteous anger, to complain
Of her, and find myself the one that's blamed!
My griefs and doubts are goaded to the utmost,

She bids me think the worst, and glories
 in it;
And yet my heart is still so base and weak
It cannot break the chains that bind me to
 her,
Nor arm itself with noble scorn, against
The ungrateful object of a love too fond!
[*To* CÉLIMÈNE.] How skilled you are to
 turn against me now,
Traitress, the weapon of my utter weakness,
And use to your own ends the strange
 excess
Of fated love sprung from your fickle
 beauty.
Defend yourself, I beg you, from a crime
That crushes me; do not pretend you 're
 guilty,
But show this letter innocent, if you can.
My love consents to help you; try to seem
Faithful, and I will try to think you so.
CÉLIMÈNE.   Fie, fie, you 're mad, with all
 your jealous frenzies,
And don't deserve the love that's given
 you.
I 'd like to know what ever could compel
 me
To stoop on your account to base dissem-
 bling?
Or why, if my heart leaned another way,
I shouldn't say so with sincerity?
What! Does the kind assurance of my feel-
 ings
Not come to my defence against your
 doubts?
Compared with such a pledge, are they of
 weight?
Do you not outrage me by heeding them?
And since it costs a woman such great
 effort
To own her love, and since our sex's
 honour,
A foe to love, opposes such avowals,
May any lover doubt the oracle
When for his sake we overpass those
 bounds?
Is he not guilty if he does not trust
What 's never said without a mighty
 struggle?
Fie on you, doubts like these deserve my
 anger.

You are not worth the least consideration.
I am a fool, and vexed at my own folly
In still retaining any kindness toward you;
I ought to fix my love on someone else,
And give you reason for a just complaint.
ALCESTE.   How strange my weakness for
 you is! No doubt
You are deceiving me with tender words;
No matter; I must undergo my fate;
My soul is wholly given to love of you;
And I must see, even to the bitter end,
What your heart is, and whether 't will
 betray me.
CÉLIMÈNE.   No, you don't love me as one
 ought to love.
ALCESTE.   Nothing can match the great-
 ness of my love.
In its excess of zeal it goes so far
As even to wish you harm; yes, I could
 wish
That no one ever thought you lovable,
That you were forced to live in misery,
That heaven at your birth had given you
 nothing,
And that you had no wealth or rank or
 station,
If so my heart, by free and full devotion,
Might make amends to you for fate's in-
 justice,
And I might have the joy and glory, then,
Of seeing you owe all to my affection.
CÉLIMÈNE.   That 's a strange way of car-
 ing for me! Heaven
Forbid your ever having cause . . . but
 here
Is your Du Bois, and strange enough he
 looks!

Scene IV

CÉLIMÈNE, ALCESTE, DU BOIS

ALCESTE.   What means this plight you 're
 in, this frightened air?
What is it?
DU BOIS.   Sir . . .
ALCESTE.   Well?
DU BOIS.   Here 's strange things have
 happened.
ALCESTE.   Well, what?
DU BOIS.   We are bad off, sir, very bad.

ALCESTE. How?

DU BOIS. Shall I speak right out?

ALCESTE. Yes, speak, and quickly.

DU BOIS. There's no one here who'll . . . ?

ALCESTE. Ah! what dallying!
Speak, will you?

DU BOIS. Sir, we've got to get away.

ALCESTE. What's that?

DU BOIS. We must decamp, and make
no noise.

ALCESTE. But why?

DU BOIS. I tell you we must leave this
place.

ALCESTE. What for?

DU BOIS. And never stop to say good-
bye.

ALCESTE. But what's the cause, the cause,
of what you tell me?

DU BOIS. The cause, the cause, sir, is, we
must be packing.

ALCESTE. Ah! I shall break your head,
beyond a doubt,
You booby, if you do not change your
style.

DU BOIS. Sir, a man dressed in black, with
blacker looks,
Came right into the kitchen, sir, and left us
A paper all so scribbled over, sir,
A man would have to be the very devil
To read the thing. I make no sort of doubt
But it's about your law-suit; still, old Nick
Himself could not make head or tail of it.

ALCESTE. Well, well, what then? What has
this scrawl to do,
You rascal, with our sudden forced departure?

DU BOIS. I'm here to tell you, sir, an hour
later
A man who often pays you visits came

To look for you, and in a hurry too;
And when he couldn't find you, asked me
kindly—
Because he knows I am your faithful
servant—
To tell you . . . wait a bit . . . what is
his name . . . ?

ALCESTE. Rogue! Never mind his name;
say what he told you!

DU BOIS. Well, he's a friend of yours, and
that's enough.
He told me you must leave here, for your
life,
And that you're liable to be arrested.

ALCESTE. But why? He told you nothing
definite?

DU BOIS. No. But he asked for ink and
paper then
And wrote a word by which you can, I
think,
Get at the bottom of this mystery.

ALCESTE. Then give it to me.

CÉLIMÈNE. What can this portend?

ALCESTE. I don't know; but I mean to
clear it up.
Will you not soon have done, you devil's
limb?

DU BOIS. [After having fumbled about for
the note a long time.] Faith, sir, I've left
it, sir, upon your table.

ALCESTE. I don't know what restrains
me . . .

CÉLIMÈNE. Keep your temper,
And go unravel this perplexing business.

ALCESTE. It seems that Fate, in spite of all
I do,
Has sworn to interrupt my talk with you;
But, madam, help me baffle Fate, I pray,
And let me see you yet again to-day.

ACT V

Scene I

ALCESTE, PHILINTE

ALCESTE. My mind's made up, I say.

PHILINTE. But must this blow,
However hard it seem, compel you to . . .

ALCESTE. No matter what you do or what
you say,

Nothing can move me from my settled pur-
pose;
The age we're living in is so depraved
That I must shun all intercourse with men.
What! Honour, justice, decency, the laws,
Are all combined against my adversary;
My rights are everywhere proclaimed; I rest
Assured upon the justice of my cause;

And yet I 'm disappointed by the outcome;
With justice on my side, I lose my case!
A knave, whose story is a public scandal,
Comes off triumphant in his treachery,
And honest truth must yield to black-
  guardism!
He cuts my throat, and proves he 's doing
  right!
That grinning face, in which his cant and
  cunning
Show clearly forth, has influence enough
To overthrow the right and ruin justice!
He gets decree of court to crown his crime!
Then, not contented with the wrong he 's
  done me,
Finding a villainous book in circulation,
A book deserving of the utmost censure,
And which it is disgraceful even to read,
The scoundrel has the face to say I wrote
  it!
And thereupon Oronte begins to mutter,
And basely tries to spread the lie! . . .
  Oronte
Who has the standing of a gentleman
At court, and whom I never wronged,
  unless
By being frank and honest, when he came
With ardent eagerness, against my will,
To ask my judgment on some rhymes he 'd
  written!
Because I treat him like an honest man
And won't betray the truth or him, he helps
To overwhelm me with a trumped-up
  crime!
Now he 's become my greatest enemy,
And never will be brought to pardon me,
All just because I didn't praise his sonnet!
And men, good heavens, are made of stuff
  like this!
These are the deeds their pride can bring
  them to!
This is the honesty, the love of virtue,
The justice, and the honour, found among
  'em!
I 've borne the plague of 'em too long; I 'll
  leave
This savage ambuscade and cut-throat hole;
And since among mankind you live like
  wolves,
You 'll never see me more in all your days.

PHILINTE.   Your plan, methinks, is just a
  little hasty;
The mischief 's not so great as you make
  out.
Your adversary's impudent accusation
Has not caused your arrest—'t is not be-
  lieved in;
We find his false report defeats itself,
And such an action well may do him harm.
ALCESTE.   Do *him* harm! He that 's known
  for scurvy tricks
Need fear no scandal. He 's a licensed
  scoundrel,
And far from being harmed by this affair,
To-morrow he 'll be found in higher credit.
PHILINTE.   In any case 't is certain few are
  fooled
By this report his malice spread against
  you,
And on that score you have no more to
  fear;
As for your law-suit, which you may com-
  plain of
With justice, you can easily appeal
And have this sentence . . .
ALCESTE.   No, I 'll hold by it.
However great the wrong this verdict does
  me,
I 'll take good care it shan't be set aside;
It is so clear a case of justice wronged,
I 'll hand it down to future generations
As signal proof and unsurpassed example
Of what men's villainy could be to-day.
The thing may cost me twenty thousand
  francs,
But for my twenty thousand francs I 'll
  have
The right to rail against the wickedness
Of human nature, and forever hate it.
PHILINTE.   But after all . . .
ALCESTE.   But after all, your trouble
Is wasted, sir; what can you find to say
About it? Will you have the impudence
To palliate these constant infamies?
PHILINTE.   No, I agree to anything you
  please.
Intrigue and selfish motives govern all,
Deceit wins every battle now-a-days,
And men should be quite other than they
  are.

But is their lack of righteousness a reason
To shun the world? These faults of human nature
But give us opportunities in life
To put in practice our philosophy;
This is the best employment virtue finds;
If everything were clothed in probity,
If all men's hearts were open, just, and gentle,
Most of our virtues would be wholly useless,
Since we employ them now, in cheerfully
Enduring wrong, with right upon our side;
And just as any heart of genuine virtue . . .

ALCESTE. I know, sir, you 're a mighty fluent talker,
Always abounding in fine arguments;
Still, you waste time, and all your dapper speeches.
Reason demands, for my own good, that I
Should quit the world; I can't control my tongue
Enough, nor answer for the things I 'd say.
I 'd have a hundred duels on my hands.
So let me wait in peace for Célimène;
She must accept the plan that brings me here;
I 'll learn in that way if she really loves me,
And here and now she must convince me of it.

PHILINTE. Let 's go see Éliante, until she comes.

ALCESTE. No, no, my heart 's too full of care. You go
Up stairs to her, and leave me here alone
In this dark corner, with my black chagrin.

PHILINTE. Strange company that is, and too austere
To wait with! I 'll bring Éliante down here.

Scene II

CÉLIMÈNE, ORONTE, ALCESTE

ORONTE. Yes, 't is for you to say, if ties so dear,
Madam, shall make me wholly yours forever.
I must have full assurance of your heart;
A lover does not like these waverings;
And if my ardent love has power to move you,
You should not hesitate to prove it to me;

And after all, the only proof I ask
Is, no more to admit Alceste's addresses,
To sacrifice him, madam, to my love,
And shut your door against him from this day.

CÉLIMÈNE. But why are you, whom I have heard so often
Lauding his merit, angry with him now?

ORONTE. There 's no need, madam, of these explanations.
The point is, what are your own sentiments?
Choose, if you please, the one you wish to keep;
My own decision only waits on yours.

ALCESTE. [Coming out of the corner to which he had withdrawn.] Yes, madam, he is right, it 's time to choose,
And his demand agrees with my desire.
The same impatience brings me here, the same
Intention; and my love demands of you
Some certain proof. Things can't drag on forever.
Now is the moment to declare your heart.

ORONTE. Sir, not for anything would I disturb
Your happy fortune by an ill-timed wooing.

ALCESTE. Sir, not for anything—jealous or not—
Would I consent to share her heart with you.

ORONTE. If she can possibly prefer your love . . .

ALCESTE. If she can feel for you the slightest leaning . . .

ORONTE. I swear she 'll have no more of my addresses.

ALCESTE. I swear I 'll ne'er set eyes on her again.

ORONTE. Now, madam, you may speak, without restraint.

ALCESTE. Now, madam, you may choose, and have no fear.

ORONTE. You only need to tell us which you love.

ALCESTE. You only need to say the word, and choose.

ORONTE. What! Can you seem to balk at such a choice!

ALCESTE. What! Can you waver and appear uncertain!

CÉLIMÈNE. Good heavens! How out of place is this insistence!
How little sense does either of you show!
'T is not but what I know which one to choose;
Of course I could not hold my heart suspended
Upon the scales, in doubt between you two;
No choice is quicker made than that of love;
But still, the truth is, I 'm too much embarrassed
To state my preference before you both;
I think that words which well may prove unpleasant,
Should not be said point blank, and publicly;
We can give hints enough of how we feel
Without your forcing us to open quarrel;
And gentler intimations are sufficient
To tell a suitor of his ill success.

ORONTE. No, I fear nothing from a frank avowal;
For my part, I consent to it.

ALCESTE.   And I
Demand it. Open declaration, now,
Is what I dare insist on most of all,
And I will have no mincing matters, either.
You 're always trying to retain them all;
But no more dallying or uncertainty!
Make now a clear and public declaration,
Or I shall take your silence for decision
And hold that it confirms my worst suspicions.

ORONTE. I thank you for your angry passion, sir,
And I repeat to her the selfsame words.

CÉLIMÈNE. How you do weary me with your caprice!
What reason is there in the thing you ask for?
Have I not told you why I can't consent?
Here 's Éliante, I 'll let her be the judge.

Scene III

ÉLIANTE, PHILINTE, CÉLIMÈNE, ORONTE, ALCESTE

CÉLIMÈNE. Dear cousin, I am being persecuted
By these two men, whose scheme seems preconcerted.
They both demand, and both insist upon it,
That I proclaim the choice I make between them,
And publicly forbid the other one
To pay me any court forever after.
Tell me if such a thing is ever done.

ÉLIANTE. You might do better not to ask my counsel;
Perhaps I am the wrong one to appeal to;
I 'm on the side of those who speak their mind.

ORONTE. Madam, it is in vain you seek evasions.

ALCESTE. Your shifts and turns are ill supported here.

ORONTE. You needs must speak, and stop this balancing.

ALCESTE. You need do nothing but continue silent.

ORONTE. I only ask one word, to settle matters.

ALCESTE. And I shall understand, if you say nothing.

Scene IV

ARSINOÉ, CELIMÈNE, ÉLIANTE, ALCESTE, PHILINTE, ACASTE, CLITANDRE, ORONTE

ACASTE. [To CÉLIMÈNE.] Madam, we both have come, by your good leave,
To clear up here a certain trifling matter.

CLITANDRE. [To ORONTE and ALCESTE.]
Your presence is right welcome, gentlemen;
You likewise are concerned in this affair.

ARSINOÉ. Madame, you 'll be surprised to see me here;
These gentlemen insisted on my coming;
Both called upon me, and complained to me
Of certain doings that I could not credit.
I feel too sure your heart at least is right,
To think you capable of such a crime;
I shut my eyes against their strongest proofs,
Forgot, for friendship's sake, our little quarrels,

And even consented to come here with
  them
To see you clear yourself of this vile slan-
  der.
ACASTE.   Yes, madam, we should like to
  have the pleasure
Of seeing how you 'll try to face it out.
You wrote this letter, did you, to Clitandre?
CLITANDRE.   You penned this sweet epistle
  to Acaste?
ACASTE. [*To* ORONTE *and* ALCESTE.] This
  writing, gentlemen, is not unknown
To you. I doubt not her civility
Has made you but too well acquainted
  with it.
Still, this is well worth reading:

"You are a strange fellow to blame me for
my gaiety, and reproach me with being never
so merry as when I am not with you. Nothing
can be more unjust, and if you don't come
very soon and entreat my pardon for this
crime, I 'll never forgive you as long as I live.
Our great gawk of a viscount . . ."

He ought to be here.

"Our great gawk of a viscount, whom you
complain of first, could never by any possibility suit my taste. Ever since I saw him for
three mortal quarters of an hour stand spitting
into a well to make rings in the water, I
haven't been able to think much of him. As
for the little marquis . . ."

Myself, sirs; with no vanity I say it.

"As for the little marquis, who held me so
long by the hand yesterday, I think there is
nothing so diminutive as his whole personality;
he is one of those gentry who have no worth
but their titles, and whose merit is all leather
and prunello.[1] As for the man with the green
ribbons . . ."

[*To* ALCESTE.] 'T is your turn now, sir.

"As for the man with the green ribbons, he
amuses me sometimes with his blunt ways and
his surly humours; but hundreds of times I
find him the most bothersome bore in the
world. And as to the sonnetteer . . ."

[*To* ORONTE.] This is your package, sir.

"And as to the sonnetteer, who has set up
for a wit, and is determined to be an author

---

[1] Costume materials. The point of the translator's phrase derives from Pope's couplet:

whether the world will or no, I can't bring
myself to listen to him, and his prose wearies
me as much as his verse. So be assured that I
am not always so merry as you think; that I
miss you greatly, and more than I could wish,
at all the entertainments they drag me to; and
that the presence of people we like gives a
marvellous relish to our pleasures."

CLITANDRE.   Now here am I, for my turn.

"Your Clitandre, that you talk to me of,
who abounds so in sweet compliments, is the
very last of human beings that I could have a
liking for. He is absurd to imagine that he is
loved, and you are equally so to believe that
you are not. Be reasonable, and exchange your
ideas for his; and come to see me as often as
you can, to help me bear the annoyance of
being beset by him."

There is a noble type of character
Set forth. You know its name perhaps, dear
  madam.
Enough. We 'll both of us be proud to show
This portrait of your heart, where'er we go.
ACASTE.   I could find much to say; the
  theme is tempting;
But I don't hold you worthy of my anger.
I 'll show you, little marquises can find
Hearts to console them, of a nobler kind.

Scene V

ARSINOÉ, CÉLIMÈNE, ÉLIANTE, ALCESTE,
ORONTE, PHILINTE

ORONTE.   What! Must I see myself thus
  torn to tatters,
After the things I 've had you write to me!
And does your heart, in love's false finery
Arrayed, plight troth with all mankind by
  turns!
I was too much the dupe, I 'm so no longer.
I owe you much for teaching me to know
  you,
I 'm richer by the heart you thus restore,
And find revenge in knowing what you lose.
[*To* ALCESTE.]   I shall oppose your love no
  longer, sir,
And now you may conclude your match
  with her.

"Worth makes the man, and want of it the
  fellow;
    The rest is all but leather or prunello."

Scene VI

CÉLIMÈNE, ÉLIANTE, ARSINOÉ, ALCESTE,
PHILINTE

ARSINOÉ [*To* CÉLIMÈNE.] This is the blackest deed I've ever known;
I can't be silent, I'm in such a ferment.
Did ever anybody see the like?
Not that I care a snap about those others;
But that this gentleman, [*Pointing to* ALCESTE] whom your good luck
Attached to you, a man of worth and honour,
Who doted on you to idolatry,
Should be so . . .
ALCESTE.   Madam, will you please allow me
To manage my affairs myself, and not
Take on yourself this quite superfluous burden?
However warmly you espouse my cause,
I'm in. no way to pay your zeal in kind;
And you are not a person I could think of
Should I seek vengeance by another choice.
ARSINOÉ.   Eh! Do you fancy, sir, I've that idea,
Or do you think I'd be so quick to have you?
I must say you are mighty vain if you
Can lay that flattering unction to your soul.
This lady's leavings are an article
'T would be a great mistake to rate so highly.
Pray undeceive yourself; don't be so proud.
People like me are not for such as you.
You'd do well still to dangle at her skirts,
And marry her—you'd get your just deserts.

Scene VII

CÉLIMÈNE, ÉLIANTE, ALCESTE, PHILINTE

ALCESTE. [*To* CÉLIMÈNE.] Well, I've kept silent, spite of what I've heard,
And let them all say out their say before me.
Have I controlled my feelings long enough,
And may I now . . . ?
CÉLIMÈNE.   Yes, yes, say all you will;
You have the right, you justly may complain
And blame me as you please. I'm wrong, I own it;
In my confusion I shall not attempt
To put you off with any vain excuse.
The others' anger I despised. But you
I must admit I've wronged; and your resentment
Beyond all doubt is just; I know how guilty
I must appear to you; how everything
Proclaims that I was ready to betray you,
And that you truly have good cause to hate me.
Do so, I must submit.
ALCESTE.   Ah! Can I, traitress?
Can I thus triumph over all my love?
And though with all my might I long to hate you,
How can I ever make my heart obey me?
[*To* ÉLIANTE *and* PHILINTE.] You see how far an abject love can go;
I call you both to witness to my weakness.
Yet, to confess the truth, this is not all,
You'll see me push it to the bitter end,
And prove that men are wrongfully called wise,
For all hearts have a touch of human nature.
[*To* CÉLIMÈNE.]   Yes, I am willing to forget your crimes;
I'll find it in my heart to pardon all,
And tell myself that they are weaknesses
To which the vices of the time misled you,
If only you'll consent to that design
Which I have formed, to flee from all mankind,
And be resolved at once to follow me
Into my desert, where I've vowed to live.
'T is only so that in the world's opinion
You can repair the mischief of your letters,
And even after scandal so abhorrent
To noble natures, I may love you still.
CÉLIMÈNE.   What, I renounce the world before I'm old,
And go be buried in your solitude!
ALCESTE.   But if your fondness equals my affection,
What matters to you all the world beside?
Will not your wishes be content with me?

CÉLIMÈNE. But solitude has terrors for a soul
Of twenty; mine's not great and firm enough,
I fear, to let me take that high resolve.
But if my hand can satisfy your wishes,
I'll bring myself to suffer such a bond,
And marriage . . .

ALCESTE. No; my heart detests you now.
This one rebuff does more than all the rest.
And since you cannot find, in that dear tie,
Your all in me, as I my all in you,
Go, I refuse you; this last sore offence
Sets me forever free from your base fetters.

[CÉLIMÈNE *goes*.]

SCENE VIII

ÉLIANTE, ALCESTE, PHILINTE

ALCESTE. [*To* ÉLIANTE.] Madam, a hundred virtues crown your beauty,
In you alone I've found sincerity,
And long I've felt for you a deep regard;
But let me still esteem you thus; and suffer
My heart, with all its varied agitations,
Not to demand the honour of your service.
I'm too unworthy, and begin to see
That heaven did not create me fit for marriage;
The leavings of a heart unworthy you
Would be an offering meaner than your due
And so . . .

ÉLIANTE. So let it be, Alceste, I pray;
I'm at no loss to give my hand away;
And here's your friend—to seek no further—he,
If I should ask him, might accept of me.

PHILINTE. That honour, madam, is my whole desire;
To win it I would go through flood and fire.

ALCESTE. May you, to taste true happiness, preserve
These feelings each for each, and never swerve.
Betrayed on all sides, overwhelmed with wrong,
I'll leave this den of thieves vice reigns among,
And find some lonely corner, if I can,
Where one is free to be an honest man.

PHILINTE. Come, madam, let us use our utmost art
To change this savage purpose of his heart.

Comedy of Manners

OMEDY OF MANNERS does not constitute a separate order of comedy in the same sense as the comic types discussed earlier. It is simply a variety of social comedy—with a difference. In most respects its subject matter, its technical methods, and its point of view conform with those met in all social comedy and call for no special attention. Its difference, however, is of such a nature, and produces so distinctive a result, that it merits independent consideration. This difference is one of degree more than of kind. It consists in a deliberate restriction of dramatic interest to the single specialized subject of manners: that is, to the characteristic mode of behavior developed by an organized society. Consequently comedy of manners addresses its appeal specifically to that civilized and discriminating segment of humanity to whom personal and social manners are a matter of genuine moment. It is from this unique and highly specialized preoccupation that the type derives its name.

The strictly selective focus of comedy of manners reflects a corresponding exclusiveness in its whole dramatic attitude. Social comedy in general tends to look upon society as a universal and more or less inevitable human phenomenon. It is concerned with society as an institution, sanctioned by collective human experience, and justified by its utilitarian expediency. Comedy of manners takes a rather different view. It conceives of society as the refined product of conscious artifice embodied in fashionable Society. It is concerned with social intercourse as a mode of artistic living, governed by conventional principles of deportment, and justified by the esthetic satisfactions which it is able to provide. As a result of these divergent views, whereas social comedy emphasizes the general virtues of sanity and reason, comedy of manners stresses the particular amenities of style and sophistication. In its evaluation of human conduct the former is fundamentally ethical; the latter is essentially esthetic. For the one, the infallible criterion is good sense; for the other, the touchstone is invariably good taste. From this brief comparison it is evident that the self-imposed restrictions of comedy of manners not only narrow its range of interest but also affect materially its whole scale of values. In effect, comedy of manners is an excursion into the esthetics of man's most exquisitely refined social art. As such, it is the most sophisticated form of all drama; it deals with the most artificial and self-conscious manifestations of human nature; and it applies to the fine art of civilized urbanity the most subtle esthetic appraisal ever attempted by critical laughter.

Obviously so esoteric a form of drama is able to flourish only in an equally rarefied cultural atmosphere. The niceties of polite deportment are usually caviare to the general: if not incomprehensible, they are likely to appear trivial. Only in a compact and homogeneous social group is it possible for kindred interests and tastes to crystallize into a mandatory code of conduct. Furthermore, the operation of such a code presupposes sufficient affluence and leisure to divert attention from the means of livelihood to the mode of living. In short, there must exist an appropriate motive and opportunity for social intercourse to take on the significance of an essential occupation. Such a combination of circumstances is, in the nature of the case, relatively rare. One of its most conspicuous occurrences took place in London during the half-century which followed the restoration of Charles II to the throne in 1660. During this Restoration period there came into existence an in-bred court and town Society which was consciously artificial in its sophistication and dedicated to the elegancies of fashion. Occupied largely with social diversion, it took over the theater as a convenient sounding-board for its congenial gossip and critical opinions. In doing so, it created a comedy of manners which, despite the ephemerality of the specific fashions dealt with, incorporates so admirably the perennial concerns of the sophisticate that it has remained ever since a model of its kind.

Since comedy of manners is more interested in the quality of social behavior than in the conditions which produce it, in conversation and deportment more than in dramatic action, it requires little in the way of special stage facilities other than space for the exhibition of human conduct. The Restoration stage was a tentative compromise between the picture-frame stage of Molière and the platform stage of Shakespeare. With the proscenium-arched setting of the one it combined an apron, or jutting forestage, borrowed from the other. Thus it was able to accommodate rapid action as well as to change scenery, although its sets were customarily simple, formal, and generalized. On the other hand, if comedy of manners makes few demands of its stage, it does require a very special equipment of intelligence and taste on the part of its creator. To be successful in the genre, it is imperative that a dramatist be sufficiently conversant with contemporary fashions to understand not only their most delicate nuances but also their fundamental significance. Moreover, he must subscribe to them as a necessary concomitant of civilized living, and in dealing with them be acute enough to discriminate between authentic excellence and specious imitation. At the same time he must be

sufficiently objective to view manners critically, recognizing that the artificiality which makes them susceptible to misconception and abuse fosters
with equal facility the fastidious and the fatuous. As an arbiter of
elegance, he must be capable of weighing the virtues and vices in terms of
the most subtle hair-line distinctions. In short, he must himself be a hyper-
sophisticate of impeccable taste whose own brilliance and wit are the
validation of his standards. One of the supreme masters of such sophistication was William Congreve (1670–1729), the brightest luminary of
the Restoration comic stage. His masterpiece, *The Way of the World*
(1700), is a superb expression of sophisticated wit and urbanity, and one
of the most brilliant comedies of manners ever written.

Because of its dedication to deliberate artifice, comedy of manners
exhibits certain idiosyncrasies which need to be understood if its virtues
are to be appreciated. In the first place, it is interested in deportment
rather than in the circumstances of dramatic action—in how people
behave rather than in what they do or why they do it. Consequently it
tends to minimize dramatic incidents, usually relegating these to occurrences off-stage, and concentrates upon the conversation and conduct
which reveal a reaction to the implied developments. In the second place,
it is particularly concerned with the question of correct deportment. But
correctness of deportment is rarely an expression of spontaneous human
impulses; it is the projection of a conscious standard of behavior which
has very little to do with either individual personality or immediate sentiments. For this reason, while most social comedy is ultimately a comedy
of character, comedy of manners confines its attention to those impersonal affectations of behavior which mask and obliterate individual character more often than they reveal it. And as it is but little concerned with
the actualities of character, it is relatively indifferent to the causes of
human behavior; its sole interest is the conformity or non-conformity of
conduct with an objective code. To this extent it is preoccupied with a
strictly intellectual activity, the precise bounds of which are prescribed
by expert knowledge and cultivated taste, and the most appropriate
expression of which is razor-keen wit.

In the domain with which comedy of manners is engaged, social
amenities acquire central importance as the means whereby life is made
artistically agreeable. Social intercourse assumes the nature of a civilized
diversion—a game of skill in which the edicts of fashion are the prescribed rules of the game. On the pragmatic ground that any game is only
a game, with no significance apart from its rules, and that all rules are
bound to be arbitrary and subject to perversion, comedy of manners is
little disposed either to question the prevailing rules or to substitute a
different kind of game. Accepting the game in progress, it concentrates
on the skill of the playing. In the intricate game of manners the objectives
are wit and charm. The point of the play is to achieve them within the
rigidly prescribed conventions—to wear, as it were, a strait jacket with

the elegant style of a dinner jacket. For success the requirements are as absolute as the conditions are arbitrary. It is the nature of wit and charm to admit of no middle ground: partial achievement is equivalent to total failure. To be partially witty or charming is as impossible as to be partially virgin; one either is altogether or one is not at all. As a result, in its distinctions, comedy of manners is as ruthless as it is rigid, and not infrequently as cruel as wit itself often is. It recognizes but two categories of human beings—those who succeed in living up to its standards and those who fail. Upon those who succeed it bestows the accolade due to taste and brilliance; those who fail it dismisses to the limbo of exploitation and ridicule. If this attitude appear harsh, its defense is quite obvious. The fine art of manners, like any other art, is justified solely by the excellence of its performance. It is an exercise for the initiate, in which no one is obliged to participate. Therefore, if one chooses to compete with professionals, one must be prepared to take the consequences.

In Congreve's comedy, the way of the world is not an issue; it is a candidly accepted mode of life. Neither is there any dispute about the code of manners upon which it rests. The question is not how virtuous or how rational the several characters are because of their code, but how felicitously they exemplify the principles which they profess. That the code itself is far from perfect is evident from the opportunities which it presents for the viciousness of Fainall and Mrs. Marwood, the follies of Lady Wishfort, Witwoud, and Petulant, and the strictures of Sir Wilfull. To rebel against it, however, as does Sir Wilfull, is to make the dubious exchange of an urbane hypocrisy for a boorish vulgarity. To succumb to it, on the other hand, is simply to be absurd with the pretentious or contemptible with the depraved. In either case, to a fastidious taste, the results are grotesque and ridiculous. The real art of social grace is the ability to function effectively within the existing medium. Millamant and Mirabell have no quarrel with the way of the world, even when it constricts their personal volitions. Both are eminently practical in their acquiescence to prevailing fashions and the financial arrangements necessary to sustain them. It is indicative that both are quite as much interested in preserving Millamant's inheritance and their own social aplomb as they are in obtaining each other. Neither is perturbed by the insincerities of affectation. To them the social graces are a matter of supreme importance. Wit, gayety, and charm of manners are their credentials of taste and cleverness. They cultivate and possess the brilliance and hardness of gems which take an added luster from the artifice of their setting. By comparison the other characters are tawdry imitations. Lady Wishfort betrays the ostentatious elegance and vulgarity of a kitchen-wench masquerading as a duchess. Petulant and Witwoud are upstart crows beguiled by their own borrowed plumage. Mrs. Marwood and Fainall are the inevitable counterfeits attracted by any established currency.

The distinctions involved in the contrast comprise the point of the play. Addressed to the connoisseur of manners, they are the vindication of his creed and the diversion of his taste. As the ludicrous absurdity of the inept argues the virtue of social finesse, the sophisticated grace of Millamant and Mirabell demonstrates that fine manners are more than facile affectation. These perfect sophisticates embody a refinement which is as intellectually perceptive as it is sensitive in spirit. Having no illusions about the game they are playing, they are able to move with exquisite precision between the pitfalls of folly and scurrility. Keenly aware of the absurdity of ineptitude, they are no less aware of the nice difference between reality and pretense. With no flaw in the brittle finish of their sophistication, they are adept at those subtle indirections which reveal the truth beneath the mask. The marriage contract in Act IV is an admirable illustration. Superficially a witty skirmish in the fashionable battle of the sexes, it is actually an astute and quite serious prescription for successful marriage; and the caution with which Millamant and Mirabell propose and subscribe to it is its own testimony to the sincerity of their sentiments. The delight of such a comedy is the amber of mannered grace and pungent ridicule in which Congreve embalms his social butterflies. Its effect is an exercise in fastidious discrimination, sparkling with agile wit, meticulous in the well-groomed phrase, and conducted with the ease of conscious style and impeccable manners.

Although incidental treatment of manners is fairly common in social comedy, pure comedy of manners is a rather rare form of drama. Most frequently it gives way to simple satire or burlesque of selected social affectations. For further acquaintance with its purer form, characteristic examples from the Restoration period may be found in Sir George Etherege's *The Man of Mode,* William Wycherley's *The Country Wife,* and George Farquhar's *The Beaux' Stratagem.* The type is anticipated in a less highly developed form in such plays of the earlier seventeenth century as Ben Jonson's *Epicoene, or The Silent Woman,* Beaumont and Fletcher's *The Scornful Lady,* and James Shirley's *The Lady of Pleasure.* Miscellaneous examples of later date are Sheridan's *The School for Scandal,* Oscar Wilde's *The Importance of Being Earnest,* Somerset Maugham's *Our Betters,* Noel Coward's *Private Lives,* and S. N. Behrman's *End of Summer.* An interesting modern variant of the type appears in the extraordinarily popular *Life With Father* by Howard Lindsay and Russel Crouse, while the tendency toward burlesque is hilariously illustrated in that farce which is a sort of backstairs comedy of manners, *You Can't Take It With You* by George S. Kaufman and Moss Hart.

THE WAY

OF

THE WORLD

by

WILLIAM CONGREVE

Dramatis Personæ

FAINALL, *in love with* MRS. [1] MAR-
  WOOD
MIRABELL, *in love with*
  MRS. MILLAMANT
WITWOUD ⎱ *followers of*
PETULANT ⎰
  MRS. MILLAMANT
SIR WILFULL WITWOUD, *half-
  brother to* WITWOUD, *and nephew
  to* LADY WISHFORT
WAITWELL, *servant to* MIRABELL
LADY WISHFORT, *enemy to* MIRA-
  BELL, *for having falsely pre-
  tended love to her*

MRS. MILLAMANT, *a fine lady, niece
  to* LADY WISHFORT, *and loves*
  MIRABELL
MRS. MARWOOD, *friend to*
  MR. FAINALL, *and likes*
  MIRABELL
MRS. FAINALL, *daughter to*
  LADY WISHFORT, *and wife to*
  FAINALL, *formerly friend to*
  MIRABELL
FOIBLE, *woman to* LADY WISHFORT
MINCING, *woman to* MRS. MILLA-
  MANT
BETTY, *servant in a chocolate-
  house*

PEG, *servant to* LADY WISHFORT

Dancers, Footmen, and Attendants.

SCENE: *London.*

The time equal to that of the presentation.[2]

---

[1] The abbreviation for *Mistress,* which is used in referring to both married and
unmarried women.
[2] Equivalent to *Time: the present.*

Scene: *A Chocolate-house*

[MIRABELL *and* FAINALL, *rising from cards.*
BETTY *waiting.*]

MIRABELL. You are a fortunate man,
Mr. Fainall.

FAINALL. Have we done?

MIRABELL. What you please. I'll play on
to entertain you.

FAINALL. No, I'll give you your revenge
another time, when you are not so indifferent; you are thinking of something else
now, and play too negligently; the coldness
of a losing gamester lessens the pleasure to
the winner. I'd no more play with a man
that slighted his ill fortune, than I'd make
love to a woman who undervalued the loss
of her reputation.

MIRABELL. You have a taste extremely
delicate, and are for refining on your
pleasures.

FAINALL. Prithee, why so reserved?
Something has put you out of humour.

MIRABELL. Not at all: I happen to be
grave to-day; and you are gay; that's all.

FAINALL. Confess, Millamant and you
quarrelled last night, after I left you; my
fair cousin has some humours that would
tempt the patience of a Stoic. What, some
coxcomb came in, and was well received by
her, while you were by?

MIRABELL. Witwoud and Petulant; and
what was worse, her aunt, your wife's
mother, my evil genius; or to sum up all in
her own name, my old Lady Wishfort
came in.

FAINALL. Oh, there it is then! She has a
lasting passion for you, and with reason.
What, then my wife was there?

MIRABELL. Yes, and Mrs. Marwood and
three or four more, whom I never saw before. Seeing me, they all put on their grave
faces, whispered one another, then complained aloud of the vapours, and after fell
into a profound silence.

FAINALL. They had a mind to be rid of
you.

MIRABELL. For which reason I resolved
not to stir. At last the good old lady broke
through her painful taciturnity, with an in-
vective against long visits. I would not have
understood her, but Millament joining in
the argument, I rose and with a constrained
smile told her I thought nothing was so easy
as to know when a visit began to be troublesome; she reddened and I withdrew, without expecting [3] her reply.

FAINALL. You were to blame to resent
what she spoke only in compliance with
her aunt.

MIRABELL. She is more mistress of herself, than to be under the necessity of such
a resignation.

FAINALL. What? though half her fortune
depends upon her marrying with my lady's
approbation?

MIRABELL. I was then in such a humour,
that I should have been better pleased if
she had been less discreet.

FAINALL. Now I remember, I wonder
not they were weary of you; last night was
one of their cabal-nights; they have 'em
three times a week, and meet by turns, at
one another's apartments, where they come
together like the coroner's inquest, to sit
upon the murdered reputations of the week.
You and I are excluded; and it was once
proposed that all the male sex should be
excepted; but somebody moved that to
avoid scandal there might be one man of
the community; upon which motion Witwoud and Petulant were enrolled members.

MIRABELL. And who may have been the
foundress of this sect? My Lady Wishfort,
I warrant, who publishes her detestation of
mankind; and full of the vigour of fifty-
five, declares for a friend and ratafia; [4] and
let posterity shift for itself, she'll breed no
more.

FAINALL. The discovery of your sham
addresses to her, to conceal your love to her
niece, has provoked this separation; had
you dissembled better, things might have
continued in the state of nature.

MIRABELL. I did as much as man could,

---

[3] Awaiting.

[4] A brandy-like liqueur.

265

with any reasonable conscience; I proceeded to the very last act of flattery with her, and was guilty of a song in her commendation. Nay, I got a friend to put her into a lampoon, and compliment her with the imputation of an affair with a young fellow, which I carried so far, that I told her the malicious town took notice that she was grown fat of a sudden; and when she lay in of a dropsy, persuaded her she was reported to be in labour. The devil's in't, if an old woman is to be flattered further, unless a man should endeavour downright personally to debauch her; and that my virtue forbade me. But for the discovery of that amour, I am indebted to your friend, or your wife's friend, Mrs. Marwood.

FAINALL. What should provoke her to be your enemy, without she has made you advances, which you have slighted? Women do not easily forgive omissions of that nature.

MIRABELL. She was always civil to me, till of late. I confess I am not one of those coxcombs who are apt to interpret a woman's good manners to her prejudice; and think that she who does not refuse 'em everything, can refuse 'em nothing.

FAINALL. You are a gallant man, Mirabell; and though you may have cruelty enough not to satisfy a lady's longing, you have too much generosity not to be tender of her honour. Yet you speak with an indifference which seems to be affected, and confesses you are conscious of a negligence.

MIRABELL. You pursue the argument with a distrust that seems to be unaffected, and confesses you are conscious of a concern for which the lady is more indebted to you than your wife.

FAINALL. Fie, fie, friend, if you grow censorious I must leave you. I'll look upon the gamesters in the next room.

MIRABELL. Who are they?

FAINALL. Petulant and Witwoud. [To BETTY.] Bring me some chocolate.

[Exit FAINALL.]

MIRABELL. Betty, what says your clock?

BETTY. Turned of the last canonical hour, sir.[5]   [Exit BETTY.]

MIRABELL. How pertinently the jade answers me! Ha! almost one o'clock! [Looking on his watch.] O, y'are come—

[Enter a SERVANT.]

Well, is the grand affair over? You have been something tedious.

SERVANT.   Sir, there's such coupling at Pancras,[6] that they stand behind one another, as 'twere in a country dance. Ours was the last couple to lead up; and no hopes appearing of dispatch, besides, the parson growing hoarse, we were afraid his lungs would have failed before it came to our turn; so we drove round to Duke's Place; and there they were riveted in a trice.

MIRABELL. So, so, you are sure they are married.

SERVANT. Married and bedded, sir: I am witness.

MIRABELL. Have you the certificate?

SERVANT. Here it is, sir.

MIRABELL. Has the tailor brought Waitwell's clothes home, and the new liveries?

SERVANT. Yes, sir.

MIRABELL. That's well. Do you go home again, d'ye hear, and adjourn the consummation till farther order; bid Waitwell shake his ears, and Dame Partlet [7] rustle up her feathers, and meet me at one o'clock by Rosamond's Pond,[8] that I may see her before she returns to her lady; and as you tender [9] your ears be secret.

[Exit SERVANT.]

[Re-enter FAINALL.]

FAINALL. Joy of your success, Mirabell; you look pleased.

MIRABELL. Ay; I have been engaged in a matter of some sort of mirth, which is not yet ripe for discovery. I am glad this is not a cabal-night. I wonder, Fainall, that you who are married, and of consequence

---

[5] Twelve o'clock noon. Canonical hours for performing marriages were eight to twelve A.M.
[6] St. Pancras and St. James (Duke's Place) were churches where marriages could be performed without publication of banns.
[7] Wife of Chantecleer the cock. The reference is, of course, to Waitwell's bride.
[8] In the fashionable St. James's Park.
[9] Value.

hould be discreet, will suffer your wife to
be of such a party.

FAINALL. Faith, I am not jealous. Besides, most who are engaged are women
and relations; and for the men, they are of
a kind too contemptible to give scandal.

MIRABELL. I am of another opinion. The
greater the coxcomb, always the more the
scandal: for a woman who is not a fool
can have but one reason for associating
with a man that is.

FAINALL. Are you jealous as often as
you see Witwoud entertained by Millamant?

MIRABELL. Of her understanding I am,
if not of her person.

FAINALL. You do her wrong; for to give
her her due, she has wit.

MIRABELL. She has beauty enough to
make any man think so, and complaisance
enough not to contradict him who shall tell
her so.

FAINALL. For a passionate lover, methinks you are a man somewhat too discerning in the failings of your mistress.

MIRABELL. And for a discerning man,
somewhat too passionate a lover; for I like
her with all her faults; nay, like her for her
faults. Her follies are so natural, or so artful, that they become her; and those affectations which in another woman would
be odious, serve but to make her more
agreeable. I'll tell thee, Fainall, she once
used me with that insolence, that in revenge
I took her to pieces; sifted her, and separated her failings; I studied 'em, and got
'em by rote. The catalogue was so large,
that I was not without hopes, one day or
other, to hate her heartily: to which end
I so used myself to think of 'em, that at
length, contrary to my design and expectation, they gave me every hour less and less
disturbance; till in a few days it became
habitual to me to remember 'em without
being displeased. They are now grown as
familiar to me as my own frailties; and in
all probability in a little time longer I shall
like 'em as well.

FAINALL. Marry her, marry her; be half
as well acquainted with her charms as you
are with her defects, and my life on't, you
are your own man again.

[*Re-enter* BETTY.]

MIRABELL. Say you so?

FAINALL. Ay, ay; I have experience: I
have a wife, and so forth.

[*Enter a* MESSENGER.]

MESSENGER. Is one Squire Witwoud
here?

BETTY. Yes; what's your business?

MESSENGER. I have a letter for him,
from his brother, Sir Wilfull, which I am
charged to deliver into his own hands.

BETTY. He's in the next room, friend—
that way.   [*Exit* MESSENGER.]

MIRABELL. What, is the chief of that
noble family in town, Sir Wilfull Witwoud?

FAINALL. He is expected to-day. Do
you know him?

MIRABELL. I have seen him; he promises
to be an extraordinary person. I think you
have the honour to be related to him.

FAINALL. Yes; he is half-brother to this
Witwoud by a former wife, who was sister
to my Lady Wishfort, my wife's mother.
If you marry Millamant, you must call
cousins too.

MIRABELL. I had rather be his relation
than his acquaintance.

FAINALL. He comes to town in order to
equip himself for travel.

MIRABELL. For travel! Why, the man
that I mean is above forty.[10]

FAINALL. No matter for that; 'tis for the
honour of England, that all Europe should
know we have blockheads of all ages.

MIRABELL. I wonder there is not an act
of Parliament to save the credit of the nation, and prohibit the exportation of fools.

FAINALL. By no means, 'tis better as 'tis;
'tis better to trade with a little loss, than to
be quite eaten up, with being overstocked.

MIRABELL. Pray, are the follies of this
knight-errant, and those of the squire his
brother, anything related?

---

[10] Mirabell is thinking of the conventional
rounding out of one's schooling with a grand
tour.

FAINALL. Not at all; Witwoud grows by the knight, like a medlar grafted on a crab.[11] One will melt in your mouth, and t'other set your teeth on edge; one is all pulp, and the other all core.

MIRABELL. So one will be rotten before he be ripe, and the other will be rotten without ever being ripe at all.

FAINALL. Sir Wilfull is an odd mixture of bashfulness and obstinacy. But when he's drunk, he's as loving as the monster in *The Tempest*,[12] and much after the same manner. To give the other his due, he has something of good nature, and does not always want wit.

MIRABELL. Not always; but as often as his memory fails him, and his commonplace of comparisons. He is a fool with a good memory, and some few scraps of other folks' wit. He is one whose conversation can never be approved, yet it is now and then to be endured. He has indeed one good quality, he is not exceptious; for he so passionately affects the reputation of understanding raillery, that he will construe an affront into a jest; and call downright rudeness and ill language, satire and fire.

FAINALL. If you have a mind to finish his picture, you have an opportunity to do it at full length. Behold the original.

[*Enter* WITWOUD.]

WITWOUD. Afford me your compassion, my dears; pity me, Fainall. Mirabell, pity me.

MIRABELL. I do from my soul.

FAINALL. Why, what's the matter?

WITWOUD. No letters for me, Betty?

BETTY. Did not the messenger bring you one but now, sir?

WITWOUD. Ay, but no other?

BETTY. No, sir.

WITWOUD. That's hard, that's very hard; —a messenger, a mule, a beast of burden, he has brought me a letter from the fool my brother, as heavy as a panegyric in a funeral sermon, or a copy of commendatory verses from one poet to another. And what's worse, 'tis as sure a forerunner of the author as an epistle dedicatory.

MIRABELL. A fool, and your brother, Witwoud!

WITWOUD. Ay, ay, my half-brother. My half-brother he is, no nearer, upon honour.

MIRABELL. Then 'tis possible he may be but half a fool.

WITWOUD. Good, good, Mirabell, *le drole!* [13] Good, good!—hang him, don't let's talk of him.—Fainall, how does your lady? Gad, I say anything in the world to get this fellow out of my head. I beg pardon that I should ask a man of pleasure, and the town, a question at once so foreign and domestic. But I talk like an old maid at a marriage, I don't know what I say: but she's the best woman in the world.

FAINALL. 'Tis well you don't know what you say, or else your commendation would go near to make me either vain or jealous.

WITWOUD. No man in town lives well with a wife but Fainall. Your judgment, Mirabell?

MIRABELL. You had better step and ask his wife, if you would be credibly informed.

WITWOUD. Mirabell—

MIRABELL. Ay?

WITWOUD. My dear, I ask ten thousand pardons—Gad, I have forgot what I was going to say to you.

MIRABELL. I thank you heartily, heartily.

WITWOUD. No, but prithee excuse me— my memory is such a memory.

MIRABELL. Have a care of such apologies, Witwoud; for I never knew a fool but he affected to complain, either of the spleen or his memory.

FAINALL. What have you done with Petulant?

WITWOUD. He's reckoning his money— my money it was; I have no luck today.

FAINALL. You may allow him to win of you at play, for you are sure to be too hard for him at repartee: since you monopolize the wit that is between you, the fortune must be his of course.

---

[11] A soft, pulpy fruit grafted on a crabapple.
[12] Referring to Caliban in Shakespeare's play.

[13] You wag!

MIRABELL. I don't find that Petulant confesses the superiority of wit to be your talent, Witwoud.

WITWOUD. Come, come, you are malicious now, and would breed debates. Petulant's my friend, and a very honest fellow, and a very pretty fellow, and has a smattering—faith and troth, a pretty deal of an odd sort of a small wit. Nay, I'll do him justice. I'm his friend, I won't wrong him, neither. And if he had but any judgment in the world, he would not be altogether contemptible. Come, come, don't detract from the merits of my friend.

FAINALL. You don't take your friend to be over-nicely bred.

WITWOUD. No, no, hang him, the rogue has no manners at all, that I must own—no more breeding than a bum-baily,[14] that I grant you. 'Tis pity, faith; the fellow has fire and life.

MIRABELL. What, courage?

WITWOUD. Hum, faith, I don't know as to that—I can't say as to that. Yes, faith, in a controversy he'll contradict anybody.

MIRABELL. Though 'twere a man whom he feared, or a woman whom he loved?

WITWOUD. Well, well, he does not always think before he speaks. We have all our failings; you're too hard upon him, you are, faith. Let me excuse him—I can defend most of his faults, except one or two; one he has, that's the truth on't, if he were my brother, I could not acquit him. That, indeed, I could wish were otherwise.

MIRABELL. Ay, marry, what's that, Witwoud?

WITWOUD. Oh, pardon me! Expose the infirmities of my friend? No, my dear, excuse me there.

FAINALL. What, I warrant he's unsincere, or 'tis some such trifle.

WITWOUD. No, no, what if he be? 'Tis no matter for that, his wit will excuse that: a wit should no more be sincere, than a woman constant; one argues a decay of parts,[15] as t'other of beauty.

MIRABELL. Maybe you think him too positive?

WITWOUD. No, no, his being positive is an incentive to argument, and keeps up conversation.

FAINALL. Too illiterate?

WITWOUD. That! that's his happiness. His want of learning gives him the more opportunities to show his natural parts.

MIRABELL. He wants words?

WITWOUD. Ay; but I like him for that now; for his want of words gives me the pleasure very often to explain his meaning.

FAINALL. He's impudent?

WITWOUD. No, that's not it.

MIRABELL. Vain?

WITWOUD. No.

MIRABELL. What, he speaks unseasonable truths sometimes, because he has not wit enough to invent an evasion?

WITWOUD. Truths! Ha, ha, ha! No, no, since you will have it—I mean, he never speaks truth at all—that's all. He will lie like a chambermaid, or a woman of quality's porter. Now that is a fault.

[*Enter a* COACHMAN.]

COACHMAN. Is Master Petulant here, mistress?

BETTY. Yes.

COACHMAN. Three gentlewomen in a coach would speak with him.

FAINALL. O brave Petulant, three!

BETTY. I'll tell him.

COACHMAN. You must bring two dishes of chocolate and a glass of cinnamon-water.

[*Exeunt* BETTY *and* COACHMAN.]

WITWOUD. That should be for two fasting strumpets, and a bawd troubled with wind. Now you may know what the three are.

MIRABELL. You are very free with your friend's acquaintance.

WITWOUD. Ay, ay, friendship without freedom is as dull as love without enjoyment, or wine without toasting; but to tell you a secret, these are trulls whom he allows coach-hire, and something more by the week, to call on him once a day at public places.

[14] Sheriff's deputy.

[15] Social talents.

MIRABELL. How!

WITWOUD. You shall see he won't go to 'em because there's no more company here to take notice of him. Why, this is nothing to what he used to do; before he found out this way, I have known him call for himself—

FAINALL. Call for himself? What dost thou mean?

WITWOUD. Mean? Why, he would slip you out of this chocolate-house, just when you had been talking to him. As soon as your back was turned—whip he was gone; then trip to his lodging, clap on a hood and scarf and mask, slap into a hackney-coach, and drive hither to the door again in a trice; where he would send in for himself —that I mean—call for himself, wait for himself, nay and what's more, not finding himself, sometimes leave a letter for himself.

MIRABELL. I confess this is something extraordinary—I believe he waits for himself now, he is so long a coming. Oh, I ask his pardon.

[Re-enter BETTY, with PETULANT.]

BETTY. Sir, the coach stays.

PETULANT. Well, well; I come.—'Sbud, a man had as good be a professed midwife as a professed whoremaster, at this rate; to be knocked up and raised at all hours, and in all places! Pox on 'em, I won't come!— D'ye hear, tell 'em I won't come.—Let 'em snivel and cry their hearts out.

[Exit BETTY.]

FAINALL. You are very cruel, Petulant.

PETULANT. All's one, let it pass—I have a humour to be cruel.

MIRABELL. I hope they are not persons of condition that you use at this rate.

PETULANT. Condition! condition's a dried fig, if I am not in humour. By this hand, if they were your—a—a—your what-d'ye-call-'ems themselves, they must wait or rub off, if I want appetite.

MIRABELL. What-d'ye-call-'ems! What are they, Witwoud?

WITWOUD. Empresses, my dear—by your what-d'ye-call-'ems he means sultana queens.

PETULANT. Ay, Roxolanas.[16]

MIRABELL. Cry you mercy.

FAINALL. Witwoud says they are—

PETULANT. What does he say th'are?

WITWOUD. I? Fine ladies, I say.

PETULANT. Pass on, Witwoud.—Hark-'ee, by this light, his relations—two co-heiresses his cousins, and an old aunt, that loves caterwauling better than a conventicle.[17]

WITWOUD. Ha, ha, ha! I had a mind to see how the rogue would come off. Ha, ha, ha! Gad, I can't be angry with him, if he had said they were my mother and my sisters.

MIRABELL. No?

WITWOUD. No; the rogue's wit and readiness of invention charm me. Dear Petulant!

[Re-enter BETTY.]

BETTY. They are gone, sir, in great anger.

PETULANT. Enough, let 'em trundle. Anger helps complexion, saves paint.

[Exit BETTY.]

FAINALL. This continence is all dissembled; this is in order to have something to brag of the next time he makes court to Millamant, and swear he has abandoned the whole sex for her sake.

MIRABELL. Have you not left out your impudent pretensions there yet? I shall cut your throat, sometime or other, Petulant, about that business.

PETULANT. Ay, ay, let that pass—there are other throats to be cut.—

MIRABELL. Meaning mine, sir?

PETULANT. Not I—I mean nobody—I know nothing. But there are uncles and nephews in the world—and they may be rivals. What then? All's one for that—

MIRABELL. How? Hark'ee, Petulant, come hither. Explain, or I shall call your interpreter.

---

[16] Roxolana is the sultana in D'Avenant's spectacular play *The Siege of Rhodes.*

[17] A nonconformist religious meeting, reputedly given to noisy psalm-singing.

PETULANT. Explain! I know nothing. Why, you have an uncle, have you not, lately come to town, and lodges by my Lady Wishfort's?

MIRABELL. True.

PETULANT. Why, that's enough. You and he are not friends; and if he should marry and have a child, you may be disinherited, ha?

MIRABELL. Where hast thou stumbled upon all this truth?

PETULANT. All's one for that; why, then, say I know something.

MIRABELL. Come, thou art an honest fellow, Petulant, and shalt make love to my mistress, thou sha't, faith. What hast thou heard of my uncle?

PETULANT. I? Nothing, I. If throats are to be cut, let swords clash; snug's the word, I shrug and am silent.

MIRABELL. O raillery, raillery. Come, I know thou art in the women's secrets. What, you're a cabalist; I know you stayed at Millamant's last night, after I went. Was there any mention made of my uncle or me? Tell me. If thou hadst but good nature equal to thy wit, Petulant, Tony Witwoud, who is now thy competitor in fame, would show as dim by thee as a dead whiting's eye by a pearl of Orient; he would no more be seen by [18] thee, than Mercury is by the sun. Come, I'm sure thou wo't tell me.

PETULANT. If I do, will you grant me common sense then, for the future?

MIRABELL. Faith, I'll do what I can for thee, and I'll pray that Heaven may grant it thee in the meantime.

PETULANT. Well, hark'ee.

[PETULANT and MIRABELL converse apart.]

FAINALL. Petulant and you both will find Mirabell as warm a rivel as a lover.

WITWOUD. Pshaw, pshaw, that she laughs at Petulant is plain. And for my part —but that it is almost a fashion to admire her, I should—hark'ee—to tell you a secret, but let it go no further—between friends, I shall never break my heart for her.

FAINALL. How!

WITWOUD. She's handsome; but she's a sort of an uncertain woman.

FAINALL. I thought you had died for her.

WITWOUD. Umh—no—

FAINALL. She has wit.

WITWOUD. 'Tis what she will hardly allow anybody else. Now, demme, I should hate that, if she were as handsome as Cleopatra. Mirabell is not so sure of her as he thinks for.

FAINALL. Why do you think so?

WITWOUD. We stayed pretty late there last night, and heard something of an uncle to Mirabell, who is lately come to town— and is between him and the best part of his estate. Mirabell and he are at some distance, as my Lady Wishfort has been told; and you know she hates Mirabell, worse than a Quaker hates a parrot, or than a fishmonger hates a hard frost. Whether this uncle has seen Mrs. Millamant or not, I cannot say; but there were items of such a treaty being in embryo; and if it should come to life, poor Mirabell wouid be in some sort unfortunately fobbed,[19] i' faith.

FAINALL. 'Tis impossible Millamant should harken to it.

WITWOUD. Faith, my dear, I can't tell; she's a woman and a kind of a humorist.

MIRABELL. [To PETULANT.] And this is the sum of what you could collect last night.

PETULANT. The quintessence. Maybe Witwoud knows more, he stayed longer. Besides, they never mind him; they say anything before him.

MIRABELL. I thought you had been the greatest favourite.

PETULANT. Ay, tête à tête; but not in public, because I make remarks.

MIRABELL. Do you?

PETULANT. Ay, ay; pox, I'm malicious, man. Now, he's soft, you know; they are not in awe of him. The fellow's well bred, he's what you call a—what-d'ye-call-'em. A fine gentleman, but he's silly withal.

MIRABELL. I thank you, I know as much

[18] Beside.

[19] Swindled.

as my curiosity requires. Fainall, are you for the Mall? [20]

FAINALL. Ay, I'll take a turn before dinner.

WITWOUD. Ay, we'll all walk in the Park; the ladies talked of being there.

MIRABELL. I thought you were obliged to watch for your brother Sir Wilfull's arrival.

WITWOUD. No, no, he comes to his aunt's, my Lady Wishfort; pox on him, I shall be troubled with him too; what shall I do with the fool?

PETULANT. Beg him for his estate, that I may beg you afterwards, and so have but one trouble with you both.

WITWOUD. O rare Petulant! thou art as quick as fire in a frosty morning; thou shalt to the Mall with us; and we'll be very severe.

PETULANT. Enough! I'm in a humour to be severe.

MIRABELL. Are you? Pray, then, walk by yourselves. Let us not be accessory to your putting the ladies out of countenance, with your senseless ribaldry, which you roar out aloud as often as they pass by you; and when you have made a handsome woman blush, then you think you have been severe.

PETULANT. What, what? Then let 'em either show their innocence by not understanding what they hear, or else show their discretion by not hearing what they would not be thought to understand.

MIRABELL. But hast not thou then sense enough to know that thou ought'st to be most ashamed of thyself when thou hast put another out of countenance?

PETULANT. Not I, by this hand—I always take blushing either for a sign of guilt, or ill breeding.

MIRABELL. I confess you ought to think so. You are in the right, that you may plead the error of your judgment in defence of your practice.

Where modesty's ill manners, 'tis but fit
That impudence and malice pass for wit.

[Exeunt.]

ACT II

Scene: St. James's Park

[Enter MRS. FAINALL and MRS. MARWOOD.]

MRS. FAINALL. Ay, ay, dear Marwood, if we will be happy, we must find the means in ourselves, and among ourselves. Men are ever in extremes, either doting or averse. While they are lovers, if they have fire and sense, their jealousies are insupportable: and when they cease to love, (we ought to think at least) they loathe; they look upon us with horror and distaste; they meet us like the ghosts of what we were, and as such, fly from us.

MRS. MARWOOD. True, 'tis an unhappy circumstance of life, that love should ever die before us; and that the man so often should outlive the lover. But say what you will, 'tis better to be left, than never to have been loved. To pass our youth in dull indifference, to refuse the sweets of life because they once must leave us, is as preposterous as to wish to have been born old, because we one day must be old. For my part, my youth may wear and waste, but it shall never rust in my possession.

MRS. FAINALL. Then it seems you dissemble an aversion to mankind, only in compliance with my mother's humour.

MRS. MARWOOD. Certainly. To be free,[1] I have no taste of those insipid dry discourses, with which our sex of force must entertain themselves, apart from men. We may affect endearments to each other, profess eternal friendships, and seem to dote like lovers; but 'tis not in our natures long to persevere. Love will resume his empire in our breasts, and every heart, or soon or late, receive and readmit him as its lawful tyrant.

[20] A walk in St. James's Park, fashionable at the time for promenading.

[1] Frank.

MRS. FAINALL. Bless me, how have I been deceived! Why you profess a libertine.

MRS. MARWOOD. You see my friendship by my freedom. Come, be as sincere, acknowledge that your sentinments agree with mine.

MRS. FAINALL. Never.

MRS. MARWOOD. You hate mankind?

MRS. FAINALL. Heartily, inveterately.

MRS. MARWOOD. Your husband?

MRS. FAINALL. Most transcendently; ay, though I say it, meritoriously.

MRS. MARWOOD. Give me your hand upon it.

MRS. FAINALL. There.

MRS. MARWOOD. I join with you. What I have said has been to try you.

MRS. FAINALL. Is it possible? Dost thou hate those vipers, men?

MRS. MARWOOD. I have done hating 'em, and am now come to despise 'em; the next thing I have to do is eternally to forget 'em.

MRS. FAINALL. There spoke the spirit of an Amazon, a Penthesilea.[2]

MRS. MARWOOD. And yet I am thinking sometimes to carry my aversion further.

MRS. FAINALL. How?

MRS. MARWOOD. Faith, by marrying. If I could but find one that loved me very well, and would be thoroughly sensible of ill usage, I think I should do myself the violence of undergoing the ceremony.

MRS. FAINALL. You would not make him a cuckold?

MRS. MARWOOD. No; but I'd make him believe I did, and that's as bad.

MRS. FAINALL. Why, had not you as good do it?

MRS. MARWOOD. Oh, if he should ever discover it, he would then know the worst, and be out of his pain; but I would have him ever to continue upon the rack of fear and jealousy.

MRS. FAINALL. Ingenious mischief! Would thou wert married to Mirabell.

MRS. MARWOOD. Would I were.

MRS. FAINALL. You change colour.

[2] The Amazons were a race of female warriors who, led by their queen, Penthesilia, aided Priam in the Trojan War.

MRS. MARWOOD. Because I hate him.

MRS. FAINALL. So do I; but I can hear him named. But what reason have you to hate him in particular?

MRS. MARWOOD. I never loved him; he is, and always was, insufferably proud.

MRS. FAINALL. By the reason you give for your aversion, one would think it dissembled; for you have laid a fault to his charge of which his enemies must acquit him.

MRS. MARWOOD. Oh, then it seems you are one of his favourable enemies. Methinks you look a little pale, and now you flush again.

MRS. FAINALL. Do I? I think I am a little sick o' the sudden.

MRS. MARWOOD. What ails you?

MRS. FAINALL. My husband. Don't you see him? He turned short upon me unawares, and has almost overcome me.

[*Enter* FAINALL *and* MIRABELL.]

MRS. MARWOOD. Ha, ha, ha! he comes opportunely for you.

MRS. FAINALL. For you, for he has brought Mirabell with him.

FAINALL. My dear.

MRS. FAINALL. My soul.

FAINALL. You don't look well to-day, child.

MRS. FAINALL. D'ye think so?

MIRABELL. He is the only man that does, madam.

MRS. FAINALL. The only man that would tell me so at least; and the only man from whom I could hear it without mortification.

FAINALL. Oh, my dear, I am satisfied of your tenderness; I know you cannot resent anything from me; especially what is an effect of my concern.

MRS. FAINALL. Mr. Mirabell, my mother interrupted you in a pleasant relation last night: I would fain hear it out.

MIRABELL. The persons concerned in that affair have yet a tolerable reputation. I am afraid Mr. Fainall will be censorious.

MRS. FAINALL. He has a humour more prevailing than his curiosity, and will willingly dispense with the hearing of one scandalous story, to avoid giving an occasion to make another by being seen to walk with his wife. This way, Mr. Mirabell, and I dare promise you will oblige us both.

[*Exeunt* MRS. FAINALL *and* MIRABELL.]

FAINALL. Excellent creature! Well, sure if I should live to be rid of my wife, I should be a miserable man.

MRS. MARWOOD. Ay!

FAINALL. For having only that one hope, the accomplishment of it, of consequence, must put an end to all my hopes; and what a wretch is he who must survive his hopes! Nothing remains when that day comes, but to sit down and weep like Alexander, when he wanted other worlds to conquer.

MRS. MARWOOD. Will you not follow 'em?

FAINALL. Faith, I think not.

MRS. MARWOOD. Pray let us; I have a reason.

FAINALL. You are not jealous?

MRS. MARWOOD. Of whom?

FAINALL. Of Mirabell.

MRS. MARWOOD. If I am, is it inconsistent with my love to you that I am tender of your honour?

FAINALL. You would intimate, then, as if there were a fellow-feeling between my wife and him.

MRS. MARWOOD. I think she does not hate him to that degree she would be thought.

FAINALL. But he, I fear, is too insensible.

MRS. MARWOOD. It may be you are deceived.

FAINALL. It may be so. I do now begin to apprehend it.

MRS. MARWOOD. What?

FAINALL. That I have been deceived, madam, and you are false.

MRS. MARWOOD. That I am false! What mean you?

FAINALL. To let you know I see through all your little arts. Come, you both love him; and both have equally dissembled your aversion. Your mutual jealousies of one another have made you clash till you have both struck fire. I have seen the warm confession reddening on your cheeks and sparkling from your eyes.

MRS. MARWOOD. You do me wrong.

FAINALL. I do not. 'Twas for my ease to oversee and wilfully neglect the gross advances made him by my wife; that by permitting her to be engaged, I might continue unsuspected in my pleasures, and take you oftener to my arms in full security. But could you think, because the nodding husband would not wake, that e'er the watchful lover slept?

MRS. MARWOOD. And wherewithal can you reproach me?

FAINALL. With infidelity, with loving another, with love of Mirabell.

MRS. MARWOOD. 'Tis false. I challenge you to show an instance that can confirm your groundless accusation. I hate him.

FAINALL. And wherefore do you hate him? He is insensible, and your resentment follows his neglect. An instance? The injuries you have done him are a proof: your interposing in his love. What cause had you to make discoveries of his pretended passion? To undeceive the credulous aunt, and be the officious obstacle of his match with Millamant?

MRS. MARWOOD. My obligations to my lady urged me: I had professed a friendship to her; and could not see her easy nature so abused by that dissembler.

FAINALL. What, was it conscience then? Professed a friendship! Oh, the pious friendships of the female sex!

MRS. MARWOOD. More tender, more sincere, and more enduring, than all the vain and empty vows of men, whether professing love to us, or mutual faith to one another.

FAINALL. Ha, ha, ha! you are my wife's friend too.

MRS. MARWOOD. Shame and ingratitude! Do you reproach me? You, you upbraid me! Have I been false to her, through strict fidelity to you, and sacrificed my friendship to keep my love inviolate? And have you the baseness to charge me with the guilt, unmindful of the merit! To you it should be meritorious, that I have been vicious. And do you reflect that guilt upon me, which should lie buried in your bosom?

FAINALL. You misinterpret my reproof. I meant but to remind you of the slight account you once could make of strictest ties, when set in competition with your love to me.

MRS. MARWOOD. 'Tis false, you urged it with deliberate malice—'twas spoke in scorn, and I never will forgive it.

FAINALL. Your guilt, not your resentment, begets your rage. If yet you loved, you could forgive a jealousy: but you are stung to find you are discovered.

MRS. MARWOOD. It shall be all discovered. You too shall be discovered; be sure you shall. I can but be exposed. If I do it myself I shall prevent [3] your baseness.

FAINALL. Why, what will you do?

MRS. MARWOOD. Disclose it to your wife; own what has passed between us.

FAINALL. Frenzy!

MRS. MARWOOD. By all my wrongs, I'll do't! I'll publish to the world the injuries you have done me, both in my fame and fortune. With both I trusted you, you bankrupt in honour, as indigent of wealth.

FAINALL. Your fame I have preserved. Your fortune has been bestowed as the prodigality of your love would have it, in pleasures which we both have shared. Yet, had not you been false, I had e'er this repaid it. 'Tis true. Had you permitted Mirabell with Millamant to have stolen their marriage, my lady had been incensed beyond all means of reconcilement: Millamant had forfeited the moiety of her fortune, which then would have descended to my wife—and wherefore did I marry, but to make lawful prize of a rich widow's wealth, and squander it on love and you?

MRS. MARWOOD. Deceit and frivolous pretence!

FAINALL. Death, am I not married? What's pretence? Am I not imprisoned, fettered? Have I not a wife? Nay, a wife that was a widow, a young widow, a handsome widow; and would be again a widow, but that I have a heart of proof, and something

[3] Anticipate.

of a constitution to bustle through the ways of wedlock and this world. Will you yet be reconciled to truth and me?

MRS. MARWOOD. Impossible. Truth and you are inconsistent. I hate you, and shall for ever.

FAINALL. For loving you?

MRS. MARWOOD. I loathe the name of love after such usage; and next to the guilt with which you would asperse me, I scorn you most. Farewell.

FAINALL. Nay, we must not part thus.

MRS. MARWOOD. Let me go.

FAINALL. Come, I'm sorry.

MRS. MARWOOD. I care not—let me go—break my hands, do—I'd leave 'em to get loose.

FAINALL. I would not hurt you for the world. Have I no other hold to keep you here?

MRS. MARWOOD. Well, I have deserved it all.

FAINALL. You know I love you.

MRS. MARWOOD. Poor dissembling! Oh, that—well, it is not yet—

FAINALL. What? What is it not? What is it not yet? It is not yet too late—

MRS. MARWOOD. No, it is not yet too late—I have that comfort.

FAINALL. It is, to love another.

MRS. MARWOOD. But not to loathe, detest, abhor mankind, myself, and the whole treacherous world.

FAINALL. Nay, this is extravagance. Come, I ask your pardon—no tears—I was to blame, I could not love you and be easy in my doubts—pray forbear—I believe you; I'm convinced I've done you wrong; and any way, every way will make amends. I'll hate my wife yet more, damn her, I'll part with her, rob her of all she's worth, and we'll retire somewhere, anywhere, to another world. I'll marry thee—be pacified. —'Sdeath, they come! Hide your face, your tears—you have a mask, wear it a moment. This way, this way—be persuaded.

[*Exeunt* FAINALL *and* MRS. MARWOOD.]

[*Re-enter* MIRABELL *and* MRS. FAINALL.]

MRS. FAINALL. They are here yet.

MIRABELL. They are turning into the other walk.

MRS. FAINALL. While I only hated my husband, I could bear to see him; but since I have despised him, he's too offensive.

MIRABELL. Oh, you should hate with prudence.

MRS. FAINALL. Yes, for I have loved with indiscretion.

MIRABELL. You should have just so much disgust for your husband as may be sufficient to make you relish your lover.

MRS. FAINALL. You have been the cause that I have loved without bounds, and would you set limits to that aversion, of which you have been the occasion? Why did you make me marry this man?

MIRABELL. Why do we daily commit disagreeable and dangerous actions? To save that idol, reputation. If the familiarities of our loves had produced that consequence, of which you were apprehensive, where could you have fixed a father's name with credit, but on a husband? I knew Fainall to be a man lavish of his morals, an interested and professing friend, a false and a designing lover; yet one whose wit and outward fair behaviour have gained a reputation with the town, enough to make that woman stand excused, who has suffered herself to be won by his addresses. A better man ought not to have been sacrificed to the occasion; a worse had not answered to the purpose. When you are weary of him, you know your remedy.

MRS. FAINALL. I ought to stand in some degree of credit with you, Mirabell.

MIRABELL. In justice to you, I have made you privy to my whole design, and put it in your power to ruin or advance my fortune.

MRS. FAINALL. Whom have you instructed to represent your pretended uncle?

MIRABELL. Waitwell, my servant.

MRS. FAINALL. He is an humble servant to Foible, my mother's woman, and may win her to your interest.

MIRABELL. Care is taken for that—she is won and worn by this time. They were married this morning.

MRS. FAINALL. Who?

MIRABELL. Waitwell and Foible. I would not tempt my servant to betray me by trusting him too far. If your mother, in hopes to ruin me, should consent to marry my pretended uncle, he might, like Mosca in *The Fox*,[4] stand upon terms; so I made him sure beforehand.

MRS. FAINALL. So, if my poor mother is caught in a contract, you will discover the imposture betimes, and release her by producing a certificate of her gallant's former marriage.

MIRABELL. Yes, upon condition she consent to my marriage with her niece, and surrender the moiety of her fortune in her possession.

MRS. FAINALL. She talked last night of endeavouring at a match between Millamant and your uncle.

MIRABELL. That was by Foible's direction, and my instruction, that she might seem to carry it more privately.

MRS. FAINALL. Well, I have an opinion of your success, for I believe my lady will do anything to get an husband; and when she has this, which you have provided for her, I suppose she will submit to anything to get rid of him.

MIRABELL. Yes, I think the good lady would marry anything that resembled a man, though 'twere no more than what a butler could 'pinch out of a napkin.

MRS. FAINALL. Female frailty! We must all come to it, if we live to be old, and feel the craving of a false appetite when the true is decayed.

MIRABELL. An old woman's appetite is depraved like that of a girl—'tis the green-sickness of a second childhood; and like the faint offer of a latter spring, serves but to usher in the fall; and withers in an affected bloom.

MRS. FAINALL. Here's your mistress.

[*Enter* MRS. MILLAMANT, WITWOUD, *and* MINCING.]

MIRABELL. Here she comes, i' faith, full sail, with her fan spread and her streamers

4 Jonson's play, *Volpone*, in which the servant Mosca outwits his master.

out, and a shoal of fools for tenders. Ha, no, I cry her mercy.

MRS. FAINALL. I see but one poor empty sculler; and he tows her woman after him.

MIRABELL. You seem to be unattended, madam. You used to have the *beau monde* throng after you; and a flock of gay fine perukes hovering round you.

WITWOUD. Like moths about a candle— I had like to have lost my comparison for want of breath.

MILLAMANT. Oh, I have denied myself airs to-day. I have walked as fast through the crowd—

WITWOUD. As a favourite in disgrace; and with as few followers.

MILLAMANT. Dear Mr. Witwoud, truce with your similitudes: for I am as sick of 'em—

WITWOUD. As a physician of a good air. I cannot help it, madam, though 'tis against myself.

MILLAMANT. Yet again! Mincing, stand between me and his wit.

WITWOUD. Do, Mrs. Mincing, like a screen before a great fire. I confess I do blaze today, I am too bright.

MRS. FAINALL. But, dear Millamant, why were you so long?

MILLAMANT. Long! Lord, have I not made violent haste? I have asked every living thing I met for you; I have enquired after you, as after a new fashion.

WITWOUD. Madam, truce with your similitudes. No, you met her husband, and did not ask him for her.

MIRABELL. By your leave, Witwoud, that were like enquiring after an old fashion, to ask a husband for his wife.

WITWOUD. Hum, a hit, a hit, a palpable hit, I confess it.

MRS. FAINALL. You were dressed before I came abroad.

MILLAMANT. Ay, that's true—oh, but then I had—Mincing, what had I? Why was I so long?

MINCING. O mem, your la'ship stayed to peruse a pecquet of letters.

MILLAMANT. Oh, ay, letters—I had letters—I am persecuted with letters—I hate letters. Nobody knows how to write letters; and yet one has 'em, one does not know why. They serve one to pin up one's hair.

WITWOUD. Is that the way? Pray, madam, do you pin up your hair with all your letters? I find I must keep copies.

MILLAMANT. Only with those in verse, Mr. Witwoud. I never pin up my hair with prose. I fancy one's hair would not curl if it were pinned up with prose. I think I tried once, Mincing.

MINCING. O mem, I shall never forget it.

MILLAMANT. Ay, poor Mincing tift and tift [5] all the morning.

MINCING. Till I had the cremp in my fingers, I'll vow, mem. And all to no purpose. But when your la'ship pins it up with poetry, it sits so pleasant the next day as anything, and is so pure and so crips.

WITWOUD. Indeed, so "crips"? [6]

MINCING. You're such a critic, Mr. Witwoud.

MILLAMANT. Mirabell, did not you take exceptions last night? Oh, ay, and went away. Now I think on't I'm angry—no, now I think on't I'm pleased—for I believe I gave you some pain.

MIRABELL. Does that please you?

MILLAMANT. Infinitely; I love to give pain.

MIRABELL. You would affect a cruelty which is not in your nature; your true vanity is in the power of pleasing.

MILLAMANT. Oh, I ask your pardon for that. One's cruelty is one's power, and when one parts with one's cruelty, one parts with one's power; and when one has parted with that, I fancy one's old and ugly.

MIRABELL. Ay, ay, suffer your cruelty to ruin the object of your power, to destroy your lover—and then how vain, how lost a thing you'll be! Nay, 'tis true. You are no longer handsome when you've lost your lover; your beauty dies upon the instant: for beauty is the lover's gift; 'tis he bestows your charms—your glass is all a cheat. The

---

[5] Arranged.
[6] Mincing, as her name implies, affects what she considers an elegant clipped enunciation, only to spoil the effect with this dialect form of *crisp*.

ugly and the old, whom the looking-glass mortifies, yet after commendation can be flattered by it, and discover beauties in it: for that reflects our praises, rather than your face.

MILLAMANT.   Oh, the vanity of these men! Fainall, d'ye hear him? If they did not commend us, we were not handsome! Now you must know they could not commend one, if one was not handsome. Beauty the lover's gift! Lord, what is a lover, that it can give? Why, one makes lovers as fast as one pleases, and they live as long as one pleases, and they die as soon as one pleases: and then if one pleases, one makes more.

WITWOUD.   Very pretty. Why, you make no more of making of lovers, madam, than of making so many card-matches.

MILLAMANT.   One no more owes one's beauty to a lover, than one's wit to an echo: they can but reflect what we look. and say; vain empty things if we are silent or unseen, and want a being.

MIRABELL.   Yet to those two vain empty things you owe two the greatest pleasures of your life.

MILLAMANT.   How so?

MIRABELL.   To your lover you owe the pleasure of hearing yourselves praised; and to an echo the pleasure of hearing yourselves talk.

WITWOUD.   But I know a lady that loves talking so incessantly, she won't give an echo fair play; she has that everlasting rotation of tongue, that an echo must wait till she dies, before it can catch her last words.

MILLAMANT.   Oh, fiction! Fainall, let us leave these men.

MIRABELL.   [*Aside to* MRS. FAINALL.] Draw off Witwoud.

MRS. FAINALL.   [*Aside.*] Immediately.— I have a word or two for Mr. Witwoud.

MIRABELL.   [*To* MRS. MILLAMANT.] I would beg a little private audience too.

[*Exeunt* WITWOUD *and* MRS. FAINALL.] You had the tyranny to deny me last night though you knew I came to impart a secret to you that concerned my love.

MILLAMANT.   You saw I was engaged.

MIRABELL.   Unkind. You had the leisure to entertain a herd of fools; things who visit you from their excessive idleness; bestowing on your easiness that time, which is the incumbrance of their lives. How can you find delight in such society? It is impossible they should admire you, they are not capable: or if they were, it should be to you as a mortification; for sure to please a fool is some degree of folly.

MILLAMANT.   I please myself—besides, sometimes to converse with fools is for my health.

MIRABELL.   Your health! Is there a worse disease than the conversation of fools?

MILLAMANT.   Yes, the vapours; fools are physic for it, next to asafetida.

MIRABELL.   You are not in a course of fools? [7]

MILLAMANT.   Mirabell, if you persist in this offensive freedom, you'll displease me. I think I must resolve, after all, not to have you. We shan't agree.

MIRABELL.   Not in our physic it may be.

MILLAMANT.   And yet our distemper in all likelihood will be the same; for we shall be sick of one another. I shan't endure to be reprimanded, nor instructed; 'tis so dull to act always by advice, and so tedious to be told of one's faults—I can't bear it. Well, I won't have you, Mirabell—I'm resolved—I think—you may go—ha, ha, ha! What would you give, that you could help loving me?

MIRABELL.   I would give something that you did not know I could not help it.

MILLAMANT.   Come, don't look grave then. Well, what do you say to me?

MIRABELL.   I say that a man may as soon make a friend by his wit, or a fortune by his honesty, as win a woman with plain dealing and sincerity.

MILLAMANT.   Sententious Mirabell! Prithee, don't look with that violent and inflexible wise face, like Solomon at the dividing of the child in an old tapestry hanging.

MIRABELL.   You are merry, madam, but

[7] *I.e.,* undergoing a course of treatment with fools.

I would persuade you for a moment to be serious.

MILLAMANT. What, with that face? No, if you keep your countenance, 'tis impossible I should hold mine. Well, after all, there is something very moving in a lovesick face —ha, ha, ha! Well, I won't laugh, don't be peevish. Heigho! Now I'll be melancholy, as melancholy as a watch-light.[8] Well, Mirabell, if ever you will win me, woo me now. Nay, if you are so tedious, fare you well. I see they are walking away.

MIRABELL. Can you not find in the variety of your disposition one moment—

MILLAMANT. To hear you tell me Foible's married, and your plot like to speed? No.

MIRABELL. But how you came to know it—

MILLAMANT. Unless by the help of the devil, you can't imagine; unless she should tell me herself. Which of the two it may have been, I will leave you to consider; and when you have done thinking of that, think of me. [*Exit* MRS. MILLAMANT.]

MIRABELL. I have something more— Gone! Think of you! To think of a whirlwind, though 'twere in a whirlwind, were a case of more steady contemplation—a very tranquillity of mind and mansion. A fellow that lives in a windmill has not a more whimsical dwelling than the heart of a man that is lodged in a woman. There is no point of the compass to which they cannot turn, and by which they are not turned, and by one as well as another; for motion, not method, is their occupation. To know this, and yet continue to be in love, is to be made wise from the dictates of reason, and yet persevere to play the fool by the force of instinct.—Oh, here come my pair of turtles![9] What, billing so sweetly! Is not Valentine's Day over with you yet?

[*Enter* WAITWELL *and* FOIBLE.]

Sirrah Waitwell, why sure you think you were married for your own recreation, and not for my conveniency.

WAITWELL. Your pardon, sir. With

submission, we have indeed been solacing in lawful delights; but still with an eye to business, sir. I have instructed her as well as I could. If she can take your directions as readily as my instructions, sir, your affairs are in a prosperous way.

MIRABELL. Give you joy, Mrs. Foible.

FOIBLE. Oh 'las, sir, I'm so ashamed— I'm afraid my lady has been in a thousand inquietudes for me. But I protest, sir, I made as much haste as I could.

WAITWELL. That she did indeed, sir. It was my fault that she did not make more.

MIRABELL. That I believe.

FOIBLE. But I told my lady as you instructed me, sir. That I had a prospect of seeing Sir Rowland, your uncle; and that I would put her ladyship's picture in my pocket to show him; which I'll be sure to say has made him so enamoured of her beauty that he burns with impatience to lie at her ladyship's feet and worship the original.

MIRABELL. Excellent Foible! Matrimony has made you eloquent in love.

WAITWELL. I think she has profited, sir. I think so.

FOIBLE. You have seen Madam Millamant, sir?

MIRABELL. Yes.

FOIBLE. I told her, sir, because I did not know that you might find an opportunity; she had so much company last night.

MIRABELL. Your diligence will merit more. In the meantime— [*Gives money.*]

FOIBLE. O dear sir, your humble servant.

WAITWELL. Spouse!

MIRABELL. Stand off, sir, not a penny.— Go on and prosper, Foible. The lease shall be made good and the farm stocked, if we succeed.

FOIBLE. I don't question your generosity, sir: and you need not doubt of success. If you have no more commands, sir, I'll be gone; I'm sure my lady is at her toilet, and can't dress till I come.—Oh dear, I'm sure that [*looking out*] was Mrs. Marwood that

8 Night-light.

9 Turtle-doves.

went by in a mask; if she has seen me with you I'm sure she'll tell my lady. I'll make haste home and prevent [10] her. Your servant, sir. B'w'y, Waitwell.

[*Exit* FOIBLE.]

WAITWELL. Sir Rowland, if you please. The jade's so pert upon her preferment she forgets herself.

MIRABELL. Come, sir, will you endeavour to forget yourself—and transform into Sir Rowland.

WAITWELL. Why, sir, it will be impossible I should remember myself—married,

knighted, and attended all in one day! 'Tis enough to make any man forget himself. The difficulty will be how to recover my acquaintance and familiarity with my former self, and fall from my transformation to a reformation into Waitwell. Nay, I shan't be quite the same Waitwell neither —for now I remember me, I am married, and can't be my own man again.

Ay there's the grief; that's the sad change of life;

To lose my title, and yet keep my wife.

[*Exeunt.*]

ACT III

Scene: *A room in* LADY WISHFORT'S *house.*

[LADY WISHFORT *at her toilet,* PEG *waiting.*]

LADY WISHFORT. Merciful, no news of Foible yet?

PEG. No, madam.

LADY WISHFORT. I have no more patience. If I have not fretted myself till I am pale again, there's no veracity in me. Fetch me the red—the red, do you hear, sweetheart? An arrant ash colour, as I'm a person. Look you how this wench stirs! Why dost thou not fetch me a little red? Didst thou not hear me, mopus? [1]

PEG. The red ratafia [2] does your ladyship mean, or the cherry-brandy?

LADY WISHFORT. Ratafia, fool! No, fool. Not the ratafia, fool—grant me patience! I mean the Spanish paper, idiot—complexion, darling. Paint, paint, paint—dost thou understand that, changeling?—dangling thy hands like bobbins before thee. Why dost thou not stir, puppet?—thou wooden thing upon wires.

PEG. Lord, madam, your ladyship is so impatient—I cannot come at the paint, madam; Mrs. Foible has locked it up, and carried the key with her.

LADY WISHFORT. A pox take you both! Fetch me the cherry-brandy then.

[*Exit* PEG.]

I'm as pale and as faint, I look like Mrs. Qualmsick the curate's wife, that's always breeding.—Wench, come, come, wench, what art thou doing? Sipping? Tasting? Save thee, dost thou not know the bottle?

[*Re-enter* PEG *with a bottle and china cup.*]

PEG. Madam, I was looking for a cup.

LADY WISHFORT. A cup, save thee, and what a cup hast thou brought! Dost thou take me for a fairy, to drink out of an acorn? Why didst thou not bring thy thimble? Hast thou ne'er a brass thimble clinking in thy pocket with a bit of nutmeg? I warrant thee. Come, fill, fill.—So—again. [*One knocks.*] See who that is.—Set down the bottle first. Here, here, under the table. What, wouldst thou go with the bottle in thy hand like a tapster?—As I'm a person, this wench has lived in an inn upon the road, before she came to me, like Maritornes the Asturian in *Don Quixote.*—No Foible yet?

PEG. Oh, madam—Mrs. Marwood.

LADY WISHFORT. Oh, Marwood! Let her come in. Come in, good Marwood.

[*Enter* MRS. MARWOOD.]

MRS. MARWOOD. I'm surprised to find your ladyship in dishabille at this time of day.

LADY WISHFORT. Foible's a lost thing; has been abroad since morning, and never heard of since.

---

[10] Forestall.

[1] Stupid.   [2] A liqueur.

MRS. MARWOOD. I saw her but now, as I came masked through the Park, in conference with Mirabell.

LADY WISHFORT. With Mirabell! You call my blood into my face, with mentioning that traitor. She durst not have the confidence. I sent her to negotiate an affair, in which if I'm detected I'm undone. If that wheedling villain has wrought upon Foible to detect me, I'm ruined. Oh, my dear friend, I'm a wretch of wretches if I'm detected.

MRS. MARWOOD. Oh, madam, you cannot suspect Mrs. Foible's integrity.

LADY WISHFORT. Oh, he carries poison in his tongue that would corrupt integrity itself. If she has given him an opportunity, she has as good as put her integrity into his hands. Ah, dear Marwood, what's integrity to an opportunity?—Hark! I hear her. [To PEG.] Go, you thing, and send her in!

[Exit PEG.]

Dear friend, retire into my closet, that I may examine her with more freedom. You'll pardon me, dear friend, I can make bold with you. There are books over the chimney—Quarles and Prynne, and *The Short View of the Stage,* with Bunyan's works, to entertain you.[3]

[Exit MRS. MARWOOD.]

[Enter FOIBLE.]

LADY WISHFORT. Oh, Foible, where hast thou been? What hast thou been doing?

FOIBLE. Madam, I have seen the party.

LADY WISHFORT. But what hast thou done?

FOIBLE. Nay, 'tis your ladyship has done, and are to do; I have only promised. But a man so enamoured—so transported! [Holding out a miniature.] Well, here it is —all that is left; all that is not kissed away. Well, if worshipping of pictures be a sin— poor Sir Rowland, I say.

LADY WISHFORT. The miniature has been counted like—But hast thou not betrayed me, Foible? Hast thou not detected me to that faithless Mirabell?—What hadst thou to do with him in the Park? Answer me, has he got nothing out of thee?

FOIBLE. [Aside.] So, the devil has been beforehand with me! What shall I say?— Alas, madam, could I help it if I met that confident thing? Was I in fault? If you had heard how he used me, and all upon your ladyship's account, I'm sure you would not suspect my fidelity. Nay, if that had been the worst I could have borne: but he had a fling at your ladyship too; and then I could not hold but, i' faith, I gave him his own.

LADY WISHFORT. Me? What did the filthy fellow say?

FOIBLE. O madam, 'tis a shame to say what he said—with his taunts and his fleers, tossing up his nose. Humh (says he), what, you are a-hatching some plot (says he), you are so early abroad, or catering (says he), ferreting for some disbanded officer, I warrant. Half-pay is but thin subsistence (says he). Well, what pension does your lady propose? Let me see (says he), what, she must come down pretty deep now— she's superannuated (says he) and—

LADY WISHFORT. Ods my life, I'll have him—I'll have him murdered! I'll have him poisoned! Where does he eat? I'll marry a drawer[4] to have him poisoned in his wine. I'll send for Robin from Locket's immediately.

FOIBLE. Poison him? Poisoning's too good for him. Starve him, madam, starve him; marry Sir Rowland, and get him disinherited. Oh, you would bless yourself, to hear what he said.

LADY WISHFORT. A villain! Superannuated!

FOIBLE. Humh (says he), I hear you are laying designs against me too (says he), and Mrs. Millamant is to marry my uncle —(he does not suspect a word of your ladyship) but (says he) I'll fit you for that, I warrant you (says he), I'll hamper you

[3] Quarles was a writer of religious verse; Prynne, a Puritan controversialist who attacked the stage. Collier's *Short View* was an indictment of the immorality of the Restoration stage. Bun-yan was a Restoration dissenting preacher and pamphleteer of most lowly station, as well as the author of *The Pilgrim's Progress.*
[4] Bartender. Locket's was a fashionable tavern.

for that (says he), you and your old frippery too (says he), I'll handle you—

LADY WISHFORT. Audacious villain! Handle me! Would he durst! Frippery! Old frippery! Was there ever such a foul-mouthed fellow? I'll be married tomorrow, I'll be contracted tonight.

FOIBLE. The sooner the better, madam.

LADY WISHFORT. Will Sir Rowland be here, say'st thou? When, Foible?

FOIBLE. Incontinently, madam. No new sheriff's wife expects the return of her husband after knighthood, with that impatience in which Sir Rowland burns for the dear hour of kissing your ladyship's hand after dinner.

LADY WISHFORT. Frippery! Superannuated frippery! I'll frippery the villain. I'll reduce him to frippery and rags—a tatterdemalion! I hope to see him hung with tatters, like a Long Lane penthouse,[5] or a gibbet-thief. A slander-mouthed railer: I warrant the spendthrift prodigal's in debt as much as the million lottery,[6] or the whole court upon a birthday.[7] I'll spoil his credit with his tailor. Yes, he shall have my niece with her fortune, he shall.

FOIBLE. He! I hope to see him lodge in Ludgate first, and angle into Blackfriars for brass farthings with an old mitten.[8]

LADY WISHFORT. Ay, dear Foible; thank thee for that, dear Foible. He has put me out of all patience. I shall never recompose my features to receive Sir Rowland with any economy of face. This wretch has fretted me that I am absolutely decayed. Look, Foible.

FOIBLE. Your ladyship has frowned a little too rashly, indeed, madam. There are some cracks discernible in the white varnish.

LADY WISHFORT. Let me see the glass. Cracks, say'st thou? Why, I am arrantly flayed. I look like an old peeled wall. Thou must repair me, Foible, before Sir Row-

land comes; or I shall never keep up to my picture.

FOIBLE. I warrant you, madam; a little art once made your picture like you; and now a little of the same art must make you like your picture. Your picture must sit for you, madam.

LADY WISHFORT. But art thou sure Sir Rowland will not fail to come? Or will 'a not fail when he does come? Will he be importunate, Foible, and push? For if he should not be importunate—I shall never break decorums—I shall die with confusion, if I am forced to advance—oh no, I can never advance—I shall swoon if he should expect advances. No, I hope Sir Rowland is better bred than to put a lady to the necessity of breaking her forms. I won't be too coy neither. I won't give him despair—but a little disdain is not amiss; a little scorn is alluring.

FOIBLE. A little scorn becomes your ladyship.

LADY WISHFORT. Yes, but tenderness becomes me best—a sort of a dyingness. You see that picture has a sort of a—ha, Foible? A swimminess in the eyes. Yes, I'll look so. My niece affects it; but she wants features. Is Sir Rowland handsome? Let my toilet be removed—I'll dress above. I'll receive Sir Rowland here. Is he handsome? Don't answer me. I won't know: I'll be surprised. I'll be taken by surprise.

FOIBLE. By storm, madam. Sir Rowland's a brisk man.

LADY WISHFORT. Is he! Oh, then he'll importune, if he's a brisk man. I shall save decorums if Sir Rowland importunes. I have a mortal terror at the apprehension of offending against decorums. Nothing but importunity can surmount decorums. Oh, I'm glad he's a brisk man. Let my things be removed, good Foible.

[*Exit* LADY WISHFORT.]

---

[5] An old-clothes shop in Long Lane.
[6] A lottery loan raised by the government in 1694.
[7] Lavish finery and gifts for the celebration of a royal birthday easily plunged spendthrift courtiers into debt.

[8] Debtors lodged in the Fleet Prison, in Ludgate, solicited charity from those passing through the Blackfriars district by letting down from the windows a mitten at the end of a cord.

[*Enter* MRS. FAINALL.]

MRS. FAINALL. Oh, Foible, I have been in a fright, lest I should come too late. That devil, Marwood, saw you in the Park with Mirabell, and I'm afraid will discover it to my lady.

FOIBLE. Discover what, madam?

MRS. FAINALL. Nay, nay, put not on that strange face. I am privy to the whole design, and know that Waitwell, to whom thou wert this morning married, is to personate Mirabell's uncle, and as such, winning my lady, to involve her in those difficulties from which Mirabell only must release her, by his making his conditions to have my cousin and her fortune left to her own disposal.

FOIBLE. Oh, dear madam, I beg your pardon. It was not my confidence in your ladyship that was deficient; but I thought the former good correspondence between your ladyship and Mr. Mirabell might have hindered his communicating this secret.

MRS. FAINALL. Dear Foible, forget that.

FOIBLE. Oh, dear madam, Mr. Mirabell is such a sweet winning gentleman—but your ladyship is the pattern of generosity. Sweet lady, to be so good! Mr. Mirabell cannot choose but be grateful. I find your ladyship has his heart still. Now, madam, I can safely tell your ladyship our success. Mrs. Marwood had told my lady; but I warrant I managed myself. I turned it all for the better. I told my lady that Mr. Mirabell railed at her. I laid horrid things to his charge, I'll vow; and my lady is so incensed, that she'll be contracted to Sir Rowland to-night, she says. I warrant I worked her up, that he may have her for asking for, as they say of a Welsh maidenhead.

MRS. FAINALL. Oh, rare Foible!

FOIBLE. Madam, I beg your ladyship to acquaint Mr. Mirabell of his success. I would be seen as little as possible to speak to him; besides, I believe Madam Marwood watches me.—She has a month's mind; [9] but I know Mr. Mirabell can't abide her.—

[*Enter a* FOOTMAN.]

John, remove my lady's toilet.—Madam, your servant. My lady is so impatient, I fear she'll come for me, if I stay.

MRS. FAINALL. I'll go with you up the back stairs, lest I should meet her.

[*Exeunt.*]

[*Re-enter* MRS. MARWOOD.]

MRS. MARWOOD. Indeed, Mrs. Engine,[10] is it thus with you? Are you become a go-between of this importance? Yes, I shall watch you. Why, this wench is the *passe-partout,* a very master-key to everybody's strong box. My friend Fainall, have you carried it so swimmingly? I thought there was something in it; but it seems it's over with you. Your loathing is not from a want of appetite then, but from a surfeit. Else you could never be so cool to fall from a principal to be an assistant, to procure for him! A pattern of generosity, that I confess. Well, Mr. Fainall, you have met with your match.—Oh, man, man! Woman, woman! The devil's an ass: if I were a painter, I would draw him like an idiot, a driveler with a bib and bells. Man should have his head and horns,[11] and woman the rest of him. Poor simple fiend!—Madam Marwood has a month's mind, but he can't abide her!—'Twere better for him you had not been his confessor in that affair, without you could have kept his counsel closer. I shall not prove another pattern of generosity, and stalk for him, till he takes his stand to aim at a fortune. He has not obliged me to that with those excesses of himself; and now I'll have none of him. Here comes the good lady, panting ripe; with a heart full of hope, and a head full of care, like any chemist upon the day of projection.[12]

---

[9] A desire for Mirabell.
[10] Mrs. Intriguer.

[11] The badge of a cuckold.
[12] Like an alchemist at the crucial moment in transmuting base metal into gold.

[*Enter* LADY WISHFORT.]

LADY WISHFORT. Oh, dear Marwood, what shall I say for this rude forgetfulness? But my dear friend is all goodness.

MRS. MARWOOD. No apologies, dear madam. I have been very well entertained.

LADY WISHFORT. As I'm a person, I am in a very chaos to think I should so forget myself—but I have such an olio [13] of affairs, really I know not what to do.—[*Calls.*] Foible!—I expect my nephew Sir Wilfull every moment too.—Why, Foible! —He means to travel for improvement.

MRS. MARWOOD. Methinks Sir Wilfull should rather think of marrying than travelling at his years. I hear he is turned of forty.

LADY WISHFORT. Oh, he's in less danger of being spoiled by his travels. I am against my nephew's marrying too young. It will be time enough when he comes back, and has acquired discretion to choose for himself.

MRS. MARWOOD. Methinks Mrs. Millamant and he would make a very fit match. He may travel afterwards. 'Tis a thing very usual with young gentlemen.

LADY WISHFORT. I promise you I have thought on't—and since 'tis your judgment, I'll think on't again. I assure you I will; I value your judgment extremely. On my word, I'll propose it.

[*Enter* FOIBLE.]

Come, come, Foible—I had forgot my nephew will be here before dinner—I must make haste.

FOIBLE. Mr. Witwoud and Mr. Petulant are come to dine with your ladyship.

LADY WISHFORT. Oh dear, I can't appear till I'm dressed. Dear Marwood, shall I be free with you again, and beg you to entertain 'em? I'll make all imaginable haste. Dear friend, excuse me.

[*Exeunt* LADY WISHFORT *and* FOIBLE.]

[*Enter* MRS. MILLAMANT *and* MINCING.]

MILLAMANT. Sure never anything was so unbred as that odious man.—Marwood, your servant.

[13] Miscellany. [14] Cheap woolen cloth.

MRS. MARWOOD. You have a colour; what's the matter?

MILLAMANT. That horrid fellow, Petulant, has provoked me into a flame. I have broke my fan.—Mincing, lend me yours.— Is not all powder out of my hair?

MRS. MARWOOD. No. What has he done?

MILLAMANT. Nay, he has done nothing; he has only talked. Nay, he has said nothing neither; but he has contradicted everything that has been said. For my part, I thought Witwoud and he would have quarrelled.

MINCING. I vow, mem, I thought once they would have fit.

MILLAMANT. Well, 'tis a lamentable thing, I'll swear, that one has not the liberty of choosing one's acquaintance as one does one's clothes.

MRS. MARWOOD. If we had that liberty, we should be as weary of one set of acquaintance, though never so good, as we are of one suit, though never so fine. A fool and a doily stuff [14] would now and then find days of grace, and be worn for variety.

MILLAMANT. I could consent to wear 'em, if they would wear alike; but fools never wear out—they are such *drap-de-Berry* [15] things! Without one could give 'em to one's chambermaid after a day or two.

MRS. MARWOOD. 'Twere better so indeed. Or what think you of the play-house? A fine gay glossy fool should be given there, like a new masking habit, after the masquerade is over, and we have done with the disguise. For a fool's visit is always a disguise, and never admitted by a woman of wit, but to blind her affair with a lover of sense. If you would but appear barefaced now, and own Mirabell, you might as easily put off Petulant and Witwoud as your hood and scarf. And indeed 'tis time, for the town has found it: the secret is grown too big for the pretence. 'Tis like Mrs. Primly's great belly; she may lace it down before, but it burnishes on her hips. Indeed, Millamant, you can no more conceal it than my Lady Strammel can her face—that goodly face, which, in defiance of her Rhenish-

[15] A heavy and more durable woolen material.

wine tea,[16] will not be comprehended in a mask.

MILLAMANT. I'll take my death, Marwood, you are more censorious than a decayed beauty or a discarded toast.—Mincing, tell the men they may come up. My aunt is not dressing.—Their folly is less provoking than your malice.

[Exit MINCING.]

The town has found it! What has it found? That Mirabell loves me is no more a secret, than it is a secret that you discovered it to my aunt, or than the reason why you discovered it is a secret.

MRS. MARWOOD. You are nettled.

MILLAMANT. You're mistaken. Ridiculous!

MRS. MARWOOD. Indeed, my dear, you'll tear another fan, if you don't mitigate those violent airs.

MILLAMANT. O silly! Ha, ha, ha! I could laugh immoderately. Poor Mirabell! His constancy to me has quite destroyed his complaisance for all the world beside. I swear, I never enjoined it him, to be so coy. If I had the vanity to think he would obey me, I would command him to show more gallantry. 'Tis hardly well bred to be so particular on one hand, and so insensible on the other. But I despair to prevail, and so let him follow his own way. Ha, ha, ha! Pardon me, dear creature, I must laugh, ha, ha, ha!—though I grant you 'tis a little barbarous, ha, ha, ha!

MRS. MARWOOD. What pity 'tis, so much fine raillery, and delivered with so significant gesture, should be so unhappily directed to miscarry.

MILLAMANT. Ha? Dear creature, I ask your pardon—I swear I did not mind you.[17]

MRS. MARWOOD. Mr. Mirabell and you both may think it a thing impossible, when I shall tell him by telling you—

MILLAMANT. O dear, what? for it is the same thing, if I hear it—ha, ha, ha!

MRS. MARWOOD. That I detest him, hate him, madam.

MILLAMANT. O madam, why so do I—

and yet the creature loves me, ha, ha, ha! How can one forbear laughing to think of it—I am a sibyl if I am not amazed to think what he can see in me. I'll take my death, I think you are handsomer—and within a year or two as young. If you could but stay for me, I should overtake you—but that cannot be. Well, that thought makes me melancholy. Now I'll be sad.

MRS. MARWOOD. Your merry note may be changed sooner than you think.

MILLAMANT. D'ye say so? Then I'm resolved I'll have a song to keep up my spirits.

[Enter MINCING.]

MINCING. The gentlemen stay but to comb, madam, and will wait on you.

MILLAMANT. Desire Mrs. —— that is in the next room to sing the song I would have learnt yesterday. [Exit MINCING.] You shall hear it, madam—not that there's any great matter in it—but 'tis agreeable to my humour.

SONG

I

Love's but the frailty of the mind,
When 'tis not with ambition joined;
A sickly flame, which if not fed expires;
And feeding, wastes in self-consuming fires.

II

'Tis not to wound a wanton boy
Or am'rous youth, that gives the joy;
But 'tis the glory to have pierced a swain,
For whom inferior beauties sighed in vain.

III

Then I alone the conquest prize,
When I insult a rival's eyes:
If there's delight in love, 'tis when I see
That heart which others bleed for, bleed for me.

[Enter PETULANT and WITWOUD.]

MILLAMANT. Is your animosity composed, gentlemen?

WITWOUD. Raillery, raillery, madam; we have no animosity. We hit off a little wit now and then, but no animosity. The falling out of wits is like the falling out of

[16] Used to aid the complexion and reduce corpulence.

[17] Was not paying attention.

lovers. We agree in the main, like treble and bass. Ha, Petulant?

PETULANT. Ay, in the main. But when I have a humour to contradict—

WITWOUD. Ay, when he has a humour to contradict, then I contradict too. What, I know my cue. Then we contradict one another like two battledores; for contradictions beget one another like Jews.

PETULANT. If he says black's black—if I have a humour to say 'tis blue—let that pass—all's one for that. If I have a humour to prove it, it must be granted.

WIWOUD. Not positively must—but it may—it may.

PETULANT. Yes, it positively must, upon proof positive.

WITWOUD. Ay, upon proof positive it must; but upon proof presumptive it only may. That's a logical distinction now, madam.

MRS. MARWOOD. I perceive your debates are of importance, and very learnedly handled.

PETULANT. Importance is one thing, and learning's another; but a debate's a debate, that I assert.

WITWOUD. Petulant's an enemy to learning; he relies altogether on his parts.

PETULANT. No, I'm no enemy to learning; it hurts not me.

MRS. MARWOOD. That's a sign indeed it's no enemy to you.

PETULANT. No, no, it's no enemy to anybody, but them that have it.

MILLAMANT. Well, an illiterate man's my aversion. I wonder at the impudence of any illiterate man, to offer to make love.

WITWOUD. That I confess I wonder at too.

MILLAMANT. Ah, to marry an ignorant that can hardly read or write!

PETULANT. Why should a man be ever the further from being married though he can't read, any more than he is from being hanged? The ordinary's [18] paid for setting the psalm, and the parish-priest for reading the ceremony. And for the rest which is to follow in both cases, a man may do it without book—so all's one for that.

MILLAMANT. D'ye hear the creature? Lord, here's company, I'll be gone.

[Exit MILLAMANT.]

[Enter a SERVANT, followed by SIR WILFULL WITWOUD in a country riding habit.]

WITWOUD. In the name of Bartlemew and his fair,[19] what have we here?

MRS. MARWOOD. 'Tis your brother, I fancy. Don't you know him?

WITWOUD. Not I. Yes, I think it is he. I've almost forgot him; I have not seen him since the Revolution.[20]

SERVANT. Sir, my lady's dressing. Here's company, if you please to walk in, in the meantime.

SIR WILFULL. Dressing! What, it's but morning here, I warrant, with you in London; we should count it towards afternoon in our parts, down in Shropshire. Why, then belike my aunt han't dined yet—ha, friend?

SERVANT. Your aunt, sir?

SIR WILFULL. My aunt, sir, yes; my aunt, sir, and your lady, sir; your lady is my aunt, sir. Why, what, dost thou not know me, friend? Why, then send somebody hither that does. How long hast thou lived with thy lady, fellow, ha?

SERVANT. A week, sir; longer than anybody in the house, except my lady's woman.

SIR WILFULL. Why, then belike thou dost not know thy lady, if thou see'st her, ha, friend?

SERVANT. Why, truly, sir, I cannot safely swear to her face in a morning, before she is dressed. 'Tis like I may give a shrewd guess at her by this time.

SIR WILFULL. Well, prithee try what thou canst do; if thou canst not guess, enquire her out, dost hear, fellow? And tell her, her nephew, Sir Wilfull Witwoud, is in the house.

SERVANT. I shall, sir.

18 Chaplain.
19 The annual Bartholomew Fair in Smithfield attracted a motley crowd of rustics.
20 Which in 1688 drove James II from the throne.

SIR WILFULL. Hold ye, hear me, friend; a word with you in your ear. Prithee, who are these gallants?

SERVANT. Really, sir, I can't tell; here come so many here, 'tis hard to know 'em all.   [Exit SERVANT.]

SIR WILFULL. Oons, this fellow knows less than a starling; I don't think 'a knows his own name.

MRS. MARWOOD. Mr. Witwoud, your brother is not behindhand in forgetfulness —I fancy he has forgot you too.

WITWOUD. I hope so—the devil take him that remembers first, I say.

SIR WILFULL. Save you, gentlemen and lady.

MRS. MARWOOD. For shame, Mr. Witwoud; why won't you speak to him?—And you, sir.

WITWOUD. Petulant, speak.

PETULANT. And you, sir.

SIR WILFULL. [Saluting MRS. MARWOOD.] No offence, I hope.

MRS. MARWOOD. No, sure, sir.

WITWOUD. This is a vile dog, I see that already. No offence! Ha, ha, ha! To him; to him, Petulant, smoke him.[21]

PETULANT. [Surveying him round.] It seems as if you had come a journey, sir; hem, hem.

SIR WILFULL. Very likely, sir, that it may seem so.

PETULANT. No offence, I hope, sir.

WITWOUD. Smoke the boots, the boots, Petulant, the boots; ha, ha, ha!

SIR WILFULL. Maybe not, sir; thereafter as 'tis meant, sir.

PETULANT. Sir, I presume upon the information of your boots.

SIR WILFULL. Why, 'tis like you may, sir. If you are not satisfied with the information of my boots, sir, if you will step to the stable, you may enquire further of my horse, sir.

PETULANT. Your horse, sir! Your horse is an ass, sir!

SIR WILFULL. Do you speak by way of offence, sir?

MRS. MARWOOD. The gentleman's merry, that's all, sir. [Aside.] 'Slife, we shall have a quarrel betwixt an horse and an ass, before they find one another out. [Aloud.] You must not take anything amiss from your friends, sir. You are among your friends here, though it may be you don't know it. If I am not mistaken, you are Sir Wilfull Witwoud.

SIR WILFULL. Right, lady; I am Sir Wilfull Witwoud, so I write myself—no offence to anybody, I hope—and nephew to the Lady Wishfort of this mansion.

MRS. MARWOOD. Don't you know this gentleman, sir?

SIR WILFULL. Hum! What, sure 'tis not— yea, by'r Lady, but 'tis. 'Sheart, I know not whether 'tis or no. Yea, but 'tis, by the Wrekin.[22] Brother Anthony! What, Tony, i' faith! What, dost thou not know me? By'r Lady, nor I thee, thou art so be-cravated, and so beperiwigged. 'Sheart, why dost not speak? Art thou o'erjoyed?

WITWOUD. Odso, brother, is it you? Your servant, brother.

SIR WILFULL. Your servant! Why, yours, sir. Your servant again. 'Sheart, and your friend and servant to that—and a—[puff] and a flap-dragon for your service, sir, and a hare's foot, and a hare's scut for your service, sir, an you be so cold and so courtly![23]

WITWOUD. No offence, I hope, brother.

SIR WILFULL. 'Sheart, sir, but there is, and much offence. A pox, is this your Inns o' Court[24] breeding, not to know your friends and your relations, your elders, and your betters?

WITWOUD. Why, brother Wilfull of Salop,[25] you may be as short as a Shrewsbury cake,[26] if you please, but I tell you 'tis not modish to know relations in town. You think you're in the country, where great lubberly brothers slabber and kiss one an-

---

[21] Give him a working-over.
[22] A hill in Shropshire.
[23] A flapdragon was a raisin used in the game of flapdragon; a scut is a tail. The general purport of Sir Wilfull's remark is "Nuts to your high-falutin airs!"
[24] The London law schools, of which Furnival's Inn, mentioned later, was one.
[25] Shropshire.   [26] Short-bread.

other when they meet, like a call of sergeants.[27] 'Tis not the fashion here; 'tis not indeed, dear brother.

SIR WILFULL. The fashion's a fool; and you're a fop, dear brother. 'Sheart, I've suspected this. By'r Lady, I conjectured you were a fop, since you began to change the style of your letters, and write in a scrap of paper gilt round the edges, no broader than a subpœna. I might expect this when you left off "Honoured Brother," and "hoping you are in good health," and so forth—to begin with a "Rat me, knight, I'm so sick of a last night's debauch"—Od's heart, and then tell a familiar tale of a cock and a bull, and a whore and a bottle, and so conclude. You could write news before you were out of your time, when you lived with honest Pumple Nose, the attorney of Furnival's Inn. You could intreat to be remembered then to your friends round the Wrekin. We could have gazettes then, and Dawks's Letter,[28] and the weekly bill,[29] till of late days.

PETULANT. 'Slife, Witwoud, were you ever an attorney's clerk? Of the family of the Furnivals? Ha, ha, ha!

WITWOUD. Ay, ay, but that was for a while. Not long, not long. Pshaw! I was not in my own power then. An orphan, and this fellow was my guardian; ay, ay, I was glad to consent to that man to come to London. He had the disposal of me then. If I had not agreed to that, I might have been bound prentice to a felt-maker in Shrewsbury; this fellow would have bound me to a maker of felts.

SIR WILFULL. 'Sheart, and better than to be bound to a maker of fops; where, I suppose, you have served your time, and now you may set up for yourself.

MRS. MARWOOD. You intend to travel, sir, as I'm informed.

SIR WILFULL. Belike I may, madam. I may chance to sail upon the salt seas, if my mind hold.

PETULANT. And the wind serve.

SIR WILFULL. Serve or not serve, I shan't ask license of you, sir; nor the weather-cock your companion. I direct my discourse to the lady, sir.—'Tis like my aunt may have told you, madam. Yes, I have settled my concerns, I may say now, and am minded to see foreign parts. If an how that the peace holds, whereby, that is, taxes abate.

MRS. MARWOOD. I thought you had designed for France at all adventures.

SIR WILFULL. I can't tell that; 'tis like I may, and 'tis like I may not. I am somewhat dainty in making a resolution, because when I make it I keep it. I don't stand shill I, shall I, then; if I say't, I'll do't. But I have thoughts to tarry a small matter in town, to learn somewhat of your lingo first, before I cross the seas. I'd gladly have a spice of your French, as they say, whereby to hold discourse in foreign countries.

MRS. MARWOOD. Here is an academy in town for that use.

SIR WILFULL. There is? 'Tis like there may.

MRS. MARWOOD. No doubt you will return very much improved.

WITWOUD. Yes, refined, like a Dutch skipper from a whale-fishing.

[Enter LADY WISHFORT and FAINALL.]

LADY WISHFORT. Nephew, you are welcome.

SIR WILFULL. Aunt, your servant.

FAINALL. Sir Wilfull, your most faithful servant.

SIR WILFULL. Cousin Fainall, give me your hand.

LADY WISHFORT. Cousin Witwoud, your servant; Mr. Petulant, your servant. Nephew, you are welcome again. Will you drink anything after your journey, nephew, before you eat? Dinner's almost ready.

SIR WILFULL. I'm very well, I thank you, aunt—however, I thank you for your courteous offer. 'Sheart, I was afraid you would have been in the fashion too, and have remembered to have forgot your relations. Here's your Cousin Tony, belike, I mayn't call him brother for fear of offence.

---

[27] Like sergeants-at-law being called to the bar.
[28] A weekly news summary of the time.

[29] Parish death list.

LADY WISHFORT. Oh, he's a rallier, nephew—my cousin's a wit; and your great wits always rally their best friends to choose.[30] When you have been abroad, nephew, you'll understand raillery better.

[FAINALL and MRS. MARWOOD talk apart.]

SIR WILFULL. Why then, let him hold his tongue in the meantime, and rail when that day comes.

[Enter MINCING.]

MINCING. Mem, I come to acquaint your la'ship that dinner is impatient.

SIR WILFULL. Impatient? Why then, be-like it won't stay till I pull off my boots. Sweetheart, can you help me to a pair of slippers? My man's with his horses, I warant.

LADY WISHFORT. Fie, fie, nephew, you would not pull off your boots here! Go down into the hall—dinner shall stay for you.—My nephew's a little unbred, you'll pardon him, madam.—Gentlemen, will you walk? Marwood?

MRS. MARWOOD. I'll follow you, ma-dam, before Sir Wilfull is ready.

[Exeunt all but MRS. MARWOOD and FAINALL.]

FAINALL. Why then, Foible's a bawd, an arrant, rank, match-making bawd. And I, it seems, am a husband, a rank husband; and my wife a very arrant, rank wife—all in the way of the world. 'Sdeath, to be an anticipated cuckold—a cuckold in embryo! Sure I was born with budding antlers[31] like a young satyr, or a citizen's child.[32] 'Sdeath, to be outwitted, to be out-jilted—out-matrimonied! If I had kept my speed like a stag, 'twere somewhat; but to crawl after with my horns like a snail, and outstripped by my wife—'tis scurvy wed-lock.

MRS. MARWOOD. Then shake it off. You have often wished for an opportunity to

part, and now you have it. But first prevent their plot. The half of Millamant's fortune is too considerable to be parted with, to a foe, to Mirabell.

FAINALL. Damn him, that had been mine, had you not made that fond discovery[33]—that had been forfeited, had they been married. My wife had added lustre to my horns by that increase of fortune; I could have worn 'em tipt with gold, though my forehead had been furnished like a deputy-lieutenant's hall.

MRS. MARWOOD. They may prove a cap of maintenance[34] to you still, if you can away with[35] your wife. And she's no worse than when you had her—I dare swear she had given up her game before she was married.

FAINALL. Hum! That may be. She might throw up her cards; but I'll be hanged if she did not put Pam[36] in her pocket.

MRS. MARWOOD. You married her to keep you; and if you contrive to have her keep you better than you expected, why should you not keep her longer than you intended?

FAINALL. The means, the means?

MRS. MARWOOD. Discover to my lady your wife's conduct; threaten to part with her. My lady loves her, and will come to any composition to save her reputation. Take the opportunity of breaking it, just upon the discovery of this imposture. My lady will be enraged beyond bounds, and sacrifice niece, and fortune, and all at that conjuncture. And let me alone to keep her warm; if she should flag in her part, I will not fail to prompt her.

FAINALL. Faith, this has an appearance.

MRS. MARWOOD. I'm sorry I hinted to my lady to endeavour a match between Milla-mant and Sir Wilfull; that may be an ob-stacle.

FAINALL. Oh, for that matter leave me to manage him; I'll disable him for that; he

[30] As they choose.
[31] A cuckold was supposed to sprout horns on his forehead.
[32] According to the jesting of the time, citizens' children were destined to have their wives seduced by courtiers.
[33] Foolish revelation.
[34] A pun based on the heraldic term *cap of maintenance*—an official cap with peaks which suggested a cuckold's horns.
[35] Put up with.
[36] The jack of clubs, high card in the game of loo.

will drink like a Dane. After dinner I'll set his hand in.

MRS. MARWOOD. Well, how do you stand affected towards your lady?

FAINALL. Why, faith, I'm thinking of it. Let me see—I am married already; so that's over. My wife has played the jade with me—well, that's over too. I never loved her, or if I had, why, that would have been over too by this time. Jealous of her I cannot be, for I am certain; so there's an end of jealousy. Weary of her I am, and shall be—no, there's no end of that; no, no, that were too much to hope. Thus far concerning my repose. Now for my reputation. As to my own, I married not for it; so that's out of the question. And as to my part in my wife's—why, she had parted with hers before; so bringing none to me, she can take none from me; 'tis against all rule of play that I should lose to one who has not wherewithal to stake.

MRS. MARWOOD. Besides, you forget, marriage is honourable.

FAINALL. Hum! Faith, and that's well thought on; marriage is honourable, as you say; and if so, wherefore should cuckoldom be a discredit, being derived from so honourable a root?

MRS. MARWOOD. Nay, I know not; if the root be honourable, why not the branches?

FAINALL. So, so, why, this point's clear. Well, how do we proceed?

MRS. MARWOOD. I will contrive a letter which shall be delivered to my lady at the time when that rascal who is to act Sir Rowland is with her. It shall come as from an unknown hand—for the less I appear to know of the truth, the better I can play the incendiary. Besides, I would not have Foible provoked if I could help it—because you know she knows some passages—nay, I expect all will come out—but let the mine be sprung first, and then I care not if I am discovered.

FAINALL. If the worst come to the worst, I'll turn my wife out to grass. I have already a deed of settlement of the best part of her estate, which I wheedled out of her; and that you shall partake at least.

MRS. MARWOOD. I hope you are convinced that I hate Mirabell now. You'll be no more jealous?

FAINALL. Jealous? No—by this kiss. Let husbands be jealous, but let the lover still believe; or if he doubt, let it be only to endear his pleasure, and prepare the joy that follows, when he proves his mistress true. But let husbands' doubts convert to endless jealousy; or if they have belief, let it corrupt to superstition, and blind credulity. I am single, and will herd no more with 'em. True, I wear the badge, but I'll disown the order. And since I take my leave of 'em, I care not if I leave 'em a common motto to their common crest:

All husbands must, or pain, or shame,
    endure;
The wise too jealous are, fools too secure.

[*Exeunt.*]

ACT IV

Scene: *The same as the preceding.*

[*Enter* LADY WISHFORT *and* FOIBLE.]

LADY WISHFORT. Is Sir Rowland coming, say'st thou, Foible? and are things in order?

FOIBLE. Yes, madam. I have put waxlights in the sconces; and placed the footmen in a row in the hall, in their best liveries, with the coachman and postilion to fill up the equipage.

LADY WISHFORT. Have you pulvilled[1] the coachman and postilion, that they may not stink of the stable when Sir Rowland comes by?

FOIBLE. Yes, madam.

LADY WISHFORT. And are the dancers and the music ready, that he may be entertained in all points with correspondence to his passion?

FOIBLE. All is ready, madam.

[1] Used scented powder on.

LADY WISHFORT. And—well—and how do I look, Foible?

FOIBLE. Most killing well, madam.

LADY WISHFORT. Well, and how shall I receive him? In what figure shall I give his heart the first impression? There is a great deal in the first impression. Shall I sit?—No, I won't sit—I'll walk—ay, I'll walk from the door upon his entrance, and then turn full upon him. No, that will be too sudden. I'll lie—ay, I'll lie down—I'll receive him in my little dressing-room; there's a couch—yes, yes, I'll give the first impression on a couch. I won't lie neither, but loll and lean upon one elbow, with one foot a little dangling off, jogging in a thoughtful way—yes—and then as soon as he appears, start, ay, start and be surprised, and rise to meet him in a pretty disorder—yes—oh, nothing is more alluring than a levee from a couch in some confusion. It shows the foot to advantage, and furnishes with blushes, and recomposing airs beyond comparison. Hark! There's a coach.

FOIBLE. 'Tis he, madam.

LADY WISHFORT. Oh, dear, has my nephew made his addresses to Millamant? I ordered him.

FOIBLE. Sir Wilfull is set in to drinking, madam, in the parlour.

LADY WISHFORT. Od's my life, I'll send him to her. Call her down, Foible; bring her hither. I'll send him as I go. When they are together, then come to me, Foible, that I may not be too long alone with Sir Rowland.

[Exit LADY WISHFORT.]

[Enter MRS. MILLAMANT and MRS. FAINALL.]

FOIBLE. Madam, I stayed here to tell your ladyship that Mr. Mirabell has waited this half-hour for an opportunity to talk with you. Though my lady's orders were to leave you and Sir Wilfull together. Shall I tell Mr. Mirabell that you are at leisure?

MILLAMANT. No. What would the dear man have? I am thoughtful, and would amuse myself—bid him come another time. [Repeating, and walking about.]

> There never yet was woman made,
> Nor shall, but to be curst.[2]

That's hard!

MRS. FAINALL. You are very fond of Sir John Suckling today, Millamant, and the poets.

MILLAMANT. Ha? Ay, and filthy verses—so I am.

FOIBLE. Sir Wilfull is coming, madam. Shall I send Mr. Mirabell away?

MILLAMANT. Ay, if you please, Foible, send him away—or send him hither—just as you will, dear Foible.—I think I'll see him.—Shall I? Ay, let the wretch come.

[Exit FOIBLE.]

[Repeating.]

> Thyrsis, a youth of the inspired train.[3]

Dear Fainall, entertain Sir Wilfull—thou hast philosophy to undergo a fool; thou art married and hast patience. I would confer with my own thoughts.

MBS. FAINALL. I am obliged to you, that you would make me your proxy in this affair; but I have business of my own.

[Enter SIR WILFULL.]

Oh, Sir Wilfull, you are come at the critical instant. There's your mistress up to the ears in love and contemplation; pursue your point, now or never.

SIR WILFULL. Yes; my aunt would have it so. I would gladly have been encouraged with a bottle or two, because I'm somewhat wary at first, before I am acquainted. [This while MILLAMANT walks about repeating to herself.] But I hope, after a time, I shall break[4] my mind—that is, upon further acquaintance.—So for the present, cousin, I'll take my leave—if so be you'll be so kind to make my excuse, I'll return to my company—

MRS. FAINALL. Oh, fie, Sir Wilfull! What, you must not be daunted.

---

[2] Troublesome. The lines are by the seventeenth-century poet Suckling.

[3] From Edmund Waller's poem, *The Story of Phoebus and Daphne, Applied.*

[4] I.e., speak.

SIR WILFULL. Daunted! no, that's not it, it is not so much for that—for if so be that I set on't, I'll do't. But only for the present, 'tis sufficient till further acquaintance, that's all—your servant.

MRS. FAINALL. Nay, I'll swear you shall never lose so favourable an opportunity, if I can help it. I'll leave you together, and lock the door.   [Exit MRS. FAINALL.]

SIR WILFULL. Nay, nay, cousin—I have forgot my gloves. What d'ye do?—'Sheart, 'a has locked the door indeed, I think. Nay, Cousin Fainall, open the door!—Pshaw, what a vixen trick is this? Nay, now 'a has seen me too.—Cousin, I made bold to pass through, as it were—I think this door's enchanted—

MILLAMANT. [Repeating.]

I prithee spare me, gentle boy,
Press me no more for that slight toy [5]—

SIR WILFULL. Anan? [6] Cousin, your servant.

MILLAMANT. [Repeating.]

That foolish trifle of a heart—

Sir Wilfull!

SIR WILFULL. Yes—your servant. No offence, I hope, cousin.

MILLAMANT. [Repeating.]

I swear it will not do its part,
Though thou dost thine, employ'st thy
    power and art.

Natural, easy Suckling!

SIR WILFULL. Anan? Suckling? No such suckling neither, cousin, nor stripling: I thank heaven, I'm no minor.

MILLAMANT. Ah, rustic, ruder than Gothic.

SIR WILFULL. Well, well, I shall understand your lingo one of these days, cousin; in the meanwhile I must answer in plain English.

MILLAMANT. Have you any business with me, Sir Wilfull?

SIR WILFULL. Not at present, cousin.— Yes, I made bold to see, to come and know if that how you were disposed to fetch a walk this evening; if so be that I might not be troublesome, I would have sought a walk with you.

MILLAMANT. A walk? What then?

SIR WILFULL. Nay, nothing—only for the walk's sake, that's all—

MILLAMANT. I nauseate walking; 'tis a country diversion; I loathe the country and everything that relates to it.

SIR WILFULL. Indeed! Hah! Look ye, look ye, you do? Nay, 'tis like you may. Here are choice of pastimes here in town, as plays and the like; that must be confessed indeed.

MILLAMANT. Ah, l'étourdie! [7] I hate the town too.

SIR WILFULL. Dear heart, that's much— hah! that you should hate 'em both! Hah! 'tis like you may; there are some can't relish the town, and others can't away with the country—'tis like you may be one of those, cousin.

MILLAMANT. Ha, ha, ha! Yes, 'tis like I may.—You have nothing further to say to me?

SIR WILFULL. Not at present, cousin. 'Tis like when I have an opportunity to be more private—I may break my mind in some measure—I conjecture you partly guess—However, that's as time shall try— but spare to speak and spare to speed, as they say.

MILLAMANT. If it is of no great importance, Sir Wilfull, you will oblige me to leave me: I have just now a little business—

SIR WILFULL. Enough, enough, cousin: yes, yes, all a case. When you're disposed, when you're disposed. Now's as well as another time; and another time as well as now. All's one for that.—Yes, yes, if your concerns call you, there's no haste; it will keep cold, as they say. Cousin, your servant.—I think this door's locked.

MILLAMANT. You may go this way, sir.

SIR WILFULL. Your servant; then with your leave I'll return to my company.

[Exit SIR WILFULL.]

---

[5] These and the following lines quoted by Millamant are again by Suckling.

[6] Equivalent to "How's that again?"
[7] Ah, the giddy whirl!

MILLAMANT. Ay, ay; ha, ha, ha!

Like Phœbus sung the no less am'rous boy,[8]

[*Enter* MIRABELL.]

MIRABELL.

Like Daphne she, as lovely and as coy.

Do you lock yourself up from me to make my search more curious? [9] Or is this pretty artifice contrived to signify that here the chase must end, and my pursuit be crowned, for you can fly no further?

MILLAMANT. Vanity! No—I'll fly and be followed to the last moment. Though I am upon the very verge of matrimony, I expect you should solicit me as much as if I were wavering at the grate of a monastery, with one foot over the threshold. I'll be solicited to the very last, nay, and afterwards.

MIRABELL. What, after the last?

MILLAMANT. Oh, I should think I was poor and had nothing to bestow, if I were reduced to an inglorious ease, and freed from the agreeable fatigues of solicitation.

MIRABELL. But do not you know that when favours are conferred upon instant and tedious solicitation, that they diminish in their value, and that both the giver loses the grace, and the receiver lessens his pleasure?

MILLAMANT. It may be in things of common application; but never sure in love. Oh, I hate a lover that can dare to think he draws a moment's air independent on the bounty of his mistress. There is not so impudent a thing in nature as the saucy look of an assured man, confident of success. The pedantic arrogance of a very husband has not so pragmatical [10] an air. Ah! I'll never marry, unless I am first made sure of my will and pleasure.

MIRABELL. Would you have 'em both before marriage? Or will you be contented with the first now, and stay for the other till after grace? [11]

MILLAMANT. Ah, don't be impertinent.

—My dear liberty, shall I leave thee? My faithful solitude, my darling contemplation, must I bid you then adieu? Ay-h, adieu—my morning thoughts, agreeable wakings, indolent slumbers, all ye *douceurs,*[12] ye *sommeils du matin,*[13] adieu?— I can't do't, 'tis more than impossible. Positively, Mirabell, I'll lie abed in a morning as long as I please.

MIRABELL. Then I'll get up in a morning as early as I please.

MILLAMANT. Ah! Idle creature, get up when you will.—And d'ye hear, I won't be called names after I'm married; positively I won't be called names.

MIRABELL. Names!

MILLAMANT. Ay, as wife, spouse, my dear, joy, jewel, love, sweetheart, and the rest of that nauseous cant, in which men and their wives are so fulsomely familiar—I shall never bear that. Good Mirabell, don't let us be familiar or fond, nor kiss before folks, like my Lady Fadler and Sir Francis: nor go to Hyde Park together the first Sunday in a new chariot, to provoke eyes and whispers; and then never to be seen there together again; as if we were proud of one another the first week, and ashamed of one another for ever after. Let us never visit together, nor go to a play together, but let us be very strange [14] and well bred: let us be as strange as if we had been married a great while; and as well bred as if we were not married at all.

MIRABELL. Have you any more conditions to offer? Hitherto your demands are pretty reasonable.

MILLAMANT. Trifles. As liberty to pay and receive visits to and from whom I please; to write and receive letters, without interrogatories or wry faces on your part. To wear what I please, and choose conversation with regard only to my own taste; to have no obligation upon me to converse with wits that I don't like because they are your acquaintance, or to be intimate with fools because they may be your relations.

---

[8] This and the following line are from Waller's poem quoted earlier.
[9] Ingenious.
[10] Matter-of-fact.

[11] Till after the nuptial blessing has been pronounced.
[12] Delights.
[13] Morning slumbers.   [14] Distant.

Come to dinner when I please, dine in my dressing-room when I'm out of humour, without giving a reason. To have my closet [15] inviolate; to be sole empress of my tea-table, which you must never presume to approach without first asking leave. And lastly, wherever I am, you shall always knock at the door before you come in. These articles subscribed, if I continue to endure you a little longer, I may by degrees dwindle into a wife.

MIRABELL. Your bill of fare is something advanced in this latter account. Well, have I liberty to offer conditions—that when you are dwindled into a wife, I may not be beyond measure enlarged into a husband?

MILLAMANT. You have free leave. Propose your utmost, speak and spare not.

MIRABELL. I thank you. *Imprimis* then, I convenant that your acquaintance be general; that you admit no sworn confident, or intimate of your own sex; no she-friend to screen her affairs under your countenance, and tempt you to make trial of a mutual secrecy. No decoy-duck to wheedle you a-fop-scrambling to the play in a mask—then bring you home in a pretended fright, when you think you shall be found out—and rail at me for missing the play, and disappointing the frolic which you had, to pick me up and prove my constancy.

MILLAMANT. Detestable *imprimis!* I go to the play in a mask!

MIRABELL. *Item,* I article, that you continue to like your own face as long as I shall; and while it passes current with me, that you endeavour not to new-coin it. To which end, together with all vizards for the day, I prohibit all masks for the night, made of oiled-skins and I know not what—hog's bones, hare's gall, pig-water, and the marrow of a roasted cat. In short, I forbid all commerce with the gentlewoman in What-d'ye-call-it Court. *Item,* I shut my doors against all bawds with baskets, and penny-worths of muslin, china, fans, atlases,[16] etc. —*Item,* when you shall be breeding—

MILLAMANT. Ah! name it not.

[15] Personal room.   [16] Satins.

MIRABELL. Which may be presumed, with a blessing on our endeavours—

MILLAMANT. Odious endeavours—

MIRABELL. I denounce against all strait lacing, squeezing for a shape, till you mould my boy's head like a sugar-loaf; and instead of a man-child, make me the father to a crooked billet. Lastly, to the dominion of the tea-table I submit; but with proviso—that you exceed not in your province, but restrain yourself to native and simple tea-table drinks, as tea, chocolate, and coffee; as likewise to genuine and authorised tea-table talk—such as mending of fashions, spoiling reputations, railing at absent friends, and so forth—but that on no account you encroach upon the men's prerogative, and presume to drink healths, or toast fellows; for prevention of which I banish all foreign forces, all auxiliaries to the tea-table, as orange-brandy, all aniseed, cinnamon, citron and Barbadoes waters, together with ratafia and the most noble spirit of clary—but for cowslip-wine, poppy-water, and all dormitives,[17] those I allow. These provisos admitted, in other things I may prove a tractable and complying husband.

MILLAMANT. Oh, horrid provisos! Filthy strong waters! I toast fellows, odious men! I hate your odious provisos.

MIRABELL. Then we're agreed. Shall I kiss your hand upon the contract? And here comes one to be a witness to the sealing of the deed.

[*Enter* MRS. FAINALL.]

MILLAMANT. Fainall, what shall I do? Shall I have him? I think I must have him.

MRS. FAINALL. Ay, ay, take him, take him, what should you do?

MILLAMANT. Well then—I'll take my death, I'm in a horrid fright—Fainall, I shall never say it—well—I think—I'll enure you.

MRS. FAINALL. Fie, fie, have him, have him, and tell him so in plain terms: for I am sure you have a mind to him.

[17] Soporific drinks.

MILLAMANT. Are you? I think I have—and the horrid man looks as if he thought so too.—Well, you ridiculous thing you, I'll have you—I won't be kissed, nor I won't be thanked—here, kiss my hand though.—So, hold your tongue now, and don't say a word.

MRS. FAINALL. Mirabell, there's a necessity for your obdience—you have neither time to talk nor stay. My mother is coming; and in my conscience, if she should see you, would fall into fits, and maybe not recover time enough to return to Sir Rowland, who, as Foible tells me, is in a fair way to succeed. Therefore spare your ecstacies for another occasion, and slip down the back stairs, where Foible waits to consult you.

MILLAMANT. Ay, go, go. In the meantime I suppose you have said something to please me.

MIRABELL. I am all obedience.

[Exit MIRABELL.]

MRS. FAINALL. Yonder Sir Wilfull's drunk, and so noisy that my mother has been forced to leave Sir Rowland to appease him; but he answers her only with singing and drinking. What they have done by this time I know not; but Petulant and he were upon quarreling as I came by.

MILLAMANT. Well, if Mirabell should not make a good husband, I am a lost thing—for I find I love him violently.

MRS. FAINALL. So it seems, when you mind not what's said to you. If you doubt him, you had best take up with Sir Wilfull.

MILLAMANT. How can you name that superannuated lubber? Foh!

[Enter WITWOUD from drinking.]

MRS. FAINALL. So, is the fray made up, that you have left 'em?

WITWOUD. Left 'em? I could stay no longer. I have laughed like ten christ'nings—I am tipsy with laughing—if I had stayed any longer I should have burst—I must have been let out and pieced in the sides like an unsized camlet.[18]—Yes, yes, the fray is composed; my lady came in like a

nolle prosequi,[19] and stopped the proceedings.

MILLAMANT. What was the dispute?

WITWOUD. That's the jest; there was no dispute. They could neither of 'em speak for rage; and so fell a sputt'ring at one another like two roasting apples.

[Enter PETULANT drunk.]

Now, Petulant, all's over, all's well?—Gad, my head begins to whim it about!—Why dost thou not speak? Thou art both as drunk and as mute as a fish.

PETULANT. Look you, Mrs. Millamant—if you can love me, dear nymph—say it—and that's the conclusion. Pass on, or pass off—that's all.

WITWOUD. Thou hast uttered volumes, folios, in less than decimo sexto,[20] my dear Lacedemonian.[21] Sirrah Petulant, thou art an epitomiser of words.

PETULANT. Witwoud—you are an annihilator of sense.

WITWOUD. Thou art a retailer of phrases; and dost deal in remnants of remnants, like a maker of pincushions—thou art in truth (metaphorically speaking) a speaker of shorthand.

PETULANT. Thou art (without a figure) just one half of an ass, and Baldwin [22] yonder, thy half-brother, is the rest—a gemini [23] of asses split would make just four of you.

WITWOUD. Thou dost bite, my dear mustard-seed; kiss me for that.

PETULANT. Stand off—I'll kiss no more males—I have kissed your twin yonder in a humour of reconciliation, till he [hiccup] rises upon my stomach like a radish.

MILLAMANT. Eh! filthy creature!—What was the quarrel?

PETULANT. There was no quarrel—there might have been a quarrel.

WITWOUD. If there had been words enow between 'em to have expressed provocation, they had gone together by the ears like a pair of castanets.

PETULANT. You were the quarrel.

18 A cloth woven of goat's hair.
19 A legal motion to drop prosecution.
20 A pocket-size volume.

21 Noted for terse speech.
22 The name of the ass in medieval beast epics.
23 Pair.

MILLAMANT. Me!

PETULANT. If I have a humour to quarrel, I can make less matters conclude premises. If you are not handsome, what then, if I have a humour to prove it? If I shall have my reward, say so; if not, fight for your face the next time yourself.—I'll go sleep.

WITWOUD. Do, wrap thyself up like a wood-louse, and dream revenge—and hear me, if thou canst learn to write by tomorrow morning, pen me a challenge—I'll carry it for thee.

PETULANT. Carry your mistress's monkey a spider—go flea dogs, and read romances—I'll go to bed to my maid.

[*Exit* PETULANT.]

MRS. FAINALL. He's horribly drunk. How came you all in this pickle?

WITWOUD. A plot, a plot, to get rid of the knight—your husband's advice; but he sneaked off.

[*Enter* LADY WISHFORT, *and* SIR WILFULL *drunk.*]

LADY WISHFORT. Out upon't, out upon't, at years of discretion, and comport yourself at this rantipole [24] rate.

SIR WILFULL. No offence, aunt.

LADY WISHFORT. Offence? As I'm a person, I'm ashamed of you. Fogh! how you stink of wine! D'ye think my niece will ever endure such a borachio? [25] You're an absolute borachio!

SIR WILFULL. Borachio!

LADY WISHFORT. At a time when you should commence an amour and put your best foot foremost—

SIR WILFULL. 'Sheart, an you grutch me your liquor, make a bill. Give me more drink, and take my purse. [*Sings.*]

> Prithee fill me the glass
> Till it laugh in my face,
> With ale that is potent and mellow;
> He that whines for a lass
> Is an ignorant ass,
> For a bumper has not its fellow.

But if you would have me marry my cousin—say the word, and I'll do't—Wilfull will do't, that's the word—Wilfull will do't, that's my crest—my motto I have forgot.

LADY WISHFORT. My nephew's a little overtaken, cousin—but 'tis with drinking your health. O' my word, you are obliged to him—

SIR WILFULL. *In vino veritas,* [26] aunt.—If I drunk your health today, cousin, I am a borachio. But if you have a mind to be married, say the word, and send for the piper—Wilfull will do't. If not, dust it away, and let's have t'other round.—Tony! 'Odsheart, where's Tony?—Tony's an honest fellow, but he spits after a bumper, and that's a fault. [*Sings.*]

> We'll drink and we'll never ha' done, boys,
> Put the glass then around with the sun, boys,
> Let Apollo's example invite us;
> For he's drunk every night,
> And that makes him so bright,
> That he's able next morning to light us.

The sun's a good pimple, an honest soaker; he has a cellar at your Antipodes. If I travel, aunt, I touch at your Antipodes. Your Antipodes are a good rascally sort of topsy-turvy fellows—if I had a bumper I'd stand upon my head and drink a health to 'em.—A match or no match, cousin with the hard name?—Aunt, Wilfull will do't. If she has her maidenhead, let her look to't; if she has not, let her keep her own counsel in the meantime, and cry out at the nine months' end.

MILLAMANT. Your pardon, madam, I can stay no longer—Sir Wilfull grows very powerful. Egh! how he smells! I shall be overcome if I stay. Come, cousin.

[*Exeunt* MILLAMANT *and* MRS. FAINALL.]

LADY WISHFORT. Smells! he would poison a tallow-chandler and his family. Beastly creature, I know not what to do with him.—Travel, quoth 'a; ay, travel, travel, get thee gone, get thee but far enough, to the

---

24 Rowdy.
25 A large wine-skin or bottle.

26 Under the influence of wine the truth comes out.

Saracens, or the Tartars, or the Turks—for thou art not fit to live in a Christian commonwealth, thou beastly pagan.

SIR WILFULL. Turks, no; no Turks, aunt; your Turks are infidels, and believe not in the grape. Your Mahometan, your Mussulman, is a dry stinkard—no offence, aunt. My map says that your Turk is not so honest a man as your Christian—I cannot find by the map that your Mufti [27] is orthodox—whereby it is a plain case, that orthodox is a hard word, aunt, and [*hiccup*] Greek for claret. [*Sings.*]

To drink is a Christian diversion
Unknown to the Turk and the Persian:
 Let Mahometan fools
 Live by heathenish rules,
And be damned over tea-cups and coffee.
 But let British lads sing,
 Crown a health to the king,
And a fig for your sultan and sophy.[28]

Ah, Tony!

[*Enter* FOIBLE *and whispers* LADY WISHFORT.]

LADY WISHFORT. Sir Rowland impatient? Good lack! what shall I do with this beastly tumbril?—Go lie down and sleep, you sot, or as I'm a person, I'll have you bastinadoed with broomsticks. Call up the wenches. [*Exit* FOIBLE.]

SIR WILFULL. Ahey? Wenches, where are the wenches?

LADY WISHFORT. Dear Cousin Witwoud, get him away, and you will bind me to you inviolably. I have an affair of moment that invades me with some precipitation. You will oblige me to all futurity.

WITWOUD. Come, knight—pox on him, I don't know what to say to him—will you go to a cock-match?

SIR WILFULL. With a wench, Tony? Is she a shakebag, sirrah? Let me bite your cheek for that.

WITWOUD. Horrible! He has a breath like a bagpipe.—Ay, ay, come, will you march, my Salopian?

SIR WILFULL. Lead on, little Tony—I'll follow thee, my Anthony, my Tantony. Sirrah, thou sha't be my Tantony, and I'll be thy pig.[29]

—And a fig for your sultan and sophy.

[*Exeunt* SIR WILFULL *and* WITWOUD.]

LADY WISHFORT. This will never do. It will never make a match—at least before he has been abroad.

[*Enter* WAITWELL, *disguised as for*
SIR ROWLAND.]

Dear Sir Rowland, I am confounded with confusion at the retrospection of my own rudeness—I have more pardons to ask than the Pope distributes in the year of jubilee. But I hope where there is likely to be so near an alliance, we may unbend the severity of decorum, and dispense with a little ceremony.

WAITWELL. My impatience, madam, is the effect of my transport; and till I have the possession of your adorable person, I am tantalized on a rack and do but hang, madam, on the tenter [30] of expectation.

LADY WISHFORT. You have excess of gallantry, Sir Rowland; and press things to a conclusion with a most prevailing vehemence.—But a day or two for decency of marriage—

WAITWELL. For decency of funeral, madam. The delay will break my heart—or if that should fail, I shall be poisoned. My nephew will get an inkling of my designs, and poison me—and I would willingly starve him before I die—I would gladly go out of the world with that satisfaction. That would be some comfort to me, if I could but live so long as to be revenged on that unnatural viper.

LADY WISHFORT. Is he so unnatural, say you? Truly I would contribute much both to the saving of your life and the accomplishment of your revenge—not that I respect [31] myself, though he has been a perfidious wretch to me.

---

[27] Mohammedan religious official.
[28] Shah of Persia.

[29] In pictures St. Anthony, as the patron of swineherds, was often accompanied by a pig.
[30] Tenter-hook.   [31] Consider.

WAITWELL. Perfidious to you!

LADY WISHFORT. Oh, Sir Rowland, the hours that he has died away at my feet, the tears that he has shed, the oaths that he has sworn, the palpitations that he has felt, the trances and the tremblings, the ardors and the ecstasies, the kneelings and the risings, the heart-heavings and the hand-gripings, the pangs and the pathetic regards of his protesting eyes—oh, no memory can register!

WAITWELL. What, my rival! Is the rebel my rival? 'A dies.

LADY WISHFORT. No, don't kill him at once, Sir Rowland; starve him gradually inch by inch.

WAITWELL. I'll do't. In three weeks he shall be barefoot; in a month out at knees with begging an alms—he shall starve upward and upward, till he has nothing living but his head, and then go out in a stink like a candle's end upon a save-all.[32]

LADY WISHFORT. Well, Sir Rowland, you have the way—you are no novice in the labyrinth of love—you have the clue. But as I am a person, Sir Rowland, you must not attribute my yielding to any sinister appetite, or indigestion of widowhood; nor impute my complacency to any lethargy of continence. I hope you do not think me prone to any iteration of nuptials—

WAITWELL. Far be it from me—

LADY WISHFORT. If you do, I protest I must recede—or think that I have made a prostitution of decorums but in the vehemence of compassion, and to save the life of a person of so much importance—

WAITWELL. I esteem it so—

LADY WISHFORT. Or else you wrong my condescension—

WAITWELL. I do not, I do not—

LADY WISHFORT. Indeed you do.

WAITWELL. I do not, fair shrine of virtue.

LADY WISHFORT. If you think the least scruple of carnality was an ingredient—

WAITWELL. Dear madam, no. You are all camphire [33] and frankincense, all chastity and odour.

LADY WISHFORT. Or that—

[Enter FOIBLE.]

FOIBLE. Madam, the dancers are ready, and there's one with a letter, who must deliver it into your own hands.

LADY WISHFORT. Sir Rowland, will you give me leave? Think favourably, judge candidly, and conclude you have found a person who would suffer racks in honour's cause, dear Sir Rowland, and will wait on you incessantly.   [Exit LADY WISHFORT.]

WAITWELL. Fie, fie! what a slavery have I undergone! Spouse, hast thou any cordial? I want spirits.

FOIBLE. What a washy rogue art thou, to pant thus for a quarter of an hour's lying and swearing to a fine lady!

WAITWELL. Oh, she is the antidote to desire. Spouse, thou wilt fare the worse for't—I shall have no appetite to iteration of nuptials this eight and forty hours. By this hand, I'd rather be a chairman in the dog-days than act Sir Rowland till this time tomorrow.

[Re-enter LADY WISHFORT with a letter.]

LADY WISHFORT. Call in the dancers.— Sir Rowland, we'll sit, if you please, and see the entertainment.

[A dance.]

Now with your permission, Sir Rowland, I will peruse my letter. I would open it in your presence because I would not make you uneasy. If it should make you uneasy I would burn it—speak if it does—but you may see by the superscription it is like a woman's hand.

FOIBLE. [Aside to WAITWELL.] By heaven! Mrs. Marwood's, I know it! My heart aches—get it from her—

WAITWELL. A woman's hand? No, madam, that's no woman's hand, I see that

[32] A holder which enables a candle to burn to the end.

[33] Believed to induce impotence.

already. That's somebody whose throat must be cut.

LADY WISHFORT. Nay, Sir Rowland, since you give me a proof of your passion by your jealousy, I promise you I'll make you a return by a frank communication. You shall see it—we'll open it together—look you here.

[*Reads.*] "Madam, though unknown to you,"—look you there, 'tis from nobody that I know—"I have that honour for your character, that I think myself obliged to let you know you are abused. He who pretends to be Sir Rowland is a cheat and a rascal—" Oh heavens! what's this?

FOIBLE. [*Aside.*] Unfortunate, all's ruined.

WAITWELL. How, how? Let me see, let me see! [*Reading.*] "A rascal and disguised and suborned for that imposture,"—O villainy! O villainy!—"by the contrivance of—"

LADY WISHFORT. I shall faint, I shall die! I shall die! Oh!

FOIBLE. [*Aside to* WAITWELL.] Say 'tis your nephew's hand. Quickly—his plot—swear, swear it!

WAITWELL. Here's a villain! Madam, don't you perceive it, don't you see it?

LADY WISHFORT. Too well, too well. I have seen too much.

WAITWELL. I told you at first I knew the hand. A woman's hand! The rascal writes a sort of a large hand—your Roman hand. I saw there was a throat to be cut presently. If he were my son, as he is my nephew, I'd pistol him—

FOIBLE. Oh, treachery! But are you sure, Sir Rowland, it is his writing?

WAITWELL. Sure? Am I here? Do I live? Do I love this pearl of India? I have twenty letters in my pocket from him, in the same character.

LADY WISHFORT. How!

FOIBLE. Oh, what luck it is, Sir Rowland, that you were present at this juncture! This was the business that brought Mr. Mirabell disguised to Madam Millamant this afternoon. I thought something was

contriving, when he stole by me and would have hid his face.

LADY WISHFORT. How, how! I heard the villain was in the house indeed, and now I remember, my niece went away abruptly, when Sir Wilfull was to have made his addresses.

FOIBLE. Then, then, madam, Mr. Mirabell waited for her in her chamber; but I would not tell your ladyship, to discompose you when you were to receive Sir Rowland.

WAITWELL. Enough, his date is short.

FOIBLE. No, good Sir Rowland, don't incur the law.

WAITWELL. Law! I care not for law. I can but die, and 'tis in a good cause—my lady shall be satisfied of my truth and innocence, though it cost me my life.

LADY WISHFORT. No, dear Sir Rowland, don't fight! If you should be killed, I must never show my face—or hanged—oh, consider my reputation, Sir Rowland! No, you shan't fight. I'll go in and examine my niece; I'll make her confess. I conjure you, Sir Rowland, by all your love, not to fight.

WAITWELL. I am charmed, madam; I obey. But some proof you must let me give you—I'll go for a black box, which contains the writings of my whole estate, and deliver that into your hands.

LADY WISHFORT. Ay, dear Sir Rowland, that will be some comfort; bring the black box.

WAITWELL. And may I presume to bring a contract to be signed this night? May I hope so far?

LADY WISHFORT. Bring what you will; but come alive, pray come alive. Oh, this is a happy discovery!

WAITWELL. Dead or alive, I'll come—and married we will be in spite of treachery; ay, and get an heir that shall defeat the last remaining glimpse of hope in my abandoned nephew. Come, my buxom widow: E'er long you shall substantial proof receive That I'm an errant knight—

FOIBLE. [*Aside.*] Or arrant knave.

[*Exeunt.*]

ACT V

Scene: *The same as the preceding.*

[*Enter* LADY WISHFORT *and* FOIBLE.]

LADY WISHFORT. Out of my house, out of my house, thou viper, thou serpent, that I have fostered! thou bosom traitress, that I raised from nothing!—begone, begone, begone, go, go!—that I took from washing of old gauze and weaving of dead hair,[1] with a bleak blue nose, over a chafing-dish of starved embers, and dining behind a traverse rag, in a shop no bigger than a bird-cage—go, go, starve again, do, do!

FOIBLE. Dear madam, I'll beg pardon on my knees.

LADY WISHFORT. Away, out, out, go set up for yourself again!—do, drive a trade, do, with your threepenny worth of small ware flaunting upon a packthread, under a brandy-seller's bulk,[2] or against a dead wall by a ballad-monger! Go, hang out an old Frisoneer gorget,[3] with a yard of yellow colberteen[4] again! do! an old gnawed mask, two rows of pins, and a child's fiddle, a glass necklace with the beads broken, and a quilted nightcap with one ear! Go, go, drive a trade! These were your commodities, you treacherous trull, this was your merchandise you dealt in, when I took you into my house, placed you next myself, and made you governante of my whole family. You have forgot this, have you, now you have feathered your nest?

FOIBLE. No, no, dear madam. Do but hear me, have but a moment's patience—I'll confess all. Mr. Mirabell seduced me. I am not the first that he has wheedled with his dissembling tongue; your ladyship's own wisdom has been deluded by him—then how should I, a poor ignorant, defend myself? O madam, if you knew but what he promised me, and how he assured me your ladyship should come to no damage—or else the wealth of the Indies should not

have bribed me to conspire against so good, so sweet, so kind a lady as you have been to me.

LADY WISHFORT. No damage? What, to betray me, to marry me to a cast serving-man; to make me a receptacle, an hospital for a decayed pimp? No damage? O thou frontless[5] impudence, more than a big-bellied actress!

FOIBLE. Pray, do but hear me, madam—he could not marry your ladyship, madam. No indeed, his marriage was to have been void in law; for he was married to me first, to secure your ladyship. He could not have bedded your ladyship; for if he had consummated with your ladyship, he must have run the risk of the law, and been put upon his clergy.[6] Yes indeed, I enquired of the law in that case before I would meddle or make.

LADY WISHFORT. What, then I have been your property, have I? I have been convenient to you, it seems—while you were catering for Mirabell, I have been broker for you? What, have you made a passive bawd of me?—This exceeds all precedent; I am brought to fine uses, to become a botcher[7] of second-hand marriages between Abigails and Andrews![8] I'll couple you! Yes, I'll baste you together, you and your Philander! I'll Duke's Place[9] you, as I'm a person! Your turtle is in custody already; you shall coo in the same cage, if there be constable or warrant in the parish.

[*Exit* LADY WISHFORT.]

FOIBLE. Oh, that ever I was born! Oh, that I was ever married! A bride—ay, I shall be a Bridewell[10] bride. Oh!

[*Enter* MRS. FAINALL.]

MRS. FAINALL. Poor Foible, what's the matter?

FOIBLE. O madam, my lady's gone for a

---

[1] *I.e.*, from laundering and wig-making.
[2] Stall.
[3] Woolen neck-cloth.
[4] Lace.
[5] Brazen.
[6] Compelled to plead benefit of clergy—an old

legal device for escaping the death penalty by proving an ability to read.
[7] Patcher.
[8] *I.e.*, maids and valets.
[9] See note 6, Act I.
[10] A London prison, largely for prostitutes.

constable; I shall be had to a justice, and put to Bridewell to beat hemp! Poor Waitwell's gone to prison already.

MRS. FAINALL. Have a good heart, Foible; Mirabell's gone to give security for him. This is all Marwood's and my husband's doing.

FOIBLE. Yes, yes; I know it, madam; she was in my lady's closet, and overheard all that you said to me before dinner. She sent the letter to my lady; and that missing effect, Mr. Fainall laid this plot to arrest Waitwell when he pretended to go for the papers; and in the meantime Mrs. Marwood declared all to my lady.

MRS. FAINALL. Was there no mention made of me in the letter? My mother does not suspect my being in the confederacy? I fancy Marwood has not told her, though she has told my husband.

FOIBLE. Yes, madam; but my lady did not see that part; we stifled the letter before she read so far. Has that mischievous devil told Mr. Fainall of your ladyship then?

MRS. FAINALL. Ay, all's out—my affair with Mirabell, everything discovered. This is the last day of our living together, that's my comfort.

FOIBLE. Indeed, madam, and so 'tis a comfort if you knew all. He has been even with your ladyship, which I could have told you long enough since, but I love to keep peace and quietness by my good will—I had rather bring friends together than set 'em at distance. But Mrs. Marwood and he are nearer related than ever their parents thought for.

MRS. FAINALL. Say'st thou so, Foible? Canst thou prove this?

FOIBLE. I can take my oath of it, madam; so can Mrs. Mincing. We have had many a fair word from Madam Marwood, to conceal something that passed in our chamber one evening when you were at Hyde Park, and we were thought to have gone a-walking—but we went up unawares —though we were sworn to secrecy too. Madam Marwood took a book and swore us upon it; but it was but a book of verses and poems. So as long as it was not a Bible oath, we may break it with a safe conscience.

MRS. FAINALL. This discovery is the most opportune thing I could wish.

[*Enter* MINCING.]

Now, Mincing?

MINCING. My lady would speak with Mrs. Foible, mem. Mr. Mirabell is with her. —He has set your spouse at liberty, Mrs. Foible, and would have you hide yourself in my lady's closet, till my old lady's anger is abated. Oh, my old lady is in a perilous passion at something Mr. Fainall has said; he swears, and my old lady cries. There's a fearful hurricane, I vow. He says, mem, how that he'll have my lady's fortune made over to him, or he'll be divorced.

MRS. FAINALL. Does your lady and Mirabell know that?

MINCING. Yes, mem; they have sent me to see if Sir Wilfull be sober, and to bring him to them. My lady is resolved to have him, I think, rather than lose such a vast sum as six thousand pound—Oh, come, Mrs. Foible, I hear my old lady.

MRS. FAINALL. Foible, you must tell Mincing that she must prepare to vouch when I call her.

FOIBLE. Yes, yes, madam.

MINCING. Oh, yes, mem, I'll vouch anything for your ladyship's service, be what it will. [*Exeunt* MINCING *and* FOIBLE.]

[*Enter* LADY WISHFORT *and* MRS. MARWOOD.]

LADY WISHFORT. Oh, my dear friend, how can I enumerate the benefits that I have received from your goodness? To you I owe the timely discovery of the false vows of Mirabell; to you the detection of the impostor Sir Rowland. And now you are become an intercessor with my son-in-law, to save the honour of my house, and compound for the frailties of my daughter. Well, friend, you are enough to reconcile me to the bad world, or else I would retire to deserts and solitudes, and feed harmless sheep by groves and purling streams. Dear

Marwood, let us leave the world, and retire by ourselves and be shepherdesses.

MRS. MARWOOD. Let us first dispatch the affair in hand, madam. We shall have leisure to think of retirement afterwards. Here is one who is concerned in the treaty.

LADY WISHFORT. O daughter, daughter, is it possible thou shouldst be my child, bone of my bone, and flesh of my flesh, and as I may say, another me, and yet transgress the most minute particle of severe virtue? Is it possible you should lean aside to iniquity, who have been cast in the direct mold of virtue? I have not only been a mold but a pattern for you, and a model for you, after you were brought into the world.

MRS. FAINALL. I don't understand your ladyship.

LADY WISHFORT. Not understand? Why, have you not been naught? [11] Have you not been sophisticated? [12] Not understand? Here I am ruined to compound for your caprices and your cuckoldoms. I must pawn my plate and my jewels, and ruin my niece, and all little enough—

MRS. FAINALL. I am wronged and abused, and so are you. 'Tis a false accusation, as false as hell, as false as your friend there, ay, or your friend's friend, my false husband.

MRS. MARWOOD. My friend, Mrs. Fainall? Your husband my friend! What do you mean?

MRS. FAINALL. I know what I mean, madam, and so do you; and so shall the world at a time convenient.

MRS. MARWOOD. I am sorry to see you so passionate, madam. More temper [13] would look more like innocence. But I have done. —I am sorry my zeal to serve your ladyship and family should admit of misconstruction, or make me liable to affronts. You will pardon me, madam, if I meddle no more with an affair in which I am not personally concerned.

LADY WISHFORT. O dear friend, I am so ashamed that you should meet with such returns! [To MRS. FAINALL.] You ought to ask pardon on your knees, ungrateful creature! She deserves more from you than all your life can accomplish. [To MRS. MARWOOD.] Oh, don't leave me destitute in this perplexity! No, stick to me, my good genius.

MRS. FAINALL. I tell you, madam, you're abused. Stick to you! Ay, like a leech, to suck your best blood—she'll drop off when she's full. Madam, you sha'not pawn a bodkin nor part with a brass counter in composition for me. I defy 'em all. Let 'em prove their aspersions: I know my own innocence, and dare stand by a trial.

[Exit MRS. FAINALL.]

LADY WISHFORT. Why, if she should be innocent, if she should be wronged after all, ha? I don't know what to think—and I promise you, her education has been unexceptionable—I may say it; for I chiefly made it my own care to initiate her very infancy in the rudiments of virtue, and to impress upon her tender years a young odium and aversion to the very sight of men—ay, friend, she would ha' shrieked if she had but seen a man, till she was in her teens. As I'm a person, 'tis true. She was never suffered to play with a male-child, though but in coats; nay, her very babies [14] were of the feminine gender. Oh, she never looked a man in the face but her own father, or the chaplain, and him we made a shift to put upon her for a woman, by the help of his long garments, and his sleek face till she was going in her fifteen.

MRS. MARWOOD. 'Twas much she should be deceived so long.

LADY WISHFORT. I warrant you, or she would never have borne to have been catechised by him; and have heard his long lectures against singing and dancing, and such debaucheries; and going to filthy plays, and profane music-meetings, where the lewd trebles squeak nothing but bawdy, and the basses roar blasphemy. Oh, she would have swooned at the sight or name of an obscene play-book—and can I think, after all this, that my daughter can be naught? What, a

[11] Bad, in the sense of immoral.
[12] Adulterated.
[13] Temperateness.
[14] Dolls.

whore? And thought it excommunication to set her foot within the door of a playhouse! Oh, my dear friend, I can't believe it, no, no! As she says, let him prove it, let him prove it.

MRS. MARWOOD.   Prove it, madam? What, and have your name prostituted in a public court; yours and your daughter's reputation worried at the bar by a pack of bawling lawyers? To be ushered in with an *Oyez* [15] of scandal; and have your case opened by an old fumbling lecher in a quoif like a man midwife, to bring your daughter's infamy to light; to be a theme for legal punsters, and quibblers by the statute; and become a jest, against a rule of court, where there is no precedent for a jest in any record, not even in Doomsday Book; to discompose the gravity of the bench, and provoke naughty interrogatories in more naughty law Latin; while the good judge, tickled with the proceeding, simpers under a grey beard, and fidges off and on his cushion as if he had swallowed cantharides,[16] or sat upon cow-itch.

LADY WISHFORT.   Oh, 'tis very hard!

MRS. MARWOOD.   And then to have my young revellers of the Temple take notes, like 'prentices at a conventicle; and after, talk it all over again in Commons, or before drawers [17] in an eating-house.

LADY WISHFORT.   Worse and worse!

MRS. MARWOOD.   Nay, this is nothing; if it would end here, 'twere well. But it must after this be consigned by the shorthand writers to the public press; and from thence be transferred to the hands, nay, into the throats and lungs of hawkers, with voices more licentious than the loud flounderman's, or the woman that cries grey-pease; and this you must hear till you are stunned; nay, you must hear nothing else for some days.

LADY WISHFORT.   Oh, 'tis insupportable! No, no, dear friend, make it up, make it up; ay, ay, I'll compound. I'll give up all, myself and my all, my niece and her all—anything, everything for composition.

MRS. MARWOOD.   Nay, madam, I advise nothing; I only lay before you, as a friend, the inconveniences which perhaps you have overseen.[18] Here comes Mr. Fainall. If he will be satisfied to huddle up all in silence, I shall be glad. You must think I would rather congratulate than condole with you.

[*Enter* FAINALL.]

LADY WISHFORT.   Ay, ay, I do not doubt it, dear Marwood; no, no, I do not doubt it.

FAINALL.   Well, madam, I have suffered myself to be overcome by the importunity of this lady your friend; and am content you shall enjoy your own proper estate during life, on condition you oblige yourself never to marry, under such penalty as I think convenient.

LADY WISHFORT.   Never to marry?

FAINALL.   No more Sir Rowlands. The next imposture may not be so timely detected.

MRS. MARWOOD.   That condition, I dare answer, my lady will consent to without difficulty; she has already but too much experienced the perfidiousness of men. Besides, madam, when we retire to our pastoral solitude we shall bid adieu to all other thoughts.

LADY WISHFORT.   Ay, that's true; but in case of necessity, as of health, or some such emergency—

FAINALL.   Oh, if you are prescribed marriage, you shall be considered; I will only reserve to myself the power to choose for you. If your physic be wholesome, it matters not who is your apothecary. Next, my wife shall settle on me the remainder of her fortune, not made over already, and for her maintenance depend entirely on my discretion.

LADY WISHFORT.   This is most inhumanly savage, exceeding the barbarity of a Muscovite husband.

FAINALL.   I learned it from his Czarish majesty's retinue,[19] in a winter evening's

---

[15] The call for the opening of court.
[16] An aphrodisiac.
[17] Waiters.

[18] Overlooked.
[19] Alluding to the visit paid to England in 1698 by Peter the Great.

conference over brandy and pepper, amongst other secrets of matrimony and policy, as they are at present practised in the northern hemisphere. But this must be agreed unto, and that positively. Lastly, I will be endowed, in right of my wife, with that six thousand pound, which is the moiety of Mrs. Millamant's fortune in your possession; and which she has forfeited (as will appear by the last will and testament of your deceased husband, Sir Jonathan Wishfort) by her disobedience in contracting herself against your consent or knowledge, and by refusing the offered match with Sir Wilfull Witwoud, which you, like a careful aunt, had provided for her.

LADY WISHFORT. My nephew was *non compos,*[20] and could not make his addresses.

FAINALL. I come to make demands—I'll hear no objections.

LADY WISHFORT. You will grant me time to consider?

FAINALL. Yes, while the instrument is drawing, to which you must set your hand till more sufficient deeds can be perfected: which I will take care shall be done with all possible speed. In the meanwhile I will go for the said instrument, and till my return you may balance this matter in your own discretion. [*Exit* FAINALL.]

LADY WISHFORT. This insolence is beyond all precedent, all parallel; must I be subject to this merciless villain?

MRS. MARWOOD. 'Tis severe indeed, madam, that you should smart for your daughter's wantonness.

LADY WISHFORT. 'Twas against my consent that she married this barbarian, but she would have him, though her year[21] was not out. Ah, her first husband, my son Languish, would not have carried it thus. Well, that was my choice, this is hers; she is matched now with a witness![22] I shall be mad, dear friend! Is there no comfort for me? Must I live to be confiscated at this rebel-rate?—Here come two more of my Egyptian plagues too.

[*Enter* MRS. MILLAMANT *and* SIR WILFULL.]

SIR WILFULL. Aunt, your servant.

LADY WISHFORT. Out, caterpillar, call not me aunt! I know thee not!

SIR WILFULL. I confess I have been a little in disguise, as they say—'sheart! and I'm sorry for't. What would you have? I hope I committed no offence, aunt—and if I did I am willing to make satisfaction; and what can a man say fairer? If I have broke anything, I'll pay for't, an it cost a pound. And so let that content for what's past, and make no more words. For what's to come, to pleasure you I'm willing to marry my cousin. So pray let's all be friends; she and I are agreed upon the matter before a witness.

LADY WISHFORT. How's this, dear niece? Have I any comfort? Can this be true?

MILLAMANT. I am content to be a sacrifice to your repose, madam. And to convince you that I had no hand in the plot, as you were misinformed, I have laid my commands on Mirabell to come in person, and be a witness that I give my hand to this flower of knighthood; and for the contract that passed between Mirabell and me, I have obliged him to make a resignation of it in your ladyship's presence. He is without, and waits your leave for admittance.

LADY WISHFORT. Well, I'll swear I am something revived at this testimony of your obedience. But I cannot admit that traitor —I fear I cannot fortify myself to support his appearance. His is as terrible to me as a Gorgon; if I see him, I fear I shall turn to stone, petrify incessantly.

MILLAMANT. If you disoblige him, he may resent your refusal, and insist upon the contract still. Then, 'tis the last time he will be offensive to you.

LADY WISHFORT. Are you sure it will be the last time? If I were sure of that—shall I never see him again?

MILLAMANT. Sir Wilfull, you and he are to travel together, are you not?

20 Not in possession of his faculties.
21 *I.e.,* of widow's mourning.

22 The sense is: She has certainly got herself a match this time!

SIR WILFULL. 'Sheart, the gentleman's a civil gentleman, aunt, let him come in; why, we are sworn brothers and fellow-travellers. We are to be Pylades and Orestes,[23] he and I. He is to be my interpreter in foreign parts. He has been over-seas once already; and with proviso that I marry my cousin, will cross 'em once again, only to bear me company. 'Sheart, I'll call him in—an I set on't once, he shall come in; and see who'll hinder him. [*Exit* SIR WILFULL.]

MRS. MARWOOD. [*Aside.*] This is precious fooling, if it would pass; but I'll know the bottom of it.

LADY WISHFORT. O dear Marwood, you are not going?

MARWOOD. Not far, madam; I'll return immediately. [*Exit* MRS. MARWOOD.]

[*Re-enter* SIR WILFULL *with* MIRABELL.]

SIR WILFULL. Look up, man, I'll stand by you; 'sbud, an she do frown, she can't kill you—besides—hark'ee, she dare not frown desperately, because her face is none of her own; 'sheart, an she should, her forehead would wrinkle like the coat of a cream-cheese; but mum for that, fellow-traveller.

MIRABELL. If a deep sense of the many injuries I have offered to so good a lady, with a sincere remorse, and a hearty contrition, can but obtain the least glance of compassion, I am too happy. Ah, madam, there was a time—but let it be forgotten—I confess I have deservedly forfeited the high place I once held, of sighing at your feet. Nay, kill me not by turning from me in disdain—I come not to plead for favour—nay, not for pardon; I am suppliant only for your pity—I am going where I never shall behold you more—

SIR WILFULL. How, fellow-traveller! You shall go by yourself then.

MIRABELL. Let me be pitied first; and afterwards forgotten—I ask no more.

SIR WILFULL. By'r Lady, a very reasonable request, and will cost you nothing, aunt. Come, come, forgive and forget, aunt—why, you must an you are a Christian.

MIRABELL. Consider, madam, in reality you could not receive much prejudice; it was an innocent device. Though I confess it had a face of guiltiness, it was at most an artifice which love contrived—and errors which love produces have ever been accounted venial. At least think it is punishment enough, that I have lost what in my heart I hold most dear; that to your cruel indignation I have offered up this beauty, and with her my peace and quiet; nay, all my hopes of future comfort.

SIR WILFULL. An he does not move me, would I might never be o' the quorum! [24] An it were not as good a deed as to drink, to give her to him again, I would I might never take shipping!—Aunt, if you don't forgive quickly, I shall melt, I can tell you that. My contract went no farther than a little mouth-glue,[25] and that's hardly dry—one doleful sigh more from my fellow-traveller and 'tis dissolved.

LADY WISHFORT. Well, nephew, upon your account. Ah, he has a false insinuating tongue!—Well, sir, I will stifle my just resentment at my nephew's request. I will endeavour what I can to forget—but on proviso that you resign the contract with my niece immediately.

MIRABELL. It is in writing and with papers of concern; but I have sent my servant for it, and will deliver it to you, with all acknowledgments for your transcendent goodness.

LADY WISHFORT. [*Aside.*] Oh, he has witchcraft in his eyes and tongue! When I did not see him, I could have bribed a villain to his assassination; but his appearance rakes the embers which have so long lain smothered in my breast.

[*Enter* FAINALL *and* MRS. MARWOOD.]

FAINALL. Your date of deliberation, madam, is expired. Here is the instrument; are you prepared to sign?

LADY WISHFORT. If I were prepared, I

[23] A classical example of friendship. Pylades accompanied Orestes in his flight from the Furies after the slaying of his mother, Clytemnestra. The story is dealt with in the *Oresteia* of Aeschylus. [24] Serve as a magistrate. [25] *I.e.*, it was only a verbal promise.

am not impowered. My niece exerts a lawful claim, having matched herself by my direction to Sir Wilfull.

FAINALL. That sham is too gross to pass on me, though 'tis imposed on you, madam.

MILLAMANT. Sir, I have given my consent.

MIRABELL. And, sir, I have resigned my pretensions.

SIR WILFULL. And, sir, I assert my right; and will maintain it in defiance of you, sir, and of your instrument. 'Sheart, an you talk of an instrument, sir, I have an old fox [26] by my thigh shall hack your instrument of ram vellum to shreds, sir. It shall not be sufficient for a mittimus [27] or a tailor's measure; therefore withdraw your instrument, sir, or by'r Lady I shall draw mine.

LADY WISHFORT. Hold, nephew, hold!

MILLAMANT. Good Sir Wilfull, respite your valour.

FAINALL. Indeed? Are you provided of a guard, with your single beefeater there? But I'm prepared for you; and insist upon my first proposal. You shall submit your own estate to my management, and absolutely make over my wife's to my sole use, as pursuant to the purport and tenor of this other covenant.—I suppose, madam, your consent is not requisite in this case; nor, Mr. Mirabell, your resignation; nor, Sir Wilfull, your right. You may draw your fox if you please, sir, and make a bear-garden flourish somewhere else; for here it will not avail. This, my Lady Wishfort, must be subscribed, or your darling daughter's turned adrift, like a leaky hulk to sink or swim, as she and the current of this lewd town can agree.

LADY WISHFORT. Is there no means, no remedy, to stop my ruin? Ungrateful wretch! dost thou not owe thy being, thy subsistence, to my daughter's fortune?

FAINALL. I'll answer you when I have the rest of it in my possession.

MIRABELL. But that you would not accept of a remedy from my hands—I own I have not deserved you should owe any ob-

[26] Sword.

ligation to me; or else perhaps I could advise—

LADY WISHFORT. Oh, what? what? To save me and my child from ruin, from want, I'll forgive all that's past; nay, I'll consent to anything to come, to be delivered from this tyranny.

MIRABELL. Ay, madam, but that is too late; my reward is intercepted. You have disposed of her, who only could have made me a compensation for all my services. But be it as it may, I am resolved I'll serve you —you shall not be wronged in this savage manner.

LADY WISHFORT. How! Dear Mr. Mirabell, can you be so generous at last! But it is not possible. Hark'ee, I'll break my nephew's match; you shall have my niece yet, and all her fortune, if you can but save me from this imminent danger.

MIRABELL. Will you? I take you at your word. I ask no more. I must have leave for two criminals to appear.

LADY WISHFORT. Ay, ay, anybody, anybody!

MIRABELL. Foible is one, and a penitent.

[*Enter* MRS. FAINALL, FOIBLE, *and* MINCING. MIRABELL *and* LADY WISHFORT *go to them and converse with them.*]

MRS. MARWOOD. [*To* FAINALL.] Oh, my shame! These corrupt things are brought hither to expose me.

FAINALL. If it must all come out, why let 'em know it; 'tis but *the way of the world.* That shall not urge me to relinquish or abate one tittle of my terms; no, I will insist the more.

FOIBLE. Yes, indeed, madam, I'll take my Bible oath of it.

MINCING. And so will I, mem.

LADY WISHFORT. O Marwood, Marwood, art thou false? my friend deceive me? Hast thou been a wicked accomplice with that profligate man?

MRS. MARWOOD. Have you so much ingratitude and injustice, to give credit against your friend, to the aspersions of two such mercenary trulls?

[27] A warrant of arrest.

MINCING. Mercenary, mem? I scorn your words. 'Tis true we found you and Mr. Fainall in the blue garret; by the same token, you swore us to secrecy upon Messalinas's poems.[28] Mercenary? No, if we would have been mercenary, we should have held our tongues; you would have bribed us sufficiently.

FAINALL. Go, you are an insignificant thing!—Well, what are you the better for this! Is this Mr. Mirabell's expedient? I'll be put off no longer.—You thing, that was a wife, shall smart for this. I will not leave thee wherewithal to hide thy shame; your body shall be naked as your reputation.

MRS. FAINALL. I despise you, and defy your malice! You have aspersed me wrongfully—I have proved your falsehood. Go, you and your treacherous—I will not name it! but starve together—perish—

FAINALL. Not while you are worth a groat, indeed, my dear. Madam, I'll be fooled no longer.

LADY WISHFORT. Ah, Mr. Mirabell, this is small comfort, the detection of this affair.

MIRABELL. Oh, in good time. Your leave for the other offender and penitent to appear, madam.

[Enter WAITWELL with a box of writings.]

LADY WISHFORT. Oh, Sir Rowland! Well, rascal!

WAITWELL. What your ladyship pleases. I have brought the black box at last, madam.

MIRABELL. Give it me—Madam, you remember your promise?

LADY WISHFORT. Ay, dear sir.

MIRABELL. Where are the gentlemen?

WAITWELL. At hand, sir, rubbing their eyes—just risen from sleep.

FAINALL. 'Sdeath, what's this to me? I'll not wait your private concerns.

[Enter PETULANT and WITWOUD.]

PETULANT. How now? What's the matter? Who's hand's out?

WITWOUD. Hey day! What, are you all got together, like players at the end of the last act?

MIRABELL. You may remember, gentlemen, I once requested your hands as witnesses to a certain parchment.

WITWOOD. Ay, I do; my hand I remember—Petulant set his mark.

MIRABELL. You wrong him; his name is fairly written, as shall appear. You do not remember, gentlemen, anything of what that parchment contained?

[Undoing the box.]

WITWOUD. No.

PETULANT. Not I. I writ; I read nothing.

MIRABELL. Very well, now you shall know.—Madam, your promise!

LADY WISHFORT. Ay, ay, sir, upon my honour.

MIRABELL. Mr. Fainall, it is now time that you should know that your lady, while she was at her own disposal, and before you had by your insinuations wheedled her out of a pretended settlement of the greatest part of her fortune—

FAINALL. Sir! pretended!

MIRABELL. Yes, sir. I say that this lady while a widow, having, it seems, received some cautions respecting your inconstancy and tyranny of temper, which from her own partial opinion and fondness of you she could never have suspected—she did, I say, by the wholesome advice of friends and of sages learned in the laws of this land, deliver this same as her act and deed to me in trust, and to the uses within mentioned. You may read if you please [holding out the parchment]—though perhaps what is inscribed on the back may serve your occasions.

FAINALL. Very likely, sir. What's here? Damnation!

[Reads.] "A deed of conveyance of the whole estate real of Arabella Languish, widow, in trust to Edward Mirabell."—Confusion!

MIRABELL. Even so, sir; 'tis the way of the world, sir—of the widows of the world. I suppose this deed may bear an elder date

[28] Messalina was the profligate wife of the Roman emperor Claudius. What Mincing refers to was probably a volume of Miscellany Poems, popular at the time.

than what you have obtained from your lady.

FAINALL. Perfidious fiend! Then thus I'll be revenged.—

[*Offers to run at* MRS. FAINALL.]

SIR WILFULL. Hold, sir! Now you may make your bear-garden flourish somewhere else, sir.

FAINALL. Mirabell, you shall hear of this, sir, be sure you shall.—Let me pass, oaf.

[*Exit* FAINALL.]

MRS. FAINALL. [*To* MRS. MARWOOD.] Madam, you seem to stifle your resentment. You had better give it vent.

MRS. MARWOOD. Yes, it shall have vent —and to your confusion, or I'll perish in the attempt.   [*Exit* MRS. MARWOOD.]

LADY WISHFORT. O daughter, daughter! 'Tis plain thou hast inherited thy mother's prudence.

MRS. FAINALL. Thank Mr. Mirabell, a cautious friend, to whose advice all is owing.

LADY WISHFORT. Well, Mr. Mirabell, you have kept your promise—and I must perform mine.—First, I pardon for your sake Sir Rowland there and Foible. The next thing is to break the matter to my nephew —and how to do that—

MIRABELL. For that, madam, give yourself no trouble. Let me have your consent. Sir Wilfull is my friend; he has had compassion upon lovers, and generously engaged a volunteer in this action, for our service, and now designs to prosecute his travels.

SIR WILFULL. 'Sheart, aunt, I have no mind to marry. My cousin's a fine lady, and the gentleman loves her, and she loves him, and they deserve one another. My resolution is to see foreign parts—I have set on't—and when I'm set on't, I must do't. And if these two gentlemen would travel too, I think they may be spared.

PETULANT. For my part, I say little—I think things are best off or on.

WITWOUD. I' gad, I understand nothing of the matter; I'm in a maze yet, like a dog in a dancing-school.

LADY WISHFORT. Well, sir, take her, and with her all the joy I can give you.

MILLAMANT. Why does not the man take me? Would you have me give myself to you over again?

MIRABELL. Ay, and over and over again; for I would have you as often as possibly I can. [*Kisses her hand.*] Well, heaven grant I love you not too well, that's all my fear.

SIR WILFULL. 'Sheart, you'll have him time enough to toy after you're married; or if you will toy now, let us have a dance in the meantime, that we who are not lovers may have some other employment besides looking on.

MIRABELL. With all my heart, dear Sir Wilfull. What shall we do for music?

FOIBLE. Oh, sir, some that were provided for Sir Rowland's entertainment are yet within call.   [*A dance.*]

LADY WISHFORT. As I am a person, I can hold out no longer; I have wasted my spirits so today already, that I am ready to sink under the fatigue; and I cannot but have some fears upon me yet, that my son Fainall will pursue some desperate course.

MIRABELL. Madam, disquiet not yourself on that account; to my knowledge his circumstances are such, he must of force comply. For my part, I will contribute all that in me lies to a reunion.—[*To* MRS. FAINALL.] In the meantime, madam, let me before these witnesses restore to you this deed of trust; it may be a means, well managed, to make you live easily together.

From hence let those be warned, who mean
    to wed;
Lest mutual falsehood stain the bridal-bed:
For each deceiver to his cost may find,
That marriage frauds too oft are paid in
    kind.

[*Exeunt omnes.*]

Tragedy of Sensibility

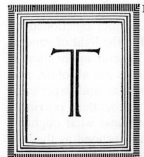HE KIND OF INTERESTS which result in comedy of manners are also responsible for a third type of tragedy. For want of a more generally accepted designation, this may be called the tragedy of sensibility. In origin an offshoot of classical tragedy, it came into existence in the seventeenth century as a product of Renaissance efforts to revive the tragic manner of the ancients. Dramatically it is important as the form in which were cast the masterpieces of French classical tragedy. In many respects it bears about the same specialized relationship to its ancient prototype as comedy of manners does to social comedy as a whole. In fact, there would be no gross distortion of its character in speaking of it as a tragedy of manners.

In order to understand the peculiar nature of this tragedy, it is perhaps best to approach it by way of its dramatic counterpart. Comedy of manners, as we have seen, is concerned with the conventions of conduct prescribed by a civilized society. Although its treatment of these amenities is light, it nevertheless recognizes that they are the outward graces of a quite serious design for living, just as the sophistication which fosters them reflects an equally sober scheme of values. The basis of both is the controlled behavior which ensues from a disciplined life. Such discipline always represents an intellectual adjustment of human nature to the requirements of an abstract code. As it demands both a conscious standard of social and moral propriety and a realistic appraisal of native human impulses, it also encounters inevitably the conflict between the two. Out of this conflict arise not only the amusing incongruities of civilized life but certain grave dilemmas as well. For to a refined sensibility the pressure of prescribed obligation is as imperative and exacting as that of a natural force and can precipitate crises which are quite as devastating. The important distinction is that such dilemmas are always consciously intellectual; they concern a mind confronted with a deliberate choice and acutely aware of the precise nature and implications of its problem. It is with the tragic potentialities of such dilemmas that tragedy

309

of sensibility essays to deal. Because these potentialities reside in the tensions peculiar to intellectual refinement and well-bred discipline, it is in essence a tragedy of sensibility.

The affinity between this tragedy and comedy of manners is reflected in its dominant characteristics. As comedy of manners emphasizes taste, tragedy of this sort emphasizes sensibility, which is the source of taste; and as the former concentrates upon manners, the latter concentrates upon discipline, which is the foundation of manners. Its prime interest is in discipline as a necessary means of cultivating the good life. Its habitual point of departure is, therefore, an intellectual problem in conduct. As the problems of widest ramification in a disciplined society, it focuses upon the intricate obligations imposed by love and honor. The invariable elements of its problem are a code of conduct sanctioned by general acceptance and individual behavior viewed in the light of general appropriateness. Because of this emphasis upon general application it regularly presupposes a scheme of life in which values are absolute, and confines its attention to those aspects of human nature and experience which may be considered universal. Within this deliberately restricted compass tragedy of sensibility raises two main questions: what ought to be done in a given situation; and why do individuals respond as they do to their admitted obligations? In other words, it sees the two aspects of its problem as moral and psychological. With respect to the first of these, however, its interest is not in the moral inferences to be drawn from a dramatic action, but in the application of an accepted code to specific test cases. Since such a process involves no serious question of principle, this aspect of the problem resolves itself to the relatively narrow question of applied ethics, or duty. Consequently the major dramatic emphasis tends to fall upon the more ample possibilities of the psychological aspect. Here the problem is much more complex. It concerns the precise nature of the experience which constrains a person of sensibility to accept or to reject deliberately the impositions of a code to which he subscribes. In the nature of the case no mere appraisal of exigent circumstances and crude passions, it calls for a delicate dissection of the whole subtle and intricate process whereby a highly civilized intellect becomes consciously operative. It is the sensitive revelation of this psychological process as an index to the universal problems of discipline which constitutes the artistic purpose of the tragedy.

The most striking feature of this kind of tragedy is its self-conscious intellectuality. Classical and romantic tragedy deal with the disastrous conflict between erratic passion and the ambiguity of ill-comprehended circumstance. Tragedy of sensibility, on the other hand, deals with the refined torture of perfect comprehension. It stems from a problem of conduct which is clearly defined and thoroughly understood by all concerned. Its dramatic conflict is a conscious clash between recognized obligations and contradictory human impulses. Its tragic irony is the suffering induced by this consciousness, whether by way of sacrifice to an obligation or remorse for repudiating it. The whole tragedy takes place upon a plane of intense intellectual awareness, in which every factor of the problem is perceived and weighed with exquisite precision. No matter how powerfully incited by passion, characters never forfeit possession of their rational faculties. Aware at all times of exactly what they are doing, they also appreciate its ultimate significance and thus are able to sit in judgment upon themselves as well as others. Consequently each emotion is explicit, each decision deliberate, and each act premeditated. Tragic error is not a flaw in knowledge or understanding; it is a lapse in proper discipline.

The sensibilities requisite for tragedy of such refinement first bore significant fruit in seventeenth-century France. Originally tragedy of sensibility was designed for much the same kind of audience and the same general stage facilities as the comedy of Molière. Its form and substance accordingly reflect the taste of the period. Dramatic structure and technique were based upon the tragic practices of the ancients, regularized to conform with neo-classical precepts concerning decorum and the unities of time, place, and action. As in classical tragedy, attention was focused upon a single dramatic crisis. On the other hand, although the general outlines of the ancient model were preserved, its choric and spectacular elements gave way to the more congenial concentration upon character psychology and the problems of behavior. To facilitate this interest, the ancient chorus was replaced by a set of individual confidants, systematically assigned to the major characters, and the whole play became much more discursive. With these changes, dramatic action resolved itself almost entirely into an inward agitation of mind and spirit. Scenes exhibited on the stage were viewed chiefly as opportunities for discourse in which characters could reveal their inner struggles. Hence their organic relationship to one another was determined less by an external progression of events than by the logical development of character analysis. In similar fashion characters were regarded less as complex individuals than as organic factors of a specific problem. Stripped of all personality except that connected with the dramatic action, they were reduced to the stark essentials of their dramatic function. As a result, both the action and the characters exhibit a singular isolation from any immediate background; they are as little native to seventeenth-century France as to the ancient world. Their sole context is the intellectual problem of which they are a part and the understanding mind which contemplates it. Thus they often create the curious effect of existing in a sort of mathematical equation outside place and time. Yet, because the mind is invited to contemplate a timeless human problem, the action in which it is couched becomes timely anywhere, and the characters inseparable from it possess the universal validity of elemental human nature.

Artificial, elegant, intellectual, tragedy of sensibility purveyed admirably to the serious interests of a consciously cultured age. It became not only the supreme expression of French classicism but the classic expression of French rationalism and artistic taste. It was brought to its peak of perfection—a perfection, indeed, beyond which it was incapable of further development—by Jean Racine (1639–1699). In his hands it achieved a precision of form, a sensitivity of insight, and a subtlety of eloquence which transmuted impassioned intellect into exquisite art. To this day the tragedies of Racine constitute the supreme achievement of French serious drama. Among them perhaps the most modern and universal in its appeal is *Phædra,* which was first produced in Paris in 1677. Although at first accorded a somewhat cool reception, it has since become one of the acknowledged masterpieces of the French stage, with a title rôle which has served as a feminine equivalent of Hamlet for Europe's greatest actresses. It is a tragedy which brought to their culmination Racine's unique dramatic powers and which illustrates the peculiar virtues of its type at their artistic best.

   Phædra is a modern version of two ancient tragedies, the *Hippolytus* of Euripides and a tragedy of the same title by Seneca. The influence of these ancient models is reflected in its general structure, its concentration of interest, its declamatory speeches, and certain technical devices like the formal narrative in which Theramenes recounts the death of Hippolytus. Apart from such deliberate imitations, however, the plays are quite different in methods and purpose. *Phædra* has been described as a succession of dramatic conversations. Superficially the description is apt. On the stage characters come and go for the express purpose of talking with each other, and especially with their respective confidants, about what is going on. There are two features of this conversation, however, which give it a peculiar dramatic force. In the first place, it is always more important for what it implies than for what it says; its essential purpose is not exposition but dramatic revelation. What it reveals is the reaction or tension produced in a character by the subject discussed. Hence dramatic action is presented indirectly by a sort of reverberation; drama is transferred from the stage to the mind of the auditor; and, as the instrument of this transfer, conversation itself is charged with dramatic intensity. In the second place, because of its emphasis on implication, conversation of this sort exhibits an extraordinary subtlety of expression. Dramatic dialogue becomes an art of intricate suggestion. Each turn of phrase is designed to convey delicate overtones of meaning. Words themselves turn actor in a rhetorical drama of intimations. For this reason the coupling of lucid precision with evocative subtlety in Racine's poetic style is not only one of his most characteristic but also one of his most important dramatic virtues. In the original French nearly every line is a marvel of exact yet irradiant eloquence. Unfortunately it is this quality of style which practically defies translation; nevertheless, although much of the poetry escapes, even the translation retains a great deal of its compact suggestiveness. In reading the play, it is important to give special attention to this particular feature of its style.

Essentially *Phædra* is a tragedy of civilized humanity snared in the meshes of its own civilization. Despite the primitive tale of passion with which it deals, the tragedy itself is far from primitive in conception. The behavior of Racine's characters and the problems which they confront alike presuppose a code of civilized decorum to which each admits an obligation. The central issues of the play have to do with duty, honor, and propriety. For example, it is illuminating to observe how much Phædra and Œnone are concerned with reputation, and with the scandal of shame rather than the iniquity of illicit love. The problem is not one of moral intelligence but one of decent conduct. Quite clearly Phædra recognizes that the evil of her plight resides not in the fact of her passion but in the danger of yielding to it. Hence, although the play presents a detailed study of passion, the passion with which it deals is not an untamed one; for, no matter how swept by passion, its characters are never the creatures of blind emotional impulse. In this respect, it is well to compare the play with such other tragedies as *Oedipus, Hamlet,* and *Desire Under the Elms.* Phædra is a consciously self-controlled individual with a profound understanding of herself and her dilemma. From the beginning she admits the evil of her unhappy infatuation and perceives the peril of her barbaric heredity. Determined to rule her conduct as decorum demands, she deliberately takes extreme measures, even resolving upon death, in order to preserve her honor and that of her husband. The irony of her struggle is the fatal hope which impels her to clutch at straws when the report of Theseus' death alters her obligations. Once her confession to Hippolytus is made, the situation is beyond retrieve. Every frantic effort to mend her broken honor but patches bad with worse. Yet, distracted as she is, she never loses the sharp clarity of her vision, and her acts remain deliberate, even when most ambiguous. Indeed, the quintessence of her tragedy is the horror with which she perceives the exact nature of her catastrophe and is compelled to pronounce judgment on herself. For Phædra, in spirit as in flesh, remains the daughter of Minos, who holds the urn of final judgment. Her tragedy is the plight of humanity between the millstones of passion and discipline. It is a tragedy of fastidious values and nice intellectual distinctions, an appreciation of which is a measure of human sensibility.

For reasons mentioned earlier, tragedy of sensibility in its pure form is so specialized a type of drama that it can flourish only under rather special conditions. While for more than a century its outward form was widely imitated throughout Europe, the imitations, lacking the inner substance of Racine, resulted in little of permanent value. In connection with *Phædra* it is desirable to read the *Hippolytus* plays of Euripides and Seneca, if only to observe the differences. Other characteristic tragedies by Racine are *Andromache, Britannicus,* and *Athaliah,* to which may be added plays like *The Cid* and *Cinna* by his contemporary Pierre Corneille. The type is affiliated with the heroic plays on love and honor produced in Restoration England, of which John Dryden's *All For Love* may serve as an example. A somewhat later derivative is Joseph Addison's *Cato,* which will probably suggest why other derivatives are as well left unmentioned. The real heirs of this type of tragedy are the modern problem play, discussed later, and the psychological drama of various forms. Of this latter category O'Neill's *Strange Interlude* is an interesting example.

PHAEDRA

by

JEAN RACINE

TRANSLATED BY

ROBERT HENDERSON

Characters

THESEUS, *son of Ægeus and King of Athens*

PHÆDRA, *wife of* THESEUS *and daughter of Minos and Pasiphaë*

HIPPOLYTUS, *son of* THESEUS *and Antiope, Queen of the Amazons*

ARICIA, *princess of the blood royal of Athens*

ŒNONE, *nurse of* PHÆDRA

THERAMENES, *tutor of* HIPPOLYTUS

ISMENE, *friend of* ARICIA

PANOPE, *waiting-woman of* PHÆDRA

GUARDS

The scene is laid in Trœzen, a town of the Peloponnesus.

Reprinted through the kind generosity of the translator.

[*Enter* HIPPOLYTUS *and* THERAMENES.]

HIPPOLYTUS. My mind is settled, dear
  Theramenes,
And I must stay no more in lovely Trœzen,
Racking my soul in doubt and mortal an-
  guish.
I am ashamed of my long idleness.
Look you, my father gone six months and
  more—
One so dear gone,—and to what fate be-
  fallen
I do not know, nor do I know what cor-
  ner
Of all the wide earth hides him!
THERAMENES.   Ah, my prince,—
And where, then, would you seek him? I
  have sailed
Over the seas on either side of Corinth.
Where Acheron [1] is lost among the Shades
I asked, indeed, if aught were known of
  Theseus!
And to content you, I have gone to Elis,
Rounded Tœnarus, sailed to the far waters
Where Icarus once fell.[2] What newer
  hope . . . ?
Under what favored sky would you think
  now
To trace his footsteps? Who knows if your
  father
Wishes the secret of his absence known?
Perhaps while we are trembling for his life
The hero calmly plots a fresh intrigue,
And only waits till the deluded lady—
HIPPOLYTUS. Peace, good Theramenes!
  Respect his name.
The waywardness of youth is his no longer,
And nothing so unworthy should detain
  him.
Now for a long time, Phædra has held that
  heart
Inconstant once, and she need fear no
  rival.
And if I seek him, it is but my duty.
I leave a place I dare no longer see!

THERAMENES. Indeed! When, prince, did
  you begin to dread
These peaceful haunts, so dear to happy
  childhood,
Where I have often known you rather stay
Than face the tumult and the pomp of
  Athens?
What danger do you shun? Or is it grief?
HIPPOLYTUS. All things are changed. That
  happy past is gone.
Since then, the gods sent Phædra!
THERAMENES.   Now I see!
It is the queen whose sight offends you.
  Yes,—
For with a step-dame's spite she schemed
  your exile
At her first sight of you. But then, her
  hatred
Is somewhat milder, if not wholly vanished.
A dying woman—one who longs for death!
What danger can she bring upon your
  head?
Weary of life, and weary of herself,—
Sick with some ill she will not ever speak
  of,—
Can Phædra then lay plots?—
HIPPOLYTUS.   I do not fear
The hatred of the queen. There is an-
  other
From whom I fly, and that is young Aricia,
The sole survivor of an impious race.
THERAMENES. What! You become her
  persecutor, too?
The gentle sister of the cruel sons
Of Pallas [3] did not share their perfidy.
Why should you hate such charming inno-
  cence?
HIPPOLYTUS. If it were hate, I should not
  need to fly.
THERAMENES. Then will you tell me what
  your flying means?
Is this the proud Hippolytus I see?
Love's fiercest foe alive?—the fiercest hater
Of Theseus' well-worn yoke?—Now can it
  be

---

[1] A river of Epirus believed to flow underground through the realm of the dead.
[2] Fleeing from Crete on wings constructed of
feathers and wax, Icarus flew too near the sun,
the wax melted, and he fell into the Aegean Sea
near Asia Minor. The several places mentioned in
this speech are in the Peloponnesus and serve to
block out the geographical setting of the play.
[3] Uncle of Theseus. His sons, the brothers of
Aricia, plotted to kill Theseus, who in turn killed
them.

That Venus, scorned, will justify your
father?
And is Hippolytus, like other mortals,
To bow, perforce, and offer incense to
her?—
And can he love? . . .
HIPPOLYTUS.   My friend, you must not
ask me.
You who have known my heart through
all my life,
And known it to be proud and most dis-
dainful,—
You will not ask that I should shame my-
self
By now disowning all that I professed.
My mother was an Amazon [4]—my wild-
ness,
Which you think strange, I suckled at her
breast,
And as I grew, why, Reason did approve
What Nature planted in me. Then you told
me
The story of my father, and you know
How, often, when I listened to your voice
I kindled, hearing of his noble acts,—
And you would tell how he brought con-
solation
To mortals for the absence of Alcides,[5]
And how he cleared the roads of monsters,
—robbers,—
Procrustes, Cercyron, Sciro, Sinnis slain,
Scattered the Epidaurian giant's bones,
And how Crete ran with blood of the
Minotaur! [6]
But when you told me of less glorious
deeds,—
Troth plighted here and there and every-
where,
Young Helen stolen from her home at
Sparta,
And Peribœa's tears in Salamis,
And many other trusting ones deceived,
Whose very names he cannot now remem-
ber,—
Lone Ariadne, crying to the rocks,—

And last of all this Phædra, bound to him
By better ties,—You know that with regret
I heard, and urged that you cut short the
tale.
I had been happier, could I erase
This one unworthy part of his bright story
Out of my memory. Must I in turn
Be made love's slave, and brought to bend
so low?
It is the more contemptible in me,
For no such brilliance clings about my
name
As to the name of Theseus,—no monsters
quelled
Have given me the right to share his weak-
ness.
And if I must be humbled for my pride,
Aricia should have been the last to tame me!
Was I not mad that I should have forgotten
Those barriers which must keep us far
apart
Eternally? For by my father's order
Her brothers' blood must never flow again
In a child of hers. He dreads a single shoot
From any stock so guilty, and would bury
Their name with her; so even to the tomb
No torch of Hymen may be lit for her.
Shall I espouse her rights against my father,
Provoke his wrath, launch on a mad
career?—
THERAMENES.   But if your time has come,
dear prince, the gods
Will care but little for your guiding reason.
Theseus would shut your eyes;—he but
unseals them.
His hatred kindles you to burn, rebellious,
And only lends his enemy new charms.
Then, too, why should you fear a guiltless
passion?
Do you not dare this once to try its sweet-
ness,
Rather than follow such a hair-drawn
scruple?—
Afraid to stray where Hercules has wan-
dered?—[7]

[4] The female warrior Antiope.
[5] Hercules, with whom Theseus vied in the performance of heroic feats.
[6] A bull-like monster slain by Theseus in one
of his greatest exploits. It was the misbegotten
offspring of Pasiphaë, who was also the mother
of Phædra. The preceding names refer to eccen-

tric brigands also put out of the way by Theseus.
Those following allude to the various ladies whom
Theseus loved and left. The hero was as non-
chalant in love as in deeds of valor.
[7] Like Theseus, Hercules was addicted to seduc-
tion.

What heart so stout that Venus has not
   won it?
And you, so long her foe, where would
   you be
Had your own mother, always scorning
   love,
Never been moved with tenderness for
   Theseus?
What good to act a pride you do not feel?
If you are changed, confess it! For some
   time
You have been seldom seen urging the car
With wild delight, rapid, along the shore,
Or, skillful in the art that Neptune taught,
Making th' unbroken steed obey the bit.
The forest has flung back our shouts less
   often.
A secret burden, cast upon your spirits,
Has dimmed your eye.—Can I then doubt
   your love?
It is in vain that you conceal your hurt.
Tell me, has not Aricia touched your
   heart?
HIPPOLYTUS.   Theramenes, I go to find my
   father.
THERAMENES.   Will you not see the queen
   before you leave?
HIPPOLYTUS.   So I intend. And you may
   tell her so.
Yes, I will see her, since it is my duty.
But what new ill vexes her dear Œnone?

[*Enter* ŒNONE.]

ŒNONE.   Alas, my lord, what grief was
   e'er like mine?
The queen has almost touched the gates of
   death.
It is in vain I watch her night and day,
In my very arms this secret malady
Is killing her—her mind is all disordered.
She rises from her bed, weary yet restless,
Pants for the outer air, yet she commands
   me
That none should see her in her misery.
She comes!
HIPPOLYTUS.   That is enough. I shall not
   vex her
Nor make her see the face of one she
   hates.

[*Exeunt* HIPPOLYTUS *and* THERAMENES.]

[*Enter* PHÆDRA.]

PHÆDRA.   Yes, this is far enough. Stay
   here, Œnone.
My strength is failing. I must rest a little.
I am dazzled with the light; it has been long
Since I have seen it. Ah, and my trembling
   knees
Are failing me—
ŒNONE.   Dear Heaven, I would our tears
Might bring relief.
PHÆDRA.   And how these clumsy trinkets,
These veils oppress me! Whose officious
   hand
Tied up these knots, and gathered all these
   coils
Over my brow? All things conspire against
   me
And would distress me more!
ŒNONE.   That which you wish
This moment, frets you next! Did you not
   ask
A minute past, that we should deck you
   out,
Saying you felt your energy return,
Saying you sickened of your idleness,
And wished to go and see the light of day?
You sought the sun, and now you see it
   here,—
And now you would be hidden from its
   shining!
PHÆDRA.   O splendid author of a hapless
   race,—
You whom my mother boasted as her
   father,—
Well may you blush to see me in such
   plight.
For the last time I look on thee, O Sun!
ŒNONE.   So! And are you still in love with
   death?
Will you not ever make your peace with
   life,
And leave these cruel accents of despair?
PHÆDRA.   I wish that I were seated in the
   forest.
When may I follow with delighted eye,
Through glorious dust, flying in full
   career,—
A chariot?
ŒNONE.   Madam?

PHÆDRA.   Have I lost my wits?
What did I say? Where am I? Ah, and
   where
Do my vain wishes wander? For the gods
Have made me mad! And now I blush,
   Œnone,—
I hide my face, for you have seen too
   clearly
The grief and shame, that, quite in spite of
   me,
Will overflow my eyes.
ŒNONE.   If you must blush,
Blush at the silence that inflames your grief.
Deaf to my voice, you will not have my
   care.
Then will you have no pity on yourself,
But let your life be ended in mid-course?
What evil spell has drained its fountains
   dry?
Night-shadows thrice have darkened all the
   heavens
Since sleep came to your eyes, and now
   three times
The dawn has chased the darkness back
   again
Since your pale lips knew food. You faint,
   are languid,—
What awful purpose have you in your
   heart?
How do you dare attempt to lose your life
And so offend the gods who gave it you,—
And so prove false to Theseus and your
   marriage?—
Yes, and betray your most unhappy chil-
   dren,
Bending their necks yourself, beneath the
   yoke?
That day, be sure, which robs them of their
   mother
Will give his high hopes back to the
   stranger's son,—
To that proud enemy of you and yours,
Born of an Amazon,—Hippolytus!—
PHÆDRA.   You gods!
ŒNONE.   Ah, this is a reproach to move
   you!
PHÆDRA.   Unhappy one, what name have
   your lips spoken?
ŒNONE.   Your anger is most just, and it is
   well

That hated name can rouse such rage!
   Then live,
And hear again the claims of love and
   duty!
Live, then,—and stop this son of Scythia
From crushing down your children by his
   sway,
Ruling the noblest offspring of the gods,—
The purest blood of Greece! Never delay!
Death threatens every moment! Now re-
   store
Your shattered strength, while the dim
   torch of life
Burns, and can yet be fanned into a flame.
PHÆDRA.   I have endured its guilt and
   shame too long.
ŒNONE.   Why? What remorse is gnawing
   at your heart?
What crime can have disturbed you so?
   Your hands
Have not been stained with the blood of
   innocence.
PHÆDRA.   No, I thank Heaven my hands
   are free from stain,—
I would my soul were innocent as they!
ŒNONE.   Why then, what awful plan have
   you been scheming,
At which your conscience still should be
   afraid?
PHÆDRA.   Have I not said enough? Spare
   me the rest!
I die to save myself a full confession.
ŒNONE.   Die, then,—and keep a silence
   more than human!—
But seek some other hand to close your
   eyes,
For I will go before you to the Shades.
There are a thousand highways always
   open,
And since you have so little faith in me,
I'll go the shortest! When has my love
   failed you?
Remember, in my arms you lay, new-born.
For you I left my country and my chil-
   dren,—
And is this payment for my service to you?
PHÆDRA.   What will you gain from words
   that are so bitter?
Were I to speak, horror would freeze your
   blood.

ŒNONE. What can you say more terrible to me
Than to behold you die before my eyes?
PHÆDRA. If you should know my sin, I still should die,
But with guilt added—
ŒNONE.   Oh, my dearest lady,
By all the tears that I have wept for you,
By these poor knees I clasp, now ease my mind
From doubt and torture!
PHÆDRA.   As you wish. Then rise.
ŒNONE. I hear you. Speak.
PHÆDRA.   Ah, how shall I begin?
ŒNONE. Leave off your fears,—you hurt me with distrust.
PHÆDRA. O malice of great Venus! Into what madness,
What wild distractions, did she cast my mother! [8]
ŒNONE. Let them be blotted from all memory,
Buried in silence, for all times to come.
PHÆDRA. My sister, Ariadne, what was the love
Which brought you death, forsaken on lone shores?
ŒNONE. Madam, what deep pain is it prompts reproaches
Thus against all your kin—?
PHÆDRA.   It is her will—
It is the will of Venus, and I perish,
Last and least happy of a family
Where all were wretched!
ŒNONE.   Do you love?
PHÆDRA.   I feel
All of its fever—
ŒNONE.   Ah! For whom?
PHÆDRA.   Now hear
The final horror. Yes, I love. My lips
Tremble to name him.
ŒNONE.   Whom?
PHÆDRA.   And do you know him?—
He whom I tortured long,—the Amazon's son!
ŒNONE. Hippolytus! Great gods!
PHÆDRA.   Yes, you have named him.

[8] Venus inspired in Pasiphaë a passion for a bull.

ŒNONE. Blood freezes in my veins! O cursed race!
Ill-omened journey! Land of misery,
Why did we ever reach these dangerous shores?
PHÆDRA. My wound is not a new one. Scarcely had I
Been bound to Theseus by our marriage tie,
With peace and happiness seeming so well secured,
Until at Athens I saw my enemy.
I looked, I first turned pale, then blushed to see him,
And all my soul was in the greatest turmoil;
A mist made dim my sight, and my voice faltered,
And now my blood ran cold, then burned like fire.
In all my fevered body I could feel
Venus, whose fury had pursued so many
Of my sad race. I sought to shun her torments
With fervent vows. I built a shrine for her,
And there, 'mid many victims did I seek
The reason I had lost; but all for nothing.
I found no remedy for pain of love!
I offered incense vainly on her altars,
I called upon her name, and while I called her,
I loved Hippolytus, always before me!
And when I made her altars smoke with victims,
'Twas for a god whose name I dared not utter,—
And still I fled his presence, only to find him—
(The worst of horrors)—in his father's features!
At last I raised revolt against myself
And stirred my courage up to persecute
The enemy I loved. To banish him
I wore a harsh and jealous step-dame's manner,
And ceaselessly I clamored for his exile,
Till I had torn him from his father's arms!
I breathed once more, Œnone. In his absence
The days passed by less troubled than before—
Innocent days! I hid my bitter grief,

Submitted to my husband, cherished the
  fruits
Of our most fatal marriage,—and in vain!
Again I saw the one whom I had banished,
Brought here by my own husband, and
  again
The old wound bled. And now it is not love
Hid in my heart, but Venus in her might
Seizing her prey. Justly I fear my sin!
I hate my life, and hold my love in horror.
I die:—I would have kept my name un-
  sullied,
Burying guilty passion in the grave;
But I have not been able to refuse you;
You weep and pray, and so I tell you all,
And I shall be content, if as I perish,
You do not vex me with unjust reproaches,
Nor vainly try to snatch away from death
The last faint sparks of life, yet lingering!

[*Enter* PANOPE.]

PANOPE. I wish that I might hide sad tid-
  ings from you,
But 'tis my duty, madam, to reveal them.
The hand of death has seized your peerless
  husband.
You are the last to hear it.

ŒNONE.   What is this?

PANOPE. The queen begs Heaven for the
  safe return
Of Theseus, but she trusts, indeed, in
  vain—
She is deceived. Hippolytus, his son,
Has learned from vessels newly come to
  port
That Theseus is dead.

PHÆDRA.   Oh gods!

PANOPE.   At Athens
Opinions are divided; some would have it
Your child should rule, and some, despite
  the law,
Are bold, and dare support the stranger's
  son,
While one presuming faction, it is said,
Would crown Aricia, and the house of
  Pallas.
I thought it well to warn you of this danger.
Hippolytus is ready, now, to start,
And if he chance to show himself in
  Athens,

The crowd, I fear, will follow in his lead.

ŒNONE. It is enough. The queen has
  heard your message,
And she will not neglect your timely warning.

[*Exit* PANOPE.]

Dear lady, I had almost ceased from urging
That you should wish to live. I thought to
  follow
My mistress to that tomb from which my
  pleading
Had failed to turn her,—but this new mis-
  fortune
Changes the aspect of affairs, and prompts
  us
To take fresh measures. Madam, Theseus
  is gone,
And you must fill his place. He leaves a
  son,—
Slave if you die, but if you live, a king!
Upon whom can he lean, but you, his
  mother?
There is no hand but yours to dry his
  tears.
Live then, for him, or else his guiltless
  weeping
Will move the gods to wrath against his
  mother.
Live, for no blame is in your passion now.
The king is dead, you bear the bonds no
  longer
Which made your love a thing of crime and
  horror.
You need no longer dread Hippolytus,
For you may see him, now, without re-
  proach.
Perhaps, if he is certain of your hatred,
He means to lead the rebels. Undeceive
  him!
Soften his callous heart, and bend his
  pride!
King of this fertile land, his portion lies
Here in his Trœzen, yet he knows the
  laws,—
They give your son these walls Minerva
  built,
Aye, and protects,—but if a common foe
Threatens you both, you had best be
  united.
For you must thwart Aricia!

PHÆDRA.   I consent.
Yes, I will live, if life can yet be mine,—
If my affection for a son has power

To rouse my sinking heart, at such a dangerous hour!

[Exeunt.]

ACT II

[Enter ARICIA and ISMENE.]

ARICIA.   Hippolytus has asked to see me
here?
Hippolytus has asked to bid farewell?
'Tis true, Ismene? You are not deceived?
ISMENE.   This is the first result of Theseus'
death,
And you may look to see from every side
Hearts that he kept away, now turning to
you.
Aricia soon shall find all Greece low-bending
To do her homage.
ARICIA.   Then it is not only
An idle tale? Am I a slave no longer?
Have I no enemies?
ISMENE.   The gods, Aricia,
Trouble your peace no more, for Theseus'
soul
Is with your brothers, now.
ARICIA.   Does rumor tell
How Theseus died?
ISMENE.   Tales most incredible
Are spread. Some say, that, seizing a new
bride,
The faithless man was swallowed by the
waves.
Others have said, and this report prevails,
That he, together with Pirithous,[1]
Went to the world below, seeking the shores
Of Cocytus,[2] showing his living self
To the pale ghosts, but could not leave the
gloom,
For they who enter there abide forever.
ARICIA.   Can I believe a mortal may descend
Into that gulf before his destined hour?
What lure could ever overcome its terrors?
ISMENE.   Nay, he is dead; 'tis only you
who doubt it.
The men of Athens all bewail his loss.

Trœzen already hails Hippolytus,
And Phædra, fearing for her children's
rights,
Asks counsel of such friends as share her
troubles,
Here in this palace!
ARICIA.   Will Hippolytus
Prove kinder than his father, make my
chains light,
And pity my misfortunes?
ISMENE.   Yes, I think so.
ARICIA.   Indeed, I think you do not know
him well,
Or you would not believe a heart so hard
Could ever pity, or could look on me
As one not sharing in the scorn he feels
For all our sex. Does he not still avoid
Whatever place we go?
ISMENE.   I know the stories
Of proud Hippolytus, but I have seen him
When he was near to you, and watched to
see
How one supposed so cold would bear himself.
I found his manners not at all like those
Which I had looked to see, for in his face
Was great confusion, at your slightest
glance.
He could not turn his languid eyes away,
But still looked back again to gaze at you.
Love is a word that may offend his pride,
But though the tongue deny it, looks betray!
ARICIA.   How eagerly my heart hears what
you say,
Though it may be delusion, dear Ismene!
Did it seem possible to you, who know me,
That I, poor toy of unrelenting fate,
Fed upon bitter tears by night and day,
Could ever taste the maddening draught of
love?
I am the last frail offspring of my race—

---

[1] In one of his exploits Theseus accompanied
his friend Pirithous to the underworld in an attempt to kidnap its queen, Persephone.

[2] Like Acheron, a river reputed to flow though
the realms of the dead.

My royal race, the Children of the Earth,[3]
And of them, I alone survive war's fury.
Yes, I have lost six brothers, in their
youth,—
Mown by the sword, cut off in their first
flower!
They were the hope of an illustrious house.
Earth drank their blood with sorrow; it was
kin
To his whom she brought forth. And well
you know,
Since then, no heart in Greece could sigh
for me,
Lest, by a sister's flame, her brother's ashes
Might chance to blaze again. And, too, you
know
How I disdained the cautions of my captor,
His care, and his suspicion, and you know
How often I have thanked the king's in-
justice,
Since I had never loved the thought of love.
He happily confirmed my inclinations,—
But then, I never yet had seen his son!
It is not merely that my eye is caught,
And that I love him for his grace and
beauty,—
Charms which he does not know, or seems
to scorn,—
I love him for a kind of wealth that's rarer.
He has his father's virtues, not his faults.
I love, and I must grant it, that high pride
Which never stooped beneath the yoke of
love.
Phædra gains little glory from a lover
Free of his sighs; I am too proud, I think,
To share devotion with a thousand others,
Or enter in a door that's never shut.
But to make one who never stooped before
Bend his proud neck,—to pierce a heart of
stone,
And bind one captive, whom his chains
astonish,
Who struggles vainly in his pleasant
bonds,—
That takes my fancy, and I long for it.
The god of strength was easier disarmed
Than this Hippolytus, for Hercules
Yielded so often to the eyes of beauty

[3] As Phædra traced her ancestry to the Sun,
Aricia was descended from Earth.

That he made triumph cheap. But, dear
Ismene,
I take too little heed of a resistance
Which I may never quell. If I am humbled,
And if I find defeat, then you will hear me
Speak ill of that same pride I so admire!
What! can he love? And have I been so
happy
That I have bent—?

ISMENE.   He comes,—and you shall
hear him.

[*Enter* HIPPOLYTUS.]

HIPPOLYTUS.   Lady, before you go, it is
my duty
To tell you of the changes of your fortune.
What I have feared is true; my sire is dead.
Yes, his long stay was what I had supposed
it.
For only death, which came to end his
labors,
Could keep him hidden from the world so
long.
The gods at last have doomed Alcides'
friend—
His friend, and his successor. Since your
hatred
I think will grant his virtues, it can hear
Some praise for him, without resenting it,
Knowing that it is due. I have one hope
To soothe me in my sorrow. I can free you.
Now I revoke the laws, whose strictness
moved me
To pity for you; you are your own mistress
Of heart and hand. Here in my heritage,
In Trœzen, here where Pittheus once
reigned,
And where I now am king, by my own
right,
I leave you free, free as myself,—and more.

ARICIA.   Your kindness is too great; it overcomes me.
A goodness which will pay disgrace with
honor
Can give a greater force than you would
think
To the harsh laws from which you would
release me.

HIPPOLYTUS.   Athens, not knowing how to
fill the throne

Left empty, speaks of you, and then of me,
And then of Phædra's son.

ARICIA.   Of me, my lord?

HIPPOLYTUS.   I know that by the law it is
not mine,
For Greece reproaches me my foreign
mother.
But if my brother were my only rival,
My rights are clearly truer ones than his,
So that I should not care for twists of the
law.
There is a juster claim to check my bold-
ness.
I yield my place to you, or rather, grant
That you should have it,—you should hold
the sceptre,
Bequeathed to you from Earth's great son,
Erectheus.
It came, then, to Ægeus, and the city
Which was protected and increased by him
Was glad to welcome such a king as The-
seus,
Leaving your luckless brothers out of mind.
Now Athens calls you back within her
walls.
Long strife has cost her groans enough
already,
Her fields are glutted with your kinsmen's
blood,
Fattening those same furrows whence it
sprang.
I will rule here in Trœzen; Phædra's son
Has his rich kingdom waiting him in Crete.
Athens is yours, and I will do my best
To bring to you the votes which are divided
Between us two.

ARICIA.   I fear a dream deceives me.
For I am stunned, my lord, at what I hear.
Am I, indeed, awake? Can I believe
Such generosity as this? What god
Has put it in your heart? Well you deserve
That fame you have, yet it falls short of
you.
For me, you will be traitor to yourself!
Was it not grace enough never to hate me,
To have been free so long from enmity,
Which some have harbored—

HIPPOLYTUS.   Hate you? I to hate you?
However darkly you have seen my pride,
Did you suppose a monster gave me birth?

What savagery, what hatred, full of venom
Would not become less evil, seeing you?
Could I resist this charm which caught my
soul—

ARICIA.   Why, what is this, sir?

HIPPOLYTUS.   I have said too much
Not to say more. No prudence can resist
The violence of passion. Now, at last,
Silence is broken. I must tell you now
The secret that my heart can hold no
longer.
You see before you an unhappy victim
Of hasty pride,—a prince who begs com-
passion.
For I was long the enemy of love.
I mocked his fetters, I despised his cap-
tives,
And while I pitied these poor, shipwrecked
mortals,
I watched the storms, and seemed quite
safe on land.
And now I find that I have such a fate,
And must be tossed upon a sea of troubles!
My boldness is defeated in a moment,
And all my boasted pride is humbleness.
For nearly six months past, ashamed, de-
spairing,
Carrying with me always that sharp arrow
Which tears my heart, I struggle quite in
vain
To free me, both from you and from my-
self.
I leave your presence;—leaving, I find you
near,
And in the forest's darkness see your
form.
Black night, no less than daylight brings the
vision
Of charms that I avoid. All things conspire
To make Hippolytus your slave. The fruit
Of all my sighs is only that I cannot
Find my own self again. My bow, my spear,
Please me no longer. I have quite forgotten
My chariot, and the teaching of the Sea
God.
The woods can only echo back my groans,
Instead of flinging back those joyous shouts
With which I urged my horses. Hearing
this,
A tale of passion so uncouth, you blush

At your own handiwork. These are wild
words
With which I offer you my heart, a captive
Held, strangely, by a silken jess. And yet
The off'ring should be dearer to your eyes,
Since such words come as strangers to my
lips.
Nor do not scorn my vows, so poorly
spoken
Since, but for you, they never had been
formed.

[Enter THERAMENES.]

THERAMENES.   My lord, I came to tell you
of the queen.
She comes to seek you.
HIPPOLYTUS.   Me?
THERAMENES.   And what she wishes
I do not know. I speak at her request,
For she would talk with you before you
go.
HIPPOLYTUS.   What shall I say to her? Can
she expect—?
ARICIA.   You cannot, noble prince, refuse
to hear her,
Though you are sure she is your enemy.
There is a shade of pity due her tears.
HIPPOLYTUS.   Shall we part so? And will
you let me leave you
Not knowing if I have offended you,—
The goddess I adore,—with all this bold-
ness?
Or if this heart, which I now leave with
you—
ARICIA.   Go now, my prince, and do what-
ever deeds
Your generosity would have you do.
Make Athens own my sceptre. All these
gifts
I will accept. But the high throne of Em-
pire
Is not the thing most precious to my eyes!
                    [Exeunt ARICIA and ISMENE.]
HIPPOLYTUS.   Friend, are we ready?—But
the queen is coming.
See that the ship is trimmed and fit to sail.
Hurry, gather the crew, and hoist the signal,
And then return, the sooner to release me
From a most irksome meeting.
                          [Exit THERAMENES.]

[Enter PHÆDRA and ŒNONE.]

PHÆDRA. [To ŒNONE.] Look, I see him!
My blood forgets to flow,—tongue will not
speak
What I have come to say!
ŒNONE.   Think of your son.
And think that all his hopes depend on
you.
PHÆDRA.   They tell me that you leave us,
hastily.
I come to add my own tears to your sorrow,
And I would plead my fears for my young
son.
He has no father, now; 'twill not be long
Until the day that he will see my death,
And even now, his youth is much imperiled
By a thousand foes. You only can defend
him.
And in my inmost heart, remorse is stir-
ring,—
Yes, and fear, too, lest I have shut your
ears
Against his cries; I fear that your just anger
May, before long, visit on him that hatred
His mother earned.
HIPPOLYTUS.   Madam, you need not fear.
Such malice is not mine.
PHÆDRA.   I should not blame you
If you should hate me; I have injured you.
So much you know;—you could not read
my heart.
Yes, I have tried to be your enemy,
For the same land could never hold us both.
In private and abroad I have declared it;—
I was your enemy! I found no peace
Till seas had parted us; and I forbade
Even your name to be pronounced to me.
And yet, if punishment be meted out
Justly, by the offense;—if only hatred
Deserves a hate, then never was there
woman
Deserved more pity, and less enmity.
HIPPOLYTUS.   A mother who is jealous for
her children
Will seldom love the children of a mother
Who came before her. Torments of suspi-
cion
Will often follow on a second marriage.
Another would have felt that jealousy

No less than you; perhaps more violently.
PHÆDRA. Ah, prince, but Heaven made
me quite exempt
From what is usual, and I can call
That Heaven as my witness! 'Tis not this—
No, quite another ill devours my heart!
HIPPOLYTUS. This is no time for self-re-
proaching, madam.
Perhaps your husband still beholds the
light,
Perhaps he may be granted safe return
In answer to our prayers; his guarding god
Is Neptune, whom he never called in vain.
PHÆDRA. He who has seen the mansions
of the dead
Returns not thence. Since Theseus has gone
Once to those gloomy shores, we need not
hope,
For Heaven will not send him back again.
Prince, there is no release from Acheron;—
It is a greedy maw,—and yet I think
He lives and breathes in you,—and still I
see him
Before me here; I seem to speak to him—
My heart—! Oh, I am mad! Do what I
will,
I cannot hide my passion.
HIPPOLYTUS. Yes, I see
What strange things love will do, for The-
seus, dead,
Seems present to your eyes, and in your
soul
A constant flame is burning.
PHÆDRA. Ah, for Thesus
I languish and I long, but not, indeed,
As the Shades have seen him, as the fickle
lover
Of a thousand forms, the one who fain
would ravish
The bride of Pluto;—but one faithful,
proud,
Even to slight disdain,—the charm of youth
That draws all hearts, even as the gods are
painted,—
Or as yourself. He had your eyes, your
manner,—
He spoke like you, and he could blush like
you,

And when he came across the waves to
Crete,
My childhood home, worthy to win the
love
Of Minos' daughters,—what were you do-
ing then?
Why did my father gather all these men,
The flower of Greece, and leave Hippoly-
tus?
Oh, why were you too young to have em-
barked
On board the ship that brought your father
there?
The monster [4] would have perished at your
hands,
Despite the windings of his vast retreat.
My sister would have armed you with the
clue
To guide your steps, doubtful within the
maze.—
But no—for Phædra would have come be-
fore her,
And love would first have given me the
thought,
And I it would have been, whose timely aid
Had taught you all the labyrinthine ways!
The care that such a dear life would have
cost me!
No thread [5] could satisfy my lover's fears.
I would have wished to lead the way my-
self,
And share the peril you were sure to face.
Yes, Phædra would have walked the maze
with you,—
With you come out in safety, or have per-
ished!
HIPPOLYTUS. Gods! What is this I hear?
Have you forgotten
That Theseus is my father and your hus-
band?
PHÆDRA. Why should you fancy I have
lost remembrance
And that I am regardless of my honor?
HIPPOLYTUS. Forgive me, madam! With
a blush I own
That I mistook your words, quite innocent.
For very shame I cannot see you longer—
Now I will go—

---

[4] The Minotaur, destroyed by Theseus.
[5] Which Ariadne, Phædra's sister, gave to Theseus to guide his return through the labyrinth of the Minotaur.

PHÆDRA. Ah, prince, you understood me,—
Too well, indeed! For I had said enough.
You could not well mistake. But do not think
That in those moments when I love you most
I do not feel my guilt. No easy yielding
Has helped the poison that infects my mind.
The sorry object of divine revenge,
I am not half so hateful to your sight
As to myself. The gods will bear me witness,—
They who have lit this fire within my veins,—
The gods who take their barbarous delight
In leading some poor mortal heart astray!
Nay, do you not remember, in the past,
How I was not content to fly?—I drove you
Out of the land, so that I might appear
Most odious—and to resist you better
I tried to make you hate me—and in vain!
You hated more, and I loved not the less,
While your misfortunes lent you newer charms.
I have been drowned in tears and scorched by fire!
Your own eyes might convince you of the truth
If you could look at me, but for a moment!
What do I say? You think this vile confession
That I have made, is what I meant to say?
I did not dare betray my son. For him
I feared,—and came to beg you not to hate him.
This was the purpose of a heart too full
Of love for you to speak of aught besides.
Take your revenge, and punish me my passion!
Prove yourself worthy of your valiant father,
And rid the world of an offensive monster!
Does Theseus' widow dare to love his son?
Monster indeed! Nay, let her not escape you!
Here is my heart! Here is the place to strike!
It is most eager to absolve itself!

It leaps impatiently to meet your blow!—
Strike deep! Or if, indeed, you find it shameful
To drench your hand in such polluted blood,—
If that be punishment too mild for you,—
Too easy for your hate,—if not your arm,
Then lend your sword to me.—Come! Give it now!—
ŒNONE. What would you do, my lady?
Oh, just gods!
But someone comes;—go quickly. Run from shame.
You cannot fly, if they should find you thus.

[*Exeunt* PHÆDRA *and* ŒNONE.]

[*Enter* THERAMENES.]

THERAMENES. Is that the form of Phædra that I see
Go hurrying? What are these signs of sorrow?
Where is your sword? Why are you pale and shaken?
HIPPOLYTUS. Friend, let us fly. Indeed, I am confused
With greatest horror and astonishment.
Phædra—but no; gods, let this dreadful secret
Remain forever buried and unknown.
THERAMENES. The ship is ready if you wish to sail,
But Athens has already cast her vote.
Their leaders have consulted all the tribes.
Your brother is elected;—Phædra wins!
HIPPOLYTUS. Phædra?
THERAMENES. A herald bringing a commission
Has come from Athens, placing the reins of power
In Phædra's hands. Her son is king.—
HIPPOLYTUS. O gods,—
O ye who know her, is it thus, indeed,
That ye reward her virtue?
THERAMENES. Meanwhile rumor
Is whispering that Theseus is not dead,—
That there are those who saw him in Epirus,—
But I have searched, and I know all too well—

HIPPOLYTUS. No matter. Let no chances
be neglected.
This rumor must be hunted to its source,
And if it be not worthy of belief

Let us then sail, and at whatever cost,
We'll trust the sceptre to deserving hands.

[*Exeunt.*]

ACT III

[*Enter* PHÆDRA *and* ŒNONE.]

PHÆDRA. Ah, let them take away the
worthless honors
They bring to me;—why urge that I should
see them?
What flattery can soothe my wounded
heart?
Far rather hide me. I have said too much.
My madness bursting like a stream in flood,
I spoke what never should have reached his
ears.
Oh gods! The way he heard me! How re-
luctant
To take my meaning,—dull and cold as
marble,
And only eager for a quick retreat!
And how his blushes made my shame the
deeper!
Why did you turn me from the death I
sought?
Ah, when his sword was pointed at my
breast,
Did he grow pale?—or try to snatch it from
me?
That I had touched it was enough for him
To make it seem forever horrible,
And to defile whatever hand should hold it.
ŒNONE. When you will brood upon your
bitter grief,
You only fan a fire that must be quenched.
Would it not more become the blood of
Minos
To find you peace in cares that are more
noble?—
And in defiance of this wretch, who flies
From what he hates, reign on the throne
you're offered?
PHÆDRA. I reign?—And shall I hold the
rod of empire,
When reason can no longer reign in me?
When I have lost control of mine own
senses?

When I do gasp beneath a shameful yoke?
When I am dying?—
ŒNONE.   Fly!
PHÆDRA.   I cannot leave him.
ŒNONE. You dare not fly from one you
dared to banish?
PHÆDRA. That time is past. He knows how
I am frenzied,
For I have overstepped my modesty,
And blazoned out my shame before his
eyes.
Against my will, hope crept into my heart.
Did you not call my failing powers to
me?
Was it not you, yourself, called back my
soul
Which fluttered on my lips, and with your
counsel
Lent me new life? Who told me I might
love him?
ŒNONE. Blame me or blame me not for
your misfortunes,—
What could I not have done if it would
save you?
But if your anger ever was aroused
By insult, can you pardon him his scorn?
How cruel were his eyes, severe and fixed,
Surveying you, half prostrate at his feet!
How hateful, then, his savage pride ap-
peared!
Why did not Phædra see as I saw then?
PHÆDRA. This pride that you detest may
yield to time.
The rudeness of the forest clings about him,
For he was bred there by the strictest laws.
Love is a word he never knew before.
Perhaps it was surprise that stunned him
so;—
There was much vehemence in all I said.
ŒNONE. Remember that his mother was
barbaric—
PHÆDRA. She was a Scythian, but she
learned to love.

ŒNONE. He has a bitter hate for all our sex.

PHÆDRA. Well, then no rival ever rules his heart.

Your counsel comes a little late, Œnone.

Now you must serve my madness, not my reason.

Love cannot find a way into his heart,

So let us take him where he has more feeling.

The lure of power seemed somewhat to touch him.

He could not hide that he was drawn to Athens,—

His vessels' prows were pointed there already,

With sails all set to run before the breeze.

Go, and on my behalf, touch his ambition,—

Dazzle his eyes with prospects of the crown.

The sacred diadem shall grace his brow,—

My highest honor is to set it there,

And he shall have the power I cannot keep.

He'll teach my son how men are ruled.— It may be

That he will deign to be a father to him.

He shall control both son and mother;— try him,—

Try every means to move him, for your words

Should meet more favor than my own could find.

Urge him with groans and tears,—say Phædra's dying,

Nor blush to speak in pleading terms with him.

My last hope is in you,—do what you will,

I'll sanction it,—the issue is my fate!

[*Exit* ŒNONE.]

PHÆDRA. [*Alone.*] Venus implacable, thou seest me shamed,

And I am sore confounded. Have I not

Been humbled yet enough? Can cruelty

Stretch farther still? Thine arrows have struck home!

It is thy victory! Wouldst gain new triumphs?—

Then seek an enemy more obdurate,—

Hippolytus neglects thee, braves thine anger.

He never bows his knee before thine altars.

Thy name offends his proud, disdainful hearing.

Our interests are alike,—avenge thyself.

Force him to love—

[*Re-enter* ŒNONE.]

But what is this, Œnone?

Already back? Then it must be he hates me,

And will not hear you speak—

ŒNONE. Yes, you must stifle

A love that's vain, and best call back your virtue.

The king we thought was dead will soon appear

Here to your eyes. Yes, Theseus will be here,

For he has come again. The eager people

Are hastening to see him. I had gone

As you commanded, seeking for the prince,

When all the air was torn,—a thousand shouts—

PHÆDRA. My husband living! 'Tis enough, Œnone.

I owned a passion that dishonors him.

He is alive. I wish to know no more.

ŒNONE. What is it?

PHÆDRA. What I prophesied to you,—

What you refused to hear, while with your weeping

You overcame repentance. Had I died

I had deserved some pity, earlier.

I took your counsel, and I die dishonored.

ŒNONE. You die?

PHÆDRA. Just Heavens! What I have done today!

My husband comes, and with him comes his son,

And I shall see the witness of my passion,

The object of my most adulterous flame

Watch with what face I make his father welcome,

Knowing my heart is big with sighs he scorned,

And my eyes wet with tears that could not move him.

Will his respect for Theseus make him hide it?—

Conceal my madness?—not disgrace his
father?
And do you think he can repress the hor-
ror
Which he must have for me? A fruitless
silence!
I know my treason, and I lack the boldness
Of those abandoned women who can feel
Tranquillity in crime,—can show a fore-
head
All unashamed. I know my madness well,
Recall it all. I think that these high roofs
And all these walls can speak. They will
accuse me.
They only wait until my husband comes,
And then they will reveal my perfidy.
'Tis death alone can take away this horror.
Is it so great an ill to cease to live?
Death holds no fear for those in misery.
I tremble only for the name I leave,—
My son's sad heritage. The blood of Jove
Might justly swell the pride of those who
boast it,
But what a heavy weight a mother's guilt
Leaves for her children! Yes, I dread that
scorn
For my disgrace, which will be cast on
them
With too much truth. I tremble when I
think
How they will never dare to raise their
heads,
Crushed with that curse.—
ŒNONE.   Nay, do not doubt my pity.
There never was a juster fear than yours.
Then why do you expose them to this
shame?
And why must you accuse yourself, de-
stroying
The one hope left. It will be said of
Phædra
That she well knows of her own perfidy,
That she has fled from out her husband's
sight,—
And proud Hippolytus may well rejoice
That, dying, you should lend his tale belief.
What answer can I make him? It will be
For him a story easy to deny,
And I shall hear him, while triumphantly
He tells your shame to every open ear.

Why, I had sooner Heaven's fire consumed
me!
Deceive me not! And do you love him
still?
What think you now of this contemptuous
prince?
PHÆDRA.   As of a monster fearful to mine
eyes!
ŒNONE.   Why do you give him easy vic-
tory?
You are afraid! Dare to accuse him first!
Say he is guilty of the charge he brings
This day against you. Who shall say it's
false?
All things conspire against him. In your
hands
His sword, which he most happily forgot,—
Your present trouble, and your past dis-
tress,—
Your warnings to his father,—and his exile
Which you accomplished with your earnest
prayers—
PHÆDRA.   So! You would have me slander
innocence!
ŒNONE.   My zeal asks nothing from you
but your silence.
I also tremble. I am loath to do it.
I'd face a thousand deaths more willingly.
But since, without this bitter deed, I lose
you,
And since, for me, your life outweighs all
else,
Why, I will speak. Theseus, however angry,
Will do no worse than banish him again.
A father, punishing, remains a father.
His anger will be soothed with easy pen-
ance.
But even if some guiltless blood be spilt,
Is not your honor of a greater worth,—
A treasure far too precious to be risked?
You must submit, no matter what is need-
ful,
For when your reputation is at stake,
Then you must sacrifice your very con-
science.
But someone comes. 'Tis Theseus—
PHÆDRA.   Look, I see
Hippolytus most stern, and in his eyes
There is my ruin written. I am helpless.
My fate is yours. Do with it as you will.

[*Enter* THESEUS, HIPPOLYTUS *and* THERAMENES.]

THESEUS.   Fortune will fight no longer with my wishes,
But to your arms it brings me back—
PHÆDRA.   Wait, Theseus.
Nay, do not hurry to profane caresses
One time so sweet, which I am now not worthy
Even to taste of, for you have been wronged.
Fortune has proved most spiteful. In your absence
It has not spared your wife. I am not fit
To meet you tenderly, and from this time
I only care how I shall bear my shame.
                    [*Exeunt* PHÆDRA *and* ŒNONE.]
THESEUS.   Strange welcome for your father, is it not?
What does it mean, my son?
HIPPOLYTUS.   Why, only Phædra
Can solve that mystery. If I can move you
By any wish, then let me never see her.
Hippolytus begs leave to disappear,—
To leave the home that holds your wife, forever.
THESEUS.   You, my son! Leave me?
HIPPOLYTUS.   'Twas not I who sought her.
You were the one to lead her to these shores!
My lord, at your departure you thought fit
To leave Aricia and the queen in Trœzen,
And I, myself, was charged with their protection.
But now, what cares will need to keep me here?
My idle youth has shown what skill it has
Over such petty foes as roam the woods.
May I not leave this life of little glory,—
Of ease—and dip my spear in nobler blood?
Before you reached my age, more than one tyrant,
More than one monster had already felt
The force of your good arm. You had succeeded
In whipping insolence; you had removed
All of the dangers lurking on our coasts.
The traveler no longer feared for outrage,

And Hercules, himself, who knew your deeds,
Relied on you, and rested from his labors.
But I—the son of such a noble father,—
I am unknown, and I am far behind
Even my mother's footsteps. Let my courage
Have scope to act. If there is yet some monster
Escaped from you, then let me seek for glory,
Bringing the spoils to you; or let it be
That memory of death well met with courage
Shall keep my name a living one,—shall prove
To all the world I am my father's son.
THESEUS.   Why, what is this? What terror can have seized you?
What makes my kindred fly before my face?
If I return to find myself so feared,
To find so little welcome in my home,
Then why did Heaven free me from my prison?
My only friend, misled by his own passion,
Set out to rob the tyrant of Epirus,—
To rob him of his wife! Regretfully
I gave the lover aid. Fate blinded us,—
Myself as well as him. The tyrant seized me,
Defenseless and unarmed. With tears I saw
Pirithous cast forth to be devoured
By savage beasts, that lapped the blood of men.
He shut me in a gloomy cave, far down,
Deep in the earth, near to the realm of Pluto.
I lay six months, before the gods had pity,
Then I escaped the eyes that guarded me.
I purged the world of this, its enemy,
And he, himself, has fed his monsters' hunger.
But when I come, with an expectant joy,
When I draw close to all that is most precious
Of what the gods have left me,—when my soul
Looks for its happiness in these dear places.

Then I am welcomed only with a shudder,
With turning from me, and with hasty
flight.
And since it seems that I inspire such
terror,
Would I were still imprisoned in Epirus!
Phædra complains that I have suffered out-
rage.
Who has betrayed me? Speak! Was I
avenged?
Why was I not? Has Greece, to whom
mine arm
Has often brought good help, sheltered my
foe?
You do not answer. Is it that my son,—
My own son—has he joined mine enemies?
I'll enter, for I cannot bear to wonder.
I'll learn at once the culprit and the crime,
And Phædra must explain her trouble to
me.   [Exit THESEUS.]

HIPPOLYTUS. What mean these words?
They freeze my very blood!
Will Phædra, in her frenzy, blame her-
self,—
Make sure of her destruction? And the
king,—
What will he say? O gods! The fatal poison
That love has spread through all my father's
house!
I burn with fires his hatred disapproves.
How changed he finds me from the son he
knew!
My mind is much alarmed with dark fore-
bodings,
But surely innocence need never fear.
Come, let us go, and in some other place
Consider how I best may move my father
To make him tender, and to tell a love
Troubled, but never vanquished, by his
frown.   [Exeunt.]

ACT IV

[Enter THESEUS and ŒNONE.]

THESEUS.   Ah, what is this I hear? Pre-
sumptuous traitor!
And would he have disgraced his father's
honor?
With what relentless footsteps Fate pursues
me!
I know not where I go, nor where I am!
My kindest love, how very ill repaid!
Bold scheme! Oh most abominable thought!
A wretch who did not shrink from vio-
lence
To reach the object of his evil passion!
I know this sword,—it served to arm his
fury,—
The sword I gave him for a nobler use!
And could the sacred ties of blood not stop
him?
And Phædra,—was she loath to have him
punished?
She held her silence. Was it to spare his
guilt?
ŒNONE.   Only to spare a most unhappy
father.
She knew it shameful that her eyes had
kindled

So infamous a love,—had prompted him
To such a crime,—and Phædra would have
died.
I saw her raise her arm, and ran to save
her.
To me alone you owe it that she lives.
And since I pity her, and pity you,
I came, unwilling, to explain her tears.
THESEUS.   The traitor! Well indeed might
he turn pale!
It was for fear he trembled when he saw
me!
I was amazed that he should show no glad-
ness.
The coldness of his greeting chilled my
love.
But was this guilty passion that consumes
him
Declared before I banished him from
Athens?
ŒNONE.   Remember, sire, how Phædra
urged it on you.
It was illicit love that caused her hatred.
THESEUS.   And then this flame burst out
again at Trœzen?
ŒNONE.   Sire, I have told you all there is.
The queen

Is left to bear her grief alone too long.
Let me now leave you. I will wait on her.

[*Exit* ŒNONE.]

[*Enter* HIPPOLYTUS.]

THESEUS. Ah, there he is! Great gods!
That noble manner
Might well deceive an eye less fond than
mine!
Why should the sacred mark of virtue
shine
Bright on the forehead of an evil wretch?
Why should the blackness of a traitor's
heart
Not show itself by sure and certain signs?
HIPPOLYTUS. My father, may I ask what
fatal cloud
Has troubled so the face of majesty?
Dare you not trust this secret to your son?
THESEUS. Traitor, how dare you show
yourself before me?
Monster, whom Heaven's bolts have spared
too long!
A last survivor of that robber band
Whereof I cleansed the earth, your brutal
lust
Scorned to respect even my marriage bed!
And now you dare,—my hated foe,—to
come
Here to my presence, here where all things
are filled
And foul with infamy, instead of seeking
Some unknown land, that never heard my
name.
Fly, traitor, fly! Stay not to tempt my
wrath!
I scare restrain it. Do not brave my hatred.
I have been shamed forever; 'tis enough
To be the father of so vile a son,
Without your death, to stain indelibly
The splendid record of my noble deeds.
Fly! And unless you yearn for punishment
To make you yet another villain slain,
Take heed that this sun, shining on us now,
Shall see your foot no more upon this soil.
I say it once again,—fly!—and in haste!
Rid all my realms of your detested person.
On thee,—on thee, great Neptune, do I
call!
If once I cleared thy shores of murderers,

Remember, then, thy promise to reward me
For these good deeds, by granting my first
prayer.
I was held long in close captivity.
I did not then demand thy mighty aid,
For I have saved so great a privilege
To use in greatest need. That time is come.
And now I ask,—avenge a wretched father!
I leave this traitor subject to thy wrath.
I ask that thou shouldst quench his fires in
blood,
And by thy fury, I will judge thy favor!
HIPPOLYTUS. Phædra accuses me of wan-
ton passion!
A final horror to confuse my soul!
Such blows, unlooked for, falling all at
once,
Have crushed me, choked me, struck me
into silence!
THESEUS. Traitor, you thought that in a
timid silence
Phædra would cover your brutality.
But, though you fled, you still should not
have left her
Holding the sword that seals your con-
demnation.
Or rather, to complete your perfidy,
You should have robbed her both of speech
and life!
HIPPOLYTUS. Most justly angered at so
black a lie,
I might be pardoned, should I speak the
truth.
But it concerns your honor to conceal it.
Welcome that reverence which stops my
tongue,
And, without seeking to increase your
troubles,
Look closely at my life, as it has been.
Great crimes come never singly; they are
linked
To sins that went before. Who once has
sinned,
May, at the last, do greater violence
To all that men hold sacred. Vice, like
virtue,
Grows in small steps, and no true inno-
cence
Can ever fall at once to deepest guilt.
No man of virtue, in a single day,

Can turn himself to treason, murder, in-
cest!
I am the son of one both chaste and brave.
I have not proved unworthy of my birth.
Pittheus, one by all men reckoned wise,
Deigned to instruct me, when I left her
keeping.
I do not wish to boast upon my merits,
But if I may lay claim to any virtue,
I think I have displayed, beyond all else,
That I abhor those sins with which you
charge me.
Look you, Hippolytus is known in Greece
As one so continent he's thought austere,
And all men know how I abstain, unbend-
ing.
The daylight is not purer than my heart.
Then how could I, if burning so pro-
fanely,—
THESEUS.   Villain, it is that very pride con-
demns you!
I see the hateful reason for your coldness,
For only Phædra charmed your shameless
eyes.
Your heart, quite cold to other witcheries,
Refused the pure flame of a lawful love.
HIPPOLYTUS.   No, father, I have hidden
it too long.
This heart has not disdained its sacred
flame.
Here, at your feet, I'll tell my real offense.
I love, and love, indeed, where you forbid
it.
My heart's devotion binds me to Aricia,—
The child of Pallas has subdued your
son!
Her I adore, rebellious to your laws.
For her alone I breathe my ardent sighs.
THESEUS.   You love her? Gods! But no,—
I see the truth.
You play this crime to justify yourself.
HIPPOLYTUS.   Sir, for six months I kept
me from her presence,
And still I love her. I have come to tell it,—
Trembling I come—! Can nothing free
your mind
Of such an error? Can my oaths not soothe
you?
By Heaven—Earth,—by all the powers of
Nature—

THESEUS.   The wicked will not ever shrink
from lying.
Be still, and spare me tiresome vows and
pleadings,
Since your false virtue knows no other way.
HIPPOLYTUS.   Although you think it false
and insincere,
Phædra has cause enough to know it true.
THESEUS.   Ah, how your boldness rouses
all my anger!
HIPPOLYTUS.   What is my term and place
of banishment?
THESEUS.   Were you beyond the Pillars of
Alcides,[1]
Your perjured presence still were far too
near me!
HIPPOLYTUS.   What friends will pity me, if
you forsake me
And think me guilty of so vile a crime?
THESEUS.   Go seek for friends who praise
adultery,
And look for those who clap their hands at
incest!—
Low traitors, lawless,—steeped in in-
famy,—
Fit comforters for such an one as you!
HIPPOLYTUS.   Are incest and adultery the
words
Which you will cast at me? I hold my peace.
Yet think what mother Phædra had—re-
member
Her blood, not mine, is tainted with these
horrors!
THESEUS.   So then! Before my eyes your
rage bursts out,
And loses all restraint. Go from my sight!—
This last time I will say it,—traitor, go!
And do not wait until a father's anger
Drives you away in public execration!
                                        [Exit HIPPOLYTUS.]
THESEUS. [Alone.] Wretch! Thou must meet
inevitable ruin!
Neptune has sworn by Styx,—an oath most
dreadful
Even to gods,—and he will keep his prom-
ise.
Thou canst not ever flee from his revenge.
I loved thee, and in spite of this offense

[1] The Pillars of Hercules were the headlands
which form the Strait of Gibraltar.

My heart is moved by what I see for thee.
Nay, but thy doom is but too fully earned.
Had father ever better cause for rage?
O you just gods, who see my crushing grief,
Why was I cursed with such an evil son?

[Enter PHÆDRA.]

PHÆDRA. I come to you, my lord, in
proper dread,
For I have heard your voice raised high in
anger,
And much I fear that deeds have followed
threats.
Oh, spare your child, if there is still some
time!
Respect your race, your blood, I do beseech you.
I would not hear that blood cry from the
earth!
Save me the horror and the lasting shame
Of having caused his father's hand to shed
it!

THESEUS. No, madam, I am free from
such a stain.
But still the wretch has not escaped my
vengeance.
The hand of an Immortal holds his doom,
And pledges his destruction. 'Tis a debt
That Neptune owes me. You shall be
avenged.

PHÆDRA. A debt to you? Prayers made in
anger—

THESEUS.   Fear not.
They will not fail. But join your prayers to
mine,
And paint his crimes for me in all their
blackness,
To fan my sluggish wrath to whitest heat.
You do not know of all his villainy.
His rage against you feeds itself on slanders.
Your words, he says, are full of all deceit.
He says Aricia has his heart and soul,
That he loves only her—

PHÆDRA.   Aricia?—

THESEUS.   Yes.
He said it to my face:—an idle pretext!
A trick I am not caught by. Let us hope
That Neptune does swift justice. I am going
Now to his altars, urging he keep his oath.

[Exit THESEUS.]

PHÆDRA. [Alone.] So he is gone! What
words have struck mine ears?
What smothered fires are burning in my
heart?
What fatal stroke falls like a thunder-bolt?
Stung with remorse that would not give me
peace,
I tore myself from out Œnone's arms
And hurried here to help Hippolytus,
With all my soul and strength. Who
knows, indeed,
But that new-found repentance might have
moved me
To speak in accusation of myself?—
And if my voice had not been choked with
shame,
Perhaps I might have told the frightful
truth.
Hippolytus can feel—but not for me!
Aricia has his heart, his plighted word!
You gods! I thought his heart could not be
touched
By any love, when, deaf to all my tears,
He armed his eye with scorn, his brow
with threats.
I thought him strong against all other
women,
And yet another has prevailed upon him!
She tamed his pride, and she has gained his
favor!
Perhaps he has a heart that's quick to
melt,
And I alone am she he cannot bear!
Then shall I charge myself with his pro-
tection?—

[Enter ŒNONE.]

Dear nurse, and do you know what I have
learned?

ŒNONE. No, but in truth I come with
trembling limbs.
I dreaded what you planned when you went
out,
And fear of fatal madness turned me pale.

PHÆDRA. Who would have thought it,
nurse? I had a rival.

ŒNONE. A rival?

PHÆDRA.   Yes, he loves. I cannot
doubt it.
This wild Hippolytus I could not tame,—

Who scorned to be admired, and who was
  wearied
With lovers' sighs,—this tiger whom I
  dreaded
Fawns on the hand of one who broke his
  pride.
Aricia found the entrance to his heart!
ŒNONE. Aricia?
PHÆDRA.   'Tis a torture yet untried!
Now for what other pains am I reserved?
All I have suffered,—ecstasies of passion,
Longings and fears, the horrors of remorse,
The shame of being spurned with con-
  tumely,
Were feeble tastes of what is now my tor-
  ment.
They love each other! By what secret
  charm
Have they deceived me? When and where
  and how
Did they contrive to meet? You knew it
  all,—
And why, then, was I kept from knowing
  of it?
You never told me of their stolen hours
Of love and of delight. Have they been
  seen
Talking together often?—did they seek
The forest shadows? Ah, they had full free-
  dom
To be together. Heaven watched their sighs.
They loved,—and never felt that they were
  guilty.
The morning sun shone always clear for
  them,
While I,—an outcast from the face of Na-
  ture,
Shunned the bright day, and would have
  hid myself,—
Death the one god whom I dared ask for
  aid!
I waited for the freedom of the grave.
My woe was fed with bitterness, and
  watered
With many tears. It was too closely
  watched.
I did not dare to weep without restraint,
And knowing it a solace perilous,
I feared it, and I hid my mortal terror
Beneath a face most tranquil. Oftentimes

I stopped my tears, and made myself to
  smile—
ŒNONE. What fruit can they desire from
  fruitless love?
For they can meet no more.
PHÆDRA.   That love will stay,
And it will stay forever. While I speak—
O dreadful thought—they laugh and scorn
  my madness
And my distracted heart. In spite of exile,
In spite of that which soon must come to
  part them,
They make a thousand oaths to bind their
  union.
Œnone, can I bear this happiness
Which so insults me? I would have your
  pity.
Yes, she must be destroyed. My husband's
  fury
Against her hated race shall be renewed.
The punishment must be a heavy one.
Her guilt outruns the guilt of all her
  brothers.
I'll plead with Theseus, in my jealousy,—
What do I say? Oh, have I lost my senses?
Is Phædra jealous? will she, then, go beg-
  ging
For Theseus' help? He lives,—and yet I
  burn.
For whom? Whose heart is this I claim as
  mine?
My hair stands up with horror at my words,
And from this time, my guilt has passed all
  bounds!
Hypocrisy and incest breathe at once
Through all I do. My hands are ripe for
  murder,
To spill the guiltless blood of innocence.
Do I still live, a wretch, and dare to face
The holy Sun, from whom I have my be-
  ing?
My father's father was the king of gods;
My race is spread through all the uni-
  verse.—
Where can I hide? In the dark realms of
  Pluto?
But there my father holds the fatal urn.
His hands award the doom irrevocable.—
Minos is judge of all the ghosts in hell.

And how his awful shade will start and shudder
When he shall see his daughter brought before him,
And made confess such many-colored sins,
Such crimes, perhaps, as hell itself knows not!
O father, what will be thy words at seeing
So dire a sight? I see thee drop the urn,
Turning to seek some punishment unheard of,—
To be, thyself, mine executioner!
Oh, spare me! For a cruel deity
Destroys thy race. Oh, look upon my madness,
And in it see her wrath. This aching heart
Gathers no fruit of pleasure from its crime.
It is a shame which hounds me to the grave,
And ends a life of misery in torment.

ŒNONE. Ah, madam, drive away this groundless fear.
Look not so hard upon a little sin.
You love. We cannot conquer destiny.
Why, you were drawn as by a fatal charm;—
Is that a marvel we have never seen?
Has love, then, come to triumph over you,
And no one else? By nature man is weak.
You are a mortal,—bow to mortal fortune.
You chafe against a yoke that many others
Have borne before you. They upon Olympus,—
The very gods themselves, who make us tremble

For our poor sins, have burned with lawless passions.

PHÆDRA. What words are these? What counsels do you give me?
Why will you still pour poison in mine ears?
You have destroyed me. You have brought me back
When I should else have left the light oɪ day.
You made me to forget my solemn duty,
And see Hippolytus, whom I had shunned.
What have you done? Why did those wicked lips
Slander his faultless life with blackest lies?
It may be you have murdered him. By now
The prayer unholy of a heartless father
May have been granted. I will have no words!
Go, monster! Leave me to my sorry fate.
May the just gods repay you properly,
And may your punishment remain forever
To strike with fear all such as you, who strive
To feed the frailty of the great with cunning,
To push them to the very brink of ruin
To which their feet incline,—to smooth the path
Of guilt. Such flatterers the gods, in anger,
Bestow on kings as their most fatal gift!
                              [Exit PHÆDRA.]
ŒNONE. [Alone.] O Gods! What is there
     I've not done to serve her?
And this is the reward that I have won!
                              [Exit.]

ACT V

[Enter HIPPOLYTUS and ARICIA.]

ARICIA. Can you keep silent in this mortal danger?
Your father loves you. Will you leave him so—
When he is thus deceived? If you are cruel,—
If, in your heart, you will not see my tears,
Why then, content,—and do not ever see me.
Abandon poor Aricia,—but at least

If you must go, make sure your life is safe.
Defend your honor from a shameful stain,
And force your father to recall his prayers.
There still is time. Why, for a mere caprice,
Should you leave open way for Phædra's slanders?
Let Theseus know the truth.

HIPPOLYTUS.   Could I say more
And not expose him to a great disgrace?
How should I dare, by speaking what I know,

To make my father's brow blush red with
shame?
You only know the hateful mystery.
I have not showed my heart to any other
But you and Heaven. Judge, then, if I love
you,
Since you have seen I could not hide from
you
All I would fain have hidden from myself!
Remember under what a seal I spoke.
Forget what I have said, if that may be,
And never let so pure a mouth give voice
To such a secret. Let us trust to Heaven
To give me justice, for the gods are just.
For their own honor they will clear the
guiltless.
The time will come for Phædra to be pun-
ished.
She cannot always flee the shame she
merits.
I ask no other favor than your silence.
In all besides, I give my wrath free scope.
Make your escape from this captivity,
Be bold, and come with me upon my flight.
Oh, do not stay on this accursèd soil
Where virtue breathes the air of pestilence.
To hide your leaving, take the good advan-
tage
Of all this turmoil, roused by my disgrace.
I promise you the means of flight are ready.
You have, as yet, no other guards than
mine.
Defenders of great strength will fight our
quarrel.
Argos has open arms, and Sparta calls us.
Let us appeal for justice to our friends,
And let us not stand by while Phædra
joins us
Together in one ruin, driving us
Down from the throne,—and swells her
son's possessions
By robbings. Come, take this happy chance.
What fear can hold you back? You seem to
pause.
Only your better fortune makes me urge
That we be bold. When I am all a-fire,
Why are you ice? Are you afraid to fol-
low
One who is banished?
ARICIA.   Ah, but such an exile

Would be most dear to me. For with what
joy
I'd live, if I could link my fate to yours,
And be forgot by all the world. But still
We are not bound by that sweet tie together.
Then how am I to steal away with you?
I know the strictest honor need not stop me
From seeking freedom from your father's
hands,
For this, indeed, is not my parents' home,
And flight is lawful, when one flies from
tyrants.
But you, sir, love me, and my virtue
shrinks—
HIPPOLYTUS.   No, no! To me your honor
is as dear
As it is to yourself. A nobler purpose
Brings me to you. I ask you leave your foes
And follow with your husband. That same
Heaven
Which sends these woes, sets free the pledge
between us
From human hands. There are not always
torches
To light the face of Hymen. Come with
me—
Beside the gates of Trœzen is a temple,
Amid the ancient tombs of princes, buried.
They who are false can never enter there,
And there no mortal dares make perjured
oaths,
For instant punishment will come on guilt.
There is not any stronger check to false-
hood
Than what is present there,—fear of a
death
That cannot be escaped. There we shall go,
If you consent, and swear eternal love,
And call the god who watches there to
witness
Our solemn vows, and ask his guarding
care.
I will invoke the holiest of powers—
The chaste Diana and the Queen of
Heaven,—
Yes, all the gods, who know my inmost
heart,
Will answer for my sacred promises.
ARICIA.   Here is the king. Away—make no
delay.

I linger yet a while to hide my flight.
Go you, and leave me with some trusted
one
To lead my timid footsteps to your side.

[*Exit* HIPPOLYTUS.]

[*Enter* THESEUS *and* ISMENE.]

THESEUS.   O gods, throw light upon my
troubled mind!
Show me the truth which I am seeking here.
ARICIA.   [*To* ISMENE.] Be ready, dear Is-
mene, for our flight.   [*Exit* ISMENE.]
THESEUS.   Your color changes, and you
seem confused.
Madam,—what dealing had my son with
you?
ARICIA.   Sire, he was bidding me his last
farewell.
THESEUS.   It seems your eyes can tame
that stubborn pride,
And the first sighs he breathes are paid to
you.
ARICIA.   I cannot well deny the truth; he
has not
Inherited your hatred and injustice,—
He does not treat me as a criminal.
THESEUS.   That is to say,—he swore eter-
nal love.
Do not depend on such a fickle heart.
He swore as much to others, long before.
ARICIA.   He, Sire?
THESEUS.   You stop the roving of
his taste.
How should you bear so vile a partnership?
ARICIA.   And how can you endure that
wicked slanders
Should make so pure a life seem black as
pitch?
How do you know so little of his heart?
Do you so ill distinguish innocence
From the worst guilt? What mist before
your eyes
Can make them blind to such an open
virtue?
Ah! 'Tis too much to let false tongues de-
fame him!
Repent! Call back again your fatal prayers.
Oh, be afraid, lest Heaven in its justice
Hate you enough to hear your wish and
grant it!

The gods, in anger, often take our vic-
tims,—
And oftentimes they punish us with gifts!
THESEUS.   No, it is vain to seek to hide his
guilt.
Your love is blind to his depravity.
But I have witnesses beyond reproach,—
Tears I have seen,—true tears, that may be
trusted.
ARICIA.   Take heed, my lord. Although
your mighty hand
Has rid the world of many beasts and
monsters,
You have not slain them all,—there's one
alive!—
Your son, himself, forbids that I say more,
And since I know how much he still reveres
you,
I know that I should cause him much dis-
tress
If I should dare to finish. I shall act
Like reverence,—and to be silent,—leave
you.

[*Exit* ARICIA.]

THESEUS.   [*Alone.*] What is there in her
mind? What hidden meaning
Lurks in a speech begun, then broken
short?
Would both deceive me with a vain pre-
tense?
Have they conspired to put me to this tor-
ture?
And yet, for all that I am most severe,
What plaintive voice is crying in my heart?
I have a secret pity that disturbs me.
Œnone must be questioned, once again,
For I must see this crime in clearer light.
Guards, bid Œnone come to me,—alone.

[*Enter* PANOPE.]

PANOPE.   I do not know the purpose of
the queen.
Yet, seeing her distress, I fear the worst;—
Despair most fatal, painted on her fea-
tures,—
Death's pallor is already in her face.
Œnone, shamed and driven from her sight,
Has thrown herself into the ocean's depths.
What moved her to so rash a deed, none
knows,

And now the waves forever hide her from us.

THESEUS. What is that you say?

PANOPE. Her sad fate adds New trouble to the queen's tempestuous soul. Sometimes, to soothe her secret pain, she clasps Her children to her, bathes them with her tears,— Then suddenly forgets her mother's love, And thrusts them from her with a look of horror. She wanders back and forth with doubtful steps, Her eye looks vacantly, and will not know us. She wrote three times, and thrice she changed her mind, And tore the letter when it scarce was started. Be willing then to see her, Sire,—to help her. [Exit PANOPE.]

THESEUS. Œnone dead, and Phædra bent on dying? Oh, call my son to me again, great Heaven! Let him defend himself, for I am ready To hear him, now. Oh, haste not to bestow Thy fatal bounty, Neptune. Rather my prayers Should stay unheard forever. Far too soon I raised too cruel hands, and I believed Lips that may well have lied! Ah, what may follow?—

[Enter THERAMENES.]

'Tis you, Theramenes? Where is my son? I gave him to your keeping in his childhood,— But why should tears be flowing from thine eyes? How is it with my son—?

THERAMENES. You worry late. It is a vain affection. He is dead.

THESEUS. O gods!

THERAMENES. Yes, I have seen the very flower Of all mankind cut down; and I am bold To say that never man deserved it less.

THESEUS. My son! My son is dead! When I was reaching My arms to him again, then why should Heaven Hasten his doom? What sudden blow was this?

THERAMENES. When we had scarcely passed the gates of Trœzen,— He, silent in his chariot, his guards Downcast and silent, too, all ranged around him,— He turned his steeds to the Mycenian road, And, lost in thought, allowed the reins to lie Loose on their backs, and his high-mettled chargers, One time so eager to obey his voice, Now seemed to know his sadness and to share it. Then, coming from the sea, a frightful cry Shatters the troubled air with sudden discord; And groaning from the bosom of the earth Answers the crying of that fearful voice. It froze the blood within our very hearts! Our horses hear, and stand with bristling manes. Meanwhile there rises on the watery plain A mountain wave, mighty, with foaming crest. It rolls upon the shore, and as it breaks It throws before our eyes a raging monster. Its brow is armed with terrifying horns And all its body clothed with yellow scales. In front it is a bull, behind, a dragon, Turning and twisting in impatient fury. It bellows till the very shores do tremble. The sky is struck with horror at the sight. The earth in terror quakes; breath of the beast Poisons the air. The very wave that brought it Runs back in fear. All fly, forgetting courage Which cannot help,—and in a nearby temple Take refuge,—all but brave Hippolytus. A hero's worthy son, he stays his horses, Seizes his darts, and rushing forward, hurls

A missile with sure aim, and wounds the
beast
Deep in the flank. It springs, raging with
pain,
Right to the horses' feet, and roaring,
falls,
Writhes in the dust, shows them his fiery
throat,
And covers them with flame and smoke
and blood.
Fear lends them wings; deaf to his voice
for once,
Heeding no curb, the horses race away.
Their master tires himself in futile efforts.
Each courser's bit is red with blood and
foam.
Some say a god, in all this wild disorder,
Is seen, pricking their dusty flanks with
goads.
They rush to jagged rocks, urged by this
terror.
The axle crashes, and the hardy youth
Sees his car broken, shattered into bits.
He himself falls, entangled in the reins.—
Forgive my grief. That cruel sight will be
For me the source of never-ending tears.
I saw thy luckless son,—I saw him, Sire,
Dragged by those horses that his hands had
fed.
He could not stop their fierce career,—his
cries
But added to their terror. All his body
Was soon a mass of wounds. Our anguished
cries
Filled the whole plain. At length the horses
slackened.
They stopped close by the ancient tombs
which mark
The place where lie the ashes of his fathers.
I ran there panting, and behind me came
His guard, along a track fresh-stained with
blood,
Reddening all the rocks; locks of his hair
Hung dripping in the briers,—gory tri-
umphs!
I came and called him. Stretching out his
hand,
He opened dying eyes, soon to be closed.
"The gods have robbed me of a guiltless
life,"

I heard him say; "Take care of sad Aricia,
When I am dead. Friend, if my father
mourn
When he shall know his son's unhappy
fate,—
One accused falsely,—then, to give me
peace,
Tell him to treat his captive tenderly,
And to restore—" The hero's breath had
failed,
And in my arms there lay a mangled
body,—
A thing most piteous, the bleeding spoil
Of Heaven's wrath,—his father could not
know him.

THESEUS. Alas, my son:—my hope, now
lost forever!
The gods are ruthless. They have served
me well,
And I am left to live a life of anguish
And of a great remorse.

THERAMENES.   And then, Aricia,
Flying from you, came timidly to take him
To be her husband, there, before the
gods.
And coming close, she saw the grass, all
reeking,
All bloody red, and (sad for a lover's
eyes!)
She saw him, lying there, disfigured,
pale,—
And for a time she knew not her mis-
fortune.
She did not know the hero she adores.
She looked and asked, "Where is Hippoly-
tus?"
Only too sure, at last, that he was lying
Before her there, with sad eyes, silently
Reproaching Heaven, she groaned, and
shuddering
Fell fainting, all but lifeless at his feet.
Ismene, all in tears, knelt down beside
her,
And called her back to life, a life of noth-
ing
But sense of pain. And I to whom the light
Is only darkness, now, come to discharge
The duty he imposed on me: to tell you
His last desire,—a melancholy task.—
But here his mortal enemy is coming.

[*Enter* PHÆDRA *and* GUARDS.]

THESEUS.   Madam, you've triumphed, and
my son is killed!
Ah, but what room have I for fear! How
justly
Suspicion racks me that in blaming him
I erred! But he is dead; accept your victim,
Rightly or wrongly slain. Your heart may
leap.
For me, my eyes shall be forever blind.
Since you have said it, I'll believe him
guilty.
His death is cause enough for me to weep.
It would be folly, should I seek a light
Which could not bring him back to soothe
my grief,
And which might only make me more un-
happy.
I will go far from you and from this shore,
For here the vision of my mangled son
Would haunt my memory, and drive me
mad.
I wish I might be banished from the world,
For all the world must rise in judgment on
me.
Even my glory weights my punishment,
For if I bore a name less known to men,
'Twere easier to hide me. Ah, I mourn
And hate all prayers the gods have granted
me.
Nor will I ever go to them again
With useless pleadings. All that they can
give
Is far outweighed by what they took from
me.
PHÆDRA.   My lord, I cannot hear you and
be silent.
I must undo the wrong that he has suf-
fered,—
Your son was innocent.
THESEUS.   Unhappy father!
And I condemned him for a word of yours!
You think I can forgive such cruelty—?
PHÆDRA.   Moments are precious to me; let
me speak.

'Twas I who cast an eye of lawless passion
On chaste and dutiful Hippolytus.
The gods had lit a baleful fire in me,
And vile Œnone's cunning did the rest.
She feared Hippolytus,—who knew my
madness,—
Would tell you of that passion which he
hated.
And so she took advantage of my weakness
And hastened, that she might accuse him
first.
She has been punished now, but all too
lightly.
She sought to flee my anger,—cast herself
Into the waves. The sword had long since
cut
My thread of life, but still I heard the cry
Of slandered innocence, and I determined
To die a slower way, and first confess
My penitence to you. There is a poison
Medea brought to Athens, in my veins.
The venom works already in my heart.
A strange and fatal chill is spreading
there.
I see already, through a gathering mist,
The husband whom I outrage with my
presence.
Death veils the light of Heaven from mine
eyes,
And gives it back its purity, defiled.
PANOPE.   She dies, my lord.
THESEUS.   I would the memory
Of her disgraceful deed might perish with
her!
Ah! I have learned too late! Come, let us
go,
And with the blood of mine unhappy son
Mingle our tears,—embrace his dear re-
mains,
Repenting deeply for a hated prayer.
Let him have honor such as he deserves,
And, to appease his sore-offended spirit,
No matter what her brothers' guilt has
been,
From this day forth, Aricia is my daughter.
                                            [*Exeunt.*]

The Problem Play

SINCE IT IS the nature of drama to deal with conflicts and tensions, every play contains problems of one sort or another. Ordinarily these problems are generated from within the play itself; they originate in a specific dramatic action and are inseparable from the unique situation with which the play deals. To the extent that they pertain to character they may imply a certain general application to human nature, but their connection with any particular context of place or time is rarely more than incidental. The type of drama which has come to be known as the problem play, however, is concerned with problems of a different sort. Its problems are generated as an oyster creates a pearl—around an external irritant. That is to say, its dramatic action is constructed around a problem of human life which exists independent of the play, and which the play is designed to illuminate. Thus the problem does not grow out of the play; the play grows out of the problem, from the significance of which it derives its own final significance. In this respect the problem play represents not only a departure from common dramatic precedent but also a deliberate subordination of drama to the performance of a social function. Its ultimate concern is not with dramatic art but with the conditions under which men live. In the nature of the case, these conditions, together with the problems which arise from them, are always specific and necessarily imply a particular context of place and time. Hence the problem play itself is always a product of special circumstances and depends for its general interest upon the timeliness and broad application of the problem with which it deals.

Historically the problem play is a direct outgrowth of the interests responsible for comedy of manners and tragedy of sensibility. All three types of drama reflect an acute consciousness of the demands imposed upon humanity by social modes of life, and all have in common a pronounced sense of social context and social obligation. The chief difference among them is that the two earlier types concentrate tentatively on the restricted interests of a select group, whereas the problem play, by broadening its base, expands these interests to a wider social application. In either case what is fundamental is the manner of viewing human life. This represents an important shift from viewing the life of an individual in terms of perennial human experience to seeing it in the context of specific temporal circumstances. As the principal agent in establishing this transfer of interest, the problem play constitutes the transition from older dramatic conceptions to those of modern times. To it belongs the distinction of launching modern drama. In addition, it has proved to be the dramatic genre most congenial to modern interests and habits of thought; and, in its various adaptations, it is by all odds the most common type of modern play. This unique eminence is largely attributable to the fact that the problem play is founded on the most potent single factor in modern drama—the awareness of environment as a dominant influence on human destiny. Under the pressure of this awareness the whole conception of dramatic conflict has undergone a significant change. To modern eyes what appears most pertinent is no longer the traditional clash of personalities but the struggle of the individual with his environment. As a major factor in this conflict, the external conditions of human existence have accordingly taken on a new reality, which is as objective as it is concrete. The problem play is an endeavor to explore the human significance of these conditions as they impinge upon the individual and the social group.

It is this choice of subject matter and purpose, rather than any singularity of form, which distinguishes the problem play as a type of drama. Actually the problem play employs a variety of techniques; it may be either comic or tragic; and it adopts any form which happens to be convenient, so long as it serves to present the problem. Its early affiliations were with such diverse exhibits as sentimental comedy, bourgeois melodrama, and neo-classical tragedy. The basis of its most common modern form was that egregious specimen of theatrical carpentry, the well-made play of Scribe and Sardou. On the contemporary stage it is practically inseparable from most of the dramatic forms cultivated. In the main, however, it tends to prefer a form of drama which is intermediate between comedy and tragedy; indeed it constitutes the most common mixed variety of modern drama. The reason for this preference is that the problem play, like a great deal of modern drama, is interested in diverting theatrical entertainment to serious ulterior purposes. In order to perform this feat successfully, it is obliged to interest and move an audience with the cogency of its problem without boring it by obtrusive didacticism or interfering with the rational detachment necessary for judicious appraisal. What it requires, therefore, is a dramatic vehicle which permits a maximum diversity of treatment, a balanced mingling of attitudes, and a ready transition from tension to relaxation.

Whatever the form adopted, the mechanics of the problem play are conditioned by an invariable threefold requirement. In order to deal with any problem satisfactorily, they must succeed in demonstrating its actual existence, its precise nature and causes, and its general human pertinence. Since a play which exists for the sake of its problem is pointless unless the problem has a reality apart from the play, this demonstration necessarily involves more than the internal logic of dramatic action. To be effective it must be immediately referable to the actual experience of the audience. Such a demonstration of a problem's reality calls for verisimilitude in the circumstances of action and for naturalness in their employment. Exposition of its nature presupposes an accurate observation and analysis of verifiable data. Establishment of its general application necessitates an emphasis upon commonplaces of familiar experience and upon characters who exemplify common human traits or typical social attitudes. In consequence, the technique of the problem play is prevailingly realistic, scientific, and sociological.

This objective analysis of familiar realities is the most conspicuous feature of true problem drama. Since successful elucidation of a problem depends upon scrupulous adherence to fact and upon the justice with which its various aspects are represented, the pure problem play endeavors to avoid overt bias or special pleading. However humanitarian its motive may be, it strives to keep its methods strictly scientific. For much the same reason it usually makes no effort to solve the problem which it raises, remaining content merely to indicate why some solution is desirable. In short, it conceives its function to be not therapy but diagnosis. Upon occasion, however, this emphasis shifts, and pure objectivity yields to partisan dialectic. When this occurs, the problem play ceases to be a dispassionate examination of evidence and takes on a radically different connotation. Substantially it becomes the defense of a thesis, in which the purpose is proof of a specific contention, and the dramatic action is an argument marshalled to that end. In effect, such thesis drama transforms a problem into a springboard for deliberate indoctrination and propaganda, as is the case with much recent Soviet drama, or for the promulgation of social ideas, as in many of the plays of Bernard Shaw.

The first to elevate the problem play to artistic distinction was the nineteenth-century Norwegian dramatist Henrik Ibsen (1828–1906). It was his achievement in the genre which not only brought the dramatist his first world-wide recognition but also made him the acknowledged father of modern drama. Ibsen's cultivation of the problem play during the last quarter of the nineteenth century established its basic principles and suggested much of its characteristic subject matter. In addition it indicated the two main applications of its interest—the sociological and the psychological. Beginning with problems of broad social import, the work of Ibsen turned more and more to the psychological problems of the individual in a complex social environment. In manner it also ranged from pungent satirical comedy to quiet but corrosive tragedy. With the realistic pertinence of his versatile interests, the breadth and depth of his human understanding, and the compelling power of his dramatic skill, Ibsen became the greatest universal dramatist since Molière. To choose among his pure problem plays on an absolute basis of immediate impact, however, is to encounter a difficulty inherent in the type. A problem play is always contemporaneous with its problem, and there is nothing more tedious than an outlived agitation. Those Ibsen plays which once threatened to blow society apart and incited every reaction from censorship to riot seem nowadays too often like a tempest in a teapot. Although in many cases their problems are not so much dead as merely sleeping, they have suffered from time's annoying habit of marching on. Fortunately, or perhaps unfortunately, the same stricture does not apply to Ibsen's very lively problem comedy *An Enemy of the People,* which first stirred up the animals (on which see Act IV) in 1882. The problems with which it deals are as vigorous now as they ever were, and mankind will probably be embarked on the millennium before the cogency of the play has faded.

An Enemy of the People is a somewhat rueful comedy of the all too commonplace. Its aim is to present a problem of wide social implication in terms of familiar everyday experience. For this purpose its attention is focused on the ordinary activities of an average small-town community. Its characters are chosen to represent the usual kinds of undistinguished people likely to be met almost anywhere. Its central issue is not, at least immediately, the fate of nations but bad drainage at the local waterworks. Its dramatic conflicts are the petty rivalries, the picayune bickerings, and the shabby maneuverings spawned by any parochial scandal. Technically, the play takes advantage of a curtained stage, with its opportunity for detailed stage sets, to surround each segment of action with the concrete tokens of its specific environment. As a corollary to this physical verisimilitude it also purges the action of stagy histrionics and confines dialogue to colloquial naturalness. The use of a separate setting and terminal curtain, which has the effect of making each act a relatively independent unit of dramatic development, provides a convenient device for systematic treatment of the problem. In particular, the conclusion of action by the fall of a curtain makes possible the use of the final tableau and curtain line to sum up the substance of an act and emphasize its special connotation. Thus each act is devoted with logical precision to a major aspect of the problem until, by the end of the play, every pertinent ramification has been explored and the vicious circle is complete.

This personally conducted tour of problem inspection constitutes the dramatic action of the play. It is designed to settle nothing, but simply to illuminate the factors which have to be taken into account before anything can be settled, and to indicate the human consequences of leaving the problem unsettled. Beginning with a commonplace incident, it traces the intricate chain-reaction which rapidly involves the most divergent personal fortunes in a common dilemma and culminates in the epidemic bigotry of panic. What starts as a straightforward question of civic health expands into a highly complex problem of private and public morality. The circumstances of the play are therefore designed to represent two levels of significance. On the one they reveal the commonplace behavior which can be paralleled from anyone's experience. On the other they embody the universal conflict between moral responsibility and practical exigency. The case of Dr. Stockmann, for example, epitomizes the perennial problem of personal integrity and social obligation. Egotistical enough to maintain his own convictions in the face of public opinion, idealistic enough to believe that truth and righteousness take precedence over all other considerations, sublimely indifferent to inevitable consequences, yet dependent for results and even subsistence upon the practicalities which he ignores, Stockmann exemplifies the eternal struggle between principle and practice, and ironically is condoned only when his virtue can be attributed to ulterior motives. In similar fashion Mrs. Stockmann prefigures the eternal matriarch, whose interest in abstract principles is strictly conditional upon conservation of the family. The Burgomaster is the perennial bureaucrat, committed to the twin principles that his policies create right and that all adverse criticism is irresponsible. Hovstad is the professional liberal who crusades with editorial fearlessness for whatever is popular enough to boost circulation. Aslaksen is the generic man of cautious good will, who stands four-square for civic righteousness, so long as it costs nothing, and nothing ever comes of it. As for "the compact majority," it is the substance of public opinion, which is the impregnable conviction that any infringement of its sovereign complacency is manifestly wicked. Upon the naturalness with which these general implications follow from the specific instances of the dramatic action, and upon the skill with which the audience is brought to recognize in these specific instances the normalities of common human experience, the success of the play depends. Furthermore, since *An Enemy of the People* treads enthusiastically on a number of sensitive toes which are common property, no small part of its particular success depends upon the shrewd comic treatment which alleviates the sting without diluting the astringency of its satire.

The problem play is so common a type of modern drama that any recommendation of examples is bound to be arbitrary. On the other hand, for reasons mentioned earlier, the mortality rate among plays of this type is high. Bearing these cautions in mind, one may begin further exploration of the type with at least three of Ibsen's more famous plays: *A Doll's House, Ghosts,* and *Hedda Gabler.* Although technically problem plays may be differentiated as social or psychological, actually the two categories overlap so much that they are to be distinguished chiefly in terms of relative emphasis. The social problem play appears in *Justice* and *Loyalties* by John Galsworthy, the chief English exponent of the type, in *The Red Robe* and *The Three Daughters of M. Dupont* by Eugène Brieux, in *Mixed Marriage* by St. John Ervine, and in such plays by Shaw as *Mrs. Warren's Profession* and *The Doctor's Dilemma*. Representatives of the more common combined variety may be found in more recent plays like *The Silver Cord* by Sidney Howard, *Craig's Wife* by George Kelly, *Hotel Universe* by Philip Barry, or *The Children's Hour* by Lillian Hellman.

AN ENEMY

OF

THE PEOPLE

by

HENRIK IBSEN

TRANSLATED BY

ELEANOR MARX-AVELING

Characters in the Play

DR. THOMAS STOCKMANN, *medical officer of the Baths.*

MRS. STOCKMANN, *his wife.*

PETRA, *their daughter, a teacher.*

EILIF ⎱ *their sons, thirteen and*
MORTEN ⎰ *ten years old respectively.*

PETER STOCKMANN, *the doctor's elder brother, Burgomaster and chief of police, chairman of the Baths Committee, etc.*

MORTEN KIIL, *master tanner, Mrs. Stockmann's adoptive father.*

HOVSTAD, *editor of the "People's Messenger."*

BILLING, *on the staff of the paper.*

HORSTER, *a ship's captain.*

ASLAKSEN, *a printer.*

Participants in a meeting of citizens: all sorts and conditions of men, some women, and a band of schoolboys.

The action passes in a town on the South Coast of Norway.

Reprinted from *The Collected Works of Henrik Ibsen,* Vol. VIII, translated by William Archer and Eleanor Marx-Aveling; used by permission of the publishers, Charles Scribner's Sons.

Evening. DR. STOCKMANN'S *sitting-room; simply but neatly decorated and furnished. In the wall to the right are two doors, the further one leading to the hall, the nearer one to the Doctor's study. In the opposite wall, facing the hall door, a door leading to the other rooms of the house. Against the middle of this wall stands the stove; further forward a sofa with a mirror above it, and in front of it an oval table with a cover. On the table a lighted lamp, with a shade. In the back wall an open door leading to the dining-room, in which is seen a supper-table, with a lamp on it.*

[BILLING *is seated at the supper-table, with a napkin under his chin.* MRS. STOCKMANN *is standing by the table and placing before him a dish with a large joint of roast beef. The other seats round the table are empty; the table is in disorder, as after a meal.*]

MRS. STOCKMANN. If you come an hour late, Mr. Billing, you must put up with a cold supper.

BILLING. [*Eating.*] It is excellent— really first rate.

MRS. STOCKMANN. You know how Stockmann insists on regular meal-hours—

BILLING. Oh, I don't mind at all. I almost think I enjoy my supper more when I can sit down to it like this, alone and undisturbed.

MRS. STOCKMANN. Oh, well, if you enjoy it— [*Listening in the direction of the hall.*] I believe this is Mr. Hovstad coming too.

BILLING. Very likely.

[BURGOMASTER STOCKMANN *enters, wearing an overcoat and an official gold-laced cap, and carrying a stick.*]

BURGOMASTER. Good evening, sister-in-law.

MRS. STOCKMANN. [*Coming forward into the sitting-room.*] Oh, good evening; is it you? It is good of you to look in.

BURGOMASTER. I was just passing, and so— [*Looks towards the drawing-room.*] Ah, I see you have company.

MRS. STOCKMANN. [*Rather embarrassed.*] Oh no, not at all; it's the merest chance. [*Hurriedly.*] Won't you sit down and have a little supper?

BURGOMASTER. I? No, thank you. Good gracious! hot meat in the evening! That wouldn't suit my digestion.

MRS. STOCKMANN. Oh, for once in a way—

BURGOMASTER. No, no,—much obliged to you. I stick to tea and bread and butter. It's more wholesome in the long run—and rather more economical, too.

MRS. STOCKMANN. [*Smiling.*] You mustn't think Thomas and I are mere spendthrifts, either.

BURGOMASTER. You are not, sister-in-law; far be it from me to say that. [*Pointing to the Doctor's study.*] Is he not at home?

MRS. STOCKMANN. No, he has gone for a little turn after supper—with the boys.

BURGOMASTER. I wonder if that is a good thing to do. [*Listening.*] There he is, no doubt.

MRS. STOCKMANN. No, that is not he. [*A knock.*] Come in!

[HOVSTAD *enters from the hall.*]

MRS. STOCKMANN. Ah, it's Mr. Hovstad—

HOVSTAD. You must excuse me; I was detained at the printer's. Good evening, Burgomaster.

BURGOMASTER. [*Bowing rather stiffly.*] Mr. Hovstad? You come on business, I presume?

HOVSTAD. Partly. About an article for the paper.

BURGOMASTER. So I supposed. I hear my brother is an extremely prolific contributor to the *People's Messenger*.

HOVSTAD. Yes, when he wants to unburden his mind on one thing or another, he gives the *Messenger* the benefit.

MRS. STOCKMANN. [*To* HOVSTAD.] But will you not—? [*Points to the dining-room.*]

BURGOMASTER. Well, well, I am far from blaming him for writing for the class of readers he finds most in sympathy with him. And, personally, I have no reason to bear your paper any ill will, Mr. Hovstad.

HOVSTAD. No, I should think not.

BURGOMASTER. One may say, on the whole, that a fine spirit of mutual tolerance prevails in our town—an excellent public spirit. And that is because we have a great common interest to hold us together—an interest in which all right-minded citizens are equally concerned—

HOVSTAD. Yes—the Baths.

BURGOMASTER. Just so. We have our magnificent new Baths. Mark my words! The whole life of the town will centre around the Baths, Mr. Hovstad. There can be no doubt of it!

MRS. STOCKMANN. That is just what Thomas says.

BURGOMASTER. How marvellously the place has developed, even in this couple of years! Money has come into circulation, and brought life and movement with it. Houses and ground-rents rise in value every day.

HOVSTAD. And there are fewer people out of work.

BURGOMASTER. That is true. There is a gratifying diminution in the burden imposed on the well-to-do classes by the poor-rates;[1] and they will be still further lightened if only we have a really good summer this year—a rush of visitors—plenty of invalids, to give the Baths a reputation.

HOVSTAD. I hear there is every prospect of that.

BURGOMASTER. Things look most promising. Inquiries about apartments and so forth keep on pouring in.

HOVSTAD. Then the Doctor's paper will come in very opportunely.

BURGOMASTER. Has he been writing again?

HOVSTAD. This is a thing he wrote in the winter; enlarging on the virtues of the Baths, and on the excellent sanitary conditions of the town. But at that time I held it over.

BURGOMASTER. Ah—I suppose there was something not quite judicious about it?

[1] Taxes for support of the poor.

HOVSTAD. Not at all. But I thought it better to keep it till the spring when people are beginning to look about them, and think of their summer quarters—

BURGOMASTER. You were right, quite right, Mr. Hovstad.

MRS. STOCKMANN. Yes, Thomas is really indefatigable where the Baths are concerned.

BURGOMASTER. It is his duty as one of the staff.

HOVSTAD. And of course he was really their creator.

BURGOMASTER. Was he? Indeed! I gather that certain persons are of that opinion. But I should have thought that I, too, had a modest share in that undertaking.

MRS. STOCKMANN. Yes, that is what Thomas is always saying.

HOVSTAD. No one dreams of denying it, Burgomaster. You set the thing going, and put it on a practical basis; everybody knows that. I only meant that the original idea was the doctor's.

BURGOMASTER. Yes, my brother has certainly had ideas enough in his time—worse luck! But when it comes to realising them, Mr. Hovstad, we want men of another stamp. I should have thought that in this house at any rate—

MRS. STOCKMANN. Why, my dear brother-in-law—

HOVSTAD. Burgomaster, how can you—?

MRS. STOCKMANN. Do go in and have your supper, Mr. Hovstad; my husband is sure to be home directly.

HOVSTAD. Thanks; just a mouthful, perhaps. [He goes into the dining-room.]

BURGOMASTER. [Speaking in a low voice.] It is extraordinary how people who spring direct from the peasant class never can get over their want of tact.

MRS. STOCKMANN. But why should you care? Surely you and Thomas can share the honour, like brothers.

BURGOMASTER. Yes, one would suppose so; but it seems a share of the honour is not enough for some persons.

MRS. STOCKMANN. What nonsense! You

and Thomas always get on so well together. [*Listening.*] There, I think I hear him.

[*Goes and opens the door to the hall.*]

DR. STOCKMANN. [*Laughing and talking loudly, without.*] Here's another visitor for you, Katrina. Isn't it capital, eh? Come in, Captain Horster. Hang your coat on that peg. What! you don't wear an overcoat? Fancy, Katrina, I caught him in the street, and I could hardly get him to come in.

[CAPTAIN HORSTER *enters and bows to* MRS. STOCKMANN.]

DR. STOCKMANN. [*In the doorway.*] In with you, boys. They're famishing again! Come along, Captain Horster; you must try our roast beef—

[*He forces* HORSTER *into the dining-room.* EILIF *and* MORTEN *follow them.*]

MRS. STOCKMANN. But, Thomas, don't you see—

DR. STOCKMANN. [*Turning round in the doorway.*] Oh, is that you, Peter! [*Goes up to him and holds out his hand.*] Now this is really capital.

BURGOMASTER. Unfortunately, I have only a moment to spare—

DR. STOCKMANN. Nonsense! We shall have some toddy [2] in a minute. You're not forgetting the toddy, Katrina?

MRS. STOCKMANN. Of course not; the water's boiling.

[*She goes into the dining-room.*]

BURGOMASTER. Toddy too—!

DR. STOCKMANN. Yes; sit down, and let's make ourselves comfortable.

BURGOMASTER. Thanks; I never join in drinking parties.

DR. STOCKMANN. But this isn't a party.

BURGOMASTER. I don't know what else— [*Looks towards the dining-room.*] It's extraordinary how they can get through all that food.

DR. STOCKMANN. [*Rubbing his hands.*] Yes, doesn't it do one good to see young people eat? Always hungry! That's as it should be. They need good, solid meat to put stamina into them! It is they that have

[2] A hot whiskey drink.

got to whip up the ferment of the future, Peter.

BURGOMASTER. May I ask what there is to be "whipped up," as you call it?

DR. STOCKMANN. You'll have to ask the young people that—when the time comes. We shan't see it, of course. Two old fogies like you and me—

BURGOMASTER. Come, come! Surely that is a very extraordinary expression to use—

DR. STOCKMANN. Oh, you mustn't mind my nonsense, Peter. I'm in such glorious spirits, you see. I feel so unspeakably happy in the midst of all this growing, germinating life. Isn't it a marvellous time we live in! It seems as though a whole new world were springing up around us.

BURGOMASTER. Do you really think so?

DR. STOCKMANN. Of course, you can't see it as clearly as I do. You have passed your life in the midst of it all; and that deadens the impression. But I who had to vegetate all those years in that little hole in the north, hardly ever seeing a soul that could speak a stimulating word to me—all this affects me as if I had suddenly dropped into the heart of some teeming metropolis.

BURGOMASTER. Well, metropolis—

DR. STOCKMANN. Oh, I know well enough that things are on a small scale here, compared with many other places. But there's life here—there's promise— there's an infinity of things to work and strive for; and that is the main point. [*Calling.*] Katrina, haven't there been any letters?

MRS. STOCKMANN. [*In the dining-room.*] No, none at all.

DR. STOCKMANN. And then a good income, Peter! That's a thing one learns to appreciate when one has lived on starvation wages—

BURGOMASTER. Good heavens—!

DR. STOCKMANN. Oh yes, I can tell you we often had hard times of it up there. And now we can live like princes! To-day, for example, we had roast beef for dinner; and we've had some of it for supper too.

Won't you have some? Come along—just look at it, at any rate—

BURGOMASTER. No, no; certainly not—

DR. STOCKMANN. Well then, look here—do you see we've bought a table-cover?

BURGOMASTER. Yes, so I observed.

DR. STOCKMANN. And a lamp-shade, too. Do you see? Katrina has been saving up for them. They make the room look comfortable, don't they? Come over here. No, no, no, not there. So—yes! Now you see how it concentrates the light—. I really think it has quite an artistic effect. Eh?

BURGOMASTER. Yes, when one can afford such luxuries—

DR. STOCKMANN. Oh, I can afford it now. Katrina says I make almost as much as we spend.

BURGOMASTER. Ah—almost!

DR. STOCKMANN. Besides, a man of science must live in some style. Why, I believe a mere sheriff [3] spends much more a year than I do.

BURGOMASTER. Yes, I should think so! A member of the superior magistracy—

DR. STOCKMANN. Well then, even a common shipowner! A man of that sort will get through many times as much—

BURGOMASTER. That is natural, in your relative positions.

DR. STOCKMANN. And after all, Peter, I really don't squander any money. But I can't deny myself the delight of having people about me. I *must* have them. After living so long out of the world, I find it a necessity of life to have bright, cheerful, freedom-loving, hard-working young fellows around me—and that's what they are, all of them, that are sitting there eating so heartily. I wish you knew more of Hovstad—

BURGOMASTER. Ah, that reminds me—Hovstad was telling me that he is going to publish another article of yours.

DR. STOCKMANN. An article of mine?

BURGOMASTER. Yes, about the Baths. An article you wrote last winter.

[3] The chief magistrate of a county; hence an official of some importance.

DR. STOCKMANN. Oh, that one! But I don't want that to appear for the present.

BURGOMASTER. Why not? It seems to me this is the very time for it.

DR. STOCKMANN. Very likely—under ordinary circumstances—

[*Crosses the room.*]

BURGOMASTER. [*Following him with his eyes.*] And what is unusual in the circumstances now?

DR. STOCKMANN. [*Standing still.*] The fact is, Peter, I really cannot tell you just now; not this evening, at all events. There may prove to be a great deal that is unusual in the circumstances. On the other hand, there may be nothing at all. Very likely it's only my fancy.

BURGOMASTER. Upon my word, you are very enigmatical. Is there anything in the wind? Anything I am to be kept in the dark about? I should think, as Chairman of the Bath Committee—

DR. STOCKMANN. And I should think that I— Well, well, don't let us get our backs up, Peter.

BURGOMASTER. God forbid! I am not in the habit of "getting my back up," as you express it. But I must absolutely insist that all arrangements shall be made and carried out in a businesslike manner, and through the properly constituted authorities. I cannot be a party to crooked or underhand courses.

DR. STOCKMANN. Have *I* ever been given to crooked or underhand courses?

BURGOMASTER. At any rate you have an ingrained propensity to taking your own course. And that, in a well-ordered community, is almost as inadmissible. The individual must subordinate himself to society, or, more precisely, to the authorities whose business it is to watch over the welfare of society.

DR. STOCKMANN. Maybe. But what the devil has that to do with me?

BURGOMASTER. Why, this is the very thing, my dear Thomas, that it seems you will never learn. But take care; you will have to pay for it—sooner or later. Now I have warned you. Good-bye.

DR. STOCKMANN. Are you stark mad? You're on a totally wrong track—

BURGOMASTER. I am not often on the wrong track. Moreover, I must protest against— [*Bowing towards dining-room.*] Good-bye, sister-in-law; good-day to you, gentlemen. [*He goes.*]

MRS. STOCKMANN. [*Entering the sitting-room.*] Has he gone?

DR. STOCKMANN. Yes, and in a fine temper, too.

MRS. STOCKMANN. Why, my dear Thomas, what have you been doing to him now?

DR. STOCKMANN. Nothing at all. He can't possibly expect me to account to him for everything—before the time comes.

MRS. STOCKMANN. What have you to account to him for?

DR. STOCKMANN. H'm; — never mind about that, Katrina.—It's very odd the postman doesn't come.

[HOVSTAD, BILLING and HORSTER *have risen from table and come forward into the sitting-room.* EILIF *and* MORTEN *presently follow.*]

BILLING. [*Stretching himself.*] Ah! Strike me dead if one doesn't feel a new man after such a meal.

HOVSTAD. The Burgomaster didn't seem in the best of tempers this evening.

DR. STOCKMANN. That's his stomach. He has a very poor digestion.

HOVSTAD. I fancy it's the staff of the *Messenger* he finds it hardest to stomach.

MRS. STOCKMANN. I thought you got on well enough with him.

HOVSTAD. Oh, yes; but it's only a sort of armistice between us.

BILLING. That's it. That word sums up the situation.

DR. STOCKMANN. We must remember that Peter is a lonely bachelor, poor devil! He has no home to be happy in; only business, business. And then all that cursed weak tea he goes and pours down his throat! Now then, chairs round the table, boys! Katrina, shan't we have the toddy now?

MRS. STOCKMANN. [*Going towards the dining-room.*] I am just getting it.

DR. STOCKMANN. And you, Captain Horster, sit beside me on the sofa. So rare a guest as you—. Sit down, gentlemen, sit down.

[*The men sit round the table;* MRS. STOCKMANN *brings in a tray with kettle, glasses, decanters, etc.*]

MRS. STOCKMANN. Here you have it: here's arrak, and this is rum, and this cognac. Now, help yourselves.

DR. STOCKMANN. [*Taking a glass.*] So we will. [*While the toddy is being mixed.*] And now out with the cigars. Eilif, I think you know where the box is. And Morten, you may fetch my pipe. [*The boys go into the room on the right.*] I have a suspicion that Eilif sneaks a cigar now and then, but I pretend not to notice. [*Calls.*] And my smoking-cap, Morten! Katrina, can't you tell him where I left it. Ah, he's got it. [*The boys bring in the things.*] Now, friends, help yourselves. I stick to my pipe, you know;—this one has been on many a stormy journey with me, up there in the north. [*They clink glasses.*] Your health! Ah, I can tell you it's better fun to sit cosily here, safe from wind and weather.

MRS. STOCKMANN. [*Who sits knitting.*] Do you sail soon, Captain Horster?

HORSTER. I hope to be ready for a start by next week.

MRS. STOCKMANN. And you're going to America?

HORSTER. Yes, that's the intention.

BILLING. But then you'll miss the election of the new Town Council.

HORSTER. Is there to be an election again?

BILLING. Didn't you know?

HORSTER. No, I don't trouble myself about those things.

BILLING. But I suppose you take an interest in public affairs?

HORSTER. No, I don't understand anything about them.

BILLING. All the same, one ought at least to vote.

HORSTER. Even those who don't understand anything about it?

BILLING. Understand? Why, what do you mean by that? Society is like a ship: every man must put his hand to the helm.

HORSTER. That may be all right on shore; but at sea it wouldn't do at all.

HOVSTAD. It's remarkable how little sailors care about public affairs as a rule.

BILLING. Most extraordinary.

DR. STOCKMANN. Sailors are like birds of passage; they are at home both in the south and in the north. So it behooves the rest of us to be all the more energetic, Mr. Hovstad. Will there be anything of public interest in the *People's Messenger* to-morrow?

HOVSTAD. Nothing of local interest. But the day after to-morrow I think of printing your article—

DR. STOCKMANN. Oh, confound it, that article! No, you'll have to hold it over.

HOVSTAD. Really? We happen to have plenty of space, and I should say this was the very time for it—

DR. STOCKMANN. Yes, yes, you may be right; but you must hold it over all the same. I shall explain to you by-and-by.

[PETRA, *wearing a hat and cloak, and with a number of exercise-books under her arm, enters from the hall.*]

PETRA. Good evening.

DR. STOCKMANN. Good evening, Petra. Is that you?

[*General greetings.* PETRA *puts her cloak, hat, and books on a chair by the door.*]

PETRA. Here you all are, enjoying yourselves, while I've been out slaving.

DR. STOCKMANN. Well then, you come and enjoy yourself too.

BILLING. May I mix you a little—?

PETRA. [*Coming towards the table.*] Thank you, I'd rather help myself—you

always make it too strong. By the way, father, I have a letter for you.

[*Goes to the chair where her things are lying.*]

DR. STOCKMANN. A letter! From whom?

PETRA. [*Searching in the pocket of her cloak.*] I got it from the postman just as I was going out—

DR. STOCKMANN. [*Rising and going towards her.*] And you only bring it me now?

PETRA. I really hadn't time to run up again. Here it is.

DR. STOCKMANN. [*Seizing the letter.*] Let me see, let me see, child. [*Reads the address.*] Yes; this is it—!

MRS. STOCKMANN. Is it the one you have been so anxious about, Thomas?

DR. STOCKMANN. Yes, it is. I must go at once. Where shall I find a light, Katrina? Is there no lamp in my study again!

MRS. STOCKMANN. Yes—the lamp is lighted. It's on the writing-table.

DR. STOCKMANN. Good, good. Excuse me one moment—

[*He goes into the room on the right.*]

PETRA. What can it be, mother?

MRS. STOCKMANN. I don't know. For the last few days he has been continually on the look-out for the postman.

BILLING. Probably a country patient—

PETRA. Poor father! He'll soon have far too much to do. [*Mixes her toddy.*] Ah, this will taste good!

HOVSTAD. Have you been teaching in the night school as well to-day?

PETRA. [*Sipping from her glass.*] Two hours.

BILLING. And four hours in the morning at the institute—

PETRA. [*Sitting down by the table*] Five hours.

MRS. STOCKMANN. And I see you have exercises to correct this evening.

PETRA. Yes, a heap of them.

HORSTER. It seems to me you have plenty to do, too.

PETRA. Yes; but I like it. You feel so delightfully tired after it.

BILLING. Do you like that?

PETRA. Yes, for then you sleep so well.

MORTEN. I say, Petra, you must be a great sinner.

PETRA. A sinner?

MORTEN. Yes, if you work so hard. Mr. Rörlund says work is a punishment for our sins.

EILIF. [Contemptuously.] Bosh! What a silly you are, to believe such stuff as that.

MRS. STOCKMANN. Come, come, Eilif.

BILLING. [Laughing.] Capital, capital!

HOVSTAD. Should you not like to work so hard, Morten?

MORTEN. No, I shouldn't.

HOVSTAD. Then what will you do with yourself in the world?

MORTEN. I should like to be a Viking.

EILIF. But then you'd have to be a heathen.

MORTEN. Well, so I would.

BILLING. There I agree with you, Morten! I say just the same thing.

MRS. STOCKMANN. [Making a sign to him.] No, no, Mr. Billing, I'm sure you don't.

BILLING. Strike me dead but I do, though. I am a heathen, and I'm proud of it. You'll see we shall all be heathens soon.

MORTEN. And shall we be able to do anything we like then?

BILLING. Well, you see, Morten—

MRS. STOCKMANN. Now run away, boys; I'm sure you have lessons to prepare for to-morrow.

EILIF. You might let me stay just a little longer—

MRS. STOCKMANN. No, you must go, too. Be off, both of you.

[The boys say good-night and go into the room on the left.]

HOVSTAD. Do you really think it can hurt the boys to hear these things?

MRS. STOCKMANN. Well, I don't know; I don't like it.

PETRA. Really, mother, I think you are quite wrong there.

MRS. STOCKMANN. Perhaps. But I don't like it—not here, at home.

PETRA. There's no end of hypocrisy both at home and at school. At home you must hold your tongue, and at school you have to stand up and tell lies to the children.

HORSTER. Have you to tell lies?

PETRA. Yes; do you think we don't have to tell them many and many a thing we don't believe ourselves?

BILLING. Ah, that's too true.

PETRA. If only I could afford it, I should start a school myself, and things should be very different there.

BILLING. Oh, afford it—!

HORSTER. If you really think of doing that, Miss Stockmann, I shall be delighted to let you have a room at my place. You know my father's old house is nearly empty; there's a great big dining-room on the ground floor—

PETRA. [Laughing.] Oh, thank you very much—but I'm afraid it won't come to anything.

HOVSTAD. No, I fancy Miss Petra is more likely to go over to journalism. By the way, have you had time to look into the English novel you promised to translate for us?

PETRA. Not yet. But you shall have it in good time.

[DR. STOCKMANN enters from his room, with the letter open in his hand.]

DR. STOCKMANN. [Flourishing the letter.] Here's news, I can tell you, that will waken up the town!

BILLING. News?

MRS. STOCKMANN. What news?

DR. STOCKMANN. A great discovery, Katrina!

HOVSTAD. Indeed?

MRS. STOCKMANN. Made by you?

DR. STOCKMANN. Precisely — by me! [Walks up and down.] Now let them go on accusing me of fads and crackbrained notions. But they won't dare to! Ha-ha! I tell you they won't dare!

PETRA. Do tell us what it is, father.

DR. STOCKMANN. Well, well, give me time, and you shall hear all about it. If only I had Peter here now! This just shows how we men can go about forming judgments like the blindest moles—

HOVSTAD. What do you mean, Doctor?

DR. STOCKMANN. [*Stopping beside the table.*] Isn't it the general opinion that our town is a healthy place?

HOVSTAD. Of course.

DR. STOCKMANN. A quite exceptionally healthy place, indeed—a place to be warmly recommended, both to invalids and people in health—

MRS. STOCKMANN. My dear Thomas—

DR. STOCKMANN. And assuredly we haven't failed to recommend and belaud it. I've sung its praises again and again, both in the *Messenger* and in pamphlets—

HOVSTAD. Well, what then?

DR. STOCKMANN. These Baths, that we have called the pulse of the town, its vital nerve, and—and the devil knows what else—

BILLING. "Our city's palpitating heart," I once ventured to call them in a convivial moment—

DR. STOCKMANN. Yes, I daresay. Well —do you know what they really are, these mighty, magnificent, belauded Baths, that have cost so much money—do you know what they are?

HOVSTAD. No, what are they?

MRS. STOCKMANN. Do tell us.

DR. STOCKMANN. Simply a pestiferous hole.

PETRA. The Baths, father?

MRS. STOCKMANN. [*At the same time.*] Our Baths!

HOVSTAD. [*Also at the same time.*] But, Doctor—!

BILLING. Oh, it's incredible!

DR. STOCKMANN. I tell you the whole place is a poisonous whited-sepulchre; noxious in the highest degree! All that filth up there in the Mill Dale—the stuff that smells so horribly—taints the water in the feed-pipes of the Pump-Room; and the same accursed poisonous refuse oozes out by the beach—

HOVSTAD. Where the sea-baths are?

DR. STOCKMANN. Exactly.

HOVSTAD. But how are you so sure of all this, Doctor?

DR. STOCKMANN. I've investigated the whole thing as conscientiously as possible. I've long had my suspicions about it. Last year we had some extraordinary cases of illness among the patients—both typhoid and gastric attacks—

MRS. STOCKMANN. Yes, I remember.

DR. STOCKMANN. We thought at the time that the visitors had brought the infection with them; but afterwards—last winter —I began to question that. So I set about testing the water as well as I could.

MRS. STOCKMANN. It was *that* you were working so hard at!

DR. STOCKMANN. Yes, you may well say I've worked, Katrina. But here, you know, I hadn't the necessary scientific appliances; so I sent samples both of our drinking-water and of our sea-water to the University, for exact analysis by a chemist.

HOVSTAD. And you have received his report?

DR. STOCKMANN. [*Showing letter.*] Here it is! And it proves beyond dispute the presence of putrefying organic matter in the water—millions of infusoria. It's absolutely pernicious to health, whether used internally or externally.

MRS. STOCKMANN. What a blessing you found it out in time!

DR. STOCKMANN. Yes, you may well say that.

HOVSTAD. And what do you intend to do now, Doctor?

DR. STOCKMANN. Why, to set things right, of course.

HOVSTAD. You think it can be done, then?

DR. STOCKMANN. It *must* be done. Else the whole Baths are useless, ruined. But there's no fear. I am quite clear as to what is required.

MRS. STOCKMANN. But, my dear Thomas, why should you have made such a secret of all this?

DR. STOCKMANN. Would you have had

me rush all over the town and chatter about it, before I was quite certain? No, thank you; I'm not so mad as that.

PETRA. But to us at home—

DR. STOCKMANN. I couldn't say a word to a living soul. But to-morrow you may look in at the Badger's—

MRS. STOCKMANN. Oh, Thomas!

DR. STOCKMANN. Well, well, at your grandfather's. The old fellow *will* be astonished! He thinks I'm not quite right in my head—yes, and plenty of others think the same, I've noticed. But now these good people shall see—yes, they shall see now! [*Walks up and down rubbing his hands.*] What a stir there will be in the town, Katrina! Just think of it! All the water-pipes will have to be relaid.

HOVSTAD. [*Rising.*] All the water-pipes?

DR. STOCKMANN. Why, of course. The intake is too low down; it must be moved much higher up.

PETRA. So you were right, after all.

DR. STOCKMANN. Yes, do you remember, Petra? I wrote against it when they were beginning the works. But no one would listen to me then. Now, you may be sure, I shall give them my full broadside —for of course I've prepared a statement for the Directors; it has been lying ready a whole week; I've only been waiting for this report. [*Points to letter.*] But now they shall have it at once. [*Goes into his room and returns with a MS. in his hand.*] See! Four closely written sheets! And I'll enclose the report. A newspaper, Katrina! Get me something to wrap them up in. There—that's it. Give it to—to— [*Stamps.*] —what the devil's her name? Give it to the girl, I mean, and tell her to take it at once to the Burgomaster.

[MRS. STOCKMANN *goes out with the packet through the dining-room.*]

PETRA. What do you think Uncle Peter will say, father?

DR. STOCKMANN. What should he say? He can't possibly be otherwise than pleased that so important a fact has been brought to light.

HOVSTAD. I suppose you will let me put a short announcement of your discovery in the *Messenger.*

DR. STOCKMANN. Yes, I shall be much obliged if you will.

HOVSTAD. It is highly desirable that the public should know about it as soon as possible.

DR. STOCKMANN. Yes, certainly.

MRS. STOCKMANN. [*Returning.*] She's gone with it.

BILLING. Strike me dead if you won't be the first man in the town, Doctor.

DR. STOCKMANN. [*Walks up and down in high glee.*] Oh, nonsense! After all, I have done no more than my duty. I've been a lucky treasure-hunter, that's all. But all the same—

BILLING. Hovstad, don't you think the town ought to get up a torchlight procession in honour of Dr. Stockmann?

HOVSTAD. I shall certainly propose it.

BILLING. And I'll talk it over with Aslaksen.

DR. STOCKMANN. No, my dear friends; let all such claptrap alone. I won't hear of anything of the sort. And if the Directors should want to raise my salary, I won't accept it. I tell you, Katrina, I will not accept it.

MRS. STOCKMANN. You are quite right, Thomas.

PETRA. [*Raising her glass.*] Your health, father!

HOVSTAD *and* BILLING. Your health, your health, Doctor!

HORSTER. [*Clinking glasses with the* DOCTOR.] I hope you may have nothing but joy of your discovery.

DR. STOCKMANN. Thanks, thanks, my dear friends! I can't tell you how happy I am—! Oh, what a blessing it is to feel that you have deserved well of your native town and your fellow citizens. Hurrah, Katrina!

[*He puts both his arms round her neck, and whirls her round with him.* MRS. STOCKMANN *screams and struggles. A burst of laughter, applause, and cheers for the* DOCTOR. *The boys thrust their heads in at the door as the curtain falls.*]

ACT SECOND

The DOCTOR'S *sitting-room. The dining-room door is closed. Morning.*

[MRS. STOCKMANN *enters from the dining-room with a sealed letter in her hand, goes to the foremost door on the right, and peeps in.*]

MRS. STOCKMANN. Are you there, Thomas?

DR. STOCKMANN. [*Within.*] Yes, I have just come in. [*Enters.*] What is it?

MRS. STOCKMANN. A letter from your brother. [*Hands it to him.*]

DR. STOCKMANN. Aha, let us see. [*Opens the envelope and reads.*] "The MS. sent me is returned herewith—" [*Reads on, mumbling to himself.*] H'm—

MRS. STOCKMANN. Well, what does he say?

DR. STOCKMANN. [*Putting the paper in his pocket.*] Nothing; only that he'll come up himself about midday.

MRS. STOCKMANN. Then be sure you remember to stay at home.

DR. STOCKMANN. Oh, I can easily manage that; I've finished my morning's visits.

MRS. STOCKMANN. I am very curious to know how he takes it.

DR. STOCKMANN. You'll see he won't be over-pleased that it is I that have made the discovery, and not he himself.

MRS. STOCKMANN. Ah, that's just what I'm afraid of.

DR. STOCKMANN. Of course at bottom he'll be glad. But still—Peter is damnably unwilling that any one but himself should do anything for the good of the town.

MRS. STOCKMANN. Do you know, Thomas, I think you might stretch a point, and share the honour with him. Couldn't it appear that it was he that put you on the track—?

DR. STOCKMANN. By all means, for aught I care. If only I can get things put straight—

[Old MORTEN KIIL *puts his head in at the hall door, and asks slyly.*]

MORTEN KIIL. Is it—is it true?

MRS. STOCKMANN. [*Going towards him.*] Father—is that you?

DR. STOCKMANN. Hallo, father-in-law! Good morning, good morning.

MRS. STOCKMANN. Do come in.

MORTEN KIIL. Yes, if it's true; if not, I'm off again.

DR. STOCKMANN. If what is true?

MORTEN KIIL. This crazy business about the water-works. Now, is it true?

DR. STOCKMANN. Why, of course it is. But how came *you* to hear of it?

MORTEN KIIL. [*Coming in.*] Petra looked in on her way to the school—

DR. STOCKMANN. Oh, did she?

MORTEN KIIL. Ay, ay—and she told me—. I thought she was only making game of me; but that's not like Petra either.

DR. STOCKMANN. No, indeed; how could you think so?

MORTEN KIIL. Oh, you can never be sure of anybody. You may be made a fool of before you know where you are. So it is true, after all?

DR. STOCKMANN. Most certainly it is. Do sit down, father-in-law. [*Forces him down on the sofa.*] Now isn't it a real blessing for the town—?

MORTEN KIIL. [*Suppressing his laughter.*] A blessing for the town?

DR. STOCKMANN. Yes, that I made this discovery in time—

MORTEN KIIL. [*As before.*] Ay, ay, ay! —Well, I could never have believed that you would play monkey-tricks with your very own brother.

DR. STOCKMANN. Monkey-tricks!

MRS. STOCKMANN. Why, father dear—

MORTEN KIIL. [*Resting his hands and chin on the top of his stick and blinking slyly at the* DOCTOR.] What was it again? Wasn't it that some animals had got into the water-pipes?

DR. STOCKMANN. Yes; infusorial animals.

MORTEN KIIL. And any number of

these animals had got in, Petra said—whole swarms of them.

DR. STOCKMANN. Certainly; hundreds of thousands.

MORTEN KIIL. But no one can see them—isn't that it?

DR. STOCKMANN. Quite right; no one can see them.

MORTEN KIIL. [*With a quiet, chuckling laugh.*] I'll be damned if that isn't the best thing I've heard of you yet.

DR. STOCKMANN. What do you mean?

MORTEN KIIL. But you'll never in this world make the Burgomaster take in anything of the sort.

DR. STOCKMANN. Well, that we shall see.

MORTEN KIIL. Do you really think he'll be so crazy?

DR. STOCKMANN. I hope the whole town will be so crazy.

MORTEN KIIL. The whole town! Well, I don't say but it may. But it serves them right; it'll teach them a lesson. They wanted to be so much cleverer than we old fellows. They hounded me out of the Town Council. Yes; I tell you they hounded me out like a dog, that they did. But now it's their turn. Just you keep up the game with them, Stockmann.

DR. STOCKMANN. Yes, but, father-in-law—

MORTEN KIIL. Keep it up, I say. [*Rising.*] If you can make the Burgomaster and his gang eat humble pie, I'll give a hundred crowns straight away to the poor.

DR. STOCKMANN. Come, that's good of you.

MORTEN KIIL. Of course, I've little enough to throw away; but if you can manage that, I shall certainly remember the poor at Christmas-time, to the tune of fifty crowns.

[HOVSTAD *enters from hall.*]

HOVSTAD. Good morning! [*Pausing.*] Oh! I beg your pardon—

DR. STOCKMANN. Not at all. Come in, come in.

MORTEN KIIL. [*Chuckling again.*] He! Is he in it, too?

HOVSTAD. What do you mean?

DR. STOCKMANN. Yes, of course he is.

MORTEN KIIL. I might have known it! It's to go into the papers. Ah, you're the one, Stockmann! Do you two lay your heads together; I'm off.

DR. STOCKMANN. Oh no; don't go yet, father-in-law.

MORTEN KIIL. No, I'm off now. Play them all the monkey-tricks you can think of. Deuce take me but you shan't lose by it.

[*He goes,* MRS. STOCKMANN *accompanying him.*]

DR. STOCKMANN. [*Laughing.*] What do you think—? The old fellow doesn't believe a word of all this about the water-works.

HOVSTAD. Was that what he—?

DR. STOCKMANN. Yes; that was what we were talking about. And I daresay you have come on the same business.

HOVSTAD. Yes. Have you a moment to spare, Doctor?

DR. STOCKMANN. As many as you like, my dear fellow.

HOVSTAD. Have you heard anything from the Burgomaster?

DR. STOCKMANN. Not yet. He'll be here presently.

HOVSTAD. I have been thinking the matter over since last evening.

DR. STOCKMANN. Well?

HOVSTAD. To you, as a doctor and a man of science, this business of the water-works appears an isolated affair. I daresay it hasn't occurred to you that a good many other things are bound up with it?

DR. STOCKMANN. Indeed! In what way? Let us sit down, my dear fellow.—No; there, on the sofa.

[HOVSTAD *sits on sofa: the* DOCTOR *in an easy-chair on the other side of the table.*]

Well, so you think—?

HOVSTAD. You said yesterday that the water is polluted by impurities in the soil.

DR. STOCKMANN. Yes, undoubtedly; the

mischief comes from that poisonous swamp up in the Mill Dale.

HOVSTAD. Excuse me, Doctor, but I think it comes from a very different swamp.

DR. STOCKMANN. What swamp may that be?

HOVSTAD. The swamp in which our whole municipal life is rotting.

DR. STOCKMANN. The devil, Mr. Hovstad! What notion is this you've got hold of?

HOVSTAD. All the affairs of the town have gradually drifted into the hands of a pack of bureaucrats—

DR. STOCKMANN. Come now, they're not all bureaucrats.

HOVSTAD. No; but those who are not are the friends and adherents of those who are. We are entirely under the thumb of a ring of wealthy men, men of old family and position in the town.

DR. STOCKMANN. Yes, but they are also men of ability and insight.

HOVSTAD. Did they show ability and insight when they laid the water-pipes where they are?

DR. STOCKMANN. No; that, of course, was a piece of stupidity. But that will be set right now.

HOVSTAD. Do you think it will go so smoothly?

DR. STOCKMANN. Well, smoothly or not, it will have to be done.

HOVSTAD. Yes, if the press exerts its influence.

DR. STOCKMANN. Not at all necessary, my dear fellow; I am sure my brother—

HOVSTAD. Excuse me, Doctor, but I must tell you that I think of taking the matter up.

DR. STOCKMANN. In the paper?

HOVSTAD. Yes. When I took over the *People's Messenger,* I was determined to break up the ring of obstinate old blockheads who held everything in their hands.

DR. STOCKMANN. But you told me yourself what came of it. You nearly ruined the paper.

HOVSTAD. Yes, at that time we had to draw in our horns, that's true enough. The whole Bath scheme might have fallen through if these men had been sent about their business. But now the Baths are an accomplished fact, and we can get on without these august personages.

DR. STOCKMANN. Get on without them, yes; but still we owe them a great deal.

HOVSTAD. The debt shall be duly acknowledged. But a journalist of my democratic tendencies cannot let such an opportunity slip through his fingers. We must explode the tradition of official infallibility. That rubbish must be got rid of, like every other superstition.

DR. STOCKMANN. There I am with you with all my heart, Mr. Hovstad. If it's a superstition, away with it!

HOVSTAD. I should be sorry to attack the Burgomaster, as he is your brother. But I know you think with me—the truth before all other considerations.

DR. STOCKMANN. Why, of course. [*Vehemently.*] But still—! but still—!

HOVSTAD. You mustn't think ill of me. I am neither more self-interested nor more ambitious than other men.

DR. STOCKMANN. Why, my dear fellow —who says you are?

HOVSTAD. I come of humble folk, as you know; and I have had ample opportunities of seeing what the lower classes really require. And that is to have a share in the direction of public affairs, Doctor. That is what develops ability and knowledge and self-respect—

DR. STOCKMANN. I understand that perfectly.

HOVSTAD. Yes; and I think a journalist incurs a heavy responsibility if he lets slip a chance of helping to emancipate the downtrodden masses. I know well enough that our oligarchy will denounce me as an agitator, and so forth; but what do I care? If only my conscience is clear, I—

DR. STOCKMANN. Just so, just so, my dear Mr. Hovstad. But still—deuce take it—! [*A knock at the door.*] Come in!

[ASLAKSEN, *the printer, appears at the door leading to the hall. He is humbly but respectably dressed in black, wears a white necktie, slightly crumpled, and has a silk hat and gloves in his hand.*]

ASLAKSEN. [*Bowing.*] I beg pardon, Doctor, for making so bold—

DR. STOCKMANN. [*Rising.*] Hallo! If it isn't Mr. Aslaksen!

ASLAKSEN. Yes, it's me, Doctor.

HOVSTAD. [*Rising.*] Is it me you want, Aslaksen?

ASLAKSEN. No, not at all. I didn't know you were here. No, it's the Doctor himself—

DR. STOCKMANN. Well, what can I do for you?

ASLAKSEN. Is it true, what Mr. Billing tells me, that you're going to get us a better set of water-works?

DR. STOCKMANN. Yes, for the Baths.

ASLAKSEN. Of course, of course. Then I just looked in to say that I'll back up the movement with all my might.

HOVSTAD. [*To the* DOCTOR.] You see!

DR. STOCKMANN. I'm sure I thank you heartily; but—

ASLAKSEN. You may find it no such bad thing to have us small middle-class men at your back. We form what you may call a compact majority in the town—when we really make up our minds, that's to say. And it's always well to have the majority with you, Doctor.

DR. STOCKMANN. No doubt, no doubt; but I can't conceive that any special measures will be necessary in this case. I should think in so clear and straightforward a matter—

ASLAKSEN. Yes, but all the same, it can do no harm. I know the local authorities very well—the powers that be are not over-ready to adopt suggestions from outsiders. So I think it wouldn't be amiss if we made some sort of a demonstration.

HOVSTAD. Precisely my opinion.

DR. STOCKMANN. A demonstration, you say? But in what way would you demonstrate?

ASLAKSEN. Of course, with great moderation, Doctor. I always insist upon moderation; for moderation is a citizen's first virtue—at least that's my way of thinking.

DR. STOCKMANN. We all know that, Mr. Aslaksen.

ASLAKSEN. Yes, I think my moderation is generally recognised. And this affair of the water-works is very important for us small middle-class men. The Baths bid fair to become, as you might say, a little gold-mine for the town. We shall all have to live by the Baths, especially we house-owners. So we want to support the Baths all we can; and as I am Chairman of the House-owners' Association—

DR. STOCKMANN. Well—?

ASLAKSEN. And as I'm an active worker for the Temperance Society—of course, you know, Doctor, that I'm a temperance man?

DR. STOCKMANN. To be sure, to be sure.

ASLAKSEN. Well, you'll understand that I come in contact with a great many people. And as I'm known to be a prudent and law-abiding citzen, as you yourself remarked, Doctor, I have a certain influence in the town, and hold some power in my hands—though I say it that shouldn't.

DR. STOCKMANN. I know that very well, Mr. Aslaksen.

ASLAKSEN. Well then, you see—it would be easy for me to get up an address, if it came to a pinch.

DR. STOCKMANN. An address.

ASLAKSEN. Yes, a kind of vote of thanks to you, from the citizens of the town, for your action in a matter of such general concern. Of course, it will have to be drawn up with all fitting moderation, so as to give no offence to the authorities and parties in power. But so long as we're careful about that, no one can take it ill, I should think.

HOVSTAD. Well, even if they didn't particularly like it—

ASLAKSEN. No, no, no; no offence to the powers that be, Mr. Hovstad. No opposition to people that can take it out of us again so easily. I've had enough of that in my time; no good ever comes of it. But no one can object to the free but temperate expression of a citizen's opinion.

DR. STOCKMANN. [*Shaking his hand.*] I

can't tell you, my dear Mr. Aslaksen, how heartily it delights me to find so much support among my fellow townsmen. I'm so happy—so happy! Come, you'll have a glass of sherry? Eh?

ASLAKSEN. No, thank you; I never touch spirituous liquors.

DR. STOCKMANN. Well, then, a glass of beer—what do you say to that?

ASLAKSEN. Thanks, not that either, Doctor. I never take anything so early in the day. And now I'll be off round the town, and talk to some of the house-owners, and prepare public opinion.

DR. STOCKMANN. It's extremely kind of you, Mr. Aslaksen; but I really cannot get it into my head that all these preparations are necessary. The affair seems to me so simple and self-evident.

ASLAKSEN. The authorities always move slowly, Doctor—God forbid I should blame them for it—

HOVSTAD. We'll stir them up in the paper to-morrow, Aslaksen.

ASLAKSEN. No violence, Mr. Hovstad. Proceed with moderation, or you'll do nothing with them. Take my advice; I've picked up experience in the school of life.—And now I'll say good morning, Doctor. You know now that at least you have us small middle-class men behind you, solid as a wall. You have the compact majority on your side, Doctor.

DR. STOCKMANN. Many thanks, my dear Mr. Aslaksen. [Holds out his hand.] Good-bye, good-bye.

ASLAKSEN. Are you coming to the office, Mr. Hovstad?

HOVSTAD. I shall come on presently. I have still one or two things to arrange.

ASLAKSEN. Very well.

[Bows and goes. DR. STOCKMANN accompanies him into the hall.]

HOVSTAD. [As the DOCTOR re-enters.] Well, what do you say to that, Doctor? Don't you think it is high time we should give all this weak-kneed, half-hearted cowardice a good shaking up?

DR. STOCKMANN. Are you speaking of Aslaksen?

HOVSTAD. Yes, I am. He's a decent enough fellow, but he's one of those who are sunk in the swamp. And most people here are just like him; they are forever wavering and wobbling from side to side: what with scruples and misgivings, they never dare advance a step.

DR. STOCKMANN. Yes, but Aslaksen seems to me thoroughly well-intentioned.

HOVSTAD. There is one thing I value more than good intentions, and that is an attitude of manly self-reliance.

DR. STOCKMANN. There I am quite with you.

HOVSTAD. So I am going to seize this opportunity, and try whether I can't for once put a little grit into their good intentions. The worship of authority must be rooted up in this town. This gross, inexcusable blunder of the water-works must be brought home clearly to every voter.

DR. STOCKMANN. Very well. If you think it's for the good of the community, so be it; but not till I have spoken to my brother.

HOVSTAD. At all events, I shall be writing my leader in the meantime. And if the Burgomaster won't take the matter up—

DR. STOCKMANN. But how can you conceive his refusing?

HOVSTAD. Oh, it's not inconceivable. And then—

DR. STOCKMANN. Well then, I promise you—; look here—in that case you may print my paper—put it in just as it is.

HOVSTAD. May I? Is that a promise?

DR. STOCKMANN. [Handing him the manuscript.] There it is; take it with you. You may as well read it in any case; you can return it to me afterwards.

HOVSTAD. Very good; I shall do so. And now, good-bye, Doctor.

DR. STOCKMANN. Good-bye, good-bye. You'll see it will all go smoothly, Mr. Hovstad—as smoothly as possible.

HOVSTAD. H'm—we shall see.

[Bows and goes out through the hall.]

DR. STOCKMANN. [Going to the dining-room door and looking in.] Katrina! Hallo! are you back, Petra?

PETRA. [*Entering.*] Yes, I've just got back from school.

MRS. STOCKMANN. [*Entering.*] Hasn't he been here yet?

DR. STOCKMANN. Peter? No; but I have been having a long talk with Hovstad. He's quite enthusiastic about my discovery. It turns out to be of much wider import than I thought at first. So he has placed his paper at my disposal, if I should require it.

MRS. STOCKMANN. Do you think you will?

DR. STOCKMANN. Not I! But at the same time, one cannot but be proud to know that the enlightened, independent press is on one's side. And what do you think? I have had a visit from the Chairman of the House-owners' Association, too.

MRS. STOCKMANN. Really? What did he want?

DR. STOCKMANN. To assure me of his support. They will all stand by me at a pinch. Katrina, do you know what I have behind me?

MRS. STOCKMANN. Behind you? No. What have you behind you?

DR. STOCKMANN. The compact majority!

MRS. STOCKMANN. Oh! Is that good for you, Thomas?

DR. STOCKMANN. Yes, indeed; I should think it *was* good. [*Rubbing his hands as he walks up and down.*] Great God! what a delight it is to feel oneself in such brotherly unison with one's fellow townsmen!

PETRA. And to do so much that's good and useful, father!

DR. STOCKMANN. And all for one's native town, too!

MRS. STOCKMANN. There's the bell.

DR. STOCKMANN. That must be he. [*Knock at the door.*] Come in!

[*Enter* BURGOMASTER STOCKMANN *from the hall.*]

BURGOMASTER. Good morning.

DR. STOCKMANN. I'm glad to see you, Peter.

MRS. STOCKMANN. Good morning, brother-in-law. How are you?

BURGOMASTER. Oh, thanks, so-so. [*To the* DOCTOR.] Yesterday evening, after office hours, I received from you a dissertation upon the state of the water at the Baths.

DR. STOCKMANN. Yes. Have you read it?

BURGOMASTER. I have.

DR. STOCKMANN. And what do you think of the affair?

BURGOMASTER. H'm—
[*With a sidelong glance.*]

MRS. STOCKMANN. Come, Petra.

[*She and* PETRA *go into the room on the left.*]

BURGOMASTER. [*After a pause.*] Was it necessary to make all these investigations behind my back?

DR. STOCKMANN. Yes, till I was absolutely certain, I—

BURGOMASTER. And are you absolutely certain now?

DR. STOCKMANN. My paper must surely have convinced you of that.

BURGOMASTER. Is it your intention to submit this statement to the Board of Directors, as a sort of official document?

DR. STOCKMANN. Of course. Something must be done in the matter, and that promptly.

BURGOMASTER. As usual, you use very strong expressions in your statement. Amongst other things, you say that what we offer our visitors is a slow poison.

DR. STOCKMANN. Why, Peter, what else can it be called? Only think—poisoned water both internally and externally! And that to poor invalids who come to us in all confidence, and pay us handsomely to cure them!

BURGOMASTER. And then you announce as your conclusion that we must build a sewer to carry off the alleged impurities from the Mill Dale, and must re-lay all the water-pipes.

DR. STOCKMANN. Yes. Can you suggest any other plan?—I know of none.

BURGOMASTER. I found a pretext for looking in at the town engineer's this morning, and—in a half-jesting way—I mentioned these alterations as things we might possibly have to consider, at some future time.

DR. STOCKMANN. At some future time!

BURGOMASTER. Of course, he smiled at what he thought my extravagance. Have you taken the trouble to think what your proposed alterations would cost? From what the engineer said, I gathered that the expenses would probably mount up to several hundred thousand crowns.

DR. STOCKMANN. So much as that?

BORGOMASTER. Yes. But that is not the worst. The work would take at least two years.

DR. STOCKMANN. Two years! Do you mean to say two whole years?

BURGOMASTER. At least. And what are we to do with the Baths in the meanwhile? Are we to close them? We should have no alternative. Do you think any one would come here, if it got abroad that the water was pestilential?

DR. STOCKMANN. But, Peter, that's precisely what it is.

BURGOMASTER. And all this now, just now, when the Baths are doing so well! Neighbouring towns, too, are not without their claims to rank as health-resorts. Do you think they would not at once set to work to divert the full stream of visitors to themselves? Undoubtedly they would; and we should be left stranded. We should probably have to give up the whole costly undertaking; and so you would have ruined your native town.

DR. STOCKMANN. I—ruined—!

BURGOMASTER. It is only through the Baths that the town has any future worth speaking of. You surely know that as well as I do.

DR. STOCKMANN. Then what do you think should be done?

BURGOMASTER. I have not succeeded in convincing myself that the condition of the water at the Baths is as serious as your statement represents.

DR. STOCKMANN. I tell you it's if anything worse—or will be in the summer, when the hot weather sets in.

BURGOMASTER. I repeat that I believe you exaggerate greatly. A competent physician should know what measures to take—he should be able to obviate deleterious influences, and to counteract them in case they should make themselves unmistakably felt.

DR. STOCKMANN. Indeed—? And then?

BURGOMASTER. The existing waterworks are, once for all, a fact, and must naturally be treated as such. But when the time comes, the Directors will probably not be indisposed to consider whether it may not be possible, without unreasonable pecuniary sacrifices, to introduce certain improvements.

DR. STOCKMANN. And do you imagine I could ever be a party to such dishonesty?

BURGOMASTER. Dishonesty?

DR. STOCKMANN. Yes, it would be dishonesty—a fraud, a lie, an absolute crime against the public, against society as a whole!

BURGOMASTER. I have not, as I before remarked, been able to convince myself that there is really any such imminent danger.

DR. STOCKMANN. You have! You must have! I know that my demonstration is absolutely clear and convincing. And you understand it perfectly, Peter, only you won't admit it. It was you who insisted that both the Bath-buildings and the waterworks should be placed where they now are; and it's that—it's that damned blunder that you won't confess. Pshaw! Do you think I don't see through you?

BURGOMASTER. And even if it were so? If I do watch over my reputation with a certain anxiety, I do it for the good of the town. Without moral authority I cannot guide and direct affairs in the way I consider most conducive to the general welfare. Therefore—and on various other grounds—it is of great moment to me that your statement should not be submitted to the Board of Directors. It must be kept back, for the good of the community. Later on I will bring up the matter for discussion, and we will do the best we can, quietly; but not a word, not a whisper, of this unfortunate business must come to the public ears.

DR. STOCKMANN. But it can't be prevented now, my dear Peter.

BURGOMASTER. It must and shall be prevented.

DR. STOCKMANN. It can't be, I tell you; far too many people know about it already.

BURGOMASTER. Know about it! Who? Surely not those fellows on the *People's Messenger*—?

DR. STOCKMANN. Oh, yes; they know. The liberal, independent press will take good care that you do your duty.

BURGOMASTER. [*After a short pause.*] You are an amazingly reckless man, Thomas. Have not you reflected what the consequences of this may be to yourself?

DR. STOCKMANN. Consequences?—Consequences to me?

BURGOMASTER. Yes—to you and yours.

DR. STOCKMANN. What the devil do you mean?

BURGOMASTER. I believe I have always shown myself ready and willing to lend you a helping hand.

DR. STOCKMANN. Yes, you have, and I thank you for it.

BURGOMASTER. I ask for no thanks. Indeed, I was in some measure forced to act as I did—for my own sake. I always hoped I should be able to keep you a little in check, if I helped to improve your pecuniary position.

DR. STOCKMANN. What! So it was only for your own sake—!

BURGOMASTER. In a measure, I say. It is painful for a man in an official position, when his nearest relative goes and compromises himself time after time.

DR. STOCKMANN. And you think I do that?

BURGOMASTER. Yes, unfortunately, you do, without knowing it. Yours is a turbulent, unruly, rebellious spirit. And then you have an unhappy propensity for rushing into print upon every possible and impossible occasion. You no sooner hit upon an idea than you must needs write a newspaper article or a whole pamphlet about it.

DR. STOCKMANN. Isn't it a citizen's duty, when he has conceived a new idea, to communicate it to the public?

BURGOMASTER. Oh, the public has no need for new ideas. The public gets on best with the good old recognised ideas it has already.

DR. STOCKMANN. You say that right out!

BURGOMASTER. Yes, I must speak frankly to you for once. Hitherto I have tried to avoid it, for I know how irritable you are; but now I must tell you the truth, Thomas. You have no conception how much you injure yourself by your officiousness. You complain of the authorities, ay, of the Government itself—you cry them down and maintain that you have been slighted, persecuted. But what else can you expect, with your impossible disposition?

DR. STOCKMANN. Oh, indeed! So I am impossible, am I?

BURGOMASTER. Yes, Thomas, you are an impossible man to work with. I know that from experience. You have no consideration for any one or any thing; you seem quite to forget that you have me to thank for your position as medical officer of the Baths—

DR. STOCKMANN. It was mine by right! Mine, and no one else's! I was the first to discover the town's capabilities as a watering-place; I saw them, and, at that time, I alone. For years I fought single-handed for this idea of mine; I wrote and wrote—

BURGOMASTER. No doubt; but then the right time had not come. Of course, in that out-of-the-world corner, you could not judge of that. As soon as the propitious moment arrived, I—and others—took the matter in hand—

DR. STOCKMANN. Yes, and you went and bungled the whole of my glorious plan. Oh, we see now what a set of wiseacres you were!

BURGOMASTER. All *I* can see is that you are again seeking an outlet for your pugnacity. You want to make an onslaught on your superiors—that is an old habit of yours. You cannot endure any authority over you; you look askance at any one who holds a higher post than your own; you regard him as a personal enemy—and then you care nothing what kind of weapon you use against him. But now I have shown you how much is at stake for the town, and consequently for me, too. And therefore I warn you, Thomas, that I am inexorable in the demand I am about to make of you!

DR. STOCKMANN. What demand?

BURGOMASTER. As you have not had the sense to refrain from chattering to outsiders about this delicate business, which should have been kept an official secret, of course it cannot now be hushed up. All sorts of rumours will get abroad, and evil-disposed persons will invent all sorts of additions to them. It will therefore be necessary for you publicly to contradict these rumours.

DR. STOCKMANN. I! How? I don't understand you?

BURGOMASTER. We expect that, after further investigation, you will come to the conclusion that the affair is not nearly so serious or pressing as you had at first imagined.

DR. STOCKMANN. Aha! So you expect that?

BURGOMASTER. Furthermore, we expect you to express your confidence that the Board of Directors will thoroughly and conscientiously carry out all measures for the remedying of any possible defects.

DR. STOCKMANN. Yes, but that you'll never be able to do, so long as you go on tinkering and patching. I tell you that, Peter; and it's my deepest, sincerest conviction—

BURGOMASTER. As an official, you have no right to hold any individual conviction.

DR. STOCKMANN. [Starting.] No right to—?

BURGOMASTER. As an official, I say. In your private capacity, of course, it is another matter. But as a subordinate official of the Baths, you have no right to express any conviction at issue with that of your superiors.

DR. STOCKMANN. This is too much! I, a doctor, a man of science, have no right to—!

BURGOMASTER. The matter in question is not a purely scientific one; it is a complex affair; it has both a technical and an economic side.

DR. STOCKMANN. What the devil do I care what it is! I will be free to speak my mind upon any subject under the sun!

BURGOMASTER. As you please—so long as it does not concern the Baths. With them we forbid you to meddle.

DR. STOCKMANN. [Shouts.] You forbid—! You! A set of—

BURGOMASTER. I forbid it—I, your chief; and when I issue an order, you have simply to obey.

DR. STOCKMANN. [Controlling himself.] Upon my word, Peter, if you weren't my brother—

[PETRA tears open the door.]

PETRA. Father, you shan't submit to this!

MRS. STOCKMANN. [Following her.] Petra, Petra!

BURGOMASTER. Ah! So we have been listening!

MRS. STOCKMANN. The partition is so thin, we couldn't help—

PETRA. I stood and listened on purpose.

BURGOMASTER. Well, on the whole, I am not sorry—

DR. STOCKMANN. [Coming nearer to him.] You spoke to me of forbidding and obeying—

BURGOMASTER. You have forced me to adopt that tone.

DR. STOCKMANN. And am I to give myself the lie, in a public declaration?

BURGOMASTER. We consider it absolutely necessary that you should issue a statement in the terms indicated.

DR. STOCKMANN. And if I do not obey?

BURGOMASTER. Then we shall ourselves put forth a statement to reassure the public.

DR. STOCKMANN. Well and good; then I shall write against you. I shall stick to my point and prove that *I* am right, and *you* wrong. And what will you do then?

BURGOMASTER. Then I shall be unable to prevent your dismissal.

DR. STOCKMANN. What—!

PETRA. Father! Dismissal!

MRS. STOCKMANN. Dismissal!

BURGOMASTER. Your dismissal from the Baths. I shall be compelled to move that notice be given you at once, and that you have henceforth no connection whatever with the Baths.

DR. STOCKMANN. You would dare to do that!

BURGOMASTER. It is you who are playing the daring game.

PETRA. Uncle, this is a shameful way to treat a man like father.

MRS. STOCKMANN. Do be quiet, Petra!

BURGOMASTER. [*Looking at* PETRA.] Aha! We have opinions of our own already, eh? To be sure, to be sure! [*To* MRS. STOCKMANN.] Sister-in-law, you are presumably the most rational member of this household. Use all your influence with your husband; try to make him realise what all this will involve both for his family—

DR. STOCKMANN. My family concerns myself alone!

BURGOMASTER. —both for his family, I say, and for the town he lives in.

DR. STOCKMANN. It is I that have the real good of the town at heart! I want to lay bare the evils that, sooner or later, must come to light. Ah! You shall see whether I love my native town.

BURGOMASTER. You, who, in your blind obstinacy, want to cut off the town's chief source of prosperity!

DR. STOCKMANN. That source is poisoned, man! Are you mad? We live by trafficking in filth and corruption! The whole of our flourishing social life is rooted in a lie!

BURGOMASTER. Idle fancies—or worse. The man who scatters broadcast such offensive insinuations against his native place must be an enemy of society.

DR. STOCKMANN. [*Going towards him.*] You dare to—!

MRS. STOCKMANN. [*Throwing herself between them.*] Thomas!

PETRA. [*Seizing her father's arm.*] Keep calm, father!

BURGOMASTER. I will not expose myself to violence. You have had your warning now. Reflect upon what is due to yourself and to your family. Good-bye.

[*He goes.*]

DR. STOCKMANN. [*Walking up and down.*] And I must put up with such treatment! In my own house, Katrina! What do you say to that!

MRS. STOCKMANN. Indeed, it's a shame and a disgrace, Thomas—

PETRA. Oh, if I could only get hold of uncle—!

DR. STOCKMANN. It's my own fault. I ought to have stood up against them long ago—to have shown my teeth—and used them, too!—And to be called an enemy of society! Me! I won't bear it; by Heaven, I won't!

MRS. STOCKMANN. But my dear Thomas, after all, your brother has the power—

DR. STOCKMANN. Yes, but I have the right.

MRS. STOCKMANN. Ah yes, right, right! What good does it do to have the right, if you haven't any might?

PETRA. Oh, mother—how can you talk so?

DR. STOCKMANN. What! No good, in a free community, to have right on your side? What an absurd idea, Katrina! And besides —haven't I the free and independent press before me—and the compact majority at my back? That is might enough, I should think!

MRS. STOCKMANN. Why, good heavens, Thomas! you're surely not thinking of—?

DR. STOCKMANN. What am I not thinking of?

MRS. STOCKMANN. —of setting yourself up against your brother, I mean.

DR. STOCKMANN. What the devil would you have me do, if not stick to what is right and true?

PETRA. Yes, that's what I should like to know?

MRS. STOCKMANN. But it will be of no earthly use. If they won't, they won't.

DR. STOCKMANN. Ho-ho, Katrina! just wait a while, and you shall see whether I can fight my battles to the end.

MRS. STOCKMANN. Yes, to the end of getting your dismissal; that is what will happen.

DR. STOCKMANN. Well then, I shall at any rate have done my duty towards the public, towards society—I who am called an enemy of society!

MRS. STOCKMANN. But towards your family, Thomas? Towards us at home? Do you think *that* is doing your duty towards those who are dependent on you?

PETRA. Oh, mother, don't always think first of us.

MRS. STOCKMANN. Yes, it's easy for you to talk; you can stand alone if need be. —But remember the boys, Thomas; and think a little of yourself, too, and of me—

DR. STOCKMANN. You're surely out of your senses, Katrina! If I were to be such a pitiful coward as to knuckle under to this Peter and his confounded crew—should I ever have another happy hour in all my life?

MRS. STOCKMANN. I don't know about that; but God preserve us from the happiness we shall all of us have if you persist in defying them. There you will be again, with nothing to live on, with no regular income. I should have thought we had had enough

of that in the old days. Remember them, Thomas; think of what it all means.

DR. STOCKMANN. [*Struggling with him-self and clenching his hands.*] And this is what these jacks-in-office can bring upon a free and honest man! Isn't it revolting, Katrina?

MRS. STOCKMANN. Yes, no doubt they are treating you shamefully. But God knows there's plenty of injustice one must just submit to in this world.—Here are the boys, Thomas. Look at them! What is to become of them? Oh no, no! you can never have the heart—

[EILIF *and* MORTEN, *with school-books, have meanwhile entered.*]

DR. STOCKMANN. The boys—! [*With a sudden access of firmness and decision.*] Never, though the whole earth should crumble, will I bow my neck beneath the yoke.   [*Goes towards his room.*]

MRS. STOCKMANN. [*Following him.*] Thomas—what are you going to do?

DR. STOCKMANN. [*At the door.*] I must have the right to look my boys in the face when they have grown into free men.
                    [*Goes into his room.*]

MRS. STOCKMANN. [*Bursts into tears.*] Ah, God help us all!

PETRA. Father is true to the core. He will never give in!

[*The boys ask wonderingly what it all means;* PETRA *signs to them to be quiet as the curtain falls.*]

ACT THIRD

The Editor's Room of the "People's Mes-senger." In the background, to the left, an entrance-door; to the right another door with glass panes, through which can be seen the composing-room. A door in the right-hand wall. In the middle of the room a large table covered with papers, newspapers, and books. In front, on the left, a window, and by it a desk with a high stool. A couple of arm-chairs beside the table; some other chairs along the walls. The room is dingy and cheer-less, the furniture shabby, the arm-chairs

dirty and torn. In the composing-room are seen a few compositors at work; fur-ther back, a hand-press in operation.

[HOVSTAD *is seated at the desk, writing. Presently* BILLING *enters from the right, with the* DOCTOR'S *manuscript in his hand.*]

BILLING. Well, I must say—!

HOVSTAD. [*Writing.*] Have you read it through?

BILLING. [*Laying the MS. on the desk.*]

Yes, I should think I had.

HOVSTAD. Don't you think the Doctor comes out strong?

BILLING. Strong! Why, strike me dead if he isn't crushing! Every word falls like a —well, like a sledge-hammer.

HOVSTAD. Yes, but these fellows won't collapse at the first blow.

BILLING. True enough; but we'll keep on hammering away, blow after blow, till the whole officialdom comes crashing down. As I sat in there reading that article, I seemed to hear the revolution thundering afar.

HOVSTAD. [*Turning round.*] Hush! Don't let Aslaksen hear that.

BILLING. [*In a lower voice.*] Aslaksen's a white-livered, cowardly fellow, without a spark of manhood in him. But this time you'll surely carry your point? Eh? You'll print the Doctor's paper?

HOVSTAD. Yes, if only the Burgomaster doesn't give in—

BILLING. That would be deuced annoying.

HOVSTAD. Well, whatever happens, fortunately we can turn the situation to account. If the Burgomaster won't agree to the Doctor's proposal, he'll have all the small middle-class down upon him—all the House-owners' Association, and the rest of them. And if he does agree to it, he'll fall out with the whole crew of big shareholders in the Baths, who have hitherto been his main support—

BILLING. Yes, of course; for no doubt they'll have to fork out a lot of money—

HOVSTAD. You may take your oath of that. And then, don't you see, when the ring is broken up, we'll din it into the public day by day that the Burgomaster is incompetent in every respect, and that all responsible positions in the town, the whole municipal government in short, must be entrusted to men of liberal ideas.

BILLING. Strike me dead if that isn't the square truth! I see it—I see it: we are on the eve of a revolution!

[*A knock at the door.*]

HOVSTAD. Hush! [*Calls*] Come in!

[DR. STOCKMANN *enters from the back, left.*]

HOVSTAD. [*Going towards him.*] Ah, here is the Doctor. Well?

DR. STOCKMANN. Print away, Mr. Hovstad!

HOVSTAD. So it has come to that?

BILLING. Hurrah!

DR. STOCKMANN. Print away, I tell you. To be sure it has come to that. Since they will have it so, they must. War is declared, Mr. Billing!

BILLING. War to the knife, say I! War to the death, Doctor!

DR. STOCKMANN. This article is only the beginning. I have four or five others sketched out in my head already. But where do you keep Aslaksen?

BILLING. [*Calling into the printing-room.*] Aslasken! just come here a moment.

HOVSTAD. Four or five more articles, eh? On the same subject?

DR. STOCKMANN. Oh no—not at all, my dear fellow. No; they will deal with quite different matters. But they're all of a piece with the water-works and sewer question. One thing leads to another. It's just like beginning to pick at an old house, don't you know?

BILLING. Strike me dead, but that's true! You feel you can't leave off till you've pulled the whole lumber-heap to pieces.

[ASLAKSEN *enters from the printing-room.*]

ASLAKSEN. Pulled to pieces! Surely the Doctor isn't thinking of pulling the Baths to pieces?

HOVSTAD. Not at all. Don't be alarmed.

DR. STOCKMANN. No, we were talking of something quite different. Well, what do you think of my article, Mr. Hovstad?

HOVSTAD. I think it's simply a masterpiece—

DR. STOCKMANN. Yes, isn't it? I'm glad you think so—very glad.

HOVSTAD. It's so clear and to the point. One doesn't in the least need to be a specialist to understand the gist of it. I am certain every intelligent man will be on your side.

ASLAKSEN. And all the prudent ones, too, I hope?

BILLING. Both the prudent and imprudent—in fact, almost the whole town.

ASLAKSEN. Then I suppose we may venture to print it.

DR. STOCKMANN. I should think so!

HOVSTAD. It shall go in to-morrow.

DR. STOCKMANN. Yes, plague take it, not a day must be lost. Look here, Mr. Aslaksen, this is what I wanted to ask you: won't you take personal charge of the article?

ASLAKSEN. Certainly I will.

DR. STOCKMANN. Be as careful as if it were gold. No printers' errors; every word is important. I shall look in again presently; perhaps you'll be able to let me see a proof. —Ah! I can't tell you how I long to have the thing in print—to see it launched—

BILLING. Yes, like a thunderbolt!

DR. STOCKMANN. —and submitted to the judgment of every intelligent citizen. Oh, you have no idea what I have had to put up with to-day. I've been threatened with all sorts of things. I was to be robbed of my clearest rights as a human being—

BILLING. What! Your rights as a human being!

DR. STOCKMANN. —I was to humble myself, and eat the dust; I was to set my personal interests above my deepest, holiest convictions—

BILLING. Strike me dead, but that's too outrageous!

HOVSTAD. Oh, what can you expect from that quarter?

DR. STOCKMANN. But they shall find they were mistaken in me; they shall learn that in black and white, I promise them! I shall throw myself into the breach every day in the *Messenger,* bombard them with one explosive article after another—

ASLAKSEN. Yes, but look here—

BILLING. Hurrah! It's war! War!

DR. STOCKMANN. I shall smite them to the earth, I shall crush them, I shall level their entrenchments to the ground in the eyes of all right-thinking men! That's what I shall do!

ASLAKSEN. But above all things be temperate, Doctor; bombard with moderation—

BILLING. Not at all, not at all! Don't spare the dynamite!

DR. STOCKMANN. [*Going on imperturbably.*] For now it's no mere question of water-works and sewers, you see. No, the whole community must be purged, disinfected—

BILLING. *There* sounds the word of salvation!

DR. STOCKMANN. All the old bunglers must be sent packing, you understand. And that in every possible department! Such endless vistas have opened out before me to-day. I am not quite clear about everything yet, but I shall see my way presently. It's young and vigorous standard-bearers we must look for, my friends; we must have new captains at all the outposts.

BILLING. Hear, hear!

DR. STOCKMANN. And if only we hold together, it will go so smoothly, so smoothly! The whole revolution will glide off the stocks just like a ship. Don't you think so?

HOVSTAD. For my part, I believe we have now every prospect of placing our municipal affairs in the right hands.

ASLAKSEN. And if only we proceed with moderation, I really don't think there can be any danger.

DR. STOCKMANN. Who the devil cares whether there's danger or not! What I do, I do in the name of truth and for conscience' sake.

HOVSTAD. You are a man to be backed up, Doctor.

ASLAKSEN. Yes, there's no doubt the Doctor is a true friend to the town; he's what I call a friend of society.

BILLING. Strike me dead if Dr. Stockmann isn't a Friend of the People, Aslaksen!

ASLAKSEN. I have no doubt the Houseowners' Association will soon adopt that expression.

DR. STOCKMANN. [*Shaking their hands, deeply moved.*] Thanks, thanks, my dear, faithful friends; it does me good to hear you. My respected brother called me something very different. Never mind! Trust me to pay him back with interest! But I must be off now to see a poor devil of a patient. I shall look in again, though. Be sure you look after the article, Mr. Aslaksen; and, whatever you do, don't leave out any of my notes of exclamation! Rather put in a few more! Well, good-bye for the present, good-bye, good-bye.

[*Mutual salutations while they accompany him to the door. He goes out.*]

HOVSTAD. He will be invaluable to us.

ASLAKSEN. Yes, so long as he confines himself to this matter of the Baths. But if he goes further, it will scarcely be advisable to follow him.

HOVSTAD. H'm—that entirely depends on—

BILLING. You're always so confoundedly timid, Aslaksen.

ASLAKSEN. Timid? Yes, when it's a question of attacking local authorities, I *am* timid, Mr. Billing; I have learnt caution in the school of experience, let me tell you. But start me on the higher politics, confront me with the Government itself, and then see if I'm timid.

BILLING. No, you're not; but that's just where your inconsistency comes in.

ASLAKSEN. The fact is, I am keenly alive to my responsibilities. If you attack the Government, you at least do society no harm; for the men attacked don't care a straw, you see—they stay where they are all the same. But local authorities can be turned out; and then we might get some incompetent set into power, to the irreparable injury both of house-owners and other people.

HOVSTAD. But the education of citizens by self-government—do you never think of *that?*

ASLAKSEN. When a man has solid interests to protect, he can't think of everything, Mr. Hovstad.

HOVSTAD. Then I hope I may never have solid interests to protect.

BILLING. Hear, hear!

ASLAKSEN. [*Smiling.*] H'm! [*Points to the desk.*] Governor Stensgård [1] sat in that editorial chair before you.

BILLING. [*Spitting.*] Pooh! A turncoat like that!

HOVSTAD. I am no weathercock—and never will be.

ASLAKSEN. A politician should never be too sure of anything on earth, Mr. Hovstad. And as for you, Mr. Billing, you ought to take in a reef or two, I should say, now that you are applying for the secretaryship to the Town Council.

BILLING. I—!

HOVSTAD. Is that so, Billing?

BILLING. Well, yes—but, deuce take it, you understand, I'm only doing it to spite their high-mightinesses.

ASLAKSEN. Well, that has nothing to do with me. But if I am to be accused of cowardice and inconsistency, I should just like to point out *this*: My political record is open to every one. I have not changed at all, except in becoming more moderate. My heart still belongs to the people; but I don't deny that my reason inclines somewhat towards the authorities—the local ones, I mean.   [*Goes into the printing-room.*]

BILLING. Don't you think we should try to get rid of him, Hovstad?

HOVSTAD. Do you know of any one else that will pay for our paper and printing?

BILLING. What a confounded nuisance it is to have no capital!

HOVSTAD. [*Sitting down by the desk.*] Yes, if we only had that—

BILLING. Suppose you applied to Dr. Stockmann?

HOVSTAD. [*Turning over his papers.*] What would be the good? He hasn't a rap.

BILLING. No; but he has a good man behind him—old Morten Kiil—"The Badger," as they call him.

[1] Stensgård is the central character in Ibsen's political satire *The League of Youth,* in which Aslaksen also appears.

HOVSTAD. [*Writing.*] Are you so sure he has money?

BILLING. Yes, strike me dead if he hasn't! And part of it must certainly go to Stockmann's family. He's bound to provide for—for the children at any rate.

HOVSTAD. [*Half turning.*] Are you counting on *that*?

BILLING. Counting? How should I be counting on it?

HOVSTAD. Best not! And that secretaryship you shouldn't count on either; for I can assure you, you won't get it.

BILLING. Do you think I don't know that? A refusal is the very thing I want. Such a rebuff fires the spirit of opposition in you, gives you a fresh supply of gall, as it were; and that's just what you need in a god-forsaken hole like this, where anything really stimulating so seldom happens.

HOVSTAD. [*Writing.*] Yes, yes.

BILLING. Well—they shall soon hear from me!—Now I'll go and write the appeal to the House-owners' Association.

[*Goes into the room on the right.*]

HOVSTAD. [*Sits at his desk, biting his penholder, and says slowly:*] H'm—so that's the way of it.—[*A knock at the door.*] Come in.

[PETRA *enters from the back, left.*]

HOVSTAD. [*Rising.*] What! Is it you? Here?

PETRA. Yes; please excuse me—

HOVSTAD. [*Offering her an arm-chair.*] Won't you sit down?

PETRA. No, thanks; I must go again directly.

HOVSTAD. Perhaps you bring a message from your father—?

PETRA. No, I have come on my own account. [*Takes a book from the pocket of her cloak.*] Here is that English story.

HOVSTAD. Why have you brought it back?

PETRA. Because I won't translate it.

HOVSTAD. But you promised—

PETRA. Yes; but then I hadn't read it. I suppose you have not read it either?

HOVSTAD. No; you know I can't read English; but—

PETRA. Exactly; and that's why I wanted to tell you that you must find something else. [*Putting the book on the table.*] This will never do for the *Messenger*.

HOVSTAD. Why not?

PETRA. Because it flies in the face of all your convictions.

HOVSTAD. Well, for that matter—

PETRA. You don't understand me. It makes out that a supernatural power looks after the so-called good people in this world, and turns everything to their advantage at last; while all the so-called bad people are punished.

HOVSTAD. Yes, but that's all right. That's the very thing the public like.

PETRA. And would *you* supply the public with such stuff? You don't believe a word of it yourself. You know well enough that things do not really happen like that.

HOVSTAD. Of course not; but an editor can't always do as he likes. He has often to humour people's fancies in minor matters. After all, politics is the chief thing in life —at any rate for a newspaper; and if I want the people to follow me along the path of emancipation and progress, I mustn't scare them away. If they find a moral story like this down in the cellar,[2] they are all the more ready to take in what we tell them above—they feel themselves safer.

PETRA. For shame! You're not such a hypocrite as to set traps like that for your readers. You're not a spider.

HOVSTAD. [*Smiling.*] Thanks for your good opinion. It's true that the idea is Billing's, not mine.

PETRA. Mr. Billing's!

HOVSTAD. Yes, at least he was talking in that strain the other day. It was Billing that was so anxious to get the story into the paper; I don't even know the book.

PETRA. But how can Mr. Billing, with his advanced views—

HOVSTAD. Well, Billing is many-sided. He's applying for the secretaryship to the Town Council, I hear.

[2] In continental newspapers literary supplements were printed at the bottom of the page.

PETRA. I don't believe that, Mr. Hovstad. How could he descend to such a thing?

HOVSTAD. That you must ask *him*.

PETRA. I could never have thought it of Billing!

HOVSTAD. [*Looking more closely at her.*] No? Is it such a surprise to you?

PETRA. Yes. And yet—perhaps not. Oh, I don't know—

HOVSTAD. We journalists are not worth much, Miss Petra.

PETRA. Do you really say that?

HOVSTAD. I think so, now and then.

PETRA. Yes, in the little every-day squabbles—that I can understand. But now that you have taken up a great cause—

HOVSTAD. You mean this affair of your father's?

PETRA. Of course. I should think you must feel yourself worth more than the general run of people now.

HOVSTAD. Yes, to-day I do feel something of the sort.

PETRA. Yes, surely you must. Oh, it's a glorious career you have chosen! To be the pioneer of unrecognised truths and new and daring ways of thought!—even, if that were all, to stand forth fearlessly in support of an injured man—

HOVSTAD. Especially when the injured man is—I hardly know how to put it—

PETRA. You mean when he is so upright and true?

HOVSTAD. [*In a low voice.*] I mean—especially when he is your father.

PETRA. [*Suddenly taken aback.*] That?

HOVSTAD. Yes, Petra—Miss Petra.

PETRA. So that is your chief thought, is it? Not the cause itself? Not the truth? Not father's great, warm heart?

HOVSTAD. Oh, that too, of course.

PETRA. No, thank you; you said too much that time, Mr. Hovstad. Now I shall never trust you again, in anything.

HOVSTAD. Can you be so hard on me because it's mainly for your sake—?

PETRA. What I blame you for is that you have not acted straightforwardly towards father. You have talked to him as if you cared only for the truth and the good of the community. You have trifled with both father and me. You are not the man you pretended to be. And that I will never forgive you—never.

HOVSTAD. You shouldn't say that so bitterly, Miss Petra—least of all now.

PETRA. Why not now?

HOVSTAD. Because your father cannot do without my help.

PETRA. [*Measuring him from head to foot.*] So you are capable of *that,* too? Oh, shame!

HOVSTAD. No, no. I spoke without thinking. You mustn't believe that of me.

PETRA. I know what to believe. Good-bye.

[ASLAKSEN *enters from printing-room, hurriedly and mysteriously.*]

ALSAKSEN. What do you think, Mr. Hovstad—[*Seeing* PETRA.] Ow, that's awkward—

PETRA. Well, there is the book. You must give it to someone else.

[*Going towards the main door.*]

HOVSTAD. [*Following her.*] But, Miss Petra—

PETRA. Good-bye.   [*She goes.*]

ASLAKSEN. I say, Mr. Hovstad!

HOVSTAD. Well, well; what is it?

ASLAKSEN. The Burgomaster's out there, in the printing-office.

HOVSTAD. The Burgomaster?

ASLAKSEN. Yes. He wants to speak to you; he came in by the back way—he didn't want to be seen, you understand.

HOVSTAD. What can be the meaning of this? Stop, I'll go myself—

[*Goes towards the printing-room, opens the door, bows and invites the* BURGO-MASTER *to enter.*]

Keep a look-out, Aslaksen, that no one—

ASLAKSEN. I understand.

[*Goes into the printing-room.*]

BURGOMASTER. You didn't expect to see me here, Mr. Hovstad.

HOVSTAD. No, I cannot say that I did.

BURGOMASTER. [*Looking about him.*] You are very comfortably installed here—capital quarters.

HOVSTAD. Oh—

BURGOMASTER. And here have I come, without with your leave or by your leave, to take up your time—

HOVSTAD. You are very welcome, Burgomaster; I am at your service. Let me take your cap and stick. [*He does so, and puts them on a chair.*] And won't you be seated?

BURGOMASTER. [*Sitting down by the table.*] Thanks. [HOVSTAD *also sits by the table.*] I have been much—very much worried to-day, Mr. Hovstad.

HOVSTAD. Really? Well, I suppose with all your various duties, Burgomaster—

BURGOMASTER. It is the Doctor that has been causing me annoyance to-day.

HOVSTAD. Indeed! The Doctor?

BURGOMASTER. He has written a sort of memorandum to the Directors about some alleged shortcomings in the Baths.

HOVSTAD. Has he really?

BURGOMASTER. Yes; hasn't he told you? I thought he said—

HOVSTAD. Oh, yes, by-the-bye, he did mention something—

ASLAKSEN. [*From the printing-office.*] I've just come for the manuscript—

HOVSTAD. [*In a tone of vexation.*] Oh! —there it is on the desk.

ASLAKSEN. [*Finding it.*] All right.

BURGOMASTER. Why, *that* is the very thing—

ASLAKSEN. Yes, this is the Doctor's article, Burgomaster.

HOVSTAD. Oh, is that what you were speaking of?

BURGOMASTER. Precisely. What do you think of it?

HOVSTAD. I have no technical knowledge of the matter, and I've only glanced through it.

BURGOMASTER. And yet you are going to print it!

HOVSTAD. I can't very well refuse a signed communication—

ASLAKSEN. I have nothing to do with the editing of the paper, Burgomaster—

BURGOMASTER. Of course not.

ASLAKSEN. I merely print what is placed in my hands.

BURGOMASTER. Quite right, quite right.

ASLAKSEN. So I must—

[*Goes towards the printing-room.*]

BURGOMASTER. No, stop a moment, Mr. Aslaksen. With your permission, Mr. Hovstad—

HOVSTAD. By all means, Burgomaster.

BURGOMASTER. You are a discreet and thoughtful man, Mr. Aslaksen.

ASLAKSEN. I am glad you think so, Burgomaster.

BURGOMASTER. And a man of very wide influence.

ASLAKSEN. Well — chiefly among the lower middle-class.

BURGOMASTER. The small taxpayers form the majority—here as everywhere.

ASLAKSEN. That's very true.

BURGOMASTER. And I have no doubt that you know the general feeling among them. Am I right?

ASLAKSEN. Yes, I think I may say that I do, Burgomaster.

BURGOMASTER. Well—since our townsfolk of the poorer class appear to be so heroically eager to make sacrifices—

ASLAKSEN. How so?

HOVSTAD. Sacrifices?

BURGOMASTER. It is a pleasing evidence of public spirit—a most pleasing evidence. I admit it is more than I should quite have expected. But, of course, you know public feeling better than I do.

ASLAKSEN. Yes, but, Burgomaster—

BURGOMASTER. And assuredly it is no small sacrifice the town will have to make.

HOVSTAD. The town?

ASLAKSEN. But I don't understand—. It's the Baths—

BURGOMASTER. At a rough provisional estimate, the alterations the Doctor thinks desirable will come to two or three hundred thousand crowns.

ASLAKSEN. That's a lot of money; but—

BURGOMASTER. Of course, we shall be obliged to raise a municipal loan.

HOVSTAD. [*Rising.*] You surely can't mean that the town—?

ASLAKSEN. Would you come upon the

rates? Upon the scanty savings of the lower middle-class?

BURGOMASTER. Why, my dear Mr. Aslaksen, where else are the funds to come from?

ASLAKSEN. The proprietors of the Baths must see to that.

BURGOMASTER. The proprietors are not in a position to go to any further expense.

ASLAKSEN. Are you quite sure of that, Burgomaster?

BURGOMASTER. I have positive information. So if these extensive alterations are called for, the town itself will have to bear the cost.

ASLAKSEN. Oh, plague take it all—I beg your pardon!—but this is quite another matter, Mr. Hovstad.

HOVSTAD. Yes, it certainly is.

BURGOMASTER. The worst of it is that we shall be obliged to close the establishment for a couple of years.

HOVSTAD. To close it? Completely?

ASLAKSEN. For two years!

BURGOMASTER. Yes, the work will require that time—at least.

ASLAKSEN. But, damn it all! we can't stand that, Burgomaster. What are we house-owners to live on in the meantime?

BURGOMASTER. It's extremely difficult to say, Mr. Aslaksen. But what would you have us do? Do you think a single visitor will come here if we go about making them fancy that the water is poisoned, that the place is pestilential, that the whole town—

ASLAKSEN. And it's all nothing but fancy?

BURGOMASTER. With the best will in the world, I have failed to convince myself that it is anything else.

ASLAKSEN. In that case it's simply inexcusable of Dr. Stockmann—I beg your pardon, Burgomaster, but—

BURGOMASTER. I'm sorry to say you are only speaking the truth, Mr. Aslaksen. Unfortunately, my brother has always been noted for his rashness.

ASLAKSEN. And yet you want to back him up in this, Mr. Hovstad!

HOVSTAD. But who could possibly imagine that—?

BURGOMASTER. I have drawn up a short statement of the facts, as they appear from a sober-minded standpoint; and I have intimated that any drawbacks that may possibly exist can no doubt be remedied by measures compatible with the finances of the Baths.

HOVSTAD. Have you the article with you, Burgomaster?

BURGOMASTER. [Feeling in his pockets.] Yes; I brought it with me, in case you—

ASLAKSEN. [Quickly.] Plague take it, there he is!

BURGOMASTER. Who? My brother?

HOVSTAD. Where? where?

ASLAKSEN. He's coming through the composing-room.

BURGOMASTER. Most unfortunate! I don't want to meet him here, and yet there are several things I want to talk to you about.

HOVSTAD. [Pointing to the door on the right.] Go in there for a moment.

BURGOMASTER. But—?

HOVSTAD. You'll find nobody but Billing there.

ASLAKSEN. Quick, quick, Burgomaster; he's just coming.

BURGOMASTER. Very well, then. But try to get rid of him quickly.

[He goes out by the door on the right, which ASLAKSEN opens, and closes behind him.]

HOVSTAD. Pretend to be busy, Aslaksen.

[He sits down and writes. ASLAKSEN turns over a heap of newspapers on a chair, right.]

DR. STOCKMANN. [Entering from the composing-room.] Here I am, back again. [Puts down his hat and stick.]

HOVSTAD. [Writing.] Already, Doctor? Make haste with what we were speaking of, Aslaksen. We've no time to lose to-day.

DR. STOCKMANN. [To ASLAKSEN.] No proof yet, I hear.

ASLAKSEN. [Without turning round.] No; how could you expect it?

DR. STOCKMANN. Of course not; but you understand my impatience. I can have no rest or peace until I see the thing in print.

HOVSTAD. H'm; it will take a good while yet. Don't you think so, Aslaksen?

ASLAKSEN. I'm afraid it will.

DR. STOCKMANN. All right, all right, my good friend; then I shall look in again. I'll look in twice if necessary. With so much at stake—the welfare of the whole town— one mustn't grudge a little trouble. [*Is on the point of going but stops and comes back.*] Oh, by the way—there's one other thing I must speak to you about.

HOVSTAD. Excuse me; wouldn't some other time—?

DR. STOCKMANN. I can tell you in two words. You see it's this: when people read my article in the paper to-morrow, and find I have spent the whole winter working quietly for the good of the town—

HOVSTAD. Yes, but, Doctor—

DR. STOCKMANN. I know what you're going to say. You don't think it was a bit more than my duty—my simple duty as a citizen. Of course, I know that, as well as you do. But you see, my fellow townsmen —good Lord! the poor souls think so much of me—

ASLAKSEN. Yes, the townspeople have hitherto thought very highly of you, Doctor.

DR. STOCKMANN. That's exactly why I'm afraid that—. What I wanted to say was this: when all this comes to them—especially to the poorer classes—as a summons to take the affairs of the town into their own hands for the future—

HOVSTAD. [*Rising.*] H'm Doctor, I won't conceal from you—

DR. STOCKMANN. Aha! I thought there was something brewing! But I won't hear of it. If they are getting up anything of that sort—

HOVSTAD. Of what sort?

DR. STOCKMANN. Well, anything of any sort—a procession with banners, or a banquet, or a subscription for a testimonial, or whatever it may be—you must give me

your solemn promise to put a stop to it. And you, too, Mr. Aslaksen; do you hear?

HOVSTAD. Excuse me, Doctor; we may as well tell you the whole truth first as last—

[MRS. STOCKMANN *enters from tne back, left.*]

MRS. STOCKMANN. [*Seeing the* DOCTOR.] Ah! just as I thought!

HOVSTAD. [*Going towards her.*] Mrs. Stockmann, too?

DR. STOCKMANN. What the devil do *you* want here, Katrina?

MRS. STOCKMANN. You know very well what I want.

HOVSTAD. Won't you sit down? Or perhaps—

MRS. STOCKMANN. Thanks, please don't trouble. And you must forgive my following my husband here; remember, I am the mother of three children.

DR. STOCKMANN. Stuff and nonsense! We all know that well enough.

MRS. STOCKMANN. Well, it doesn't look as if you thought very much about your wife and children to-day, or you wouldn't be so ready to plunge us all into ruin.

DR. STOCKMANN. Are you quite mad, Katrina! Has a man with a wife and children no right to proclaim the truth? Has he no right to be an active and useful citizen? Has he no right to do his duty by the town he lives in?

MRS. STOCKMANN. Everything in moderation, Thomas!

ASLAKSEN. That's just what I say. Moderation in everything.

MRS. STOCKMANN. You are doing us a great wrong, Mr. Hovstad, in enticing my husband away from house and home, and befooling him in this way.

HOVSTAD. I am not befooling any one—

DR. STOCKMANN. Befooling! Do you think I should let myself be befooled?

MRS. STOCKMANN. Yes, that's just what you do. I know very well that you are the cleverest man in the town; but you're very easily made a fool of, Thomas. [*To* HOV-

STAD.] Remember that he loses his post at the Baths if you print what he has written—

ASLAKSEN. What!

HOVSTAD. Well, now, really, Doctor—

DR. STOCKMANN. [*Laughing.*] Ha, ha! just let them try—! No, no, my dear, they'll think twice about that. I have the compact majority behind me, you see!

MRS. STOCKMANN. That's just the misfortune, that you should have such a horrid thing behind you.

DR. STOCKMANN. Nonsense, Katrina;—you go home and look after your house, and let me take care of society. How can you be in such a fright when you see me so confident and happy? [*Rubbing his hands and walking up and down.*] Truth and the People must win the day; you may be perfectly sure of that. Oh! I can see all our free-souled citizens standing shoulder to shoulder like a conquering army—! [*Stopping by a chair.*] Why, what the devil is *that*?

ASLAKSEN. [*Looking at it.*] Oh Lord!

HOVSTAD. [*The same.*] H'm—

DR. STOCKMANN. Why, here's the top-knot of authority!

[*He takes the* BURGOMASTER'S *official cap carefully between the tips of his fingers and holds it up.*]

MRS. STOCKMANN. The Burgomaster's cap!

DR. STOCKMANN. And here's the staff of office, too! But how in the devil's name did they—?

HOVSTAD. Well, then—

DR. STOCKMANN. Ah, I understand! He has been here to talk you over. Ha, ha! He reckoned without his host that time! And when he caught sight of me in the printing-room—[*Bursts out laughing*]—he took to his heels, eh, Mr. Aslaksen?

ASLAKSEN. [*Hurriedly.*] Exactly; he took to his heels, Doctor.

DR. STOCKMANN. Made off without his stick and— No, that won't do! Peter never left anything behind him. But where the devil have you stowed him? Ah—in here, of course. Now you shall see, Katrina!

MRS. STOCKMANN. Thomas—I implore you—!

ASLAKSEN. Take care, Doctor!

[DR. STOCKMANN *has put on the* BURGO-MASTER'S *cap and grasped his stick; he now goes up to the door, throws it open, and makes a military salute. The* BURGOMASTER *enters, red with anger. Behind him comes* BILLING.]

BURGOMASTER. What is the meaning of these antics?

DR. STOCKMANN. Respect, my good Peter! Now, it's I that am in power in this town.   [*He struts up and down.*]

MRS. STOCKMANN. [*Almost in tears.*] Oh, Thomas!

BURGOMASTER. [*Following him.*] Give me my cap and stick!

DR. STOCKMANN. [*As before.*] You may be Chief of Police, but I am Burgomaster. I am master of the whole town, I tell you!

BURGOMASTER. Put down my cap, I say. Remember it is an official cap, as by law prescribed!

DR. STOCKMANN. Pshaw! Do you think the awakening lion of the democracy will let itself be scared by a gold-laced cap? There's to be a revolution in the town to-morrow, let me tell you. You threatened me with dismissal; but now *I* dismiss *you*—dismiss you from all your offices of trust—. You think I can't do it?—Oh, yes, I can! I have the irresistible forces of society on my side. Hovstad and Billing will thunder in the *People's Messenger,* and Aslaksen will take the field at the head of the House-owners' Association—

ASLAKSEN. No, Doctor, I shall not.

DR. STOCKMANN. Why, of course, you will—

BURGOMASTER. Aha! Perhaps Mr. Hovstad would like to join the agitation after all?

HOVSTAD. No, Burgomaster.

ASLAKSEN. No, Mr. Hovstad isn't such a fool as to ruin both himself and the paper for the sake of a delusion.

DR. STOCKMANN. [*Looking about him.*] What does all this mean?

HOVSTAD. You have presented your case

in a false light, Doctor; therefore I am unable to give you my support.

BILLING. And after what the Burgomaster has been so kind as to explain to me, I—

DR. STOCKMANN. In a false light! Well, I am responsible for that. Just you print my article, and I promise you I shall prove it up to the hilt.

HOVSTAD. I shall not print it. I cannot, and will not, and dare not print it.

DR. STOCKMANN. You dare not? What nonsense is this? You are editor; and I suppose it's the editor that controls a paper.

ASLAKSEN. No, it's the subscribers, Doctor.

BURGOMASTER. Fortunately.

ASLAKSEN. It's public opinion, the enlightened majority, the house-owners and all the rest. It's *they* who control a paper.

DR. STOCKMANN. [*Calmly.*] And all these powers I have against me?

ASLAKSEN. Yes, you have. It would mean absolute ruin for the town if your article were inserted.

DR. STOCKMANN. So *that* is the way of it!

BURGOMASTER. My hat and stick!

[DR. STOCKMANN *takes off the cap and lays it on the table along with the stick.*]

BURGOMASTER. [*Taking them both.*] Your term of office has come to an untimely end.

DR. STOCKMANN. The end is not yet. [*To* HOVSTAD.] So you are quite determined not to print my article in the *Messenger?*

HOVSTAD. Quite; for the sake of your family, if for no other reason.

MRS. STOCKMANN. Oh, be kind enough to leave his family out of the question, Mr. Hovstad.

BURGOMASTER. [*Takes a manuscript from his pocket.*] When this appears, the public will be in possession of all necessary information; it is an authentic statement. I place it in your hands.

HOVSTAD. [*Taking the MS.*] Good. It shall appear in due course.

DR. STOCKMANN. And not mine! You imagine you can kill me and the truth by a conspiracy of silence! But it won't be so easy as you think. Mr. Aslaksen, will you be good enough to print my article at once, as a pamphlet? I'll pay for it myself, and be my own publisher. I'll have four hundred copies—no, five—six hundred.

ASLAKSEN. No. If you offered me its weight in gold, I dare not lend my press to such a purpose, Doctor. I daren't fly in the face of public opinion. You won't get it printed anywhere in the whole town.

DR. STOCKMANN. Then give it me back.

HOVSTAD. [*Handing him the MS.*] By all means.

DR. STOCKMANN. [*Taking up his hat and cane.*] It shall be made public all the same. I shall read it at a great mass meeting; all my fellow citizens shall hear the voice of truth!

BURGOMASTER. Not a single society in the town would let you their hall for such a purpose.

ASLAKSEN. Not one, I'm quite certain.

BILLING. No, strike me dead if they would!

MRS. STOCKMANN. That would be too disgraceful! Why do they turn against you like this, every one of them?

DR. STOCKMANN. [*Irritated.*] I'll tell you why. It's because in this town all the men are old women—like you. They all think of nothing but their families, not of the general good.

MRS. STOCKMANN. [*Taking his arm.*] Then I'll show them that an—an old woman can be a man for once in a way. For now I'll stand by you, Thomas.

DR. STOCKMANN. Bravely said, Katrina! I swear by my soul and conscience the truth shall out! If they won't let me a hall, I'll hire a drum and march through the town with it; and I'll read my paper at every street corner.

BURGOMASTER. You can scarcely be such a raving lunatic as that?

DR. STOCKMANN. I am.

ASLAKSEN. You would not get a single man in the whole town to go with you.

BILLING. No, strike me dead if you would!

MRS. STOCKMANN. Don't give in, Thomas. I'll ask the boys to go with you.

DR. STOCKMANN. That's a splendid idea!

MRS. STOCKMANN. Morten will be delighted; and Eilif will go, too, I daresay.

DR. STOCKMANN. Yes, and so will Petra! And you yourself, Katrina!

MRS. STOCKMANN. No, no, not I. But I'll stand at the window and watch you—that I will.

DR. STOCKMANN. [*Throwing his arms about her and kissing her.*] Thank you for that! Now, my good sirs, we're ready for the fight! Now we shall see whether your despicable tactics can stop the mouth of the patriot who wants to purge society!

[*He and his wife go out together by the door in the back, left.*]

BURGOMASTER. [*Shaking his head dubiously.*] Now he has turned *her* head too!

[CURTAIN.]

ACT FOURTH

A large old-fashioned room in CAPTAIN HORSTER'S *house. An open folding-door in the background leads to an anteroom. In the wall on the left are three windows. About the middle of the opposite wall is a platform, and on it a small table, two candles, a water-bottle and glass, and a bell. For the rest, the room is lighted by sconces placed between the windows. In front, on the left, is a table with a candle on it, and by it a chair. In front, to the right, a door, and near it a few chairs.*

[*Large assemblage of all classes of townsfolk. In the crowd are a few women and schoolboys. More and more people gradually stream in from the back until the room is quite full.*]

FIRST CITIZEN. [*To another standing near him.*] So you're here too, Lamstad?

SECOND CITIZEN. I never miss a public meeting.

A BYSTANDER. I suppose you've brought your whistle?

SECOND CITIZEN. Of course I have; haven't you?

THIRD CITIZEN. I should think so. And Skipper Evensen said he'd bring a thumping big horn.

SECOND CITIZEN. He's a good 'un, is Evensen!   [*Laughter in the group.*]

A FOURTH CITIZEN. [*Joining them.*] I say, what's it all about? What's going on here to-night?

SECOND CITIZEN. Why, it's Dr. Stockmann that's going to lecture against the Burgomaster.

FOURTH CITIZEN. But the Burgomaster's his brother.

FIRST CITIZEN. That makes no difference. Dr. Stockmann's not afraid of him.

THIRD CITIZEN. But he's all wrong; the *People's Messenger* says so.

SECOND CITIZEN. Yes, he must be wrong this time; for neither the House-owners' Association nor the Citizens' Club would let him have a hall.

FIRST CITIZEN. They wouldn't even lend him the hall at the Baths.

SECOND CITIZEN. No, you may be sure they wouldn't.

A MAN. [*In another group.*] Now, who's the one to follow in this business, eh?

ANOTHER MAN. [*In the same group.*] Just keep your eye on Aslaksen, and do as he does.

BILLING. [*With a portfolio under his arm, makes his way through the crowd.*] Excuse me, gentlemen. Will you allow me to pass? I'm here to report for the *People's Messenger.* Many thanks.

[*Sits by the table on the left.*]

A WORKING-MAN. Who's he?

ANOTHER WORKING-MAN. Don't you know him? It's that fellow Billing that writes for Aslaksen's paper.

[CAPTAIN HORSTER *enters by the door in front on the right, escorting* MRS. STOCK-

MANN *and* PETRA. EILIF *and* MORTEN *follow them.*]

HORSTER. This is where I thought you might sit; you can so easily slip out if anything should happen.

MRS. STOCKMANN. Do you think there will be any disturbance?

HORSTER. One can never tell—with such a crowd. But there's no occasion for anxiety.

MRS. STOCKMANN. [*Sitting down.*] How kind it was of you to offer Stockmann this room.

HORSTER. Since no one else would, I—

PETRA. [*Who has also seated herself.*] And it was brave too, Captain Horster.

HORSTER. Oh, I don't see where the bravery comes in.

[HOVSTAD *and* ASLAKSEN *enter at the same moment, but make their way through the crowd separately.*]

ASLAKSEN. [*Going up to* HORSTER.] Hasn't the Doctor come yet?

HORSTER. He's waiting in there.
　　　[*A movement at the door in the background.*]

HOVSTAD. [*To* BILLING.] There's the Burgomaster! Look!

BILLING. Yes, strike me dead if he hasn't put in an appearance after all!

[BURGOMASTER STOCKMANN *makes his way blandly through the meeting, bowing politely to both sides, and takes his stand by the wall on the left. Soon afterwards,* DR. STOCKMANN *enters by the door on the right. He wears a black frock-coat and white necktie. Faint applause, met by a subdued hissing. Then silence.*]

DR. STOCKMANN. [*In a low tone.*] How do you feel, Katrina?

MRS. STOCKMANN. Quite comfortable, thank you. [*In a low voice.*] Now do keep your temper, Thomas.

DR. STOCKMANN. Oh, I shall keep myself well in hand. [*Looks at his watch, ascends the platform, and bows.*] It's a quarter past the hour, so I shall begin—
　　　[*Takes out his MS.*]

ASLAKSEN. But surely a chairman must be elected first.

DR. STOCKMANN. No, that's not at all necessary.

SEVERAL GENTLEMEN. [*Shouting.*] Yes, yes.

BURGOMASTER. I should certainly say that a chairman ought to be elected.

DR. STOCKMANN. But I've called this meeting to give a lecture, Peter!

BURGOMASTER. Dr. Stockmann's lecture may possibly lead to differences of opinion.

SEVERAL VOICES IN THE CROWD. A chairman! A chairman!

HOVSTAD. The general voice of the meeting seems to be for a chairman!

DR. STOCKMANN. [*Controlling himself.*] Very well, then; let the meeting have its way.

ASLAKSEN. Will not the Burgomaster take the chair?

THREE GENTLEMEN. [*Clapping.*] Bravo! Bravo!

BURGOMASTER. For reasons you will easily understand, I must decline. But, fortunately, we have among us one whom I think we can all accept. I allude to the president of the House-owners' Association, Mr. Aslaksen.

MANY VOICES. Yes, yes! Bravo, Aslaksen! Hurrah for Aslaksen!
　　　[DR. STOCKMANN *takes his MS. and descends from the platform.*]

ASLAKSEN. Since my fellow citizens repose this trust in me, I cannot refuse—
　　　[*Applause and cheers.* ASLAKSEN *ascends the platform.*]

BILLING. [*Writing.*] So—"Mr. Aslaksen was elected by acclamation—"

ASLAKSEN. And now, as I have been called to the chair, I take the liberty of saying a few brief words. I am a quiet, peace-loving man; I am in favour of discreet moderation, and of—and of moderate discretion. Every one who knows me knows that.

MANY VOICES. Yes, yes, Aslaksen!

ASLAKSEN. I have learnt in the school of life and of experience that moderation is the virtue in which the individual citizen finds his best advantage—

BURGOMASTER. Hear, hear!

ASLAKSEN. —and it is discretion and moderation, too, that best serve the community. I could therefore suggest to our respected fellow citizen, who has called this meeting, that he should endeavour to keep within the bounds of moderation.

A MAN. [By the door.] Three cheers for the Temperance Society!

A VOICE. Go to the devil!

VOICES. Hush! hush!

ASLAKSEN. No interruptions, gentlemen!—Does any one wish to offer any observations?

BURGOMASTER. Mr. Chairman!

ASLAKSEN. Burgomaster Stockmann will address the meeting.

BURGOMASTER. On account of my close relationship—of which you are probably aware—to the present medical officer of the Baths, I should have preferred not to speak here this evening. But my position as chairman of the Baths, and my care for the vital interests of this town, force me to move a resolution. I may doubtless assume that not a single citizen here present thinks it desirable that untrustworthy and exaggerated statements should get abroad as to the sanitary condition of the Baths and of our town.

MANY VOICES. No, no, no! Certainly not! We protest!

BURGOMASTER. I therefore beg to move, "That this meeting declines to hear the proposed lecture or speech on the subject by the medical officer of the Baths."

DR. STOCKMANN. [Flaring up.] Declines to hear—! What do you mean?

MRS. STOCKMANN. [Coughing.] H'm! h'm!

DR. STOCKMANN. [Controlling himself.] So I am not to be heard?

BURGOMASTER. In my statement in the People's Messenger I have made the public acquainted with the essential facts, so that all well-disposed citizens can easily form their own judgment. From that statement it will be seen that the medical officer's proposal—besides amounting to a vote of censure upon the leading men of the town—at bottom only means saddling the ratepayers [1] with an unnecessary outlay of at least a hundred thousand crowns.

[Sounds of protest and some hissing.]

ASLAKSEN. [Ringing the bell.] Order, gentlemen! I must beg leave to support the Burgomaster's resolution. I quite agree with him that there is something beneath the surface of the Doctor's agitation. In all his talk about the Baths, it is really a revolution he is aiming at; he wants to effect a redistribution of power. No one doubts the excellence of Dr. Stockmann's intentions—of course, there cannot be two opinions as to that. I, too, am in favour of self-government by the people, if only it doesn't cost the ratepayers too much. But in this case it would do so; and therefore I'll be hanged if—excuse me—in short, I cannot go with Dr. Stockmann upon this occasion. You can buy even gold too dear; that's my opinion. [Loud applause on all sides.]

HOVSTAD. I, too, feel bound to explain my attitude. Dr. Stockmann's agitation seemed at first to find favour in several quarters, and I supported it as impartially as I could. But it presently appeared that we had been misled by a false representation of the facts—

DR. STOCKMANN. False—!

HOVSTAD. Well, then, an untrustworthy representation. This the Burgomaster's report has proved. I trust no one here present doubts my liberal principles; the attitude of the Messenger on all great political questions is well known to you all. But I have learned from men of judgment and experience that in purely local matters a paper must observe a certain amount of caution.

ASLAKSEN. I entirely agree with the speaker.

HOVSTAD. And in the matter under discussion it is quite evident that Dr. Stockmann has public opinion against him. But,

[1] Taxpayers.

gentlemen, what is an editor's clearest and most imperative duty? Is it not to work in harmony with his readers? Has he not in some sort received a tacit mandate to further assiduously and unweariedly the interests of his constituents? Or am I mistaken in this?

MANY VOICES. No, no, no! Hovstad is right!

HOVSTAD. It has cost me a bitter struggle to break with a man in whose house I have of late been a frequent guest—with a man who, up to this day, has enjoyed the unqualified good will of his fellow citizens —with a man whose only, or, at any rate, whose chief fault is that he consults his heart rather than his head.

A FEW SCATTERED VOICES. That's true! Hurrah for Dr. Stockmann!

HOVSTAD. But my duty towards the community has constrained me to break with him. Then, too, there is another consideration that impels me to oppose him, and, if possible, to block the ill-omened path upon which he is entering: consideration for his family—

DR. STOCKMANN. Keep to the waterworks and sewers!

HOVSTAD. —consideration for his wife and his unprotected children.

MORTEN. Is that us, mother?

MRS. STOCKMANN. Hush!

ASLAKSEN. I will now put the Burgomaster's resolution to the vote.

DR. STOCKMANN. You need not. I have no intention of saying anything this evening of all the filth at the Baths. No! You shall hear something quite different.

BURGOMASTER. [Half aloud.] What next, I wonder?

A DRUNKEN MAN. [At the main entrance.] I'm a ratepayer, so I've a right to my opinion! And it's my full, firm, incomprehensible opinion that—

SEVERAL VOICES. Silence up there!

OTHERS. He's drunk! Turn him out!

[The drunken man is turned out.]

DR. STOCKMANN. Can I speak?

ASLAKSEN. [Ringing the bell.] Dr. Stockmann will address the meeting.

DR. STOCKMANN. A few days ago, I should have liked to see any one venture upon such an attempt to gag me as has been made here to-night! I would have fought like a lion for my sacred rights! But now I care little enough; for now I have more important things to speak of.

[The people crowd closer round him. MORTEN KIIL comes in sight among the bystanders.]

DR. STOCKMANN. [Continuing.] I have been pondering a great many things during these last days—thinking such a multitude of thoughts, that at last my head was positively in a whirl—

BURGOMASTER. [Coughing.] H'm—!

DR. STOCKMANN. But presently things seemed to straighten themselves out, and I saw them clearly in all their bearings. That is why I stand here this evening. I am about to make great revelations, my fellow citizens! I am going to announce to you a far-reaching discovery, beside which the trifling fact that our water-works are poisoned, and that our health-resort is built on pestilential ground, sinks into insignificance.

MANY VOICES. [Shouting.] Don't speak about the Baths! We won't listen to that! No more of that!

DR. STOCKMANN. I have said I would speak of the great discovery I have made within the last few days—the discovery that all our sources of spiritual life are poisoned, and that our whole society rests upon a pestilential basis of falsehood.

SEVERAL VOICES. [In astonishment and half aloud.] What's he saying?

BURGOMASTER. Such an insinuation—!

ASLAKSEN. [With his hand on the bell.] I must call upon the speaker to moderate his expressions.

DR. STOCKMANN. I have loved my native town as dearly as any man can love the home of his childhood. I was young when I left our town, and distance, homesickness and memory threw, as it were, a glamour over the place and its people.

[Some applause and cries of approval.]

DR. STOCKMANN. Then for years I was imprisoned in a horrible hole, far away in the north. As I went about among the people scattered here and there over the stony wilderness, it seemed to me, many a time, that it would have been better for these poor famishing creatures to have had a cattle-doctor to attend them, instead of a man like me.

[*Murmurs in the room.*]

BILLING. [*Laying down his pen.*] Strike me dead if I've ever heard—!

HOVSTAD. What an insult to an estimable peasantry!

DR. STOCKMANN. Wait a moment!—I don't think any one can reproach me with forgetting my native town up there. I sat brooding like an eider duck, and what I hatched was—the plan of the Baths.

[*Applause and expressions of dissent.*]

DR. STOCKMANN. And when, at last, fate ordered things so happily that I could come home again—then, fellow citizens, it seemed to me that I hadn't another desire in the world. Yes, one desire I had: an eager, constant, burning desire to be of service to my birthplace, and to its people.

BURGOMASTER. [*Gazing into vacancy.*] A strange method to select—!

DR. STOCKMANN. So I went about revelling in my happy illusions. But yesterday morning—no, it was really two nights ago—my mind's eyes were opened wide, and the first thing I saw was the colossal stupidity of the authorities—

[*Noise, cries, and laughter.* MRS. STOCKMANN *coughs repeatedly.*]

BURGOMASTER. Mr. Chairman!

ASLAKSEN. [*Ringing his bell.*] In virtue of my position—!

DR. STOCKMANN. It's petty to catch me up on a word, Mr. Aslaksen! I only mean that I became alive to the extraordinary muddle our leading men had been guilty of, down at the Baths. I cannot for the life of me abide leading men—I've seen enough of them in my time. They are like goats in a young plantation: they do harm at every point; they block the path of a free man wherever he turns—and I should be glad if we could exterminate them like other noxious animals— [*Uproar in the room.*]

BURGOMASTER. Mr. Chairman, are such expressions permissible?

ASLAKSEN. [*With his hand on the bell.*] Dr. Stockmann—

DR. STOCKMANN. I can't conceive how it is that I have only now seen through these gentry; for haven't I had a magnificent example before my eyes here every day—my brother Peter—slow of understanding, tenacious in prejudice—

[*Laughter, noise, and whistling.* MRS. STOCKMANN *coughs.* ASLAKSEN *rings violently.*]

THE DRUNKEN MAN. [*Who has come in again.*] Is it me you're alluding to? Sure enough, my name's Petersen; but devil take me if—

ANGRY VOICES. Out with that drunken man! Turn him out!

[*The man is again turned out.*]

BURGOMASTER. Who is that person?

A BYSTANDER. I don't know him, Burgomaster.

ANOTHER. He doesn't belong to the town.

A THIRD. I believe he's a timber-dealer from— [*The rest is inaudible.*]

ASLAKSEN. The man was evidently intoxicated.—Continue, Dr. Stockmann; but pray endeavour to be moderate.

DR. STOCKMANN. Well, fellow citizens, I shall say no more about our leading men. If any one imagines, from what I have just said, that it's these gentlemen I want to make short work of to-night, he is mistaken—altogether mistaken. For I cherish the comfortable conviction that these laggards, these relics of a decaying order of thought, are diligently cutting their own throats. They need no doctor to hasten their end. And it is not people of *that* sort that constitute the real danger to society; it is not they who are most active in poisoning the sources of our spiritual life and making a plague-spot of the ground beneath our feet; it is not *they* who are the most dangerous enemies of truth and freedom in our society.

CRIES FROM ALL SIDES. Who, then? Who is it? Name, name!

DR. STOCKMANN. Yes, you may be sure I shall name them! For *this* is the great discovery I made yesterday. [*In a louder tone.*] The most dangerous foe to truth and freedom in our midst is the compact majority. Yes, it's the confounded, compact, liberal majority—that, and nothing else! There, I've told you.

[*Immense disturbance in the room. Most of the audience are shouting, stamping, and whistling. Several elderly gentlemen exchange furtive glances and seem to be enjoying the scene.* MRS. STOCKMANN *rises in alarm.* EILIF *and* MORTEN *advance threateningly toward the schoolboys, who are making noises.* ASLAKSEN *rings the bell and calls for order.* HOVSTAD *and* BILLING *both speak, but nothing can be heard. At last quiet is restored.*]

ASLAKSEN. I must request the speaker to withdraw his ill-considered expressions.

DR. STOCKMANN. Never, Mr. Aslaksen! For it's this very majority that robs me of my freedom, and wants to forbid me to speak the truth.

HOVSTAD. The majority always has right on its side.

BILLING. Yes, and truth too, strike me dead!

DR. STOCKMANN. The majority *never* has right on its side. Never, I say! That is one of the social lies that a free, thinking man is bound to rebel against. Who make up the majority in any given country? Is it the wise men or the fools? I think we must agree that the fools are in a terrible, overwhelming majority, all the wide world over. But how in the devil's name can it ever be right for the fools to rule over the wise men? [*Uproar and yells.*]

DR. STOCKMANN. Yes, yes, you can shout me down, but you cannot gainsay me. The majority has *might*—unhappily—but *right* it has not. It is I, and the few, the individuals, that are in the right. The minority is always right.

[*Renewed uproar.*]

HOVSTAD. Ha ha! Dr. Stockmann has turned aristocrat since the day before yesterday!

DR. STOCKMANN. I have said that I have no words to waste on the little, narrow-chested, short-winded crew that lie in our wake. Pulsating life has nothing more to do with them. I am speaking of the few, the individuals among us, who have made all the new, germinating truths their own. These men stand, as it were, at the outposts, so far in the van that the compact majority has not yet reached them—and *there* they fight for truths that are too lately born into the world's consciousness to have won over the majority.

HOVSTAD. So the Doctor's a revolutionist now!

DR. STOCKMANN. Yes, by Heaven, I am, Mr. Hovstad! I am going to revolt against the lie that truth belongs exclusively to the majority. What sort of truths do the majority rally round? Truths so stricken in years that they are sinking into decrepitude. When a truth is so old as that, gentlemen, it's in a fair way to become a lie.

[*Laughter and jeers.*]

DR. STOCKMANN. Yes, yes, you may believe me or not, as you please; but truths are by no means the wiry Methuselahs some people think them. A normally constituted truth lives—let us say—as a rule, seventeen or eighteen years; at the outside twenty; very seldom more. And truths so patriarchal as that are always shockingly emaciated; yet it's not till then that the majority takes them up and recommends them to society as wholesome food. I can assure you there's not much nutriment in that sort of fare; you may take my word as a doctor for that. All these majority-truths are like last year's salt pork; they're like rancid, mouldy ham, producing all the moral scurvy that devastates society.

ASLAKSEN. It seems to me that the honourable speaker is wandering rather far from the subject.

BURGOMASTER. I beg to endorse the Chairman's remark.

DR. STOCKMANN. Why, you're surely mad, Peter! I'm keeping as closely to my text as I possibly can; for my text is precisely this—that the masses, the majority, this devil's own compact majority—it's that, I say, that's poisoning the sources of our spiritual life, and making a plague-spot of the ground beneath our feet.

HOVSTAD. And you make this charge against the great, independent majority, just because they have the sense to accept only certain and acknowledged truths?

DR. STOCKMANN. Ah, my dear Mr. Hovstad, don't talk about certain truths! The truths acknowledged by the masses, the multitude, were certain truths to the vanguard in our grandfathers' days. We, the vanguard of to-day, don't acknowledge them any longer; and I don't believe there exists any other certain truth but this— that no society can live a healthy life upon truths so old and marrowless.

HOVSTAD. But instead of all this vague talk, suppose you were to give us some specimens of these old marrowless truths that we are living upon.

[Approval from several quarters.]

DR. STOCKMANN. Oh, I could give you no end of samples from the rubbish-heap; but, for the present, I shall keep to one acknowledged truth, which is a hideous lie at bottom, but which Mr. Hovstad, and the Messenger, and all adherents of the Messenger, live on all the same.

HOVSTAD. And that is—?

DR. STOCKMANN. That is the doctrine you have inherited from your forefathers, and go on thoughtlessly proclaiming far and wide—the doctrine that the multitude, the vulgar herd, the masses, are the pith of the people—that they are the people—that the common man, the ignorant, undeveloped member of society, has the same right to sanction and to condemn, to counsel and to govern, as the intellectually distinguished few.

BILLING. Well, now, strike me dead—!

HOVSTAD. [Shouting at the same time.] Citizens, please note this!

ANGRY VOICES. Ho-ho! Aren't we the people? Is it only the grand folks that are to govern?

A WORKING MAN. Out with the fellow that talks like that!

OTHERS. Turn him out!

A CITIZEN. [Shouting.] Blow your horn, Evensen!

[The deep notes of a horn are heard; whistling, and terrific noise in the room.]

DR. STOCKMANN. [When the noise has somewhat subsided.] Now do be reasonable! Can't you bear even for once in a way to hear the voice of truth? I don't ask you all to agree with me on the instant. But I certainly should have expected Mr. Hovstad to back me up, as soon as he had collected himself a bit. Mr. Hovstad sets up to be a freethinker—

SEVERAL VOICES. [Subdued and wondering.] Freethinker, did he say? What? Mr. Hovstad a freethinker?

HOVSTAD. [Shouting.] Prove it, Dr. Stockmann. When have I said so in print?

DR. STOCKMANN. [Reflecting.] No, upon my soul, you're right there; you've never had the frankness to do that. Well, well, I won't put you on the rack, Mr. Hovstad. Let me be the freethinker then. And now I'll make it clear to you all, and on scientific grounds too, that the Messenger is leading you shamefully by the nose, when it tells you that you, the masses, the crowd, are the true pith of the people. I tell you that's only a newspaper lie. The masses are nothing but the raw material that must be fashioned into a People.

[Murmurs, laughter, and disturbance in the room.]

DR. STOCKMANN. Is it not so with all other living creatures? What a difference between a cultivated and an uncultivated breed of animals! Just look at a common barn-door hen. What meat do you get from such a skinny carcase? Not much, I can tell you! And what sort of eggs does she lay? A decent crow or raven can lay nearly as good. Then take a cultivated Spanish or Japanese hen, or take a fine pheasant or turkey—ah! then you'll see the difference! And now look at the dog, our near relation. Think first of an ordinary vulgar cur—I mean one of those wretched, ragged, plebeian mongrels that haunt the gutters, and soil the sidewalks. Then place such a mongrel by the side of a poodle-dog, descended through many generations from an aristocratic stock, who have lived on delicate food, and heard harmonious voices and music. Do you think the brain of the poodle isn't very differently developed from that of the mongrel? Yes, you may be sure it is! It's well-bred poodle-pups like this that jugglers train to perform the most marvellous tricks. A common peasant-cur could never learn anything of the sort—not if he tried till doomsday.

[Noise and laughter are heard all round.]

A CITIZEN. [Shouting.] Do you want to make dogs of us now?

ANOTHER MAN. We're not animals, Doctor!

DR. STOCKMANN. Yes, on my soul, but we *are* animals, my good sir! We're one and all of us animals, whether we like it or not. But truly there are few enough aristocratic animals among us. Oh, there's a terrible difference between poodle-men and mongrel-men! And the ridiculous part of it is that Mr. Hovstad quite agrees with me so long as it's four-legged animals we're talking of—

HOVSTAD. Oh, beasts are only beasts.

DR. STOCKMANN. Well and good—but no sooner do I apply the law to two-legged animals, than Mr. Hovstad stops short; then he daren't hold his own opinions, or think out his own thoughts; then he turns the whole principle upside down, and proclaims in the *People's Messenger* that the barn-door hen and the gutter-mongrel are precisely the finest specimens in the menagerie. But that's always the way, so long as the commonness still lingers in your system, and you haven't worked your way up to spiritual distinction.

HOVSTAD. I make no pretence to any sort of distinction. I come of simple peasant folk, and I am proud that my root should lie deep down among the common people, who are here being insulted.

WORKMEN. Hurrah for Hovstad! Hurrah! hurrah!

DR. STOCKMANN. The sort of common people I am speaking of are not found among the lower classes alone; they crawl and swarm all around us—up to the very summits of society. Just look at your own smug, respectable Burgomaster! Why, my brother Peter belongs as clearly to the common people as any man that walks on two legs— [Laughter and hisses.]

BURGOMASTER. I protest against such personalities.

DR. STOCKMANN. [Imperturbably.] —and that not because, like myself, he's descended from a good-for-nothing old pirate from Pomerania, or thereabouts—for that's our ancestry—

BURGOMASTER. An absurd tradition! Utterly groundless.

DR. STOCKMANN. —but he is so because he thinks the thoughts and holds the opinions of his official superiors. Men who do that belong, intellectually speaking, to the common people; and that is why my distinguished brother Peter is at bottom so undistinguished,—and consequently so illiberal.

BURGOMASTER. Mr. Chairman—!

HOVSTAD. So that the distinguished people in this country are the Liberals? That's quite a new light on the subject.

[Laughter.]

DR. STOCKMANN. Yes, that is part of my new discovery. And this, too, follows: that liberality of thought is almost precisely the same thing as morality. Therefore I say it's absolutely unpardonable of the *Messenger* to proclaim, day out, day in, the false doctrine that it's the masses, the multitude, the compact majority, that monopolise liberality and morality,—and that vice and corruption and all sorts of spiritual uncleanness ooze out of culture, as all that filth oozes down to the Baths from the Mill Dale tan-works!

[Noise and interruptions.]

DR. STOCKMANN. [Goes on imperturbably, smiling in his eagerness.] And yet this same *Messenger* can preach about elevating the masses and the multitude to a higher level of well-being! Why, deuce take it, if the *Messenger's* own doctrine holds good, the elevation of the masses would simply mean hurling them straight to perdition! But, happily, the notion that culture demoralises is nothing but an old traditional lie. No, it's stupidity, poverty, the ugliness of life, that do the devil's work! In a house that isn't aired and swept every day—my wife maintains that the floors ought to be scrubbed, too, but perhaps that is going too far;—well,—in such a house, I say, within two or three years, people lose the power of thinking or acting morally. Lack of oxygen enervates the conscience. And there seems to be precious little oxygen in many and many a house in this town, since the whole compact majority is unscrupulous enough to want to found its future upon a quagmire of lies and fraud.

ASLAKSEN. I cannot allow so gross an insult to be levelled against a whole community.

A GENTLEMAN. I move that the Chairman order the speaker to sit down.

EAGER VOICES. Yes, yes! That's right! Sit down! Sit down!

DR. STOCKMANN. [*Flaring up.*] Then I shall proclaim the truth at every street corner! I shall write to newspapers in other towns! The whole country shall know how matters stand here!

HOVSTAD. It almost seems as if the Doctor's object were to ruin the town.

DR. STOCKMANN. Yes, so well do I love my native town that I would rather ruin it than see it flourishing upon a lie.

ASLAKSEN. That's plain speaking.

[*Noise and whistling.* MRS. STOCKMANN *coughs in vain; the* DOCTOR *no longer heeds her.*]

HOVSTAD. [*Shouting amid the tumult.*] The man who would ruin a whole community must be an enemy to his fellow citizens!

DR. STOCKMANN. [*With growing excitement.*] What does it matter if a lying community is ruined! Let it be levelled to the ground, say I! All men who live upon a lie ought to be exterminated like vermin! You'll end by poisoning the whole country; you'll bring it to such a pass that the whole country will deserve to perish. And if ever it comes to that, I shall say, from the bottom of my heart: Perish the country! Perish all its people!

A MAN. [*In the crowd.*] Why, he talks like a regular enemy of the people!

BILLING. Strike me dead but there spoke the people's voice!

THE WHOLE ASSEMBLY. [*Shouting.*] Yes! yes! yes! He's an enemy of the people! He hates his country! He hates the whole people!

ASLAKSEN. Both as a citizen of this town and as a human being, I am deeply shocked at what it has been my lot to hear to-night. Dr. Stockmann has unmasked himself in a manner I should never have dreamt of. I must reluctantly subscribe to the opinion just expressed by some estimable citizens; and I think we ought to formulate this opinion in a resolution. I therefore beg to move, "That this meeting declares the medical officer of the Baths, Dr. Thomas Stockmann, to be an enemy of the people."

[*Thunders of applause and cheers. Many form a circle round the* DOCTOR *and hoot at him.* MRS. STOCKMANN *and* PETRA *have risen.* MORTEN *and* EILIF *fight the other school-boys, who have also been hooting. Some grown-up persons separate them.*]

DR. STOCKMANN. [*To the people hooting.*] Ah, fools that you are! I tell you that—

ASLAKSEN. [*Ringing.*] The Doctor is out of order in speaking. A formal vote must be taken; but out of consideration for personal feelings, it will be taken in writing and without names. Have you any blank paper, Mr. Billing?

BILLING. Here's both blue and white paper—

ASLAKSEN. Capital; that will save time. Cut it up into slips. That's it. [*To the meet-*

ing.] Blue means no, white means aye. I myself will go round and collect the votes.

[*The* BURGOMASTER *leaves the room.* ASLAKSEN *and a few others go round with pieces of paper in hats.*]

A GENTLEMAN. [*To* HOVSTAD.] What can be the matter with the Doctor? What does it all mean?

HOVSTAD. Why, you know what a harebrained creature he is.

ANOTHER GENTLEMAN. [*To* BILLING.] I say, you're often at his house. Have you ever noticed if the fellow drinks?

BILLING. Strike me dead if I know what to say. The toddy's always on the table when any one looks in.

A THIRD GENTLEMAN. No, I should rather say he went off his head at times.

FIRST GENTLEMAN. I wonder if there's madness in the family?

BILLING. I shouldn't be surprised.

A FOURTH GENTLEMAN. No, it's pure malice. He wants to be revenged for something or other.

BILLING. He was certainly talking about a rise in his salary the other day; but he didn't get it.

ALL THE GENTLEMEN. [*Together.*] Aha! That explains everything.

THE DRUNKEN MAN. [*In the crowd.*] I want a blue one, I do! And I'll have a white one, too.

SEVERAL PEOPLE. There's the tipsy man again! Turn him out.

MORTEN KIIL. [*Approaching the* DOCTOR.] Well, Stockmann, you see now what such monkey-tricks lead to?

DR. STOCKMANN. I have done my duty.

MORTEN KIIL. What was that you said about the Mill Dale tanneries?

DR. STOCKMANN. You heard what I said —that all the filth comes from them.

MORTEN KIIL. From my tannery as well?

DR. STOCKMANN. I'm sorry to say yours is the worst of all.

MORTEN KIIL. Are you going to put *that* in the papers, too?

DR. STOCKMANN. I can't gloze anything over.

MORTEN KIIL. This may cost you dear, Stockmann! [*He goes out.*]

A FAT GENTLEMAN. [*Goes up to* HORSTER, *without bowing to the ladies.*] Well, Captain, so you lend your house to enemies of the people.

HORSTER. I suppose I can do as I please with my own property, Sir.

THE GENTLEMAN. Then of course you can have no objection if I follow your example?

HORSTER. What do you mean, Sir?

THE GENTLEMAN. You shall hear from me to-morrow. [*Turns away and goes out.*]

PETRA. Wasn't that the owner of your ship, Captain Horster?

HORSTER. Yes, that was Mr. Vik.

ASLAKSEN. [*With the voting papers in his hands, ascends the platform and rings.*] Gentlemen! I have now to announce the result of the vote. All the voters, with one exception—

A YOUNG GENTLEMAN. That's the tipsy man!

ASLAKSEN. With the exception of one intoxicated person, this meeting of citizens unanimously declares the medical officer of the Baths, Dr. Thomas Stockmann, to be an enemy of the people. [*Cheers and applause.*] Three cheers for our fine old municipality! [*Cheers.*] Three cheers for our able and energetic Burgomaster, who has so loyally set family prejudice aside! [*Cheers.*] The meeting is dissolved. [*He descends.*]

BILLING. Three cheers for the Chairman!

ALL. Hurrah for Aslaksen!

DR. STOCKMANN. My hat and coat, Petra. Captain, have you room for passengers to the new world?

HORSTER. For you and yours, Doctor, we'll make room.

DR. STOCKMANN. [*While* PETRA *helps him to put on his coat.*] Good! Come, Katrina; come, boys!

[*He gives his wife his arm.*]

MRS. STOCKMANN. [*In a low voice.*] Thomas, dear, let us go out by the back way.

DR. STOCKMANN. No back ways, Katrina! [*In a loud voice.*] You shall hear from the enemy of the people, before he shakes the dust from his feet! I am not so forbearing as a certain person; I don't say: I forgive you, for you know not what you do.

ASLAKSEN. [*Shouts.*] This is a blasphemous comparison, Dr. Stockmann!

BILLING. Strike me—! This is more than a serious man can stand!

A COARSE VOICE. And he threatens us into the bargain!

ANGRY CRIES. Let's smash his windows! Duck him in the fiord!

A MAN. [*In the crowd.*] Blow your horn, Evensen! Blow, man, blow!

[*Horn-blowing, whistling, and wild shouting. The* DOCTOR, *with his family, goes towards the door.* HORSTER *clears the way for them.*]

ALL. [*Yelling after them as they go out.*] Enemy of the people! Enemy of the people! Enemy of the people!

BILLING. Strike me dead if I'd care to drink toddy at Stockmann's to-night!

[*The people throng towards the door; the shouting is taken up by others outside; from the street are heard cries of "Enemy of the people! Enemy of the people!" Curtain.*]

ACT FIFTH

DR. STOCKMANN'S *Study. Bookshelves and glass cases with various collections along the walls. In the back, a door leading to the hall; in front, on the left, a door to the sitting-room. In the wall to the right are two windows, all the panes of which are smashed. In the middle of the room is the* DOCTOR'S *writing-table, covered with books and papers. The room is in disorder. It is forenoon.*

[DR. STOCKMANN, *in dressing-gown, slippers, and skull-cap, is bending down and raking with an umbrella under one of the cabinets; at last he rakes out a stone.*]

DR. STOCKMANN. [*Speaking through the sitting-room doorway.*] Katrina, I've found another!

MRS. STOCKMANN. [*In the sitting-room.*] Oh, I'm sure you'll find plenty more.

DR. STOCKMANN. [*Placing the stone on a pile of others on the table.*] I shall keep these stones as sacred relics. Eilif and Morten shall see them every day, and when I die they shall be heirlooms. [*Raking under the bookcase.*] Hasn't—what the devil is her name?—the girl—hasn't she been for the glazier yet?

MRS. STOCKMANN. [*Coming in.*] Yes, but he said he didn't know whether he would be able to come to-day.

DR. STOCKMANN. I believe, if the truth were told, he daren't come.

MRS. STOCKMANN. Well, Randina, too, had an idea he was afraid to come, because of the neighbours. [*Speaks through the sitting-room doorway.*] What is it, Randina? —Very well. [*Goes out, and returns immediately.*] Here is a letter for you, Thomas.

DR. STOCKMANN. Let me see. [*Opens the letter and reads.*] Aha!

MRS. STOCKMANN. Who is it from?

DR. STOCKMANN. From the landlord. He gives us notice.

MRS. STOCKMANN. Is it possible? He is such a nice man—

DR. STOCKMANN. [*Looking at the letter.*] He daren't do otherwise, he says. He is very unwilling to do it; but he daren't do otherwise—on account of his fellow citizens—out of respect for public opinion—is in a dependent position—doesn't dare to offend certain influential men—

MRS. STOCKMANN. There, you see, Thomas.

DR. STOCKMANN. Yes, yes, I see well enough; they are all cowards, every one of them, in this town; no one dares do anything for fear of all the rest. [*Throws the letter on the table.*] But it's all the same to us, Katrina. We will shape our course for the new world, and then—

MRS. STOCKMANN. But are you sure this

idea of going abroad is altogether wise, Thomas?

DR. STOCKMANN. Would you have me stay here, where they have pilloried me as an enemy of the people, branded me, smashed my windows! And look here, Katrina, they've torn a hole in my black trousers, too.

MRS. STOCKMANN. Oh dear; and these are the best you have!

DR. STOCKMANN. A man should never put on his best trousers when he goes out to battle for freedom and truth. Well, I don't care so much about the trousers; them you can always patch up for me. But that the mob, the rabble, should dare to attack me as if they were my equals—*that* is what I can't, for the life of me, stomach!

MRS. STOCKMANN. Yes, they have behaved abominably to you here, Thomas; but is that any reason for leaving the country altogether?

DR. STOCKMANN. Do you think the plebeians aren't just as insolent in other towns? Oh yes, they are, my dear; it's six of one and half a dozen of the other. Well, never mind; let the curs yelp; *that's* not the worst; the worst is that every one, all over the country, is the slave of his party. Not that I suppose—very likely it's no better in the free West either; the compact majority, and enlightened public opinion, and all the other devil's trash is rampant there too. But you see the conditions are larger there than here; they may kill you, but they don't slow-torture you; they don't screw up a free soul in a vise, as they do at home here. And then, if need be, you can keep out of it all. [*Walks up and down.*] If I only knew of any primeval forest, or a little South Sea island to be sold cheap—

MRS. STOCKMANN. Yes, but the boys, Thomas.

DR. STOCKMANN. [*Comes to a standstill.*] What an extraordinary woman you are, Katrina! Would you rather have the boys grow up in such a society as ours? Why, you could see for yourself yesterday evening that one half of the population is stark mad, and if the other half hasn't lost its wits, that's only because they are brute beasts who haven't any wits to lose.

MRS. STOCKMANN. But really, my dear Thomas, you do say such imprudent things.

DR. STOCKMANN. What! Isn't it the truth that I tell them? Don't they turn all ideas upside down? Don't they stir up right and wrong into one hotch-potch? Don't they call lies everything that I know to be the truth? But the maddest thing of all is to see crowds of grown men, calling themselves Liberals, go about persuading themselves and others that they are friends of freedom! Did you ever hear anything like it, Katrina?

MRS. STOCKMANN. Yes, yes, no doubt. But—

[PETRA *enters from the sitting-room.*]

MRS. STOCKMANN. Back from school already?

PETRA. Yes; I have been dismissed.

MRS. STOCKMANN. Dismissed?

DR. STOCKMANN. You, too!

PETRA. Mrs. Busk gave me notice, and so I thought it best to leave there and then.

DR. STOCKMANN. You did perfectly right!

MRS. STOCKMANN. Who could have thought Mrs. Busk was such a bad woman!

PETRA. Oh, mother, Mrs. Busk isn't bad at all; I saw clearly how sorry she was. But she dared not do otherwise, she said; and so I am dismissed.

DR. STOCKMANN. [*Laughing and rubbing his hands.*] She dared not do otherwise —just like the rest! Oh, it's delicious.

MRS. STOCKMANN. Oh well, after that frightful scene last night—

PETRA. It wasn't only that. What do you think, father—?

DR. STOCKMANN. Well?

PETRA. Mrs. Busk showed me no fewer than three letters she had received this morning—

DR. STOCKMANN. Anonymous, of course?

PETRA. Yes.

DR. STOCKMANN. They never dare give their names, Katrina!

PETRA.   And two of them stated that a gentleman who is often at our house said at the club last night that I held extremely advanced opinions upon various things—

DR. STOCKMANN.   Of course, you didn't deny it.

PETRA.   Of course not. You know Mrs. Busk herself is pretty advanced in her opinions when we're alone together; but now that this has come out about me, she dared not keep me on.

MRS. STOCKMANN.   Some one that is often at our house, too. There, you see, Thomas, what comes of all your hospitality.

DR. STOCKMANN.   We won't live any longer in such a pig-sty! Pack up as quickly as you can, Katrina; let's get away—the sooner the better.

MRS. STOCKMANN.   Hush! I think there is some one in the passage. See who it is, Petra.

PETRA.   [Opening the door.] Oh, is it you, Captain Horster? Please come in.

HORSTER.   [From the hall.] Good morning. I thought I might just look in and ask how you are.

DR. STOCKMANN.   [Shaking his hand.] Thanks; that's very good of you.

MRS. STOCKMANN.   And thank you for helping us through the crowd last night, Captain Horster.

PETRA.   How did you ever get home again?

HORSTER.   Oh, that was all right. I am tolerably able-bodied, you know; and those fellows' bark is worse than their bite.

DR. STOCKMANN.   Yes, isn't it extraordinary, this piggish cowardice? Come here, and let me show you something! Look, here are all the stones they threw in at us. Only look at them! Upon my soul, there aren't more than two decent-sized lumps in the whole heap; the rest are nothing but pebbles—mere gravel. They stood down there, and yelled, and swore they'd half kill me; —but as for really doing it—no, there's mighty little fear of *that* in this town!

HORSTER.   You may thank your stars for that this time, Doctor.

DR. STOCKMANN.   So I do, of course. But it's depressing all the same; for if ever it should come to a serious national struggle, you may be sure public opinion would be for taking to its heels, and the compact majority would scamper for their lives like a flock of sheep, Captain Horster. *That* is what's so melancholy to think of; it grieves me to the heart.—But deuce take it—it's foolish of me to feel anything of the sort! They have called me an enemy of the people; well then, let me *be* an enemy of the people!

MRS. STOCKMANN.   That you'll never be, Thomas.

DR. STOCKMANN.   You'd better not take your oath of it, Katrina. A bad name may act like a pin-scratch in the lung. And that confounded word—I can't get rid of it; it has sunk deep into my heart; and there it lies gnawing and sucking like an acid. And no magnesia can cure me.

PETRA.   Pooh; you should only laugh at them, father.

HORSTER.   People will think differently yet, Doctor.

MRS. STOCKMANN.   Yes, Thomas, that's as certain as that you are standing here.

DR. STOCKMANN.   Yes, perhaps, when it is too late. Well, as they make their bed so they must lie! Let them go on wallowing here in their pig-sty, and learn to repent having driven a patriot into exile. When do you sail, Captain Horster?

HORSTER.   Well—that's really what I came to speak to you about—

DR. STOCKMANN.   What? Anything wrong with the ship?

HORSTER.   No; but the fact is, I shan't be sailing in her.

PETRA.   Surely *you* have not been dismissed?

HORSTER.   [Smiling.] Yes, I have.

PETRA.   You, too!

MRS. STOCKMANN.   There, you see, Thomas.

DR. STOCKMANN.   And for the truth's sake! Oh, if I could possibly have imagined such a thing—

HORSTER.   You mustn't be troubled

about this; I shall soon find a berth with some other company, elsewhere.

DR. STOCKMANN. And this is that man Vik! A wealthy man, independent of every one! Faugh!

HORSTER. Oh, for that matter, he's a very well-meaning man. He said himself he would gladly have kept me on if only he dared—

DR. STOCKMANN. But he didn't dare? Of course not!

HORSTER. It's not so easy, he said, when you belong to a party—

DR. STOCKMANN. My gentleman has hit it there! A party is like a sausage-machine; it grinds all the brains together in one mash; and that's why we see nothing but porridge-heads and pulp-heads all around!

MRS. STOCKMANN. Now really, Thomas!

PETRA. [To HORSTER.] If only you hadn't seen us home, perhaps it would not have come to this.

HORSTER. I don't regret it.

PETRA. [Gives him her hand.] Thank you for that!

HORSTER. [To DR. STOCKMANN.] And then, too, I wanted to tell you this: if you are really determined to go abroad, I've thought of another way—

DR. STOCKMANN. That's good—if only we can get off quickly—

MRS. STOCKMANN. Hush! Isn't that a knock?

PETRA. I believe it is uncle.

DR. STOCKMANN. Aha! [Calls.] Come in!

MRS. STOCKMANN. My dear Thomas, now do promise me—

[The BURGOMASTER enters from the hall.]

BURGOMASTER. [In the doorway.] Oh, you are engaged. Then I'd better—

DR. STOCKMANN. No, no; come in.

BURGOMASTER. But I wanted to speak to you alone.

MRS. STOCKMANN. We can go into the sitting-room.

HORSTER. And I shall look in again presently.

DR. STOCKMANN. No, no; go with the ladies, Captain Horster; I must hear more about—

HORSTER. All right, then I'll wait.

[He follows MRS. STOCKMANN and PETRA into the sitting-room. The BURGOMAS-TER says nothing, but casts glances at the windows.]

DR. STOCKMANN. I daresay you find it rather draughty here to-day? Put on your cap.

BURGOMASTER. Thanks, if I may. [Does so.] I fancy I caught cold yesterday evening. I stood there shivering—

DR. STOCKMANN. Really? On my soul, now, I found it quite warm enough.

BURGOMASTER. I regret that it was not in my power to prevent these nocturnal excesses.

DR. STOCKMANN. Have you anything else in particular to say to me?

BURGOMASTER. [Producing a large letter.] I have this document for you from the Directors of the Baths.

DR. STOCKMANN. My dismissal?

BURGOMASTER. Yes; dated from to-day. [Places the letter on the table.] We are very sorry—but frankly, we dared not do otherwise, on account of public opinion.

DR. STOCKMANN. [Smiling.] Dared not? I've heard that phrase already to-day.

BURGOMASTER. I beg you to realise your position clearly. For the future, you cannot count upon any sort of practice in the town.

DR. STOCKMANN. Devil take the practice! But how can you be so sure of that?

BURGOMASTER. The House-owners' Association is sending round a circular from house to house, in which all well-disposed citizens are called upon not to employ you; and I dare swear that not a single head of a family will venture to refuse his signature; he simply dare not.

DR. STOCKMANN. Well, well; I don't doubt that. But what then?

BURGOMASTER. If I might advise, I would suggest that you should leave the town for a time—

DR. STOCKMANN. Yes, I've had some such idea in my mind already.

BURGOMASTER. Good. And when you have had six months or so for mature deliberation, if you could make up your mind to acknowledge your error, with a few words of regret—

DR. STOCKMANN. I might perhaps be reinstated, you think?

BURGOMASTER. Perhaps it's not quite out of the question.

DR. STOCKMANN. Yes, but how about public opinion? You daren't, on account of public opinion.

BURGOMASTER. Opinion is extremely variable. And, to speak candidly, it is of the greatest importance for us to have such an admission under your own hand.

DR. STOCKMANN. Yes, I daresay it would be mightily convenient for you! But you remember what I've said to you before about such foxes' tricks!

BURGOMASTER. At that time your position was infinitely more favourable; at that time you thought you had the whole town at your back—

DR. STOCKMANN. Yes, and now I have the whole town on my back— [*Flaring up.*] But no—not if I had the devil and his dam on my back!— Never—never, I tell you!

BURGOMASTER. The father of a family has no right to act as you are doing. You have no right to do it, Thomas.

DR. STOCKMANN. I have no right! There's only one thing in the world that a free man has no right to do; and do you know what that is?

BURGOMASTER. No.

DR. STOCKMANN. Of course not; but *I* will tell you. A free man has no right to wallow in filth like a cur; he has no right to act so that he ought to spit in his own face!

BURGOMASTER. That sounds extremely plausible; and if there were not another explanation of your obstinacy—but we all know there is—

DR. STOCKMANN. What do you mean by that?

BURGOMASTER. You understand well enough. But as your brother, and as a man who knows the world, I warn you not to build too confidently upon prospects and

expectations that may very likely come to nothing.

DR. STOCKMANN. Why, what on earth are you driving at?

BURGOMASTER. Do you really want me to believe that you are ignorant of the terms of old Morten Kiil's will?

DR. STOCKMANN. I know that the little he has is to go to a home for old and needy artisans. But what has that got to do with me?

BURGOMASTER. To begin with, "the little he has" is no trifle. Morten Kiil is a tolerably wealthy man.

DR. STOCKMANN. I have never had the least notion of that!

BURGOMASTER. H'm—really? Then I suppose you have no notion that a not inconsiderable part of his fortune is to go to your children, you and your wife having a life-interest in it. Has he not told you that?

DR. STOCKMANN. No, I'll be hanged if he has! On the contrary, he has done nothing but grumble about being so preposterously over-taxed. But are you really sure of this, Peter?

BURGOMASTER. I have it from a thoroughly trustworthy source.

DR. STOCKMANN. Why, good heavens, then Katrina's provided for—and the children, too! Oh, I must tell her—[*Calls.*] Katrina, Katrina!

BURGOMASTER. [*Holding him back.*] Hush! don't say anything about it yet.

MRS. STOCKMANN. [*Opening the door.*] What is it?

DR. STOCKMANN. Nothing, my dear; go in again.

[MRS. STOCKMANN *closes the door.*]

DR. STOCKMANN. [*Pacing up and down.*] Provided for! Only think—all of them provided for! And for life! After all, it's a grand thing to feel yourself secure!

BURGOMASTER. Yes, but that is just what you are not. Morten Kiil can revoke his will any day or hour he chooses.

DR. STOCKMANN. But he won't, my good Peter. The Badger is only too delighted to see me fall foul of you and your wiseacre friends.

BURGOMASTER. [Starts and looks searchingly at him.] Aha! That throws a new light on a good many things.

DR. STOCKMANN. What things?

BURGOMASTER. So the whole affair has been a carefully-concocted intrigue. Your recklessly violent onslaught—in the name of truth—upon the leading men of the town—

DR. STOCKMANN. Well, what of it?

BURGOMASTER. It was nothing but a preconcerted requital for that vindictive old Morten Kiil's will.

DR. STOCKMANN. [Almost speechless.] Peter—you are the most abominable plebeian I have ever known in all my born days.

BURGOMASTER. All is over between us. Your dismissal is irrevocable—for now we have a weapon against you. [He goes out.]

DR. STOCKMANN. Shame! shame! shame! [Calls.] Katrina! The floor must be scrubbed after him! Tell her to come here with a pail—what's her name? confound it —the girl with the smudge on her nose—

MRS. STOCKMANN. [In the sitting-room doorway.] Hush, hush, Thomas!

PETRA. [Also in the doorway.] Father, here's grandfather; he wants to know if he can speak to you alone.

DR. STOCKMANN. Yes, of course he can. [By the door.] Come in, father-in-law.

[MORTEN KIIL enters. DR. STOCKMANN closes the door behind him.]

DR. STOCKMANN. Well, what is it? Sit down.

MORTEN KIIL. I won't sit down. [Looking about him.] It looks cheerful here to-day, Stockmann.

DR. STOCKMANN. Yes, don't you think so?

MORTEN KIIL. Sure enough. And you've plenty of fresh air, too; you've got your fill of that oxygen you were talking about yesterday. You must have a rare good conscience to-day, I should think.

DR. STOCKMANN. Yes, I have.

MORTEN KIIL. So I should suppose. [Tapping himself on the breast.] But do you know what I have got here?

DR. STOCKMANN. A good conscience, too, I hope.

MORTON KIIL. Pooh! No; something far better than that.

[Takes out a large pocket-book, opens it, and shows STOCKMANN a bundle of papers.]

DR. STOCKMANN. [Looking at him in astonishment.] Shares in the Baths!

MORTEN KIIL. They weren't difficult to get to-day.

DR. STOCKMANN. And you've gone and bought these up—?

MORTEN KIIL. All I had the money to pay for.

DR. STOCKMANN. Why, my dear sir,— just when things are in such a desperate way at the Baths—

MORTEN KIIL. If you behave like a reasonably being, you can soon set the Baths all right again.

DR. STOCKMANN. Well, you can see for yourself I'm doing all I can. But the people of this town are mad!

MORTEN KIIL. You said yesterday that the worst filth came from my tannery. Now, if that's true, then my grandfather, and my father before me, and I myself, have for ever so many years been poisoning the town with filth, like three destroying angels. Do you think I'm going to sit quiet under such a reproach?

DR. STOCKMANN. Unfortunately, you can't help it.

MORTEN KIIL. No, thank you. I hold fast to my good name. I've heard that people call me "the Badger." A badger's a sort of a pig, I know; but I'm determined to give them the lie. I will live and die a clean man.

DR. STOCKMANN. And how will you manage that?

MORTEN KIIL. You shall make me clean, Stockmann.

DR. STOCKMANN. I!

MORTEN KIIL. Do you know what money I've used to buy these shares with? No, you can't know; but now I'll tell you. It's the money Katrina and Petra and the boys are to have after my death. For, you see, I've laid by something after all.

DR. STOCKMANN. [*Flaring up.*] And you've taken Katrina's money and done *this* with it!

MORTEN KIIL. Yes; the whole of it is invested in the Baths now. And now I want to see if you're really so stark, staring mad, after all, Stockmann. If you go on making out that these beasts and other abominations dribble down from my tannery, it'll be just as if you were to flay broad stripes of Katrina's skin—and Petra's too, and the boys'. No decent father would ever do that —unless he were a madman.

DR. STOCKMANN. [*Walking up and down.*] Yes, but I *am* a madman; I *am* a madman!

MORTEN KIIL. You surely can't be so raving, ramping mad where your wife and children are concerned.

DR. STOCKMANN. [*Stopping in front of him.*] Why couldn't you have spoken to me before you went and bought all that rubbish?

MORTEN KIIL. What's done can't be undone.

DR. STOCKMANN. [*Walking restlessly about.*] If only I weren't so certain about the affair—! But I am absolutely convinced that I'm right.

MORTEN KIIL. [*Weighing the pocketbook in his hand.*] If you stick to this lunacy, these aren't worth much.

[*Puts the book into his pocket.*[

DR. STOCKMANN. But, deuce take it! surely science ought to be able to hit upon some antidote, some sort of prophylactic—

MORTEN KIIL. Do you mean something to kill the beasts?

DR. STOCKMANN. Yes, or at least to make them harmless.

MORTEN KIIL. Couldn't you try ratsbane?

DR. STOCKMANN. Oh, nonsense, nonsense!—But since every one declares it's nothing but fancy, why fancy let it be! Let them have it their own way! Haven't the ignorant, narrow-hearted curs reviled me as an enemy of the people?—and weren't they

on the point of tearing the clothes off my back?

MORTEN KIIL. And they've smashed all your windows for you, too!

DR. STOCKMANN. Yes, and then there's one's duty to one's family! I must talk that over with Katrina; such things are more in her line.

MORTEN KIIL. That's right! You just follow the advice of a sensible woman.

DR. STOCKMANN. [*Turning upon him angrily.*] How could you act so preposterously! Risking Katrina's money, and putting me to this horrible torture! When I look at you, I seem to see the devil himself—!

MORTEN KIIL. Then I'd better be off. But I must hear from you, yes or no, by two o'clock. If it's no, all the shares go to the Hospital—and that this very day.

DR. STOCKMANN. And what will Katrina get?

MORTEN KIIL. Not a rap.

[*The door leading to the hall opens.* HOVSTAD *and* ASLAKSEN *are seen outside it.*]

MORTEN KIIL. Hullo! look at these two.

DR. STOCKMANN. [*Staring at them.*] What! Do *you* actually venture to come here?

HOVSTAD. Why, to be sure we do.

ASLAKSEN. You see, we've something to discuss with you.

MORTEN KIIL. [*Whispers.*] Yes or no— by two o'clock.

ASLAKSEN. [*With a glance at* HOVSTAD.] Aha! [MORTEN KIIL *goes out.*]

DR. STOCKMANN. Well, what do you want with me? Be brief.

HOVSTAD. I can quite understand that you resent our attitude at the meeting yesterday—

DR. STOCKMANN. Your attitude, you say? Yes, it was a pretty attitude! I call it the attitude of cowards—of old women— Shame upon you!

HOVSTAD. Call it what you will; but we *could* not act otherwise.

DR. STOCKMANN. You *dared* not, I suppose? Isn't that so?

HOVSTAD. Yes, if you like to put it so.

ASLAKSEN. But why didn't you just say a word to us beforehand? The merest hint to Mr. Hovstad or to me—

DR. STOCKMANN. A hint? What about?

ASLAKSEN. About what was really behind it all.

DR. STOCKMANN. I don't in the least understand you.

ASLAKSEN. [Nods confidentially.] Oh, yes, you do, Dr. Stockmann.

HOVSTAD. It's no good making a mystery of it any longer.

DR. STOCKMANN. [Looking from one to the other.] Why, what in the devil's name—!

ASLAKSEN. May I ask—isn't your father-in-law going about the town buying up all the Bath stock?

DR. STOCKMANN. Yes, he has been buying Bath stock to-day but—

ASLAKSEN. It would have been more prudent to let somebody else do that—some one not so closely connected with you.

HOVSTAD. And then you ought not to have appeared in the matter under your own name. No one need have known that the attack on the Baths came from you. You should have taken me into your counsels, Dr. Stockmann.

DR. STOCKMANN. [Stares straight in front of him; a light seems to break in upon him, and he says as though thunderstruck.] Is this possible? Can such things be?

ASLAKSEN. [Smiling.] It's plain enough that they can. But they ought to be managed delicately, you understand.

HOVSTAD. And there ought to be more people in it; for the responsibility always falls more lightly when there are several to share it.

DR. STOCKMANN. [Calmly] In one word, gentlemen—what is it you want?

ASLAKSEN. Mr. Hovstad can best—

HOVSTAD. No, you explain, Aslaksen.

ASLAKSEN. Well, it's this: now that we know how the matter really stands, we believe we can venture to place the People's Messenger at your disposal.

DR. STOCKMANN. You can venture to now, eh? But how about public opinion? Aren't you afraid of bringing down a storm upon us?

HOVSTAD. We must manage to ride out the storm.

ASLAKSEN. And you must be ready to put about quickly, Doctor. As soon as your attack has done its work—

DR. STOCKMANN. As soon as my father-in-law and I have bought up the shares at a discount, you mean?

HOVSTAD. I presume it is mainly on scientific grounds that you want to take the management of the Baths into your own hands.

DR. STOCKMANN. Of course; it was on scientific grounds that I got the old Badger to stand in with me. And then we'll tinker up the water-works a little, and potter about a bit down at the beach, without its costing the town sixpence. That ought to do the business? Eh?

HOVSTAD. I think so—if you have the Messenger to back you up.

ASLAKSEN. In a free community the press is a power, Doctor.

DR. STOCKMANN. Yes, indeed; and so is public opinion. And you, Mr. Aslaksen— I suppose you will answer for the House-owners' Association?

ASLAKSEN. Both for the House-owners' Association and the Temperance Society. You may make your mind easy.

DR. STOCKMANN. But, gentlemen—really I'm quite ashamed to mention such a thing —but—what return—?

HOVSTAD. Of course, we should prefer to give you our support for nothing. But the Messenger is not very firmly established; it's not getting on as it ought to; and I should be very sorry to have to stop the paper just now, when there's so much to be done in general politics.

DR. STOCKMANN. Naturally; that would be very hard for a friend of the people like you. [Flaring up.] But I—I am an enemy of the people! [Striding about the room.] Where's my stick? Where the devil is my stick?

HOVSTAD. What do you mean?

ASLAKSEN. Surely you wouldn't—

DR. STOCKMANN. [*Standing still.*] And suppose I don't give you a single farthing out of all my shares? You must remember we rich folk don't like parting with our money.

HOVSTAD. And you must remember that this business of the shares can be represented in two ways.

DR. STOCKMANN. Yes, you are the man for that; if I don't come to the rescue of the *Messenger,* you'll manage to put a vile complexion on the affair; you'll hunt me down, I suppose—bait me—try to throttle me as a dog throttles a hare!

HOVSTAD. That's a law of nature—every animal fights for its own subsistence.

ASLAKSEN. And must take its food where it can find it, you know.

DR. STOCKMANN. Then see if you can't find some out in the gutter; [*Striding about the room*] for now, by heaven! we shall see which is the strongest animal of us three. [*Finds his umbrella and brandishes it.*] Now, look here—!

HOVSTAD. You surely don't mean to assault us!

ASLAKSEN. I say, be careful with that umbrella!

DR. STOCKMANN. Out at the window with you, Mr. Hovstad!

HOVSTAD. [*By the hall door.*] Are you utterly crazy?

DR. STOCKMANN. Out at the window, Mr. Aslaksen! Jump, I tell you! Be quick about it!

ASLAKSEN. [*Running round the writing-table.*] Moderation, Doctor; I'm not at all strong; I can't stand much— [*Screams.*] Help! help!

[MRS. STOCKMANN, PETRA, *and* HORSTER *enter from sitting-room.*]

MRS. STOCKMANN. Good heavens, Thomas! what *can* be the matter?

DR. STOCKMANN. [*Brandishing the umbrella.*] Jump, I tell you! Out into the gutter!

HOVSTAD. An unprovoked assault! I call you to witness, Captain Horster.

[*Rushes off through the hall.*]

ASLAKSEN. [*Bewildered.*] If one only knew the local situation—!

[*He slinks out by the sitting-room door.*]

MRS. STOCKMANN. [*Holding back the* DOCTOR.] Now, do restrain yourself, Thomas!

DR. STOCKMANN. [*Throwing down the umbrella.*] I'll be hanged if they haven't got off after all.

MRS. STOCKMANN. Why, what can they have wanted with you?

DR. STOCKMANN. I'll tell you afterwards; I have other things to think of now. [*Goes to the table and writes on a visiting-card.*] Look here, Katrina: what's written here?

MRS. STOCKMANN. Three big *Noes;* what does that mean?

DR. STOCKMANN. That I'll tell you afterwards, too. [*Handing the card.*] There, Petra; let smudgy-face run to the Badger's with this as fast as she can. Be quick!

[PETRA *goes out through the hall with the card.*]

DR. STOCKMANN. Well, if I haven't had visits to-day from all the emissaries of the devil! But now I'll sharpen my pen against them till it becomes a goad; I'll dip it in gall and venom; I'll hurl my inkstand straight at their skulls.

MRS. STOCKMANN. You forget we are going away, Thomas.

[PETRA *returns.*]

DR. STOCKMANN. Well?

PETRA. She has gone.

DR. STOCKMANN. Good. Going away, do you say? No, I'll be damned if we do; we stay where we are, Katrina!

PETRA. Stay!

MRS. STOCKMANN. Here in the town?

DR. STOCKMANN. Yes, here; the field of battle is here; here the fight must be fought; here I will conquer! As soon as my trousers are mended, I shall go out into the town and look for a house; we must have a roof over our heads for the winter.

HORSTER. That you can have in my house.

DR. STOCKMANN. Can I?

HORSTER. Yes, there's no difficulty about that. I have room enough, and I'm hardly ever at home myself.

MRS. STOCKMANN. Oh, how kind of you, Captain Horster!

PETRA. Thank you!

DR. STOCKMANN. [Shaking his hand.] Thanks, thanks! So that is off my mind. And this very day I shall set to work in earnest. Oh, there's no end of work to be done here, Katrina! It's a good thing I shall have all my time at my disposal now; for you must know I've had notice from the Baths—

MRS. STOCKMANN. [Sighing.] Oh, yes, I was expecting that.

DR. STOCKMANN. —And now they want to take away my practice as well. But let them! The poor I shall keep anyhow—those that can't pay; and, good Lord! it's they that need me most. But by heaven! I'll make them listen to me; I'll preach to them in season and out of season, as the saying goes.

MRS. STOCKMANN. My dear Thomas, I should have thought you had learnt what good preaching does.

DR. STOCKMANN. You really are absurd, Katrina. Am I to let myself be beaten off the field by public opinion, and the compact majority, and all that sort of devilry? No, thank you! Besides, my point is so simple, so clear and straightforward. I only want to drive it into the heads of these curs that the Liberals are the craftiest foes free men have to face; that party programmes wring the necks of all young and living truths; that considerations of expediency turn justice and morality upside down, until life here becomes simply unlivable. Come, Captain Horster, don't you think I shall be able to make the people understand that?

HORSTER. Maybe; I don't know much about these things myself.

DR. STOCKMANN. Well, you see—this is the way of it! It's the party leaders that must be exterminated. For a party leader is just like a wolf, you see—like a ravening wolf; he must devour a certain number of smaller animals a year, if he's to exist at all. Just look at Hovstad and Aslaksen! How many small animals they polish off—or at least mangle and maim, so that they're fit for nothing else but to be house-owners and subscribers to the *People's Messenger*! [Sits on the edge of the table.] Just come here, Katrina—see how bravely the sun shines to-day! And how the blessed fresh spring air blows in upon me!

MRS. STOCKMANN. Yes, if only we could live on sunshine and spring air, Thomas.

DR. STOCKMANN. Well, you'll have to pinch and save to eke them out—and then we shall get on all right. That's what troubles me least. No, what *does* trouble me is that I don't see any man free enough and high-minded enough to dare to take up my work after me.

PETRA. Oh, don't think about that, father; you have time enough before you.— Why, see, there are the boys already.

[EILIF and MORTEN enter from the sitting-room.]

MRS. STOCKMANN. Have you a holiday to-day?

MORTEN. No; but we had a fight with the other fellows in play-time—

EILIF. That's not true; it was the other fellows that fought us.

MORTEN. Yes, and then Mr. Rörlund said we had better stop at home for a few days.

DR. STOCKMANN. [Snapping his fingers and springing down from the table.] Now I have it! Now I have it, on my soul! You shall never set foot in school again!

THE BOYS. Never go to school!

MRS. STOCKMANN. Why, Thomas—

DR. STOCKMANN. Never, I say! I shall teach you myself—that's to say, I won't teach you any mortal thing—

MORTEN. Hurrah!

DR. STOCKMANN. —But I shall help you

to grow into free, high-minded men.—Look here, you'll have to help me, Petra.

PETRA. Yes, father, you may be sure I will.

DR. STOCKMANN. And we'll have our school in the room where they reviled me as an enemy of the people. But we must have more pupils. I must have at least a dozen boys to begin with.

MRS. STOCKMANN. You'll never get them in this town.

DR. STOCKMANN. We shall see. [*To the boys.*] Don't you know any street urchins— any regular ragamuffins—?

MORTEN. Yes, father, I know lots!

DR. STOCKMANN. That's all right; bring me a few of them. I shall experiment with the street-curs for once in a way; there are sometimes excellent heads amongst them.

MORTEN. But what are we to do when we've grown into free and high-minded men!

DR. STOCKMANN. Drive all the wolves out to the far west, boys!

[EILIF *looks rather doubtful;* MORTEN *jumps about shouting "Hurrah!"*]

MRS. STOCKMANN. If only the wolves don't drive you out, Thomas.

DR. STOCKMANN. Are you quite mad, Katrina! Drive me out! Now that I am the strongest man in the town?

MRS. STOCKMANN. The strongest—now?

DR. STOCKMANN. Yes, I venture to say this: that now I am one of the strongest men in the whole world.

MORTEN. I say, what fun!

DR. STOCKMANN. [*In a subdued voice.*] Hush; you mustn't speak about it yet; but I have made a great discovery.

MRS. STOCKMANN. What, another?

DR. STOCKMANN. Yes, of course! [*Gathers them about him, and speaks confidentially.*] This is what I have discovered, you see: the strongest man in the world is he who stands most alone.

MRS. STOCKMANN. [*Shakes her head, smiling.*] Ah, Thomas dear—!

PETRA. [*Grasping his hands cheerily.*] Father!

[CURTAIN.]

Courtesy of the Ohio State University Theater

THIRD-ACT SET FOR "THE SEA GULL"

A period production in the Ohio State University Theater, illustrating the modern illusionistic stage.

Realistic Drama

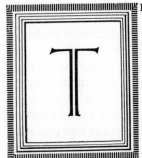HERE IS ALWAYS A CERTAIN human interest in seeing familiar realities depicted on the stage, and a certain advantage in equating drama with everyday life. For purposes of comedy and satire in particular a degree of verisimilitude is practically obligatory. From its very beginning, therefore, European drama gives evidence of an intermittent interest in realism which more or less approximates the facts of common experience. During the nineteenth century, however, this sporadic impulse was intensified by the increasing preoccupation with social conditions and the material aspects of life. As we have seen, it is impossible to deal seriously with social problems unless the circumstances presented coincide with the testimony of actual experience. Scientific analyses of psychology or environment are equally fruitless unless they postulate a similar truth to life. What is imperative in either case is not so much a creative imagination as an accurate perception and a scrupulous fidelity to fact. The effect upon drama has been a promotion of methods which simulate the appearance of actuality and thus create an illusion that what appears on the stage is identical with what occurs in real life. While the creation of this illusion does not preclude the selection and arrangement of materials necessary to any work of art—in fact, the whole impression of reality is quite as illusory, and is produced quite as artificially, as any other dramatic illusion—it does demand that the methods employed in no way violate the normal impressions created by common human experience. The result, therefore, is a deliberate effort to supplant the traditional make-believe of the theater with a veracious transcript from life and, in so doing, to impress dramatic art into the service of scientific exposition. As a reflection of modern sensitivity to the importance of environment, this realistic treatment of subject matter has become the most characteristic feature of modern drama.

Because of this prevalence of realistic methods the several types of drama produced by the modern theater exhibit little difference in general technique. What serves to distinguish them as separate types is their choice of subject matter and the purpose for which their technique is employed. Among these the realistic impulse is responsible for a type of drama in which realism constitutes not so much a means to an end as an end in itself. It is a type of drama designed to create a realistic illusion strictly for its own sake. As such, this realistic drama is something new in the theater and reflects an interest which is less moral or esthetic than it is scientific. Its sole object is to set before an audience a recognizable cross-section of life with a minimum of distortion and with only such heightening of salient features as is necessary to bring out their significance. The motive behind this endeavor is a conviction that the bald facts of life are more dramatic and meaningful than any fabrication of art, and that the supreme function of art is to bring home to human understanding the true purport of these realities. The most characteristic feature of this realistic drama is its resolute adherence to things as they are, or, perhaps more accurately, as one may perceive them to be. As an earnest of this dedication, it prefers to choose its subject matter from the familiar and the commonplace, even going out of its way at times to stress the drab, the mean, and the sordid. In order to maintain the true proportions of life, it also tends to minimize the exceptional or unrepresentative and to concentrate upon a norm of average and ordinary experience. Its aim is not to create drama out of these raw materials, but to expose the drama inherent in them. Thus the point of departure is not art but life; the ultimate objective is revelation of scientific truth; and the artistic function of such drama is simply to present the substance of life as accurately and unobtrusively as possible so that the facts may speak for themselves. For this reason realistic drama strives to eliminate the more obvious artifices of dramatic convention. The overt structure of an organic plot it avoids in favor of a dramatic action which apparently begins at random, develops casually, and ends without finality. In place of the arbitrary restrictions of pure comedy and tragedy it prefers the conglomerate neutrality of a serio-comic drama which, because it lacks the sustained effect of the former, reflects more accurately the indeterminate composition of life and its abortive vacillations. Its artistic function it confines to sensitivity of perception, judicious selection of materials, and skill in investing factual accuracy with appropriate dramatic power. Essentially its art is the art of concealing art.

The final virtue of any drama engaged in a simulation of real life depends in large measure upon its success in surmounting certain liabilities inherent in the undertaking. To begin with, the very nature of the project involves something of a dilemma. On the one hand, if realistic drama is guilty of distorting life, it obviously falsifies its effect and forfeits its chief claim to attention. On the other hand, if it succeeds in becoming an exact duplicate of life, the precise utility of the duplication, to say nothing of the competitive advantage of a substitute over the original, remains somewhat obscure. Between the horns of this major dilemma appear other difficulties no less vexing. Photographic reproduction of reality tends to become a sort of animated journalism with a value much like that of a newsreel. Its documentary contribution is of interest chiefly to the sociologist or the statistician, while its popular appeal is likely to be no more than an ephemeral one to idle or morbid curiosity. When this report concentrates on familiar commonplaces, particularly if they happen at the same time to be disagreeable ones, whatever novelty it may possess quickly evaporates, and the residue may merely serve to confirm prior impressions that life in the main is dull. The awkward difficulty is that to most human beings the commonplace routines of life are singularly undramatic, if not downright tedious, and a clinical exploration of the boring simply results in boredom. If realistic drama averts these perils, it is still susceptible to a more insidious one. Since so much of its effect depends upon reproducing the appearance of things, it runs the constant risk of becoming a drama of surfaces. In its solicitude for appearances the danger is that it may fail to reflect anything but the surface of life and thus represent a reality which is purely superficial. In order to minimize these occupational hazards, realistic drama takes refuge in a variety of subterfuges. Most commonly it falls back upon the inherent tensions of a social problem to lend its materials dramatic interest. Sometimes it follows the lead of the newspaper headline and deliberately chooses sensational subjects. At other times it stimulates interest by the suspense of intricate character analysis or by the timeliness of social satire. In rarer instances, however, it faces the issue squarely and, while maintaining a strict verisimilitude, succeeds in revealing beneath the rags of the commonplace a throb of authentic and vital drama.

Dramatic realism of this latter sort affords no greater achievement than the subtle art of the Russian dramatist and master of the short story Anton Chekhov (1860–1904). This eminence Chekhov owes in part to the good fortune of producing his best plays in close coöperation with the Moscow Art Theatre, the most famous theatrical institution of modern times. This superb acting company, organized in 1898 under the guidance of such celebrated artists as Stanislavsky and Nemirovitch-Dantchenko, was committed to the same dramatic ideals as Chekhov himself. By an absolute realism of detail it strove to make the background of action authentic in every respect. Acting it sought to transform from the external representation of a rôle into an actual assumption of the personality called for. Through a complex fusion of setting, properties, lighting, action, and dialogue into a unique and self-contained fabric of reality, it endeavored to create an independent unit of existence with the same validity as actual experience, and thus to banish completely any apparent difference between drama and life. Finally, to its minute surface realism it sought to add the depth of spiritual reality in order to suggest the elaborate texture of connotation attached to the most casual incidents. With the fortunes of this enterprise Chekhov's realistic comedy

The Sea Gull is uniquely identified. Coldly received upon its first presentation in 1896 under other auspices, when produced by the Moscow Art Theatre shortly after its organization two years later, the play established at one stroke the reputation of its author and the company. It became a classic expression of their combined ideals of dramatic art, and in the sequel remained practically a symbol of their dedication to realistic drama at its best.

The Sea Gull, while more complex and highly integrated than most realistic drama, illustrates well the essential features of the type and especially its artistic possibilities. As may be seen in the illustration facing page 405, it is designed for a realistic stage: that is, for a picture-frame stage with a curtain which may be drawn to reveal a setting of detailed verisimilitude. So far as theatrical resources permit, it presupposes scenery, properties, and costumes which reproduce explicit realities; lighting effects which create an atmosphere of appropriate naturalness; and a theater small enough for details of setting and stage business to register, and for lines to be spoken in a normal conversational manner. The characters of the play are conceived as a group of unique human beings belonging to a particular context of time, place, and social station. Each is imbedded in a peculiar history of his own and is distinguished by his own personal idiosyncrasies. They are represented as typical of humanity only in so far as their individuality chances to repeat a familiar pattern. In similar fashion the dramatic action concerns the particular activities connected with a specific country estate in Czarist Russia. These activities are carefully selected to create an impression of humdrum everyday existence. They comprise such unexceptional items as the routine of farming, fishing, neighborhood visits, idle pastimes, tepid flirtations, and endless languid conversations. Apart from Trepleff's periodic bouts with suicide, the most spectacular events are amateur theatricals, a lotto game, and an occasional family row. Furthermore, the method of presentation is equally commonplace. The dialogue is casual and desultory. The stage business is made up of those incidental and spontaneous acts which constitute so much of common behavior. The whole action reflects the haphazard drift of ordinary experience. The final purpose, however, is to present this transcript of life on two levels of significance. On the one, it is a conscientious reproduction of the superficial appearances which identify it with recognizable reality. On the other, it is an endeavor to suggest the attractions, the repulsions, and the tensions which exist beneath these surface appearances and, as in life, can only be inferred.

This conception of drama is very similar to that appearing in tragedy of sensibility. In both cases the real drama is submerged and appears only by reflection. Between the two, however, there is a wide difference in subject matter. Whereas tragedy of sensibility is concerned with general human experience and typical human beings, realistic drama deals with the unique experience of specific individuals. There is also an important difference in the means used to express this submerged drama. In tragedy of sensibility the expression is direct and formal, with little regard for the naturalness of the method; in *The Sea Gull* the method of expression is as indirect and inferential as life itself. Essentially it is a method of elaborately calculated juxtaposition. While the various details of speech and action are introduced in a manner which appears to be quite incidental and fortuitous, to each is imparted a subtle irradiation of meaning by the special context in which it is placed. Thus the apparent casualness of the dramatic action is in reality a closely wrought tissue of cross-references and implied relationships. In many respects the technique resembles the orchestration of a symphony. Like musical sounds possessed of overtones and capable of combination into melodic phrases and harmonic patterns, the separate details of setting, speech, and action are used to weave themes and variations into an intricate fabric of counterpoint and chorded harmony. For example, the note of frustration sounded by Masha at the very opening of the play introduces a theme which progresses from character to character and from context to context with subtly varying connotations in much the same way that a musical theme is announced and developed, now by solo instruments, now by full ensemble, through all the shifting tonal values of strings, woodwinds, and brasses. The acts of the play, like symphonic movements, represent progressive permutations of these themes in terms of a prevailing mood and tempo. The final meaning is the total effect: not the individual melody nor the isolated theme, but the ultimate synthesis of every suspended element in one harmonious and organic design.

Because of the intricacy and indirectness of this artistic method a play like *The Sea Gull* demands a constant attention to each minute detail. For the audience this is not so much a matter of conscious consideration as of an alert sensitivity to nuances of connotation. As the play expresses itself, like music, through incremental suggestion and association, one assimilates it in the same way, by a half-intuitive apprehension. But the process is successful only to the extent that one is aware of the suggestions afforded. Such details as the appurtenances of setting, the incidental use of properties, casual references to the weather, allusions to contemporary writers, or apparently irrelevant bits of stage business are designed to perform a definite dramatic function and to contribute to the cumulative effect. They are not merely embellishments of action and dialogue, but essential factors in the dramatic development with an independent value of their own. There is a tacit eloquence in such incidentals as Masha's taking of snuff or her waltzing, Trigorin's ubiquitous notebook, the wrangling over horses, the lotto game in Trepleff's study, or the insistent presence of the lake. Taken by itself, a gesture or a comment may seem inconsequential; but in its proper context it gives off expanding overtones of implication. The wanton shooting of the sea gull is but an obvious instance of this tangential meaning. Of particular importance in this connection are the frequent and carefully indicated pauses. Here for a moment time is allowed to tick away while a host of clustered associations flood into the vacuum until silence itself becomes reverberant with unspoken meaning. The technique is a delicate and subtle one, but it is by no means merely a complicated method of performing the simple. The task to which it addresses itself is both difficult and elusive. This is no less than to present life in all the complexity and relativity of its meaning; indeed, to present more than the dramatist is prepared to elucidate. It attempts to provide not only a scrupulously exact reproduction of life, but one so rich and suggestive that it induces an actual experience of living. Thus it aims at a result which exceeds the dramatist's interpretation. By creating a living semblance of reality and indicating its salient features it strives to promote an insight into life which transcends the play's immediate meaning and even the possibility of explicit statement.

Further reading in realistic drama may well begin with Chekhov's other great play, *The Cherry Orchard,* or with *The Lower Depths* by his fellow-countryman Maxim Gorky. In English drama attempts at realism go as far back as the medieval miracle play, as may be seen in the so-called *Second Shepherds' Play.* Elizabethan examples may be found in *Eastward Ho!* by Ben Jonson, George Chapman, and John Marston, or in *A Trick to Catch the Old One* by Thomas Middleton; and an eighteenth-century example in George Lillo's *The London Merchant.* Well-known representatives of modern realistic drama are *What Price Glory* by Laurence Stallings and Maxwell Anderson, *Street Scene* by Elmer Rice, *Dead End* by Sidney Kingsley, *Awake and Sing* by Clifford Odets, and the Chekhovian *The Time of Your Life* by William Saroyan. An interesting attempt to combine poetry and realism, together with other matters, appears in Maxwell Anderson's *Winterset.*

THE SEA GULL

A COMEDY IN FOUR ACTS

by

ANTON CHEKHOV

TRANSLATED BY

STARK YOUNG

Characters in the Play

IRINA NICOLAYEVNA ARCADINA, MADAME TREPLEFF, *an actress*

CONSTANTINE GAVRILOVITCH TREPLEFF, *her son*

PETER NICOLAYEVITCH SORIN, *her brother*

NINA MIKHAILOVNA ZARYECHNY, *a young girl, the daughter of a wealthy landowner*

ILYA AFANASYEVITCH SHAMREYEFF, *a retired lieutenant*, SORIN'S *steward*

PAULINE ANDREYEVNA, *his wife*

MASHA (MARYA ILYINISHNA), *his daughter*

BORIS ALEXEYEVITCH TRIGORIN, *a literary man*

EUGENE SERGEYEVITCH DORN, *a doctor*

SEMYON SEMYONOVITCH MEDVEDENKO, *a schoolmaster*

YAKOV, *a servant*

A MAID

A COOK

The action is laid at SORIN'S *country place. Between the Third and Fourth Acts two years elapse.*

Reprinted from *The Sea Gull* by Anton Chekhov; copyright 1939 by Stark Young, translator; used by permission of the publishers, Charles Scribner's Sons.

A section of the park on SORIN'S *estate. The wide avenue leading away from the spectators into the depths of the park toward the lake is closed by a platform hurriedly put together for private theatricals, so that the lake is not seen at all. To left and right of the platform there are bushes. A few chairs, a small table.*

[*The sun has just set. On the platform behind the curtain are* YAKOV *and other workmen; sounds of coughing and hammering are heard.* MASHA *and* MEDVEDENKO *enter on the left, returning from a walk.*]

MEDVEDENKO.   Why do you always wear black?

MASHA.   I am in mourning for my life. I'm unhappy.

MEDVEDENKO.   You unhappy? I can't understand it. Your health is good, and your father is not rich but he's well enough off. My life is much harder to bear than yours. I get twenty-three roubles a month, and that's all, and then out of that the pension fund has to be deducted, but I don't wear mourning.   [*They sit down.*]

MASHA.   It isn't a question of money. Even a beggar can be happy.

MEDVEDENKO.   Yes, theoretically he can, but not when you come right down to it. Look at me, with my mother, my two sisters and my little brother, and my salary twenty-three roubles in all. Well, people have to eat and drink, don't they? Have to have tea and sugar? Have tobacco? So it just goes round and round.

MASHA.   [*Glancing towards the stage.*] The play will begin soon.

MEDVEDENKO.   Yes. The acting will be done by Nina Zaryechny and the play was written by Constantine Gavrilovitch. They are in love with each other, and today their souls are mingled in a longing to create some image both can share and true to both. But my soul and your soul can't find any ground to meet on. You see how it is. I love you; I can't stay at home because I keep wishing so for you; and so every day I walk four miles here and four miles back and meet with nothing but indifference on

your side. That's only natural. I've got nothing, we're a big family. Who wants to marry a man who can't even feed himself?

MASHA.   Fiddlesticks! [*She takes snuff.*] Your love touches me, but I can't return it, that's all. [*Offers him snuff.*] Help yourself.

MEDVEDENKO.   I'd as soon not. [*A pause.*]

MASHA.   My, how close it is! It must be going to storm tonight. All you do is philosophise or talk about money. You think the worst misery we can have is poverty. But I think it's a thousand times easier to go ragged and beg for bread than— But you'd never understand that—

[*Enter* SORIN, *leaning on his walking stick, and* TREPLEFF.]

SORIN.   For some reason, who knows, my dear boy, the country's not my style. Naturally. You can't teach an old horse new tricks. Last night I went to bed at ten o'clock, and at nine this morning I awoke feeling as if my brain stuck to my skull, and so on. [*Laughing.*] And then on top of all that I fell asleep after dinner just the same. And so now I'm a wreck, I'm still lost in a nightmare, and all the rest of it.

TREPLEFF.   That's true, Uncle, you really ought to live in town. [*Sees* MASHA *and* MEDVEDENKO.] Look, my friends, we'll call you when the play starts, but don't stay here now. I'll have to ask you to go.

SORIN.   [*To* MASHA.] Marya Ilyinishna, won't you kindly ask your father to leave that dog unchained, to stop that howling? All last night again my sister couldn't sleep.

MASHA.   You'll have to tell my father yourself. I shan't do it, so please don't ask me to. [*To* MEDVEDENKO.] Let's go.

MEDVEDENKO.   Then you'll let us know before the play starts.

[MASHA *and* MEDVEDENKO *go out.*]

SORIN.   That just means the dog will howl all night again. You see how 'tis; in the country I have never had what I wanted. It used to be I'd get leave for twenty-eight days, say, and come down here to recoup, and so on; but they plagued me so with one silly piece of nonsense after another that the very first day I wanted to be out of it. [*Laughs.*] I've always left here with relish. Well, now that I'm retired, I have nowhere to go and all the rest of it. Like it—like it not, I live—

YAKOV. We're going for a swim, Constantine Gavrilovitch.

TREPLEFF. So long as you are back in ten minutes. [*Looks at his watch.*] We're about to begin.

YAKOV. Yes, sir.

TREPLEFF. Here's your theatre. The curtain, then the first wing, then the second wing, and still farther open space. No scenery at all. You see what the background is—it stretches to the lake and on to the horizon. And the curtain will go up at 8:30, just when the moon's rising.

SORIN. Magnificent!

TREPLEFF. If Nina's late, then, of course, the whole effect will be spoilt. It's time she were here now. But her father and mother watch her so she can hardly get out of the house, it's like escaping from prison. [*Straightening his uncle's tie.*] Uncle, your hair and beard are rumpled up—oughtn't you to have them trimmed?

SORIN. [*Combing his beard.*] It's the tragedy of my life. I always look as if I'd been drunk, even when I was young I did—and so on. Women never have loved me. [*Sits down.*] Why is my sister in such a bad humour?

TREPLEFF. Why? Bored. [*Sits down by* SORIN.] Jealous. She's set against me, against the performance and against my play, because Nina's going to act in it and she's not. She's never read my play but she hates it.

SORIN. You [*laughing*] imagine things, really.

TREPLEFF. Yes, she's furious because even on this little stage it's Nina will have a success and not she. [*Looks at his watch.*] A psychological case, my mother: She's undeniably talented, intelligent, capable of

sobbing over a novel; she recites all of Nekrasov's [1] poetry by heart; she nurses the sick like an angel; but you just try praising Duse! [2] Oh, ho! You praise nobody but her, write about her, rave about her, go into ecstasies over her marvellous performance in "La Dame Aux Camélias" or in "The Fumes of Life." [3] But all that is a drug she can't get in the country, so she's bored and cross. We are all her enemies—it's all our fault. And then she's superstitious—afraid of three candles or number thirteen. She's stingy. She's got seventy thousand roubles in an Odessa bank, I know that for a fact. But ask her for a loan, she'll burst into tears.

SORIN. You've got it into your head your play annoys your mother, and that upsets you, and so forth. Don't worry, your mother worships the ground you walk on.

TREPLEFF. [*Picking petals from a flower.*] Loves me—loves me not, loves me—loves me not, loves me—loves me not. [*Laughing.*] You see, my mother doesn't love me, of course not. I should say not! What she wants is to live, and love, and wear pretty clothes; and here I am twenty-five years old and a perpetual reminder that she's no longer young. You see when I'm not there she's only thirty-two, and when I am she's forty-three—and for that she hates me. She knows too that I refuse to admit the theatre. She loves the theatre; it seems to her that she's working for humanity, for holy art. But to my thinking her theatre today is nothing but routine, convention. When the curtain goes up, and by artificial light in a room with three walls, these great geniuses, these priests of holy art, show how people eat, drink, make love, move about and wear their jackets; when they try to fish a moral out of these flat pictures and phrases, some sweet little bit anybody could understand and any fool take home; when in a thousand different dishes they serve me the same thing over

[1] A Russian poet (1821–1877) noted for the artistic perfection of his lyrics.
[2] Eleonora Duse (1859–1924), the celebrated Italian actress.
[3] The first is the famous play by Alexandre Dumas the younger, and the second a play by the obscure Russian playwright B. Markevitch.

and over, over and over, over and over—well, it's then I run and run like Maupassant [4] from the Eiffel Tower and all that vulgarity about to bury him.

SORIN. But we can't do without the theatre.

TREPLEFF. We must have new forms. New forms we must have, and if we can't get them we'd better have nothing at all. [*He looks at his watch.*] I love my mother —I love her very much—but she leads a senseless life, always making a fuss over this novelist, her name forever chucked about in the papers—it disgusts me. It's just the simple egotism of an ordinary mortal, I suppose, stirring me up sometimes that makes me wish I had somebody besides a famous actress for a mother, and fancy if she had been an ordinary woman I'd have been happier. Uncle, can you imagine anything more hopeless than my position is in her house? It used to be she'd entertain, all famous people—actors and authors—and among them all I was the only one who was nothing, and they put up with me only because I was her son. Who am I? What am I? I left the university in my third year, owing to circumstances, as they say, for which the editors are not responsible; I've no talent at all, not a kopeck [5] on me; and according to my passport I am—a burgher of Kiev. [6] My father was a burgher of Kiev, though he was also a famous actor. So when these actors and writers of hers bestowed on me their gracious attentions, it seemed to me their eyes were measuring my insignificance. I guessed their thoughts and felt humiliated.

SORIN. By the by, listen, can you please tell me what sort of man this novelist is. You see I can't make him out. He never opens his mouth.

TREPLEFF. He's an intelligent man, he's simple, apt to be melancholy. Quite decent. He's well under forty yet but he's already

celebrated, he's had more than enough of everything. As for his writings—well, we'll say charming, full of talent, but after Tolstoy or Zola, [7] of course, a little of Trigorin goes a long way.

SORIN. My boy, I'm fond of writers, you know. Once there were two things I wanted passionately. To marry and to be an author. I never succeeded in doing either. It must be pleasant being a minor writer even, and all the rest of it.

TREPLEFF. I hear footsteps. [*Embraces his uncle.*] I can't live without her. Just the sound of her footsteps is lovely.

[*Goes to meet* NINA ZARYECHNY *as she enters.*]

TREPLEFF. I'm insanely happy! My enchantress! My dream!

NINA. I'm not late, surely I'm not late.

TREPLEFF. [*Kissing her hands.*] No, no, no.

NINA. All day I—I was so afraid father wouldn't let me come. But at last he's gone out. He went out just now with my stepmother. The sky has turned red, the moon will soon be up, and I raced the horse, raced him. [*Laughs.*] But I'm so happy.

[*Warmly shaking* SORIN'S *hand.*]

SORIN. [*Laughing.*] You've been crying, I see by your little eyes. Too bad!

NINA. That's so. You can see how out of breath I am. Do let's hurry. I've got to go in half an hour. I must. Don't ask me to stay, my father doesn't know I'm here.

TREPLEFF. It's time to begin anyhow—I'll go call them.

SORIN. I'll go. I'll go this minute. [*Begins to sing* "The Two Grenadiers" *then stops.*] Once I started singing like that and a deputy who was standing by said, "Your Excellency has a very strong voice"—then he thought awhile and said, "Strong but unpleasant." [*Exit* SORIN, *laughing.*]

NINA. My father and his wife won't let

---

[4] Guy de Maupassant (1850–1893), the great French master of the realistic short story.

[5] A Russian coin, one-hundredth of a rouble: here used as about the equivalent in meaning of an American cent.

[6] The implication is roughly: a solid citizen from the sticks.

[7] The great Russian and French realistic novelists.

me come here; they say it's Bohemia. They are afraid I'll go on the stage. But I am drawn here to this lake like a sea gull. My heart is full of you.

TREPLEFF. We're alone.

NINA. Isn't that some one over there?

TREPLEFF. No, nobody. [Kisses her.]

NINA. What kind of tree is that?

TREPLEFF. It's an elm.

NINA. Why does it look so dark?

TREPLEFF. Because it's evening and everything looks darker. Don't go away early, please don't.

NINA. I must.

TREPLEFF. But if I should follow you, Nina? I'll stand all night in the garden, looking up at your window.

NINA. Oh, no! You mustn't. The watchman would see you and Treasure doesn't know you yet, he'd bark.

TREPLEFF. I love you.

NINA. Ssh—!

TREPLEFF. Who's that?—You, Yakov?

YAKOV. [From behind stage.] Yes, sir.

TREPLEFF. You must get to your seats, it's time to begin. The moon's coming up.

YAKOV. Yes, sir.

TREPLEFF. Have you got that methylated spirit? Is the sulphur ready? [To NINA.] You see when the red eyes appear there must be a smell of sulphur around. You'd better go now, everything's ready. Do you feel nervous?

NINA. Yes, awfully. It's not that I'm afraid of your mother so much, it's Boris Trigorin terrifies me, acting before him, a famous author like him. Tell me, is he young?

TREPLEFF. Yes.

NINA. What marvellous stories he writes!

TREPLEFF. [Coldly.] I don't know. I don't read them.

NINA. It's hard to act in your play. There are no living characters in it.

TREPLEFF. Living characters! I must represent life not as it is and not as it should be, but as it appears in my dreams.

NINA. In your play there's no action; it's all recitation. It seems to me a play must have some love in it.

[They go out by way of the stage.]

[Enter PAULINE ANDREYEVNA and DORN.]

PAULINE. It's getting damp, go back and put on your galoshes.

DORN. I'm hot.

PAULINE. You don't take any care of yourself and it's just contrariness. You're a doctor and know very well how bad damp air is for you, but you like to make me miserable. You sat out on that terrace all last evening on purpose.

DORN. [Sings low.] Oh, never say that I—

PAULINE. You were so enchanted by Madame Arcadina's conversation you didn't even notice the cold. You may as well own up—she charms you.

DORN. I'm fifty-five.

PAULINE. Fiddlesticks! What's that for a man, it's not old. You're still young enough looking—women still like you.

DORN. [Gently.] Tell me, what is it you want?

PAULINE. Before an actress you are all ready to kiss the ground. All of you!

DORN. [Sings low.] Once more I stand before thee— If society does make a fuss over actors, treats them differently from, say, shopkeepers—it's only right and natural. That's the pursuit of the ideal.

PAULINE. Women have always fallen in love with you and hung on your neck. Is that the pursuit of the ideal too?

DORN. [Shrugs his shoulders.] Why? In the relations women have had with me there has been a great deal that was fine. What they chiefly loved in me was the fact that I was a first-class doctor. Ten or fifteen years ago, you remember, I was the only decent accoucheur [8] they had in all this part of the country. Besides, I've always been an honorable man.

PAULINE. [Clasping his hand.] My dear!

DORN. Ssh—here they come!

[8] Obstetrician, or, more exactly, male midwife.

[*Enter* MADAME ARCADINA *on* SORIN'S *arm,* TRIGORIN, SHAMREYEFF, MEDVEDENKO, *and* MASHA.]

SHAMREYEFF. In '73 at the Poltava Fair I can assure you she was magnificent, ah, magnificent! Pure delight! But tell me if you know where Chadin, Paul Semyonovitch, the comedian, is now? Take his Raspluyef [9]—'twas better than Sadovsky's, I can assure you, most esteemed lady. But what's become of him?

ARCADINA. You keep asking me about someone before the flood—how should I know? [*Sits down.*]

SHAMREYEFF. Ah, [*Sighs.*] Paulie Chadin! Nobody like that now. The stage is not what it was, Irina Nikolayevna, ah no! In those days there were mighty oaks, now we have nothing but stumps.

DORN. There are not many brilliant talents nowadays, it's true, but the general average of the acting is much higher.

SHAMREYEFF. I can't agree with you there. However, that's a matter of taste, *De gustibus aut bene, aut nihil.* [10]

[TREPLEFF *comes out from behind the stage.*]

ARCADINA. My dear son, when does it begin?

TREPLEFF. Please be patient. It's only a moment.

ARCADINA. [*Reciting from* Hamlet.] My son!
"Thou turnst mine eyes into my very soul,
And there I see such black and grained spots
As will not leave their tinct."

TREPLEFF. [*Paraphrasing from* Hamlet.] Nay, but to live in wickedness, seek love in the depths of sin— [*Behind the stage a horn blows.*] Ladies and gentlemen, we begin! I beg your attention. [*A pause.*] I begin. [*Tapping the floor with a stick. In a loud voice.*] Harken, ye mists, out of ancient time, that drift by night over the bosom of this lake, darken our eyes with

sleep and in our dream show us what will be in 200,000 years.

SORIN. In 200,000 years nothing will be.

TREPLEFF. Then let them present to us that nothing.

ARCADINA. Let them. We are asleep.

[*The curtain rises. Vista opens across the lake. Low on the horizon the moon hangs, reflected in the water.* NINA ZARYECHNY *all in white, seated on a rock.*]

NINA. Men and beasts, lions, eagles and partridges, antlered deer, mute fishes dwelling in the water, star-fish and small creatures invisible to the eye—these and all life have run their sad course and are no more. Thousands of creatures have come and gone since there was life on the earth. Vainly now the pallid moon doth light her lamp. In the meadows the cranes wake and cry no longer; and the beetles' hum is silent in the linden groves. Cold, cold, cold. Empty, empty, empty! Terrible, terrible, terrible. [*A pause.*] Living bodies have crumbled to dust, and Eternal Matter has changed them into stones and water and clouds, and there is one soul of many souls. I am that soul of the world. . . . In me the soul of Alexander the Great, of Cæsar, of Shakespeare, of Napoleon and of the lowest worm. The mind of man and the brute's instinct mingle in me. I understand all, all, and in me lives each several life again.

[*The will-o'-the-wisps appear.*]

ARCADINA. [*In a stage whisper.*] We're in for something decadent.

TREPLEFF. [*Imploring and reproaching.*] Mother!

NINA. I am alone. Once in a hundred years I open my lips to speak, and in this void my sad echo is unheard. And you, pale fires, you do not hear me. . . . Before daybreak the putrid marsh begets you, and you wander until sunrise, but without

---

[9] A low-comedy rôle. Shamreyeff's dramatic criticism is unconsciously grotesque.

[10] Either good or worthless—it's a question of tastes.

thought, without will, without the throb of life. For fear life should spring in you, the father of eternal matter, the Devil, causes every instant in you, as in stones and in water, an interchange of the atoms, and you are changing endlessly. I, only, the world's soul, remain unchanged and am eternal. [*A pause.*] I am like a prisoner cast into a deep, empty well, and know not where I am nor what awaits me. One thing only is not hidden from me: in the stubborn, savage fight with the Devil, the principle of material forces, I am destined to conquer; and when that has been, matter and spirit shall be made one in the shadow of my soul forever. And lo, the kingdom of universal will is at hand. But that cannot be before long centuries of the moon, the shining dog star, and the earth, have run to dust. And till that time horror shall be, horror, horror, horror! [*A pause; upon the background of the lake appear two red spots.*] Behold, my mighty adversary, the Devil, approaches. I see his awful, blood-red eyes.

ARCADINA.   I smell surphur, is that necessary?

TREPLEFF.   Yes, it is.

ARCADINA.   Oh, I see [*Laughing.*]—it's a stage effect!

TREPLEFF.   Mother!

NINA.   But without man he is lost—

PAULINE.   [*To* DORN.] You're taking your hat off. Put it on, you'll catch cold.

ARCADINA.   The doctor has taken off his hat to the Devil, the father of Eternal Matter!

TREPLEFF.   [*Blazing up, in a loud voice.*] The play's over! That's enough! Curtain!

ARCADINA.   Why are you angry?

TREPLEEF.   That's enough! Curtain! Drop the curtain! [*Stamping his foot.*] Curtain! [*The curtain falls.*] You must excuse me! I don't know how it was but I forgot somehow that only a chosen few can write plays and act them. I was infringing on a monopoly—My—I— [*Instead of saying more he makes a gesture of having done with it and goes out to the left.*]

ARCADINA.   What's the matter with him?

SORIN.   Irina, my dear, you mustn't treat a young man's pride like that.

ARCADINA.   Now what have I said?

SORIN.   You've hurt his feelings.

ARCADINA.   But he told us beforehand it was all in fun, that's the way I took it—of course.

SORIN.   Just the same—

ARCADINA.   And now it appears he's produced a masterpiece. Evidently he had no intention of amusing us, not at all; he got up this performance and fumigated us with sulphur to demonstrate to us how plays should be written and what's worth acting in. I'm sick of him. Nobody could stand his everlasting digs and outbursts. He's an unruly, conceited boy.

SORIN.   He was only hoping to give you some pleasure.

ARCADINA.   Yes? I notice he didn't choose some familiar sort of play, but forced his own decadent raving on us. I can listen to raving. I don't mind listening to it, so long as I'm not asked to take it seriously; but this of his is not like that. Not at all, it's introducing us to a new epoch in art, inaugurating a new era in art. But to my mind it's not new forms or epochs, it's simply bad temper.

TRIGORIN.   Every one writes as he wants to and as he can.

ARCADINA.   Well, let him write as he wants to and as he can, so long as he leaves me out of it.

DORN.   Great Jove angry is no longer Jove.

ARCADINA.   I'm not Jove, I'm a woman. [*Lighting a cigarette.*] I'm not angry—I'm merely vexed to see a young man wasting his time. I didn't mean to hurt him.

MEDVEDENKO.   Nobody has any grounds for separating matter from spirit, for it may be this very spirit itself is a union of material atoms. [*Excitedly, to* TRIGORIN.] You know, somebody ought to put in a play, and then act on the stage, how we poor schoolmasters live. It's a hard, hard life.

ARCADINA.   That's so, but we shan't talk

of plays or atoms. The evening is so lovely. Listen—they're singing! [*Pausing to listen.*] How good it is!

PAULINE. It's on the other side of the lake. [*A pause.*]

ARCADINA. Sit down by me here. [*To* TRIGORIN.] You know, ten or fifteen years ago we had music on this lake every night almost. There were six big country houses then around the shore; and it was all laughter, noise, shooting and lovemaking—making love without end. The *jeune premier* [11] and the idol of all six houses was our friend here, I must present [*Nods toward* DORN.] Doctor Eugene Sergeyevitch. He's charming now, but then he was irresistible. Why did I hurt my poor boy's feelings? I'm worried about him. [*Calls.*] Kostya! [12] Son! Kostya!

MASHA. I'll go look for him.

ARCADINA. Would you, my dear?

MASHA. [*Calling.*] Ah-oo! Constantine. Ah-oo!   [*She goes out.*]

NINA. [*Coming from behind the stage.*] Evidently we're not going on, so I may as well come out. Good evening! [*Kisses* MADAME ARCADINA *and* PAULINE ANDREYEVNA.]

SORIN. Bravo! Bravo!

ARCADINA. Bravo! Bravo! We were all enchanted. With such looks and such a lovely voice, it's a sin for you to stay here in the country. You have talent indeed. Do you hear? You owe it to yourself to go on the stage.

NINA. Oh, that's my dream. [*Sighing.*] But it will never come true.

ARCADINA. Who can tell? Let me present Boris Alexeyevitch Trigorin.

NINA. Oh, I'm so glad— [*Much embarrassed.*] I'm always reading your—

ARCADINA. [*Drawing* NINA *down beside her.*] Don't be shy, dear. He may be a famous author, but his heart's quite simple. Look, he's embarrassed too.

DORN. I suppose we may raise the curtain now. This way it's frightening.

SHAMREYEFF. [*Loudly.*] Yakov, my man, raise the curtain. [*The curtain is raised.*]

NINA. [*To* TRIGORIN.] It's a strange play, isn't it?

TRIGORIN. I didn't understand a word of it. However, I enjoyed watching it. You acted with so much sincerity, and the scenery was so lovely. [*A pause.*] I dare say there are quantities of fish in this lake.

NINA. Yes.

TRIGORIN. I love fishing. I can think of no greater pleasure than to sit along towards evening by the water and watch a float.

NINA. But, I'd have thought that for any one who had tasted the joy of creation, no other pleasures could exist.

ARCADINA. [*Laughing.*] Don't talk like that. When people make him pretty speeches he simply crumples up.

SHAMREYEFF. I remember one evening at the Opera in Moscow when the celebrated Silva was singing, how delighted we were when he took low C. Imagine our surprise—it so happened the bass from our church choir was there and all at once we heard "Bravo Silva" from the gallery a whole octave lower—like this—"Bravo Silva." The audience was thunderstruck. [*A pause.*]

DORN. The angel of silence is flying over us.

NINA. Oh, I must go. Goodbye.

ARCADINA. Where to? Where so early? We won't allow it.

NINA. Papa is waiting for me.

ARCADINA. What a man, really! [*Kissing her.*] Well, there's no help for it. It's too sad losing you.

NINA. If you only knew how I don't want to go.

ARCADINA. Somebody must see you home, child.

NINA. [*Frightened.*] Oh, no, no.

SORIN. [*Imploring her.*] Don't go.

NINA. I must, Peter Nicolayevitch.

SORIN. Stay an hour more, and so on. Come now, really!

---

[11] A theatrical term referring to the actor who plays the romantic lead.

[12] Diminutive for Constantine.

NINA. [*Hesitating with tears in her eyes.*] I can't.

[*She shakes hands and hurries out.*]

ARCADINA. Now there's a really poor, unfortunate girl. They say her mother when she died willed the husband all her immense fortune, everything to the very last kopeck, and now this little girl is left with nothing, since her father has already willed everything he has to the second wife. That's shocking.

DORN. Yes, her papa is rather a beast, I must grant him that.

SORIN. [*Rubbing his hands to warm them.*] What do you say, we'd better go in too, it's getting damp. My legs ache.

ARCADINA. It's like having wooden legs, you can hardly walk on them. Come on, you poor old patriarch. [*She takes his arm.*]

SHAMREYEFF. [*Offering his arm to his wife.*] Madame?

SORIN. There's that dog howling again. [*To* SHAMREYEFF.] Be good enough, Ilya Afanasyevitch, to tell them to let that dog off the chain.

SHAMREYEFF. It can't be done, Peter Nikolayevitch, or we'll be having thieves in the barn, and the millet's there. [*To* MEDVEDENKO *walking beside him.*] Yes, a whole octave lower "Bravo Silva"! And not your concert singer, mind you, just ordinary church choir.

MEDVEDENKO. And what salary does a church singer get?

[*All except* DORN *go out.*]

DORN. [*Alone.*] I don't know—maybe I'm no judge, I may be going off my head, but I liked that play. There's something in it. When the girl spoke of the vast solitude, and afterward when the Devil's eyes appeared, I could feel my hands trembling. It was all so fresh and naïve. But here he comes. I want to say all the nice things I can to him.

[*Enter* TREPLEFF.]

TREPLEFF. They've all gone.

DORN. I'm here.

TREPLEFF. Masha's been hunting for me all over the park. Repulsive creature!

DORN. Constantine Gavrilovitch, I admired your play extremely. It's a curious kind of thing and I haven't heard the end, but still it made a deep impression on me. You've got great talent. You must keep on! [CONSTANTINE *presses his hand and embraces him impulsively.*] Phew, what a nervous fellow! Tears in his eyes! What I wanted to say is you chose your subject from the realm of abstract ideas, and that's right—a work of art should express a great idea. There is no beauty without seriousness. My, you are pale!

TREPLEFF. So you think—I ought to go on?

DORN. Yes. But write only of what is profound and eternal. You know how I have lived my life, I have lived it with variety and choiceness; and I have enjoyed it; and I am content. But if ever I had felt the elevation of spirit that comes to artists in their creative moments I believe I should have despised this body and all its usages, and tried to soar above all earthly things.

TREPLEFF. Forgive me, where's Nina?

DORN. And another thing. In a work of art there must be a clear, definite idea. You must know what your object is in writing, for if you follow that picturesque road without a definite aim, you will go astray and your talent will be your ruin.

TREPLEFF. [*Impatiently.*] Where is Nina?

DORN. She's gone home.

TREPLEFF. [*In despair.*] What shall I do? I want to see her. I must see her. I'm going—

[MASHA *enters.*]

DORN. Calm yourself, my friend!

TREPLEFF. But all the same I'm going. I must go.

MASHA. Constantine Gavrilovitch, come indoors. Your mother wants you. She's anxious.

TREPLEFF. Tell her I've gone—and please—all of you let me alone! Don't follow me around.

DORN. Come, come, come, boy, you mustn't act like this—it won't do.

TREPLEFF. [*In tears.*] Goodbye, Doctor —and thank you—

[*Exit* TREPLEFF.]

DORN. [*Sighing.*] Ah, youth, youth—

MASHA. When there is nothing else left to say, people always say, "Ah, youth, youth." [*Takes a pinch of snuff.*]

DORN. [*Takes snuff-box out of her hand and flings it into the bushes.*] It's disgusting. [*A pause.*] There in the house they seem to be playing. We'd better go in.

MASHA. No, no, wait a minute.

DORN. What is it?

MASHA. Let me talk to you—I don't love my father, I can't talk to him, but I feel with all my heart that you are near me— Help me—help me— [*Starts to sob.*] or I shall do something silly, I'll make my life a mockery, ruin it—I can't keep on—

DORN. How? Help you how?

MASHA. I'm tortured. No one, no one knows what I'm suffering— [*Laying her head on his breast, softly.*] I love Constantine.

DORN. How nervous they all are! How nervous they all are! And so much love! O magic lake! [*Tenderly.*] What can I do for you, child? What, what?

[CURTAIN.]

ACT TWO

A croquet lawn. In the background on the right is the house with a large terrace; on the left is seen the lake, in which the blazing sun is reflected. Flowerbeds. Noon. Hot.

[*On one side of the croquet lawn, in the shade of an old linden tree,* MADAME ARCADINA, DORN *and* MASHA *are sitting on a garden bench.* DORN *has an open book on his knees.*]

ARCADINA. [*To* MASHA.] Here, let's stand up. [*They both stand up.*] Side by side. You are twenty-two and I am nearly twice that. Doctor Dorn, tell us, which one of us looks the younger?

DORN. You, of course.

ARCADINA. There you are—you see? . . . And why is it? Because I work, I feel, I'm always on the go, but you sit in the same spot all the time, you're not living. I make it a rule never to look ahead into the future. I let myself think neither of old age nor of death. What will be will be.

MASHA. But I feel as if I were a thousand, I trail my life along after me like an endless train. . . . Often I have no wish to be living at all. [*Sits down.*] Of course that's all nonsense. I ought to shake myself and throw it all off.

DORN. [*Sings softly.*] *Tell her, pretty flowers*—[1]

ARCADINA. Then I'm correct as an Englishman. I'm always dressed and my hair always *comme il faut.*[2] Would I permit myself to leave the house, even to come out here in the garden, in a dressing-gown or with my hair undone? Never, I should say not! The reason I have kept my looks is because I've never been a frump, never let myself go, as some do. [*Arms akimbo, she walks up and down the croquet green.*] Here I am, light as a bird. Ready to play a girl of fifteen any day.

DORN. Well, at any rate, I'll go on with my reading. [*Takes up the book.*] We stopped at the corn merchants and the rats.

ARCADINA. And the rats. Go on. [*Sits.*] Let me have it, I'll read. It's my turn anyhow. [*She takes the book and looks for the place.*] And the rats—here we are— [*Reads.*] "And certainly, for people of the world to pamper the romantics and make them at home in their houses is as dangerous as for corn merchants to raise rats in their granaries. And yet they are beloved. And so when a woman has picked out the author she wants to entrap, she besieges him with compliments, amenities and favors." Well, among the French that may

[1] From Gounod's opera *Faust.*

[2] Properly styled.

be, but certainly here with us there's nothing of the kind, we've no set program. Here with us a woman before she ever sets out to capture an author is usually head over heels in love with him herself. To go no further, take me and Trigorin . . .

[*Enter* SORIN, *leaning on a stick, with* NINA *at his side.* MEDVEDENKO *follows him, pushing a wheel chair.*]

SORIN. [*Caressingly, as if to a child.*] Yes? We're all joy, eh? We're happy today after all. [*To his sister.*] We're all joy. Father and stepmother are gone to Tver, and we are free now for three whole days.

NINA. [*Sits down beside* ARCADINA *and embraces her.*] I am so happy! I belong now to you.

SORIN. [*Sitting down in the wheel chair.*] She looks lovely today.

ARCADINA. Beautifully dressed, intriguing—that's a clever girl. [*She kisses* NINA.] We mustn't praise her too much. It's bad luck. Where's Boris Alexeyevitch?

NINA. He's at the bath-house fishing.

ARCADINA. You'd think he'd be sick of it. [*She begins reading again.*]

NINA. What is that you have?

ARCADINA. Maupassant's "On The Water," darling. [*Reads a few lines to herself.*] Well, the rest is uninteresting and untrue. [*Shutting the book.*] I'm troubled in my soul. Tell me, what's the matter with my son? Why is he so sad and morose? He spends day after day on the lake and I hardly ever see him any more.

MASHA. His heart's troubled. [*To* NINA *timidly.*] Please, Nina, read something out of his play, won't you?

NINA. [*Shrugging her shoulders.*] You really want me to? It's so uninteresting.

MASHA. [*With restrained eagerness.*] When he recites anything his eyes shine and his face grows pale. He has a beautiful sad voice, and a manner like a poet's.

[*Sound of* SORIN'S *snoring.*]

DORN. Pleasant dreams.

ARCADINA. [*To* SORIN.] Petrusha!

SORIN. Eh?

ARCADINA. Are you asleep?

SORIN. Not at all. [*A pause.*]

ARCADINA. You are not following any treatment for yourself; that's not right, brother.

SORIN. I'd be glad to follow a treatment, but the doctor won't give me any.

DORN. Take care of yourself at sixty!

SORIN. Even at sixty a man wants to live.

DORN. [*Impatiently.*] Bah! Take your valerian [3] drops.

ARCADINA. I'd think it would do him good to take a cure at some springs.

DORN. Well—he might take it. He might not take it.

ARCADINA. Try and understand that!

DORN. Nothing to understand. It's all clear. [*A pause.*]

MEDVEDENKO. Peter Nikolayevitch ought to give up smoking.

SORIN. Fiddlesticks!

DORN. No, it's not fiddlesticks! Wine and tobacco rob us of our personality. After a cigar or a vodka, you're not Peter Nikolayevitch, you're Peter Nikolayevitch plus somebody else; your ego splits up, and you begin to see yourself as a third person.

SORIN. Fine [*Laughs.*] for you to argue! You've lived your life, but what about me? I've served the Department of Justice twenty-eight years, but I've never lived, never seen anything, and all the rest of it, so naturally I want to have my life. You've had your fill and that's why you turn to philosophy. I want to live, and that's why I turn to sherry after dinner and smoking cigars, and so on. And that's that.

DORN. One must look seriously at life, but to go in for cures at sixty and regret the pleasures you missed in your youth is, if you'll forgive me, frivolous.

MASHA. [*Gets up.*] It must be time for lunch. [*Walking slow and hobbling.*] My foot's gone to sleep. [*Exit* MASHA.]

DORN. She'll down a couple of glasses before lunch.

SORIN. The poor thing gets no happiness of her own.

[3] An herb tonic.

DORN. Fiddlesticks, your Excellency.

SORIN. You argue like a man who's had his fill.

ARCADINA. Oh, what can be duller than this darling country dullness is! Hot, quiet, nobody ever does anything, everybody philosophises. It's good to be here with you, my friends, delightful listening to you, but —sitting in my hotel room, all by myself, studying my part—how much better!

NINA. [Ecstatically.] Good! I understand you.

SORIN. Of course, in town's better. You sit in your library, the footman lets nobody in without announcing them, there's the telephone—on the street cabs and so on. . . .

DORN. [Singing sotto voce.] Tell her, my flowers—

[Enter SHAMREYEFF, behind him PAULINE.]

SHAMREYEFF. Here they are. Good morning! [Kisses MADAME ARCADINA'S hand, then NINA'S.] Very glad to see you looking so well. [To MADAME ARCADINA.] My wife tells me you are thinking of driving into town with her today. Is that so?

ARCADINA. Yes, we are thinking of it.

SHAMREYEFF. Hm! That's magnificent, but what will you travel on, my most esteemed lady? Today around here we are hauling rye, all the hands are busy. And what horses would you take, may I ask?

ARCADINA. What horses? How should I know—what horses!

SORIN. There are carriage horses here!

SHAMREYEFF. [Flaring up.] Carriage horses? But where do I get the harness? Where do I get the harness? It's amazing. It's incomprehensible! Most esteemed lady! Excuse me, I am on my knees before your talent, I'd gladly give ten years of my life for you, but I cannot let you have the horses!

ARCADINA. But what if I have to go? It's a fine business!

SHAMREYEFF. Most esteemed lady! You don't know what a farm means.

ARCADINA. [Flaring up.] The same old

story! In that case I'll start for Moscow today. Order me horses from the village, or I'll walk to the station.

SHAMREYEFF. [Flaring up.] In that case I resign my position! Find yourself another steward! [Exit SHAMREYEFF.]

ARCADINA. Every summer it's like this, every summer here they insult me! I'll never put my foot here again!

[She goes out in the direction of the bathhouse. Presently she is seen going into the house. TRIGORIN follows, with fishing rods and a pail.]

SORIN. [Flaring up.] This is insolent! The devil knows what it is! I'm sick of it, and so on. Bring all the horses here this very minute!

NINA. [To PAULINE.] To refuse Irina Nikolayevna, the famous actress! Any little wish of hers, the least whim, is worth more than all your farm. It's simply unbelievable!

PAULINE. [In despair.] What can I do? Put yourself in my shoes, what can I do?

SORIN. [To NINA.] Let's go find my sister. We'll all beg her not to leave us. Isn't that so? [Looking in the direction SHAMREYEFF went.] You insufferable man! Tyrant!

NINA. [Prevents his getting up.] Sit still, sit still. We'll wheel you. [She and MEDVEDENKO push the wheel chair.] Oh, how awful it is!

SORIN. Yes, yes, it's awful. But he won't leave, I'll speak to him right off.

[They go out, leaving DORN and PAULINE.]

DORN. People are certainly tiresome. Really the thing to do, of course, is throw that husband of yours out by the neck; but it will all end by this old woman, Peter Nicolayevitch, and his sister begging him to pardon them. See if they don't.

PAULINE. He has put the carriage horses in the fields, too. And these misunderstandings happen every day. If you only knew how it all upsets me. It's making me ill; you see how I'm trembling. I can't bear his coarseness. [Entreating.] Eugene, my darling, my dearest—take me with you. Our time is passing, we're not young any longer; if—if only we could—for the rest of our lives at least—stop hiding, stop pretending. [*A pause.*]

DORN. I am fifty-five, it's too late to change now.

PAULINE. I know, and you refuse me because there are other women close to you. It's impossible for you to take them all with you. I understand. I apologise! Forgive me, you are tired of me.

[NINA *appears before the house picking a bunch of flowers.*]

DORN. No, not at all.

PAULINE. I am miserable with jealousy. Of course you are a doctor. You can't escape women. I understand.

DORN. [*To* NINA, *as she joins them.*] What's happening?

NINA. Irina Nikolayevna is crying and Peter Nikolayevitch having his asthma.

DORN. [*Rising.*] I must go and give them both some valerian drops.

NINA. [*Giving him the flowers.*] Won't you?

DORN. *Merci bien.* [*Goes toward the house.*]

PAULINE. What pretty flowers! [*Nearing the house, in a low voice.*] Give me those flowers! Give me those flowers!

[*He hands her the flowers, she tears them to pieces and flings them away. They go into the house.*]

NINA [*Alone.*] How strange it is seeing a famous actress cry, and about such a little nothing! And isn't it strange that a famous author should sit all day long fishing? The darling of the public, his name in the papers every day, his photograph for sale in shop windows, his book translated into foreign languages, and he's delighted because he's caught two chub. I imagined famous people were proud and distant, and that they despised the crowd, and used their fame and the glamor of their names to revenge themselves on the world for putting birth and money first. But here I see them crying or fishing, playing cards, laughing or losing their tempers, like everybody else.

[TREPLEFF *enters, without a hat, carrying a gun and a dead sea gull.*]

TREPLEFF. Are you here alone?

NINA. Alone. [TREPLEFF *lays the sea gull at her feet.*] What does that mean?

TREPLEFF. I was low enough today to kill this sea gull. I lay it at your feet.

NINA. What's the matter with you? [*Picks up the sea gull and looks at it.*]

TREPLEFF. [*Pause.*] It's the way I'll soon end my own life.

NINA. I don't recognize you.

TREPLEFF. Yes, ever since I stopped recognizing you. You've changed toward me. Your eyes are cold. You hate to have me near you.

NINA. You are so irritable lately, and you talk—it's as if you were talking in symbols. And this sea gull, I suppose that's a symbol, too. Forgive me, but I don't understand it. [*Lays the sea gull on the seat.*] I'm too simple to understand you.

TREPLEFF. This began that evening when my play failed so stupidly. Women will never forgive failure. I've burnt it all, every scrap of it. If you only knew what I'm going through! Your growing cold to me is terrible, unbelievable; it's as if I had suddenly waked and found this lake dried up and sunk in the ground. You say you are too simple to understand me. Oh, what is there to understand? My play didn't catch your fancy, you despise my kind of imagination, you already consider me commonplace, insignificant, like so many others. [*Stamping his foot.*] How well I understand it all, how I understand it. It's like a spike in my brain, may it be damned along with my pride, which is sucking my blood, sucking it like a snake.

[*He sees* TRIGORIN, *who enters reading a book.*]

Here comes the real genius, he walks like Hamlet, and with a book too. [*Mimicking.*] "Words, words, words." This sun has hardly reached you, and you are already smiling, your glance is melting in his rays. I won't stand in your way. [*He goes out.*]

TRIGORIN. [*Making notes in a book.*]

Takes snuff and drinks vodka, always wears black. The schoolmaster in love with her.

NINA. Good morning, Boris Alexeyevitch!

TRIGORIN. Good morning. It seems that things have taken a turn we hadn't expected, so we are leaving today. You and I aren't likely to meet again. I'm sorry. I don't often meet young women, young and charming. I've forgotten how one feels at eighteen or nineteen, I can't picture it very clearly, and so the girls I draw in my stories and novels are mostly wrong. I'd like to be in your shoes for just one hour, to see things through your eyes, and find out just what sort of a little person you are.

NINA. And how I'd like to be in your shoes!

TRIGORIN. Why?

NINA. To know how it feels being a famous genius. What's it like being famous? How does it make you feel?

TRIGORIN. How? Nohow, I should think. I'd never thought about it. [Reflecting.] One of two things: either you exaggerate my fame, or else my fame hasn't made me feel it.

NINA. But if you read about yourself in the papers?

TRIGORIN. When they praise me I'm pleased; when they abuse me, I feel whipped for a day or so.

NINA. It's a marvellous world! If you only knew how I envy you! Look how different people's lots are! Some have all they can do to drag through their dull, obscure lives; they are all just alike, all miserable; others—well, you, for instance—have a bright, interesting life that means something. You are happy.

TRIGORIN. I? [Shrugging his shoulders.] H'm—I hear you speak of fame and happiness, of a bright, interesting life, but for me that's all words, pretty words that—if you'll forgive my saying so—mean about the same to me as candied fruits, which I never eat. You are very young and very kind.

NINA. Your life is beautiful.

TRIGORIN. I don't see anything so very beautiful about it. [Looks at his watch.] I must get to my writing. Excuse me, I'm busy— [Laughs.] You've stepped on my pet corn, as they say, and here I am, beginning to get excited and a little cross. At any rate, let's talk. Let's talk about my beautiful, bright life. Well, where shall we begin? [After reflecting a moment.] You know, sometimes violent obsessions take hold of a man, some fixed idea pursues him, the moon for example, day and night he thinks of nothing but the moon. Well, I have just such a moon. Day and night one thought obsesses me: I must be writing, I must be writing, I must be—I've scarcely finished one novel when somehow I'm driven on to write another, then a third, and after the third a fourth. I write incessantly, and always at a breakneck speed, and that's the only way I can write. What's beautiful and bright about that, I ask you? Oh, what a wild life! Why, now even, I'm here talking to you, I'm excited, but every minute I remember that the story I haven't finished is there waiting for me. I see that cloud up there, it's shaped like a grand piano—instantly a mental note—I must remember to put that in my story—a cloud sailing by—grand piano. A whiff of heliotrope. Quickly I make note of it: cloying smell, widow's color—put that in next time I describe a summer evening. Every sentence, every word I say and you say, I lie in wait for it, snap it up for my literary storeroom—it might come in handy— As soon as I put my work down, I race off to the theatre or go fishing, hoping to find a rest, but not at all—a new idea for a story comes rolling around in my head like a cannon ball, and I'm back at my desk and writing and writing and writing. And it's always like that, everlastingly. I have no rest from myself, and I feel that I am consuming my own life, that for the honey I'm giving to someone in the void, I rob my best flowers of their pollen, I tear up those flowers and trample on their roots. Do I seem mad? Do my friends seem to talk with me as they would to a sane man? "What are you writing at now? What shall we have next?" Over and over it's like that, till I think all this attention and praise is said only out of kindness to a sick man—deceive him, soothe him, and then any minute come stealing up behind and pack him off to the madhouse. And in those years, my young best years, when I was beginning, why then writing made my life a torment. A minor writer, especially when he's not successful, feels clumsy, he's all thumbs, the world has no need for him; his nerves are about to go; he can't resist hanging around people in the arts, where nobody knows him, or takes any notice of him, and he's afraid to look them straight in the eyes, like a man with a passion for gambling who hasn't any money to play with. I'd never seen my readers but for some reason or other I pictured them as hating me and mistrusting me, I had a deathly fear of the public, and when my first play was produced it seemed to me all the dark eyes in the audience were looking at it with hostility and all the light eyes with frigid indifference. Oh, how awful that was! What torment it was!

NINA. But surely the inspiration you feel and the creation itself of something must give you a moment of high, sweet happiness, don't they?

TRIGORIN. Yes. When I'm writing I enjoy it and I enjoy reading my proofs, but the minute it comes out I detest it; I see it's not what I meant it to be; I was wrong to write it at all, and I'm vexed and sick at heart about it. [Laughs.] Then the public reads it. "Yes, charming, clever—Charming but nothing like Tolstoy: A very fine thing, but Turgenev's 'Fathers and Sons' is finer." To my dying day that's what it will be, clever and charming, charming and clever—nothing more. And when I'm dead they'll be saying at my grave, "Here lies Trigorin, a delightful writer but not so good as Turgenev."

NINA. Excuse me, but I refuse to understand you. You are simply spoiled by success.

TRIGORIN. What success? I have never pleased myself. I don't like myself as a writer. The worst of it is that I am in a sort of daze and often don't understand what I write—I love this water here, the trees, the sky, I feel nature, it stirs in me a passion, an irresistible desire to write. But I am not only a landscape painter, I am a citizen too, I love my country, the people, I feel that if I am a writer I ought to speak also of the people, of their sufferings, of their future, speak of science, of the rights of man, and so forth; and I speak of everything, I hurry up, on all sides they are after me, are annoyed at me, I dash from side to side like a fox the hounds are baiting, I see life and science getting always farther and farther ahead as I fall always more and more behind, like a peasant, missing his train, and the upshot is I feel that I can write only landscape, and in all the rest I am false and false to the marrow of my bones.

NINA. You work too hard, and have no time and no wish to feel your own importance. You may be dissatisfied with yourself, of course, but other people think you are great and excellent. If I were such a writer as you are I'd give my whole life to the people, but I should feel that the only happiness for them would be in rising to me; and they should draw my chariot.

TRIGORIN. Well, in a chariot—Agamemnon[4] am I, or what. [They both smile.]

NINA. For the happiness of being an author or an actress I would bear any poverty, disillusionment, I'd have people hate me. I'd live in a garret and eat black bread, I'd endure my own dissatisfaction with myself and all my faults, but in return I should ask for fame—real resounding fame. [Covers her face with her hands.] My head's swimming— Ouf!

ARCADINA. [From within the house.] Boris Alexeyevitch!

TRIGORIN. She's calling me. I dare say, to come and pack. But I don't feel like going away. [He glances at the lake.] Look, how beautiful it is! Marvellous!

NINA. Do you see over there that house and garden?

[4] Leader of the Greeks in the Trojan War.

TRIGORIN. Yes.

NINA. It used to belong to my dear mother. I was born there. I've spent all my life by this lake and I know every little island on it.

TRIGORIN. It's all very charming. [*Seeing the sea gull.*] What is that?

NINA. A sea gull. Constantine shot it.

TRIGORIN. It's a lovely bird. Really, I don't want to leave here. Do try and persuade Irina Nikolayevna to stay. [*Makes a note in his book.*]

NINA. What is it you're writing?

TRIGORIN. Only a note. An idea struck me. [*Putting the notebook away.*] An idea for a short story: a young girl, one like you, has lived all her life beside a lake; she loves the lake like a sea gull and is happy and free like a sea gull. But by chance a man comes, sees her, and out of nothing better to do, destroys her, like this sea gull here. [*A pause.*]

[MADAME ARCADINA *appears at the window.*]

ARCADINA. Boris Alexeyevitch, where are you?

TRIGORIN. Right away! [*Goes toward the house, looking back at* NINA; MADAME ARCADINA *remains at the window.*] What is it?

ARCADINA. We're staying.

[TRIGORIN *enters the house.*]

NINA. [*Coming forward, standing lost in thought.*] It's a dream!

[CURTAIN.]

ACT THREE

The dining-room in SORIN'S *house. On the right and left are doors. A sideboard. A medicine cupboard. In the middle of the room a table. A small trunk and hat-boxes, signs of preparations for leaving.*

[TRIGORIN *is at lunch,* MASHA *standing by the table.*]

MASHA. I tell you this because you're a writer. You might use it. I tell you the truth: if he had died when he shot himself I wouldn't live another minute. Just the same I'm getting braver; I've just made up my mind to tear this love out of my heart by the roots.

TRIGORIN. How will you do it?

MASHA. I'm going to get married. To Medvedenko.

TRIGORIN. Is that the schoolmaster?

MASHA. Yes.

TRIGORIN. I don't see why you must do that.

MASHA. Loving without hope, waiting the whole year long for something—but when I'm married I won't have any time for love, there'll be plenty of new things I'll have to do to make me forget the past. Anyhow it will be a change, you know. Shall we have another?

TRIGORIN. Haven't you had about enough?

MASHA. Ah! [*Pours two glasses.*] Here! Don't look at me like that! Women drink oftener than you imagine. Not so many of them drink openly like me. Most of them hide it. Yes. And it's always vodka or cognac. [*Clinks glasses.*] Your health. You're a decent sort, I'm sorry to be parting from you. [*They drink.*]

TRIGORIN. I don't want to leave here myself.

MASHA. You should beg her to stay.

TRIGORIN. She'd never do that now. Her son is behaving himself very tactlessly. First he tries shooting himself and now, they say, he's going to challenge me to a duel. But what for? He sulks, he snorts, he preaches new art forms—but there's room for all, the new and the old—why elbow?

MASHA. Well, and there's jealousy. However, that's not my business. [*Pause.*]

[YAKOV *crosses right to left with a piece of luggage.* NINA *enters, stops near window.*]

MASHA. That schoolmaster of mine is none too clever, but he's a good man and he's poor, and he loves me dearly. I'm sorry for him, and I'm sorry for his old mother. Well, let me wish you every happiness. Think kindly of me. [*Warmly shakes his hand.*] Let me thank you for your friendly interest. Send me your books, be sure to write in them. Only don't put "esteemed lady," but simply this: "To Marya, who, not remembering her origin, does not know why she is living in this world." Goodbye. [MASHA *goes out.*]

NINA. [*Holding out her hand close to* TRIGORIN.] Even or odd?

TRIGORIN. Even.

NINA. [*Sighing.*] No. I had only one pea in my hand. I was trying my fortune: To be an actress or not. I wish somebody would advise me.

TRIGORIN. There's no advice in this sort of thing. [*A pause.*]

NINA. We are going to part—I may never see you again. Won't you take this little medal to remember me? I've had it engraved with your initials and on the other side the title of your book: *Days and Nights.*

TRIGORIN. What a graceful thing to do! [*Kisses the medal.*] It's a charming present.

NINA. Sometimes think of me.

TRIGORIN. I'll think of you. I'll think of you as I saw you that sunny day—do you remember—a week ago when you had on your white dress—we were talking—a white sea gull was lying on the bench beside us.

NINA. [*Pensive.*] Yes, the sea gull. [*A pause.*] Some one's coming—let me see you two minutes before you go, won't you?

[*Goes out on the left as* MADAME ARCADINA *and* SORIN, *in full dress, with a star, enter, then* YAKOV, *busy with the packing.*]

ARCADINA. Stay at home, old man. How could you be running about with your rheumatism? [*To* TRIGORIN.] Who was it just went out? Nina?

TRIGORIN. Yes.

ARCADINA. *Pardon!* We intruded. [*Sits down.*] I believe everything's packed. I'm exhausted.

TRIGORIN. *Days and Nights,* page 121, lines eleven and twelve.[1]

YAKOV. [*Clearing the table.*] Shall I pack your fishing rods as well?

TRIGORIN. Yes, I'll want them again. But the books you can give away.

YAKOV. Yes, sir.

TRIGORIN. [*To himself.*] Page 121, lines eleven and twelve. What's in those lines? [*To* ARCADINA.] Have you my works here in the house?

ARCADINA. Yes, in my brother's study, the corner bookcase.

TRIGORIN. Page 121.

[*Exit* TRIGORIN.]

ARCADINA. Really, Petrusha, you'd better stay at home.

SORIN. You're going away. It's dreary for me here at home without you.

ARCADINA. But what's there in town?

SORIN. Nothing in particular, but all the same. [*Laughs.*] There's the laying of the foundation stone for the town hall, and all that sort of thing. A man longs if only for an hour or so to get out of this gudgeon existence, and it's much too long I've been lying around like an old cigarette holder. I've ordered the horses around at one o'clock, we'll set off at the same time.

ARCADINA. [*After a pause.*] Oh, stay here, don't be lonesome, don't take cold. Look after my son. Take care of him. Advise him. [*A pause.*] Here I am leaving and so shall never know why Constantine tried to kill himself. I have a notion the main reason was jealousy, and the sooner I take Trigorin away from here the better.

SORIN. How should I explain it to you? There were other reasons beside jealousy. Here we have a man who is young, intelligent, living in the country in solitude, without money, without position, without a future. He has nothing to do. He is ashamed and afraid of his idleness. I love him very much and he's attached to me, but he feels just the same that he's superfluous in this house, and a sort of dependent here, a poor

---

[1] Trigorin is reading the inscription on the medal which Nina has just given him.

relation. That's something we can understand, it's pride of course.

ARCADINA. I'm worried about him. [*Reflecting.*] He might go into the service, perhaps.

SORIN. [*Whistling, then hesitatingly.*] It seems to me the best thing you could do would be to let him have a little money. In the first place he ought to be able to dress himself like other people, and so on. Look how he's worn that same old jacket these past three years; he runs around without an overcoat. [*Laughs.*] Yes, and it wouldn't harm him to have a little fun—he might go abroad, perhaps—it wouldn't cost much.

ARCADINA. Perhaps I could manage a suit, but as for going abroad—no. Just at this moment I can't even manage the suit. [*Firmly.*] I haven't any money! [SORIN *laughs.*] No.

SORIN. [*Whistling.*] Forgive me, my dear, don't be angry. You're a generous, noble woman.

ARCADINA. [*Weeping.*] I haven't any money.

SORIN. Of course if I had any money, I'd give him some myself, but I haven't anything, not a kopek. [*Laughs.*] My manager takes all my pension and spends it on agriculture, cattle-raising, bee-keeping, and my money goes for nothing. The bees die, the cows die, horses they never let me have.

ARCADINA. Yes, I have some money, but I'm an actress, my costumes alone are enough to ruin me.

SORIN. You are very good, my dear. I respect you. Yes— But there again something's coming over me— [*Staggers.*] My head's swimming. [*Leans on table.*] I feel faint, and so on.

ARCADINA. [*Alarmed.*] Petrusha! [*Trying to support him.*] Petrusha, my darling! [*Calls.*] Help me! Help!

[*Enter* TREPLEFF, *his head bandaged, and* MEDVEDENKO.]

ARCADINA. He feels faint.

SORIN. It's nothing, it's nothing— [*Smiles and drinks water.*] It's gone already—and so on.

TREPLEFF. [*To his mother.*] Don't be alarmed, mother, it's not serious. It often happens now to my uncle. Uncle, you must lie down.

SORIN. A little, yes. All the same I'm going to town— I'm lying down and I'm going to town—that's clear.

[*He goes, leaning on his stick.*]

MEDVEDENKO. [*Gives him his arm.*] There's a riddle: in the morning it's on four legs, at noon on two, in the evening on three.[2]

SORIN. [*Laughs.*] That's it. And on the back at night. Thank you, I can manage alone.

MEDVEDENKO. My, what ceremony!

[*He and* SORIN *go out.*]

ARCADINA. How he frightened me!

TREPLEFF. It's not good for him to live in the country. He's low in his mind. Now, mother, if you'd only have a burst of sudden generosity and lend him a thousand or fifteen hundred, he could spend a whole year in town.

ARCADINA. I haven't any money. I'm an actress, not a banker. [*A pause.*]

TREPLEFF. Mother, change my bandage. You do it so well.

ARCADINA. [*Takes bottle of iodoform and a box of bandages from cupboard.*] And the doctor's late.

TREPLEFF. He promised to be here at ten, but it's already noon.

ARCADINA. Sit down. [*Takes off bandage.*] You look as if you were in a turban. Some man who came by the kitchen yesterday asked what nationality you were. But it's almost entirely healed. What's left is nothing. [*Kisses him on the head.*] While I'm away, you won't do any more click-click?

TREPLEFF. No, mother. That was a moment when I was out of my head with despair, and couldn't control myself. It won't happen again. [*Kisses her fingers.*]

---

2 Alluding to the riddle of the Sphinx, by solving which Oedipus saved Thebes and became its king. Sorin's cane suggests the three legs, by which the creature man walks in the evening of his life.

You have clever fingers. I remember long, long ago when you were still playing at the Imperial Theatre—there was a fight one day in our court, and a washerwoman who was one of the tenants got beaten almost to death. Do you remember? She was picked up unconscious—you nursed her, took medicines to her, bathed her children in the washtub. Don't you remember?

ARCADINA. No. [*Puts on fresh bandage.*]

TREPLEFF. Two ballet dancers were living then in the same house we did, they used to come and drink coffee with you.

ARCADINA. That I remember.

TREPLEFF. They were very pious. [*A pause.*] Lately, these last days, I have loved you as tenderly and fully as when I was a child. Except for you, there's nobody left me now. Only why, why do you subject yourself to the influence of that man?

ARCADINA. You don't understand him, Constantine. He's a very noble character.

TREPLEFF. Nevertheless, when he was told I was going to challenge him to a duel, nobility didn't keep him from playing the coward. He's leaving. Ignominious retreat!

ARCADINA. Such tosh! I myself beg him to leave here.

TREPLEFF. Noble character! Here we both are nearly quarrelling over him, and right now very likely he's in the drawing-room or in the garden laughing at us— developing Nina, trying once and for all to convince her he's a genius.

ARCADINA. For you it's a pleasure—saying disagreeable things to me. I respect that man and must ask you not to speak ill of him in my presence.

TREPLEFF. And I don't respect him. You want me too to think he's a genius, but, forgive me, I can't tell lies—his creations make me sick.

ARCADINA. That's envy. People who are not talented but pretend to be have nothing better to do than to disparage real talents. It must be a fine consolation!

TREPLEFF. [*Sarcastically.*] Real talents! [*Angrily.*] I'm more talented than both of you put together, if it comes to that! [*Tears off the bandage.*] You two, with your stale routine, have grabbed first place in art and think that only what you do is real or legitimate; the rest you'd like to stifle and keep down. I don't believe in you two. I don't believe in you or in him.

ARCADINA. Decadent!

TREPLEFF. Go back to your darling theatre and act there in trashy, stupid plays!

ARCADINA. Never did I act in such plays. Leave me alone! You are not fit to write even wretched vaudeville. Kiev burgher! Sponge!

TREPLEFF. Miser!

ARCADINA. Beggar! [*He sits down, cries softly.*] Nonentity! [*Walks up and down.*] Don't cry! You mustn't cry! [*Weeps. Kisses him on his forehead, his cheeks, his head.*] My dear child, forgive me! Forgive me, your wicked mother! Forgive miserable me!

TREPLEFF. [*Embracing her.*] If you only knew! I've lost everything. She doesn't love me, now I can't write. All my hopes are gone.

ARCADINA. Don't despair. It will all pass. He's leaving right away. She'll love you again. [*Dries his tears.*] That's enough. We've made it up now.

TREPLEFF. [*Kissing her hands.*] Yes, mother.

ARCADINA. [*Tenderly.*] Make it up with him, too. You don't want a duel. You don't, do you?

TREPLEFF. Very well, only, mother, don't let me see him. It's painful to me. It's beyond me.

[TRIGORIN *comes in.*]

There he is. I'm going. [*Quickly puts dressings away in cupboard.*] The doctor will do my bandage later.

TRIGORIN. [*Looking through a book.*] Page 121—lines eleven and twelve. Here it is. [*Reads.*] "If you ever, ever need my life, come and take it."

[TREPLEFF *picks up the bandage from the floor and goes out.*]

ARCADINA. [*Looking at her watch.*] The horses will be here soon.

TRIGORIN. [*To himself.*] If you ever, ever need my life, come and take it.

ARCADINA. I hope you are all packed.

TRIGORIN. [*Impatiently.*] Yes, yes— [*In deep thought.*] Why is it I thought I felt sadness in that call from a pure soul, and my heart aches so with pity? If you ever, ever need my life, come and take it. [*To* MADAME ARCADINA.] Let's stay just one more day.

[*She shakes her head.*]

TRIGORIN. Let's stay!

ARCADINA. Darling, I know what keeps you here. But have some self-control. You're a little drunk, be sober.

TRIGORIN. You be sober, too, be understanding, reasonable, I beg you; look at all this like a true friend— [*Presses her hand.*] You are capable of sacrificing. Be my friend, let me be free.

ARCADINA. [*Excited.*] Are you so infatuated?

TRIGORIN. I am drawn to her! Perhaps this is just what I need.

ARCADINA. The love of some provincial girl? Oh, how little you know yourself!

TRIGORIN. Sometimes people talk but are asleep. That's how it is now—I'm talking to you but in my dream see her. I'm possessed by sweet, marvellous dreams. Let me go—

ARCADINA. [*Trembling.*] No, no, I'm an ordinary woman like any other woman, you shouldn't talk to me like this. Don't torture me, Boris. It frightens me.

TRIGORIN. If you wanted to, you could be far from ordinary. There is a kind of love that's young, and beautiful, and is all poetry, and carries us away into a world of dreams; on earth it alone can ever give us happiness. Such a love I still have never known. In my youth there wasn't time, I was always around some editor's office, fighting off starvation. Now it's here, that love, it's come, it beckons me. What sense, then, is there in running away from it?

ARCADINA. [*Angry.*] You've gone mad.

TRIGORIN. Well, let me!

ARCADINA. You've all conspired today just to torment me. [*Weeps.*]

TRIGORIN. [*Clutching at his breast.*] She doesn't understand. She doesn't want to understand.

ARCADINA. Am I so old or ugly that you don't mind talking to me about other women? [*Embracing and kissing him.*] Oh, you madman! My beautiful, my marvel— you are the last chapter of my life. [*Falls on knees.*] My joy, my pride, my blessedness! [*Embracing his knees.*] If you forsake me for one hour even, I'll never survive it, I'll go out of my mind, my wonderful, magnificent one, my master.

TRIGORIN. Somebody might come in. [*Helps her to rise.*]

ARCADINA. Let them, I am not ashamed of my love for you. [*Kisses his hands.*] My treasure! You reckless boy, you want to be mad, but I won't have it, I won't let you. [*Laughs.*] You are mine—you are mine. This brow is mine, and the eyes mine, and this beautiful silky hair, too, is mine. You are all mine. You are so talented, so intelligent, the best of all modern writers; you are the one and only hope of Russia— you have such sincerity, simplicity, healthy humor. In one stroke you go to the very heart of a character or a scene; your people are like life itself. Oh, it's impossible to read you without rapture! Do you think this is only incense? I'm flattering you? Come, look me in the eyes—Do I look like a liar? There you see, only I can appreciate you; only I tell you the truth, my lovely darling.—You are coming? Yes? You won't leave me?

TRIGORIN. I have no will of my own— I've never had a will of my own. Flabby, weak, always submitting! Is it possible that might please women? Take me, carry me away, only never let me be one step away from you.

ARCADINA. [*To herself.*] Now he's mine. [*Casually, as if nothing had happened.*] However, if you like you may stay. I'll go by myself, and you come later, in a week. After all, where would you hurry to?

TRIGORIN. No, let's go together.

ARCADINA. As you like. Together, together then. [*A pause.* TRIGORIN *writes in notebook.*] What are you writing?

TRIGORIN. This morning I heard a happy expression, one I'd heard so long ago that I'd forgotten it: "Virgin forest." It might be useful in a story. [*Yawns.*] So, we're off. Once more the cars, stations, station buffets, stews and conversations!

[SHAMREYEFF *enters.*]

SHAMREYEFF. I have the honor with deep regret to announce that the horses are ready. It's time, most esteemed lady, to be off to the station; the train arrives at five minutes after two. So will you do me the favor, Irina Nikolayevna, not to forget to inquire about this: Where's the actor Suzdaltsev now? Is he alive? Is he well? We used to drink together once upon a time. In "The Stolen Mail" he was inimitable. In the same company with him at Elisavetograd, I remember, was the tragedian Izmailov, also a remarkable personality. Don't hurry, most esteemed lady, there are five minutes still. Once in some melodrama they were playing conspirators, and when they were suddenly discovered, he had to say, "We are caught in a trap," but Izmailov said, "We are traught in a clap." [*Laughs.*] Clap!

[YAKOV *is busy with luggage.* MAID *brings* ARCADINA'S *hat, coat, parasol, gloves. All help her put them on. The* COOK *peers through door on left, as if hesitating, then he comes in. Enter* PAULINE, SORIN *and* MEDVEDENKO.]

PAULINE. [*With basket.*] Here are some plums for the journey. They are sweet ones. In case you'd like some little thing.

ARCADINA. You are very kind, Pauline Andreyevna.

PAULINE. Goodbye, my dear. If anything has been not quite so, forgive it. [*Cries.*]

ARCADINA. [*Embracing her.*] Everything has been charming, everything's been charming. Only you mustn't cry.

PAULINE. Time goes so.

ARCADINA. There's nothing we can do about that.

[SORIN, *in a greatcoat with a cape, his hat on and his stick in his hand, crosses the stage.*]

SORIN. Sister, you'd better start if you don't want to be late. I'll go get in the carriage. [*Exit* SORIN.]

MEDVEDENKO. And I'll walk to the station—to see you off. I'll step lively. [*Exit* MEDVEDENKO.]

ARCADINA. Goodbye, my friends. If we are alive and well next summer we'll meet again. [*The* MAID, COOK *and* YAKOV *kiss her hand.*] Don't forget me. [*Gives* COOK *a rouble.*] Here's a rouble for the three of you.

COOK. We humbly thank you, madam. Pleasant journey to you. Many thanks to you.

YAKOV. God bless you!

SHAMREYEFF. Make us happy with a letter. Goodbye, Boris Alexeyevitch.

ARCADINA. Where's Constantine? Tell him I'm off now. I must say goodbye to him. Well, remember me kindly. [*To* YAKOV.] I gave the cook a rouble. It's for the three of you.

[*All go out, the stage is empty. Off-stage are heard the usual sounds when people are going away. The* MAID *comes back for the basket of plums from the table and goes out again.* TRIGORIN *returns.*]

TRIGORIN. I forgot my stick. It's out there on the terrace, I think.

[*As he starts to go out by the door on the left, he meets* NINA *coming in.*] Is it you? We are just going—

NINA. I felt we should meet again. [*Excited.*] Boris Alexeyevitch, I've come to a decision, the die is cast. I am going on the stage. Tomorrow I shall not be here. I am leaving my father, deserting everything, beginning a new life. I'm off like you—for Moscow—we shall meet there.

TRIGORIN. [*Glancing around him.*] Stay at Hotel Slavyansky Bazaar. Let me know at once. Molchanovka, Groholsky House. I must hurry. [*A pause.*]

NINA. One minute yet.

TRIGORIN. [*In a low voice.*] You are so beautiful— Oh, how happy to think we'll be meeting soon. [*She puts her head on his breast.*] I shall see those lovely eyes again, that ineffably beautiful, tender smile—those gentle features, their pure, angelic expression—my darling— [*A long kiss.*]

[CURTAIN.]

ACT FOUR

One of the drawing-rooms in SORIN'S *house, turned by* CONSTANTINE TREPLEFF *into a study. On the right and left, doors leading into other parts of the house. Facing us, glass doors on to the terrace. Beside the usual furniture of a drawing-room, there is a writing-table in the corner to the right; near the door on the left, a sofa, a bookcase full of books, and books in the windows and on the chairs. Evening. A single lamp with a shade is lighted. Semi-darkness. The sound from outside of trees rustling and the wind howling in the chimney.*

[*The night watchman is knocking.* MED-VEDENKO *and* MASHA *come in.*]

MASHA. Constantine Gavrilovitch! Constantine Gavrilovitch! [*Looking around.*] Nobody here. Every other minute all day long the old man keeps asking, "Where's Kostya, where's Kostya?" He can't live without him.

MEDVEDENKO. He's afraid to be alone. [*Listening.*] What terrible weather! It's two days now.

MASHA. [*Turning up the lamp.*] Out on the lake there are waves. Tremendous.

MEDVEDENKO. The garden's black. We ought to have told them to pull down that stage. It stands all bare and hideous, like a skeleton, and the curtain flaps in the wind. When I passed there last night it seemed to me that in the wind I heard some one crying.

MASHA. Well, here—[*Pause.*]

MEDVEDENKO. Masha, let's go home.

MASHA. [*Shakes her head.*] I'm going to stay here tonight.

MEDVEDENKO. [*Imploring.*] Masha, let's go. Our baby must be hungry.

MASHA. Nonsense. Matriona will feed it. [*A pause.*]

MEDVEDENKO. It's hard on him. He's been three nights now without his mother.

MASHA. You're getting just too tiresome. In the old days you'd at least philosophise a little, but now it's all baby, home, baby, home—and that's all I can get out of you.

MEDVEDENKO. Let's go, Masha.

MASHA. Go yourself.

MEDVEDENKO. Your father won't let me have a horse.

MASHA. He will if you just ask him.

MEDVEDENKO. Very well, I'll try. Then you'll come tomorrow.

MASHA. [*Taking snuff.*] Well, tomorrow. Stop bothering me.

[*Enter* TREPLEFF *and* PAULINE; TREPLEFF *carries pillows and a blanket,* PAULINE *sheets and pillowcases; they lay them on the sofa, then* TREPLEFF *goes and sits down at his desk.*]

MASHA. Why's that, mama?

PAULINE. Peter Nikolayevitch asked to sleep in Kostya's room.

MASHA. Let me— [*She makes the bed.*]

PAULINE. [*Sighing.*] Old people, what children—

[*Goes to the desk; leaning on her elbows she gazes at the manuscript; a pause.*]

MEDVEDENKO. So I'm going. Goodbye, Masha. [*Kisses her hand.*] Goodbye, mother. [*Tries to kiss her hand.*]

PAULINE. [*With annoyance.*] Well, go if you're going.

MEDVEDENKO. Goodbye, Constantine Gavrilovitch.

[TREPLEFF *without speaking gives him his hand;* MEDVEDENKO *goes out.*]

PAULINE. [*Gazing at manuscript.*] Nobody ever thought or dreamed that some day, Kostya, you'd turn out to be a real author. But now, thank God, the magazines send you money for your stories. [*Passing her hand over his hair.*] And you've grown handsome—dear, good Kostya, be kind to my little Masha.

MASHA. [*Making the bed.*] Let him alone, mama.

PAULINE. She's a sweet little thing. [*A pause.*] A woman, Kostya, doesn't ask much—only kind looks. As I well know.

[TREPLEFF *rises from the desk and without speaking goes out.*]

MASHA. You shouldn't have bothered him.

PAULINE. I feel sorry for you, Masha.

MASHA. Why should you?

PAULINE. My heart aches and aches for you. I see it all, I understand everything.

MASHA. It's all foolishness! Hopeless love—that's only in novels. No matter. Only you mustn't let yourself go, and be always waiting for something, waiting for fine weather by the sea. If love stirs in your heart, stamp it out. Now they've promised to transfer my husband to another district. As soon as we get there—I'll forget it all—I'll tear it out of my heart by the roots.

[*Two rooms off is heard a melancholy waltz.*]

PAULINE. Kostya is playing. That means he's feeling sad.

[MASHA *waltzes silently a few turns.*]

MASHA. The great thing, mama, is to be where I don't see him. If only my Semyon could get his transfer, I promise you I'd forget in a month. It's all nonsense.

[*Door on left opens,* DORN *and* MEDVEDENKO *come in, wheeling* SORIN *in his chair.*]

MEDVEDENKO. I have six souls at home now. And flour at seventy kopeks.

DORN. So it just goes round and round.

MEDVEDENKO. It's easy for you to smile. You've got more money than the chickens could pick up.

DORN. Money! After practicing medicine thirty years, my friend, so driven day and night that I could never call my soul my own, I managed to save up at last two thousand roubles; and I've pust spent all that on a trip abroad. I've got nothing at all.

MASHA. [*To her husband.*] Aren't you gone yet?

MEDVEDENKO. [*Apologizing.*] How can I, when they won't let me have a horse!

MASHA. [*Under her breath angrily.*] I wish I'd never lay eyes on you again.

[SORIN'S *wheel-chair remains left center;* PAULINE, MASHA, *and* DORN *sit down beside him.* MEDVEDENKO *stands to one side gloomily.*]

DORN. Look how many changes they have made here! The drawing-room is turned into a study.

MASHA. Constantine Gavrilovitch likes to work in here. He can go into the garden whenever he likes and think. [*A watchman's rattle sounds.*]

SORIN. Where's my sister?

DORN. She went to the station to meet Trigorin. She'll be right back.

SORIN. If you thought you had to send for my sister, that shows I'm very ill. [*Reflecting.*] Now that's odd, isn't it? I'm very ill, but they won't let me have any medicine around here.

DORN. And what would you like? Valerian drops? Soda? Quinine?

SORIN. So it's more philosophy, I suppose. Oh, what an affliction! [*He motions with his head toward the sofa.*] Is that for me?

PAULINE. Yes, for you, Peter Nikolayevitch.

SORIN. Thank you.

DORN. [*Singing sotto voce.*] *The moon drifts in the sky tonight.*

SORIN. Listen, I want to give Kostya a subject for a story. It should be called: "The Man Who Wanted To"—*L'homme qui a voulu.* In my youth long ago wanted to become an author—and never became one; wanted to speak eloquently—and spoke execrably [*Mimicking himself.*] and so on and so forth, and all the rest of it, yes and no, and in the résumé would drag on, drag on, till the sweat broke out; wanted to marry—and never married;

wanted always to live in town—and now am ending up my life in the country, and so on.

DORN. Wanted to become a State Counsellor—and became one.

SORIN. [*Laughing.*] For that I never longed. That came to me of itself.

DORN. Come now, to be picking faults with life at sixty-two, you must confess, that's not magnanimous.

SORIN. How bullheaded you are! Can't you take it in? I want to live.

DORN. That's frivolous, it's the law of nature that every life must come to an end.

SORIN. You argue like a man who's had his fill. You've had your fill and so you're indifferent to living, it's all one to you. But at that even you will be afraid to die.

DORN. The fear of death—a brute fear. We must overcome it. The fear of death is reasonable only in those who believe in an eternal life, and shudder to think of the sins they have committed. But you in the first place don't believe, in the second place what sins have you? For twenty-five years you served as State Counsellor—and that's all.

SORIN. [*Laughing.*] Twenty-eight.

[TREPLEFF *enters and sits on the stool beside* SORIN. MASHA *never takes her eyes off his face.*]

DORN. We are keeping Constantine Gavrilovitch from his work.

TREPLEFF. No, it's nothing. [*A pause.*]

MEDVEDENKO. Permit me to ask you, Doctor, what town in your travels did you most prefer?

DORN. Genoa.

TREPLEFF. Why Genoa?

DORN. Because of the marvellous street crowd. When you go out of your hotel in the evening you find the whole street surging with people. You let yourself drift among the crowd, zigzagging back and forth, you live its life, its soul pours into you, until finally you begin to believe there might really be a world spirit after all, like that Nina Zaryechny acted in your play.

By the way, where is Nina just now? Where is she and how is she?

TREPLEFF. Very well, I imagine.

DORN. I've been told she was leading rather an odd sort of life. How's that?

TREPLEFF. It's a long story, Doctor.

DORN. You can shorten it. [*A pause.*]

TREPLEFF. She ran away from home and joined Trigorin. That you knew?

DORN. I know.

TREPLEFF. She had a child. The child died. Trigorin got tired of her, and went back to his old ties, as might be expected. He'd never broken these old ties anyhow, but flitted in that backboneless style of his from one to the other. As far as I could say from what I know, Nina's private life didn't quite work out.

DORN. And on the stage?

TREPLEFF. I believe even worse. She made her debut in Moscow at a summer theatre, and afterward a tour in the provinces. At that time I never let her out of my sight, and wherever she was I was. She always attempted big parts, but her acting was crude, without any taste, her gestures were clumsy. There were moments when she did some talented screaming, talented dying, but those were only moments.

DORN. It means, though, she has talent?

TREPLEFF. I could never make out. I imagine she has. I saw her, but she didn't want to see me, and her maid wouldn't let me in her rooms. I understood how she felt, and never insisted on seeing her. [*A pause.*] What more is there to tell you? Afterward, when I'd come back home here, she wrote me some letters. They were clever, tender, interesting; she didn't complain, but I could see she was profoundly unhappy; there was not a word that didn't show her exhausted nerves. And she'd taken a strange fancy. She always signed herself The Sea Gull. In "The Mermaid" the miller says that he's a crow; the same way in all her letters she kept repeating she was a sea gull. Now she's here.

DORN. How do you mean, here?

TREPLEFF. In town, staying at the inn. She's already been here five days, living there in rooms. Masha drove in, but she never sees anybody. Semyon Semyonovich declares that last night after dinner he saw her in the fields, a mile and a half from here.

MEDVEDENKO. Yes, I saw her. [*A pause.*] Going in the opposite direction from here, toward town. I bowed to her, asked why she had not been out to see us. She said she'd come.

TREPLEFF. Well, she won't. [*A pause.*] Her father and stepmother don't want to know her. They've set watchmen to keep her off the grounds. [*Goes toward the desk with* DORN.] How easy it is, Doctor, to be a philosopher on paper, and how hard it is in life!

SORIN. She was a beautiful girl.

DORN. How's that?

SORIN. I say she was a beautiful girl. State Counsellor Sorin was downright in love with her himself once for a while.

DORN. You old Lovelace! [1] [*They hear* SHAMREYEFF'S *laugh.*]

PAULINE. I imagine they're back from the station.

TREPLEFF. Yes, I hear mother.

[*Enter* MADAME ARCADINA *and* TRIGORIN, SHAMREYEFF *following.*]

SHAMREYEFF. We all get old and fade with the elements, esteemed lady, but you, most honored lady, are still young . . . white dress, vivacity—grace.

ARCADINA. You still want to bring me bad luck,[2] you tiresome creature!

TRIGORIN. [*To* SORIN.] Howdy do, Peter Nikolayevitch. How is it you are still indisposed? That's not so good. [*Pleased at seeing* MASHA.] Masha Ilyinishna!

MASHA. You know me? [*Grasps his hand.*]

TRIGORIN. Married?

MASHA. Long ago.

TRIGORIN. Are you happy? [*Bows to*

DORN *and* MEDVEDENKO, *then hesitatingly goes to* TREPLEFF.] Irina Nikolayevna tells me you have forgotten the past and given up being angry. [TREPLEFF *holds out his hand.*]

ARCADINA. [*To her son.*] Look, Boris Alexeyevitch has brought you the magazine with your last story.

TREPLEFF. [*Taking the magazine. To* TRIGORIN.] Thank you. You're very kind. [*They sit down.*]

TRIGORIN. Your admirers send their respects to you. In Petersburg and in Moscow, everywhere, there's a great deal of interest in your work, and they all ask me about you. They ask: what is he like, what age is he, is he dark or fair? For some reason they all think you are no longer young. And nobody knows your real name, since you always publish under a pseudonym. You're a mystery, like the Man in the Iron Mask.[3]

TREPLEFF. Will you be with us long?

TRIGORIN. No, tomorrow I think I'll go to Moscow. I must. I'm in a hurry to finish a story, and besides I've promised to write something for an annual. In a word, it's the same old thing.

[MADAME ARCADINA *and* PAULINE *have set up a card table.* SHAMREYEFF *lights candles, arranges chairs, gets box of lotto from a cupboard.*]

TRIGORIN. The weather's given me a poor welcome. The wind is ferocious. Tomorrow morning if it dies down I'm going out to the lake to fish. And I want to look around the garden and the place where— do you remember?—your play was done. The idea for a story is all worked out in my mind, I want only to refresh my memory of the place where it's laid.

MASHA. Papa, let my husband have a horse! He must get home.

SHAMREYEFF. [*Mimics.*] A horse— home. [*Sternly.*] See for yourself: they are

---

[1] In Samuel Richardson's novel *Clarissa Harlowe*, Robert Lovelace is a character who became something of a type for the seducer of innocent maidens.

[2] *I.e.*, by paying her compliments and thus attracting the evil eye. See her similar remark about Nina in Act II.

[3] A state prisoner during the reign of Louis XIV of France. His identity was concealed by an iron mask and remains a famous historical mystery. He figures in Dumas' romance *The Man in the Iron Mask.*

just back from the station. They'll not go out again.

MASHA. They're not the only horses. . . . [*Seeing that he says nothing, she makes an impatient gesture.*] Nobody can do anything with you—

MEDVEDENKO. I can walk, Masha. Truly—

PAULINE. [*Sighs.*] Walk, in such weather! [*Sits down at card table.*] Sit down, friends.

MEDVEDENKO. It's only four miles. . . . Goodbye. [*Kisses wife's hand.*] Goodbye, mama. [*His mother-in-law puts out her hand reluctantly.*] I should not have troubled anybody, but the little baby— [*Bowing to them.*] Goodbye.

[*He goes out as if apologising.*]

SHAMREYEFF. He'll make it. He's not a general.

PAULINE. [*Taps on table.*] Sit down, friends. Let's not lose time, they'll be calling us to supper soon.

[SHAMREYEFF, MASHA *and* DORN *sit at the card table.*]

ARCADINA. [*To* TRIGORIN.] When these long autumn evenings draw on we pass the time out here with lotto. And look: the old lotto set we had when my mother used to play with us children. Don't you want to take a hand with us till supper time? [*She and* TRIGORIN *sit down at the table.*] It's a tiresome game, but it does well enough when you're used to it. [*She deals three cards to each one.*]

TREPLEFF. [*Turns magazine pages.*] He's read his own story, but mine he hasn't even cut. [*He lays the magazine on the desk; on his way out, as he passes his mother, he kisses her on the head.*]

ARCADINA. But you, Kostya?

TREPLEFF. Sorry, I don't care to. I'm going for a walk. [*Goes out.*]

ARCADINA. Stake—ten kopeks. Put it down for me, Doctor.

DORN. Command me.

MASHA. Has everybody bet? I'll begin. Twenty-two.

ARCADINA. I have it.

MASHA. Three.

DORN. Here you are.

MASHA. Did you put down three? Eight! Eighty-one! Ten!

SHAMREYEFF. Not so fast.

ARCADINA. What a reception they gave me at Kharkoff! Can you believe it, my head's spinning yet.

MASHA. Thirty-four. [*A sad waltz is heard.*]

ARCADINA. The students gave me an ovation, three baskets of flowers, two wreaths and look— [*She takes off a brooch and puts it on the table.*]

SHAMREYEFF. Yes, that's the real—

MASHA. Fifty!

DORN. Fifty, you say?

ARCADINA. I had a superb costume. Say what you like but really when it comes to dressing myself I am no fool.

PAULINE. Kostya is playing. The poor boy's sad.

SHAMREYEFF. In the papers they often abuse him.

MASHA. Seventy-seven.

ARCADINA. Who cares what they say?

TRIGORIN. He hasn't any luck. He still can't discover how to write a style of his own. There is something strange, vague, at times even like delirious raving. Not a single character that is alive.

MASHA. Eleven!

ARCADINA. [*Glancing at* SORIN.] Petrusha, are you bored? [*A pause.*] He's asleep.

DORN. He's asleep, the State Counsellor.

MASHA. Seven! Ninety!

TRIGORIN. Do you think if I lived in such a place as this and by this lake, I would write? I should overcome such a passion and devote my life to fishing.

MASHA. Twenty-eight!

TRIGORIN. To catch a perch or a bass— that's something like happiness!

DORN. Well, I believe in Constantine Gavrilovitch. He has something! He has something! He thinks in images, his stories are bright and full of color, I always feel them strongly. It's only a pity that he's got no definite purpose. He creates impressions, never more than that, but on mere impressions you don't go far. Irina Nikolayevna, are you glad your son is a writer?

ARCADINA. Imagine, I have not read him yet. There's never time.

MASHA. Twenty-six!

[TREPLEFF *enters without saying anything, sits at his desk.*]

SHAMREYEFF. And, Boris Alexeyevitch, we've still got something of yours here.

TRIGORIN. What's that?

SHAMREYEFF. Somehow or other Constantine Gavrilovitch shot a sea gull, and you asked me to have it stuffed for you.

TRIGORIN. I don't remember. [*Reflecting.*] I don't remember.

MASHA. Sixty-six! One!

TREPLEFF. [*Throwing open the window, stands listening.*] How dark! I don't know why I feel so uneasy.

ARCADINA. Kostya, shut the window, there's a draught. [TREPLEFF *shuts window.*]

MASHA. Ninety-eight.

TRIGORIN. I've made a game.

ARCADINA. [*Gaily.*] Bravo! Bravo!

SHAMREYEFF. Bravo!

ARCADINA. This man's lucky in everything, always. [*Rises.*] And now let's go have a bite of something. Our celebrated author didn't have any dinner today. After supper we'll go on. Kostya, leave your manuscript, come have something to eat.

TREPLEFF. I don't want to, mother, I've had enough.

ARCADINA. As you please. [*Wakes* SORIN.] Petrusha, supper! [*Takes* SHAMREYEFF'S *arm.*] I'll tell you how they received me in Kharkoff.

[PAULINE *blows out candles on table; she and* DORN *wheel* SORIN'S *chair out of the room. All but* TREPLEFF *go out. He gets ready to write. Runs his eye over what's already written.*]

TREPLEFF. I've talked so much about new forms, but now I feel that little by little I am slipping into mere routine myself. [*Reads.*] "The placards on the wall proclaimed"—"pale face in a frame of dark hair"—frame—that's flat. [*Scratches out*

what he's written.] I'll begin again where the hero is awakened by the rain, and throw out all the rest. This description of a moonlight night is too long and too precious. Trigorin has worked out his own method, it's easy for him. With him a broken bottle-neck lying on the dam glitters in the moonlight and the mill wheel casts a black shadow—and there before you is the moonlit night; but with me it's the shimmering light, and the silent twinkling of the stars, and the far-off sound of a piano dying away in the still, sweet-scented air. It's painful. [*A pause.*] Yes, I'm coming more and more to the conclusion that it's a matter not of old forms and not of new forms, but that a man writes, not thinking at all of what form to choose, writes because it comes pouring out from his soul. [*A tap at the window nearest the desk.*] What's that? [*Looks out.*] I don't see anything. [*Opens the door and peers into the garden.*] Someone ran down the steps. [*Calls.*] Who's there? [*Goes out. The sound of his steps along the veranda. A moment later returns with* NINA. Nina! Nina! [*She lays her head on his breast, with restrained sobbing.*]

TREPLEFF. [*Moved.*] Nina! Nina! It's you—you. I had a presentiment, all day my soul was tormented. [*Takes off her hat and cape.*] Oh, my sweet, my darling, she has come! Let's not cry, let's not.

NINA. There's someone here.

TREPLEFF. No one.

NINA. Lock the doors. Someone might come in.

TREPLEFF. Nobody's coming in.

NINA. I know Irina Nikolayevna is here. Lock the doors.

TREPLEFF. [*Locks door on right. Goes to door on left.*] This one doesn't lock. I'll put a chair against it. [*Puts chair against door.*] Don't be afraid, nobody's coming in.

NINA. [*As if studying his face.*] Let me look at you. [*Glancing around her.*] It's warm, cozy— This used to be the drawing-room. Am I very much changed?

TREPLEFF. Yes . . . you are thinner

and your eyes are bigger. Nina, how strange it is I'm seeing you. Why wouldn't you let me come to see you? Why didn't you come sooner? I know you've been here now for nearly a week. I have been every day there where you were, I stood under your window like a beggar.

NINA. I was afraid you might hate me. I dream every night that you look at me and don't recognize me. If you only knew! Ever since I came I've been here walking about—by the lake. I've been near your house often, and couldn't make up my mind to come in. Let's sit down. [*They sit.*] Let's sit down and let's talk, talk. It's pleasant here, warm, cozy— You hear—the wind? There's a place in Turgenev: "Happy is he who on such a night is under his own roof, who has a warm corner." I—a sea gull—no, that's not it. [*Rubs her forehead.*] What was I saying? Yes—Turgenev. "And may the Lord help all homeless wanderers." It's nothing. [*Sobs.*]

TREPLEFF. Nina, again—Nina!

NINA. It's nothing. It will make me feel better. I've not cried for two years. Last night I came to the garden to see whether our theatre was still there, and it's there still. I cried for the first time in two years, and my heart grew lighter and my soul was clearer. Look, I'm not crying now. [*Takes his hand.*] You are an author, I—an actress. We have both been drawn into the whirlpool. I used to be as happy as a child. I used to wake up in the morning singing. I loved you and dreamed of being famous, and now? Tomorrow early I must go to Yelets in the third class—with peasants, and at Yelets the cultured merchants will plague me with attentions. Life's brutal!

TREPLEFF. Why Yelets?

NINA. I've taken an engagement there for the winter. It's time I was going.

TREPLEFF. Nina, I cursed you and hated you. I tore up all your letters, tore up your photograph, and yet I knew every minute that my heart was bound to yours forever. It's not in my power to stop loving you, Nina. Ever since I lost you and began to get my work published, my life has been unbearable—I am miserable— All of a sudden my youth was snatched from me, and now I feel as if I'd been living in the world for ninety years. I call out to you, I kiss the ground you walk on, I see your face wherever I look, the tender smile that shone on me those best years of my life.

NINA. [*In despair.*] Why does he talk like that? Why does he talk like that?

TREPLEFF. I'm alone, not warmed by anybody's affection. I'm all chilled—it's cold like living in a cave. And no matter what I write it's dry, gloomy and harsh. Stay here, Nina, if you only would! and if you won't, then take me with you.

[NINA *quickly puts on her hat and cape.*]

TREPLEFF. Nina, why? For God's sake, Nina! [*He is looking at her as she puts her things on. A pause.*]

NINA. My horses are just out there. Don't see me off. I'll manage by myself. [*Sobbing.*] Give me some water. [*He gives her a glass of water.*]

TREPLEFF. Where are you going now?

NINA. To town. [*A pause.*] Is Irina Nikolayevna here?

TREPLEFF. Yes, Thursday my uncle was not well, we telegraphed her to come.

NINA. Why do you say you kiss the ground I walk on? I ought to be killed. [*Bends over desk.*] I'm so tired. If I could rest—rest. I'm a sea gull. No, that's not it. I'm an actress. Well, no matter— [*Hears* ARCADINA *and* TRIGORIN *laughing in the dining-room. She listens, runs to the door on the left and peeps through the keyhole.*] And he's here too. [*Goes to* TREPLEFF.] Well, no matter. He didn't believe in the theatre, all my dreams he'd laugh at, and little by little I quit believing in it myself, and lost heart. And there was the strain of love, jealousy, constant anxiety about my little baby. I got to be small and trashy, and played without thinking. I didn't know what to do with my hands, couldn't stand properly on the stage, couldn't control my voice. You can't imagine the feeling when you are acting and know it's dull. I'm a sea gull. No, that's not it. Do you remember, you shot a sea gull? A man comes by chance, sees it, and out of nothing else to do, destroys it. That's not it— [*Puts her hand to her forehead.*] What was I—? I was talking about the stage. Now I'm not like that. I'm a real actress, I act with delight, with rapture, I'm drunk when I'm on the stage, and feel that I am beautiful. And now, ever since I've been here, I've kept walking about, kept walking and thinking, thinking and believing my soul grows stronger every day. Now I know, I understand, Kostya, that in our work—acting or writing—what matters is not fame, not glory, not what I used to dream about, it's how to endure, to bear my cross, and have faith. I have faith and it all doesn't hurt me so much, and when I think of my calling I'm not afraid of life.

TREPLEFF. [*Sadly.*] You've found your way, you know where you are going, but I still move in a chaos of images and dreams, not knowing why or who it's for. I have no faith, and I don't know where my calling lies.

NINA. [*Listening.*] Ssh — I'm going. Goodbye. When I'm a great actress, come and look at me. You promise? But now [*Takes his hand.*]—It's late. I can hardly stand on my feet, I feel faint. I'd like something to eat.

TREPLEFF. Stay, I'll bring you some supper here.

NINA. No, no—I can manage by myself. The horses are just out there. So, she brought him along with her? But that's all one. When you see Trigorin—don't ever tell him anything. I love him. I love him even more than before. "An idea for a short story." I love, I love passionately, I love to desperation. How nice it used to be, Kostya! You remember? How gay and warm and pure our life was; what things we felt, tender, delicate like flowers. Do you remember? "Men and beasts, lions, eagles and partridges, antlered deer, mute fishes dwelling in the water, star-fish and small creatures invisible to the eye—these and all life have run their sad course and are no more. Thousands of creatures have come and gone since there was life on the earth. Vainly now the pallid moon doth light her lamp. In the meadows the cranes wake and cry no longer; and the beetles' hum is silent in the linden groves." [*Impulsively embraces* TREPLEFF, *and runs out by the terrace door.*]

TREPLEFF. [*A pause.*] Too bad if any one meets her in the garden and tells mother. That might upset mother.

[*He stands for two minutes tearing up all his manuscripts and throwing them under the desk, then unlocks door on right, and goes out.*]

DORN. [*Trying to open the door on the left.*] That's funny. This door seems to be locked. [*Enters and puts chair back in its place.*] A regular hurdle race—

[*Enter* MADAME ARCADINA *and* PAULINE, *behind them* YAKOV *with a tray and bottles;* MASHA, *then* SHAMREYEFF *and* TRIGORIN.]

ARCADINA. Put the claret and the beer for Boris Alexandreyevitch here on the table. We'll play and drink. Let's sit down, friends.

PAULINE. [*To* YAKOV.] Bring the tea now, too. [*Lights the candles and sits down.*]

SHAMREYEFF. [*Leading* TRIGORIN *to the cupboard.*] Here's the thing I was telling you about just now. By your order.

TRIGORIN. [*Looking at the sea gull.*] I don't remember. [*Reflecting.*] I don't remember.

[*Sound of a shot offstage right; everybody jumps.*]

ARCADINA. [*Alarmed.*] What's that?

DORN. Nothing. It must be—in my medicine case—something blew up. Don't you worry. [*He goes out right, in a moment returns.*] So it was. A bottle of ether blew up. [*Sings.*] Again I stand before thee.

ARCADINA. [*Sitting down at the table.*] Phew, I was frightened! It reminded me of how— [*Puts her hands over her face.*] Everything's black before my eyes.

DORN. [*Turning through the magazine, to* TRIGORIN.] About two months ago in this magazine there was an article—a letter from America—and I wanted to ask you among other things— [*Puts his arm around* TRIGORIN'S *waist and leads him toward the front of the stage.*] since I'm very much interested in this question. [*Dropping his voice.*] Get Irina Nikolayevna somewhere away from here. The fact is Constantine Gavrilovitch has shot himself.

[CURTAIN.]

Folk Drama

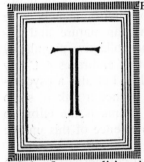

THEATRICAL REALISM is a profession of faith in the dramatic value of the facts of life. If this faith is vain, the descriptive methods of realistic drama possess little merit apart from novelty. On the other hand, if it is to carry much conviction, the drama which it produces is obliged to satisfy at least two conditions: the facts presented must warrant the attention devoted to them, and the representation of common reality must amount to more than a laboring of the obvious. The effect of the first condition is to make the value of realistic drama contingent ultimately on the value of its subject matter. For this reason most modern types of drama reflect the adventures of a technique in search of a subject. The second condition implies an approach to common reality which reveals a fresh meaning in a familiar experience. In practice such a reappraisal amounts to an attempt to view the customary in an unaccustomed perspective, to probe the essential nature of an experience, to isolate the qualities which give it a special connotation, and by a process of microscopic analysis to lay bare the unique and perhaps unsuspected truth beneath a commonplace appearance. Its effect is a pronounced tendency on the part of realism to stress the importance of the particular instance, and especially the distinctive features which define this importance. The operation of these two factors is apparent in such characteristic products of the modern theater as the problem play and the realistic drama of Chekhov. A further manifestation is the modern interest in folk drama.

Modern folk drama is a sophisticated version of a primitive folk expression, which, although a far cry from its naïve prototype, interestingly enough retains much of the original motive and content. In its modern incarnation it is an outgrowth of the scientific search for significant reality. As such, its basic motive is that illumination of the particular so dear to realism, and its content is that universal obsession of the modern mind, the importance of environment. Its point of departure is a recognition of the fact that many peculiarities of individual personality and behavior are attributable to environmental influence. More significantly it recognizes that, as various individuals fall subject to a common environment, this influence also produces collective idiosyncrasies; and, as various environments differ among themselves, it is responsible finally for important group differences. The effect is evident in drama itself; for in the general uniformity imposed by realism on the modern drama it is precisely the differences in material and cultural environment which, more than anything else, serve to distinguish the contribution of one country or region from that of another. What is important about these environmental differences is the disparity which they introduce in human nature—a disparity which obviously increases in interest and importance as the singularities of environment become more pronounced. This relationship between human nature and environment is reflected most conspicuously in the collective singularity of the folk, or ethnic group. The concept of the folk embraces not only a special environment and a distinctive mode of life, but also a psychology and temperament which are equally unique. Hence a folk is, so to speak, an animate environment in action. Folk drama is the effort to recreate on the stage both the substance and the essence of this unique entity.

In many respects folk drama is the theatrical counterpart of genre painting. Representational and realistic, it endeavors to portray the true likeness of an ethnic type and mode of life in such a manner that one may perceive their essential spirit. Since this endeavor may be addressed either to the folk portrayed or to the interested alien, its attitude may range from pointing with pride to viewing with alarm or, as is more often the case, with simple curiosity. Frequently it reflects a strong local self-consciousness; at other times, what amounts to a tourist's fascination with the queer customs of the quaint natives. In either case it flourishes best in connection with a cohesive group whose folkways are sufficiently pronounced and distinctive to create a cultural island in the midst of humanity. In the modern theater the most conspicuous and impressive product of the folk impulse is the Irish drama which, toward the turn of the present century, came into being on a wave of resurgent Irish nationalism. Most of this drama reflects a deliberate effort to create a representative Irish theater and to exploit an indigenous Irish culture. For this reason it is primarily designed for home consumption. At the same time it has endeavored to hold a critical mirror up to typical Irish life and character. It is the high degree of vitality and art attained in performing this function which has attracted the widest attention abroad.

Although during the past half-century Irish drama has put forth a rich variety of plays and a goodly number of able playwrights, perhaps its greatest glory still remains that brief but brilliant genius of its youth, John Millington Synge (1871–1909). As in the case of Chekhov and the Moscow Art Theatre, the fortunes of Synge are inseparably linked with the famous Abbey Theatre, which was established in Dublin in 1904. As the Moscow Art Theatre was dedicated to realism, the Abbey was dedicated to an exploration of Ireland's cultural heritage and national character. Under the influence of its devoted founders Synge was inspired to live among the Irish peasantry and to study intimately its folk habits and disposition. The half-dozen plays of his brief career are a vivid expression of this awakened folk-consciousness. Not only do they capture the surface appearance and prevailing manner of Irish life, but in their earthy themes, in their imaginative beauty, and particularly in their lilting and pungent idiom they also distill the inner essence of the Irish spirit. Among them are two authentic masterpieces: the superb genre study *Riders to the Sea,* which is one of the most moving of modern tragedies, and the robust *Playboy of the Western World,* which is a landmark of modern comedy. The tempestuous career of this latter play, the disturbances which greeted its first Dublin performance on January 26, 1907, and the riots which pursued it elsewhere bear redoubtable testimony to the astuteness with which Synge sounded the Irish temperament.

The Playboy of the Western World is a folk comedy of peasant life in the western counties of Ireland. Although its comedy is lively enough to entertain in its own right without need of further connotation, as folk drama its success naturally depends on the skill and fidelity with which it reflects the authentic conditions of this life. Initially this is a matter of selecting and introducing a body of circumstantial details which are both revelatory and scrupulously true to fact. In this matter Synge exercised conscientious care. He drew his materials from personal observation, and based the central situation of the play on an actual occurrence. Regarding their authenticity he notes: "Anyone who has lived in real intimacy with the Irish peasantry will know that the wildest sayings and ideas in this play are tame indeed, compared with the fancies one may hear in any little hillside cabin in Geesala, or Carraroe, or Dingle Bay." As for the dialogue, he adds: "I have used one or two words only that I have not heard among the country people of Ireland, or spoken in my own nursery before I could read the newspapers." The final test of this authenticity is, of course, the extent to which such realistic details coincide with the actual experience of those familiar with the circumstances. For the sake of general dramatic plausibility, however, the materials are also selected with an eye to the common assumptions of a less expert audience. For example, the play deliberately exploits such popular impressions of the Irish scene as the prevailing poverty, the antipathy to English law, or the boisterous spirits and romantic propensities of the people. Furthermore, since the object of the play is a portrayal of collective rather than individual truth, these materials are chosen primarily on the basis of their broadly representative nature. Thus the behavior of Pegeen is an expression not so much of unique personality as of qualities common to all the women in the play; and, for all their superficial differences, both Christy and Shawn exemplify the same incongruous mingling of complacency, propriety, and veneration of the violent which is endemic in the whole community. Finally, such materials are selected as coalesce naturally to account for the life and temperament depicted. Folk drama is both an exhibition and an explanation; but it is an explanation which is valid only for a special combination of circumstances. Therefore, whatever may be their incidental implications for humanity in general, the materials of *The Playboy* are selected for the express purpose of making clear the inherent connection between Christy's fantastic adventure and a specific folk situation.

The general method of dealing with these materials is an arrangement of typical instances and adroit suggestions in such a manner that they create a cumulative and self-explanatory pattern of life. The setting in the isolated public house, with its redolence of illicit whiskey, shabby vagrancy, simmering gossip, and noisy brawls, serves to establish the dominant atmosphere. Imitation of the native idiom, imagery, and speech rhythms transforms the dialogue into an automatic articulation of the folk spirit and point of view which mold the turn of phrase. Furthermore, its systematic introduction of local allusions brings into a sort of hovering impingement a whole implied setting of wild uplands, peat bogs, potato patches, and lonely lanes among the furze, together with the off-stage peasants, peddlers, poachers, and peelers who inhabit them. Incidents and characters are employed with a comparable suggestiveness. For example, the wake which initiates proceedings emphasizes the curious mixture of grim reality and primitive revelry in the whole situation. The very betrothal of a girl like Pegeen to the pusillanimous Shawn testifies to a scarcity of eligible males which goes far to explain Christy's meteoric career. Similarly the shifty conniving of the Widow Quin, the paltry bribes of the relatively affluent Shawn, and the irresistible appeal of Christy as a combination pot-boy and husband reiterate the meager meanness of a life constricted by penury, hardship, and isolation. By a careful juxtaposition of such exemplary evidence the play builds up its impression of a definite environment and folk temper. At the same time, by means of this evidence it endeavors to make comprehensible the grotesque union of romantic yearning and crude animal spirits which attributes glamor to the winner of a donkey race and epic splendor to the cleaving of an old man's skull.

The final aim of this endeavor, and perhaps the final justification of folk drama as a whole, is an interpretation which goes beyond the mere display of folk vagaries. Beneath its surface realism and ribaldry *The Playboy of the Western World* embodies a serious critical and at times satirical purpose; it has something of profound importance to suggest about Irish life and temperament. Indeed, its very choice of subject matter and the attitude which it adopts are part of what it is trying to say. It is no accident that the central situation with which the play deals is ironically grotesque. Equally relevant is the fact that this situation, for all its aspects of pathos, its streaks of ugliness, and its touches of lyrical beauty, is viewed as essentially comic. To be sure, the inflation of a voluble loafer, prude, and coward into a complacent hero of romantic lawlessness is richly farcical in any case. This is precisely the point that Synge wishes to make. For it is not a whit more farcical than the condition responsible for it—the preposterous welter of fawning and bluster, of propriety and truculence, of mercurial spirits, extravagant sentiment, and petty egotism which epitomizes the whole folk temperament. Its absurd corollary is the consternation and resentment provoked by Old Mahon's uncoöperative reluctance to remain dead and the consequent collapse of Christy's synthetic glamor. At the core of the fiasco is the congenital propensity to evade unwelcome fact in flamboyant and sentimental fiction. In singling out this source of temperamental ineffectuality, Synge's intimation is clear: if conditions are lamentable or ludicrous, not only does Ireland make the Irish, but the converse is also true. Hence the play, despite its strictures, remains quite properly a comedy. If it contains adversities and absurdities, it also holds the reassurance of a potentially satisfactory ending. Even for the susceptible peasants fraud and crime lose their romantic aura when stripped to their naked reality, and in the general disillusionment Christy is rudely awakened to the treachery of vagrant impulses. This awakening to truth is at once the theme, the hope, and the dramatic function of the play. If the village as a whole learns only to rue its volatile emotions, Pegeen in her belated lament recognizes the loss of a promising reality for a sentimental delusion. More fortunate, Christy arises from the shards of his shattered romancing to a new appreciation of his real potentialities. In the headiness of this discovery he turns his back on the past and goes swaggering into the future as lusty, as assured, and as irrepressible as, perhaps, an awakened Ireland herself.

Folk drama, as noted earlier, flourishes most naturally in association with ethnic groups which exhibit pronounced and distinctive folkways. In modern drama two of the most productive associations have been with the Irish and the American Negro. The first may be further illustrated by Synge's *Riders to the Sea,* Sean O'Casey's *Juno and the Paycock,* and Lennox Robinson's *The White Headed Boy.* The second is responsible for such folk plays as *Porgy* by Dorothy and DuBose Hayward, *In Abraham's Bosom* by Paul Green, and the impressive modern miracle play, *The Green Pastures* by Marc Connelly. A Welsh example is *The Corn is Green* by Emlyn Williams. Interesting variants of the folk impulse also appear in Hatcher Hughes's *Hell Bent fer Heaven,* Thornton Wilder's *Our Town,* Eugene O'Neill's *Ah, Wilderness!,* and the notorious *Tobacco Road,* adapted by Jack Kirkland from Erskine Caldwell's novel.

THE PLAYBOY
OF THE
WESTERN WORLD

A PLAY IN THREE ACTS

by

JOHN MILLINGTON SYNGE

Characters in the Play

CHRISTOPHER MAHON
OLD MAHON, *his father, a squatter*
MICHAEL JAMES FLAHERTY, *called*
MICHAEL JAMES, *a publican* [1]
MARGARET FLAHERTY, *called* PE-
GEEN MIKE, *his daughter*
WIDOW QUIN, *a woman of about
thirty*

SHAWN KEOGH, *her cousin, a young
farmer*
PHILLY CULLEN *and* JIMMY FAR-
RELL, *small farmers*
SARA TANSEY, SUSAN BRADY, HONOR
BLAKE *and* NELLY, *village girls*
A BELLMAN [2]
SOME PEASANTS

*The action takes place near a village, on a wild coast of Mayo.
The first Act passes on an evening of autumn, the other two
Acts on the following day.*

Copyright, 1935, by the Modern Library. Reprinted by permission of Random House, Inc.
[1] Proprietor of a public house, or tavern.
[2] Town crier.

SCENE. *Country public house or she-been, very rough and untidy. There is a sort of counter on the right with shelves, holding many bottles and jugs, just seen above it. Empty barrels stand near the counter. At back, a little to left of counter, there is a door into the open air, then, more to the left, there is a settle with shelves above it, with more jugs, and a table beneath a window. At the left there is a large open fire-place, with turf fire, and a small door into inner room. Pegeen, a wild-looking but fine girl of about twenty, is writing at table. She is dressed in the usual peasant dress.*

PEGEEN. [*Slowly as she writes.*] Six yards of stuff for to make a yellow gown. A pair of lace boots with lengthy heels on them and brassy eyes. A hat is suited for a wedding-day. A fine tooth comb. To be sent with three barrels of porter in Jimmy Farrell's creel cart on the evening of the coming Fair to Mister Michael James Flaherty. With the best compliments of this season. Margaret Flaherty.

[SHAWN KEOGH, *a fat and fair young man, comes in as she signs, looks round awkwardly, when he sees she is alone.*]

SHAWN. Where's himself?

PEGEEN. [*Without looking at him.*] He's coming. [*She directs the letter.*] To Master Sheamus Mulroy, Wine and Spirit Dealer, Castlebar.

SHAWN. [*Uneasily.*] I didn't see him on the road.

PEGEEN. How would you see him [*Licks stamp and puts it on letter.*] and it dark night this half hour gone by?

SHAWN. [*Turning towards the door again.*] I stood a while outside wondering would I have a right to pass on or to walk in and see you, Pegeen Mike, [*Comes to fire.*] and I could hear the cows breathing, and sighing in the stillness of the air, and not a step moving any place from this gate to the bridge.

PEGEEN. [*Putting letter in envelope.*] It's above at the cross-roads he is, meeting Philly Cullen; and a couple more are going along with him to Kate Cassidy's wake.

SHAWN. [*Looking at her blankly.*] And he's going that length in the dark night?

PEGEEN. [*Impatiently.*] He is surely, and leaving me lonesome on the scruff of the hill. [*She gets up and puts envelope on dresser, then winds clock.*] Isn't it long the nights are now, Shawn Keogh, to be leaving a poor girl with her own self counting the hours to the dawn of day?

SHAWN. [*With awkward humour.*] If it is, when we're wedded in a short while you'll have no call to complain, for I've little will to be walking off to wakes or weddings in the darkness of the night.

PEGEEN. [*With rather scornful good humour.*] You're making mighty certain, Shaneen, that I'll wed you now.

SHAWN. Aren't we after making a good bargain, the way we're only waiting these days on Father Reilly's dispensation from the bishops, or the Court of Rome?

PEGEEN. [*Looking at him teasingly, washing up at dresser.*] It's a wonder, Shaneen, the Holy Father'd be taking notice of the likes of you; for if I was him I wouldn't bother with this place where you'll meet none but Red Linahan, has a squint in his eye, and Patcheen is lame in his heel, or the mad Mulrannies were driven from California and they lost in their wits. We're a queer lot these times to go troubling the Holy Father on his sacred seat.

SHAWN. [*Scandalized.*] If we are, we're as good this place as another, maybe, and as good these times as we were for ever.

PEGEEN. [*With scorn.*] As good, is it? Where now will you meet the like of Daneen Sullivan knocked the eye from a peeler,[3] or Marcus Quin, God rest him, got six months for maiming ewes, and he a great warrant to tell stories of holy Ireland till he'd have the old women shedding down tears about their feet. Where will you find the like of them, I'm saying?

SHAWN. [*Timidly.*] If you don't, it's a

---

[3] A police constable, representing, of course, the English law.

good job, maybe; for [*With peculiar emphasis on the words.*] Father Reilly has small conceit to have that kind walking around and talking to the girls.

PEGEEN. [*Impatiently, throwing water from basin out of the door.*] Stop tormenting me with Father Reilly [*Imitating his voice.*] when I'm asking only what way I'll pass these twelve hours of dark, and not take my death with the fear. [*Looking out of door.*]

SHAWN. [*Timidly.*] Would I fetch you the Widow Quin, maybe?

PEGEEN. Is it the like of that murderer? You'll not, surely.

SHAWN. [*Going to her, soothingly.*] Then I'm thinking himself will stop along with you when he sees you taking on, for it'll be a long night-time with great darkness, and I'm after feeling a kind of fellow above in the furzy ditch, groaning wicked like a maddening dog, the way it's good cause you have, maybe, to be fearing now.

PEGEEN. [*Turning on him sharply.*] What's that? Is it a man you seen?

SHAWN. [*Retreating.*] I couldn't see him at all; but I heard him groaning out, and breaking his heart. It should have been a young man from his words speaking.

PEGEEN. [*Going after him.*] And you never went near to see was he hurted or what ailed him at all?

SHAWN. I did not, Pegeen Mike. It was a dark, lonesome place to be hearing the like of him.

PEGEEN. Well, you're a daring fellow, and if they find his corpse stretched above in the dews of dawn, what'll you say then to the peelers, or the Justice of the Peace?

SHAWN. [*Thunderstruck.*] I wasn't thinking of that. For the love of God, Pegeen Mike, don't let on I was speaking of him. Don't tell your father and the men is coming above; for if they heard that story, they'd have great blabbing this night at the wake.

PEGEEN. I'll maybe tell them, and I'll maybe not.

SHAWN. They are coming at the door. Will you whisht,[4] I'm saying?

PEGEEN. Whisht yourself.

[*She goes behind counter.* MICHAEL JAMES, *fat jovial publican, comes in followed by* PHILLY CULLEN, *who is thin and mistrusting, and* JIMMY FARRELL, *who is fat and amorous, about forty-five.*]

MEN. [*Together.*] God bless you. The blessing of God on this place.

PEGEEN. God bless you kindly.

MICHAEL. [*To men who go to the counter.*] Sit down now, and take your rest. [*Crosses to* SHAWN *at the fire.*] And how is it you are, Shawn Keogh? Are you coming over the sands to Kate Cassidy's wake?

SHAWN. I am not, Michael James. I'm going home the short cut to my bed.

PEGEEN. [*Speaking across the counter.*] He's right too, and have you no shame, Michael James, to be quitting off for the whole night, and leaving myself lonesome in the shop?

MICHAEL. [*Good-humouredly.*] Isn't it the same whether I go for the whole night or a part only? and I'm thinking it's a queer daughter you are if you'd have me crossing backward through the Stooks [5] of the Dead Women, with a drop taken.

PEGEEN. If I am a queer daughter, it's a queer father'd be leaving me lonesome these twelve hours of dark, and I piling the turf with the dogs barking, and the calves mooing, and my own teeth rattling with the fear.

JIMMY. [*Flatteringly.*] What is there to hurt you, and you a fine, hardy girl would knock the head off any two men in the place?

PEGEEN. [*Working herself up.*] Isn't there the harvest boys with their tongues red for drink, and the ten tinkers is camped in the east glen, and the thousand militia— bad cess [6] to them!—walking idle through the land. There's lots surely to hurt me, and I won't stop alone in it, let himself do what he will.

4 Keep silent.
5 Sheaves.

6 Luck.

MICHAEL. If you're that afeard, let Shawn Keogh stop along with you. It's the will of God, I'm thinking, himself should be seeing to you now.

[*They all turn on* SHAWN.]

SHAWN. [*In horrified confusion.*] I would and welcome, Michael James, but I'm afeared of Father Reilly; and what at all would the Holy Father and the Cardinals of Rome be saying if they heard I did the like of that?

MICHAEL. [*With contempt.*] God help you! Can't you sit in by the hearth with the light lit and herself beyond in the room? You'll do that surely, for I've heard tell there's a queer fellow above, going mad or getting his death, maybe, in the gripe [7] of the ditch, so she'd be safer this night with a person here.

SHAWN. [*With plaintive despair.*] I'm afeard of Father Reilly, I'm saying. Let you not be tempting me, and we near married itself.

PHILLY. [*With cold contempt.*] Lock him in the west room. He'll stay then and have no sin to be telling to the priest.

MICHAEL. [*To* SHAWN, *getting between him and the door.*] Go up now.

SHAWN. [*At the top of his voice.*] Don't stop me, Michael James. Let me out of the door, I'm saying, for the love of the Almighty God. Let me out. [*Trying to dodge past him.*] Let me out of it, and may God grant you His indulgence in the hour of need.

MICHAEL. [*Loudly.*] Stop your noising, and sit down by the hearth.

[*Gives him a push and goes to counter laughing.*]

SHAWN. [*Turning back, wringing his hands.*] Oh, Father Reilly and the saints of God, where will I hide myself to-day? Oh, St. Joseph and St. Patrick and St. Brigid, and St. James, have mercy on me now!

[SHAWN *turns round, sees door clear, and makes a rush for it.*]

MICHAEL. [*Catching him by the coat-tail.*] You'd be going, is it?

SHAWN. [*Screaming.*] Leave me go,

[7] Trough.

Michael James, leave me go, you old Pagan, leave me go, or I'll get the curse of the priests on you, and of the scarlet-coated bishops of the courts of Rome.

[*With a sudden movement he pulls himself out of his coat, and disappears out of the door, leaving his coat in* MICHAEL'S *hands.*]

MICHAEL. [*Turning round, and holding up coat.*] Well, there's the coat of a Christian man. Oh, there's sainted glory this day in the lonesome west; and by the will of God I've got you a decent man, Pegeen, you'll have no call to be spying after if you've a score of young girls, maybe, weeding in your fields.

PEGEEN. [*Taking up the defence of her property.*] What right have you to be making game of a poor fellow for minding the priest, when it's your own the fault is, not paying a penny pot-boy to stand along with me and give me courage in the doing of my work?

[*She snaps the coat away from him, and goes behind counter with it.*]

MICHAEL. [*Taken aback.*] Where would I get a pot-boy? Would you have me send the bellman screaming in the streets of Castlebar?

SHAWN. [*Opening the door a chink and putting in his head, in a small voice.*] Michael James!

MICHAEL. [*Imitating him.*] What ails you?

SHAWN. The queer dying fellow's beyond looking over the ditch. He's come up, I'm thinking, stealing your hens. [*Looks over his shoulder.*] God help me, he's following me now [*He runs into room.*], and if he's heard what I said, he'll be having my life, and I going home lonesome in the darkness of the night.

[*For a perceptible moment they watch the door with curiosity. Some one coughs outside. Then* CHRISTY MAHON, *a slight young man, comes in very tired and frightened and dirty.*]

CHRISTY. [*In a small voice.*] God save all here!

MEN. God save you kindly.

CHRISTY. [*Going to the counter.*] I'd trouble you for a glass of porter, woman of the house. [*He puts down coin.*]

PEGEEN. [*Serving him.*] You're one of the tinkers, young fellow, is beyond camped in the glen?

CHRISTY. I am not; but I'm destroyed walking.

MICHAEL. [*Patronizingly.*] Let you come up then to the fire. You're looking famished with the cold.

CHRISTY. God reward you. [*He takes up his glass and goes a little way across to the left, then stops and looks about him.*] Is it often the police do be coming into this place, master of the house?

MICHAEL. If you'd come in better hours, you'd have seen "Licensed for the sale of Beer and Spirits, to be consumed on the premises," written in white letters above the door, and what would the polis want spying on me, and not a decent house within four miles, the way every living Christian is a bona fide, saving one widow alone?

CHRISTY. [*With relief.*] It's a safe house, so.

[*He goes over to the fire, sighing and moaning. Then he sits down, putting his glass beside him and begins gnawing a turnip, too miserable to feel the others staring at him with curiosity.*]

MICHAEL. [*Going after him.*] Is it yourself is fearing the polis? You're wanting,[8] maybe?

CHRISTY. There's many wanting.

MICHAEL. Many surely with the broken harvest and the ended wars. [*He picks up some stockings, etc., that are near the fire, and carries them away furtively.*] It should be larceny, I'm thinking.

CHRISTY. [*Dolefully.*] I had it in my mind it was a different word and a bigger.

PEGEEN. There's a queer lad. Were you never slapped in school, young fellow, that you don't know the name of your deed?

CHRISTY. [*Bashfully.*] I'm slow at learning, a middling scholar only.

MICHAEL. If you're a dunce itself, you'd have a right to know that larceny's robbing and stealing. Is it for the like of that you're wanting?

CHRISTY. [*With a flash of family pride.*] And I the son of a strong farmer, [*With a sudden qualm.*] God rest his soul, could have bought up the whole of your old house awhile since, from the butt of his tailpocket, and not have missed the weight of it gone.

MICHAEL. [*Impressed.*] If it's not stealing, it's maybe something big.

CHRISTY. [*Flattered.*] Aye; it's maybe something big.

JIMMY. He's a wicked-looking young fellow. Maybe he followed after a young woman on a lonesome night.

CHRISTY. [*Shocked.*] Oh, the saints forbid, mister; I was all times a decent lad.

PHILLY. [*Turning on JIMMY.*] You're a silly man, Jimmy Farrell. He said his father was a farmer a while since, and there's himself now in a poor state. Maybe the land was grabbed from him, and he did what any decent man would do.

MICHAEL. [*To CHRISTY, mysteriously.*] Was it bailiffs?[9]

CHRISTY. The divil a one.

MICHAEL. Agents?

CHRISTY. The divil a one.

MICHAEL. Landlords?

CHRISTY. [*Peevishly.*] Ah, not at all, I'm saying. You'd see the like of them stories on any little paper of a Munster town. But I'm not calling to mind any person, gentle, simple, judge or jury, did the like of me.

[*They all draw nearer with delighted curiosity.*]

PHILLY. Well, that lad's a puzzle-the-world.

JIMMY. He'd beat Dan Davies' circus, or the holy missioners[10] making sermons on the villainy of man. Try him again, Philly.

PHILLY. Did you strike golden guineas

---

8 *I.e.,* wanted by the police.
9 The references here are to the hereditary enemies of the Irish peasants, the agents of absentee landlords.
10 Priests on a preaching mission.

out of solder, young fellow, or shilling coins itself?

CHRISTY. I did not, mister, not sixpence nor a farthing coin.

JIMMY. Did you marry three wives maybe? I'm told there's a sprinkling have done that among the holy Luthers of the preaching north.

CHRISTY. [Shyly.] I never married with one, let alone with a couple or three.

PHILLY. Maybe he went fighting for the Boers,[11] the like of the man beyond, was judged to be hanged, quartered and drawn. Were you off east, young fellow, fighting bloody wars for Kruger and the freedom of the Boers?

CHRISTY. I never left my own parish till Tuesday was a week.

PEGEEN. [Coming from counter.] He's done nothing, so. [To CHRISTY.] If you didn't commit murder or a bad, nasty thing, or false coining, or robbery, or butchery, or the like of them, there isn't anything that would be worth your troubling for to run from now. You did nothing at all.

CHRISTY. [His feelings hurt.] That's an unkindly thing to be saying to a poor orphaned traveller, has a prison behind him, and hanging before, and hell's gap gaping below.

PEGEEN. [With a sign to the men to be quiet.] You're only saying it. You did nothing at all. A soft lad the like of you wouldn't slit the windpipe of a screeching sow.

CHRISTY. [Offended.] You're not speaking the truth.

PEGEEN. [In mock rage.] Not speaking the truth, is it? Would you have me knock the head off you with the butt of the broom?

CHRISTY. [Twisting round on her with a sharp cry of horror.] Don't strike me. I killed my poor father, Tuesday was a week, for doing the like of that.

PEGEEN. [With blank amazement.] Is it killed your father?

CHRISTY. [Subsiding.] With the help of God I did surely, and that the Holy Immaculate Mother may intercede for his soul.

PHILLY. [Retreating with JIMMY.] There's a daring fellow.

JIMMY. Oh, glory be to God!

MICHAEL. [With great respect.] That was a hanging crime, mister honey. You should have had good reason for doing the like of that.

CHRISTY. [In a very reasonable tone.] He was a dirty man, God forgive him, and he getting old and crusty, the way I couldn't put up with him at all.

PEGEEN. And you shot him dead?

CHRISTY. [Shaking his head.] I never used weapons. I've no license, and I'm a law-fearing man.

MICHAEL. It was with a hilted knife maybe? I'm told, in the big world it's bloody knives they use.

CHRISTY. [Loudly, scandalized.] Do you take me for a slaughter-boy?

PEGEEN. You never hanged him, the way Jimmy Farrell hanged his dog from the license, and had it screeching and wriggling three hours at the butt of a string, and himself swearing it was a dead dog, and the peelers swearing it had life?

CHRISTY. I did not then. I just riz the loy [12] and let fall the edge of it on the ridge of his skull, and he went down at my feet like an empty sack, and never let a grunt or groan from him at all.

MICHAEL. [Making a sign to PEGEEN to fill CHRISTY's glass.] And what way weren't you hanged, mister? Did you bury him then?

CHRISTY. [Considering.] Aye. I buried him then. Wasn't I digging spuds in the field?

MICHAEL. And the peelers never followed after you the eleven days that you're out?

CHRISTY. [Shaking his head.] Never a one of them, and I walking forward facing hog, dog, or divil on the highway of the road.

[11] Dutch colonists in South Africa, whose republic under Paul Kruger was conquered by Great Britain in the Boer War of 1899–1902.

[12] Raised up the spade.

PHILLY. [*Nodding wisely.*] It's only with a common week-day kind of a murderer them lads would be trusting their carcase, and that man should be a great terror when his temper's roused.

MICHAEL. He should then. [*To* CHRISTY.] And where was it, mister honey, that you did the deed?

CHRISTY. [*Looking at him with suspicion.*] Oh, a distant place, master of the house, a windy corner of high, distant hills.

PHILLY. [*Nodding with approval.*] He's a close man, and he's right, surely.

PEGEEN. That'd be a lad with the sense of Solomon to have for a pot-boy, Michael James, if it's the truth you're seeking one at all.

PHILLY. The peelers is fearing him, and if you'd that lad in the house there isn't one of them would come smelling around if the dogs itself were lapping poteen [13] from the dung-pit of the yard.

JIMMY. Bravery's a treasure in a lonesome place, and a lad would kill his father, I'm thinking, would face a foxy divil with a pitchpike [14] on the flags of hell.

PEGEEN. It's the truth they're saying, and if I'd that lad in the house, I wouldn't be fearing the loosèd kharki [15] cut-throats, or the walking dead.

CHRISTY. [*Swelling with surprise and triumph.*] Well, glory be to God!

MICHAEL. [*With deference.*] Would you think well to stop here and be pot-boy, mister honey, if we gave you good wages, and didn't destroy you with the weight of work?

SHAWN. [*Coming forward uneasily.*] That'd be a queer kind to bring into a decent quiet household with the like of Pegeen Mike.

PEGEEN. [*Very sharply.*] Will you whisht? Who's speaking to you?

SHAWN. [*Retreating.*] A bloody-handed murderer the like of . . .

PEGEEN. [*Snapping at him.*] Whisht I am saying; we'll take no fooling from your

like at all. [*To* CHRISTY *with a honeyed voice.*] And you, young fellow, you'd have a right to stop, I'm thinking, for we'd do our all and utmost to content your needs.

CHRISTY. [*Overcome with wonder.*] And I'd be safe in this place from the searching law?

MICHAEL. You would, surely. If they're not fearing you, itself, the peelers in this place is decent droughty [16] poor fellows, wouldn't touch a cur dog and not give warning in the dead of night.

PEGEEN. [*Very kindly and persuasively.*] Let you stop a short while anyhow. Aren't you destroyed walking with your feet in bleeding blisters, and your whole skin needing washing like a Wicklow sheep?

CHRISTY. [*Looking round with satisfaction.*] It's a nice room, and if it's not humbugging me you are, I'm thinking that I'll surely stay.

JIMMY. [*Jumps up.*] Now, by the grace of God, herself will be safe this night, with a man killed his father holding danger from the door, and let you come on, Michael James, or they'll have the best stuff drunk at the wake.

MICHAEL. [*Going to the door with the men.*] And begging your pardon, mister, what name will we call you, for we'd like to know?

CHRISTY. Christopher Mahon.

MICHAEL. Well, God bless you, Christy, and a good rest till we meet again when the sun'll be rising to the noon of day.

CHRISTY. God bless you all.

MEN. God bless you.

[*They go out except* SHAWN, *who lingers at door.*]

SHAWN. [*To* PEGEEN.] Are you wanting me to stop along with you and keep you from harm?

PEGEEN. [*Gruffly.*] Didn't you say you were fearing Father Reilly?

SHAWN. There'd be no harm staying now, I'm thinking, and himself in it too.

PEGEEN. You wouldn't stay when there

---

[13] Illicitly distilled whiskey.
[14] Pitchfork.

[15] Khaki, *i.e.,* soldiers.
[16] *I.e.,* thirsty.

was need for you, and let you step off nimble this time when there's none.

SHAWN. Didn't I say it was Father Reilly . . .

PEGEEN. Go on, then, to Father Reilly [In a jeering tone.], and let him put you in the holy brotherhoods, and leave that lad to me.

SHAWN. If I meet the Widow Quin . . .

PEGEEN. Go on, I'm saying, and don't be waking this place with your noise. [She hustles him out and bolts the door.] That lad would wear the spirits from the saints of peace. [Bustles about, then takes off her apron and pins it up in the window as a blind. CHRISTY watching her timidly. Then she comes to him and speaks with bland good-humour.] Let you stretch out now by the fire, young fellow. You should be destroyed travelling.

CHRISTY. [Shyly again, drawing off his boots.] I'm tired, surely, walking wild eleven days, and waking fearful in the night.

[He holds up one of his feet, feeling his blisters, and looking at them with compassion.]

PEGEEN. [Standing beside him, watching him with delight.] You should have had great people in your family, I'm thinking, with the little, small feet you have, and you with a kind of a quality name, the like of what you'd find on the great powers and potentates of France and Spain.

CHRISTY. [With pride.] We were great surely, with wide and windy acres of rich Munster land.

PEGEEN. Wasn't I telling you, and you a fine, handsome young fellow with a noble brow?

CHRISTY. [With a flash of delighted surprise.] Is it me?

PEGEEN. Aye. Did you never hear that from the young girls where you come from in the west or south?

CHRISTY. [With venom.] I did not then. Oh, they're bloody liars in the naked parish where I grew a man.

PEGEEN. If they are itself, you've heard it these days, I'm thinking, and you walking the world telling out your story to young girls or old.

CHRISTY. I've told my story no place till this night, Pegeen Mike, and it's foolish I was here, maybe, to be talking free, but you're decent people, I'm thinking, and yourself a kindly woman, the way I wasn't fearing you at all.

PEGEEN. [Filling a sack with straw.] You've said the like of that, maybe, in every cot and cabin where you've met a young girl on your way.

CHRISTY. [Going over to her, gradually raising his voice.] I've said it nowhere till this night, I'm telling you, for I've seen none the like of you the eleven long days I am walking the world, looking over a low ditch or a high ditch on my north or my south, into stony scattered fields, or scribes [17] of bog, where you'd see young, limber girls, and fine prancing women making laughter with the men.

PEGEEN. If you weren't destroyed travelling, you'd have as much talk and streeleen,[18] I'm thinking, as Owen Roe O'Sullivan or the poets of the Dingle Bay, and I've heard all times it's the poets are your like, fine fiery fellows with great rages when their temper's roused.

CHRISTY. [Drawing a little nearer to her.] You've a power of rings, God bless you, and would there be any offence if I was asking are you single now?

PEGEEN. What would I want wedding so young?

CHRISTY. [With relief.] We're alike, so.

PEGEEN. [She puts sack on settle and beats it up.] I never killed my father. I'd be afeard to do that, except I was the like of yourself with blind rages tearing me within, for I'm thinking you should have had great tussling when the end was come.

CHRISTY. [Expanding with delight at the first confidential talk he has ever had with a woman.] We had not then. It was a hard woman was come over the hill, and if he was always a crusty kind when he'd a hard woman setting him on, not the divil himself

[17] Patches.

[18] Palaver.

or his four fathers could put up with him at all.

PEGEEN. [*With curiosity.*] And isn't it a great wonder that one wasn't fearing you?

CHRISTY. [*Very confidentially.*] Up to the day I killed my father, there wasn't a person in Ireland knew the kind I was, and I there drinking, waking, eating, sleeping, a quiet, simple poor fellow with no man giving me heed.

PEGEEN. [*Getting a quilt out of the cupboard and putting it on the sack.*] It was the girls were giving you heed maybe, and I'm thinking it's most conceit [19] you'd have to be gaming with their like.

CHRISTY. [*Shaking his head, with simplicity.*] Not the girls itself, and I won't tell you a lie. There wasn't anyone heeding me in that place saving only the dumb beasts of the field.

[*He sits down at fire.*]

PEGEEN. [*With disappointment.*] And I thinking you should have been living the like of a king of Norway or the Eastern world.

[*She comes and sits beside him after placing bread and mug of milk on the table.*]

CHRISTY. [*Laughing piteously.*] The like of a king, is it? And I after toiling, moiling, digging, dodging from the dawn till dusk with never a sight of joy or sport saving only when I'd be abroad in the dark night poaching rabbits on hills, for I was a divil to poach, God forgive me, [*Very naïvely.*] and I near got six months for going with a dung fork and stabbing a fish.

PEGEEN. And it's that you'd call sport, is it, to be abroad in the darkness with yourself alone?

CHRISTY. I did, God help me, and there I'd be as happy as the sunshine of St. Martin's Day, watching the light passing the north or the patches of fog, till I'd hear a rabbit starting to screech and I'd go running in the furze. Then when I'd my full share I'd come walking down where you'd see the ducks and geese stretched sleeping on the highway of the road, and before I'd pass the dunghill, I'd hear himself snoring out, a loud lonesome snore he'd be making all times, the while he was sleeping, and he a man 'd be raging all times, the while he was waking, like a gaudy officer you'd hear cursing and damning and swearing oaths.

PEGEEN. Providence and Mercy, spare us all!

CHRISTY. It's that you'd say surely if you seen him and he after drinking for weeks, rising up in the red dawn, or before it maybe, and going out into the yard as naked as an ash tree in the moon of May, and shying clods against the visage of the stars till he'd put the fear of death into the banbhs [20] and the screeching sows.

PEGEEN. I'd be well-nigh afeard of that lad myself, I'm thinking. And there was no one in it but the two of you alone?

CHRISTY. The divil a one, though he'd sons and daughters walking all great states and territories of the world, and not a one of them, to this day, but would say their seven curses on him, and they rousing up to let a cough or sneeze, maybe, in the deadness of the night.

PEGEEN. [*Nodding her head.*] Well, you should have been a queer lot. I never cursed my father the like of that, though I'm twenty and more years of age.

CHRISTY. Then you'd have cursed mine, I'm telling you, and he a man never gave peace to any, saving when he'd get two months or three, or be locked in the asylums for battering peelers or assaulting men [*With depression.*] the way it was a bitter life he led me till I did up a Tuesday and halve his skull.

PEGEEN. [*Putting her hand on his shoulder.*] Well, you'll have peace in this place, Christy Mahon, and none to trouble you, and it's near time a fine lad like you should have your good share of the earth.

CHRISTY. It's time surely, and I a seemly fellow with great strength in me and bravery of . . .

[*Someone knocks.*]

[19] Inclination.

[20] Suckling pigs.

CHRISTY. [*Clinging to* PEGEEN.] Oh, glory! it's late for knocking, and this last while I'm in terror of the peelers, and the walking dead.

[*Knocking again.*]

PEGEEN. Who's there?

VOICE. [*Outside.*] Me.

PEGEEN. Who's me?

VOICE. The Widow Quin.

PEGEEN. [*Jumping up and giving him bread and milk.*] Go on now with your supper, and let on to be sleepy, for if she found you were such a warrant to talk, she'd be stringing gabble till the dawn of day.

[*He takes bread and sits shyly with his back to the door.*]

PEGEEN. [*Opening door, with temper.*] What ails you, or what is it you're wanting at this hour of the night?

WIDOW QUIN. [*Coming in a step and peering at* CHRISTY.] I'm after meeting Shawn Keogh and Father Reilly below, who told me of your curiosity man, and they fearing by this time he was maybe roaring, romping on your hands with drink.

PEGEEN. [*Pointing to* CHRISTY.] Look now is he roaring, and he stretched away drowsy with his supper and his mug of milk. Walk down and tell that to Father Reilly and to Shaneen Keogh.

WIDOW QUIN. [*Coming forward.*] I'll not see them again, for I've their word to lead that lad forward for to lodge with me.

PEGEEN. [*In blank amazement.*] This night, is it?

WIDOW QUIN. [*Going over.*] This night. "It isn't fitting," says the priesteen, "to have his likeness lodging with an orphaned girl." [*To* CHRISTY.] God save you, mister!

CHRISTY. [*Shyly.*] God save you kindly.

WIDOW QUIN. [*Looking at him with half-amazed curiosity.*] Well, aren't you a little smiling fellow? It should have been great and bitter torments did rouse your spirits to a deed of blood.

CHRISTY. [*Doubtfully.*] It should, maybe.

21 Pa.

WIDOW QUIN. It's more than "maybe" I'm saying, and it'd soften my heart to see you sitting so simple with your cup and cake, and you fitter to be saying your catechism than slaying your da.[21]

PEGEEN. [*At counter, washing glasses.*] There's talking when any'd see he's fit to be holding his head high with the wonders of the world. Walk on from this, for I'll not have him tormented and he destroyed travelling since Tuesday was a week.

WIDOW QUIN. [*Peaceably.*] We'll be walking surely when his supper's done, and you'll find we're great company, young fellow, when it's of the like of you and me you'd hear the penny poets [22] singing in an August Fair.

CHRISTY. [*Innocently.*] Did you kill your father?

PEGEEN. [*Contemptuously.*] She did not. She hit himself with a worn pick, and the rusted poison did corrode his blood the way he never overed it, and died after. That was a sneaky kind of murder did win small glory with the boys itself.

[*She crosses to* CHRISTY'S *left.*]

WIDOW QUIN. [*With good-humour.*] If it didn't, maybe all knows a widow woman has buried her children and destroyed her man is a wiser comrade for a young lad than a girl, the like of you, who'd go helter-skeltering after any man would let you a wink upon the road.

PEGEEN. [*Breaking out into wild rage.*] And you'll say that, Widow Quin, and you gasping with the rage you had racing the hill beyond to look on his face.

WIDOW QUIN. [*Laughing derisively.*] Me, is it? Well, Father Reilly has cuteness to divide you now. [*She pulls* CHRISTY *up.*] There's great temptation in a man did slay his da, and we'd best be going, young fellow; so rise up and come with me.

PEGEEN. [*Seizing his arm.*] He'll not stir. He's pot-boy in this place, and I'll not have him stolen off and kidnabbed while himself's abroad.

22 Singers of sentimental love-songs.

WIDOW QUIN. It'd be a crazy pot-boy'd lodge him in the shebeen where he works by day, so you'd have a right to come on, young fellow, till you see my little houseen, a perch off on the rising hill.

PEGEEN. Wait till morning, Christy Mahon. Wait till you lay eyes on her leaky thatch is growing more pasture for her buck goat than her square of fields, and she without a tramp itself to keep in order her place at all.

WIDOW QUIN. When you see me contriving in my little gardens, Christy Mahon, you'll swear the Lord God formed me to be living lone, and that there isn't my match in Mayo for thatching, or mowing, or shearing a sheep.

PEGEEN. [With noisy scorn.] It's true the Lord God formed you to contrive indeed. Doesn't the world know you reared a black lamb at your own breast, so that the Lord Bishop of Connaught felt the elements of a Christian, and he eating it after in a kidney stew? Doesn't the world know you've been seen shaving the foxy skipper from France for a threepenny bit and a sop of grass tobacco would wring the liver from a mountain goat you'd meet leaping the hills?

WIDOW QUIN. [With amusement.] Do you hear her now, young fellow? Do you hear the way she'll be rating at your own self when a week is by?

PEGEEN. [To CHRISTY.] Don't heed her. Tell her to go into her pigsty and not plague us here.

WIDOW QUIN. I'm going; but he'll come with me.

PEGEEN. [Shaking him.] Are you dumb, young fellow?

CHRISTY. [Timidly, to WIDOW QUIN.] God increase you; but I'm pot-boy in this place, and it's here I'd liefer stay.

PEGEEN. [Triumphantly.] Now you have heard him, and go on from this.

WIDOW QUIN. [Looking round the room.] It's lonesome this hour crossing the hill, and if he won't come along with me, I'd have a right maybe to stop this night with yourselves. Let me stretch out on the settle, Pegeen Mike; and himself can lie by the hearth.

PEGEEN. [Short and fiercely.] Faith, I won't. Quit off or I will send you now.

WIDOW QUIN. [Gathering her shawl up.] Well, it's a terror to be aged a score. [To CHRISTY.] God bless you now, young fellow, and let you be wary, or there's right torment will await you here if you go romancing with her like, and she waiting only, as they bade me say, on a sheepskin parchment to be wed with Shawn Keogh of Killakeen.

[The WIDOW QUIN goes out.]

CHRISTY. [Going to PEGEEN as she bolts the door.] What's that she's after saying?

PEGEEN. Lies and blather, you've no call to mind. Well, isn't Shawn Keogh an impudent fellow to send up spying on me? Wait till I lay hands on him. Let him wait, I'm saying.

CHRISTY. And you're not wedding him at all?

PEGEEN. I wouldn't wed him if a bishop came walking for to join us here.

CHRISTY. That God in glory may be thanked for that.

PEGEEN. There's your bed now. I've put a quilt upon you I'm after quilting a while since with my own two hands, and you'd best stretch out now for your sleep, and may God give you a good rest till I call you in the morning when the cocks will crow.

CHRISTY. [As she goes to inner room.] May God and Mary and St. Patrick bless you and reward you, for your kindly talk.

[She shuts the door behind her. He settles his bed slowly, feeling the quilt with immense satisfaction.]

Well, it's a clean bed and soft with it, and it's great luck and company I've won me in the end of time—two fine women fighting for the likes of me—till I'm thinking this night wasn't I a foolish fellow not to kill my father in the years gone by.

[CURTAIN.]

ACT TWO

SCENE. *As before. Brilliant morning light.* CHRISTY, *looking bright and cheerful, is cleaning a girl's boots.*

CHRISTY. [*To himself, counting jugs on dresser.*] Half a hundred beyond. Ten there. A score that's above. Eighty jugs. Six cups and a broken one. Two plates. A power of glasses. Bottles, a school-master'd be hard set to count, and enough in them, I'm thinking, to drunken all the wealth and wisdom of the County Clare. [*He puts down the boot carefully.*] There's her boots now, nice and decent for her evening use, and isn't it grand brushes she has? [*He puts them down and goes by degrees to the looking-glass.*] Well, this'd be a fine place to be my whole life talking out with swearing Christians, in place of my old dogs and cat, and I stalking around, smoking my pipe and drinking my fill, and never a day's work but drawing a cork an odd time, or wiping a glass, or rinsing out a shiny tumbler for a decent man. [*He takes the looking-glass from the wall and puts it on the back of a chair; then sits down in front of it and begins washing his face.*] Didn't I know rightly I was handsome, though it was the divil's own mirror we had beyond, would twist a squint across an angel's brow; and I'll be growing fine from this day, the way I'll have a soft lovely skin on me and won't be the like of the clumsy young fellows do be ploughing all times in the earth and dung. [*He starts.*] Is she coming again? [*He looks out.*] Stranger girls. God help me, where'll I hide myself away and my long neck naked to the world? [*He looks out.*] I'd best go to the room maybe till I'm dressed again.

[*He gathers up his coat and the looking-glass, and runs into the inner room. The door is pushed open, and SUSAN BRADY looks in, and knocks on door.*]

SUSAN. There's nobody in it.
                              [*Knocks again.*]
NELLY. [*Pushing her in and following her, with HONOR BLAKE and SARA TANSEY.*]

It'd be early for them both to be out walking the hill.

SUSAN. I'm thinking Shawn Keogh was making game of us and there's no such man in it at all.

HONOR. [*Pointing to straw and quilt.*] Look at that. He's been sleeping there in the night. Well, it'll be a hard case if he's gone off now, the way we'll never set our eyes on a man killed his father, and we after rising early and destroying ourselves running fast on the hill.

NELLY. Are you thinking them's his boots?

SARA. [*Taking them up.*] If they are, there should be his father's track on them. Did you never read in the papers the way murdered men do bleed and drip?

SUSAN. Is that blood there, Sara Tansey?

SARA. [*Smelling it.*] That's bog water, I'm thinking, but it's his own they are surely, for I never seen the like of them for whity mud, and red mud, and turf on them, and the fine sands of the sea. That man's been walking, I'm telling you.

[*She goes down right, putting on one of his boots.*]

SUSAN. [*Going to window.*] Maybe he's stolen off to Belmullet with the boots of Michael James, and you'd have a right so to follow after him, Sara Tansey, and you the one yoked the ass cart and drove ten miles to set your eyes on the man bit the yellow lady's nostril on the northern shore.

[*She looks out.*]

SARA. [*Running to window with one boot on.*] Don't be talking, and we fooled to-day. [*Putting on other boot.*] There's a pair do fit me well, and I'll be keeping them for walking to the priest, when you'd be ashamed this place, going up winter and summer with nothing worth while to confess at all.

HONOR. [*Who has been listening at the door.*] Whisht! there's someone inside the room. [*She pushes door a chink open.*] It's a man.

[SARA *kicks off boots and puts them where they were. They all stand in a line looking through chink.*]

SARA. I'll call him. Mister! Mister! [*He puts in his head.*] Is Pegeen within?

CHRISTY. [*Coming in as meek as a mouse, with the looking-glass held behind his back.*] She's above on the cnuceen,[1] seeking the nanny goats, the way she'd have a sup of goat's milk for to colour my tea.

SARA. And asking your pardon, is it you's the man killed his father?

CHRISTY. [*Sidling toward the nail where the glass was hanging.*] I am, God help me!

SARA. [*Taking eggs she has brought.*] Then my thousand welcomes to you, and I've run up with a brace of duck's eggs for your food to-day. Pegeen's ducks is no use, but these are the real rich sort. Hold out your hand and you'll see it's no lie I'm telling you.

CHRISTY. [*Coming forward shyly, and holding out his left hand.*] They're a great and weighty size.

SUSAN. And I run up with a pat of butter, for it'd be a poor thing to have you eating your spuds dry, and you after running a great way since you did destroy your da.

CHRISTY. Thank you kindly.

HONOR. And I brought you a little cut of cake, for you should have a thin stomach on you, and you that length walking the world.

NELLY. And I brought you a little laying pullet—boiled and all she is—was crushed at the fall of night by the curate's car. Feel the fat of that breast, mister.

CHRISTY. It's bursting, surely.

[*He feels it with the back of his hand, in which he holds the presents.*]

SARA. Will you pinch it? Is your right hand too sacred for to use at all? [*She slips round behind him.*] It's a glass he has. Well, I never seen to this day a man with a looking-glass held to his back. Them that kills their fathers is a vain lot surely.

[*Girls giggle.*]

CHRISTY. [*Smiling innocently and piling*

[1] Hill.

presents on glass.*] I'm very thankful to you all to-day . . .

WIDOW QUIN. [*Coming in quickly, at door.*] Sara Tansey, Susan Brady, Honor Blake! What in glory has you here at this hour of day?

GIRLS. [*Giggling.*] That's the man killed his father.

WIDOW QUIN. [*Coming to them.*] I know well it's the man; and I'm after putting him down in the sports below for racing, leaping, pitching, and the Lord knows what.

SARA. [*Exuberantly.*] That's right, Widow Quin. I'll bet my dowry that he'll lick the world.

WIDOW QUIN. If you will, you'd have a right to have him fresh and nourished in place of nursing a feast. [*Taking presents.*] Are you fasting or fed, young fellow?

CHRISTY. Fasting, if you please.

WIDOW QUIN. [*Loudly.*] Well, you're the lot. Stir up now and give him his breakfast. [*To CHRISTY.*] Come here to me [*She puts him on bench beside her while the girls make tea and get his breakfast.*] and let you tell us your story before Pegeen will come, in place of grinning your ears off like the moon of May.

CHRISTY. [*Beginning to be pleased.*] It's a long story; you'd be destroyed listening.

WIDOW QUIN. Don't be letting on to be shy, a fine, gamey, treacherous lad the like of you. Was it in your house beyond you cracked his skull?

CHRISTY. [*Shy but flattered.*] It was not. We were digging spuds in his cold, sloping, stony, divil's patch of a field.

WIDOW QUIN. And you went asking money of him, or making talk of getting a wife would drive him from his farm?

CHRISTY. I did not, then; but there I was, digging and digging, and "You squinting idiot," says he, "let you walk down now and tell the priest you'll wed the Widow Casey in a score of days."

WIDOW QUIN. And what kind was she?

CHRISTY. [*With horror.*] A walking terror from beyond the hills, and she two score and five years, and two hundredweights and five pounds in the weighing scales, with a limping leg on her, and a blinded eye, and she a woman of noted misbehavior with the old and young.

GIRLS. [*Clustering round him, serving him.*] Glory be.

WIDOW QUIN. And what did he want driving you to wed with her?

[*She takes a bit of the chicken.*]

CHRISTY. [*Eating with growing satisfaction.*] He was letting on I was wanting a protector from the harshness of the world, and he without a thought the whole while but how he'd have her hut to live in and her gold to drink.

WIDOW QUIN. There's maybe worse than a dry hearth and a widow woman and your glass at night. So you hit him then?

CHRISTY. [*Getting almost excited.*] I did not. "I won't wed her," says I, "when all knows she did suckle me for six weeks when I came into the world, and she a hag this day with a tongue on her has the crows and seabirds scattered, the way they would cast a shadow on her garden with the dread of her curse."

WIDOW QUIN. [*Teasingly.*] That one should be right company.

SARA. [*Eagerly.*] Don't mind her. Did you kill him then?

CHRISTY. "She's too good for the like of you," says he, "and go on now or I'll flatten you out like a crawling beast has passed under a dray." "You will not if I can help it," says I. "Go on," says he, "or I'll have the divil making garters of your limbs to-night." "You will not if I can help it," says I.

[*He sits up, brandishing his mug.*]

SARA. You were right surely.

CHRISTY. [*Impressively.*] With that the sun came out between the cloud and the hill, and it shining green in my face. "God have mercy on your soul," says he, lifting a scythe; "or on your own," says I, raising the loy.

SUSAN. That's a grand story.

HONOR. He tells it lovely.

CHRISTY. [*Flattered and confident, waving bone.*] He gave a drive with the scythe,

and I gave a lep to the east. Then I turned around with my back to the north, and I hit a blow on the ridge of his skull, laid him stretched out, and he split to the knob of his gullet.

[*He raises the chicken bone to his Adam's apple.*]

GIRLS. [*Together.*] Well, you're a marvel! Oh, God bless you! You're the lad surely!

SUSAN. I'm thinking the Lord God sent him this road to make a second husband to the Widow Quin, and she with a great yearning to be wedded, though all dread her here. Lift him on her knee, Sara Tansey.

WIDOW QUIN. Don't tease him.

SARA. [*Going over to dresser and counter very quickly, and getting two glasses and porter.*] You're heroes surely, and let you drink a supeen with your arms linked like the outlandish lovers in the sailor's song. [*She links their arms and gives them the glasses.*] There now. Drink a health to the wonders of the western world, the pirates, preachers, poteen-makers, with the jobbing jockies,[2] parching peelers, and the juries fill their stomachs selling judgments of the English law.

[*Brandishing the bottle.*]

WIDOW QUIN. That's a right toast, Sara Tansey. Now, Christy.

[*They drink with their arms linked, he drinking with his left hand, she with her right. As they are drinking,* PEGEEN MIKE *comes in with a milk can and stands aghast. They all spring away from* CHRISTY. *He goes down left.* WIDOW QUIN *remains seated.*]

PEGEEN. [*Angrily, to* SARA.] What is it you're wanting?

SARA. [*Twisting her apron.*] An ounce of tobacco.

PEGEEN. Have you tuppence?

SARA. I've forgotten my purse.

PEGEEN. Then you'd best be getting it and not fooling us here. [*To the* WIDOW QUIN, *with more elaborate scorn.*] And what is it you're wanting, Widow Quin?

2 Swindling peddlers.

WIDOW QUIN. [*Insolently.*] A penn'orth of starch.

PEGEEN. [*Breaking out.*] And you without a white shift or a shirt in your whole family since the drying of the flood. I've no starch for the like of you, and let you walk on now to Killamuck.

WIDOW QUIN. [*Turning to* CHRISTY, *as she goes out with the girls.*] Well, you're mighty huffy this day, Pegeen Mike, and you, young fellow, let you not forget the sports and racing when the noon is by.

[*They go out.*]

PEGEEN. [*Imperiously.*] Fling out that rubbish and put them cups away. [CHRISTY *tidies away in great haste.*] Shove in the bench by the wall. [*He does so.*] And hang that glass on the nail. What disturbed it at all?

CHRISTY. [*Very meekly.*] I was making myself decent only, and this a fine country for young lovely girls.

PEGEEN. [*Sharply.*] Whisht your talking of girls.   [*Goes to counter—right.*]

CHRISTY. Wouldn't any wish to be decent in a place . . .

PEGEEN. Whisht I'm saying.

CHRISTY. [*Looks at her face for a moment with great misgivings, then as a last effort, takes up a loy, and goes towards her, with feigned assurance.*] It was with a loy the like of that I killed my father.

PEGEEN. [*Still sharply.*] You've told me that story six times since the dawn of day.

CHRISTY. [*Reproachfully.*] It's a queer thing you wouldn't care to be hearing it and them girls after walking four miles to be listening to me now.

PEGEEN. [*Turning around astonished.*] Four miles.

CHRISTY. [*Apologetically.*] Didn't himself say there were only four bona fides living in the place?

PEGEEN. It's bona fides by the road they are, but that lot came over the river lepping the stones. It's not three perches when you go like that, and I was down this morning looking on the papers the post-boy does have in his bag. [*With meaning and emphasis.*] For there was great news this day, Christopher Mahon.

[*She goes into room left.*]

CHRISTY. [*Suspiciously.*] Is it news of my murder?

PEGEEN. [*Inside.*] Murder, indeed.

CHRISTY. [*Loudly.*] A murdered da?

PEGEEN. [*Coming in again and crossing right.*] There was not, but a story filled half a page of the hanging of a man. Ah, that should be a fearful end, young fellow, and it worst of all for a man who destroyed his da, for the like of him would get small mercies, and when it's dead he is, they'd put him in a narrow grave, with cheap sacking wrapping him round, and pour down quicklime on his head, the way you'd see a woman pouring any frish-frash [3] from a cup.

CHRISTY. [*Very miserably.*] Oh, God help me. Are you thinking I'm safe? You were saying at the fall of night, I was shut [4] of jeopardy and I here with yourselves.

PEGEEN. [*Severely.*] You'll be shut of jeopardy in no place if you go talking with a pack of wild girls the like of them do be walking abroad with the peelers, talking whispers at the fall of night.

CHRISTY. [*With terror.*] And you're thinking they'd tell?

PEGEEN. [*With mock sympathy.*] Who knows, God help you.

CHRISTY. [*Loudly.*] What joy would they have to bring hanging to the likes of me?

PEGEEN. It's queer joys they have, and who knows the thing they'd do, if it'd make the green stones cry itself to think of you swaying and swiggling at the butt of a rope, and you with a fine, stout neck, God bless you! the way you'd be a half an hour, in great anguish, getting your death.

CHRISTY. [*Getting his boots and putting them on.*] If there's that terror of them, it'd be best, maybe, I went on wandering like Esau or Cain and Abel on the sides of Neifin or the Erris plain.[5]

PEGEEN. [*Beginning to play with him.*]

---

[3] Dregs.
[4] Free.

[5] A mountain ridge and neighboring plain in County Mayo.

It would, maybe, for I've heard the Circuit Judges this place is a heartless crew.

CHRISTY. [Bitterly.] It's more than Judges this place is a heartless crew. [Looking up at her.] And isn't it a poor thing to be starting again and I a lonesome fellow will be looking out on women and girls the way the needy fallen spirits do be looking on the Lord?

PEGEEN. What call have you to be that lonesome when there's poor girls walking Mayo in their thousands now?

CHRISTY. [Grimly.] It's well you know what call I have. It's well you know it's a lonesome thing to be passing small towns with the lights shining sideways when the night is down, or going in strange places with a dog noising before you and a dog noising behind, or drawn to the cities where you'd hear a voice kissing and talking deep love in every shadow of the ditch, and you passing on with an empty, hungry stomach failing from your heart.

PEGEEN. I'm thinking you're an odd man, Christy Mahon. The oddest walking fellow I ever set my eyes on to this hour to-day.

CHRISTY. What would any be but odd men and they living lonesome in the world?

PEGEEN. I'm not odd, and I'm my whole life with my father only.

CHRISTY. [With infinite admiration.] How would a lovely handsome woman the like of you be lonesome when all men should be thronging around to hear the sweetness of your voice, and the little infant children should be pestering your steps I'm thinking, and you walking the roads.

PEGEEN. I'm hard set to know what way a coaxing fellow the like of yourself should be lonesome either.

CHRISTY. Coaxing?

PEGEEN. Would you have me think a man never talked with the girls would have the words you've spoken to-day? It's only letting on you are to be lonesome, the way you'd get around me now.

CHRISTY. I wish to God I was letting on; but I was lonesome all times, and born

⁶ Switch.

lonesome, I'm thinking, as the moon of dawn.   [Going to door.]

PEGEEN. [Puzzled by his talk.] Well, it's a story I'm not understanding at all why you'd be worse than another, Christy Mahon, and you a fine lad with the great savagery to destroy your da.

CHRISTY. It's little I'm understanding myself, saving only that my heart's scalded this day, and I am going off stretching out the earth between us, the way I'll not be waking near you another dawn of the year till the two of us do arise to hope or judgment with the saints of God, and now I'd best be going with my wattle ⁶ in my hand, for hanging is a poor thing [Turning to go.], and it's little welcome only is left me in this house to-day.

PEGEEN. [Sharply.] Christy! [He turns round.] Come here to me. [He goes toward her.] Lay down that switch and throw some sods on the fire. You're pot-boy in this place, and I'll not have you mitch ⁷ off from us now.

CHRISTY. You were saying I'd be hanged if I stay.

PEGEEN. [Quite kindly at last.] I'm after going down and reading the fearful crimes of Ireland for two weeks or three, and there wasn't a word of your murder. [Getting up and going over to the counter.] They've likely not found the body. You're safe so with ourselves.

CHRISTY. [Astonished, slowly.] It's making game of me you were [Following her with fearful joy.], and I can stay so, working at your side, and I not lonesome from this mortal day.

PEGEEN. What's to hinder you from staying, except the widow woman or the young girls would inveigle you off?

CHRISTY. [With rapture.] And I'll have your words from this day filling my ears, and that look is come upon you meeting my two eyes, and I watching you loafing around in the warm sun, or rinsing your ankles when the night is come.

PEGEEN. [Kindly, but a little embarrassed.] I'm thinking you'll be a loyal young

⁷ Sneak.

lad to have working around, and if you vexed me a while since with your leaguing with the girls, I wouldn't give a thraneen [8] for a lad hadn't a mighty spirit in him and a gamey heart.

[SHAWN KEOGH *runs in carrying a cleeve* [9] *on his back, followed by the* WIDOW QUIN.]

SHAWN. [*To* PEGEEN.] I was passing below, and I seen your mountain sheep eating cabbages in Jimmy's field. Run up or they'll be bursting surely.

PEGEEN. Oh, God mend them!

[*She puts a shawl over her head and runs out.*]

CHRISTY. [*Looking from one to the other. Still in high spirits.*] I'd best go to her aid maybe. I'm handy with ewes.

WIDOW QUIN. [*Closing the door.*] She can do that much, and there is Shaneen has long speeches for to tell you now.

[*She sits down with an amused smile.*]

SHAWN. [*Taking something from his pocket and offering it to* CHRISTY.] Do you see that, mister?

CHRISTY. [*Looking at it.*] The half of a ticket to the Western States!

SHAWN. [*Trembling with anxiety.*] I'll give it to you and my new hat [*Pulling it out of hamper.*]; and my breeches with the double seat [*Pulling it off.*]; and my new coat is woven from the blackest shearings for three miles around [*Giving him the coat.*]; I'll give you the whole of them, and my blessing, and the blessing of Father Reilly itself, maybe, if you'll quit from this and leave us in the peace we had till last night at the fall of dark.

CHRISTY. [*With a new arrogance.*] And for what is it you're wanting to get shut of me?

SHAWN. [*Looking to the* WIDOW *for help.*] I'm a poor scholar with middling faculties to coin a lie, so I'll tell you the truth, Christy Mahon. I'm wedding with Pegeen beyond, and I don't think well of having a clever fearless man the like of you dwelling in her house.

[8] Straw.
[9] Basket.

CHRISTY. [*Almost pugnaciously.*] And you'd be using bribery for to banish me?

SHAWN. [*In an imploring voice.*] Let you not take it badly, mister honey: isn't beyond the best place for you where you'll have golden chains and shiny coats and you riding upon hunters with the ladies of the land?

[*He makes an eager sign to the* WIDOW QUIN *to come to help him.*]

WIDOW QUIN. [*Coming over.*] It's true for him, and you'd best quit off and not have that poor girl setting her mind on you, for there's Shaneen thinks she wouldn't suit you though all is saying that she'll wed you now.

[CHRISTY *beams with delight.*]

SHAWN. [*In terrified earnest.*] She wouldn't suit you, and she with the divil's own temper the way you'd be strangling one another in a score of days. [*He makes the movement of strangling with his hands.*] It's the like of me only that she's fit for, a quiet simple fellow wouldn't raise a hand upon her if she scratched itself.

WIDOW QUIN. [*Putting* SHAWN'S *hat on* CHRISTY.] Fit them clothes on you anyhow, young fellow, and he'd maybe loan them to you for the sports. [*Pushing him towards inner door.*] Fit them on and you can give your answer when you have them tried.

CHRISTY. [*Beaming, delighted with the clothes.*] I will then. I'd like herself to see me in them tweeds and hat.

[*He goes into room and shuts the door.*]

SHAWN. [*In great anxiety.*] He'd like herself to see them. He'll not leave us, Widow Quin. He's a score of divils in him the way it's well nigh certain he will wed Pegeen.

WIDOW QUIN. [*Jeeringly.*] It's true all girls are fond of courage and do hate the like of you.

SHAWN. [*Walking about in desperation.*] Oh, Widow Quin, what'll I be doing now? I'd inform again him, but he'd burst from Kilmainham [10] and he'd be sure and certain to destroy me. If I wasn't so God-fearing,

[10] A prison near Dublin where Charles Parnell, the famous Irish patriot, was imprisoned.

I'd near have courage to come behind him and run a pike into his side. Oh, it's a hard case to be an orphan and not to have your father that you're used to, and you'd easy kill and make yourself a hero in the sight of all. [*Coming up to her.*] Oh, Widow Quin, will you find me some contrivance when I've promised you a ewe?

WIDOW QUIN.   A ewe's a small thing, but what would you give me if I did wed him and did save you so?

SHAWN.   [*With astonishment.*] You?

WIDOW QUIN.   Aye. Would you give me the red cow you have and the mountainy ram, and the right of way across your rye path, and a load of dung at Michaelmas, and turbary [11] upon the western hill?

SHAWN.   [*Radiant with hope.*] I would surely, and I'd give you the wedding-ring I have, and the loan of a new suit, the way you'd have him decent on the wedding-day. I'd give you two kids for your dinner, and a gallon of poteen, and I'd call the piper on the long car to your wedding from Crossmolina or from Ballina. I'd give you . . .

WIDOW QUIN.   That'll do so, and let you whisht, for he's coming now again.

[CHRISTY *comes in very natty in the new clothes.* WIDOW QUIN *goes to him admiringly.*]

WIDOW QUIN.   If you seen yourself now, I'm thinking you'd be too proud to speak to us at all, and it'd be a pity surely to have your like sailing from Mayo to the Western World.

CHRISTY.   [*As proud as a peacock.*] I'm not going. If this is a poor place itself, I'll make myself contented to be lodging here.

[WIDOW QUIN *makes a sign to* SHAWN *to leave them.*]

SHAWN.   Well, I'm going measuring the race-course while the tide is low, so I'll leave you the garments and my blessing for the sports to-day. God bless you!

[*He wriggles out.*]

WIDOW QUIN.   [*Admiring* CHRISTY.] Well, you're mighty spruce, young fellow. Sit

[11] The right to cut turf.

down while you're quiet till you talk with me.

CHRISTY.   [*Swaggering.*] I'm going abroad on the hillside for to seek Pegeen.

WIDOW QUIN.   You'll have time and plenty for to seek Pegeen, and you heard me saying at the fall of night the two of us should be great company.

CHRISTY.   From this out I'll have no want of company when all sorts is bringing me their food and clothing [*He swaggers to the door, tightening his belt.*], the way they'd set their eyes upon a gallant orphan cleft his father with one blow to the breeches belt. [*He opens door, then staggers back.*] Saints of glory! Holy angels from the throne of light!

WIDOW QUIN.   [*Going over.*] What ails you?

CHRISTY.   It's the walking spirit of my murdered da?

WIDOW QUIN.   [*Looking out.*] Is it that tramper?

CHRISTY.   [*Wildly.*] Where'll I hide my poor body from that ghost of hell?

[*The door is pushed open, and* OLD MAHON *appears on threshold.* CHRISTY *darts in behind door.*]

WIDOW QUIN.   [*In great amusement.*] God save you, my poor man.

MAHON.   [*Gruffly.*] Did you see a young lad passing this way in the early morning or the fall of night?

WIDOW QUIN.   You're a queer kind to walk in not saluting at all.

MAHON.   Did you see the young lad?

WIDOW QUIN.   [*Stiffly.*] What kind was he?

MAHON.   An ugly young streeler [12] with a murderous gob [13] on him, and a little switch in his hand. I met a tramper seen him coming this way at the fall of night.

WIDOW QUIN.   There's harvest hundreds do be passing these days for the Sligo boat. For what is it you're wanting him, my poor man?

MAHON.   I want to destroy him for breaking the head on me with the clout of

[12] "Big mouth."   [13] "Mug."

a loy. [*He takes off a big hat and shows his head in a mass of bandages and plaster, with some pride.*] It was he did that, and amn't I a great wonder to think I've traced him ten days with that rent in my crown?

WIDOW QUIN. [*Taking his head in both hands and examining it with extreme delight.*] That was a great blow. And who hit you? A robber maybe?

MAHON. It was my own son hit me, and the divil a robber, or anything else, but a dirty, stuttering lout.

WIDOW QUIN. [*Letting go his skull and wiping her hands in her apron.*] You'd best be wary of a mortified scalp, I think they call it, lepping around with that wound in the splendour of the sun. It was a bad blow surely, and you should have vexed him fearful to make him strike that gash in his da.

MAHON. Is it me?

WIDOW QUIN. [*Amusing herself.*] Aye. And isn't it a great shame when the old and hardened do torment the young?

MAHON. [*Raging.*] Torment him, is it? And I after holding out with the patience of a martyred saint till there's nothing but destruction on, and I'm driven out in my old age with none to aid me.

WIDOW QUIN. [*Greatly amused.*] It's a sacred wonder the way that wickedness will spoil a man.

MAHON. My wickedness, is it? Amn't I after saying it is himself has me destroyed, and he a lier on walls, a talker of folly, a man you'd see stretched the half of the day in the brown ferns with his belly to the sun.

WIDOW QUIN. Not working at all?

MAHON. The divil a work, or if he did itself, you'd see him raising up a haystack like the stalk of a rush, or driving our last cow till he broke her leg at the hip, and when he wasn't at that he'd be fooling over little birds he had—finches and felts [14]—or making mugs at his own self in the bit of a glass we had hung on the wall.

WIDOW QUIN. [*Looking at* CHRISTY.]

[14] Thrushes.

What way was he so foolish? It was running wild after the girls maybe?

MAHON. [*With a shout of derision.*] Running wild, is it? If he seen a red petticoat coming swinging over the hill, he'd be off to hide in the sticks, and you'd see him shooting out his sheep's eyes between the little twigs and the leaves, and his two ears rising like a hare looking through a gap. Girls, indeed!

WIDOW QUIN. It was drink maybe?

MAHON. And he a poor fellow would get drunk on the smell of a pint. He'd a queer rotten stomach, I'm telling you, and when I gave him three pulls from my pipe a while since, he was taken with contortions till I had to send him in the ass cart to the females' nurse.

WIDOW QUIN. [*Clasping her hands.*] Well, I never till this day heard tell of a man the like of that!

MAHON. I'd take a mighty oath you didn't surely, and wasn't he the laughing joke of every female woman where four baronies [15] meet, the way the girls would stop their weeding if they seen him coming the road to let a roar at him, and call him the looney of Mahon's.

WIDOW QUIN. I'd give the world and all to see the like of him. What kind was he?

MAHON. A small low fellow.

WIDOW QUIN. And dark?

MAHON. Dark and dirty.

WIDOW QUIN. [*Considering.*] I'm thinking I seen him.

MAHON. [*Eagerly.*] An ugly young blackguard.

WIDOW QUIN. A hideous, fearful villain, and the spit of you.

MAHON. What way is he fled?

WIDOW QUIN. Gone over the hills to catch a coasting steamer to the north or south.

MAHON. Could I pull up on him now?

WIDOW QUIN. If you'll cross the sands below where the tide is out, you'll be in it as soon as himself, for he had to go round ten miles by the top of the bay. [*She points to the door.*] Strike down by the head be-

[15] Sections of land.

yond and then follow on the roadway to the north and east.

[MAHON *goes abruptly.*]

WIDOW QUIN. [*Shouting after him.*] Let you give him a good vengeance when you come up with him, but don't put yourself in the power of the law, for it'd be a poor thing to see a judge in his black cap reading out his sentence on a civil warrior the like of you.

[*She swings the door to and looks at* CHRISTY, *who is cowering in terror, for a moment, then she bursts into a laugh.*]

WIDOW QUIN. Well, you're the walking Playboy of the Western World, and that's the poor man you had divided to his breeches belt.

CHRISTY. [*Looking out: then, to her.*] What'll Pegeen say when she hears that story? What'll she be saying to me now?

WIDOW QUIN. She'll knock the head of you, I'm thinking, and drive you from the door. God help her to be taking you for a wonder, and you a little schemer making up the story you destroyed your da.

CHRISTY. [*Turning to the door, nearly speechless with rage, half to himself.*] To be letting on he was dead, and coming back to his life, and following after me like an old weasel tracing a rat, and coming in here laying desolation between my own self and the fine women of Ireland, and he a kind of carcase that you'd fling upon the sea . . .

WIDOW QUIN. [*More soberly.*] There's talking for a man's one only son.

CHRISTY. [*Breaking out.*] His one son, is it? May I meet him with one tooth and it aching, and one eye to be seeing seven and seventy divils in the twists of the road, and one old timber leg on him to limp into the scalding grave. [*Looking out.*] There he is now crossing the strands, and that the Lord God would send a high wave to wash him from the world.

WIDOW QUIN. [*Scandalized.*] Have you no shame? [*Putting her hand on his shoulder and turning him round.*] What ails you? Near crying, is it?

CHRISTY. [*In despair and grief.*] Amn't I after seeing the love-light of the star of knowledge shining from her brow, and hearing words would put you thinking on the holy Brigid speaking to the infant saints, and now she'll be turning again, and speaking hard words to me, like an old woman with a spavindy ass she'd have, urging on a hill.

WIDOW QUIN. There's poetry talk for a girl you'd see itching and scratching, and she with a stale stink of poteen on her from selling in the shop.

CHRISTY. [*Impatiently.*] It's her like is fitted to be handling merchandise in the heavens above, and what'll I be doing now, I ask you, and I a kind of wonder was jilted by the heavens when a day was by.

[*There is a distant noise of girls' voices.* WIDOW QUIN *looks from window and comes to him, hurriedly.*]

WIDOW QUIN. You'll be doing like myself, I'm thinking, when I did destroy my man, for I'm above many's the day, odd times in great spirits, abroad in the sunshine, darning a stocking or stitching a shift; and odd times again looking out on the schooners, hookers, trawlers is sailing the sea, and I thinking on the gallant hairy fellows are drifting beyond, and myself long years living alone.

CHRISTY. [*Interested.*] You're like me, so.

WIDOW QUIN. I am your like, and it's for that I'm taking a fancy to you, and I with my little houseen above where there'd be myself to tend you, and none to ask were you a murderer or what at all.

CHRISTY. And what would I be doing if I left Pegeen?

WIDOW QUIN. I've nice jobs you could be doing, gathering shells to make a whitewash for our hut within, building up a little goose-house, or stretching a new skin on an old curragh [16] I have, and if my hut is far from all sides, it's there you'll meet the wisest old men, I tell you, at the corner of my wheel, and it's there yourself and me will have great times whispering and hugging. . . .

[16] Boat.

VOICES. [*Outside, calling far away.*] Christy! Christy Mahon! Christy!

CHRISTY. Is it Pegeen Mike?

WIDOW QUIN. It's the young girls, I'm thinking, coming to bring you to the sports below, and what is it you'll have me to tell them now?

CHRISTY. Aid me for to win Pegeen. It's herself only that I'm seeking now. [WIDOW QUIN *gets up and goes to window.*] Aid me for to win her, and I'll be asking God to stretch a hand to you in the hour of death, and lead you short cuts through the Meadows of Ease, and up the floor of Heaven to the Footstool of the Virgin's Son.

WIDOW QUIN. There's praying.

VOICES. [*Nearer.*] Christy! Christy Mahon!

CHRISTY. [*With agitation.*] They're coming. Will you swear to aid and save me for the love of Christ?

WIDOW QUIN. [*Looks at him for a moment.*] If I aid you, will you swear to give me a right of way I want, and a mountainy ram, and a load of dung at Michaelmas, the time that you'll be master here?

CHRISTY. I will, by the elements and stars of night.

WIDOW QUIN. Then we'll not say a word of the old fellow, the way Pegeen won't know your story till the end of time.

CHRISTY. And if he chances to return again?

WIDOW QUIN. We'll swear he's a maniac and not your da. I could take an oath I seen him raving on the sands to-day.

[*Girls run in.*]

SUSAN. Come on to the sports below. Pegeen says you're to come.

SARA TANSEY. The lepping's beginning, and we've a jockey's suit to fit upon you for the mule race on the sands below.

HONOR. Come on, will you?

CHRISTY. I will then if Pegeen's beyond.

SARA TANSEY. She's in the boreen [17] making game of Shaneen Keogh.

CHRISTY. Then I'll be going to her now.

[*He runs out followed by the girls.*]

WIDOW QUIN. Well, if the worst comes in the end of all, it'll be great game to see there's none to pity him but a widow woman, the like of me, has buried her children and destroyed her man.

[*She goes out.*]

[CURTAIN.]

ACT THREE

SCENE. *As before. Later in the day.* JIMMY *comes in, slightly drunk.*

JIMMY. [*Calls.*] Pegeen! [*Crosses to inner door.*] Pegeen Mike! [*Comes back again into the room.*] Pegeen!

[PHILLY *comes in in the same state.*] [*To* PHILLY.] Did you see herself?

PHILLY. I did not; but I sent Shawn Keogh with the ass cart for to bear him home. [*Trying cupboards which are locked.*] Well, isn't he a nasty man to get into such staggers at a morning wake? and isn't herself the divil's daughter for locking, and she so fussy after that young gaffer, you might take your death with drought and none to heed you?

[17] Lane.

JIMMY. It's little wonder she'd be fussy, and he after bringing bankrupt ruin on the roulette man, and the trick-o'-the-loop man, and breaking the nose of the cockshot-man, and winning all in the sports below, racing, lepping, dancing, and the Lord knows what! He's right luck, I'm telling you.

PHILLY. If he has, he'll be rightly hobbled yet, and he not able to say ten words without making a brag of the way he killed his father, and the great blow he hit with the loy.

JIMMY. A man can't hang by his own informing, and his father should be rotten by now.

[OLD MAHON *passes window slowly.*]

PHILLY. Supposing a man's digging

spuds in that field with a long spade, and supposing he flings up the two halves of that skull, what'll be said then in the papers and the courts of law?

JIMMY. They'd say it was an old Dane,[1] maybe, was drowned in the flood.

[OLD MAHON *comes in and sits down near door listening.*]

Did you never hear tell of the skulls they have in the city of Dublin, ranged out like blue jugs in a cabin of Connaught?[2]

PHILLY. And you believe that?

JIMMY. [*Pugnaciously.*] Didn't a lad see them and he after coming from harvesting in the Liverpool boat? "They have them there," says he, "making a show of the great people there was one time walking the world. White skulls and black skulls and yellow skulls, and some with full teeth, and some haven't only but one."

PHILLY. It was no lie, maybe, for when I was a young lad there was a graveyard beyond the house with the remnants of a man who had thighs as long as your arm. He was a horrid man, I'm telling you, and there was many a fine Sunday I'd put him together for fun, and he with shiny bones, you wouldn't meet the like of these days in the cities of the world.

MAHON. [*Getting up.*] You wouldn't, is it? Lay your eyes on that skull, and tell me where and when there was another the like of it, is splintered only from the blow of a loy.

PHILLY. Glory be to God! And who hit you at all?

MAHON. [*Triumphantly.*] It was my own son hit me. Would you believe that?

JIMMY. Well, there's wonders hidden in the heart of man!

PHILLY. [*Suspiciously.*] And what way was it done?

MAHON. [*Wandering about the room.*] I'm after walking hundreds and long scores of miles, winning clean beds and the fill of my belly four times in the day, and I doing nothing but telling stories of that naked truth. [*He comes to them a little aggres-*

sively.] Give me a supeen and I'll tell you now.

[WIDOW QUIN *comes in and stands aghast behind him. He is facing* JIMMY *and* PHILLY, *who are on the left.*]

JIMMY. Ask herself beyond. She's the stuff hidden in her shawl.

WIDOW QUIN. [*Coming to* MAHON *quickly.*] You here, is it? You didn't go far at all?

MAHON. I seen the coasting steamer passing, and I got a drought upon me and a cramping leg, so I said, "The divil go along with him," and turned again. [*Looking under her shawl.*] And let you give me a supeen, for I'm destroyed travelling since Tuesday was a week.

WIDOW QUIN. [*Getting a glass, in a cajoling tone.*] Sit down then by the fire and take your ease for a space. You've a right to be destroyed indeed, with your walking, and fighting, and facing the sun. [*Giving him poteen from a stone jar she has brought in.*] There now is a drink for you, and may it be to your happiness and length of life.

MAHON. [*Taking glass greedily and sitting down by fire.*] God increase you!

WIDOW QUIN. [*Taking men to the right stealthily.*] Do you know what? That man's raving from his wound to-day, for I met him a while since telling a rambling tale of a tinker had him destroyed. Then he heard of Christy's deed, and he up and says it was his son had cracked his skull. Oh, isn't madness a fright, for he'll go killing someone yet, and he thinking it's the man has struck him so?

JIMMY. [*Entirely convinced.*] It's a fright, surely. I knew a party was kicked in the head by a red mare, and he went killing horses a great while, till he eat the insides of a clock and died after.

PHILLY. [*With suspicion.*] Did he see Christy?

WIDOW QUIN. He didn't. [*With a warning gesture.*] Let you not be putting him in mind of him, or you'll be likely summoned if there's murder done. [*Looking round at*

---

[1] The Danes invaded Ireland in the ninth century.

[2] *I.e.,* here at home. Mayo is a county of Connaught.

MAHON.] Whisht! He's listening. Wait now till you hear me taking him easy and un-ravelling all. [*She goes to* MAHON.] And what way are you feeling, mister? Are you in contentment now?

MAHON. [*Slightly emotional from his drink.*] I'm poorly only, for it's a hard story the way I'm left to-day, when it was I did tend him from his hour of birth, and he a dunce never reached his second book, the way he'd come from school, many's the day, with his legs lamed under him, and he blackened with his beatings like a tinker's ass. It's a hard story, I'm saying, the way some do have their next and nigh-est raising up a hand of murder on them, and some is lonesome getting their death and lamentation in the dead of night.

WIDOW QUIN. [*Not knowing what to say.*] To hear you talking so quiet, who'd know you were the same fellow we seen pass to-day?

MAHON. I'm the same surely. The wrack and ruin of three score years; and it's a terror to live that length, I tell you, and to have your sons going to the dogs against you, and you wore out scolding them, and skelping [3] them, and God knows what.

PHILLY. [*To* JIMMY.] He's not raving. [*To* WIDOW QUIN.] Will you ask him what kind was his son?

WIDOW QUIN. [*To* MAHON, *with a pecul-iar look.*] Was your son that hit you a lad of one year and a score maybe, a great hand at racing and lepping and licking the world?

MAHON. [*Turning on her with a roar of rage.*] Didn't you hear me say he was the fool of men, the way from this out he'll know the orphan's lot with old and young making game of him and they swearing, raging, kicking at him like a mangy cur.

[*A great burst of cheering outside, some way off.*]

MAHON. [*Putting his hands to his ears.*] What in the name of God do they want roaring below?

[3] Beating.

WIDOW QUIN. [*With the shade of a smile.*] They're cheering a young lad, the champion Playboy of the Western World.

[*More cheering.*]

MAHON. [*Going to window.*] It'd split my heart to hear them, and I with pulses in my brain-pan for a week gone by. Is it rac-ing they are?

JIMMY. [*Looking from door.*] It is then. They are mounting him for the mule race will be run upon the sands. That's the play-boy on the winkered [4] mule.

MAHON. [*Puzzled.*] That lad, is it? If you said it was a fool he was, I'd have laid a mighty oath he was the likeness of my wandering son. [*Uneasily, putting his hand to his head.*] Faith, I'm thinking I'll go walking for to view the race.

WIDOW QUIN. [*Stopping him, sharply.*] You will not. You'd best take the road to Belmullet, and not be dilly-dallying in this place where there isn't a spot you could sleep.

PHILLY. [*Coming forward.*] Don't mind her. Mount there on the bench and you'll have a view of the whole. They're hurrying before the tide will rise, and it'd be near over if you went down the pathway through the crags below.

MAHON. [*Mounts on bench,* WIDOW QUIN *beside him.*] That's a right view again the edge of the sea. They're coming now from the point. He's leading. Who is he at all?

WIDOW QUIN. He's the champion of the world, I tell you, and there isn't a hop'orth [5] isn't falling lucky to his hands today.

PHILLY. [*Looking out, interested in the race.*] Look at that. They're pressing him now.

JIMMY. He'll win it yet.

PHILLY. Take your time, Jimmy Farrell. It's too soon to say.

WIDOW QUIN. [*Shouting.*] Watch him taking the gate. There's riding.

JIMMY. [*Cheering.*] More power to the young lad!

MAHON. He's passing the third.

JIMMY. He'll lick them yet!

[4] Fitted with blinders.　　　[5] Trifle.

WIDOW QUIN. He'd lick them if he was running races with a score itself.

MAHON. Look at the mule he has, kicking the stars.

WIDOW QUIN. There was a lep! [*Catching hold of* MAHON *in her excitement.*] He's fallen! He's mounted again! Faith, he's passing them all!

JIMMY. Look at him skelping her!

PHILLY. And the mountain girls hooshing him on!

JIMMY. It's the last turn! The post's cleared for them now!

MAHON. Look at the narrow place. He'll be into the bogs! [*With a yell.*] Good rider! He's through it again!

JIMMY. He's neck and neck!

MAHON. Good boy to him! Flames, but he's in!

[*Great cheering, in which all join.*]

MAHON. [*With hesitation.*] What's that? They're raising him up. They're coming this way. [*With a roar of rage and astonishment.*] It's Christy! by the stars of God! I'd know his way of spitting and he astride the moon.

[*He jumps down and makes for the door, but* WIDOW QUIN *catches him and pulls him back.*]

WIDOW QUIN. Stay quiet, will you. That's not your son. [*To* JIMMY.] Stop him, or you'll get a month for the abetting of manslaughter and be fined as well.

JIMMY. I'll hold him.

MAHON. [*Struggling.*] Let me out! Let me out, the lot of you! till I have my vengeance on his head to-day.

WIDOW QUIN. [*Shaking him, vehemently.*] That's not your son. That's a man is going to make a marriage with the daughter of this house, a place with fine trade, with a license, and with poteen too.

MAHON. [*Amazed.*] That man marrying a decent and moneyed girl! Is it mad yous are? Is it in a crazy-house for females that I'm landed now?

WIDOW QUIN. It's mad yourself is with the blow upon your head. That lad is the wonder of the Western World.

⁶ Lobe of my ear.   ⁷ Paralytic.

MAHON. I seen it's my son.

WIDOW QUIN. You seen that you're mad. [*Cheering outside.*] Do you hear them cheering him in the zig-zags of the road? Aren't you after saying that your son's a fool, and how would they be cheering a true idiot born?

MAHON. [*Getting distressed.*] It's maybe out of reason that that man's himself. [*Cheering again.*] There's none surely will go cheering him. Oh, I'm raving with a madness that would fright the world. [*He sits down with his hand to his head.*] There was one time I seen ten scarlet divils letting on they'd cork my spirit in a gallon can; and one time I seen rats as big as badgers sucking the life blood from the butt of my lug; ⁶ but I never till this day confused that dribbling idiot with a likely man. I'm destroyed surely.

WIDOW QUIN. And who'd wonder when it's your brain-pan that is gaping now?

MAHON. Then the blight of the sacred drought upon myself and him, for I never went mad to this day, and I not three weeks with the Limerick girls drinking myself silly, and parlatic ⁷ from the dusk to dawn. [*To* WIDOW QUIN, *suddenly.*] Is my visage astray?

WIDOW QUIN. It is then. You're a sniggering maniac, a child could see.

MAHON. [*Getting up more cheerfully.*] Then I'd best be going to the Union ⁸ beyond, and there'll be a welcome before me, I tell you, [*With great pride.*] and I a terrible and fearful case, the way that there I was one time, screeching in a straitened waistcoat,⁹ with seven doctors writing out my sayings in a printed book. Would you believe that?

WIDOW QUIN. If you're a wonder itself, you'd best be hasty, for them lads caught a maniac one time and pelted the poor creature till he ran out, raving and foaming, and was drowned in the sea.

MAHON. [*With philosophy.*] It's true mankind is the divil when your head's astray. Let me out now and I'll slip down the boreen, and not see them so.

⁸ Asylum.   ⁹ Strait jacket.

WIDOW QUIN. [*Showing him out.*] That's it. Run to the right, and not a one will see. [*He runs off.*]

PHILLY. [*Wisely.*] You're at some gaming, Widow Quin; but I'll walk after him and give him his dinner and a time to rest, and I'll see then if he's raving or as sane as you.

WIDOW QUIN. [*Annoyed.*] If you go near that lad, let you be wary of your head, I'm saying. Didn't you hear him telling he was crazed at times?

PHILLY. I heard him telling a power; and I'm thinking we'll have right sport, before night will fall. [*He goes out.*]

JIMMY. Well, Philly's a conceited and foolish man. How could that madman have his senses and his brain-pan slit? I'll go after them and see him turn on Philly now.

[*He goes;* WIDOW QUIN *hides poteen behind counter. Then hubbub outside.*]

VOICES. There you are! Good jumper! Grand lepper! Darlint boy! He's the racer! Bear him on, will you!

[CHRISTY *comes in, in jockey's dress, with* PEGEEN MIKE, SARA, *and other girls, and men.*]

PEGEEN. [*To crowd.*] Go on now and don't destroy him and he drenching with sweat. Go along, I'm saying, and have your tug-of-warring till he's dried his skin.

CROWD. Here's his prizes! A bagpipes! A fiddle was played by a poet in the years gone by! A flat and three-thorned blackthorn would lick the scholars out of Dublin town!

CHRISTY. [*Taking prizes from the men.*] Thank you kindly, the lot of you. But you'd say it was little only I did this day if you'd seen me a while since striking my one single blow.

TOWN CRIER. [*Outside, ringing a bell.*] Take notice, last event of this day! Tug-of-warring on the green below! Come on, the lot of you! Great achievements for all Mayo men!

PEGEEN. Go on, and leave him for to rest and dry. Go on, I tell you, for he'll do no more.

[*She hustles crowd out;* WIDOW QUIN *following them.*]

MEN. [*Going.*] Come on, then. Good luck for the while!

PEGEEN. [*Radiantly, wiping his face with her shawl.*] Well, you're the lad, and you'll have great times from this out when you could win that wealth of prizes, and you sweating in the heat of noon!

CHRISTY. [*Looking at her with delight.*] I'll have great times if I win the crowning prize I'm seeking now, and that's your promise that you'll wed me in a fortnight, when our banns is called.

PEGEEN. [*Backing away from him.*] You've right daring to go ask me that, when all knows you'll be starting to some girl in your own townland, when your father's rotten in four months, or five.

CHRISTY. [*Indignantly.*] Starting from you, is it? [*He follows her.*] I will not, then, and when the airs is warming in four months, or five, it's then yourself and me should be pacing Neifin in the dews of night, the times sweet smells do be rising, and you'd see a little shiny new moon, maybe, sinking on the hills.

PEGEEN. [*Looking at him playfully.*] And it's that kind of a poacher's love you'd make, Christy Mahon, on the sides of Neifin, when the night is down?

CHRISTY. It's little you'll think if my love's a poacher's, or an earl's itself, when you'll feel my two hands stretched around you, and I squeezing kisses on your puckered lips, till I'd feel a kind of pity for the Lord God in all ages sitting lonesome in his golden chair.

PEGEEN. That'll be right fun, Christy Mahon, and any girl would walk her heart out before she'd meet a young man was your like for eloquence, or talk, at all.

CHRISTY. [*Encouraged.*] Let you wait, to hear me talking, till we're astray in Erris, when Good Friday's by, drinking a sup from a well, and making mighty kisses with out wetted mouths, or gaming in a gap or sunshine, with yourself stretched back unto your necklace, in the flowers of the earth.

PEGEEN. [*In a lower voice, moved by his tone.*] I'd be nice so, is it?

CHRISTY. [*With rapture.*] If the mitred bishops seen you that time, they'd be the like of the holy prophets, I'm thinking, do be straining the bars of Paradise to lay eyes on the Lady Helen of Troy, and she abroad, pacing back and forward, with a nosegay in her golden shawl.

PEGEEN. [*With real tenderness.*] And what is it I have, Christy Mahon, to make me fitting entertainment for the like of you, that has such poet's talking, and such bravery of heart?

CHRISTY. [*In a low voice.*] Isn't there the light of seven heavens in your heart alone, the way you'll be an angel's lamp to me from this out, and I abroad in the darkness, spearing salmons in the Owen, or the Carrowmore? [10]

PEGEEN. If I was your wife, I'd be along with you those nights, Christy Mahon, the way you'd see I was a great hand at coaxing bailiffs, or coining funny nick-names for the stars of night.

CHRISTY. You, is it? Taking your death in the hailstones, or in the fogs of dawn.

PEGEEN. Yourself and me would shelter easy in a narrow bush, [*With a qualm of dread.*] but we're only talking, maybe, for this would be a poor, thatched place to hold a fine lad is the like of you.

CHRISTY. [*Putting his arm around her.*] If I wasn't a good Christian, it's on my naked knees I'd be saying my prayers and paters [11] to every jackstraw you have roofing your head, and every stony pebble is paving the laneway to your door.

PEGEEN. [*Radiantly.*] If that's the truth, I'll be burning candles from this out to the miracles of God that have brought you from the south to-day, and I, with my gowns bought ready, the way that I can wed you, and not wait at all.

CHRISTY. It's miracles, and that's the truth. Me there toiling a long while, and walking a long while, not knowing at all I was drawing all times nearer to this holy day.

[10] A river and a lake of Mayo.

PEGEEN. And myself, a girl, was tempted often to go sailing the seas till I'd marry a Jew-man, with ten kegs of gold, and I not knowing at all there was the like of you drawing nearer, like the stars of God.

CHRISTY. And to think I'm long years hearing women talking that talk, to all bloody fools, and this the first time I've heard the like of your voice talking sweetly for my own delight.

PEGEEN. And to think it's me is talking sweetly, Christy Mahon, and I the fright of seven townlands for my biting tongue. Well, the heart's a wonder; and, I'm thinking, there won't be our like in Mayo, for gallant lovers, from this hour, to-day. [*Drunken singing is heard outside.*] There's my father coming from the wake, and when he's had his sleep we'll tell him, for he's peaceful then.

[*They separate.*]

MICHAEL. [*Singing outside.*]
  The jailor and the turnkey
    They quickly ran us down,
  And brought us back as prisoners
    Once more to Cavan town.

[*He comes in supported by* SHAWN.]
  There we lay bewailing
    All in a prison bound. . . .

[*He sees* CHRISTY. *Goes and shakes him drunkenly by the hand, while* PEGEEN *and* SHAWN *talk on the left.*]

MICHAEL. [*To* CHRISTY.] The blessing of God and the holy angels on your head, young fellow. I hear tell you're after winning all in the sports below; and wasn't it a shame I didn't bear you along with me to Kate Cassidy's wake, a fine, stout lad, the like of you, for you'd never see the match of it for flows of drink, the way when we sunk her bones at noonday in her narrow grave, there were five men, aye, and six men, stretched out retching speechless on the holy stones.

CHRISTY. [*Uneasily, watching* PEGEEN.] Is that the truth?

MICHAEL. It is then, and aren't you a louty schemer to go burying your poor father unbeknownst when you'd a right to

[11] Paternosters: Lord's prayer.

throw him on the crupper of a Kerry mule and drive him westwards, like holy Joseph in the days gone by, the way we could have given him a decent burial, and not have him rotting beyond, and not a Christian drinking a smart drop to the glory of his soul?

CHRISTY. [*Gruffly.*] It's well enough he's lying, for the likes of him.

MICHAEL. [*Slapping him on the back.*] Well, aren't you a hardened slayer? It'll be a poor thing for the household man where you go sniffing for a female wife; and [*Pointing to* SHAWN.] look beyond at that shy and decent Christian I have chosen for my daughter's hand, and I after getting the gilded dispensation this day for to wed them now.

CHRISTY. And you'll be wedding them this day, is it?

MICHAEL. [*Drawing himself up.*] Aye. Are you thinking, if I'm drunk itself, I'd leave my daughter living single with a little frisky rascal is the like of you?

PEGEEN. [*Breaking away from* SHAWN.] Is it the truth the dispensation's come?

MICHAEL. [*Triumphantly.*] Father Reilly's after reading it in gallous [12] Latin, and "It's come in the nick of time," says he; "so I'll wed them in a hurry, dreading that young gaffer who'd capsize the stars."

PEGEEN. [*Fiercely.*] He's missed his nick of time, for it's that lad, Christy Mahon, that I'm wedding now.

MICHAEL. [*Loudly with horror.*] You'd be making him a son to me, and he wet and crusted with his father's blood?

PEGEEN. Aye. Wouldn't it be a bitter thing for a girl to go marrying the like of Shaneen, and he a middling kind of a scarecrow, with no savagery or fine words in him at all?

MICHAEL. [*Gasping and sinking on a chair.*] Oh, aren't you a heathen daughter to go shaking the fat of my heart, and I swamped and drownded with the weight of drink? Would you have them turning on me the way that I'd be roaring to the dawn of day with the wind upon my heart? Have

you not a word to aid me, Shaneen? Are you not jealous at all?

SHAWN. [*In great misery.*] I'd be afeard to be jealous of a man did slay his da.

PEGEEN. Well, it'd be a poor thing to go marrying your like. I'm seeing there's a world of peril for an orphan girl, and isn't it a great blessing I didn't wed you, before himself came walking from the west or south?

SHAWN. It's a queer story you'd go picking a dirty tramp up from the highways of the world.

PEGEEN. [*Playfully.*] And you think you're a likely beau to go straying along with, the shiny Sundays of the opening year, when it's sooner on a bullock's liver you'd put a poor girl thinking than on the lily or the rose?

SHAWN. And have you no mind of my weight of passion, and the holy dispensation, and the drift [13] of heifers I am giving, and the golden ring?

PEGEEN. I'm thinking you're too fine for the like of me, Shawn Keogh of Killakeen, and let you go off till you'd find a radiant lady with droves of bullocks on the plains of Meath, and herself bedizened in the diamond jewelries of Pharaoh's ma. That'd be your match, Shaneen. So God save you now!

[*She retreats behind* CHRISTY.]

SHAWN. Won't you hear me telling you . . . ?

CHRISTY. [*With ferocity.*] Take yourself from this, young fellow, or I'll maybe add a murder to my deeds to-day.

MICHAEL. [*Springing up with a shriek.*] Murder is it? Is it mad yous are? Would you go making murder in this place, and it piled with poteen for our drink to-night? Go on to the fore-shore if it's fighting you want, where the rising tide will wash all traces from the memory of man.

[*Pushes* SHAWN *towards* CHRISTY.]

SHAWN. [*Shaking himself free, and getting behind* MICHAEL.] I'll not fight him, Michael James. I'd liefer live a bachelor, simmering in passions to the end of time,

---

[12] Villainous.

[13] Drove.

than face a lepping savage the like of him has descended from the Lord knows where. Strike him yourself, Michael James, or you'll lose my drift of heifers and my blue bull from Sneem.

MICHAEL. Is it me fight him, when it's father-slaying he's bred to now? [*Pushing* SHAWN.] Go on you fool and fight him now.

SHAWN. [*Coming forward a little.*] Will I strike him with my hand?

MICHAEL. Take the loy is on your western side.

SHAWN. I'd be afeard of the gallows if I struck him with that.

CHRISTY. [*Taking up the loy.*] Then I'll make you face the gallows or quit off from this.   [SHAWN *flies out of the door.*]

CHRISTY. Well, fine weather be after him, [*Going to* MICHAEL, *coaxingly.*] and I'm thinking you wouldn't wish to have that quaking blackguard in your house at all. Let you give us your blessing and hear her swear her faith to me, for I'm mounted on the springtide of the stars of luck, the way it'll be good for any to have me in the house.

PEGEEN. [*At the other side of* MICHAEL.] Bless us now, for I swear to God I'll wed him, and I'll not renege.

MICHAEL. [*Standing up in the centre, holding on to both of them.*] It's the will of God, I'm thinking, that all should win an easy or a cruel end, and it's the will of God that all should rear up lengthy families for the nurture of the earth. What's a single man, I ask you, eating a bit in one house and drinking a sup in another, and he with no place of his own, like an old braying jackass strayed upon the rocks? [*To* CHRISTY.] It's many would be in dread to bring your like into their house for to end them, maybe, with a sudden end; but I'm a decent man of Ireland, and I liefer face the grave untimely and I seeing a score of grandsons growing up little gallant swearers by the name of God, than go peopling my bedside with puny weeds the like of what you'd breed, I'm thinking, out of Shaneen Keogh. [*He joins their hands.*] A daring

fellow is the jewel of the world, and a man did split his father's middle with a single clout, should have the bravery of ten, so may God and Mary and St. Patrick bless you, and increase you from this mortal day.

CHRISTY *and* PEGEEN. Amen, O Lord!

[*Hubbub outside.* OLD MAHON *rushes in, followed by all the crowd, and* WIDOW QUIN. *He makes a rush at* CHRISTY, *knocks him down, and begins to beat him.*]

PEGEEN. [*Dragging back his arm.*] Stop that, will you? Who are you at all?

MAHON. His father, God forgive me!

PEGEEN. [*Drawing back.*] Is it rose from the dead?

MAHON. Do you think I look so easy quenched with the tap of a loy?

[*Beats* CHRISTY *again.*]

PEGEEN. [*Glaring at* CHRISTY.] And it's lies you told, letting on you had him slitted, and you nothing at all.

CHRISTY. [*Catching* MAHON'S *stick.*] He's not my father. He's a raving maniac would scare the world. [*Pointing to* WIDOW QUIN.] Herself knows it is true.

CROWD. You're fooling Pegeen! The Widow Quin seen him this day, and you likely knew! You're a liar!

CHRISTY. [*Dumfounded.*] It's himself was a liar, lying stretched out with an open head on him, letting on he was dead.

MAHON. Weren't you off racing the hills before I got my breath with the start I had seeing you turn on me at all?

PEGEEN. And to think of the coaxing glory we had given him, and he after doing nothing but hitting a soft blow and chasing northward in a sweat of fear. Quit off from this.

CHRISTY. [*Piteously.*] You've seen my doings this day, and let you save me from the old man; for why would you be in such a scorch of haste to spur me to destruction now?

PEGEEN. It's there your treachery is spurring me, till I'm hard set to think you're the one I'm after lacing in my heart-strings half-an-hour gone by. [*To* MAHON.] Take him on from this, for I think bad the world should see me raging for a Munster liar, and the fool of men.

MAHON. Rise up now to retribution, and come on with me.

CROWD. [*Jeeringly.*] There's the playboy! There's the lad thought he'd rule the roost in Mayo. Slate him now, mister.

CHRISTY. [*Getting up in shy terror.*] What is it drives you to torment me here, when I'd asked the thunders of the might of God to blast me if I ever did hurt to any saving only that one single blow.

MAHON. [*Loudly.*] If you didn't, you're a poor good-for-nothing, and isn't it by the like of you the sins of the whole world are committed?

CHRISTY. [*Raising his hands.*] In the name of the Almighty God. . . .

MAHON. Leave troubling the Lord God. Would you have him sending down droughts, and fevers, and the old hen and the cholera morbus?

CHRISTY. [*To* WIDOW QUIN.] Will you come between us and protect me now?

WIDOW QUIN. I've tried a lot, God help me, and my share is done.

CHRISTY. [*Looking round in desperation.*] And I must go back into my torment is it, or run off like a vagabond straying through the Unions [14] with the dusts of August making mudstains in the gullet of my throat, or the winds of March blowing on me till I'd take an oath I felt them making whistles of my ribs within?

SARA. Ask Pegeen to aid you. Her like does often change.

CHRISTY. I will not then, for there's torment in the splendour of her like, and she a girl any moon of midnight would take pride to meet, facing southwards on the heaths of Keel. But what did I want crawling forward to scorch my understanding at her flaming brow?

PEGEEN. [*To* MAHON, *vehemently, fearing she will break into tears.*] Take him on from this or I'll set the young lads to destroy him here.

MAHON. [*Going to him, shaking his*

14 Parish workhouses.

stick.] Come on now if you wouldn't have the company to see you skelped.

PEGEEN. [*Half laughing, through her tears.*] That's it, now the world will see him pandied,[15] and he an ugly liar was playing off the hero, and the fright of men.

CHRISTY. [*To* MAHON, *very sharply.*] Leave me go!

CROWD. That's it. Now, Christy. If them two set fighting, it will lick the world.

MAHON. [*Making a grab at* CHRISTY.] Come here to me.

CHRISTY. [*More threateningly.*] Leave me go, I'm saying.

MAHON. I will maybe, when your legs is limping, and your back is blue.

CROWD. Keep it up, the two of you. I'll back the old one. Now the playboy.

CHRISTY. [*In low and intense voice.*] Shut your yelling, for if you're after making a mighty man of me this day by the power of a lie, you're setting me now to think if it's a poor thing to be lonesome, it's worse maybe to go mixing with the fools of earth.

[MAHON *makes a movement towards him.*]

CHRISTY. [*Almost shouting.*] Keep off . . . lest I do show a blow unto the lot of you would set the guardian angels winking in the clouds above.

[*He swings round with a sudden rapid movement and picks up a loy.*]

CROWD. [*Half frightened, half amused.*] He's going mad! Mind yourselves! Run from the idiot!

CHRISTY. If I am an idiot, I'm after hearing my voice this day saying words would raise the topknot on a poet in a merchant's town. I've won your racing, your lepping, and . . .

MAHON. Shut your gullet and come on with me.

CHRISTY. I'm going, but I'll stretch you first.

[*He runs at old* MAHON *with the loy, chases him out of the door, followed by crowd and* WIDOW QUIN. *There is a great noise outside, then a yell, and*

15 Beaten.

dead silence for a moment. CHRISTY *comes in, half dazed, and goes to fire.*]

WIDOW QUIN. [*Coming in, hurriedly, and going to him.*] They're turning again you. Come on, or you'll be hanged, indeed.

CHRISTY. I'm thinking, from this out, Pegeen'll be giving me praises the same as in the hours gone by.

WIDOW QUIN. [*Impatiently.*] Come by the back-door. I'd think bad to have you stifled on the gallows tree.

CHRISTY. [*Indignantly.*] I will not, then. What good'd be my life-time, if I left Pegeen?

WIDOW QUIN. Come on, and you'll be no worse than you were last night; and you with a double murder this time to be telling to the girls.

CHRISTY. I'll not leave Pegeen Mike.

WIDOW QUIN. [*Impatiently.*] Isn't there the match of her in every parish public, from Binghamstown unto the plain of Meath? Come on, I tell you, and I'll find you finer sweethearts at each waning moon.

CHRISTY. It's Pegeen I'm seeking only, and what'd I care if you brought me a drift of chosen females, standing in their shifts itself, maybe, from this place to the Eastern World?

SARA. [*Runs in, pulling off one of her petticoats.*] They're going to hang him. [*Holding out petticoat and shawl.*] Fit these upon him, and let him run off to the east.

WIDOW QUIN. He's raving now; but we'll fit them on him, and I'll take him, in the ferry, to the Achill boat.

CHRISTY. [*Struggling feebly.*] Leave me go, will you? when I'm thinking of my luck to-day, for she will wed me surely, and I a proven hero in the end of all.

[*They try to fasten petticoat round him.*]

WIDOW QUIN. Take his left hand, and we'll pull him now. Come on, young fellow.

CHRISTY. [*Suddenly starting up.*] You'll be taking me from her? You're jealous, is it, of her wedding me? Go on from this.

[*He snatches up a stool, and threatens them with it.*]

WIDOW QUIN. [*Going.*] It's in the madhouse they should put him, not in jail, at all. We'll go by the back-door, to call the doctor, and we'll save him so.

[*She goes out, with* SARA, *through inner room. Men crowd in the doorway.* CHRISTY *sits down again by the fire.*]

MICHAEL. [*In a terrified whisper.*] Is the old lad killed surely?

PHILLY. I'm after feeling the last gasps quitting his heart.

[*They peer in at* CHRISTY.]

MICHAEL. [*With a rope.*] Look at the way he is. Twist a hangman's knot on it, and slip it over his head, while he's not minding at all.

PHILLY. Let you take it, Shaneen. You're the soberest of all that's here.

SHAWN. Is it me to go near him, and he the wickedest and worst with me? Let you take it, Pegeen Mike.

PEGEEN. Come on, so.

[*She goes forward with the others, and they drop the double hitch over his head.*]

CHRISTY. What ails you?

SHAWN. [*Triumphantly, as they pull the rope tight on his arms.*] Come on to the peelers, till they stretch you now.

CHRISTY. Me!

MICHAEL. If we took pity on you, the Lord God would, maybe, bring us ruin from the law to-day, so you'd best come easy, for hanging is an easy and speedy end.

CHRISTY. I'll not stir. [*To* PEGEEN.] And what is it you'll say to me, and I after doing it this time in the face of all?

PEGEEN. I'll say, a strange man is a marvel, with his mighty talk; but what's a squabble in your back-yard, and the blow of a loy, have taught me that there's a great gap between a gallous story and a dirty deed. [*To* MEN.] Take him on from this, or the lot of us will be likely put on trial for his deed to-day.

CHRISTY. [*With horror in his voice.*] And it's yourself will send me off, to have a horny-fingered hangman hitching his bloody slip-knots at the butt of my ear.

MEN. [*Pulling rope.*] Come on, will you?

[*He is pulled down on the floor.*]

CHRISTY. [*Twisting his legs round the table.*] Cut the rope, Pegeen, and I'll quit the lot of you, and live from this out, like the madmen of Keel, eating muck and green weeds, on the faces of the cliffs.

PEGEEN. And leave us to hang, is it, for a saucy liar, the like of you? [*To* MEN.] Take him on, out from this.

SHAWN. Pull a twist on his neck, and squeeze him so.

PHILLY. Twist yourself. Sure he cannot hurt you, if you keep your distance from his teeth alone.

SHAWN. I'm afeard of him. [*To* PEGEEN.] Lift a lighted sod, will you, and scorch his leg.

PEGEEN. [*Blowing the fire, with a bellows.*] Leave go now, young fellow, or I'll scorch your shins.

CHRISTY. You're blowing for to torture me. [*His voice rising and growing stronger.*] That's your kind, is it? Then let the lot of you be wary, for, if I've to face the gallows, I'll have a gay march down, I tell you, and shed the blood of some of you before I die.

SHAWN. [*In terror.*] Keep a good hold, Philly. Be wary, for the love of God. For I'm thinking he would liefest wreak his pains on me.

CHRISTY. [*Almost gaily.*] If I do lay my hands on you, it's the way you'll be at the fall of night, hanging as a scarecrow for the fowls of hell. Ah, you'll have a gallous jaunt I'm saying, coaching out through Limbo [16] with my father's ghost.

SHAWN. [*To* PEGEEN.] Make haste, will you? Oh, isn't he a holy terror, and isn't it true for Father Reilly, that all drink's a curse that has the lot of you so shaky and uncertain now?

CHRISTY. If I can wring a neck among you, I'll have a royal judgment looking on the trembling jury in the courts of law. And won't there be crying out in Mayo the day I'm stretched upon the rope with ladies in their silks and satins snivelling in their lacy kerchiefs, and they rhyming songs and ballads on the terror of my fate?

[*He squirms round on the floor and bites* SHAWN'S *leg.*]

SHAWN. [*Shrieking.*] My leg's bit on me. He's the like of a mad dog, I'm thinking, the way that I will surely die.

CHRISTY. [*Delighted with himself.*] You will then, the way you can shake out hell's flags of welcome for my coming in two weeks or three, for I'm thinking Satan hasn't many have killed their da in Kerry, and in Mayo too.

[OLD MAHON *comes in behind on all fours and looks on unnoticed.*]

MEN. [*To* PEGEEN.] Bring the sod, will you?

PEGEEN. [*Coming over.*] God help him so. [*Burns his leg.*]

CHRISTY. [*Kicking and screaming.*] Oh, glory be to God!

[*He kicks loose from the table, and they all drag him towards the door.*]

JIMMY. [*Seeing* OLD MAHON.] Will you look what's come in?

[*They all drop* CHRISTY *and run left.*]

CHRISTY. [*Scrambling on his knees face to face with old* MAHON.] Are you coming to be killed a third time, or what ails you now?

MAHON. For what is it they have you tied?

CHRISTY. They're taking me to the peelers to have me hanged for slaying you.

MICHAEL. [*Apologetically.*] It is the will of God that all should guard their little cabins from the treachery of law, and what would my daughter be doing if I was ruined or was hanged itself?

MAHON. [*Grimly, loosening* CHRISTY.] It's little I care if you put a bag on her back, and went picking cockles till the hour of death; but my son and myself will be going our own way, and we'll have great times from this out telling stories of the villainy of Mayo, and the fools is here. [*To* CHRISTY, *who is freed.*] Come on now.

CHRISTY. Go with you, is it? I will then, like a gallant captain with his heathen

16 The place of lost souls.

slave. Go on now and I'll see you from this day stewing my oatmeal and washing my spuds, for I'm master of all fights from now. [*Pushing* MAHON.] Go on, I'm saying.

MAHON.   Is it me?

CHRISTY.   Not a word out of you. Go on from this.

MAHON.   [*Walking out and looking back at* CHRISTY *over his shoulder*.] Glory be to God! [*With a broad smile*.] I am crazy again!   [*Goes*.]

CHRISTY.   Ten thousand blessings upon all that's here, for you've turned me a likely gaffer in the end of all, the way I'll go romancing through a romping lifetime from this hour to the dawning of the judgment day.   [*He goes out*.]

MICHAEL.   By the will of God, we'll have peace now for our drinks. Will you draw the porter, Pegeen?

SHAWN.   [*Going up to her*.] It's a miracle Father Reilly can wed us in the end of all, and we'll have none to trouble us when his vicious bite is healed.

PEGEEN.   [*Hitting him a box on the ear*.] Quit my sight. [*Putting her shawl over her head and breaking out into wild lamentations*.] Oh, my grief, I've lost him surely. I've lost the only Playboy of the Western World.

[CURTAIN.]

Naturalistic Tragedy

EVERY TRAGIC INTERPRETATION of human experience postulates a general philosophy of life. Because of this fact a distinctive type of tragedy always represents the culmination of a cultural epoch, and these basic types are no more numerous than the distinctive epochs which have molded dramatic thought. Thus far western drama has evolved four major types of tragedy. The three already considered are products respectively of the ancient world, the Renaissance, and the seventeenth century. The one remaining type is a development of roughly the last half-century. Known as naturalistic tragedy, it represents the endeavor of the modern world to express the tragic implications of its characteristic outlook on life.

In this latest endeavor to create a representative form of tragedy, however, the results to date have been none too impressive in either quantity or quality. As a matter of fact, the modern temper has proved singularly unpropitious for tragedy of any sort. The difficulty is that its prevailing realistic and scientific bias runs counter to the considerations on which tragedy is based. Realism, for example, places its emphasis on the ordinary life of average humanity. On the contrary, there is nothing ordinary about tragedy; the experiences with which it deals are exceptional and highly personal, and a genuine tragic figure, by virtue of his experience, cannot possibly be average or commonplace. Hence tragedy always amounts to a distortion of the normal which is diametrically opposed to the canons of realism. The further realistic tendency to regard human life as a casual by-product of nature and environment also has the awkward effect of reducing individual disaster to relative insignificance. As a mere incident of cosmic mechanics, individual destiny recedes to only peripheral importance. Moreover, the individual himself forfeits his capacity for both personal volition and moral responsibility. Considered, after the fashion of modern psychology, as a stream of consciousness, rippled by vagrant impulses and muddied by upheavals from the subconscious, he becomes too insubstantial and elusive for his vicissi-

tudes to be of much moment; and viewed as an impotent victim of circumstance, he is even less capable of tragic struggle or meaning. Under
conditions of this sort a realistic spectacle of life's ruthless attrition is the
breaking of a butterfly upon a wheel; for where there exists no real contest there can be no tragic struggle, and sordid misery is by no means the
same as tragic passion. While it may afford a certain pathos or horror, its
final effect is merely painful and revolting. In any case, to add to the
difficulty, the modern temper, for all its interest in stark realities, is not
particularly hospitable to the insoluble dilemmas with which tragedy is
concerned. Modern realism is essentially pragmatic and utilitarian; its
motive for exploring reality is to discover effective means of coping with
it. Since there is no utility in mere contemplation of the objectionable, its
interest in life's adversities is ultimately corrective. Viewed in this light,
an indulgence in tragedy is neither practical nor very realistic. For its
most congenial expression, therefore, modern realism prefers such con-
structive forms of drama as the problem play, the critical satire, or the
dramatic analysis of social and psychological processes.

Perhaps the most serious complication, however, arises from the
scientific cast of modern thought. The scientific attitude, with its devotion
to dispassionate objectivity, not only militates against the subjective sympathies requisite for an emotional identification with tragic experience,
but calls into question the very validity of a tragic view of life. As a
dramatic concept, tragedy is frankly humanistic; it interprets catastrophe
from the special viewpoint of humanity; and, as befits a purview scaled
to distinctive human considerations, its final concern is with moral values.
The bias of modern culture, on the other hand, has been predominantly
naturalistic; it has conceived of all existence as a natural phenomenon
to be interpreted in the impartial perspective of nature as a whole; and
its consequent concern has been with scientific truth. From the standpoint
of natural science man's place in nature is without special priority. His
sole recognizable prerogative is the functional one of learning to control an intractable existence or of adapting himself to its conditions. His
responses to this situation, his individual success or failure in dealing
with it, and his personal sentiments concerning the process, like all other
realities, are simply scientific facts. Their possible tragic aspect is an
irrelevant human distinction. Paradoxically, therefore, any tragedy which
accurately reflects the modern temper is obliged to represent an attitude
which is fundamentally incompatible with its own artistic premises.

The attempt of the modern theater to assimilate this scientific spirit
has resulted in what is known as naturalistic drama. Dramatic naturalism
is an endeavor to interpret human life according to the prescriptions of
natural science. Like science it is interested in reducing the data of
experience to general principles and inherent laws. Its aim is to penetrate the surface appearance of reality to its organic structure and process
of operation. Hence its final concern is not phenomena but the essential

nature of life and of man. As a dramatic method, naturalism possesses the virtue of combining a realistic fidelity to fact with a revelation of scientific truth which goes beyond the superficiality of mere verisimilitude. In its result, naturalistic drama becomes a presentation of human existence in terms of the mechanistic processes which seem to account for it. While this interpretation merges humanity with nature, and thus effectually strips it of its last vestige of unique significance, at the same time it also endows human experience with a compensating and peculiarly modern dramatic value. As part of a universal organism, human life is seen to be a manifestation of elemental forces working out the ineluctable laws of nature. So conceived, it assumes a new immensity of meaning. Its mechanics become one with the dynamics of all existence; its vicissitudes take on the inherent magnitude of life itself; and its issues acquire a literally vital significance. In the unfolding of this cosmic drama the human individual sustains a comparable expansion from unique to universal dimensions, being at once a stage on which it is enacted in miniature and the actor of an involuntary rôle. In the latter capacity particularly, his unequal struggle for personal survival and fulfilment takes on the proportions of Greek tragedy. Indeed, it is tantamount to the ancient tragic struggle with destiny restated in terms of modern science.

Although naturalistic drama is not necessarily tragic, the human condition which it presents is precarious enough to occasion a prevailing sobriety of treatment and to suggest, perhaps, an ultimate tragic implication. In this instance, however, the tragedy is one not of the isolated individual but of the race. Considered in human terms, it is fundamentally the fact of human existence in a universe which affords it no special dispensation; and the supreme tragic irony is the human consciousness which apprises man of this fact. Inherently, therefore, naturalistic tragedy involves two somewhat inconsistent factors: on the one hand, an acceptance of materialistic determinism as a rational and scientifically adequate explanation of human existence; and, on the other, a compassion for human egotism and irrationality sufficient to induce a tragic sense of life. The difficulty of reconciling this incongruity accounts in large measure for the fact that the modern naturalistic theater has been more a chamber of horrors than a temple of authentic tragedy. Among the more conspicuous exceptions to this fate is the work of Eugene O'Neill (1888–   ), the most distinguished American dramatist to date, and one of the giants of the modern theater. As a confirmed naturalist, O'Neill has dedicated a versatile and consistently experimental career to a resolution of the dilemmas inherent in his method. Although his work exhibits a corresponding unevenness of quality, which causes it to vacillate between an almost clinical analysis of fact and a deliberate escape into symbolistic experiment, no modern dramatist has been more assiduous in his devotion to the natural science of man, and none has incorporated in his interpretation of life a more pervasive sense of man's tragic destiny. Of his several tragedies in the naturalistic manner, *Desire Under the Elms* (1924) most completely realizes its tragic intention and illustrates the nature and possibilities of the genre. It is perhaps the most impressive naturalistic tragedy which the modern theater has produced.

Desire Under the Elms, as its stage directions indicate, is conceived as no mere replica of surface reality; it is a grim portrayal of crude lusts and elemental passions dredged from the depths of human experience. Although it uses a realistic stage setting to present a reasonable likeness of a New England farmhouse, and there is a conscientious effort to imitate the speech and mannerisms appropriate to people like the Cabots, this show of versimilitude is frankly eclectic and goes no further than is necessary to relate the subject matter to recognizable fact. Beyond this requirement the play employs realistic methods with considerable freedom, and less for the purpose of creating an illusion of outward naturalness than as a means of externalizing concretely the inner nature of its materials. Its manipulation of the farmhouse architecture is symptomatic. Just as it ignores normal reality by removing the farmhouse façade to expose the action taking place inside, it takes similar liberties with the normal façade of life in order to get at the vital mechanism housed within. Thus the picture of life which it presents is not so much a photographic reproduction of surface appearances as an X-ray exposure of anatomical structure. The immediate tensions of the Cabot household are used to reveal the congenital struggle of human nature with the forces which, operating upon and within it, make it what it is and determine its destiny. While the external shell of action roughly approximates a particular aspect of rural New England life in the mid-nineteenth century, the core of drama is a general life process which exists outside specific place or time. In a way, therefore, the true substance of the play possesses the isolated and universal validity of a laboratory demonstration. The subject is a clinical case history. The focus of interest is, not the fortunes of any individual, but the experience of a group. The real protagonist is composite: it is humanity itself, as exemplified collectively by all the characters of the play.

In presenting this case history the play endeavors to be scrupulously scientific. It treats both events and characters as natural phenomena resulting automatically from an organic life process. Individual consciousness it regards as a complex product of environmental influences and subliminal impulses which are rooted in the deepest instincts of human nature and obey the compulsions of natural law. In effect, therefore, its analysis of natural functions constitutes an inquiry into the fundamental chemistry of life—a study, as it were, of human destiny in terms of basal metabolism. In order to isolate more readily the basic elements of human behavior, uncontaminated by the inhibitions and sublimations of civilized decorum, the play chooses to deal with rudimentary characters in a relatively primitive environment. To their elucidation it marshals all the formal disciplines of modern natural and social science, with particular attention to biology and economics, and with a liberal admixture of post-Freudian psychology. Thus it presents the antagonism between Eben and his father as a consequence of harsh economic pressure combined with hereditary temperament and the sexual jealousy induced by an Oedipus complex. Old Cabot's marriage it interprets according to such diverse factors as an economic urge to possession, a biologic need for survival in offspring, a social craving for congenial companionship and understanding, a confused religious fervor compounded of camp-meeting evangelism and primitive fertility rites, and finally a simple mating instinct engendered by the advent of spring. The fate of Abbie it traces to the spiritual anarchy which ensues when her desperate bid for material security encounters economic competition, domestic and biologic frustration, and the psychological ambiguities of her dual mother-mistress relationship with Eben. Reducing these miscellaneous phenomena to their lowest common denominator, the play resolves the dynamics of human life to an operation of certain imperious urges or basic desires, generated by the most vital needs of human nature, yet often exceeding its physical capacity for fulfilment. In terms of the evidence afforded by its dramatic action the play endeavors to examine scientifically the tragic conflicts and frustrations precipitated by these elemental desires under the elms of one exemplary New England farmstead.

Such a scientific probing of the tragic evils which destroy mankind lays an inevitable stress upon the ugly, sordid, and vicious aspects of human experience. This is especially so because the naturalistic approach to the problem tends to emphasize the physical nature of man and the animal instincts which mold his desires. Since the desires which end in tragedy are destructive of human well-being, it is evident that they represent impulses beyond man's comprehension or his rational control. Hence the picture of tragic man which emerges is that of a more or less rational animal goaded to his own destruction by such blind and primal instincts as self-preservation, sex, and the pursuit of some modicum of happiness. The attempt to view such matters with scientific objectivity results in a clinical frankness which is as unsettling to conventional notions of propriety as to some tastes it is inexcusably offensive. Doubtless the matter-of-fact candor of *Desire Under the Elms* smacks more of the research laboratory, the dissecting-room, or the stud-farm than of the drawing-room or, for that matter, the public stage; nevertheless, in extenuation it must be recognized that the concern of the play is not with human ideals or illusions but with scientific truth. In a matter as vital as human tragedy it is the actual facts in the case that count; and the facts of life are singularly inconsiderate of polite decorum. Indeed, the physical facts of neither birth nor death are especially prepossessing, nor are the manifestations of disease. To a naturalist like O'Neill tragic evil is a disease of human life as virulent, and as obscene, as any other fatal malady. From this scientific point of view, a fastidious reticence toward the lust that rots the soul is as out of place and perilous as toward the cancer that consumes the flesh.

At the same time the play recognizes in human desire a range which extends from the lust of the rutting beast to the desire of the moth for the star. Something of this polarity of human nature is intimated at the very outset, as the two elder brothers come in from the fields, their feet heavy with the muck of earth but their eyes irresistibly drawn to the luminous sky. Its essence is summed up in a single word—"Purty!" The scientific mystery, as well as perhaps the ultimate tragedy, which the play perceives in human life is that from the stony soil of human nature, under the inexorable elms of a natural universe, are conceived desires which are not of nature but of the human spirit. They represent a hunger which at once sets man apart from nature and exceeds the power of nature to gratify. Out of this hunger grow the bitter loneliness of Ephraim Cabot, which can find surcease only in brute communion with the cattle, the tormented quest of Eben for a consummation he cannot define, and the terrible transfiguration of Abbie, which leads to unnatural crime. To this capacity of the natural creature for more than nature can supply the play attributes both the calamity and the sublimity of human life. As it is the source of Ephraim's tragic frustration, it also accounts for the maimed exaltation of Eben and Abbie. For, although the latter succumb to the frailty of flesh, their very defeat before the forces of nature is a triumph for the human spirit. In the fires of lust, hatred, and crime are purified a compassion for human needs and an understanding of human values which endow them with a spiritual refinement and dignity denied the others. It is the realization of this vital fact which brings Eben back to share the redemption of Abbie's guilt and which constitutes the final ironic purgation of the tragedy.

As mentioned earlier, naturalistic drama is more conspicuous for noble intention than for notable achievement. Perhaps the truth is that naturalism is dramatically impressive only as an instrument of tragedy; that its prime function is to supply a scientifically valid approach to the tragic aspects of realism; and that its final effect depends upon the quality of its tragic concept. However that may be, the dividing line between naturalistic and realistic intentions is shadowy at best, as may be seen in such a classic ambiguity as Maxim Gorky's The Lower Depths, which may be considered either realistic or naturalistic according to where one places the emphasis. Within more narrow limitations, a fair idea of naturalistic possibilities and accomplishments may be gained from the following examples: O'Neill's Beyond the Horizon and Strange Interlude, The Father by August Strindberg, The Power of Darkness by Leo Tolstoy, The Weavers by Gerhardt Hauptmann, and The Passion Flower by Jacinto Benavente.

DESIRE UNDER THE ELMS

by

EUGENE O'NEILL

Characters

EPHRAIM CABOT
SIMEON ⎫
PETER ⎬ *his sons*
EBEN ⎭
ABBIE PUTNAM

*Young Girl, Two Farmers, The Fiddler, A Sheriff,
and other folk from the neighboring farms.*

The action of the entire play takes place in, and immediately outside of, the Cabot farmhouse in New England, in the year 1850. The south end of the house faces front to a stone wall with a wooden gate at center opening on a country road. The house is in good condition but in need of paint. Its walls are a sickly grayish, the green of the shutters faded. Two enormous elms are on each side of the house. They bend their trailing branches down over the roof. They appear to protect and at the same time subdue. There is a sinister maternity in their aspect, a crushing, jealous absorption. They have developed from their intimate contact with the life of man in the house an appalling humaneness. They brood oppressively over the house. They are like exhausted women resting their sagging breasts and hands and hair on its roof, and when it rains their tears trickle down monotonously and rot on the shingles.

There is a path running from the gate around the right corner of the house to the front door. A narrow porch is on this side. The end wall facing us has two windows in its upper story, two larger ones on the floor below. The two upper are those of the father's bedroom and that of the brothers. On the left, ground floor, is the kitchen—on the right, the parlor, the shades of which are always drawn down.

Copyright, 1931, by Eugene O'Neill. Reprinted by permission of Random House, Inc.

PART ONE

SCENE ONE

Exterior of the Farmhouse. It is sunset of a day at the beginning of summer in the year 1850. There is no wind and everything is still. The sky above the roof is suffused with deep colors, the green of the elms glows, but the house is in shadow, seeming pale and washed out by contrast.

A door opens and EBEN CABOT *comes to the end of the porch and stands looking down the road to the right. He has a large bell in his hand and this he swings mechanically, awakening a deafening clangor. Then he puts his hands on his hips and stares up at the sky. He sighs with a puzzled awe and blurts out with halting appreciation.*

EBEN. God! Purty!

[His eyes fall and he stares about him frowningly. He is twenty-five, tall and sinewy. His face is well-formed, good-looking, but its expression is resentful and defensive. His defiant, dark eyes remind one of a wild animal's in captivity. Each day is a cage in which he finds himself trapped but inwardly unsubdued. There is a fierce repressed vitality about him. He has black hair, mustache, a thin curly trace of beard. He is dressed in rough farm clothes. He spits on the ground with intense disgust, turns and goes back into the house.

SIMEON *and* PETER *come in from their work in the fields. They are tall men, much older than their half-brother (*SIMEON *is thirty-nine and* PETER *thirty-seven), built on a squarer, simpler model, fleshier in body, more bovine and homelier in face, shrewder and more practical. Their shoulders stoop a bit from years of farm work. They clump heavily along in their clumsy thick-soled boots caked with earth. Their clothes, their faces, hands, bare arms and throats are earth-stained. They smell of earth. They stand together for a moment in front* of the house and, as if with the one impulse, stare dumbly up at the sky, leaning on their hoes. Their faces have a compressed, unresigned expression. As they look upward, this softens.]*

SIMEON. [*Grudgingly.*] Purty.

PETER. Ay-eh.

SIMEON. [*Suddenly.*] Eighteen year ago.

PETER. What?

SIMEON. Jenn. My woman. She died.

PETER. I'd fergot.

SIMEON. I rec'lect—now an' agin. Makes it lonesome. She'd hair long's a hoss' tail—an' yaller like gold!

PETER. Waal—she's gone. [*This with indifferent finality—then after a pause.*] They's gold in the West, Sim.

SIMEON. [*Still under the influence of sunset—vaguely.*] In the sky?

PETER. Waal—in a manner o' speakin' —thar's the promise. [*Growing excited.*] Gold in the sky—in the West—Golden Gate—Californi-a!—Goldest West!—fields o' gold!

SIMEON. [*Excited in his turn.*] Fortunes layin' just atop o' the ground waitin' t' be picked! Solomon's mines, they says!

[For a moment they continue looking up at the sky—then their eyes drop.]

PETER. [*With sardonic bitterness.*] Here —it's stones atop o' the ground—stones atop o' stones—makin' stone walls—year atop o' year—him 'n' yew 'n' me 'n' then Eben—makin' stone walls fur him to fence us in!

SIMEON. We've wuked. Give our strength. Give our years. Plowed 'em under in the ground,—[*He stamps rebelliously.*]— rottin'—makin' soil for his crops! [*A pause.*] Waal—the farm pays good for hereabouts.

PETER. If we plowed in Californi-a, they'd be lumps o' gold in the furrow!

SIMEON. Californi-a's t'other side o' earth, a'most. We got t' calc'late—

PETER. [*After a pause.*] 'Twould be hard fur me, too, to give up what we've 'arned here by our sweat.

[A pause. EBEN *sticks his head out of the dining-room window, listening.]*

491

SIMEON. Ay-eh. [*A pause.*] Mebbe—he'll die soon.

PETER. [*Doubtfully.*] Mebbe.

SIMEON. Mebbe—fur all we knows—he's dead now.

PETER. Ye'd need proof.

SIMEON. He's been gone two months—with no word.

PETER. Left us in the fields an evenin' like this. Hitched up an' druv off into the West. That's plumb onnateral. He hain't never been off this farm 'ceptin' t' the village in thirty year or more, not since he married Eben's maw. [*A pause. Shrewdly.*] I calc'late we might git him declared crazy by the court.

SIMEON. He skinned 'em too slick. He got the best o' all on 'em. They'd never b'lieve him crazy. [*A pause.*] We got t' wait—till he's under ground.

EBEN. [*With a sardonic chuckle.*] Honor thy father! [*They turn, startled, and stare at him. He grins, then scowls.*] I pray he's died. [*They stare at him. He continues matter-of-factly.*] Supper's ready.

SIMEON *and* PETER. [*Together.*] Ay-eh.

EBEN. [*Gazing up at the sky.*] Sun's downin' purty.

SIMEON *and* PETER. [*Together.*] Ay-eh. They's gold in the West.

EBEN. Ay-eh. [*Pointing.*] Yonder atop o' the hill pasture, ye mean?

SIMEON *and* PETER. [*Together.*] In Californi-a!

EBEN. Hunh? [*Stares at them indifferently for a second, then drawls.*] Waal—supper's gittin' cold.

[*He turns back into kitchen.*]

SIMEON. [*Startled—smacks his lips.*] I air hungry!

PETER. [*Sniffing.*] I smells bacon!

SIMEON. [*With hungry appreciation.*] Bacon's good!

PETER. [*In same tone.*] Bacon's bacon! [*They turn, shouldering each other, their bodies bumping and rubbing together as they hurry clumsily to their food, like two friendly oxen toward their evening meal. They disappear around the right corner of house and can be heard entering the door.*]

[CURTAIN]

SCENE TWO

The color fades from the sky. Twilight begins. The interior of the kitchen is now visible. A pine table is at center, a cook-stove in the right rear corner, four rough wooden chairs, a tallow candle on the table. In the middle of the rear wall is fastened a big advertising poster with a ship in full sail and the word "California" in big letters. Kitchen utensils hang from nails. Everything is neat and in order but the atmosphere is of a men's camp kitchen rather than that of a home.

Places for three are laid. EBEN *takes boiled potatoes and bacon from the stove and puts them on the table, also a loaf of bread and a crock of water.* SIMEON *and* PETER *shoulder in, slump down in their chairs without a word.* EBEN *joins them. The three eat in silence for a moment, the two elder as naturally unrestrained as beasts of the field,* EBEN *picking at his food without appetite, glancing at them with a tolerant dislike.*

SIMEON. [*Suddenly turns to* EBEN.] Looky here! Ye'd oughtn't t' said that, Eben.

PETER. 'Twa'n't righteous.

EBEN. What?

SIMEON. Ye prayed he'd died.

EBEN. Waal—don't yew pray it?

[*A pause.*]

PETER. He's our Paw.

EBEN. [*Violently.*] Not mine!

SIMEON. [*Dryly.*] Ye'd not let no one else say that about yer Maw! Ha! [*He gives one abrupt sardonic guffaw.* PETER *grins.*]

EBEN. [*Very pale.*] I meant—I hain't his'n—I hain't like him—he hain't me!

PETER. [*Dryly.*] Wait till ye've growed his age!

EBEN. [*Intensely.*] I'm Maw—every drop o' blood! [*A pause. They stare at him with indifferent curiosity.*]

PETER. [*Reminiscently*.] She was good t' Sim 'n' me. A good Step-maw's scurse.

SIMEON. She was good t' everyone.

EBEN. [*Greatly moved, gets to his feet and makes an awkward bow to each of them—stammering*.] I be thankful t' ye. I'm her—her heir. [*He its down in confusion*.]

PETER. [*After a pause—judicially*.] She was good even t' him.

EBEN. [*Fiercely*.] An' fur thanks he killed her!

SIMEON. [*After a pause*.] No one never kills nobody. It's allus somethin'. That's the murderer.

EBEN. Didn't he slave Maw t' death?

PETER. He's slaved himself t' death. He's slaved Sim 'n' me 'n' yew t' death— on'y none o' us hain't died—yit.

SIMEON. It's somethin'—drivin' him—t' drive us!

EBEN. [*Vengefully*.] Waal—I hold him t' jedgment! [*Then scornfully*.] Somethin'! What's somethin'?

SIMEON. Dunno.

EBEN. [*Sardonically*.] What's drivin' yew to Californi-a, mebbe? [*They look at him in surprise*.] Oh, I've heerd ye! [*Then, after a pause*.] But ye'll never go t' the gold fields!

PETER. [*Assertively*.] Mebbe!

EBEN. Whar'll ye git the money?

PETER. We kin walk. It's an a'mighty ways—Californi-a—but if yew was t' put all the steps we've walked on this farm end t' end we'd be in the moon!

EBEN. The Injuns'll skulp ye on the plains.

SIMEON. [*With grim humor*.] We'll mebbe make 'em pay a hair fur a hair!

EBEN. [*Decisively*.] But t'aint that. Ye won't never go because ye'll wait here fur yer share o' the farm, thinkin' allus he'll die soon.

SIMEON. [*After a pause*.] We've a right.

PETER. Two-thirds belongs t'us.

EBEN. [*Jumping to his feet*.] Ye've no right! She wa'n't yewr Maw! It was her farm! Didn't he steal it from her? She's dead. It's my farm.

SIMEON. [*Sardonically*.] Tell that t' Paw when he comes! I'll bet ye a dollar he'll laugh—fur once in his life. Ha! [*He laughs himself in one single mirthless bark*.]

PETER. [*Amused in turn, echoes his brother*.] Ha!

SIMEON. [*After a pause*.] What've ye got again us, Eben? Year arter year it's skulked in yer eye—somethin'.

PETER. Ay-eh.

EBEN. Ay-eh. They's somethin'. [*Suddenly exploding*.] Why didn't ye never stand between him 'n' my Maw when he was slavin' her to her grave—t' pay her back fur the kindness she done t' yew? [*There is a long pause. They stare at him in surprise*.]

SIMEON. Waal—the stock'd got t' be watered.

PETER. 'R they was woodin' t' do.

SIMEON. 'R plowin'.

PETER. 'R hayin'.

SIMEON. 'R spreadin' manure.

PETER. 'R weedin'.

SIMEON. 'R prunin'.

PETER. 'R milkin'.

EBEN. [*Breaking in harshly*.] An' makin' walls—stone atop o' stone—makin' walls till yer heart's a stone ye heft up out o' the way o' growth onto a stone wall t' wall in yer heart!

SIMEON. [*Matter-of-factly*.] We never had no time t' meddle.

PETER. [*To* EBEN.] Yew was fifteen afore yer Maw died—an' big fur yer age. Why didn't ye never do nothin'?

EBEN. [*Harshly*.] They was chores t' do, wa'n't they? [*A pause—then slowly*.] It was on'y arter she died I come to think o' it. Me cookin'—doin' her work—that made me know her, suffer her sufferin'—she'd come back t' help—come back t' bile potatoes—come back t' fry bacon—come back t' bake biscuits—come back all cramped up t' shake the fire, an' carry ashes, her eyes weepin' an' bloody with smoke an' cinders same's they used t' be. She still comes back —stands by the stove thar in the evenin'— she can't find it nateral sleepin' an' restin' in peace. She can't git used t' bein' free—even in her grave.

SIMEON. She never complained none.

EBEN. She'd got too tired. She'd got too used t' bein' too tired. That was what he done. [*With vengeful passion.*] An' sooner'r later, I'll meddle. I'll say the thin's I didn't say then t' him! I'll yell 'em at the top o' my lungs. I'll see t' it my Maw gits some rest an' sleep in her grave! [*He sits down again, relapsing into a brooding silence. They look at him with a queer indifferent curiosity.*]

PETER. [*After a pause.*] Whar in tarnation d'ye s'pose he went, Sim?

SIMEON. Dunno. He druv off in the buggy, all spick an' span, with the mare all breshed an' shiny, druv off clackin' his tongue an' wavin' his whip. I remember it right well. I was finishin' plowin', it was spring an' May an' sunset, an' gold in the West, an' he druv off into it. I yells "Whar ye goin', Paw?" an' he hauls up by the stone wall a jiffy. His old snake's eyes was glitterin' in the sun like he'd been drinkin' a jugful an' he says with a mule's grin: "Don't ye run away till I come back!"

PETER. Wonder if he knowed we was wantin' fur Californi-a?

SIMEON. Mebbe. I didn't say nothin' and he says, lookin' kinder queer an' sick: "I been hearin' the hens cluckin' an' the roosters crowin' all the durn day. I been listenin' t' the cows lowin' an' everythin' else kickin' up till I can't stand it no more. Its spring an' I'm feelin' damned," he says. "Damned like an old bare hickory tree fit on'y fur burnin'," he says. An' then I calc'late I must've looked a mite hopeful, fur he adds real spry and vicious: "But don't git no fool idee I'm dead. I've sworn t' live a hundred an' I'll do it, if on'y t' spite yer sinful greed! An' now I'm ridin' out t' learn God's message t' me in the spring, like the prophets done. An' yew git back t' yer plowin'," he says. An' he druv off singin' a hymn. I thought he was drunk—'r I'd stopped him goin'.

EBEN. [*Scornfully.*] No, ye wouldn't!

Ye're scared o' him. He's stronger—inside—than both o' ye put together!

PETER. [*Sardonically.*] An' yew—be yew Samson?

EBEN. I'm gittin' stronger. I kin feel it growin' in me—growin' an' growin'—till it'll bust out—! [*He gets up and puts on his coat and a hat. They watch him, gradually breaking into grins.* EBEN *avoids their eyes sheepishly.*] I'm goin' out fur a spell—up the road.

PETER. T' the village?

SIMEON. T' see Minnie?

EBEN. [*Defiantly.*] Ay-eh!

PETER. [*Jeeringly.*] The Scarlet Woman!

SIMEON. Lust—that's what's growin' in ye!

EBEN. Waal—she's purty!

PETER. She's been purty fur twenty year!

SIMEON. A new coat o' paint'll make a heifer out of forty.

EBEN. She hain't forty!

PETER. If she hain't, she's teeterin' on the edge.

EBEN. [*Desperately.*] What d'yew know—

PETER. All they is . . . Sim knew her—an' then me arter—

SIMEON. An' Paw kin tell yew somethin' too! He was fust!

EBEN. D'ye mean t' say he . . . ?

SIMEON. [*With a grin.*] Ay-eh! We air his heirs in everythin'!

EBEN. [*Intensely.*] That's more to it! That grows on it! It'll bust soon! [*Then violently.*] I'll go smash my fist in her face! [*He pulls open the door in rear violently.*]

SIMEON. [*With a wink at* PETER—*drawlingly.*] Mebbe—but the night's wa'm—purty—by the time ye git thar mebbe ye'll kiss her instead!

PETER. Sart'n he will!

[*They both roar with coarse laughter.* EBEN *rushes out and slams the door—then the outside front door—comes around the corner of the house and stands still by the gate, staring up at the sky.*]

SIMEON. [*Looking after him.*] Like his Paw.

PETER. Dead spit an' image!

SIMEON. Dog'll eat dog!

PETER. Ay-eh! [*Pause. With yearning.*] Mebbe a year from now we'll be in Californ-i-a.

SIMEON. Ay-eh! [*A pause. Both yawn.*] Let's git t'bed.

[*He blows out the candle. They go out door in rear.* EBEN *stretches his arms to the sky—rebelliously.*]

EBEN. Waal—thar's a star, an' somewhar's they's him, an' here's me, an' thar's Min up the road—in the same night. What if I does kiss her? She's like t'night, she's soft 'n' wa'm, her eyes kin wink like a star, her mouth's wa'm, her arms're wa'm, she smells like a wa'm plowed field, she's purty. . . . Ay-eh! By God A'mighty she's purty, an' I don't give a damn how many sins she's sinned afore mine or who she's sinned 'em with, my sin's as purty as any one on 'em!

[*He strides off down the road to the left.*]

[CURTAIN]

SCENE THREE

It is the pitch darkness just before dawn. EBEN *comes in from the left and goes around to the porch, feeling his way, chuckling bitterly and cursing half-aloud to himself.*

EBEN. The cussed old miser! [*He can be heard going in the front door. There is a pause as he goes upstairs, then a loud knock on the bedroom door of the brothers.*] Wake up!

SIMEON. [*Startledly.*] Who's thar?

EBEN. [*Pushing open the door and coming in, a lighted candle in his hand. The bedroom of the brothers is revealed. Its ceiling is the sloping roof. They can stand upright only close to the center dividing wall of the upstairs.* SIMEON *and* PETER *are in a double bed, front.* EBEN'S *cot is to the rear.* EBEN *has a mixture of silly grin and vicious scowl on his face.*] I be!

PETER. [*Angrily.*] What in hell's-fire . . . ?

EBEN. I got news fur ye! Ha! [*He gives one abrupt sardonic guffaw.*]

SIMEON. [*Angrily.*] Couldn't ye hold it 'til we'd got our sleep?

EBEN. It's nigh sunup. [*Then explosively.*] He's gone an' married agen!

SIMEON and PETER. [*Explosively.*] Paw?

EBEN. Got himself hitched to a female 'bout thirty-five—an' purty, they says . . .

SIMEON. [*Aghast.*] It's a durn lie!

PETER. Who says?

SIMEON. They been stringin' ye!

EBEN. Think I'm a dunce, do ye? The hull village says. The preacher from New Dover, he brung the news—told it t'our preacher—New Dover, that's whar the old loon got himself hitched—that's whar the woman lived—

PETER. [*No longer doubting—stunned.*] Waal . . . !

SIMEON. [*The same.*] Waal . . . !

EBEN. [*Sitting down on a bed—with vicious hatred.*] Ain't he a devil out o' hell? It's jest t' spite us—the damned old mule!

PETER. [*After a pause.*] Everythin'll go t' her now.

SIMEON. Ay-eh! [*A pause — dully.*] Waal—if it's done—

PETER. It's done us. [*Pause—then persuasively.*] They's gold in the fields o' Californ-i-a, Sim. No good a-stayin' here now.

SIMEON. Jest what I was a-thinkin'. [*Then with decision.*] S'well fust's last! Let's light out and git this mornin'.

PETER. Suits me.

EBEN. Ye must like walkin'.

SIMEON. [*Sardonically.*] If ye'd grow wings on us we'd fly thar!

EBEN. Ye'd like ridin' better—on a boat, wouldn't ye? [*Fumbles in his pocket and takes out a crumpled sheet of foolscap.*] Waal, if ye sign this ye kin ride on a boat. I've had it writ out an' ready in case ye'd ever go. It says fur three hundred dollars t' each ye agree yewr shares o' the farm is sold t' me. [*They look suspiciously at the paper. A pause.*]

SIMEON. [*Wonderingly.*] But if he's hitched agen—

PETER. An' whar'd yew git that sum o' money, anyways?

EBEN. [*Cunningly.*] I know whar it's

hid. I been waitin'—Maw told me. She knew whar it lay fur years, but she was waitin' . . . It's her'n—the money he hoarded from her farm an' hid from Maw. It's my money by rights now.

PETER. Whar's it hid?

EBEN. [Cunningly.] Whar yew won't never find it without me. Maw spied on him—'r she'd never knowed. [A pause. They look at him suspiciously, and he at them.] Waal, is it fa'r trade?

SIMEON. Dunno.

PETER. Dunno.

SIMEON. [Looking at window.] Sky's grayin'.

PETER. Ye better start the fire, Eben.

SIMEON. An' fix some vittles.

EBEN. Ay-eh. [Then with a forced jocular heartiness.] I'll git ye a good one. If ye're startin' t' hoof it t' Californi-a ye'll need somethin' that'll stick t' yer ribs. [He turns to the door, adding meaningly.] But ye kin ride on a boat if ye'll swap. [He stops at the door and pauses. They stare at him.]

SIMEON. [Suspiciously.] Whar was ye all night?

EBEN. [Defiantly.] Up t' Min's. [Then slowly.] Walkin' thar, fust I felt 's if I'd kiss her; then I got a-thinkin' o' what ye'd said o' him an' her an' I says, I'll bust her nose fur that. Then I got t' the village an' heerd the news an' I got madder'n hell an' run all the way t' Min's not knowin' what I'd do— [He pauses—then sheepishly but more defiantly.] Waal—when I seen her, I didn't hit her—nor I didn't kiss her nuther—I begun t' beller like a calf an' cuss at the same time, I was so durn mad—an' she got scared—an' I jest grabbed holt an' tuk her! [Proudly.] Yes, sirree! I tuk her. She may've been his'n—an' your'n, too—but she's mine now!

SIMEON. [Dryly.] In love, air yew?

EBEN. [With lofty scorn.] Love! I don't take no stock in sech slop!

PETER. [Winking at SIMEON.] Mebbe Eben's aimin' t' marry, too.

SIMEON. Min'd make a true faithful he'pmeet! [They snicker.]

EBEN. What do I care fur her—'ceptin'

she's round an' wa'm? The p'int is she was his'n—an' now she b'longs t' me! [He goes to the door—then turns—rebelliously.] An' Min hain't sech a bad un. They's worse'n Min in the world, I'll bet ye! Wait'll we see this cow the Old Man's hitched t'! She'll beat Min, I got a notion. [He starts to go out.]

SIMEON. [Suddenly.] Mebbe ye'll try t' make her your'n, too?

PETER. Ha! [He gives a sardonic laugh of relish at this idea.]

EBEN. [Spitting with disgust.] Her—here — sleepin' with him — stealin' my Maw's farm! I'd as soon pet a skunk 'r kiss a snake! [He goes out. The two stare after him suspiciously. A pause. They listen to his steps receding.]

PETER. He's startin' the fire.

SIMEON. I'd like t' ride t' Californi-a—but—

PETER. Min might o' put some scheme in his head.

SIMEON. Mebbe it's all a lie 'bout Paw marryin'. We'd best wait an' see the bride.

PETER. An' don't sign nothin' till we does!

SIMEON. Nor till we've tested it's good money! [Then with a grin.] But if Paw's hitched we'd be sellin' Eben somethin' we'd never git nohow!

PETER. We'll wait an' see. [Then with sudden vindictive anger.] An' till he comes, let's yew 'n' me not wuk a lick, let Eben tend to thin's if he's a mind t', let's us jest sleep an eat an' drink likker, an' let the hull damned farm go t' blazes!

SIMEON. [Excitedly.] By God, we've 'arned a rest! We'll play rich fur a change. I hain't a-going to stir outa bed till breakfast's ready.

PETER. An' on the table!

SIMEON. [After a pause—thoughtfully.] What d'ye calc'late she'll be like—our new Maw? Like Eben thinks?

PETER. More'n' likely.

SIMEON. [Vindictively.] Waal—I hope she's a she-devil that'll make him wish he was dead an' livin' in the pit o' hell fur comfort!

PETER. [*Fervently.*] Amen!

SIMEON. [*Imitating his father's voice.*] "I'm ridin' out t' learn God's message t' me in the spring like the prophets done," he says. I'll bet right then an' thar he knew plumb well he was goin' whorin', the stinkin' old hypocrite!

[CURTAIN]

SCENE FOUR

Same as Scene Two—shows the interior of the kitchen with a lighted candle on table. It is gray dawn outside. SIMEON *and* PETER *are just finishing their breakfast.* EBEN *sits before his plate of untouched food, brooding frowningly.*

PETER. [*Glancing at him rather irritably.*] Lookin' glum don't help none.

SIMEON. [*Sarcastically.*] Sorrowin' over his lust o' the flesh!

PETER. [*With a grin.*] Was she yer fust?

EBEN. [*Angrily.*] None o' yer business. [*A pause.*] I was thinkin' o' him. I got a notion he's gittin' near—I kin feel him comin' on like yew kin feel malaria chill afore it takes ye.

PETER. It's too early yet.

SAMEON. Dunno. He'd like t' catch us nappin'—jest t' have somethin' t' hoss us 'round over.

PETER. [*Mechanically gets to his feet.* SIMEON *does the same.*] Waal—lets git t' wuk.

[*They both plod mechanically toward the door before they realize. Then they stop short.*]

SIMEON. [*Grinning.*] Ye're a cussed fool, Pete—and I be wuss! Let him see we hain't wukin'! We don't give a durn!

PETER. [*As they go back to the table.*] Not a damned durn! It'll serve t' show him we're done with him.

[*They sit down again.* EBEN *stares from one to the other with surprise.*]

SIMEON. [*Grins at him.*] We're aimin' t' start bein' lilies o' the field.

PETER. Nary a toil 'r spin 'r lick o' wuk do we put in!

SIMEON. Ye're sole owner—till he comes—that's what ye wanted. Waal, ye got t' be sole hand, too.

PETER. The cows air bellerin'. Ye better hustle at the milkin'.

EBEN. [*With excited joy.*] Ye mean ye'll sign the paper?

SIMEON. [*Dryly.*] Mebbe.

PETER. Mebbe.

SIMEON. We're considerin'. [*Peremptorily.*] Ye better git t' wuk.

EBEN. [*With queer excitement.*] It's Maw's farm agen! It's my farm! Them's my cows! I'll milk my durn fingers off fur cows o' mine!

[*He goes out door in rear; they stare after him indifferently.*]

SIMEON. Like his Paw.

PETER. Dead spit 'n' image!

SIMEON. Waal—let dog eat dog!

[EBEN *comes out of front door and around the corner of the house. The sky is beginning to grow flushed with sunrise.* EBEN *stops by the gate and stares around him with glowing, possessive eyes. He takes in the whole farm with his embracing glance of desire.*]

EBEN. It's purty! It's damned purty! It's mine! [*He suddenly throws his head back boldly and glares with hard, defiant eyes at the sky.*] Mine, d'ye hear? Mine!

[*He turns and walks quickly off left, rear, toward the barn. The two brothers light their pipes.*]

SIMEON. [*Putting his muddy boots up on the table, tilting back his chair, and puffing defiantly.*] Waal—this air solid comfort—fur once.

PETER. Ay-eh. [*He follows suit. A pause. Unconsciously they both sigh.*]

SIMEON. [*Suddenly.*] He never was much o' a hand at milkin', Eben wa'n't.

PETER. [*With a snort.*] His hands air like hoofs! [*A pause.*]

SIMEON. Reach down the jug thar! Let's take a swaller. I'm feelin' kind o' low.

PETER. Good idee! [*He does so—gets two glasses—they pour out drinks of whisky.*] Here's t' the gold in Californi-a!

SIMEON. An' luck t' find it!

[*They drink—puff resolutely—sigh—take their feet down from the table.*]

PETER. Likker don't pear t' sot right.

SIMEON. We hain't used t' it this early.

[*A pause. They become very restless.*]

PETER. Gittin' close in this kitchen.

SIMEON. [*With immense relief.*] Let's git a breath o' air.

[*They arise briskly and go out rear—appear around house and stop by the gate. They stare up at the sky with a numbed appreciation.*]

PETER. Purty!

SIMEON. Ay-eh. Gold's t' the East now.

PETER. Sun's startin' with us fur the Golden West.

SIMEON. [*Staring around the farm, his compressed face tightened, unable to conceal his emotion.*] Waal—it's our last mornin'—mebbe.

PETER. [*The same.*] Ay-eh.

SIMEON. [*Stamps his foot on the earth and addresses it desperately.*] Waal—ye've thirty year o' me buried in ye—spread out over ye—blood an' bone an' sweat—rotted away—fertilizin' ye—richin' yer soul—prime manure, by God, that's what I been t' ye!

PETER. Ay-eh! An' me!

SIMEON. An' yew, Peter. [*He sighs—then spits.*] Waal—no use'n cryin' over spilt milk.

PETER. They's gold in the West—an' freedom, mebbe. We been slaves t' stone walls here.

SIMEON. [*Defiantly.*] We hain't nobody's slaves from this out—nor no thin's slaves nuther. [*A pause—restlessly.*] Speakin' o' milk, wonder how Eben's managin'?

PETER. I s'pose he's managin'.

SIMEON. Mebbe we'd ought t' help—this once.

PETER. Mebbe. The cows knows us.

SIMEON. An' likes us. They don't know him much.

PETER. An' the hosses, an' pigs, an' chickens. They don't know him much.

SIMEON. They knows us like brothers—an' likes us! [*Proudly.*] Hain't we raised 'em t' be fust-rate, number one prize stock?

PETER. We hain't—not no more.

SIMEON. [*Dully.*] I was fergittin'. [*Then resignedly.*] Waal, let's go help Eben a spell an' git waked up.

PETER. Suits me.

[*They are starting off down left, rear, for the barn when* EBEN *appears from there hurrying toward them, his face excited.*]

EBEN. [*Breathlessly.*] Waal—har they be! The old mule an' the bride! I seen 'em from the barn down below at the turnin'.

PETER. How could ye tell that far?

EBEN. Hain't I as far-sight as he's nearsight? Don't I know the mare 'n' buggy, an' two people settin' in it? Who else . . . ? An' I tell ye I kin feel 'em a-comin', too!

[*He squirms as if he had the itch.*]

PETER. [*Beginning to be angry.*] Waal—let him do his own unhitchin'!

SIMEON. [*Angry in his turn.*] Let's hustle in an' git our bundles an' be a-goin' as he's a-comin'. I don't want never t' step inside the door agen arter he's back.

[*They both start back around the corner of the house.* EBEN *follows them.*]

EBEN. [*Anxiously.*] Will ye sign it afore ye go?

PETER. Let's see the color o' the old skinflint's money an' we'll sign.

[*They disappear left. The two brothers clump upstairs to get their bundles.* EBEN *appears in the kitchen, runs to window, peers out, comes back and pulls up a strip of flooring in under stove, takes out a canvas bag and puts it on table, then sets the floorboard back in place. The two brothers appear a moment after. They carry old carpet bags.*]

EBEN. [*Puts his hand on bag guardingly.*] Have ye signed?

SIMEON. [*Shows paper in his hand.*] Ay-eh. [*Greedily.*] Be that the money?

EBEN. [*Opens bag and pours out pile of twenty-dollar gold pieces.*] Twenty-dollar pieces—thirty on 'em. Count 'em. [PETER *does so, arranging them in stacks of five, biting one or two to test them.*]

PETER. Six hundred. [*He puts them in bag and puts it inside his shirt carefully.*]

SIMEON. [*Handing paper to* EBEN.] Har ye be.

EBEN. [*After a glance, folds it carefully and hides it under his shirt—gratefully.*] Thank yew.

PETER. Thank yew fur the ride.

SIMEON. We'll send ye a lump o' gold fur Christmas.

[*A pause.* EBEN *stares at them and they at him.*]

PETER. [*Awkwardly.*] Waal — we're a-goin'.

SIMEON. Comin' out t' the yard?

EBEN. No. I'm waitin' in here a spell.

[*Another silence. The brothers edge awkwardly to door in rear—then turn and stand.*]

SIMEON. Waal—good-by.

PETER. Good-by.

EBEN. Good-by.

[*They go out. He sits down at the table, faces the stove and pulls out the paper. He looks from it to the stove. His face, lighted up by the shaft of sunlight from the window, has an expression of trance. His lips move. The two brothers come out to the gate.*]

PERER. [*Looking off toward barn.*] Thar he be—unhitchin'.

SIMEON. [*With a chuckle.*] I'll bet ye he's riled!

PETER. An' thar she be.

SIMEON. Let's wait 'n' see what our new Maw looks like.

PETER. [*With a grin.*] An' give him our partin' cuss!

SIMEON. [*Grinning.*] I feel like raisin' fun. I feel light in my head an' feet.

PETER. Me, too. I feel like laffin' till I'd split up the middle.

SIMEON. Reckon it's the likker?

PETER. No. My feet feel itchin' t' walk an' walk—an' jump high over thin's—an' . . .

SIMEON. Dance? [*A pause.*]

PETER. [*Puzzled.*] It's plumb onnateral.

SIMEON. [*A light coming over his face.*] I calc'late it's 'cause school's out. It's holiday. Fur once we're free!

PETER. [*Dazedly.*] Free?

SIMEON. The halter's broke—the harness is busted—the fence bars is down—the stone walls air crumblin' an' tumblin'! We'll be kickin' up an' tearin' away down the road!

PETER. [*Drawing a deep breath—oratorically.*] Anybody that wants this stinkin' old rock-pile of a farm kin hev it. T'ain't our'n, no sirree!

SIMEON. [*Takes the gate off its hinges and puts it under his arm.*] We harby 'bolishes shet gates, an' open gates, an' all gates, by thunder!

PETER. We'll take it with us fur luck an' let 'er sail free down some river.

SIMEON. [*As a sound of voices comes from left, rear.*] Har they comes!

[*The two brothers congeal into two stiff, grim-visaged statues.* EPHRAIM CABOT *and* ABBIE PUTNAM *come in.* CABOT *is seventy-five, tall and gaunt, with great, wiry, concentrated power, but stoop-shouldered from toil. His face is as hard as if it were hewn out of a boulder, yet there is a weakness in it, a petty pride in its own narrow strength. His eyes are small, close together, and extremely near-sighted, blinking continually in the effort to focus on objects, their stare having a straining, ingrowing quality. He is dressed in his dismal black Sunday suit.* ABBIE *is thirty-five, buxom, full of vitality. Her round face is pretty but marred by its rather gross sensuality. There is strength and obstinacy in her jaw, a hard determination in her eyes, and about her whole personality the same unsettled, untamed, desperate quality which is so apparent in* EBEN.]

CABOT. [*As they enter — a queer strangled emotion in his dry cracking voice.*] Har we be t' hum, Abbie.

ABBIE. [*With lust for the word.*] Hum! [*Her eyes gloating on the house without seeming to see the two stiff figures at the* gate.] It's purty—purty! I can't b'lieve it's r'ally mine.

CABOT. [Sharply.] Yewr'n? Mine! [He stares at her penetratingly. She stares back. He adds relentingly.] Our'n—mebbe! It was lonesome too long. I was growin' old in the spring. A hum's got t' hev a woman.

ABBIE. [Her voice taking possession.] A woman's got t' hev a hum!

CABOT. [Nodding uncertainly.] Ay-eh. [Then irritably.] Whar be they? Ain't thar nobody about—'r wukin'—'r nothin'?

ABBIE. [Sees the brothers. She returns their stare of cold appraising contempt with interest—slowly.] Thar's two men loafin' at the gate an' starin' at me like a couple o' strayed hogs.

CABOT. [Straining his eyes.] I kin see 'em—but I can't make out. . . .

SIMEON. It's Simeon.

PETER. It's Peter.

CABOT. [Exploding.] Why hain't ye wukin'?

SIMEON. [Dryly.] We're waitin' t' welcome ye hum—yew an' the bride!

CABOT. [Confusedly.] Huh? Waal—this be yer new Maw, boys.

[She stares at them and they at her.]

SIMEON. [Turns away and spits contemptuously.] I see her!

PETER. [Spits also.] An' I see her!

ABBIE. [With the conqueror's conscious superiority.] I'll go in an' look at my house. [She goes slowly around to porch.]

SIMEON. [With a snort.] Her house!

PETER. [Calls after her.] Ye'll find Eben inside. Ye better not tell him it's yewr house.

ABBIE. [Mouthing the name.] Eben. [Then quietly.] I'll tell Eben.

CABOT. [With a contemptuous sneer.] Ye needn't heed Eben. Eben's a dumb fool —like his Maw—soft an' simple!

SIMEON. [With his sardonic burst of laughter.] Ha! Eben's a chip o' yew—spit 'n' image—hard 'n' bitter's a hickory tree! Dog'll eat dog. He'll eat ye yet, old man!

CABOT. [Commandingly.] Ye git t' wuk!

SIMEON. [As ABBIE disappears in house —winks at PETER and says tauntingly.] So

that thar's our new Maw, be it? Whar in hell did ye dig her up? [He and PETER laugh.]

PETER. Ha! Ye'd better turn her in the pen with the other sows. [They laugh uproariously, slapping their thighs.]

CABOT. [So amazed at their effrontery that he stutters in confusion.] Simeon! Peter! What's come over ye? Air ye drunk?

SIMEON. We're free, old man—free o' yew an' the hull damned farm! [They grow more and more hilarious and excited.]

PETER. An' we're startin' out fur the gold fields o' Californi-a!

SIMEON. Ye kin take this place an' burn it!

PETER. An' bury it—fur all we cares!

SIMEON. We're free, old man! [He cuts a caper.]

PETER. Free! [He gives a kick in the air.]

SIMEON. [In a frenzy.] Whoop!

PETER. Whoop!

[They do an absurd Indian war dance about the old man who is petrified between rage and the fear that they are insane.]

SIMEON. We're free as Injuns! Lucky we don't skulp ye!

PETER. An' burn yer barn an' kill the stock!

SIMEON. An' rape yer new woman! Whoop! [He and PETER stop their dance, holding their sides, rocking with wild laughter.]

CABOT. [Edging away.] Lust fur gold— fur the sinful, easy gold o' Californi-a! It's made ye mad!

SIMEON. [Tauntingly.] Wouldn't ye like us to send ye back some sinful gold, ye old sinner?

PETER. They's gold besides what's in Californi-a! [He retreats back beyond the vision of the old man and takes the bag of money and flaunts it in the air above his head, laughing.]

SIMEON. And sinfuller, too!

PETER. We'll be voyagin' on the sea! Whoop! [He leaps up and down.]

SIMEON. Livin' free! Whoop! [*He leaps in turn.*]

CABOT. [*Suddenly roaring with rage.*] My cuss on ye!

SIMEON. Take our'n in trade fur it! Whoop!

CABOT. I'll hev ye both chained up in the asylum!

PETER. Ye old skinflint! Good-by!

SIMEON. Ye old blood-sucker! Good-by!

CABOT. Go afore I . . . !

PETER. Whoop! [*He picks a stone from the road.* SIMEON *does the same.*]

SIMEON. Maw'll be in the parlor.

PETER. Ay-eh! One! Two!

CABOT. [*Frightened.*] What air ye . . . ?

PETER. Three! [*They both throw, the stones hitting the parlor window with a crash of glass, tearing the shade.*]

SIMEON. Whoop!

PETER. Whoop!

CABOT. [*In a fury now, rushing toward them.*] If I kin lay hands on ye—I'll break yer bones fur ye!

[*But they beat a capering retreat before him,* SIMEON *with the gate still under his arm.* CABOT *comes back, panting with impotent rage. Their voices as they go off take up the song of the gold-seekers to the old tune of "Oh, Susannah!"*]

"I jumped aboard the Liza ship,
And traveled on the sea,
And every time I thought of home
I wished it wasn't me!
Oh! Californi-a,
That's the land fur me!
I'm off to Californi-a!
With my wash bowl on my knee."

[*In the meantime, the window of the upper bedroom on right is raised and* ABBIE *sticks her head out. She looks down at* CABOT—*with a sigh of relief.*]

ABBIE. Waal—that's the last o' them two, hain't it? [*He doesn't answer. Then in possessive tones.*] This here's a nice bedroom, Ephraim. It's a r'al nice bed. Is it my room, Ephraim?

CABOT. [*Grimly—without looking up.*] Our'n! [*She cannot control a grimace of aversion and pulls back her head slowly and shuts the window. A sudden horrible thought seems to enter* CABOT'S *head.*] They been up to somethin'! Mebbe—mebbe they've pizened the stock—'r somethin'!

[*He almost runs off down toward the barn. A moment later the kitchen door is slowly pushed open and* ABBIE *enters. For a moment she stands looking at* EBEN. *He does not notice her at first. Her eyes take him in penetratingly with a calculating appraised of his strength as against hers. But under this her desire is dimly awakened by his youth and good looks. Suddenly he becomes conscious of her presence and looks up. Their eyes meet. He leaps to his feet, glowering at her speechlessly.*]

ABBIE. [*In her most seductive tones which she uses all through this scene.*] Be you—Eben? I'm Abbie— [*She laughs.*] I mean, I'm yer new Maw.

EBEN. [*Viciously.*] No, damn ye!

ABBIE. [*As if she hadn't heard—with a queer smile.*] Yer Paw's spoke a lot o' yew. . . .

EBEN. Ha!

ABBIE. Ye mustn't mind him. He's an old man. [*A long pause. They stare at each other.*] I don't want t' pretend playin' Maw t' ye, Eben. [*Admiringly.*] Ye're too big an' too strong fur that. I want t' be frens with ye. Mebbe with me fur a fren ye'd find ye'd like livin' here better. I kin make it easy fur ye with him, mebbe. [*With a scornful sense of power.*] I calc'late I kin git him t' do most anythin' fur me.

EBEN. [*With bitter scorn.*] Ha! [*They stare again,* EBEN *obscurely moved, physically attracted to her—in forced stilted tones.*] Yew kin go t' the devil!

ABBIE. [*Calmly.*] If cussin' me does ye good, cuss all ye've a mind t'. I'm all prepared t' have ye agin me—at fust. I don't blame ye nuther. I'd feel the same at any stranger comin' t' take my Maw's place. [*He shudders. She is watching him care-*

fully.] Yew must've cared a lot fur yewr Maw, didn't ye? My Maw died afore I'd growed. I don't remember her none. [*A pause.*] But yew won't hate me long, Eben. I'm not the wust in the world—an' yew an' me've got a lot in common. I kin tell that by lookin' at ye. Waal—I've had a hard life, too—oceans o' trouble an' nuthin' but wuk fur reward. I was a orphan early an' had t' wuk fur others in other folks' hums. Then I married an' he turned out a drunken spreer an' so he had to wuk fur others an' me too agen in other folks' hums, an' the baby died, an' my husband got sick an' died too, an' I was glad sayin' now I'm free fur once, on'y I diskivered right away all I was free fur was t' wuk agen in other folks' hums, doin' other folks' wuk till I'd most give up hope o' ever doin' my own wuk in my own hum, an' then your Paw come. . . .

[CABOT *appears returning from the barn. He comes to the gate and looks down the road the brothers have gone. A faint strain of their retreating voices is heard: "Oh, Californi-a! That's the place for me." He stands glowering, his fist clenched, his face grim with rage.*]

EBEN. [*Fighting against his growing attraction and sympathy — harshly.*] An' bought yew—like a harlot! [*She is stung and flushes angrily. She has been sincerely moved by the recital of her troubles. He adds furiously.*] An' the price he's payin' ye—this farm—was my Maw's, damn ye! —an' mine now!

ABBIE. [*With a cool laugh of confidence.*] Yewr'n? We'll see 'bout that! [*Then strongly.*] Waal—what if I did need a hum? What else'd I marry an old man like him fur?

EBEN. [*Maliciously.*] I'll tell him ye said that!

ABBIE. [*Smiling.*] I'll say ye're lyin' a-purpose—an' he'll drive ye off the place!

EBEN. Ye devil!

ABBIE. [*Defying him.*] This be my farm —this be my hum—this be my kitchen—!

EBEN. [*Furiously, as if he were going to attack her.*] Shut up, damn ye!

ABBIE. [*Walks up to him—a queer coarse expression of desire in her face and body—slowly.*] An' upstairs—that be my bedroom—an' my bed! [*He stares into her eyes, terribly confused and torn. She adds softly.*] I hain't bad nor mean—'ceptin' fur an enemy—but I got t' fight fur what's due me out o' life, if I ever 'spect t' git it. [*Then putting her hand on his arm—seductively.*] Let's yew 'n' me be frens, Eben.

EBEN. [*Stupidly — as if hypnotized.*] Ay-eh. [*Then furiously flinging off her arm.*] No, ye durned old witch! I hate ye!
[*He rushes out the door.*]

ABBIE. [*Looks after him smiling satisfiedly—then half to herself, mouthing the word.*] Eben's nice. [*She looks at the table, proudly.*] I'll wash up *my* dishes now.

[EBEN *appears outside, slamming the door behind him. He comes around corner, stops on seeing his father, and stands staring at him with hate.*]

CABOT. [*Raising his arms to heaven in the fury he can no longer control.*] Lord God o' Hosts, smite the undutiful sons with Thy wust cuss!

EBEN. [*Breaking in violently.*] Yew 'n' yewr God! Allus cussin' folks—allus naggin' 'em!

CABOT. [*Oblivious to him—summoningly.*] God o' the old! God o' the lonesome!

EBEN. [*Mockingly.*] Naggin' His sheep t' sin! T' hell with yewr God!

[CABOT *turns. He and* EBEN *glower at each other.*]

CABOT. [*Harshly.*] So it's yew. I might've knowed it. [*Shaking his finger threateningly at him.*] Blasphemin' fool! [*Then quickly.*] Why hain't ye t' wuk?

EBEN. Why hain't yew? They've went. I can't wuk it all alone.

CABOT. [*Contemptuously.*] Nor noways! I'm wuth ten o' ye yit, old's I be! Ye'll never be more'n half a man! [*Then, matter-of-factly.*] Waal—let's git t' the barn.

[*They go. A last faint note of the "Californi-a" song is heard from the distance.* ABBIE *is washing her dishes.*]

[CURTAIN]

PART TWO

SCENE ONE

The exterior of the farmhouse, as in Part One—a hot Sunday afternoon two months later. ABBIE, *dressed in her best, is discovered sitting in a rocker at the end of the porch. She rocks listlessly, enervated by the heat, staring in front of her with bored, half-closed eyes.*

EBEN *sticks his head out of his bedroom window. He looks around furtively and tries to see—or hear—if anyone is on the porch, but although he has been careful to make no noise,* ABBIE *has sensed his movement. She stops rocking, her face grows animated and eager, she waits attentively.* EBEN *seems to feel her presence, he scowls back his thoughts of her and spits with exaggerated disdain—then withdraws back into the room.* ABBIE *waits, holding her breath as she listens with passionate eagerness for every sound within the house.*

EBEN *comes out. Their eyes meet. His falter, he is confused, he turns away and slams the door resentfully. At this gesture,* ABBIE *laughs tantalizingly, amused but at the same time piqued and irritated. He scowls, strides off the porch to the path and starts to walk past her to the road with a grand swagger of ignoring her existence. He is dressed in his store suit, spruced up, his face shines from soap and water.* ABBIE *leans forward on her chair, her eyes hard and angry now, and, as he passes her, gives a sneering, taunting chuckle.*

EBEN. [*Stung—turns on her furiously.*] What air yew cacklin' 'bout?

ABBIE. [*Triumphant.*] Yew!

EBEN. What about me?

ABBIE. Ye look all slicked up like a prize bull.

EBEN. [*With a sneer.*] Waal—ye hain't so durned purty yerself, be ye?

[*They stare into each other's eyes, his held by hers in spite of himself, hers glowingly possessive. Their physical attraction becomes a palpable force quivering in the hot air.*]

ABBIE. [*Softly.*] Ye don't mean that, Eben. Ye may think ye mean it, mebbe, but ye don't. Ye can't. It's agin nature, Eben. Ye been fightin' yer nature ever since the day I come—tryin' t' tell yerself I hain't purty t' ye. [*She laughs a low humid laugh without taking her eyes from his. A pause—her body squirms desirously—she murmurs languorously.*] Hain't the sun strong an' hot? Ye kin feel it burnin' into the earth—Nature—makin' thin's grow—bigger 'n' bigger—burnin' inside ye—makin' ye want t' grow—into somethin' else—till ye're jined with it—an' it's your'n—but it owns ye, too—an' makes ye grow bigger—like a tree—like them elums— [*She laughs again softly, holding his eyes. He takes a step toward her, compelled against his will.*] Nature'll beat ye, Eben. Ye might's well own up t' it fust 's last.

EBEN. [*Trying to break from her spell—confusedly.*] If Paw'd hear ye goin' on. . . . [*Resentfully.*] But ye've made such a damned idjit out o' the old devil . . . ! [ABBIE *laughs.*]

ABBIE. Waal—haint' it easier fur yew with him changed softer?

EBEN. [*Defiantly.*] No, I'm fightin' him—fightin' yew—fightin' fur Maw's rights t' her hum! [*This breaks her spell for him. He glowers at her.*] An' I'm onto ye. Ye hain't foolin' me a mite. Ye're aimin' t' swaller up everythin' an' make it your'n. Waal, you'll find I'm a heap sight bigger hunk nor yew kin chew! [*He turns from her with a sneer.*]

ABBIE. [*Trying to regain her ascendancy—seductively.*] Eben!

EBEN. Leave me be! [*He starts to walk away.*]

ABBIE. [*More commandingly.*] Eben!

EBEN. [*Stops—resentfully.*] What d'ye want?

ABBIE. [*Trying to conceal a growing excitement.*] Whar air ye goin'?

EBEN. [*With malicious nonchalance.*] Oh—up the road a spell.

ABBIE. T' the village?

EBEN. [*Airily.*] Mebbe.

ABBIE. [*Excitedly.*] T' see that Min, I s'pose?

EBEN. Mebbe.

ABBIE. [*Weakly.*] What d'ye want t' waste time on her fur?

EBEN. [*Revenging himself now—grinning at her.*] Ye can't beat Nature, didn't ye say? [*He laughs and again starts to walk away.*]

ABBIE. [*Bursting out.*] An ugly old hake!

EBEN. [*With a tantalizing sneer.*] She's purtier'n yew be!

ABBIE. That every wuthless drunk in the country has . . .

EBEN. [*Tauntingly.*] Mebbe—but she's better'n yew. She owns up fa'r 'n' squar' t' her doin's.

ABBIE. [*Furiously.*] Don't ye dare compare . . .

EBEN. She don't go sneakin' an' stealin' what's mine.

ABBIE. [*Savagely seizing on his weak point.*] Your'n? Yew mean—my farm?

EBEN. I mean the farm yew sold yerself fur like any other old whore—my farm!

ABBIE. [*Stung—fiercely.*] Ye'll never live t' see the day when even a stinkin' weed on it 'll belong t' ye! [*Then in a scream.*] Git out o' my sight! Go on t' yer slut—disgracin' yer Paw 'n' me! I'll git yer Paw t' horsewhip ye off the place if I want t'! Ye're only livin' here 'cause I tolerate ye! Git along! I hate the sight o' ye! [*She stops, panting and glaring at him.*]

EBEN. [*Returning her glance in kind.*] An' I hate the sight o' yew.

[*He turns and strides off up the road. She follows his retreating figure with concentrated hate. Old* CABOT *appears coming up from the barn. The hard, grim expression of his face has changed. He seems in some queer way softened, mellowed. His eyes have taken on a strange, incongruous dreamy quality. Yet there is no hint of physical weakness about him—rather* he looks more robust and younger. ABBIE *sees him and turns away quickly with unconcealed aversion. He comes slowly up to her.*]

CABOT. [*Mildly.*] War yew an' Eben quarrelin' agen?

ABBIE. [*Shortly.*] No.

CABOT. Ye was talkin' a'mighty loud. [*He sits down on the edge of porch.*]

ABBIE. [*Snappishly.*] If ye heerd us they hain't no need askin' questions.

CABOT. I didn't hear what ye said.

ABBIE. [*Relieved.*] Waal — it wa'n't nothin' t' speak on.

CABOT. [*After a pause.*] Eben's queer.

ABBIE. [*Bitterly.*] He's the dead spit 'n' image o' yew!

CABOT. [*Queerly interested.*] D'ye think so, Abbie? [*After a pause, ruminatingly.*] Me 'n' Eben's allus fit 'n' fit. I never could b'ar him noways. He's so thunderin' soft—like his Maw.

ABBIE. [*Scornfully.*] Ay-eh! 'Bout as soft as yew be!

CABOT. [*As if he hadn't heard.*] Mebbe I been too hard on him.

ABBIE. [*Jeeringly.*] Waal—ye're gittin' soft now—soft as slop! That's what Eben was sayin'.

CABOT. [*His face instantly grim and ominous.*] Eben was sayin'? Waal, he'd best not do nothin' t' try me 'r he'll soon diskiver. . . . [*A pause. She keeps her face turned away. His gradually softens. He stares up at the sky.*] Purty, hain't it?

ABBIE. [*Crossly.*] I don't see nothin' purty.

CABOT. The sky. Feels like a wa'm field up thar.

ABBIE. [*Sarcastically.*] Air yew aimin' t' buy up over the farm too? [*She snickers contemptuously.*]

CABOT. [*Strangely.*] I'd like t' own my place up thar. [*A pause.*] I'm gittin' old, Abbie. I'm gittin' ripe on the bough. [*A pause. She stares at him mystified. He goes on.*] It's allus lonesome cold in the house —even when it's bilin' hot outside. Hain't yew noticed?

ABBIE. No.

CABOT. It's wa'm down t' the barn—nice smellin' an' warm—with the cows. [*A pause.*] Cows is queer.

ABBIE. Like yew?

CABOT. Like Eben. [*A pause.*] I'm gittin' t' feel resigned t' Eben—jest as I got t' feel 'bout his Maw. I'm gittin' t' learn to b'ar his softness—jest like her'n. I calc'late I c'd a'most take t' him—if he wa'n't sech a dumb fool! [*A pause.*] I s'pose it's old age a-creepin' in my bones.

ABBIE. [*Indifferently.*] Waal—ye hain't dead yet.

CABOT. [*Roused.*] No, I hain't, yew bet —not by a hell of a sight—I'm sound 'n' tough as hickory! [*Then moodily.*] But arter three score and ten the Lord warns ye t' prepare. [*A pause.*] That's why Eben's come in my head. Now that his cussed sinful brothers is gone their path t' hell, they's no one left but Eben.

ABBIE. [*Resentfuly.*] They's me, hain't they? [*Agitatedly.*] What's all this sudden likin' ye've tuk to Eben? Why don't ye say nothing' 'bout me? Hain't I yer lawful wife?

CABOT. [*Simply.*] Ay-eh. Ye be. [*A pause—he stares at her desirously—his eyes grow avid—then with a sudden movement he seizes her hands and squeezes them, declaiming in a queer camp meeting preacher's tempo.*] Yew air my Rose o' Sharon! Behold, yew air fair; yer eyes air doves; yer lips air like scarlet; yer two breasts air like two fawns; yer navel be like a round goblet; yer belly be like a heap o' wheat. . . . [*He covers her hand with kisses. She does not seem to notice. She stares before her with hard angry eyes.*]

ABBIE. [*Jerking her hands away—harshly.*] So ye're plannin' t' leave the farm t' Eben, air ye?

CABOT. [*Dazedly.*] Leave . . . ? [*Then with resentful obstinacy.*] I hain't a-givin' it t' no one!

ABBIE. [*Remorselessly.*] Ye can't take it with ye.

CABOT. [*Thinks a moment—then reluctantly.*] No, I calc'late not. [*After a pause —with a strange passion.*] But if I could, I would, by the Etarnal! 'R if I could, in my

dyin' hour, I'd set it afire an' watch it burn —this house an' every ear o' corn an' every tree down t' the last blade o' hay! I'd sit an' know it was all a-dying with me an' no one else'd ever own what was mine, what I'd made out o' nothin' with my own sweat 'n' blood! [*A pause—then he adds with a queer affection.*] 'Ceptin' the cows. Them I'd turn free.

ABBIE. [*Harshly.*] An' me?

CABOT. [*With a queer smile.*] Ye'd be turned free, too.

ABBIE. [*Furiously.*] So that's the thanks I git fur marryin' ye—t' have ye change kind to Eben who hates ye an' talk o' turnin' me out in the road.

CABOT. [*Hastily.*] Abbie! Ye know i wa'n't . . .

ABBIE. [*Vengefully.*] Just let me tell ye a thing or two 'bout Eben! Whar's he gone? T' see that harlot, Min! I tried fur t' stop him. Disgracin' yew an' me—on the Sabbath, too!

CABOT. [*Rather guiltily.*] He's a sinner —nateral-born. It's lust eatin' his heart.

ABBIE. [*Enraged beyond endurance—wildly vindictive.*] An' his lust fur me! Kin ye find excuses fur that?

CABOT. [*Stares at her—after a dead pause.*] Lust—fur yew?

ABBIE. [*Defiantly.*] He was tryin' t' make love t' me—when ye heerd us quarrelin'.

CABOT. [*Stares at her—then a terrible expression of rage comes over his face—he springs to his feet shaking all over.*] By the A'mighty God—I'll end him!

ABBIE. [*Frightened now for* EBEN.] No! Don't ye!

CABOT. [*Violently.*] I'll git the shotgun an' blow his soft brains t' the top o' them elums!

ABBIE. [*Throwing her arms around him.*] No, Ephraim!

CABOT. [*Pushing her away violently.*] I will, by God!

ABBIE. [*In a quieting tone.*] Listen, Ephraim. 'Twa'n't nothin' bad—on'y a boy's foolin'—'twa'n't meant serious--jest jokin' an' teasin'. . . .

CABOT. Then why did ye say—lust?

ABBIE. It must hev sounded wusser'n I meant. An' I was mad at thinkin'—ye'd leave him the farm.

CABOT. [*Quieter but still grim and cruel.*] Waal then, I'll horsewhip him off the place if that much'll content ye.

ABBIE. [*Reaching out and taking his hand.*] No. Don't think o' me! Ye mustn't drive him off. 'Tain't sensible. Who'll ye get to help ye on the farm? They's no one hereabouts.

CABOT. [*Considers this—then nodding his appreciation.*] Ye got a head on ye. [*Then irritably.*] Waal, let him stay. [*He sits down on the edge of the porch. She sits beside him. He murmurs contemptuously.*] I oughtn't t' git riled so—at that 'ere fool calf. [*A pause.*] But har's the p'int. What son o' mine'll keep on here t' the farm—when the Lord does call me? Simeon an' Peter air gone t' hell—an' Eben's follerin' 'em.

ABBIE. They's me.

CABOT. Ye're on'y a woman.

ABBIE. I'm yewr wife.

CABOT. That hain't me. A son is me—my blood—mine. Mine ought t' git mine. An' then it's still mine—even though I be six foot under. D'ye see?

ABBIE. [*Giving him a look of hatred.*] Ay-eh. I see. [*She becomes very thoughtful, her face growing shrewd, her eyes studying* CABOT *craftily.*]

CABOT. I'm gittin' old—ripe on the bough. [*Then with a sudden forced reassurance.*] Not but what I hain't a hard nut t' crack even yet—an' fur many a year t' come! By the Eternal, I kin break most o' the young fellers' backs at any kind o' work any day o' the year!

ABBIE. [*Suddenly.*] Mebbe the Lord'll give *us* a son.

CABOT. [*Turns and stares at her eagerly.*] Ye mean—a son—t' me 'n' yew?

ABBIE. [*With a cajoling smile.*] Ye're a strong man yet, hain't ye? 'Tain't noways impossible, be it? We know that. Why d'ye stare so? Hain't ye never thought o' that

afore? I been thinkin' o' it all along. Ay-eh—an' I been prayin' it'd happen, too.

CABOT. [*His face growing full of joyous pride and a sort of religious ecstasy.*] Ye been prayin', Abbie?—fur a son?—t' us?

ABBIE. Ay-eh. [*With a grim resolution.*] I want a son now.

CABOT. [*Excitedly clutching both of her hands in his.*] It'd be the blessin' o' God, Abbie—the blessin' o' God A'mighty on me—in my old age—in my lonesomeness! They hain't nothin' I wouldn't do fur ye then, Abbie. Ye'd hev on'y t' ask it—anythin' ye'd a mind t'!

ABBIE. [*Interrupting.*] Would ye will the farm t' me then—t' me an' it . . . ?

CABOT. [*Vehemently.*] I'd do anythin' ye axed, I tell ye! I swar it! May I be everlastin' damned t' hell if I wouldn't! [*He sinks to his knees pulling her down with him. He trembles all over with the fervor of his hopes.*] Pray t' the Lord agen, Abbie. It's the Sabbath! I'll jine ye! Two prayers air better nor one. "An' God hearkened unto Rachel"! An' God hearkened unto Abbie! Pray, Abbie! Pray fur him to hearken!

[*He bows his head, mumbling. She pretends to do likewise but gives him a side glance of scorn and triumph.*]

[CURTAIN]

SCENE TWO

About eight in the evening. The interior of the two bedrooms on the top floor is shown. EBEN *is sitting on the side of his bed in the room on the left. On account of the heat he has taken off everything but his undershirt and pants. His feet are bare. He faces front, brooding moodily, his chin propped on his hands, a desperate expression on his face.*

In the other room CABOT *and* ABBIE *are sitting side by side on the edge of their bed, an old four-poster with feather mattress. He is in his night shirt, she in her nightdress. He is still in the queer, excited mood into which the notion of a son has thrown him. Both rooms are lighted dimly and flickeringly by tallow candles.*

CABOT. The farm needs a son.

ABBIE. I need a son.

CABOT. Ay-eh. Sometimes ye air the farm an' sometimes the farm be yew. That's why I clove t' ye in my lonesomeness. [*A pause. He pounds his knee with his fist.*] Me an' the farm has got t' beget a son!

ABBIE. Ye'd best go t' sleep. Ye're gittin' thin's all mixed.

CABOT. [*With an impatient gesture.*] No, I hain't. My mind's clear's a well. Ye don't know me, that's it. [*He stares hopelessly at the floor.*]

ABBIE. [*Indifferently.*] Mebbe.

[*In the next room* EBEN *gets up and paces up and down distractedly.* ABBIE *hears him. Her eyes fasten on the intervening wall with concentrated attention.* EBEN *stops and stares. Their hot glances seem to meet through the wall. Unconsciously he stretches out his arms for her and she half rises. Then aware, he mutters a curse at himself and flings himself face downward on the bed, his clenched fists above his head, his face buried in the pillow.* ABBIE *relaxes with a faint sigh but her eyes remain fixed on the wall; she listens with all her attention for some movement from* EBEN.]

CABOT. [*Suddenly raises his head and looks at her—scornfully.*] Will ye ever know me—'r will any man 'r woman? [*Shaking his head.*] No. I calc'late 't wa'n't t' be. [*He turns away.* ABBIE *looks at the wall. Then, evidently unable to keep silent about his thoughts, without looking at his wife, he puts out his hand and clutches her knee. She starts violently, looks at him, sees he is not watching her, concentrates again on the wall and pays no attention to what he says.*] Listen, Abbie. When I come here fifty odd year ago—I was jest twenty an' the strongest an' hardest ye ever seen—ten times as strong an' fifty times as hard as Eben. Waal—this place was nothin' but fields o' stones. Folks laughed when I tuk it. They couldn't know what I knowed. When ye kin make corn sprout out o' stones, God's livin' in yew! They wa'n't strong enuf fur that! They reckoned God was easy. They laughed. They don't laugh no more. Some died hereabouts. Some went West an' died. They're all under ground—fur follerin' arter an easy God. God hain't easy. [*He shakes his head slowly.*] An' I growed hard. Folks kept allus sayin' he's a hard man like 'twas sinful t' be hard, so's at last I said back at 'em: Waal then, by thunder, ye'll git me hard an' see how ye like it! [*Then suddenly.*] But I give in t' weakness once. 'Twas arter I'd been here two year. I got weak—despairful—they was so many stones. They was a party leavin', givin' up, goin' West. I jined 'em. We tracked on 'n on. We come t' broad medders, plains, whar the soil was black an' rich as gold. Nary a stone. Easy. Ye'd on'y to plow an' sow an' then set an' smoke yer pipe an' watch thin's grow. I could o' been a rich man—but somethin' in me fit me an' fit me —the voice of God sayin': "This hain't wuth nothin' t' Me. Git ye back t' hum!" I got afeerd o' that voice an' I lit out back t' hum here, leavin' my claim an' crops t' whoever'd a mind t' take em. Ay-eh. I actoolly give up what was rightful mine! God's hard, not easy! God's in the stones! Build my church on a rock—out o' stones an' I'll be in them! That's what He meant t' Peter. [*He sighs heavily—a pause.*] Stones. I picked 'em up an' piled 'em into walls. Ye kin read the years o' my life in them walls, every day a hefted stone, climbin' over the hills up and down, fencin' in the fields that was mine, whar I'd made thin's grow out o' nothin'—like the will o' God, like the servant o' His hand. It wa'n't easy. It was hard an' He made me hard fur it. [*He pauses.*] All the time I kept gittin' lonesomer. I tuk a wife. She bore Simeon an' Peter. She was a good woman. She wuked hard. We was married twenty year. She never knowed me. She helped but she never knowed what she was helpin'. I was allus lonesome. She died. After that it wa'n't so lonesome fur a spell. [*A pause.*] I lost count o' the years. I had no time t' fool away countin' 'em. Sim an' Peter helped. The farm growed. It was all mine! When I thought o' that I didn't feel lonesome. [*A pause.*] But ye can't hitch yer mind t' one thin' day an' night. I tuk another wife—Eben's Maw. Her folks was contestin' me at law over my deeds t' the farm—my farm! That's why Eben keeps a-talkin' his fool talk o' this bein' his Maw's farm. She bore Eben. She was purty—but soft. She tried t' be hard. She couldn't. She never knowed me nor nothin'. It was lonesomer 'n hell with her. After a matter o' sixteen odd years, she died. [*A pause.*] I lived with the boys. They hated me 'cause I was hard. I hated them 'cause they was soft. They coveted the farm without knowin' what it meant. It made me bitter 'n wormwood. It aged me—them coveting what I'd made fur mine. Then this spring the call come—the voice o' God cryin' in my wilderness, in my lonesomeness—t' go out an' seek an' find! [*Turning to her with strange passion.*] I sought ye an' I found ye! Yew air my Rose o' Sharon! Yer eyes air like. . . . [*She has turned a blank face, resentful eyes to his. He stares at her for a moment—then harshly.*] Air ye any the wiser fur all I've told ye?

ABBIE. [*Confusedly.*] Mebbe.

CABOT. [*Pushing her away from him—angrily.*] Ye don't know nothin'—nor never will. If ye don't hev a son t' redeem ye. . . . [*This in a tone of cold threat.*]

ABBIE. [*Resentfully.*] I've prayed, hain't I?

CABOT. [*Bitterly.*] Pray agen—fur understandin'!

ABBIE. [*A veiled threat in her tone.*] Ye'll have a son out o' me, I promise ye.

CABOT. How kin ye promise?

ABBIE. I got second-sight mebbe. I kin foretell. [*She gives a queer smile.*]

CABOT. I believe ye have. Ye give me the chills sometimes. [*He shivers.*] It's cold in this house. It's oneasy. They's thin's pokin' about in the dark—in the corners.

[*He pulls on his trousers, tucking in his night shirt, and pulls on his boots.*]

ABBIE. [*Surprised.*] Whar air ye goin'?

CABOT. [*Queerly.*] Down whar it's restful—whar it's warm—down t' the barn. [*Bitterly.*] I kin talk t' the cows. They know. They know the farm an' me. They'll give me peace. [*He turns to go out the door.*]

ABBIE. [*A bit frightenedly.*] Air ye ailin' tonight, Ephraim?

CABOT. Growin'. Growin' ripe on the bough. [*He turns and goes, his boots clumping down the stairs.* EBEN *sits up with a start, listening.* ABBIE *is conscious of his movement and stares at the wall.* CABOT *comes out of the house around the corner and stands by the gate, blinking at the sky. He stretches up his hands in a tortured gesture.*] God A'mighty, call from the dark!

[*He listens as if expecting an answer. Then his arms drop, he shakes his head and plods off toward the barn.* EBEN *and* ABBIE *stare at each other through the wall.* EBEN *sighs heavily and* ABBIE *echoes it. Both become terribly nervous, uneasy. Finally* ABBIE *gets up and listens, her ear to the wall. He acts as if he saw every move she was making, he becomes resolutely still. She seems driven into a decision —goes out the door in rear determinedly. His eyes follow her. Then as the door of his room is opened softly, he turns away, waits in an attitude of strained fixity.* ABBIE *stands for a second staring at him, her eyes burning with desire. Then with a little cry she runs over and throws her arms about his neck, she pulls his head back and covers his mouth with kisses. At first, he submits dumbly; then he puts his arms about her neck and returns her kisses, but finally, suddenly aware of his hatred, he hurls her away from him, springing to his feet. They stand speechless and breathless, panting like two animals.*]

ABBIE. [*At last—painfully.*] Ye shouldn't, Eben—ye shouldn't—I'd make ye happy!

EBEN. [*Harshly.*] I don't want t' be happy—from yew!

ABBIE. [*Helplessly.*] Ye do, Eben! Ye do! Why d'ye lie?

EBEN. [*Viciously.*] I don't take t'ye, I tell ye! I hate the sight o' ye!

ABBIE. [*With an uncertain troubled laugh.*] Waal, I kissed ye anyways—an' ye kissed back—yer lips was burnin'—ye can't lie 'bout that! [*Intensely.*] If ye don't care, why did ye kiss me back—why was yer lips burnin'?

EBEN. [*Wiping his mouth.*] It was like pizen on 'em. [*Then tauntingly.*] When I kissed ye back, mebbe I thought 'twas someone else.

ABBIE. [*Wildly.*] Min?

EBEN. Mebbe.

ABBIE. [*Torturedly.*] Did ye go t' see her? Did you r'ally go? I thought ye mightn't. Is that why ye throwed me off jest now?

EBEN. [*Sneeringly.*] What if it be?

ABBIE. [*Raging.*] Then ye're a dog, Eben Cabot!

EBEN. [*Threateningly.*] Ye can't talk that way t' me!

ABBIE. [*With a shrill laugh.*] Can't I? Did ye think I was in love with ye—a weak thin' like yew? Not much! I on'y wanted ye fur a purpose o' my own—an' I'll hev ye fur it yet 'cause I'm stronger'n yew be!

EBEN. [*Resentfully.*] I knowed well it was on'y part o' yer plan t' swaller every-thin'!

ABBIE. [*Tauntingly.*] Mebbe!

EBEN. [*Furious.*] Git out o' my room!

ABBIE. This air my room an' ye're on'y hired help!

EBEN. [*Threateningly.*] Git out afore I murder ye!

ABBIE. [*Quite confident now.*] I hain't a mite afeerd. Ye want me, don't ye? Yes, ye do! An' yer Paw's son'll never kill what he wants! Look at yer eyes! They's lust fur me in 'em, burnin' 'em up! Look at yer lips now! They're tremblin' an' longin' t' kiss me, an' yer teeth t' bite! [*He is watching her now with a horrible fascination. She laughs a crazy triumphant laugh.*] I'm

a-goin' t' make all o' this hum my hum! They's one room hain't mine yet, but it's a-goin' t' be tonight. I'm a-goin' down now an' light up! [*She makes him a mocking bow.*] Won't ye come courtin' me in the best parlor, Mister Cabot?

EBEN. [*Staring at her—horribly con-fused—dully.*] Don't ye dare! It hain't been opened since Maw died an' was laid out thar! Don't ye . . . ! [*But her eyes are fixed on his so burningly that his will seems to wither before hers. He stands swaying toward her helplessly.*]

ABBIE. [*Holding his eyes and putting all her will into her words as she backs out the door.*] I'll expect ye afore long, Eben.

EBEN. [*Stares after her for a while, walking toward the door. A light appears in the parlor window. He murmurs.*] In the parlor? [*This seems to arouse connotations, for he comes back and puts on his white shirt, collar, half ties the tie mechanically, puts on coat, takes his hat, stands bare-footed looking about him in bewilderment, mutters wonderingly.*] Maw! Whar air yew? [*Then goes slowly toward the door in rear.*]

[CURTAIN]

SCENE THREE

A few minutes later. The interior of the parlor is shown. A grim, repressed room like a tomb in which the family has been interred alive. ABBIE *sits on the edge of the horsehair sofa. She has lighted all the can-dles and the room is revealed in all its pre-served ugliness. A change has come over the woman. She looks awed and frightened now, ready to run away.*

The door is opened and EBEN *appears. His face wears an expression of obsessed confusion. He stands staring at her, his arms hanging disjointedly from his shoul-ders, his feet bare, his hat in his hand.*

ABBIE. [*After a pause—with a nervous, formal politeness.*] Won't ye set?

EBEN. [*Dully.*] Ay-eh.

[*Mechanically he places his hat carefully on the floor near the door and sits stiffly beside her on the edge of the sofa. A pause. They both remain rigid, looking straight ahead with eyes full of fear.*]

ABBIE. When I fust come in—in the dark—they seemed somethin' here.

EBEN. [*Simply.*] Maw.

ABBIE. I kin still feel—somethin'. . . .

EBEN. It's Maw.

ABBIE. At fust I was feered o' it. I wanted t' yell an' run. Now—since yew come—seems like it's growin' soft an' kind t' me. [*Addressing the air—queerly.*] Thank yew.

EBEN. Maw allus loved me.

ABBIE. Mebbe it knows I love yew, too. Mebbe that makes it kind t' me.

EBEN. [*Dully.*] I dunno. I should think she'd hate ye.

ABBIE. [*With certainty.*] No. I kin feel it don't—not no more.

EBEN. Hate ye fur stealin' her place—here in her hum—settin' in her parlor whar she was laid—

[*He suddenly stops, staring stupidly before him.*]

ABBIE. What is it, Eben?

EBEN. [*In a whisper.*] Seems like Maw didn't want me t' remind ye.

ABBIE. [*Excitedly.*] I knowed, Eben! It's kind t' me! It don't b'ar me no grudges fur what I never knowed an' couldn't help!

EBEN. Maw b'ars him a grudge.

ABBIE. Waal, so does all o' us.

EBEN. Ay-eh. [*With passion.*] I does, by God!

ABBIE. [*Taking one of his hands in hers and patting it*] Thar! Don't git riled thinkin o' him. Think o' yer Maw who's kind t' us. Tell me about yer Maw, Eben.

EBEN. They hain't nothin' much. She was kind. She was good.

ABBIE. [*Putting one arm over his shoulder. He does not seem to notice—passionately.*] I'll be kind an' good t' ye!

EBEN. Sometimes she used t' sing fur me.

ABBIE. I'll sing fur ye!

EBEN. This was her hum. This was her farm.

ABBIE. This is my hum! This is my farm!

EBEN. He married her t' steal 'em. She was soft an' easy. He couldn't 'preciate her.

ABBIE. He can't 'preciate me!

EBEN. He murdered her with his hardness.

ABBIE. He's murderin' me!

EBEN. She died. [*A pause.*] Sometimes she used to sing fur me.

[*He bursts into a fit of sobbing.*]

ABBIE. [*Both her arms around him—with wild passion.*] I'll sing fur ye! I'll die fur ye! [*In spite of her overwhelming desire for him, there is a sincere maternal love in her manner and voice—a horribly frank mixture of lust and mother love.*] Don't cry, Eben! I'll take yer Maw's place! I'll be everythin' she was t' ye! Let me kiss ye, Eben! [*She pulls his head around. He makes a bewildered pretense of resistance. She is tender.*] Don't be afeered! I'll kiss ye pure, Eben—same 's if I was a Maw t' ye—an' ye kin kiss me back 's if yew was my son—my boy—sayin' good-night t' me! Kiss me, Eben.

[*They kiss in restrained fashion. Then suddenly wild passion overcomes her. She kisses lustfully again and again and he flings his arms about her and returns her kisses. Suddenly, as in the bedroom, he frees himself from her violently and springs to his feet. He is trembling all over, in a strange state of terror.* ABBIE *strains her arms toward him with fierce pleading.*]

Don't ye leave me, Eben! Can't ye see it hain't enuf—lovin' ye like a Maw—can't ye see it's got t' be that an' more—much more—a hundred times more—fur me t' be happy—fur yew t' be happy?

EBEN. [*To the presence he feels in the room.*] Maw! Maw! What d'ye want? What air ye tellin' me?

ABBIE. She's tellin' ye t' love me. She knows I love ye an' I'll be good t' ye. Can't ye feel it? Don't ye know? She's tellin' ye t' love me, Eben!

EBEN. Ay-eh. I feel—mebbe she—but

—I can't figger out—why—when ye've stole her place—here in her hum—in the parlor whar she was—

ABBIE. [*Fiercely.*] She knows I love ye!

EBEN. [*His face suddenly lighting up with a fierce, triumphant grin.*] I see it! I sees why. It's her vengeance on him—so's she kin rest quiet in her grave!

ABBIE. [*Wildly.*] Vengeance o' God on the hull o' us! What d'we give a durn? I love ye, Eben! God knows I love ye!

[*She stretches out her arms for him.*]

EBEN. [*Throws himself on his knees beside the sofa and grabs her in his arms—releasing all his pent-up passion.*] An' I love yew, Abbie!—now I kin say it! I been dyin' fur want o' ye—every hour since ye come! I love ye!

[*Their lips meet in a fierce, bruising kiss.*]

[CURTAIN]

SCENE FOUR

Exterior of the farmhouse. It is just dawn. The front door at right is opened and EBEN *comes out and walks around to the gate. He is dressed in his working clothes. He seems changed. His face wears a bold and confident expression, he is grinning to himself with evident satisfaction. As he gets near the gate, the window of the parlor is heard opening and the shutters are flung back and* ABBIE *sticks her head out. Her hair tumbles over her shoulders in disarray, her face is flushed, she looks at* EBEN *with tender, languorous eyes and calls softly.*

ABBIE. Eben. [*As he turns—playfully.*] Jest one more kiss afore ye go. I'm goin' to miss ye fearful all day.

EBEN. An' me yew, ye kin bet! [*He goes to her. They kiss several times. He draws away, laughing.*] Thar. That's enuf, hain't it? Ye won't hev none left fur next time.

ABBIE. I got a million o' 'em left fur yew! [*Then a bit anxiously.*] D'ye r'ally love me, Eben?

EBEN. [*Emphatically.*] I like ye better'n any gal I ever knowed! That's gospel!

ABBIE. Likin' hain't lovin'.

EBEN. Waal then—I love ye. Now air yew satisfied?

ABBIE. Ay-eh, I be.

[*She smiles at him adoringly.*]

EBEN. I better git t' the barn. The old critter's liable t' suspicion an' come sneakin' up.

ABBIE. [*With a confident laugh.*] Let him! I kin allus pull the wool over his eyes. I'm goin' t' leave the shutters open and let in the sun 'n' air. This room's been dead long enuf. Now it's goin' t' be my room!

EBEN. [*Frowning.*] Ay-eh.

ABBIE. [*Hastily.*] I meant—our room.

EBEN. Ay-eh.

ABBIE. We made it our'n last night, didn't we? We give it life—our lovin' did.

[*A pause.*]

EBEN. [*With a strange look.*] Maw's gone back t' her grave. She kin sleep now.

ABBIE. May she rest in peace! [*Then tenderly rebuking.*] Ye oughtn't t' talk o' sad thin's—this mornin'.

EBEN. It jest come up in my mind o' itself.

ABBIE. Don't let it. [*He doesn't answer. She yawns.*] Waal, I'm a-goin' t' steal a wink o' sleep. I'll tell the Old Man I hain't feelin' pert. Let him git his own vittles.

EBEN. I see him comin' from the barn. Ye better look smart an' git upstairs.

ABBIE. Ay-eh. Good-by. Don't ferget me.

[*She throws him a kiss. He grins—then squares his shoulders and awaits his father confidently.* CABOT *walks slowly up from the left, staring up at the sky with a vague face.*]

EBEN. [*Jovially.*] Mornin', Paw. Stargazin' in daylight?

CABOT. Purty, hain't it?

EBEN. [*Looking around him possessively.*] It's a durned purty farm.

CABOT. I mean the sky.

EBEN. [*Grinning.*] How d'ye know? Them eyes o' your'n can't see that fur. [*This tickles his humor and he slaps his* thigh and laughs.] Ho-ho! That's a good un!

CABOT. [Grimly sarcastic.] Ye're feelin' right chipper, hain't ye? Whar'd ye steal the likker?

EBEN. [Good-naturedly.] 'Tain't likker. Jest life. [Suddenly holding out his hand—soberly.] Yew 'n' me is quits. Let's shake hands.

CABOT. [Suspiciously.] What's come over ye?

EBEN. Then don't. Mebbe it's jest as well. [A moment's pause.] What's come over me? [Queerly.] Didn't ye feel her passin'—goin' back t' her grave?

CABOT. [Dully.] Who?

EBEN. Maw. She kin rest now an' sleep content. She's quits with ye.

CABOT. [Confusedly.] I rested. I slept

good—down with the cows. They know how t' sleep. They're teachin' me.

EBEN. [Suddenly jovial again.] Good fur the cows! Waal—ye better git t' work.

CABOT. [Grimly amused.] Air yew bossin' me, ye calf?

EBEN. [Beginning to laugh.] Ay-eh! I'm bossin' yew! Ha-ha-ha! See how ye like it! Ha-ha-ha! I'm the prize rooster o' this roost. Ha-ha-ha!

[He goes off toward the barn laughing.]

CABOT. [Looks after him with scornful pity.] Soft-headed. Like his Maw. Dead spit 'n' image. No hope in him! [He spits with contemptuous disgust.] A born fool! [Then matter-of-factly.] Waal—I'm gittin' peckish.

[He goes toward door.]

[CURTAIN]

PART THREE

SCENE ONE

A night in late spring the following year. The kitchen and the two bedrooms upstairs are shown. The two bedrooms are dimly lighted by a tallow candle in each. EBEN is sitting on the side of the bed in his room, his chin propped on his fists, his face a study of the struggle he is making to understand his conflicting emotions. The noisy laughter and music from below where a kitchen dance is in progress annoy and distract him. He scowls at the floor.

In the next room a cradle stands beside the double bed.

In the kitchen all is festivity. The stove has been taken down to give more room to the dancers. The chairs, with wooden benches added, have been pushed back against the walls. On these are seated squeezed in tight against one another, farmers and their wives and their young folks of both sexes from the neighboring farms. They are all chattering and laughing loudly. They evidently have some secret joke in common. There is no end of winking, of nudging, of meaning nods of the head toward CABOT who, in a state of extreme

hilarious excitement increased by the amount he has drunk, is standing near the rear door where there is a small keg of whisky and serving drinks to all the men. In the left corner, front, dividing the attention with her husband, ABBIE is sitting in a rocking chair, a shawl wrapped about her shoulders. She is very pale, her face is thin and drawn, her eyes are fixed anxiously on the open door in rear as if waiting for someone.

The musician is tuning up his fiddle, seated in the far right corner. He is a lanky young fellow with a long, weak face. His pale eyes blink incessantly and he grins about him slyly with a greedy malice.

ABBIE. [Suddenly turning to a young girl on her right.] Whar's Eben?

YOUNG GIRL. [Eying her scornfully.] I dunno, Mrs. Cabot. I hain't seen Eben in ages. [Meaningly.] Seems like he's spent most o' his time t' hum since yew come.

ABBIE. [Vaguely.] I tuk his Maw's place.

YOUNG GIRL. Ay-eh. So I've heerd.

[She turns away to retail this bit of gossip to her mother sitting next to her. ABBIE turns to her left to a big stout-

ish middle-aged man whose flushed face and starting eyes show the amount of "likker" he has consumed.]

ABBIE. Ye hain't seen Eben, hev ye?

MAN. No, I hain't. [*Then he adds with a wink.*] If yew hain't, who would?

ABBIE. He's the best dancer in the county. He'd ought t' come an' dance.

MAN. [*With a wink.*] Mebbe he's doin' the dutiful an' walkin' the kid t' sleep. It's a boy, hain't it?

ABBIE. [*Nodding vaguely.*] Ay-eh—born two weeks back—purty's a picter.

MAN. They all is—t' their Maws. [*Then in a whisper, with a nudge and a leer.*] Listen, Abbie—if ye ever git tired o' Eben, remember me! Don't fergit now! [*He looks at her uncomprehending face for a second —then grunts disgustedly.*] Waal—guess I'll likker agin.

[*He goes over and joins* CABOT, *who is arguing noisily with an old farmer over cows. They all drink.*]

ABBIE. [*This time appealing to nobody in particular.*] Wonder what Eben's a-doin'?

[*Her remark is repeated down the line with many a guffaw and titter until it reaches the fiddler. He fastens his blinking eyes on* ABBIE.]

FIDDLER. [*Raising his voice.*] Bet I kin tell ye, Abbie, what Eben's doin'! He's down t' the church offerin' up prayers o' thanksgivin'.

[*They all titter expectantly.*]

A MAN. What fur? [*Another titter.*]

FIDDLER. 'Cause unto him a—[*He hesitates just long enough.*] brother is born!

[*A roar of laughter. They all look from* ABBIE *to* CABOT. *She is oblivious, staring at the door.* CABOT, *although he hasn't heard the words, is irritated by the laughter and steps forward, glaring about him. There is an immediate silence.*]

CABOT. What're ye all bleatin' about— like a flock o' goats? Why don't ye dance, damn ye? I axed ye here t' dance—t' eat, drink an' be merry—an' thar ye set cacklin' like a lot o' wet hens with the pip! Ye've swilled my likker an' guzzled my vittles like

hogs, hain't ye? Then dance fur me, can't ye? That's fa'r an' squar', hain't it?

[*A grumble of resentment goes around but they are all evidently in too much awe of him to express it openly.*]

FIDDLER. [*Slyly.*] We're waitin' fur Eben.
[*A suppressed laugh.*]

CABOT. [*With a fierce exultation.*] T' hell with Eben! Eben's done fur now! I got a new son! [*His mood switching with drunken suddenness.*] But ye needn't t' laugh at Eben, none o' ye! He's my blood, if he be a dumb fool. He's better nor any o' yew! He kin do a day's work a'most up t' what I kin—an' that'd put any o' yew pore critters t' shame!

FIDDLER. An' he kin do a good night's work, too! [*A roar of laughter.*]

CABOT. Laugh, ye damn fools! Ye're right jist the same, Fiddler. He kin work day an' night too, like I kin, if need be!

OLD FARMER. [*From behind the keg where he is weaving drunkenly back and forth—with great simplicity.*] They hain't many t' touch ye, Ephraim—a son at seventy-six. That's a hard man fur ye! I be on'y sixty-eight an' I couldn't do it.

[*A roar of laughter in which* CABOT *joins uproariously.*]

CABOT. [*Slapping him on the back.*] I'm sorry fur ye, Hi. I'd never suspicion sech weakness from a boy like yew!

OLD FARMER. An' I never reckoned yew had it in ye nuther, Ephraim.
[*There is another laugh.*]

CABOT. [*Suddenly grim.*] I got a lot in me—a hell of a lot—folks don't know on. [*Turning to the fiddler.*] Fiddle 'er up, durn ye! Give 'em somethin' t' dance t'! What air ye, an ornament? Hain't this a celebration? Then grease yer elbow an' go it!

FIDDLER. [*Seizes a drink which the* OLD FARMER *holds out to him and downs it.*] Here goes!

[*He starts to fiddle "Lady of the Lake." Four young fellows and four girls form in two lines and dance a square dance. The* FIDDLER *shouts directions for the different movements, keeping his words in the rhythm of the music* and interspersing them with jocular personal remarks to the dancers themselves. The people seated along the walls stamp their feet and clap their hands in unison. CABOT is especially active in this respect. Only ABBIE remains apathetic, staring at the door as if she were alone in a silent room.]

FIDDLER. Swing your partner t' the right! That's it, Jim! Give her a b'ar hug! Her Maw hain't lookin'. [Laughter.] Change partners! That suits ye, don' it, Essie, now ye got Reub afore ye? Look at her redden up, will ye? Waal, life is short an' so's love, as the feller says. [Laughter.]

CABOT. [Excitedly, stamping his foot.] Go it, boys! Go it, gals!

FIDDLER. [With a wink at the others.] Ye're the spryest seventy-six ever I sees, Ephraim! Now if ye'd on'y good eyesight . . . ! [Suppressed laughter. He gives CABOT no chance to retort but roars.] Promenade! Ye're walkin' like a bride down the aisle, Sarah! Waal, while they's life they's allus hope, I've heerd tell. Swing your partner to the left! Gosh A'mighty, look at Johnny Cook high-steppin'! They hain't goin' t' be much strength left fur hoein' in the corn lot t'morrow. [Laughter.]

CABOT. Go it! Go it! [Then suddenly, unable to restrain himself any longer, he prances into the midst of the dancers, scattering them, waving his arms about wildly.] Ye're all hoofs! Git out o' my road! Give me room! I'll show ye dancin'. Ye're all too soft!

[He pushes them roughly away. They crowd back toward the walls, muttering, looking at him resentfully.]

FIDDLER. [Jeeringly.] Go it, Ephraim! Go it!

[He starts "Pop, Goes the Weasel," increasing the tempo with every verse until at the end he is fiddling crazily as fast as he can go.]

CABOT. [Starts to dance, which he does very well and with tremendous vigor. Then he begins to improvise, cuts incredibly grotesque capers, leaping up and cracking his heels together, prancing around in a circle with body bent in an Indian war dance, then suddenly straightening up and kicking as high as he can with both legs. He is like a monkey on a string. And all the while he intersperses his antics with shouts and derisive comments.] Whoop! Here's dancin' fur ye! Whoop! See that! Seventy-six, if I'm a day! Hard as iron yet! Beatin' the young 'uns like I allus done! Look at me! I'd invite ye t' dance on my hundredth birthday on'y ye'll all be dead by then. Ye're a sickly generation! Yer hearts air pink, not red! Yer veins is full o' mud an' water! I be the on'y man in the county! Whoop! See that! I'm a Injun! I've killed Injuns in the West afore ye was born—an skulped 'em too! They's a arrer wound on my backside I c'd show ye! The hull tribe chased me. I outrun 'em all—with the arrer stuck in me! An' I tuk vengeance on 'em. Ten eyes fur an eye, that was my motter! Whoop! Look at me! I kin kick the ceilin' off the room! Whoop!

FIDDLER. [Stops playing—exhaustedly.] God A'mighty, I got enuf. Ye got the devil's strength in ye.

CABOT. [Delightedly.] Did I beat yew, too? Wa'al, ye played smart. Hev a swig. [He pours whisky for himself and FIDDLER. They drink. The others watch CABOT silently with cold, hostile eyes. There is a dead pause. The FIDDLER rests. CABOT leans against the keg, panting, glaring around him confusedly. In the room above, EBEN gets to his feet and tiptoes out of the door in rear, appearing a moment later in the other bedroom. He moves silently, even frightenedly, toward the cradle and stands there looking down at the baby. His face is as vague as his reactions are confused, but there is a trace of tenderness, of interested discovery. At the same moment that he reaches the cradle, ABBIE seems to sense something. She gets up weakly and goes to CABOT.]

ABBIE. I'm goin' up t' the baby.

CABOT. [With real solicitation.] Are ye

able fur the stairs? D'ye want me t' help ye, Abbie?

ABBIE. No. I'm able. I'll be down agen soon.

CABOT. Don't ye git wore out! He needs ye, remember—our son does!

[*He grins affectionately, patting her on the back. She shrinks from his touch.*]

ABBIE. [*Dully.*] Don't—tech me. I'm goin'—up.

[*She goes. CABOT looks after her. A whisper goes around the room. CABOT turns. It ceases. He wipes his forehead streaming with sweat. He is breathing pantingly.*]

CABOT. I'm a-goin' out t' git fresh air. I'm feelin' a mite dizzy. Fiddle up thar! Dance, all o' ye! Here's likker fur them as wants it. Enjoy yerselves. I'll be back.

[*He goes, closing the door behind him.*]

FIDDLER. [*Sarcastically.*] Don't hurry on our account! [*A suppressed laugh. He imitates ABBIE.*] Whar's Eben?

[*More laughter.*]

A WOMAN. [*Loudly.*] What's happened in this house is plain as the nose on yer face!

[ABBIE *appears in the doorway upstairs and stands looking in surprise and adoration at* EBEN *who does not see her.*]

A MAN. Ssshh! He's li'ble t' be listenin' at the door. That'd be like him.

[*Their voices die to an intensive whispering. Their faces are concentrated on this gossip. A noise as of dead leaves in the wind comes from the room. CABOT has come out from the porch and stands by the gate, leaning on it, staring at the sky blinkingly. ABBIE comes across the room silently. EBEN does not notice her until quite near.*]

EBEN. [*Starting.*] Abbie!

ABBIE. Ssshh! [*She throws her arms around him. They kiss—then bend over the cradle together.*] Ain't he purty?—dead spit 'n' image o' yew!

EBEN. [*Pleased.*] Air he? I can't tell none.

ABBIE. E-zactly like!

EBEN. [*Frowningly.*] I don't like this. I don't like lettin' on what's mine's his'n. I been doin' that all my life. I'm gittin' t' the end o' b'arin' it!

ABBIE. [*Putting her finger on his lips.*] We're doin' the best we kin. We got t' wait. Somethin's bound t' happen. [*She puts her arms around him.*] I got t' go back.

EBEN. I'm goin' out. I can't b'ar it with the fiddle playin' an' the laughin'.

ABBIE. Don't git feelin' low. I love ye, Eben. Kiss me.

[*He kisses her. They remain in each other's arms.*]

CABOT. [*At the gate, confusedly.*] Even the music can't drive it out—somethin'. Ye kin feel it droppin' off the elums, climbin' up the roof, sneakin' down the chimney, pokin' in the corners! They's no peace in houses, they's no rest livin' with folks. Somethin's always livin' with ye. [*With a deep sigh.*] I'll go t' the barn an' rest a spell. [*He goes wearily toward the barn.*]

FIDDLER. [*Tuning up.*] Let's celebrate the old skunk gittin' fooled! We kin have some fun now he's went.

[*He starts to fiddle "Turkey in the Straw." There is real merriment now. The young folks get up to dance.*]

[CURTAIN]

SCENE TWO

*A half hour later—Exterior—*EBEN *is standing by the gate looking up at the sky, an expression of dumb pain bewildered by itself on his face.* CABOT *appears, returning from the barn, walking wearily, his eyes on the ground. He sees* EBEN *and his whole mood immediately changes. He becomes excited, a cruel, triumphant grin comes to his lips, he strides up and slaps* EBEN *on the back. From within comes the whining of the fiddle and the noise of stamping feet and laughing voices.*

CABOT. So har ye be!

EBEN. [*Startled, stares at him with hatred for a moment—then dully.*] Ay-eh.

CABOT. [*Surveying him jeeringly.*] Why

hain't ye been in t' dance? They was all axin' fur ye.

EBEN. Let 'em ax!

CABOT. They's a hull passel o' purty gals.

EBEN. T' hell with 'em!

CABOT. Ye'd ought t' be marryin' one o' 'em soon.

EBEN. I hain't marryin' no one.

CABOT. Ye might 'arn a share o' a farm that way.

EBEN. [With a sneer.] Like yew did, ye mean? I hain't that kind.

CABOT. [Stung.] Ye lie! 'Twas yer Maw's folks aimed t' steal my farm from me.

EBEN. Other folks don't say so. [After a pause—defiantly.] An' I got a farm, anyways!

CABOT. [Derisively.] Whar?

EBEN. [Stamps a foot on the ground.] Har!

CABOT. [Throws his head back and laughs coarsely.] Ho-ho! Ye hev, hev ye? Waal, that's a good un!

EBEN. [Controlling himself—grimly.] Ye'll see!

CABOT. [Stares at him suspiciously, trying to make him out—a pause—then with scornful confidence.] Ay-eh. I'll see. So'll ye. It's ye that's blind—blind as a mole underground. [EBEN suddenly laughs, one short sardonic bark: "Ha." A pause. CABOT peers at him with renewed suspicion.] Whar air ye hawin' 'bout? [EBEN turns away without answering. CABOT grows angry.] God A'mighty, yew air a dumb dunce! They's nothin' in that thick skull o' your'n but noise—like a empty keg it be! [EBEN doesn't seem to hear. CABOT'S rage grows.] Yewr farm! God A'mighty! If ye wa'n't a born donkey ye'd know ye'll never own stick nor stone on it, specially now arter him bein' born. It's his'n, I tell ye—his'n arter I die—but I'll live a hundred jest t' fool ye all—an' he'll be growed then —yewr age a'most! [EBEN laughs again his sardonic "Ha." This drives CABOT into a fury.] Ha? Ye think ye kin git 'round that someways, do ye? Waal, it'll be her'n, too —Abbie's—ye won't git 'round her—she knows yer tricks—she'll be too much fur

ye—she wants the farm her'n—she was afeerd o' ye—she told me ye was sneakin' 'round tryin' t' make love t' her t' git her on yer side . . . ye . . . ye mad fool, ye! [He raises his clenched fists threateningly.]

EBEN. [Is confronting him, choking with rage.] Ye lie, ye old skunk! Abbie never said no sech thing!

CABOT. [Suddenly triumphant when he sees how shaken EBEN is.] She did. An' I says, I'll blow his brains t' the top o' them elums—an' she says, no, that hain't sense, who'll ye git t'help ye on the farm in his place—an' then she says yew'n me ought t' have a son—I know we kin, she says— an' I says, if we do, ye kin have anythin' I've got ye've a mind t'. An' she says, I wants Eben cut off so's this farm'll be mine when ye die! [With terrible gloating.] An' that's what's happened, hain't it? An' the farm's her'n! An' the dust o' the road— that's your'n! Ha! Now who's hawin'?

EBEN. [Has been listening, petrified with grief and rage—suddenly laughs wildly and brokenly.] Ha-ha-ha! So that's her sneakin' game—all along!—like I suspicioned at fust —t' swaller it all—an' me, too . . . ! [Madly.] I'll murder her!

[He springs toward the porch but CABOT is quicker and gets in between.]

CABOT. No, ye don't!

EBEN. Git out o' my road!

[He tries to throw CABOT aside. They grapple in what becomes immediately a murderous struggle. The old man's concentrated strength is too much for EBEN. CABOT gets one hand on his throat and presses him back across the stone wall. At the same moment, ABBIE comes out on the porch. With a stifled cry she runs toward them.]

ABBIE. Eben! Ephraim! [She tugs at the hand on EBEN's throat.] Let go, Ephraim! Ye're chokin' him!

CABOT. [Removes his hand and flings EBEN sideways full length on the grass, gasping and choking. With a cry, ABBIE kneels beside him, trying to take his head on her lap, but he pushes her away. CABOT

stands looking down with fierce triumph.]
'Ye needn't t've fret, Abbie, I wa'n't aimin'
t' kill him. He hain't wuth hangin' fur—not
by a hell of a sight! [*More and more triumphantly.*] Seventy-six an' him not thirty
yit—an' look whar he be fur thinkin' his
Paw was easy! No, by God, I hain't easy!
An' him upstairs, I'll raise him t' be like
me! [*He turns to leave them.*] I'm goin' in
an' dance!—sing an' celebrate! [*He walks
to the porch—then turns with a great grin.*]
I don't calc'late it's left in him, but if he
gets pesky, Abbie, ye jest sing out. I'll come
a-runnin' an', by the Etarnal, I'll put him
across my knee an' birch him! Ha-ha-ha!

[*He goes into the house laughing. A moment later his loud "whoop" is heard.*]

ABBIE. [*Tenderly.*] Eben. Air ye hurt?

[*She tries to kiss him but he pushes her
violently away and struggles to a sitting position*]

EBEN. [*Gaspingly.*] T'hell—with ye!

ABBIE. [*Not believing her ears.*] It's me,
Eben—Abbie—don't ye know me?

EBEN. [*Glowering at her with hatred.*]
Ay-eh—I know ye—now!

[*He suddenly breaks down, sobbing
weakly.*]

ABBIE. [*Fearfully.*] Eben—what's happened t' ye—why did ye look at me 's if
ye hated me?

EBEN. [*Violently, between sobs and
gasps.*] I do hate ye! Ye're a whore—a
damn trickin' whore!

ABBIE. [*Shrinking back horrified.*] Eben!
Ye don't know what ye're sayin'!

EBEN. [*Scrambling to his feet and following her—accusingly.*] Ye're nothin' but a
stinkin' passel o' lies! Ye've been lyin' t' me
every word ye spoke, day an' night, since
we fust—done it. Ye've kept sayin' ye
loved me. . . .

ABBIE. [*Frantically.*] I do love ye!

[*She takes his hand but he flings hers
away.*]

EBEN. [*Unheeding.*] Ye've made a fool o'
me—a sick, dumb fool—a-purpose! Ye've
been on'y playin' yer sneakin', stealin' game
all along—gittin' me t' lie with ye so's ye'd
hev a son he'd think was his'n, an' makin'

him promise he'd give ye the farm and let
me eat dust, if ye did git him a son! [*Staring
at her with anguished, bewildered eyes.*]
They must be a devil livin' in ye! T'ain't
human t' be as bad as that be!

ABBIE. [*Stunned—dully.*] He told
yew . . . ?

EBEN. Hain't it true? It hain't no good
in yew lyin'.

ABBIE. [*Pleadingly.*] Eben, listen—ye
must listen—it was long ago—afore we
done nothin'—yew was scornin' me—goin'
t' see Min—when I was lovin' ye—an' I
said it t' him t' git vengeance on ye!

EBEN. [*Unheedingly. With tortured passion.*] I wish ye was dead! I wish I was
dead along with ye afore this come! [*Rag-
ingly.*] But I'll git my vengeance too! I'll
pray Maw t' come back t' help me—t' put
her cuss on yew an' him!

ABBIE. [*Brokenly.*] Don't ye, Eben!
Don't ye! [*She throws herself on her knees
before him, weeping.*] I didn't mean t' do
bad t'ye! Fergive me, won't ye?

EBEN. [*Not seeming to hear her—
fiercely.*] I'll git squar' with the old skunk—
an' yew! I'll tell him the truth 'bout the
son he's so proud o'! Then I'll leave ye here
t' pizen each other—with Maw comin' out
o' her grave at nights—an' I'll go t' the
gold fields o' Californi-a whar Sim an'
Peter be!

ABBIE. [*Terrified.*] Ye won't—leave me?
Ye can't!

EBEN. [*With fierce determination.*] I'm
a-goin', I tell ye! I'll git rich thar an' come
back an' fight him fur the farm he stole—
an' I'll kick ye both out in the road—t' beg
an' sleep in the woods—an' yer son along
with ye—t' starve an' die!

[*He is hysterical at the end.*]

ABBIE. [*With a shudder—humbly.*] He's
yewr son, too, Eben.

EBEN. [*Torturedly.*] I wish he never was
born! I wish he'd die this minit! I wish I'd
never sot eyes on him! It's him—yew havin'
him—a-purpose t' steal—that's changed
everythin'!

ABBIE. [*Gently.*] Did ye believe I loved
ye—afore he come?

EBEN. Ay-eh—like a dumb ox!

ABBIE. An' ye don't believe no more?

EBEN. B'lieve a lyin' thief! Ha!

ABBIE. [Shudders—then humbly.] An' did ye r'ally love me afore?

EBEN. [Brokenly.] Ay-eh—an' ye was trickin' me!

ABBIE. An' ye don't love me now!

EBEN. [Violently.] I hate ye, I tell ye!

ABBIE. An' ye're truly goin' West—goin' t' leave me—all account o' him being born?

EBEN. I'm a-goin' in the mornin'—or may God strike me t' hell!

ABBIE. [After a pause—with a dreadful cold intensity—slowly.] If that's what his comin's done t' me—killin' yewr love—takin' yew away—my on'y joy—the on'y joy I ever knowed—like heaven t' me—purtier'n heaven—then I hate him, too, even if I be his Maw!

EBEN. [Bitterly.] Lies! Ye love him! He'll steal the farm fur ye! [Brokenly.] But t'ain't the farm so much—not no more —it's yew foolin' me—gittin' me t' love ye —lyin' yew loved me—jest t' git a son t' steal!

ABBIE. [Distractedly.] He won't steal! I'd kill him fust! I do love ye! I'll prove t' ye . . . !

EBEN. [Harshly.] T'ain't no use lyin' no more. I'm deaf t' ye! [He turns away.] I hain't seein' ye agen. Good-by!

ABBIE. [Pale with anguish.] Hain't ye even goin' t' kiss me—not once—arter all we loved?

EBEN. [In a hard voice.] I hain't wantin' t' kiss ye never agen! I'm wantin' t' forgit I ever sot eyes on ye!

ABBIE. Eben!—ye mustn't—wait a spell —I want t' tell ye . . .

EBEN. I'm a-goin' in t' git drunk. I'm a-goin' t' dance.

ABBIE. [Clinging to his arm—with passionate earnestness.] If I could make it—'s if he'd never come up between us—if I could prove t' ye I wa'n't schemin' t' steal from ye—so's everythin' could be jest the same with us, lovin' each other jest the same, kissin' an' happy the same's we've been happy afore he come—if I could do it—ye'd love me agen, wouldn't ye? Ye'd kiss me agen? Ye wouldn't never leave me, would ye?

EBEN. [Moved.] I calc'late not. [Then shaking her hand off his arm—with a bitter smile.] But ye hain't God, be ye?

ABBIE. [Exultantly.] Remember ye've promised! [Then with strange intensity.] Mebbe I kin take back one thin' God does!

EBEN. [Peering at her.] Ye're gittin' cracked, hain't ye? [Then going towards door.] I'm a-goin' t' dance.

ABBIE. [Calls after him intensely.] I'll prove t' ye! I'll prove I love ye better'n . . . [He goes in the door, not seeming to hear. She remains standing where she is, looking after him—then she finishes desperately.] Better'n everythin' else in the world!

[CURTAIN]

SCENE THREE

Just before dawn in the morning—shows the kitchen and CABOT's bedroom. In the kitchen, by the light of a tallow candle on the table, EBEN is sitting, his chin propped on his hands, his drawn face blank and expressionless. His carpetbag is on the floor beside him. In the bedroom, dimly lighted by a small whale-oil lamp, CABOT lies asleep. ABBIE is bending over the cradle, listening, her face full of terror yet with an undercurrent of desperate triumph. Suddenly, she breaks down and sobs, appears about to throw herself on her knees beside the cradle; but the old man turns restlessly, groaning in his sleep, and she controls herself, and, shrinking away from the cradle with a gesture of horror, backs swiftly toward the door in rear and goes out. A moment later she comes into the kitchen and, running to EBEN, flings her arms about his neck and kisses him wildly. He hardens himself, he remains unmoved and cold, he keeps his eyes straight ahead.

ABBIE. [Hysterically.] I done it, Eben! I told ye I'd do it! I've proved I love ye—

better'n everythin'—so's ye can't never doubt me no more!

EBEN. [*Dully.*] Whatever ye done, it hain't no good now.

ABBIE. [*Wildly.*] Don't ye say that! Kiss me, Eben, won't ye? I need ye t' kiss me arter what I done! I need ye t' say you love me!

EBEN. [*Kisses her without emotion—dully.*] That's fur good-by. I'm a-goin' soon.

ABBIE. No! No! Ye won't go—not now!

EBEN. [*Going on with his own thoughts.*] I been a-thinkin'—an' I hain't goin' t' tell Paw nothin'. I'll leave Maw t' take vengeance on ye. If I told him, the old skunk'd jest be stinkin' mean enuf to take it out on that baby. [*His voice showing emotion in spite of him.*] An' I don't want nothin' bad t' happen t' him. He hain't t' blame fur yew. [*He adds with a certain queer pride.*] An' he looks like me! An' by God, he's mine! An' some day I'll be a-comin' back an' . . . !

ABBIE. [*Too absorbed in her own thoughts to listen to him—pleadingly.*] They's no cause fur ye t' go now—they's no sense—it's all the same's it was—they's nothin' come b'tween us now—arter what I done!

EBEN. [*Something in her voice arouses him. He stares at her a bit frightenedly.*] Ye look mad, Abbie. What did ye do?

ABBIE. I—I killed him, Eben.

EBEN. [*Amazed.*] Ye killed him?

ABBIE. [*Dully.*] Ay-eh.

EBEN. [*Recovering from his astonishment—savagely.*] An' serves him right! But we got t' do somethin' quick t' make it look s'if the old skunk'd killed himself when he was drunk. We kin prove by 'em all how drunk he got.

ABBIE. [*Wildly.*] No! No! Not him! [*Laughing distractedly.*] But that's what I ought t' done, hain't it? I oughter killed him instead! Why didn't ye tell me?

EBEN. [*Appalled.*] Instead? What d'ye mean?

ABBIE. Not him.

EBEN. [*His face grown ghastly.*] Not—not that baby!

ABBIE. [*Dully.*] Ay-eh!

EBEN. [*Falls to his knees as if he'd been struck—his voice trembling with horror.*] Oh, God A'mighty! A'mighty God! Maw, whar was ye, why didn't ye stop her?

ABBIE. [*Simply.*] She went back t' her grave that night we fust done it, remember? I hain't felt her about since. [*A pause. EBEN hides his head in his hands, trembling all over as if he had the ague. She goes on dully.*] I left the piller over his little face. Then he killed himself. He stopped breathin'. [*She begins to weep softly.*]

EBEN. [*Rage beginning to mingle with grief.*] He looked like me! He was mine, damn ye!

ABBIE. [*Slowly and brokenly.*] I didn't want t' do it. I hated myself fur doin' it. I loved him. He was so purty—dead spit 'n' image o' yew. But I loved yew more—an' yew was goin' away—far off whar I'd never see ye agen, never kiss ye, never feel ye pressed agin me agen—an' ye said ye hated me fur havin' him—ye said ye hated him an' wished he was dead—ye said if it hadn't been fur him comin' it'd be the same's afore between us.

EBEN. [*Unable to endure this, springs to his feet in a fury, threatening her, his twitching fingers seeming to reach out for her throat.*] Ye lie! I never said—I never dreamed ye'd— I'd cut off my head afore I'd hurt his finger!

ABBIE. [*Piteously, sinking on her knees.*] Eben, don't ye look at me like that—hatin' me—not after what I done fur ye—fur us—so's we could be happy agen—

EBEN. [*Furiously now.*] Shut up, or I'll kill ye! I see yer game now—the same old sneakin' trick—ye're aimin' t' blame me fur the murder ye done!

ABBIE. [*Moaning—putting her hands over her ears.*] Don't ye, Eben! Don't ye! [*She grasps his legs.*]

EBEN. [*His mood suddenly changing to horror, shrinks away from her.*] Don't ye tech me! Ye're pizen! How could ye—t' murder a pore little critter— Ye must've swapped yer soul t' hell! [*Suddenly raging.*]

Ha! I kin see why ye done it! Not the lies ye jest told—but 'cause ye wanted t' steal agen—steal the last thin' ye'd left me—my part o' him—no, the hull o' him—ye saw he looked like me—ye knowed he was all mine—an' ye couldn't b'ar it—I know ye! Ye killed him fur bein' mine! [*All this has driven him almost insane. He makes a rush past her for the door—then turns—shaking both fists at her, violently.*] But I'll take vengeance now! I'll git the Sheriff! I'll tell him everythin'! Then I'll sing "I'm off to Californi-a!" an' go—gold—Golden Gate —gold sun—fields o' gold in the West! [*This last he half shouts, half croons incoherently, suddenly breaking off passionately.*] I'm a-goin' fur the Sheriff t' come an' git ye! I want ye tuk away, locked up from me! I can't stand t' luk at ye! Murderer an' thief 'r not, ye still tempt me! I'll give ye up t' the Sheriff!

[*He turns and runs out, around the corner of house, panting and sobbing, and breaks into a swerving sprint down the road.*]

ABBIE. [*Struggling to her feet, runs to the door, calling after him.*] I love ye, Eben! I love ye! [*She stops at the door weakly, swaying, about to fall.*] I don't care what ye do—if ye'll on'y love me agen—

[*She falls limply to the floor in a faint.*]

[CURTAIN]

SCENE FOUR

About an hour later. Same as Scene Three. Shows the kitchen and CABOT's *bedroom. It is after dawn. The sky is brilliant with the sunrise. In the kitchen,* ABBIE *sits at the table, her body limp and exhausted, her head bowed down over her arms, her face hidden. Upstairs,* CABOT *is still asleep but awakens with a start. He looks toward the window and gives a snort of surprise and irritation—throws back the covers and begins hurriedly pulling on his clothes. Without looking behind him, he begins talking to* ABBIE *whom he supposes beside him.*

CABOT. Thunder 'n' lightin', Abbie! I hain't slept this late in fifty year! Looks 's if the sun was full riz a'most. Must've been the dancin' an' likker. Must be gittin' old. I hope Eben's t' wuk. Ye might've tuk the trouble t' rouse me, Abbie. [*He turns—sees no one there—surprised.*] Waal—whar air she? Gittin' vittles, I calc'late. [*He tiptoes to the cradle and peers down—proudly.*] Mornin', sonny. Purty's a picter! Sleepin' sound. He don't beller all night like most o' 'em. [*He goes quietly out the door in rear—a few moments later enters kitchen —sees* ABBIE—*with satisfaction.*] So thar ye be. Ye got any vittles cooked?

ABBIE. [*Without moving.*] No.

CABOT. [*Coming to her, almost sympathetically.*] Ye feelin' sick?

ABBIE. No.

CABOT. [*Pats her on shoulder. She shudders.*] Ye'd best lie down a spell. [*Half jocularly.*] Yer son'll be needin' ye soon. He'd ought t' wake up with a gnashin' appetite, the sound way he's sleepin'.

ABBIE. [*Shudders—then in a dead voice.*] He hain't never goin' t' wake up.

CABOT. [*Jokingly.*] Takes after me this mornin'. I hain't slept so late in . . .

ABBIE. He's dead.

CABOT. [*Stares at her—bewilderedly.*] What . . .

ABBIE. I killed him.

CABOT. [*Stepping back from her— aghast.*] Air ye drunk—'r crazy—'r . . . !

ABBIE. [*Suddenly lifts her head and turns on him—wildly.*] I killed him, I tell ye! I smothered him. Go up an' see if ye don't b'lieve me!

[CABOT *stares at her a second, then bolts out the rear door, can be heard bounding up the stairs, and rushes into the bedroom and over to the cradle.* ABBIE *has sunk back lifelessly into her former position.* CABOT *puts his hand down on the body in the crib. An expression of fear and horror comes over his face.*]

CABOT. [*Shrinking away—tremblingly.*] God A'mighty! God A'mighty. [*He stum-*

bles out the door—in a short while returns to the kitchen—comes to ABBIE, *the stunned expression still on his face—hoarsely.*] Why did ye do it? Why? [*As she doesn't answer, he grabs her violently by the shoulders and shakes her.*] I ax ye why ye done it! Ye'd better tell me 'r . . . !

ABBIE. [*Gives him a furious push which sends him staggering back and springs to her feet—with wild rage and hatred.*] Don't ye dare tech me! What right hev ye t' question me 'bout him? He wa'n't yewr son! Think I'd have a son by yew? I'd die fust! I hate the sight o' ye an' allus did! It's yew I should've murdered, if I'd had good sense! I hate ye! I love Eben. I did from the fust. An' he was Eben's son—mine an' Eben's—not your'n!

CABOT. [*Stands looking at her dazedly—a pause—finding his words with an effort—dully.*] That was it—what I felt—pokin' round the corners—while ye lied—holdin' yerself from me—sayin' ye'd a'ready conceived— [*He lapses into crushed silence—then with a strange emotion.*] He's dead, sart'n. I felt his heart. Pore little critter! [*He blinks back one tear, wiping his sleeve across his nose.*]

ABBIE. [*Hysterically.*] Don't ye! Don't ye! [*She sobs unrestrainedly.*]

CABOT. [*With a concentrated effort that stiffens his body into a rigid line and hardens his face into a stony mask—through his teeth to himself.*] I got t' be—like a stone—a rock o' jedgment! [*A pause. He gets complete control over himself—harshly.*] If he was Eben's, I be glad he air gone! An' mebbe I suspicioned it all along. I felt they was somethin' onnateral—somewhars—the house got so lonesome—an' cold—drivin' me down t' the barn—t' the beasts o' the field. . . . Ay-eh. I must've suspicioned—somethin'. Ye didn't fool me—not altogether, leastways—I'm too old a bird—growin' ripe on the bough. . . . [*He becomes aware he is wandering, straightens again, looks at* ABBIE *with a cruel grin.*] So ye'd liked t' hev murdered me 'stead o' him, would ye? Waal, I'll live to a hundred! I'll live t' see ye hung! I'll deliver ye up t' the

jedgment o' God an' the law! I'll git the Sheriff now. [*Starts for the door.*]

ABBIE. [*Dully.*] Ye needn't. Eben's gone fur him.

CABOT. [*Amazed.*] Eben—gone fur the Sheriff?

ABBIE. Ay-eh.

CABOT. T' inform agen ye?

ABBIE. Ay-eh.

CABOT. [*Considers this—a pause—then in a hard voice.*] Waal, I'm thankful fur him savin' me the trouble. I'll git t' wuk. [*He goes to the door—then turns—in a voice full of strange emotion.*] He'd ought t' been my son, Abbie. Ye'd ought t' loved me. I'm a man. If ye'd love me, I'd never told no Sheriff on ye no matter what ye did, if they was t' brile me alive!

ABBIE. [*Defensively.*] They's more to it nor yew know, makes him tell.

CABOT. [*Dryly.*] Fur yewr sake, I hope they be. [*He goes out—comes around to the gate—stares up at the sky. His control relaxes. For a moment he is old and weary. He murmurs despairingly.*] God A'mighty, I be lonesomer'n ever! [*He hears running footsteps from the left, immediately is himself again.* EBEN *runs in, panting exhaustedly, wild-eyed and mad looking. He lurches through the gate.* CABOT *grabs him by the shoulder.* EBEN *stares at him dumbly.*] Did ye tell the Sheriff?

EBEN. [*Nodding stupidly.*] Ay-eh.

CABOT. [*Gives him a push away that sends him sprawling—laughing with withering contempt.*] Good fur ye! A prime chip o' yer Maw ye be! [*He goes toward the barn, laughing harshly.* EBEN *scrambles to his feet. Suddenly* CABOT *turns—grimly threatening.*] Git off this farm when the Sheriff takes her—or, by God, he'll have t' come back an' git me fur murder, too!

[*He stalks off.* EBEN *does not appear to have heard him. He runs to the door and comes into the kitchen.* ABBIE *looks up with a cry of anguished joy.* EBEN *stumbles over and throws himself on his knees beside her—sobbing brokenly.*]

EBEN.   Fergive me!

ABBIE. [*Happily.*] Eben! [*She kisses him and pulls his head over against her breast.*]

EBEN. I love ye! Fergive me!

ABBIE. [*Ecstatically.*] I'd fergive ye all the sins in hell fur sayin' that! [*She kisses his head, pressing it to her with a fierce passion of possession.*]

EBEN. [*Brokenly.*] But I told the Sheriff. He's comin' fur ye!

ABBIE. I kin b'ar what happens t' me—now!

EBEN. I woke him up. I told him. He says, wait 'til I git dressed. I was waiting. I got to thinkin' o' yew. I got to thinkin' how I'd loved ye. It hurt like somethin' was bustin' in my chest an' head. I got t' cryin'. I knowed sudden I loved ye yet, an' allus would love ye!

ABBIE. [*Caressing his hair—tenderly.*] My boy, hain't ye?

EBEN. I begun t' run back. I cut across the fields an' through the woods. I thought ye might have time t' run away—with me—an' . . .

ABBIE. [*Shaking her head.*] I got t' take my punishment—t' pay fur my sin.

EBEN. Then I want t' share it with ye.

ABBIE. Ye didn't do nothin'.

EBEN. I put it in yer head. I wisht he was dead! I as much as urged ye t' do it!

ABBIE. No. It was me alone!

EBEN. I'm as guilty as yew be! He was the child o' our sin.

ABBIE. [*Lifting her head as if defying God.*] I don't repent that sin! I hain't askin' God t' fergive that!

EBEN. Nor me—but it led up t' the other—an' the murder ye did, ye did 'count o' me—an' it's my murder, too, I'll tell the Sheriff—an' if ye deny it, I'll say we planned it t'gether—an' they'll all be'lieve me, fur they suspicion everythin' we've done, an' it'll seem likely an' true to 'em. An' it is true—way down. I did help ye—somehow.

ABBIE. [*Laying her head on his—sobbing.*] No! I don't want yew t' suffer!

EBEN. I got t' pay fur my part o' the sin! An' I'd suffer wuss leavin' ye, goin' West, thinkin' o' ye day an' night, bein' out when yew was in— [*Lowering his voice.*] 'r bein' alive when yew was dead. [*A pause.*] I want t' share with ye, Abbie—prison 'r death 'r hell 'r anythin'! [*He looks into her eyes and forces a trembling smile.*] If I'm sharin' with ye, I won't feel lonesome, leastways.

ABBIE. [*Weakly.*] Eben! I won't let ye! I can't let ye!

EBEN. [*Kissing her — tenderly.*] Ye can't he'p yerself. I got ye beat fur once!

ABBIE. [*Forcing a smile—adoringly.*] I hain't beat—s'long's I got ye!

EBEN. [*Hears the sound of feet outside.*] Ssshh! Listen! They've come t' take us!

ABBIE. No, it's him. Don't give him no chance to fight ye, Eben. Don't say nothin' —no matter what he says. An' I won't neither.

[*It is* CABOT. *He comes up from the barn in a great state of excitement and strides into the house and then into the kitchen.* EBEN *is kneeling beside* ABBIE, *his arm around her, hers around him. They stare straight ahead.*]

CABOT. [*Stares at them, his face hard. A long pause—vindictively.*] Ye make a slick pair o' murderin' turtle doves! Ye'd ought t' be both hung on the same limb an' left thar t' swing in the breeze an' rot—a warnin' t' old fools like me t' b'ar their lonesomeness alone—an' fur young fools like ye t' hobble their lust. [*A pause. The excitement returns to his face, his eyes snap, he looks a bit crazy.*] I couldn't work today. I couldn't take no interest. T' hell with the farm! I'm leavin' it! I've turned the cows an' other stock loose! I've druv 'em into the woods whar they kin be free! By freein' 'em, I'm freein' myself! I'm quittin' here today! I'll set fire t' house an' barn an' watch 'em burn, an' I'll leave yer Maw t' haunt the ashes, an' I'll will the fields back t' God, so that nothin' human kin never touch 'em! I'll be a'goin' to Californi-a—t' jine Simeon an' Peter—true sons o' mine if they be dumb fools—an' the Cabots'll find Solomon's Mines t'gether! [*He suddenly cuts a mad caper.*] Whoop!

What was the song they sung? "Oh, Califor-ni-a! That's the land fur me." [*He sings this—then gets on his knees by the floorboard under which the money was hid.*] An' I'll sail thar on one o' the finest clippers I kin find! I've got the money! Pity ye didn't know whar this was hidden so's ye could steal . . . [*He has pulled up the board. He stares—feels—stares again. A pause of dead silence He slowly turns, slumping into a sitting position on the floor, his eyes like those of a dead fish, his face the sickly green of an attack of nausea. He swallows painfully several times—forces a weak smile at last.*] So—ye did steal it!

EBEN. [*Emotionlessly.*] I swapped it t' Sim an' Peter fur their share o' the farm—t' pay their passage t' Californi-a.

CABOT. [*With one sardonic*] Ha! [*He begins to recover. Gets slowly to his feet—strangely.*] I calc'late God give it to 'em—not yew! God's hard, not easy! Mebbe they's easy gold in the West but it hain't God's gold. It hain't fur me. I kin hear His voice warnin' me agen t' be hard an' stay on my farm. I kin see his hand usin' Eben t' steal t' keep me from weakness. I kin feel I be in the palm o' His hand, His fingers guidin' me. [*A pause—then he mutters sadly.*] It's a-goin' t' be lonesomer now than ever it war afore—an' I'm gittin' old, Lord—ripe on the bough. . . . [*Then stiffening.*] Waal—what d'ye want? God's lonesome, hain't He? God's hard an' lonesome!

[*A pause. The* SHERIFF *with two men comes up the road from the left. They move cautiously to the door. The* SHERIFF *knocks on it with the butt of his pistol.*]

SHERIFF. Open in the name o' the law! [*They start.*]

CABOT. They've come fur ye. [*He goes to the rear door.*] Come in, Jim! [*The three men enter.* CABOT *meets them in doorway.*] Jest a minit, Jim. I got 'em safe here. [*The* SHERIFF *nods. He and his companions remain in the doorway.*]

EBEN. [*Suddenly calls.*] I lied this mornin', Jim. I helped her to do it. Ye kin take me, too.

ABBIE. [*Brokenly.*] No!

CABOT. Take 'em both. [*He comes forward—stares at* EBEN *with a trace of grudging admiration.*] Purty good—fur yew! Waal, I got t' round up the stock. Good-by.

EBEN. Good-by.

ABBIE. Good-by.

[CABOT *turns and strides past the men—comes out and around the corner of the house, his shoulders squared, his face stony, and stalks grimly toward the barn. In the meantime the* SHERIFF *and men have come into the room.*]

SHERIFF. [*Embarrassedly.*] Waal—we'd best start.

ABBIE. Wait. [*Turns to* EBEN.] I love ye, Eben.

EBEN. I love ye, Abbie. [*They kiss. The three men grin and shuffle embarrassedly.* EBEN *takes* ABBIE'S *hand. They go out the door in rear, the men following, and come from the house, walking hand in hand to the gate.* EBEN *stops there and points to the sunrise sky.*] Sun's a-rizin'. Purty, hain't it?

ABBIE. Ay-eh.

[*They both stand for a moment looking up raptly in attitudes strangely aloof and devout.*]

SHERIFF. [*Looking around at the farm enviously—to his companion.*] It's a jim-dandy farm, no denyin'. Wished I owned it!

[CURTAIN]

Symbolistic Drama

SYMBOLISM IS A DEVICE of expression by means of images which are employed, not for the sake of their immediate value as percepts, but for the sake of the concepts which they suggest. Its function is to afford a means of representing tangibly concepts which are otherwise difficult to express in concrete form. As such, it is the property of no particular age or art. On the contrary, it is perhaps the most ancient and common device of artistic expression, if not actually the primitive basis of all human communication. Indeed, art itself may be said to be in essence a symbol of life. Since drama, by the nature of its medium, is primarily a representational art, a certain amount of symbolism is virtually inherent in its technique, although in most instances the appearance of this element is no more than sporadic and incidental. As an incidental feature, however, symbolism may occur in any kind of drama belonging to any period. For example, among the plays contained in the present volume, the blinding of Oedipus is used to symbolize physically the spiritual defect which has caused his disaster; Hamlet's "customary suits of solemn black" reflect visually the qualitative difference which sets him apart from his associates; Chekhov's dead sea gull epitomizes the wanton vandalism of spirit with which the play is largely concerned; and amid the abundant symbolism of *Desire Under the Elms,* as the farm is an obvious symbol of material achievement, the child is a more complex symbol of the various fulfilments of desire.

While for the most part dramatic use of symbolism is incidental, upon occasion the practice becomes so comprehensive and so integral to the whole dramatic intention that it creates a distinctive type of drama. Symbolistic drama of this sort is usually a response to certain rather specialized artistic exigencies. From what has been said above it is evident that the functional value of symbolism is largely determined by two factors: a desire for a concrete vehicle of representation, and a need to express subject matter which either has no objective existence or else is inadequately represented by its external manifestations. Whenever, therefore, drama endeavors to deal in terms of realistic verisimilitude with matters which pass beyond the realm of the tangible, it tends inevitably to fall back upon symbolism as its most appropriate recourse. As the demand grows more imperative, the dependence upon this sort of artistic solution increases correspondingly, until at last symbolism ceases to be an incidental expedient and becomes the entire mode of expression. Twice in the history of western drama such a general development has taken place. During the Middle Ages drama engaged in an effort to reduce the precepts of contemporary moral and religious doctrine to terms of common human experience. This embodiment of abstract concepts in realistic personification and concrete example resulted in the systematic symbolism of allegory which is known as the morality play. More recently, during the last three-quarters of a century, and under rather different auspices, somewhat similar impulses have prompted a comparable excursion into symbolistic drama. This modern venture is part of a larger symbolistic movement which has affected most of the arts. Its origin is the modern dedication to realism. Like naturalism, with which it has much in common, it reflects an effort to extend the scope of verisimilitude to include those realities which do not immediately meet the eye. It differs from naturalism, however, in that the realities with which it is primarily concerned are neither material nor objective but spiritual and subjective. Consequently, whereas naturalism concentrates on the social and physical aspects of human existence, symbolism addresses itself to the individual and psychological aspects. To the extent that this symbolistic drama has dealt with moral and philosophical ideas it has produced what is substantially a modern equivalent of the morality play. As it has endeavored, on the other hand, to explore and to express scientifically the psychology of subjective experience, it has resulted in the distinctive modern phenomenon known as expressionistic drama.

Expressionism is the most extreme, complex, and bizarre form thus far adopted by symbolism in the theater. Because of its modernity, its comprehensiveness, and its disconcerting disparity with usual dramatic effects it offers a good point of departure for considering the principles and practices of symbolistic drama as a whole. Expressionism is largely a product of the twentieth century. It is also a direct outgrowth of the century's scientific preoccupation with experimental truth. Hence its fundamental aims are both realistic and scientific. As the term indicates, however, it is a technique not of imitation but of expression; that is to say, it is designed, not to reproduce the external circumstances of human life, but to communicate their inner significance for those who are subjected to them. Specifically, it is an effort to express the realities of subjective experience. A by-product of the modern scientific interest in psychology, expressionism endeavors to embody with scientific accuracy the impressions which life makes upon man's consciousness, the conceptions which influence his behavior, and the unordered welter of memories and associations which impinge upon him from the realm of the subconscious. Its technique is devised to project upon the stage with realistic verisimilitude an objective and concrete representation of this subjective psychological reality.

In so far as its purpose is to present this sort of experience with realistic fidelity to fact, expressionism is tantamount, therefore, to what may be described as subjective realism. In the sense that it involves a rebellion against the superficiality of absolute verisimilitude, as well as an endeavor to explore the nature of realities which have no adequate external manifestation, it also represents a logical extension of the interests which are embodied in naturalism. What most conspicuously differentiates it from these theatrical affiliates is its choice of symbolism as the most appropriate mode of expression for its peculiar concerns. Hence, whereas realism and naturalism restrict themselves to methods which preserve an illusion of normal objective reality, expressionism frankly abandons all such inhibitions; its use of symbolistic devices is validated, not by their conformity with external fact, but solely by the accuracy and efficacy with which they communicate its special subject matter. Since this procedure amounts, in effect, to a realistic treatment of naturalistic interests by symbolistic methods, the result on the stage, quite understandably, is often a disparity between matter and manner which is not only startling but at times fantastic. Despite this fantastic appearance, nevertheless, it should be noted that the apparent fantasy, like that of a nightmare, is always realistic both in circumstance and in force. In other words, the fantasy presented by expressionism is always designed to be a faithful reproduction of authentic subjective experience.

As symbolism in general is a device of expression, expressionism in particular is a technique of representation. As such, it has had its most pronounced effect on dramatic and theatrical design. Abandoning the practices whereby such dramatists as Chekhov and Synge strove to create an illusion of normal reality, it has deliberately reshuffled the raw materials of sensuous perception and rearranged them in new and bizarre patterns according to a different conception of realism, the aim of which is to reflect, not the outward semblance of common life, but the inward nature of psychological experience. The final value of such a technique obviously depends on the value of what it is used to express. Since technical facility is ever a more prevalent virtue than intellectual profundity, the unfortunate truth is that a great deal of modern expressionism is more interesting as technical experiment than important as artistic achievement. As a matter of fact, its most fruitful accomplishments have been in methods of staging rather than in dramatic composition. At the same time, among serious modern dramatists, a trend toward some form of symbolism has been an almost inevitable concomitant of the restrictions imposed by factual realism, as may be seen in such symptomatic work as that of Ibsen, Strindberg, and O'Neill. The tendency is well illustrated by the case of

August Strindberg (1849–1912), the intense, half-mad Swedish genius who is the generally accepted father of modern expressionistic drama. Influenced by the realistic and scientific temper of the last century, Strindberg gained his international reputation first as a writer of naturalistic plays. In exploring the final causes of human behavior, however, he was led so far into the hidden recesses of human nature that, in order to reveal this submerged truth satisfactorily, he found himself obliged to supplement his usual realistic practices with the more expressive resources of symbolism. As he probed more deeply into the psychological profundities of consciousness and the subconscious, his search for an adequate means of expressing this sub-surface reality eventually prompted the experiments which have resulted in dramatic expressionism. *The Dream Play* (1902) is one of the more influential of these experiments. It provides an excellent introduction to symbolistic drama in that, without being extreme or too confusing, it not only exemplifies the basic principles and practices of the genre but also applies them to subject matter which is of broad and genuine human significance.

The artistic purpose of *The Dream Play* is to represent in objective and realistic terms the nature of a subjective experience: that is, a coordination of those impressions and reactions which constitute a state of mind and emotion. Since the constituents of such an experience are not material objects, but the immaterial ideas, mental images, and personal feelings which result from such stimuli, the order of reality with which the play deals is substantially different from that of the material universe. The laws of its being are not physical but psychological. For example, differentials of space and time do not exist: past and present, near and far, are devoid of meaning; the sole dimensions are appropriateness of association and immediacy. Similarly in the mind's eye objects do not necessarily appear as they present themselves to the senses, but rather in the form of their interpretation. And in the ordering of these materials logic often yields to an imaginative association which is as irrational as it is uninhibited. Hence, in comparison with the objective world of sensuous realities, the realm of subjective experience is one of strange discrepancies, of fantastic dislocations and juxtapositions, which at times takes on the illusory quality of a dream—unless one accepts the dream as the true reality, and the external world as the illusion. In order to represent this subjective reality at all on the stage, it is necessary to employ means which depart radically from custom. In order to reproduce it faithfully, it is necessary to create a verisimilitude which has little resemblance to the world of sense impressions.

As a means of bridging this inconsistency and imparting a superficial plausibility and naturalness to its vagaries, the play is cast in the form of a dream. The device is used, however, not as an excuse for anarchic eccentricity, but to provide a systematic and scientific delineation of the actual dream process. Thus from modern dream psychology the play borrows both a sanction for the symbolic nature of dreams and a scientific scheme for its own structure and mechanics. From the same source it also adopts certain working principles: that the substance of a dream, however fantastic its manifestations, is essential truth; that repressed truths, when released from the censorship of consciousness, emerge in their real proportions; and that truths thus released often masquerade under grotesque disguises. The design of the play, therefore, represents a scientifically planned distortion of normal order, the aim of which is not chaos but a reordering of experience according to essential relationships rather than the accidents of place or time. The general intention Strindberg has described in a prefatory note to the play: "the author has tried to imitate the disconnected but seemingly logical form of the dream. Anything may happen; everything is possible and probable. Time and space do not exist. On an insignificant background of reality, imagination designs and embroiders novel patterns: a medley of memories, experiences, free fancies, absurdities, and improvisations. The characters split, double, multiply, vanish, solidify, blur, clarify. But one consciousness reigns above them all—that of the dreamer; and before it there are no secrets, no incongruities, no scruples, no laws. There is neither judgment nor exoneration, but merely narration."

In order to realize this effect on the stage, the play strives above all for the factual, if grotesque, vividness and the fluid continuity of a dream. As in a motion picture, formal act and scene divisions are replaced by a casual and unbroken sequence of plastic dream images. Scene flows into scene without interruption; situation merges with situation; widely separated incidents are telescoped like double exposures on a film. With complete disregard of normal verisimilitude incongruous properties are brought into startling juxtaposition. Settings consist only of arbitrary essentials presented with the matter-of-fact unnaturalness of a dream, and change their appearance and value with a similar abrupt caprice. Against this kaleidoscopic representation of vagrant impressions, memories, and associations the characters of the play carry on a correspondingly protean existence. Their state is one of continual flux: not only do they change, divide, and fuse, but the same characters reappear in different guise. Moreover, as in a dream the central figure is always the dreamer himself, the protagonist of every dramatic situation, despite the shifting variety of rôles, is always the same—that is, the dreamer, whose dream constitutes the fabric of the play. For example, the Officer, the Lawyer, and the Poet are at once different and the same: actually they are the dreamer himself in different rôles, which in turn are but different aspects or functions of the same personality. In similar fashion the Daughter of Indra merges with the Portress, Victoria, Christine, and other female characters. As a matter of fact, in the last analysis not even the male and female characters are to be too sharply differentiated, except as the two sexes represent complementary principles in human nature. In other words, considered psychologically, all the characters of the play are but aspects of a single experience and personality, momentarily detached and objectified in a specific type of situation. Similarly all the situations of the play are but the fragments of experience which coalesce to form that personality. The assimilation of these fragments, by a process which detaches them from their original context yet retains its essential significance, constitutes the psychological pattern of personality reflected in the dream.

The symbolic nature of dreams provides the play with a scientific psychological foundation for its philosophical superstructure. The bizarre symbols which the dream uses to mask truth the play uses to reveal it. Hence the play exists on two levels of meaning. On the one level, the dream is an expressionistic representation of psychological reality; on the other, it becomes a symbol of philosophical truth. In this symbolic sense, the dream itself is conceived as a synoptic apologue of human life. Its texture is the ironic experience of immortal spirit immersed in the heavy atmosphere of mortality. The resulting struggle between the spiritual and the material, between the eternal and the temporal, is symbolized in the experiences of Indra's Daughter and the earthbound dreamer in his several functions as Officer, Lawyer, and Poet. The machinery of this dream symbolism is provided by assigning to all the events, characters, objects, and settings in the play a definite symbolic value and function, for the elucidation of which each member of the audience is called upon to be his own psychoanalyst. Its basis is, of course, simply figurative expression. Its frame of reference, however, lies both within and without the confines of the play: that is, in the interpretations explicitly provided, and in the experience of the audience itself. In general, the clue to symbolic meaning is either a careful parallelism with familiar experience or an emphasis on selected identifying features. Many of the specific symbols—for example, the Growing Castle of mortal existence, the shawl of human sorrows worn by the Portress, Fairhaven and Foulstrand, or the locked door behind which lies the secret of life—are fairly obvious. Others—like the Billposter's fishing-basket of heart's desire, which must of course be green to be perfectly satisfactory, and which, as is so often the case, turns out to be less satisfying in possession than in anticipation—readily yield their meaning to a little ingenious reflection. On the other hand, much of the symbolism is a good deal more subtle and complex. A relatively simple example occurs in the schoolroom episode, where the dreamer finds himself in the embarrassing position of being the Officer-pupil and the Teacher at the same time. Beneath the apparent absurdity of this situation is cloaked a very real human predicament, in which man is obliged to remain the perennial bewildered pupil of life, yet at the same time to expound learnedly his half-digested knowledge, to the ultimate confounding of all sense and intelligence.

On the whole, whatever symbolism is not immediately transparent is explained ultimately in the course of the play. It is necessary to recognize, however, that in dealing with all symbolistic drama the degree of one's comprehension depends upon the alertness and sensitivity which one brings to an identifying of the familiar fact or experience in its unfamiliar, and often fantastic, figurative representation. This matter is especially important since the very unfamiliarity of the symbolic expression is often designed to add an unsuspected dimension to the experience itself. For the final symbolic significance of *The Dream Play* derives not alone from the simple identification of specific symbols or from any explicit explanations, but from the effect of the total design. Like a musical composition, its symbolism is a tissue of themes, developments, variations, recapitulations, and final resolution. By means of repeated patterns, incremental amplifications and juxtapositions, and the presentation of the same characters and objects in shifting contexts the play endeavors to enhance its basic design with an ever richer texture of implication, and thus to accord its symbols an increasingly more complete and exact definition. One's capacity to perceive the justice of this symbolistic representation not only enriches the inherent value of the play, but in an even more significant manner illuminates the resources of one's own experience.

Further acquaintance with symbolistic drama should include representatives of its several forms. The morality play is best illustrated by its finest English example, the anonymous and justly famous *Everyman*. The more conventional form of modern symbolism is well exemplified in Maurice Maeterlinck's *Pelleas and Melisande* and Paul Claudel's *The Tidings Brought to Mary*. Various interpretations of expressionism appear in such plays as *From Morn Till Midnight* by Georg Kaiser, *Man and the Masses* by Ernst Toller, *The Adding Machine* by Elmer Rice, *Beggar On Horseback* by George S. Kaufman and Marc Connelly, *The Great God Brown* by Eugene O'Neill, and *The Skin of Our Teeth* by Thornton Wilder. Finally, while not strictly expressionistic, the following plays illustrate some of the collateral possibilities of symbolistic methods: O'Neill's *The Emperor Jones,* Karel Capek's *R. U. R.,* Ferenc Molnar's *Liliom,* and Luigi Pirandello's *Six Characters in Search of an Author.*

THE DREAM PLAY

by

AUGUST STRINDBERG

TRANSLATED BY

EDWIN BJÖRKMAN

Reprinted from *Plays—First Series* by August Strindberg, translated by Edwin Bjorkman; used by permission of the publishers, Charles Scribner's Sons.

PROLOGUE

The background represents cloud banks that resemble corroding slate cliffs with ruins of castles and fortresses.

The constellations of Leo, Virgo, and Libra are visible, and from their midst the planet Jupiter is shining with a strong light.

[THE DAUGHTER OF INDRA [1] *stands on the topmost cloud.*]

THE VOICE OF INDRA. [*From above.*]
Where are you, daughter, where?

THE DAUGHTER.
Here, father, here.

THE VOICE.
You've lost your way, my child—beware, you sink—
How got you there?

THE DAUGHTER.
I followed from ethereal heights the ray
Of lightning, and for car a cloud I took—
It sank, and now my journey downward tends.
O, noble father, Indra, tell what realms
I now draw near? The air is here so close,
And breathing difficult.

THE VOICE.
Behind you lies the second world; the third
Is where you stand. From Cukra, morning star,
You have withdrawn yourself to enter soon
The vapory circle of the earth. For mark,
The Seventh House you take. It's Libra called:
There stands the day-star in the balanced hour
When Fall gives equal weight to night and day.

THE DAUGHTER.
You named the earth—is that the ponderous world
And dark, that from the moon must take its light?

THE VOICE.
It is the heaviest and densest sphere
Of all that travel through the space.

THE DAUGHTER.
And is it never brightened by the sun?

THE VOICE.
Of course, the sun does reach it—now and then—

THE DAUGHTER.
There is a rift, and downward goes my glance—

THE VOICE.
What sees my child?

THE DAUGHTER.
I see—O beautiful!—with forest green,
With waters blue, white peaks, and yellow fields—

THE VOICE.
Yes, beautiful as all that Brahma [2] made—
But still more beautiful it was of yore,
In primal morn of ages. Then occurred
Some strange mishap; the orbit was disturbed;
Rebellion led to crime that called for check—

THE DAUGHTER.
Now from below I hear some sounds arise—
What sort of race is dwelling there?

THE VOICE.
See for yourself—Of Brahma's work no ill
I say: but what you hear, it is their speech.

THE DAUGHTER.
It sounds as if—it has no happy ring!

THE VOICE.
I fear me not—for even their mother-tongue
Is named complaint. A race most hard to please,
And thankless, are the dwellers on the earth—

THE DAUGHTER.
O, say not so—for I hear cries of joy,
Hear noise and thunder, see the lightnings flash—

[1] In Hindu mythology Indra is the supreme god and symbol of divine beneficence.

[2] The Hindu god who represents divinity in its creative aspect.

535

Now bells are ringing, fires are lit,
And thousand upon thousand tongues
Sing praise and thanks unto the heavens
  on high—
Too harshly, father, you are judging
  them.

THE VOICE.

Descend, that you may see and hear, and
  then
Return and let me know if their complaints
And wailings have some reasonable
  ground—

THE DAUGHTER.

Well then, I go; but, father, come with
  me.

THE VOICE.

No, there below I cannot breathe—

THE DAUGHTER.

Now sinks the cloud—what sultriness—I
  choke!

I am not breathing air, but smoke and
  steam—
With heavy weight it drags me down,
And I can feel already how it rolls—
Indeed, the best of worlds is not the
  third—

THE VOICE.

The best I cannot call it, nor the worst.
Its name is Dust; and like them all, it
  rolls:
And therefore dizzy sometimes grows
  the race,
And seems to be half foolish and half
  mad—
Take courage, child—a trial, that is
  all!

THE DAUGHTER.

[Kneeling as the cloud sinks downward.]
I sink!

[CURTAIN.]

THE DREAM PLAY [1]

The background represents a forest of gigantic hollyhocks in bloom. They are white, pink, crimson, sulphureous, violet; and above their tops is seen the gilded roof of a castle, the apex of which is formed by a bud resembling a crown. At the foot of the castle walls stand a number of straw ricks, and around these stable litter is scattered. The side-scenes, which remain unchanged throughout the play, show conventionalised frescoes, suggesting at once internal decoration, architecture, and landscape.

[Enter THE GLAZIER and THE DAUGHTER.]

THE DAUGHTER. The castle is growing higher and higher above the ground. Do you see how much it has grown since last year?

THE GLAZIER. [To himself.] I have never seen this castle before—have never heard of a castle that grew, but—[To THE DAUGHTER, with firm conviction.] Yes, it has grown two yards, but that is because they have manured it—and if you notice, it has put out a wing on the sunny side.

THE DAUGHTER. Ought it not to be blooming soon, as we are already past midsummer?

THE GLAZIER. Don't you see the flower up there?

THE DAUGHTER. Yes, I see! [Claps her hands.] Say, father, why do flowers grow out of dirt?

THE GLAZIER. [Simply.] Because they do not feel at home in the dirt, and so they make haste to get up into the light in order to blossom and die.

[1] The play has no listing of Dramatis Personæ because the various characters do not represent separable individuals; they are actually various aspects of human nature or represent different phases of the same personality. Although there is no specific designation, the play is divided into four parts or episodes, here for the sake of convenience referred to as acts. The act divisions are indicated by the fall of the curtain. Unlike conventional acts, however, these divisions do not constitute logical stages in the development of the dramatic action; rather, they reflect varying moods or impressions in a momentarily interrupted sequence of dream images. Within each act are various scenes which shift abruptly and merge with one another after the irrational logic of dream phantasmagoria. In order not to interrupt this fluid development, the play does not indicate scene divisions, which, however, need to be kept in mind if the structure and meaning of the play are to be followed satisfactorily.

THE DAUGHTER. Do you know who lives in that castle?

THE GLAZIER. I have known it, but cannot remember.

THE DAUGHTER. I believe a prisoner is kept there—and he must be waiting for me to set him free.

THE GLAZIER. And what is he to pay for it?

THE DAUGHTER. One does not bargain about one's duty. Let us go into the castle.

THE GLAZIER. Yes, let us go in.

[*They go toward the background, which opens and slowly disappears on either side.*

The stage shows now a humble, bare room, containing only a table and a few chairs. On one of the chairs sits an OFFICER, *dressed in a very unusual yet modern uniform. He is tilting the chair backward and beating the table with his sabre.*]

THE DAUGHTER. [*Goes to the* OFFICER, *from whose hand she gently takes the sabre.*] Don't! Don't!

THE OFFICER. Oh, Agnes dear, let me keep the sabre.

THE DAUGHTER. No, you break the table. [*To* THE GLAZIER.] Now you go down to the harness-room and fix that window pane. We'll meet later.

[THE GLAZIER *goes out.*]

THE DAUGHTER. You are imprisoned in your own rooms—I have come to set you free.

THE OFFICER. I have been waiting for you, but I was not sure you were willing to do it.

THE DAUGHTER. The castle is strongly built; it has seven walls, but—it can be done!—Do you want it, or do you not?

THE OFFICER. Frankly speaking, I cannot tell—for in either case I shall suffer pain. Every joy that life brings has to be paid for with twice its measure of sorrow. It is hard to stay where I am, but if I buy the sweets of freedom, then I shall have to suffer twice as much—Agnes, I'd rather endure it as it is, if I can only see you.

THE DAUGHTER. What do you see in me?

THE OFFICER. Beauty, which is the harmony of the universe—There are lines of your body which are nowhere to be found, except in the orbits of the solar system, in strings that are singing softly, or in the vibrations of light—You are a child of heaven—

THE DAUGHTER. So are you.

THE OFFICER. Why must I then keep horses, tend stable, and cart straw?

THE DAUGHTER. So that you may long to get away from here.

THE OFFICER. I am longing, but it is so hard to find one's way out.

THE DAUGHTER. But it is a duty to seek freedom in the light.

THE OFFICER. Duty? Life has never recognised any duties toward me.

THE DAUGHTER. You feel yourself wronged by life?

THE OFFICER. Yes, it has been unjust—

[*Now voices are heard from behind a partition, which a moment later is pulled away.* THE OFFICER *and* THE DAUGHTER *look in that direction and stop as if paralysed in the midst of a gesture.*

At a table sits THE MOTHER, *looking very sick. In front of her a tallow candle is burning, and every little while she trims it with a pair of snuffers. The table is piled with new-made shirts, and these she is marking with a quill and ink. To the left stands a brown-colored wardrobe.*]

THE FATHER. [*Holds out a silk mantilla toward* THE MOTHER *and says gently.*] You don't want it?

THE MOTHER. A silk mantilla for me, my dear—of what use would that be when I am going to die shortly?

THE FATHER. Do you believe what the doctor says?

THE MOTHER. Yes, I believe also what he says, but still more what the voice says in here.

THE FATHER. [*Sadly.*] It is true then?—

And you are thinking of your children first and last.

THE MOTHER. That has been my life and my reason for living—my joy and my sorrow—

THE FATHER. Christine, forgive me—everything!

THE MOTHER. What have I to forgive? Dearest, you forgive *me!* We have been tormenting each other. Why? That we may not know. We couldn't do anything else—However, here is the new linen for the children. See that they change twice a week—Wednesdays and Sundays—and that Louise washes them—their whole bodies—Are you going out?

THE FATHER. I have to be in the Department at eleven o'clock.

THE MOTHER. Ask Alfred to come in before you go.

THE FATHER. [*Pointing to* THE OFFICER.] Why, he is standing right there, dear heart.

THE MOTHER. So my eyes are failing, too—Yes, it is turning dark. [*Trims the candle.*] Come here, Alfred.

[THE FATHER *goes out through the middle of the wall, nodding good-bye as he leaves.* THE OFFICER *goes over to* THE MOTHER.]

THE MOTHER. Who is that girl?

THE OFFICER. [*Whispers.*] It is Agnes.

THE MOTHER. Oh, is that Agnes?—Do you know what they say?—That she is a daughter of the god Indra who has asked leave to descend to the earth in order that she may find out what the conditions of men are—But don't say anything about it.

THE OFFICER. A child of the gods, indeed!

THE MOTHER. [*Aloud.*] My Alfred, I must soon part from you and from the other children—But let me first speak a word to you that bears on all the rest of your life.

THE OFFICER. [*Sadly.*] Speak, mother.

THE MOTHER. Only a word: don't quarrel with God!

THE OFFICER. What do you mean, mother?

THE MOTHER. Don't go around feeling that life has wronged you.

THE OFFICER. But when I am treated unjustly—

THE MOTHER. You are thinking of the time when you were unjustly punished for having taken a penny that later turned up?

THE OFFICER. Yes, and that one wrong gave a false twist to my whole life—

THE MOTHER. Perhaps. But please take a look into that wardrobe now—

THE OFFICER. [*Embarrassed.*] You know, then? It is—

THE MOTHER. The *Swiss Family Robinson*—for which—

THE OFFICER. Don't say any more!

THE MOTHER. For which your brother was punished—and which you had torn and hidden away.

THE OFFICER. Just think that the old wardrobe is still standing there after twenty years— We have moved so many times, and my mother died ten years ago.

THE MOTHER. Yes, and what of it? You are always asking all sorts of questions, and in that way you spoil the better part of your life—There is Lena, now.

LENA. [*Enters.*] Thank you very much, ma'am, but I can't go to the baptism.

THE MOTHER. And why not, my girl?

LENA. I have nothing to put on.

THE MOTHER. I'll let you use my mantilla here.

LENA. Oh, no, ma'am, that wouldn't do!

THE MOTHER. Why not?—It is not likely that I'll go to any more parties.

THE OFFICER. And what will father say? It is a present from him—

THE MOTHER. What small minds—

THE FATHER. [*Puts his head through the wall.*] Are you going to lend my present to the servant girl?

THE MOTHER. Don't talk that way! Can you not remember that I was a servant girl also? Why should you offend one who has done nothing?

THE FATHER. Why should you offend me, your husband?

THE MOTHER. Oh, this life! If you do anything nice, there is always somebody who finds it nasty. If you act kindly to one, it hurts another. Oh, this life!

[*She trims the candle so that it goes out. The stage turns dark and the partition is pushed back to its former position.*]

THE DAUGHTER. Men are to be pitied.

THE OFFICER. You think so?

THE DAUGHTER. Yes, life is hard—but love overcomes everything. You shall see for yourself.

[*They go toward the background.*]

[*The background is raised and a new one revealed, showing an old, dilapidated party-wall. In the centre of it is a gate closing a passageway. This opens upon a green, sunlit space, where is seen a tremendous blue monk's-hood (aconite). To the left of the gate sits* THE PORTRESS. *Her head and shoulders are covered by a shawl, and she is crocheting at a bedspread with a star-like pattern. To the right of the gate is a billboard, which* THE BILLPOSTER *is cleaning. Beside him stands a dipnet with a green pole. Further to the right is a door that has an air-hole shaped like a four-leaved clover. To the left of the gate stands a small linden tree with coal-black trunk and a few pale-green leaves. Near it is a small air-hole leading into a cellar.*] [2]

THE DAUGHTER. [*Going to* THE PORTRESS.] Is the spread not done yet?

THE PORTRESS. No, dear. Twenty-six years on such a piece of work is not much.

THE DAUGHTER. And your lover never came back?

THE PORTRESS. No, but it was not his fault. He had to go—poor thing! That was thirty years ago now.

THE DAUGHTER. [*To* THE BILLPOSTER.] She belonged to the ballet? Up there in the opera-house?

THE BILLPOSTER. She was number one—but when *he* went, it was as if her dancing

[2] As indicated in later stage directions, behind The Portress are also a door and window which lead into her lodge.

had gone with him—and so she didn't get any more parts.

THE DAUGHTER. Everybody complains—with their eyes, at least, and often with words also—

THE BILLPOSTER. I don't complain very much—not now, since I have a dipnet and a green cauf [3]—

THE DAUGHTER. And that can make you happy?

THE BILLPOSTER. Oh, I'm so happy, so— It was the dream of my youth and now it has come true. Of course, I have grown to be fifty years—

THE DAUGHTER. Fifty years for a dipnet and a cauf—

THE BILLPOSTER. A *green* cauf—mind you, *green*—

THE DAUGHTER. [*To* THE PORTRESS.] Let me have the shawl now, and I shall sit here and watch the human children. But you must stand behind me and tell me about everything.

[*She takes the shawl and sits down at the gate.*]

THE PORTRESS. This is the last day, and the house will be closed up for the season. This is the day when they learn whether their contracts are to be renewed.

THE DAUGHTER. And those that fail of engagement—

THE PORTRESS. Oh, Lord have mercy! I pull the shawl over my head not to see them.

THE DAUGHTER. Poor human creatures!

THE PORTRESS. Look, here comes one— She's not one of the chosen. See, how she cries.

[THE SINGER *enters from the right; rushes through the gate with her handkerchief to her eyes; stops for a moment in the passageway beyond the gate and leans her head against the wall; then out quickly.*]

THE DAUGHTER. Men are to be pitied!

THE PORTRESS. But look at this one. That's the way a happy person looks.

[THE OFFICER *enters through the passage-*

[3] A perforated wooden box to hold fish.

way; dressed in Prince Albert coat and high hat, and carrying a bunch of roses in one hand; he is radiantly happy.]

THE PORTRESS. He's going to marry Miss Victoria.

THE OFFICER. [*Far down on the stage, looks up and sings.*] Victoria!

THE PORTRESS. The young lady will be coming in a moment.

THE OFFICER. Good! The carriage is waiting, the table is set, the wine is on ice— Oh, permit me to embrace you, ladies! [*He embraces* THE PORTRESS *and* THE DAUGHTER. *Sings.*] Victoria!

A WOMAN'S VOICE FROM ABOVE. [*Sighs.*] I am here!

THE DAUGHTER. Do you know me?

THE OFFICER. No, I know one woman only—Victoria. Seven years I have come here to wait for her—at noon, when the sun touched the chimneys, and at night, when it was growing dark. Look at the asphalt here, and you will see the path worn by the steps of a faithful lover. Hooray! She is mine. [*Sings.*] Victoria! [*There is no reply.*] Well, she is dressing, I suppose. [*To* THE BILLPOSTER.] There is the dipnet, I see. Everybody belonging to the opera is crazy about dipnets—or rather about fishes—because the fishes are dumb and cannot sing!— What is the price of a thing like that?

THE BILLPOSTER. It is rather expensive.

THE OFFICER. [*Sings.*] Victoria! [*Shakes the linden tree.*] Look, it is turning green once more. For the eighth time. [*Sings.*] Victoria!— Now she is fixing her hair. [*To* THE DAUGHTER.] Look here, Madam, could I not go up and get my bride?

THE PORTRESS. Nobody is allowed on the stage.

THE OFFICER. Seven years I have been coming here. Seven times three hundred and sixty-five makes two thousand five hundred and fifty-five. [*Stops and pokes at the door with the four-leaved clover hole.*] And I have been looking two thousand five hundred and fifty-five times at that door without discovering where it leads. And that clover leaf which is to let in light—for whom is the light meant? Is there anybody within? Does anybody live there?

THE PORTRESS. I don't know. I have never seen it opened.

THE OFFICER. It looks like a pantry door which I saw once when I was only four years old and went visiting with the maid on a Sunday afternoon. We called at several houses—on other maids—but I did not get beyond the kitchen anywhere, and I had to sit between the water barrel and the salt box. I have seen so many kitchens in my days, and the pantry was always just outside, with small round holes bored in the door, and one big hole like a clover leaf— But there cannot be any pantry in the opera-house as they have no kitchen. [*Sings.*] Victoria!— Tell me, Madam, could she have gone out any other way?

THE PORTRESS. No, there is no other way.

THE OFFICER. Well, then, I shall see her here.

[STAGE PEOPLE *rush out and are closely watched by* THE OFFICER *as they pass.*]

THE OFFICER. Now she must soon be coming—Madam, that blue monk's-hood outside—I have seen it since I was a child. Is it the same?— I remember it from a country rectory where I stopped when I was seven years old— There are two doves, two blue doves, under the hood—but that time a bee came flying and went into the hood. Then I thought: now I have you! And I grabbed hold of the flower. But the sting of the bee went through it, and I cried—but then the rector's wife came and put damp dirt on the sting—and we had strawberries and cream for dinner— I think it is getting dark already. [*To* THE BILLPOSTER.] Where are you going?

THE BILLPOSTER. Home for supper.

THE OFFICER. [*Draws his hand across his eyes.*] Evening? At this time?— O, please may I go in and telephone to the Growing Castle?

THE DAUGHTER. What do you want there?

THE OFFICER. I am going to tell the Glazier to put in double windows, for it will soon be winter, and I am feeling horribly cold.

[*Goes into the gatekeeper's lodge.*]

THE DAUGHTER. Who is Miss Victoria?

THE PORTRESS. His sweetheart.

THE DAUGHTER. Right said! What she is to us and others matters nothing to him. And what she is to him, that alone is her real self. [*It is suddenly turning dark.*]

THE PORTRESS. [*Lights a lantern.*] It is growing dark early to-day.

THE DAUGHTER. To the gods a year is as a minute.

THE PORTTRESS. And to men a minute may be as long as a year.

THE OFFICER. [*Enters again, looking dusty; the roses are withered.*] She has not come yet?

THE PORTRESS. No.

THE OFFICER. But she will come— She will come! [*Walks up and down.*] But come to think of it, perhaps I had better call off the dinner after all—as it is late? Yes, I will do that.

[*Goes back into the lodge and telephones.*]

THE PORTRESS. [*To THE DAUGHTER.*] Can I have my shawl back now?

THE DAUGHTER. No, dear, be free a while. I shall attend to your duties—for I want to study men and life, and see whether things really are as bad as they say.

THE PORTRESS. But it won't do to fall asleep here—never sleep night or day—

THE DAUGHTER. No sleep at night?

THE PORTRESS. Yes, if you are able to get it, but only with the bell string tied around the wrist—for there are night watchmen on the stage, and they have to be relieved every third hour.

THE DAUGHTER. But that is torture!

THE PORTRESS. So you think, but people like us are glad enough to get such a job, and if you only knew how envied I am—

THE DAUGHTER. Envied?— Envy for the tortured?

THE PORTRESS. Yes— But I can tell you what is harder than all drudging and keeping awake nights, harder to bear than

draught and cold and dampness—it is to receive the confidences of all the unhappy people up there— They all come to me. Why? Perhaps they read in the wrinkles of my face some runes that are graved by suffering and that invite confessions— In that shawl, dear, lie hidden thirty years of my own and other people's agonies.

THE DAUGHTER. It is heavy, and it burns like nettles.

THE PORTRESS. As it is your wish, you may wear it. When it grows too burdensome, call me, and I shall relieve you.

THE DAUGHTER. Good-bye. What can be done by you ought not to surpass my strength.

THE PORTRESS. We shall see!—But be kind to my poor friends, and don't grow impatient of their complaints.

[*She disappears through the passageway.*]

[*Complete darkness covers the stage, and while it lasts the scene is changed so that the linden tree appears stripped of all its leaves. Soon the blue monk's-hood is withered, and when the light returns, the verdure in the open space beyond the passageway has changed into autumnal brown.*]

THE OFFICER. [*Enters when it is light again. He has gray hair and a gray beard. His clothes are shabby, his collar is soiled and wrinkled. Nothing but the bare stems remain of the bunch of roses. He walks to and fro.*] To judge by all signs, Summer is gone and Fall has come. The linden shows it, and the monk's-hood also. [*Walks.*] But the Fall is *my* Spring, for then the opera begins again, and then she must come. Please, Madam, may I sit down a little on this chair?

THE DAUGHTER. Yes, sit down, friend— I am able to stand.

THE OFFICER. [*Sits down.*] If I could only get some sleep, then I should feel better—[*He falls asleep for a few moments. Then he jumps up and walks back and forth again. Stops at last in front of the door with the clover leaf and pokes at it.*]

This door here will not leave me any peace—what is behind it? There must be something. [*Faint dance music is heard from above.*] Oh, now the rehearsals have begun. [*The light goes out and flares up again, repeating this rhythmically as the rays of a lighthouse come and go.*] What does this mean? [*Speaking in time with the blinkings of the light.*] Light and dark—light and dark?

THE DAUGHTER. [*Imitating him.*] Night and day—night and day! A merciful Providence wants to shorten your wait. Therefore the days are flying in hot pursuit of the nights.

[*The light shines unbrokenly once more. THE BILLPOSTER enters with his dipnet and his implements.*]

THE OFFICER. There is the Billposter with his dipnet. Was the fishing good?

THE BILLPOSTER. I should say so. The Summer was hot and a little long—the net turned out pretty good, but not as I had expected.

THE OFFICER. [*With emphasis.*] Not as I had expected!— That is well said. Nothing ever was as I expected it to be—because the thought is more than the deed, more than the thing.

[*Walks to and fro, striking at the wall with the rose stems so that the last few leaves fall off.*]

THE BILLPOSTER. Has she not come down yet?

THE OFFICER. Not yet, but she will soon be here— Do you know what is behind that door, Billposter?

THE BILLPOSTER. No, I have never seen that door open yet.

THE OFFICER. I am going to telephone for a locksmith to come and open it.

[*Goes into the lodge. THE BILLPOSTER posts a bill and goes toward the right.*]

THE DAUGHTER. What is the matter with the dipnet?

THE BILLPOSTER. Matter? Well, I don't know as there is anything the matter with it—but it just didn't turn out as I had expected, and the pleasure of it was not so much after all.

THE DAUGHTER. How did you expect it to be?

THE BILLPOSTER. How?— Well, I couldn't tell exactly—

THE DAUGHTER. I can tell you! You had expected it to be what it was not. It had to be green, but not that kind of green.

THE BILLPOSTER. You have it, Madam. You understand it all—and that is why everybody goes to you with his worries. If you would only listen to me a little also—

THE DAUGHTER. Of course, I will!— Come in to me and pour out your heart.

[*She goes into the lodge. THE BILLPOSTER remains outside, speaking to her.*]

[*The stage is darkened again. When the light is turned on, the tree has resumed its leaves, the monk's-hood is blooming once more, and the sun is shining on the green space beyond the passageway.*]

[THE OFFICER *enters. Now he is old and white-haired, ragged, and wearing worn-out shoes. He carries the bare remnants of the rose stems. Walks to and fro slowly, with the gait of an aged man. Reads on the posted bill.* A BALLET GIRL *comes in from the right.*]

THE OFFICER. Is Miss Victoria gone?

THE BALLET GIRL. No, she has not gone yet.

THE OFFICER. Then I shall wait. She will be coming soon, don't you think?

THE BALLET GIRL. Oh, yes, I am sure.

THE OFFICER. Don't go away now, for I have sent word to the locksmith, so you will soon see what is behind that door.

THE BALLET GIRL. Oh, it will be awfully interesting to see that door opened. That door, there, and the Growing Castle—have you heard of the Growing Castle?

THE OFFICER. Have I?— I have been a prisoner in it.

THE BALLET GIRL. No, was that you? But why do they keep such a lot of horses there?

THE OFFICER. Because it is a stable castle, don't you know.

THE BALLET GIRL. [*With confusion.*] How stupid of me not to guess that!

[A MALE CHORUS SINGER *enters from the right.*]

THE OFFICER. Has Miss Victoria gone yet?

THE CHORUS SINGER. [*Earnestly.*] No, she has not. She never goes away.

THE OFFICER. That is because she loves me— See here, don't go before the locksmith comes to open the door here.

THE CHORUS SINGER. No, is the door going to be opened? Well, that will be fun!— I just want to ask the Portress something.

[THE PROMPTER *enters from the right.*]

THE OFFICER. Is Miss Victoria gone yet?

THE PROMPTER. Not that I know of.

THE OFFICER. Now, didn't I tell you she was waiting for me?— Don't go away, for the door is going to be opened.

THE PROMPTER. Which door?

THE OFFICER. Is there more than one door?

THE PROMPTER. Oh, I know—that one with the clover leaf. Well, then I have got to stay— I am only going to have a word with the Portress.

[THE BALLET GIRL, THE CHORUS SINGER, *and* THE PROMPTER *gather beside* THE BILLPOSTER *in front of the lodge window and talk by turns to* THE DAUGHTER. THE GLAZIER *enters through the gate.*]

THE OFFICER. Are you the locksmith?

THE GLAZIER. No, the locksmith had visitors, and a glazier will do just as well.

THE OFFICER. Yes, of course, of course —but did you bring your diamond along?

THE GLAZIER. Why, certainly!— A glazier without his diamond, what would that be?

THE OFFICER. Nothing at all!— Let us get to work then.

[*Claps his hands together. All gather in a ring around the door. Male members of the chorus dressed as Master Singers and Ballet Girls in costumes from*

the opera "Aïda" enter from the right and join the rest.]

THE OFFICER. Locksmith—or glazier— do your duty!

[THE GLAZIER *goes up to the door with the diamond in his hand.*]

THE OFFICER. A moment like this will not occur twice in a man's life. For this reason, my friends, I ask you—please consider carefully—

A POLICEMAN. [*Enters.*] In the name of the law, I forbid the opening of that door!

THE OFFICER. Oh, Lord! What a fuss there is as soon as anybody wants to do anything new or great. But we will take the matter into court—let us go to the Lawyer. Then we shall see whether the laws still exist or not— Come along to the Lawyer.

[*Without lowering of the curtain, the stage changes to a lawyer's office, and in this manner. The gate remains, but as a wicket in the railing running clear across the stage. The gatekeeper's lodge turns into the private enclosure of the Lawyer, and it is now entirely open to the front. The linden, leafless, becomes a hat tree. The billboard is covered with legal notices and court decisions. The door with the four-leaved clover hole forms part of a document chest.*]

[THE LAWYER, *in evening dress, and white necktie, is found sitting to the left, inside the gate, and in front of him stands a desk covered with papers. His appearance indicates enormous sufferings. His face is chalk-white and full of wrinkles, and its shadows have a purple effect. He is ugly, and his features seem to reflect all the crimes and vices with which he has been forced by his profession to come into contact. Of his two clerks, one has lost an arm, the other an eye.*

The people gathered to witness "the opening of the door" remain as before, but they appear now to be waiting for an audience with THE LAWYER.*]

Judging by their attitudes, one would think they had been standing there forever.

THE DAUGHTER, *still wearing the shawl, and* THE OFFICER *are near the footlights.*]

THE LAWYER. [*Goes over to* THE DAUGHTER.] Tell me, sister, can I have that shawl? I shall keep it here until I have a fire in my grate, and then I shall burn it with all its miseries and sorrows.

THE DAUGHTER. Not yet, brother. I want it to hold all it possibly can, and I want it above all to take up your agonies—all the confidences you have received about crime, vice, robbery, slander, abuse—

THE LAWYER. My dear girl, for such a purpose your shawl would prove totally insufficient. Look at these walls. Does it not look as if the wall-paper itself had been soiled by every conceivable sin? Look at these documents into which I write tales of wrong. Look at myself— No smiling man ever comes here; nothing is to be seen here but angry glances, snarling lips, clenched fists— And everybody pours his anger, his envy, his suspicions, upon me. Look—my hands are black, and no washing will clean them. See how they are chapped and bleeding— I can never wear my clothes more than a few days because they smell of other people's crimes— At times I have the place fumigated with sulphur, but it does not help. I sleep near by, and I dream of nothing but crimes— Just now I have a murder case in court—oh, I can stand that, but do you know what is worse than anything else?— That is to separate married people! Then it is as if something cried way down in the earth and up there in the sky—as if it cried treason against the primal force, against the source of all good, against love— And do you know, when reams of paper have been filled with mutual accusations, and at last a sympathetic person takes one of the two apart and asks, with a pinch of the ear or a smile, the simple question: what have you really got against your husband?—or your wife?—then he, or she, stands perplexed and cannot give

the cause. Once—well, I think a lettuce salad was the principal issue; another time it was just a word—mostly it is nothing at all. But the tortures, the sufferings—these I have to bear— See how I look! Do you think I could ever win a woman's love with this countenance so like a criminal's? Do you think anybody dares to be friendly with me, who have to collect all the debts, all the money obligations, of the whole city?— It is a misery to be man!

THE DAUGHTER. Men are to be pitied!

THE LAWYER. They are. And what people are living on puzzles me. They marry on an income of two thousand, when they need four thousand. They borrow, of course—everybody borrows. In some sort of happy-go-lucky fashion, by the skin of their teeth, they manage to pull through— and thus it continues to the end, when the estate is found to be bankrupt. Who pays for it at last no one can tell.

THE DAUGHTER. Perhaps He who feeds the birds.

THE LAWYER. Perhaps. But if He who feeds the birds would only pay a visit to this earth of His and see for Himself how the poor human creatures fare—then His heart would surely fill with compassion.

THE DAUGHTER. Men are to be pitied!

THE LAWYER. Yes, that is the truth!— [*To* THE OFFICER.] What do you want?

THE OFFICER. I just wanted to ask if Miss Victoria has gone yet.

THE LAWYER. No, she has not; you can be sure of it— Why are you poking at my chest over there?

THE OFFICER. I thought the door of it looked exactly—

THE LAWYER. Not at all! Not at all!

[*All the church bells begin to ring.*]

THE OFFICER. Is there going to be a funeral?

THE LAWYER. No, it is graduation day —a number of degrees will be conferred, and I am going to be made a Doctor of Laws. Perhaps you would also like to be graduated and receive a laurel wreath?

THE OFFICER. Yes, why not? That would be a diversion, at least.

THE LAWYER. Perhaps then we may begin upon this solemn function at once— But you had better go home and change your clothes.   [THE OFFICER *goes out*.]

[*The stage is darkened and the following changes are made. The railing stays, but it encloses now the chancel of a church. The billboard displays hymn numbers. The linden hat tree becomes a candelabrum.* THE LAWYER'*s desk is turned into the desk of the presiding functionary, and the door with the clover leaf leads to the vestry.*

The chorus of MASTER SINGERS *become heralds with staffs, and the* BALLET GIRLS *carry laurel wreaths. The rest of the people act as spectators.*

The background is raised, and the new one thus discovered represents a large church organ, with the keyboards below and the organist's mirror above.

Music is heard. At the sides stand figures symbolising the four academic faculties: Philosophy, Theology, Medicine, and Jurisprudence.

At first the stage is empty for a few moments.]

[HERALDS *enter from the right.* BALLET GIRLS *follow with laurel wreaths carried high before them.* THREE GRADUATES *appear one after another from the left, receive their wreaths from the* BALLET GIRLS, *and go out to the right.* THE LAWYER *steps forward to get his wreath.* THE BALLET GIRLS *turn away from him and refuse to place the wreath on his head. Then they withdraw from the stage.* THE LAWYER, *shocked, leans against a column. All the others withdraw gradually until only* THE LAWYER *remains on the stage.*]

THE DAUGHTER. [*Enters, her head and shoulders covered by a white veil.*] Do you see, I have washed the shawl! But why are you standing there? Did you get your wreath?

THE LAWYER. No, I was not held worthy.

THE DAUGHTER. Why? Because you have defended the poor, put in a good word for the wrong-doing, made the burden easier for the guilty, obtained a respite for the condemned? Woe upon me: they are not angels—but they are to be pitied!

THE LAWYER. Say nothing evil of men —for after all it is my task to voice their side.

THE DAUGHTER. [*Leaning against the organ.*] Why do they strike their friends in the face?

THE LAWYER. They know no better.

THE DAUGHTER. Let us enlighten them. Will you try? Together with me?

THE LAWYER. They do not accept enlightenment— Oh, that our plaint might reach the gods of heaven!

THE DAUGHTER. It shall reach the throne— [*Turns toward the organ.*] Do you know what I see in this mirror?— The world turned the right way!— Yes indeed, for naturally we see it upside down.

THE LAWYER. How did it come to be turned the wrong way?

THE DAUGHTER. When the copy was taken—

THE LAWYER. You have said it! The copy— I have always had the feeling that it was a spoiled copy. And when I began to recall the original images, I grew dissatisfied with everything. But men called it soreheadedness, looking at the world through the devil's eyes, and other such things.

THE DAUGHTER. It is certainly a crazy world! Look at the four faculties here. The government, to which has fallen the task of preserving society, supports all four of them. Theology, the science of God, is constantly attacked and ridiculed by philosophy, which declares itself to be the sum of all wisdom. And medicine is always challenging philosophy, while refusing entirely to count theology a science and even insisting on calling it a mere superstition. And they belong to a common Academic Council, which has been set to teach the young respect—for the university. It is a bedlam. And woe unto him who first recovers his reason!

THE LAWYER. Those who find it out first are the theologians. As a preparatory study, they take philosophy, which teaches them that theology is nonsense. Later they learn from theology that philosophy is nonsense. Madmen, I should say!

THE DAUGHTER. And then there is jurisprudence which serves all but the servants.

THE LAWYER. Justice, which, when it wants to do right, becomes the undoing of men. Equity, which so often turns into iniquity!

THE DAUGHTER. What a mess you have made of it, you man-children. Children, indeed!— Come here, and I will give you a wreath—one that is more becoming to you. [*Puts a crown of thorns on his head.*] And now I will play for you.

[*She sits down at the keyboards, but instead of organ-notes human voices are heard.*]

VOICES OF CHILDREN. O Lord everlasting. [*Last note sustained.*]

VOICES OF WOMEN. Have mercy upon us! [*Last note sustained.*]

VOICES OF MEN. [*Tenors.*] Save us for thy mercy's sake! [*Last note sustained.*]

VOICES OF MEN. [*Basses.*] Spare Thy Children, O Lord, and deliver us from Thy wrath!

ALL. Have mercy upon us! Hear us! Have pity upon the mortals!— O Lord eternal, why art Thou afar?— Out of the depths we call unto Thee: Make not the burden of Thy children too heavy! Hear us! Hear us!

[*The stage turns dark.* THE DAUGHTER *rises and draws close to* THE LAWYER. *By a change of light, the organ becomes Fingal's Cave.*[4] *The ground*

swell of the ocean, which can be seen rising and falling between the columns of basalt, produces a deep harmony that blends the music of winds and waves.]

THE LAWYER. Where are we, sister?

THE DAUGHTER. What do you hear?

THE LAWYER. I hear drops falling—

THE DAUGHTER. Those are the tears that men are weeping— What more do you hear?

THE LAWYER. There is sighing—and whining—and wailing—

THE DAUGHTER. Hither the plaint of the mortals has reached—and no farther. But why this never-ending wailing? Is there then nothing in life to rejoice at?

THE LAWYER. Yes, what is most sweet, and what is also most bitter—love—wife and home—the highest and the lowest!

THE DAUGHTER. May I try it?

THE LAWYER. With me?

THE DAUGHTER. With you— You know the rocks, the stumbling-stones. Let us avoid them.

THE LAWYER. I am so poor.

THE DAUGHTER. What does that matter if we only love each other? And a little beauty costs nothing.

THE LAWYER. I have dislikes which may prove your likes.

THE DAUGHTER. They can be adjusted.

THE LAWYER. And if we tire of it?

THE DAUGHTER. Then come the children and bring with them a diversion that remains for ever new.

THE LAWYER. You, you will take me, poor and ugly, scorned and rejected?

THE DAUGHTER. Yes—let us unite our destinies.

THE LAWYER. So be it then!

[CURTAIN.]

An extremely plain room inside THE LAWYER'S *office. To the right, a big double bed covered by a canopy and curtained*

in. Next to it, a window. To the left, an iron heater with cooking utensils on top of it. CHRISTINE *is pasting paper strips*

[4] A famous sea-swept cavern on the rocky shore of a small uninhabited island off the west coast of Scotland. Fingal, or Finn, was an ancient hero of Celtic legend.

along the cracks of the double windows. In the background, an open door to the office. Through the door are visible a number of poor clients waiting for admission.

CHRISTINE. I paste, I paste.

THE DAUGHTER. [*Pale and emaciated, sits by the stove.*] You shut out all the air. I choke!

CHRISTINE. Now there is only one little crack left.

THE DAUGHTER. Air, air—I cannot breathe!

CHRISTINE. I paste, I paste.

THE LAWYER. That's right, Christine! Heat is expensive.

THE DAUGHTER. Oh, it feels as if my lips were being glued together.

THE LAWYER. [*Standing in the doorway, with a paper in his hand.*] Is the child asleep?

THE DAUGHTER. Yes, at last.

THE LAWYER. [*Gently.*] All this crying scares away my clients.

THE DAUGHTER. [*Pleasantly.*] What can be done about it?

THE LAWYER. Nothing.

THE DAUGHTER. We shall have to get a larger place.

THE LAWYER. We have no money for it.

THE DAUGHTER. May I open the window —this bad air is suffocating.

THE LAWYER. Then the heat escapes, and we shall be cold.

THE DAUGHTER. It is horrible!— May we clean up out there?

THE LAWYER. You have not the strength to do any cleaning, nor have I, and Christine must paste. She must put strips through the whole house, on every crack, in the ceiling, in the floor, in the walls.

THE DAUGHTER. Poverty I was prepared for, but not for dirt.

THE LAWYER. Poverty is always dirty, relatively speaking.

THE DAUGHTER. This is worse than I dreamed!

THE LAWYER. We are not the worst off by far. There is still food in the pot.

THE DAUGHTER. But what sort of food?

THE LAWYER. Cabbage is cheap, nourishing, and good to eat.

THE DAUGHTER. For those who like cabbage—to me it is repulsive.

THE LAWYER. Why didn't you say so?

THE DAUGHTER. Because I loved you. I wanted to sacrifice my own taste.

THE LAWYER. Then I must sacrifice my taste for cabbage to you—for sacrifices must be mutual.

THE DAUGHTER. What are we to eat, then? Fish? But you hate fish.

THE LAWYER. And it is expensive.

THE DAUGHTER. This is worse than I thought it!

THE LAWYER. [*Kindly.*] Yes, you see how hard it is— And the child that was to become a link and a blessing—it becomes our ruin.

THE DAUGHTER. Dearest, I die in this air, in this room, with its backyard view, with its baby cries and endless hours of sleeplessness, with those people out there, and their whinings, and bickerings, and incriminations— I shall die here!

THE LAWYER. My poor little flower, that has no light and no air—

THE DAUGHTER. And you say that people exist who are still worse off?

THE LAWYER. I belong with the envied ones in this locality.

THE DAUGHTER. Everything else might be borne if I could only have some beauty in my home.

THE LAWYER. I know you are thinking of flowers—and especially of heliotropes— but a plant costs half a dollar, which will buy six quarts of milk or a peck of potatoes.

THE DAUGHTER. I could gladly get along without food if I could only have some flowers.

THE LAWYER. There is a kind of beauty that costs nothing—but the absence of it in the home is worse than any other torture to a man with a sense for the beautiful.

THE DAUGHTER. What is it?

THE LAWYER. If I tell you, you will get angry.

THE DAUGHTER. We have agreed not to get angry.

THE LAWYER. We have agreed— Everything can be overcome, Agnes, except the short, sharp accents— Do you know them? Not yet!

THE DAUGHTER. They will never be heard between us.

THE LAWYER. Not as far as it lies on me!

THE DAUGHTER. Tell me now.

THE LAWYER. Well—when I come into a room, I look first of all at the curtains— [*Goes over to the window and straightens out the curtains.*] If they hang like ropes or rags, then I leave soon. And next I take a glance at the chairs—if they stand straight along the wall, then I stay. [*Puts a chair back against the wall.*] Finally I look at the candles in their sticks—if they point this way and that, then the whole house is askew. [*Straightens up a candle on the chest of drawers.*] This is the kind of beauty, dear heart, that costs nothing.

THE DAUGHTER. [*With bent head.*] Beware of the short accents, Axel!

THE LAWYER. They were not short.

THE DAUGHTER. Yes, they were.

THE LAWYER. Well, I'll be—

THE DAUGHTER. What kind of language is that?

THE LAWYER. Pardon me, Agnes! But I have suffered as much from your lack of orderliness as you have suffered from dirt. And I have not dared to set things right myself, for when I do so, you get as angry as if I were reproaching you—ugh! Hadn't we better quit now?

THE DAUGHTER. It is very difficult to be married—it is more difficult than anything else. One has to be an angel, I think!

THE LAWYER. I think so, too.

THE DAUGHTER. I fear I shall begin to hate you after this!

THE LAWYER. Woe to us then! —But let us forestall hatred. I promise never again to speak of any untidiness—although it is torture to me!

THE DAUGHTER. And I shall eat cabbage though it means agony to me.

THE LAWYER. A life of common suffering, then! One's pleasure, the other one's pain!

THE DAUGHTER. Men are to be pitied!

THE LAWYER. You see that?

THE DAUGHTER. Yes, but for heaven's sake, let us avoid the rocks, now when we know them so well.

THE LAWYER. Let us try! Are we not decent and intelligent persons? Able to forbear and forgive?

THE DAUGHTER. Why not smile at mere trifles?

THE LAWYER. We—only we—can do so. Do you know, I read this morning—by the bye, where is the newspaper?

THE DAUGHTER. [*Embarrassed.*] Which newspaper?

THE LAWYER. [*Sharply.*] Do I keep more than one?

THE DAUGHTER. Smile now, and don't speak sharply—I used your paper to make the fire with—

THE LAWYER. [*Violently.*] Well, I'll be damned!

THE DAUGHTER. Why don't you smile?— I burned it because it ridiculed what is holy to me.

THE LAWYER. Which is unholy to me! Yah! [*Strikes one clenched fist against the open palm of the other hand.*] I smile, I smile so that my wisdom teeth show— Of course, I am to be nice, and I am to swallow my own opinions, and say yes to everything, and cringe and dissemble! [*Tidies the curtains around the bed*] That's it! Now I am going to fix things until you get angry again— Agnes, this is simply impossible!

THE DAUGHTER. Of course it is!

THE LAWYER. And yet we must endure —not for the sake of our promises, but for the sake of the child!

THE DAUGHTER. You are right—for the sake of the child. Oh, oh—we have to endure!

THE LAWYER. And now I must go out to my clients. Listen to them—how they growl with impatience to tear each other, to get each other fined and jailed— Lost souls!

THE DAUGHTER. Poor, poor people! And this pasting!

[*She drops her head forward in dumb despair.*]

CHRISTINE. I paste, I paste.

[THE LAWYER *stands at the door, twisting the doorknob nervously.*]

THE DAUGHTER. How that knob squeaks! It is as if you were twisting my heart-strings—

THE LAWYER. I twist, I twist!

THE DAUGHTER. Don't!

THE LAWYER. I twist!

THE DAUGHTER. No!

THE LAWYER. I—

THE OFFICER. [*In the office, on the other side of the door, takes hold of the knob.*] Will you permit me?

THE LAWYER. [*Lets go his hold.*] By all means. Seeing that you have your degree!

THE OFFICER. Now all life belongs to me. Every road lies open. I have mounted Parnassus. The laurel is won. Immortality, fame, all is mine!

THE LAWYER. And what are you going to live on?

THE OFFICER. Live on?

THE LAWYER. You must have a home, clothes, food—

THE OFFICER. Oh, that will come—if you can only find somebody to love you!

THE LAWYER. You don't say so!— You don't— Paste, Christine, paste until they cannot breathe.

[*Goes out backward, nodding.*]

CHRISTINE. I paste, I paste—until they cannot breathe.

THE OFFICER. Will you come with me now?

THE DAUGHTER. At once! But where?

THE OFFICER. To Fairhaven. There it is summer; there the sun is shining; there we find youth, children, and flowers, singing and dancing, feasting and frolicking.

THE DAUGHTER. Then I will go there.

THE OFFICER. Come!

THE LAWYER. [*Enters again.*] Now I go back to my first hell—this was the second and greater. The sweeter the hell, the greater— And look here, now she has been dropping hair-pins on the floor again.

[*He picks up some hair-pins.*]

THE OFFICER. My! but he has discovered the pins also.

THE LAWYER. Also?— Look at this one. You see two prongs, but it is only one pin. It is two, yet only one. If I bend it open, it is a single piece. If I bend it back, there are two, but they remain one for all that. It means: these two are one. But if I break—like this!—then they become two.

[*Breaks the pin and throws the pieces away.*]

THE OFFICER. All that he has seen!— But before breaking, the prongs must diverge. If they point together, then it holds.

THE LAWYER. And if they are parallel, then they will never meet—and it neither breaks nor holds.

THE OFFICER. The hair-pin is the most perfect of all created things. A straight line which equals two parallel ones.

THE LAWYER. A lock that shuts when it is open.

THE OFFICER. And thus shuts in a braid of hair that opens up when the lock shuts.

THE LAWYER. It is like this door. When I close it, then I open—the way out—for you, Agnes!

[*Withdraws and closes the door behind him.*]

THE DAUGHTER. Well then?

[*The stage changes. The bed with its curtains becomes a tent. The stove stays as it was. The background is raised. To the right, in the foreground, are seen hills stripped of their trees by fire, and red heather growing between the blackened tree stumps. Red-painted pig-sties and outhouses. Beyond these, in the open, apparatus for mechanical gymnastics, where sick persons are being treated on machines resembling instruments of torture. To the left, in the foreground, the quarantine station, consisting of open sheds, with ovens, furnaces, and pipe coils. In the middle distance, a narrow strait. The back-*

*ground shows a beautiful wooded
shore. Flags are flying on its piers,
where ride white sailboats, some with
sails set and some without. Little Italian villas, pavilions, arbors, marble
statues are glimpsed through the foliage along the shore.*]

[*The* MASTER OF QUARANTINE, *made up
like a blackamoor, is walking along the
shore.*]

THE OFFICER. [*Meets him and they
shake hands.*] Why, Ordström! [1] Have you
landed here?

MASTER OF QUARANTINE. Yes, here I
am.

THE OFFICER. Is this Fairhaven?

MASTER OF QUARANTINE. No, that is on
the other side. This is Foulstrand.

THE OFFICER. Then we have lost our
way.

MASTER OF QUARANTINE. We?— Won't
you introduce me?

THE OFFICER. No, that wouldn't do. [*In
a lowered voice.*] It is Indra's own daughter.

MASTER OF QUARANTINE. Indra's? And I
was thinking of Varuna [2] himself— Well,
are you not surprised to find me black in
the face?

THE OFFICER. I am past fifty, my boy,
and at that age one has ceased to be surprised. I concluded at once that you were
bound for some fancy ball this afternoon.

MASTER OF QUARANTINE. Right you
were! And I hope both of you will come
along.

THE OFFICER. Why, yes—for I must say
—the place does not look very tempting.
What kind of people live here anyhow?

MASTER OF QUARANTINE. Here you find
the sick; over there, the healthy.

THE OFFICER. Nothing but poor folk on
this side, I suppose.

MASTER OF QUARANTINE. No, my boy,
it is here you find the rich. Look at that

---

one on the rack. He has stuffed himself
with paté de foie gras and truffles and Burgundy until his feet have grown knotted.

THE OFFICER. Knotted?

MASTER OF QUARANTINE. Yes, he has a
case of knotted feet. And that one who lies
under the guillotine—he has swilled brandy
so that his backbone has to be put through
the mangle.

THE OFFICER. There is always something amiss!

MASTER OF QUARANTINE. Moreover,
everybody living on this side has some kind
of canker to hide. Look at the fellow coming here, for instance.

[*An old dandy is pushed on the stage in
a wheel-chair. He is accompanied by
a gaunt and grisly coquette in the six-
ties, to whom* THE FRIEND, *a man of
about forty, is paying court.*]

THE OFFICER. It is the major—our
schoolmate!

MASTER OF QUARANTINE. Don Juan. [3]
Can you see that he is still enamored of
that old spectre beside him? He does not
notice that she has grown old, or that she
is ugly, faithless, cruel.

THE OFFICER. Why, that is love! And I
couldn't have dreamt that a fickle fellow
like him would prove capable of loving so
deeply and so earnestly.

MASTER OF QUARANTINE. That is a
mighty decent way of looking at it.

THE OFFICER. I have been in love with
Victoria myself—in fact I am still waiting
for her in the passageway—

MASTER OF QUARANTINE. Oh, you are
the fellow who is waiting in the passageway?

THE OFFICER. I am the man.

MASTER OF QUARANTINE. Well, have you
got that door opened yet?

THE OFFICER. No, the case is still in
court— The Billposter is out with his dipnet, of course, so that the taking of evidence is always being put off—and in the
meantime the Glazier has mended all the

---

[1] The literal meaning of the name is "word-
spout."
[2] The Hindu god of the physical universe, one
of whose functions was the meting out of rewards and punishments.
[3] A legendary Spanish nobleman whose name
has become proverbial for cynical sensuality.

THE DREAM PLAY

551

window panes in the castle, which has grown half a story higher— This has been an uncommonly good year—warm and wet—

MASTER OF QUARANTINE. But just the same you have had no heat comparing with what I have here.

THE OFFICER. How much do you have in your ovens?

MASTER OF QUARANTINE. When we fumigate cholera suspects, we run it up to one hundred and forty degrees.

THE OFFICER. Is the cholera going again?

MASTER OF QUARANTINE. Don't you know that?

THE OFFICER. Of couse, I know it, but I forget so often what I know.

MASTER OF QUARANTINE. I wish often that I could forget—especially myself. That is why I go in for masquerades and carnivals and amateur theatricals.

THE OFFICER. What have you been up to, then?

MASTER OF QUARANTINE. If I told they would say that I was boasting; and if I don't tell, then they call me a hypocrite.

THE OFFICER. That is why you blackened your face?

MASTER OF QUARANTINE. Exactly— making myself a shade blacker than I am.

THE OFFICER. Who is coming there?

MASTER OF QUARANTINE. Oh, a poet who is going to have his mud bath.

[THE POET enters with his eyes raised toward the sky and carrying a pail of mud in one hand.]

THE OFFICER. Why, he ought to be having light baths and air baths.

MASTER OF QUARANTINE. No, he is roaming about the higher regions so much that he gets homesick for the mud—and wallowing in the mire makes the skin callous like that of a pig. Then he cannot feel the stings of the wasps.

THE OFFICER. This is a queer world, full of contradictions.

THE POET. [Ecstatically.] Man was created by the god Phtah [4] out of clay on a

[4] The Egyptian god regarded as the creator of the world.

potter's wheel, or a lathe— [Sceptically.] or any damned old thing! [Ecstatically.] Out of clay does the sculptor create his more or less immortal masterpieces— [Sceptically.] which mostly are pure rot. [Ecstatically.] Out of clay they make those utensils which are so indispensable in the pantry and which generically are named pots and plates— [Sceptically.] but what in thunder does it matter to me what they are called anyhow? [Ecstatically.] Such is the clay! When clay becomes fluid, it is called mud— C'est mon affaire!— [Shouts.] Lena!

[LENA enters with a pail in her hand.]

THE POET. Lena, show yourself to Miss Agnes— She knew you ten years ago, when you were a young, happy and, let us say, pretty girl— Behold how she looks now. Five children, drudgery, baby-cries, hunger, ill-treatment. See how beauty has perished and joy vanished in the fulfilment of duties which should have brought that inner satisfaction which makes each line in the face harmonious and fills the eye with a quiet glow.

MASTER OF QUARANTINE. [Covering THE POET'S mouth with his hand.] Shut up! Shut up!

THE POET. That is what they all say. And if you keep silent, then they cry: speak! Oh, restless humanity!

THE DAUGHTER. [Goes to LENA.] Tell me your troubles.

LENA. No, I dare not, for then they will be made worse.

THE DAUGHTER. Who could be so cruel?

LENA. I dare not tell, for if I do, I shall be spanked.

THE POET. That is just what will happen. But I will speak, even though the blackamoor knock out all my teeth—I will tell that justice is not always done—Agnes, daughter of the gods, do you hear music and dancing on the hill over there?— Well, it is Lena's sister who has come home from the city where she went astray—you understand? Now they are killing the fatted calf; but Lena, who stayed at home, has to carry slop pails and feed the pigs.[5]

THE DAUGHTER. There is rejoicing at home because the stray has left the paths of evil, and not merely because she has come back. Bear that in mind.

THE POET. But then they should give a ball and banquet every night for the spotless worker that never strayed into paths of error— Yet they do nothing of the kind, but when Lena has a free moment, she is sent to prayer-meetings where she has to hear reproaches for not being perfect. Is this justice?

THE DAUGHTER. Your question is so difficult to answer because— There are so many unforeseen cases—

THE POET. That much the Caliph, Haroun the Just,[6] came to understand. He was sitting on his throne, and from its height he could never make out what happened below. At last complaints penetrated to his exalted ears. And then, one fine day, he disguised himself and descended unobserved among the crowds to find out what kind of justice they were getting.

THE DAUGHTER. I hope you don't take me for Haroun the Just!

THE OFFICER. Let us talk of something else— Here come visitors.

[A white boat, shaped like a viking ship, with a dragon for figure-head, with a pale-blue silken sail on a gilded yard, and with a rose-red standard flying from the top of a gilded mast, glides through the strait from the left. HE and SHE are seated in the stern with their arms around each other.]

THE OFFICER. Behold perfect happiness, bliss without limits, young love's rejoicing!

[The stage grows brighter.]

HE. [Stands up in the boat and sings.]

Hail, beautiful haven,
Where the Springs of my youth were spent,
Where my first sweet dreams were dreamt—

To thee I return
But lonely no longer!

Ye hills and groves,
Thou sky o'erhead,
Thou mirroring sea,
Give greeting to her:
My love, my bride,
My light and my life!

[The flags at the landings of Fairhaven are dipped in salute; white handkerchiefs are waved from verandahs and boats, and the air is filled with tender chords from harps and violins.]

THE POET. See the light that surrounds them! Hear how the air is ringing with music!— Eros![7]

THE OFFICER. It is Victoria.

MASTER OF QUARANTINE. Well, what of it?

THE OFFICER. It is his Victoria— My own is still mine. And nobody can see her— Now you hoist the quarantine flag, and I shall pull in the net.

[THE MASTER OF QUARANTINE waves a yellow flag.]

THE OFFICER. [Pulling a rope that turns the boat toward Foulstrand.] Hold on there!

[HE and SHE become aware of the hideous view and give vent to their horror.]

MASTER OF QUARANTINE. Yes, it comes hard. But here every one must stop who hails from plague-stricken places.

THE POET. The idea of speaking in such a manner, or acting in such a way, within the presence of two human beings united in love! Touch them not! Lay not hands on love! It is treason!— Woe to us! Everything beautiful must now be dragged down —dragged into the mud!

[HE and SHE step ashore, looking sad and shamefaced.]

HE. Woe to us! What have we done?

MASTER OF QUARANTINE. It is not nec-

---

[5] The parallel here is obviously with the parable of the Prodigal Son.
[6] Caliph of Bagdad (763–809) who figures in many tales of the *Arabian Nights*. He was reputed

to go among the common people in disguise to observe the functioning of justice.
[7] Love.

essary to have done anything in order to encounter life's little pricks.

SHE. So short-lived are joy and happiness!

HE. How long must we stay here?

MASTER OF QUARANTINE. Forty days and nights.

SHE. Then rather into the water!

HE. To live here—among blackened hills and pig-sties?

THE POET. Love overcomes all, even sulphur fumes and carbolic acid.

MASTER OF QUARANTINE. [*Starts a fire in the stove; blue, sulphurous flames break forth.*] Now I set the sulphur going. Will you please step in?

SHE. Oh, my blue dress will fade.

MASTER OF QUARANTINE. And become white. So your roses will also turn white in time.

HE. Even your cheeks—in forty days!

SHE. [*To* THE OFFICER.] That will please you.

THE OFFICER. No, it will not!— Of course, your happiness was the cause of my suffering, but—it doesn't matter—for I am graduated and have obtained a position over there—heigh-ho and alas! And in the Fall I shall be teaching school—teaching boys the same lessons I myself learned during my childhood and youth—the same lessons throughout my manhood and, finally, in my old age—the self-same lessons! What does twice two make? How many times can four be evenly divided by two?—Until I get a pension and can do nothing at all—just wait around for meals and the newspapers—until at last I am carted to the crematorium and burned to ashes— Have you nobody here who is entitled to a pension? Barring twice two makes four, it is probably the worst thing of all—to begin school all over again when one already is graduated; to ask the same questions until death comes—

[*An elderly man goes by, with his hands folded behind his back.*]

THE OFFICER. There is a pensioner now, waiting for himself to die. I think he must be a captain who missed the rank of major; or an assistant judge who was not made a chief justice. Many are called but few are chosen— He is waiting for his breakfast now.

THE PENSIONER. No, for the newspaper —the morning paper.

THE OFFICER. And he is only fifty-four years old. He may spend twenty-five more years waiting for meals and newspapers— is it not dreadful?

THE PENSIONER. What is not dreadful? Tell me, tell me!

THE OFFICER. Tell that who can!— Now I shall have to teach boys that twice two makes four. And how many times four can be evenly divided by two. [*He clutches his head in despair.*] And Victoria, whom I loved and therefore wished all the happiness life can give—now she has her happiness, the greatest one known to her, and for this reason I suffer—suffer, suffer!

SHE. Do you think I can be happy when I see you suffering? How can you think it? Perhaps it will soothe your pains that I am to be imprisoned here for forty days and nights? Tell me, does it soothe your pains?

THE OFFICER. Yes and no. How can I enjoy seeing you suffer? Oh!

SHE. And do you think my happiness can be founded on your torments?

THE OFFICER. We are to pitied—all of us!

ALL. [*Raise their arms toward the sky and utter a cry of anguish that sounds like a dissonant chord.*] Oh!

THE DAUGHTER. Everlasting One, hear them! Life is evil! Men are to be pitied!

ALL. [*As before.*] Oh!

[*For a moment the stage is completely darkened, and during that moment everybody withdraws or takes up a new position. When the light is turned on again, Foulstrand is seen in the background, lying in deep shadow. The strait is in the middle distance and Fairhaven in the foreground, both steeped in light. To the right, a corner of the Casino, where dancing couples are visible through the open windows.*]

Three servant maids are standing outside on top of an empty box, with arms around each other, staring at the dancers within. On the verandah of the Casino stands a bench, where "PLAIN" EDITH *is sitting. She is bareheaded, with an abundance of tousled hair, and looks sad. In front of her is an open piano. To the left a frame house painted yellow. Two children in light dresses are playing ball outside. In the centre of the middle distance, a pier with white sailboats tied to it, and flagpoles with hoisted flags. In the strait is anchored a naval vessel, brig-rigged, with gun ports. But the entire landscape is in winter dress, with snow on the ground and on the bare trees.]*

[THE DAUGHTER *and* THE OFFICER *enter.*]

THE DAUGHTER. Here is peace, and happiness, and leisure. No more toil; every day a holiday; everybody dressed up in his best; dancing and music in the early morning. [*To the maids.*] Why don't you go in and have a dance, girls?

THE MAIDS. We?

THE OFFICER. They are servants, don't you see!

THE DAUGHTER. Of course!— But why is Edith sitting there instead of dancing?

[EDITH *buries her face in her hands.*]

THE OFFICER. Don't question her! She has been sitting there three hours without being asked for a dance.

[*Goes into the yellow house on the left.*]

THE DAUGHTER. What a cruel form of amusement!

THE MOTHER. [*In a low-necked dress, enters from the Casino and goes up to* EDITH.] Why don't you go in as I told you?

EDITH. Because—I cannot throw myself at them. That I am ugly I know, and I know that nobody wants to dance with me, but I might be spared from being reminded of it.

[*Begins to play on the piano, the Toccata Con Fuga, Op. 10, by Sebastian Bach.*

The waltz music from within is heard faintly at first. Then it grows in strength, as if to compete with the Bach Toccata. EDITH *prevails over it and brings it to silence. Dancers appear in the doorway to hear her play. Everybody on the stage stands still and listens reverently.*]

A NAVAL OFFICER. [*Takes* ALICE, *one of the dancers, around the waist and drags her toward the pier.*] Come quick!

[EDITH *breaks off abruptly, rises and stares at the couple with an expression of utter despair; stands as if turned to stone.*

Now the front wall of the yellow house disappears, revealing three benches full of schoolboys. Among these THE OFFICER *is seen, looking worried and depressed. In front of the boys stands* THE TEACHER, *bespectacled and holding a piece of chalk in one hand, a rattan cane in the other.*]

THE TEACHER. [*To* THE OFFICER.] Well, my boy, can you tell me what twice two makes?

[THE OFFICER *remains seated while he racks his mind without finding an answer.*]

THE TEACHER. You must rise when I ask you a question.

THE OFFICER. [*Harassed, rises.*] Two—twice—let me see. That makes two-two.

THE TEACHER. I see! You have not studied your lesson.

THE OFFICER. [*Ashamed.*] Yes, I have, but—I know the answer, but I cannot tell it—

THE TEACHER. You want to wriggle out of it, of course. You know it, but you cannot tell. Perhaps I may help you. [*Pulls his hair.*]

THE OFFICER. Oh, it is dreadful, it is dreadful!

THE TEACHER. Yes, it is dreadful that such a big boy lacks all ambition—

THE OFFICER. [*Hurt.*] Big boy—yes, I am big—bigger than all these others—I am full-grown, I am done with school— [*As if waking up*] I have graduated—why am I then sitting here? Have I not received my doctor's degree?

THE TEACHER. Certainly, but you are to sit here and mature, you know. You have to mature—isn't that so?

THE OFFICER. [*Feels his forehead.*] Yes, that is right, one must mature— Twice two —makes two—and this I can demonstrate by analogy, which is the highest form of all reasoning. Listen!— Once one makes one; consequently twice two must make two. For what applies in one case must also apply in another.

THE TEACHER. Your conclusion is based on good logic, but your answer is wrong.

THE OFFICER. What is logical cannot be wrong. Let us test it. One divided by one gives one, so that two divided by two must give two.

THE TEACHER. Correct according to analogy. But how much does once three make?

THE OFFICER. Three, of course.

THE TEACHER. Consequently twice three must also make three.

THE OFFICER. [*Pondering.*] No, that cannot be right—it cannot—or else— [*Sits down dejectedly.*] No, I am not mature yet.

THE TEACHER. No, indeed, you are far from mature.

THE OFFICER. But how long am I to sit here, then?

THE TEACHER. Here—how long? Do you believe that time and space exist?— Suppose that time does exist, then you should be able to say what time is. What is time?

THE OFFICER. Time— [*Thinks.*] I cannot tell, but I know what it is. Consequently I may also know what twice two is without being able to tell it. And, teacher, can you tell what time is?

THE TEACHER. Of course I can.

ALL THE BOYS. Tell us then!

THE TEACHER. Time — let me see. [*Stands immovable with one finger on his nose.*] While we are talking, time flies. Consequently time is something that flies while we talk.

A BOY. [*Rising.*] Now you are talking, teacher, and while you are talking, I fly: consequently I am time.

[*Runs out.*]

THE TEACHER. That accords completely with the laws of logic.

THE OFFICER. Then the laws of logic are silly, for Nils, who ran away, cannot be time.

THE TEACHER. That is also good logic, although it is silly.

THE OFFICER. Then logic itself is silly.

THE TEACHER. So it seems. But if logic is silly, then all the world is silly—and then the devil himself wouldn't stay here to teach you more silliness. If anybody treats me to a drink, we'll go and take a bath.

THE OFFICER. That is a *posterus prius*,[8] or the world turned upside down, for it is customary to bathe first and have the drink afterward. Old fogy!

THE TEACHER. Beware of a swelled head, doctor!

THE OFFICER. Call me captain, if you please. I am an officer, and I cannot understand why I should be sitting here to get scolded like a schoolboy—

THE TEACHER. [*With raised index finger.*] We were to mature!

MASTER OF QUARANTINE. [*Enters.*] The quarantine begins.

THE OFFICER. Oh, there you are. Just think of it, this fellow makes me sit among the boys although I am graduated.

MASTER OF QUARANTINE. Well, why don't you go away?

THE OFFICER. Heaven knows!— Go away? Why, that is no easy thing to do.

THE TEACHER. I guess not—just try!

THE OFFICER. [*To* MASTER OF QUARANTINE.] Save me! Save me from his eye!

MASTER OF QUARANTINE. Come on. Come and help us dance— We have to dance before the plague breaks out. We must!

THE OFFICER. Is the brig leaving?

MASTER OF QUARANTINE. Yes, first of all the brig must leave— Then there will be a lot of tears shed, of course.

THE OFFICER. Always tears: when she

8 *I.e.*, putting the cart before the horse.

comes and when she goes— Let us get out of here.

[*They go out.* THE TEACHER *continues his lesson in silence.*

THE MAIDS *that were staring through the window of the dance hall walk sadly down to the pier.* EDITH, *who has been standing like a statue at the piano, follows them.*]

THE DAUGHTER. [*To* THE OFFICER.] Is there not one happy person to be found in this paradise?

THE OFFICER. Yes, there is a newly married couple. Just watch them.

[THE NEWLY MARRIED COUPLE *enter.*]

HUSBAND. [*To his* WIFE.] My joy has no limits, and I could now wish to die—

WIFE. Why die?

HUSBAND. Because at the heart of happiness grows the seed of disaster. Happiness devours itself like a flame—it cannot burn for ever, but must go out some time. And this presentiment of the coming end destroys joy in the very hour of its culmination.

WIFE. Let us then die together—this moment!

HUSBAND. Die? All right! For I fear happiness—that cheat!

[*They go toward the water.*]

THE DAUGHTER. Life is evil! Men are to be pitied!

THE OFFICER. Look at this fellow. He is the most envied mortal in this neighborhood.

[THE BLIND MAN *is led in.*]

THE OFFICER. He is the owner of these hundred or more Italian villas. He owns all these bays, straits, shores, forests, together with the fishes in the water, the birds in the air, the game in the woods. These thousand or more people are his tenants. The sun rises upon his sea and sets upon his land—

THE DAUGHTER. Well—is he complaining also?

THE OFFICER. Yes, and with right, for he cannot see.

MASTER OF QUARANTINE. He is blind.

THE DAUGHTER. The most envied of all!

THE OFFICER. Now he has come to see the brig depart with his son on board.

THE BLIND MAN. I cannot see, but I hear. I hear the anchor bill claw the clay bottom as when the hook is torn out of a fish and brings up the heart with it through the neck— My son, my only child, is going to journey across the wide sea to foreign lands, and I can follow him only in my thought! Now I hear the clanking of the chain—and—there is something that snaps and cracks like clothes drying on a line— wet handkerchiefs perhaps. And I hear it blubber and snivel as when people are weeping—maybe the splashing of the wavelets among the seines—or maybe girls along the shore, deserted and disconsolate— Once I asked a child why the ocean is salt, and the child, who had a father on a long trip across the high seas, said immediately: the ocean is salt because the sailors shed so many tears into it. And why do the sailors cry so much then?— Because they are always going away, replied the child; and that is why they are always drying their handkerchiefs in the rigging— And why does man weep when he is sad? I asked at last— Because the glass in the eyes must be washed now and then, so that he can see clearly, said the child.

[*The brig has set sail and is gliding off. The girls along the shore or alternately waving their handkerchiefs and wiping off their tears with them. Then a signal is set on the foremast—a red ball in a white field, meaning "yes." In response to it* ALICE *waves her handkerchief triumphantly.*]

THE DAUGHTER. [*To* THE OFFICER.] What is the meaning of that flag?

THE OFFICER. It means "yes." It is the lieutenant's troth—red as the red blood of the arteries, set against the blue cloth of the sky.

THE DAUGHTER. And how does "no" look?

THE OFFICER. It is blue as the spoiled blood in the veins—but look, how jubilant Alice is.

THE DAUGHTER. And how Edith cries.

THE BLIND MAN. Meet and part. Part and meet. That is life. I met his mother. And then she went away from me. He was left to me; and now he goes.

THE DAUGHTER. But he will come back.

THE BLIND MAN. Who is speaking to me? I have heard that voice before—in my dreams; in my youth, when vacation began; in the early years of my marriage, when my child was born. Every time life smiled at me, I heard that voice, like a whisper of the south wind, like a chord of harps from above, like what I feel the angels' greeting must be in the Holy Night—

[THE LAWYER enters and goes up to whisper something into THE BLIND MAN'S ear.]

THE BLIND MAN. Is that so?

THE LAWYER. That's the truth. [Goes to THE DAUGHTER.] Now you have seen most of it, but you have not yet tried the worst of it.

THE DAUGHTER. What can that be?

THE LAWYER. Repetition—recurrence. To retrace one's own tracks; to be sent back to the task once finished—come!

THE DAUGHTER. Where?

THE LAWYER. To your duties.

THE DAUGHTER. What does that mean?

THE LAWYER. Everything you dread. Everything you do not want but must. It means to forgo, to give up, to do without, to lack—it means everything that is unpleasant, repulsive, painful.

THE DAUGHTER. Are there no pleasant duties?

THE LAWYER. They become pleasant when they are done.

THE DAUGHTER. When they have ceased to exist—Duty is then something unpleasant. What is pleasant then?

THE LAWYER. What is pleasant is sin.

THE DAUGHTER. Sin?

THE LAWYER. Yes, something that has to be punished. If I have had a pleasant day or night, then I suffer infernal pangs and a bad conscience the next day.

THE DAUGHTER. How strange!

THE LAWYER. I wake up in the morning with a headache; and then the repetitions begin, but so that everything becomes perverted. What the night before was pretty, agreeable, witty, is presented by memory in the morning as ugly, distasteful, stupid. Pleasure seems to decay, and all joy goes to pieces. What men call success serves always as a basis for their next failure. My own successes have brought ruin upon me. For men view the fortune of others with an instinctive dread. They regard it unjust that fate should favor any one man, and so they try to restore balance by piling rocks on the road. To have talent is to be in danger of one's life, for then one may easily starve to death!—However, you will have to return to your duties, or I shall bring suit against you, and we shall pass through every court up to the highest—one, two, three!

THE DAUGHTER. Return?— To the iron stove, and the cabbage pot, and the baby clothes—

THE LAWYER. Exactly! We have a big wash to-day, for we must wash all the handkerchiefs—

THE DAUGHTER. Oh, must I do it all over again?

THE LAWYER. All life is nothing but doing things over again. Look at the teacher in there— He received his doctor's degree yesterday, was laurelled and saluted, climbed Parnassus and was embraced by the monarch—and to-day he starts school all over again, asks how much twice two makes, and will continue to do so until his death— However, you must come back to your home!

THE DAUGHTER. I would rather die!

THE LAWYER. Die?— That is not allowed. First of all, it is a disgrace—so much so that even the dead body is subjected to insults; and secondly, one goes to hell—it is a mortal sin!

THE DAUGHTER. It is not easy to be human!

ALL. Hear!

THE DAUGHTER. I shall not go back

with you to humiliation and dirt— I am longing for the heights whence I came— but first the door must be opened so that I may learn the secret— It is my will that the door be opened!

THE LAWYER. Then you must retrace your own steps, cover the road you have already travelled, suffer all annoyances, repetitions, tautologies, recopyings, that a suit will bring with it—

THE DAUGHTER. May it come then— But first I must go into the solitude and the wilderness to recover my own self. We shall meet again! [*To* THE POET.] Follow me.

[*Cries of anguish are heard from a distance.* Woe! Woe! Woe!]

THE DAUGHTER. What is that?

THE LAWYER. The lost souls at Foulstrand.

THE DAUGHTER. Why do they wail more loudly than usual to-day?

THE LAWYER. Because the sun is shining here; because here we have music, dancing, youth. And it makes them feel their own sufferings more keenly.

THE DAUGHTER. We must set them free.

THE LAWYER. Try it! Once a liberator appeared, and he was nailed to a cross.

THE DAUGHTER. By whom?

THE LAWYER. By all the right-minded.

THE DAUGHTER. Who are they?

THE LAWYER. Are you not acquainted with all the right-minded? Then you must learn to know them.

THE DAUGHTER. Were they the ones that prevented your graduation?

THE LAWYER. Yes.

THE DAUGHTER. Then I know them!

[CURTAIN.]

On the shores of the Mediterranean. To the left, in the foreground, a white wall, and above it branches of an orange tree with ripe fruit on them. In the background, villas and a Casino placed on a terrace. To the right, a huge pile of coal and two wheelbarrows. In the background, to the right, a corner of blue sea.

[*Two coalheavers, naked to the waist, their faces, hands, and bodies blackened by coal dust, are seated on the wheelbarrows. Their expressions show intense despair.*

THE DAUGHTER *and* THE LAWYER *in the background.*]

THE DAUGHTER. This is paradise!

FIRST COALHEAVER. This is hell!

SECOND COALHEAVER. One hundred and twenty degrees in the shadow.

FIRST HEAVER. Let's have a bath.

SECOND HEAVER. The police won't let us. No bathing here.

FIRST HEAVER. Couldn't we pick some fruit off that tree?

SECOND HEAVER. Then the police would get after us.

FIRST HEAVER. But I cannot do a thing in this heat—I'll just chuck the job—

SECOND HEAVER. Then the police will get you for sure!— [*Pause.*] And you wouldn't have anything to eat anyhow.

FIRST HEAVER. Nothing to eat? We, who work hardest, get least food; and the rich, who do nothing, get most. Might one not—without disregard of truth—assert that this is injustice?— What has the daughter of the gods to say about it?

THE DAUGHTER. I can say nothing at all— But tell me, what have you done that makes you so black and your lot so hard?

FIRST HEAVER. What have we done? We have been born of poor and perhaps not very good parents— Maybe we have been punished a couple of times.

THE DAUGHTER. Punished?

FIRST HEAVER. Yes, the unpunished hang out in the Casino up there and dine on eight courses with wine.

THE DAUGHTER. [*To* THE LAWYER.] Can that be true?

THE LAWYER. On the whole, yes.

THE DAUGHTER. You mean to say that

every man at some time has deserved to go to prison?

THE LAWYER. Yes.

THE DAUGHTER. You, too?

THE LAWYER. Yes.

THE DAUGHTER. Is it true that the poor cannot bathe in the sea?

THE LAWYER. Yes. Not even with their clothes on. None but those who intend to take their own lives escape being fined. And those are said to get a good drubbing at the police station.

THE DAUGHTER. But can they not go outside of the city, out into the country, and bathe there?

THE LAWYER. There is no place for them—all the land is fenced in.

THE DAUGHTER. But I mean in the free, open country.

THE LAWYER. There is no such thing—it all belongs to somebody.

THE DAUGHTER. Even the sea, the great, vast sea—

THE LAWYER. Even that! You cannot sail the sea in a boat and land anywhere without having it put down in writing and charged for. It is lovely!

THE DAUGHTER. This is not paradise.

THE LAWYER. I should say not!

THE DAUGHTER. Why don't men do something to improve their lot?

THE LAWYER. Oh, they try, of course, but all the improvers end in prison or in the madhouse—

THE DAUGHTER. Who puts them in prison?

THE LAWYER. All the right-minded, all the respectable—

THE DAUGHTER. Who sends them to the madhouse?

THE LAWYER. Their own despair when they grasp the hopelessness of their efforts.

THE DAUGHTER. Has the thought not occurred to anybody, that for secret reasons it must be as it is?

THE LAWYER. Yes, those who are well off always think so.

THE DAUGHTER. That it is all right as it is?

FIRST HEAVER. And yet we are the foundations of society. If the coal is not unloaded, then there will be no fire in the kitchen stove, in the parlor grate, or in the factory furnace; then the light will go out in the streets and shops and homes; then darkness and cold will descend upon you —and, therefore, we have to sweat as in hell so that the black coals may be had— And what do you do for us in return?

THE LAWYER. [To THE DAUGHTER.] Help them!— [Pause.] That conditions cannot be quite the same for everybody, I understand, but why should they differ so widely?

[A GENTLEMAN and A LADY pass across the stage.]

THE LADY. Will you come and play a game with us?

THE GENTLEMAN. No, I must take a walk, so I can eat something for dinner.

FIRST HEAVER. So that he can eat something?

SECOND HEAVER. So that he can—?

[Children enter and cry with horror when they catch sight of the grimy workers.]

FIRST HEAVER. They cry when they see us. They cry—

SECOND HEAVER. Damn it all!— I guess we'll have to pull out the scaffolds soon and begin to operate on this rotten body—

FIRST HEAVER. Damn it, I say, too!

[Spits.]

THE LAWYER. [To THE DAUGHTER.] Yes, it is all wrong. And men are not so very bad—but—

THE DAUGHTER. But—?

THE LAWYER. But the government—

THE DAUGHTER. [Goes out, hiding her face in her hands.] This is not paradise.

COALHEAVERS. No, hell, that's what it is!

[CURTAIN.]

Fingal's Cave. Long green waves are roll-
ing slowly into the cave. In the fore-
ground, a siren buoy is swaying to and
fro in time with the waves, but without
sounding except at the indicated mo-
ment. Music of the winds. Music of the
waves.

[THE DAUGHTER *and* THE POET.]

THE POET. Where are you leading me?

THE DAUGHTER. Far away from the
noise and lament of the man-children, to
the utmost end of the ocean, to the cave
that we name Indra's Ear because it is the
place where the king of the heavens is said
to listen to the complaints of the mortals.

THE POET. What? In this place?

THE DAUGHTER. Do you see how this
cave is built like a shell? Yes, you can see
it. Do you know that your ear, too, is built
in the form of a shell? You know it, but
have not thought of it. [*She picks up a shell*
from the beach.] Have you not as a child
held such a shell to your ear and listened—
and heard the ripple of your heart-blood,
the humming of your thoughts in the brain,
the snapping of a thousand little worn-out
threads in the tissues of your body? All that
you hear in this small shell. Imagine then
what may be heard in this larger one!

THE POET. [*Listening.*] I hear nothing
but the whispering of the wind.

THE DAUGHTER. Then I shall interpret
it for you. Listen. The wail of the winds.

[*Recites to subdued music.*]

Born beneath the clouds of heaven,
Driven we were by the lightnings of Indra
Down to the sand-covered earth.
Straw from the harvested fields soiled our
        feet;
Dust from the high-roads,
Smoke from the cities,
Foul-smelling breaths,
Fumes from cellars and kitchens,
All we endured.
Then to the open sea we fled,
Filling our lungs with air,
Shaking our wings,
And laving our feet.

Indra, Lord of the Heavens,
Hear us!
Hear our sighing!
Unclean is the earth;
Evil is life;
Neither good nor bad
Can men be deemed.
As they can, they live,
One day at a time.
Sons of dust, through dust they journey;
Born out of dust, to dust they return.
Given they were, for trudging,
Feet, not wings for flying.
Dusty they grew—
Lies the fault then with them,
Or with Thee?

THE POET. Thus I heard it once—

THE DAUGHTER. Hush! The winds are
still singing.

[*Recites to subdued music.*]

We, winds that wander,
We, the air's offspring,
Bear with us men's lament.
Heard us you have
During gloom-filled Fall nights,
In chimneys and pipes,
In key-holes and door cracks,
When the rain wept on the roof:
Heard us you have
In the snowclad pine woods
Midst wintry gloom:
Heard us you have,
Crooning and moaning
In ropes and rigging
On the high-heaving sea.

It was we, the winds,
Offspring of the air,
Who learned how to grieve
Within human breasts
Through which we passed—
In sick-rooms, on battle-fields,
But mostly where the newborn
Whimpered and wailed
At the pain of living.

We, we the winds,
We are whining and whistling:
Woe! Woe! Woe!

THE POET. It seems to me that I have already—

THE DAUGHTER. Hush! Now the waves are singing.

[*Recites to subdued music.*]

We, we waves,
That are rocking the winds
To rest—-
Green cradles, we waves!
Wet are we, and salty;
Leap like flames of fire—
Wet flames are we:
Burning, extinguishing;
Cleansing, replenishing;
Bearing, engendering.

We, we waves,
That are rocking the winds
To rest!

THE DAUGHTER. False waves and faithless! Everything on earth that is not burned, is drowned—by the waves. Look at this. [*Pointing to pile of débris.*] See what the sea has taken and spoiled! Nothing but the figure-heads remain of the sunken ships— and the names: *Justice, Friendship, Golden Peace, Hope*—this is all that is left of *Hope* —of fickle *Hope*—railings, tholes, bails! And lo: the life buoy—which saved itself and let distressed men perish.

THE POET. [*Searching the pile.*] Here is the nameboard of the ship *Justice*. Tnat was the one which left Fairhaven with the Blind Man's son on board. It is lost then! And with it are gone the lover of Alice, the hopeless love of Edith.

THE DAUGHTER. The blind man? Fairhaven? I must have been dreaming of them. And the lover of Alice, "Plain" Edith, Foulstrand and the Quarantine, sulphur and carbolic acid, the graduation in the church, the Lawyer's office, the passageway and Victoria, the Growing Castle and the Officer— All this I have been dreaming—

THE POET. It was in one of my poems.

THE DAUGHTER. You know then what poetry is—

THE POET. I know then what dreaming is— But what is poetry?

THE DAUGHTER. Not reality, but more than reality—not dreaming, but daylight dreams—

THE POET. And the man-children think that we poets are only playing—that we invent and make believe.

THE DAUGHTER. And fortunate it is, my friend, for otherwise the world would lie fallow for lack of ministration. Everybody would be stretched on his back, staring into the sky. Nobody would be touching plough or spade, hammer or plane,

THE POET. And you say this, Indra's daughter, you who belong in part up there—

THE DAUGHTER. You do right in reproaching me. Too long have I stayed down here taking mud baths like you— My thoughts have lost their power of flight; there is clay on their wings—mire on their feet—and I myself— [*Raising her arms.*] I sink, I sink— Help me, father, Lord of the Heavens! [*Silence.*] I can no longer hear his answer. The ether no longer carries the sound from his lips to my ear's shell—the silvery thread has snapped— Woe is me, I am earthbound!

THE POET. Do you mean to ascend— soon?

THE DAUGHTER. As soon as I have consigned this mortal shape to the flames— for even the waters of the ocean cannot cleanse me. Why do you question me thus?

THE POET. Because I have a prayer—

THE DAUGHTER. What kind of prayer?

THE POET. A written supplication from humanity to the ruler of the universe, formulated by a dreamer.

THE DAUGHTER. To be presented by whom?

THE POET. By Indra's daughter.

THE DAUGHTER. Can you repeat what you have written?

THE POET. I can.

THE DAUGHTER. Speak it then.

THE POET. Better that you do it.

THE DAUGHTER. Where can I read it?

THE POET. In my mind—or here.

[*Hands her a roll of paper.*]

THE DAUGHTER. [*Receives the roll, but reads without looking at it.*] Well, by me it shall be spoken then:

"Why must you be born in anguish?
Why, O man-child, must you always
Wring your mother's heart with tor-
  ture
When you bring her joy maternal,
Highest happiness yet known?
Why to life must you awaken,
Why to light give natal greeting,
With a cry of anger and of pain?
Why not meet it smiling, man-child,
When the gift of life is counted
In itself a boon unmatched?
Why like beasts should we be coming,
We of race divine and human?
Better garment craves the spirit
Than one made of filth and blood!
Need a god his teeth be changing—"

—Silence, rash one! Is it seemly
For the work to blame its maker?
No one yet has solved life's riddle.

"Thus begins the human journey
O'er a road of thorns and thistles;
If a beaten path be offered,
It is named at once forbidden;
If a flower you covet, straightway
You are told it is another's;
If a field should bar your progress,
And you dare to break across it,
You destroy your neighbour's harvest;
Others then your own will trample,
That the measure may be evened!
Every moment of enjoyment
Brings to some one else a sorrow,
But your sorrow gladdens no one,
For from sorrow naught but sorrow
  springs.

"Thus you journey till you die,
And your death brings others' bread."

—Is it thus that you approach,
Son of Dust, the One Most High?

THE POET.

Could the son of dust discover
Words so pure and bright and simple
That to heaven they might ascend—?

Child of gods, wilt thou interpret
Mankind's grievance in some language
That immortals understand?

THE DAUGHTER. I will.

THE POET. [*Pointing to the buoy.*] What is that floating there?— A buoy?

THE DAUGHTER. Yes.

THE POET. It looks like a lung with a windpipe.

THE DAUGHTER. It is the watchman of the seas. When danger is abroad, it sings.

THE POET. It seems to me as if the sea were rising and the waves growing larger—

THE DAUGHTER. Not unlikely.

THE POET. Woe! What do I see? A ship bearing down upon the reef.

THE DAUGHTER. What ship can that be?

THE POET. The ghost ship of the seas, I think.

THE DAUGHTER. What ship is that?

THE POET. The *Flying Dutchman.*[1]

THE DAUGHTER. Oh, that one. Why is he punished so hard, and why does he not seek harbor?

THE POET. Because he has seven faith-less wives.

THE DAUGHTER. And for this he should be punished?

THE POET. Yes, all the right-minded condemned him—

THE DAUGHTER. Strange world, this!— How can he then be freed from his curse?

THE POET. Freed?— Oh, they take good care that none is set free.

THE DAUGHTER. Why?

THE POET. Because— No, it is not the *Dutchman!* It is an ordinary ship in distress. Why does not the buoy cry out now? Look, how the sea is rising—how high the waves are—soon we shall be unable to get out of the cave! Now the ship's bell is ringing— Soon we shall have another figure-

[1] A legendary phantom ship doomed to haunt the seas eternally unable to make port.

head. Cry out, buoy! Do your duty, watch-man. [*The buoy sounds a four-voice chord of fifths and sixths, reminding one of fog horns.*] The crew is signalling to us—but we are doomed ourselves.

THE DAUGHTER. Do you not wish to be set free?

THE POET. Yes, of course—of course, I wish it—but not just now, and not by water.

THE CREW. [*Sings in quartet.*] Christ Kyrie! [2]

THE POET. Now they are crying aloud, and so is the sea, but no one gives ear.

THE CREW. [*As before.*] Christ Kyrie!

THE DAUGHTER. Who is coming there?

THE POET. Walking on the waters? There is only one who does that—and it is not Peter, the Rock, for he sank like a stone—[3]

[*A white light is seen shining over the water at some distance.*]

THE CREW. Christ Kyrie!

THE DAUGHTER. Can this be He?

THE POET. It is He, the crucified—

THE DAUGHTER. Why—tell me—why was He crucified?

THE POET. Because He wanted to set free—

THE DAUGHTER. Who was it—I have forgotten—that crucified Him?

THE POET. All the right-minded.

THE DAUGHTER. What a strange world!

THE POET. The sea is rising. Darkness is closing in upon us. The storm is grow-ing—

[THE CREW *set up a wild outcry.*]

THE POET. The crew scream with hor-ror at the sight of their Saviour—and now—they are leaping overboard for fear of the Redeemer—

[THE CREW *utter another cry.*]

THE POET. Now they are crying be-cause they must die. Crying when they are born, and crying when they pass away!

[*The rising waves threaten to engulf the two in the cave.*]

THE DAUGHTER. If I could only be sure that it is a ship—

THE POET. Really—I don't think it is a ship— It is a two-storied house with trees in front of it—and—a telephone tower—a tower that reaches up into the skies— It is the modern Tower of Babel [4] sending wires to the upper regions—to communicate with those above—

THE DAUGHTER. Child, the human thought needs no wires to make a way for itself—the prayers of the pious penetrate the universe. It cannot be a Tower of Babel, for if you want to assail the heavens, you must do so with prayer.

THE POET. No, it is no house—no tele-phone tower:—don't you see?

THE DAUGHTER. What are you seeing?

THE POET. I see an open space covered with snow—a drill ground— The winter sun is shining from behind a church on a hill, and the tower is casting its long shadow on the snow— Now a troop of sol-diers come marching across the grounds. They march up along the tower, up the spire. Now they have reached the cross, but I have a feeling that the first one who steps on the gilded weathercock at the top must die. Now they are near it—a corporal is leading them—ha-ha! There comes a cloud sweeping across the open space, and right in front of the sun, of course—now everything is gone—the water in the cloud put out the sun's fire!—The light of the sun created the shadow picture of the tower, but the shadow picture of the cloud swal-lowed the shadow picture of the tower—

[*While* THE POET *is still speaking, the stage is changed and shows once more the passageway outside the opera-house.*]

THE DAUGHTER. [*To* THE PORTRESS.] Has the Lord Chancellor arrived yet?

THE PORTRESS. No.

THE DAUGHTER. And the Deans of the Faculties?

<hr>

[2] Christ, O Lord! The term is used to suggest the *Kyrie Eleison*, the liturgical chant which be-gins "O Lord, have mercy on us!"

[3] The reference is to Christ's walking on the sea. For the account see *St. Matthew*, xiv, 22–33.
[4] See *Genesis*, xi, 4–9.

THE PORTRESS. No.

THE DAUGHTER. Call them at once, then, for the door is to be opened—

THE PORTRESS. Is it so very pressing?

THE DAUGHTER. Yes, it is. For there is a suspicion that the solution of the world-riddle may be hidden behind it. Call the Lord Chancellor, and the Deans of the Four Faculties also.

[THE PORTRESS blows a whistle.]

THE DAUGHTER. And do not forget the Glazier and his diamond, for without them nothing can be done.

[STAGE PEOPLE enter from the left as in the earlier scene.]

THE OFFICER. [Enters from the background, in Prince Albert and high hat, with a bunch of roses in his hand, looking radiantly happy.] Victoria!

THE PORTRESS. The young lady will be coming in a moment.

THE OFFICER. Good! The carriage is waiting, the table is set, the wine is on ice— Permit me to embrace you, Madam! [Embraces THE PORTRESS.] Victoria!

A WOMAN'S VOICE FROM ABOVE. [Sings.] I am here!

THE OFFICER. [Begins to walk to and fro.] Good! I am waiting.

THE POET. It seems to me that all this has happened before—

THE DAUGHTER. So it seems to me also.

THE POET. Perhaps I have dreamt it.

THE DAUGHTER. Or put it in a poem, perhaps.

THE POET. Or put it in a poem.

THE DAUGHTER. Then you know what poetry is.

THE POET. Then I know what dreaming is.

THE DAUGHTER. It seems to me that we have said all this to each other before, in some other place.

THE POET. Then you may soon figure out what reality is.

THE DAUGHTER. Or dreaming!

THE POET. Or poetry!

[Enter the LORD CHANCELLOR and the DEANS of the THEOLOGICAL, PHILOS-OPHICAL, MEDICAL, and LEGAL FACULTIES.]

LORD CHANCELLOR. It is about the opening of that door, of course— What does the Dean of the Theological Faculty think of it?

DEAN OF THEOLOGY. I do not think—I believe—Credo—

DEAN OF PHILOSOPHY. I hold—

DEAN OF MEDICINE. I know—

DEAN OF JURISPRUDENCE. I doubt until I have evidence and witnesses.

LORD CHANCELLOR. Now they are fighting again!— Well, what does Theology believe?

THEOLOGY. I believe that this door must not be opened, because it hides dangerous truths—

PHILOSOPHY. Truth is never dangerous.

MEDICINE. What is truth?

JURISPRUDENCE. What can be proved by two witnesses.

THEOLOGY. Anything can be proved by two false witnesses—thinks the pettifogger.

PHILOSOPHY. Truth is wisdom; and wisdom, knowledge, is philosophy itself— Philosophy is the science of sciences, the knowledge of knowing, and all other sciences are its servants.

MEDICINE. Natural science is the only true science—and philosophy is no science at all. It is nothing but empty speculation.

THEOLOGY. Good!

PHILOSOPHY. [To THEOLOGY.] Good, you say! And what are you, then? You are the arch-enemy of all knowledge; you are the very antithesis of knowledge; you are ignorance and obscurantism—

MEDICINE. Good!

THEOLOGY. [To MEDICINE.] You cry "good," you, who cannot see beyond the length of your own nose in the magnifying glass; who believe in nothing but your own unreliable senses—in your vision, for instance, which may be far-sighted, near-sighted, blind, purblind, cross-eyed, one-eyed, color-blind, red-blind, green-blind—

MEDICINE. Idiot!

THEOLOGY. Ass! [They fight.]

LORD CHANCELLOR. Peace! One crow does not peck out the other's eye.

PHILOSOPHY. If I had to choose between those two, Theology and Medicine, I should choose—neither!

JURSIPRUDENCE. And if I had to sit in judgment on the three of you, I should find —all guilty! You cannot agree on a single point, and you never could. Let us get back to the case in court. What is the opinion of the Lord Chancellor as to this door and its opening?

LORD CHANCELLOR. Opinion? I have no opinion whatever. I am merely appointed by the government to see that you don't break each other's arms and legs in the Council—while you are educating the young! Opinion? Why, I take mighty good care to avoid everything of the kind. Once I had one or two, but they were refuted at once. Opinions are always refuted—by their opponents, of course— But perhaps we might open the door now, even with the risk of finding some dangerous truths behind it?

JURISPRUDENCE. What is truth? What is truth?

THEOLOGY. I am the truth and the life—

PHILOSOPHY. I am the science of sciences—

MEDICINE. I am the only exact science—

JURISPRUDENCE. I doubt—

[*They fight.*]

THE DAUGHTER. Instructors of the young, take shame!

JURISPRUDENCE. Lord Chancellor, as representative of the government, as head of the corps of instructors, you must prosecute this woman's offence. She has told all of you to take shame, which is an insult; and she has—in a sneering, ironical sense —called you instructors of the young, which is a slanderous speech.

THE DAUGHTER. Poor youth!

JURISPRUDENCE. She pities the young, which is to accuse us. Lord Chancellor, you must prosecute the offence.

THE DAUGHTER. Yes, I accuse you— you in a body—of sowing doubt and discord in the minds of the young.

JURSIPRUDENCE. Listen to her—she herself is making the young question our authority, and then she charges us with sowing doubt. Is it not a criminal act, I ask all the right-minded?

ALL RIGHT-MINDED. Yes, it is criminal.

JURISPRUDENCE. All the right-minded have condemned you. Leave in peace with your lucre, or else—

THE DAUGHTER. My lucre? Or else? What else?

JURISPRUDENCE. Else you will be stoned.

THE POET. Or crucified.

THE DAUGHTER. I leave. Follow me, and you shall learn the riddle.

THE POET. Which riddle?

THE DAUGHTER. What did he mean by "my lucre"?

THE POET. Probably nothing at all. That kind of thing we call talk. He was just talking.

THE DAUGHTER. But it was what hurt me more than anything else!

THE POET. That is why he said it, I suppose— Men are that way.

ALL RIGHT-MINDED. Hooray! The door is open.

LORD CHANCELLOR. What was behind the door?

THE GLAZIER. I can see nothing.

LORD CHANCELLOR. He cannot see anything—of course, he cannot! Deans of the Faculties: what was behind that door?

THEOLOGY. Nothing! That is the solution of the world-riddle. In the beginning God created heaven and earth out of nothing—

PHILOSOPHY. Out of nothing comes nothing.

MEDICINE. Yes, bosh—which is nothing!

JURISPRUDENCE. I doubt. And this is a case of deception. I appeal to all the right-minded.

THE DAUGHTER. [*To* THE POET.] Who are the right-minded?

THE POET. Who can tell? Frequently all the right-minded consist of a single person. To-day it is me and mine; to-morrow it is you and yours. To that position you are appointed—or rather, you appoint yourself to it.

ALL RIGHT-MINDED. We have been deceived.

LORD CHANCELLOR. Who has deceived you?

ALL RIGHT-MINDED. The Daughter!

LORD CHANCELLOR. Will the Daughter please tell us what she meant by having this door opened?

THE DAUGHTER. No, friends. If I did, you would not believe me.

MEDICINE. Why, then, there is nothing there.

THE DAUGHTER. You have said it—but you have not understood.

MEDICINE. It is bosh, what she says!

ALL. Bosh!

THE DAUGHTER. [To THE POET.] They are to be pitied.

THE POET. Are you in earnest?

THE DAUGHTER. Always in earnest.

THE POET. Do you think the right-minded are to be pitied also?

THE DAUGHTER. They most of all, perhaps.

THE POET. And the four faculties, too?

THE DAUGHTER. They also, and not the least. Four heads, four minds, and one body. Who made that monster?

ALL. She has not answered!

LORD CHANCELLOR. Stone her then!

THE DAUGHTER. I have answered.

LORD CHANCELLOR. Hear—she answers.

ALL. Stone her! She answers!

THE DAUGHTER. Whether she answer or do not answer, stone her! Come, prophet, and I shall tell you the riddle—but far away from here—out in the desert, where no one can hear us, no one see us, for—

THE LAWYER. [Enters and takes THE DAUGHTER by the arm.] Have you forgotten your duties?

THE DAUGHTER. Oh, heavens, no! But I have higher duties.

THE LAWYER. And your child?

THE DAUGHTER. My child—what of it?

THE LAWYER. Your child is crying for you.

THE DAUGHTER. My child! Woe, I am earthbound! And this pain in my breast, this anguish—what is it?

THE LAWYER. Don't you know?

THE DAUGHTER. No.

THE LAWYER. It is remorse.

THE DAUGHTER. Is that remorse?

THE LAWYER. Yes, and it follows every neglected duty; every pleasure, even the most innocent, if innocent pleasures exist, which seems doubtful; and every suffering inflicted upon one's fellow beings.

THE DAUGHTER. And there is no remedy?

THE LAWYER. Yes, but only one. It consists in doing your duty at once—

THE DAUGHTER. You look like a demon when you speak that word duty— And when, as in my case, there are two duties to be met?

THE LAWYER. Meet one first, and then the other.

THE DAUGHTER. The highest first—therefore, you look after my child, and I shall do my duty—

THE LAWYER. Your child suffers because it misses you—can you bear to know that a human being is suffering for your sake?

THE DAUGHTER. Now strife has entered my soul—it is rent in two, and the halves are being pulled in opposite directions!

THE LAWYER. Such, you know, are life's little discords.

THE DAUGHTER. Oh, how it is pulling!

THE POET. If you could only know how I have spread sorrow and ruin around me by the exercise of my calling—and note that I say calling, which carries with it the highest duty of all—then you would not even touch my hand.

THE DAUGHTER. What do you mean?

THE POET. I had a father who put his whole hope on me as his only son, destined to continue his enterprise. I ran away from the business college. My father grieved himself to death. My mother wanted me to be religious, and I could not do what she wanted—and she disowned me. I had a friend who assisted me through trying days of need—and that friend acted as a tyrant against those on whose behalf I was speaking and writing. And I had to strike down my friend and benefactor in order to save my soul. Since then I have had no peace. Men call me devoid of honor, infamous— and it does not help that my conscience says, "You have done right," for in the next moment it is saying, "You have done wrong." Such is life.

THE DAUGHTER. Come with me into the desert.

THE LAWYER. Your child!

THE DAUGHTER. [Indicating all those present.] Here are my children. By themselves they are good, but if they only come together, then they quarrel and turn into demons—Farewell!

[Outside the castle. The same scenery as in the first scene of the first act. But now the ground in front of the castle wall is covered with flowers—blue monk's-hood or aconite. On the roof of the castle, at the very top of its lantern, there is a chrysanthemum bud ready to open. The castle windows are illuminated with candles.]

[THE DAUGHTER and THE POET.]

THE DAUGHTER. The hour is not distant when, with the help of the flames, I shall once more ascend to the ether. It is what you call to die, and what you approach in fear.

THE POET. Fear of the unknown.

THE DAUGHTER. Which is known to you.

THE POET. Who knows it?

THE DAUGHTER. All! Why do you not believe your prophets?

THE POET. Prophets have always been disbelieved. Why is that so? And "if God has spoken, why will men not believe then?" His convincing power ought to be irresistible.

THE DAUGHTER. Have you always doubted?

THE POET. No. I have had certainty many times. But after a while it passed away, like a dream when you wake up.

THE DAUGHTER. It is not easy to be human!

THE POET. You see and admit it?

THE DAUGHTER. I do.

THE POET. Listen! Was it not Indra that once sent his son down here to receive the complaints of mankind?

THE DAUGHTER. Thus it happened— and how was he received?

THE POET. How did he fill his mission? —to answer with another question.

THE DAUGHTER. And if I may reply with still another—was not man's position bettered by his visit to the earth? Answer truly!

THE POET. Bettered?— Yes, a little. A very little— But instead of asking questions —will you not tell the riddle?

THE DAUGHTER. Yes. But to what use? You will not believe me.

THE POET. In you I shall believe, for I know who you are.

THE DAUGHTER. Then I shall tell! In the morning of the ages, before the sun was shining, Brahma, the divine primal force, let himself be persuaded by Maya, the world-mother, to propagate himself. This meeting of the divine primal matter with the earth-matter was the fall of heaven into sin. Thus the world, existence, mankind, are nothing but a phantom, an appearance, a dream-image—

THE POET. My dream!

THE DAUGHTER. A dream of truth! But in order to free themselves from the earth-matter, the offspring of Brahma seek privation and suffering. There you have suffering as a liberator. But this craving for suffering comes into conflict with the craving for enjoyment, or love—do you now understand what love is, with its utmost joys merged into its utmost sufferings, with its mixture of what is most sweet and most bitter? Can you now grasp what woman is? Woman, through whom sin and death found their way into life?

THE POET. I understand!— And the end?

THE DAUGHTER. You know it: conflict between the pain of enjoyment and the pleasure of suffering—between the pangs of the penitent and the joys of the prodigal—

THE POET. A conflict it is then?

THE DAUGHTER. Conflict between opposites produces energy, as fire and water give the power of steam—

THE POET. But peace? Rest?

THE DAUGHTER. Hush! You must ask no more, and I can no longer answer. The altar is already adorned for the sacrifice—the flowers are standing guard—the candles are lit—there are white sheets in the windows—spruce boughs have been spread in the gateway—

THE POET. And you say this as calmly as if for you suffering did not exist!

THE DAUGHTER. You think so? I have suffered all your sufferings, but in a hundredfold degree, for my sensations were so much more acute—

THE POET. Relate your sorrow!

THE DAUGHTER. Poet, could you tell yours so that not one word went too far? Could your word at any time approach your thought?

THE POET. No, you are right! To myself I appeared like one struck dumb, and when the mass listened admiringly to my song, I found it mere noise— For this reason, you see, I have always felt ashamed when they praised me.

THE DAUGHTER. And then you ask me— Look me straight in the eye!

THE POET. I cannot bear your glance—

THE DAUGHTER. How could you bear my word then, were I to speak in your tongue?

THE POET. But tell me at least before you go: from what did you suffer most of all down here?

THE DAUGHTER. From—being: to feel my vision weakened by an eye, my hearing blunted by an ear, and my thought, my bright and buoyant thought, bound in labyrinthine coils of fat. You have seen a brain—what roundabout and sneaking paths—

THE POET. Well, that is because all the right-minded think crookedly!

THE DAUGHTER. Malicious, always malicious, all of you!

THE POET. How could one possibly be otherwise?

THE DAUGHTER. First of all I now shake the dust from my feet—the dirt and the clay—

[Takes off her shoes and puts them into the fire.]

THE PORTRESS. [Puts her shawl into the fire.] Perhaps I may burn my shawl at the same time? [Goes out.]

THE OFFICER. [Enters.] And I my roses, of which only the thorns are left.

[Goes out.]

THE BILLPOSTER. [Enters.] My bills may go, but never the dipnet! [Goes out.]

THE GLAZIER. [Enters.] The diamond that opened the door—good-bye!

[Goes out.]

THE LAWYER. [Enters.] The minutes of the great process concerning the pope's beard or the water loss in the sources of the Ganges. [Goes out.]

MASTER OF QUARANTINE. [Enters.] A small contribution in shape of the black mask that made me a blackamoor against my will! [Goes out.]

VICTORIA. [Enters.] My beauty, my sorrow! [Goes out.]

EDITH. [Enters.] My plainness, my sorrow! [Goes out.]

THE BLIND MAN. [Enters; puts his hand into the fire.] I give my hand for my eye.

[Goes out.]

[DON JUAN in his wheel chair; SHE and THE FRIEND.]

DON JUAN. Hurry up! Hurry up! Life is short! [Leaves with the other two.]

THE POET. I have read that when the end of life draws near, everything and everybody rushes by in continuous review— Is this the end?

THE DAUGHTER. Yes, it is my end. Farewell!

THE POET. Give us a parting word.

THE DAUGHTER. No, I cannot. Do you believe that your words can express our thoughts?

DEAN OF THEOLOGY. [Enters in a rage.]

I am cast off by God and persecuted by man; I am deserted by the government and scorned by my colleagues! How am I to believe when nobody else believes? How am I to defend a god that does not defend his own? Bosh, that's what it is!

[*Throws a book on the fire and goes out.*]

THE POET. [*Snatches the book out of the fire.*] Do you know what it is? A martyrology, a calendar with a martyr for each day of the year.

THE DAUGHTER. Martyr?

THE POET. Yes, one that has been tortured and killed on account of his faith! Tell me, why?— Do you think that all who are tortured suffer, and that all who are killed feel pain? Suffering is said to be salvation, and death a liberation.

CHRISTINE. [*With slips of paper.*] I paste, I paste until there is nothing more to paste—

THE POET. And if heaven should split in twain, you would try to paste it together— Away!

CHRISTINE. Are there no double windows in this castle?

THE POET. Not one, I tell you.

CHRISTINE. Well, then I'll go.

[*Goes out.*]

THE DAUGHTER.

The parting hour has come, the end draws near.

And now farewell, thou dreaming child of man,

Thou singer, who alone know'st how to live!

When from thy winged flight above the earth

At times thou sweepest downward to the dust,

It is to touch it only, not to stay!

And as I go—how, in the parting hour,

As one must leave for e'er a friend, a place,

The heart with longing swells for what one loves,

And with regret for all wherein one failed!

O, now the pangs of life in all their force

I feel: I know at last the lot of man—

Regretfully one views what once was scorned;

For sins one never sinned remorse is felt;

To stay one craves, but equally to leave:

As if to horses tied that pull apart,

One's heart is split in twain, one's feelings rent,

By indecision, contrast, and discord.

Farewell! To all thy fellow-men make known

That where I go I shall forget them not;

And in thy name their grievance shall be placed

Before the throne. Farewell!

[*She goes into the castle. Music is heard. The background is lit up by the burning castle and reveals a wall of human faces, questioning, grieving, despairing. As the castle breaks into flames, the bud on the roof opens into a gigantic chrysanthemum flower.*]

[CURTAIN.]

The Virtuoso Play

NO SURVEY of dramatic achievement can be complete without some attention to its most common, if least memorable, manifestation. This category of drama, unlike the others discussed earlier, is not distinguished by any special features of form or technique; parasitically it uses any established type of drama as its host. Its unique character is simply a product of its underlying purpose. For lack of a more generally accepted name, it may be described as virtuoso drama. The nature of this particular phenomenon is attributable to a peculiarity of art itself. In general, the development of any art may be said to represent an evolution from ritual toward virtuosity. That is to say, art begins as a functional adjunct to the process of living, often in connection with religious or magical practices; as it develops it evolves an increasingly elaborate and refined technique, the skill and effectivenes of which are capable of affording an increment of aesthetic pleasure; and it culminates in such a proficiency and subtlety of technique that the very exercise of it constitutes its own aesthetic justification. In other words, the inevitable trend of the process is from art for life's sake toward art for art's sake. From this trend derives a common duality in artistic achievement. For example, in the realm of music, a composer may draw upon all the resources of an orchestra to give substance to an important musical conception; on the other hand, he may deliberately contrive a musical composition for the sake of entertaining with an ingenious display of his own technical facility, the possibilities of the instruments, and the virtuosity of the performers. As employments of genuine art, both are eminently legitimate and enjoyable; but in their ultimate value there is a vast difference. The first provides a significant human experience; the second, a momentarily exhilarating diversion. Virtuoso drama is the theatrical version of this second artistic category.

Every successful play is a product of skilled craftsmanship. Whatever its final intention or value, its artistic achievement is a matter of calculated theatrical effect. What is known as "good theater," therefore, is an essential element of all dramatic art. Moreover, good theater remains good theater regardless of the uses to which it is put; for one's response to skilfully contrived theatrical effects and the immediate satisfaction one derives from them have very little to do with their inherent justification. For this reason it is possible to divorce good theater from significant drama and still retain a quite acceptable form of entertainment. One is not referring here to specious and pretentious drama, which is simply an example of bad dramatic art; for pretentious profession of what is never intended is intellectually and artistically as meretricious in the theater as in life. Dramatic virtuosity is an entirely different affair. As a business enterprise and an entertainment facility, the theater has always been a wholesale dispenser of this commodity; nor is there anything especially reprehensible about the practice. Pretending to be no more than it is, at its best it affords an innocuous and quite legitimate delight in artistic dexterity, and at its worst it is no worse than an amiable method of killing time. In dealing with a play of this sort, however, it is always advisable to bear in mind one important characteristic: while it does not necessarily present "a tale told by an idiot," it is by nature largely "full of sound and fury, signifying nothing," or, at most, not very much.

All serious dramatic art, whether tragic or comic, involves a basic relationship between drama and life; that is, there is always an inherent correlation between what it presents on the stage and the actualities of human experience, so that its creation of theatrical effects is always a means to a larger end. In contrast, the most distinctive feature of the virtuoso play is its exclusive theatricality. The production of amusing or sensational effects is its sole concern. Not only are these effects regarded as a sufficient end in themselves, but they constitute the whole reason for the play's existence. Removed from their immediate impact, the play becomes a bloodless phantom. Designed as strictly a theater piece, it is a performance calculated in terms of production opportunities. Its situations are contrived of factitious artifices to create a predetermined effect; its characters are conceived histrionically; its criterion of artistic excellence is the successfully manipulated *coup de théâtre*. Whereas serious drama strives for an effect which is appropriate to the circumstances with which it deals, the virtuoso play reverses the process; beginning with a desirable effect, it works backward to a mechanical pretext for producing it. Because of this subordination of cause to effect, it is inevitably more concerned with sensations and sentiments than with reality or authentic emotion. Correspondingly its chief virtue is not revelation of truth but the clever ingenuity with which it contrives artful impressions. Superficial as mere mechanical dexterity and momentary brilliance may be, within their limitations they are none the less capable of a considerable novelty, suspense, excitement, and sentimental pleasure. Their greatest liability is their ephemerality. Not only do such superficial appeals by nature lack the substance necessary to sustain them beyond their appointed theatrical moment, but where no great value is at stake, replacement is cheap. The result is that plays of this sort are notoriously short lived. Having served their purpose of transitory enjoyment, they are readily supplanted by fresh competitors, no better in their kind, but with the advantage of novelty and more immediate interest.

One of the most conspicuous exceptions thus far to this rule is the so-called heroic comedy *Cyrano de Bergerac,* by the French dramatist Edmond Rostand (1868–1918). Something of an international sensation when it first appeared in 1897, the play has enjoyed in several versions, both on the stage and in print, a sustained success and durability which are by way of making it a modern classic of its genre. The tremendous success of the play, its unquestionable dramatic effectiveness, its appealing idealism, and its sensitive poetic expression, however, do not alter the fact that it is fundamentally a masterpiece of theatrical virtuosity. As a matter of fact, it is a veritable mosaic of tested devices, infallible situations, sanctified conventions, well-worn themes, stereotyped sentiments, and approved stylistic artifices. In its inception it was deliberately designed as a vehicle to exploit the versatile talents of the celebrated French actor Constant Coquelin. From beginning to end it is skilfully contrived to exhibit a fascinating personality in a variety of piquant situations. In the process the whole storehouse of theatrical tradition is ransacked to furnish situations of demonstrated effectiveness, characters of certified interest, and sentiments of guaranteed appeal. The historical subject matter is chosen for its glamor and quaintness. The settings are ostentatiously picturesque. Characters are tailor-made to standard romantic measurements. Incidents are prefabricated to provide a dazzling array of gallant feats, stirring crises, noble gestures, tender moments, witty exchanges, and bravura rhapsodies. Spectacle follows on spectacle, and each act brings down the curtain on a stunning tableau. With a masterly touch on the strings of human susceptibility, the play runs the whole gamut of heroic valor, exalted passion, impudent gayety, astringent wit, graceful sentiment, idyllic yearning, tender compassion, and ironic pathos. Everything is deliberately calculated; every scene, every speech, every gesture is expertly contrived, but with such impeccable style and such exquisite theatrical finesse that, under the spell of its illusion, one is ready to swear it the very stuff of life. Yet a moment's more sober reflection will testify that it is actually as false and factitious as the nose without which no actor could possibly be Cyrano. It is a fabric manufactured of whole cloth—a tissue of magnificent artifice, conceived in the essential spirit of Cyrano himself, and dedicated to the principle which Cyrano has so admirably expressed—"what a gesture!"

The virtues of such a play are those of a luxurious motorcar or any other piece of fine machinery. They afford pleasure by their smooth efficiency, sleek beauty, and capacity to minister to one's comfort and civilized enjoyment. They serve their purpose so admirably because they are features built in to satisfy the customer. For touring pleasure, what is more engaging than picturesque terrain and glamorous inhabitants? For ease, pick-up, and smooth performance, what more reassuring than gallant spirit, agile wit, and dashing valor? For relaxed comfort, what more delightful than love, especially hapless and deathless love, designed with exquisite sentiment and trimmed in impassioned eloquence? And for sheer power when needed, what more satisfying than heroic honor with over-drive of impregnable integrity and noble renunciation? These custom-built appointments there is no effort to conceal; on the contrary, awareness of them is designed to add to the customer's pleasure. One misses the whole brilliance of Rostand's virtuosity unless one recognizes the delicate balance of wit and sentiment, the intricate counterpoint of humor and heroics, the adroit manipulation of suspense, reversal of situation, parallelism and contrast of themes, preparation of theatrical effects, and timing of surprise. The fact that these features are strictly machine-made, are quite unnatural, and coincide with the probabilities of neither reality nor romance has nothing whatever to do with the case. Their justification is their immediate theatrical effectiveness. Their art is the magical virtuosity with which they enchant the passing moment.

The ability to perform this feat calls attention to a curious factor in drama, without which the virtuoso play would lose most of its effectiveness. On the face of it, there is scarcely a scene in *Cyrano de Bergerac* which is not highly implausible. The duel of the ballade, the celebrated balcony scene, the ebbing of Cyrano's life in a symbolic autumn twilight, with the leaves falling and the light fading, to one last white plume of expiring defiance—these are figments of the artistic fancy rather than probabilities of any human experience. As for the gaudy events of the climactic fourth act, they are not only incredible but patently preposterous. Yet no play can possibly capture the imagination of an audience unless it creates an illusion of some kind of reality. To this inexorable law the play of theatrical virtuosity is as much subject as any other drama. The reality which it seeks in its illusion, however, is based not on human existence, whether conceived realistically or romantically, objectively or subjectively, but on life as it exists in the theater. For the curious fact is that the theater actually does possess a life of its own, different in many respects from that beyond its doors, but amazingly comprehensive and sufficient unto itself. As drama is the creator of this life, to a certain extent all drama is also its creature. Being entirely a product of it, the drama of pure artifice owes its whole effectiveness to its expression of this theatrical reality.

As the basis of all theatrical art is the will to make believe, the reality of every theatrical illusion is to a greater or less extent the reality of make-believe. Now, make-believe is simply a process of asserting that things are so because it is convenient that they should be so. The end result is the only relevant consideration, and the only requisite is that matters be understood. Without this initial profession of faith the world of theatrical art could not exist. Nevertheless, theatrical belief is by no means the same as simple credulity, nor is the world which it creates a haphazard one. Its conventions of make-believe are quite systematic and orderly; they are the product of practical expediency; and in their operation they exercise the force of logical law. By a process of trial and error the theater has hit upon its own way of arranging human affairs plausibly, agreeably, and artistically. It has identified situations which may be considered properly dramatic, codified human motives, stereotyped modes of speaking and acting, and prescribed the methods by which it is to be interpreted. By adapting the materials of life to the exigencies of art it has evolved an ordered and rationalized form of existence in which the distinction between truth and accepted pretense has become increasingly tenuous. The inherent conservatism of dramatic art and its tenacity of precedent have further consolidated this material into a continuing body of established principles and practices. The result is that over the centuries the theater has accumulated a heritage of tradition and convention which amounts in effect to an independent record of human experience. While in many respects this theatrical pageant parallels the course of actual life, there are also important differences; for men do not always behave the same on the stage as in the street, nor do events fall out in exactly the same way. For purposes of dramatic plausibility, however, the sanction of theatrical precedent is often quite as persuasive as the testimony of life. It is upon this traditional life of the theater that a play like *Cyrano de Bergerac* bases its illusion of reality, and it is from the accumulated sanction of this theatrical reality that it derives its momentary semblance of truth.

To this general category belong those two hardy perennials of the theater, farce and melodrama. Indeed, it is in these forms that it flourishes most extensively, although it is equally adept at aping the manners of more serious drama, and accounts for the great majority of musical plays. Despite the prevalence and popularity of this kind of drama, however, its limited longevity leaves little of more than historical interest to the modern reader. Perhaps the most ancient durable farce is the *Amphitryon* of Plautus, which might be supplemented by Noel Coward's *Blithe Spirit* or *The Man Who Came to Dinner* by Moss Hart and George Kaufman. Elizabethan varieties may be sampled in Shakespeare's *The Taming of the Shrew*, *Philaster* by Francis Beaumont and John Fletcher, and *The Cardinal* by James Shirley. To these may be added Molière's amusing *The Bourgeois Gentleman* and the younger Dumas' long popular *Camille*, or *The Lady of the Camellias*. Of more recent vintage are J. M. Barrie's *Alice-sit-by-the-Fire* and Ferenc Molnar's *The Guardsman*. Straightforward melodrama appears in *The Green Goddess* by William Archer, *Margin for Error* by Clare Boothe, *Angel Street* by Patrick Hamilton, and *Ladies in Retirement* by Reginald Denham and

Edward Percy. In conclusion, the following more ambitious plays will illustrate some of the variant uses of the type: *The Philadelphia Story* by Philip Barry, *Outward Bound* by Sutton Vane, *The Front Page* by Ben Hecht and Charles MacArthur, *The Petrified Forest* by Robert Sherwood, and *The Little Foxes* by Lillian Hellman.

CYRANO DE BERGERAC

by

EDMUND ROSTAND

TRANSLATED BY

BRIAN HOOKER

THE PERSONS

CYRANO DE BERGERAC
CHRISTIAN DE NEUVILLETTE
COMTE DE GUICHE
RAGUENEAU
LE BRET
CARBON DE CASTEL-JALOUX
The Cadets
LIGNIÈRE
VICOMTE DE VALVERT
A Marquis
Second Marquis
Third Marquis
MONTFLEURY
BELLEROSE
JODELET
CUIGY
BRISSAILLE
A Meddler
A Musketeer
Another Musketeer
A Spanish Officer
A Cavalier

The Porter
A Citizen
His Son
A Cut-Purse
A Spectator
A Sentry
BERTRANDOU *the Fifer*
A Capuchin
Two Musicians
The Poets
The Pastrycooks
The Pages
ROXANE
HER DUENNA
LISE
The Orange-Girl
MOTHER MARGUÉRITE DE JÉSUS
SISTER MARTHE
SISTER CLAIRE
An Actress
A Soubrette
The Flower-Girl

The Crowd, Citizens, Marquis, Musketeers, Thieves, Pastrycooks, Poets, Cadets of Gascoyne, Actors, Violins, Pages, Children, Spanish Soldiers, Spectators, Intellectuals, Academicians, Nuns, etc.

[*The first four Acts in 1640; the fifth in 1655.*]

From *Cyrano de Bergerac* by Edmond Rostand, translated by Brian Hooker. Copyright, 1923, by Henry Holt and Company.

CYRANO DE BERGERAC

by

EDMUND ROSTAND

TRANSLATED BY

BRIAN HOOKER

THE PERSONS

CYRANO DE BERGERAC	The Porter
CHRISTIAN DE NEUVILLETTE	A Citizen
COMTE DE GUICHE	His Son
RAGUENEAU	A Cut-Purse
LE BRET	A Spectator
CARBON DE CASTEL-JALOUX	A Sentry
The Cadets	BERTRANDOU the Fifer
LIGNIÈRE	A Capuchin
VICOMTE DE VALVERT	Two Musicians
A Marquis	The Poets
Second Marquis	The Pastrycooks
Third Marquis	The Pages
MONTFLEURY	ROXANE
BELLEROSE	HER DUENNA
JODELET	LISE
CUIGY	The Orange-Girl
BRISSAILLE	MOTHER MARGUERITE DE JÉSUS
A Meddler	SISTER MARTHE
A Musketeer	SISTER CLAIRE
Another Musketeer	An Actress
A Spanish Officer	A Soubrette
A Cavalier	The Flower-Girl

The Crowd, Citizens, Marquis, Musketeers, Thieves, Pastrycooks, Poets, Cadets of Gascoyne, Actors, Violins, Pages, Children, Spanish Soldiers, Spectators, Intellectuals, Academicians, Nuns, etc.

[The first four Acts in 1640; the fifth in 1655].

From Cyrano de Bergerac by Edmond Rostand, translated by Brian Hooker.
Copyright 1923, by Henry Holt and Company.

THE FIRST ACT

A PERFORMANCE AT THE HÔTEL DE BOURGOGNE

The Hall of the Hôtel de Bourgogne [1] *in 1640. A sort of Tennis Court, arranged and decorated for Theatrical productions.*

The Hall is a long rectangle; we see it diagonally, in such a way that one side of it forms the back scene, which begins at the First Entrance on the Right and runs up to the Last Entrance on the Left, where it makes a right angle with the Stage which is seen obliquely.

This Stage is provided on either hand with benches placed along the wings. The curtain is formed by two lengths of Tapestry which can be drawn apart. Above a Harlequin cloak, the Royal Arms. Broad steps lead from the Stage down to the floor of the Hall. On either side of these steps, a place for the Musicians. A row of candles serves as footlights. Two tiers of Galleries along the side of the Hall; the upper one divided into boxes.

There are no seats upon the Floor, which is the actual stage of our theatre; but toward the back of the Hall, on the right, a few benches are arranged; and underneath a stairway on the extreme right, which leads up to the galleries, and of which only the lower portion is visible, there is a sort of Sideboard, decorated with little tapers, vases of flowers, bottles and glasses, plates of cake, et cetera.

Farther along, toward the centre of our stage, is the Entrance to the Hall: a great double door which opens only slightly to admit the Audience. On one of the panels of this door, as also in other places about the Hall, and in particular just over the Sideboard, are Playbills in red, upon which we may read the title LA CLORISE.

As the Curtain Rises, the Hall is dimly lighted and still empty. The Chandeliers are lowered to the floor, in the middle of the Hall, ready for lighting.

[Sounds of voices outside the door. Then a Cavalier enters abruptly.]

THE PORTER. *[Follows him.]* Hallo there!—Fifteen sols!

THE CAVALIER. I enter free.

THE PORTER. Why?

THE CAVALIER. Soldier of the Household of the King!

THE PORTER. *[Turns to another Cavalier who has just entered.]* You?

SECOND CAVALIER. I pay nothing.

THE PORTER. Why not?

SECOND CAVALIER. Musketeer!

FIRST CAVALIER. *[To the Second.]* The play begins at two. Plenty of time— And here's the whole floor empty. Shall we try Our exercise?

[They fence with the foils which they have brought.]

A LACKEY. *[Enters.]* —Pst! . . . Flanquin! . . .

ANOTHER. *[Already on stage.]* What, Champagne?

FIRST LACKEY. *[Showing games which he takes out of his doublet.]* Cards. Dice. Come on. *[Sits on the floor.]*

SECOND LACKEY. *[Same action.]* Come on, old cock!

FIRST LACKEY. *[Takes from his pocket a bit of candle, lights it, sets it on the floor.]* I have stolen A little of my master's fire.

A GUARDSMAN. *[To a* FLOWER GIRL *who comes forward.]* How sweet Of you, to come before they light the hall! *[Puts his arm around her.]*

FIRST CAVALIER. *[Receives a thrust of the foil.]* A hit!

SECOND LACKEY. A club!

THE GUARDSMAN. *[Pursuing the girl.]* A kiss!

THE FLOWER GIRL. *[Pushing away from him.]* They'll see us!—

THE GUARDSMAN. *[Draws her into a dark corner.]* No danger!

A MAN. *[Sits on the floor, together with*

[1] The leading Paris theater in the early seventeenth century. Here was presented Racine's *Phædra*. The setting of this act gives an excellent and authentic reproduction of general theatrical conditions in the time of Racine and Molière.

several others who have brought packages of food.]
When we come early, we have time to eat.
A CITIZEN. [*Escorting his son, a boy of sixteen.*] Sit here, my son.
FIRST LACKEY.   Mark the Ace!
ANOTHER MAN. [*Draws a bottle from under his cloak and sits down with the others.*]   Here's the spot
For a jolly old sot to suck his Burgundy—
[*Drinks.*]
Here—in the house of the Burgundians! [2]
THE CITIZEN. [*To his son.*] Would you not think you were in some den of vice?
[*Points with his cane at the drunkard.*]
Drunkards—
[*In stepping back, one of the cavaliers trips him up.*]
Bullies!—
[*He falls between the lackeys.*]
Gamblers!—
THE GUARDSMAN. [*Behind him as he rises still struggling with the* FLOWER GIRL.]
One kiss—
THE CITIZEN.   Good God—
[*Draws his son quickly away.*]
Here!—And to think, my son, that in this hall
They play Rotrou! [3]
THE BOY.   Yes, father—and Corneille!
THE PAGES. [*Dance in, holding hands and singing.*] Tra-la-la-la-la-la-la-la-la-lère . . .
THE PORTER. You pages there—no nonsense!
FIRST PAGE. [*With wounded dignity.*]
Oh, Monsieur!
Really! How could you?
[*To the Second, the moment* THE PORTER *turns his back.*]
Pst!—a bit of string?
SECOND PAGE. [*Shows fishline with hook.*]
Yes—and a hook.
FIRST PAGE.   Up in the gallery,
And fish for wigs!

A CUT-PURSE. [*Gathers around him several evil-looking young fellows.*]
Now then, you picaroons,
Perk up, and hear me mutter. Here's your bout—
Bustle around some cull,[4] and bite his bung [5] . . .
SECOND PAGE. [*Calls to other pages already in the gallery.*]
Hey! Brought your pea-shooters?
THIRD PAGE. [*From above.*]
And our peas, too!
[*Blows, and showers them with peas.*]
THE BOY. What is the play this afternoon?
THE CITIZEN.   Clorise.[6]
THE BOY. Who wrote that?
THE CITIZEN. Balthasar Baro. What a play! . . . [*He takes* THE BOY'S *arm and leads him upstage.*]
THE CUT-PURSE. [*To his pupils.*]
Lace now, on those long sleeves, you cut it off— [*Gesture with thumb and finger, as if using scissors.*]
A SPECTATOR. [*To another, pointing upward toward the gallery.*]
Ah, Le Cid! [7] —Yes, the first night, I sat there—
THE CUT-PURSE. Watches— [*Gesture as of picking a pocket.*]
THE CITIZEN. [*Coming down with his son.*]
Great actors we shall see to-day—
THE CUT-PURSE. Handkerchiefs—
[*Gesture of holding the pocket with left hand, and drawing out handkerchief with right.*]
THE CITIZEN.   Montfleury—[8]
A VOICE. [*In the gallery.*]
Lights! Light the lights!
THE CITIZEN. Bellerose, l'Épy, Beaupré, Jodelet—[9]
A PAGE. [*On the floor.*]
Here comes the orange-girl.
THE ORANGE-GIRL.   Oranges, milk,
Raspberry syrup, lemonade—
[*Noise at the door.*]

---

[2] Referring, of course, to the name of the theater.
[3] Jean Rotrou (1609–1650) and Pierre Corneille (1606–1684) were the two leading dramatists of the time.
[4] Easy mark.   [5] *I.e.*, lift his purse.
[6] A play in the then fashionable pastoral mode.

[7] Corneille's most famous play, which, however, was not first produced in this theater.
[8] A prominent, and obese, actor of the period, who was lampooned by both Molière and the historical Cyrano.
[9] Other members of the Hôtel de Bourgogne company, the last an especially noted actor.

A FALSETTO VOICE. [*Outside.*] Make way, Brutes!

FIRST LACKEY. What, the Marquis—on the floor?

[*The* MARQUIS [10] *enter in a little group.*]

SECOND LACKEY. Not long— Only a few moments; they'll go and sit On the stage presently.

FIRST MARQUIS. [*Seeing the hall half empty.*] How now! We enter Like tradespeople—no crowding, no disturbance!— No treading on the toes of citizens? Oh fie! Oh fie! [*He encounters two gentlemen who have already arrived.*] Cuigy! Brissaille! [*Great embracings.*]

CUIGY. The faithful! [*Looks around him.*] We are here before the candles.

FIRST MARQUIS. Ah, be still! You put me in a temper.

SECOND MARQUIS. Console yourself, Marquis—The lamplighter!

THE CROWD. [*Applauding the appearance of the lamplighter.*] Ah! . . .

[*A group gathers around the chandelier while he lights it. A few people have already taken their place in the gallery.* LIGNIÈRE [11] *enters the hall, arm in arm with* CHRISTIAN DE NEUVILLETTE. LIGNIÈRE *is a slightly disheveled figure, dissipated and yet distinguished looking.* CHRISTIAN, *elegantly but rather unfashionably dressed, appears pre-occupied and keeps looking up at the boxes.*]

CUIGY. Lignière!—

BRISSAILLE. [*Laughing.*] Still sober—at this hour?

LIGNIÈRE. [*To* CHRISTIAN.] May I present you? [CHRISTIAN *assents.*] Baron Christian de Neuvillette. [*They salute.*]

THE CROWD. [*Applauding as the lighted chandelier is hoisted into place.*] Ah!—

CUIGY. [*Aside to* BRISSAILLE, *looking at* CHRISTIAN.] Rather A fine head, is it not? The profile . . .

FIRST MARQUIS. [*Who has overheard.*] Peuh!

LIGNIÈRE. [*Presenting them to* CHRISTIAN.] Messieurs de Cuigy . . . de Brissaille . . .

CHRISTIAN. [*Bows.*] Enchanted!

FIRST MARQUIS. [*To the second.*] He is not ill-looking; possibly a shade Behind the fashion.

LIGNIÈRE. [*To* CUIGY.] Monsieur is recently From the Touraine.

CHRISTIAN. Yes, I have been in Paris Two or three weeks only. I join the Guards To-morrow.

FIRST MARQUIS. [*Watching the people who come into the boxes.*] Look—Madame la Présidente Aubry!

THE ORANGE-GIRL. Oranges, milk—

THE VIOLINS. [*Tuning up.*] La . . . la . . .

CUIGY. [*To* CHRISTIAN, *calling his attention to the increasing crowd.*] We have An audience to-day!

CHRISTIAN. A brilliant one.

FIRST MARQUIS. Oh, yes, all our own people—the gay world!

[*They name the ladies who enter the boxes elaborately dressed. Bows and smiles are exchanged.*]

SECOND MARQUIS. Madame de Guéméné . . .

CUIGY. De Boist-Dauphin . . .

FIRST MARQUIS. Whom we adore—

BRISSAILLE. Madame de Chavigny . . .

SECOND MARQUIS. Who plays with all our hearts—

LIGNIÈRE. Why, there's Corneille Returned from Rouen!

THE BOY. [*To his father.*] Are the Academy [12] All here?

THE CITIZEN. I see some of them . . . there's Boudu—

---

[10] Traditionally, the "little Marquis" of the period was an affected fop.
[11] A contemporary writer of epigrams. It should be noted that nearly all the principal characters are historical, and are represented according to their generally reputed personality. Similarly the general events of the play accord with historical fact.
[12] *I.e.,* the members of the French Academy, founded by Richelieu in 1635.

Boissat—Cureau—Porchères—Colomby—
Bourzeys—Bourdon—Arbaut—
　　　　　　　　　Ah, those great names,
Never to be forgotten! [13]

FIRST MARQUIS.　　　　　Look—at last!
Our Intellectuals! Barthénoide,
Urimédonte, Félixérie [14] . . .

SECOND MARQUIS.　　[*Languishing.*]
　　　　　　　　　Sweet heaven!
How exquisite their surnames are! Mar-
　quis,
You know them all?

FIRST MARQUIS.　I know them all, Mar-
　quis!

LIGNIÈRE.　[*Draws* CHRISTIAN *aside.*]
My dear boy, I came here to serve you—
　Well,
But where's the lady? I'll be going.

CHRISTIAN.　　　　　　Not yet—
A little longer! She is always here.
Please! I must find some way of meeting
　her.
I am dying of love! And you—you know
Everyone, the whole court and the whole
　town,
And put them all into your songs—at least
You can tell me her name!

THE FIRST VIOLIN.　[*Raps on his desk with
　his bow.*]　　　　　Pst— Gentlemen!
　　　　　　　[*Raises his bow.*]

THE ORANGE-GIRL.　Macaroons, lemon-
　ade—

CHRISTIAN.　　　　　Then she may be
One of those æsthetes . . . Intellectuals,
You call them— How can I talk to a
　woman
In that style? I have no wit. This fine
　manner
Of speaking and of writing nowadays—
Not for me! I am a soldier—and afraid.
That's her box, on the right—the empty
　one.

LIGNIÈRE.　[*Starts for the door.*]
I am going.

CHRISTIAN.　[*Restrains him.*] No—wait!

LIGNIÈRE.　　　　Not I. There's a tavern
Not far away—and I am dying of thirst.

THE ORANGE-GIRL.　[*Passes with her tray.*]
Orange juice?

LIGNIÈRE.　No!

THE ORANGE-GIRL.　Milk?

LIGNIÈRE.　　　　Pouah!

THE ORANGE-GIRL.　　　　Muscatel?

LIGNIÈRE.　Here! Stop! [*To* CHRISTIAN.]
I'll stay a little. [*To the Girl.*] Let me see
Your Muscatel.
　　[*He sits down by the sideboard. The* GIRL
　　　pours out wine for him.]

VOICES.　[*In the crowd about the door,
　upon the entrance of a spruce little man,
　rather fat, with a beaming smile.*]
　　　　　　　Ragueneau!

LIGNIÈRE.　[*To* CHRISTIAN.] Ragueneau,
Poet and pastrycook—a character!

RAGUENEAU.　[*Dressed like a confectioner
　in his Sunday clothes, advances quickly
　to* LIGNIÈRE.]
Sir, have you seen Monsieur de Cyrano?

LIGNIÈRE.　[*Presents him to* CHRISTIAN.]
Permit me . . . Ragueneau, confectioner,
The chief support of modern poetry.

RAGUENEAU.　[*Bridling.*]
Oh—too much honor!

LIGNIÈRE.　　　　Patron of the Arts—
Mæcenas! [15] Yes, you are—

RAGUENEAU.　　　　　Undoubtedly,
The poets gather round my hearth.

LIGNIÈRE.　　　　　On credit—
Himself a poet—

RAGUENEAU.　So they say—

LIGNIÈRE.　　　　　Maintains
The Muses.

RAGUENEAU.　It is true that for an ode---

LIGNIÈRE.　You give a tart—

RAGUENEAU.　　　A tartlet—

LIGNIÈRE.　　　　　　Modesty!
And for a triolet you give—

RAGUENEAU.　　　　Plain bread!

LIGNIÈRE.　[*Severely.*] Bread and milk!
And you love the theatre?

RAGUENEAU.　I adore it!

LIGNIÈRE.　　　Well, pastry pays for all.
Your place to-day now—Come, between
　ourselves,

[13] The irony being that they *have* been practically forgotten.
[14] Samples of the fanciful names adopted by
the exquisite female counterparts of the Marquis.

[15] The famous Roman patron of poetry and the
arts.

What did it cost you?

RAGUENEAU. Four pies; fourteen cakes.
[*Looking about.*]
But— Cyrano not here? Astonishing!

LIGNIÈRE. Why so?

RAGUENEAU. Why— Montfleury plays!

LIGNIÈRE. Yes, I hear
That hippopotamus assumes the rôle
Of Phédon.[16] What is that to Cyrano?

RAGUENEAU. Have you not heard? Monsieur de Bergerac
So hates Montfleury, he has forbidden him
For three weeks to appear upon the stage.

LIGNIÈRE. [*Who is, by this time, at his fourth glass.*] Well?

RAGUENEAU. Montfleury plays!—

CUIGY. [*Strolls over to them.*]
Yes—what then?

RAGUENEAU. Ah! That
Is what I came to see.

FIRST MARQUIS. This Cyrano—
Who is he?

CUIGY. Oh, he is the lad with the long sword.

SECOND MARQUIS. Noble?

CUIGY. Sufficiently; he is in the Guards.
[*Points to a gentleman who comes and goes about the hall as though seeking for someone.*]
His friend Le Bret [17] can tell you more.
[*Calls to him.*] Le Bret!
[LE BRET *comes down to them.*]
Looking for Bergerac?

LE BRET. Yes. And for trouble.

CUIGY. Is he not an extraordinary man?

LE BRET. The best friend and the bravest soul alive!

RAGUENEAU. Poet—

CUIGY. Swordsman—

LE BRET. Musician—

BRISSAILLE. Philosopher—

LIGNIÈRE. Such a remarkable appearance, too!

RAGUENEAU. Truly, I should not look to find his portrait

By the grave hand of Philippe de Champagne.[18]
He might have been a model for Callot—[19]
One of those wild swashbucklers in a masque—
Hat with three plumes, and doublet with six points—
His cloak behind him over his long sword
Cocked, like the tail of strutting Chanticleer—
Prouder than all the swaggering Tamburlaines [20]
Hatched out of Gascony.[21] And to complete
This Punchinello figure—such a nose!—
My lords, there is no such nose as that nose—
You cannot look upon it without crying:
"Oh, no,
Impossible! Exaggerated!" Then
You smile, and say: "Of course— I might have known;
Presently he will take it off." But that
Monsieur de Bergerac will never do.

LIGNIÈRE. [*Grimly.*] He keeps it—and God help the man who smiles!

RAGUENEAU. His sword is one half of the shears of Fate!

FIRST MARQUIS. [*Shrugs.*]
He will not come.

RAGUENEAU. Will he not? Sir, I'll lay you
A pullet à la Ragueneau!

FIRST MARQUIS. [*Laughing.*] Done!
[*Murmurs of admiration;* ROXANE *has just appeared in her box. She sits at the front of the box, and her Duenna takes a seat toward the rear.* CHRISTIAN, *busy paying the* ORANGE-GIRL, *does not see her at first.*]

SECOND MARQUIS. [*With little excited cries.*] Ah!
Oh! Oh! Sweet sirs, look yonder! Is she not
Frightfully ravishing?

FIRST MARQUIS. Bloom of the peach—
Blush of the strawberry—

SECOND MARQUIS. So fresh—so cool,

---

[16] The idyllic shepherd of *Clorise*.
[17] Henri Le Bret was the life-long friend and biographer of Cyrano.
[18] A celebrated portrait painter.
[19] An engraver who excelled in the fantastic.

[20] The swaggering hero of Marlowe's famous play—here substituted for the original French equivalent.
[21] Traditionally the home of hot heads and touchy pride.

That our hearts, grown all warm with lov-
    ing her,
May catch their death of cold!
CHRISTIAN. [*Looks up, sees* ROXANE, *and
    seizes* LIGNIÈRE *by the arm.*]
                    There! Quick—up there—
In the box! Look!—
LIGNIÈRE. [*Coolly.*] Herself?
CHRISTIAN.   Quickly— Her name?
LIGNIÈRE. [*Sipping his wine, and speaking
    between sips.*] Madeleine Robin, called
    Roxane . . . refined . . .
Intellectual . . .
CHRISTIAN. Ah!—
LIGNIÈRE.   Unmarried . . .
CHRISTIAN.   Oh!—
LIGNIÈRE. No title . . . rich enough . . .
    an orphan . . . cousin
To Cyrano . . . of whom we spoke just
    now . . .
    [*At this point, a very distinguished look-
    ing gentleman, the Cordon Bleu* [22]
    *around his neck, enters the box, and
    stands a moment talking with* ROXANE.]
CHRISTIAN. [*Starts.*] And the man? . . .
LIGNIÈRE. [*Beginning to feel his wine a
    little; cocks his eye at them.*] Oho! That
    man? . . . Comte de Guiche . . .
In love with her . . . married himself, how-
    ever,
To the niece of the Cardinal—Riche-
    lieu [23] . . .
Wishes Roxane, therefore, to marry one
Monsieur de Valvert . . . Vicomte . . .
    friend of his . . .
A somewhat melancholy gentleman . . .
But . . . well, accommodating! . . . She
    says No . . .
Nevertheless, de Guiche is powerful . . .
Not above persecuting . . .
    [*He rises, swaying a little, and very
    happy.*]
                    I have written
A little song about his little game . . .
Good little song, too . . . Here, I'll sing it
    for you . . .
Make de Guiche furious . . . naughty little
    song . . .

Not so bad, either— Listen! . . .
    [*He stands with his glass held aloft,
    ready to sing.*]
CHRISTIAN.   No. Adieu.
LIGNIÈRE. Whither away?
CHRISTIAN.   To Monsieur de Valvert!
LIGNIÈRE. Careful! The man's a swords-
    man . . . [*Nods toward* ROXANE, *who is
    watching* CHRISTIAN.] Wait! Someone
Looking at you—
CHRISTIAN. Roxane! . . .
    [*He forgets everything, and stands spell-
    bound, gazing toward* ROXANE. *The*
    CUT-PURSE *and his crew, observing
    him transfixed, his eyes raised and his
    mouth half open, begin edging in his
    direction.*]
LIGNIÈRE.   Oh! Very well,
Then I'll be leaving you . . . Good day . . .
    Good day! . . .
    [CHRISTIAN *remains motionless.*]
Everywhere else, they like to hear me
    sing!—
Also, I am thirsty.
    [*He goes out, navigating carefully.* LE
    BRET, *having made the circuit of the
    hall, returns to* RAGUENEAU, *somewhat
    reassured.*]
LE BRET.   No sign anywhere
Of Cyrano!
RAGUENEAU. [*Incredulous.*] Wait and see!
LE BRET.   Humph! I hope
He has not seen the bill.
THE CROWD.   The play!— The play!—
FIRST MARQUIS. [*Observing* DE GUICHE, *as
    he descends from* ROXANE'S *box and
    crosses the floor, followed by a knot of
    obsequious gentlemen, the* VICOMTE DE
    VALVERT *among them.*]
This man de Guiche—what ostentation!
SECOND MARQUIS.   Bah!—
Another Gascon!
FIRST MARQUIS. Gascon, yes—but cold
And calculating—certain to succeed—
My word for it. Come, shall we make our
    bow?
We shall be none the worse, I promise
    you . . .   [*They go toward* DE GUICHE.]

[22] The blue ribbon of the Order of the Holy
Ghost, the highest order of Bourbon chivalry.

[23] The famous prime minister of France.

SECOND MARQUIS. Beautiful ribbons,
Count! That color, now,
What is it—*Kiss-me-Dear* or *Startled-Fawn?*
DE GUICHE. I call that shade *The Dying
Spaniard.*
FIRST MARQUIS. Ha!
And no false colors either—thanks to you
And your brave troops, in Flanders before
long
The Spaniard will die daily.
DE GUICHE. Shall we go
And sit upon the stage? Come, Valvert.
CHRISTIAN. [*Starts at the name.*] Valvert!—
The Vicomte— Ah, that scoundrel! Quick
—my glove—
I'll throw it in his face—
[*Reaching into his pocket for his glove,
he catches the hand of* THE CUT-PURSE.]
THE CUT-PURSE. Oh!—
CHRISTIAN. [*Holding fast to the man's
wrist.*] Who are you?
I was looking for a glove—
THE CUT-PURSE. [*Cringing.*] You found a
hand. [*Hurriedly.*]
Let me go—I can tell you something—
CHRISTIAN. [*Still holding him.*] Well?
THE CUT-PURSE. Lignière—that friend of
yours—
CHRISTIAN. [*Still holding him.*] Well?
THE CUT-PURSE. Good as dead—
Understand? Ambuscaded. Wrote a song
About—no matter. There's a hundred men
Waiting for him to-night—I'm one of them.
CHRISTIAN. A hundred! Who arranged
this?
THE CUT-PURSE. Secret.
CHRISTIAN. Oh!
THE CUT-PURSE. [*With dignity.*]
Professional secret.
CHRISTIAN. Where are they to be?
THE CUT-PURSE. Porte de Nesle. On his
way home. Tell him so.
Save his life.
CHRISTIAN. [*Releases the man.*]
Yes, but where am I to find him?
THE CUT-PURSE. Go round the taverns.
There's The Golden Grape,
The Pineapple, The Bursting Belt, The Two

Torches, The Three Funnels—in every one
You leave a line of writing—understand?
To warn him.
CHRISTIAN. [*Starts for the door.*]
I'll go! God, what swine—a hundred
Against one man! . . .
[*Stops and looks longingly at* ROXANE.]
Leave *her* here!—
[*Savagely, turning toward* VALVERT.]
And leave *him!*—
[*Decidedly.*]
I must save Lignière! [*Exit.*]
[DE GUICHE, VALVERT, *and all the Mar-
quis have disappeared through the
curtains, to take their seats upon the
stage. The floor is entirely filled; not
a vacant seat remains in the gallery or
in the boxes.*]
THE CROWD. The play! The play!
Begin the play!
A CITIZEN. [*As his wig is hoisted into the
air on the end of a fishline, in the hands
of a page in the gallery.*] My wig!!
CRIES OF JOY. He's bald! Bravo,
You pages! Ha ha ha!
THE CITIZEN. [*Furious, shakes his fist at
the boy.*] Here, you young villain!
CRIES AND LAUGHTER. [*Beginning very
loud, then suddenly repressed.*]
HA HA! Ha Ha! ha ha! . . .
[*Complete silence.*]
LE BRET. [*Surprised.*] That sudden hush!
[*A* SPECTATOR *whispers in his ear.*]
Yes?
THE SPECTATOR. I was told on good
authority . . .
MURMURS. [*Here and there.*] What? . . .
Here? . . . No . . . Yes . . . Look—in
the latticed box—
The Cardinal! . . . The Cardinal! . . .
A PAGE. The Devil!—
Now we shall all have to behave ourselves!
[*Three raps on the stage. The audience
becomes motionless. Silence.*]
THE VOICE OF A MARQUIS. [*From the
stage, behind the curtains.*]
Snuff that candle!
ANOTHER MARQUIS. [*Puts his head out
through the curtains.*] A chair! . . .
[*A chair is passed from hand to hand*

over the heads of the crowd. He takes it, and disappears behind the curtains, not without having blown a few kisses to the occupants of the boxes.]

A SPECTATOR.   Silence!

VOICES.   Hssh! . . . Hssh! . . .

[Again the three raps on the stage. The curtains part. TABLEAU. *The Marquis seated on their chairs to right and left of the stage, insolently posed. Back drop representing a pastoral scene, bluish in tone. Four little crystal chandeliers light up the stage. The violins play softly.]*

LE BRET. *[In a low tone to* RAGUENEAU.] Montfleury enters now?

RAGUENEAU. *[Nods.]*   Opens the play.

LE BRET. *[Much relieved.]* Then Cyrano is not here!

RAGUENEAU.   I lose . . .

LE BRET.   Humph! So much the better!

[The melody of a Musette is heard. MONTFLEURY *appears upon the scene, a ponderous figure in the costume of a rustic shepherd, a hat garlanded with roses tilted over one ear, playing upon a beribboned pastoral pipe.]*

THE CROWD. *[Applauds.]* Montfleury! . . . Bravo! . . .

MONTFLEURY. *[After bowing to the applause, begins the rôle of Phédon.]* "Thrice happy he who hides from pomp and power In sylvan shade or solitary bower; Where balmy zephyrs fan his burning cheeks—"

A VOICE. *[From the midst of the hall.]* Wretch! Have I not forbade you these three weeks? *[Sensation. Every one turns to look. Murmurs.]*

SEVERAL VOICES. What? . . . Where? . . . Who is it? . . .

CUIGY.   Cyrano!

LE BRET. *[In alarm.]*   Himself!

THE VOICE. King of clowns! Leave the stage—*at once!*

THE CROWD.   Oh!

MONTFLEURY.   Now, Now, now—

THE VOICE. You disobey me?

SEVERAL VOICES. *[From the floor, from the boxes.]*   Hsh! Go on— Quiet!—Go on, Montfleury!—Who's afraid?—

MONTFLEURY. *[In a voice of no great assurance.]* "Thrice happy he who hides from . . ."

THE VOICE. *[More menacingly.]*   Well? Well? Well? . . . Monarch of mountebanks! Must I come and plant A forest on your shoulders?

[A cane at the end of a long arm shakes above the heads of the crowd.]

MONTFLEURY. *[In a voice increasingly feeble.]*   "Thrice hap—"

[The cane is violently agitated.]

THE VOICE.   GO!!!

THE CROWD. Ah! . . .

CYRANO.[24] *[Arises in the centre of the floor, erect upon a chair, his arms folded, his hat cocked ferociously, his moustache bristling, his nose terrible.]* Presently I shall grow angry!

[Sensation at his appearance.]

MONTFLEURY. *[To the Marquis.]*   Messieurs, If you protect me—

A MARQUIS. *[Nonchalantly.]*   Well—proceed!

CYRANO.   Fat swine! If you dare breathe one balmy zephyr more, I'll fan your cheeks for you!

THE MARQUIS.   Quiet down there!

CYRANO. Unless these gentlemen retain their seats, My cane may bite their ribbons!

ALL THE MARQUIS. *[On their feet.]*   That will do!— Montfleury—

CYRANO. Fly, goose! Shoo! Take to your wings, Before I pluck your plumes, and draw your gorge!

A VOICE. See here!—

[24] Savinien Cyrano de Bergerac (1619–1655), of a noble Gascon family, was a soldier, noted swordsman, student of physics and philosophy, dramatist, and author of a celebrated satire, *The Comic Histories of the States and Empires in the Moon and Sun.*

CYRANO.   Off stage!

ANOTHER VOICE.   One moment—

CYRANO.   What—still there?
[*Turns back his cuffs deliberately.*]
Very good—then I enter—*Left*—with
knife—
To carve this large Italian sausage.

MONTFLEURY. [*Desperately attempting dignity.*]   Sir,
When you insult me, you insult the Muse!

CYRANO. [*With great politeness.*] Sir, if the
Muse, who never knew your name,
Had the honor to meet you—then be sure
That after one glance at that face of yours,
That figure of a mortuary urn—
She would apply her buskin—toward the
rear!

THE CROWD. Montfleury! . . . Montfluery!
The play! The play!

CYRANO. [*To those who are shouting and
crowding about him.*] Pray you, be gentle with my scabbard here—
She'll put her tongue out at you presently!—
[*The circle enlarges.*]

THE CROWD. [*Recoiling.*] Keep back—

CYRANO. [*To* MONTFLEURY.] Begone!

THE CROWD. [*Pushing in closer, and growling.*]   Ahr! . . . ahr! . . .

CYRANO. [*Turns upon them.*]
                        Did some one speak?
[*They recoil again.*]

A VOICE. [*In the back of the hall, sings.*]
            Monsieur de Cyrano
            Must be another Cæsar—
        Let Brutus lay him low,
            And play us La Clorise!

ALL THE CROWD. [*Singing.*]
            La Clorise! La Clorise!

CYRANO. Let me hear one more word of
that same song,
And I destroy you all!

A CITIZEN.   Who might you be?
Samson?—

CYRANO. Precisely. Would you kindly lend
me
Your jawbone? [25]

A LADY. [*In one of the boxes.*]
                    What an outrage!

---

[25] Samson slew the Philistines with the jawbone of an ass.

A NOBLE.   Scandalous!

A CITIZEN. Annoying!

A PAGE.   What a game!

THE CROWD.   Kss! Montfleury!
Cyrano!

CYRANO. Silence!

THE CROWD. [*Delirious.*]
            Woof! Woof! Baaa! Cockadoo!

CYRANO. I—

A PAGE.   Meow!

CYRANO.   I say be silent!—
[*His voice dominates the uproar. Mo-
mentary hush.*]
                            And I offer
One universal challenge to you all!
Approach, young heroes—I will take your
names.
Each in his turn—no crowding! One, two,
three—
Come, get your numbers—who will head
the list—
You, sir? No— You? Ah, no. To the first
man
Who falls I'll build a monument! . . . Not
one?
Will all who wish to die, please raise their
hands? . . .
I see. You are so modest, you might
blush
Before a sword naked. Sweet innocence! . . .
Not one name? Not one finger? . . . Very
well,
Then I go on:
[*Turning back toward the stage, where*
MONTFLEURY *waits in despair.*]
                    I'd have our theatre cured
Of this carbuncle. Or if not, why then—
[*His hand on his sword hilt.*]
The lancet!

MONTFLEURY. I—

CYRANO. [*Descends from his chair, seats
himself comfortably in the centre of the
circle which has formed around him, and
makes himself quite at home.*]
                    Attend to me—full moon!
I clap my hands, three times—thus. At the
third
You will eclipse yourself.

THE CROWD. [*Amused.*] Ah!

CYRANO.   Ready? One.

MONTFLEURY. I—

A VOICE. [*From the boxes.*] No!

THE CROWD. He'll go— He'll stay—

MONTFLEURY. I really think, Gentlemen—

CYRANO. *Two.*

MONTFLEURY. Perhaps I had better—

CYRANO. *Three!*

[MONTFLEURY *disappears, as if through a trap-door. Tempest of laughter, hoots and hisses.*]

THE CROWD. Yah!—Coward—Come back—

CYRANO. [*Beaming, drops back in his chair and crosses his legs.*] Let him—if he dare!

A CITIZEN. The Manager! Speech! Speech!

[BELLEROSE *advances and bows.*]

THE BOXES. Ah! Bellerose!

BELLEROSE. [*With elegance.*] Most noble—most fair—

THE CROWD. No! The Comedian— Jodelet!—

JODELET. [*Advances, and speaks through his nose.*] Lewd fellows of the baser sort—

THE CROWD. Ha! Ha! Not bad! Bravo!

JODELET. No Bravos here! Our heavy tragedian with the voluptuous bust Was taken suddenly—

THE CROWD. Yah! Coward!

JODELET. I mean . . . He had to be excused—

THE CROWD. Call him back— No!— Yes!—

THE BOY. [*To* CYRANO.] After all, Monsieur, what reason have you To hate this Montfluery?

CYRANO. [*Graciously, still seated.*] My dear young man, I have two reasons, either one alone Conclusive. *Primo:* A lamentable actor, Who mouths his verse and moans his tragedy, And heaves up—Ugh!—like a hod-carrier, lines That ought to soar on their own wings. *Secundo:*— Well—that's my secret.

THE OLD CITIZEN. [*Behind him.*] But you close the play— *La Clorise*—by Baro! Are we to miss Our entertainment, merely—

CYRANO. [*Respectfully, turns his chair toward the old man.*] My dear old boy, The poetry of Baro being worth Zero, or less, I feel that I have done Poetic justice!

THE INTELLECTUALS. [*In the boxes.*] Really!—our Baro!— My dear!—Who ever?—Ah, dieu! The idea!—

CYRANO. [*Gallantly, turns his chair toward the boxes.*] Fair ladies—shine upon us like the sun, Blossom like flowers around us—be our songs, Heard in a dream— Make sweet the hour of death, Smiling upon us as you close our eyes— Inspire, but do not try to criticize!

BELLEROSE. Quite so!—and the mere money—possibly You would like that returned— Yes?

CYRANO. Bellerose, You speak the first word of intelligence! I will not wound the mantle of the Muse— Here, catch!— [*Throws him a purse.*] And hold your tongue.

THE CROWD. [*Astonished.*] Ah! Ah!

JODELET. [*Deftly catches the purse, weighs it in his hand.*] Monsieur, You are hereby authorized to close our play Every night, on the same terms.

THE CROWD. Boo!

JODELET. And welcome! Let us be booed together, you and I!

BELLEROSE. Kindly pass out quietly . . .

JODELET. [*Burlesquing* BELLROSE.] Quietly . . .

[*They begin to go out, while* CYRANO *looks about him with satisfaction. But the exodus ceases presently during the ensuing scene. The ladies in the boxes who have already risen and put on their wraps, stop to listen, and finally sit down again.*]

LE BRET. [*To* CYRANO.] Idiot!

A MEDDLER. [*Hurries up to* CYRANO.]
    But what a scandal! Montfleury—
The great Montfleury! Did you know the
    Duc
De Candale was his patron? Who is yours?
CYRANO. No one.
THE MEDDLER. No one—no patron?
CYRANO.   I said no.
THE MEDDLER. What, no great lord, to
    cover with his name—
CYRANO. [*With visible annoyance.*]
No, I have told you twice. Must I repeat?
No sir, no patron—
                [*His hand on his sword.*]
                    But a patroness!
THE MEDDLER. And when do you leave
    Paris?
CYRANO.   That's as may be.
THE MEDDLER. The Duc de Candale has a
    long arm.
CYRANO.   Mine.
Is longer, [*Drawing his sword.*] by three
    feet of steel.
THE MEDDLER.   Yes, yes,
But do you dream of daring—
CYRANO.   I do dream
Of daring . . .
THE MEDDLER. But—
CYRANO.   You may go now.
THE MEDDLER.   But—
CYRANO.   You may go—
Or tell me why are you staring at my nose!
THE MEDDLER. [*In confusion.*]
No—I—
CYRANO. [*Stepping up to him.*]
            Does it astonish you?
THE MEDDLER. [*Drawing back.*]
                    Your grace
Misunderstands my—
CYRANO.   Is it long and soft
And dangling, like a trunk?
THE MEDDLER. [*Same business.*]
                    I never said—
CYRANO. Or crooked, like an owl's beak?
THE MEDDLER.   I—
CYRANO.   Perhaps
A pimple ornaments the end of it?
THE MEDDLER. No—
CYRANO. Or a fly parading up and down?
What is this portent?

THE MEDDLER.   Oh!—
CYRANO.   This phenomenon?
THE MEDDLER. But I have been careful
    not to look—
CYRANO.   And why
Not, if you please?
THE MEDDLER. Why—
CYRANO.   It disgusts you, then?
THE MEDDLER. My dear sir—
CYRANO.   Does its color appear to you
Unwholesome?
THE MEDDLER. Oh, by no means!
CYRANO.   Or its form
Obscene?
THE MEDDLER. Not in the least—
CYRANO.   Then why assume
This deprecating manner? Possibly
You find it just a trifle large?
THE MEDDLER. [*Babbling.*] Oh, no!—
Small, very small, infinitesimal—
CYRANO. [*Roars.*]   What!
How? You accuse me of absurdity?
Small—*my nose?* Why—
THE MEDDLER. [*Breathless.*] My God!—
CYRANO.   Magnificent,
My nose! . . . You pug, you knob, you
    button-head,
Know that I glory in this nose of mine,
For a great nose indicates a great man—
Genial, courteous, intellectual,
Virile, courageous—as I am—and such
As you—poor wretch—will never dare to
    be
Even in imagination. For that face—
That blank, inglorious concavity
Which my right hand finds—
                [*He strikes him.*]
THE MEDDLER.   Ow!
CYRANO.   —on top of you,
Is as devoid of pride, of poetry,
Of soul, of picturesqueness, of contour,
Of character, of NOSE in short—as that
    [*Takes him by the shoulders and turns
    him around, suiting the action to the
    word.*]
Which at the end of that limp spine of
    yours
My left foot—
THE MEDDLER. [*Escaping.*]
        Help! The Guard!

CYRANO. Take notice, all
Who find this feature of my countenance
A theme for comedy! When the humorist
Is noble, then my custom is to show
Appreciation proper to his rank—
More heartfelt . . . and more pointed. . . .
DE GUICHE. [Who has come down from the stage, surrounded by the Marquis.]
Presently
This fellow will grow tiresome.
VALVERT. [Shrugs.] Oh, he blows
His trumpet!
DE GUICHE. Well—will no one interfere?
VALVERT. No one? [Looks round.]
Observe I myself will proceed
To put him in his place.
[He walks up to CYRANO, who has been watching him, and stands there, looking him over with an affected air.]
Ah . . . your nose . . . hem! . . .
Your nose is . . . rather large!
CYRANO. [Gravely.] Rather.
VALVERT. [Simpering.] Oh well—
CYRANO. [Coolly.] Is that all?
VALVERT. [Turns away, with a shrug.]
Well, of course—
CYRANO. Ah, no, young sir!
You are too simple. Why, you might have said—
Oh, a great many things! Mon dieu, why waste
Your opportunity? For example, thus:—
Aggressive: I, sir, if that nose were mine,
I'd have it amputated—on the spot!
Friendly: How do you drink with such a nose?
You ought to have a cup made specially.
Descriptive: 'Tis a rock—a crag—a cape—
A cape? say rather, a peninsula!
Inquisitive: What is that receptacle—
A razor-case or a portfolio?
Kindly: Ah, do you love the little birds
So much that when they come and sing to you,
You give them this to perch on? Insolent:
Sir, when you smoke, the neighbors must suppose
Your chimney is on fire. Cautious: Take care—

A weight like that might make you top-heavy.
Thoughtful: Somebody fetch my parasol—
Those delicate colors fade so in the sun!
Pedantic: Does not Aristophanes
Mention a mythologic monster called
Hippocampelephantocamelos?
Surely we have here the original!
Familiar: Well, old torchlight! Hang your hat
Over that chandelier—it hurts my eyes.
Eloquent: When it blows, the typhoon howls,
And the clouds darken. Dramatic: When it bleeds—
The Red Sea! Enterprising: What a sign
For some perfumer! Lyric: Hark—the horn
Of Roland calls to summon Charlemagne!—
Simple: When do they unveil the monument?
Respectful: Sir, I recognize in you
A man of parts, a man of prominence—
Rustic: Hey? What? Call that a nose? Na, na—
I be no fool like what you think I be—
That there's a blue cucumber! Military:
Point against cavalry! Practical: Why not
A lottery with this for the grand prize?
Or—parodying Faustus in the play—
"Was this the nose that launched a thousand ships
And burned the topless towers of Ilium?"
These, my dear sir, are things you might have said
Had you some tinge of letters, or of wit
To color your discourse. But wit,—not so,
You never had an atom—and of letters,
You need but three to write you down—an Ass.
Moreover,—if you had the invention, here
Before these folk to make a jest of me—
Be sure you would not then articulate
The twentieth part of half a syllable
Of the beginning! For I say these things
Lightly enough myself, about myself,
But I allow none else to utter them.

DE GUICHE. [*Tries to lead away the amazed* VALVERT.] Vicomte—come.

VALVERT. [*Choking.*]

Oh— These arrogant grand airs!—
A clown who—look at him—not even
gloves!
No ribbons—no lace—no buckles on his
shoes—

CYRANO. I carry my adornments on my
soul.
I do not dress up like a popinjay;
But inwardly, I keep my daintiness.
I do not bear with me, by any chance,
An insult not yet washed away—a con-
science
Yellow with unpurged bile—an honor
frayed
To rags, a set of scruples badly worn.
I go caparisoned in gems unseen,
Trailing white plumes of freedom, gar-
landed
With my good name—no figure of a man,
But a soul clothed in shining armor, hung
With deeds for decorations, twirling—
thus—
A bristling wit, and swinging at my side
Courage, and on the stones of this old town
Making the sharp truth ring, like golden
spurs!

VALVERT. But—

CYRANO. But I have no gloves! A pity too!
I had one—the last one of an old pair—
And lost that. Very careless of me. Some
Gentleman offered me an impertinence.
I left it—in his face.

VALVERT. Dolt, bumpkin, fool,
Insolent puppy, jobbernowl!

CYRANO. [*Removes his hat and bows.*]

Ah, yes?
And I—Cyrano-Savinien-Hercule
De Bergerac!

VALVERT. [*Turns away.*] Buffoon!

CYRANO. [*Cries out as if suddenly taken
with a cramp.*] Oh!

VALVERT. [*Turns back.*] Well, what now?

CYRANO. [*With grimaces of anguish.*]
I must do something to relieve these
cramps—
This is what comes of lack of exercise—
Ah!—

VALVERT. What is all this?

CYRANO. My sword has gone to sleep!

VALVERT. [*Draws.*] So be it!

CYRANO. You shall die exquisitely.

VALVERT. [*Contemptuously.*] Poet!

CYRANO. Why, yes, a poet, if you will;
So while we fence, I'll make you a Ballade
Extempore.

VALVERT. A Ballade?

CYRANO. Yes. You know
What that is?

VALVERT. I—

CYRANO. The Ballade, sir, is formed
Of three stanzas of eight lines each—

VALVERT. Oh, come!

CYRANO. And a refrain of four.

VALVERT. You—

CYRANO. I'll compose
One, while I fight with you; and at the end
Of the last line—thrust home!

VALVERT. Will you?

CYRANO. I will.
[*Declaims.*]
"*Ballade of the duel at the Hôtel de Bour-
gogne
Between de Bergerac and a Bœotian.*" 26

VALVERT. [*Sneering.*] What do you mean
by that?

CYRANO. Oh, that? The title.

THE CROWD. [*Excited.*] Come on—
A circle—
Quiet—
Down in front!
[TABLEAU. *A ring of interested spectators
in the centre of the floor, the Marquis
and the Officers mingling with the citizens and common folk. Pages swarm-
ing up on men's shoulders to see better; the Ladies in the boxes standing
and leaning over. To the right,* DE
GUICHE *and his following; to the left,*
LE BRET, CUIGY, RAGUENEAU, *and
others of* CYRANO'S *friends.*]

CYRANO. [*Closes his eyes for an instant.*]
Stop . . . Let me choose my rimes. . . .
Now! Here we go—
[*He suits the action to the word, through-
out the following:*]

26 The inhabitants of ancient Bœotia were regarded as stupid yokels.

Lightly I toss my hat away,
Languidly over my arm let fall
The cloak that covers my bright array—
Then out swords, and to work withal!
A Launcelot,[27] in his Lady's hall . . .
A Spartacus,[28] at the Hippodrome! . . .
I dally awhile with you, dear jackal,
Then, as I end the refrain, thrust home.

[*The swords cross—the fight is on.*]

Where shall I skewer my peacock? . . . Nay,
Better for you to have shunned this
brawl!—
Here, in the heart, thro' your ribbons gay?
—In the belly, under your silken shawl?
Hark, how the steel rings musical!
Mark how my point floats, light as the
foam,
Ready to drive you back to the wall,
Then, as I end the refrain, thrust home!

Ho, for a rime! . . . You are white as
whey—
You break, you cower, you cringe, you
. . . crawl!
Tac!—and I parry your last essay:
So may the turn of a hand forestall
Life with its honey, death with its gall;
So may the turn of my fancy roam
Free, for a time, till the rimes recall,
Then, as I end the refrain, thrust home!

[*He announces solemnly.*]

REFRAIN

Prince! Pray God, that is Lord of all,
Pardon your soul, for your time has come!
Beat—pass—fling you aslant, asprawl—
Then, as I end the refrain . . .

[*He lunges; VALVERT staggers back and falls into the arms of his friends. CYRANO recovers, and salutes.*]
—Thrust home!

[*Shouts. Applause from the boxes. Flowers and handkerchiefs come fluttering down. The Officers surround*

CYRANO *and congratulate him.* RAGUENEAU *dances for joy.* LE BRET *is unable to conceal his enthusiasm. The friends of* VALVERT *hold him up and help him away.*]

THE CROWD. [*In one long cry.*] Ah-h!
A CAVALIER. Superb!
A WOMAN. Simply sweet!
RAGUENEAU. Magnelephant!
A MARQUIS. A novelty!
LE BRET. Bah!
THE CROWD. [*Thronging around* CYRANO.] Compliments—regards—Bravo!—
A WOMAN'S VOICE. Why, he's a hero!
A MUSKETEER. [*Advances quickly to* CYRANO, *with outstretched hands.*] Monsieur, will you Permit me?—It was altogether fine! I think I may appreciate these things—Moreover, I have been stamping for pure joy! [*He retires quickly.*]
CYRANO. [*To* CUIGY.] What was that gentleman's name?
CUIGY. Oh . . . D'Artagnan.[29]
LE BRET. [*Takes* CYRANO'S *arm.*] Come here and tell me—
CYRANO. Let this crowd go first—
[*To* BELLEROSE.] May we stay?
BELLEROSE. [*With great respect.*] Certainly! [*Cries and cat-calls off stage.*]
JODELET. [*Comes down from the door where he has been looking out.*] Hark!— Montfleury—They are hooting him.
BELLEROSE. [*Solemnly.*] Sic transit gloria![30] [*Changes his tone and shouts to the porter and the lamplighter.*] —Strike! . . . Close the house! . . . Leave the lights— We rehearse The new farce after dinner.
[JODELET *and* BELLEROSE *go out after elaborately saluting* CYRANO.]
THE PORTER. [*To* CYRANO.] You do not dine?
CYRANO. I?—No!
[THE PORTER *turns away.*]

[27] The model of chivalry in the Arthurian romances.
[28] Leader of the revolt of the Roman gladiators, 73–71 B.C.
[29] The historical adventurer who is best known as the hero of Dumas' romance, *The Three Musketeers.*
[30] Thus passes fame!

LE BRET. Why not?

CYRANO. [*Haughtily.*] Because—

[*Changing his tone when he sees* THE PORTER *has gone.*] Because I have No money.

LE BRET. [*Gesture of tossing.*] But—the purse of gold?

CYRANO. Farewell, Paternal pension!

LE BRET. So you have, until The first of next month—?

CYRANO. Nothing.

LE BRET. What a fool!—

CYRANO. But—what a gesture!

THE ORANGE-GIRL. [*Behind her little counter; coughs.*] Hem!

[CYRANO *and* LE BRET *look around; she advances timidly.*] Pardon, Monsieur . . . A man ought never to go hungry . . . [*Indicating the sideboard.*] See, I have everything here . . . [*Eagerly.*] Please!—

CYRANO. [*Uncovers.*] My dear child, I cannot bend this Gascon pride of mine To accept such a kindness— Yet, for fear That I may give you pain if I refuse, I will take . . . [*He goes to the sideboard and makes his selection.*] Oh, not very much! A grape . . . [*She gives him the bunch; he removes a single grape.*] One only! And a glass of water . . . [*She starts to pour wine into it; he stops her.*] Clear! And . . . half a macaroon! [*He gravely returns the other half.*]

LE BRET. Old idiot!

THE ORANGE-GIRL. Please!—Nothing more?

CYRANO. Why, yes— Your hand to kiss. [*He kisses the hand which she holds out, as he would the hand of a princess.*]

THE ORANGE-GIRL. Thank you, sir. [*She curtseys.*] Good-night. [*She goes out.*]

CYRANO. Now, I am listening. [*Plants himself before the sideboard and arranges thereon—*]

Dinner!— [*the macaroon.*] Drink!— [*the glass of water.*] Dessert!— [*the grape.*] There—now I'll sit down. [*Seats himself.*] Lord, I was hungry! Abominably! [*Eating.*] Well!

LE BRET. These fatheads with the bellicose grand airs Will have you ruined if you listen to them; Talk to a man of sense and hear how all Your swagger impresses him.

CYRANO. [*Finishes his macaroon.*] Enormously.

LE BRET. The Cardinal—

CYRANO. [*Beaming.*] Was he there?

LE BRET. He must have thought you—

CYRANO. Original.

LE BRET. Well, but—

CYRANO. He is himself A playwright. He will not be too displeased That I have closed another author's play.

LE BRET. But look at all the enemies you have made!

CYRANO. [*Begins on the grape.*] How many—do you think?

LE BRET. Just forty-eight Without the women.

CYRANO. Count them.

LE BRET. Montfleury, Baro, de Guiche, the Vicomte, the Old Man, All the Academy—

CYRANO. Enough! You make me Happy!

LE BRET. But where is all this leading you? What is your plan?

CYRANO. I have been wandering— Wasting my force upon too many plans. Now I have chosen one.

LE BRET. What one?

CYRANO. The simplest— To make myself in all things admirable!

LE BRET. Hmph!—Well, then, the real reason why you hate Montfleury— Come, the truth, now!

CYRANO. [*Rises.*] That Silenus, Who cannot hold his belly in his arms, Still dreams of being sweetly dangerous Among the women—sighs and languishes,

Making sheeps' eyes out of his great frog's face—
I hate him ever since one day he dared
Smile upon—
Oh, my friend, I seemed to see
Over some flower a great snail crawling!
LE BRET. [Amazed.] How,
What? Is it possible?—
CYRANO. [With a bitter smile.]
For me to love? . . .
[Changing his tone; seriously.]
I love.
LE BRET. May I know? You have never said—
CYRANO. Whom I love? Think a moment.
Think of me—
Me, whom the plainest woman would despise—
Me, with this nose of mine that marches on
Before me by a quarter of an hour!
Whom should I love? Why—of course—it must be
The woman in the world most beautiful.
LE BRET. Most beautiful?
CYRANO. In all this world—most sweet
Also; most wise; most witty, and most fair!
LE BRET. Who and what is this woman?
CYRANO. Dangerous
Mortally, without meaning; exquisite
Without imagining. Nature's own snare
To allure manhood. A white rose wherein
Love lies in ambush for his natural prey.
Who knows her smile has known a perfect thing.
She creates grace in her own image, brings
Heaven to earth in one movement of her hand—
Nor thou, O Venus! balancing thy shell
Over the Mediterranean blue, nor thou,
Diana! marching through broad, blossoming woods,
Art so divine as when she mounts her chair,
And goes abroad through Paris!
LE BRET. Oh, well—of course,
That makes everything clear!
CYRANO. Transparently.
LE BRET. Madeleine Robin—your cousin?
CYRANO. Yes; Roxane.
LE BRET. And why not? If you love her, tell her so!

You have covered yourself with glory in her eyes
This very day.
CYRANO. My old friend—look at me,
And tell me how much hope remains for me
With its protuberance! Oh, I have no more
Illusions! Now and then—bah! I may grow
Tender, walking alone in the blue cool
Of evening, through some garden fresh with flowers
After the benediction of the rain;
My poor big devil of a nose inhales
April . . . and so I follow with my eyes
Where some boy, with a girl upon his arm,
Passes a patch of silver . . . and I feel
Somehow, I wish I had a woman too,
Walking with little steps under the moon,
And holding my arm so, and smiling. Then
I dream—and I forget. . . .
And then I see
The shadow of my profile on the wall!
LE BRET. My friend! . . .
CYRANO. My friend, I have my bitter days,
Knowing myself so ugly, so alone.
Sometimes—
LE BRET. You weep?
CYRANO. [Quickly.] Oh, not that ever! No,
That would be too grotesque—tears trickling down
All the long way along this nose of mine?
I will not so profane the dignity
Of sorrow. Never any tears for me!
Why, there is nothing more sublime than tears,
Nothing!—Shall I make them ridiculous
In my poor person?
LE BRET. Love's no more than chance!
CYRANO. [Shakes his head.] No. I love
Cleopatra; do I appear
Cæsar? I adore Beatrice; have I
The look of Dante?
LE BRET. But your wit—your courage—
Why, that poor child who offered you just now
Your dinner!—She—you saw with your own eyes,
Her eyes did not avoid you.
CYRANO. [Thoughtful.] That is true . . .
LE BRET. Well then! Roxane herself, watching your duel,

Paler than—
CYRANO.   Pale?—
LE BRET.   Her lips parted, her hand
Thus at her breast— I saw it! Speak to her,
Speak, man!
CYRANO. Through my nose? She might
laugh at me;
That is the one thing in this world I fear!
THE PORTER. [Followed by THE DUENNA,
approaches CYRANO respectfully.]
A lady asking for Monsieur.
CYRANO.   Mon dieu . . .
Her Duenna!—
THE DUENNA. [A sweeping curtsey.]
Monsieur . . .
A message for you:
From our good cousin we desire to know
When and where we may see him privately.
CYRANO. [Amazed.] To see me?
THE DUENNA. [An elaborate reverence.]
To see you. We have certain things
To tell you.
CYRANO. Certain—
THE DUENNA. Things.
CYRANO. [Trembling.] Mon dieu! . . .
THE DUENNA.   We go
To-morrow, at the first flush of the dawn,
To hear Mass at St. Roch. Then afterwards,
Where can we meet and talk a little?
CYRANO. [Catching LE   BRET'S   arm.]
Where?
I— Ah, mon dieu! . . . mon dieu! . . .
THE DUENNA.   Well?
CYRANO.   I am thinking . . .
THE DUENNA. And you think?
CYRANO. I . . . The Shop of Ragueneau . . .
Ragueneau—pastrycook . . .
THE DUENNA. Who dwells?—
CYRANO.   Mon dieu! . . .
Oh, yes . . . Ah, mon dieu! . . . Rue
St.-Honoré.
THE DUENNA. We are agreed. Remember
—seven o'clock.   [Reverence.]
Until then—
CYRANO. I'll be there.
[THE DUENNA goes out.]
CYRANO. [Falls into the arms of LE BRET.]
Me . . . to see me! . . .
LE BRET. You are not quite so gloomy.
CYRANO.   After all,

She knows that I exist—no matter why!
LE BRET. So now, you are going to be
happy.
CYRANO.   Now! . . . [Beside himself.]
I—I am going to be a storm—a flame—
I need to fight whole armies all alone;
I have ten hearts; I have a hundred arms;
I feel
Too strong to war with mortals—
[He shouts at the top of his voice.]
BRING ME GIANTS!
[A moment since, the shadows of the
comedians have been visible moving
and posturing upon the stage. The
violins have taken their places.]
A VOICE. [From the stage.] Hey—pst—
less noise! We are rehearsing here!
CYRANO. [Laughs.] We are going.
[He turns up stage. Through the street
door enter CUIGY, BRISSAILLE, and a
number of officers, supporting LI-
GNIÈRE, who is now thoroughly
drunk.]
CUIGY.   Cyrano
CYRANO.   What is it?
CUIGY.   Here—
Here's your stray lamb!
CYRANO. [Recognizes LIGNIÈRE.]
Lignière— What's wrong with him?
CUIGY. He wants you.
BRISSAILLE. He's afraid to go home.
CYRANO.   Why?
LIGNIÈRE. [Showing a crumpled scrap of
paper and speaking with the elaborate
logic of profound intoxication.] This let-
ter—hundred against one—that's me—
I'm the one—all because of little song—
Good song— Hundred men, waiting, un-
derstand?
Porte de Nesle—way home— Might be
dangerous—
Would you permit me spend the night with
you?
CYRANO. A hundred—is that all? You are
going home!
LIGNIÈRE. [Astonished.] Why—
CYRANO. [In a voice of thunder, indicating
the lighted lantern which THE PORTER
holds up curiously as he regards the
scene.]   Take that lantern!

[LIGNIÈRE *precipitately seizes the lan-*
tern.]

Forward march! I say
I'll be the man to-night that sees you home.
[*To the officers.*]
You others follow—I want an audience!
CUIGY. A hundred against one—
CYRANO.   Those are the odds
To-night!
[*The Comedians in their costumes are*
descending from the stage and joining
the group.]
LE BRET. But why help this—
CYRANO.   There goes Le Bret
Growling!
LE BRET. —This drunkard here?
CYRANO. [*His hand on* LE BRET'S *shoul-*
der.]   Because this drunkard—
This tun of sack, this butt of Burgundy—
Once in his life has done one lovely thing:
After the Mass, according to the form,
He saw, one day, the lady of his heart
Take holy water for a blessing. So
This one, who shudders at a drop of rain,
This fellow here—runs headlong to the
font,
Bends down and drinks it dry!
A SOUBRETTE.   I say that was
A pretty thought!
CYRANO. Ah, was it not?
THE SOUBRETTE. [*To the others.*] But why
Against one poor poet, a hundred men?
CYRANO. March!   [*To the officers.*]
And you gentlemen, remember now,
No rescue— Let me fight alone.
A COMEDIENNE. [*Jumps down from the*
stage.]   Come on!
I'm going to watch—
CYRANO.   Come along!
ANOTHER COMEDIENNE. [*Jumps down,*
speaks to a Comedian costumed as an
old man.]   You, Cassandre?
CYRANO. Come all of you—the Doctor,
Isabelle,
Léandre—the whole company—a swarm
Of murmuring, golden bees—we'll parody
Italian farce and Tragedy-of-Blood;
Ribbons for banners, masks for blazonry,
And tambourines to be our rolling drums!
ALL THE WOMEN. [*Jumping for joy.*]

Bravo!—My hood— My cloak— Hurry!
JODOLET. [*Mock heroic.*]   Lead on!—
CYRANO. [*To the violins.*] You violins—
play us an overture—
[*The violins join the procession which is*
forming. The lighted candles are
snatched from the stage and distrib-
uted; it becomes a torchlight proces-
sion.]
Bravo!—Officers— Ladies in costume—
And twenty paces in advance. . . .
[*He takes his station as he speaks.*]
Myself,
Alone, with glory fluttering over me,
Alone as Lucifer at war with heaven!
Remember—no one lifts a hand to help—
Ready there? One . . . two . . . three! Porter,
the doors! . . .
[*The Porter flings wide the great doors.*
We see in the dim moonlight a corner
of old Paris, purple and picturesque.]
Look—Paris dreams—nocturnal, nebulous,
Under blue moonbeams hung from wall to
wall—
Nature's own setting for the scene we
play!—
Yonder, behind her veil of mist, the Seine,
Like a mysterious and magic mirror
Trembles—
And you shall see what you shall see!
ALL. To the Porte de Nesle!
CYRANO. [*Erect upon the threshold.*]
To the Porte de Nesle!
[*He turns back for a moment to the*
Soubrette.]
Did you not ask, my dear, why against one
Singer they send a hundred swords?
[*Quietly, drawing his own sword.*]
Because
They know this one man for a friend of
mine!
[*He goes out. The procession follows:*
LIGNIÈRE *zigzagging at its head, then,*
the Comediennes on the arms of the
Officers, then the Comedians, leaping
and dancing as they go. It vanishes
into the night to the music of the
violins, illuminated by the flickering
glimmer of the candles.]
[CURTAIN.]

THE SECOND ACT

THE BAKERY OF THE POETS

The Shop of RAGUENEAU, *Baker and Pastrycook: a spacious affair at the corner of the Rue St.-Honoré and the Rue de l'Arbre Sec. The street, seen vaguely through the glass panes in the door at the back, is grey in the first light of dawn.*

In the foreground, at the Left, a Counter is surmounted by a Canopy of wrought iron from which are hanging ducks, geese, and white peacocks. Great crockery jars hold bouquets of common flowers, yellow sunflowers in particular. On the same side farther back, a huge fireplace; in front of it, between great andirons, of which each one supports a little saucepan, roast fowls revolve and weep into their dripping-pans. To the Right at the First Entrance, a door. Beyond it, Second Entrance, a staircase leads up to a little dining-room under the eaves, its interior visible through open shutters. A table is set there and a tiny Flemish candlestick is lighted; there one may retire to eat and drink in private. A wooden gallery, extending from the head of the stairway, seems to lead to other little dining-rooms.

In the centre of the shop, an iron ring hangs by a rope over a pulley so that it can be raised or lowered; adorned with game of varius kinds hung from it by hooks, it has the appearance of a sort of gastronomic chandelier.

In the shadow under the staircase, ovens are glowing. The spits revolve; the copper pots and pans gleam ruddily. Pastries in pyramids. Hams hanging from the rafters. The morning baking is in progress: a bustle of tall cooks and timid scullions and scurrying apprentices; a blossoming of white caps adorned with cock's feathers or the wings of guinea fowl. On wicker trays or on great metal platters they bring in rows of pastries and fancy dishes of various kinds.

Tables are covered with trays of cakes and rolls; others with chairs placed about them are set for guests.

One little table in a corner disappears under a heap of papers. At the Curtain Rise RAGUENEAU *is seated there. He is writing poetry.*

A PASTRYCOOK. [*Brings in a dish.*]
Fruits *en gelée!*

SECOND PASTRYCOOK. [*Brings dish.*]
    Custard!

THIRD PASTRYCOOK. [*Brings roast peacock ornamented with feathers.*] Peacock *roti!*

FOURTH PASTRYCOOK. [*Brings tray of cakes.*] Cakes and confections!

FIFTH PASTRYCOOK. [*Brings earthen dish.*]
    Beef *en casserole!*

RAGUENEAU. [*Raises his head; returns to mere earth.*]
Over the coppers of my kitchen flows
The frost-silver dawn. Silence awhile
The god who sings within thee, Ragueneau!
Lay down the lute—the oven calls for thee!
  [*Rises; goes to one of the cooks.*]
Here's a hiatus in your sauce; fill up
The measure.

THE COOK. How much?

RAGUENEAU. [*Measures on his finger.*]
    One more dactyl.

THE COOK.   Huh? . . .

FIRST PASTRYCOOK. Rolls!

SECOND PASTRYCOOK. Roulades! [1]

RAGUENEAU. [*Before the fireplace.*]
    Veil, O Muse, thy virgin eyes
From the lewd gleam of these terrestrial fires! [*To* FIRST PASTRYCOOK.]
Your rolls lack balance. Here's the proper form—
An equal hemistich on either side,
And the cæsura in between.
[*To another, pointing out an unfinished pie.*]
    Your house
Of crust should have a roof upon it.
[*To another, who is seated on the hearth, placing poultry on a spit.*]
    And you—

---

[1] Fruit turnovers.

Along the interminable spit, arrange
The modest pullet and the lordly Turk
Alternately, my son—as great Malherbe [2]
Alternates male and female rimes. Remember,
A couplet, or a roast, should be well turned.

AN APPRENTICE. [Advances with a dish covered by a napkin.]
Master, I thought of you when I designed
This, hoping it might please you.

RAGUENEAU. Ah! A Lyre—

THE APPRENTICE. In puff-paste—

RAGUENEAU. And the jewels—
candied fruit!

THE APPRENTICE. And the strings, barley-sugar!

RAGUENEAU. [Gives him money.]
Go and drink
My health.

[LISE enters.]
St!—My wife— Circulate, and hide
That money!
[Shows the Lyre to LISE, with a languid air.]
Graceful—yes?

LISE. Ridiculous!
[She places on the counter a pile of paper bags.]

RAGUENEAU. Paper bags? Thank you . . .
[He looks at them.]
Ciel! My manuscripts!
The sacred verses of my poets—rent
Asunder, limb from limb—butchered to make
Base packages of pastry! Ah, you are one
Of those insane Bacchantes [3] who destroyed
Orpheus!

LISE. Your dirty poets left them here
To pay for eating half our stock-in-trade:
We ought to make some profit out of them!

RAGUENEAU. Ant! Would you blame the locust for his song?

LISE. I blame the locust for his appetite!
There used to be a time—before you had
Your hungry friends—you never called me
Ants—

No, nor Bacchantes!

RAGUENEAU. What a way to use
Poetry!

LISE. Well, what is the use of it?

RAGUENEAU. But, my dear girl, what
would you do with prose?
[Two Children enter.]
Well, dears?

A CHILD. Three little patties.

RAGUENEAU. [Serves them.] There we are!
All hot and brown.

THE CHILD. Would you mind wrapping
them?

RAGUENEAU. One of my paper bags! . . .
Oh, certainly.
[Reads from the bag, as he is about to
wrap the patties in it.]
"Ulysses, when he left Penelope"—
Not that one! [Takes another bag; reads.]
"Phœbus, golden-crowned"—
Not that one.

LISE. Well? They are waiting!

RAGUENEAU. Very well, very well!—
The Sonnet to Phyllis . . .
Yet—it does seem hard . . .

LISE. Made up your mind—at last! Mph!
Jack-o'-Dreams!

RAGUENEAU. [As her back is turned, calls
back the Children, who are already at
the door.] Pst!—Children— Give me
back the bag. Instead
Of three patties, you shall have six of them!
[Makes the exchange. The Children go
out. He reads from the bag, as he
smooths it out tenderly.]
"Phyllis"—
A spot of butter on her name!—
"Phyllis"—

CYRANO. [Enters hurriedly.]
What is the time?

RAGUENEAU. Six o'clock.

CYRANO. One
Hour more . . .

RAGUENEAU. Felicitations!

CYRANO. And for what?

RAGUENEAU. Your victory! I saw it all—

CYRANO. Which one?

---

[2] Celebrated French poet and critic (1555–1628).

[3] Priestesses of Bacchus.

RAGUENEAU. At the Hôtel de Bourgogne.

CYRANO.   Oh—the duel!

RAGUENEAU. The duel in Rime!

LISE.   He talks of nothing else.

CYRANO. Nonsense!

RAGUENEAU. [*Fencing and foining with a spit, which he snatches up from the hearth.*]
"*Then, as I end the refrain, thrust home!*"
"*Then, as I end the refrain*"—
                    Gods! What a line!
"*Then, as I end*"—

CYRANO.   What time now, Ragueneau?

RAGUENEAU. [*Petrified at the full extent of a lunge, while he looks at the clock.*]
Five after six—   [*Recovers.*]
              "*—thrust home!*"
                    A Ballade, too!

LISE. [*To* CYRANO, *who in passing has mechanically shaken hands with her.*]
Your hand—what have you done?

CYRANO.   Oh, my hand?—Nothing.

RAGUENEAU. What danger now—

CYRANO.   No danger.

LISE.   I believe
He is lying.

CYRANO. Why? Was I looking down my nose?
That must have been a devil of a lie!

[*Changing his tone; to* RAGUENEAU.]
I expect someone. Leave us here alone,
When the time comes.

RAGUENEAU.   How can I? In a moment,
My poets will be here.

LISE.   To break their . . . fast!

CYRANO. Take them away, then, when I give the sign.
—What time?

RAGUENEAU. Ten minutes after.

CYRANO.   Have you a pen?

RAGUENEAU. [*Offers him a pen.*]
An eagle's feather!

A MUSKETEER. [*Enters, and speaks to* LISE *in a stentorian voice.*] Greeting!

CYRANO. [*To* RAGUENEAU.] Who is this?

RAGUENEAU. My wife's friend. A terrific warrior,
So he says.

CYRANO. Ah— I see.

[*Takes up the pen; waves* RAGUENEAU *away.*]
                    Only to write—
To fold— To give it to her—and to go . . .
          [*Throws down the pen.*]
Coward! And yet—the Devil take my soul
If I dare speak one word to her . . .
      [*To* RAGUENEAU.]   What time now?

RAGUENEAU. A quarter after six.

CYRANO. [*Striking his breast.*]
              —One little word
Of all the many thousand I have here!
Whereas in writing . . .
                    [*Takes up the pen.*]
              Come, I'll write to her
That letter I have written on my heart,
Torn up, and written over many times—
So many times . . . that all I have to do
Is to remember, and to write it down.

[*He writes. Through the glass of the door appear vague and hesitating shadows. The Poets enter, clothed in rusty black and spotted with mud.*]

LISE. [*To* RAGUENEAU.] Here come your scarecrows!

FIRST POET. Comrade!

SECOND POET. [*Takes both* RAGUENEAU'S *hands.*]   My dear brother!

THIRD POET. [*Sniffing.*] O Lord of Roasts, how sweet thy dwellings are!

FOURTH POET.   Phoebus Apollo of the Silver Spoon!

FIFTH POET.   Cupid of Cookery!

RAGUENEAU. [*Surrounded, embraced, beaten on the back.*]   These geniuses,
They put one at one's ease!

FIRST POET.   We were delayed
By the crowd at the Porte de Nesle.

SECOND POET.   Dead men
All scarred and gory, scattered on the stones,
Villainous-looking scoundrels — eight of them.

CYRANO. [*Looks up an instant.*]
Eight? I thought only seven—

RAGUENEAU.   Do you know
The hero of this hecatomb?

CYRANO.   I? . . . No.

LISE. [*To the* MUSKETEER.] Do you?

THE MUSKETEER. Hmm—perhaps!

FIRST POET. They say one man alone
Put to flight all this crowd.

SECOND POET. Everywhere lay
Swords, daggers, pikes, bludgeons—

CYRANO. [Writing.] "Your eyes . . ."

THIRD POET. As far
As the Quai des Orfevres, hats and cloaks—

FIRST POET. Why, that man must have
been the devil!

CYRANO. "Your lips . . ."

FIRST POET. Some savage monster might
have done this thing!

CYRANO. "Looking upon you, I grow faint
with fear . . ."

SECOND POET. What have you written
lately, Ragueneau?

CYRANO. "Your Friend — Who loves
you . . ."
So. No signature;
I'll give it to her myself.

RAGUENEAU. A Recipe
In Rime.

THIRD POET. Read us your rimes!

FOURTH POET. Here's a brioche
Cocking its hat at me.
[He bites off the top of it.]

FIRST POET. Look how those buns
Follow the hungry poet with their eyes—
Those almond eyes!

SECOND POET. We are listening—

THIRD POET. See this cream-puff—
Fat little baby, drooling while it smiles!

SECOND POET. [Nibbling at the pastry
Lyre.]
For the first time, the Lyre is my support.

RAGUENEAU. [Coughs, adjusts his cap,
strikes an attitude.] A Recipe in Rime—

SECOND POET. [Gives FIRST POET a dig
with his elbow.] Your breakfast?

FIRST POET. Dinner!

RAGUENEAU. [Declaims.]

A Recipe for Making Almond Tarts.

Beat your eggs, the yolk and white,
Very light;
Mingle with their creamy fluff
Drops of lime-juice, cool and green;
Then pour in
Milk of Almonds, just enough.

Dainty patty-pans, embraced
In puff-paste—
Have these ready within reach;
With your thumb and finger, pinch
Half an inch
Up around the edge of each—

Into these, a score or more,
Slowly pour
All your store of custard; so
Take them, bake them golden-brown—
Now sit down! . . .
Almond tartlets, Ragueneau!

THE POETS. Delicious! Melting!

A POET. [Chokes.] Humph!

CYRANO. [TO RAGUENEAU.] Do you not see
Those fellows fattening themselves?—

RAGUENEAU. I know.
I would not look—it might embarrass
them—
You see, I love a friendly audience.
Besides—another vanity—I am pleased
When they enjoy my cooking.

CYRANO. [Slaps him on the back.]
Be off with you!—
[RAGUENEAU goes up stage.]
Good little soul! [Calls to LISE.] Madame!—
[She leaves the MUSKETEER and comes
down to him.] This musketeer—
He is making love to you?

LISE. [Haughtily.] If any man
Offends my virtue—all I have to do
Is look at him—once!

CYRANO. [Looks at her gravely; she drops
her eyes.] I do not find
Those eyes of yours unconquerable.

LISE. [Panting.] —Ah!

CYRANO. [Raising his voice a little.]
Now listen— I am fond of Ragueneau;
I allow no one—do you understand?—
To . . . take his name in vain!

LISE. You think—

CYRANO. [Ironic emphasis.] I think
I interrupt you.
[He salutes the MUSKETEER, who has
heard without daring to resent the warning. LISE goes to the MUSKETEER as he
returns CYRANO'S salute.]

LISE. You—you swallow that?—

You ought to have pulled his nose!

THE MUSKETEER. His nose?—His nose! . . .

[*He goes out hurriedly.* ROXANE *and* THE DUENNA *appear outside the door.*]

CYRANO. [*Nods to* RAGUENEAU.] Pst!—

RAGUENEAU. [*To the Poets.*]
                    Come inside—

CYRANO. [*Impatient.*] Pst! . . . Pst! . . .

RAGUENEAU.   We shall be more Comfortable . . .

[*He leads the Poets into inner room.*]

FIRST POET. The cakes!

SECOND POET.   Bring them along!
                              [*They go out.*]

CYRANO. If I can see the faintest spark of hope,

Then—   [*Throws door open—bows.*]
      Welcome!

[ROXANE *enters, followed by* THE DUENNA, *whom* CYRANO *detains.*]
                    Pardon me—one word—

THE DUENNA.   Take two.

CYRANO. Have you a good digestion?

THE DUENNA.   Wonderful!

CYRANO. Good. Here are two sonnets, by Benserade [4]—

THE DUENNA. Euh?

CYRANO. Which I fill for you with éclairs.

THE DUENNA.   Ooo!

CYRANO. Do you like cream-puffs?

THE DUENNA. Only with whipped cream.

CYRANO. Here are three . . . six—embosomed in a poem

By Saint-Amant. This ode of Chapelin Looks deep enough to hold—a jelly roll.

—Do you love Nature?

THE DUENNA.   Mad about it.

CYRANO.   Then

Go out and eat these in the street. Do not Return—

THE DUENNA. Oh, but—

CYRANO.   Until you finish them.
                    [*Down to* ROXANE.]

Blessed above all others be the hour

When you remembered to remember me,

And came to tell me . . . what?

ROXANE. [*Takes off her mask.*[5]]
                    First let me thank you

Because . . . That man . . . that creature, whom your sword

Made sport of yesterday— His patron, one—

CYRANO. De Guiche?—

ROXANE. —who thinks himself in love with me

Would have forced that man upon me for —a husband—

CYRANO. I understand—so much the better then!

I fought, not for my nose, but your bright eyes.

ROXANE. And then, to tell you—but before I can

Tell you— Are you, I wonder, still the same

Big brother—almost—that you used to be

When we were children, playing by the pond

In the old garden down there—

CYRANO.   I remember—

Every summer you came to Bergerac! . . .

ROXANE. You used to make swords out of bulrushes—

CYRANO. You dandelion-dolls with golden hair—

ROXANE. And those green plums—

CYRANO.   And those black mulberries—

ROXANE. In those days, you did everything I wished!

CYRANO. Roxane, in short skirts, was called Madeleine.

ROXANE. Was I pretty?

CYRANO.   Oh—not too plain!

ROXANE.   Sometimes

When you had hurt your hand you used to come

Running to me—and I would be your mother,

And say— Oh, in a very grown-up voice:
                    [*She takes his hand.*]

"*Now,* what have you been doing to yourself?

Let me see—" [*She sees the hand—starts.*]
      Oh!—

                    Wait—I said *Let me see!*

Still—at your age! How did you do that?

---

[4] A minor poet and composer of ballets (1612–91). Those mentioned later are similarly poets of the period.

[5] Worn by ladies when abroad in the streets.

CYRANO. Playing
With the big boys, down by the Porte de
Nesle.

ROXANE. [Sits at a table and wets her
handkerchief in a glass of water.]
Come here to me.

CYRANO. —Such a wise little mother!

ROXANE. And tell me, while I wash this
blood away,
How many you—played with?

CYRANO. Oh, about a hundred.

ROXANE. Tell me.

CYRANO. No. Let me go. Tell me what you
Were going to tell me—if you dared?

ROXANE. [Still holding his hand.] I think
I do dare—now. It seems like long ago
When I could tell you things. Yes—I
dare . . .
Listen:
I . . . love someone.

CYRANO. Ah! . . .

ROXANE. Someone who does not know.

CYRANO. Ah! . . .

ROXANE. At least—not yet.

CYRANO. Ah! . . .

ROXANE But he will know
Some day.

CYRANO. Ah! . . .

ROXANE A big boy who loves me too,
And is afraid of me, and keeps away,
And never says one word.

CYRANO. Ah! . . .

ROXANE. Let me have
Your hand a moment—why, how hot it
is!—
I know. I see him trying . . .

CYRANO. Ah! . . .

ROXANE There now!
Is that better?—
[She finishes bandaging the hand with
her handkerchief.]
Besides—only to think—
(This is a secret.) He is a soldier too,
In your own regiment—

CYRANO. Ah! . . .

ROXANE. Yes, in the Guards.
Your company too.

CYRANO. Ah! . . .

ROXANE. And such a man!—
He is proud—noble—young—brave—
beautiful—

CYRANO. [Turns pale; rises.] Beautiful!—

ROXANE. What's the matter?

CYRANO. [Smiling.] Nothing—this—
My sore hand!

ROXANE. Well, I love him. That is all.
Oh—and I never saw him anywhere
Except the Comédie.

CYRANO. You have never spoken?—

ROXANE. Only our eyes . . .

CYRANO. Why, then—
How do you know?—

ROXANE. People talk about people; and I
hear
Things . . . and I know.

CYRANO. You say he is in the Guards:
His name?

ROXANE. Baron Christian de Neuvillette.

CYRANO. He is not in the Guards.

ROXANE. Yes. Since this morning.
Captain Carbon de Castel-Jaloux.

CYRANO. So soon! . . .
So soon we lose our hearts!—
But, my dear child,—

THE DUENNA. [Opens the door.] I have
eaten the cakes, Monsieur de Bergerac!

CYRANO. Good! Now go out and read the
poetry! [THE DUENNA disappears.]
—But, my dear child! You, who love only
words,
Wit, the grand manner— Why, for all you
know,
The man may be a savage, or a fool.

ROXANE. His curls are like a hero from
D'Urfé.[6]

CYRANO. His mind may be as curly as his
hair.

ROXANE. Not with such eyes. I read his
soul in them.

CYRANO. Yes, all our souls are written in
our eyes!
But—if he be a bungler?

ROXANE. Then I shall die—

[6] Author of the pastoral romance L'Astrée,
which was a sort of devotional manual for exqui-
sites like Roxane.

There!

CYRANO. [*After a pause.*] And you brought me here to tell me this?
I do not yet quite understand, Madame,
The reason for your confidence.

ROXANE. They say
That in your company— It frightens me—
You are all Gascons . . .

CYRANO. And we pick a quarrel
With any flat-foot who intrudes himself,
Whose blood is not pure Gascon like our own?
Is this what you have heard?

ROXANE. I am so afraid
For him!

CYRANO. [*Between his teeth.*]
Not without reason!—

ROXANE. And I thought
You . . . You were so brave, so invincible
Yesterday, against all those brutes!—If you,
Whom they all fear—

CYRANO. Oh, well—I will defend
Your little Baron.

ROXANE. Will you? Just for me?
Because I have always been—your friend!

CYRANO. Of course . . .

ROXANE. Will you be *his* friend?

CYRANO. I will be his friend.

ROXANE. And never let him fight a duel?

CYRANO. No—never.

ROXANE. Oh, but you are a darling!—I must go—
You never told me about last night— Why,
You must have been a hero! Have him write
And tell me all about it—will you?

CYRANO. Of course . . .

ROXANE. [*Kisses her hand.*] I always did love you!—A hundred men
Against one— Well. . . . Adieu. We are great friends,
Are we not?

CYRANO. Of course . . .

ROXANE. He *must* write to me—
A hundred— You shall tell me the whole story
Some day, when I have time. A hundred men—

What courage!

CYRANO. [*Salutes as she goes out.*]
Oh . . . I have done better since!
[*The door closes after her.* CYRANO *remains motionless, his eyes on the ground. Pause. The other door opens;* RAGUENEAU *puts in his head.*]

RAGUENEAU. May I come in?

CYRANO. [*Without moving.*] Yes . . .
[RAGUENEAU *and his friends re-enter. At the same time,* CARBON DE CASTEL-JALOUX *appears at the street door in uniform as Captain of the Guards; recognizes* CYRANO *with a sweeping gesture.*]

CARBON. Here he is!—Our hero!

CYRANO. [*Raises his head and salutes.*]
Our Captain!

CARBON. We know! All our company
Are here—

CYRANO. [*Recoils.*] No—

CARBON. Come! They are waiting for you.

CYRANO. No!

CARBON. [*Tries to lead him out.*]
Only across the street— Come!

CYRANO. Please—

CARBON. [*Goes to the door and shouts in a voice of thunder.*] Our champion
Refuses! He is not feeling well to-day!

A VOICE OUTSIDE. Ah! Sandious!
[*Noise outside of swords and trampling feet approaching.*]

CARBON. Here they come now!

THE CADETS. [*Entering the shop.*]
Mille dious!—
Mordious!—Capdedious!—Pocapdedious!

RAGUENEAU. [*In astonishment.*]
Gentlemen—
You are all Gascons?

THE CADETS. All!

FIRST CADET. [*To* CYRANO.] Bravo!

CYRANO. Baron!

ANOTHER CADET. [*Takes both his hands.*]
Vivat!

CYRANO. Baron!

THIRD CADET. Come to my arms!

CYRANO. Baron!

OTHERS. To mine!—To mine!—

CYRANO.   Baron . . .
Baron . . . Have mercy—
RAGUENEAU.   You are all Barons too?
THE CADETS.   *Are* we?
RAGUENEAU.   Are they?. . .
FIRST CADET.   Our coronets would star the
midnight sky!
LE BRET.   [*Enters; hurries to* CYRANO.]
The whole Town's looking for you! Rav-
ing mad—
A triumph! Those who saw the fight—
CYRANO.   I hope
You have not told them where I—
LE BRET.   [*Rubbing his hand.*]   Certainly
I told them!
CITIZEN.   [*Enters, followed by a group.*]
Listen! Shut the door!—Here comes
All Paris!
[*The street outside fills with a shouting
crowd. Chairs and carriages stop at
the door.*]
LE BRET.   [*Aside to* CYRANO, *smiling.*]
And Roxane?
CYRANO.   [*Quickly.*]   Hush!
THE CROWD OUTSIDE.   Cyrano!
[*A mob bursts into the shop. Shouts,
acclamations, general disturbance.*]
RAGUENEAU.   [*Standing on a table.*]
My shop invaded— They'll break every-
thing—
Glorious!
SEVERAL MEN.   [*Crowding about* CYRANO.]
My friend! . . . My friend! . . .
CYRANO.   Why, yesterday
I did not have so many friends!
LE BRET.   Success
At last!
A MARQUIS.   [*Runs to* CYRANO, *with out-
stretched hands.*] My dear—really!—
CYRANO.   [*Coldly.*]   So? And how long
Have I been dear to you?
ANOTHER MARQUIS.   One moment—pray!
I have two ladies in my carriage here;
Let me present you—
CYRANO.   Certainly! And first,
Who will present you, sir,—to me?
LE BRET.   [*Astounded.*]   Why, what
The devil?—

CYRANO.   Hush!
A MAN OF LETTERS.   [*With a portfolio.*]
May I have the details? . . .
CYRANO.   You may not.
LE BRET.   [*Plucking* CYRANO'S *sleeve.*]
Theophraste Renaudot! [7]—Editor
Of the *Gazette*—your reputation! . . .
CYRANO.   No!
A POET.   [*Advances.*] Monsieur—
CYRANO.   Well?
THE POET.   Your full name?
I will compose
A pentacrostic [8]—
ANOTHER.   Monsieur—
CYRANO.   That will do!
[*Movement. The crowd arranges itself.*
DE GUICHE *appears, escorted by* CUIGY,
BRISSAILLE, *and the other officers who
were with* CYRANO *at the close of the
First Act.*]
CUIGY.   [*Goes to* CYRANO.] Monsieur de
Guiche!—
[*Murmur. Everyone moves.*]
A message from the Marshal
De Gassion [9]—
DE GUICHE.   [*Saluting* CYRANO.]
Who wishes to express
Through me his admiration. He has heard
Of your affair—
THE CROWD.   Bravo!
CYRANO.   [*Bowing.*] The Marshal speaks
As an authority.
DE GUICHE.   He said just now
The story would have been incredible
Were it not for the witness—
CUIGY.   Of our eyes!
LE BRET.   [*Aside to* CYRANO.] What is it?
CYRANO.   Hush!—
LE BRET.   Something is wrong with you;
Are you in pain?
CYRANO.   [*Recovering himself.*]
In pain? Before this crowd?
[*His moustache bristles. He throws out
his chest.*]
I? In pain? You shall see!
DE GUICHE.   [*To whom* CUIGY *has been
whispering.*]   Your name is known
Already as a soldier. You are one

---

[7] Founder in 1631 of the first French newspaper, the *Gazette de France*, which collected
weekly the current news and gossip.

[8] An acrostic poem in five stanzas.
[9] A famous general of the period.

Of those wild Gascons, are you not?

CYRANO. The Guards,
Yes. A Cadet.

A CADET. [*In a voice of thunder.*]
One of ourselves!

DE GUICHE. Ah! So
Then all these gentlemen with the haughty
  air,
These are the famous—

CARBON. Cyrano!

CYRANO. Captain?

CARBON. Our troop being all present, be so
  kind
As to present them to the Comte de
  Guiche!

CYRANO. [*With a gesture presenting the
  Cadets to* DE GUICHE, *declaims:*]

The Cadets of Gascoyne—the defenders
  Of Carbon de Castel-Jaloux:
Free fighters, free lovers, free spenders—
The Cadets of Gascoyne—the defenders
Of old homes, old names, and old splen-
  dors—
  A proud and a pestilent crew!
The Cadets of Gascoyne, the defenders
Of Carbon de Castel-Jaloux.

Hawk-eyed, they stare down all contend-
  ers—
  The wolf bares his fangs as they do—
Make way there, you fat money-lenders!
(Hawk-eyed, they stare down all con-
  tenders)
Old boots that have been to the menders,
  Old cloaks that are worn through and
    through—
Hawk-eyed, they stare down all contend-
  ers—
  The wolf bares his fangs as they do!

Skull-breakers they are, and sword-benders;
  Red blood is their favorite brew;
Hot haters and loyal befrienders,
Skull-breakers they are, and sword-benders.
Wherever a quarrel engenders,
  They're ready and waiting for you!
Skull-breakers they are, and sword-benders;
  Red blood is their favorite brew!

Behold them, our Gascon defenders
  Who win every woman they woo!

There's never a dame but surrenders—
Behold them, our Gascon defenders!
Young wives who are clever pretenders—
  Old husbands who house the cuckoo [10]—
Behold them—our Gascon defenders
Who win every woman they woo!

DE GUICHE. [*Languidly, sitting in a chair.*]
Poets are fashionable nowadays
To have about one. Would you care to join
My following?

CYRANO. No, sir. I do not follow.

DE GUICHE. Your duel yesterday amused
  my uncle
The Cardinal. I might help you there.

LE BRET. Grand Dieu!

DE GUICHE. I suppose you have written a
  tragedy—
They all have.

LE BRET. [*Aside to* CYRANO.]
Now at last you'll have it played—
Your *Agrippine!*

DE GUICHE. Why not? Take it to him.

CYRANO. [*Tempted.*] Really—

DE GUICHE. He is himself a dramatist;
Let him rewrite a few lines here and there,
And he'll approve the rest.

CYRANO. [*His face falls again.*] Impossible.
My blood curdles to think of altering
One comma.

DE GUICHE. Ah, but when he likes a thing
He pays well.

CYRANO. Yes—but not so well as I—
When I have made a line that sings itself
So that I love the sound of it—I pay
Myself a hundred times.

DE GUICHE. You are proud, my friend.

CYRANO. You have observed that?

A CADET. [*Enters with a drawn sword,
  along the whole blade of which is trans-
  fixed a collection of disreputable hats,
  their plumes draggled, their crowns cut
  and torn.*] Cyrano! See here—
Look what we found this morning in the
  street—

The plumes dropped in their flight by those
  fine birds
Who showed the white feather!

[10] *I.e.*, are cuckolds, or husbands of unfaithful
wives.

CARBON.   Spoils of the hunt—
Well mounted!

THE CROWD.   Ha-ha-ha!

CUIGY.   Whoever hired
Those rascals, he must be an angry man
To-day!

BRISSAILLE.   Who was it? Do you know?

DE GUICHE.   Myself!—
          [*The laughter ceases.*]
I hired them to do the sort of work
We do not soil our hands with—punishing
A drunken poet. . . .
          [*Uncomfortable silence.*]

THE CADET.   [*To* CYRANO.] What shall we
do with them?
They ought to be preserved before they
spoil—

CYRANO.   [*Takes the sword, and in the gesture of saluting* DE GUICHE *with it, makes
all the hats slide off at his feet.*] Sir, will
you not return these to your friends?

DE GUICHE.   My chair—my porters here
—immediately! [*To* CYRANO *violently.*]
—As for you, sir!—

A VOICE.   [*In the street.*]
          The chair of Monseigneur
Le Comte de Guiche!—

DE GUICHE.   [*Who has recovered his self-
control; smiling.*]
          Have you read *Don Quixote*? [11]

CYRANO.   I have—and found myself the
hero.

A PORTER.   [*Appears at the door.*]   Chair
Ready!

DE GUICHE.   Be so good as to read once
more
The chapter of the windmills. [12]

CYRANO.   [*Gravely.*]   Chapter Thirteen.

DE GUICHE.   Windmills, remember, if you
fight with them—

CYRANO.   My enemies change, then, with
every wind?

DE GUICHE.   —May swing round their huge
arms and cast you down
Into the mire.

CYRANO.   Or up—among the stars!
[DE GUICHE *goes out. We see him get into
the chair. The Officers follow murmur-*
ing among themselves. LE BRET *goes
up with them. The crowd goes out.*]

CYRANO.   [*Saluting with burlesque politeness those who go out without daring
to take leave of him.*]
Gentlemen . . . Gentlemen. . . .

LE BRET.   [*As the door closes, comes down,
shaking his clenched hands to heaven.*]
          You have done it now—
You have made your fortune!

CYRANO.   There you go again,
Growling!—

LE BRET.   At least this latest pose of
yours—
Ruining every chance that comes your
way—
Becomes exaggerated—

CYRANO.   Very well,
Then I exaggerate!

LE BRET.   [*Triumphantly.*] Oh, you do!

CYRANO.   Yes;
On principle. There are things in this world
A man does well to carry to extremes.

LE BRET.   Stop trying to be Three Musketeers in one!
Fortune and glory—

CYRANO.   What would you have me do?
Seek for the patronage of some great man,
And like a creeping vine on a tall tree
Crawl upward, where I cannot stand alone?
No, thank you! Dedicate, as others do,
Poems to pawnbrokers? Be a buffoon
In the vile hope of teasing out a smile
On some cold face? No, thank you! Eat a
toad
For breakfast every morning? Make my
knees
Callous, and cultivate a supple spine,—
Wear out my belly grovelling in the dust?
No, thank you! Scratch the back of any
swine
That roots up gold for me? Tickle the horns
Of Mammon with my left hand, while my
right,
Too proud to know his partner's business,
Takes in the fee? No, thank you! Use the
fire
God gave me to burn incense all day long

---

[11] The novel by Cervantes which satirizes
chivalric extravagance.

[12] Dealing with the absurdity of gallant folly.

Under the nose of wood and stone? No,
  thank you!
Shall I go leaping into ladies' laps
And licking fingers?—or—to change the
  form—
Navigating with madrigals for oars,
My sails full of the sighs of dowagers?
No, thank you! Publish verses at my own
Expense? No, thank you! Be the patron
  saint
Of a small group of literary souls
Who dine together every Tuesday? No,
I thank you! Shall I labor night and day
To build a reputation on one song,
And never write another? Shall I find
True genius only among Geniuses,
Palpitate over little paragraphs,
And struggle to insinuate my name
Into the columns of the *Mercury?* [13]
No, thank you! Calculate, scheme, be
  afraid,
Love more to make a visit than a poem,
Seek introductions, favors, influences?—
No, thank you! No, I thank you! And again
I thank you!—But . . .
              To sing, to laugh, to dream,
To walk in my own way and be alone,
Free, with an eye to see things as they are,
A voice that means manhood—to cock my
  hat
Where I choose—At a word, a *Yes,* a *No,*
To fight—or write. To travel any road
Under the sun, under the stars, nor doubt
If fame or fortune lie beyond the bourne—
Never to make a line I have not heard
In my own heart; yet, with all modesty
To say: "My soul, be satisfied with flowers,
With fruit, with weeds even; but gather
  them
In the one garden you may call your own."
So, when I win some triumph, by some
  chance,
Render no share to Cæsar—in a word,
I am too proud to be a parasite,
And if my nature wants the germ that
  grows
Towering to heaven like the mountain pine,
Or like the oak, sheltering multitudes—

[13] The *Mercure François,* a literary periodical founded in 1605.

I stand, not high it may be—but alone!
LE BRET.   Alone, yes!—but why stand
  against the world?
What devil has possessed you now, to go
Everywhere making yourself enemies?
CYRANO.   Watching you other people mak-
  ing friends
Everywhere—as a dog makes friends! I
  mark
The manner of these canine courtesies
And think: "My friends are of a cleaner
  breed;
Here comes—thank God!—another en-
  emy!"
LE BRET.   But this is madness!
CYRANO.   Method, let us say.
It is my pleasure to displease. I love
Hatred. Imagine how it feels to face
The volley of a thousand angry eyes—
The bile of envy and the froth of fear
Spattering little drops about me— You—
Good nature all around you, soft and
  warm—
You are like those Italians, in great cowls
Comfortable and loose— Your chin sinks
  down
Into the folds, your shoulders droop. But
  I—
The Spanish ruff I wear around my throat
Is like a ring of enemies; hard, proud,
Each point another pride, another thorn—
So that I hold myself erect perforce,
Wearing the hatred of the common herd
Haughtily, the harsh collar of Old Spain,
At once a fetter and—a halo!
LE BRET.   Yes . . .
[*After a silence, draws* CYRANO'S *arm
    through his own.*]
Tell this to all the world— And then to me
Say very softly that . . . She loves you
  not.
CYRANO.   [*Quickly.*] Hush!
[*A moment since,* CHRISTIAN *has entered
    and mingled with the Cadets, who do
    not offer to speak to him. Finally, he
    sits down at a small table, where he is
    served by* LISE.]
A CADET.   [*Rises from a table up stage, his
    glass in his hand.*] Cyrano!—Your story!
CYRANO.   Presently . . .

[*He goes up, on the arm of* LE BRET, *talking to him. The Cadets come down stage.*]

THE CADET. The story of the combat! An example

For—

[*He stops by the table where* CHRISTIAN *is sitting.*]

—this young tadpole here.

CHRISTIAN. [*Looks up.*] Tadpole?

ANOTHER CADET. Yes, you!— You narrow-gutted Northerner!

CHRISTIAN. Sir?

FIRST CADET. Hark ye, Monsieur de Neuvillette: You are to know There is a certain subject—I would say, A certain object—never to be named Among us: utterly unmentionable!

CHRISTIAN. And that is?

THIRD CADET. [*In an awful voice.*]
Look at me! . . .

[*He strikes his nose three times with his finger, mysteriously.*]
You understand?

CHRISTIAN. Why, yes; the—

FOURTH CADET. Sh! . . . We never speak that word—

[*Indicating* CYRANO *by a gesture.*]
To breathe it is to have to do with HIM!

FIFTH CADET. [*Speaks through his nose.*] He has exterminated several Whose tone of voice suggested . . .

SIXTH CADET. [*In a hollow tone; rising from under the table on all fours.*]
Would you die Before your time? Just mention anything Convex . . . or cartilaginous . . .

SEVENTH CADET. [*His hand on* CHRISTIAN'S *shoulder.*] One word— One syllable—one gesture—nay, one sneeze— Your handkerchief becomes your winding-sheet!

[*Silence. In a circle around* CHRISTIAN, *arms crossed, they regard him expectantly.*]

CHRISTIAN. [*Rises and goes to* CARBON, *who is conversing with an officer, and pretending not to see what is taking place.*] Captain!

CARBON. [*Turns and looks him over.*] Sir?

CHRISTIAN. What is the proper thing to do When Gascons grow too boastful?

CARBON. Prove to them That one may be a Norman, and have courage. [*Turns his back.*]

CHRISTIAN. I thank you.

FIRST CADET. [*To* CYRANO.]
Come—the story!

ALL. The story!

CYRANO. [*Comes down.*] Oh, My story? Well . . .

[*They all draw up their stools and group themselves around him, eagerly.* CHRISTIAN *places himself astride of a chair, his arms on the back of it.*]
I marched on, all alone To meet those devils. Overhead, the moon Hung like a gold watch at the fob of heaven, Till suddenly some Angel rubbed a cloud, As it might be his handkerchief, across The shining crystal, and—the night came down. No lamps in those back streets— It was so dark— Mordious! You could not see beyond—

CHRISTIAN. Your nose.

[*Silence. Every man slowly rises to his feet. They look at* CYRANO *almost with terror. He has stopped short, utterly astonished. Pause.*]

CYRANO. Who is that man there?

A CADET. [*In a low voice.*]
A recruit—arrived This morning.

CYRANO. [*Takes a step toward* CHRISTIAN.] A recruit—

CARBON. [*In a low voice.*]
His name is Christian De Neuvil—

CYRANO. [*Suddenly motionless.*] Oh . . .

[*He turns pale, flushes, makes a movement as if to throw himself upon* CHRISTIAN.]
I—

[*Controls himself, and goes on in a choking voice.*]
I see. Very well,

As I was saying—

>[*With a sudden burst of rage.*]

Mordious! . . .

>[*He goes on in a natural tone.*]

It grew dark,
You could not see your hand before your
eyes.
I marched on, thinking how, all for the sake
Of one old souse—

>[*They slowly sit down, watching him.*]

who wrote a bawdy song
Whenever he took—

CHRISTIAN. A noseful—

>[*Everyone rises.* CHRISTIAN *balances himself on two legs of his chair.*]

CYRANO. [*Half strangled.*]

—Took a notion . . .
Whenever he took a notion— For his sake,
I might antagonize some dangerous man,
One powerful enough to make me pay—

CHRISTIAN. Through the nose—

CYRANO. [*Wipes the sweat from his forehead.*] —Pay the Piper. After all,
I thought, why am I putting in my—

CHRISTIAN. Nose—

CYRANO. —My oar . . . Why am I putting
in my oar?
The quarrel's none of mine. However—
now
I am here, I may as well go through with it.
Come, Gascon—do your duty!—Suddenly
A sword flashed in the dark. I caught it
fair—

CHRISTIAN. On the nose—

CYRANO. On my blade. Before I knew it,
There I was—

CHRISTIAN. Rubbing noses—

CYRANO. [*Pale and smiling.*]

Crossing swords
With half a score at once. I handed one—

CHRISTIAN. A nosegay—

CYRANO. [*Leaping at him.*]

Ventre-Saint-Gris! . . .

>[*The Gascons tumble over each other to get a good view. Arrived in front of* CHRISTIAN, *who has not moved an inch,* CYRANO *masters himself again, and continues.*]

He went down;
The rest gave way; I charged—

CHRISTIAN. Nose in the air—

CYRANO. I skewered two of them—disarmed a third—
Another lunged— Paf! And I countered—

CHRISTIAN. Pif!

CYRANO. [*Bellowing.*] TONNERRE! Out of
here—All of you!

>[*All the Cadets rush for the door.*]

FIRST CADET. At last—
The old lion wakes!

CYRANO. All of you! Leave me here
Alone with that man!

>[*The lines following are heard brokenly, in the confusion of getting through the door.*]

SECOND CADET. Bigre! He'll have the fellow
Chopped into sausage—

RAGUENEAU. Sausage?—

THIRD CADET. Mince-meat, then—
One of your pies!—

RAGUENEAU. Am I pale? You look white
As a fresh napkin—

CARBON. [*At the door.*] Come!

FOURTH CADET. He'll never leave
Enough of him to—

FIFTH CADET. Why, it frightens ME
To think of what will—

SIXTH CADET. [*Closing the door.*]

Something horrible
Beyond imagination . . .

>[*They are all gone: some through the street door, some by the inner doors to right and left. A few disappear up the staircase.* CYRANO *and* CHRISTIAN *stand face to face a moment, and look at each other.*]

CYRANO. To my arms!

CHRISTIAN. Sir? . . .

CYRANO. You have courage!

CHRISTIAN. Oh, that! . . .

CYRANO. You are brave—
That pleases me.

CHRISTIAN. You mean? . . .

CYRANO. Do you not know
I am her brother? Come!

CHRISTIAN. Whose?—

CYRANO. Hers—Roxane!

CHRISTIAN. Her . . . brother? You?

>[*Hurries to him.*]

CYRANO. Her cousin. Much the same.

CHRISTIAN. And she has told you? . . .

CYRANO. Everything.

CHRISTIAN. She loves me?

CYRANO. Perhaps.

CHRISTIAN. [*Takes both his hands.*] My dear sir— more than I can say, I am honored—

CYRANO. This is rather sudden.

CHRISTIAN. Please Forgive me—

CYRANO. [*Holds him at arm's length, looking at him.*] Why, he is a handsome devil, This fellow!

CHRISTIAN. On my honor—if you knew How much I have admired—

CYRANO. Yes, yes—and all Those Noses which—

CHRISTIAN. Please! I apologize.

CYRANO. [*Change of tone.*] Roxane expects a letter—

CHRISTIAN. Not from me?—

CYRANO. Yes. Why not?

CHRISTIAN. Once I write, that ruins all!

CYRANO. And why?

CHRISTIAN. Because . . . because I am a fool! Stupid enough to hang myself!

CYRANO. But no— You are no fool; you call yourself a fool, There's proof enough in that. Besides, you did not Attack me like a fool.

CHRISTIAN. Bah! Anyone Can pick a quarrel. Yes, I have a sort Of rough and ready soldier's tongue. I know That. But with any woman—paralyzed, Speechless, dumb. I can only look at them. Yet sometimes, when I go away, their eyes . . .

CYRANO. Why not their hearts, if you should wait and see?

CHRISTIAN. No. I am one of those— I know—those men Who never can make love.

CYRANO. Strange. . . . Now it seems I, if I gave my mind to it, I might Perhaps make love well.

CHRISTIAN. Oh, if I had words To say what I have here!

CYRANO. If I could be A handsome little Musketeer with eyes!—

CHRISTIAN. Besides—you know Roxane— how sensitive— One rough word, and the sweet illusion— gone!

CYRANO. I wish you might be my interpreter.

CHRISTIAN. I wish I had your wit—

CYRANO. Borrow it, then!— Your beautiful young manhood—lend me that, And we two make one hero of romance!

CHRISTIAN. What?

CYRANO. Would you dare repeat to her the words I gave you, day by day?

CHRISTIAN. You mean?

CYRANO. I mean Roxane shall have no disillusionment! Come, shall we win her both together? Take The soul within this leathern jack of mine, And breathe it into you? [*Touches him on the breast.*] So—there's my heart Under your velvet, now!

CHRISTIAN. But— Cyrano!—

CYRANO. But— Christian, why not?

CHRISTIAN. I am afraid—

CYRANO. I know— Afraid that when you have her all alone, You lose all. Have no fear. It is yourself She loves—give her yourself put into words— My words, upon your lips!

CHRISTIAN. But . . . but your eyes! . . . They burn like—

CYRANO. Will you? . . . Will you?

CHRISTIAN. Does it mean So much to you?

CYRANO. [*Beside himself.*] It means— [*Recovers, changes tone.*] A Comedy, A situation for a poet! Come, Shall we collaborate? I'll be your cloak Of darkness, your enchanted sword, your ring To charm the fairy Princess!

CHRISTIAN. But the letter— I cannot write—

CYRANO. Oh, yes, the letter.

[*He takes from his pocket the letter which he has written.*] Here.

CHRISTIAN. What is this?

CYRANO. All there; all but the address.

CHRISTIAN. I—

CYRANO. Oh, you may send it. It will serve.

CHRISTIAN. But why Have you done this?

CYRANO. I have amused myself As we all do, we poets—writing vows To Chloris, Phyllis—any pretty name— You might have had a pocketful of them! Take it, and turn to facts my fantasies— I loosed these loves like doves into the air; Give them a habitation and a home. Here, take it— You will find me all the more Eloquent, being insincere! Come!

CHRISTIAN. First, There must be a few changes here and there— Written at random, can it fit Roxane?

CYRANO. Like her own glove.

CHRISTIAN. No, but—

CYRANO. My son, have faith— Faith in the love of women for themselves— Roxane will know this letter for her own!

CHRISTIAN. [*Throws himself into the arms of* CYRANO. *They stand embraced.*]

My friend!

[*The door up stage opens a little. A Cadet steals in.*]

THE CADET. Nothing. A silence like the tomb . . . I hardly dare look— [*He sees the two.*] Wha-at?

[*The Other Cadets crowd in behind him and see.*]

THE CADETS. No!—No!

SECOND CADET. Mon dieu!

THE MUSKETEER. [*Slaps his knee.*] Well, well, well!

CARBON. Here's our devil . . . Christianized! Offend one nostril, and he turns the other.

THE MUSKETEER. Now we are allowed to talk about his nose! [*Calls.*] Hey, Lise! Come here— [*Affectedly.*] Snf! What a horrid smell! What is it? . . .

[*Plants himself in front of* CYRANO, *and looks at his nose in an impolite manner.*]

You ought to know about such things; What seems to have died around here?

CYRANO. [*Knocks him backward over a bench.*] Cabbage-heads!

[*Joy. The Cadets have found their old* CYRANO *again. General disturbance.*]

[CURTAIN.]

THE THIRD ACT

ROXANE'S KISS

A little square in the old Marais: old houses, and a glimpse of narrow streets. On the Right THE HOUSE OF ROXANE *and her garden wall, overhung with tall shrubbery. Over the door of the house a balcony and a tall window; to one side of the door, a bench.*

Ivy clings to the wall; jasmine embraces the balcony, trembles, and falls away.

By the bench and the jutting stonework of the wall one might easily climb up to the balcony.

Opposite, an ancient house of the like character, brick and stone, whose front door forms an Entrance. The knocker on this door is tied up in linen like an injured thumb.

At the Curtain Rise THE DUENNA *is seated on the bench beside the door. The window is wide open on* ROXANE'S *balcony; a light within suggests that is is early evening. By* THE DUENNA *stands* RAGUENEAU *dressed in what might be the livery of one attached to the household. He is by way of*

*telling her something, and wiping his eyes
meanwhile.*

RAGUENEAU.   —And so she ran off with a
  Musketeer!
I was ruined— I was alone— Remained
Nothing for me to do but hang myself,
So I did that. Presently along comes
Monsieur de Bergerac, and cuts me down,
And makes me steward to his cousin.
THE DUENNA.   Ruined?—
I thought your pastry was a great success!
RAGUENEAU. [*Shakes his head.*] Lise loved
  the soldiers, and I loved the poets—
Mars ate up all the cakes Apollo left;
It did not take long. . . .
THE DUENNA. [*Calls up to window.*]
                     Roxane! Are you ready?
We are late!
VOICE OF ROXANE. [*Within.*]
            Putting on my cape—
THE DUENNA. [*To RAGUENEAU, indicating
  the house opposite.*]   Clomire
Across the way receives on Thursday
  nights—
We are to have a psycho-colloquy
Upon the Tender Passion.
RAGUENEAU.   Ah—the Tender . . .
THE DUENNA. [*Sighs.*] —Passion! . . .
                     [*Calls up to window.*]
     Roxane!—Hurry, dear—we shall miss
The Tender Passion!
ROXANE.   Coming!—
  [*Music of stringed instruments off-stage
    approaching.*]
THE VOICE OF CYRANO. [*Singing.*]
                     La, la, la!—
THE DUENNA. A serenade?—How pleas-
  ant—
CYRANO.   No, no, no!—
F natural, you natural born fool!
  [*Enters, followed by two pages, carrying
    theorbos.*]
FIRST PAGE. [*Ironically.*] No doubt your
  honor knows F natural
When he hears—
CYRANO.   I am a musician, infant!—
A pupil of Gassendi.[1]

----
[1] One of the most eminent philosophers of the
seventeenth century, who actually was a teacher
of Cyrano.

THE PAGE.   [*Plays and sings.*] La, la,—
CYRANO.   Here—
Give me that—
  [*He snatches the instrument from* THE
    PAGE *and continues the tune.*]
                 La, la, la, la—
ROXANE. [*Appears on the Balcony.*]
                          Is that you
Cyrano?
CYRANO.   [*Singing.*]
            I, who praise your lilies fair,
But long to love your ro . . . ses!
ROXANE.   I'll be down—
Wait—   [*Goes in through window.*]
THE DUENNA.   Did you train these virtuosi?
CYRANO.   No—
I won them on a bet from D'Assoucy.[2]
We were debating a fine point of grammar
When, pointing out these two young night-
  ingales
Dressed up like peacocks, with their instru-
  ments,
He cries: "No, but I KNOW! I'll wager you
A day of music." Well, of course he lost;
And so until to-morrow they are mine,
My private orchestra. Pleasant at first,
But they become a trifle—
  [*To the Pages.*]   Here! Go play
A minuet to Montfleury—and tell him
I sent you!
  [*The* PAGES *go up to the exit.* CYRANO
    turns to THE DUENNA.]
                 I came here as usual
To inquire after our friend—
  [*To* PAGES.]   Play out of tune.
And keep on playing!
  [*The* PAGES *go out. He turns to* THE
    DUENNA.]
            —Our friend with the great soul.
ROXANE. [*Enters in time to hear the last
  words.*] He is beautiful and brilliant—
and I love him!
CYRANO.   Do you find Christian . . . intel-
  lectual?
ROXANE.   More so than you, even.
CYRANO.   I am glad.
ROXANE.   No man
Ever so beautifully said those things—

----
[2] A poetaster with whom Cyrano quarreled.

Those pretty nothings that are everything.
Sometimes he falls into a reverie;
His inspiration fails—then all at once,
He will say something absolutely . . .
Oh! . . .
CYRANO.   Really!
ROXANE.   How like a man! You
think a man
Who has a handsome face must be a fool.
CYRANO.   He talks well about . . . matters
of the heart?
ROXANE.   He does not *talk;* he rhapsodizes
. . . dreams . . .
CYRANO.   [*Twisting his moustache.*]
He . . . writes well?
ROXANE.   Wonderfully. Listen now:
          [*Reciting as from memory.*]
"Take my heart; I shall have it all the more;
Plucking the flowers, we keep the plant in
bloom—"
Well?
CYRANO.   Pooh!
ROXANE.   And this:
          "Knowing you have in store
More heart to give than I to find heart-
room—"
CYRANO.   First he has too much, then too
little; just
How much heart does he need?
ROXANE.   [*Tapping her foot.*]
          You are teasing me!
You are jealous!
CYRANO.   [*Startled.*] Jealous?
ROXANE.   Of his poetry—
You poets are like that . . .
          And these last lines
Are they not the last word in tenderness?—
"There is no more to say: only believe
That unto you my whole heart gives one
cry,
And writing, writes down more than you
receive;
Sending you kisses through my finger-
tips—
Lady, O read my letter with your lips!"
CYRANO.   H'm, yes—those last lines . . .
but he overwrites!
ROXANE.   Listen to this—
CYRANO.   You know them all by heart?
ROXANE.   Every one!

CYRANO.   [*Twisting his moustache.*]
          I may call that flattering . . .
ROXANE.   He is a master!
CYRANO.   Oh—come!
ROXANE.   Yes—a master!
CYRANO.   [*Bowing.*] A master—if you
will!
THE DUENNA.   [*Comes down stage quickly.*]
          Monsieur de Guiche!—
[*To* CYRANO, *pushing him toward the
house.*]
Go inside—If he does not find you here,
It may be just as well. He may suspect—
ROXANE.   —My secret! Yes; he is in love
with me
And he is powerful. Let him not know—
One look would frost my roses before
bloom.
CYRANO.   [*Going into house.*]
Very well, very well!
ROXANE.   [*To* DE GUICHE, *as he enters.*]
          We were just going—
DE GUICHE.   I came only to say farewell.
ROXANE.   You leave
Paris?
DE GUICHE.   Yes—for the front.
ROXANE.   Ah!
DE GUICHE.   And to-night!
ROXANE.   Ah!
DE GUICHE.   We have orders to besiege
Arras.
ROXANE.   Arras?
DE GUICHE.   Yes. My departure leaves you
. . . cold?
ROXANE.   [*Politely.*] Oh! Not that.
DE GUICHE.   It has left me desolate—
When shall I see you? Ever? Did you know
I was made Colonel?
ROXANE.   [*Indifferent.*] Bravo!
DE GUICHE.   Regiment
Of the Guards.
ROXANE.   [*Catching her breath.*]
          Of the Guards?—
DE GUICHE.   *His* regiment,
Your cousin, the mighty man of words!—
          [*Grimly.*]   Down there
We may have an accounting.
ROXANE.   [*Suffocating.*]   Are you sure
The Guards are ordered?
DE GUICHE.   Under my command!

ROXANE. [*Sinks down, breathless, on the bench; aside.*] Christian!—

DE GUICHE.   What is it?

ROXANE. [*Losing control of herself.*] To the war—perhaps Never again to— When a woman cares, Is that nothing?

DE GUICHE. [*Surprised and delighted.*] You say this now—to me— Now, at the very moment?—

ROXANE. [*Recovers—changes her tone.*] Tell me something: My cousin— You say you mean to be revenged On him. Do you mean that?

DE GUICHE. [*Smiles.*] Why? Would you care?

ROXANE.   Not for him.

DE GUICHE.   Do you see him?

ROXANE.   Now and then.

DE GUICHE. He goes about everywhere nowadays With one of the Cadets--de Neuve— Neuville— Neuvillers—

ROXANE. [*Coolly.*] A tall man?—

DE GUICHE.   Blond—

ROXANE.   Rosy cheeks?—

DE GUICHE. Handsome!—

ROXANE.   Pooh!—

DE GUICHE.   And a fool.

ROXANE. [*Languidly.*] So he appears . . . [*Animated.*] But Cyrano? What will you do to him? Order him into danger? He loves that! I know what *I* should do.

DE GUICHE.   What?

ROXANE.   Leave him here With his Cadets, while all the regiment Goes on to glory! That would torture him— To sit all through the war with folded arms— I know his nature. If you hate that man, Strike at his self-esteem.

DE GUICHE.   Oh woman—woman! Who but a woman would have thought of this?

ROXANE. He'll eat his heart out, while his Gascon friends

Bite their nails all day long in Paris here. And you will be avenged!

DE GUICHE.   You love me then, A little? . . . [*She smiles.*] Making my enemies your own, Hating them—I should like to see in that A sign of love, Roxane.

ROXANE.   Perhaps it is one . . .

DE GUICHE. [*Shows a number of folded despatches.*] Here are the orders—for each company— Ready to send . . . [*Selects one.*] So— This is for the Guards— I'll keep that. Aha, Cyrano! [*To* ROXANE.] You too, You play your little games, do you?

ROXANE. [*Watching him.*] Sometimes . . .

DE GUICHE. [*Close to her, speaking hurriedly.*] And you!—Oh, I am mad over you!— Listen— I leave to-night—but—let you through my hands Now, when I feel you trembling?—Listen —Close by, In the Rue d'Orleans, the Capuchins Have their new convent. By their law, no layman May pass inside those walls. I'll see to that— Their sleeves are wide enough to cover me— The servants of my Uncle-Cardinal Will fear his nephew. So—I'll come to you Masked, after everyone knows I have gone— Oh, let me wait one day!—

ROXANE.   If this be known, Your honor—

DE GUICHE. Bah!

ROXANE.   The war—your duty—

DE GUICHE. [*Blows away an imaginary feather.*]   Phoo! Only say yes!

ROXANE. No!

DE GUICHE   Whisper . . .

ROXANE. [*Tenderly.*]   I ought not To let you . . .

DE GUICHE. Ah! . . .

ROXANE. [*Pretends to break down.*]
                    Ah, go!
    [*Aside.*]   —Christian remains—
                    [*Aloud—heroically.*]
I must have you a hero—Antoine . . .
DE GUICHE.   Heaven! . . .
So you can love—
ROXANE.   One for whose sake I fear.
DE GUICHE. [*Triumphant.*] I go!
          Will that content you?
                    [*Kisses her hand.*]
ROXANE.   Yes—my friend!
                    [*He goes out.*]
THE DUENNA. [*As* DE GUICHE *disappears,
    making a deep curtsey behind his back,
    and imitating* ROXANE'S *intense tone.*]
Yes—my friend!
ROXANE. [*Quickly, close to her.*]
                    Not a word to Cyrano—
He would never forgive me if he knew
I stole his war! [*She calls toward the house.*]
                    Cousin!
    [CYRANO *comes out of the house; she
    turns to him, indicating the house op-
    posite.*]
                    We are going over—
Alcandre speaks to-night—and Lysimon.
THE DUENNA. [*Puts finger in her ear.*]
                    My little finger says we shall not hear
Everything.
CYRANO.   Never mind me—
THE DUENNA. [*Across the street.*]
                    Look— Oh, look!
The knocker tied up in a napkin— Yes,
They muzzled you because you bark too
    loud
And interrupt the lecture—little beast!
ROXANE. [*As the door opens.*] Enter . . .
    [*To* CYRANO.] If Christian comes, tell
    him to wait.
CYRANO. Oh—   [ROXANE *returns.*]
When he comes, what will you talk
    about?
You always know beforehand.
ROXANE.   About . . .
CYRANO.   Well?
ROXANE. You will not tell him, will you?
CYRANO.   I am dumb.
ROXANE. About nothing! Or about every-
    thing—

I shall say: "Speak of love in your own
    words—
Improvise! Rhapsodize! Be eloquent!"
CYRANO. [*Smiling.*] Good!
ROXANE.   Sh!—
CYRANO.   Sh!—
ROXANE.   Not a word!
          [*She goes in; the door closes.*]
CYRANO. [*Bowing.*] Thank you so much—
ROXANE. [*Opens door and puts out her
    head.*] He must be unprepared—
CYRANO.   Of course!
ROXANE.   Sh!— [*Goes in again.*]
CYRANO. [*Calls.*]   Christian!

          [CHRISTIAN *enters.*]

I have your theme—bring on your mem-
    ory!—
Here is your chance now to surpass your-
    self,
No time to lose— Come! Look intelligent—
Come home and learn your lines.
CHRISTIAN.   No.
CYRANO.   What?
CHRISTIAN.   I'll wait
Here for Roxane.
CYRANO.   What lunacy is this?
Come quickly!
CHRISTIAN. No, I say! I have had enough—
Taking my words, my letters, all from
    you—
Making our love a little comedy!
It was a game at first; but now—she
    cares . . .
Thanks to you. I am not afraid. I'll speak
For myself now.
CYRANO.   Undoubtedly!
CHRISTIAN.   I will!
Why not? I am no such fool—you shall see!
Besides—my dear friend—you have taught
    me much:
I ought to know something . . . By God, I
    know
Enough to take a woman in my arms!
    [ROXANE *appears in the doorway, oppo-
    site.*]
There she is now . . . Cyrano, wait! Stay
    here!
CYRANO. [*Bows.*] Speak for yourself, my
    friend!   [*He goes out.*]

ROXANE. [*Taking leave of the company.*]
                —Barthénoide!
Alcandre! . . . Grémione! . . .
THE DUENNA.   I told you so—
We missed the Tender Passion!
            [*She goes into* ROXANE'S *house.*]
ROXANE.   Urimédonte!—
Adieu!
    [*As the guests disappear down the street,
    she turns to* CHRISTIAN.]
            Is that you, Christian? Let us stay
Here, in the twilight. They are gone. The
    air
Is fragrant. We shall be alone. Sit down
There—so . . .   [*They sit on the bench.*]
            Now tell me things.
CHRISTIAN. [*After a silence.*] I love you.
ROXANE. [*Closes her eyes.*]   Yes,
Speak to me about love . . .
CHRISTIAN.   I love you.
ROXANE.   Now
Be eloquent! . . .
CHRISTIAN. I love—
ROXANE. [*Opens her eyes.*]
                You have your theme—
Improvise! Rhapsodize!
CHRISTIAN.   I love you so!
ROXANE. Of course. And then? . . .
CHRISTIAN. And then . . . Oh, I should be
So happy if you loved me too! Roxane,
Say that you love me too!
ROXANE. [*Making a face.*]
                I ask for cream—
You give me milk and water. Tell me first
A little, how you love me.
CHRISTIAN.   Very much.
ROXANE. Oh—tell me how you *feel!*
CHRISTIAN. [*Coming nearer, and devour-
ing her with his eyes.*]
                Your throat . . . If only
I might . . . kiss it—
ROXANE.   Christian!
CHRISTIAN.   I love you so!
ROXANE. [*Makes as if to rise.*] Again?
CHRISTIAN. [*Desperately, restraining her.*]
    No, not again— I do not love you—
ROXANE. [*Settles back.*] That is better . . .
CHRISTIAN. I adore you!
ROXANE.   Oh!—
            [*Rises and moves away.*]

CHRISTIAN.   I know;
I grow absurd.
ROXANE. [*Coldly.*] And that displeases me
As much as if you had grown ugly.
CHRISTIAN.   I—
ROXANE. Gather your dreams together
    into words!
CHRISTIAN. I love—
ROXANE. I know; you love me. Adieu.
            [*She goes to the house.*]
CHRISTIAN.   No,
But wait—please—let me— I was going to
    say—
ROXANE. [*Pushes the door open.*]
That you adore me. Yes; I know that too.
No! . . . Go away! . . .
    [*She goes in and shuts the door in his
    face.*]
CHRISTIAN.   I . . . I . . .
CYRANO. [*Enters.*]   A great success!
CHRISTIAN. Help me!
CYRANO.   Not I.
CHRISTIAN.   I cannot live unless
She loves me—now, this moment!
CYRANO.   How the devil
Am I to teach you now—this moment?
CHRISTIAN. [*Catches him by the arm.*]
                —Wait!—
Look! Up there!—Quick—
    [*The light shows in* ROXANE'S *window.*]
CYRANO.   Her window—
CHRISTIAN. [*Wailing.*]   I shall die!
CYRANO. Less noise!
CHRISTIAN.   Oh, I—
CYRANO.   It does seem fairly dark—
CHRISTIAN. [*Excitedly.*]
Well?—Well?—Well?—
CYRANO.   Let us try what can be done;
It is more than you deserve—stand over
    there,
Idiot—there!—before the balcony—
Let me stand underneath. I'll whisper you
What to say.
CHRISTIAN. She may hear—she may—
CYRANO.   Less noise!
            [*The* PAGES *appear up stage.*]
FIRST PAGE. Hep!—
CYRANO. [*Finger to lips.*] Sh!—
FIRST PAGE. [*Low voice.*]
            We serenaded Montfleury!—

What next?

CYRANO. Down to the corner of the street—
One this way—and the other over there—
If anybody passes, play a tune!

PAGE. What tune, O musical Philosopher?

CYRANO. Sad for a man, or merry for a woman—
Now go!

[*The* PAGES *disappear, one toward each corner of the street.*]

CYRANO. [*To* CHRISTIAN.] Call her!

CHRISTIAN. Roxane!

CYRANO. Wait . . .
[*Gathers up a handful of pebbles.*]
Gravel . . .
[*Throws it at the window.*] There!—

ROXANE. [*Opens the window.*]
Who is calling?

CHRISTIAN. I—

ROXANE. Who?

CHRISTIAN. Christian.

ROXANE. You again?

CHRISTIAN. I had to tell you—

CYRANO. [*Under the balcony.*]
Good— Keep your voice down.

ROXANE. No. Go away. You tell me nothing.

CHRISTIAN. Please!—

ROXANE. You do not love me any more—

CHRISTIAN. [*To whom* CYRANO *whispers his words.*] No—no—
Not any more— I love you . . . ever more . . .
And ever . . . more and more!

ROXANE. [*About to close the window— pauses.*] A little better . . .

CHRISTIAN. [*Same business.*] Love grows and struggles like . . . an angry child . . .
Breaking my heart . . . his cradle . . .

ROXANE. [*Coming out on the balcony.*]
Better still—
But . . . such a babe is dangerous; why not
Have smothered it new-born?

CHRISTIAN. [*Same business.*]
And so I do . . .
And yet he lives . . . I found . . . as you shall find . . .
This new-born babe . . . an infant . . . Hercules!

ROXANE. [*Further forward.*] Good!—

CHRISTIAN. [*Same business.*] Strong enough . . . at birth . . . to strangle those
Two serpents—Doubt and . . . Pride.

ROXANE. [*Leans over balcony.*]
Why, very well!
Tell me now why you speak so haltingly—
Has your imagination gone lame?

CYRANO. [*Thrusts* CHRISTIAN *under the balcony, and stands in his place.*] Here—
This grows too difficult!

ROXANE. Your words to-night
Hesitate. Why?

CYRANO. [*In a low tone, imitating* CHRISTIAN.] Through the warm summer gloom
They grope in darkness toward the light of you.

ROXANE. My words, well aimed, find you more readily.

CYRANO. My heart is open wide and waits for them—
Too large a mark to miss! My words fly home,
Heavy with honey like returning bees,
To your small secret ear. Moreover—yours
Fall to me swiftly. Mine more slowly rise.

ROXANE. Yet not so slowly as they did at first.

CYRANO. They have learned the way, and you have welcomed them.

ROXANE. [*Softly.*] Am I so far above you now?

CYRANO. So far—
If you let fall upon me one hard word,
Out of that height—you crush me!

ROXANE. [*Turns.*] I'll come down—

CYRANO. [*Quickly.*] No!

ROXANE. [*Points out the bench under the balcony.*] Stand you on the bench. Come nearer!

CYRANO. [*Recoils into the shadow.*] No!—

ROXANE. And why—so great a *No*?

CYRANO. [*More and more overcome by emotion.*] Let me enjoy
The one moment I ever—my one chance
To speak to you . . . unseen!

ROXANE. Unseen?—

CYRANO. Yes!—yes . . .
Night, making all things dimly beautiful,
One veil over us both— You only see

The darkness of a long cloak in the gloom,
And I the whiteness of a summer gown—
You are all light— I am all shadow! . . .
How
Can you know what this moment means
  to me?
If I was ever eloquent—
ROXANE.   You were
Eloquent—
CYRANO.   —You have never heard till now
My own heart speaking!
ROXANE.   Why not?
CYRANO.   Until now,
I spoke through . . .
ROXANE. Yes?—
CYRANO.   —through that sweet drunken-
  ness
You pour into the world out of your eyes!
But to-night . . . But to-night, I indeed
  speak
For the first time!
ROXANE. For the first time— Your voice,
Even, is not the same.
CYRANO.   [Passionately; moves nearer.]
                     How should it be?
I have another voice to-night—my own,
Myself, daring—
[He stops, confused; then tries to recover
  himself.]
                Where was I? . . . I forget! . . .
Forgive me. This is all sweet like a
  dream . . .
Strange—like a dream . . .
ROXANE.   How, strange?
CYRANO.   Is it not so
To be myself to you, and have no fear
Of moving you to laughter?
ROXANE.   Laughter—why?
CYRANO. [Struggling for an explanation.]
Because . . . What am I . . . What is any
  man,
That he dare ask for you? Therefore my
  heart
Hides behind phrases. There's a modesty
In these things too— I come here to pluck
  down
Out of the sky the evening star—then
  smile,
And stoop to gather little flowers.
ROXANE.   Are they

Not sweet, those little flowers?
CYRANO.   Not enough sweet
For you and me, to-night!
ROXANE. [Breathless.] You never spoke
To me like this . . .
CYRANO.   Little things, pretty things—
Arrows and hearts and torches—roses red,
And violets blue—are these all? Come
  away,
And breathe fresh air! Must we keep on
  and on
Sipping stale honey out of tiny cups
Decorated with golden tracery,
Drop by drop, all day long? We are alive;
We thirst— Come away, plunge, and drink,
  and drown
In the great river flowing to the sea!
ROXANE. But . . . Poetry?
CYRANO.   I have made rimes for you—
Not now— Shall we insult Nature, this
  night,
These flowers, this moment—shall we set
  all these
To phrases from a letter by Voiture? [3]
Look once at the high stars that shine in
  heaven,
And put off artificiality!
Have you not seen great gaudy hothouse
  flowers,
Barren, without fragrance?—Souls are like
  that:
Forced to show all, they soon become all
  show—
The means to Nature's end ends meaning-
  less!
ROXANE. But . . . Poetry?
CYRANO. Love hates that game of words!
It is a crime to fence with life— I tell you,
There comes one moment, once—and God
  help those
Who pass that moment by!—when Beauty
  stands
Looking into the soul with grave, sweet
  eyes
That sicken at pretty words!
ROXANE.   If that be true—
And when that moment comes to you and
  me—

[3] A clever stylist who was the idol of the salons
and epitomized the elegant taste of the age.

What words will you? . . .

CYRANO.   All those, all those, all those
That blossom in my heart, I'll fling to
   you—
Armfuls of loose bloom! Love, I love
   beyond
Breath, beyond reason, beyond love's own
   power
Of loving! Your name is like a golden bell
Hung in my heart; and when I think of
   you,
I tremble, and the bell swings and rings—
                              Roxane! . . .
Roxane! . . . along my veins, Roxane! . . .
                              I know
All small forgotten things that once meant
   You—
I remember last year, the First of May,
A little before noon, you had your hair
Drawn low, that one time only. Is that
   strange?
You know how, after looking at the sun,
One sees red suns everywhere—so, for
   hours
After the flood of sunshine that you are,
My eyes are blinded by your burning hair!

ROXANE. [Very low.] Yes . . . that is . . .
   Love—

CYRANO.   Yes, that is Love—that wind
Of terrible and jealous beauty, blowing
Over me—that dark fire, that music . . .
                              Yet
Love seeketh not his own! Dear, you may
   take
My happiness to make you happier,
Even though you never know I gave it
   you—
Only let me hear sometimes, all alone,
The distant laughter of your joy! . . .
                              I never
Look at you, but there's some new virtue
   born
In me, some new courage. Do you begin
To understand, a little? Can you feel
My soul, there in the darkness, breathe on
   you?
—Oh, but to-night, now, I dare say these
   things—
I . . . to you . . . and you hear them! . . .
   It is too much!

In my most sweet unreasonable dreams,
I have not hoped for this! Now let me die,
Having lived. It is my voice, mine, my own,
That makes you tremble there in the green
   gloom
Above me—for you do tremble, as a blos-
   som
Among the leaves— You tremble, and I
   can feel,
All the way down along these jasmine
   branches,
Whether you will or no, the passion of you
Trembling . . .

[He kisses wildly the end of a drooping
   spray of jasmine.]

ROXANE.   Yes, I do tremble . . . and I
   weep . . .
And I love you . . . and I am yours . . .
   and you
Have made me thus!

CYRANO. [After a pause; quietly.]
              What is death like, I wonder?
I know everything else now . . .
                              I have done
This, to you—I, myself . . .
                              Only let me
Ask one thing more—

CHRISTIAN. [Under the balcony.] One kiss!

ROXANE. [Startled.] One?—

CYRANO. [To CHRISTIAN.] You! . . .

ROXANE.   You ask me
For—

CYRANO.   I . . . Yes, but—I mean—
   [To CHRISTIAN.]   You go too far!

CHRISTIAN. She is willing!—Why not
   make the most of it?

CYRANO. [To ROXANE.] I did ask . . . but I
   know I ask too much . . .

ROXANE.   Only one— Is that all?

CYRANO.   All!—How much more
Than all!—I know—I frighten you—I
   ask . . .
I ask you to refuse—

CHRISTIAN. [To CYRANO.]
                    But why? Why? Why?

CYRANO.   Christian, be quiet!

ROXANE. [Leaning over.]
                    What is that you say
To yourself?

CYRANO.   I am angry with myself

Because I go too far, and so I say
To myself: "Christian, be quiet!"

[*The theorbos begin to play.*]

                                    Hark—someone
Is coming—

[ROXANE *closes her window.* CYRANO *listens to the theorbos, one of which plays a gay melody, the other a mournful one.*]

                    A sad tune, a merry tune—
Man, woman—what do they mean?

[*A* CAPUCHIN *enters; he carries a lantern, and goes from house to house, looking at the doors.*]

                              Aha!—a priest!

[*To the* CAPUCHIN.]

What is this new game of Diogenes? [4]

THE CAPUCHIN.   I am looking for the house of Madame—

CHRISTIAN.   [*Impatient.*]   Bah!—

THE CAPUCHIN.   Madeleine Robin—

CHRISTIAN.   What does he want?

CYRANO.   [*To the* CAPUCHIN; *points out a street.*]   This way—
To the right—keep to the right—

THE CAPUCHIN.   I thank you, sir!—
I'll say my beads for you to the last grain.

CYRANO.   Good fortune, father, and my service to you!

[*The* CAPUCHIN *goes out.*]

CHRISTIAN.   Win me that kiss!

CYRANO.   No.

CHRISTIAN.   Sooner or later—

CYRANO.   True . . .
That is true . . . Soon or late, it will be so
Because you are young and she is beautiful—   [*To himself.*]
Since it must be, I had rather be myself

[*The window re-opens.* CHRISTIAN *hides under the balcony.*]

The cause of . . . what must be.

ROXANE.   [*Out on the balcony.*]
                    Are you still there?
We were speaking of—

CYRANO.   A kiss. The word is sweet—
What will the deed be? Are your lips afraid
Even of its burning name? Not much
afraid—

Not too much! Have you not unwittingly
Laid aside laughter, slipping beyond speech
Insensibly, already, without fear,
From words to smiles . . . from smiles to
   sighs . . . from sighing,
Even to tears? One step more—only one—
From a tear to a kiss—one step, one thrill!

ROXANE.   Hush!—

CYRANO.   And what is a kiss,
   when all is done?
A promise given under seal—a vow
Taken before the shrine of memory—
A signature acknowledged—a rosy dot
Over the i of Loving—a secret whispered
To listening lips apart—a moment made
Immortal, with a rush of wings unseen—
A sacrament of blossoms, a new song
Sung by two hearts to an old simple tune—
The ring of one horizon around two souls
Together, all alone!

ROXANE.   Hush! . . .

CYRANO.   Why, what shame?—
There was a Queen of France, not long ago,
And a great lord of England [5]—a queen's
   gift,
A crown jewel!—

ROXANE.   Indeed!

CYRANO.   Indeed, like him,
I have my sorrows and my silences;
Like her, you are the queen I dare adore;
Like him I am faithful and forlorn—

ROXANE.   Like him,
Beautiful—

CYRANO.   [*Aside.*] So I am—I forgot that!

ROXANE.   Then—Come! . . . Gather your
   sacred blossom . . .

CYRANO.   [*To* CHRISTIAN.]   Go!—

ROXANE.   Your crown jewel . . .

CYRANO.   Go on!—

ROXANE.   Your old new song . . .

CYRANO.   Climb!—

CHRISTIAN.   [*Hesitates.*]
        No— Would you?—not yet—

ROXANE.   Your moment made
Immortal . . .

CYRANO.   [*Pushing him.*]
            Climb up, animal!

[CHRISTIAN *springs on the bench, and*

---

[4] A Greek who, when asked why he went about in daylight carrying a lantern, replied that he sought an honest man.

[5] Anne of Austria, Queen of Louis XIII, and the Duke of Buckingham were principals in a famous romance.

climbs by the pillars, the branches, the vines, until he bestrides the balcony railing.]

CHRISTIAN.   Roxane! . . .
[*He takes her in his arms and bends over her.*]
CYRANO. [*Very low.*] Ah! . . . Roxane! . . .
                    I have won what I have won—
The feast of love—and I am Lazarus! [6]
Yet . . . I have something here that is mine now
And was not mine before I spoke the words
That won her—not for me! . . . Kissing my words,
My words, upon your lips!
                    [*The theorbos begin to play.*]
                              A merry tune—
A sad tune— So! The Capuchin!
[*He pretends to be running, as if he had arrived from a distance; then calls up to the balcony.*]
                                        Holo!
ROXANE.   Who is it?
CYRANO.   I. Is Christian there with you?
CHRISTIAN. [*Astonished.*] Cyrano!
ROXANE.   Good morrow, Cousin!
CYRANO.   Cousin, . . . good morrow!
ROXANE.   I am coming down.
[*She disappears into the house. The* CAPUCHIN *enters up stage.*]
CHRISTIAN. [*Sees him.*] Oh—again!
THE CAPUCHIN. [*To* CYRANO.]
                              She lives *here*,
Madeleine Robin!
CYRANO.   You said RO-LIN.
THE CAPUCHIN.   No—
R-O-B-I-N—
ROXANE. [*Appears on the threshold of the house, followed by* RAGUENEAU *with a lantern, and by* CHRISTIAN.]
              What is it?
THE CAPUCHIN.   A letter.
CHRISTIAN.   Oh! . . .
THE CAPUCHIN. [*To* ROXANE.]
Some matter profitable to the soul—
A very noble lord gave it to me!
ROXANE. [*To* CHRISTINE.] De Guiche!
CHRISTIAN.   He dares?—

---

[6] The beggar in *St. Luke*, xvi, who fed on the crumbs which fell from the rich man's table.

ROXANE.   It will not be for long;
When he learns that I love you . . .
[*By the light of the lantern which* RAGUE-NEAU *holds, she reads the letter in a low tone, as if to herself.*]
                              "Mademoiselle
The drums are beating, and the regiment
Arms for the march. Secretly I remain
Here, in the Convent. I have disobeyed;
I shall be with you soon. I send this first
By an old monk, as simple as a sheep,
Who understands nothing of this. Your smile
Is more than I can bear, and seek no more.
Be alone to-night, waiting for one who dares
To hope you will forgive . . .—" etcetera—
                    [*To the* CAPUCHIN.]
Father, this letter concerns you . . .
                    [*To* CHRISTIAN.]
                              —and you.
Listen:
[*The others gather around her. She pretends to read from the letter, aloud.*]
              "Mademoiselle:
                              The Cardinal
Will have his way, although against your will;
That is why I am sending this to you
By a most holy man, intelligent,
Discreet. You will communicate to him
Our order to perform, here and at once
The rite of . . .   [*Turns the page.*]
                    —Holy Matrimony. You
And Christian will be married privately
In your house. I have sent him to you. I know
You hesitate. Be resigned, nevertheless,
To the Cardinal's command, who sends herewith
His blessing. Be assured also of my own
Respect and high consideration—*signed*,
Your very humble and—etcetera—"
THE CAPUCHIN.   A noble lord! I said so— never fear—
A worthy lord!—a very worthy lord!—
ROXANE. [*To* CHRISTIAN.]
Am I a good reader of letters?
CHRISTIAN. [*Motions toward the* CAPU-CHIN.]   Careful!—

ROXANE. [*In a tragic tone.*]
Oh, this is terrible!

THE CAPUCHIN. [*Turns the light of his lantern on* CYRANO.] You are to be—

CHRISTIAN. *I* am the bridegroom!

THE CAPUCHIN. [*Turns his lantern upon* CHRISTIAN; *then, as if some suspicion crossed his mind, upon seeing the young man so handsome.*] Oh—why, *you* . . .

ROXANE. [*Quickly.*]   Look here—
"*Postscript:* Give to the Convent in my name
One hundred and twenty pistoles"—

THE CAPUCHIN.   Think of it!
A worthy lord—a very worthy lord! . . .
                    [*To* ROXANE, *solemnly.*]
Daughter, resign yourself!

ROXANE. [*With an air of martyrdom.*]
                    I am resigned . . .
[*While* RAGUENEAU *opens the door for the* CAPUCHIN *and* CHRISTIAN *invites him to enter, she turns to* CYRANO.]
De Guiche may come. Keep him out here
with you.
Do not let him—

CYRANO. I understand! [*To the* CAPUCHIN.]
                    How long
Will you be?—

THE CAPUCHIN. Oh, a quarter of an hour.

CYRANO. [*Hurrying them into the house.*]
Hurry—I'll wait here—

ROXANE. [*To* CHRISTIAN.] Come!
                    [*They go into the house.*]

CYRANO.   Now then, to make
His Grace delay that quarter of an hour . . .
I have it!—up here—
[*He steps on the bench, and climbs up the wall toward the balcony. The theorbos begin to play a mournful melody.*]
                    Sad music— Ah, a man! . . .
[*The music pauses on a sinister tremolo.*]
Oh—very much a man!
[*He sits astride of the railing, and, drawing toward him a long branch of one of the trees which border the garden wall, he grasps it with both hands, ready to swing himself down.*]
                    So—not too high—
[*He peers down at the ground.*]

I must float gently through the atmosphere—

DE GUICHE. [*Enters, masked, groping in the dark toward the house.*]
Where is that cursed, bleating Capuchin?

CYRANO. What if he knows my voice?—
the devil!—Tic-tac,
Bergerac—we unlock our Gascon tongue;
A good strong accent—

DE GUICHE. Here is the house—all dark—
Damn this mask!—
[*As he is about to enter the house,* CYRANO *leaps from the balcony, still holding fast to the branch, which bends and swings him between* DE GUICHE *and the door; then he releases the branch and pretends to fall heavily as though from a height. He lands flat-long on the ground, where he lies motionless, as if stunned.* DE GUICHE *leaps back.*]
                    What is that?
[*When he lifts his eyes, the branch has sprung back into place. He can see nothing but the sky; he does not understand.*]
                    Why . . . where did this man
Fall from?

CYRANO. [*Sits up, and speaks with a strong accent.*] —The moon!

DE GUICHE.   You—

CYRANO.   From the moon, the moon!
I fell out of the moon!

DE GUICHE.   The fellow is mad—

CYRANO. [*Dreamily.*] Where am I?

DE GUICHE.   Why—

CYRANO.   What time is it? What place
Is this? What day? What season?

DE GUICHE.   You—

CYRANO.   I am stunned!

DE GUICHE. My dear sir—

CYRANO.   Like a bomb—a bomb—I fell
From the moon!

DE GUICHE. Now, see here—

CYRANO. [*Rising to his feet, and speaking in a terrible voice.*] I say, the moon!

DE GUICHE. [*Recoils.*] Very well—if you say so—
[*Aside.*] Raving mad!—

CYRANO. [*Advancing upon him.*] I am not speaking metaphorically!

DE GUICHE. Pardon.

CYRANO. A hundred years—an hour ago—
I really cannot say how long I fell—
I was in yonder shining sphere—

DE GUICHE. [*Shrugs.*] Quite so. Please let me pass.

CYRANO. [*Interposes himself.*] Where am I? Tell the truth—
I can bear it. In what quarter of the globe
Have I descended like a meteorite?

DE GUICHE. Morbleu!

CYRANO. I could not choose my place to fall—
The earth spun round so fast— Was it the Earth,
I wonder?—Or is this another world?
Another moon? Whither have I been drawn
By the dead weight of my posterior?

DE GUICHE. Sir, I repeat—

CYRANO. [*With a sudden cry, which causes* DE GUICHE *to recoil again.*]
His face! My God—black!

DE GUICHE. [*Carries his hand to his mask.*] Oh—

CYRANO. [*Terrified.*] Are you a native? Is this Africa?

DE GUICHE. —This mask!

CYRANO. [*Somewhat reassured.*] Are we in Venice? Genoa?

DE GUICHE. [*Tries to pass him.*] A lady is waiting for me.

CYRANO. [*Quite happy again.*] So this is Paris!

DE GUICHE. [*Smiling in spite of himself.*] This fool becomes amusing.

CYRANO. Ah! You smile?

DE GUICHE. I do. Kindly permit me—

CYRANO. [*Delighted.*] Dear old Paris— Well, well!—
[*Wholly at his ease, smiles, bows, arranges his dress.*]
Excuse my appearance. I arrive
By the last thunderbolt—a trifle singed
As I came through the ether. These long journeys—
You know! There are so few conveniences!
My eyes are full of star-dust. On my spurs,

Some sort of fur . . . Planet's apparently . . .
[*Plucks something from his sleeve.*]
Look—on my doublet— That's a Comet's hair!
[*He blows something from the back of his hand.*]
Phoo!

DE GUICHE. [*Grows angry.*] Monsieur—

CYRANO. [*As* DE GUICHE *is about to push past, thrusts his leg in the way.*]
Here's a tooth, stuck in my boot,
From the Great Bear.[7] Trying to get away,
I tripped over the Scorpion and came down
Slap, into one scale of the Balances—
The pointer marks my weight this moment . . . [*Pointing upward.*]
See?
[DE GUICHE *makes a sudden movement.* CYRANO *catches his arm.*]
Be careful! If you struck me on the nose,
It would drip milk!

DE GUICHE. Milk?

CYRANO. From the Milky Way!

DE GUICHE. Hell!

CYRANO. No, no—Heaven.
[*Crossing his arms.*]
Curious place up there—
Did you know Sirius wore a nightcap? True!
[*Confidentially.*]
The Little Bear is still too young to bite.
[*Laughing.*]
My foot caught in the Lyre, and broke a string. [*Proudly.*]
Well—when I write my book, and tell the tale
Of my adventures—all these little stars
That shake out of my cloak—I must save those
To use for asterisks!

DE GUICHE. That will do now—
I wish—

CYRANO. Yes, yes—I know—

DE GUICHE. Sir—

CYRANO. You desire
To learn from my own lips the character
Of the moon's surface—its inhabitants
If any—

---

[7] The constellation of the Big Dipper. The following references are, of course, to other constellations.

DE GUICHE. [*Loses patience and shouts.*]
        I desire no such thing! I—
CYRANO. [*Rapidly.*] You wish to know by
    what mysterious means
I reached the moon?—well—confiden-
    tially—
It was a new invention of my own.
DE GUICHE. [*Discouraged.*] Drunk too—as
    well as mad!
CYRANO.   I scorned the eagle
Of Regiomontanus,[8] and the dove
Of Archytas! [9]
DE GUICHE. A learned lunatic!—
CYRANO. I imitated no one. I myself
Discovered not one scheme merely, but
    six—
Six ways to violate the virgin sky!
    [DE GUICHE *has succeeded in passing
    him, and moves toward the door of*
    ROXANE'S *house.* CYRANO *follows,
    ready to use violence if necessary.*]
DE GUICHE. [*Looks around.*] Six?
CYRANO. [*With increasing volubility.*] As
    for instance—Having stripped myself
Bare as a wax candle, adorn my form
With crystal vials filled with morning
    dew,
And so be drawn aloft, as the sun rises
Drinking the mist of dawn!
DE GUICHE. [*Takes a step toward* CYRANO.]
            Yes—that makes one.
CYRANO. [*Draws back to lead him away
    from the door; speaks faster and
    faster.*]
Or, sealing up the air in a cedar chest,
Rarefy it by means of mirrors, placed
In an icosahedron.[10]
DE GUICHE. [*Takes another step.*] Two.
CYRANO. [*Still retreating.*]   Again,
I might construct a rocket, in the form
Of a huge locust, driven by impulses
Of villainous saltpetre from the rear,
Upward, by leaps and bounds.
DE GUICHE. [*Interested in spite of himself,
    and counting on his fingers.*] Three.
CYRANO. [*Same business.*]   Or again,

Smoke having a natural tendency to rise,
Blow in a globe enough to raise me.
DE GUICHE. [*Same business, more and
    more astonished.*]   Four!
CYRANO. Or since Diana,[11] as old fables
    tell,
Draws forth to fill her crescent horn, the
    marrow
Of bulls and goats—to anoint myself there-
    with.
DE GUICHE. [*Hypnotized.*] Five!—
CYRANO. [*Has by this time led him all
    the way across the street, close to a
    bench.*]
            Finally—seated on an iron plate,
To hurl a magnet in the air—the iron
Follows—I catch the magnet—throw
    again—
And so proceed indefinitely.
DE GUICHE.   Six!—
All excellent,—and which did you adopt?
CYRANO. [*Coolly.*] Why, none of them. . . .
    A seventh.
DE GUICHE. Which was?—
CYRANO.   Guess!—
DE GUICHE. An interesting idiot, this!
CYRANO. [*Imitates the sound of waves
    with his voice, and their movement by
    large, vague gestures.*] Hoo! . . . Hoo! . . .
DE GUICHE. Well?
CYRANO.   Have you guessed it yet?
DE GUICHE.   Why, no.
CYRANO. [*Grandiloquent.*] The ocean! . . .
What hour its rising tide seeks the full
    moon,
I laid me on the strand, fresh from the
    spray,
My head fronting the moonbeams, since
    the hair
Retains moisture—and so I slowly rose
As upon angels' wings, effortlessly,
Upward—then suddenly I felt a shock!—
And then . . .
DE GUICHE. [*Overcome by curiosity, sits
    down on the bench.*] And then?
CYRANO.   And then—

[8] A fifteenth-century German philosopher who invented a flying machine shaped like an eagle.
[9] A Greek philosopher who invented a mechanical dove.
[10] A solid with twenty faces.
[11] Goddess of the moon.

[*Changes abruptly to his natural voice.*]
                    The time is up!—
Fifteen minutes, your Grace!—You are
now free;
And—they are bound—in wedlock.
DE GUICHE. [*Leaping up.*]   Am *I* drunk?
That voice . . .
    [*The door of* ROXANE'S *house opens;*
    lackeys appear, bearing lighted can-
    dles. Lights up. CYRANO *removes his*
    hat.]
                And that nose!—Cyrano!
CYRANO. [*Saluting.*]   Cyrano! . . .
This very moment, they have exchanged
rings.
DE GUICHE.   Who?
    [*He turns up stage.* TABLEAU: *between*
    the lackeys, ROXANE *and* CHRISTIAN
    appear, hand in hand. The CAPUCHIN
    follows them, smiling. RAGUENEAU
    holds aloft a torch. The DUENNA *brings*
    up the rear, in a negligée, and a pleas-
    ant flutter of emotion.]
                    Zounds!
    [*To* ROXANE.]   You?—
    [*Recognizes* CHRISTIAN.]   He?—
    [*Saluting* ROXANE.]   My sincere
compliments!
                        [*To* CYRANO.]
You also, my inventor of machines!
Your rigmarole would have detained a saint
Entering Paradise—decidedly
You must not fail to write that book some
day!
CYRANO. [*Bowing.*] Sir, I engage myself to
do so.[12]
THE CAPUCHIN. [*Leads the bridal pair*
    down to DE GUICHE *and strokes with*
    great satisfaction his long white beard.]
                        My lord,
The handsome couple you—and God—
have joined
Together!
DE GUICHE. [*Regarding him with a frosty*
    eye.]   Quite so. [*Turns to* ROXANE.]
                Madame, kindly bid

[12] Eventually he did, the *Comic History* referred to earlier, from which Rostand derived
some of the preceding material.

Your . . . husband farewell.
ROXANE.   Oh!—
DE GUICHE. [*To* CHRISTIAN.]
                    Your regiment
Leaves to-night, sir. Report at once!
ROXANE.   You mean
For the front? The war?
DE GUICHE.   Certainly!
ROXANE.   I thought
The Cadets were not going—
DE GUICHE.   Oh yes, they are!
    [*Taking out the despatch from his*
    pocket.]
Here is the order—
                    [*To* CHRISTIAN.]
                Baron! Deliver this.
ROXANE. [*Throws herself into* CHRISTIAN'S
    arms.] Christian!
DE GUICHE. [*To* CYRANO, *sneering.*]
            The bridal night is not so near!
CYRANO. [*Aside.*] Somehow that news
fails to disquiet me.
CHRISTIAN. [*To* ROXANE.] Your lips
again . . .
CYRANO.   There . . . That will do now—
Come!
CHRISTIAN. [*Still holding* ROXANE.]
You do not know how hard it is—
CYRANO. [*Tries to drag him away.*]
                        I know!
    [*The beating of drums is heard in the*
    distance.]
DE GUICHE. [*Up stage.*] The regiment—on
the march!
ROXANNE. [*As* CYRANO *tries to lead*
    CHRISTIAN *away, follows, and detains*
    them.]
                Take care of him
For me—   [*Appealingly.*]
            Promise me never to let him do
Anything dangerous!
CYRANO.   I'll do my best—
I cannot promise—
ROXANE. [*Same business.*]
                Make him be careful!
CYRANO.   Yes—
I'll try—
ROXANE. [*Same business.*]
    Be sure you keep him dry and warm!

CYRANO. Yes, yes—if possible—

ROXANE. [*Same business; confidentially, in his ear.*] See that he remains Faithful—

CYRANO. Of course! If—

ROXANE. [*Same business.*] And have him write to me Every single day!

CYRANO. [*Stops.*] That, I promise you!

[CURTAIN.]

THE FOURTH ACT

THE CADETS OF GASCOYNE

The Post occupied by the Company of CARBON DE CASTEL-JALOUX *at The Siege of Arras.*[1]

In the background, a Rampart traversing the entire scene; beyond this, and apparently below, a Plain stretches away to the horizon. The country is cut up with earthworks and other suggestions of the siege. In the distance against the sky-line, the houses and the walls of Arras.

Tents; scattered Weapons; Drums, etcetera. It is near day-break, and the East is yellow with approaching dawn. Sentries at intervals. Camp-fires.

Curtain Rise discovers the Cadets asleep, rolled in their cloaks. CARBON DE CASTEL-JALOUX *and* LE BRET *keep watch. They are both very thin and pale.* CHRISTIAN *is asleep among the others, wrapped in his cloak, in the foreground, his face lighted by the flickering fire. Silence.*

LE BRET. Horrible!

CARBON. Why, yes. All of that.

LE BRET. Mordious!

CARBON. [*Gesture toward the sleeping Cadets.*] Swear gently— You might wake them.

[*To Cadets.*] Go to sleep— Hush!

[*To* LE BRET.] Who sleeps dines.

LE BRET. I have insomnia. God! What a famine. [*Firing off stage.*]

CARBON. Curse that musketry! They'll wake my babies.

[*To the men.*] Go to sleep!—

A CADET. [*Rouses.*] Diantre! Again?

CARBON. No—only Cyrano coming home. [*The heads which have been raised sink back again.*]

A SENTRY. [*Off stage.*] Halt! Who goes there?

VOICE OF CYRANO. Bergerac!

THE SENTRY ON THE PARAPET. Halt! Who goes?—

CYRANO. [*Appears on the parapet.*] Bergerac, idiot!

LE BRET. [*Goes to meet him.*] Thank God again!

CYRANO. [*Signs to him not to wake anyone.*] Hush!

LE BRET. Wounded?—

CYRANO. No— They always miss me—quite A habit by this time!

LE BRET. Yes— Go right on— Risk your life every morning before breakfast To send a letter!

CYRANO. [*Stops near* CHRISTIAN.] I promised he should write Every single day . . .

[*Looks down at him.*] Hm— The boy looks pale When he is asleep—thin too—starving to death— If that poor child knew! Handsome, none the less . . .

LE BRET. Go and get some sleep!

CYRANO. [*Affectionately.*] Now, now—you old bear, No growling!—I am careful—you know I am— Every night, when I cross the Spanish lines I wait till they are all drunk.

LE BRET. You might bring Something with you.

---

[1] A city in northern France held by the Spanish and captured by the French in 1640.

CYRANO.   I have to travel light
To pass through— By the way, there will
be news
For you to-day; the French will eat or
die,
If what I saw means anything.

LE BRET.   Tell us!

CYRANO.   No—
I am not sure—we shall see!

CARBON.   What a war,
When the besiegers starve to death!

LE BRET.   Fine war—
Fine situation! We besiege Arras—
The Cardinal Prince of Spain besieges
us—
And—here we are!

CYRANO.   Someone might besiege him.

CARBON.   A hungry joke!

CYRANO.   Ho, ho!

LE BRET.   Yes, you can laugh—
Risking a life like yours to carry letters—
Where are you going now?

CYRANO.   [At the tent door.] To write another.   [Goes into tent.]
[A little more daylight. The clouds redden. The town of Arras shows on the
horizon. A cannon shot is heard, followed immediately by a roll of drums,
far away to the left. Other drums beat
a little nearer. The drums go on
answering each other here and there,
approach, beat loudly almost on the
stage, and die away toward the right,
across the camp. The camp awakes.
Voices of officers in the distance.]

CARBON.   [Sighs.] Those drums!—another
good nourishing sleep
Gone to the devil.
            [The CADETS rouse themselves.]
                    Now then!—

FIRST CADET.   [Sits up, yawns.]
                    God! I'm hungry!

SECOND CADET.   Starving!

ALL.   [Groan.]   Aoh!

CARBON.   Up with you!

THIRD CADET.   Not another step!

FOURTH CADET.   Not another movement!

FIRST CADET.   Look at my tongue—

I said this air was indigestible!

FIFTH CADET.   My coronet for half a pound
of cheese!

SIXTH CADET.   I have no stomach for this
war— I'll stay
In my tent—like Achilles.[2]

ANOTHER.   Yes—no bread,
No fighting—

CARBON.   Cyrano!

OTHER.   May as well die—

CARBON.   Come out here!—You know
how to talk to them.
Get them laughing—

SECOND CADET.   [Rushes up to FIRST CADET
who is eating something.]
            What are you gnawing there?

FIRST CADET.   Gun wads and axle-grease.
Fat country this
Around Arras.

ANOTHER.   [Enters.]
            I have been out hunting!

ANOTHER.   [Enters.]   I
Went fishing, in the Scarpe! [3]

ALL.   [Leaping up and surrounding the
newcomers.]   Find anything?
Any fish? Any game? Perch? Partridges?
Let me look!

THE FISHERMAN.   Yes—one gudgeon.
                    [Shows it.]

THE HUNTER.   One fat . . . sparrow.
                    [Shows it.]

ALL.   Ah!—See here, this—mutiny!—

CARBON.   Cyrano!
Come and help!

CYRANO.   [Enters from tent.] Well?
    [Silence. To the FIRST CADET who is
    walking away, with his chin on his
    chest.]
            You there, with the long face?

FIRST CADET.   I have something on my
mind that troubles me.

CYRANO.   What is that?

FIRST CADET.   My stomach.

CYRANO.   So have I.

FIRST CADET.   No doubt
You enjoy this!

CYRANO.   [Tightens his belt.]
            It keeps me looking young.

---

[2] The Greek warrior whose sulking in his tent
created a crisis during the Trojan War.

[3] A river adjacent to Arras.

SECOND CADET. My teeth are growing rusty.

CYRANO. Sharpen them!

THIRD CADET. My belly sounds as hollow as a drum.

CYRANO. Beat the long roll on it!

FOURTH CADET. My ears are ringing.

CYRANO. Liar! A hungry belly has no ears.

FIFTH CADET. Oh, for a barrel of good wine!

CYRANO. [Offers him his own helmet.] Your casque.

SIXTH CADET. I'll swallow anything!

CYRANO. [Throws him the book which he has in his hand.] Try the Iliad.

SEVENTH CADET. The Cardinal, he has four meals a day— What does he care!

CYRANO. Ask him; he really ought To send you . . . a spring lamb out of his flock, Roasted whole—

THE CADET. Yes, and a bottle—

CYRANO. [Exaggerates the manner of one speaking to a servant.] If you please, Richelieu—a little more of the Red Seal . . . Ah, thank you!

THE CADET. And the salad—

CYRANO. Of course—Romaine!

ANOTHER CADET. [Shivering.] I am as hungry as a wolf.

CYRANO. [Tosses him a cloak.] Put on Your sheep's clothing.

FIRST CADET. [With a shrug.] Always the clever answer.

CYRANO. Always the answer—yes! Let me die so— Under some rosy-golden sunset, saying A good thing, for a good cause! By the sword, The point of honor—by the hand of one Worthy to be my foeman, let me fall— Steel in my heart, and laughter on my lips!

VOICES HERE AND THERE. All very well— We are hungry!

CYRANO. Bah! You think Of nothing but yourselves.

[His eye singles out the old fifer in the background.]

Here, Bertrandou,

You were a shepherd once— Your pipe now! Come, Breathe, blow,—Play to these belly-worshippers The old airs of the South—

Airs with a smile in them,
Airs with a sigh in them, airs with the breeze
And the blue of the sky in them—

Small, demure tunes Whose every note is like a little sister— Songs heard only in some long silent voice Not quite forgotten— Mountain melodies Like thin smoke rising from brown cottages In the still noon, slowly— Quaint lullabies, Whose very music has a Southern tongue—

[The old man sits down and prepares his fife.]

Now let the fife, that dry old warrior, Dream, while over the stops your fingers dance A minuet of little birds—let him Dream beyond ebony and ivory; Let him remember he was once a reed Out of the river, and recall the spirit Of innocent, untroubled country days . . .

[The fifer begins to play a Provençal melody.]

Listen, you Gascons! Now it is no more The shrill fife— It is the flute, through woodlands far Away, calling—no longer the hot battle-cry, But the cool, quiet pipe our goatherds play! Listen—the forest glens . . . the hills . . . the downs . . . The green sweetness of night on the Dordogne [4] . . . Listen, you Gascons! It is all Gascoyne! . . .

[Every head is bowed; every eye cast down. Here and there a tear is furtively brushed away with the back of a hand, the corner of a cloak.]

CARBON. [Softly to CYRANO.] You make them weep—

CYRANO. For homesickness—a hunger More noble than that hunger of the flesh; It is their hearts now that are starving.

---

[4] A river of southern France flowing by the town of Bergerac.

CARBON.   Yes,
But you melt down their manhood.

CYRANO. [*Motions the drummer to approach.*]   You think so?
Let them be. There is iron in their blood
Not easily dissolved in tears. You need
Only—
      [*He makes a gesture; the drum beats.*]

ALL. [*Spring up and rush toward their weapons.*]
What's that? Where is it?— What?—

CYRANO. [*Smiles.*]   You see—
Let Mars snore in his sleep once—and farewell
Venus—sweet dreams—regrets—dear thoughts of home—
All the fife lulls to rest wakes at the drums!

A CADET. [*Looks up stage.*]
Aha— Monsieur de Guiche!

THE CADETS. [*Mutter among themselves.*]
                        Ugh! . . .

CYRANO. [*Smiles.*]   Flattering Murmur!

A CADET. He makes me weary!

ANOTHER.   With his collar
Of lace over his corselet—

ANOTHER.   Like a ribbon
Tied round a sword!

ANOTHER.   Bandages for a boil
On the back of his neck—

SECOND CADET.   A courtier always!

ANOTHER. The Cardinal's nephew!

CARBON.   None the less—a Gascon.

FIRST CADET. A counterfeit! Never you trust that man—
Because we Gascons, look you, are all mad—
This fellow is reasonable—nothing more
Dangerous than a reasonable Gascon!

LE BRET. He looks pale.

ANOTHER.   Oh, he can be hungry too,
Like any other poor devil—but he wears
So many jewels on that belt of his
That his cramps glitter in the sun!

CYRANO. [*Quickly.*]   Is he
To see us looking miserable? Quick—
Pipes!—Cards!—Dice!—
      [*They all hurriedly begin to play, on their stools, on the drums, or on their cloaks spread on the ground, lighting their long pipes meanwhile.*]
            As for me, I read Descartes.[5]
[*He walks up and down, reading a small book which he takes from his pocket.* TABLEAU: DE GUICHE *enters, looking pale and haggard. All are absorbed in their games. General air of contentment.* DE GUICHE *goes to* CARBON. *They look at each other askance, each observing with satisfaction the condition of the other.*]

DE GUICHE. Good morning!
[*Aside.*]   He looks yellow.

CARBON. [*Same business.*] He is all eyes.

DE GUICHE. [*Looks at the* CADETS.]
What have we here? Black looks? Yes, gentlemen—
I am informed I am not popular;
The hill-nobility, barons of Béarn,
The pomp and pride of Périgord—I learn
They disapprove their colonel; call him courtier,
Politician—they take it ill that I
Cover my steel with lace of Genoa.
It is a great offense to be a Gascon
And not to be a beggar!
      [*Silence. They smoke. They play.*]
                  Well— Shall I have
Your captain punish you? . . . No.

CARBON.   As to that,
It would be impossible.

DE GUICHE.   Oh?

CARBON.   I am free;
I pay my company; it is my own;
I obey military orders.

DE GUICHE.   Oh!
That will be quite enough.
      [*To the* CADETS.]   I can afford
Your little hates. My conduct under fire
Is well known. It was only yesterday
I drove the Count de Bucquoi from Bapaume,
Pouring my men down like an avalanche,
I myself led the charge—

CYRANO. [*Without looking up from his book.*]   And your white scarf?

DE GUICHE. [*Surprised and gratified.*]

[5] The great French philosopher, whose *Discourse on Method* was published in 1637.

You heard that episode? Yes—rallying
My men for the third time, I found myself
Carried among a crowd of fugitives
Into the enemy's lines. I was in danger
Of being shot or captured; but I thought
Quickly—took off and flung away the scarf
That marked my military rank—and so
Being inconspicuous, escaped among
My own force, rallied them, returned again
And won the day! . . .

[*The* CADETS *do not appear to be listening, but here and there the cards and
the dice boxes remain motionless, the
smoke is retained in their cheeks.*]

               What do you say to that?
Presence of mind—yes?

CYRANO.   Henry of Navarre [6]
Being outnumbered, never flung away
His white plume.

[*Silent enjoyment. The cards flutter, the
dice roll, the smoks puffs out.*]

DE GUICHE.   My device was a success,
However!

[*Same attentive pause, interrupting the
games and the smoking.*]

CYRANO.   Possibly . . . An officer
Does not lightly resign the privilege
Of being a target.

[*Cards, dice, and smoke fall, roll, and
float away with increasing satisfaction.*]

                Now, if I had been there—
Your courage and my own differ in this—
When your scarf fell, I should have put
    it on.

DE GUICHE.   Boasting again!

CYRANO.   Boasting? Lend it to me
To-night; I'll lead the first charge, with
    your scarf
Over my shoulder!

DE GUICHE.   Gasconnade once more!
You are safe making that offer, and you
    know it—
My scarf lies on the river bank between
The lines, a spot swept by artillery
Impossible to reach alive!

CYRANO. [*Produces the scarf from his
pocket.*]   Yes. Here . . .

[6] King of France, 1589–1610, who happened
to come from Béarn.

[*Silence. The* CADETS *stifle their laughter
behind their cards and their dice
boxes.* DE GUICHE *turns to look at
them. Immediately they resume their
gravity and their game. One of them
whistles carelessly the mountain air
which the fifer was playing.*]

DE GUICHE. [*Takes the scarf.*] Thank you!
That bit of white is what I need
To make a signal. I was hesitating—
You have decided me.

[*He goes up to the parapet, climbs upon
it, and waves the scarf at arm's length
several times.*]

ALL.   What is he doing?—
What?—

THE SENTRY ON THE PARAPET.   There's a
man down there running away!

DE GUICHE. [*Descending.*]
A Spaniard. Very useful as a spy
To both sides. He informs the enemy
As I instruct him. By his influence
I can arrange their dispositions.

CYRANO.   Traitor!

DE GUICHE. [*Folding the scarf.*]
A traitor, yes; but useful . . .
             We were saying? . . .
Oh, yes— Here is a bit of news for you:
Last night we had hopes of reprovisioning
The army. Under cover of the dark,
The Marshal moved to Dourlens. Our sup-
    plies
Are there. He may reach them. But to
    return
Safely, he needs a large force—at least half
Our entire strength. At present, we have
    here
Merely a skeleton.

CARBON.   Fortunately,
The Spaniards do not know that.

DE GUICHE.   Oh, yes; they know.
They will attack.

CARBON.   Ah!

DE GUICHE.   From that spy of mine
I learned of their intention. His report
Will determine the point of their advance.
The fellow asked me what to say! I told
    him:
"Go out between the lines; watch for my
    signal;

Where you see that, let them attack there."

CARBON. [*To the* CADETS.]   Well,
Gentlemen!

[*All rise. Noise of sword belts and breast-
     plates being buckled on.*]

DE GUICHE.   You may have perhaps an
hour.

FIRST CADET.   Oh— An hour!

[*They all sit down and resume their
     games once more.*]

DE GUICHE.   [*To* CARBON.]
          The great thing is to gain time.
Any moment the Marshal may return.

CARBON.   And to gain time?

DE GUICHE.   You will all be so kind
As to lay down your lives!

CYRANO.   Ah! Your revenge?

DE GUICHE.   I make no great pretense of
loving you!
But—since you gentlemen esteem your-
     selves
Invincible, the bravest of the brave,
And all that—why need we be personal?
I serve the king in choosing . . . as I
     choose!

CYRANO.   [*Salutes.*] Sir, permit me to offer
—all our thanks.

DE GUICHE.   [*Returns the salute.*]
You love to fight a hundred against one;
Here is your opportunity!

[*He goes up stage with* CARBON.]

CYRANO.   [*To the* CADETS.]   My friends,
We shall add now to our old Gascon arms
With their six chevrons, blue and gold, a
     seventh—
Blood-red!

[DE GUICHE *talks in a low tone to* CAR-
     BON *up stage. Orders are given. The
     defense is arranged.* CYRANO *goes to*
     CHRISTIAN, *who has remained motion-
     less with folded arms.*]
          Christian?

[*Lays a hand on his shoulder.*]

CHRISTIAN.   [*Shakes his head.*] Roxane . . .

CYRANO.   Yes.

CHRISTIAN.   I should like
To say farewell to her, with my whole heart
Written for her to keep.

CYRANO.   I thought of that—
[*Takes a letter from his doublet.*]

I have written your farewell.

CHRISTIAN.   Show me!

CYRANO.   You wish
To read it?

CHRISTIAN.   Of course!

[*He takes the letter; begins to read, looks
     up suddenly.*]
                                        What?—

CYRANO.   What is it?

CHRISTIAN.   Look—
This little circle—

CYRANO.   [*Takes back the letter quickly,
     and looks innocent.*] Circle?—

CHRISTIAN.   Yes—a tear!

CYRANO.   So it is! . . . Well—a poet while
he writes
Is like a lover in his lady's arms,
Believing his imagination—all
Seems true—you understand? There's half
     the charm
Of writing— Now, this letter as you see
I have made so pathetic that I wept
While I was writing it!

CHRISTIAN.   You—wept?

CYRANO.   Why, yes—
Because . . . it is a little thing to die,
But—not to see her . . . that is terrible!
And I shall never—
                              [CHRISTIAN *looks at him.*]
                              We shall never—
[*Quickly.*]   You
Will never—

CHRISTIAN.   [*Snatches the letter.*]
                    Give me that!

[*Noise in the distance on the outskirts
     of the camp.*]

VOICE OF A SENTRY.
                    Halt—who goes there?
     [*Shots, shouting, jingle of harness.*]

CARBON.   What is it?—

THE SENTRY ON THE PARAPET.
                    Why, a coach.
                    [*They rush to look.*]

CONFUSED VOICES.   What? In the Camp?
A coach? Coming this way— It must have
     driven
Through the Spanish lines—what the
     devil— Fire!—
No— Hark! The driver shouting—what
     does he say?

Wait— He said: "On the service of the King!"

[*They are all on the parapet looking over. The jingling comes nearer.*]

DE GUICHE.   Of the King?

[*They come down and fall into line.*]

CARBON.   Hats off, all!

DE GUICHE.   [*Speaks off stage.*]
                    The King! Fall in, Rascals!—

[*The coach enters at full trot. It is covered with mud and dust. The curtains are drawn. Two footmen are seated behind. It stops suddenly.*]

CARBON.   [*Shouts.*] Beat the assembly—

[*Roll of drums. All the* CADETS *uncover.*]

DE GUICHE.   Two of you
Lower the steps—open the door—

[*Two men rush to the coach. The door opens.*]

ROXANE.   [*Comes out of the coach.*]
                    Good morning!

[*At the sound of a woman's voice, every head is raised. Sensation.*]

DE GUICHE.   On the King's service— You?

ROXANE.   Yes—my own king—
Love!

CYRANO.   [*Aside.*] God is merciful . . .

CHRISTIAN.   [*Hastens to her.*]
                    You! Why have you—

ROXANE.   Your war lasted so long!

CHRISTIAN.   But why?—

ROXANE.   Not now—

CYRANO.   [*Aside.*] I wonder if I dare to look at her . . .

DE GUICHE.   You cannot remain here!

ROXANE.   Why, certainly!
Roll that drum here, somebody . . .

[*She sits on the drum, which is brought to her.*]
                    Thank you— There!
                    [*She laughs.*]
Would you believe—they fired upon us?
                    —My coach
Looks like the pumpkin in the fairy tale,
Does it not? And my footmen—

[*She throws a kiss to* CHRISTIAN.]
                    How do you do?
                    [*She looks about.*]
How serious you all are! Do you know,

It is a long drive here—from Arras?
[*Sees* CYRANO.]   Cousin,
I am glad to see you!

CYRANO.   [*Advances.*]
                    Oh— How did you come?

ROXANE.   How did I find you? Very easily—
I followed where the country was laid waste
—Oh, but I saw such things! I had to see
To believe. Gentlemen, is that the service
Of your King? I prefer my own!

CYRANO.   But how
Did you come through?

ROXANE.   Why, through the Spanish lines
Of course!

FIRST CADET.   They let you pass?—

DE GUICHE.   What did you say?
How did you manage?

LE BRET.   Yes, that must have been
Difficult!

ROXANE.   No— I simply drove along.
Now and then some hidalgo scowled at me
And I smiled back—my best smile; whereupon,
The Spaniards being (without prejudice
To the French) the most polished gentlemen
In the world—I passed!

CARBON.   Certainly that smile
Should be a passport! Did they never ask
Your errand or your destination?

ROXANE.   Oh,
Frequently! Then I drooped my eyes and said:
"I have a lover . . ." Whereupon, the Spaniard
With an air of ferocious dignity
Would close the carriage door—with such a gesture
As any king might envy, wave aside
The muskets that were levelled at my breast,
Fall back three paces, equally superb
In grace and gloom, draw himself up, thrust forth
A spur under his cloak, sweeping the air
With his long plumes, bow very low, and say:
"Pass, Señorita!"

CHRISTIAN.   But, Roxane—

ROXANE.   I know—
I said "a lover"—but you understand—
Forgive me!—If I said "I am going to meet
My husband," no one would believe me!
CHRISTIAN.   Yes,
But—
ROXANE. What then?
DE GUICHE. You must leave this place.
CYRANO.   At once.
ROXANE. I?
LE BRET. Yes—immediately.
ROXANE.   And why?
CHRISTIAN. [*Embarrassed.*] Because . . .
CYRANO. [*Same.*] In half an hour . . .
DE GUICHE. [*Same.*] Or three quarters . . .
CARBON. [*Same.*]   Perhaps
It might be better . . .
LE BRET.   If you . . .
ROXANE.   Oh— I see!
You are going to fight. I remain here.
ALL.   No—no!
ROXANE. He is my husband—
     [*Throws herself in* CHRISTIAN'S *arms.*]
                    I will die with you!
CHRISTIAN. Your eyes! . . . Why do you?—
ROXANE.   You know why . . .
DE GUICHE. [*Desperate.*]   This post
Is dangerous—
ROXANE. [*Turns.*] How—dangerous?
CYRANO.   The proof
Is, we are ordered—
ROXANE. [*To* DE GUICHE.]
              Oh—you wish to make
A widow of me?
DE GUICHE.   On my word of honor—
ROXANE. No matter. I am just a little
  mad—
I will stay. It may be amusing.
CYRANO.   What,
A heroine—our intellectual?
ROXANE. Monsieur de Bergerac, I am
  your cousin!
A CADET. We'll fight now! Hurrah!
ROXANE. [*More and more excited.*]
           I am safe with you—my friends!
ANOTHER. [*Carried away.*]
The whole camp breathes of lilies!—
ROXANE.   And I think,
This hat would look well on the battle-
field! . . .

But perhaps—   [*Looks at* DE GUICHE.]
           The Count ought to leave
  us. Any moment
Now, there may be danger.
DE GUICHE.   This is too much!
I must inspect my guns. I shall return—
You may change your mind— There will
  yet be time—
ROXANE. Never!
                    [DE GUICHE *goes out.*]
CHRISTIAN. [*Imploring.*] Roxane! . . .
ROXANE.   No!
FIRST CADET. [*To the rest.*] She stays here!
ALL. [*Rushing about, elbowing each other,
  brushing off their clothes.*]   A comb!—
Soap!—Here's a hole in my— A needle!—
Who
Has a ribbon?—Your mirror, quick!—My
  cuffs—
A razor—
ROXANE. [*To* CYRANO, *who is still urging
  her.*]   No! I shall not stir one step!
CARBON. [*Having, like the others, tight-
  ened his belt, dusted himself, brushed off
  his hat, smoothed out his plume and put
  on his lace cuffs, advances to* ROXANE
  ceremoniously.]
In that case, may I not present to you
Some of these gentlemen who are to have
The honor of dying in your presence?
ROXANE. [*Bows.*]   Please!—
  [*She waits, standing, on the arm of* CHRIS-
  TIAN, *while*
CARBON. [*—presents.*] Baron de Peyres-
  cous de Colignac!
THE CADET. [*Salutes.*] Madame . . .
ROXANE.   Monsieur . . .
CARBON. [*Continues.*] Baron de Casterac
De Cahuzac— Vidame de Malgouyre
Estressac Lésbas d'Escarabiot—
THE VIDAME. Madame . . .
CARBON.   Chevalier d'Antignac-Juzet—
Baron Hillot de Blagnac-Saléchan
De Castel-Crabioules—
THE BARON.   Madame . . .
ROXANE.   How many
Names you all have!
THE BARON. Hundreds!
CARBON. [*To* ROXANE.] Open the hand
That holds your handkerchief.

ROXANE. [*Opens her hand; the handkerchief falls.*] Why?
[*The whole company makes a movement toward it.*]

CARBON. [*Picks it up quickly.*]
My company
Was in want of a banner. We have now
The fairest in the army!

ROXANE. [*Smiling.*] Rather small—

CARBON. [*Fastens the handkerchief to his lance.*] Lace—and embroidered!

A CADET. [*To the others.*]
With her smiling on me,
I could die happy, if I only had
Something in my—

CARBON. [*Turns upon him.*]
Shame on you! Feast your eyes
And forget your—

ROXANE. [*Quickly.*] It must be this fresh air—
I am starving! Let me see . . .
Cold partridges,
Pastry, a little white wine—that would do.
Will someone bring that to me?

A CADET. [*Aside.*] Will someone!—

ANOTHER. Where the devil are we to find—

ROXANE. [*Overhears; sweetly.*]
Why, there—
In my carriage.

ALL. Wha-at?

ROXANE. All you have to do
Is to unpack, and carve, and serve things.
Oh,
Notice my coachman; you may recognize
An old friend.

THE CADETS. [*Rush to the coach.*]
Ragueneau!

ROXANE. [*Follows them with her eyes.*]
Poor fellows . . .

THE CADETS. [*Acclamations.*] Ah!
Ah!

CYRANO. [*Kisses her hand.*]
Our good fairy!

RAGUENEAU. [*Standing on his box, like a mountebank before a crowd.*]
Gentlemen!—
[*Enthusiasm.*]

THE CADETS. Bravo!
Bravo!

RAGUENEAU. The Spaniards, basking in our smiles,
Smiled on our baskets!
[*Applause.*]

CYRANO. [*Aside to* CHRISTIAN.]
Christian!—

RAGUENEAU. They adored
The Fair, and missed—
[*He takes from under the seat a dish, which he holds aloft.*]
the Fowl!
[*Applause. The dish is passed from hand to hand.*]

CYRANO. [*As before, to* CHRISTIAN.]
One moment—

RAGUENEAU. Venus
Charmed their eyes while Adonis quietly
[*Brandishing a ham.*]
Brought home the Boar! [7]
[*Applause; the ham is seized by a score of hands outstretched.*]

CYRANO. [*As before.*]
Pst— Let me speak to you—

ROXANE. [*As the* CADETS *return, their arms full of provisions.*]
Spread them out on the ground. [*Calls.*]
Christian! Come here;
Make yourself useful.
[CHRISTIAN *turns to her, at the moment when* CYRANO *was leading him aside. She arranges the food, with his aid and that of the two imperturbable footmen.*]

RAGUENEAU. Peacock, *aux truffes!*

FIRST CADET. [*Comes down, cutting a huge slice of the ham.*] Tonnerre!
We are not going to die without a gorge—
[*Sees* ROXANE; *corrects himself hastily.*]
Pardon—a banquet!

RAGUENEAU. [*Tossing out the cushions of the carriage.*] Open these—they are full
Of ortolans!
[*Tumult; laughter; the cushions are eviscerated.*]

THIRD CADET. Lucullus! [8]

---

[7] Adonis, beloved of Venus, was killed by a boar.

[8] A famous Roman epicure noted for luxurious living.

RAGUENEAU. [*Throws out bottles of red wine.*] Flasks of ruby—
[*And of white.*]
Flasks of topaz—
ROXANE. [*Throws a tablecloth at the head of* CYRANO.]
Come back out of your dreams!
Unfold this cloth—
RAGUENEAU. [*Takes off one of the lanterns of the carriage, and flourishes it.*]
Our lamps are bonbonnières!
CYRANO. [*To* CHRISTIAN.] I must see you before you speak with her—
RAGUENEAU. [*More and more lyrical.*]
My whip-handle is one long sausage!
ROXANE. [*Pouring wine; passing the food.*]
We
Being about to die, first let us dine!
Never mind the others—all for Gascoyne!
And if de Guiche comes, he is not invited!
[*Going from one to another.*]
Plenty of time—you need not eat so fast—
Hold your cup—
[*To another.*]
What's the matter?
THE CADET. [*Sobbing.*] You are so good
To us . . .
ROXANE. There, there! Red or white wine?
—Some bread
For Monsieur de Carbon!—Napkins— A knife—
Pass your plate— Some of the crust? A little more—
Light or dark?—Burgundy?—
CYRANO. [*Follows her with an armful of dishes, helping to serve.*] Adorable!
ROXANE. [*Goes to* CHRISTIAN.]
What would you like?
CHRISTIAN. Nothing.
ROXANE. Oh, but you must!—
A little wine? A biscuit?
CHRISTIAN. Tell me first
Why you came—
ROXANE. By and by. I must take care
Of these poor boys—
LE BRET. [*Who has gone up stage to pass up food to the sentry on the parapet, on the end of a lance.*] De Guiche!
CYRANO. Hide everything

Quick!—Dishes, bottles, tablecloth—
Now look
Hungry again— [*To* RAGUENEAU.]
You there! Up on your box—
—Everything out of sight?—
[*In a twinkling, everything has been pushed inside the tents, hidden in their hats or under their cloaks.* DE GUICHE *enters quickly, then stops, sniffing the air. Silence.*]
DE GUICHE. It smells good here.
A CADET. [*Humming with an air of great unconcern.*]
Sing ha-ha-ha and ho-ho-ho—
DE GUICHE. [*Stares at him; he grows embarrassed.*] You there—
What are you blushing for?
THE CADET. Nothing—my blood
Stirs at the thought of battle.
ANOTHER. *Pom . . . pom . . . pom!* . . .
DE GUICHE. [*Turns upon him.*]
What is that?
THE CADET. [*Slightly stimulated.*]
Only song—only little song—
DE GUICHE. You appear happy!
THE CADET. Oh, yes—always happy
Before a fight—
DE GUICHE. [*Calls to* CARBON, *for the purpose of giving him an order.*]
Captain! I—
[*Stops and looks at him.*]
What the devil—
You are looking happy too!—
CARBON. [*Pulls a long face and hides a bottle behind his back.*] No!
DE GUICHE. Here—I had
One gun remaining. I have had it placed
[*He points off stage.*]
There—in that corner—for your men.
A CADET. [*Simpering.*] So kind!—
Charming attention!
ANOTHER. [*Same business; burlesque.*]
Sweet solicitude!—
DE GUICHE. [*Contemptuous.*]
I believe you are both drunk—
[*Coldly.*]
Being unaccustomed
To guns—take care of the recoil!
FIRST CADET. [*Gesture.*] Ah-h . . . Pfft!
DE GUICHE. [*Goes up to him, furious.*]

How dare you?

FIRST CADET. A Gascon's gun never re-coils!

DE GUICHE. [Shakes him by the arm.]
You *are* drunk—

FIRST CADET. [Superbly.]
     With the smell of powder!

DE GUICHE. [Turns away with a shrug.]
     Bah! [To ROXANE.]
Madame, have you decided?

ROXANE.   I stay here.

DE GUICHE. You have time to escape—

ROXANE.   No!

DE GUICHE.   Very well—
Someone give me a musket!

CARBON.   What!

DE GUICHE.   *I* stay
Here also.

CYRANO. [Formally.]
     Sir, you show courage!

FIRST CADET.   A Gascon
In spite of all that lace!

ROXANE.   Why—

DE GUICHE.   Must I run
Away, and leave a woman?

SECOND CADET. [To FIRST CADET.]
     We might give him
Something to eat—what do you say?

[All the food reappears, as if by magic.]

DE GUICHE. [His face lights up.] A feast!

THIRD CADET. Here a little, there a little—

DE GUICHE. [Recovers his self-control;
haughtily.]   Do you think
I want your leavings?

CYRANO. [Saluting.]
     Colonel—you improve!

DE GUICHE. I can fight as I am!

FIRST CADET. [Delighted.] Listen to him—
He has an accent!

DE GUICHE. [Laughs.] Have I so?

FIRST CADET.   A Gascon!—
A Gascon, after all.
     [They all begin to dance.]

CARBON. [Who has disappeared for a moment behind the parapet, reappears on top of it.] I have placed my pikemen
Here.

[Indicates a row of pikes showing above the parapet.]

DE GUICHE. [Bows to ROXANE.]
We'll review them; will you take my arm?
     [She takes his arm; they go up on the parapet. The rest uncover, and follow them up stage.]

CHRISTIAN. [Goes hurriedly to CYRANO.]
Speak quickly!
     [At the moment when ROXANE appears on the parapet the pikes are lowered in salute, and a cheer is heard. She bows.]

THE PIKEMEN. [Off stage.] Hurrah!

CHRISTIAN.   What is it?

CYRANO.   If Roxane . . .

CHRISTIAN. Well?

CYRANO. Speaks about your letters . . .

CHRISTIAN.   Yes—I know!

CYRANO. Do not make the mistake of showing . . .

CHRISTIAN.   What?

CYRANO. Showing surprise.

CHRISTIAN. Surprise—why?

CYRANO.   I must tell you! . . .
It is quite simple—I had forgotten it
Until just now. You have . . .

CHRISTIAN.   Speak quickly!

CYRANO.   You
Have written oftener than you think.

CHRISTIAN.   Oh—have I!

CYRANO. I took upon me to interpret you;
And wrote—sometimes . . . without . . .

CHRISTIAN.   My knowing. Well?

CYRANO. Perfectly simple!

CHRISTIAN.   Oh, yes, perfectly!—
For a month, we have been blockaded here!—
How did you send all these letters?

CYRANO.   Before
Daylight, I managed—

CHRISTIAN.   I see. That was also
Perfectly simple!
     —So I wrote to her,
How many times a week? Twice? Three times? Four?

CYRANO. Oftener.

CHRISTIAN.   Every day?

CYRANO.   Yes,—every day . . .
Every single day . . .

CHRISTIAN. [Violently.]
     And that wrought you up
Into such a flame that you faced death—

CYRANO. [*Sees* ROXANE *returning.*] Hush—
Not before her!

[*He goes quickly into the tent.* ROXANE
comes up to CHRISTIAN.]

ROXANE.   Now—Christian!

CHRISTIAN. [*Takes her hands.*] Tell me now
Why you came here—over these ruined
  roads—
Why you made your way among moss-
  troopers
And ruffians—you—to join me here?

ROXANE.   Because—
Your letters . . .

CHRISTIAN.   Meaning?

ROXANE.   It was your own fault
If I ran into danger! I went mad—
Mad with you! Think what you have writ-
  ten me,
How many times, each one more wonderful
Than the last!

CHRISTIAN.   All this for a few absurd
Love-letters—

ROXANE. Hush—absurd! How can you
  know?
I thought I loved you, ever since one night
When a voice that I never would have
  known
Under my window breathed your soul to
  me . . .
But—all this time, your letters—every one
Was like hearing your voice there in the
  dark,
All around me, like your arms around
  me . . .   [*More lightly.*]
                          At last,
I came. Anyone would! Do you suppose
The prim Penelope had stayed at home
Embroidering,—if Ulysses wrote like you?
She would have fallen like another Helen—
Tucked up those linen petticoats of hers
And followed him to Troy!

CHRISTIAN.   But you—

ROXANE.   I read them
Over and over. I grew faint reading them.
I belonged to you. Every page of them
Was like a petal fallen from your soul—
Like the light and the fire of a great love,
Sweet and strong and true—

CHRISTIAN.   Sweet . . . and
  strong . . . and true . . .

You felt that, Roxane?—

ROXANE.   You know how I feel! . . .

CHRISTIAN. So you came . . .

ROXANE. Oh, my Christian, oh my king,—
Lift me up if I fall upon my knees—
It is the heart of me that kneels to you,
And will remain forever at your feet—
You cannot lift that!—

                I came here to say
'Forgive me'—(It is time to be forgiven
Now, when we may die presently)—forgive
  me
For being light and vain and loving you
Only because you were beautiful.

CHRISTIAN. [*Astonished.*]   Roxane! . . .

ROXANE. Afterwards I knew better. Afterwards
(I had to learn to use my wings) I loved
  you
For yourself too—knowing you more, and
  loving
More of you. And now—

CHRISTIAN.   Now? . . .

ROXANE.   It is yourself
I love now: your own self.

CHRISTIAN. [*Taken aback.*] Roxane!

ROXANE. [*Gravely.*]   Be happy!—
You must have suffered; for you must have
  seen
How frivolous I was; and to be loved
For the mere costume, the poor casual body
You went about in—to a soul like yours,
That must have been torture! Therefore
  with words
You revealed your heart. Now that image
  of you
Which filled my eyes first—I see better
  now,
And I see it no more!

CHRISTIAN.   Oh!—

ROXANE.   You still doubt
Your victory?

CHRISTIAN. [*Miserably.*] Roxane!—

ROXANE.   I understand:
You cannot perfectly believe in me—
A love like this—

CHRISTIAN.   I want no love like this!
I want love only for—

ROXANE.   Only for what
Every woman sees in you? I can do

Better than that!

CHRISTIAN. No— it was best before!

ROXANE. You do not altogether know
me . . . Dear,

There is more of me than there was—with
this,

I can love more of you—more of what
makes

You your own self—Truly! . . . If you
were less

Lovable—

CHRISTIAN. No!

ROXANE. —Less charming—ugly even—
I should love you still.

CHRISTIAN. You mean that?

ROXANE. I do
Mean that!

CHRISTIAN. Ugly? . . .

ROXANE. Yes. Even then!

CHRISTIAN. [*Agonized.*] Oh . . . God! . . .

ROXANE. Now are you happy?

CHRISTIAN. [*Choking.*] Yes . . .

ROXANE. What is it?

CHRISTIAN. [*Pushes her away gently.*]
Only . . .

Nothing . . . one moment . . .

ROXANE. But—

CHRISTIAN. [*Gesture toward* THE CADETS.]
I am keeping you

From those poor fellows— Go and smile
at them;

They are going to die!

ROXANE. [*Softly.*] Dear Christian!

CHRISTIAN. Go—

[*She goes up among the Gascons, who
gather round her respectfully.*]

Cyrano!

CYRANO. [*Comes out of the tent, armed for
the battle.*] What is wrong? You look—

CHRISTIAN. She does not
Love me any more.

CYRANO. [*Smiles.*] You think not?

CHRISTIAN. She loves
You.

CYRANO. No!—

CHRISTIAN. [*Bitterly.*]
She loves only my soul.

CYRANO. No!

CHRISTIAN. Yes—
That means you. And you love her.

CYRANO. I?

CHRISTIAN. I see—
I know!

CYRANO. That is true . . .

CHRISTIAN. More than—

CYRANO. [*Quietly.*] More than that.

CHRISTIAN. Tell her so!

CYRANO. No.

CHRISTIAN. Why not?

CYRANO. Why—look at me!

CHRISTIAN. She would love me if I were
ugly.

CYRANO. [*Startled.*] She—
Said that?

CHRISTIAN. Yes. Now then!

CYRANO. [*Half to himself.*]
It was good of her

To tell you that . . .

[*Change of tone.*]
Nonsense! Do not believe

Any such madness—
It was good of her

To tell you . . .
Do not take her at her word!

Go on—you never will be ugly— Go!

She would never forgive me.

CHRISTIAN. That is what
We shall see.

CYRANO. No, no—

CHRISTIAN. Let her choose between us!—
Tell her everything!

CYRANO. No—you torture me—

CHRISTIAN. Shall I ruin your happiness,
because

I have a cursed pretty face? That seems
Too unfair!

CYRANO. And am I to ruin yours
Because I happen to be born with power

To say what you—perhaps—feel?

CHRISTIAN. Tell her!

CYRANO. Man—
Do not try me too far!

CHRISTIAN. I am tired of being
My own rival!

CYRANO. Christian!—

CHRISTIAN. Our secret marriage—
No witnesses—fraudulent—that can be
Annulled—

CYRANO. Do not try me—

CHRISTIAN. I want her love

For the poor fool I am—or not at all!
Oh, I am going through with this! I'll know,
One way or the other. Now I shall walk
  down
To the end of the post. Go tell her. Let her
  choose
One of us.

CYRANO.   It will be you.

CHRISTIAN.   God—I hope so!
        [He turns and calls.]
Roxane!

CYRANO.   No—no—

ROXANE.   *[Hurries down to him.]*
                Yes, Christian?

CHRISTIAN.   Cyrano
Has news for you—important.
        [She turns to CYRANO. CHRISTIAN *goes
        out.]*

ROXANE.   *[Lightly.]*   Oh—important?

CYRANO.   He is gone . . .
                        [To ROXANE.*]*
        Nothing—only Christian thinks
You ought to know—

ROXANE.   I do know. He still doubts
What I told him just now. I saw that.

CYRANO.   *[Takes her hand.]*   Was it
True—what you told him just now?

ROXANE.   It was true!
I said that I should love him even . . .

CYRANO.   *[Smiling sadly.]*   The word
Comes hard—before me?

ROXANE.   Even if he were . . .

CYRANO.   Say it—
I shall not be hurt!—Ugly?

ROXANE.   Even then
I should love him.

        *[A few shots, off stage, in the direction
        in which* CHRISTIAN *disappeared.]*
                Hark! The guns—

CYRANO.   Hideous?

ROXANE.   Hideous.

CYRANO.   Disfigured?

ROXANE.   Or disfigured.

CYRANO.   Even
Grotesque?

ROXANE.   How could he ever be grotesque—
Ever—to me!

CYRANO.   But you could love him so,
As much as?—

ROXANE.   Yes—and more!

CYRANO.   *[Aside, excitedly.]*
                It is true—true!—
Perhaps—God! This is too much happi-
  ness . . .
                [To ROXANE.*]*
I—Roxane—listen—

LE BRET.   *[Enters quickly; calls to* CYRANO
        in a low tone.]   Cyrano—

CYRANO.   *[Turns.]*   Yes?

LE BRET.   Hush! . . .
        [Whispers a few words to him.]

CYRANO.   *[Lets fall* ROXANE'S *hand.]* Ah!

ROXANE.   What is it?

CYRANO.   *[Half stunned, and aside.]*
                All gone . . .

ROXANE.   *[More shots.]*   What is it? Oh,
They are fighting!—
        [She goes up to look off stage.]

CYRANO.   All gone. I cannot ever
Tell her, now . . . ever . . .

ROXANE.   *[Starts to rush away.]*
                What has happened?

CYRANO.   *[Restrains her.]*   Nothing.
        [Several CADETS *enter. They conceal
        something which they are carrying,
        and form a group so as to prevent*
        ROXANE *from seeing their burden.]*

ROXANE.   These men—

CYRANO.   Come away . . .
        [He leads her away from the group.]

ROXANE.   You were telling me
Something—

CYRANO.   Oh, that? Nothing . . .
                        [Gravely.]
                        I swear to you
That the spirit of Christian—that his soul
Was—   *[Corrects himself quickly.]*
        That his soul is no less great—

ROXANE.   *[Catches at the word.]* Was?
                        [Crying out.]
                                Oh!—
        *[She rushes among the men, and scatters
        them.]*

CYRANO.   All gone . . .

ROXANE.   *[Sees* CHRISTIAN *lying upon his
        cloak.]*   Christian!

LE BRET.   *[To* CYRANO.*]* At the first volley.
        *[*ROXANE *throws herself upon the body of*
        CHRISTIAN. *Shots; at first scattered,
        then increasing. Drums. Voices shout-
        ing.]*

CARBON. [*Sword in hand.*] Here They come!—Ready!—

[*Followed by the* CADETS, *he climbs over the parapet and disappears.*]

ROXANE. Christian!

CARBON. [*Off stage.*] Come on, there, you!

ROXANE. Christian!

CARBON. Fall in!

ROXANE. Christian!

CARBON. *Measure your fuse!*

[RAGUENEAU *hurries up, carrying a helmet full of water.*]

CHRISTIAN. [*Faintly.*] Roxane! . . .

CYRANO. [*Low and quick, in* CHRISTIAN'S *ear, while* ROXANE *is dipping into the water a strip of linen torn from her dress.*] I have told her; she loves you.

[CHRISTIAN *closes his eyes.*]

ROXANE. [*Turns to* CHRISTIAN.] Yes, My darling?

CARBON. *Draw your ramrods!*

ROXANE. [*To* CYRANO.] He is not dead? . . .

CARBON. *Open your charges!*

ROXANE. I can feel his cheek Growing cold against mine—

CARBON. *Take aim!*

ROXANE. A letter— Over his heart—

[*She opens it.*] For me.

CYRANO. [*Aside.*] My letter . . .

CARBON. *Fire!*

[*Musketry, cries and groans. Din of battle.*]

CYRANO. [*Trying to withdraw his hand, which* ROXANE, *still upon her knees, is holding.*]

But, Roxane—they are fighting—

ROXANE. Wait a little . . . He is dead. No one else knew him but you . . . [*She weeps quietly.*] Was he not a great lover, a great man, A hero?

CYRANO. [*Standing, bareheaded.*] Yes, Roxane.

ROXANE. A poet, unknown, Adorable?

CYRANO. Yes, Roxane.

ROXANE. A fine mind?

CYRANO. Yes, Roxane.

ROXANE. A heart deeper than we knew— A soul magnificently tender?

CYRANO. [*Firmly.*] Yes, Roxane!

ROXANE. [*Sinks down upon the breast of* CHRISTIAN.] He is dead now . . .

CYRANO. [*Aside; draws his sword.*] Why, so am I— For I am dead, and my love mourns for me And does not know . . .

[*Trumpets in distance.*]

DE GUICHE. [*Appears on the parapet, disheveled, wounded on the forehead, shouting.*] The signal—hark—the trumpets! The army has returned— Hold them now! —Hold them! The army!—

ROXANE. On his letter—blood . . . and tears.

A VOICE. [*Off stage.*] Surrender!

THE CADETS. No!

RAGUENEAU. This place is dangerous!—

CYRANO. [*To* DE GUICHE.] Take her away—I am going—

ROXANE. [*Kisses the letter; faintly.*] His blood . . . his tears . . .

RAGUENEAU. [*Leaps down from the coach and runs to her.*] She has fainted—

DE GUICHE. [*On the parapet; savagely, to the* CADETS.] Hold them!

VOICE OFF STAGE. Lay down your arms!

VOICES. No! No!

CYRANO. [*To* DE GUICHE.] Sir, you have proved yourself— Take care of her.

DE GUICHE. [*Hurries to* ROXANE *and takes her up in his arms.*] As you will—we can win, if you hold on A little longer—

CYRANO. Good!

[*Calls out to* ROXANE, *as she is carried away, fainting, by* DE GUICHE *and* RAGUENEAU.] Adieu, Roxane!

[*Tumult, outcries. Several* CADETS *come back wounded and fall on the stage.* CYRANO, *rushing to the fight, is stopped on the crest of the parapet by* CARBON, *covered with blood.*]

CARBON. We are breaking—I am twice
wounded—
CYRANO. [*Shouts to the Gascons.*] *Hardi!
Reculez pas, Drollos!* [9]
[*To* CARBON, *holding him up.*]
So—never fear!
I have two deaths to avenge now—Chris-
tian's
And my own!
[*They come down.* CYRANO *takes from
him the lance with* ROXANE'S *hand-
kerchief still fastened to it.*]
Float, little banner, with her name!
[*He plants it on the parapet; then shouts
to the* CADETS.]
Toumbé dessus! Escrasas lous! [10]
[*To the fifer.*]
Your fife!
Music!
[*Fife plays. The wounded drag them-
selves to their feet. Other* CADETS
*scramble over the parapet and group
themselves around* CYRANO *and his
tiny flag. The coach is filled and
covered with men, bristling with
muskets, transformed into a re-
doubt.*]

A CADET. [*Reels backward over the wall,
still fighting, shouts.*]
They are climbing over!—
[*And falls dead.*]
CYRANO.   Very good—
Let them come!— A salute now—
[*The parapet is crowned for an instant
with a rank of enemies. The imperial
banner of Spain is raised aloft.*]
Fire!
[*General volley.*]
VOICE. [*Among the ranks of the enemy.*]
Fire!
[*Murderous counter-fire; the* CADETS *fall
on every side.*]
A SPANISH OFFICER. [*Uncovers.*] Who are
these men who are so fond of death?
CYRANO. [*Erect amid the hail of bullets,
declaims.*]
The Cadets of Gascoyne, the defenders
Of Carbon de Castel-Jaloux—
Free fighters, free lovers, free spenders—
[*He rushes forward, followed by a few
survivors.*]
The Cadets of Gascoyne . . .
[*The rest is lost in the din of battle.*]
[CURTAIN]

THE FIFTH ACT

CYRANO'S GAZETTE

*Fifteen years later, in 1655. The Park
of the Convent occupied by the Ladies of
the Cross, at Paris.*

*Magnificent foliage. To the Left, the
House upon a broad Terrace at the head
of a flight of steps, with several Doors
opening upon the Terrace. In the centre
of the scene an enormous Tree alone in
the centre of a little open space. Toward
the Right, in the foreground, among Box-
wood Bushes, a semicircular Bench of
stone.*

*All the way across the Background of
the scene, an Avenue overarched by the
chestnut trees, leading to the door of a
Chapel on the Right, just visible among the
branches of the trees. Beyond the double*
*curtain of the trees, we catch a glimpse of
bright lawns and shaded walks, masses of
shrubbery; the perspective of the Park; the
sky.*

*A little side door of the Chapel opens
upon a Colonnade, garlanded with Autumnal vines, and disappearing on the
Right behind the box-trees.*

*It is late October. Above the still living
green of the turf all the foliage is red and
yellow and brown. The evergreen masses
of Box and Yew stand out darkly against
this Autumnal coloring. A heap of dead
leaves under every tree. The leaves are
falling everywhere. They rustle underfoot
along the walks; the Terrace and the Bench
are half covered with them.*

[9] Go to it! No yielding, you rogues!

[10] Roll over them! Smear them!

Before the Bench on the Right, on the side toward the Tree, is placed a tall embroidery frame and beside it a little Chair. Baskets filled with skeins of many-colored silks and balls of wool. Tapestry unfinished on the Frame.

At the Curtain Rise the nuns are coming and going across the Park; several of them are seated on the Bench around MOTHER MARGUÉRITE DE JÉSUS. *The leaves are falling.*

SISTER MARTHE [*To* MOTHER MARGUÉRITE.]
Sister Claire has been looking in the glass
At her new cap; twice!

MOTHER MARGUÉRITE. [*To* SISTER CLAIRE.]
              It is very plain;
Very.

SISTER CLAIRE. And Sister Marthe stole a plum
Out of the tart this morning!

MOTHER MARGUÉRITE. [*To* SISTER MARTHE.]
              That was wrong;
Very wrong.

SISTER CLAIRE. Oh, but such a little look!

SISTER MARTHE. Such a little plum!

MOTHER MARGUÉRITE. [*Severely.*]
              I shall tell Monsieur
De Cyrano, this evening.

SISTER CLAIRE.   No! Oh no!—
He will make fun of us.

SISTER MARTHE.   He will say nuns
Are so gay!

SISTER CLAIRE. And so greedy!

MOTHER MARGUÉRITE. [*Smiling.*]
              And so good . . .

SISTER CLAIRE. It must be ten years, Mother Marguérite,
That he has come here every Saturday, Is it not?

MOTHER MARGUÉRITE.
        More than ten years; ever since
His cousin came to live among us here—
Her worldly weeds among our linen veils,
Her widowhood and our virginity—
Like a black dove among white doves.

SISTER MARTHE.   No one
Else ever turns that happy sorrow of hers
Into a smile.

ALL THE NUNS.
      He is such fun!—He makes us
Almost laugh!—And he teases everyone—
And pleases everyone— And we all love him—
And he likes our cake, too—

SISTER MARTHE.   I am afraid
He is not a good Catholic.

SISTER CLAIRE.   Some day
We shall convert him.

THE NUNS.   Yes—yes!

MOTHER MARGUÉRITE.   Let him be;
I forbid you to worry him. Perhaps
He might stop coming here.

SISTER MARTHE. But . . . God?

MOTHER MARGUÉRITE.   You need not
Be afraid. God knows all about him.

SISTER MARTHE.   Yes . . .
But every Saturday he says to me,
Just as if he were proud of it: "Well, Sister,
I ate meat yesterday!"

MOTHER MARGUÉRITE. He tells you so?
The last time he said that, he had not eaten
Anything for two days.

SISTER MARTHE. Mother!—

MOTHER MARGUÉRITE.   He is poor;
Very poor.

SISTER MARTHE. Who said so?

MOTHER MARGUÉRITE. Monsieur Le Bret.

SISTER MARTHE. Why does not someone help him?

MOTHER MARGUÉRITE.   He would be
Angry; very angry . . .

[*Between the trees up stage,* ROXANE *appears, all in black, with a widow's cap and long veils.* DE GUICHE, *magnificently grown old, walks beside her. They move slowly.* MOTHER MARGUÉRITE *rises.*]
             Let us go in—
Madame Madeleine has a visitor.

SISTER MARTHE. [*To* SISTER CLAIRE.]
The Duc de Grammont, is it not? The Marshal?

SISTER CLAIRE. [*Looks toward* DE GUICHE.]
I think so—yes.

SISTER MARTHE. He has not been to see her
For months—

THE NUNS. He is busy—the Court!—The Camp!—

SISTER CLAIRE. The world . . .

[*They go out.* DE GUICHE *and* ROXANE *come down in silence, and stop near the embroidery frame. Pause.*]

DE GUICHE. And you remain here, wasting all that gold—
For ever in mourning?

ROXANE. For ever.

DE GUICHE. And still faithful?

ROXANE. And still faithful . . .

DE GUICHE. [*After a pause.*]
Have you forgiven me?

ROXANE. [*Simply, looking up at the cross of the Convent.*]
I am here. [*Another pause.*]

DE GUICHE. Was Christian . . . all that?

ROXANE. If you knew him.

DE GUICHE. Ah? We were not precisely . . . intimate . . .
And his last letter—always at your heart?

ROXANE. It hangs here, like a holy reliquary.

DE GUICHE. Dead—and you love him still!

ROXANE. Sometimes I think
He has not altogether died; our hearts
Meet, and his love flows all around me, living.

DE GUICHE. [*After another pause.*]
You see Cyrano often?

ROXANE. Every week.
My old friend takes the place of my Gazette,
Brings me all the news. Every Saturday,
Under that tree where you are now, his chair
Stands, if the day be fine. I wait for him,
Embroidering; the hour strikes; then I hear,
(I need not turn to look!) at the last stroke,
His cane tapping the steps. He laughs at me
For my eternal needlework. He tells
The story of the past week—
[LE BRET *appears on the steps.*]
There's Le Bret!—
[LE BRET *approaches.*]
How is it with our friend?

LE BRET. Badly.

DE GUICHE. Indeed?

ROXANE. [*To* DE GUICHE.]

Oh, he exaggerates!

LE BRET. Just as I said—
Loneliness, misery—I told him so!—
His satires make a host of enemies—
He attacks the false nobles, the false saints,
The false heroes, the false artists—in short,
Everyone!

ROXANE. But they fear that sword of his—
No one dare touch him!

DE GUICHE. [*With a shrug.*]
H'm—that may be so.

LE BRET. It is not violence I fear for him,
But solitude—poverty—old gray December,
Stealing on wolf's feet, with a wolf's green eyes,
Into his darkening room. Those bravoes yet
May strike our Swordsman down! Every day now,
He draws his belt up one hole; his poor nose
Looks like old ivory; he has one coat
Left—his old black serge.

DE GUICHE. That is nothing strange
In this world! No, you need not pity him
Overmuch.

LE BRET. [*With a bitter smile.*]
My lord Marshal! . . .

DE GUICHE. I say, do not
Pity him overmuch. He lives his life,
His own life, his own way—thought, word, and deed
Free!

LE BRET. [*As before.*] My lord Duke! . . .

DE GUICHE. [*Haughtily.*]
Yes, I know—I have all;
He has nothing. Nevertheless, to-day
I should be proud to shake his hand . . .
[*Saluting* ROXANE.]
Adieu.

ROXANE. I will go with you.

[DE GUICHE *salutes* LE BRET, *and turns with* ROXANE *toward the steps.*]

DE GUICHE. [*Pauses on the steps, as she climbs.*] Yes—I envy him
Now and then . . .
Do you know, when a man wins
Everything in this world, when he succeeds
Too much—he feels, having done nothing wrong

Especially, Heaven knows!—he feels some-
how
A thousand small displeasures with himself,
Whose whole sum is not quite Remorse,
but rather
A sort of vague disgust . . . The ducal robes
Mounting up, step by step, to pride and
power,
Somewhere among their folds draw after
them
A rustle of dry illusions, vain regrets
As your veil, up the stairs here, draws
along
The whisper of dead leaves.

ROXANE. [*Ironical.*] The sentiment
Does you honor.

DE GUICHE. Oh, yes . . .

[*Pausing suddenly.*]
Monsieur Le Bret!—
[*To* ROXANE.]
You pardon us?—

[*He goes to* LE BRET, *and speaks in a low
tone.*]
One moment— It is true
That no one dares attack your friend. Some
people
Dislike him, none the less. The other day
At Court, such a one said to me: "This
man
Cyrano may die—accidentally."

LE BRET. [*Coldly.*] Thank you.

DE GUICHE. You may thank me.
Keep him at home
All you can. Tell him to be careful.

LE BRET. [*Shaking his hands to heaven.*]
Careful!—
He is coming here. I'll warn him—yes,
but! . . .

ROXANE. [*Still on the steps, to a* NUN *who
approaches her.*] Here
I am—what is it?

THE NUN. Madame, Ragueneau
Wishes to see you.

ROXANE. Bring him here.
[*To* LE BRET *and* DE GUICHE.]
He comes
For sympathy—having been first of all
A Poet, he became since then, in turn,
A Singer—

LE BRET. Bath-house keeper—

ROXANE. Sacristan—

LE BRET. Actor—

ROXANE. Hairdresser—

LE BRET. Music-master—

ROXANE. Now,
To-day—

RAGUENEAU. [*Enters hurriedly.*]
Madame! [*He sees* LE BRET.]
Monsieur!—

ROXANE. [*Smiling.*] First tell your troubles
To Le Bret for a moment.

RAGUENEAU. But, Madame—
[*She goes out, with* DE GUICHE, *not hear-
ing him.* RAGUENEAU *comes to* LE
BRET.]
After all, I had rather— You are here—
She need not know so soon— I went to see
him
Just now— Our friend— As I came near
his door,
I saw him coming out. I hurried on
To join him. At the corner of the street,
As he passed— Could it be an accident?—
I wonder!—At the window overhead,
A lackey with a heavy log of wood
Let it fall—

LE BRET. Cyrano!

RAGUENEAU. I ran to him—

LE BRET. God! The cowards!

RAGUENEAU. I found him lying there—
A great hole in his head—

LE BRET. Is he alive?

RAGUENEAU. Alive—yes. But . . . I had
to carry him
Up to his room—Dieu! Have you seen his
room?—

LE BRET. Is he suffering?

RAGUENEAU. No; unconscious.

LE BRET. Did you
Call a doctor?

RAGUENEAU. One came—for charity.

LE BRET. Poor Cyrano!—We must not tell
Roxane
All at once . . . Did the doctor say —

RAGUENEAU. He said
Fever, and lesions of the— I forget
Those long names— Ah, if you had seen
him there,
His head all white bandages!—Let us go
Quickly—there is no one to care for him—

All alone— If he tries to raise his head,
He may die!

LE BRET. [*Draws him away to the Right.*]
        This way— It is shorter—through
The Chapel!—

ROXANE. [*Appears on the stairway, and
    calls* LE BRET *as he is going out by the
    colonnade which leads to the small door
    of the Chapel.*]
        Monsieur Le Bret!—
[LE BRET *and* RAGUENEAU *rush off with-
    out hearing.*]
                        Running away
When I call to him? Poor dear Ragueneau
Must have been very tragic!
[*She comes slowly down the stair, toward
    the tree.*]
                        What a day! . . .
Something in these bright Autumn after-
noons
Happy and yet regretful—an old sorrow
Smiling . . . as though poor little April
    dried
Her tears long ago—and remembered . . .
[*She sits down at her work. Two Nuns
    come out of the house carrying a great
    chair and set it under the tree.*]
                                Ah—
The old chair, for my old friend!—

SISTER MARTHE.   The best one
In our best parlor!—

ROXANE. Thank you, Sister—
            [*The Nuns withdraw.*]
                            There—
[*She begins embroidering. The clock
    strikes.*]
The hour!—He will be coming now—my
    silks—
All done striking? He never was so late
Before! The sister at the door—my thim-
ble . . .
Here it is—she must be exhorting him
To repent all his sins . . .   [*A pause.*]
                        He ought to be
Converted, by this time— Another leaf—
[*A dead leaf falls on her work; she
    brushes it away.*]
Certainly nothing could—my scissors—
    ever
Keep him away—

A NUN. [*Appears on the steps.*]
                Monsieur de Bergerac.

ROXANE. [*Without turning.*] What was I
    saying? . . . Hard, sometimes, to match
These faded colors! . . .

[*While she goes on working,* CYRANO *ap-
    pears at the top of the steps, very pale,
    his hat drawn over his eyes. The Nun
    who has brought him in goes away.
    He begins to descend the steps leaning
    on his cane, and holding himself on
    his feet only by an evident effort.*
    ROXANE *turns to him, with a tone of
    friendly banter.*]
                    After fourteen years,
Late—for the first time!

CYRANO. [*Reaches the chair, and sinks
    into it; his gay tone contrasting with his
    tortured face.*]   Yes, yes—maddening!
I was detained by—

ROXANE.   Well?

CYRANO.   A visitor,
Most unexpected.

ROXANE. [*Carelessly, still sewing.*]
                        Was your visitor
Tiresome?

CYRANO. Why, hardly that—inopportune,
Let us say—an old friend of mine—at
    least
A very old acquaintance.

ROXANE.   Did you tell him
To go away?

CYRANO.   For the time being, yes.
I said: "Excuse me—this is Saturday—
I have a previous engagement, one
I cannot miss, even for you— Come back
An hour from now."

ROXANE. Your friend will have to wait;
I shall not let you go till dark.

CYRANO. [*Very gently.*]   Perhaps
A little before dark, I must go . . .
[*He leans back in the chair, and closes
    his eyes.* SISTER MARTHE *crosses above
    the stairway.* ROXANE *sees her, motions
    her to wait, then turns to* CYRANO.]

ROXANE.   Look—
Somebody waiting to be teased.

CYRANO. [*Quickly, opens his eyes.*]
                            Of course!
            [*In a big, comic voice.*]

Sister, approach!

[SISTER MARTHE *glides toward him.*]
                    Beautiful downcast eyes!—
So shy—

SISTER MARTHE. [*Looks up, smiling.*]
        You—   [*She sees his face.*]
                    Oh!—

CYRANO. [*Indicates* ROXANE.]
                    Sh!—Careful!

[*Resumes his burlesque tone.*]
                    Yesterday,
I ate meat again!

SISTER MARTHE.   Yes, I know.

[*Aside.*]   That is why
He looks so pale . . .

            [*To him: low and quickly.*]
                    In the refectory,
Before you go—come to me there—
                    I'll make you
A great bowl of hot soup—will you come?

CYRANO. [*Boisterously.*]   Ah—
Will I come!

SISTER MARTHE.   You are quite reasonable
To-day!

ROXANE.   Has she converted you?

SISTER MARTHE.   Oh, no—
Not for the world!—

CYRANO.   Why, now I think of it,
That is so— You, bursting with holiness,
And yet you never preach! Astonishing
I call it . . .

            [*With burlesque ferocity.*]
            Ah—now I'll astonish you—
I am going to—
[*With the air of seeking for a good joke
and finding it.*]
            —let you pray for me
To-night, at vespers!

ROXANE.   Aha!

CYRANO.   Look at her—
Absolutely struck dumb!

SISTER MARTHE. [*Gently.*] I did not wait
For you to say I might.   [*She goes out.*]

CYRANO. [*Returns to* ROXANE, *who is
bending over her work.*]
            Now, may the devil
Admire me, if I ever hope to see
The end of that embroidery.

ROXANE. [*Smiling.*]   I thought
It was time you said that.

[*A breath of wind causes a few leaves to
fall.*]

CYRANO.   The leaves—

ROXANE. [*Raises her head and looks away
through the trees.*]   What color—
Perfect Venetian red! Look at them fall.

CYRANO.   Yes—they know how to die. A
little way
From the branch to the earth, a little fear
Of mingling with the common dust—and
yet
They go down gracefully—a fall that seems
Like flying!

ROXANE.   Melancholy—you?

CYRANO.   Why, no,
Roxane!

ROXANE.   Then let the leaves fall. Tell me
now
The Court news—my Gazette!

CYRANO.   Let me see—

ROXANE.   Ah!

CYRANO. [*More and more pale, struggling
against pain.*]
Saturday, the nineteenth: The King fell ill,
After eight helpings of grape marmalade.
His malady was brought before the court,
Found guilty of high treason; whereupon
His Majesty revived. The royal pulse
Is now normal. *Sunday, the twentieth:*
The Queen gave a grand ball, at which they
burned
Seven hundred and sixty-three wax candles,
Note:
They say our troops have been victorious
In Austria. *Later:* Three sorcerers
Have been hung. *Special post:* The little dog
Of Madame d'Athis was obliged to take
Four pills before—

ROXANE.   Monsieur de Bergerac,
Will you kindly be quiet!

CYRANO.   *Monday . . .* nothing.
Lygdamire has a new lover.

ROXANE.   Oh!

CYRANO. [*His face more and more al-
tered.*]   *Tuesday,*
The twenty-second: All the court has gone
To Fontainebleau. *Wednesday:* The Comte
de Fiesque
Spoke to Madame de Montglat; she said
No.

Thursday: Mancini [1] was the Queen of
France
Or—very nearly! *Friday:* La Montglat
Said Yes. *Saturday, twenty-sixth.* . . .
[*His eyes close; his head sinks back;
silence.*]

ROXANE. [*Surprised at not hearing any
more, turns, looks at him, and rises,
frightened.*]   He has fainted—
            [*She runs to him, crying out.*]
Cyrano!

CYRANO. [*Opens his eyes.*]
            What . . . What is it? . . .
[*He sees* ROXANE *leaning over him, and
quickly pulls his hat down over his
head and leans back away from her in
the chair.*]   No—oh no—
It is nothing—truly!

ROXANE.   But—

CYRANO.   My old wound—
At Arras—sometimes—you know. . . .

ROXANE.   My poor friend!

CYRANO. Oh it is nothing; it will soon be
    gone. . . .   [*Forcing a smile.*]
There! It is gone!

ROXANE. [*Standing close to him.*]
            We all have our old wounds—
I have mine—here . . .
            [*Her hand at her breast.*]
            under this faded scrap
Of writing. . . . It is hard to read now—all
But the blood—and the tears. . . .
            [*Twilight begins to fall.*]

CYRANO.   His letter! . . . Did you
Not promise me that some day . . . that
    some day
You would let me read it?

ROXANE.   His letter?—You . . .
You wish—

CYRANO. I do wish it—to-day.

ROXANE. [*Gives him the little silken bag
from around her neck.*]   Here. . . .

CYRANO. May I . . . open it?

ROXANE.   Open it, and read.
[*She goes back to her work, folds it
again, rearranges her silks.*]

CYRANO. [*Unfolds the letter; reads.*]
"Farewell Roxane, because to-day I die—"

[1] Marie Mancini, whom Louis XIV wished to
marry.

ROXANE. [*Looks up, surprised.*] Aloud?

CYRANO. [*Reads.*]
            "I know that it will be to-day,
My own dearly beloved—and my heart
Still so heavy with love I have not told,
And I die without telling you! No more
Shall my eyes drink the sight of you like
    wine,
Never more, with a look that is a kiss,
Follow the sweet grace of you—"

ROXANE.   How you read it—
His letter!

CYRANO. [*Continues.*]
            "I remember now the way
You have, of pushing back a lock of hair
With one hand, from your forehead—and
    my heart
Cries out—"

ROXANE.   His letter . . . and you read it
so . . .
[*The darkness increases imperceptibly.*]

CYRANO. "Cries out and keeps crying:
'Farewell, my dear,
My dearest—' "

ROXANE. In a voice. . . .

CYRANO.   "—My own heart's own,
My own treasure—"

ROXANE. [*Dreamily.*] In such a voice. . . .

CYRANO.   —"My love—"

ROXANE.   —As I remember hearing . . .
[*She trembles.*]   —long ago. . .
[*She comes near him, softly, without his
seeing her; passes the chair, leans over
silently, looking at the letter. The darkness increases.*]

CYRANO. "—I am never away from you.
    Even now,
I shall not leave you. In another world,
I shall be still that one who loves you,
    loves you
Beyond measure, beyond—"

ROXANE. [*Lays her hand on his shoulder.*]
            How can you read
Now? It is dark. . . .

[*He starts, turns, and sees her there close
to him. A little movement of surprise,
almost of fear; then he bows his head.
A long pause; then in the twilight now
completely fallen, she says very softly,
clasping her hands.*]

And all these fourteen years,
He has been the old friend, who came to
me
To be amusing.

CYRANO.   Roxane!—

ROXANE.   It was you.

CYRANO. No, no, Roxane, no!

ROXANE.   And I might have known,
Every time that I heard you speak my
name! . . .

CYRANO. No— It was not I—

ROXANE.   It was . . . you!

CYRANO.   I swear—

ROXANE. I understand everything now:
The letters—
That was you . . .

CYRANO.   No!

ROXANE. And the dear, foolish words—
That was you. . . .

CYRANO.   No!

ROXANE.   And the voice . . .
in the dark. . . .
That was . . . you!

CYRANO.   On my honor—

ROXANE.   And . . . the Soul!—
That was all you.

CYRANO.   I never loved you—

ROXANE.   Yes,
You loved me.

CYRANO. [Desperately.]
                    No— He loved you—

ROXANE.   Even now,
You love me!

CYRANO. [His voice weakens.] No!

ROXANE. [Smiling.]
                    And why . . . so great a No?

CYRANO. No, no, my own dear love, I
love you not! . . .   [Pause.]

ROXANE. How many things have died . . .
and are new-born! . . .
Why were you silent for so many years,
All the while, every night and every day,
He gave me nothing—you knew that—
    You knew
Here, in this letter lying on my breast,
Your tears— You knew they were your
    tears—

CYRANO. [Holds the letter out to her.]
                              The blood
Was his.

ROXANE. Why do you break that silence
now,
To-day?

CYRANO. Why? Oh, because—
    [LE BRET and RAGUENEAU enter, run-
    ning.]

LE BRET.   What recklessness—
I knew it! He is here!

CYRANO. [Smiling, and trying to rise.]
                              Well? Here I am!

RAGUENEAU. He has killed himself, Madame, coming here!

ROXANE. He— Oh, God. . . . And that
faintness . . . was that?—

CYRANO.   No,
Nothing! I did not finish my Gazette—
Saturday, twenty-sixth: An hour or so
Before dinner, Monsieur de Bergerac
Died, foully murdered.
    [He uncovers his head, and shows it
    swathed in bandages.]

ROXANE.   Oh, what does he mean?—
Cyrano!—What have they done to you?—

CYRANO.   "Struck down
By the sword of a hero, let me fall—
Steel in my heart, and laughter on my lips!"
Yes, I said that once. How Fate loves a
jest!—
Behold me ambushed—taken in the rear—
My battlefield a gutter—my noble foe
A lackey, with a log of wood! . . .
                              It seems
Too logical—I have missed everything,
Even my death!

RAGUENEAU. [Breaks down.]
                    Ah, Monsieur!—

CYRANO.   Ragueneau,
Stop blubbering!   [Takes his hand.]
                    What are you writing nowadays,
Old poet?

RAGUENEAU. [Through his tears.]
                    I am not a poet now;
I snuff the—light the candles—for Molière!

CYRANO. Oh—Molière!

RAGUENEAU.   Yes, but I am leaving him
To-morrow. Yesterday they played Sca-
pin—[2]
He has stolen your scene—

[2] One of Molière's popular farces, into which
is actually inserted some material from a comedy
by Cyrano.

LE BRET.   The whole scene—
word for word!
RAGUENEAU.   Yes: "What the devil was he
doing there"—
That one!
LE BRET.   [*Furious.*]
          And Molière stole it all from you—
Bodily!—
CYRANO.   Bah— He showed good taste. . . .
     [*To* RAGUENEAU.]   The Scene
Went well? . . .
RAGUENEAU.   Ah, Monsieur, they laughed
—and laughed—
How they did laugh!
CYRANO.   Yes—that has been my life. . . .
Do you remember that night Christian
spoke
Under your window? It was always so!
While I stood in the darkness underneath,
Others climbed up to win the applause—
the kiss!—
Well—that seems only justice— I still say,
Even now, on the threshold of my tomb—
"Molière has genius—Christian had good
looks—"
     [*The chapel bell is ringing. Along the
     avenue of trees above the stairway, the
     Nuns pass in procession to their
     prayers.*]
They are going to pray now; there is the
bell.
ROXANE.   [*Raises herself and calls to
them.*] Sister!—Sister!—
CYRANO.   [*Holding on to her hand.*]
                    No,—do not go away—
I may not still be here when you return. . . .
     [*The Nuns have gone into the chapel.
     The organ begins to play.*]
A little harmony is all I need—
Listen. . . .
ROXANE.   You shall not die! I love you!—
CYRANO.   No—
That is not in the story! You remember
When Beauty said "I love you" to the
Beast
That was a fairy prince, his ugliness
Changed and dissolved, like magic. . . .
     But you see

I am still the same.
ROXANE.   And I—I have done
This to you! All my fault—mine!
CYRANO.   You? Why, no,
On the contrary! I had never known
Womanhood and its sweetness but for
you.
My mother did not love to look at me—
I never had a sister— Later on,
I feared the mistress with a mockery
Behind her smile. But you—because of
you
I have had one friend not quite all a
friend—
Across my life, one whispering silken
gown! . . .
LE BRET.   [*Points to the rising moon which
begins to shine down between the trees.*]
Your other friend is looking at you.
CYRANO.   [*Smiling at the moon.*] I see. . . .
ROXANE.   I never loved but one man in
my life,
And I have lost him—twice. . . .
CYRANO.   Le Bret—I shall be up there
presently
In the moon—without having to invent
Any flying-machines!
ROXANE.   What are you saying? . . .
CYRANO.   The moon—yes, that would be
the place for me—
My kind of paradise! I shall find there
Those other souls who should be friends
of mine—
Socrates [3]—Galileo [4]—
LE BRET.   [*Revolting.*] No! No! No!
It is too idiotic—too unfair—
Such a friend—such a poet—such a man
To die so—to die so!—
CYRANO.   [*Affectionately.*]
                    There goes Le Bret,
Growling!
LE BRET.   [*Breaks down.*] My friend!—
CYRANO.   [*Half raises himself, his eye wan-
ders.*]   The Cadets of Gascoyne,
The Defenders. . . . The elementary mass—
Ah—there's the point! Now, then . . .
LE BRET.   Delirious—
And all that learning—

[3] The Athenian philosopher (469–399 B.C.) who
was the teacher of Plato and figures prominently
in the latter's dialogues.

[4] A famous astronomer (1564–1642).

CYRANO. On the other hand,
We have Copernicus [5]—
ROXANE. Oh!
CYRANO. [More and more delirious.]
"Very well,
But what the devil was he doing there?—
What the devil was he doing there, up
there?" . . .
[He declaims.]
Philosopher and scientist,
Poet, musician, duellist—
He flew high, and fell back again!
A pretty wit—whose like we lack—
A lover . . . not like other men. . . .
Here lies Hercule-Savinien
De Cyrano de Bergerac—
Who was all things—and all in vain!
Well, I must go—pardon—I cannot stay!
My moonbeam comes to carry me away. . . .
[He falls back into the chair, half faint-
ing. The sobbing of ROXANE recalls
him to reality. Gradually his mind
comes back to him. He looks at her,
stroking the veil that hides her hair.]
I would not have you mourn any the less
That good, brave, noble Christian; but per-
haps—
I ask you only this—when the great cold
Gathers around my bones, that you may
give
A double meaning to your widow's weeds
And the tears you let fall for him may be
For a little—my tears. . . .
ROXANE. [Sobbing.] Oh, my love! . . .
CYRANO. [Suddenly shaken as with a fever
fit, he raises himself erect and pushes her
away.] —Not here!—
Not lying down! . . .
[They spring forward to help him; he
motions them back.]
Let no one help me—no one!—
Only the tree. . . .
[He sets his back against the trunk.
Pause.]
It is coming . . . I feel
Already shod with marble . . . gloved with
lead . . . [Joyously.]

[5] The founder of modern astronomy (1473–
1543).

Let the old fellow come now! He shall find
me
On my feet—sword in hand—
[Draws his sword.]
LE BRET. Cyrano!
ROXANE. [Half fainting.] Oh,
Cyrano!
CYRANO. I can see him there—he grins—
He is looking at my nose—that skeleton
—What's that you say? Hopeless?—Why,
very well!—
But a man does not fight merely to win!
No—no—better to know one fights in
vain! . . .
You there— Who are you? A hundred
against one—
I know them now, my ancient enemies—
[He lunges at the empty air.]
Falsehood! . . . There! There! Prejudice—
Compromise—
Cowardice— [Thrusting.]
What's that? No! Surrender? No!
Never—never! . . .
Ah, you too, Vanity!
I knew you would overthrow me in the
end—
No! I fight on! I fight on! I fight on!
[He swings the blade in great circles,
then pauses, gasping. When he speaks
again, it is another tone.]
Yes, all my laurels you have riven away
And all my roses; yet in spite of you,
There is one crown I bear away with me,
And to-night, when I enter before God,
My salute shall sweep all the stars away
From the blue threshold! One thing without
stain,
Unspotted from the world, in spite of doom
Mine own!—
[He springs forward, his sword aloft.]
And that is . . .
[The sword escapes from his hand; he
totters, and falls into the arms of LE
BRET and RAGUENEAU.]
ROXANE. [Bends over him and kisses him
on the forehead.] —That is . . .
CYRANO. [Opens his eyes and smiles up at
her.] My white plume. . . .
[CURTAIN.]

SUPPLEMENT

Guide for Intensive Study

The following pages are intended to supply practical guidance for an intensive study of the plays contained in this volume. In order to avoid the intrusion of ready-made interpretations and to stimulate independent critical analysis, this guidance is couched in the form of questions. If at first glance such assistance appears to be a sort of Indian gift, it should be remarked that only in popular superstition is the beginning of wisdom a matter of knowing the right answers. Actually it is a matter of knowing the right questions to raise concerning the subject at hand. As a suggestive aid toward this end, the following pages offer some frankly leading questions, so phrased as to indicate the nature of the materials which bear upon the answer. Without pretending to present the only pertinent questions or necessarily the most important ones, and without endeavoring to prompt any specific interpretation, they are designed simply to suggest the sort of questions which have to be taken into account if the play is to be understood at all. Since certain of these questions are fundamental to all drama, these are collected in one general list at the beginning and should be applied to all the plays. The remaining questions are devised to emphasize the special features of the individual plays with which they deal.

GENERAL QUESTIONS

1. To what particular category of drama does the play belong, and what special considerations are necessitated by the fact?
2. With what is the play essentially concerned, and what is its apparent dramatic intention?
3. What is the precise nature of the dramatic conflict or tension presented by the play?
4. What kinds of characters are involved, and what is the dramatic function of each?
5. Of what does the plot consist, and how does the dramatic structure relate to the aims of the play?
6. What, if anything, is contributed by the setting?
7. What specific expository information is supplied to clarify the initial dramatic situation?

653

8.   What motivates the dramatic action, and how satisfactory is this motivation?

9.   What tempo is implied by each scene, and what is the theatrical effect of this tempo?

10.   What stage business and spectacle are required by the text of the play, and what is their theatrical value?

11.   What is the prevailing tone of tne play, and how does it affect the play's significance?

12.   What is the dramatist's attitude toward his material, and how valid is it?

13.   What specific guidance does the dramatist provide toward an understanding of his intentions?

14.   What does the play finally succeed in accomplishing, and what is the value of this achievement?

15.   What bearing does the play have upon one's personal design for living?

OEDIPUS THE KING

1.   What specific expository purposes are served by the Prologue? What significant facts define the dramatic situation? What particular features of his position and past history involve Oedipus in this situation? What is ironic about the knowledge and motives which impel his initial acts? Why is this preliminary knowledge on the part of the audience necessary for the tragic effects aimed at?

2.   Of what does the dramatic action of the First Episode consist? How much of its value depends upon what the audience knows about the situation and its outcome? Why is the first speech of Oedipus given such length and prominence? Is the attitude of Oedipus toward Tiresias convincingly motivated? Why does he dismiss the seer's accusations so readily? Is his rationalization of them convincing? Why is his bitter resentment dangerous?

3.   How is the blindness of Tiresias used to intensify the irony of the situation? Why is his prophecy of the truth dramatically necessary? What is the artistic value of this foreshadowing? Why does it not destroy the suspense? In summarizing the situation at the end of this episode, what features are emphasized by the First Stasimon?

4.   In the Second Episode what contrast between Oedipus and Creon is emphasized? How does Oedipus become increasingly responsible for his own destruction? Is there any excuse for his rash accusations? In the long speech of Creon, which again deals with important subject matter, what deficiencies of Oedipus are deliberately brought to attention? What decisive developments warrant the heightened emotional use of the *kommos*?

5. Why does Jocasta's scepticism about prophecy fail to reassure Oedipus? What light do his sensitive suspicions throw upon his earlier behavior? Is Jocasta aware of the indictment she is building up against him? What creates the tragic irony of the situation? How does the Second Stasimon guide the audience toward the significance of the dramatic action? What ethical criteria does it advance for evaluating the play?

6. In the Third Episode what contradictions appear in Jocasta's reasoning and counsel? During the First Messenger's conversation with Oedipus, what accounts for her long silence and subsequent evasiveness? In what way does Oedipus misunderstand her attitude? At the close of this episode why does his dedication to Fortune mark the climax of the dramatic action and the delineation of his character? In this episode what use is made of peripety, or sudden reversal of fortunes? As a favorite device of classical tragedy, what purpose does it serve throughout the play?

7. Compare the length and dramatic methods of the Fourth Episode and the Exodus. What is the artistic reason for the differences? What is the purpose of the stylistic devices used in the Fourth Episode? Is the Fourth Stasimon a relaxation of emotional tension or an expansion of Oedipus' cry of horror?

8. In the Exodus what is gained or lost dramatically by having the off-stage events reported by the Second Messenger? Upon the final appearance of Oedipus, what is the value of the shift from spoken dialogue to chant? What artistic effects are aimed at in this concluding scene?

9. What are the dramatic purposes revealed by the play? What specific uses of irony occur in it? To what extent is this irony an essential part of the tragedy? How does this feature affect the structure and technique of the play?

10. What is the attitude of the tragedy toward the guilt of Oedipus? What is its conception of justice? Is this attitude defensible? In general, what are the ethical views of the play?

HAMLET

1. Since romantic tragedy presents the cumulative development of a dramatic story, it is best to study *Hamlet* in terms of its incremental development. From this point of view, what is the dramatic function of the first act? What is the mood established by the first scene? What specific exposition is provided by the scene, and by what means? What is the purpose of Horatio's scepticism? How is the forward movement of time managed plausibly through the continuous scenes of the act?

2. In Act I, Scene ii, what specific qualities of character are stressed in Claudius, Gertrude, and Hamlet? What is the basic irony of the situation, and how is it pointed up by Hamlet's outburst to his mother?

What attitudes are revealed by the King and Queen toward Hamlet, and by Hamlet toward them? What is the significance of Hamlet's questions and the speculations about the Ghost?

3. What specific information does Hamlet's first soliloquy reveal concerning his state of mind at the opening of the play, the reasons for it, and the temperament and habits of thought characteristic of him? Why is the use of soliloquy necessary? Throughout the play how do Hamlet's several soliloquies clarify the dramatic action? What is the significance of their location in the play?

4. What special characteristics of Laertes and Polonius are their speeches of advice in Scene iii designed to emphasize? What do they have in common? What is their standard of judgment? How does Ophelia react to each? What motivates Polonius' instructions to her?

5. What misgivings are betrayed in Hamlet's conversation with Horatio as they await the Ghost? How do they foreshadow Hamlet's personal tragedy? What new information does the Ghost impart to Hamlet? What specific injunctions and warnings does he issue? How does this visit of the Ghost alter the dramatic situation and precipitate the action of the play? How do you explain Hamlet's behavior when he is rejoined by his friends? What intimations of subsequent action appear in the first act? What is the importance of Hamlet's concluding comment?

6. What is Hamlet's initial attitude toward the Ghost? In what respects and for what reasons does it alter subsequently? Why is Hamlet's attitude dramatically important?

7. How much time elapses between Acts I and II? How is this information conveyed? What has taken place in the interval?

8. What is the significance of Hamlet's behavior which Ophelia reports to her father? What are the advantages in reporting rather than staging his pantomime? What pressure does this report exert on Polonius?

9. Beginning with Act II, why is it urgent that Claudius discover what is wrong with Hamlet? Why are Rosencrantz and Guildenstern willing to aid him throughout the play? What governs Hamlet's attitude toward them? How do you view their behavior?

10. What grounds does Polonius have for his explanation of Hamlet's madness? How far does Claudius agree with him? Why does he acquiesce to Polonius' schemes? What light is thrown on the situation by the letter to Ophelia which Polonius reads? When Hamlet appears for the first time after initiating his reputation for madness, what clues are given about his condition? What circumstances govern his behavior? How do his comments to Polonius reveal the conclusions to which he has come about Polonius and Ophelia?

11. What suggests to Hamlet the staging of the "mouse-trap" play? What is the significance of the particular speech which Hamlet asks the player to recite, and how does it affect him? Is there any consistency in

what happens to Hamlet during the course of the act? Why does it result in a changed attitude toward the Ghost? What special dramatic functions are performed by the soliloquy which concludes the act?

12. The third act, which brings the events of the play to a crisis, is prefaced by Hamlet's most famous soliloquy. What state of mind does it reveal? With what considerations is Hamlet preoccupied? The following conversation with Ophelia falls into two parts. What causes the break? What governs Hamlet's behavior in each part? What is his attitude toward Ophelia? How do you explain the deliberate obscenity of his subsequent remarks to her at the play?

13. In what ways does Hamlet's staging of his play provide the turning point of the dramatic action? In his preliminary comments to Horatio, what is implied by the particular quality of Horatio's character which he praises? Why does Hamlet require the corroboration of Horatio in judging the King's guilt? Assuming that Hamlet is responsible for the tenor of the speeches presented, against whom are the opening ones directed? What does this fact indicate about Hamlet's strongest motives? What does the King's behavior indicate? How much does it actually reveal guilt? How does Hamlet interpret it? What does Horatio think, and how much attention does Hamlet give to his views? What is the general effect on Claudius? What motives and pretexts for action does the play provide him?

14. Observe the intentional parallelism of the two following scenes. What is the purpose of this parallelism? What reasons does Hamlet advance for not killing the King? How convincing are they? Why is the time really inopportune for action against Claudius? With respect to the action called for, what is the emphasized contrast between Hamlet and Claudius? In view of Hamlet's attitude, how do you explain the contrast of his behavior in killing Polonius in the next scene? How does his treatment of his mother also contrast with his behavior toward Claudius? What is his attitude toward her? What is he trying to accomplish? To what extent does the Queen understand the situation? What is her response to the insinuation that she is implicated in the murder of Hamlet's father? What are the principal tragic ironies of the scene? In what way does it mark the emotional climax of Hamlet's struggle? What effect does it have on his subsequent manner and behavior?

15. Having supplied Claudius with an urgent motive for his elimination, how does Hamlet also provide an opportunity? What is the dramatic purpose of the abortive trip to England? What explanation exists for Hamlet's conduct throughout the last two acts?

16. What are the dramatic functions of Ophelia's madness? What light does it throw on Hamlet's condition? What do her songs and disconnected remarks indicate of what is preying on her mind? Is her mental collapse adequately prepared for? What is there about her situation which enables Claudius to turn it to his own account? To what extent does

Ophelia's pathetic incoherence and distraction serve to symbolize this whole stage of the dramatic action?

17.   How does Laertes' reaction to the murder of a father compare with Hamlet's? What accounts for the difference? What specific factors bend Laertes to the King's purpose? How much is true and how much false in the King's self-defense for having done nothing about the murder of Polonius? To what extent are Laertes' villainous proposals against Hamlet, as well as his later swift repentance, credible and consistent with his nature?

18.   How does the scene with the grave-diggers set the tone for the last act of the play? What is it designed to emphasize? What information does it give about Hamlet's age? What is the importance of Hamlet's encounter with Laertes at Ophelia's grave?

19.   Is Hamlet's early success in the fencing bout to be attributed entirely to his superior skill? What is Laertes' attitude throughout, and how do you account for it? Why has he decided to go through with the plot? What is the special combination of circumstances which brings about Hamlet's revenge? As he is dying, what is characteristic about his chief concerns? Is Horatio's explanation to the English Ambassador an accurate résumé of the play's dramatic action? What light does it cast on the irony of the tragedy?

20.   What precisely is the nature of the tragedy dealt with in the play? To what extent are the several characters at fault? How much of the tragedy is occasioned by deliberate evil intention? How much is the result of good intention or the pressure of circumstances? How far is it inevitable? In what respects does it exhibit pathos and irony and inspire awe?

TWELFTH NIGHT

1.   At the opening of the play how is the appropriate mood established? What is this mood? What is the value of the frequent use of song and music?

2.   What different varieties of comic entertainment are provided by the opening scenes? What is the respective value of each? To what extent is each identified with a particular group of characters? What is the purpose of this distinction?

3.   Into what groups are the characters divided? What are the special interests of each? How are the several strands of interest unified?

4.   What are the initial impressions created by Orsino, Olivia, and Viola? What are the dominant characteristics of Orsino? What is his condition? How serious is Olivia's grief, and what opportunities are given for judging it? Is it a reason or a pretext for her aloofness from Orsino?

5.   Why is the first meeting between Olivia and Viola amusing? What

specific motives prompt the behavior of each? What special kinds of incongruity are involved? What is Viola's method and intention in discharging her mission? Why does she insist on following a prepared routine? Why is she pert and brusque? What causes her wariness to change as the scene progresses?

6.   How does Olivia's conversation with the Clown in Act I, Scene v, aid in establishing a comic point of view? What is the Clown's general function? What is provided by his jesting beyond idle banter? Why is a witty and trenchant fool particularly appropriate to comedy?

7.   What varieties of entertainment are contributed by Sir Toby, Sir Andrew, and Maria? What are their special functions, and why are these important? Why are Sir Toby and Sir Andrew comic? What is the difference between them, and what light do they throw on the nature of comedy?

8.   What is the first impression created by Malvolio? Why does this immediately differentiate him from all the other characters? Why is this distinction of major significance in a play of this sort? What special deficiency in him does Olivia associate with his lack of humor? To what does Maria attribute it? What is Shakespeare's implication about it?

9.   What mechanical devices are used to develop the plot? In what respects is this development natural or conventional? How much does the shifting connotation of scenes depend upon the interchange of Viola and Sebastian? Why are the artificialities of plot both acceptable and desirable?

10.   As the play progresses, what incongruities appear in Orsino's behavior? What do they indicate about him? What is his attitude toward Viola? As a man presumably in love, what characteristics does he exhibit? How do these serve Viola's purpose? What is incongruous about the relations of the two? What makes Viola's situation amusing? Why does it arouse sympathy?

11.   What motivates the plot against Malvolio? What particular weakness, emphasized earlier, betrays him? Why is Maria's trick appropriate to Malvolio's character? What methods does Shakespeare use to prepare the audience to approve of Malvolio's discomfiture? Why does Malvolio arouse antipathy? How does the garden scene (II, v) contribute to this control of the audience? In this scene what stage business accompanies the eavesdropping? What general applications give a special piquancy to Malvolio's day-dreaming? What qualities of character make plausible his acceptance of the anonymous letter? Why is the conduct recommended in the letter particularly grotesque? What is the precise point of the joke?

12.   In the climactic scenes of Act III, concerned with the exhibition of Malvolio and the duel, what are the sources of the comedy? In what respects are the two scenes similar and different? How do they differ in effect? Are Malvolio, Viola, and Sir Andrew aware of the joke played

on them? How do the reasons for the deception differ in each case, and how does this alter the effect? What bearing does this difference have upon the attitude of the audience toward each?

13.   What makes Malvolio's conduct in the dark closet toward the Clown and Sir Topas plausible? Is his treatment unjust and inhuman? Is it compatible with comedy? How is his plight treated by the others? Are his own final sentiments to be considered as justified, pathetic, or ludicrous? On what grounds?

14.   Is the marriage between Olivia and Sebastian merely an implausible convenience of plot? Is there any satisfactory explanation of Olivia's ready acquiescence? To what extent does it coincide with earlier evidences of her love? What preparation is given for Sebastian's facile compliance? Are his reactions acceptable? Exactly what are they?

15.   The masterly last scene illustrates admirably how romantic comedy is able to present the absurd yet remain consistent with idealized life. How is this achievement managed? Structurally, how is the increasing confusion built up? Why does each perfectly truthful explanation appear false and contradictory? Why does Antonio's attempt to substantiate his claims convince Orsino that he is lying? What does Orsino's bitterness reveal of his real feelings toward Viola, and how does this prepare for the happy ending? What is the purpose of concentrating the accusations on Viola? Why is it desirable to emphasize her? What is the effect on the sympathies of the audience? Why is it possible to resolve all the confusions at one stroke without tedious explanations? What basic contrasts are the source of the incongruities?

16.   To what extent does the effect of the comedy depend on irony? How much does the play emphasize the danger of appearances? How much of the comic effect results from logical reasoning based on false premises? How far does the play support the contention that the basis of comedy is a false situation?

17.   In what respects is the play's treatment of life selective? To what extent does it falsify human experience? What elements are idealized? What particular features may be considered romantic? What is the play's final truth to life?

THE MISANTHROPE

1.   How does the opening scene define the central conflict of the play? Precisely what is it? How do the attitudes of Alceste and Philinte differ? In terms of the issues involved, which is the more rational?

2.   What are the evidences of Philinte's urbanity? What is to be thought of his defense of tolerance toward human failings? What is the respective appropriateness of such an attitude to comedy and to tragedy? Is there any reason for associating Alceste's intolerant virtue with simple egotism?

3.   To what extent does Molière try to establish a point of view for the play? What is it? How does he introduce the criterion of common sense?

4.   Exactly what foibles of society are satirized throughout the play? Are they truly representative? How are they shown to be ludicrous? To what extent do they defeat their own purposes?

5.   What dramatic purpose is served by Molière's trick of briefly sketching a character just before his appearance? Do the frequent character sketches scattered throughout the dialogue represent anything more than examples of malicious slander? What is their comic purpose and value?

6.   What social defects does Oronte exemplify? Is he actually a fool? Does Alceste exhibit much good sense in dealing with him? What puts Alceste at a disadvantage? Why are his efforts to reconcile politeness and honesty comic? In the progress of their differences (II, vii and IV, i) why does the comic balance turn against Alceste and make his indignation grotesque?

7.   To what extent do the quarrels between Alceste and Célimène in Act II arise from the fact that each insists upon being reasonable? Wherein lies the discrepancy? Why does Alceste's effort at reasonableness turn out comic? Is his reaction to Célimène's series of verbal portraits justified? Is her description of him accurate? How much is he a victim of wit? What wit?

8.   Why is Acaste's frank estimate of himself at the beginning of Act III fatuous? To what extent is it a witty and tacit criticism of human nature in general? What does it reveal about Acaste? Does it throw any light on Alceste?

9.   How does Arsinoé's warning to Célimène betray its real motives? What are they? What is Arsinoé's nature? Does she justify what Célimène says of her earlier? How is her envious malice kept within the bounds of comedy?

10.   What qualities differentiate Célimène from her associates? On what grounds can you explain her attraction for Alceste? How does Molière endeavor to protect her sharp-tongued irresponsibility from serious censure? To what extent do the following extenuate her behavior: cleverness, sufficient provocation, lack of intent to harm, willingness to admit faults, honest effort to be just? Does she ever appear ludicrous?

11.   The first three acts of the play present a complex pattern of contrasts. The fourth act, in preparing for the climax, reduces these various contrasts to a common denominator and thus supplies a standard for judging them. How do Philinte and Éliante contribute to this purpose? Compare Philinte with Alceste, and Éliante with Arsinoé and Célimène. In this connection, what is the effect of Alceste's proposed revenge on Célimène immediately after Éliante's confession? What makes it grotesque? How does it compare with what Alceste objects to in Célimène?

How does Scene iv bring into sharp contrast the two basic viewpoints of the play? What is to be said for each?

12.   Why is Act V actually the climax of Alceste's confused indignation and absurdity? As an example of high comedy, what are its specific virtues? Upon what does its incongruity depend? How does Molière maintain its comic tone? What final motives account for Alceste's behavior? Earlier Célimène has differentiated between superficial words and actions and more subtle indications of true feeling. In Scene vi, when she is caught in her own insincerities, does her treatment of the various suitors bear out her contention? Is Alceste capable of making this distinction? Why does he reject Célimène? Does his earlier refusal to save his 20,000 francs thrown any light on his attitude?

13.   How does the comedy of Act IV, Scene iv differ from the rest of the play? What does it depend on? In Act V, Scene ii much of the comic effect depends on stage business, especially that of Célimène. What is the stage business required?

14.   Is the conclusion of the play comically appropriate? Why does Molière avoid the conventional happy ending of a reconciliation between Alceste and Célimène? What is the purpose of the contrasted union of Philinte and Éliante?

15.   Throughout the play Molière states his social views through the mouth of various characters. What are these principles? What is the dramatic purpose of stating them? Are they introduced obtrusively or with dramatic appropriateness? Does the comedy vindicate them?

THE WAY OF THE WORLD

1.   How does the setting for Act I aid in establishing the general atmosphere of the play? What is the effect of the other settings? How are the point of view and tone of the play established?

2.   What specific exposition of plot and character is contributed by Act I? Is it introduced naturally? How is it made theatrically entertaining? How much depends upon the dialogue? What is the nature of the wit displayed? What qualitative differences appear in its several varieties? How much characterization is actually supplied? To what aspects of character is it devoted? In what respects are Mirabell and Fainall contrasted with Witwoud and Petulant?

3.   The first two acts appear to be chiefly occupied with gossip and repartee. Why is this emphasis appropriate to the interests of the play? Although little action appears on the stage, how is the dramatic action of the play kept from being static and given a steady forward movement? Are characters excluded from participation in the plot because they are absent from the stage? To what extent does the indirect revelation of character relationships and motives actually constitute an advancement of the plot? What are the motives behind each relationship? At the end

of each of the first two acts actually how much more complex is the plot than it was at the beginning? By what devices has this increase in complexity been achieved?

4.   What are the chief interests of the society depicted? Its values? Its criteria of excellence? What is the prevailing attitude toward love and marriage? Are the proponents of this attitude to be considered disreputable, cynical, or realistic? How much weight do they give to emotion? To rationality? Is it possible to make distinctions among attitudes in terms of the motives which inspire each? Note that love, as a private communion between two individuals, is a profound emotional experience; as a social activity, it is a competitive sport. Similarly marriage may be a sacrament or a social institution. Upon what level are these matters dealt with in the play? How does the song in Act III help to establish the tone? To what extent is love treated as a battle between the sexes? Why is there a reluctance to admit being in love? A desire to create suspicion of insincerity or infidelity? An ambition to achieve conquest and cause pain? What are the objectives of the game? Do they explain the treachery and callousness of the participants? What bearing do they have on the interest which Mirabell inspires in all the ladies?

5.   Upon her belated appearance does Millamant live up to her advance notices? Of what does her charm consist? How does she compare with Mrs. Fainall and Mrs. Marwood? Is she to be considered superficial, self-centered, and hard-hearted? Why does she ridicule Mirabell? Does she give any indication of more tender sentiments?

6.   Besides his wit, does anything differentiate Mirabell from Fainall in their relations with the ladies? Does his intrigue for Millamant's fortune make him an unprincipled scoundrel? Do Mirabell and Millamant contrast favorably or unfavorably with the others? What are their special virtues? Why are they to be considered virtues?

7.   In Act III Mirabell and Millamant are practically excluded from the stage. How are they kept in the center of dramatic interest? In what respects does the dramatic emphasis shift in this act? What are the important plot developments? How do these developments depend upon the sort of activities dominated by Lady Wishfort and her circle?

8.   What element of society is represented by Lady Wishfort? Why is she ludicrous? What social tone does she impart to her associates? What is her claim to attention? What is the quality of her manners? What is the significance of her library? Is there any indication of her breeding? What light is thrown on the matter by her relatives Witwoud and Sir Wilfull?

9.   In Act III Sir Wilfull supplies a double-edged contrast for purposes of social criticism. In what respects, and from what point of view, is he himself ludicrous? To what extent, and on what grounds, does he reveal the absurdity of others? Does his censure apply to Millamant and Mirabell?

10.   More than any other part of the play, Act III directs satire against

the manners of fashionable society. What specific features are selected for ridicule, and what is the principle of selection? How does the satire divide the characters into differentiated groups? Which characters escape satire? Is the satire skillfully managed? Is it effective? To what extent does it serve to palliate the tricks perpetrated by Mirabell and Millamant and to keep them within the bounds of comedy? Why is this act important in controlling the sympathies of the audience?

11.   Act IV is constructed around a contrast between the love affair of Millamant and Mirabell and that of Lady Wishfort and Sir Rowland. It is concerned with love and marriage as a part of a social pattern. In what ways do both affairs reflect the influence of the code of manners, and how does the fashionable code interfere with each? What is the difference in effect? What attitude does Congreve take toward the conventional pattern? To what extent is the question one of manners? How is Sir Wilfull used to emphasize this feature?

12.   How do Millamant and Mirabell reconcile the conflict between sophistication and love? Despite their flippant manner, do they indicate any serious devotion to each other? What is the dramatic purpose of Millamant's quotations of poetry? In their bargain, which parodies the letter of a marriage contract and the spirit of a marriage-of-convenience, how is sincerity of purpose made compatible with sophistication of manner? Are the stipulations simply frivolous? To what extent do they imply a criticism of prevailing fashions? How do they compare with the concerns of Lady Wishfort? How do they differentiate Mirabell and Millamant from the other characters? How does this affect one's attitude toward them?

13.   Act V contains more swift plot development than all the rest of the play, although the elaborate preparations which precede it make possible the rapid shifts in situation. For all the speeded action, however, the purpose remains to exhibit manners as they operate under stress in a test case. In this act what varieties of attitude toward the social code are reflected in the several characters? How does each behave under stress? Which appear ridiculous, contemptible, or admirable? What justification and what censure of manners are implied? How does the conduct of Lady Wishfort maintain the action on a comic level? How does the trickery of Mirabell differ from the other intrigues? By what means is sympathy enlisted for its success? What are the final values implied by the comedy?

PHÆDRA

1.   In the opening conversation between Hippolytus and Theramenes what salient facts of the existing situation are revealed? What is the attitude of Hippolytus toward them? What is the nature of the inner conflict suggested by his attitude? Are his expressed sentiments about

Aricia to be taken at face value? Why does he argue so strongly against love? With whom is he arguing? Why is the revelation of his attitude a desirable beginning?

2. Upon her first appearance, what is the point of stressing Phædra's physical condition? What does it reveal of her mental state? Why does she reveal her secret? What is the precise nature of her problem? How clearly does she appreciate the issues involved? Is her emotionalism extravagant? What is the chief cause of her anguish?

3. In what respects is there a difference in sensibility between Phædra and Œnone? What sentiments motivate Œnone's conduct? Does she remain a consistent character throughout the play? To what extent is her character a factor in the plot development? What kind of considerations regularly govern her counsel to Phædra?

4. How does the report of Theseus' death activate the dramatic situation? What periodic changes in its significance are introduced by the varying rumors and final appearance of Theseus? How much of the plot depends upon this factor?

5. What sort of a person is Aricia? Is her character conceived in the mold of an ancient heroic age? What kind of a society does she reflect? What considerations dominate her behavior throughout the play? Is she a coquette? What is the nature of her interest in Hippolytus? How well does Hippolytus understand her demureness? How does he happen to declare his love? Is there any significance in Aricia's final disposition? Why do her feelings toward Hippolytus provide a necessary and important contrast to those of Phædra?

6. What traits are emphasized throughout the play in the character of Hippolytus? From what point of view do such traits appear admirable? What bearing do they have upon his susceptibility to Aricia and his revulsion from Phædra? Why do they exercise so strong an appeal to Phædra? Why is Hippolytus so deeply shocked by Phædra's confession? When later he is accused by his father, what constitutes the reality of his predicament? What is ironic about his defense? What code dictates his behavior? Is he the victim of false delicacy or of a genuine dilemma?

7. The core of the play is a subtle delineation of Phædra's tragic passion through the various phases of the psychological conflict which it precipitates. What fundamental characteristics differentiate Phædra from Hippolytus and Aricia? What is the basic irony of her plight? Throughout Acts II, III, and IV observe carefully the progress of her psychological struggle and the variations in her emotional state. What brings about her confession of love to Hippolytus? What effect is produced by the report of Theseus's death? By his unexpected return? By the advice of Œnone? By the behavior of Hippolytus? By the discovery of his love for Aricia? Does Phædra initially expect Hippolytus to condone her passion? When Theseus returns, what is ironic about the evasions of Phædra and Hippolytus? How do you explain the ambiguity

of her greeting? Is it deliberate? Does she deliberately plan to accuse Hippolytus? What are her initial motives for interceding with Theseus in his behalf? Does she finally seek death because Hippolytus is dead?

8.   What accounts for the violent extremity of Phædra's behavior? Is it to be regarded as a fault? On what grounds? What gives it emotional depth and tragic dignity? What causes the peculiar complexity of Phædra's situation? Does she herself understand it clearly? What is the effect of her capacity for self-judgment? To what extent does her thinking coincide with and differ from that of Œnone? To what extent are the reactions of the two governed by emotional impulse, moral conviction, or logical reasoning? What concerns dominate their thinking? At its climax in Act IV, what produces the particular bitterness of Phædra's distraction? What changes occur in her moral stature? Why is her tragedy a tragedy of sensibility?

9.   What are the specific dramatic functions of the plot? What structural devices are used to advance the action? How does Theseus serve this purpose? What is the importance of the political issues introduced? How do they affect the action? What is the contribution of the several confidants? What is their special relationship to the characters whom they attend? Are they always to be viewed as separate characters? What is the purpose of representing so much of the action indirectly?

10.   How does *Phædra* compare with classical tragedy? What are the specific similarities and dissimilarities? What are the differences in fundamental purpose, and how do these affect the final nature of the play? In the light of the dramatic purpose which it is intended to serve, what are the particular virtues of the form? What are its distinctive artistic features?

AN ENEMY OF THE PEOPLE

1.   In comparison with earlier plays, what effect is created by the use of detailed stage settings? How much use is made of special properties? What is the importance of the minute directions for stage business? Why is it desirable to be so specific? What proportions of the dramatic effect depend upon dialogue, stage business, and setting? How does this distribution affect the total impression made by the play? How does it affect the dialogue?

2.   What are the special characteristics of the dialogue? Upon what does its effect of naturalness depend? Is its apparent casualness actual? In the first act test a few passages to see how many speeches you consider superfluous; then examine the rest of the play to see how many of these speeches could be omitted without loss. Among the speeches which you consider necessary, in each case explain why.

3.   What distinctive features appear in the structural organization of the play? What is the function of the plot? Is the dramatic conflict resolved? What conclusions are reached? How is the dramatic action rounded out and completed? How is the play's structure affected by the use of special stage sets and a curtain? What is the structural conception of the act? How is the end of each act affected by the use of the curtain? What use is made of final tableau and curtain line, and what is its effect?

4.   Itemize the specific information supplied by the first act, and observe how it is used in the play. Is this exposition managed naturally or with patent artificiality? Is the introduction of the characters plausible? How do these introductions aid the naturalness of the exposition? What are the qualities emphasized in each of the characters? To what extent are these characteristics referable to familiar types? What are the dominant traits of the Burgomaster, Stockmann, and Mrs. Stockmann? What is the chief cause of difference between the Stockmann brothers? Why is Stockmann especially pleased with the report on the Baths? What is your impression of him as a person? Do you notice anything deliberately ironic about the conclusion of the act?

5.   Act II is devoted chiefly to illustrating the nature of the play's problem. What is it? Is it simple or complex? What are its major components? Besides the difficulty with the Baths, what occasions it? Is it a genuine problem or a simple question of right and wrong? Under the circumstances, what do you think ought to be done? On what grounds and from what point of view would you justify your recommendation?

6.   The problem of the polluted Baths produces a variety of reactions, which should be considered in detail. What are these specific reactions? What is the motive which governs each? Are the reactions typical, and, if so, typical of what?

7.   Why does the major clash occur between Stockmann and his brother? What are their dominant characteristics and the fundamental differences in their points of view? How do these clarify the central problem? Is the Burgomaster simply a smug reactionary? Is Stockmann simply an impractical visionary? What explains his innocent confidence? How is he ironically reduced to much the same dilemma as his brother? In this conflict what is the dramatic function of Mrs. Stockmann?

8.   At the end of Act II Stockmann is confident of public support, the various motives for which have been suggested. Act III examines the reality behind the appearance and the operation of the motives under pressure. Why is it appropriate for the scene to shift to the newspaper office? How is it shown that the several characters are caught by the same pressures? What are the real sources of the liberalism professed by Hovstad, Billing, and Aslaksen? What causes their abrupt change in sentiment? What is particularly grotesque about Aslaksen's position? How is the scene maintained on a level of comedy? What technical

features of the situation make Stockmann a comic figure? What is comic about Mrs. Stockmann's attitude?

9.   Since the problem of the play concerns public welfare, and Stockmann considers himself a champion of the people, the meeting of Stockmann and the people face to face in Act IV is not only the climax of the action but practically an obligatory scene. Is the chosen scene well adapted to the purpose? How are the various members of the crowd used for expository purposes? What functions are performed by the crowd as a unit? In what respects do these functions resemble those of the chorus in classical tragedy? Although a major purpose of the act is the expression of Stockmann's views, how is his speech made dramatic? What devices are used to enhance its theatrical effectiveness? How is suspense maintained? To what extent does the scene represent an actual dramatic conflict?

10.   What is the validity of the views expressed in Stockmann's speech? Are they presented as gratuitous opinions or do they grow out of the play? What personal justification does Stockmann have for holding them? To what extent does the behavior of the people in this scene provide a commentary on them? What is the basic difference in attitude between Stockmann and his audience? In what ways are his views and behavior open to criticism? What dramatic devices are used to retain sympathy for him?

11.   Does Stockmann's tirade on public opinion and the compact majority constitute an attack on democracy? What bearing do the parliamentary maneuvers just before the speech have upon democratic processes? Is the indignation of the crowd justified? What confuses the whole issue? Is Stockmann actually an enemy of the people?

12.   What particular aspects of the problem are dealt with in the last act? Why is this test of Stockmann's sincerity necessary? Exactly what is his response to the dilemma created by Morten Kiil? What saves him from succumbing? Why is the material of the act treated comically? What absurdities are stressed in the operation of public opinion? How do his opponents rationalize Stockmann's behavior? Why is this rationalization an effective means of satire?

13.   Ibsen once referred to Stockmann as "muddle-headed." Is this a just description of him? What qualities interfere with his effectuality? Are these all to be attributed to his idealism? What is the connection between his idealism and his rashness? Is he himself guilty of any inconsistencies? What difficulties of social reform does he illustrate? Is the play a satire on idealism or pragmatism or both? How does this question relate to the realism of the play?

14.   Why is it advisable to treat the problems of the play in comic terms? What would be the effect of treating Stockmann and his situation with complete gravity? How are the respective virtues of treating the problems of the play by denunciation or comic satire illuminated by

Stockmann's speech in Act IV? What is the value of Stockmann's sense of humor, and what is its general bearing on the play?

THE SEA GULL

1.   What do the visual setting and tangible properties of the play contribute to its total effect? What specific features of the setting are referred to in the dialogue? What dramatic use is made of lighting effects, of weather conditions, of the storm in the last act? What continuing use is made of the principal background feature, the lake?

2.   Is the detailed stage business noted in the directions a natural corollary of the dialogue or an independent contribution to the total effect? What is its relation to the dialogue? In each instance what does it contribute to the specific context? What particular meaning is conveyed by silence, as indicated by the frequent pauses?

3.   What is the nature of the dialogue? Is its effect natural? Is it incoherent? In its specific context how does it imply character and situation? To what extent does the manner of speaking reveal the personality of the speaker?

4.   What is the organic structure of the first act, and what is it trying to accomplish? Divide the act into the major scenes, or blocks of dramatic action, of which it is composed. What is the dramatic function of each, and how is it connected with the others? What precise information is provided about the characters and their interrelationship? What uses are made of dramatic contrast? Why is the staging of Trepleff's play given the central position in the act?

5.   Act II emphasizes the various frustrations of the different characters. What specifically are these frustrations, and from what do they arise? Which characters are envied as exceptions? Are they exceptions? Are they to be envied? What important differences exist between the two famous persons, Arcadina and Trigorin? What are the dominant interests and character qualities of Arcadina? How is she sharply contrasted with Trigorin? What is fundamentally wrong with the society and life depicted by the act?

6.   What sort of person is Nina? Why is it unfortunate that Trepleff is in love with such a person? Why is she attracted to Trigorin? What impels him to reveal himself so intimately to her? What is the effect on her? What is ironic about the attitudes expressed by each in the closing speeches of the act?

7.   What symbolism does Trepleff imply when he lays the sea gull at Nina's feet? What symbolism is suggested to Trigorin? What does the sea gull mean to Nina? How do these responses reflect important differences in the three characters? How does the episode of the sea gull relate to the play's general theme?

8.   In Act III the frustrations of the preceding act reach a climactic

state of desperation. Beginning with Trepleff's attempt at suicide, what specific instances of this desperation are presented? What is the effect on the general emotional tone? To what extent is this emotional stress used to lay bare the essential qualities of personality? Under the spur of emotion how are the speech and sentiments of Arcadina and Trigorin affected by the fact that one is a popular actress and the other a fashionable novelist? In general, what qualities of the several characters are stressed? How are the respective reactions kept short of tragedy? Can such characters be tragic?

9.   What is the peculiar irony of Trigorin's position? How complex are the motives for his designs on Nina? To what extent is he a victim of circumstances? Of his own shoddy mediocrity of spirit? Is he pathetic or ludicrous or despicable?

10.   How far do the events of Act III represent a struggle between the influences of the two women Arcadina and Nina? What are the major contrasts between them? In what ways do they resemble each other in character, desires, and attitude toward others? To what extent are they essentially the same person at different ages and stages of experience? Consider this question in the light of the attitude of the others toward them and of their own attitude toward each other. What is the cause of Arcadina's particular desperation? Has it any similarity to that of Nina?

11.   The first three acts present all the strands of Chekhov's pattern and show how they intertwine. After a lapse of two years, Act IV reveals the design which they have woven. To what extent does the act deliberately echo earlier themes? What use is made of these recurrences? How much has the lapse of time altered their significance? In which cases and in what respects? What is the dramatic value of this detailed parallelism with earlier acts?

12.   In what specific ways does the dramatic action of Act IV parallel the pattern of the first two acts? What features create a difference in effect? How does the first part of the act, through the device of the lotto game, explain what happens later? What dramatic effects are aimed at in Masha's calling of the numbers during the game? What is the dramatic significance of Masha's waltzing, of Trepleff's efforts to work in the midst of the chattering crowd, of Nina's obsession with the sea gull, of Trepleff's final and deliberate destruction of his manuscripts? What is ironic about the reactions to the sea gull exhibited by the three persons originally concerned with it? As a symbol, does the sea gull refer only to Nina? What are the causes which lead Trepleff to kill himself? In the state of life depicted what sort of people survive and what sort are destroyed? What makes the difference?

13.   What is the point of the manner in which the play is concluded? What is the total effect of the play and how is it produced? Is the illusion created realistic and true to life? Is the technical structure natural or artificial? What is the justification for calling the play a comedy?

THE PLAYBOY OF THE WESTERN WORLD

1.   What constitutes the comic situation of the play? How complex is it? What is the basis of its incongruity? In what ways does this incongruity change as the play progresses? By what means is the plot developed? What gives it suspense and variety? What specific phases of development are represented by the three acts?

2.   What is the nature of the comedy? Is it subtle or farcical, natural or fabricated? To what extent is it inherent in the situation? In what respects does it derive from character? What particular qualities of human nature are drawn on? Why are these comic? What are the advantages and disadvantages of murder as a subject of comedy? How is it treated in this play?

3.   What promotes the romance between Pegeen and Christy? What motives govern Pegeen's behavior? What is the source of her interest in Christy? What factors stimulate its development? To what extent is love involved? Why does the romance collapse? Why is this collapse comic rather than pathetic? What is the effect of the final sentiments expressed by Christy and Pegeen? In what way are the characteristics of romance and realism reflected in the situation?

4.   What sort of a person is Christy? What is ironic about his meteoric career? What makes him a comic character? In what ways does he afford a commentary on human nature? To what extent does his character change and remain the same? Why is he the protagonist of the play? How does this fact bear upon the final effect of the play? Of what does his ultimate triumph consist? In what respects may he be considered a symbolic figure?

5.   What specific dramatic functions are performed by the other characters? How much is Shawn responsible for the developments of the play? What governs the Widow Quin's conduct? How do you explain her various shifts of allegiance? What is the point of the bargains which she strikes? Why is she a good foil to Pegeen?

6.   To what extent is the play realistic? Are the situations plausible? Are the characters credible? What means are used to establish the atmosphere of the play? How do these affect the treatment of themes and characters? How much of the play possesses a universal application?

7.   List the features of the play which are peculiar to its Irish setting. How are they introduced? What particular aspects of Irish life are stressed? How does this special background affect the credibility of the play? How is it related to the play's realism?

8.   More than in a distinctive environment, folk drama is interested in the distinctive psychology and temperament of a people. What particular traits of Irish temperament does the play emphasize? To what extent may the characters be considered typical? In what degree are the traits of individuals characteristic of the whole group? To what extent

do these traits reflect the conditions of living depicted? To what extent are they responsible for the conditions? To what extent are they seriously criticized? On what grounds? Why are they suitable for comic treatment? Why may the play be considered a distinctively Irish comedy?

9.   One of the most notable features of the play is its use of Irish dialect and speech rhythms. What are the distinguishing features of this speech? What does its use contribute to the atmosphere of the play? What is its general effect? What are its special artistic values? In particular, what is its bearing on such matters as truth to life and beauty, or realistic diction and poetic eloquence?

DESIRE UNDER THE ELMS

1.   In the general setting of the play what effects are aimed at? What particular details of setting are stressed in the opening scenes? To what special features of life is attention directed? To what extent does the play strive for an impression of ordinary reality? What sort of reality? How natural is the dialogue? To what extent is it thematic? In what respects is the play realistic in method, and in what respects naturalistic? What is the difference in effect? Compare the realism of the play with that of *The Sea Gull*.

2.   What is the general dramatic purpose of the scenes in Part One? What matters of dramatic importance are introduced? What aspects of character and sources of behavior are emphasized? In what terms is human nature interpreted? What is the bearing on the situation of such considerations as the following: environment, heredity, biology, psychology, physics, chemistry, economics, geography.

3.   In a play avowedly concerned with desire, what specific kinds of desire does Part One attempt to identify and define? How are these desires accounted for? On what grounds may such explanation be considered natural and satisfactory? In what respects are these desires related to environment? To what extent do they reflect the operation of natural processes? To what extent do they represent a conflict with nature? What is the source of the conflict?

4.   What is the dramatic significance of the attitudes exhibited by the three brothers toward their father's behavior, toward his treatment of Eben's mother, and toward their own situation? What is the importance of Simeon's remark in Scene Two that "No one never kills nobody. It's allus somethin' "? Of the brothers' reiteration that Eben is "Like his Paw"?

5.   What are the dominant desires of Abbie? How do her desires compare with those of the others? What new factors does she introduce into the situation? Why do these factors precipitate a dramatic conflict? What explains Abbie's attitude toward Eben? In what terms are the relations between Abbie, Eben, and Old Cabot dealt with? To what

extent is their behavior natural? In what respects is their relationship unnatural?

6.   Part Two traces the interaction of the forces which are defined in Part One. What are the specific sources of conflict? What psychological, biological, and social factors are involved in the development of the dramatic action? To what extent are the characters victims of nature? How much of the action represents a struggle between spirit and matter?

7.   Cabot's long speech in the second scene of this part reveals much of the psychology which accounts for his behavior as well as for the tragedy of his frustrated loneliness. How well does he understand himself and the nature of his plight? What is your interpretation? Why does he seek consolation in the barn with the cows? What psychological explanation is suggested for his religious strain? What is tragic about his condition? What parallels exist between it and the respective conditions of Abbie and Eben? Why are Abbie's impulsions as confused as those of Cabot? What is the significance of the recurring themes of love and hate, softness and hardness, possession and loss? What ironies do they produce?

8.   In the complex design of the climactic fourth scene, what are the various forces which impel Abbie and Eben to their adultery? How much of their former antagonism is revealed as inverted attraction? How much of this attraction is a recoil from their mutual hatred of Cabot? How much is attributable to loneliness? To what extent is the basic motive lust? What deeper motives does the scene reveal? What explains the identification of Abbie with Eben's mother? Why is the element of sex stressed in the several relationships of the play?

9.   Part Three deals with the inevitable and ironic results produced by the operation of the forces delineated in the preceding scenes. In what ways does the baby serve to focus and symbolize these results? How does it serve to victimize Cabot? How does it change the situation for Abbie and Eben? How does it enhance their status as tragic figures?

10.   What does Scene One of Part Three reveal of the basic cause of Cabot's tragic loneliness? What natural laws operate to produce the ironies of Scene Two? What occasions the conflict between these laws and human nature? How it this conflict related to the underlying concept of tragedy in the play?

11.   What important change in Abbie's character is involved in her murder of the child? Is this change for the better or the worse? What particular aspect of her deed causes Eben to recoil from her? Is his reason of the same sort as that which caused his earlier revulsion? What is the basic difference in significance between the adultery and the murder? What paradox in the murder explains Eben's subsequent attitude?

12.   At the conclusion of the play what important transformation has taken place in Abbie and Eben? Why do they differ fundamentally from Cabot? Why does Eben prefer to share Abbie's guilt and punishment?

What is signified by the fact that they admit their conduct is a sin, are ready to suffer for it, yet do not regret it? To what extent is their redemption dependent upon their sin? What is ironic about their case? Why is this irony tragic?

13.   What is the scientific significance of Cabot's devotion to the farm? Of his interest in Abbie? Of his dedication to hardness? Of his loneliness? Of his defeat? In each case what is the symbolic significance? What light is thrown on the play by the masterly irony of the last speech?

THE DREAM PLAY

1.   A symbolistic work like *The Dream Play* confronts the reader with a special problem. The understanding of its thought content and artistic merits depends chiefly on the sensitivity with which one recognizes the symbols used and identifies their human significance. This is a matter not only of constant alertness to the possible implications of objects, persons, and actions, but also of skill in following the clues to meaning which are provided by such technical devices as juxtaposition, parallelism, and association. The combination of realism with an expressionistic technique, which is given plausibility by the dream illusion, makes possible a free arrangement of these symbolic relationships. On the whole, the symbolism of the play is either transparent or specifically explained in the course of the action. Nevertheless, one must realize that one's first task is to identify the symbols; for the whole technique is fruitless unless one recognizes, for example, that the Officer, the Lawyer, and the Poet are not three persons, but three aspects of one personality, or that the several rôles assumed by the Daughter of Indra are actually variant manifestations of the basic quality which she symbolizes.

2.   In the Prologue what preparation is provided for the nature of the symbolism to follow? What special qualities of earthly existence are stressed? What clues are given to the conception embodied in the Daughter of Indra?

3.   In the first act what technical devices are used to create the effect of dream? What specific realistic features of dream are employed? What methods are used to dislocate normal time and place relationships? To what extent is the apparent disorder of the action logical? What links of association keep it from becoming chaotic? How consistently is the dream pattern maintained throughout the play? Where do the chief lapses occur? What purpose, if any, accounts for these lapses?

4.   What clues suggest the meaning of the growing castle? What particular properties of monkshood give it a symbolic value, and what is its significance in the play? Who is the Officer? What prompts the episode of the Mother and the Father? What is the dramatic purpose of indicating characters by means of a descriptive title rather than a specific name? Where exceptions occur, is there any significance in the name assigned?

In the scene in the passageway, what objects are introduced as symbols? What psychological explanation is suggested for their presence and emphasis in the dream? What distinctive properties indicate their symbolic significance?

5.   In the scenes of the passageway, the law office, and the church, what specific aspects of human experience are dealt with? Why are the Officer and the Lawyer the central figures? What is the relation between them? What is the connection between the Daughter and the Portress? Why do the Daughter and the Lawyer address each other as brother and sister? What general impressions of human experience are stressed? What special characteristics indicate the nature of human life? What specific themes are introduced and repeated? In this connection, observe throughout the play the development of themes as in a musical composition, and especially the use of the recurring "Men are to be pitied" as a leitmotif. As the play progresses, what modulations of meaning occur in this theme? To what extent does the first act represent a systematic survey of human ills? From what sources do these ills arise? How is the mirror on the church organ used to illuminate the meaning of the act? What is the dramatic value, and the interpretative significance, of the ending of the act?

6.   While retaining the bizarre juxtaposition and overlapping of dream images, the second act is in the main a straightforward symbolic representation of ordered reality. What typical aspects of human experience are dealt with? In the first scene what is implied by presenting the Lawyer as the husband? How is his function connected with that of the Officer? Who is Christine, and how is she related to the Daughter? What ironies of marriage are emphasized? In what connotations is this matter of marriage to be interpreted? What is the symbolic purport of the hairpin and the door? Why are they appropriate symbols?

7.   The Foulstrand and Fairhaven scenes systematically pass in synoptic review the major features of human existence as seen from contrasting points of view. What devices are used to maintain the dream effect? What special features of human life are stressed? How are the various characters related to one another? To what extent do they form a coordinated pattern of personality in the same manner that the incidents form a pattern of life? What is the point of the constant contrasts? What is the appropriateness of the quarantine symbol? How is emphasis directed to such themes as justice, mutability, frustration, the cancelling effect of contrasts? What other themes do you observe? How far does the evidence of these scenes sustain the thesis that joy is always balanced by sorrow and that anyone's gain is paid by another's loss? What is the special function of the schoolroom scene? Why is the Poet associated with mud? What is his relation to the Officer and the Lawyer? In facing the general irony of human life, with which particular matters does each of the three concern himself?

8. In the scenes just considered how convincing is the representation of human experience? By what means does it strive for credibility and acceptance? How far is it intended as an objective and proportioned report on life? As the expression of a unified mood and impression of human experience, how satisfactorily does it explain the mood and impression in terms of the evidence?

9. How does the short episode on the Mediterranean shore relate to the preceding scenes? How does it differ from them in technique and effect? What is its climactic and explanatory value? How does it serve to sum up the thought of the play thus far?

10. What is the significance of the setting in Fingal's Cave? What shift in interest and point of view does it indicate? Why is it appropriate that this scene concerns the Daughter and the Poet? What transitional function is performed by the poetic interlude which introduces the scene? In the ensuing action what particular aspect of human life is considered? What basic cause of human misery is suggested?

11. Structurally, what is the value of the cyclical repetitions in the last act? To what extent do the last scenes draw together and interpret the vagrant strands of the whole dream? What light is thrown on the sources of human distress and on the human responsibility for it? What is signified by the disputes of the four Faculties? Why are the Faculties chosen for this function? What clues are provided to explain the secret of the opened door? What is suggested concerning the interpretation of "the right-minded"?

12. The last two scenes are largely devoted to transparent symbolism and to overt explanation of the play's basic ideas. What are these ideas? How well do they clarify the action of the play? How far are they sustained by the matter of the play? To what extent does the structure of the play illustrate and reenforce its thought content? Why is the dream effect appropriate? Why is the expressionistic method desirable? What are its advantages and its disadvantages? What is the dramatic value of the symbolism?

CYRANO DE BERGERAC

1. As an exercise in technical virtuosity, Rostand's "heroic comedy" affords an excellent opportunity to review one's acquaintance with the mechanics of stagecraft. Also, since it draws heavily on established dramatic tradition and convention, it invites comparisan with one's recollections of other plays. With what plays in this book has it most in common? In what respects? What formal types of drama does it most resemble? With what sort of reality does it deal? What is its attitude toward human experience? How does it gain its plausibility?

2. In Act I how does Rostand establish the atmosphere of the play? What is the advantage of the theatrical setting? What is gained by using

as background this particular historical period? What features of the period are stressed? How are the mood and the cultural tone built up? What is the value of stressing the artificial affectations of the period? Why is so much emphasis given to matters of art, manners, and cultural taste? What is the effect of the constant allusions to historical persons and circumstances of the time?

3.   Trace the detailed process by which an effective first entrance is provided for Cyrano. How are interest and suspense maintained during the lengthy exposition? How is interest focused on Cyrano? How are the essential traits of his personality revealed? What are they? What specific appeals are made to enlist one's sympathy and admiration for Cyrano? Is he a credible character? Why does one accept him? On what grounds is he represented as admirable? To what extent are these grounds valid?

4.   How much of the first act is devoted to theatrical effects? What specifically are these? To what extent are they contrived chiefly for the immediate effect? In what respects do they contribute to the development of the drama? Consider the following episodes in the light of their naturalness, motivation, dramatic purpose, and theatrical value: the introduction of Cyrano, his discourse on his nose, the duel of the ballade, the incident with the orange girl, the conclusion of the act. How is the conclusion of the act constructed for theatrical effect? What is the effect aimed at?

5.   To what extent is Act II constructed on a scheme of contrasts? What specific contrasts are used? What constitutes the general irony of the situation? How is the heroic stature of Cyrano built up? What methods are used to prevent the process from becoming absurd or offensive? What traits of character are specifically stressed? How do they motivate Cyrano's conduct? What makes the interview between Cyrano and Roxane theatrically effective? Note its carefully contrived suspense and climax. Why is Roxane presented as insensitive and essentially self-centered? Why is the fact ironic? How does she compare with Célimène in *The Misanthrope*? What is the effect aimed at by Cyrano's subsequent arrogance? Is it dramatically justified? What is the effect of reducing it to wounded love? What is the purpose of the emphasis on irony and pathos? How is it saved from obvious sentimentality? What is accomplished by the encounter with Christian? How is Cyrano's agreement to aid him prepared for? In what way does this agreement bring to a culmination the contrasts of the act?

6.   How does the mood of Act III differ from those of the preceding acts? By what theatrical devices is it created and sustained? What are the reasons for its deliberate vacillations between intense feeling and comedy? What is the value of the wit which permeates the act? How does the balcony scene in this act compare with the famous one in *Romeo and Juliet*? What is the difference in effect? What makes this, the principal love scene, especially "good theater"? What betrays its essentially

theatrical conception? To what extent is the scene deliberately contrived to play on the emotions? In what respects is the following scene with De Guiche designed to serve as a parallel to it? In what ways do the two scenes resemble and contrast with each other? Upon what do the theatrical values of the latter depend? What is the particular value of the final curtain line as a summation of the act?

7.   The theatrical effects of Act IV are deliberately conceived according to the principles of romance in the grand manner. How many of the melodramatic incidents and instances of gallant behavior stand the test of reasonable probability? Why are they theatrically acceptable? What is the basis of their romantic appeal? To what extent is the act dominated by traditional romantic ideals of love and honor? To what extent is the conduct of the characters dictated by the sentiments and obligations of a social code? How does the opening scene establish this atmosphere? What effect has the atmosphere on plausibility? What is contributed to the general effect by the following: wit, grace and gallantry of tone, conscious style in deportment, chivalric sentiment, melodramatic incidents? What devices are employed to temper the somewhat extravagant heroics and sentimentality of the act?

8.   Examine the sequence of individual theatrical effects of which Act IV is composed. How do they differ from and complement one another? How does each serve both to sustain and to restrain the mood of the act? What are the technical reasons for directing attention to Christian's last letter to Roxane? What is gained by setting the crisis of the love story against a background of crowded action and confusion? Why is the heroic setting appropriate? How does the device promote suspense, tension, pathos, credibility, irony?

9.   In Act IV Rostand brings the preceding ironies of the play to a brilliantly manipulated climax. How much of the ironic result derives from a skillful use of peripety? To what extent is the peripety motivated by the pressures of love and honor? As fortunes change, what changes occur in the character of Roxane, of Christian, of De Guiche, of Cyrano? How are these changes made plausible? By what means is the epidemic of noble sentiments made to appear inevitable? In what respects does Christian's situation deliberately parallel that of Cyrano in Act II? How does his response to it affect one's view of his character? Is his death a simple casualty of battle or a deliberate sacrifice? Why does his reacttion affect Cyrano's subsequent behavior as it does? What are the complex factors which constitute the irony of Cyrano's climactic frustration? Why is this frustration inescapable for Cyrano? What is the thematic appropriateness of the act's conclusion?

10.   Act V has in many respects the nature of an epilogue. Why is this act dramatically necessary? Why is the intervening lapse of time essential? In what respects does the mood of the act differ from the rest of the play? What is its dominant tone? By what theatrical devices is this

tone created and modulated? What devices of symbolism are employed? Why is symbolism appropriate to the effect intended? How much of the total effect depends upon a proper preparation for Cyrano's last entrance? How is this preparation managed? Is the necessary exposition introduced naturally? What does the visit of De Guiche contribute to the total dramatic design? What is the appropriateness of the setting?

11.   Cyrano's last visit to Roxane is devised to recapitulate, by a systematic process of suggestion, the major themes of the play. What themes and dominant traits of Cyrano's character are restated? In terms of the play's romantic basis, why is the revelation of Cyrano's secret dramatically necessary? Is his secret betrayed or discovered? What is the difference in the significance? How is the revelation contrived plausibly? How does it affect the fundamental irony of the play? By what means does Rostand achieve his effect of pathos? Is the scene exclusively a contrived "tear-jerker"? Besides pathos, what other elements are present? Why is the conclusion of the play diverted to another note? In what respects is this conclusion a deliberate *coup de théâtre*? In what respects is it designed to represent more than a mere theatrical effect? To what extent is the final curtain line a thematic summation of the entire play?

12.   On what grounds is Rostand justified in describing his play as a comedy? What is the effect of his extensive use of irony? Why is the effect not tragic? Why is so much of the play's success dependent on its delicate balance of wit and sentiment? To what extent does its effectiveness derive from its romantic atmosphere? Select from the play several incidents which impress you with their theatrical effectiveness. From exactly what does their effectiveness derive? Is there any technical evidence that these incidents are deliberately contrived for their immediate effect? What is the nature of this evidence? What warrants Rostand's assumption that his devices will be effective? What features impart to the artifice of the play an illusion of reality? What virtues endow it with artistic validity?

A Drama Bookshelf

THE following two lists of books have been prepared, not as a general bibliography of drama, but strictly as a working supplement to the introductory aims of the present volume. The first consists of play collections which afford a compact but comprehensive library of drama for supplementary reading. The second contains a rigorously selective group of sound first books on the major aspects of drama and the theater. In both cases titles have been deliberately kept to a minimum in order to avoid embarrassing the beginner with more materials than he can use and with choices among them which he is ill prepared to make. For more detailed study of special subjects abundant guidance is afforded by the comprehensive bibliographies to be found in many of the books listed.

COLLECTIONS OF DRAMA

OATES, W. J., AND O'NEILL, E., JR. *The Complete Greek Drama*, 2 v. New York: Random House, 1938.

DUCKWORTH, G. E. *The Complete Roman Drama*, 2 v. New York: Random House, 1942.

CLARK, B. H. *World Drama*, 2 v. New York: Appleton-Century, 1932.

MANTLE, B., AND GASSNER, J. *A Treasury of the Theater*, rev. ed., 2 v. New York: Simon and Schuster, 1940.

CLARK, W. S. *Chief Patterns of World Drama*. Boston: Houghton, Mifflin, 1946.

ADAMS, J. Q. *Chief Pre-Shakespearean Dramas*. Boston: Houghton, Mifflin, 1924.

SPENCER, H. *Elizabethan Plays*. Boston: Little, Brown 1933.

MACMILLAN, D., AND JONES, H. M. *Plays of the Restoration and Eighteenth Century*. New York: Holt, 1931.

QUINN, A. H. *Representative American Plays*, rev. ed. New York: Appleton-Century, 1938.

DICKINSON, T. H. *Chief Contemporary Dramatists*, 3 series. Boston: Houghton, Mifflin, 1915, 1921, 1930.

681

HATCHER, H. *Modern American, British and Continental Dramas,* 3 v. New York: Harcourt, Brace, 1941.

WATSON, E. B., AND PRESSEY, B. *Contemporary Drama.* New York: Scribner, 1941.

GASSNER, J. *Twenty Best Plays of the Modern American Theatre,* 2 series. New York: Crown, 1939, 1947.

CERF, B. A., AND CARTMELL, V. H. *Sixteen Famous American Plays.* New York: Modern Library, 1942.

———— *Sixteen Famous British Plays.* New York: Modern Library, 1943.

———— *Sixteen Famous European Plays.* New York: Modern Library, 1947.

CRITICAL STUDIES

MATTHEWS, B. *A Study of the Drama.* Boston: Houghton, Mifflin, 1910.
Although a pioneer volume, still perhaps the most illuminating general introduction to the subject.

BROWN, J. M. *The Art of Playgoing.* New York: Norton, 1936.
A lively and stimulating discussion of dramatic principles in terms of the theater and with reference to the audience.

NICOLL, A. *The Theory of Drama.* London: Harrap, 1931.
An excellent study of the scope and principles of the major kinds of drama.

STUART, D. C. *The Development of Dramatic Art.* New York: Appleton, 1928.
An analysis of the historical growth of dramatic concepts and practices.

CLARK, B. H. *European Theories of the Drama,* rev. ed. New York: Crown, 1947.
A comprehensive collection of the major critical pronouncements from Aristotle to the present.

GASSNER, J. *Masters of the Drama,* new ed. New York: Dover, 1945.
The best single-volume account of world drama.

HARSH, P. W. *A Handbook of Classical Drama.* Stanford University Press, 1944.
The best succinct guide to the essentials of ancient drama.

CLARK, B. H., AND FREEDLEY, G. *A History of Modern Drama.* New York: Appleton-Century, 1947.
Although inclined to be factual, the most comprehensive survey of modern drama.

NICOLL, A. *The Development of the Theater,* 3d ed. New York: Harcourt, Brace, 1947.
The standard book on the subject, particularly valuable for its copious illustrations.

FREEDLEY, G., AND REEVES, J. A. *A History of the Theatre*. New York: Crown, 1941.

A comprehensive factual record of theatrical and dramatic history, profusely illustrated.

SIMONSON, L. *The Stage is Set*. New York: Harcourt, Brace, 1932.

Perhaps the most informative and stimulating single volume in English on the history, theory, and practice of theatrical art. Well illustrated.

Index

i

SUBJECTS

Act, 23, 100, 348, 409, 529, 536n, 665

Action, 4, 16, 18, 24, 25, 26, 29, 30, 45, 48, 55, 64, 65, 66, 68, 100, 101, 102, 103, 171, 172, 219, 220, 258, 348, 407, 409, 575. *See also* Action, Dramatic, *and* Stage business

Action, Dramatic, 18–19, 21, 22, 23, 25, 27, 28, 29, 31, 34, 52, 55, 56, 57, 66, 68, 80n, 83n, 100, 102, 220, 258, 259, 311, 312, 345, 347, 348, 406, 408, 409, 487, 539n, 652, 653, 654, 655, 656, 660, 662, 663, 664, 665, 666, 667, 668, 671, 674

Actors and acting, 7, 11, 16, 24, 31, 41, 48, 52, 54, 55, 63, 64, 65, 68, 102, 103, 407, 573

Ancient drama, *see* Drama, Ancient

Anticlimax, 22

Antipathy, 34, 657. *See also* Empathy *and* Sympathy

Appropriateness, 17, 28, 30, 36, 38, 45, 528, 657, 658, 660, 665, 666, 673, 674, 676, 677

Aristotle, 13, 17, 21, 67

Artificiality of drama, 9, 12, 14, 16, 17, 20, 311, 405, 657, 675

Aside, 16, 24, 101, 102

Atmosphere, 26, 31, 68, 408, 446, 530, 660, 669, 670, 674, 676, 677

Attitude, 30, 31, 33–36, 37, 38, 43, 44, 45, 46, 67, 68, 99, 173, 174, 217, 218, 257, 260, 346, 347, 444, 446, 484, 652, 653, 654, 655, 656, 657, 658, 660, 661, 662, 663, 666, 667, 668, 670, 671, 674

Audience, The theater, 8, 9, 11, 12, 13, 14, 15, 23, 24, 27, 28, 29, 30, 31, 33, 34, 35, 41, 42, 43, 48, 55, 63, 64, 65, 66, 68, 69, 101, 102, 103, 104, 311, 347, 349, 530, 652, 658,

662. *See also* Guidance of the audience

Ballet, 4, 64

Behavior, 44, 57, 217, 218, 257, 258, 259, 260, 261, 309, 310, 311, 313, 486, 654, 655, 662, 663, 670, 671, 676. *See also* Deportment

Bourgeois drama, 54, 346

Burlesque, 14, 261

Business, Stage, *see* Stage business

Catastrophe, 67, 68, 100, 313, 484

Causation in drama, 27, 28, 29, 57. *See also* Motivation

Chance occurrences in drama, 27–28

Character comedy, *see* Comedy, Character

Character, Dramatic, 7, 10, 13, 16, 18, 23, 28, 29, 31, 47, 49, 56, 57, 66, 104, 173, 174, 219, 259, 311, 313, 345, 347, 348, 407, 408, 446, 486, 529, 536n, 572, 573, 651, 653, 656, 657, 659, 660, 661, 662, 663, 664, 665, 666, 667, 668, 669, 670, 671, 672, 673, 675, 676, 677. *See also* Character types

Character types: antagonist, 34; background characters, 23, 666; confidant, 16, 23, 24, 311, 312, 664; messenger or nuntius, 66, 68, 93n, 653; mutes, 68; protagonist, 34, 104, 486, 529, 669; raisonneur, 24; stock characters, 16, 23, 52, 93n, 172, 173; type characters, 16, 23, 28, 49, 67, 172, 219, 347, 349, 665, 669

Chorus, 24, 48, 63, 64, 65, 68–69, 77n, 80n, 311, 666

Clarity, Dramatic, 7–9

Classical drama, 24, 47–49, 51, 52, 53,

687

PLAYWRIGHTS

III

PLAYS

697